The Development of
Children

To our parents and children, to whom we owe a debt of gratitude for our own development.

The Development of
Children

Fifth Edition

Michael Cole

University of California, San Diego

Sheila R. Cole

Cynthia Lightfoot

Pennsylvania State University, Delaware County

Worth Publishers

The Development of Children, Fifth edition

© 2005, 2001, 1996, 1993, 1989 by Michael Cole, Sheila R. Cole, and Cynthia Lightfoot

ISBN-13: 978-0-7167-5555-5
ISBN-10: 0-7167-5555-6
Third printing

Sponsoring Editor: Jessica Bayne
Development Editor: Jennifer Ahrend
Associate Managing Editor: Tracey Kuehn
Project Editor: Kerry O'Shaughnessy
Marketing Manager: Katherine Nurre
Production Manager: Barbara Anne Seixas
Art Director, Cover Designer: Babs Reingold
Interior Text Designer: Lissi Sigillo
Layout Design: Paul Lacy
Cover photo: © Greg Pease
Illustration Coordinator: Bill Page
Illustrations: Chris Notarile, Fineline Inc., Tomo Narashima
Photo Manager: Trish Marx
Photo Research: Nicole Villamora
Composition: Progressive Information Technologies
Printing and Binding: R. R. Donnelley and Sons Company

Library of Congress Control Number: 2004107443

Worth Publishers
41 Madison Avenue
New York, NY 10010
www.worthpublishers.com

brief contents

contents

PART I   IN THE BEGINNING

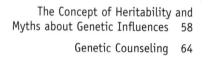

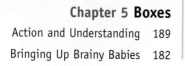
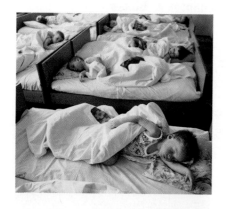

Chapter 7 **Boxes**

PART III   EARLY CHILDHOOD

Chapter 8 **Boxes**

PART IV   MIDDLE CHILDHOOD

Chapter 13 Boxes
Computers in Schools 498
Comparing Mathematics Instruction
across Cultures 520

PART V   ADOLESCENCE

Preface

Our task in writing this textbook about human development poses a special challenge. Everyone who opens this book has had extensive firsthand experience with the process of growing up. In addition, each reader has had many opportunities to witness and to think about the development of other people—parents and grandparents, brothers or sisters, friends. In this sense, students no less than their professors are already experts on the topic of human development. But, this kind of expertise is subjective, intuitive, and limited to each person's own experience of the world.

We take it as our challenge to enable you to bring together your own personal experience with the best scientific thinking in the field so that both perspectives, the personal and the scientific, inform and enrich each other. We want to dispel the idea that because information about development comes from a textbook and not one's personal life it is dry and uninteresting—information to be memorized for an examination, rather than material that provides a means for thinking about important matters such as how to improve one's own life and the lives of others.

A remarkable example of how scientific observation and personal experience can come together in the study of development comes from a report about an extraordinary moment in the otherwise perfectly ordinary life of a fish. The fish himself was nothing special—just one of many other fish kept in an aquarium by Konrad Lorenz, a student of development who was a wonderful storyteller and a brilliant researcher of the role of evolution in development.

As Lorenz tells the story, this particular fish was a Jewel fish, and a father. Jewel fish fathers participate actively in family life: they are responsible, for example, for putting their young to bed. To accomplish this task, the father inhales each youngster into his large mouth, swims to the nest, and blows the baby into the nesting hollow. One evening, the fish in Lorenz's aquarium were fed later than usual, and the father was already busy tucking his children into bed. Then Lorenz observed an astonishing event:

> As I approached the container, I saw that most of the young were already in the nesting hollow over which the mother was hovering. She refused to come for the food when I threw pieces of earthworm into the tank. The father, however, who, in great excitement, was dashing backwards and forwards searching for truants, allowed himself to be diverted from his duty by a nice hind-end of earthworm. He swam up and seized the worm, but owing to its size, was unable to swallow it. As he was in the act of chewing this mouthful, he saw a baby fish swimming by itself across the tank; he raced after the baby and took it into his already filled mouth. It was a thrilling moment. The fish had in its mouth two different things of which one must go into the stomach and the other into the nest. What would he do? If ever I have seen a fish think, it was in that moment!

The story ends happily. The fish spat out the entire contents of his mouth, completed his fatherly duty, and then had his dinner.

There are several lessons in this fish story that connect with what we hope students will learn from this book. For example, like Jewel fish babies, human children require parents to provide for their survival and well-being, sometimes in self-sacrificing ways. Like Jewel fish parents, human parents may find that their own desires and their responsibilities to their children may conflict, requiring hard decisions about what to do.

Of course, human beings are different not only from fish but from all other creatures, in many ways. Humans evolved eons after fish made their appearance on the earth, and whereas Jewel fish babies mature in a matter of weeks, human babies cannot begin life on their own for many years following birth. Once Jewel fish babies leave the nest, they must learn on their own how to find food and avoid predators, whereas human babies inherit a rich cultural tradition which allows them to benefit from the untold labors of prior generations as they move slowly from infancy through childhood and adolescence to adulthood. Both the similarities and the differences are instructive about the processes of development.

In the chapters to follow, our focus will be on human children, but we will not ignore the evidence obtained from other species, whether fish, ducks, or chimpanzees, because the modern study of development takes place within a broad, evolutionary framework. If we have been successful, you will discover that such a broad scientific framework for understanding children's development can enrich your understanding both of your own life, and of the general processes of development. Our greatest aspiration is to bring intellectual excitement to your learning about human development so that the research and theorizing we write about will guide the practical applications of scientific knowledge for those of you who will become parents and practitioners.

Our own interest in children's development is the result of years of personal and professional experience. Michael and Sheila Cole have known each other since adolescence. They have shared a personal interest in children's development from the time they were teenagers, first as camp counselors working with young children, then as parents raising children of their own, and now as grandparents, regularly called upon to help out overburdened parents or to enjoy vacations as an extended family. Both have a deep professional interest in child development: Michael Cole specializes in the study of the role of culture in contributing to children's learning and cognitive development; Sheila Cole is a journalist who has written articles about children and books for children.

Coming from a family that moved around a lot, both in the United States and abroad, Cynthia Lightfoot often feels as if she grew up in the back of a station wagon. She went to high school in Japan, began her college years at an international university in Tokyo, and returned to the United States wanting to study the relationship between culture and psychology. Her experiences working in a program for teen mothers, many of whom were Vietnamese and Cambodian refugees, focused her interest more particularly on the relationships among children's development, culture, and issues affecting minority and immigrant families.

Three Orientations: Practice, Theory, and Research

Throughout our work on this text, we have been guided by the belief that it is a mistake to make sharp distinctions between practical, theoretical, and research orientations in studying development. This belief comes not only from the modern concerns of developmental science but also from our own personal and professional experience. We are all actively interested in discovering practical approaches for fostering the development of children, so it is natural that our book should focus continually on issues such as the benefits of special nutrition programs for children who have experienced malnutrition early in life; methods for assessing the quality of out-of-home care for young children; the importance of extended families in ameliorating the problems facing poor children; the challenges of learning to read and to do arithmetic in school; ways to foster emotional self-regulation and reduce aggression among children; the special hazards of teenage pregnancy; and effective means of parenting teenagers. We also include many examples drawn from the everyday lives of children to show how a society's beliefs influence its children's development by shaping both the laws and the social norms that govern child-rearing practices.

However, there is much truth to the saying that nothing is so practical as a good theory. A deep understanding of how children develop requires familiarity not only with the everyday lives of children but also with theories that provide coherent interpretations of the facts derived from scientific research. Such understanding is an essential foundation for attempts to create and guide practical courses of action. To help guide you through the major theories of development, we focus on some of the enduring issues that all theories of development must resolve: how biological and environmental contributions—nature and nurture—are woven together; the extent to which the interaction of these factors results in continuities and discontinuities in the dynamic process of development; and the reasons for the individual differences among people. In addition, to help you build an appreciation for the significance of theoretical diversity, we present competing theories in a constant dialogue with one another, and then try to move beyond the differences to show how each theory contributes to an overall understanding of development.

The dialogue between theory and practice leads naturally to disputes about the facts of development as well as about the methodologies used to marshal facts in support of one perspective or another. Therefore it is essential to understand research methods both as a means of judging the merits of the evidence that developmentalists gather and as a means of thinking critically about the conclusions they draw. What is the evidence that sparing the rod spoils the child? How might we determine whether the differences between boys' and girls' games result from social forces or from biological predispositions? Are the links that have been found between watching violent programs on television and subsequent aggressive behavior necessarily causal? And why is it so difficult for developmentalists to answer enduring questions about development once and for all? Only through an awareness of the logic, methods, and, indeed, the shortcomings of developmental research will you come away from a course on development with the ability to evaluate for yourself the relative merits of different scientists' conclusions.

A Focus on Culture

In our view, development is best understood as a fusion of biological, social, and psychological processes interacting in the unique medium of human culture. We have tried to show not only the role of each of these factors considered separately but also how they interact in diverse cultural contexts to create whole, unique human beings.

Over the years, our work has taken us to live in many parts of the world: West Africa, Mexico, Brazil, Russia, Israel, Japan, and Great Britain. In the United States, we have lived and worked in affluent suburbs and in inner-city ghettos. Often our children have accompanied us, providing us with even richer opportunities for getting to know children in a wide variety of circumstances. Such experiences have led us to believe that culture must be included in any comprehensive theory of development.

For us to appreciate this truth fully, it is necessary for us to overcome as much as possible any ethnocentrism we may have in our view of children's development. The task is by no means an easy one. For many Americans, the initial reaction to daily life in an African village, an Asian metropolis, or the impoverished neighborhoods of a large U.S. city is likely to be "culture shock," a sense of disorientation that stems from the difficulty of understanding the way of life of people in other cultures or foreign circumstances. Very often, culture shock is accompanied by a sense of cultural superiority; the way "we" do it (prepare our food, build our houses, care for our children) seems superior to the way "they" do it. In addition, appreciation of the contribution of culture to development requires more than attention to the ways people far away raise their children. Culture is fundamental to children's experience in any society—not something added on to the process of development, but an essential part of that process, for "us" as well as for "them."

Recognizing how difficult it is to think objectively about the nature of development in unfamiliar cultures, we have tried to keep you constantly aware of the diversity of the cultural contexts in which children grow up and of the variations that exist in human child-rearing practices. Only by considering a culture as but one alternative among many designs for living can we arrive at a valid understanding of the principles that guide the development of all human beings.

A Focus on Biology

It may seem surprising that authors who profess a special interest in culture would simultaneously underscore, as we do, the importance of biological factors to human development. Often the two sources of human variability are discussed as opposing each other, as if by virtue of living within a culture, we have ceased to be biologically evolving creatures. However, modern research on development has shown this to be a false opposition. Not only is the ability to create and use culture one of the most striking biological facts about our species, but there would be no development at all without biological maturation. Advances in the biological sciences have profoundly influenced human development through improved health care and advanced medical procedures. In addition, the biological sciences have increased our understanding of development by shedding light on critical issues such as the intimate links between biological changes in the brain and changes in children's cognitive capacities. The importance of the biological domain in development is made clear throughout this book.

A Focus on Dynamic Interaction

The Development of Children combines traditional chronological and topical approaches to development in a deliberate attempt to make as clear as possible the idea that development is a process involving the whole child in a dynamically changing set of cultural contexts. Although the book is chronological in its overall structure and adopts traditional stage boundaries for each of its major sections, the organization of the text is also topical in two respects. First, within broad, conventionally defined stages, it describes developments as occurring in the biological domain, the social domain, or the psychological domain (including emotion and cognition), while at the same time tracing the ways in which these developments interweave with development in other domains. Second, it focuses on the way stagelike changes emerge from the convergence of events in the various developmental domains.

Chronological and topical perspectives correspond to the warp and the woof of development. The pattern that is woven from their combination is the story of development. It is that story that we have attempted to tell in this book.

New to the Fifth Edition

It has been almost 20 years since we undertook the first edition of this book. Over that time there has been a constantly increasing stream of scientific research that has made each revision a real challenge. Some topics that were of central interest to developmentalists have receded from the spotlight and been replaced by new findings. For example, 20 years ago research on middle childhood was particularly dominant, while both infancy and adolescence were relatively neglected areas of research. Today the study of infancy and adolescence draw the lion's share of interest.

In attempting to ensure that the presentation in this edition is as up to date as possible, we have carefully documented major new developments in the field, as attested to by the 600 or more new references. We have also used the vantage point of our long experience in surveying the field to weed out research that, while authoritative in earlier decades, has been superseded because of more powerful methods or new theoretical insights.

Readers familiar with previous editions will find that their distinctive features have been built upon, streamlined, and better integrated. These include

- **Enhanced coverage of cultural topics.** Like its predecessors, this edition of *The Development of Children* places special emphasis on the importance of understanding and appreciating the diversity of development as it occurs in many parts of the world and among different populations in North America. We have added more in-depth coverage of cultural issues throughout the text, including: cultural transmission practices (Chapter 2); children and war (Chapter 7); mathematics instruction across cultures (Chapter 13); and development of ethnic identity (Chapters 10 and 16.)

- **Expanded coverage of brain development.** In the fifth edition we continue to highlight cutting-edge research on the impact of biology and the brain on children's development. New topics include: techniques for measuring and researching brain activity (Chapter 1); brain development in late infancy (Chapter 6); biology and language acquisition (Chapter 8); brain development in early childhood (Chapter 9); and brain development during adolescence (Chapter 15).

- **Reworked sections on adolescence.** Cynthia Lightfoot's research on adolescent development allows her to bring a fresh perspective and new research to the chapters on adolescence (Chapters 15 and 16). The fifth edition includes completely revised coverage reflecting changes in the field of adolescent development, including sections on brain development in adolescence; the timing of puberty; moral reasoning; social status and peer relations; sexual identity and decision-making; and identity development.

- **Additional student support.** As with previous editions, we continue to strive to improve the accessibility of our presentation without reducing its rigor. Every chapter now begins with a vignette or story to bring the topic to life. Special topics boxes illuminate new research, spark students' curiosity, and help connect science with students' everyday lives. Among the topics covered: contemporary efforts by affluent parents to create "smarter" children (Chapter 5); the development of sign language among hearing-impaired children in Nicaragua (Chapter 8); children's methods of dealing with illness (Chapter 10); and the development of children's spirituality and understanding of ideas about God (Chapter 14). In addition, we have continued our efforts to clarify and make connections between key points whenever possible. We have devoted additional attention to examining how changes in social, biological, emotional, and cognitive domains occur as part of a single life process. In an effort to highlight the key events, tables listing the bio-social-behavioral shifts characteristic of each stage have been reproduced in the introduction to each of the text's five parts.

A Note to Instructors

The Development of Children has been designed to be taught within either a quarter or a semester system. For classes taught on the quarter system in which the curriculum is restricted to childhood, the final section of the book can be left to students to read or not, as they choose, and the remainder can be fitted comfortably into a 10-week course. For 10-week courses that include adolescence, sections rather than whole chapters in Part I can be read; Chapter 7 (on the way infant experience shapes later development) and Chapter 8 (on language) could also be skipped or assigned selectively without disrupting the general flow of the presentation.

Instructors who prefer to organize this course in a topical fashion may also wish to assign segments rather than entire chapters in Part I: these chapters present important foundational issues that can be explored to any depth that is deemed appropriate. Chapters 4 through 6 can be read in sequence, or topical issues from each can be abstracted for reading in connection with corresponding chapters in Parts III, IV, and V. The natural sequence of chapters for the remainder of the course then becomes 9, 12, 13, and 16, which emphasize cognitive development, and 10, 14, and 15, which emphasize social and personality development. Instructors planning to use this textbook in conjunction with a topical course will find it helpful to turn to the Appendix on page A-1, "Guide to Discussions of Specific Aspects of Development."

Supplements

An extensive package of supplements has been prepared, each corresponding to the fifth edition of *The Development of Children* in content, level, and organization.

Exploring Child Development MEDIA TOOL KITS

The *Instructor Toolkit,* customized for the fifth edition, includes a set of CD-ROMs with more than 100 digitized video clips, animations, and PowerPoint slides covering an array of topics from genetics to the timing of puberty. The toolkit includes a special set of videos focusing on the importance of culture in development. It features interviews with key researchers, including Patricia Greenfield and Michael Cole, and investigations of the work of Geoffrey Saxe, Gilda Morelli, and Barbara Rogoff, among others. The accompanying PowerPoint slides present detailed lecture outlines, text illustrations, and video clips. The video clips are available in VHS or DVD.

The *Student Toolkit* provides a balance of observation activities and classic experiments. Each of the 30 activities—covering areas from prenatal development, the visual cliff, the classic Piaget conservation experiments, to adolescent identity—helps illustrate key concepts as well as reinforces text material through short-answer questions. Students can print or email their answers to these questions. The CD also includes quizzes, summaries, and interactive flashcards for every chapter.

Readings on the Development of Children, Fourth Edition

This reader, by Mary Gauvain, University of California, Riverside, and Michael Cole, is newly updated for this edition of the text and includes 20 new articles.

Instructor's Resource Manual

The *Instructor's Resource Manual* by Jennifer Coots, California State University, Long Beach, features chapter-by-chapter previews and lecture guides, learning objectives, topics for discussion and debate, handouts for student projects, and supplementary readings from journals. Course planning suggestions and ideas for term projects are also included.

Study Guide

The carefully crafted *Study Guide* by Stephanie Stolarz-Fantino, University of California, San Diego, helps students to read and retain the text material at a higher level than they are likely to achieve by reading the text alone. Each chapter includes a variety of practice tests and exercises to help integrate themes that reappear in various chapters. Each chapter also includes a review of key concepts, guided study questions, and section reviews that encourage students' active participation in learning.

Test Bank

Thoroughly revised, the *Test Bank* by S. Stavros Valenti, Hofstra University, includes approximately 60 multiple-choice and 70 fill-in, true–false, matching, and essay questions for every chapter. Each question is keyed to the textbook by topic and page number and indicates level of difficulty.

Computerized Test Bank CD-ROM

This computerized test bank CD-ROM, on dual platform for Windows and Macintosh, offers an easy-to-use test-generation system, allowing instructors to add an unlimited number of questions, select specific questions, edit or scramble questions, format a test, and include pictures, equations, and multimedia links over a secure network. The CD-ROM is also the access point for online testing, as well as Blackboard- and WebCT-formatted versions of the Test Bank.

The accompanying gradebook enables instructors to record students' grades throughout the course and includes the capacity to track student records and view detailed analyses of test items, curve tests, generate reports, add weights to grades, and more.

Online Testing and Quizzing

Online testing, powered by Diploma (www.brownstone.net), gives instructors the ability to create and administer secure exams over a network and over the Internet with questions that incorporate multimedia and interactive exercises. The program allows instructors to restrict tests to specific computers or time blocks and includes a suite of grade-book and result-analysis features.

Online quizzing, powered by Questionmark, can be accessed via the companion Web site at www.worthpublishers.com/developmentofchildren5e. Instructors can quiz students online using prewritten multiple-choice questions for each text chapter (not from the test bank). Students receive instant feedback and can take the quizzes more than once. Instructors may then view results by quiz, student, or question, and get weekly results via email.

Transparency Set

A set of 50 full-color transparencies offers key illustrations, charts, graphs, and tables from the textbook.

Companion Web Site

The *Cole/Cole/Lightfoot Companion Web Site* at www.worthpublishers.com/coledevelopmentofchildren5e offers a variety of simulations, tutorials, and study aids organized by chapter with periodic updates of new Web links, exercises, and developments in developmental psychology. In addition to the online testing, syllabus posting, and Web site building services, the *Companion Web Site* offers the following features:

- Annotated Web Links
- Chapter Outlines
- Online Quizzes

- Simulations and Demonstrations
- Frequently Asked Questions about Developmental Psychology
- Interactive Flashcards

A password-protected Instructor Site offers a full array of teaching resources, including PowerPoint slides, an online quiz gradebook, and links to additional tools such as WebCT, Blackboard, and the Image and Lecture Gallery.

Journey through Childhood Developmental Psychology Video Series

Designed for both in-class demonstration and at-home viewing, these two videos with accompanying student and instructor workbooks will enable development students to observe the activities, responses, and behaviors of children of various ages and ethnicities in a variety of naturalistic environments: school, home, day-care, and health-care settings. The videos include interviews with noted researchers and child development experts, including Patricia Greenfield, Barbara Rogoff, and Gilda Morelli. The instructor's observation guide offers teaching and activity suggestions, while the student observation guide hones observational skills and shows links between segments.

The Scientific American Frontiers Video Collection for Developmental Psychology

This renowned collection comprises seventeen video segments of approximately 15 minutes each covering topics ranging from language development to nature–nurture. The videos can be used to launch classroom lectures or to emphasize and clarify course material. The accompanying *Faculty Guide* by Richard O. Straub, University of Michigan, describes and relates each segment to specific topics in the text.

Acknowledgments

A book of this scope and complexity could not be produced without the help of others. A great many people gave generously of their time and experience to deepen our treatment of various areas of development, particularly the many scholars who consented to review drafts of our manuscript and make suggestions for improvement. The remaining imperfections exist despite their best efforts.

For the foundations laid in earlier editions, we gratefully acknowledge the help of **Curt Acredolo,** University of California, Davis; **Karen Adolph,** Carnegie Mellon University; **Margarita Azmitia,** University of California, Santa Cruz; **MaryAnn Baenninger,** Trenton State College; **Ann E. Bigelow,** St. Francis Xavier University; **Gay L. Bisanz,** University of Alberta, Edmonton; **Jeffrey Bisanz,** University of Alberta; **Kathryn N. Black,** Purdue University; **Patricia C. Broderick,** Villanova University; **Urie Bronfenbrenner,** Cornell University; **Gordon Bronson,** University of California, Berkeley; **Ann L. Brown,** University of California, Berkeley; **Michaelanthony Brown-Cheatham,** San Diego State University; **Angela Buchanan,** De Anza College; **Tara C. Callaghan,** St. Francis Xavier University; **Richard Canfield,** Cornell University; **William B. Carey,** Children's Hospital of Philadelphia; **Robbie Case,** OISE; **David B. Conner,** Northeast Missouri State University; **Andrew C. Coyne,** Ohio State University; **William E. Cross, Jr.,** Cornell University; **Frank Curcio,** Boston University; **David M. Day,** University of Toronto; **Anthony De Casper,** University of North Carolina, Greensboro; **Judy S. DeLoache,** University of Illinois at Urbana-Champaign; **Cathy Dent-Read,** University of California, Irvine; **Don Devers,**

North Virginia Community College, Annandale; **Rosanne K. Dlugosz,** Scottsdale Community College; **Rebecca Eder,** University of California, Davis; **Gregory T. Eells,** Oklahoma State University; **Peter Eimas,** Brown University; **Jeffrey W. Elias,** Texas Tech University; **Beverly Fagot,** University of Oregon; **Sylvia Farnham-Diggory,** University of Delaware; **David H. Feldman,** Tufts University; **Mark Feldmen,** Stanford University; **Kurt Fischer,** Harvard University; **Brenda K. Fleming,** Family Service Agency, Phoenix; **Herbert P. Ginsburg,** Teachers College, Columbia University; **Sam Glucksberg,** Princeton University; **Kathleen S. Gorman,** University of Vermont; **Mark Grabe,** University of North Dakota; **Steve Greene,** Princeton University; **Harold D. Grotevant,** University of Minnesota; **William S. Hall,** University of Maryland, College Park; **Paul Harris,** University of Oxford; **Janis E. Jacobs,** University of Nebraska, Lincoln; **Jeannette L. Johnson,** University of Maryland, College Park; **Daniel P. Keating,** Ontario Institute for Studies in Education; **Claire Kopp,** University of California, Los Angeles; **Gisela Labouvie-Vief,** Wayne State University; **Alan W. Lanning,** College of DuPage; **Kathleen L. Lemanek,** University of Kansas; **Jacqueline Lerner,** Michigan State University; **Elizabeth Levin,** Laurentian University; **Zella Luria,** Tufts University; **Sandra Machida,** California State University, Chico; **Jean Mandler,** University of California, San Diego; **Sarah Mangelsdorf,** University of Illinois at Urbana-Champaign; **Michael Maratsos,** University of Minnesota; **Patricia H. Miller,** University of Florida; **Shitala P. Mishra,** University of Arizona; **Joan Moyer,** Arizona State University; **Frank B. Murray,** University of Delaware; **Sharon Nelson-LeGall,** University of Pittsburgh; **Nora Newcombe,** Temple University; **Ageliki Nicolopoulou,** Smith College; **Elizabeth Pemberton,** University of Delaware; **Herbert L. Pick, Jr.,** University of Minnesota; **Ellen F. Potter,** University of South Carolina, Columbia; **David E. Powley,** University of Mobile; **Thomas M. Randall,** Rhode Island College; **LeRoy P. Richardson,** Montgomery County Community College; **Christine M. Roberts,** University of Connecticut; **Barbara Rogoff,** University of California, Santa Cruz; **Marnie Roosevelt,** Santa Monica Community College; **Karl Rosengren,** University of Illinois at Urbana-Champaign; **Carolyn Saarni,** Sonoma State University; **Arnold Sameroff,** University of Michigan; **Sylvia Scribner,** City University of New York; **Felicísima C. Seráfica,** Ohio State University; **Robert S. Siegler,** Carnegie Mellon University; **Jerome L. Singer,** Yale University; **Elizabeth Spelke,** Cornell University; **Catherine Sophion,** University of Hawaii at Manoa; **Doreen Steg,** Drexel University; **Stephanie Stolarz-Fantino,** San Diego State University; **Evelyn Thoman,** University of Connecticut; **Michael Tomasello,** Emory University; **Katherine Van Giffen,** California State University, Long Beach; **Terrie Varga,** Oklahoma State University; **Billy E. Vaughn,** California School of Professional Psychology, San Diego; **Lawrence J. Walker,** University of British Columbia; **Harriet S. Waters,** State University of New York at Stony Brook; **Nanci Weinberger,** Bryant College; **Thomas S. Weisner,** University of California, Los Angeles; **Patricia E. Worden,** California State University at San Marcos; **Phillip Sanford Zeskind,** Virginia Polytechnic University; **Patricia Zukow-Goldring,** University of California, Irvine.

    Paul Baltes (Max Planck Institute for Human Development, Berlin), **Joe Campos** (University of California, Berkeley), **Robbie Case** (Stanford University), **Carol Izard** (University of Delaware), and **Larry Nucci** (University of Illinois, Chicago) merit special thanks for providing us with valuable illustrative material and special advice for our various editions.

For the fifth edition, we thank **Farell Ackerman,** University of California, San Diego; **Jackie Adamson,** South Dakota School of Mines and Technology; **Eric Amsel,** Weber State University; **Gene Anderson,** Case Western Reserve University; **Janet Astington,** University of Toronto; **Lorraine E. Bahrick,** Florida International University; **William Barowy,** Leslie College; **Elizabeth Bates,** University of California, San Diego; **Ann C. Benjamin,** University of Massachusetts, Lowell; **Margaret S. Benson,** Pennsylvania State University, Altoona College; **Gary E. Bingham,** Washington State University; **Barry Bogin,** University of Michigan; **Chris J. Boyatzis,** Bucknell University; **Michael Casey,** College of Wooster; **Joseph Campos,** University of California, Berkeley; **Leslie Carver,** University of California, San Diego; **Mark A. Casteel,** Pennsylvania State University, York; **Michael Chandler,** University of British Columbia, Vancouver; **Cindy Clark,** Pennsylvania State University, Delaware County; **Denise Davidson,** Loyola University, Chicago; **Colette Daiute,** Graduate Center, City University of New York; **Gideon Deak,** University of California, San Diego; **Imma De Stefanis,** Manhattanville College; **Jeffrey Elman,** University of California, San Diego; **Bronwyn Fees,** Kansas State University; **Gwen Fischer,** Hiram College; **Kurt Fischer,** Harvard University; **Cheryl Fortner-Wood,** Winthrop University; **Suzanne Gaskins,** Northern Illinois University; **Mary Gauvain,** University of California, Riverside; **Rochel Gelman,** Rutgers University; **Susan Gelman,** University of Michigan; **Dale Goldhaber,** University of Vermont; **Patricia Greenfield,** University of California, Los Angeles; **Karin and Klauss Grossmann,** Bielefeld University, Germany; **Larry Harper,** University of California, Davis; **Giyoo Hatano,** University of the Air, Tokyo; **Heather Henderson,** University of Maryland; **Gail Heyman,** University of California, San Diego; **Yo Jackson,** University of Kansas; **Robert D. Kavanaugh,** Williams College; **Julie Klunk,** University of Massachusetts, Boston; **Carol Lee,** Northwestern University; **James Levin,** University of California, San Diego; **Angeline Lillard,** University of Virginia; **Shirley McGuire,** University of San Francisco; **Jack Meacham,** State University of New York, Buffalo; **Susan Goldin Meadow,** University of Chicago; **Bud Mehan,** University of California, San Diego; **Patricia H. Miller,** University of Georgia; **Scott A. Miller,** University of Florida; **Eleanor Nicholson,** Erikson Institute; **Paul C. Notaro,** University of Missouri, St. Louis; **Barbara Rogoff,** University of California, Santa Cruz; **Anne M. Sebanc,** Whittier College; **Richard A. Sebby,** Southeast Missouri State University; **Anna Sfard,** University of Haifa, Israel; **Robert Siegler,** Carnegie Mellon University; **Virginia Slaughter,** University of Queensland; **Colleen Smith,** University of Wisconsin, Madison; **James Stigler,** University of California, Los Angeles; **Joan Stiles,** University of California, San Diego; **Paula Tallal,** Rutgers University; **Esther Thelen,** University of Indiana; **Thomas L. Toleno,** Marlboro College; **Michael Tomasello,** Leipzig University, Germany; **Edward Tronick,** Harvard University; **Sandra Twardosz,** University of Tennessee; **Stavros Valenti,** Hofstra University; **Marinus van IJzendoorn,** Leiden University; **Penelope Vinden,** Clark University; **Claes von Hofsten,** Uppsala University, Sweden; **Jerina Wainwright,** Anne Arundel Community College; **Alida Westman,** Eastern Michigan University; **David Witherington,** University of New Mexico.

We are also grateful to Jennifer Ahrend, Stacey Alexander, Jessica Bayne, Mary Louise Byrd, Matthew Driskill, Tracey Kuehn, Patricia Marx, Mimi Melek, Andrea Musick, Kerry O'Shaughnessy, Anna Paganelli, Barbara Anne Seixas, Martha Solonche, Nicole Villamora, Eleanor Wedge, and Catherine Woods of Worth Publishers.

The Development of
Children

The Study of Human Development

> "*The mature person is one of the most remarkable products that any society can bring forth. He or she is a living cathedral, the handiwork of many individuals over many years.*"
> —David W. Plath, Long Engagements

Early one morning in the cold winter of 1800, a dirty, naked boy wandered into a hut at the edge of a tiny French hamlet in the province of Aveyron to beg for food. In the months before this appearance, some of the people in the area had caught glimpses of the boy digging for roots, climbing trees, swimming in a stream, running rapidly on all fours. They thought he was inhuman, a wild beast, so word spread quickly when the boy appeared in the village; everyone came to see him.

Among the curious was a government commissioner, who took the boy home and fed him. The child, who appeared to be about 12 years old, seemed ignorant of the civilized comforts that the people offered to him. When clothes were put on him, he tore them off. He would not eat meat, only raw potatoes, roots, and nuts. He rarely made a sound and seemed indifferent to human voices. The local commissioner, in his report to the government, concluded that the boy had lived alone since early childhood, "a stranger to social needs and practices. . . . [T]here is . . . something extraordinary in his behavior, which makes him seem close to the state of wild animals" (quoted in Lane, 1976, pp. 8–9).

The commissioner's report caused a public sensation when it reached Paris. Newspapers hailed the child as the "Wild Boy of Aveyron." France had recently overthrown its king and become the first country in Europe to embrace a democratic form of government. Many supporters of the new republic hoped that the boy could rapidly develop intellectually and socially to demonstrate that even the poor and outcast members of society are as capable as children of the wealthy as long as they are provided with a proper education. The Wild Boy seemed a perfect test case because his life had been so devoid of supportive human contact.

Unfortunately, plans to study the Wild Boy soon ran into trouble. The first physicians to examine him concluded that he was mentally deficient and speculated that he had been put out to die by his parents for that reason. (In France in the late eighteenth century, as many as one in three normal children and a greater percentage of abnormal children were abandoned by their parents, usually because the family was too poor to support another child (Heywood, 2001).

The doctors recommended that the boy be placed in an asylum. But a young physician, Jean-Marc Itard (1744–1838), disputed the diagnosis of retardation. Itard argued that the boy only appeared to be mentally deficient because he had been isolated from society and thereby prevented from developing normally. Itard pointed to the fact that the boy had been able to survive on his own in the forest as evidence against his being mentally impaired.

Victor, the Wild Boy of Aveyron.

Jean-Marc Itard, who tried to transform the Wild Boy into a civilized Frenchman.

Itard took personal charge of the boy. He thought that he could teach him to become fully competent, to master the French language, and to acquire the best of civilized knowledge. To test his theory that the social environment has the power to shape children's development, Itard devised an elaborate set of experimental training procedures to teach the Wild Boy how to categorize objects, to reason, and to communicate (Itard, 1801/1982).

At first, Victor, as Itard named the Wild Boy, made rapid progress. He learned to communicate simple needs as well as to recognize and write a few words. He learned to use a chamber pot. He also developed affection for the people who took care of him. But Victor never learned to speak and interact with other people normally.

After 5 years of intense work, Itard abandoned his experiment. Victor had not made enough progress to satisfy Itard's superiors, and Itard himself was unsure about how much more progress the boy could make. Victor was sent to live with a woman who was paid to care for him. He died in 1828, still referred to as the Wild Boy of Aveyron. His unusual experiences in life left unanswered the large questions about human nature, the influence of civilized society, and the degree to which individuals are shaped by one or other of these forces that scholars had hoped would be answered by his discovery.

Most physicians and scholars of the time eventually concluded that Victor had indeed been mentally defective from birth. But doubts remain to this day. Some modern scholars think that Itard may have been right in his belief that Victor was normal at birth but was stunted in his development as a result of his social isolation (Lane, 1976). When he was found, Victor had spent many of his formative years alone. He had already passed the age when most children have acquired language. Others believed that Victor suffered from autism, a pathological mental condition whose symptoms include a deficit in language and an inability to interact normally with others (Frith, 1989). It is also possible that Itard's teaching methods failed where different approaches might have succeeded. We cannot be sure.

The Study of Child Development

Although there was no scientific specialty called *developmental science* in Itard's day, interest in children and their development had already begun to grow among philosophers and social reformers as well as scientists (Hartup & Silbereisen, 2002). Eventually, the study of **child development** came to encompass the physical, cognitive, social, and emotional changes that children undergo from the moment of conception onward. The basic task of the developmental sciences is to understand how these remarkable changes come about.

The Rise of the New Discipline

Philosophical questions about the nature of children and their development played a central role in the earliest stages of the scientific study of children. These questions were soon supplemented by practical concerns about the welfare of children. Attempts to address these concerns gave rise to scientific methods for studying children and new theories of child development.

Philosophical Origins

More than a century before Itard encountered Victor, John Locke (1632–1704), an English philosopher, had proposed that infants enter the world as "blank slates" or, as he phrased it, their minds are a *tabula rasa*. He believed that in the course of experiencing their environments, the guidance of their elders shapes children's natures. Locke

child development The sequence of physical, cognitive, psychological, and social changes that children undergo as they grow older.

Children's labor provided a vital contribution to family income in many nineteenth-century households. These boys and girls, photographed in a New York apartment around 1890, made artificial flowers. If they worked steadily from early morning until late evening, they could make $1.20 per day.

strongly believed that early experiences are especially important in shaping the psychological properties children later acquire. Although Locke did not deny that children are born with different "temperaments and propensities," he insisted that instruction, begun at an early age, exerts the greatest influence. Itard's faith in his ability to civilize Victor, through carefully designing an educational regime, is traceable directly to Locke. This idea has remained central to modern theories of education, for example, the strong support shown for programs like Head Start, which seek to shape children's development well before they begin to attend elementary school.

Also influential to the developmental sciences were the ideas of Jean-Jacques Rousseau (1712–1778), an eighteenth-century French philosopher who argued that children are born "pure," with a natural goodness that is either gradually enriched through caring and careful education or is corrupted by civilization. In *Emile* (1762/1911), a book that was part novel and part treatise on education, Rousseau provided a vision of childhood and education in which the role of the caretaker is to protect the child from the pressures of adult society. Emile, who stands for *Everychild,* passes through several natural stages of development. During each stage an adult ensures that he receives educational activities that are attuned to his current developmental needs. Rousseau's ideas regarding developmental stages and developmentally appropriate education continue to influence today's child-rearing practices as well as developmental theories. They underpin the widespread belief that children's development is marked by a series of qualitatively distinct stages, and they are invoked by educators who warn that it is harmful to seek to pressure children into accomplishments for which they are not yet prepared.

Children provided essential labor in many industries well into the twentieth century. These boys worked in the coal mines of Pennsylvania in 1911. Some of them were as young as 6.

Practical Concerns about Children

During the nineteenth century, philosophical questions about children's nature and development merged with more practical issues involving their welfare. Interest in child development was spurred by the larger economic and social changes occurring in Europe, America, and many other parts of the world that became ever more pronounced in the years following Victor's death. During the nineteenth century, the industrialization of Europe and North America transformed the social organization of people's lives. Industrialization also transformed the role of children in society and the settings within which they developed. Instead of growing up on farms, where they contributed their labor and were cared for by their mothers and fathers until they reached adulthood, many children were employed in factories in sprawling cities, alongside, and sometimes in place of, their parents (Heywood, 2001).

Many children in the labor force worked long hours in factories or mines under dangerous and unhealthy conditions. As political control shifted from the landed aristocracy to the urban middle classes, these conditions became a matter of social concern and they soon sparked increased scientific activity. The Factories Inquiries Committee in England, for instance, conducted a study in 1833 to discover whether children could work 12 hours a day without suffering damage. The majority of the committee members decided that 12 hours was an acceptable workday for children. Others who thought a 10-hour workday would be preferable were concerned less with children's physical, intellectual, or emotional well-being than with their morals. They recommended that the remaining 2 hours be devoted to the children's religious and moral education (Hindman, 2002).

The Beginnings of Developmental Science

Developmentalists and physicians soon began to use the data they collected to clarify basic questions about human development and how to study it. The studies of children's growth and work capacity, for example, supported Locke's philosophical assertions that the environment affects development in measurable ways. Researchers found that because of long hours and inadequate rest and nutrition, children who worked in textile mills were shorter and weighed less than local nonworking children of corresponding ages. Surveys of intellectual growth showed wide variations in children's achievements that seemed to depend on family background and individual experience. These findings fueled the continuing scientific and social debate about the factors that are primarily responsible for development. A crucial event that spurred further interest in the scientific study of children was the publication of Charles Darwin's *Origin of Species,* in 1859. Darwin's thesis that human beings had evolved from earlier species fundamentally changed the way people thought about children. Instead of being viewed as imperfect adults to be seen and not heard, children came to be viewed as scientifically interesting because their behavior provided clues to the ways in which human beings are related to other species. It became fashionable, for example, to compare the behavior of children with the behavior of higher, nonhuman primates to see if individual children went through a "chimpanzee stage" similar to the one through which the human species was thought to have evolved (see Figure 1.1). Although such parallels between species proved oversimplified, the idea that human development must be studied as a part of human evolution won general acceptance (Bjorklund & Pellegrini, 2002).

As a result of the excitement generated by Darwin's theory of evolution, much of the early science of human development involved comparing our species with other "animal" species (which we will discuss further in the section on continuity). Scientists sought to discover how current human abilities and behaviors are

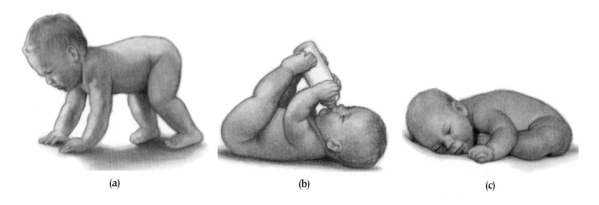

(a)   (b)   (c)

Figure 1.1 Early evolutionists scrutinized the motor development of children for evidence that it recapitulated evolutionary stages. Here an infant (a) crawls about on all fours like many animals, (b) uses its feet for grasping as primates do, and (c) sleeps in an animal-like crouch.

influenced by our evolutionary past. Wilhelm Preyer (1841–1897), a leader in comparative embryology and physiology, wrote the first textbook in child development (Preyer, 1888). He felt that fuller understanding of human development also requires the "methodical investigation" of the mind of the child. Everything should be recorded, even behaviors that seem uninteresting at the time. (See Table 1.1.)

Using his rules of observation, summarized in Table 1.1, Preyer examined the development of emotion, intention, mind, and language. He was particularly keen to establish *sequences of behavior* because he believed that they would show *how* certain behavioral patterns arose, as well as the extent to which they were organized by biological or environmental processes. For example, around 9 months of age babies become capable of pointing as a means of signaling their wants and needs to others. Preyer argued that pointing follows naturally from unsuccessful attempts to seize or grasp desired objects.

Whereas Preyer's greatest contributions to the developmental sciences were his methods of study, James Mark Baldwin (1861–1934) offered a theoretical framework that focused directly on the process of child development. Developmentalists of Preyer's day believed that adult abilities are present and fully formed in the child, just waiting "off stage" for their cue to appear. In effect, the "child mind" was defined in terms of the "adult mind." In contrast, the new, developmental perspective promoted by Baldwin reversed this logic. He believed that abilities progress through a series of specific stages that take on different forms and undergo systematic changes throughout childhood before they reach their mature state. Within the new discipline, Baldwin was the first stage theorist of note, and among the first to argue that the adult mind can be understood only in terms of the child mind that precedes it.

table 1.1

Preyer's Rules of Observation

- Rely only on direct observations; avoid the reports of "persons not practiced in scientific observing."
- Record observations immediately so that details are not forgotten.
- Make every effort to be unobtrusive, to "observe without the child's noticing the observer at all."
- Avoid any "training" of the young child in order to observe "unadulterated mental development."
- If regular observations are interrupted for more than 1 day, another observer must be substituted, and his or her observations should be checked for accuracy. (Preyer observed and recorded his child's behavior two to three times every day!)
- Everything should be recorded, even behaviors that seem uninteresting at the time.

Source: Preyer, 1890, pp. 187–188.

Ever since developmental science came to public attention, parents have relied on advice books to help them deal with the uncertainties of parenting. Shifting cultural fashions as well as new scientific knowledge have resulted in many changes in the advice parents receive. (Hulbert, 2003.)

The Norman Rockwell Museum

Late in the nineteenth century, owing in no small measure to the efforts of scholars such as Preyer and Baldwin, the study of human development became a recognized field of scientific inquiry. Special institutes and departments in universities devoted to the study of development began to spring up in major U.S. universities. Both government agencies and philanthropic foundations began to support research on child development. Specialized magazines on infant care and parenting were published and widely circulated. To this day, research on children's development continues to be motivated by twin concerns that were present at the discipline's origins. One is the scientific and philosophic interest in the question of how our biological and cultural heritages combine to determine what it means to be human. The other is the more practical concern of understanding how best to promote the health and well-being of children. Both of these motives merge in the popular idea that conducting scientific research can make the world a better place by promoting the development of our children (Hulbert, 2003).

Modern Developmental Science

Since becoming established as a discipline at the start of the twentieth century, the study of children's development has been dominated by psychologists, following in the footsteps of scholars such as Preyer and Baldwin. In recent decades, however, the study of development has become increasingly *interdisciplinary.* That is, research on development has contributed to, and profited from, the insights of a wide range of disciplines, such as anthropology, biology, linguistics, neuroscience, and sociology. Studies of development have also become increasingly *international,* reflecting a growing appreciation of the importance of cultural context in the developmental process and recognition of the increasing interaction among the world's people. As a result of the broad scope of modern studies of development, we have adopted the term *developmentalist* to describe its practitioners and the term *developmental science* to designate the discipline to which they contribute.

Not only has the scope of developmental science increased, but so have the pace and complexity of research. A rapid increase in the number of scholars who study development partly explains this change. There were only 500 members of the Society for Research in Child Development in 1960, at present there are more than 5000, and the number of new practitioners is increasing rapidly every year.

The pace and complexity of research have also been driven by important advances in technology. The ability to record children's behaviors with video cameras, to obtain images of their brain activity, and to analyze data with high-speed computers has revolutionized the way developmentalists do research. Growing concerns about the welfare of children have created new questions for researchers—questions encompassing topics such as the influence of maternal stress and nutrition on fetal brain growth, the effects of neighborhoods on family dynamics, the risks attached to medicating children who experience difficulty in school, and the special challenges facing children of immigrant families in their attempts to deal with an alien culture and unfamiliar language. The title of a recent report prepared for the National Research Council, *From Neurons to Neighborhoods,* captures the breadth of contemporary developmental science.

In addition to their roles as researchers looking for answers to these complex questions, developmentalists are often practitioners who work to promote the healthy development of children. They work in hospitals, child-care centers, schools, recreational facilities, and clinics. They assess children's developmental status and prescribe procedures for assisting children who are in difficulty. They design special environments, such as cribs that allow premature babies to develop normally outside the womb. They devise therapies for children who have difficulty controlling their tempers, and they develop techniques for teaching children how to read more effectively (Lerner et al., 2003).

As you read about the research, methods, and practical applications of developmental science, it is essential to keep in mind the general goal of developmental inquiry: to assemble the facts into larger patterns, called **theories.** A theory is a framework of ideas or body of principles that can be used to guide the collection and interpretation of a set of facts in order to increase our understanding of human nature and its development as a whole.

theory A broad framework or set of principles that can be used to guide the collection and interpretation of a set of facts.

The Central Questions of Developmental Science

Despite great variety in the work they do, and in the theories that guide their research, developmentalists share an interest in four fundamental questions about the process of development:

1. *Continuity.* Is development a gradual, continuous process of change, or is it punctuated by periods of rapid change and the sudden emergence of new forms of thought and behavior? The question of continuity applies to changes within the lifetime of a single person and to comparisons between humans and other species.

2. *Sources of development.* What are the contributions of genetic heredity and the environment to the process of developmental change, and how do they interact?

3. *Plasticity.* To what extent and under what conditions is it possible for the course of development to change, as the result of either deliberate intervention or accidental experience?

4. *Individual differences.* No two human beings are exactly alike. How does a person come to have stable individual characteristics that make him or her different from all other people?

As researchers and practitioners, developmentalists are strongly committed to exploring these questions. The answers provide insight into principles of development, as well as guidelines for how to promote development.

Questions about Continuity

Developmentalists ask two basic questions about continuity: (1) How similar are the principles of development in humans to those in other species? In other words, how much continuity is there between human beings and other animal life? (2) To what extent is individual development continuous, consisting of the gradual accumulation of small quantitative changes, and to what extent is development discontinuous, involving a series of qualitative transformations as we grow older?

Karen Huntt Mason/Corbis

These two individuals are watching a ladybug make its way along a leaf. Chimpanzees and human beings share more than 99 percent of their genetic material. Although similar in many ways, the differences between the two species are enormous.

Is Human Development Distinctive?

For centuries people have debated the extent to which humans differ from other creatures and the extent to which we are subject to the same natural laws as other forms of life. The study of human uniqueness focuses on **phylogeny,** the evolutionary history of a species. When Charles Darwin (1809–1882) published *Origin of Species,* the idea of evolution was already a subject of widespread speculation. Darwin was a firm believer in continuity among species. He saw evolution as a process of small, accumulating changes. As he put it, the difference between humans and our near evolutionary neighbors is "one of degree, not of kind" (Darwin, 1859/1958, p. 107).

To test Darwin's claim that our species evolved continuously as a part of the natural order, scientists have searched for evidence of *evolutionary links*—intermediate forms that connect us with other forms of life—and have compared our genetic makeup and behavior with those of other organisms. On the side of continuity between ourselves and other animals, it has been established that we share at least 99 percent of our genetic material with chimpanzees (Marks, 2002). There is also abundant evidence regarding behavioral similarities between humans and a variety of species—ranging from chimpanzees to wolves. For example, like many other animal species, we play, we communicate with each other, and we develop relatively stable social hierarchies. Even our facial expressions show remarkable continuity with the facial expressions of nonhuman primates (de Waal, 2001).

Despite the obvious similarities, it is nevertheless clear that there is something distinctive about our species. The difficult question is, What is that something?

Two general phenomena have long been associated with human distinctiveness. First, humans develop in a unique environment that has been shaped by countless earlier generations of people in their struggle for survival (Bruner, 1996; Cole, 1999). This special environment consists of *artifacts* (such as tools, clothing, words), *knowledge* about how to construct and use those artifacts, *beliefs* about the world, and *values* (ideas about what is worthwhile, right, and wrong) (Kagan, 2001), all of which guide adults' interactions with the physical world and with each other and their children. Anthropologists call this accumulation of artifacts, knowledge, beliefs, and values, **culture.** Culture is the "man-made" part of the environment that greets all human beings at birth (Herskovitz, 1948) and provides each developing individual with a "design for living" that he or she acquires from the community (Kluckhohn & Kelly, 1945).

Second, humans shape and pass on their culture to succeeding generations largely through their use of language. It is not surprising, then, that since antiquity, language has been proposed as a defining characteristic of our species. In the seventeenth century the philosopher René Descartes stated the traditional view eloquently:

> Language is in effect the sole sure sign of latent thought in the body; all men use it, even those who are dull or deranged, who are missing a tongue, or who lack the voice organs, but no animal can use it, and this is why it is permissible to take language as the true difference between man and beast. (Quoted in Lane, 1976, p. 23)

Even Charles Darwin, who believed strongly in the continuity of species, agreed that our distinctiveness, insofar as humans are distinct, is the result of our capacity to communicate through language. In recent years, scientists have demonstrated that chimpanzees and other primates have rudiments of culture and language (Bekoff & Colin, 2002). However, as we shall see in later chapters, the capacities for using culture and language, considered as an ensemble, are far greater in humans than in other species. Nonhuman primates in their natural habitats rarely, if ever, show objects to each other or bring others to locations to observe things there. Nor do they intentionally teach others (Tomasello, 1999).

phylogeny The evolutionary history of a species.

culture A people's design for living as encoded in their language and seen in the physical artifacts, beliefs, values, customs, and activities that have been passed down from one generation to the next.

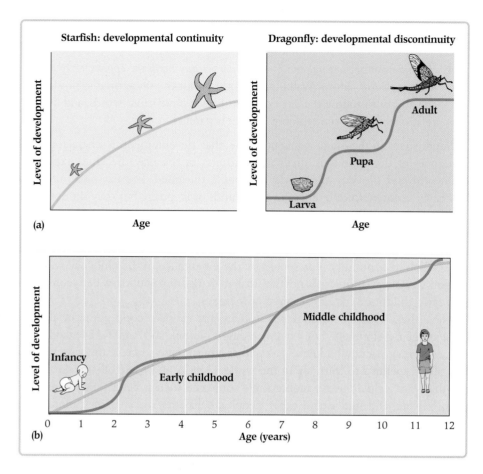

Figure 1.2 (a) The contrasting courses of development of starfish and insects provide idealized examples of continuous and discontinuous development. In the continuity view, development is a process of gradual growth (small starfish, medium-size starfish, large starfish). In the discontinuity view, development is a series of stagelike transformations (larva, pupa, adult). (b) Human development includes elements of both continuity and discontinuity.

Is Individual Development Continuous?

The second major question about continuity concerns **ontogeny,** the development of an individual organism during its lifetime. As a rule, developmentalists who believe that ontogeny is primarily a process of continuous, gradual accumulation of small changes emphasize *quantitative* change, such as growth in the number of brain cells, in vocabulary, or in memory capacity. Those who view ontogeny as a process punctuated by abrupt, discontinuous changes emphasize the emergence of *qualitative change.* Qualitative change is seen in the emergence of new patterns of behavior at specific points in development, such as the change from babbling to talking or from crawling to walking. Qualitatively new patterns that emerge during development are referred to as **developmental stages.** The contrast between the continuity and discontinuity views is illustrated in Figure 1.2.

The psychologist John Flavell (1971) suggests four criteria that are central to the concept of a developmental stage:

1. *Stages of development are distinguished by qualitative changes.* The change in motor activity associated with the transition from crawling to walking upright illustrates what is meant by a qualitative change to a new stage of development. Walking does not arise from the perfection of the movements used to crawl. Rather, the child undergoes a total reorganization of movement, using different muscles in different combinations.

2. *The transition from one stage to the next is marked by simultaneous changes in a great many, if not all, aspects of a child's behavior.* The transition from crawling to walking is accompanied by a new quality of emotional attachment between children and their caregivers as well as the new forms of child–caregiver relations that the child's greater mobility requires.

ontogeny The development of an individual organism during its lifetime.

developmental stage A qualitatively distinctive, coherent pattern of behavior that emerges during the course of development.

3. *When the change from one stage to the next occurs, it is rapid.* The transition from crawling to walking typically takes place within the space of about 90 days.

4. *The numerous behavioral and physical changes that mark the appearance of a stage form a coherent pattern.* Walking occurs at about the same time as pointing, the ability to follow the gaze of another, the child's first words, and a new relationship between children and their parents.

Supporters of the stage concept argue that development is characterized by sequences of discontinuous, qualitative changes in the way the child experiences the world and the way the world influences the child. For example, infants are especially sensitive to differences in the sounds of language but they do not understand what is being said (Karmiloff & Karmiloff-Smith, 2001). Once they begin to understand and produce language themselves, the way they learn about the world appears to change fundamentally, and so does the nature of their interaction with others. The discontinuity represented by the emergence of the child's active participation in conversation is so notable that it marks the boundary between infancy and early childhood in a great range of societies.

Nevertheless, some developmentalists deny that the stage concept is crucial for understanding development. For example, Allison Gopnik and Andrew Meltzoff believe that even very young childrenn—as well as adults—use some of the same methods that allow scientists to learn about the world. Gopnik and Meltzoff argue, for example, that young children use unobservable constructs such as beliefs and desires to explain, predict, and understand other people's behaviors and that they modify their theories when their predictions are incorrect (Gopnik, Meltzoff & Kuhl, 1999). In a similar spirit, Elizabeth Spelke and her colleagues have argued that "infants perceive fundamentally the same world as adults" (Condry, Smith & Spelke, 2000).

During most of the twentieth century, stage theories of development have been more numerous and more influential than continuity theories. Yet stage theories are confronted with a variety of facts that appear to violate one or more of the criteria for developmental stages proposed by Flavell.

One acute problem for modern stage theories is that, contrary to their depiction of qualitatively consistent, across-the-board shifts in behavior and thinking, children often appear to be in one stage on one occasion and in a different stage on another. According to one influential stage theory of cognitive development, for example, 4-year-olds are in a stage in which their thinking is largely egocentric, making it very difficult for them to see anything from a point of view other than their own. And, in fact, 4-year-olds frequently do seem limited to their own perspective—they often fail to appreciate that someone looking at an object from a location different from their own may not see the object as they themselves see it or that someone who has just returned to the room doesn't know, as they do, what has transpired while he or she was gone. Yet when they are talking to a 2-year-old, they usually simplify their speech, apparently taking the younger child's perspective and realizing that he or she might otherwise have difficulty understanding them. The fact that at a given point in development a child can exhibit behaviors associated with different stages seems to undercut the idea that being in a particular stage defines the child's general capabilities and psychological makeup.

Questions about the Sources of Development

The second major question that preoccupies developmentalists is the way in which genetically directed biological factors interact with environmental factors to influence development. This issue is often posed as a debate about the relative importance of "nature" and "nurture." **Nature** refers to the inherited biological predispositions of the individual; **nurture** refers to the influences of the social and cultural environment on the individual, particularly those of the family and the community.

nature The inherited biological predispositions of the individual.

nurture The influences of the social and cultural environment on the individual.

Much of the argument about Victor, the Wild Boy of Aveyron, was about the relative influences of nature and nurture: Was Victor incapable of speech and other behaviors normal for a boy his age because of a defective biological endowment (nature) or because of inadequate nurturing?

The extent to which development is linked to nature or nurture can have far-reaching effects on the way society treats children. If, for example, it is assumed that girls, by *nature,* lack interest and ability in mathematics and science, they are not likely to be encouraged by their parents, teachers, and other members of society to become mathematicians or scientists. If, on the other hand, it is assumed that mathematical and scientific talent are largely a result of *nurture,* a society may train girls and boys equally in these activities.

Modern developmentalists emphasize that we cannot adequately describe development by considering nature and nurture in isolation from each other because the organism and its environment constitute a single life process (Gottlieb, 2002). Nevertheless, as you shall see, debates about the relative roles of genetic inheritance and experience as sources of development have by no means ceased to preoccupy developmental science.

Questions about Plasticity

The third major question follows from the second and concerns **plasticity**—the degree to which, and the conditions under which, development is open to change and intervention. Early ideas about plasticity were influenced by researchers who identified certain "critical periods" in several nonhuman species. A **critical period** is a period of growth—in some cases only a few hours long—during which specific environmental or biological events *must* occur if development is to proceed normally. For example, certain birds that can walk at birth run the risk of being separated from their mothers. It is therefore important for the chicks to have a critical period just after hatching during which they become attached to the first moving object they see, which is usually their mother. Thereafter, they follow the object wherever it goes. If the chicks are prevented from seeing any moving object for a certain number of hours after hatching, they fail to become attached to anything at all and may wander around alone. As you can imagine, lost chicks have little chance for survival (see Figure 1.3) (Izawa, Yanagihara, Atsumi & Matsushima, 2001).

Examples of "all-or-nothing" critical periods in any species are rare. In our own species they tend to be limited to fetal development. For example, during a specific period in prenatal development, the presence or absence of certain hormones will determine whether the fetus becomes male or female. Although evidence that specific experiences actually *induce* specific developments is rather thin, there is abundant evidence pointing to periods of plasticity during which development can be *facilitated* through certain experiences (Gottlieb, 2002). For example, in order for children to develop normal language abilities, it is essential that they be exposed to language during childhood, but there is no specific period during childhood in which language input is known to be essential. Children seem to be most sensitive to language input in the first few years of life, but even if they are not regularly exposed to language until the age of 6 or 7, it appears that they are still capable of acquiring it. Thereafter, the risk of failing to acquire language increases (Newport, Bavelier & Neville, 2001). For this reason, the periods of plasticity are often called *sensitive periods* rather than critical periods. **Sensitive periods** are defined as times in an organism's development when a particular experience (or lack of it) has a more pronounced effect on the organism than does exposure to that same experience at another time (Bruer, 2001).

plasticity The degree to which, and the conditions under which, development is open to change and intervention.

critical period A period during which specific biological or environmental events are required for normal development to occur.

sensitive period A time in an organism's development when a particular experience has an especially profound effect.

Figure 1.3 Ethologist Konrad Lorenz proposed the existence of a critical period in the development of newly hatched geese during which they form an attachment to the first moving thing they see. These goslings, which were allowed to see Lorenz rather than an adult goose when they hatched, follow him in the water as he swims.

Nina Leen, *Life Magazine* ©Time Inc.

Sensitive periods may not be limited to development that involves biological readiness. Yasuko Minoura (1992) reports the existence of a "cultural sensitive period." She found that Japanese children who had resided in the United States for the 4 years between the ages of 9 and 13 had great difficulty reincorporating themselves into Japanese society when they returned to their native land as teenagers. They had learned and accepted an American way of thinking and feeling that made the Japanese way of interacting and thinking seem strange. For example, the returnees reported that they found it difficult to hide their feelings, which made them unpopular with the Japanese children they met. The same was not true of younger children who had spent an equal amount of time in the United States but returned to Japan before they were 11 years old. The younger children's reentry into Japanese culture, while not trouble-free, was rapid and thorough.

Questions about Individual Differences

In some respects, you are like all other people, like some other people, and like no other person. You are like all humans because we are all members of the same species; you are like some people but not others insofar as you share important biological characteristics (males are like each other and different from females) or cultural characteristics (Australian Aborigines are alike in comparison with the Inuit people of North America); and you are psychologically and physically unique. As you shall see in Chapter 2 (p. 50), even identical twins, who have exactly the same genetic constitutions, are not alike in every respect.

Two questions about individual differences must be taken into account in trying to understand the nature of development: (1) What makes individuals different from one another, and (2) to what extent are individual characteristics stable over time?

The question of what makes individuals different from one another is really another form of the question about the sources of development: Are we different from one another primarily because of our nature or because of our nurture? If baby Sam is unusually fussy, is it because he inherited a tendency to be easily upset or because his parents continually overstimulate him? If baby Soon-Jae becomes an accomplished pianist, is it because she inherited musical talent from her parents or because she grows up in a family that values and promotes the development of musical skills? Although powerful statistical techniques and ingenious methods of data collection have been used in an effort to tease apart the fundamental sources of variation among individuals, disagreements of theory and fact remain (Emde & Hewitt, 2001; Joseph, 2001).

Insofar as individual characteristics are innate and stable, they provide a glimpse of what children will be like in the future. If baby Sam is innately fussy, perhaps he will be an irritable child. If baby Georgia has inherited a low metabolism rate, maybe she will be overweight as a teenager.

Determining the extent to which the past provides a guide to the future is a major task facing developmentalists, so the idea that some of our psychological characteristics remain stable over extended periods of time is an appealing one. Parents sometimes remark that their children have been friendly or shy since infancy. However, demonstrating such stability scientifically—at least from an early age—has proved difficult. The problem is that measures that seem appropriate for assessing psychological traits such as memory or affability during infancy are not likely to be appropriate for assessing the same traits in an 8-year-old or in a teenager. Perhaps for this reason, many studies have observed only moderate stability of psychological traits in childhood (Caspi & Roberts, 2001). Nevertheless, some investigators do find moderately stable individual differences in a number of psychological characteristics. There is evidence, for example, that children who were shy and uncertain at 21 months of age are still likely to be timid and cautious at age 12 or later and that infants who rapidly processed visual information at 7 months of age display rapid perceptual processing when tested at the age of 11 years (Emde & Hewitt, 2001).

The stability of children's psychological characteristics over time depends on stability in their environment in addition to any stability that might be attributed to their genetic makeup. Studies have found that children who remain in an orphanage that provides only minimal care from infancy through adolescence are lethargic and unintelligent. But if they are given extra, stimulating care by the orphanage staff or if they are adopted into caring families, their condition improves markedly, and many of them become intellectually normal adults (Clarke & Clarke, 2000).

The Discipline of Developmental Science

There are two broad approaches to the study of human development. One is to seek out intimate knowledge of specific individuals and their biographies. The other is to focus on identifying and understanding characteristics common to groups of people—to all 4-year-olds, or girls, or Europeans, or Asians, or Native Americans, for example.

The difference between these two ways of knowing is a source of constant tension in scientific attempts to understand development (Valsiner & van der Veer, 2000). It is also an ongoing source of difficulty in bringing together the two roles of developmentalist as researcher and developmentalist as practitioner. The more developmentalists want to know about individuals, the more they need to know about each person's life history and current circumstances. But the more they concentrate on unique histories and patterns of influence, the less they can generalize their findings to other individuals. Uncertainties about how to draw correct conclusions concerning the relationship between general trends and individual cases occur across the broad spectrum of methods that psychologists use in their research.

The Goals of Scientific Description

Whether dealing with an individual or a group of children, developmentalists, like any other scientists, begin their research with particular goals in mind. The goals can range widely. Some seem "purely scientific"—for example, the desire to know whether the ability to perceive depth is inborn or learned. Other goals, however, are inspired by more practical considerations, such as how to assess the effectiveness of different kinds of violence prevention programs in schools.

It is helpful to consider three categories of research that differ according to the particular goals that motivate the researcher.

The goal of *basic research* is to advance basic, scientific knowledge of human development. Although the results of basic research might be used to help solve practical problems, it is often undertaken simply to satisfy a thirst for new knowledge. Basic research often explores major theoretical issues, such as questions of developmental continuity, plasticity, and the sources of development. Scientists engaged in basic research go to great lengths to control the variables and conditions affecting the process they are studying. However, absolute precision and control are difficult, and sometimes impossible, to achieve. (It is impossible, for example, to control the entire language environments of different groups of children in a precise manner to determine how language input influences language development.)

Applied research is designed to answer practical questions that arise in the course of trying to improve children's lives and experiences. In many cases, it also borrows from and extends our basic scientific knowledge. The primary

Margaret Beale Spencer conducts basic research on how contextual factors such as minority group status, poverty, and neighborhood dangers influence the learning attitudes of African American youth. She then seeks out the coping mechanisms that such youth develop in order to improve their attitudes and subsequent success in important learning activities.

Chris Hondros/Getty Images

Figure 1.4 Sallie Motch is a psychologist with Doctors Without Borders, an organization that recently won the Nobel Peace Prize. She addresses mental stress and trauma issues with Palestinian youths in the area of Hebron in the West Bank. Developmentalists like Motch engage in action research to help government and other organizations develop scientifically based programs that protect children from harm and promote their well-being.

goal, however, is to benefit society by generating knowledge that can be put to use in solving specific problems. Because applied research addresses issues that arise within the complexities of "real-life" circumstances, it is often unable to achieve the same degree of experimental control and precision that is characteristic of basic research.

Action research is a close cousin of applied research. Also known as *mission-oriented research,* action research is designed primarily to provide data that can be used in social policy decision making (Denzin & Lincoln, 2000). Examples include the Head Start program, various federal regulations regarding educational services for children with special needs, standards for the safety of toys, requirements for foster care, and legislation concerning how to prosecute minors who have committed crimes. In contrast to basic and applied research, whose intended audience usually includes scientists and other developmental practitioners, action research is often meant to sway the opinions of nonscientist legislators and government officials (see Figure 1.4).

In recent years, action research has captured a lot of attention from developmentalists. To some extent, this attention is due to an increasing commitment and sense of social obligation on the part of universities to better recognize and serve the needs of their communities (Greenwood & Levin, 2000). Universities and communities across the nation are forging partnerships around specific local issues. For example, the University of California at San Diego has created a charter school both to assist children from poor families that have never had access to higher education and to understand instructional formats that are most helpful to these children (Jones et al., 2002).

While it can be helpful to categorize research into the three different types, it is important to recognize that the boundaries between basic, applied, and action research cannot be sharply drawn. For example, research on the effectiveness of Head Start programs is *basic* in the sense of addressing questions of plasticity, *applied* in the sense of being motivated to improve the lives of socially disadvantaged children, and *action-oriented* in its implications for social policy decisions to continue funding programs and program development.

Criteria of Scientific Description

Whether engaged in basic, applied, or action research, developmentalists usually begin their work with common-sense observation and speculation. In this respect, they are not unlike anyone else who might be thinking about or offering opinions on some interesting or puzzling aspect of children's behavior. Unlike laypersons, however, developmental researchers go beyond opinion and speculation to test their ideas according to specific scientific criteria.

A moment's reflection will underscore how important it is to separate opinion and casual observation from scientific evidence. You may remember all the media attention — the TV talk shows, documentaries, and newspaper articles — devoted to adolescent problem behavior that followed in the wake of the Columbine school shooting in 2001. This concern arose in spite of a wealth of poorly publicized scientific evidence documenting marked *decreases* in adolescent problem behavior at the time (U.S. Department of Health and Human Services, 1999). Another example of how opinion can be disconnected from scientific evidence in ways that are potentially harmful to children comes from the mass media's depiction of the relationship between aggressive behavior and exposure to media violence. This relationship has been the focus of much public and scientific discussion. Looking at historical trends, Brad Bushman and Craig Anderson (2001) compared scientific reports and news reports about the effect of media violence on aggressive behavior. Their analysis shows that between 1980 and 2000, while the scientific community continued to amass increasingly *stronger* evidence indicating that exposure to violent media creates significant risk for the development of aggressive behavior, the media described the link as increasingly *weaker* and were less likely over time to urge parents to protect their children from exposure.

The relationship between social science and society is complex, and it raises a host of issues for developmentalists that you will encounter in the chapters to come. For now, it is important to understand how to recognize scientific evidence and how to separate it from speculation and casual observation. Four of the most common criteria used to judge scientific research are *objectivity, reliability, replicability,* and *validity.*

To be useful in constructing a disciplined account of human development, data should be collected and analyzed with **objectivity;** that is, the results should not be biased by the investigators' preconceptions. Total objectivity is impossible to achieve in practice because all human beings—developmentalists included—come to the study of human beings with beliefs that influence how they interpret what they see. But objectivity remains an important ideal toward which to strive.

The second criterion, **reliability,** refers to the consistency of the research findings. Research data should exhibit the property of reliability in two senses. First, investigators should be able to obtain the same results each time they collect data under a specific set of conditions. Second, independent observers should be able to agree in their descriptions of the results. Suppose that one wants to know how upset infants become when a pacifier is taken from them while they are sucking on it (Goldsmith & Campos, 1982). Statements about the degree of an infant's distress are considered reliable in the first sense if the level of distress (measured in terms of crying or thrashing about) is found to be the same on successive occasions when the baby's sucking is interrupted in a carefully controlled setting. The statements are considered reliable in the second sense if independent observers agree on how distressed the baby becomes each time the pacifier is taken away.

Replicability, the third criterion, means that other researchers can independently create the same procedures as an initial investigator did and then obtain the same results. In studies of newborns' ability to imitate, for example, some researchers report that newborns will imitate certain exaggerated facial expressions that they see another person making directly in front of them. However, using the same methods, other investigators have failed to find evidence of such imitation in newborns (see Chapter 4, p. 131). Only if the same finding, under the same conditions, is obtained repeatedly by different investigators is it likely to be considered firmly established by the scientific community.

Of all the criteria of scientific description, the fourth, **validity,** is in certain respects the most important. Validity means that the data being collected actually reflect the phenomenon that the researcher claims to be studying. A study may meet all the other criteria of being objective, reliable, and replicable but still may not meet the condition of validity, in which case it is of no value. Imagine, for example, a study of infant intelligence. The researchers may be using a particular scale to measure intelligence that is not biased by the researcher's preconceptions (it is objective), that produces the same results when given under similar conditions or when scored by different raters (it is reliable), and that can be used by other researchers to yield the same results (it is replicable). However, imagine that the scale used to measure intelligence measures the hair color on the baby's head. Obviously, if hair color is used as a measure of intelligence, then the study lacks validity and has no meaning, even though the other scientific criteria have been met.

objectivity The requirement that scientific knowledge not be distorted by the investigator's preconceptions.

reliability The scientific requirement that when the same behavior is measured on two or more occasions by the same or different observers, the measurements be consistent with each other.

replicability The scientific requirement that other researchers can use the same procedures as an initial investigator did and obtain the same results.

validity The scientific requirement that the data being collected actually reflect the phenomenon being studied.

triangulation When two or more methods are combined to confirm conclusions about factors causing a particular behavior.

naturalistic observation Observation of the actual behavior of people in the course of their everyday lives.

ethology An interdisciplinary science that studies the biological and evolutionary foundations of behavior.

ethnography The study of the cultural organization of behavior.

Methods of Data Collection

Over the past century, developmentalists have refined a variety of methods for gathering information about the development of children. Among the most widely used are naturalistic observations, experiments, and clinical interviews. No single method can answer every question about human development. Each has a strategic role to play, depending on the topic and the goal of the researcher. Often researchers use a process called **triangulation,** in which two or more methods are combined, to confirm their conclusions.

Naturalistic Observation

The most direct way to gather objective information about children is to study them through **naturalistic observation,** that is, to watch them in the course of their everyday lives and record what happens.

Naturalistic observation is a major research tool in the field of **ethology,** an interdisciplinary science that studies the biological, evolutionary foundations of behavior (Archer, 1992; Tonneau & Thompson, 2000). Ethologists place great emphasis on naturalistic observation because they believe that biologically important behaviors affecting human development are best studied in the settings that are significant to people's daily lives (Savin-Williams, 2001; Tonneau & Thompson, 2000).

For example, F. Francis Strayer and A. J. Santos (1996) carried out naturalistic observations in this tradition when they studied the way children interact in preschool classrooms. By observing and recording who interacted with whom and the nature of the interactions, Strayer and Santos discovered that social hierarchies develop spontaneously in preschool classes much as they do in certain other species of social animals. Once developed, these social hierarchies regulate the interactions that children engage in with each other and can serve to reduce aggression.

Naturalistic observation is also favored in **ethnography,** the study of the cultural organization of behavior. In the hands of developmentalists, ethnographic descriptions provide detailed knowledge of the ways that children's experiences are organized by parents and communities, as well as the many ways that children respond to such organization. For example, researchers have documented how young infants born to the Efe foragers of the Congo's Ituri forest are routinely cared for by several people and are likely to be nursed by several women. This pattern, which seems so at odds with Western ideas about child rearing, is essential to the Efe's foraging way of life and is accepted by Efe children as a matter of course (Ivey, 2000).

Naturalistic observations can be confined to a single context or can be employed to gather data in many contexts. The latter type of observational strategy is often used to study a child's *ecology,* a term derived from the Greek word for "house." In the

DOONESBURY By Garry Trudeau

Cartoonist Gary Trudeau comments on the phenomenon, established in observational research, that teachers respond differently to boys and girls in their classrooms.

biological sciences, the "house" is the habitat of a population of plants or animals, and the ecology of that population is the pattern of its relationship with its environment. In the case of human development, **ecology** has come to refer to the range of situations in which people act (see Figure 1.5) (Bronfenbrenner & Morris, 1998).

Charles Super and Sarah Harkness (2002), who have studied children's development in several countries, emphasize the links between children's development and the community within which they are born. They refer to the child's place within the community as a **developmental niche,** which can be analyzed in terms of three components: (1) the physical and social context in which the child lives, (2) the culturally determined child-rearing and educational practices of the child's society, and (3) the psychological characteristics of the child's parents. Thorough descriptions of children's real-life experiences in their sociocultural contexts provide a sense of the whole child and the many influences that act on children. Such descriptions can tell us what opportunities and difficulties children face in their lives and how circumstances might be changed to foster children's development.

Probably the most ambitious study of the ecology of human development ever to be undertaken was conducted by Roger Barker and Herbert Wright (1951, 1955). These researchers spent hundreds of hours observing and describing the natural ecology of schoolchildren in various communities in the United States and abroad. In one such study, they observed a 7-year-old American boy named Raymond from the time he awoke on April 26, 1949, until he went to sleep that night. Barker and Wright found that in this single day Raymond participated in approximately 1300 distinct activities in a wide variety of settings involving hundreds of objects and dozens of people.

For a variety of practical reasons, few ecological studies approach the scope of Barker and Wright's. Most investigators who study children across a range of

ecology The range of situations in which people are actors, the roles they play, the predicaments they encounter, and the consequences of those encounters.

developmental niche The physical and social context in which a child lives, including the child-rearing and educational practices of the society and the psychological characteristics of the parents.

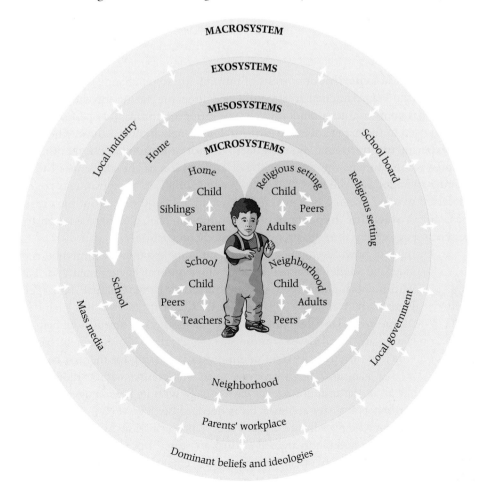

Figure 1.5 The ecological approach sees children in the context of all the various settings they inhabit on a daily basis (microsystems). These settings are related to one another in a variety of ways (mesosystems), which are in turn linked to settings and social institutions where the children are not present but which have an important influence on their development (exosystems). All of these systems are organized in terms of the culture's dominant beliefs and ideologies (the macrosystem).

In many parts of the world, including this Mexican community, children begin to take an active role in daily chores at a very early age. This little girl is learning how to sort tomatillos.

contexts are forced to be more selective about the behaviors observed and the contexts of children's behavior. For example, in a study of the role of play in the lives of young Mayan children of different ages living in a remote farming village in southeastern Mexico, Susan Gaskins (1999) made "spot observations," recording what the children were doing at different times of the day in order to make sure that she captured the full range of children's activities. She found that compared with children living in the United States, young rural Mayan children spend a great deal of time observing the routine activities of the adults and begin to take an active role in daily chores at an early age by gathering wood, hauling water, and assisting in the preparation of food. As a result, Mayan children spend considerably less time engaged in pretend play, which is perhaps the dominant activity of young children in industrialized societies.

As is true for all methods of data collection, there are limitations involved in observational research. You may recall that Wilhelm Preyer anticipated many of the potential pitfalls of using observational methods and designed his rules of observation to circumvent them (see Table 1.1, p. 5). Nevertheless, it has been demonstrated that when people know they are being watched, they often behave differently than they normally would (Hoff-Ginsberg & Tardiff, 1995). In addition, despite our best intentions to be objective, as observers we enter the scene with expectations about what we are going to see and we tend to observe selectively in accordance with those expectations. An observer cannot write down everything, so some information is inevitably lost. In some studies, prearranged note-taking schemes specify what to look for and how to report it. Recordings of behavior on videotape or film are useful, but they are extremely time-consuming to analyze. Nevertheless, observational studies are a keystone of child development research and a crucial source of data about children's development.

Experiments

A psychological **experiment** consists of introducing some change in a person's experience (the "experimental treatment") and then measuring any effect that the change has compared to a randomly chosen group of comparable people who are not exposed to the experimental treatment. Differences between those who receive the experimental treatment and those who do not provide evidence that the treatment was the cause of the difference. (For a discussion of the challenges to determining causation, see the box "Correlation and Causation.") Experiments are often preferred in basic research designed to test scientific hypotheses about the causes of behavior. A **scientific hypothesis** is an assumption that is precise enough to be tested as true or false through properly planned comparisons.

An example of how developmentalists can apply the experimental method is provided by studies that seek to determine optimal environments for babies who are born prematurely or with low birth weight (Charpak, Ruiz-Pelaez, Figueroa de Calume & Charpak, 2001). One hypothesis is that such babies, if kept in skin-to-skin contact with their mothers (a practice dubbed "kangaroo care") will develop more successfully than babies kept in bassinets, which is currently the most common way of caring for them. A baby who receives kangaroo care is kept in skin-to-skin contact with its mother virtually all of the time for several days, usually with its head snuggled between her breasts for easy access to breast-feeding (see Figure 1.6). Kangaroo care has gained especially widespread acceptance in regions where sophisticated incubators and highly trained nursing are scarce. But is it really effective?

Early research documented marked changes in newborns' breathing and heartbeats when they were moved from bassinets to kangaroo care and back again, using a *pneumogram,* a special device to record heart and

Figure 1.6 Keeping newborn babies in constant skin-to-skin contact with their mothers for several days after birth has proved to be an effective way to help low-birthweight babies survive.

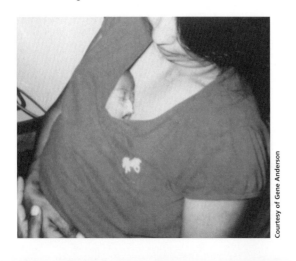

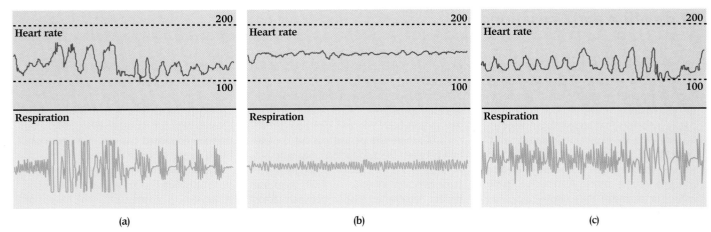

Figure 1.7 (a) The pneumogram of a newborn in a bassinet during the pre-kangaroo care period. Note the frequent episodes of low heart rate and some crying (rapid high amplitude respiration traces) followed by periodic breathing. (b) Pneumogram of the same infant during kangaroo care time. Note how regular the heartbeat and respiration are and that the heart rate is consistently well above 100. (c) Pneumogram of the same infant back in the bassinet during post-kangaroo care. Heart rate and respiration are similar to those in (a). (From Anderson, 1995.)

lung function. The pneumograms shown in Figure 1.7 depict changes in the heart and lung function of the same infant in different conditions. Note that both breathing and heart rate are irregular in the bassinet, then become stable during kangaroo care, and become unstable again when the infant is moved back to the bassinet. These data suggest that kangaroo care might promote children's overall well-being; however, proper experimental demonstration comparing children who were assigned at random to receive regular or kangaroo care would be required to document that kangaroo care is the *cause* of the long-term benefits.

In a formal experimental test of the benefits of kangaroo care, Nathalie Charpak and her colleagues (Charpak et al., 2001) compared children who received kangaroo care with those receiving traditional care in a Colombian hospital serving primarily poor and working-class mothers. A total of 746 babies born at less than or equal to 2000 grams, or 4.5 pounds, were divided at random into one of two groups (approximately 3200 grams, or 7 pounds, is the expected weight for a healthy full-term baby; babies weighing less than 2500, or 5.5 pounds, at birth are considered low birth weight). One group was designated as the **experimental group**—the group in an experiment whose environment is changed. In this study, infants in the experimental group received kangaroo care. The other infants were assigned to the **control group**—the group in an experiment that is as similar as possible to the experimental group but does not receive the experimental manipulation. In the study of kangaroo care, infants in the control group received traditional care, which meant being placed in a bassinet in warm, sanitary conditions.

In the short term, the babies assigned to the control group showed more irregular breathing and were slower to master breast-feeding compared to babies in the experimental group, who received kangaroo care. In the long term, the control-group babies showed significantly longer hospital stays, greater likelihood of illness or death, and slower growth rates. They were also slower than the experimental group to reach important developmental milestones, such as raising the head spontaneously while lying on the stomach. At present kangaroo care is used in many countries around the world, including the United States (Kirsten, Bergman & Hann, 2001).

The clear strength of the experimental method is its unique ability to isolate causal factors. However, experiments also have limitations. A major drawback to experimental research is that the very control of the environment that the experiments require may distort the validity of the results obtained. As we noted earlier, sometimes people behave differently in an artificial, experimental situation than they would normally. Children are particularly likely to behave unnaturally in an unfamiliar laboratory setting with researchers they have never met before. This, of course, raises doubts about the value of experimental results. Indeed, this problem is so pervasive that psychologist Urie Bronfenbrenner (1979) has described typical laboratory experiments involving children as studies of "the strange behavior of children in

experiment In psychology, research in which a change is introduced in a person's experience and the effect of that change is measured.

scientific hypothesis An assumption that is precise enough to be tested as true or false through properly planned comparison.

experimental group The persons in an experiment whose experience is changed as part of the experiment.

control group The group in an experiment that is treated as much as possible like the experimental group except that it does not participate in the experimental manipulation.

Correlation and Causation

In their attempts to identify the specific factors that influence a particular aspect of development, researchers often begin by determining if there is a correlation between factors that appear to be associated with the development in question. A **correlation** is said to exist between two factors when changes in one are related to changes in the other. As children grow older, for example, they display increased ability to remember lists of words; that is, children's age is correlated with their ability to remember. Similarly, the higher the social class of parents, the greater the achievement of their children in school; that is, school achievement is correlated with social class. Correlations such as these can provide hints about **causation,** which is indicated when the occurence of one event depends upon the occurence of a prior event. Despite their importance, correlations fall short of specifying actual causation.

The first step in determining the possible importance of a correlation is to establish its strength. To do this, researchers use a *correlation coefficient* (symbolized as *r*), which provides a quantitative index of the degree of association between two factors. A correlation coefficient enables developmentalists to distinguish between relationships that occur with significant regularity and those that occur by chance.

A correlation coefficient that describes the relationship between factor X and factor Y can vary in both size and direction. When $r = 1.00$, there is a perfect positive correlation between the two factors, meaning that as factor X changes, factor Y changes in the same direction. When $r = -1.00$, there is a perfect negative correlation between factor X and factor Y, meaning that as factor X changes, factor Y changes in the opposite direction. If every increase in age in a population were accompanied by an increase in weight, for example, the correlation between age and weight would be 1.00. If, instead, people always lost weight as they aged, the correlation would be −1.00. If age and weight were not related at all, the correlation would be .00. Intermediate positive or negative values of a coefficient of correlation indicate intermediate levels of association. For example, there is a correlation of approximately .50 between the heights of parents and their offspring, indicating that tall parents tend to have tall offspring (Tanner, 1990). A correlation may point to a causal relationship between two events, but, as noted above, correlation is not the same as causation. That is, correlation does not establish that the occurrence of one event causes the occurrence of the other. In some cases it may be just as likely that factor X is caused by factor Y as it is that factor X is causing factor Y. In other cases, it may be that the correlated changes in X and Y are being caused by some third factor.

The difficulty of distinguishing correlation from causation is often a source of scientific controversy. In a case such as the heights of parents and their children, the problem is not serious. The child's height obviously does not cause the height of the parents. Nor is confusion likely to arise about the relationship between a child's age and his or her weight. Age by itself cannot cause increases in weight because *age* is simply another term for the time that has elapsed since an agreed-upon starting point; and, certainly, weight cannot cause an increase in age. Other cases are less clear-cut. Among schoolchildren, for example, a correlation of about .30 has been found between height and scores on tests of mental ability; that is, taller children tend to score higher on intelligence tests than do their shorter peers (Tanner, 1990). Since nothing about children's height can plausibly be said to be a cause of their intelligence, and nothing about children's intelligence can be said to cause their

---

strange situations with strange adults for the briefest possible periods of time" (p. 19). An experiment is said to lack **ecological validity** when it creates an artificial setting that diverges so completely from children's natural environment that children behave differently than they would ordinarily, so the results cannot be put to proper use.

Clinical Interviews

The research methods discussed thus far are designed to apply uniform procedures of data collection to every individual observed. In this respect, clinical interview methods differ fundamentally from the others. The essence of the **clinical method** is to tailor questions to the individual subject. Each question depends on the answer to the one that precedes it, allowing the researcher to follow up on any given question, verify his or her understanding of the subject's responses, and probe more deeply into the subject's thoughts and feelings.

Through his extensive development and use of the clinical interview, Jean Piaget laid a foundation for an entirely new way of understanding the intellectual development of the child. His goal was to provide an account of how children's thinking becomes reorganized over time. In one of his early studies, he used a clinical interview procedure to focus on children's understanding of the idea of "thinking." In the examples that follow, note that it would have been impossible for Piaget to anticipate exactly how the children would respond. Therefore, he adapted his questions to the flow of the conversation.

ecological validity The extent to which behavior studied in one environment (such as a psychological test) is characteristic of behavior exhibited by the same person in a range of other environments.

clinical method A research method in which questions are tailored to the individual, with each question depending on the answer to the preceding one.

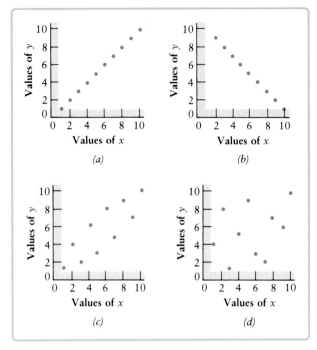

(a) *(b)* *(c)* *(d)*

Four possible relationships between two variables: (a) As values of *x* increase, values of *y* increase, producing a correlation of 1.00. (b) As values of *x* increase, values of *y* decrease, producing a correlation of -1.00. (c) As values of *x* increase, values of *y* often increase, but there are some exceptions, producing a correlation of .84. (d) As values of *x* increase, values of *y* show a weak but noticeable tendency to increase, producing a correlation of .33.

to conclude that intelligence causes school achievement. Although that explanation fits many people's notions about school achievement, it can just as plausibly be argued that students who get good grades do so by working hard and learning more, thereby boosting their IQ scores.

The use of correlation coefficients to describe relationships among phenomena is important in the study of human development because so many of the factors of interest to developmentalists (such as social class, ethnic origin, and genetic constitution) cannot be controlled experimentally. Because correlations often suggest causal relationships but do not provide crucial evidence of causation, controversies that have no clear resolution may arise, requiring developmentalists to exercise caution in interpreting their data.

correlation The condition that exists between two factors when changes in one factor are associated with changes in the other.

causation When the occurrence of one event depends upon the occurrence of a prior event.

heights, some other factor (such as nutrition, for example) must be the cause of both.

The slipperiest cases are those in which the possible cause-and-effect relationship between two variables could plausibly work in either direction. For example, there is a correlation of .50 between children's current grades in school and their scores on standard IQ tests (Minton & Schneider, 1980). On the basis of this association, it might be tempting

7-YEAR-OLD
Piaget: . . . You know what it means to think?
Child: Yes.
Piaget: Then think of your house. What do you think with?
Child: With the mouth.

(Adapted from Piaget, 1929/1979, p. 39)

11-YEAR-OLD
Piaget: Where is thought?
Child: In the head.
Piaget: If someone opened your head, would he see your thought?
Child: No.
[At this point Piaget changes his line of questioning to get at the child's conception of thinking from a different direction.]
Piaget: What is a dream?
Child: It's a thought.
Piaget: What do you dream with?
Child: With the head.
Piaget: Are the eyes open or shut?
Child: Shut.
Piaget: Where is the dream whilst you are dreaming?
Child: In the head.
Piaget: Not in front of you?
Child: It's as if (!) you could see it.

(From Piaget, 1929/1979, p. 54)

Jean Piaget, whose work has had a profound influence on developmental psychology.

Piaget's probing interviews of these children revealed two age-related patterns of understanding what thinking is. For the younger child, thinking is a bodily process—the act of speaking. You can see it happening. In contrast, the older child conceives of thinking as something invisible and unobservable, a mental process. Piaget used such data to argue for the existence of a stagelike developmental change in the way children understand and experience the world. He believed that about the age of 10 to 11 is when children first become able to think about thinking as a mental process that cannot be seen. Therefore, younger children should be unable to think about mental states as internal processes, even if they are given explicit hints, as below:

5-YEAR-OLD
Piaget: When you are in bed and you dream, where is the dream?
Child: In my bed, under the blanket.
Piaget: Is the dream there when you sleep?
Child: Yes, it is in my bed beside me.
[Piaget writes: "We tried suggestion:"] Is the dream in your head?
[The child explicitly rejects the possibility]: It is I that am in the dream: it isn't in my head.

(From Piaget, 1929/1979, p. 97)

The strong point of clinical interviews is that they provide insight into the dynamics of individual development. Every person interviewed provides a distinctive pattern of responses that corresponds to his or her individual experiences. But the clinical interview method has its limitations. First, to arrive at general conclusions on the interview topic, the clinician must ignore individual differences across interviews in order to distill the general pattern. But as the general pattern appears, the individual picture disappears. Second, because the method relies heavily on verbal expression, it is inappropriate for use with very young children, who have difficulty expressing themselves fully or precisely. This is especially the case in trying to assess children's cognitive abilities, since young children often understand things well before they can explain their understanding.

research design The overall plan describing how a study is put together; it is developed before conducting research.

longitudinal design A research design in which data are gathered about the same group of children as they grow older over an extended period of time.

cross-sectional design A research design in which children of various ages are studied at the same time.

microgenetic design A research method in which children's development is studied intensively over a relatively short period of time.

Research Designs

Before conducting research, developmentalists must not only select a method of data collection but develop an overall plan. This plan, referred to as the **research design,** describes how the study is put together. A wide range of designs is used in the social sciences, although developmentalists tend to favor those that is best suited to studying change over time—that is, how change is brought about at different ages.

Although you will be introduced to a few other research designs in later chapters, we will describe here the three most basic designs that developmentalists use—longitudinal, cross-sectional, and microgenetic. Each design takes the passage of time into account in a distinctive way.

The researcher who uses the **longitudinal design** collects information about a group of children as they grow older over an extended span of time. The researcher

High-Tech Research on Brain Development and Disorders

In the not so distant past, the only way to examine the brain was to surgically remove it from the patient's skull. Neuroscientists have been conducting postmortem research for more than a century in an effort to discover how the brain is designed, how the brain changes as we grow and age, and how it responds to injury. Although this research has generated a wealth of information on the anatomy of the brain, it is limited in at least two ways. First, although postmortem research can reveal data about brain *structure* or anatomy, it cannot provide insight on living brain *functions*. Second, because of the time lag between observing a person's behavior and examining his or her brain after death, interpreting the link between brain and behavior is necessarily fraught with uncertainty (Damasio, 1999).

Although autopsy specimens continue to provide significant information about the brain and its role in human behavior and development, neuroscientists have benefit-ed from the development of several other research technologies (Nelson & Bloom, 1997). Among the high-tech methods, *magnetic resonance imaging (MRI)* has captured the most attention. MRI techniques allow scientists to see neural structures in living patients. The procedure involves a magnetic resonance scan that provides input to a computer program. The computer uses the data to construct a three-dimensional image of the brain. The MRI procedure has paved the way for important advances in understanding the development and functions of neural structures (Sowell et al., 2002). It has also cleared a path for the early diagnosis and risk estimation of certain disorders, such as attention deficit hyperactivity disorder (ADHD) and childhood psychosis (Kumra et al., 2000; Rapoport et al., 2001).

More recent technologies have enabled neuroscientists to track actual changes in brain activity under different experimental or disease conditions. Positron emission

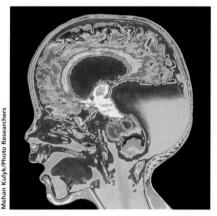

This brain scan of an 11-month-old child clearly reveals a large kidney-shaped cyst (the large red area) in the center of the baby's cerebral cortex. Seeing the cyst helps developmentalists to pinpoint its location and size and determine if surrounding brain structures are injured. This information is then used to assist them in devising a plan for treating the child.

tomography (PET) scans, as well as functional magnetic resonance imaging (fMRI) scans, are used to test hypotheses about links between brain functioning and behavior. Other ways of tracking the ebb and flow of neural activity include electrical conductance response, which is measured through the skin, and electrical potentials and magnetic fields, measured through the scalp (Damasio, 1999).

Interest in neuroscience rose so sharply in the 1990s that the era has been described as the "Decade of the Brain" (Thompson & Nelson, 2001). The discoveries of that period, emerging from the use of high-tech methods and equipment, have provided fascinating insights into the brain, its development, and its disorders, from infancy to adolescence (Tager-Flusberg, 1999). Despite these great strides in observing the living brain, our knowledge of treatment remains limited, as does our understanding of the complex relationships between mind, brain, and behavior (Trevarthen, 2001).

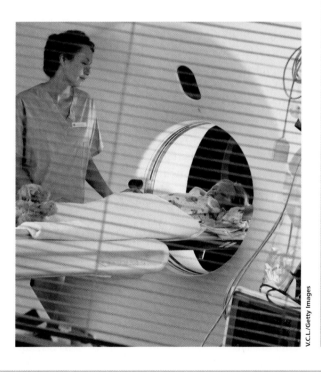

Even adults find it frightening to be inside a tunnel-shaped magnetic resonance imaging (MRI) machine where they must lie perfectly still for as long as 30 minutes. Developmentalists have worked to make the experience as comfortable as possible—in this case by allowing the child to see its parents, who are just outside the room.

who uses the **cross-sectional design** collects information about children of various ages at one time. The **microgenetic design** requires that the researcher study children's development intensely over short periods of time. These designs can be used in conjunction with each other and with any of the techniques of data collection just discussed. Each design has its own advantages and disadvantages (see Table 1.2, p. 24).

table 1.2

Research Techniques and Designs		
	Advantages	**Disadvantages**
Technique		
Naturalistic observation	Reveals full complexity of behavior and its ecology	Difficult to establish causal relations
Experiment	Best method of testing causal hypotheses	Sometimes impossible for ethical reasons Artificial procedures may distort validity of results
Clinical interview	Focuses on dynamics of individual development	Difficult to generalize beyond unique case or to establish causal relations
Design		
Longitudinal	Traces development as a process occurring over time	Repeat testing may invalidate results Costly and difficult to use Results may be confounded with historical time
Microgenetic	Observes process of change over short periods of time	Results may not be generalizable to developmental change over longer time periods
Cross-sectional	Takes relatively little time to administer Reveals age trends	Loses sense of continuity in development Findings are vulnerable to confounding with variables other than age

Longitudinal Designs

Researchers who choose a longitudinal design select a representative sample of the population they want to study and gather data from each person at two or more ages. For example, Jerome Kagan (2001) led a research team at Harvard University that traced the behavior of a group of children from shortly after birth into early adolescence. This study provided the evidence, mentioned earlier, that children who are shy and uncertain at 21 months are likely to be timid and cautious at 12 to 14 years. Without longitudinal measurements, it would be impossible to discover if there is continuity in behavior patterns as children grow older. Other influential longitudinal studies have focused on such varied topics as personality, mental health, temperament and intelligence, language development, and social adjustment (Cairns & Cairns, 1994; Emde & Hewitt, 2001; Fenson et al., 1994).

Longitudinal designs would seem to be an ideal way to study development because they fit the requirement that development be studied over time. Unfortunately, longitudinal research designs have some practical and methodological drawbacks that have restricted their use. To begin with, they are expensive to carry out and require the researcher's long-term commitment to an uncertain venture. In addition, some parents refuse to allow their children to participate in a lengthy study or may move from one location to another making it difficult for the researcher to stay in touch with them for later assessments. If such difficulties are more frequent in one social, economic, or ethnic group than in others, they may make the sample unrepresentative of the study population as a whole. Longitudinal studies frequently experience *selective dropout,* in which people who are lost from the longitudinal project differ in some significant way from those who continue to participate. Selective dropout creates a biased sample that can greatly reduce the validity of longitudinal work.

Another threat to the validity of longitudinal designs is that the people in the sample may become used to the various testing and interviewing procedures. In other

Longitudinal designs follow the same persons through the years as they age.

words, they may learn how to respond as expected. As a consequence, it is difficult to know whether changes in a person's responses over time represent normal development or simply the effect of practice in taking the tests and responding to interviews.

Finally, longitudinal designs sometimes confound (mix together) the influence of age-related changes and the influence of factors related specifically to the sample group's cohort. A **cohort** is a group of persons born about the same time who are therefore likely to share certain experiences that differ from those of people born earlier or later. In longitudinal research, differences that appear to be related to differences in age may actually arise because of differences in cohort. Consider, for example, a longitudinal study of the development of children's fears from birth onward that began in London in 1932. In their early years, the children in this study would have been living through the Great Depression. At the age of 9 or 10, many of these children would have lost one or both parents in World War II, and many others would have been sent away from their parents to the countryside in an effort to keep them safe from nightly bombings of the city. If the results of such a study indicated that the children's fears centered on hunger in their first years and that later, around the age of 9, they began to fear that they would lose their parents, it would not be possible to determine whether the observed age trends reflected general laws of development, true at any time and in any place, or whether they were the result of growing up in a particular time and place, or both (Elder, 1998).

Resources permitting, researchers can use various means to overcome these shortcomings. Some have used a **cohort sequential design,** in which the longitudinal method is replicated with several cohorts, each of which is studied longitudinally. This modification of the longitudinal design allows age-related factors in developmental change to be separated from cohort-related factors.

Cross-Sectional Designs

The most widely used developmental research design is called the *cross-sectional design* because groups representing several different ages are studied at a single time. To study the development of memory, for example, one might first test samples of 4-year-olds, 10-year-olds, 20-year-olds, and 60-year-olds to see how well they remember a list of familiar words. By comparing how people in the four age groups go about the task and what the results of their efforts are, one could then form hypotheses about developmental changes in memory processes. (Figure 1.8 on p. 26 compares longitudinal and cross-sectional research designs.) In fact, researchers have carried out a great many cross-sectional studies of memory development demonstrating both quantitative and qualitative developmental changes that we will examine in later chapters (Schneider & Bjorklund, 1998).

cohort A group of persons born about the same time who are therefore likely to share certain experiences.

cohort sequential design An experimental design in which the longitudinal method is replicated with several cohorts.

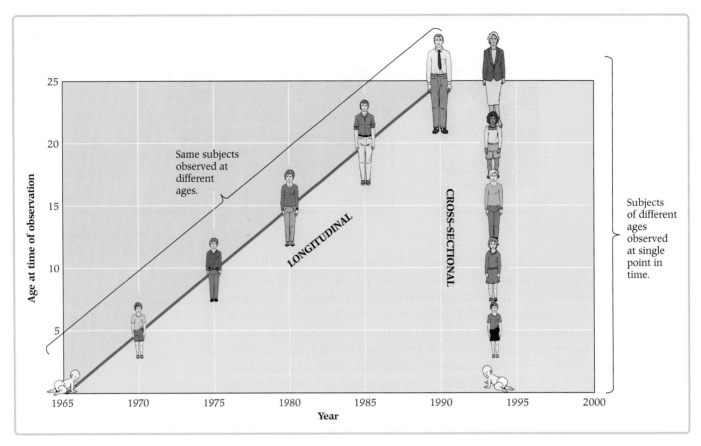

Figure 1.8 The difference between longitudinal and cross-sectional research designs.

The advantages of the cross-sectional design are readily apparent. Because it samples several age levels at once, this design is less time-consuming and less expensive than a longitudinal approach. The short time commitment required of the participants also makes it more likely that a representative sample will be recruited and that few participants will drop out of the study.

Despite these attractive features, cross-sectional designs also have drawbacks. In order to be properly conducted, such studies need to ensure that all relevant factors other than age are kept constant. That is, the makeup of all the age groups should be the same in terms of sex, ethnicity, amount of education, socioeconomic status, and so on. However, like longitudinal designs, cross-sectional designs can confound age-related changes and characteristics particular to a specific cohort. Suppose that a study of memory development was conducted in 2000. Suppose further that the study showed that the 70-year-olds performed significantly more poorly than the 20-year-olds. These results might reflect a universal tendency for memory to decline with age. But the difference might also be caused by differences in childhood nutrition, which has been shown to affect intellectual development (Pollitt, 2001). The 70-year-olds are also likely to have received less education than the 20-year-olds and to have been out of school for a long time; both education and practice have been shown to increase performance on memory tests (Rogoff, 2003). The possible presence of such confounding cohort effects means that great care must be taken when interpreting cross-sectional studies.

A second difficulty with cross-sectional designs is that by sampling the behavior of different-age people at one time, they inappropriately slice up the ongoing process of development into a series of disconnected snapshots. While such a design may be used to contrast the general ways in which 4- and 10-year-olds remember a list of words, for example, it cannot take into account the developmental process by which memory abilities and strategies change over time because it doesn't follow the same children over time. Therefore, cross-sectional designs are not able to address the continuity of development within individuals. Moreover, because cross-sectional designs cannot assess developmental change directly, when theorists formulate hypotheses about development on the basis of cross-sectional designs, they must engage in a good deal of extrapolation and guesswork about processes of change.

Microgenetic Designs

A common concern with both longitudinal and cross-sectional designs is that they do not provide direct evidence about the process of developmental change. To try to get closer to observing change processes, developmentalists sometimes use microgenetic designs, which focus on children's development over relatively short periods of time, sometimes only a few hours or days (Schlagmueller & Schneider, 2002; Vygotsky, 1978). As a rule, microgenetic designs are used with children who are thought to be on the threshold of a significant developmental change such as the ability to use a new memory strategy or to add numbers such as 6 + 2 by counting up from 6 instead of starting at 1 and counting all the way to 8. If children are provided concentrated experience in figuring out the right way to deal with a complex developmental challenge, it becomes possible for them to develop more sophisticated forms of behavior right before the observer's eyes.

Robert Siegler (1996) offers a useful analogy for understanding how microgenetic methods differ from studies that sample children's behavior at intervals of months or years. Standard methods, he writes, provide us with discontinuous snapshots of development. By contrast, microgenetic designs provide us with a movie, a more or less continuous record of change. In later chapters we will encounter specific examples of what can be learned about children's development through microgenetic designs.

Ethical Standards

In conducting worthwhile research, developmentalists make a number of important decisions. Should the study be cross-sectional or longitudinal? Should it be observational, experimental, or microgenetic? Who should be included? Children from different ethnic groups? Children from different family structures? Children from different socioeconomic backgrounds? Answers to these questions will impact the types of conclusions that can be drawn from the study and influence its potential contribution to developmental science.

John B. Watson and Rosalie Rayner conducted early experiments in which they induced fear in infants, which they subsequently sought to eliminate through learning. Such research, because it puts the infant at risk should the experimenters fail to extinguish the infant's fears, are no longer considered ethically acceptable.

Today research is evaluated not only for its scientific merit but also for its ethical soundness. Worldwide, many universities and governmental agencies that conduct research with human subjects have institutional review boards (IRBs) that are responsible for evaluating and overseeing the ethical soundness of research practices at their institutions. This wasn't always the case. Until fairly recently such decisions were left to the judgment and conscience of the individual scientist.

In no small part, the development of uniform ethical standards was prompted by the revelation of horrific experiments conducted in concentration camps by Nazi German physicians. In the name of science, thousands of Jewish, Polish, Russian, and Gypsy prisoners were forced to participate in medical experiments, most of which resulted in permanent disability or death. After the war, an international council convened in Nuremberg, Germany. Known as the *Nuremberg Tribunal,* the council brought to trial and eventually sentenced 16 German doctors for crimes against humanity.

The Nuremberg Code, the first formal, international standard for evaluating the ethics of research involving human subjects, was developed after the verdict. Since then, numerous guidelines have been developed at the international, national, state, and institutional levels. Most of the ethical guidelines share a few fundamental concerns:

- *Freedom from harm.* Above all, scientists need to ensure that their participants will not be harmed through their involvement in research. The Nuremberg Code was developed as a response to harm inflicted in medical studies. Much of the harm was of a physical nature and easy to detect. But what about psychological harm? This is more difficult to identify. Typically, two questions are asked to ascertain the potential psychological harm of any study:

  1. Does the research expose participants to experiences that are significantly different from those they encounter in their daily lives?

  2. If there are psychological effects, is it likely that they will disappear once the study is concluded, or are more lasting, even permanent effects possible?

- *Informed consent.* Participants must agree to be in the study. They must be given a reasonable understanding of what their participation entails, and it must be voluntary, meaning that they have not been forced, coerced, or offered inappropriate incentives (e.g., offering money to low-income participants or higher grades to students). When the participants are young children, "informed" consent becomes more difficult because they rarely understand complicated research procedures. With child participants, parental consent is usually required, as well as consent from other child advocates, such as school officials.

- *Confidentiality.* The information obtained must be kept confidential, that is, confined to scientific uses and not made publicly available in a way that might embarrass or harm the participant. Often, investigators will assign a code number to the participant for record-keeping purposes. This ensures the participant's anonymity. However, the investigator may uncover some serious problem that threatens the well-being of the participant, such as when a child reports abuse or seems suicidal. Under such circumstances, the higher ethic of the participant's welfare requires that the researcher break confidentiality and inform authorities who are in a position to intervene and protect the child.

Freedom from harm, informed consent, and confidentiality are not accomplished easily. This is particularly true in the case of children. For example, what may be psychologically harmful for a 2-year-old is quite different from what may be harmful for a 12-year-old. In recognition of the unique issues involved in conducting research with child participants, a special set of ethical standards has been devised by the Society for Research in Child Development (see *www.srcd.org*). Institutional review boards in the United States use these guidelines to determine the ethical soundness of all research on children conducted at their universities or agencies.

The Role of Theory

While there is general consensus among developmentalists about appropriate methods and ethical standards for research, there is less agreement about how to interpret research results. Contrary to widely held belief, facts do not "speak for themselves." The facts that developmental psychologists collect help us understand development only when they are brought together and interpreted in terms of a theory, a framework of ideas or body of principles that can be used to guide the collection and interpretation of a set of facts. Like heredity and environment, facts and theories go together. Neither comes "first"; they arise and exist together.

To draw upon an example to which we return in Chapter 11 (p. 415), people from two cultures may observe a little boy running around a preschool classroom, hitting the other children and grabbing toys away from them. They may agree that he is behaving inappropriately but interpret the same facts in very different ways. Developmentalists (as well as parents) from Japan and the United States hold different theories of what causes children to misbehave. These theories get them to notice and emphasize different aspects of the same behavior. Where an American teacher (or developmental scientist) is likely to see uncontrolled aggression, a Japanese observer is likely to see a child who has failed to develop a proper sense of how he is dependent on others for his well-being. Their different theories and the data they focus on to evaluate those theories lead, in turn, to different prescriptions about how to deal with this behavior.

Albert Einstein pointed out that theory is silently present even when we think that we are "objectively observing the world." Observation of the world may be useful, he said, "but on principle, it is quite wrong to try founding a theory on observable magnitudes alone. In reality the very opposite occurs. It is the theory which decides what we can observe" (quoted in Sameroff, 1983, p. 243).

Einstein's point applies to developmentalists' attempts to understand the human world just as forcefully as it applies to investigations of the physical world. A deeper understanding of human development will not automatically come from the continuous accumulation of facts. Rather, it will come through new attempts to make sense of the accumulating evidence on development in the light of a relevant theory.

At the present time, there is no single broad theoretical perspective that unifies the entire body of relevant scientific knowledge on human development. Instead, the field is approached from several theoretical perspectives. These perspectives can be grouped into four broad frameworks, according to the basic answers they give to the four central questions of development cited earlier: (1) Is the process of developmental change continuous or discontinuous? (2) What are the relative contributions of nature and nurture to development? (3) To what extent is development open to change and intervention? (4) What accounts for individual differences? Throughout this book we refer to these four broad frameworks as the biological-maturation, the environmental-learning, the constructivist, and the cultural-context frameworks (see Figure 1.9, p. 30).

Each of the broad frameworks encompasses many specific theories that focus on particular aspects of human development. They all provide distinctive, valuable ways of looking at the overall process of development. What follows below is only a brief overview of the four frameworks. In subsequent chapters we will return to them to explore what they can tell us about particular aspects of developmental change.

Figure 1.9 Four frameworks for interpreting the influence of nature and nurture. In the first three frameworks, biological and environmental factors directly interact with each other to shape the individual. In the fourth, the cultural-context framework, biological inheritance, and universal features of the environment act indirectly through the medium of culture.

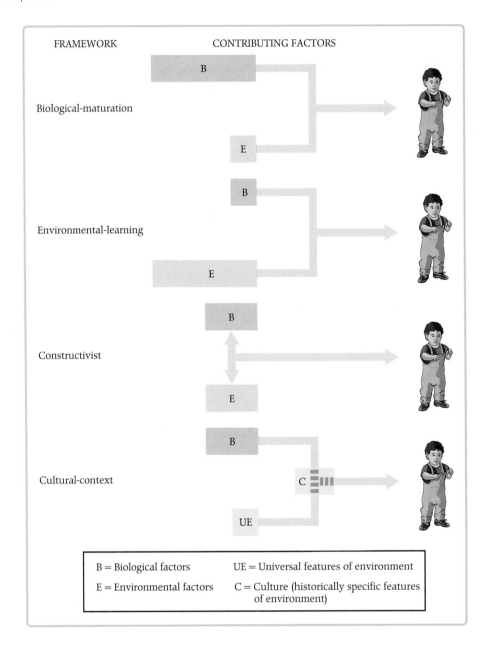

FRAMEWORK   CONTRIBUTING FACTORS

Biological-maturation

Environmental-learning

Constructivist

Cultural-context

B = Biological factors   UE = Universal features of environment

E = Environmental factors   C = Culture (historically specific features of environment)

The Biological-Maturation Framework

All the theories within the biological-maturation framework share a central view that the source of changes that characterize human development is **endogenous;** that is, change arises from inside the organism as a consequence of the organism's biological heritage. The major cause of development from this viewpoint is **maturation,** a sequence of changes that are strongly influenced by genetic inheritence and that occur as individuals age from their immature starting point at conception to full adulthood. In this view, the role of the environment is secondary in influencing the basic course of development. The biological-maturation view was clearly expressed by Arnold Gesell (1880–1961), one of the most influential developmentalists of the early twentieth century:

> Environment . . . determines the occasion, the intensity, and the correlation of many aspects of behavior, but it does not engender the basic progressions of behavior development. These are determined by inherent, maturational mechanisms. (1940, p. 13)

Among biological-maturation theorists, Sigmund Freud (1856–1939) was the first to emphasize the centrality of emotional life to the formation and function

endogenous The term applied to causes of development that arise as a consequence of the organism's biological heritage.

maturation A sequence of changes that are strongly influenced by genetic inheritance and that occur as individuals grow older.

Arnold Gesell testing a child in the observation room at the Yale Child Study Center.

Herb Gehr, *Life Magazine* ©Time Inc.

of human personality. He developed a *psychodynamic theory* of development, rooted in the idea that biological instincts generate a dynamic energy that stimulates behavior, as well as development, through a sequence of stages. When he considered the process of individual development, however, Freud, like Gesell, accorded some role to the environment. "The constitutional factor," he wrote, "must await experiences before it can make itself felt" (Freud, 1905/1953a, p. 239). In other words, the basic human drives are biologically determined, but the social environment directs the way these drives will be satisfied, thereby shaping individual personalities. Erik Erikson, another psychodynamic theorist (and student of Freud), placed a much greater emphasis on the role of culture in the process of developmental change. The differences between their two approaches are highlighted in the box "Psychodynamic Theory: Freud and Erikson" (p. 32).

The biological-maturation perspective on human development fell out of favor in the middle of the twentieth century, but in recent decades it has enjoyed renewed attention. The study of *evolutionary developmental psychology* has yielded evidence of ways in which the evolutionary past continues to influence individual development (Hernandez Blasi & Bjorklund, 2003). For example, certain evolutionary pressures have resulted in a situation where human females have a larger investment in supporting their offspring. This places females in the position of needing to inhibit aggressive impulses when their infants behave in unpleasant ways. Researchers have also shown that human females from early childhood onward are more successful than males at inhibiting aggressive responses, delaying gratification of their desires, and controlling emotional expression. The resurgence of biological-maturation theorizing has also been advanced by the development of sophisticated technologies and research methods that permit more direct measurements of biological processes (see the box "High-Tech Research on Brain Development and Disorders," p. 23).

The Environmental-Learning Framework

Theories that fall into the environmental-learning perspective do not deny that biological factors provide a basic foundation for development, but they argue that the major causes of developmental change are **exogenous;** that is, they come from the environment, particularly from the adults who shape children's behavior and beliefs by the way they reward and punish children's actions. According to theories in this

exogenous The term applied to causes of development that come from the environment, particularly from the adults who shape children's behavior and beliefs.

Psychodynamic Theory: Freud and Erikson

Psychodynamic theory claims a particularly significant place in the history of the developmental sciences. One of its unique contributions has been to show how universal developmental processes and stages can be understood by exploring the specific life experiences of particular individuals. First developed by Sigmund Freud, psychodynamic theory has been adopted and modified by numerous developmentalists, including Freud's own daughter, Anna. The best-known innovator of Freud's original theory is probably Erik Erikson, who infused traditional psychodynamic theory with his own view of how culture, in addition to biology, shapes the path of development.

Trained as a neurologist, Freud (1856–1939) sought to create a theory of personality that would enable him to cure the patients who came to him with such symptoms as extreme fear, emotional trauma, and an inability to cope with everyday life. Although many of these symptoms appeared similar to neurological disorders, Freud found that he could best understand his patients' problems by tracing their symptoms back to traumatic, unresolved experiences in early childhood.

On the basis of his clinical data, Freud constructed a general theory of development that gave primacy to the manner in which children satisfy their basic drives—the drives that act to guarantee survival. Influenced by Charles Darwin's theory of evolution, Freud reasoned that whatever their significance for individual adaptation, all biological drives have but a single goal: the survival and propagation of the species. Since reproduction, the necessary condition for the continuation of the species, is accomplished through sexual intercourse, it followed for Freud that all biological drives must ultimately serve the fundamental sex drive.

Although Freud believed that gratification remains sexual in nature throughout life, the forms of that gratification change. Sexual gratification passes through an orderly series of stages defined in terms of the parts of the body that people use to satisfy their drives. Human beings strive to satisfy the drives that dominate the stage they are in at the moment. The drives that define each stage of development are identified and described in the table below. Note that these stages end in adolescence, with the advent of adult sexuality and the potential for reproduction.

Freud (1920/1955) held that the way children experience the conflicts they encounter in each of the early stages of development determines their later personality. He also believed that from childhood onward the personality is made up of three mental structures: the id, the ego, and the superego (we will return to a discussion of these structures in Chapter 10). These three structures are rarely, if ever, in perfect equilibrium. The constant battle between them is the engine of developmental change, which Freud spoke of as *ego development*. The patterns of individual behavior that arise in this process constitute the personality.

Freud's theory of infantile sexuality provoked outrage when he proposed it, and it has remained controversial to this day. Freud is certainly vulnerable to criticism on both methodological and theoretical grounds, yet he remains one of the most influential forces in contemporary developmental theorizing for

several reasons (Miller, 2002). First, he was among the most influential champions of the view that understanding adult personality must rely on a developmental analysis. Second, he emphasized the need to arrive at scientific generalization through intensive study of individual human beings. Third, he was among the first psychologists to point out and study the complex dynamics between unconscious motives and conscious understanding, between fantasy and reality. Finally, he insisted that a human being is a complex, dynamic creature who can only be understood by study of the person as a whole.

Although few contemporary developmentalists adhere to the original psychodynamic theory devised by Freud, you will see in later chapters that many of Freud's basic ideas are still relevant to understanding gender differences and self-control (Chapter 10) and adolescent "storm and stress" and sexual development (Chapter 15).

In contrast to Freud's medical background, Erik Erikson (1902–1994) combined experience in art, teaching, psychoanalysis, and anthropology. While Erikson built on many of Freud's basic ideas of development, including the importance of early childhood in the formation of personality, the existence of the

Sigmund Freud.

Erik Erikson.

learning The process by which an organism's behavior is modified as a result of experience.

framework, **learning,** defined as the process by which an organism's behavior is modified by experience, is the major mechanism of development. John B. Watson (1878–1958), an early learning theorist, was so certain of the prime role of learning in human development that he boasted:

Freud's Psychosexual Stages and Erikson's Psychosocial Stages Compared

Approximate Age	Freud (Psychosexual)	Erikson (Psychosocial)
First year	*Oral stage* The mouth is the focus of pleasurable sensations as the baby sucks and bites.	*Trust versus mistrust* Infants learn to trust others to care for their basic needs, or to mistrust them.
Second year	*Anal stage* The anus is the focus of pleasurable sensations as the baby learns to control elimination.	*Autonomy versus shame and doubt* Children learn to exercise their will and to control themselves, or they become uncertain and doubt that they can do things by themselves.
Third to sixth year	*Phallic stage* Children develop sexual curiosity and obtain gratification when they masturbate. They have sexual fantasies about the parent of the opposite sex and feel guilt about their fantasies.	*Initiative versus guilt* Children learn to initiate their own activities, enjoy their accomplishments, and become purposeful. If they are not allowed to follow their own initiative, they feel guilty for their attempts to become independent.
Seventh year through puberty	*Latency* Sexual urges are submerged. Children focus on mastery of skills valued by adults.	*Industry versus inferiority* Children learn to be competent and effective at activities valued by adults and peers, or they feel inferior.
Adolescence	*Genital stage* Adolescents have adult sexual desires, and they seek to satisfy them.	*Identity versus role confusion* Adolescents establish a sense of personal identity as part of their social group, or they become confused about who they are and what they want to do in life.
Early adulthood		*Intimacy versus isolation* Young adults find an intimate life companion, or they risk loneliness and isolation.
Middle age		*Generativity versus stagnation* Adults must be productive in their work and willing to raise a next generation, or they risk stagnation.
Old age		*Integrity versus despair* People try to make sense of their prior experience and to assure themselves that their lives have been meaningful, or they despair over their unachieved goals and ill-spent lives.

three basic psychological structures (id, ego, superego), and the existence of unconscious drives, he differed from his teacher in two significant ways. First, Erikson emphasized social and cultural interaction, rather than biological drives, as the force behind development. Second, he viewed the developmental process as continuing throughout the life span, rather than ending in adolescence (the age of sexual maturity).

Instead of biological survival of the species, the main challenge of life, according to Erikson, is the quest for identity, which he conceived of as the stable core of personality. *Identity* in Erikson's terms can be thought of as a relatively stable mental picture of the relation between the self and the social world in various contexts. Throughout their lives people ask themselves "Who am I?" and at each stage of life they arrive at a different answer (Erikson, 1963, 1968b).

Each stage, Erikson believed, embodies a particular "main task" that the individual must accomplish in order to move on to the next stage of development. Erikson referred to these tasks as "crises" because they are the sources of conflict within the person experiencing them. Each person's sense of identity is formed in the resolution of these crises.

Erikson believed that each crisis provides the individual with a "succession of potentialities," new ways of experiencing and interacting with the world. At the same time, these potentialities are continuously being shaped by other individuals, who in turn are shaped by their culture and social institutions. The personality undergoes changes appropriate to the person's widening contacts with social institutions and cultural practices.

According to Erikson, each individual's life cycle unfolds in the context of a specific culture. While physical maturation writes the general timetable according to which a particular component of personality matures, culture provides the interpretive tools and the shape of social situations in which the crises and resolutions must be worked out.

Give me a dozen healthy infants, well-formed, and my own specified world to bring them up in and I'll guarantee to take any one at random and train him to become any type of specialist I might select—doctor, lawyer, artist, merchant-chief, and, yes, even beggar-man and thief, regardless of his talents, penchants, tendencies, abilities, vocations, and race of his ancestors. (1930, p. 104)

Because of a birth defect requiring her to be fed through a tube directly into the stomach, Monica was never fed orally or held in arms while she was fed as a baby. When she was older, she fed her dolls and, later, bottlefed her daughter, who had no such defect, in the same position as she had been fed in. The persistence of her unique behavior reflects the enduring importance of children's earliest learning experience.

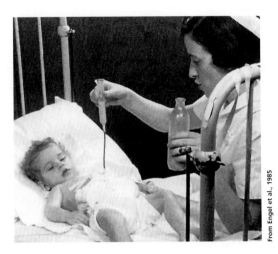

Although modern environmental-learning theories no longer share Watson's extreme view, they do assert that the environment, acting through learning mechanisms, is overwhelmingly important in shaping development (Gewirtz & Pelaez-Nogueras, 1992). Perhaps the most compelling evidence in support of such theories comes from studies done on children who have lived in near isolation owing to some quirk of circumstances or who have been brought up in orphanages with little intellectual stimulation. This research shows that enriching the social and cognitive experiences of such children dramatically improves their later social and cognitive development (Clarke & Clarke, 2000). Research has also shown that learning plays a significant role in such "biological" processes as gender development and aggressiveness (Maccoby, 1998; Patterson et al., 1998).

Their focus on the environment as the primary influence on development leads many environmental-learning theorists to emphasize the gradual and continuous nature of developmental change. This intuition is captured nicely by B. F. Skinner's metaphorical description of how the environment shapes behavior as a sculptor shapes a lump of clay:

> Although at some point the sculptor seems to have produced an entirely novel object, we can always follow the process back to the original undifferentiated lump, and we can make the successive stages by which we return to this condition as small as we wish. At no point does anything emerge which is very different from what preceded it. The final product seems to have a special unity or integrity of design, but we cannot find a point at which this suddenly appears. (1953, p. 91)

The Constructivist Framework

In contrast to the biological-maturation and environmental-learning theorists, developmentalists whose theories fall into the constructivist view find it inappropriate to attribute more importance to either nature or nurture. They assert that nature and nurture are equally necessary for development. A leading adherent of this view was the Swiss developmentalist Jean Piaget (1896–1980), who remarked:

> The human being is immersed right from birth in a social environment which affects him just as much as his physical environment. Society, even more, in a sense, than the physical environment, changes the very structure of the individual . . . Every relation between individuals (from two onwards) literally modifies them. (1973, p. 156)

What especially distinguishes constructivist theories from the biological-maturation and environmental-learning frameworks is the importance constructivists attach to children's active role in shaping their own development. Jean Piaget argued that "knowledge is not a copy of reality" (1964, p. 8), emphasizing the fact that the knowledge we acquire results from the way we modify and transform the world. According to the constructivist way of thinking, children *construct* successively higher levels of knowledge, such as the understanding that objects continue to exist when they are no longer in sight, by actively striving to master their environments.

Piaget and his followers also maintain that the environment does not influence children in the same way at all ages. Instead, the influences of the environment depend on the child's current stage of development. The size, gender mix, and influence of the peer group, for example, depend very much on whether it is a peer group of 4-year-olds or 14-year-olds.

On the basis of data from other cultures, Piaget (1966/1974) also believed that development can be speeded up or slowed down by variations in the environment (such as the presence or absence of formal schooling) but that all children go through the same basic sequence of changes. In this important sense, a constructivist approach assumes that the processes of developmental change are the same in all human groups: They are universal in the species.

As you will see in later chapters, contemporary developmentalists who follow in the tradition established by Piaget have refined or amended a number of his ideas. Nevertheless, these investigators agree with Piaget's emphasis on the central role of children's active engagement with the world and with his insistence that biology and the environment play reciprocal roles in developmental change.

The Cultural-Context Framework

Developmentalists whose work falls within the three theoretical frameworks just described assume that development arises from the interaction of two factors: children's biological heritage and their environment. The frameworks diverge in the relative weight they give to each of these two sources of influence on development and also in the way they see them interacting to produce development.

Developmentalists who work within the cultural-context framework also concur that biological and experiential factors have reciprocal roles to play in development and, like the constructivists, believe that children construct their own development through active engagement with the world. But they differ from the other theorists by asserting that a third force — culture — is part of the mixture. As indicated at the bottom of Figure 1.9 (p. 30), according to the cultural-context view, nature and nurture do not interact directly. Rather, they interact indirectly

The ways that children manipulate a stick depend greatly on the cultural context that specifies how the stick is to be used. Note the differences associated with cultural context among three Pacific island nations: Japan, Indonesia, and Tonga.

Mike Yamashita/Woodfin Camp & Associates

Lindsay Hebberd/Woodfin Camp & Associates

Jack Fields/Photo Researchers

Michael Benanav

© Michel Szulc-Krzyzanowski/The Image Works

© Journal-Courier/Steve Warmowski/The Image Works

According to the cultural-context framework, children's development is organized by their culture's "design for living." For these children living in Tibet, Bangladesh, and the United States, such influences as their culture's religious beliefs, educational system, and patterns of family interaction will significantly affect the paths of their development.

through culture, the designs for living that we discussed earlier (Greenfield, Keller, Fugigni & Maynard, 2003; Rogoff, 2003; Valsiner, 1998; Vygotsky, 1978).

One way culture influences development can be seen in children's acquisition of mathematical understanding. The kinds of mathematical thinking children develop do not depend only on their ability to deal with abstractions and on adults' efforts to arrange for them to learn mathematical concepts. They also depend on the adults' own knowledge of mathematics, which in turn depends on their cultural heritage. Children growing up among the Oksapmin, a group living in the jungles of New Guinea, appear to have the same universal ability to grasp basic number concepts as children growing up in Paris or Pittsburgh; but instead of learning to use a number system to count, they learn to count by using the parts of their bodies. This system would be unwieldy for children who must solve arithmetic problems in school and later in the money economy of Western culture, but it is perfectly adequate for dealing with the tasks of everyday life in traditional Oksapmin culture (Saxe, 2002). The development of mathematical knowledge is also influenced by the contexts in which the knowledge is used. In Brazil, for example, child street vendors develop remarkable mathematical skills in the course of everyday buying and selling. But while these children can handle mathematical problems in the marketplace with ease, they have difficulties with the same problems when they are presented to them in a school-like format (Nuñes et al., 1993). In each of these cases, culture has contributed to the course of development by arranging the conditions under which biological and environmental factors interact.

The cultural-context and constructivist points of view are similar in several respects. Both hold that the individual undergoes qualitative changes in the course of development, and both emphasize that development is impossible without the individual's active participation. They differ, however, in three important respects. First, the cultural-context framework assumes that both children and their caretakers are active agents in the process of development. Development is, in this sense, "co-constructed." Second, the cultural-context framework does not look for stagelike consistency in abilities and behavior. It anticipates wide variability in a given individual's performance as the person moves from one kind of activity to another. Third, the cultural-context framework is more open to the idea that the sequence of developmental changes a child experiences—and, indeed, even the existence or nonexistence of a particular stage of development—may depend on the child's cultural-historical circumstances (Rogoff, 2003).

None of the four theoretical frameworks we have outlined is sufficiently comprehensive to provide a full picture of all the complexities of human development. Indeed, these frameworks might best be thought of as filters, with each highlighting certain features of the overall process of development. The full picture, if one were to be achieved, would be a perfect coordination of the pictures seen through all the different filters.

Lev Vygotsky, a prominent theorist of the role of culture in development, and his daughter.

This Book and the Field of Developmental Science

Given the lack of a comprehensive and widely accepted developmental theory that unifies the field, this book adopts an integrative approach that makes it possible to present and evaluate different theorists' claims in a systematic way. And since development is a process that emerges over time, this book also adopts a chronological approach as the best way to understand the processes involved.

Telling the story of development chronologically presents two major difficulties, however. The first is how to segment the story of development into specific periods and how much significance to attribute to each of these periods. The second is how to keep track of the many aspects of development that are occurring simultaneously, how to depict the ways they combine and recombine to constitute a whole, living person.

Our solution to these difficulties has been to adopt a perspective that provides a principled way of looking at the periods of childhood and at the same time emphasizes the simultaneous action of many factors. This perspective, put forth by Robert Emde and his colleagues (Emde et al., 1976), emphasizes key stagelike changes that Emde and his colleagues refer to as *bio-behavioral shifts*—points in development at which the interaction of biological maturation and experience induces a reorganization of the child's behavioral functioning. The prototype for such a shift is the transition that occurs when, at 2 to 3 months of age, infants first make concentrated eye contact and smile in response to the smile of another person. This first "reciprocal smile" is also the first truly social smile; it creates a new quality of emotional contact between infant and parents and is recognized in several societies as an indicator of a new stage of development. There is no one cause for reciprocal, social smiling. It emerges from changes occurring in the neural fibers connecting the eye to the brain, increased density of cells in the retina of the eye, the presence of adults ready to smile at the child, and the special emotional response that this new form of connectedness evokes.

In adopting the idea of a bio-behavioral shift, we add the social dimension of development because, as Emde and his colleagues themselves note, every bio-behavioral shift involves a change in the relationship between children and their social worlds. As the onset of social smiling indicates, not only do children experience the social environment in new ways as a result of the changes in their behavior and biological makeup; they also are treated differently by other people. We therefore use the term **bio-social-behavioral shift** to refer to a major transition point in

bio-social-behavioral shift A transition point in development during which a convergence of biological, social, and behavioral changes gives rise to cause distinctively new forms of behavior.

table 1.3

Prominent Bio-Social-Behavioral Shifts in Development	
Shift Point	**New Developmental Period**
Conception: genetic material of parents combines to form unique individual →	*Prenatal period:* formation of basic organs
Birth: transition to life outside the womb →	*Early infancy:* becoming coordinated with the environment
2½ months: cortical-subcortical brain connections form; social smiling; new quality of maternal feeling →	*Middle infancy:* increased memory and sensorimotor abilities
7–9 months: wariness of novelty; fear of strangers; attachment →	*Late infancy:* symbolic thought; distinct sense of self
End of infancy (24–30 months): grammatical language →	*Early childhood (2½–6 years):* strikingly uneven levels of performance; sex-role identity; sociodramatic play
5–7 years: assigned responsibility for tasks outside of adult supervision; deliberate instruction →	*Middle childhood:* peer-group activity; rule-based games; systematic instruction
11–12 years: sexual maturation →	*Adolescence:* sex-oriented social activity; identity integration; formal reasoning
19–21 years: shift toward primary responsibility for self and raising of next generation →	*Adulthood (19+)*

development during which a convergence of biological, social, and behavioral changes gives rise to distinctively new forms of behavior. (Table 1.3 outlines the bio-social-behavioral shifts that appear to be prominent in the development of the child from conception to adulthood. Although not all of the shift points have been equally well established, they nevertheless provide a fruitful means of organizing discussions of development because they require us to consider both the sources of change and the evidence concerning developmental continuity and discontinuity in a systematic way.)

In addition, we take into account how the cultural context of children's development enters into the timing and organization not only of bio-social-behavioral shifts but of developmental processes at all ages. From the earliest hours of life, cultural conceptions of what children are and what the future holds for them influence the way parents interpret their children's behavior and shape their experience. For example, parents who believe that men have to be aggressive and tough to survive in the world are more likely to treat their baby boys differently than do those parents who believe that male aggression is a problem. And, as mentioned earlier, in some cases the timing, the essential character, and even the existence of a developmental period may be strongly influenced by cultural factors (Rogoff, 2003).

The notion of bio-social-behavioral shifts fits reasonably well with a traditional convention that divides the time between conception and the start of adulthood into five broad periods: the prenatal period, infancy, early childhood, middle childhood, and adolescence. Each period is accorded a major section of this text. Within this chronological framework, our aim is to make clear how the fundamental biological, social, behavioral, and cultural aspects of development are woven together in the process of change from one period to the next. The text subdivides infancy, a period in which change is particularly rapid, into three sub-periods marked by important transitions durin which distinctively new and significant forms of behavior emerge.

Our adoption of a bio–social–behavioral framework for the study of development does not imply a commitment to a strict stage theory. Rather, it provides a systematic way to keep in mind the intricate play of forces that combine to produce development. Nor does it imply a uniform "direction of causality" from biological characteristics of the individual to social and cultural factors or the other way around. Rather, it emphasizes the emergent nature of developmental change as a consequence of the unceasing interplay between the biological, social, individual, and cultural sources of development.

Throughout the chapters that follow, the large questions of development that captivated Itard and his contemporaries are constantly recurring themes: What makes us human? Can our natures be remolded by experience, or are the characteristics inscribed in our genes at conception relatively fixed? Can we use our knowledge of development to help us plan our futures and guide the growth of our children? Because the issues are so complex and the field's knowledge is still limited, we have tried to design each chapter to set forth basic facts, methods, and theories in a manner that will help the reader think usefully about the fundamental questions of the field.

S U M M A R Y

- One of the earliest efforts in the study of child development involved Jean Marc Itard's work with the Wild Boy of Aveyron. This unusual case posed fundamental questions about human nature:

  1. What distinguishes humans from other animals?

  2. What would we be like if we grew up isolated from society?

  3. To what degree are we the product of our upbringing and experience, and to what degree is our character the product of inborn traits?

- Both Itard's faith in the promise of scientific methods to resolve enduring questions about human nature and many of his specific techniques served as models for the scientific study of human development.

The Study of Child Development

- The study of child development is the study of the changes that children undergo starting from the moment of conception until they are teens.

- The early rise of the discipline of developmental science is closely linked to social changes wrought by industrialization that fundamentally altered the nature of family life, education, and work.

- Darwin's thesis that human beings evolved from previously existing species furthered the scientific interest in children, inspiring scientists to study children for evidence of evolution.

- Modern developmentalists study the origins of human behavior and the sequence of physical, cognitive, and psychosocial changes that children undergo as they grow older.

- An important task for developmentalists is to apply the knowledge they acquire to the promotion of healthy development.

The Central Questions of Developmental Science

- Many scientific and social questions about development revolve around four fundamental concerns:

  1. Is the process of development gradual and continuous, or is it marked by abrupt, stagelike discontinuities?

  2. How do nature and nurture interact to produce development?

  3. How plastic is development? Is it possible to change the course of development through deliberate or accidental intervention?

  4. How do people come to have stable characteristics that differentiate them from one another?

- Questions about continuity branch into more specific questions:

  1. How alike and how different are we from our near neighbors in the animal kingdom?

  2. Does development involve the gradual accumulation of small quantitative changes, or are there qualitatively distinct stages of development?

- Questions about sources of development have given rise to competing views about the contributions of biology (nature) and the environment (nurture) to the process of development.

- Questions about plasticity seek to define critical or sensitive periods in development.

- The issue of individual differences focuses on two questions:

  1. What makes individuals different from one another?

  2. To what extent are individual characteristics stable over time?

The Discipline of Developmental Science

- Developmentalists use several data-collection methods in their efforts to connect abstract theories to the concrete realities of people's everyday experience. These methods are designed to ensure that the data used to explain development are objective, reliable, valid, and replicable.

- Prominent among the methods of data collection used by developmentalists are (a) naturalistic observations, (b) experiments, and (c) clinical interviews.

- Research designs that include systematic comparisons between children of different ages enable researchers to establish relationships among developmental phenomena. Some basic research designs are:

  1. Longitudinal designs—the same children are studied repeatedly over a period of time.

  2. Cross-sectional designs—different children of different ages are studied at a single time.

  3. Cohort sequential designs—the longitudinal method is repeated with several cohorts, each of which is studied longitudinally.

  4. Microgenetic designs—the same children are studied repeatedly over a short span of time during a period of rapid change.

- No one method or research design can supply the answers to all the questions that developmentalists seek to resolve. The choice of research design depends on the specific issue being addressed.

- Theory plays an important role in developmental science by providing a broad conceptual framework within which methods and research designs are organized and facts can be interpreted.

- Four major theoretical frameworks organize a large proportion of research in children's development:

  1. According to the biological-maturation framework, the sources of development are primarily endogenous, arising from the organism's biological heritage.

  2. According to the environmental-learning framework, developmental change is caused primarily by exogenous factors arising in the environment.

  3. According to the constructivist framework, development arises from the active adaptation of the organism to the environment. The roles of environmental and biological factors are of equal magnitude.

  4. Like the constructivist framework, the cultural-context framework accords importance to both biological and environmental factors in development, but it also emphasizes that the interactions out of which development emerges are crucially shaped by the designs for living that make up the culture of any given group.

This Book and the Field of Developmental Science

- The concept of the bio-social-behavioral shift highlights the ways in which biological, social, and behavioral factors interact in a cultural context to produce developmental change. Keeping these factors in mind helps us maintain a picture of the whole developing child.

Key Terms

bio–social–behavioral shift, p. 37

causation, p. 20

child development, p. 2

clinical method, p. 20

cohort, p. 25

cohort sequential design, p. 25

control group, p. 19

correlation, p. 20

critical period, p. 11

cross-sectional design, p. 23

culture, p. 8

developmental niche, p. 17

developmental stage, p. 9

ecological validity, p. 20

ecology, p. 17

endogenous, p. 30

ethnography, p. 16

ethology, p. 16

exogenous, p. 31

experiment, p. 18

experimental group, p. 19

learning, p. 32

longitudinal design, p. 22

maturation, p. 30

microgenetic design, p. 23

naturalistic observation, p. 16

nature, p. 10

nurture, p. 10

objectivity, p. 15

ontogeny, p. 9

phylogeny, p. 8

plasticity, p. 11

reliability, p. 15

replicability, p. 15

research design, p. 22

scientific hypothesis, p. 18

sensitive period, p. 11

theory, p. 7

triangulation, p. 16

validity, p. 15

Thought Questions

1. Using arguments from the four theoretical perspectives described in this chapter, give four possible explanations for the appearance and behavior of the Wild Boy of Aveyron.

2. On the basis of your own experience, give an example of how the scientific study of child development has affected the way the current-generation children in your neighborhood are being raised.

3. What is one question you have about the development of children? How do you think scientists might go about finding the answer?

4. List three ways in which the person you were at the age of 5 differed from the person you were at the age of 15. Label those differences as either qualitative or quantitative.

5. List two major ways in which you are like your best friend and two major ways in which the two of you are different. What causal factors do you think are primarily responsible for each of these similarities and differences?

part I In the Beginning

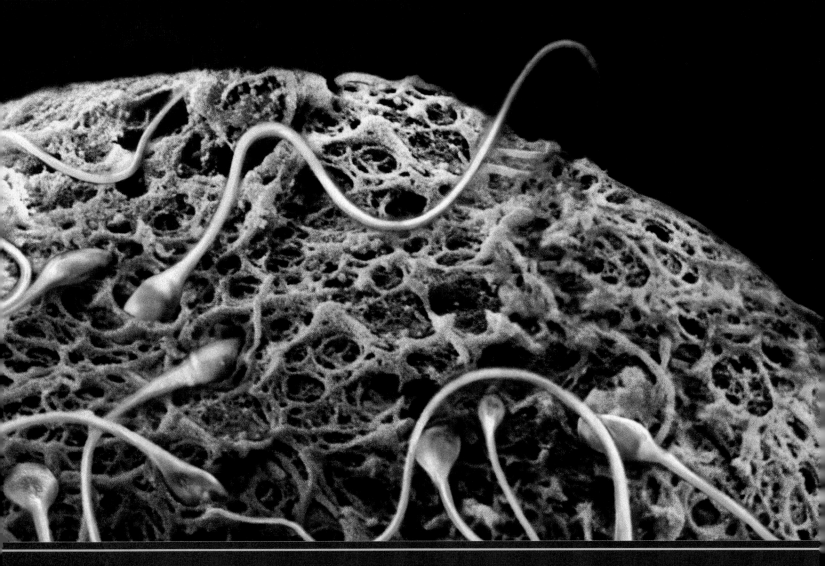

Bio-Social-Behavioral Shifts

Biological Domain

Central Nervous System
- Myelination of cortical and subcortical neural pathways
- Myelination of primary neural pathways in some sensory systems
- Increased cortical control of subcortical activity
- Increases in the number and diversity of brain cells

Psychophysiology
- Increases in amount of wakefulness
- Decreases in active (REM) sleep as a proportion of total sleep time
- Shift in pattern of sleep; quiet (NREM) sleep begins to come first

Social Domain
- New quality of coordination and emotional contact between infants and caretakers
- Beginning of "crying on purpose"

Behavioral Domain
- Learning is retained better between episodes
- Increases in visual acuity
- More complete visual scanning of objects
- Onset of social smiling
- Decreases in generalized fussiness and crying
- Visually initiated reaching becomes visually guided reaching

The development of every human being starts with the formation of a single cell at the time of conception. However, each individual human life is but a tiny drop in the vast stream of life that reaches back through thousands of generations and unimaginable millennia of time. As a result, every human being is a product of the evolutionary past of our species. Moreover, the environment each baby experiences is a product of the earth's history, including the development of its culture and society.

Science views the life process as a constant interplay of forces that create order and pattern, on the one hand, and of forces that create variation and disorder, on the other. In the modern scientific view, the interaction of these competing forces is the engine of developmental change.

What forces create order and diversity in human development? In Chapter 2 you will see that part of the answer to that question can be found in our biological inheritance. Order, the ways in which all human beings are alike, initially arises from the fact that all human beings share a finite pool of genetic possibilities and a common biosphere—the planet Earth. Variation initially arises through sexual reproduction, which in virtually every instance ensures that each individual will inherit a unique combination of genes from the common pool and

continues as each organism goes through a unique sequence of encounters with its own physical and cultural environment.

Chapter 2 describes the basic mechanisms of genetic transmission, processes of gene—environment interaction, and some of the diseases that result from genetic abnormalities. It also discusses the contribution to our development of cultural evolution, a distinctly human mode of inheritance that contributes to both order and variation in each individual's environment.

Chapter 3 discusses prenatal development and birth. It traces the changes that transform the single cell created at conception into a newborn infant with millions of cells of many kinds. It also includes a description of the conditions that greet the newborn upon emergence into the world.

The process of prenatal development illustrates many of the basic questions about development discussed in Chapter 1. For example, the process of gene—environment interaction speaks directly to questions about sources of development; the changes in form and activity that distinguish the organism 5 days following conception from the organism 5 weeks or 5 months later raise questions about developmental continuity. You will also see examples addressing issues of plasticity—critical periods during prenatal growth when the embryo is highly

sensitive to hormonal secretions and to such external agents as drugs.

After 9 months of growth and nurturing within the mother's body, chemical changes initiate the birth process. Birth constitutes the first major biosocial-behavioral shift in development. The baby is no longer able to obtain life-giving oxygen and nutrients automatically from the mother's body. Instead, the newborn must use the biological capacities that it developed during the prenatal period to breathe and eat. Other behavioral changes that occur at birth are no less remarkable, as babies gain direct access to the sights, sounds, and smells around them and begin to provide some sights, sounds, and smells of their own! Still, the newborn is completely dependent on others. Without the support of parents who structure their baby's interactions with the environment according to culturally prescribed patterns, the baby would not survive. Parents must feed, clothe, and protect their offspring for many years before they are able to take care of themselves.

Thus begins the lifelong process in which the biological forces that created the new organism at conception interact with the forces of the culturally organized environment that greets the child at birth. Barring unforeseen calamities, in about 20 years the process will begin again with a new generation.

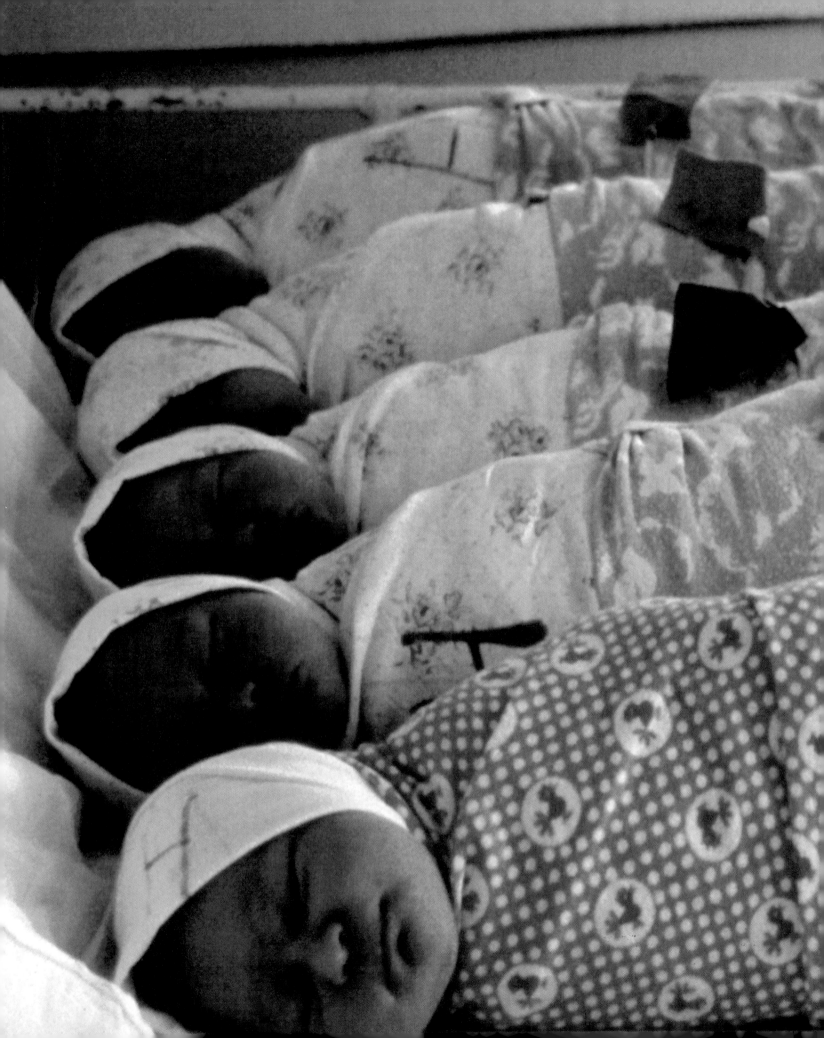

The Human Heritage: Genes and the Environment

> "*Every child conceived by a given couple is the result of a genetic lottery. He is merely one out of a large crowd of possible children, any one of whom might have been conceived on the same occasion if another of the millions of sperm cells emitted by the father had happened to fertilize the egg cell of the mother—an egg cell which is itself one among many . . . If we go to all the trouble it takes to mix our genes with those of somebody else, it is in order to make sure that our child will be different from ourselves and from all our other children.*"
>
> —François Jacob, The Possible and the Actual

Susan was a sophomore in college when she learned that her cousin Sam had been diagnosed with Wiskott–Aldrich syndrome, a rare genetic disorder in which a boy is born without a functioning immune system and with blood that does not clot normally. Babies born with this syndrome rarely live more than eight years; Sam was 3 years old when he died.

Sam had been sickly since birth, but the news about the nature of his illness provided the first evidence that some members of Susan's family were the carriers of a genetic disease. Wiskott–Aldrich syndrome is passed from mothers to sons. Each son conceived by a woman who is a carrier has a 50-50 chance of being born with the syndrome. Each daughter has a 50-50 chance of inheriting the defective gene that causes the syndrome and passing it on to her children, though the daughters are not affected by the syndrome themselves.

Sam's parents had another child who also suffered from Wiskott–Aldrich syndrome. However, with the help of more advanced medical technologies, they were able to obtain a bone marrow transplant, and the baby lived. But his life is by no means normal. His growth is stunted, he has learning disabilities, and he often has to be hospitalized.

When Susan married George three years later, they decided that they would wait to have children until they knew whether or not Susan was a carrier of Wiskott–Aldrich syndrome. She had watched her aunt and uncle struggle to keep their sons alive, shared their sorrow at Sam's death, and witnessed the devastating effects this ordeal had on the whole family. As a result, she and George decided not to carry a baby with Wiskott–Aldrich syndrome to term. "I can't see having a baby that's going to be sick its whole life only to die before the age of 5," she explained.

Susan and George began to search for a laboratory that could run tests to see if she carried the disease. It took 2 years before they found out that not only Susan's mother but two of her five sisters and Susan herself were carriers of Wiskott–Aldrich syndrome. It was bad news, but Susan said: "I was just relieved to know. Now we knew what we were up against." Susan became pregnant. At 11 weeks a genetic test revealed that the fetus was female—good news, since girls are not affected. Two years later, Susan and George decided to try to have a second child. This time, testing indicated that the fetus was a male and that it carried the deadly genetic defect. Susan and George decided to terminate the pregnancy. "It was devastating getting pregnant and knowing that you might not be able to carry the baby to term. Trying not to get too attached to the baby . . . and all . . . it was hard."

A few years later, Susan and George decided to try again to have a second child. "I felt like we were taking such a huge risk to have a second child," Susan confessed. "No matter what kind of genetic disease you are talking about, you are not making a choice just to have a baby. You are making a choice *for* them. Whether they are going to have a disease, what kind of life they will lead, whether they will live long. It's all very hard."

This time, the fetus was a girl and she was born in perfect health. Since then, both of Susan and George's daughters have been tested, and neither carries the defective gene that gives rise to Wiskott–Aldrich syndrome.

The new medical technologies that make testing for genetic diseases possible are both a burden and a blessing. They are a burden because they confront parents like Susan and George with difficult choices: Should they have any children at all, given the risks? Might it not be better to adopt children? Is it fair to bring a child into the world only to watch it suffer and die after a few years? But is it fair to conceive a child and then terminate the pregnancy through abortion? Might still newer technologies lead to a cure in time? On the other hand, genetic testing can be a blessing. As Susan put it, "I am thankful on a daily basis that I had the testing available to me so I could make an intelligent decision."

Susan and George's predicament illustrates just one aspect of the "genetic lottery." Every time an egg and sperm unite, millions of different combinations are created that influence everything from eye color to predisposition for certain diseases. But people are also more than the sum of their genetic heritage. As you will learn in this chapter, an individual's environment and culture also play a role in what he or she will become.

This continuous interaction between biological, cultural, and environmental influences is responsible for the remarkable differences—and similarities—between individuals. The similarities that mark us as members of a single species arise both because we inherit our genes from other human beings and because, over the course of human evolution, those genes have interacted within the common environment of the planet Earth. The differences among us come from the same two sources—our biological heritage and the environments, physical and cultural, in which we grow up. Owing to the process of sexual reproduction, each of us inherits a combination of genes that is, with rare exceptions, unique. The specific environments with which these genes interact also contribute to variations among people by promoting the development of certain characteristics and discouraging that of others. For example, children born into families living deep in the forests of the Amazon basin, where people still live by hunting and gathering, must develop physical endurance and become close observers of nature. Conversely, children born into families living in a North American suburb must develop the ability to sit still for long hours in school to acquire the knowledge and skills they will need for economic success as adults. In addition to being shaped by the historical and cultural circumstances in which they live, children are also shaped by their more immediate environments. Within a particular family, and even when they go to the same school, for example, each child lives through a unique set of experiences that further influences the characteristics he or she develops (Deater-Deckard et al., 2001; McGuire & Roch-Levecq, 2001).

We begin this chapter by discussing sexual reproduction, the mechanism for the genetic lottery—the chances of any given individual's being conceived. We will also consider the basic laws of genetic inheritance to which that lottery is subject. Next we will discuss genetic influences and the lifelong process of interaction between genes and environment that shapes development. To illustrate the crucial importance of an individual's genetic constitution and the principles of gene–environment interaction, we will then discuss the origins and effects of genetic abnormalities. Finally, we will take a look at the way biology and culture interact in the process of human development.

Sexual Reproduction and Genetic Transmission

At his climax during sexual intercourse, a man ejaculates about 350 million sperm into a woman's vagina. The head of each tadpole-shaped sperm contains 23 chromosomes. Each **chromosome** is a single molecule of **deoxyribonucleic acid (DNA).** DNA exists as two long, paired strands that form a spiral that creates the famous double helix. Each strand is made up of millions of chemical building blocks called *bases*. While there are only four different chemical bases in DNA (adenine, thymine, cytosine, and guanine), the sequences in which the bases occur determine the information available, much as individual letters of the alphabet combine to form words and sentences. DNA is a vast chemical information database that carries the complete set of instructions for making all the proteins a cell will ever need.

Each chromosome, in turn, contains thousands of segments called **genes.** Genes are the working subunits of DNA made up of specific sequences of bases. They are the basic physical and functional units of heredity. Each gene contains a particular set of instructions, usually coding for a particular protein from which the body's cells are created, as well as the enzymes that regulate the cells' functioning (see Figure 2.1). The 23 chromosomes carried by the sperm provide half of the genetic information necessary for the development of a new individual. The other half is provided by the woman's ovum (egg), which also has 23 chromosomes and genes that correspond with those carried by the sperm.

Following ejaculation, the sperm swim up the woman's uterus and into the fallopian tubes. This perilous journey is completed by only a few hundred of the millions of sperm that begin it. Should one of those surviving sperm encounter an ovum and penetrate its membranes, the result is conception: the ovum and sperm fuse to form a **zygote,** a single cell containing 46 chromosomes—23 from the father and 23 from the mother—that are arranged in pairs. All the cells that the child will have at birth come from this single cell with its 23 pairs of chromosomes.

chromosome A threadlike structure made up of genes. In humans, there are 46 chromosomes in every cell, except sperm and ova.

deoxyribonucleic acid (DNA) A long double-stranded molecule that makes up chromosomes.

genes The segments on a DNA molecule that act as hereditary blueprints for the organism's development.

zygote The single cell formed at conception from the union of the sperm and the ovum.

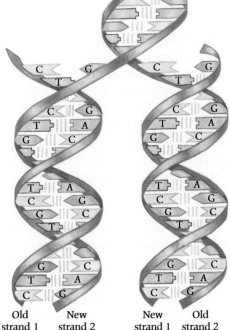

Strand 1

Strand 2

C G C G
T T
C G C G
T A T A
G C G C
T A T A
C G C G
G C G C
T T
G C G C
T A T A
C G C G

Old New New Old
strand 1 strand 2 strand 1 strand 2

(a)

Figure 2.1 (a) A strand of DNA (top) replicates by splitting down the middle of the rungs of its ladderlike structure. Each free base (center) picks up a new complementary partner: cytosine (C) pairs with guanine (G), and adenine (A) pairs with thymine (T). (b) A computer-generated, color-coded model of DNA allows researchers to rotate the image and study it from various angles.

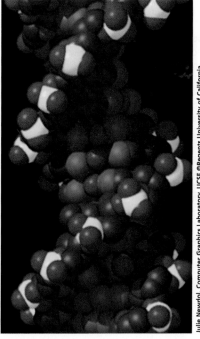

Julie Newdol, Computer Graphics Laboratory, UCSF ©Regents University of California

(b)

Figure 2.2 Mitosis is the process of cell division that generates all the cells of the body except the germ cells. During mitosis each chromosome in the cell replicates, producing a new chromosome identical to the first. The cell then splits, the chromosomes separating so that one of them goes to each new cell. Mitosis ensures that identical genetic information is maintained in the body cells over the life of the organism.

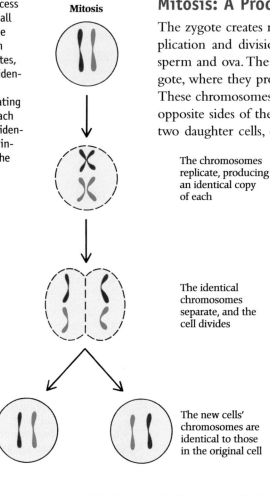

Mitosis

The chromosomes replicate, producing an identical copy of each

The identical chromosomes separate, and the cell divides

The new cells' chromosomes are identical to those in the original cell

Mitosis: A Process of Cell Replication

The zygote creates new cells through **mitosis,** the process of cell duplication and division that generates all the individual's cells except sperm and ova. The 46 chromosomes move to the middle of the zygote, where they produce exact copies of themselves (see Figure 2.2). These chromosomes separate into two identical sets, which migrate to opposite sides of the cell. The cell then divides in the middle to form two daughter cells, each of which contains 23 pairs of chromosomes (46 chromosomes in all) identical to those inherited at conception. These two daughter cells go through the same process to create two new cells each, which themselves divide as the process repeats itself again and again.

Mitosis continues throughout the life of an individual, creating new **somatic (body) cells** and replacing old ones. Each new somatic cell contains copies of the original 46 chromosomes inherited at conception. Under the ordinary conditions of life, the genetic material carried by our chromosomes is not altered by the passage of time or by the experiences that shape our minds and bodies but is faithfully copied in each instance of mitosis. (Genes can be altered by direct exposure to radiation and to certain chemicals, however. As you will see later in this chapter, the consequences of such changes can be disastrous.)

Meiosis: A Source of Genetic Variation

Although mitosis is responsible for the replication of somatic (body) cells, it is not involved in the replication of **germ cells**—the sperm and ova. If mitosis did govern the production of sperm and ova, the total number of chromosomes inherited by the offspring would double in each succeeding generation. Instead, the germ cells are formed by a cell-*division* process called **meiosis,** which ensures that the normal zygote contains only 46 chromosomes.

Meiosis represents the initial stage of the genetic lottery. In the first phase of this process, the 23 pairs of chromosomes in the cells that produce sperm or ova duplicate themselves, just as in mitosis. But then the cell divides not once, as in mitosis, but twice, creating four daughter cells (see Figure 2.3). Each of these daughter cells contains only 23 unpaired chromosomes—half the original set from the parent cell. Thus when the ovum and sperm fuse at conception, the zygote receives a full complement of 46 chromosomes (23 pairs).

Because half of the zygote's chromosomes come from each parent, each newly conceived individual is genetically different from both the father and the mother. This reproductive process creates genetic diversity across generations, enhancing the chances for the species to survive in the face of environmental changes. Genetic diversity is further increased by a process called **crossing over,** in which genetic material is exchanged between a pair of chromosomes during the first phase of meiosis. While the pair of chromosomes, each containing genes that influence the same particular characteristics, lie side by side, a section of one of the chromosomes may change places with the corresponding section of the other chromosome. Genes originally carried on one chromosome are now carried on the other.

mitosis The process of cell duplication and division that generates all the individual's cells except sperm and ova.

somatic (body) cells All the cells in the body except for the germ cells (ova and sperm).

germ cells The sperm and ova, which are specialized for sexual reproduction and have half the number of chromosomes normal for a species.

meiosis The process that produces sperm and ova, each of which contains only half of the parent cell's original complement of 46 chromosomes.

crossing over The process in which genetic material is exchanged between chromosomes containing genes for the same characteristic.

monozygotic twins Twins that come from one zygote and therefore have identical genotypes.

dizygotic twins Twins that come from two zygotes.

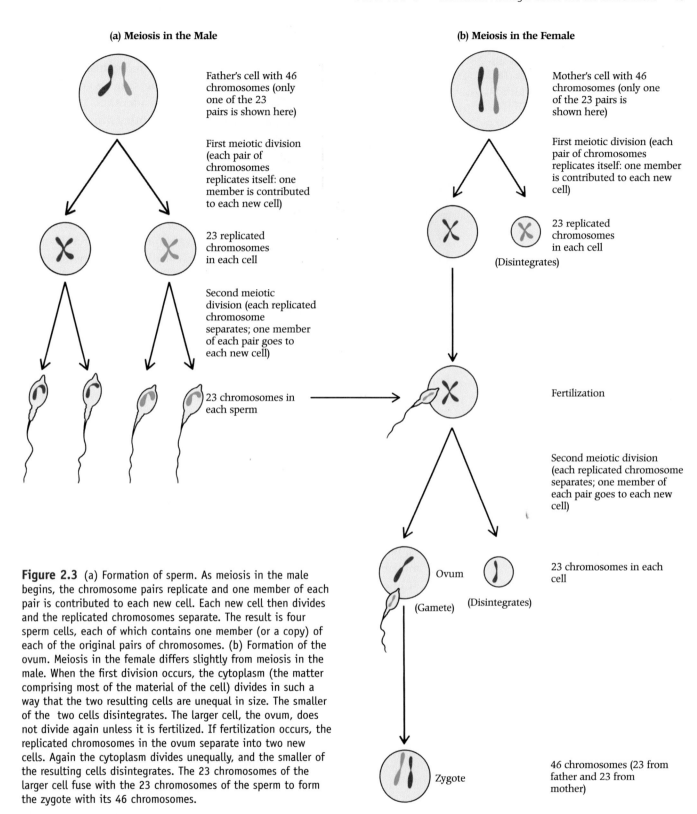

(a) Meiosis in the Male

Father's cell with 46 chromosomes (only one of the 23 pairs is shown here)

First meiotic division (each pair of chromosomes replicates itself: one member is contributed to each new cell)

23 replicated chromosomes in each cell

Second meiotic division (each replicated chromosome separates; one member of each pair goes to each new cell)

23 chromosomes in each sperm

(b) Meiosis in the Female

Mother's cell with 46 chromosomes (only one of the 23 pairs is shown here)

First meiotic division (each pair of chromosomes replicates itself: one member is contributed to each new cell)

23 replicated chromosomes in each cell

(Disintegrates)

Fertilization

Second meiotic division (each replicated chromosome separates; one member of each pair goes to each new cell)

Ovum

(Gamete)   (Disintegrates)

23 chromosomes in each cell

Zygote

46 chromosomes (23 from father and 23 from mother)

Figure 2.3 (a) Formation of sperm. As meiosis in the male begins, the chromosome pairs replicate and one member of each pair is contributed to each new cell. Each new cell then divides and the replicated chromosomes separate. The result is four sperm cells, each of which contains one member (or a copy) of each of the original pairs of chromosomes. (b) Formation of the ovum. Meiosis in the female differs slightly from meiosis in the male. When the first division occurs, the cytoplasm (the matter comprising most of the material of the cell) divides in such a way that the two resulting cells are unequal in size. The smaller of the two cells disintegrates. The larger cell, the ovum, does not divide again unless it is fertilized. If fertilization occurs, the replicated chromosomes in the ovum separate into two new cells. Again the cytoplasm divides unequally, and the smaller of the resulting cells disintegrates. The 23 chromosomes of the larger cell fuse with the 23 chromosomes of the sperm to form the zygote with its 46 chromosomes.

You can now better appreciate the extreme improbability that genes of any two children, even siblings, will be exactly alike, except in the special case of **monozygotic twins,** which come from a single fertilized egg. (Twins that come from two ova that have been fertilized at the same time are referred to as **dizygotic twins** and are no more alike than any two siblings.) For reasons that are still not well understood, sometimes during the first few mitotic divisions after

Figure 2.4 Monozygotic twin boys. Despite inhabiting a very similar environment before and after birth they have distinguishably different facial features. This clearly shows the way in which the phenotype is influenced by the environment.

Dana Shannahan

the zygote is formed, the daughter cells separate completely and develop into totally separate individuals. Having originated from the same zygote, monozygotic twins inherit identical genetic information. Monozygotic twins occur about once in every 250 conceptions. Because their genetic material is identical, monozygotic twins potentially have the same physical and psychological makeup, which is why they are often referred to as "identical twins"; but as you can see in Figure 2.4, monozygotic twins, as a result of their encounters with their environments, are never exactly alike in every detail and may even appear far from identical.

Although we receive 23 chromosomes from each of our parents, it is a matter of chance which member of any pair of chromosomes ends up in a given germ cell during meiosis. According to the laws of probability, there are 2^{23}, or about 8 million, possible genetic combinations for each sperm and ovum. Consequently, the probability that exactly the same genes will be inherited from both parents is at best 1 chance in 64 trillion!

Sexual Determination: Another Source of Variation

In 22 of the 23 pairs of chromosomes found in a human cell, the two chromosomes are of the same size and shape and they carry corresponding genes. Chromosomes of the twenty-third pair usually differ, however. This pair of chromosomes determines a person's genetic sex, a crucial source of variety in our species. In normal females, both members of the twenty-third pair of chromosomes are of the same type and are called **X chromosomes** (see Figure 2.5). The normal male, however, has just one X chromosome that is paired with a different, much smaller chromosome called a **Y chromosome.** Since a female is always XX, each of her eggs contains an X chromosome. In contrast, half of a man's sperm carry an X chromosome and half carry a Y chromosome. If a sperm containing an X chromosome fertilizes the egg, the resulting child will be XX, a female. If the sperm contains a Y chromosome, the child will be XY, a male. The genetic determination of a person's sex is controlled by a single chromosome; however, other aspects of biology and behavior have more complex origins.

Figure 2.5 Human X (above) and Y (below) chromosomes. Note how much larger the X chromosome is. Males have both an X and a Y chromosome, but females have two X chromosomes.

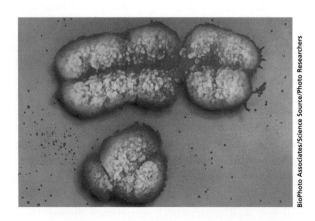

BioPhoto Associates/Science Source/Photo Researchers

Genotype and Phenotype

The ways in which genes influence development must be understood at two levels. One level is the **genotype,** the individual's genetic endowment or, in other words, the particular gene forms that the individual has inherited. The genotype is constant over the lifetime of the individual. The second level is the **phenotype,** the observable characteristics of individuals—their physical and psychological traits, health, and behavior. The phenotype develops through interactions between the genotype and the **environment**—the totality of conditions and circumstances that surround the individual. We will turn our attention first to the mechanisms of genotypic inheritance and to the laws that govern them; then we will consider the ways in which genetic inheritance expresses itself through interaction with the environment to create the phenotype.

The Laws of Genetic Inheritance

Scientific understanding of the mechanisms by which parents transmit their genetic material to the next generation dates from the pioneering studies by Gregor Mendel (1822–1884). Through experiments in which he cross-bred varieties of garden peas, Mendel deduced that parents transmit certain traits to their offspring through discrete physical entities that he referred to as "characters." It was not until many years later that Mendel's hypothetical characters were shown to operate in humans and to correspond to actual physical structures—gene-carrying chromosomes in the nucleus of the cell.

In the simplest form of hereditary transmission, a single pair of genes, one from each parent, contributes to a particular inherited characteristic. A gene that influences a specific trait (for example, the presence or absence of a cleft in the chin) can have the same or different forms. This specific form of a gene is called an **allele.** When the corresponding genes inherited from the two parents are of the same allelic form (both "cleft" or both "noncleft"), the person is said to be **homozygous** for the trait. When the alleles are different (one "cleft" and one "noncleft"), the person is said to be **heterozygous** for the trait. The distinction between homozygous and heterozygous allele pairing is essential for understanding how different genotypic combinations produce different characteristics in the phenotype.

Dominant Genes, Recessive Genes, and Codominance

When a child is homozygous for a trait with particular characteristics that is affected by a single pair of alleles, only one outcome is possible: the child will display the particular characteristics associated with that allele. When a child is heterozygous for such a trait, one of three outcomes is possible:

1. The child will display the particular characteristics that are associated with only one of the two alleles. The allele whose characteristics are expressed is referred to as a **dominant allele,** and the allele whose characteristics are not expressed is called a **recessive allele.**

2. The child will be affected by both alleles and will display characteristics that are intermediate between those "called for" by the two alleles. This may occur, for example, with respect to skin color.

3. The child will display characteristics that are affected by both alleles, but rather than being intermediate, the characteristics will be distinctively different from those linked to either contributing allele. This outcome is **codominance.**

X and Y chromosomes The two chromosomes that determine the sex of the individual. Normal females have two X chromosomes, while normal males have one Y chromosome inherited from their fathers and one X chromosome inherited from their mothers.

genotype The genetic endowment of an individual.

phenotype The organism's observable characteristics that result from the interaction of the genotype with the environment.

environment The totality of conditions and circumstances that surround the organism.

allele The specific form of a gene coded for a particular trait.

homozygous Having inherited two genes of the same allelic form for a trait.

heterozygous Having inherited two genes of different allelic forms for a trait.

dominant allele The allele that is expressed when an individual possesses two different alleles for the same trait.

recessive allele The allele that is not expressed when an individual possesses two different alleles for the same trait.

codominance Outcome in which a trait that is determined by two alleles is different from the trait produced by either of the contributing alleles alone.

Gregor Mendel.

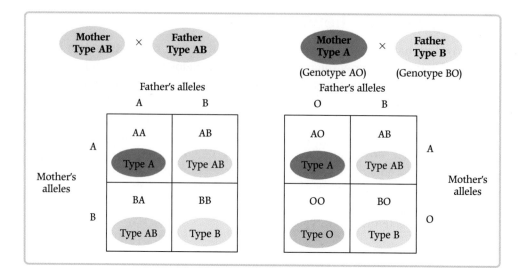

Figure 2.6 Inheritance of alleles for blood type. The alternative forms of a gene for blood type, inherited in various combinations from the parents, produce different blood phenotypes. The combination of one allele from each parent is the genotype, and the resulting blood type of the child is the phenotype.

The inheritance of blood type illustrates the homozygous outcome and two of the heterozygous outcomes. There are three alleles for blood type—A, B, and O—and four basic blood types—A, B, AB, and O. If children receive two type A, two type B, or two type O alleles, they are homozygous for the trait and will have type A, type B, or type O blood, respectively. But if they inherit either the type A or the type B allele from one parent and the type O allele from the other, they will have type A or type B blood, even though their genetic code for blood type is AO or BO. The O allele is recessive, so it does not affect the exhibited blood type. Finally, if children inherit one type A allele and one type B allele, they will exhibit a codominant outcome—type AB blood, which is qualitatively different from either type A or type B blood. Figure 2.6 shows some of the outcomes of various combinations of the three alleles for blood type.

The case of blood type provides a good way to illustrate the study of the laws of genetic inheritance because it is a discrete trait that involves a single gene. **Discrete traits** are considered "either-or" traits because a person either has one or does not. This is true of certain genetic diseases (see Table 2.2, p. 62). However, the example of blood type also oversimplifies the picture of human genetic inheritance because most traits are *polygenic*. A **polygenic trait** involves not two or three genes but several—perhaps even hundreds in the case of complex behavioral traits such as verbal skill or shyness.

Sex-Linked Genetic Effects

Some inherited human characteristics are affected by genes found on only the X or the Y chromosome, so they are called **sex-linked characteristics.** Most of these inherited sex-linked characteristics are carried on the X chromosome (it is much larger than the Y chromosome). Because females receive two X chromosomes, they get two sets of corresponding X-chromosome sex-linked genes, one from each of their parents. But because normal males receive only one X chromosome, they have only one of each gene that is on the X chromosome, which always comes from their mothers.

This difference in genetic material makes males more susceptible to genetic defects that ordinarily do not affect females. If a daughter has a harmful recessive gene on one X chromosome, she will usually have a normal dominant gene on the other X chromosome to override it. The presence of a counteracting, dominant gene ensures that the recessive gene is not expressed at the phenotypic level, so it does not cause a disease. However, a son who inherits a harmful recessive gene on his X chromosome has no such complementary allele to override the recessive gene's harmful effects. Or, if a gene is missing from the X chromosome, males do not have another copy to code for the trait in question.

Red-green color blindness is an example of such a sex-linked recessive trait. It is caused by the absence of genetic material that codes for color-absorbing pigments in the retina of the eye. For a daughter to exhibit this trait, she must be homozygous for it; that is, she must have a father who is red-green color blind and a mother who is either color blind or heterozygous for the trait. However, if a son receives the gene for red-green color blindness on the X chromosome he inherits from his mother, he will be unable to distinguish red from green because there is no corresponding gene on the Y chromosome that will enable him to see red and green.

Other sex-linked recessive traits include hemophilia, a disease in which the blood does not clot readily, and muscular dystrophy, which results in the weakening and wasting away of muscles.

Genes, the Person, and the Environment

Understanding the laws of genetic inheritance may help us describe how a person comes to have brown eyes or a certain disease, but the laws are insufficient to explain fully how genes influence the development of individual characteristics. Only through the interaction of genes with their environments—in all their many varieties—will the phenotype, the actual person, develop.

Studying Gene–Environment Interactions

Genes interact with their environments in complex and multileveled ways. As we mentioned at the beginning of the chapter, genes are merely chemical codes that specify the sequences of amino acids in the proteins produced by cells. Cells, in turn, provide the immediate environments in which the genes exist. The genes and the cell material are in constant interaction. The system of cells as a whole—the individual—is also in constant interaction with its environment. The interactions of individuals with their larger environment determine the conditions of the individual cells and hence the immediate environments of the genes (Futuyma, 1998).

Behavioral geneticists, developmentalists who seek to understand how genetic and environmental factors combine to produce individual differences in behavior, have identified several principles that apply to these interactions (Rutter et al., 1997). The first principle is that interactions between organisms and their environments need to be studied in a broad, ecological framework because variations in the environment can have profound effects on the development of the phenotype. For example, temperament is known to have a significant genetic component, but the expression of negative emotionality (such as crying, pouting, or depression), which is one of the major dimensions of temperament, depends upon family circumstances (Belsky, Fish & Isabella, 1991). Behavioral geneticists studied a large group of young infants who displayed low levels of negative emotionality early in the first year of life. If the children lived in families where the father was rarely involved with them and expressed negative feelings toward his relationship with his wife, the children's level of negative emotional displays increased over the course of the first year. But if such infants lived in families where there was a high level of marital satisfaction and the mothers were sensitive to their needs, their levels of negative emotional display remained low.

A second principle of gene–environment interaction that influences the nature of the phenotype is that gene–environment interaction is a two-way process. For example, over time, mothers of irritable infants in the United States show less visual

discrete traits Traits involving a single gene that operate as "either-or" traits because a person either has one or does not.

polygenic trait A genetic trait that is determined by the interaction of several genes.

sex-linked characteristics Traits determined by genes that are found on only the X or the Y chromosome.

behavioral geneticist A researcher who studies how genetic and environmental factors combine to produce individual differences in behavior.

The two-way interaction between genes and environment is illustrated by these Japanese teenagers playing in a highly stimulating, fast action game. On the one hand, genetic factors may influence their enjoyment of high stimulation environments or the development of sensorimotor skills. On the other hand, their enjoyment of high stimulation environments and the exercise of sensorimotor skills may lead them to seek our environments where these factors are involved.

AFP Photo/Toru Yamanaka/Getty Images

and physical contact with them, less effective stimulation, and less involvement overall than parents of less irritable children. This change in parental behavior serves to stimulate the children's expression of irritability (van den Boom & Hoeksma, 1995). However, in the shantytowns of metropolitan areas in Brazil, irritable infants who cry a lot and make strong demands for attention are more likely to survive than those who are quiet and undemanding (Scheper-Hughes, 1992). Clearly, both directions of influence, person → environment and environment → person, must be taken into account, as well as the specific characteristics of both the children and their environments.

A third principle of gene–environment interaction is that genetic factors often play a role in determining what environments individuals inhabit and how individuals shape and select their own experiences (Wachs, 1999). Children who, partly for genetic reasons, respond positively to high levels of stimulation may like to listen to music that is loud and raucous. This disposition, in turn, can influence their choice of peers with whom to spend time, as well as which peers choose to spend time with them.

These principles make it clear that developmentalists must keep a multitude of factors in mind as they seek to understand the dynamic process by which genes and the environment interact over the course of development.

Range of Reaction

In order to encompass the full variety of interaction that can occur between genes and environment, developmentalists seek to investigate as many combinations of gene–environment interactions as possible. When conducting research on gene–environment interactions, developmentalists use two approaches to meet this goal. In the first they attempt to keep the environment constant so that any variation in phenotype can be attributed to variations in the genes. In the other they keep the genotype constant while they vary the environment so that variations in the phenotype can be attributed to variations in the environment. The first procedure highlights genetic influences on development; the second highlights the influences of the environment. Either approach by itself would give us only a partial picture of gene–environment interaction, but the combination of the two approaches reveals the double-sided nature of gene–environment interactions.

By charting the changes that occur in the phenotype as the environment of a particular genotype is varied, researchers can discover the **range of reaction** for that genotype. Ideally, this range represents all the possible gene–environment

range of reaction All the possible phenotypes for a single genotype that are compatible with the continued life of the organism.

canalization The process that makes some traits relatively invulnerable to environmental events.

(a)

(b)

(c)

Figure 2.7 The effect of environment on the expression of a gene for fur color in the Himalayan rabbit. Under normal conditions (a) only the rabbit's feet, tail, ears, and nose are black. If fur is removed from a patch on the rabbit's back and an ice pack is placed there, creating a cold local environment (b), the new fur that grows in is black (c). (Adapted from Winchester, 1972.)

relationships that can sustain the continued life of the organism, so it includes all the possible developmental outcomes. For example, the color of the fur of Himalayan rabbits is influenced by temperature (see Figure 2.7). The colder the temperature, the darker the rabbit's fur becomes. The range of reaction for the expression of fur color in this creature is bounded at one end by the temperature at which the rabbit would freeze to death and at the other end by the temperature that would be too high to permit it to live. As the temperature approaches the lower boundary, the rabbit's fur becomes predominantly black. As the temperature approaches the higher boundary, even the rabbit's extremities, which get the least blood flow and are the coolest, remain white. The variations in the phenotypic expression of fur color as the temperature is varied from one extreme to the other is the range of reaction for the Himalayan rabbit's genotype for fur color.

The task of applying the range of reaction to human behavior is both ethically and scientifically difficult. Ethically, the study of human genetics is restricted by the impossibility of carrying out the experiments needed to establish a range of reaction. Such experiments would require totalitarian control over the lives of research participants and would expose some children to certain death purely for the purpose of scientific interest. Obviously, such experiments would be immoral and should not be carried out. Scientifically, the impossibility of using such experimental controls to measure the ranges of reaction in humans means that behavioral geneticists cannot rely upon strict causal analysis of human behaviors. Instead, they must rely on other organisms (mostly mice, fruit flies, and plants) for causal analyses and use weaker methods in their research with humans.

Clearly developmentalists must be cautious when applying inferences drawn from research with insects, plants, or other animals to explanations of human characteristics.

Canalization

The concept of the range of reaction focuses attention on the wide array of possible phenotypes that can result from the combination of a given genotype and the range of environments that can sustain the life of the organism. The notion of **canalization** highlights another aspect of gene–environment interactions: the fact that certain characteristics typical of a species may be restricted to a narrow range despite wide variations in environmental conditions (Waddington, 1947) (see Figure 2.8).

Just as a canal channels the flow of water into a narrow range, the genes affecting canalized traits channel the development of those traits so that they remain stable despite all but major changes in the environment. The capacity of children to acquire language is often cited as an example of a canalized develop-

Figure 2.8 Waddington's landscape. The rolling ball represents the developing organism. At each decision point, the organism can move forward along one of two diverging pathways. As development proceeds, it becomes increasingly difficult to move to a different pathway. (Adapted from Fishbein, 1976.)

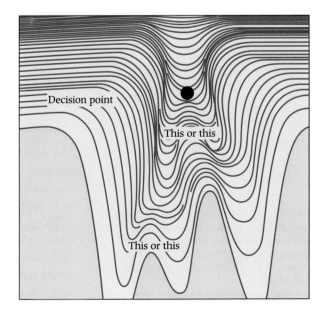

Decision point

This or this

This or this

mental process in humans. Only the most severe and prolonged deprivation of language input seems capable of deflecting language development from its species-typical developmental path.

Canalized processes also exhibit a strong tendency to self-correct after the organism is exposed to deviant experiences. Physical growth is an example of this principle. During an illness or a period of starvation, children's physical growth slows down, but when they recover or begin eating again, they grow at a faster rate than usual until they catch up with their original growth curves (Bogin, 2001). When development is not highly canalized, variability in the environment produces more frequent and more marked differences between individuals, and self-correction is less likely to occur in the wake of any unusual experiences.

The Study of Genetic Influences on Human Behavior

Although it is tempting to look for genetic "causes" to explain human characteristics—from physical traits such as height and weight to personality traits such as aggressiveness and intelligence—behavioral geneticists have long understood that this is an incorrect approach to understanding human development. Consequently, their conclusions about the role of genes with respect to behavioral characteristics such as mental retardation, language delay, temperament, and so on, are likely to use the phrase "genetically *influenced*" or "*heritable*" rather than "genetically *caused*." There are good reasons for this care in the use of terms.

Heritability

Behavioral geneticists know that any behavior that shows a large range of individual differences—shyness, say—is almost certainly influenced by multiple genes in interaction with the environment. Consequently, when they say that a characteristic such as shyness is "genetically influenced," this does not mean that a gene or set of genes that corresponds to shyness has been discovered. Nor does it mean that the environment plays no role in producing shyness. Rather, it means that there is a statistical correlation between a behavioral characteristic called shyness and the genetic variation in the population being studied. This correlation is called **heritability,** the degree to which variation in a particular characteristic (such as shyness) among individuals in a specific population is related to genetic differences among those individuals. Heritability is often represented by a statistical measure called a *heritability coefficient,* referred to as h^2. In mathematical terms, h^2 is defined as the proportion of variation in a behavior or trait, within a population, that can be attributed to genetic variation. As a formula, it is written

$$h^2 = \frac{\text{Variance due to genes}}{\text{Total variance}}$$

The total variance can be calculated directly from the measurements of the trait in question obtained from all the individuals in the sample. Genetic variation cannot be directly calculated. It must be estimated by comparing individuals who differ in their degrees of genetic relationship to each other (Plomin et al., 2001).

Using this formula, behavioral geneticists have calculated h^2 for a number of human characteristics. Consider the example of height, which for North Americans has a heritability of about 90 percent. Again, bear in mind that heritability is a *population* statistic. It does *not* apply to individual cases. To say that height is 90 percent heritable does not mean that in someone who is 72 inches tall, 64 of those inches

heritability A measure of the degree to which a variation in a particular trait among individuals in a specific population is related to genetic differences among those individuals.

are attributable to genes and the rest to the environment. Rather, it means that for the population as a whole, 90 percent of the variation in people's average height is the result of genetic factors. The reason for the high heritability of height in the United States is the relative lack of environmental diversity; in particular, nutritional levels are relatively similar throughout the population.

Finding significant heritability for a trait does *not* mean that the trait has some "true" level of heritability that holds true for all times, places, and populations. As Rutter and Plomin (1997) explain, "Estimates of heritability apply only to the population studied at that particular time, and under the environmental conditions that prevail at that point" (p. 209). For example, in studies conducted in the United States, estimates of the heritability of intelligence (as measured by IQ scores) increase between the ages of 16 and 20 presumably because young people often leave home at this time and there is a change in the environments they inhabit during this period of their lives (McGue, 1995).

Another misconception is that high heritability means that environmental interventions will be ineffective. Many people have argued that a trait that is highly heritable is relatively immune to environmental influences. This is simply not true. Height is the most prominent example of a highly heritable trait associated with strikingly different phenotypes. Although the heritability for height in North America at present is 90 percent, there has been a large increase in height in many nations during the twentieth century owing to improved nutrition (Tanner, 1990). Other misconceptions and myths about heritability are discussed in the box "The Concept of Heritability and Myths about Genetic Influences."

While it is generally true that human behavioral characteristics result from the action of many genes, in some cases geneticists have been able to identify individual genes that are responsible for a particular trait. Such traits are referred to as *discrete;* we can expect the discovery of more discrete genes as the science of molecular genetics identifies specific genes that can be closely tied to particular phenotypic characteristics across all known human environments. Williams syndrome, which produces a unique set of characteristics including extreme sociability, the likelihood of heart disease, and unusual language abilities, is one such discrete condition that we will discuss further in Chapter 8 (Bellugi & St. George, 2001). Geneticists have been able to locate the exact position where damage to a specific chromosome will result in this rare disease. In the vast majority of cases involving human characteristics, however, genetic influences are polygenic and continuous, requiring that behavioral geneticists rely on kinship studies, which allow them to specify correlations between behavioral characteristics and genetic variation in the population.

Kinship Studies

When conducting **kinship studies,** behavioral geneticists make use of the naturally occurring conditions provided by kinship relationships to estimate the genetic and environmental contributions to a particular phenotypic trait (Emde & Hewitt, 2001). That is, they determine the degree to which relatives of varying degrees of genetic closeness are similar on a given trait. Parents and their children share 50 percent of their genes; siblings also share 50 percent of their genes—except for identical twins, who share 100 percent of their genes; half siblings share 25 percent of their genes; and so on. If the degree of similarity on the trait correlates with the degree of genetic closeness, it can be inferred that the trait is heritable. Behavioral geneticists examine the similarity among relatives using three types of kinship designs: family, twin, and adoption.

kinship studies The use of naturally occurring conditions provided by kinship relations to estimate genetic and environmental contributions to a phenotypic trait.

The Concept of Heritability and Myths about Genetic Influences

In 1990 a consortium of institutions in the United States and other countries initiated the Human Genome Project. The ultimate goal of the project was to identify the physical makeup of every human gene (estimated to be 30 to 40 thousand in number), and to specify the identity and function of the approximately 3 billion base pairs strung along the chromosomes in human beings. (See Figure 2.1 to remind yourself how the four bases are combined in pairs along a ladderlike sequence on each chromosome.) The work of identifying the basic sequence of gene distribution along the chromosome was completed in April 2003. As a result, geneticists now have an invaluable tool for understanding the processes through which genes and combinations of gene sequences produce the proteins and other molecules that determine how an organism builds, operates, maintains, and reproduces itself as it responds to various environmental conditions (Office of Science, 2003).

Although only a relatively small number of genome sequences have been worked out, existing results are already beginning to identify sequences that are associated with diseases such as cancer, heart disease, and some forms of mental illness.

The increasing use of quantitative knowledge of the genetic makeup of individuals has led to an unprecedented interest in the role genes play in human development. But it has also led to confusions surrounding their role, such as recent press reports about

finding a "language gene" when, in fact, no gene that codes specifically for the ability to acquire language has been found. Rather, a gene has been identified that appears to be associated with increased clarity of verbal pronunciation, a part of what is necessary for oral speech. (Enard et al., 2002).

Worried about these confusions, Michael Rutter and Robert Plomin have warned against a number of widespread misconceptions about the nature of genetic influences on behavior that arise when enthusiasm for advances in identifying the human genome are applied uncritically (Rutter et al., 1997). Among the myths they identify are the following:

1. *Myth: Differences between populations are genetically determined.* Estimates of genetic variation within a population cannot legitimately be used to conclude that differences between populations are also genetically determined. Yet it is often assumed that high heritability on a given trait within a group means that differences between two groups on that trait are genetically based. This mistake is often made in discussions of IQ (which we deal with at length in Chapter 13). The heritability for IQ test performance during childhood is approximately 0.50, and there are significant differences between various population groups in their average IQ test performances (Japanese as a group, for example, score higher than

North Americans, and white North Americans as a group score higher than African Americans). Knowing the heritability of individual differences within the groups tells you nothing about the cause of the average differences between these groups because they are likely to differ in their environmental circumstances.

2. *Myth: Genetic effects are determinative.* It is an error to assume that there is a one-to-one correspondence between a gene and a disorder associated with it. Put differently, if you inherit the gene, you inherit the disorder. There are examples of this kind of correspondence, such as Huntington's disease, but such cases are rare. Even if only a few genes are associated with a disorder and the environment is held constant, the effects from person to person are likely to vary at the level of the phenotype. In addition, most disorders are determined by many genes acting in concert with an ensemble of environmental influences; this is the case for common medical conditions such as diabetes, hypertension, and asthma, as well as for such mental illnesses as depression.

3. *Myth: Genes associated with a disease must be bad.* Although it seems natural to suppose that genes associated with a disease are bad for development, this idea is incorrect for two reasons. First, some genes associated with a disease actually operate protectively. For example, about half the

---

family study A study that compares members of the same family to determine how similar they are on a given trait.

twin study A study in which groups of monozygotic (identical) and dizygotic (fraternal) twins of the same sex are compared to each other and to other family members for similarity on a given trait.

In the typical **family study,** relatives who live together in a household—parents, offspring, half offspring—are compared with one another to determine how similar they are on a given trait. The shortcoming of family studies for estimating the degree of genetic influence is the obvious fact that parents and siblings not only share genes but also participate in the same family environment. Thus whatever similarities are found among them could be attributed to environmental influences as well as to hereditary ones.

In order to obtain more precise estimates of genetic and environmental contributions to individual differences, behavioral geneticists capitalize on two other designs. One is the **twin study,** in which groups of monozygotic (identical) twins and dizygotic (fraternal) twins of the same sex are compared with each other and to family members for similarity on a given trait. Since monozygotic twins have 100 percent of their genes in common, whereas dizygotic twins (and other siblings) share 50 percent of their genes, monozygotic twins raised together should show greater similarity than dizygotic twins or siblings, insofar as genetic differences contribute to the trait being compared. By the same logic, dizygotic twins and siblings should be more similar than half sisters and half brothers.

"The good news is you will have a healthy baby girl. The bad news is she is a congenital liar."

Drawing by Handelsmann; © 1996. The New Yorker Magazine, Inc.

people in China and Japan possess an allele that blocks the metabolism of alcohol if the person is homozygous for it. If a person carrying this form of the gene drinks alcohol, the disruption of alcohol metabolism results in unpleasant symptoms such as flushing and nausea (McGue, 1993). It is believed that this genetic variant is responsible for the relatively low rates of alcoholism in Asian populations (Hodgkinson et al., 1991). Second, the same genetic influence may be a risk factor for certain behav-

ioral outcomes but a protective factor for others. This is true of shyness, which is a risk factor for anxiety disorder but a protective factor against antisocial behavior (Biederman et al., 1995).

4. *Myth: "Bad" genes justify both eugenics programs and termination of pregnancy.* **Eugenics** is the policy of attempting to rid the gene pool of genes considered undesirable by preventing individuals who have the genes from reproducing or by aborting fetuses known to carry particular genes, thereby ensuring that these genes are not passed on to the next generation. Eugenics is a bad idea based on a basic misunderstanding of the nature of how genes function. First, many genetically related diseases arise from genetic anomalies and mutations that are not inherited (for example, Down syndrome). Second, as we have seen, genes are only probabilistically related to phenotypes and are only one of many risk factors for any disease. That eugenics is an ill-conceived notion is highlighted by the fact that we all carry some "risk" genes that make us more susceptible to harmful phenotypes. We usually do not realize we carry such risk genes because they have not led to a particular disease—either because we do not have the other required risk genes or we have not encountered the specific environment that would lead to their expression.

5. *Myth: Gene therapy will be widely available.* It is often assumed that once the

genetic basis of many diseases has been determined, it will be possible to modify the involved genes early in development. However, to date the Food and Drug Administration (FDA) has not approved any human gene therapy product for sale. According to official publications of the Human Genome Project (2004), current gene therapy is experimental and has not proved very successful in clinical trials. Project directors report that little progress has been made since the first gene therapy clinical trial began in 1990. In 1999, gene therapy suffered a major setback with the death of 18-year-old Jesse Gelsinger, who participated in a gene therapy trial. He died from multiple organ failures 4 days after starting the treatment. His death is believed to have been triggered by a severe immune response. When we take into account that many of the diseases for which gene therapy might be sought (such as Alzheimer's and diabetes, which arise from the joint action of many different genes), it should be clear that effective gene therapies will be difficult to devise.

---

eugenics A policy of attempting to rid the gene pool of genes considered undesirable by preventing individuals who have the genes from reproducing, thereby ensuring that these genes are not passed on to the next generation.

The third design is the **adoption study,** which compares children who have been reared apart from their biological parents. Some adoption studies compare twins or siblings who have been adopted into different families. Other adoption studies compare biologically unrelated parents and children living in the same family. The basic purpose of this strategy is to determine if adopted children are more similar to their biological parents and siblings, who share their genes, or to their adoptive parents and siblings, with whom they share a common family environment.

Many studies using family, twin, and adoption strategies have shown that the degree of similarity among kin decreases as the degree of genetic similarity decreases. This pattern has been obtained for such varied characteristics as personality (Jang et al., 1998), IQ scores (Jacobs, et al., 2001), cheerfulness (Robinson, Emde & Corley, 2001), and susceptibility to schizophrenia (Gottesman & Erlenmeyer-Kimling, 2001). The typical results of these studies are reflected in Table 2.1 (p. 60), which presents results from a massive study of the correlations between the personalities of family members who differ in their degree of genetic relatedness (Loehlin, 1992). The personality trait under investigation is called "extroversion," which includes general sociability, impulsiveness, and liveliness.

---

adoption study A study in which genetically related individuals who are raised in different family environments or genetically unrelated individuals living in the same family are compared to determine the extent to which heredity or environment controls a given trait.

table 2.1

Family and Adoption Results for Extroversion		
Type of Relative	**Actual Correlation**	**Percentage of Shared Genes**
MZ twins raised together	.51	100
DZ twins raised together	.18	50
MZ twins raised apart	.38	100
DZ twins raised apart	.05	50
Parents/children living together	.16	50
Adoptive parents and children	.01	00
Siblings raised together	.20	50
Siblings raised apart	-.07	50

Source: Loehlin, 1992.

Both genetic and environmental influences are evident in the table. If you focus first on genetic influences, you will see that the correlations for monozygotic (MZ) twins are markedly greater than those for dizygotic (DZ) twins or siblings, whether they are raised together in a single family or apart in different families. You can also see that the degree of correlation between personality scores decreases consistently with decreasing degrees of family relationship. Environmental influences clearly play a role as well. The correlation between test scores for the monozygotic twins is well below 1.0, although these twins share 100 percent of their genes. Finally, the correlation between biological relatives who are raised together is higher than that between biological relatives raised apart.

Despite their usefulness, kinship studies are not without problems. It is possible, for example, that monozygotic twins may be treated more similarly than dizygotic twins or other siblings, and to the extent that they are, monozygotic twins may be more alike than dizygotic twins for environmental rather than genetic reasons (Segal, 1999). Even when siblings are adopted by different families and raised apart, the rearing environments may be similar because adoption agencies are likely to make every attempt to place children in secure, loving homes, often with people whose social and cultural backgrounds match those of the biological parents (Joseph, 2001). Thus the extent to which adopted children are similar to their biological families cannot be attributed entirely to the similarity of their genes; it may also be due to the similarity of the environments in which the families live.

At the same time, it cannot be assumed that children in a given family necessarily share the same environment. Some researchers have drawn attention to the fact that the family environment is not identical for all family members and that differences in the family-linked experiences of children living in the same home create differences between them (McGuire, 2002; Segal, 1999). These researchers point to a variety of factors that contribute to differences in the environments of siblings raised in the same family. For example, not only do parents treat each of their children differently, but siblings offer different environments for each other, and they are likely to have different teachers at school and different friends. The fact that the distinctive environments experienced by different children in the same family can lead to differences in their development in no way minimizes the importance of genetic factors. Rather, it affirms the principle that genes and the environment are two aspects of a single process of development. In later chapters, when we begin to examine the effects of the environment on development, it will be important to keep in mind that each of us experiences the world in a distinctive way that depends not only on the unique combination of genes we inherit from our parents but also on the unique environment each of us inhabits.

Mutations and Genetic Abnormalities

Despite its fantastic power to produce diversity in human beings, sexual reproduction is restricted to recombining genes that are already present in the human **gene pool,** the total variety of genetic information possessed by a sexually reproducing population. The gene pool can change, however, through **mutation,** an error in the process of gene replication that results in an alteration in the molecular structure of the DNA. A mutation can affect a particular gene or a sequence of genes on a chromosome. A mutation also results when only part of a chromosome is duplicated or when a part is lost. Mutations change the overall set of genetic possibilities that sexual reproduction then rearranges.

Mutations sometimes occur in the somatic (body) cells, but these changes affect only the person in whom they occur; they are not passed on to following generations. When mutations occur in a parent's sperm or ovum, the changed genetic information may be passed on to the next generation. Geneticists assume that spontaneous mutations have been occurring in germ cells constantly and randomly since life on earth began, introducing new genes into the gene pool of every species. Indeed, mutation is part of the evolutionary processes by which new subspecies and species are formed. The fact that mutations are a natural and fundamental part of life does not, however, mean that they usually benefit the individual organisms in which they occur. Each living organism is an intricate whole in which the functioning of the separate parts is interdependent. It is little wonder, then, that the introduction of even a small change in the genes can have serious repercussions for the individual.

It is estimated that as many as half of all human conceptions have some sort of genetic or chromosomal abnormality. The majority of these mutations and abnormalities are lethal and result in early miscarriage (Connor & Ferguson-Smith, 1993). Still, about 3.5 percent of all babies are born with some kind of genotypic aberration (Ward, 1994). Many of the more serious genetic abnormalities tend to be recessive, and an individual who receives a gene associated with an abnormality from one parent usually receives a normal gene or chromosome from the other parent that counteracts it. Some of the more commonly occurring disorders related to genetic abnormalities are listed in Table 2.2.

Developmentalists are interested in studying mutations and genetic abnormalities for three reasons:

1. Because mutations disturb the well-integrated mechanisms of development, an understanding of mutations can help reveal the intricate ways in which heredity and the environment interact.

2. If the existence of genetic abnormalities can be detected at a very early stage of development, ways may be found to prevent or ameliorate the birth defects that would normally result.

3. When children are born with genetic abnormalities, developmentalists are often responsible for finding ways to reduce the impact of the abnormalities on the children and their families.

These concerns can be illustrated in the current research being conducted on Down syndrome, phenylketonuria, sickle-cell anemia, and Klinefelter syndrome.

gene pool The total variety of genetic information possessed by a sexually reproducing population.

mutation An error in the process of gene replication that results in a change in the molecular structure of the DNA.

table 2.2

Common Genetic Diseases and Conditions

Disease or Condition	Description	Mode of Transmission	Incidence	Prognosis	Prenatal/Carrier Detection Possible?
Cystic fibrosis	Lack of an enzyme causes mucus obstruction, es-pecially in lungs and digestive tract	Recessive gene	1 in 3000 Caucasian births in U.S.; 1 in 17,000 African American births	Few victims survive to adulthood	Yes/Yes
Down syndrome	See text				
Hemophilia (bleeding disease)	Blood does not clot readily	X-linked gene; also occurs by spontaneous mutation	1 in 10,000 live births of males	Possible crippling and death from internal bleeding; transfusions ameliorate effects	Yes/Yes
Klinefelter syndrome	Males fail to develop secondary sex characteristics	Extra X chromosome	1 in 1000 U.S. white males	? Treatable?	Yes/No
Muscular dystrophy (Duchenne's type)	Weakening and wasting away of muscles	X-linked gene	1 in 3500 males under age 20	Crippling; often fatal by age 20	Yes/Yes
Neuro-fibromatosis	Highly variable; includes café au lait spots, benign tumors on periph-eral nerves, optic nerve tumors, learning disabilities	Dominant gene; 50% of cases are new mutations	1 in 3000 births	Variable depending on severity of disease; treated by surgery	No in case of spontaneous mutations/ No
Phenylketon-uria (PKU)	Lack of an enzyme causes buildup of substances in bloodstream that inhibit brain development	Recessive gene	1 in 15,000 U.S. white infants	Severe retarda-tion; treatable by restricted diet	No/Yes
Sickle-cell anemia	Abnormal blood cells cause circulatory problems and severe anemia	Recessive gene (victims are homo-zygous, but heterozygous subjects are mildly affected)	8–9% of U.S. blacks	Crippling; treatable with medication	Yes/Yes
Tay-Sachs disease	Lack of an enzyme causes buildup of waste in brain	Recessive gene	1 in 3600 among Ashkenazi Jews in U.S.	Neurological de-generation leading to death before age 4	Yes/Yes
Thalassemia (Cooley's anemia)	Abnormal red blood cells	Recessive gene	1 in 500 births in populations from subtropical areas of Europe, Africa, Asia	Listlessness, en-larged liver and spleen, occasion-ally death; treat-able by blood transfusions	Yes/Yes
Turner syndrome	Females fail to develop secondary sex characteristics	Lack of an X chromosome	1 in 5000 females	? Treatable?	Yes/No

Sources: Jorde et al., 1999; Rimoin et al., 1997; Simpson & Golbus, 1993.

Down Syndrome: A Chromosomal Error

Down syndrome was the first human disease to be linked with a specific chromo-somal disorder. More than 95 percent of the children born with Down syndrome have three copies of chromosome 21 instead of two. (For this reason, the disorder is sometimes called *trisomy 21*). Most children with Down syndrome are mentally and physically retarded and have several distinctive physical characteristics: slanting eyes; a fold on the eyelids; a rather flat facial profile; ears lower than normal; a short neck; a protruding tongue; dental irregularities; short, broad hands; a crease running all the way across the palm; small curved fingers; and abnormally wide-spaced toes (see Figure 2.9). On the average, children with this disorder are more likely than other children to suffer from heart, ear, and eye problems, and they are more susceptible to leukemia and to respiratory infections. As a result, they are more likely to die young (Frid et al., 1999).

Down syndrome occurs in about 1 of every 1000 births in the United States (Pueschel, 1992). A strong relationship has been found between the incidence of Down syndrome and the age of the parents, particularly the mother. Up to the age of 30 a woman's risk of giving birth to a live Down syndrome infant is less than 1 in 800. The risk increases to 1 in 100 by age 40, to 1 in 32 by age 45, and to 1 in 12 by age 49 (Chan et al., 1998). The risk is thought to increase with age because the human female is born with all the potential egg cells that she will ever produce. Thus older women have more time to be exposed to such environmental agents as viruses, radiation, and certain chemicals that can damage the chromosomes or interfere with the process of meiosis.

Figure 2.9 Individuals with Down syndrome can benefit from education and supportive activities tailored to their needs, such as the Special Olympics.

Over 10 percent of the people in institutions for the retarded suffer from Down syndrome (Plomin et al., 1997), but how effectively Down syndrome children function as they grow up depends not only on the severity of their disorder but also on the environment in which they are raised. Supportive intervention that includes special education by concerned adults can markedly improve the intellectual functioning of some of these children. Thus this genotype apparently has a wide range of reaction.

Phenylketonuria: A Treatable Genetic Disease

The modern history of phenylketonuria (PKU), an inherited metabolic disorder that leads to severe mental retardation if it is not treated, shows how the effects of a genetic defect can be reduced by changing the environment in which a child develops. PKU is caused by a defective recessive gene that reduces the body's ability to convert one amino acid (phenylalanine) into another (tyrosine). As a result, PKU children produce too much phenylalanine in their bloodstreams, which retards development of brain cells located in the prefrontal cortex (Diamond, 2002). It is estimated that 1 in every 10,000 infants born each year in the United States has PKU and that 1 in 100 people of European descent is a carrier of the recessive mutant gene (Guttler, 1988). The incidence of PKU is lower among blacks than among whites (Connor & Ferguson-Smith, 1993).

Knowledge of the abnormal biochemistry of PKU led researchers to hypothesize that if the accumulation of phenylalanine and phenylpyruvic acid could be prevented, infants with PKU might develop normally. Physicians have tested this hypothesis by feeding PKU infants a diet low in phenylalanine. (Phenylalanine is highly concentrated in such basic foods as milk, eggs, bread, and fish.) Such treatment reduces the severity of mental retardation significantly below that characteristic of untreated children with PKU, although current treatments are not sufficient to eradicate PKU's effects entirely (Diamond, 2002). The timing of the intervention is crucial. If phenylalanine intake is not restricted by the time a PKU infant is 1 to 3 months of age, the brain will already have suffered irreversible damage.

Most states require that newborns be given a blood test for PKU. This PKU screening is not infallible, however, and some PKU babies are not identified in time. PKU can be detected prenatally (Fan et al., 1999), and genetic testing can identify people who carry the recessive PKU gene, allowing carriers of the gene to decide whether they want to risk having a child with the disease. (See the box "Genetic Counseling.")

Genetic Counseling

Although effective gene therapies appear still to be well beyond the horizon of contemporary medicine, thanks to recent advances in the field of genetics many potential genetic problems can be avoided through genetic testing and counseling (Csaba, 2003). Genetic counselors inform expectant parents about the information they have concerning diagnosed genetic conditions that will put their child at risk. The counseling should be done in a way that allows the parents to decide as autonomously as possible about the choices confronting them and the child they are expecting.

Several situations are likely to signal that a couple needs genetic counseling:

1. They have one child with a disorder and are worried that any future children may have the same disorder.
2. They are close relatives of someone who has a genetic disorder.
3. They have had two or more miscarriages, a stillbirth, or an early infant death.
4. The woman has been exposed to infections, drugs, or other potentially dangerous substances during pregnancy.
5. They are in their mid-thirties or older and want to have children.

Several inherited disorders are especially likely to be found in specific groups of people. For example, the recessive allele for Tay-Sachs disease, in which a missing enzyme inevitably leads to death before the age of 4, is carried by 1 in 30 Ashkenazi Jews in the United States. Potential parents with genetic links to such a group can clearly benefit from genetic counseling.

In gene tests, DNA in cells taken from a person's blood, body fluids, or tissues is examined for an abnormality that flags a disease or disorder. The abnormality can be relatively large—a piece of a chromosome, or even an entire chromosome, missing or added. Sometimes the change is very small—as little as one extra, missing, or altered chemical base within the DNA strand. Genes can be amplified (too many copies), overexpressed (too active), inactivated, or lost altogether. Sometimes pieces of chromosomes become switched, transposed, or discovered in an incorrect location.

The alternatives or options that must be explained during genetic counseling often involve important ethical questions, depending upon the particular genetic abnormality, its treatability, and its likely consequences if there is no treatment (Mappes & DeGrazia, 2001). When a genetic disorder is detected, parents usually have only two alternatives: the woman can carry the pregnancy to term and give birth to a child who is genetically defective in some way, or she can terminate the pregnancy. This is not an easy choice, especially since the diagnosis often fails to predict the degree of disability the affected child will suffer or the quality of life that can be expected. The severity of a neural-tube defect, for example, can vary greatly, and many people who suffer from such defects have lived productive lives. In some cases, fetal surgery and other kinds of prenatal and postnatal interventions, such as a special diet or blood transfusions, can ameliorate the effects of a defect (as in the case of PKU).

In recent years, genetic counselors have become sensitive to the fact that the decisions parents face depend importantly on their cultural beliefs, such as the relative roles of men and women in family decision making and the ways in which delicate subjects are most effectively discussed. This recognition has given rise to a new subspecialty of multicultural genetic counseling (Penchaszadeh, 2001; Wang, 2001).

Prenatal diagnosis is a constantly changing field with expanding knowledge and new technologies; thus any attempt to define the state of the art rapidly becomes outdated. Health-care providers must be aware of the likelihood of changes and the importance of obtaining access to the latest information. For up-to-date information check the relevant entries at *www.thedevelopmentofchildren.com*.

Sickle-Cell Anemia:
An Example of Gene–Environment Interaction

The mutation that gives rise to the sickle-cell trait provides a good illustration of the interaction of heredity and environment. People who inherit the recessive gene for the sickle-cell trait from both of their parents, and thus are homozygous for it, suffer from sickle-cell anemia, a serious abnormality of the red blood cells. Normal red blood cells are round. In people with sickle-cell anemia, however, these cells take on a curved, sickle shape when the supply of oxygen to the blood is reduced, as it may be at high altitudes, after heavy physical exertion, or while under anesthesia (see Figure 2.10). These abnormal blood cells tend to clump together and clog the body's smaller blood vessels, causing people to experience pain. The disease causes the heart to enlarge and deprives the brain of blood. The deformed blood cells rupture easily, and the rupturing may lead to severe anemia and even to early death. However, people who are heterozygous for the sickle-cell gene usually do not suffer the severe symptoms. They may encounter some circulatory problems (40 percent of their red blood cells may assume the sickle shape when the supply of oxygen to the blood is reduced), but they are not at risk of death from the trait, as are those who are homozygous for it.

Sickle-cell anemia is found largely among people of African descent. In the United States, the incidence of the sickle-cell trait among African Americans is about 8 to 9 percent. But in West Africa, the incidence of the sickle-cell trait is

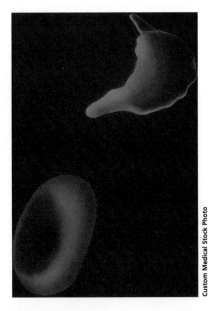

Custom Medical Stock Photo

Figure 2.10 A normal, round, red blood cell (bottom) and a sickle-shaped red blood cell (top) from a person with sickle-cell anemia.

greater than 20 percent (Connor & Ferguson-Smith, 1991). This difference is explained by the fact that heterozygous carriers of the sickle-cell trait are highly resistant to the parasite that causes malaria. Thus, in malaria-infested areas, such as the West African coast, people who carry the gene are at a selective advantage because they are less likely to suffer from malaria, which can be deadly, and are more likely to survive to reproduce. Because of this selective advantage, the frequency of the sickle-cell gene has been maintained in the West African population despite the losses caused by the deaths of homozygous carriers. In the United States, where the sickle-cell trait confers no advantage, it is gradually being eliminated from the gene pool.

Klinefelter Syndrome: A Sex-Linked Chromosomal Abnormality

Half of all chromosomal abnormalities in newborns involve the twenty-third pair of chromosomes—the X and Y chromosomes that determine the baby's sex. Occasionally a boy is born with an extra X or Y chromosome and has either an XXY or XYY genotype. Girls are sometimes born with only one X chromosome (XO) or three X chromosomes (XXX). Additionally, the X chromosome, which carries many genes, may be brittle and break into two or more pieces. Each of these chromosomal abnormalities has different implications for development.

The most common sex-linked chromosomal abnormality is Klinefelter syndrome, a condition in which males are born with an extra X chromosome (XXY). It is estimated that this abnormality occurs in about 1 of every 900 males born in the United States (Smyth & Bremmer, 1998). Males who have XXY appear to develop normally until adolescence, when they fail to show the typical signs of maturity: their sex organs do not mature; they do not acquire facial hair; their voices do not change; they have low levels of the male hormone, testosterone; and they are sterile. Most have speech and language problems and, as a result, have problems in school (Mandoki et al., 1991).

The most prevalent therapy for Klinefelter's syndrome is to begin testosterone replacement therapy at age 11 or 12, when testosterone levels begin to rise. The syndrome is not often diagnosed that early, but even if therapy is started later, it can have positive effects. The benefits include increased facial and pubic hair, a more masculine deposition of body fat, increased strength and bone density, and increased sexual functioning (Smyth, 1998).

Biology and Culture

In the absence of knowledge about genetics, many prominent biologists in the nineteenth and early twentieth centuries hypothesized that characteristics acquired by individuals during their lifetimes (what we now understand to be their phenotypes) are transmitted biologically to the next generation. This belief raised concerns that parents who engaged in criminal activity, for example, would pass on a tendency to criminality to their children in the same way that they passed on the genes that determined the colors of their children's eyes and hair (Gould, 1977).

Although the inheritance of acquired characteristics has been discredited as a mechanism of *biological* evolution, the idea behind it is not irrelevant to the study of development: cultural evolution does operate in a way that results in passing the experiences of one generation on to the next. Consider how the habit of making marks on objects has gradually evolved into symbol systems for writing and numerical calculation. Today the millions of children who are learning to read and do arithmetic in schools all over the world are mastering symbol systems that are vastly more complex than those used by any humans as recently as 10,000 years ago. This increased sophistication is not a consequence of biological evolutionary change

meme A basic unit of cultural inheritance. Like genes, memes evolve and are transmitted over time, but they are passed down through social, rather than biological, processes.

through the action of genes. Rather, it is the result of *cultural evolution*, in which the successful innovations of earlier generations—knowledge of when to hunt deer or to plant a field, of the alphabet, of the theorems of geometry—are passed on to succeeding generations through language, by example, and through deliberate instruction (Donald, 1991). There is little evidence that innovative forms of behavior are passed on from one generation to the next in nonhuman species (Tomasello, 1999).

Developmentalists are in the process of identifying ways to talk about how cultural practices—writing, hunting, mathematics—are passed on from one generation to the next. The term meme has been introduced as the cultural counterpart to the gene. While a gene is a basic unit of biological inheritance, a meme is a basic unit of cultural inheritance. Just as there is a gene that codes for eye color, so there is a meme that carries knowledge of how to hunt large game or how to study for an examination. Like genes, memes evolve and are transmitted over time, but they do so as a part of cultural, not biological, evolution (Massimini & Delle Fave, 2000). Many scholars are now examining the relationship between genetic evolution and cultural evolution (Plotkin, 2001).

Biology, Culture, and Survival Strategies

Practices that ensure survival often arise out of the interaction between biology and culture. Cultural evolution and transmission of information about how to obtain and preserve food, how to make shelters, and how to heal the sick and injured are obvious examples. Individuals who have access to these types of cultural tools are more likely to live to reproductive maturity and to pass on both their genes and their cultural knowledge to the next generation. This basic principle also applies to specific child-rearing practices, as argued by the anthropologist Robert Le Vine (1998).

Le Vine refers to the universal existence of cultural "hazard prevention strategies" that optimize the probability that children will grow to maturity and be able to raise children of their own. The strategies evolve over time in response to specific threats to the survival and well-being of children. For example, in places where the postweaning diet is low in protein and high in contaminants, many babies die when they are weaned from the breast. Following Le Vine's line of thinking, it is not surprising to find that in such environments, which exist in many parts of the world, breast-feeding typically extends well into the second year of life (Ahiadeke, 2000).

The Quechua people, who live at an altitude of 12,000 or more feet in the Andes Mountains of Peru, provide another example of a cultural hazard prevention strategy. The average daily temperature hovers around the freezing level for 340 days a year in this part of the world. To protect their children, Quechua mothers place their newborn infants in specially designed "manta pouches" that protect the baby from the cold temperatures and thin air of their surroundings. As the baby grows stronger, the thickness of the pouch is reduced accordingly. People's experience has taught them that the infants would be placed at great risk, and would be unlikely to survive, if their caregivers fail to practice the technique or implement it improperly (Tronick, et al., 1994).

The threat extends well beyond the infants themselves. Because the reproduction of genetic material is reduced if infants do not grow up and reproduce, the family line and the society as a whole would be placed at risk.

Coevolution

For many years it was believed that the biological and cultural characteristics of humans developed in a strict sequence: first the biological capacities we associate with humanity evolved to a critical point, and then an additional biological change occurred that allowed humans to use language and generate culture. Now, however,

Because Quechua babies live in an extremely cold environment, Quechua culture has elaborated modes of infant care which protect them from the cold, dry air. This practice illustrates how cultural factors modify the circumstances under which genes and the environment interact to create the phenotype in these extreme environmental conditions.

E. Z. Tronick, Child Development Unit, Harvard Medical School

the situation is believed to have been far more complicated. Contemporary studies of human origins have found evidence that rudimentary forms of culture were already present during early phases of human evolution. *Australopithecus* (one of our primitive ancestors, who lived some 3 million years ago) domesticated fire, built shelters, engaged in organized hunting, and used tools—flint knives, cooking utensils, and notation systems (Casper, 1997) (Figure 2.11).

Such findings indicate that the biological evolution of our species did not end with the appearance of culture. The brain of a modern person is about three times larger than the brain of *Australopithecus.* Most of this increase has occurred in the frontal lobes, those areas that govern complex, specifically human capacities (Donald, 2001). Insofar as the capacity to engage in cultural activities and to reason through the use of cultural tools—such as calendars, which permit people to know at what time of year their hunting, fishing, or planting is most likely to be successful—confers a selective reproductive advantage, it is probable that the more effective users of culture have been more successful in passing on their genes to succeeding generations. In short, culture has influenced biology, and the two forms of evolution, biological and cultural, have interacted with each other in a process called **coevolution** (Futuyma, 1998).

As a consequence of the coevolution of human physical and cultural characteristics, attempts to separate the influences of nature and nurture on the development of group differences between contemporary children are even more problematic than our earlier discussion of heritability suggests. The physical demands placed on people vary dramatically in different parts of the world. Furthermore, the cultural histories, as well as the gene pools, of people living in different locales have differed greatly for tens of thousands of years. These differences in environment and culture have clearly contributed to the physical differences among people, but whether they have also resulted in mental differences is by no means certain. When Japanese children excel at mathematics, for example, their performance might be attributed to a combination of genetically transmitted characteristics that have been shaped by Japanese culture (Stevenson, Chen & Lee, 1993). There are no general formulas for determining the precise contributions of culture and genes in shaping group differences in human abilities.

The complex interactions between genetic heritage, cultural heritage, and the physical environment are present at the very beginning, when genes in the zygote

coevolution The combined process that emerges from the interaction of biological evolution and cultural evolution.

Figure 2.11 The coevolution of toolmaking abilities and *Homo sapiens*. Rudimentary forms of culture were already present during early phases of human evolution.

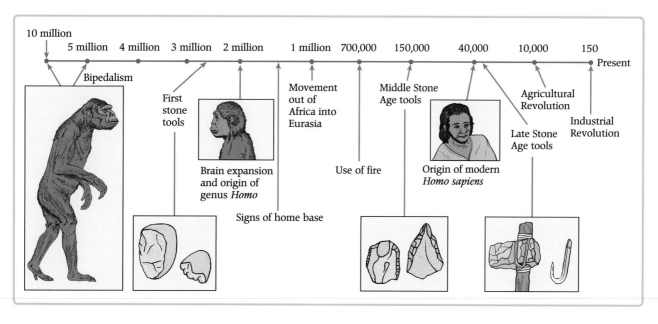

start to express themselves and guide the creation of new cells. Each new human being is but one variant within the overall range of possibilities that defines human beings. Chapter 3 follows the course of gene–environment interaction from the moment the genetic material of the mother and father come together. In later chapters, as we follow the general patterns of the development of children, you will repeatedly see instances of gene–environment interaction, with culture always playing a mediating role.

S U M M A R Y

Sexual Reproduction and Genetic Transmission

- The particular set of genes each human being inherits comes from his or her parents. Sexual reproduction rearranges the genetic combination in each new individual. With the exception of monozygotic twins, every person inherits a unique combination of genes, so great diversity among people is guaranteed.

- Throughout the life cycle new body cells are created by mitosis, a copying process that replicates the genetic material inherited at birth.

- The germ cells (sperm and ova) that unite at conception are formed by meiosis, a process of cell division that maintains a constant total of 46 chromosomes in each new individual.

- The sexes differ genetically in the composition of one pair of chromosomes. In females, the two chromosomes that make up the twenty-third pair are both X chromosomes (XX). Males have one X and one Y chromosome (XY).

Genotype and Phenotype

- The influence of genes on development must be studied at two levels—the individual's genetic constitution (genotype) and the individual's visible characteristics (phenotype)— because some genes are dominant and others are recessive and because a genotype can result in a wide variety of phenotypes, depending on the environment in which it develops.

- Genes associated with a particular characteristic can take different forms. If the corresponding genes inherited from two parents have the same form, the child will develop that form's associated characteristics. If the genes have two different forms, one may dominate the other, there may be an intermediate outcome, or an entirely new characteristic may emerge.

- The genes carried by the twenty-third pair of chromosomes give rise to sex-linked characteristics. Because females receive two X chromosomes, they get two doses of X-linked genes, one from each parent. Normal males receive only one X chromosome, and therefore only one dose of genes on the X chromosome, which always comes from the mother. Thus men are susceptible to genetic defects that usually do not affect females.

- In the study of gene–environment interactions several principles are widely used: (1) Many levels of the environment, from the local to the global, must be taken into account. (2) The notion of gene–environment interaction means that influences work in both directions. (3) Children actively shape the environments that influence their development.

- The overall relationship between genotype and phenotype can be established only by exposure of the genotype to a variety of environments. By charting the changes that occur in the phenotype as the environment is varied, geneticists can establish a range of reaction. Ideally, such a range specifies all possible phenotypes that are compatible with life for a single genotype.

- The range of reaction of most human characteristics has not been established because moral precepts and ethical standards make it impossible to carry out investigations that would expose people to all the environments that are compatible with human life.

- Some characteristics, such as language development in human beings, appear to be canalized; that is, they are restricted to a narrow range of variation and show a strong tendency to self-correction after the organism is exposed to deviant experiences.

- Only in cases where it has been possible to identify a specific gene that controls a specific pattern of phenotypes across all known environments where humans live has it been possible to make clear causal inferences from genes to behavior.

- As a substitute in the vast majority of cases where multiple, unknown, genes are likely to be involved, behavioral geneticists rely on the study of various kinship relations to estimate the relative influences of the genotype and the environment on the phenotype.

- Three types of kinship methods are widely used by behavioral geneticists: (1) In family studies, relatives who live together in a household are compared. (2) In twin studies, monozygotic and dizygotic twins are compared. (3) In adoption studies, children living apart from their biological parents are studied.

- Results of large-scale studies using family, twin, and adoption methods demonstrate the heritability of a wide range of traits, as well as the influence of the environment on development, but methods for estimating how much genetic and environmental factors contribute to the phenotype remain controversial.

Mutations and Genetic Abnormalities

- Mutation is a major source of variability in living organisms. Some mutations are compatible with normal life. Often, however, the changes brought about by mutation result in death or disorders.

- Studies of mutations and genetic abnormalities are of interest to developmentalists both for what they reveal about the process of gene–environment interaction in development and because of the need to devise preventive techniques and methods of therapy.

Biology and Culture

- Culture provides human beings with a mode of adaptation that other species do not have. Cultural evolution occurs when adaptations that arise in one generation are learned and modified by the next.

- Cultural artifacts such as tools and clothing greatly extend the range of environments in which human beings can reproduce and thrive.

- Cultural knowledge, such as the creation of "hazard prevention strategies," serves to protect and support children to enable them to mature and reproduce.

- Cultural evolution and biological evolution of human beings have interacted with each other in a process called coevolution, which greatly complicates attempts to separate the influences of nature and nurture in development.

Key Terms

adoption study, p. 59
allele, p. 51
behavioral geneticist, p. 53
canalization, p. 55
chromosome, p. 47
codominance, p. 51
coevolution, p. 67
crossing over, p. 48
deoxyribonucleic acid (DNA), p. 47
discrete traits, p. 52
dizygotic twins, p. 49
dominant allele, p. 51
environment, p. 51

eugenics, p. 59
family study, p. 58
gene pool, p. 61
genes, p. 47
genotype, p. 51
germ cells, p. 48
heritability, p. 56
heterozygous, p. 51
homozygous, p. 51
kinship studies, p. 57
meiosis, p. 48
meme, p. 66
mitosis, p. 48

monozygotic twins, p. 49
mutation, p. 61
phenotype, p. 51
polygenic trait, p. 52
range of reaction, p. 54
recessive allele, p. 51
sex-linked characteristics, p. 52
somatic (body) cells, p. 48
twin study, p. 58
X chromosome, p. 50
Y chromosome, p. 50
zygote, p. 47

Thought Questions

1. Can you think of a way in which the cultural values and preferences of your own ancestors may have influenced your genetic makeup?

2. Describe the complementary roles of mitosis and meiosis in the process of reproduction.

3. Name a behavioral tendency that you believe you have inherited. In what ways do you think this trait has been affected by your environment? Has it affected the way you have experienced your environment?

4. Why might the genetic disorder known as PKU be of special interest to researchers studying child development?

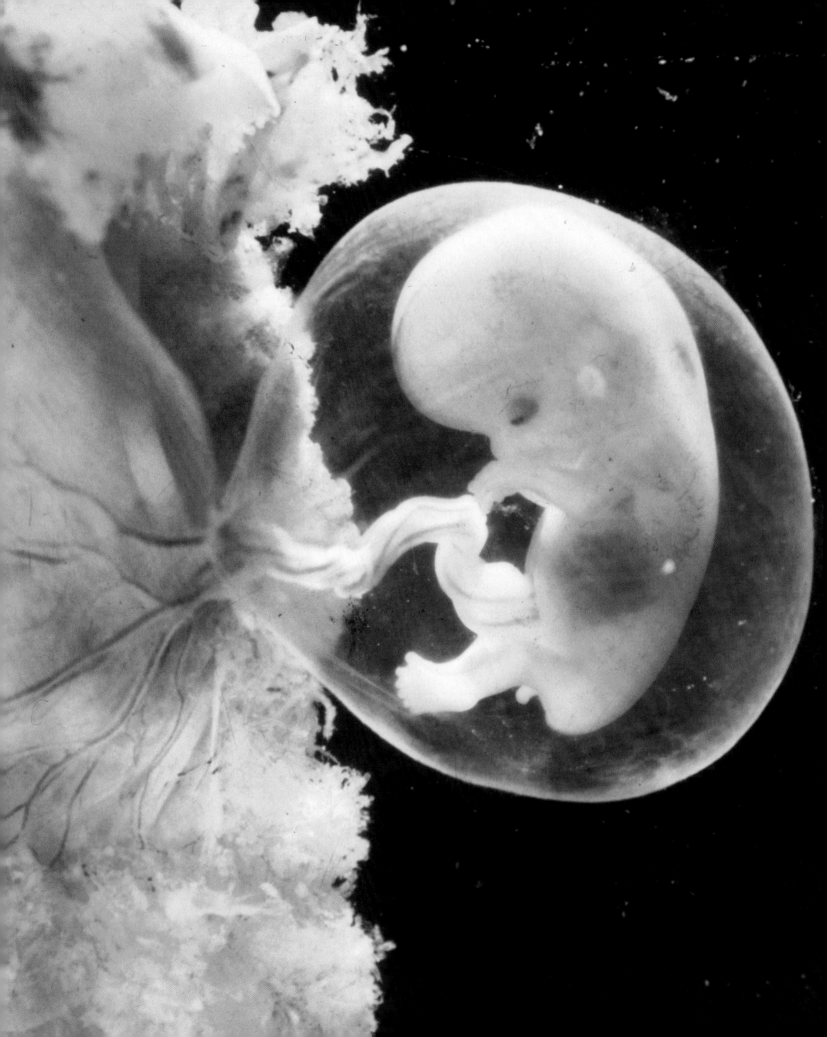

Prenatal Development and Birth

> "*Every man is some months older than he bethinks him, for we live, move, have being, and are subject to the actions of the elements and the malice of disease, in that other world, the truest Microcosm, the womb of our mother.*"
> —Sir Thomas Browne, Religio Medici, 1642

DELLA'S STORY

> *everything out of sync*
> *lights on and off*
> *contractions on top of each other . . .*
> *nurse never really there—and when she was, she wasn't, reprimanding . . .*
> *everybody talked to me while I'm blind—increasingly frozen with pain.*
> *Even Dr. A trying to extricate himself from my grasp: "you're breaking my hand and if you don't let go I won't be able to deliver your baby". . . .*
>
> *then the order to move my legs "square up your knees" the giant operating lights suddenly descending from the ceiling behind Dr. A's head. where am I? my head won't talk to my legs—can't make them move—can't breathe for the pain. . . .*
>
> *blue rubbery wet doll on my chest—I wish this gown was off. much to my amazement you are blond! (From Pollock, 1999.)*

NISA'S STORY

> *Mother's stomach grew very large. The first labor pains came at night and stayed with her until dawn. That morning, everyone went gathering. Mother and I stayed behind. We sat together for a while, then I went and played with the other children. Later, I came back and ate the nuts she had cracked for me. She got up and started to get ready. I said, "Mommy, let's go to the water well, I'm thirsty." She said, "Uhn, uhn, I'm going to gather some mongongo nuts." I told the children that I was going and we left; there were no other adults around. We walked a short way, then she sat down by the base of a large nehn tree, leaned back against it, and little Kumsa was born. (From Shostak, 1981.)*

These two descriptions of giving birth are from two vastly different cultures. The first describes the experience of a highly educated, middle-class, urban American woman. The second is provided by Nisa, a woman of the !Kung, a hunting-and-gathering society living in the Kalahari Desert of southern Africa. Each story is unusual in its own way, but neither is unique. In some societies, giving birth unassisted is treated as a cultural ideal that displays the mother's fearlessness and self-confidence. In other societies, birthing has become highly medicalized, while in still others the process is supported by other members of the community, particularly the women in the mother-to-be's family. No matter what the cultural circumstances, birth is the endpoint of a lengthy and crucial period of development that begins at conception.

Of all our existence, the 9 months we live inside our mother's womb are the most eventful for our growth and development. We begin as a zygote, a single cell the size of a period on this page, weighing approximately fifteen-millionths of a gram. At birth we consist of some 2 billion cells and weigh, on the average, 7 pounds. The changes that occur in our form are no less remarkable than the increase in our size (see Figure 3.1). The first few cells to develop from the zygote are all identical, but in a few weeks many different kinds of cells will be arranged in intricately structured, interdependent organs. In a few months, the baby-to-be will move and respond actively to its environment.

The study of prenatal development seeks to explain how these changes in form, size, and behavior take place. Understanding prenatal development is important for both theoretical and practical reasons. Many developmentalists consider prenatal development to be a theoretical model for development during all subsequent periods, from birth to death. Indeed, several principles of development are first seen in action during the prenatal period. For example, stagelike changes occur in which the organism acquires qualitatively distinct new physical forms that follow each other in a regular sequence. Each new stage is associated with distinct kinds of interaction between the developing organism and its changing environment. We will return to these principles later in the chapter.

On the practical side, understanding the prenatal period is important because the developing organism can be positively or adversely affected by the mother-to-be's nutritional status, health, and habits, including whether or not she uses drugs or alcohol. Considerable research is devoted to promoting healthy prenatal development and preventing damage to the growing organism.

Figure 3.1 Changes in the size and form of the human body from 14 days to 15 weeks after conception. (Adapted from Arey, 1974.)

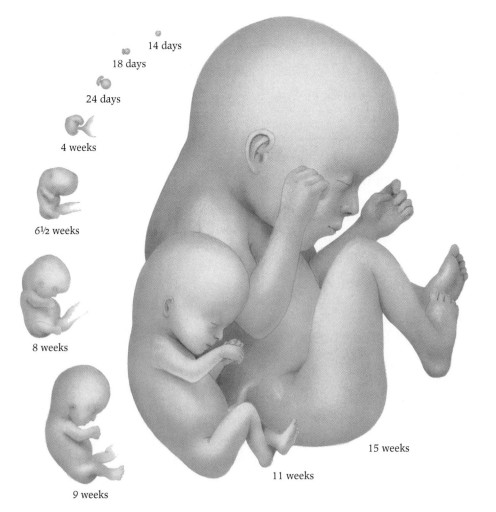

14 days

18 days

24 days

4 weeks

6½ weeks

8 weeks

9 weeks

11 weeks

15 weeks

In order to understand the relation of prenatal development in the womb to later development in the world, we first must trace the changes that take place as the organism progresses from zygote to newborn and examine the environmental factors that support or threaten development. Then we can consider the circumstances surrounding the newborn's entrance into the world.

The Periods of Prenatal Development

The transformations that occur during prenatal development are nothing short of amazing. Through a microscope, the fertilized ovum, or zygote, appears to be made up of small particles inside larger ones. The chromosomes bearing the genes are contained within the nucleus at the center of the cell. Surrounding the nucleus is the cell matter, which serves as the raw material for the first few cell divisions. The entire zygote is contained within a thin, delicate envelope called the **zona pellucida**. Within the first few weeks after conception, this single cell subdivides many times to form many kinds of cells with vastly different destinies. In approximately 266 days these cells will have been transformed into a wriggling, crying infant.

Developmental scientists often divide prenatal development into three broad periods, each characterized by distinctive patterns of growth and interaction between the organism and its environment: the germinal period, the embryonic period, and the fetal period.

1. The **germinal period** begins when the mother's and father's germ cells are joined at conception and lasts until the developing organism becomes attached to the wall of the uterus, about 8 to 10 days later.

2. The **embryonic period** extends from the time the organism becomes attached to the uterus until the end of the eighth week, when all the major organs have taken primitive shape.

3. The **fetal period** begins the ninth week after conception, with the first signs of the hardening of the bones, and continues until birth. During this period, the primitive organ systems develop to the point where the baby can exist outside the mother without medical support.

At any step in these prenatal periods, the process of development may stop. One study estimates that approximately 25 percent of all pregnancies end before the woman even recognizes that she is pregnant (Wilcox et al., 1999). If all goes well, however, the creation of a new human being is under way.

The Germinal Period

During the first 8 to 10 days after conception, the zygote moves slowly through the fallopian tube and into the uterus (see Figure 3.2). The timing of this journey is crucial. If the zygote enters the uterus too soon or too late, the uterine environment will not be hormonally prepared and the organism will be destroyed.

The First Cells of Life

Recall from Chapter 2 (p. 48) that all body cells reproduce through the process of duplication and cell division known as mitosis. **Cleavage,** the mitotic division of the zygote into several cells, begins about 24 hours after conception as

zona pellucida The thin envelope that surrounds the zygote and later the morula.

germinal period The period that begins at conception and lasts until the developing organism becomes attached to the wall of the uterus about 8 to 10 days later.

embryonic period The period that extends from the time the organism becomes attached to the uterus until the end of the eighth week of pregnancy, when all the major organs have taken primitive shape.

fetal period This period begins the ninth week after conception, with the first signs of the hardening of the bones, and continues until birth.

cleavage The series of mitotic cell divisions that transform the zygote into the blastocyst.

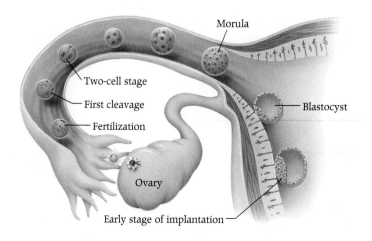

Figure 3.2 Development of the human embryo in the mother's reproductive tract from fertilization to implantation. (Adapted from Tuchmann-Duplessis et al., 1971.)

Morula

Two-cell stage

First cleavage

Fertilization

Blastocyst

Ovary

Early stage of implantation

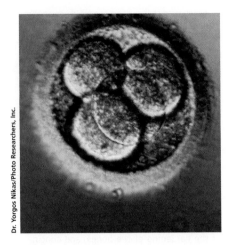

Dr. Yorgos Nikas/Photo Researchers, Inc.

Figure 3.3 A zygote after two cleavages, resulting in four cells of equal size and appearance.

the zygote travels down the fallopian tube. Thanks to the periodic doubling of each cell in the zygote, the developing organism will already consist of hundreds of cells by the time it reaches the uterus (see Figure 3.3).

An important characteristic of cleavage is that the cells existing at any given moment do not all divide at the same time. Instead of proceeding in an orderly fashion from a two-cell stage to a four-cell stage and so on, cells divide at different rates (Gilbert, 2001). This is the first instance of developmental **heterochrony,** whereby different parts of the organism develop at different rates. *Heterochrony* literally means "variability in time." This unevenness in rates of development gives rise to **heterogeneity**—variability in the *levels* of development of different parts of the organism at a given time. The fact that a newborn baby's sense of hearing is more advanced than its ability to see, for example, means that it will recognize its mother more readily by the sound of her voice than the way she looks. Both kinds of variability play an important role in the process of development throughout the life of the child.

The Emergence of New Forms in New Environments

As the first several cleavages occur, a cluster of cells called the **morula** takes shape inside the zona pellucida. For the first 4 or 5 days after conception, the cells in the morula become smaller and smaller with each cleavage until they are all approximately the size of the average body cell. Apart from being smaller, they look identical to their parent cells and resemble a large number of Ping-Pong balls crowded into a balloon. At this very early stage of development, every one of these cells, called **stem cells,** has the potential to grow into an embryo and a normal, healthy baby. (See the box "Stem Cells.")

As the cells in the morula completely pack its insides and reach the size of average body cells, the morula enters the uterus (often referred to as the *womb*), a new environment in which it will reside until birth. In the uterus, a new form of interaction between the organism and its environment begins: fluid passes from the uterus into the morula. The first noticeable changes in the morula's internal form emerge simultaneously with this interaction. As the fluid increases in the morula, it separates into two parts—an outer layer of cells and a group of centrally located cells—transforming it into the **blastocyst** (see Figure 3.4).

The two kinds of cells in the blastocyst play different roles in development because of the different ways they relate to each other and the environment of the blastocyst. The **inner cell mass,** the small knot of cells clustered along one side of the central cavity of the blastocyst, gives rise to the embryo. A layer of large, flat cells called the **trophoblast** forms a protective barrier between the inner cell mass and the environment. Later the trophoblast will develop into the membranes

Figure 3.4 Two stages in the development of the blastocyst: (a) the formation of the inner cell mass in the early blastocyst stage, and (b) the differentiation of the trophoblast cells in the late blastocyst stage. By the late blastocyst stage, the zona pellucida has disappeared. (Adapted from Moore & Persaud, 1993.)

that will protect the developing organism and transmit nutrients to it. (Appropriately, "trophoblast" comes from the Greek word, *trophe,* which means "nourishment.") As the cells of the blastocyst differentiate, the zona pellucida surrounding it disintegrates. The trophoblast now serves as a kind of pump, filling the inner cavity with life-giving fluid from the uterus and removing waste products, which enables the cells to continue to divide and the organism to grow. Although it is easy enough to describe the transformations of the undifferentiated cells of the

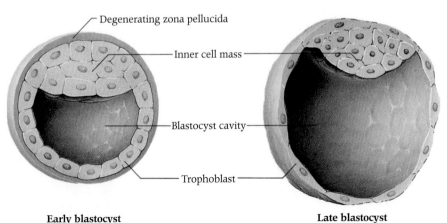

Degenerating zona pellucida

Inner cell mass

Blastocyst cavity

Trophoblast

Early blastocyst
(a)

Late blastocyst
(b)

Stem Cells

Stem cells are specialized kinds of cells that have the unique ability to renew themselves for long periods of time and to give rise to a wide variety of other specialized cells, in some cases to all of the 200 or so kinds of cells that make up a mature human body (Thomson, 2001). The form of stem cell that has attracted the most attention arises early in the first week following conception in the inner cell mass of the blastocyst. Any of such cells, if placed into a woman's uterus, has the potential to develop into a fully formed, normal baby. These stem cells are called *totipotent* (totally potent) to indicate that they have total flexibility to become any other kind of cell. In fact, identical twins develop when two such totipotent cells separate and develop into two individual, genetically identical human beings.

Stem cells still exist several days after the blastocyst has differentiated into the three germ layers called the mesoderm, endoderm, and ectoderm. At this point, however, they are no longer able to form a complete new organism. They are referred to as *pluripotent* (multiply potent) because they can give rise to many types of cells that each of the three layers will give rise to but not all types of cells necessary for fetal development (Turksen, 2002).

Research on stem cells has generated great interest among developmentalists, politicians, and the public alike. Stem cells are important to the study of development because they provide a tool for understanding the complex events that occur during the differentiation and reintegration of cells that are central to understanding all developmental processes. They are of equally great interest to politicians and the public because they

offer the possibility of a renewable source of replacement cells and tissue to treat myriad diseases and disabilities including Parkinson's and Alzheimer's diseases, spinal cord injury, stroke, burns, heart disease, diabetes, and rheumatoid arthritis (NIH, 2002). But research with stem cells raises troubling ethical issues because they must either be harvested through deliberate abortion (in the case of totipotent cells) or from fetuses who are spontaneously aborted later in pregnancy (in the case of pluripotent stem cells). A major challenge facing developmentalists is to find ways to continue to learn more about stem cells—because of their importance for understanding general principles of development and their enormous potential for improving human health and development—but to do so in a way that is both ethically acceptable and practical.

---

zygote, first into the two kinds of cells in the blastocyst and eventually into the multitudes of kinds of cells present at birth, the mechanisms by which these changes occur remain perhaps *the* central puzzle of development. What makes the different groups of cells take on different forms?

Current explanations emphasize the idea that each new form emerges as a result of the interactions that take place between the preceding form and its environment, a process called **epigenesis** (from a Greek expression meaning "at the time of generation") (Gottlieb, 2002). In the case of the morula, the "environment" varies according to the location of the two different kinds of cells inside the morula. The cells at the center of the morula are surrounded by other morula cells. Those on the outside have some contact with other morula cells, but on one side they are also in contact with the zona pellucida, which in turn is in contact with the mother's reproductive tract and its fluids. When the morula begins to exchange fluids with its environment, those nutrients and waste products must pass through the outer layer of cells. As a result, the outside cells are subject to different environmental influences than are the cells on the inside. According to the epigenetic explanation of embryonic development, the different interactions that cells have with their environmental conditions (including each other) is what leads to the creation of new kinds of cells and subsequent new forms of interaction between the organism and the environment (Gilbert, 2001).

Implantation

As the blastocyst moves farther into the uterus, the outer cells put out tiny branches that burrow into the spongy wall of the uterus until they come in contact with the mother's blood vessels. Thus begins **implantation,** the process by which the blastocyst becomes attached to the uterus. Implantation marks the transition between the germinal and the embryonic periods. Like many of life's transitions (birth being an especially dramatic example), implantation is hazardous for the organism and pregnancy loss is common during this process.

heterochrony Variability in the rates of development of different parts of the organism.

heterogeneity Variability in the levels of development of different parts of the organism at a given time.

morula The cluster of cells inside the zona pellucida.

stem cells The cells of the morula, every one of which has the potential to grow into an embryo and a normal, healthy baby.

blastocyst The hollow sphere of cells that results from the differentiation of the morula into the trophoblast and the inner cell mass.

inner cell mass The collection of cells inside the blastocyst that eventually becomes the embryo.

trophoblast The outer layer of cells of the blastocyst that develop into the membranes that protect and support the developing organism.

epigenesis The process by which a new form emerges through the interactions of the preceding form and its current environment.

implantation The process by which the blastocyst becomes attached to the uterus.

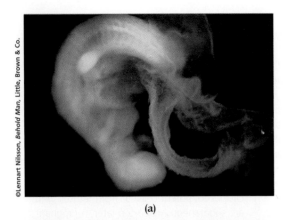

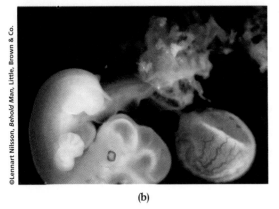

(a)

(b)

The human embryo at (a) 3 and (b) 5 weeks after conception.

The Embryonic Period

If the blastocyst is successfully implanted, the developing organism enters the period of the embryo, which lasts for about 6 weeks. During this time, all the basic organs of the body take shape, and the organism begins to respond to direct stimulation. The organism's rapid growth during this period is facilitated by the efficient way the mother now supplies it with nutrition and protects it from harmful environmental influences.

Sources of Nutrition and Protection

Early in the embryonic period, the **amnion,** a thin, tough, transparent membrane that holds the amniotic fluid ("bag of waters"), surrounds the embryo. The amniotic fluid cushions the organism as the mother moves about, provides liquid support for its weak muscles and soft bones, and gives it a medium in which it can move and change position.

Surrounding the amnion is another membrane, the **chorion,** which later becomes the fetal component of the **placenta,** a complex organ made up of tissue from both the mother and the embryo. The placenta and the embryo are linked by the **umbilical cord.** Until birth, the placenta acts simultaneously as a barrier that prevents the bloodstreams of the mother and the infant from coming into direct contact and as a filter that allows nutrients and oxygen to be exchanged. It converts nutrients carried by the mother's blood into food for the embryo. It also enables the embryo's waste products to be absorbed by the mother's bloodstream, from which they are eventually extracted by her kidneys. Thus the mother literally eats, breathes, and urinates for two (see Figure 3.5).

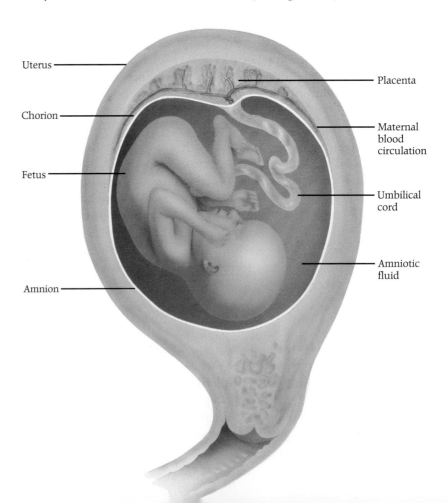

Figure 3.5 The fetus in its protective environment. (Adapted from Curtis, 1979.)

Embryonic Growth

While the outer cells of the blastocyst are forming the placenta and the other membranes that will supply and protect the embryo, the growing number of cells in the inner cell mass begin to differentiate into the various kinds of cells that eventually will become all the organs of the body. The first step in this process is the separation of the inner cell mass into two layers. The **ectoderm,** the outer layer, gives rise to the outer surface of the skin, the nails, part of the teeth, the lens of the eye, the inner ear, and the nervous system (the brain, the spinal cord, and the nerves). The **endoderm,** the inner layer, develops into the digestive system and the lungs. Shortly after these two layers form, a middle layer appears, the **mesoderm,** which will eventually become the muscles, the bones, the circulatory system, and the inner layers of the skin (Gilbert, 2001).

The embryo develops at a breathtaking pace, as you can see in Table 3.1. The table also reflects two patterns of body development that are maintained until the organism reaches adolescence. In the first, the **cephalocaudal pattern,** development proceeds from the head down. The arm buds, for instance, appear before the leg buds. In the second, the **proximodistal pattern,** development proceeds from the middle of the organism out to the periphery. Thus, the spinal cord develops before the arm buds; the upper arm develops before the forearm; and so on. In general, the process of organ formation is the same for all human embryos, but in one major respect—sexual differentiation—it varies.

table 3.1

Growth and Development of the Embryo

Days 10–13
Cells separate into ectoderm, endoderm, and mesoderm layers. The neural plate, which eventually will become the brain and the spinal cord, forms out of the ectoderm.

Third Week
The three major divisions of the brain—the hindbrain, the midbrain, and the forebrain—begin to differentiate by the end of the third week. Primitive blood cells and blood vessels are present. The heart comes into being, and by the end of the week it is beating.

Fourth Week
Limb buds are visible. Eyes, ears, and a digestive system begin to take form. The major veins and arteries are completed. Vertebrae are present, and nerves begin to take primitive form.

Fifth Week
The umbilical cord takes shape. Bronchial buds, which eventually will become the lungs, take form. Premuscle masses are present in the head, trunk, and limbs. The hand plates are formed.

Sixth Week
The head becomes dominant in size. The halves of the lower jawbone meet and fuse, and the components of the upper jaw are present. The external ear makes its appearance. The three main parts of the brain are distinct.

Seventh Week
The face and neck are beginning to take form. Eyelids take shape. The stomach is taking its final shape and position. Muscles are rapidly differentiating throughout the body and are assuming their final shapes and relationships. The brain is developing thousands of nerve cells per minute.

Eighth Week
The growth of the gut makes the body evenly round. The head is elevated and the neck is distinct. The external, middle, and inner ears assume their final forms. By the end of this week the fetus is capable of some movement and responds to stimulation around the mouth.

amnion A thin, tough, transparent membrane that holds the amniotic fluid.

chorion One of the membranes that develops out of the trophoblast. It forms the fetal component of the placenta.

placenta An organ made up of tissue from both the mother and the fetus that serves as a barrier and filter between their bloodstreams.

umbilical cord A soft tube containing blood vessels that connects the developing organism to the placenta.

ectoderm Cells of the inner cell mass that develop into the outer surface of the skin, the nails, part of the teeth, the lens of the eye, the inner ear, and the central nervous system.

endoderm Cells of the inner cell mass that develop into the digestive system and the lungs.

mesoderm The cells of the inner cell mass that give rise to the muscles, the bones, the circulatory system, and the inner layers of the skin.

cephalocaudal pattern The pattern of development that proceeds from the head down.

proximodistal pattern The pattern of development that proceeds from the middle of the organism out to the periphery.

Sexual Differentiation

As we described in Chapter 2 (p. 50), the genes that influence sexual determination are located on the X and Y chromosomes inherited at conception. Zygotes with one X and one Y chromosome are genetically male, whereas zygotes with two X chromosomes are genetically female. For the first 6 weeks after conception, however, there is no structural difference between genetically male and genetically female embryos. Both males and females have two ridges of tissue, called *gonadal ridges,* from which the male and female sex organs (gonads) will develop. Initially, these ridges give no clue to the sex of the embryo.

The genes inherited at the moment of conception determine whether the sex glands that develop from the gonadal ridges will be male testes or female ovaries. If the embryo is genetically male (XY), the process of sexual differentiation begins during the seventh week of life, in the transition to the fetal period, when the gonadal ridges begin to form testes. If the embryo is genetically female (XX), no changes are apparent in the gonadal ridges until several weeks later, when ovaries begin to form.

At the end of the seventh week after conception, genetically male and genetically female embryos still look the same. From this point on, though, it is not the presence of the Y chromosome itself but rather the presence or absence of male gonads that determines whether the embryo will develop male or female genitals. The male hormones produced by the male gonads, called *androgens,* determine maleness. Chief among the androgens is testosterone. If testosterone is present, the membranes are transformed into the male penis and scrotum. If testosterone is not present, female external genitalia are formed. Femaleness, then, depends on the *absence* of testosterone, not on the secretion of hormones by the ovaries. The influence of androgens is not limited to the gonads and the genital tract. During the last 6 months of prenatal development, the presence of testosterone suppresses the natural rhythmic activity of the *pituitary gland,* located in the brain. If testosterone is absent, the pituitary gland establishes the cyclical pattern of hormone secretion that is characteristic of the female and eventually comes to control her menstrual cycle (Wilson, 1995). Because the embryo has the potential to develop into either a male or a female, errors in sex development sometimes result in a baby's having sex organs that show characteristics of both sexes. A baby with this condition is called a *hermaphrodite.*

The Fetal Period

The fetal period begins once all the basic tissues and organs exist in rudimentary form and the tissue that will become the skeleton begins to harden, or ossify (Gilbert, 2001). During the fetal period, which lasts from the eighth or ninth week of pregnancy until birth, the fetus increases in length from approximately $1\frac{1}{2}$ inches to 20 inches and in weight from approximately 0.02 to 7.1 pounds (see Figure 3.6).

Over the course of the fetal period, each of the organ systems increases in complexity. By the tenth week after conception, the intestines have assumed their characteristic position in the body. Two weeks later, the fetus's external sexual characteristics are visible and its neck is well defined. By the end of 16 weeks, the head is erect, the lower limbs are well developed, and the ears, which began to take form in the fourth week, migrate from the neck to the sides of the head. By the end of the fifth month, the fetus has almost as many nerve cells as it will ever have as a person. By the end of the seventh month, the lungs are capable of breathing air, and the eyes, which have been closed, open and can respond to light. By the end of the eighth month, many folds of the brain are present, enabling brain cells to be packed more efficiently within the skull, and during the ninth month, the brain becomes considerably more wrinkled. In the final weeks before birth, the fetus doubles in weight.

The fetal period marks a critical stage during which the baby-to-be becomes responsive to its environment in new ways. Development is influenced by factors both inside and outside the uterus. Events inside the uterine environment affect the organism in a variety of ways. The mother's digestive system and heart are sources of noise, and her movements provide motion stimuli. The fetus comes in contact with the world outside the mother through the wall of her abdomen and, less directly, through the placenta and umbilical cord. Nutrients, oxygen, some viruses, and some potentially harmful chemicals all cross the placenta to the fetus. Through these various routes, a mother's experiences, illnesses, diet, and social circumstances can affect the child before it is born.

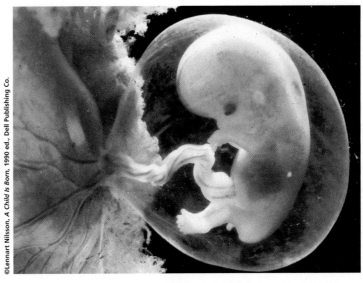

©Lennart Nilsson, *A Child Is Born*, 1990 ed., Dell Publishing Co.

Figure 3.6 The fetus at the beginning of the fetal period (approximately 9 weeks). The way the umbilical cord is attached to the placenta is clearly visible.

Sensory Capacities

Using modern techniques of measurement and recording, researchers have begun to produce a detailed picture of the development of sensory capacities before birth (Lecanuet, Graniere-Deferre, Jacquet & DeCasper, 2000). This information is essential for determining how the fetus is influenced by its uterine environment. Scientists have discovered the following about the fetus's sensory capacities:

- *Sensing motion.* The vestibular system of the middle ear, which controls the sense of balance, begins to function in the human fetus about 5 months after conception and is fully mature at birth (Lecanuet & Jacquet, 2002). This early maturity means that the fetus is capable of sensing changes in the mother's posture and orienting itself as it floats inside the fluid-filled amniotic sac.

- *Seeing.* Little is known for certain about the extent of the fetus's visual experience. At 26 weeks following conception, fetuses respond to light; it causes their heart rates to change, and it causes them to move (Lecanuet & Schaal, 1996). Aidan Macfarlane (1977) suggested that toward the end of pregnancy, the fetus may be able to see light that has penetrated the mother's stretched stomach wall. He likens the fetus's visual experience to the glow seen when the palm of the hand covers the bulb of a flashlight.

- *Hearing.* The fetus is able to respond to sound at 5 to 6 months after conception (Abrams, Gerhardt & Antonelli, 1998). Studies in which tiny microphones have been inserted into the uterus adjacent to the fetus's head reveal that the average sound level inside the womb is approximately 75 decibels, about the level at which we hear the outside world when we ride in a car with the windows up. This background noise is punctuated by the sound of air passing through the mother's stomach and, every second or so, by the more intense sound of the mother's heartbeat. Of all such sounds, the mother's voice is heard best because it is also transmitted as vibrations through her body. When sounds of moderate intensity are presented, it is possible to detect changes in the fetus's heart rate (Kisilevsky, Hains & Low, 2001; Lecanuet & Schaal, 1996).

Because external sounds must pass through the mother's abdomen and the amniotic fluid before the fetus can hear them, things sound different in the womb than they do outside it. In experiments using recordings of the mother's natural voice and her voice when it has been filtered to resemble how it sounded to the fetus while in the womb, newborns prefer the latter (Fifer & Moon, 1995).

table 3.2

Appearance of Fetal Movements in Early Pregnancy	
Movement	**Gestational Age (weeks)**
Any movement	7
Startle	8
Generalized movements	8
Hiccups	8
Isolated arm movements	9
Head retroflexion	9
Hand–face contact	10
Breathing	10
Jaw opening	10
Stretching	10
Head anteflexion	10
Yawn	11
Suck and swallow	12

Source: De Vries et al., 1982. Adapted by permission.

Fetal Activity

You might think of the fetus as floating passively in the amniotic fluid as its organs grow. But within 8 weeks following conception, the embryo begins to become active, and this activity is important to its development.

As the embryo enters the fetal stage, its body movements become increasingly varied and coordinated (see Table 3.2). At 15 weeks of age, the fetus is capable of all the movements observable in newborn infants such as head turning and leg flexing (James et al., 1995). Toward the end of the fourth month, the fetus is big enough for the mother to feel its movements.

Research has also shown that fetal *inactivity* is important to development. From 24 to 32 weeks after conception, the relatively high rate of fetal activity begins to be interrupted by quiet periods, and there is a gradual decrease in the fetus's movements (Kisilevsky & Low, 1998). These quiet periods are believed to reflect the development of neural pathways that inhibit movement. The appearance of these inhibitory pathways is related to maturation in the higher regions of the brain (see Figure 3.7).

Evidence indicates that spontaneous fetal activity plays a significant role in development (Smotherman & Robinson, 1996). Experiments with chick embryos, for example, suggest that prenatal activity is crucial to normal limb development. Under normal circumstances, the spinal cord sends out neurons, or nerve cells, to connect the limbs to the brain—many more neurons than the animal will need when it is fully coordinated. Many of these neurons die off, while the remainder are connected to muscles in an efficient way. If chick embryos are treated with drugs that prevent them from moving, the elimination of excess neurons that ordinarily accompanies neuromuscular development fails to occur. The results are disastrous. In as little as 1 or 2 days, the failure to prune away all but the neurons compatible with coordinated movement causes the joints of the chick embryos to become fixed into rigid structures, a result showing that movement is necessary for normal limb development (Pittman & Oppenheim, 1979). Fetal movements are believed to play a similar role in establishing basic neuronal connections in humans.

Breathing movements are another good example of the importance of prenatal activity to the human fetus. The fetus does not breathe in utero. It obtains oxygen through the placenta. Yet certain "breathing" movements with its chest and lungs increase at this time. Without these movements the muscles necessary for respiration after birth would be insufficiently developed (Natali et al., 1988).

Learning in the Womb

The folklore of many societies includes the belief that the fetus can learn sound patterns of stories and songs while in the womb (Lefeber & Voorhoeve, 1998). Although such beliefs have met with considerable skepticism, there is evidence that the fetus learns from at least some events both inside and outside the mother (Hepper & Shahidullah, 1994; van Heteren, Boekkooi, Jongsma & Nijhuis, 2000).

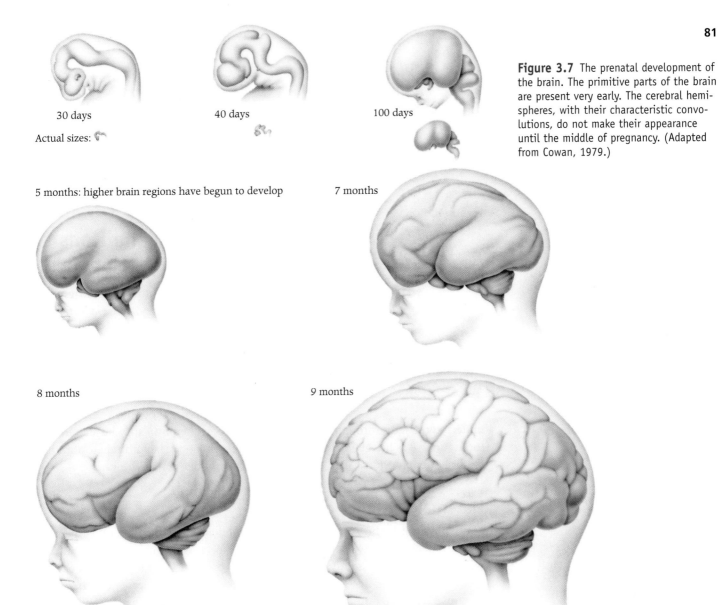

30 days

40 days

100 days

Actual sizes:

Figure 3.7 The prenatal development of the brain. The primitive parts of the brain are present very early. The cerebral hemispheres, with their characteristic convolutions, do not make their appearance until the middle of pregnancy. (Adapted from Cowan, 1979.)

5 months: higher brain regions have begun to develop

7 months

8 months

9 months

In a particularly well-known study, Anthony DeCasper and Melanie Spence (1986) asked 16 pregnant women to read aloud a particular passage from *The Cat in the Hat*, a rhyming children's story by Dr. Seuss, twice a day for the last month and a half before their babies were due. By the time the babies were born, the passage had been read to them for a total of about $3^{1}/_{2}$ hours.

Two or three days after the babies were born, DeCasper and Spence tested them with a pacifier that had been wired to record sucking rates (see Figure 3.8). First the babies were allowed to suck for 2 minutes to establish a baseline sucking rate. Afterward, changes in the rate of sucking turned on or off a tape recording of their mothers reading a story. For half of the babies, increasing their sucking rates turned on the passage from *The Cat in the Hat* that their mothers had previously read aloud, while decreasing their sucking rate turned on a story their mothers had not read. For the other half, increased sucking turned on the new story, while decreased sucking produced *The Cat in the Hat*. The key finding was that the infants modified their rates of sucking to produce *The Cat in the Hat*. The investigators concluded that the babies had indeed heard the stories being read to them by their mothers and that their learning in the womb influenced the sounds they found

Melanie Spence, University of Texas

Figure 3.8 This baby is listening to a recording of its mother telling a story. The apparatus records changes in sucking to determine how newborns react to stories read to them while they were in the womb.

The fetus evokes intense interest from its parents and siblings. The fetus is affected by this attention because it is sensitive to sounds from outside the womb.

Ericka McConnell/Getty Images

rewarding after birth. Later research has shown that in the weeks before birth, fetuses are sensitive to small differences in musical notes and prefer the sounds of their native language, even though it will be many months before they begin to speak it (Lecanuet et al., 2000).

Maternal Conditions and Prenatal Development

Although the mother's womb provides a protective and supportive environment for prenatal growth, the baby-to-be is influenced by the larger world. Outside influences are not restricted to hearing but include different sources of environmental influence that reach the organism through changes in the mother that are then transmitted to the fetus through the placenta. Her body chemistry may be altered by factors as diverse as her general environmental circumstances, her attitude toward having the baby, her emotional state, the food she eats, and her general health.

Maternal Attitudes and Stress

Many physicians who care for pregnant women and newborn infants suspect that a woman's feelings of well-being and her attitude toward her pregnancy affect the well-being of the fetus and of the child after its birth. The clearest evidence that a mother-to-be's negative attitudes can affect her baby's development comes from an extensive investigation conducted in Czechoslovakia in the 1960s and 1970s. Henry David (1981) studied the lives of 220 children whose mothers indicated strong negative attitudes toward having them by twice asking for an abortion. The refusal of the abortion was an indication that medical authorities believed these women to be capable of carrying through the pregnancy and raising the child.

The unwanted children were compared with a carefully matched control group of children whose mothers either had planned for or had accepted their pregnancies. The mothers in the two groups were matched for socioeconomic status and age; the children were matched for sex, birth order, number of siblings, and date of birth. At birth, the unwanted children weighed less and needed more medical help than the children in the control group, even though their mothers had ready access to medical care and were judged to be in good health themselves.

Even when a child is wanted and a pregnant woman has a supportive family, a moderate amount of stress can be expected during pregnancy. The mother-to-be has to adjust her life to accommodate new responsibilities. One who decides to quit her job may have to cope with a reduced income. Another may be working so hard that she feels she does not have enough time to take care of herself, let alone her expected child. And if the pregnancy was unplanned, as many are, the stress that normally accompanies pregnancy may be magnified.

Studies have shown that a mother who is under stress or becomes emotionally upset secretes hormones, such as adrenaline and cortisol, that pass through the placenta and have a measurable effect on the fetus's motor activity (Relier, 2001).

These effects can be long-lasting. Elizabeth Susman and her colleagues report that mothers who experienced more stressful environments during pregnancy produced elevated levels of cortisol and that at 3 years of age their children were more aggressive than children of mothers who experienced low stress and produced lower levels of cortisol while pregnant (Susman, Schmeelk, Ponirakis & Gariepy, 2001). Stress during pregnancy is also associated with premature delivery and **low birth weight** (a weight of less than 5 pounds) (Chicz-DeMet et al., 2001).

Nutritional Influences

Fetuses depend on their mothers for the nutrients that keep them alive and allow them to develop. By eating the right foods—in the right amounts—a mother can contribute to her baby's healthy development. In contrast, a deficient diet can have adverse consequences that are difficult or impossible to overcome.

Good Nutrition

Research indicates that whether pregnant or not a woman who gets moderate amounts of exercise needs to consume between 2000 and 2800 calories daily in a well-balanced diet that includes all the essential vitamins and minerals (Christian, 2002). In addition, pregnant women are advised to increase their intake of folic acid (a member of the vitamin B complex group commonly found in green vegetables and fruit), calcium, and iron to prevent certain birth defects (Van Der Put et al., 1997).

The foods believed to be good for pregnant women are determined by cultural beliefs and practices (Rosso, 1990). In the United States, for example, the increased consumption of foods rich in calcium is widely believed to prevent the loss of "one tooth per pregnancy" (Adair, 1987). Milk is a good source of calcium, and in the United States physicians recommend that pregnant women drink several glasses a day. In China, by contrast, milk is not a part of people's everyday diets, so other foods rich in calcium must be substituted for it (Lefeber & Voorhoeve, 2001).

Undernourishment, Malnourishment, and Related Factors

Pregnant women with deficient diets often suffer from either *undernourishment*—insufficient food intake to develop or function normally—or *malnutrition*—the imbalance between the body's needs and the intake of nutrients even when calorie intake is within the normal range.

In catastrophic conditions that accompany war and famine (which often occur at the same time) the effects on prenatal development can be profound. The clearest evidence of this effect comes from studies of sudden periods of famine. In September 1941 Leningrad (now St. Petersburg) was encircled by the German army, and no supplies reached the city until February 1942. The standard daily food ration in late November 1941 was 250 grams of bread (four slices) for factory workers and 125 grams (two slices) for everybody else. The bread was 25 percent sawdust. The number of infants born in the first half of 1942 was much lower than normal, and stillbirths doubled. Very few infants were born in the second half of 1942, all of them to couples who had better access to food than did the rest of the population. These babies were, on the average, more than a pound lighter than babies born before the siege, and they were much more likely to be premature. They were also in very poor condition at birth; they had little vitality and were unable to maintain body temperature adequately (Antonov, 1947). The sudden famine in Leningrad produced nutritional variations so extreme that normal environmental

low birth weight The term used to describe babies weighing 2500 grams or less at birth whether or not they are premature.

influences on prenatal development were dwarfed by comparison. Consequently, the specific effects of maternal undernourishment combined with malnutrition on the developing fetus during particular segments of the prenatal period could be isolated with a high degree of certainty. Severe nutritional deprivation during the first 3 months of pregnancy was most likely to result in abnormalities of the central nervous system, premature birth, and death. Deprivation during the last 3 months of pregnancy was more likely to retard fetal growth and result in low birth weight.

Studies of the relation between maternal nutrition, prenatal development, and neonatal health suggest that lesser degrees of undernourishment and malnourishment also increase risks to the fetus. Poor maternal nutrition can lead to low birth weight and even miscarriage (Mora & Nestel, 2000). There is also some evidence that poor nutrition puts fetuses at greater risk for heart disease, strokes, and other illnesses in later life (Godfrey & Barker, 2000). This association is thought to result from the fetus's adaptation to an inadequate supply of nutrients during a sensitive period in early prenatal life that leads to permanent changes in physiology and metabolism.

However, it is often difficult to isolate the effects of poor nutrition, because undernourished and malnourished mothers frequently live in impoverished environments where housing, sanitation, education, and medical care, including prenatal care, are also inadequate. Expectant mothers with low incomes are more likely to suffer from diseases or simply to be in a weakened state than are women who live in better material circumstances. Their babies are more likely to suffer from a wide variety of birth defects and illnesses and to be born prematurely (Vintzileos, Ananth, Smulian, Scorza & Knuppel, 2001, 2002). According to a variety of studies conducted in many parts of the world, including the United States, low-income mothers are also more likely to have babies who die at birth or soon after birth (United Nations Children's Fund, 2003).

Several studies demonstrate that it is possible to prevent or reduce the damaging effects of malnutrition and an impoverished environment. One of the largest intervention programs designed to assess the effects of a massive supplemental food program for women, infants, and children—dubbed WIC—was initiated by the U.S. government in 1972. Low-income women in the program are given vouchers for such staples as milk, eggs, fruit juices, and dried beans. Women who have participated in the WIC program have been found to lose fewer babies during infancy than do comparable women who have not participated in the program (Moss & Carver, 1998). Food supplements during pregnancy have also been found to be important to the baby's postnatal intellectual development. In a study carried out in Louisiana, schoolchildren whose mothers had participated in the WIC program were evaluated on a variety of intellectual measures when they were 6 or 7 years old. Those children whose mothers had received food supplements during the last 3 months of their pregnancies—the period in which the fetal brain undergoes especially rapid development—outperformed the children of mothers who did not receive food supplements until after their children were born (Hicks et al., 1982). Similar results were obtained in studies of food supplement programs in rural Guatemala and Zanzibar (Pollitt, Saco-Pollitt, Jahari, Husaini & Huang, 2000; Stoltzfus et al., 2001).

These conclusions concerning poor maternal and fetal nutrition must be considered with some caution because it is not possible to conduct carefully controlled studies for ethical reasons. However, the overall evidence strongly suggests that millions of children throughout the world are damaged by undernourishment and malnourishment both before and after birth. Most of these children do not receive food supplements, and even fewer receive high-quality medical and educational help. In fact, they experience a cascade of risk factors, of which poor nutrition is only one (see Figure 3.9). Together, such conditions lead to high rates of infant mortality and shorter life expectancies (Pollitt, 2001).

teratogens Environmental agents that cause deviations from normal development and can lead to abnormalities or death.

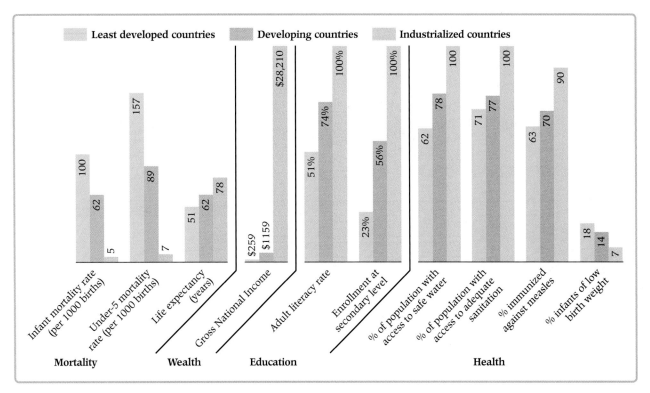

	Least developed countries	Developing countries	Industrialized countries

Mortality
- Infant mortality rate (per 1000 births): 100, 62, 5
- Under-5 mortality rate (per 1000 births): 157, 89, 7
- Life expectancy (years): 51, 62, 78

Wealth
- Gross National Income: $259, $1159, $28,210

Education
- Adult literacy rate: 51%, 74%, 100%
- Enrollment at secondary level: 23%, 56%, 100%

Health
- % of population with access to safe water: 62, 78, 100
- % of population with access to adequate sanitation: 71, 77, 100
- % immunized against measles: 63, 70, 90
- % infants of low birth weight: 18, 14, 7

Figure 3.9 In many countries of the world, poor economic conditions create a set of risk factors. For example, poor health conditions and parents' lack of education negatively influence child health and welfare. (Adapted from United Nations Children's Fund [UNICEF], 1999.)

Teratogens: Environmental Sources of Birth Defects

Other threats to the prenatal organism come from **teratogens**—environmental agents that can cause deviations in normal development and can lead to serious abnormalities or death (see Figure 3.10). Although the effects of teratogens on the developing organism vary with the specific agent involved, six general principles apply to all of them (Moore & Persaud 1998):

1. A developing organism's susceptibility to a teratogenic agent depends on its developmental stage at the time of exposure. Overall, the gravest danger to life comes during the first 2 weeks, before the cells of the organism have undergone extensive differentiation and before most women are even aware that they are pregnant (see Figure 3.11, p. 86). During this critical period, a teratogenic agent may completely destroy the organism. Once the various body systems have begun to form, each is most vulnerable at the time of its initial growth spurt. As Figure 3.11 indicates, the most vulnerable period for the central nervous system is from 15 to 36 days after conception, whereas the upper and lower limbs are most vulnerable from 24 to 49 days after conception.

2. A teratogenic agent's effects are likely to be specific to a particular organ. Therefore, each teratogen causes a particular pattern of abnormal development. The drug thalidomide, for example, causes deformation of the legs and arms, and mercury compounds cause brain damage that is manifested as cerebral palsy.

3. Individual organisms vary in their susceptibility to teratogens. The way a developing organism responds to teratogenic agents depends to some degree on its genetic vulnerability to these agents. Fewer than one-quarter of the pregnant women who used thalidomide during the period when the embryo's limbs were forming gave birth to malformed babies.

Figure 3.10 This young woman demonstrates some of the devastating effects of Agent Orange, an environmental pollutant used during the Vietnam War.

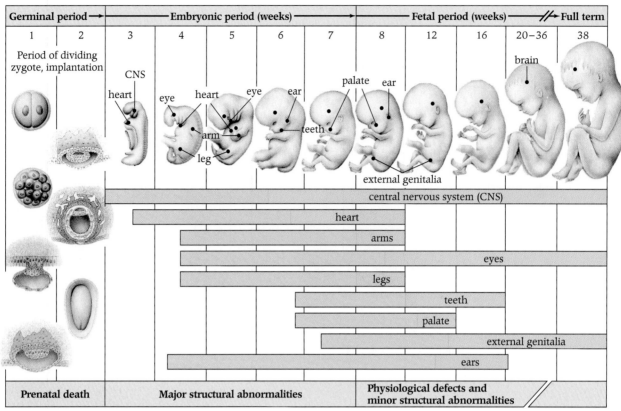

Germinal period →		Embryonic period (weeks) →					Fetal period (weeks) →			⫽→ Full term	
1	2	3	4	5	6	7	8	12	16	20–36	38

• Indicates common site of action of teratogen

Figure 3.11 The critical periods in human prenatal development occur when the organs and other body parts are forming and therefore are most vulnerable to teratogens. Before implantation, teratogens either damage all or most of the cells of the organism, causing its death, or damage only a few cells, allowing the organism to recover without developing defects. In the figure, the blue portions of the bars represent periods of highest risk of major structural abnormalities; the yellow portions represent periods of reduced sensitivity to teratogens. (Adapted from Moore & Persaud, 1993.)

4. Susceptibility to teratogenic agents depends on the mother's physiological state. The mother's age, nutrition, uterine condition, and hormonal balance all affect the action of teratogens on the developing organism. The risk of malformation is highest when the mother is younger than 20 or older than 40. The precise reason is not known. Nutritional deficiency in the mother intensifies the adverse effects of some teratogens. The impact of teratogens also appears to increase if the mother suffers from diabetes, a metabolic imbalance, or liver dysfunction, among other disorders.

5. In general, the greater the concentration of teratogenic agents such as thalidomide or mercury, the greater the risk of abnormal development.

6. Some teratogens such as rubella that have little or only a temporary effect on the mother can lead to serious abnormalities during prenatal development.

The most common teratogens include certain drugs and infections, radiation, and pollution.

Drugs

Most pregnant women in the United States take some medication during pregnancy, primarily over-the-counter pain relievers, antinauseants, or sleep aids. Fortunately, most of these drugs do not appear to harm the fetus, but there are some that do. It is also estimated that a sizable minority of women use nonmedical substances during pregnancy, ranging from caffeine, alcohol, and tobacco to "hard" drugs such as cocaine and heroin. While most of these drugs appear harmful to prenatal development, it is often hard to isolate the effects of specific drugs because drug-abusing mothers often abuse multiple drugs or are generally poor and undernourished (Orioli & Castilla, 2000).

Prescription Drugs

The potential teratogenic effects of prescription drugs first came to light with the drug thalidomide. From 1956 until 1961, thalidomide was used in Europe as a sedative and to control nausea in the early stages of pregnancy. The women who took the drug were unharmed by it, and many of the children they bore suffered no ill effects. Some children, however, were born without arms and legs; their hands and feet were attached directly to their torsos like flippers. Some had defects of sight and hearing as well. About 8000 children with deformities were born before their problems were traced to the drug and it was removed from the market (Persaud, 1977).

Since the disastrous effects of thalidomide were discovered, other prescription drugs have been found to cause abnormalities in the developing organism, including the antibiotics streptomycin and tetracycline, anticoagulants, anticonvulsants, most artificial hormones, Thorazine (used in the treatment of schizophrenia), Valium (a tranquilizer), and Accutane (used to treat difficult cases of acne).

Caffeine

Caffeine, found in coffee, tea, and cola, is the most common drug used by pregnant women. There is no evidence that caffeine causes malformations in the fetus (Clausson et al., 2002). However, some studies have found that caffeine in large doses is associated with an increased rate of spontaneous abortion and with low birth weight (Klebanoff, Levine, Clemens & Wilkins, 2002). On this basis, women are advised to limit their caffeine intake during pregnancy.

Tobacco

Smoking tobacco is not known to produce birth defects, but it has been found to harm the fetus in a variety of ways. Smoking is related to an increase in the rate of spontaneous abortion, stillbirth, and neonatal death (Chan, Keane & Robinson, 2001). Nicotine, the addictive substance in tobacco, causes abnormal growth of the placenta, resulting in a reduction in the transfer of nutrients to the fetus. It also reduces the oxygen and increases the carbon monoxide in the bloodstreams of both mother and fetus. As a result, mothers who smoke usually have babies whose birth weights are lower than those of infants born to women who do not smoke. The effects of cigarette smoke seem to be dose-related: mothers who smoke more have babies who weigh less (Chan et al., 2001; Wang et al., 2002). Recent findings suggest that even if a mother does not smoke herself, the health of her baby can be significantly affected by the cigarette smoke of others (Wang et al., 2002).

Alcohol

After smoking and caffeine, alcohol is the most commonly abused drug. About 4 percent of all U.S. women of childbearing age suffer from alcoholism, and many more are "social drinkers" who consume alcohol on a regular basis (Stratton et al., 1996). Women who drink substantial amounts of alcohol while they are pregnant are in danger of having a baby with serious birth defects. Many studies have found that infants born to mothers who were heavy drinkers during pregnancy—that is, who drank 3 ounces or more of 100-proof liquor a day (the equivalent of 3 shot glasses of whiskey)—were abnormal in some way (Kesmodel, Wisborg, Olsen, Henriksen & Secher, 2002). Many of these babies suffered from **fetal alcohol syndrome,** a set of symptoms that includes an abnormally small head and underdeveloped brain, eye abnormalities, congenital heart disease, joint anomalies, and malformations of the face (see Figure 3.12, p. 88).

fetal alcohol syndrome A syndrome found in babies whose mothers were heavy consumers of alcohol while pregnant. Symptoms include an abnormally small head and underdeveloped brain, eye abnormalities, congenital heart disease, joint anomalies, and malformations of the face.

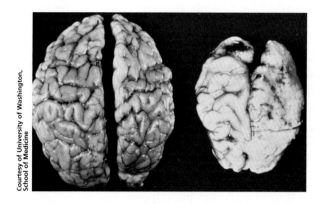

Courtesy of University of Washington, School of Medicine

George Steinmetz

Figure 3.12 Children who suffer from fetal alcohol syndrome do not merely look abnormal (right); their brains are underdeveloped, and many are severely retarded. The brain of a child who suffered from fetal alcohol syndrome (above right) lacks the convolutions characteristic of the brain of a normal child (above left).

The physical growth and mental development of children with this syndrome are likely to be retarded. Women who drink heavily during the first trimester of pregnancy and then reduce their consumption of alcohol during the next 3 months do not reduce the risk of having children with this affliction. Binge drinking—that is, the periodic consumption of 5 or more drinks on a single occasion—early in pregnancy has been found to be associated with a subtle impairment of learning and behavior in adolescence (Kesmodel, 2001). The effects of lower levels of alcohol consumption on development are currently in dispute. Research has found that in some cases the equivalent of one or two glasses of wine, either occasionally or daily, causes no discernible harm to the fetus. In other cases, such drinking results in "fetal alcohol effects," which include subtle but measurable deficits in cognitive and motor functioning. These effects will vary with both the amount of prenatal exposure to alcohol and the timing of the exposure.

Marijuana

A national survey of 4 million U.S. women who gave birth in 1992 found that 2.9 percent had used marijuana at some time during their pregnancies (Lee & Woods, 1998). Marijuana has not been definitely found to cause birth defects, but its use is associated with low birth weight. Some researchers have also found an increase in premature delivery among women who use marijuana more than once a week. However, it is uncertain whether these effects can be solely attributed to the use of marijuana. Women in the United States who use marijuana during pregnancy tend to be poorer, less educated, younger, single, and more likely to use other illegal drugs than mothers who do not use marijuana. They also receive less prenatal care and gain less weight.

Cocaine

Cocaine is a stimulant that rapidly produces addiction in the user. It may result in numerous medical complications for the mother-to-be, including heart attacks, strokes, rupture of the aorta, and seizures (Cunningham et al., 2001). Babies born to cocaine-addicted mothers have a variety of problems. These babies are more likely to be stillborn or premature, to have low birth weights, to suffer from strokes, and to exhibit birth defects (Ursitti et al., 2001). Babies born to cocaine-addicted mothers are described as being irritable, liable to react excessively to stimulation, unco-ordinated, and slow learners (Bendersky & Lewis, 1998).

Residual effects of cocaine exposure during the prenatal period may last for several years. For example, preschool-age children prenatally exposed to cocaine exhibit de-layed language development and are likely to experience difficulty regulating them-selves when presented with novel tasks (Morrow et al., 2003; Noland et al., 2003).

Despite the justified concern about the effects of prenatal exposure to cocaine, some researchers have been critical of claims that cocaine itself is the cause of these problems (Lester & Tronick, 1994). These researchers note that many mothers who use cocaine also drink alcohol and use other drugs. In addition, many of them are poor and live in stressful circumstances. All these factors are known to contribute to symp-toms such as those attributed to prenatal cocaine exposure. Consequently, while recent research continues to show negative impacts on later development, a causal link between prenatal cocaine exposure and later behavior is still not considered ironclad (Bandstra, Morrow, Anthony, Accornero & Fried, 2001; Morrow et al., 2003).

Heroin and Methadone

Babies of mothers who are addicted to either heroin or methadone are born addicted themselves and must be given heroin or methadone shortly after birth to avoid the often life-threatening ordeal of withdrawal. These babies are more likely to be prema-ture, underweight, and vulnerable to respiratory illnesses (Kaltenbach et al., 1998).

While these babies are being weaned from the drugs to which they were born addicted, they are irritable and have tremors, their cries are abnormal, their sleep is disturbed, and their motor control is diminished. The effects of the addiction are still apparent in their motor control 4 months later. Even after a year, their ability to pay attention is impaired (Yanai et al., 2000).

Several studies have also reported long-term developmental problems in children exposed to heroin, methadone, or opiate derivatives in utero, but as with cocaine, whether these problems can be solely attributed to the mother's drug use is still open to question (Eyler & Behnke, 1999).

Infections and Other Conditions

A variety of infection-causing microorganisms can endanger the embryo, the fetus, and the newborn. Most infections spread from the mother to the unborn child across the placental barrier. In a few instances, however, the baby may become infected during the passage through the birth canal. Some of the more common infections and other maternal conditions that may affect the developing human organism are summarized below; Table 3.3 (p. 90) summarizes others.

Rubella

Rubella, commonly referred to as German measles, is a condition in which an expectant mother exhibits a mild rash, swollen lymph glands, and a low fever. Researchers have found that rubella also can cause a syndrome of congenital heart disease, cataracts, deafness, and mental retardation in more than half of all babies born to mothers who suffer from the disease during the first 12 weeks of preg-nancy (Bale, 2002). (Thereafter, rubella infections are less likely to cause congenital malformations.) The development of a vaccine for rubella in 1969 has greatly reduced the incidence of the disease, but it has not been eradicated. Women are advised to avoid becoming pregnant for at least 6 months after they receive the vaccine. A few states offer a test for immunity to rubella as part of the blood test given before a marriage license is issued.

table 3.3

Some Maternal Diseases and Conditions That May Affect Prenatal Development	
Sexually Transmitted Diseases	
Genital herpes	Infection usually occurs at birth as the baby comes in contact with herpes lesions on the mother's genitals, although the virus may also cross the placental barrier to infect the fetus. Infection can lead to blindness and serious brain damage. There is no cure for the disease. Mothers with active genital herpes often have a cesarean delivery to avoid infecting their babies.
Gonorrhea	The gonococcus organism may attack the eyes while the baby is passing through the infected birth canal. Silver nitrate or erythromycin eyedrops are administered immediately after birth to prevent blindness.
Syphilis	The effects of syphilis on the fetus can be devastating. An estimated 25 percent of infected fetuses are born dead. Those who survive may be deaf, mentally retarded, or deformed. Syphilis can be diagnosed by a blood test and can be cured before the fetus is affected, since the syphilis spirochete cannot penetrate the placental membrane before the twenty-first week of gestation.
Other Diseases and Maternal Conditions	
Chicken pox	Chicken pox may lead to spontaneous abortion or premature delivery, but it does not appear to cause malformations.
Cytomegalovirus	The most common source of prenatal infection, cytomegalovirus produces no symptoms in adults, but it may be fatal to the embryo. Infection later in intrauterine life has been related to brain damage, deafness, blindness, and cerebral palsy (a defect of motor coordination caused by brain damage).
Diabetes	Diabetic mothers face a greater risk of having a stillborn child or one who dies shortly after birth. Babies of diabetics are often very large because of the accumulation of fat during the third trimester. Diabetic mothers require special care to prevent these problems.
Hepatitis	Mothers who have hepatitis are likely to pass it on to their infants during birth.
Hypertension	Hypertension (chronic high blood pressure) increases the probability of miscarriage and infant death.
Influenza	The more virulent forms of influenza may lead to spontaneous abortion or may cause abnormalities during the early stages of pregnancy.
Mumps	Mumps is suspected of causing spontaneous abortion in the first trimester of pregnancy.
Toxemia	About 5 percent of pregnant women in the United States are affected during the third trimester by this disorder of unknown origin. Most common during first pregnancies, the condition mainly affects the mother. Symptoms are water retention, high blood pressure, rapid weight gain, and protein in the urine. If untreated, toxemia may cause convulsions, coma, and even death for the mother. Death of the fetus is not uncommon.
Toxoplasmosis	A mild disease in adults with symptoms similar to those of the common cold, toxoplasmosis is caused by a parasite that is present in raw meat and cat feces. It may cause spontaneous abortion or death. Babies who survive may have serious eye or brain damage.

Sources: Moore & Persaud, 1993; Stevenson, 1977.

Acquired Immunodeficiency Syndrome (AIDS)

Approximately 30 percent of the babies born to mothers who test positive for the AIDS virus acquire this disease (UNICEF, 2003). The virus may be transmitted from the mother to her baby either by the virus's passing through the placental barrier or by the baby's exposure to the mother's infected blood during delivery. More than 800,000 children were infected in this way in 2001. The risk of transmission increases with the length of time the mother has been infected. There is no known cure for AIDS, now the seventh leading cause of death in children under the age of 4. However, if HIV-positive women receive the drug zidovudine

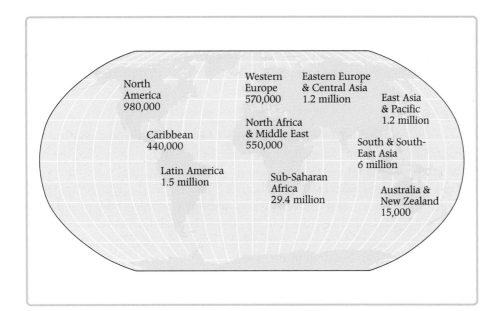

A total of 42 million adults and children were estimated to be living with HIV/AIDS at the end of 2002. (Adapted from World Health Organization, 2002.)

(AZT) during pregnancy and at the time of delivery, the chances of their passing the virus on to their children are reduced by as much as 50 percent (UNICEF, 2003).

Rh Incompatibility

Rh is a complex substance on the surface of the red blood cells. One of its components is determined by a dominant gene, and people who have this component are said to be Rh-positive. Fewer than one in ten people inherit the two recessive genes that make them Rh negative (de Vrijer et al., 1999).

When an Rh-negative woman conceives a child with an Rh-positive man, the child is likely to be Rh-positive. During the birth of the baby, some of its blood cells usually pass into the mother's bloodstream while the placenta is separating from the uterine wall. The mother's immune system creates antibodies to fight this foreign substance, which remains in her bloodstream. If the mother becomes pregnant again with another Rh-positive child, these antibodies will enter the fetus's bloodstream and attack its red blood cells.

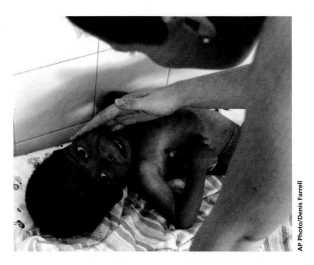

Whether or not they are infected with AIDS themselves, young children from families in which the parents have AIDS are at risk of homelessness, malnutrition, and disease, in addition to the psychological trauma of losing their parents at an early age.

Rh disease can lead to serious birth defects and even death. Fortunately, physicians can prevent Rh disease by giving the Rh-negative mother an injection of anti-Rh serum within 72 hours of the delivery of an Rh-positive child. The serum kills any Rh-positive blood cells in the mother's bloodstream so that she will not develop antibodies to attack them. Children who are born with Rh disease can be treated with periodic blood transfusions (Fanaroff & Martin, 1997).

Radiation

Massive doses of radiation often lead to serious malformations of the developing organism and in many cases cause prenatal death or spontaneous abortion (Moore & Persaud, 1993). Somewhat lower doses may spare the life of the organism, but they may have a profound effect on its development. Many of the pregnant women who were within 1500 meters of the atomic blasts at Hiroshima and Nagasaki in 1945 survived, but they later lost their babies. Of the babies who appeared to be normal at birth, 64 percent were later diagnosed as mentally retarded.

The effects of low doses of radiation on human beings have not been firmly established. Because X rays may cause malformations in the embryo, women who are pregnant, or who have been trying to become pregnant, should inform their doctors of this when they need to be X-rayed.

Pollution

Most of the thousands of chemicals that are used in industrial production and in the preparation of foods and cosmetics have never been tested to see if they are harmful to prenatal development, although some of these substances reach the embryo or fetus through the placenta (Jones, 1997). Some herbicides and pesticides have been shown to be harmful or even fatal to unborn rats, mice, rabbits, and chicks. Several pollutants sometimes found in the atmosphere and drinking water also appear to be teratogenic. Moreover, some of the effects are cumulative, as concentrations of the chemicals build up in the body.

In 1953 it was discovered that the consumption of large quantities of fish from Minamata Bay in Japan was associated with a series of symptoms that have come to be known as Minamata disease. The symptoms include cerebral palsy (a disorder of the central nervous system), deformation of the skull, and sometimes an abnormally small head. The bay was polluted by mercury from waste discharged from nearby industrial plants. The mercury passed in increasingly concentrated amounts through the food chain from the organisms eaten by fish to humans who ate the fish. Pregnant women who ate the contaminated fish then passed the mercury on to their unborn babies. Minamata disease has since become synonymous with mercury poisoning (Tuchmann-Duplessis, 1975).

The incidence of birth defects is also known to be abnormally high in areas of heavy atmospheric pollution. In the Brazilian industrial city of Cubatão, for instance, the air pollution from petrochemical and steel plants alone exceeds that generated by all the combined industries in the Los Angeles basin of California. During the 1970s, 65 of every 1000 babies born in Cubatão died shortly after birth because their brains had failed to develop—double the rate of this defect in neighboring communities that were not so heavily polluted (Freed, 1983). Fortunately, strong environmental safety efforts have greatly reduced the pollution in Cubatão, and the death rate of infants there has declined remarkably (Brooke, 1991). However, contaminants still remain in the ground, poisoning local forests (Klumpp, Domingos & Klumpp, 2002).

Atmospheric pollution in U.S. cities is not as high as it used to be in Cubatão, but it is high enough in many of them to cause concern about its effects on prenatal

The tragic consequences of prenatal mercury poisoning, or Minamata disease. This disease first came to the world's attention in the 1950s because of the pollution in Minamata Bay, Japan.

Aileen & W. Eugene Smith/Black Star

development. There is also a good deal of concern about the risk to pregnant women and their unborn children who live near chemical dumps. Unfortunately, much more research is required before it is known what actual risks these environmental hazards pose for prenatal development.

Reconsidering Prenatal Development

As you will recall, many developmentalists view the prenatal period as a model for all subsequent development because many of the principles that apply to prenatal development also explain development after birth. Before we move on to birth and life outside the uterus, it is worthwhile to review these explanatory principles as they apply to the prenatal period. You will see these ideas return throughout our study of child development.

1. *Sequence is fundamental.* One cell must exist before there can be two. Muscles and bones must be present before nerves can coordinate movement. Gonads must secrete testosterone before further sexual differentiation can occur.

2. *Timing is crucial to development.* If the ovum moves too rapidly or too slowly down the fallopian tube, pregnancy is terminated. If exposure to a particular teratogen occurs during a particular stage of development, the impact on the organism may be devastating. If the exposure occurs before or after this particular stage, there may be little or no impact. The importance of timing implies the existence of sensitive periods for the formation of new organ systems.

3. *Development consists of a process of differentiation and integration.* The single cell of the zygote becomes the many identical cells of the morula. These cells then *differentiate* into two distinct kinds of cells, which later are *integrated* into a new configuration of cells called the blastocyst. Similarly, arm buds will later differentiate to form fingers, which will differ from each other in ways that make possible the finely articulate movements of the human hand.

4. *Development is characterized by stagelike changes.* These changes occur both in the form of the organism and in the ways it interacts with its environment. The embryo not only looks altogether different from the blastocyst but also interacts with its environment in a qualitatively different way.

5. *Development proceeds unevenly.* From the earliest steps of cleavage, the various subsystems that make up the organism develop at their own rates. An important special case of such unevenness is physical development, which follows a cephalocaudal (from the head down) and proximodistal (from the center to the periphery) sequence.

6. *Development is punctuated by periods of apparent regression.* Although development generally appears to progress through time, there are also periods of apparent regression. Regressions appear to reflect a process of reorganization, as when fetal activity decreases as higher regions of the brain are beginning to become active.

7. *Development is still a mystery.* The process by which the human organism develops from a single cell into a squalling newborn baby continues to mystify investigators. In one sense, the results of development are present at the beginning, coded in the genetic materials of the zygote, which constrain the kinds of forms that can emerge out of the interactions between the organism and its environment. But new forms are constantly emerging out of the organism—environment interactions that sustain and propel development. In this sense, development is epigenetic.

Figure 3.13 During the first stage of labor, which usually lasts several hours, the cervix dilates, often to 9 or 10 centimeters in diameter. During the second stage, the birth canal widens, permitting the baby to emerge. The final stage (not shown) occurs when the placenta is delivered. (Adapted from Clarke-Stewart & Koch, 1983.)

FIRST STAGE OF LABOR

Cervix   Birth canal

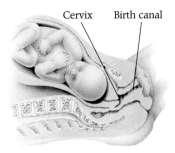

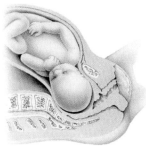

START OF SECOND STAGE
(Transition)

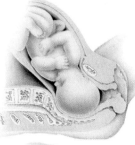

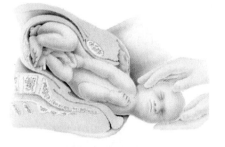

Birth: The First Bio-Social-Behavioral Shift

Among all of life's transitions, birth is the most radical. Before birth, the amniotic fluid provides a wet, warm environment, and the fetus receives continuous oxygen and nourishment through the umbilical cord. At birth, the lungs inflate to take in oxygen and exhale carbon dioxide for the first time. The first breath of oxygen acts to shut off the bypass that shunts blood away from the lungs to the placenta. It also causes the umbilical arteries to close down, cutting off fetal circulation to the placenta. Now the baby must obtain oxygen through the lungs, must work for nourishment by sucking, and no longer has the placenta to provide protection against disease-causing organisms.

The social and behavioral changes that occur at birth are no less pronounced than the biological ones, marking birth as the first bio-social-behavioral shift in human development. The newborn encounters other human beings directly for the first time, and the parents get their first glimpse of their child. From the moment of birth, infants and parents begin to construct a social relationship.

The Stages of Labor

The biological process of birth begins with a series of changes in the mother's body that forces the fetus through the birth canal. It ends when the mother expels the placenta after the baby has emerged. Labor normally begins approximately 280 days after the first day of a woman's last menstrual period, or 266 days after conception. It is customarily divided into three overlapping stages (see Figure 3.13).

The first stage of labor begins when uterine contractions of sufficient frequency, intensity, and duration begin to cause the cervix (the narrow outer end of the uterus) to dilate. This initial stage continues until the opening of the uterus into the vagina is fully dilated and the connections between the bones of the mother's pelvis become more flexible (Cunningham et al., 2001). The length of this stage varies from woman to woman and from pregnancy to pregnancy: it may last anywhere from less than an hour to several days. The norm for first births is about 14 hours. At the beginning of labor, contractions come 15 to 20 minutes apart and last anywhere from 15 to 60 seconds. As labor proceeds, the contractions become more frequent, more intense, and longer in duration.

The second stage of labor begins as the baby is pushed headfirst through the fully dilated cervix into the vagina. (This passage is facilitated by the fact that the baby's head is comparatively soft because the bones of the skull have not yet fused.) The contractions now usually come no more than a minute apart and last about a minute. The pressure of the baby in the birth canal and the powerful contractions of the uterus typically cause the mother to bear down and push the baby out.

Usually the top of the baby's head and the brow are the first to emerge. Occasionally babies emerge in other positions, the most common being the breech position, with the feet or buttocks emerging first. In cases where babies are born in a breech position, which occurs in 3 to 4 percent of single births, both mother and fetus are at considerably increased risk of serious complications or death (Nkata, 2001).

The third stage of labor, the final one, occurs as the baby emerges from the vagina and the uterus contracts around its diminished contents. The placenta buckles and separates from the uterine wall, pulling the other fetal membranes with it. Contractions quickly expel them, and they are delivered as the afterbirth.

Cultural Variations in Childbirth

As a biological process, labor occurs in roughly the same way everywhere. However, as you saw at the beginning of this chapter, there are wide variations in birthing practices. Giving birth unassisted with no special preparations is relatively rare, but by no means unique (Lefeber & Voorhoeve, 1998). In the remote Bajura district of eastern Nepal, for example, women stay in an animal shed for childbirth. The shed is separate from the main home and is usually small and dirty. During deliveries, no one helps or touches the mother. The mother must cut and tie the umbilical cord, wash clothes, and care for the baby herself. People believe that if a woman gives birth to a baby inside her home, then God will be displeased and will make family members and cattle sicken and die (CARE, 2003). The same beliefs and practices were common in rural France as late as the end of the nineteenth century (Gelis, 1991).

It is far more common to find several people attending the mother during labor and delivery, although who actually gets to play a role varies across cultures. Among the Ngoni of East Africa, for example, men are totally excluded from the process. The women even conceal the fact that they are pregnant from their husbands as long as they can. "Men are little children. They are not able to hear those things which belong to pregnancy," the women claim (Read, 1968, p. 20). When a woman learns that her daughter-in-law's labor has begun, she and other female kin move into the woman's hut, banish the husband, and take charge of the preparations. They remove everything that belongs to the husband—clothes, tools, and weapons—and all household articles except old mats and pots to be used during labor. Men are not allowed back into the hut until after the baby is born. By contrast, among the Maya of the Yucatán peninsula, in addition to a trained midwife being present to help, the husband is also expected to be present both to help his wife and to bear witness to the pain she feels (Jordan, 1993). If the husband is absent and the child dies, its death is likely to be attributed to his failure to participate.

In all industrialized countries, a large proportion of births take place in hospitals where the process is assisted by a physician or a trained midwife (Gelis, 1991). However, there are wide cultural variations in such matters as the use of medication, reliance on trained midwives rather than physicians, and the place of delivery. For example, in Holland, where roughly one-third of births take place at home, the rate of infant mortality is actually lower for home births than hospital births (Jordan, 1993).

Childbirth in the United States

In the United States there is a strong preference for giving birth in a hospital with the assistance of a physician. According to most recent estimates, 99 percent of all babies in the United States are born in hospitals, and 92 percent are delivered by a physician (Centers for Disease Control and Prevention, 2000). Two major factors underlie this preference. First, hospitals staffed by trained physicians and nurses are better equipped to provide both antiseptic surroundings and specialized help to deal with any complications that might arise during labor and delivery. Second, many drugs have been developed to relieve the pain of childbirth, and by law such drugs can be administered only by physicians.

Figure 3.14 Over the course of the twentieth century, the death rate among children in the United States under 1 year of age dropped dramatically.

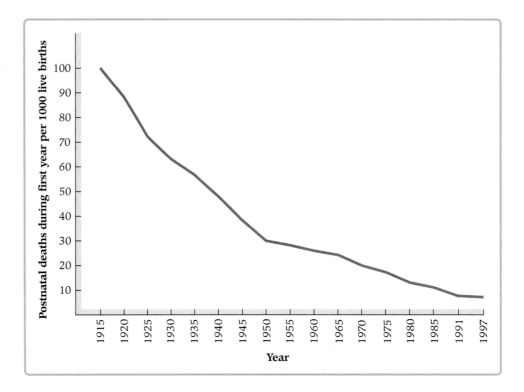

There is no doubt that the lives of thousands of babies and mothers are saved each year by the intervention of doctors and nurses using modern drugs and special medical procedures (Figure 3.14). For example, in 1915, when more than half of all babies were born at home, approximately 100 of every 1000 babies died in their first year, and almost 7 of 1000 mothers died giving birth. By 1997 (the last year for which data are available), infant deaths had been reduced to 7.2 of every 1000 babies born (Centers for Disease Control and Prevention, 2004). In the same year, only 7.7 women of every 100,000 died of causes related to pregnancy, childbirth, or postnatal complications (Centers for Disease Control and Prevention, 2004).

Despite the reductions in maternal and infant mortality, health-care professionals and parents alike have pointed to problems arising from medical intervention during normal, uncomplicated births (Martin, 1998). These concerns center on two questions: (1) What is the safest method for dealing with pain during childbirth? (2) What precautions are necessary to ensure the health of the mother and the baby?

Childbirth Pain and Its Medication

In industrialized nations, a variety of drugs are used to lessen the pain of labor and delivery when birth takes place at a hospital. They include anesthetics (which dull overall feeling), analgesics (which reduce the perception of pain), and sedatives (which reduce anxiety). Medications seldom threaten the lives of healthy, full-term babies, but the newborns of mothers who receive one or another of a variety of drugs during labor and delivery are less attentive and more irritable, have poorer muscle tone and less vigorous sucking responses, and are weaker than those whose mothers receive no medication (Jones, 1997).

Because of their concern about the possible adverse effects of drugs on the newborn, many women are turning to alternative methods of controlling the pain of labor. Typically these methods include educational classes that give the mother-to-be an idea of what to expect during labor and delivery and teach her relaxation and breathing exercises to help counteract pain. Often they also involve having someone—the baby's father, a sympathetic friend, or a midwife—be at the woman's side during labor to provide comfort and emotional support.

For many American couples, childbirth education has become a traditional part of pregnancy.

Courtesy of Lincoln General Hospital, Ruston, LA

Medical Interventions

In addition to administering drugs to ease the pain of labor, doctors may use medical procedures to safeguard the lives of mother and child. For example, when the baby is significantly overdue or when the mother is confronted with some life-threatening situation, physicians commonly induce labor, either by rupturing the membranes of the amniotic sac or by giving the mother some form of the hormone oxytocin, which initiates contractions.

Another commonly used procedure is the cesarean section, or surgical removal of the baby from the mother's uterus. This procedure has typically been used in cases of difficult labor, when the baby is in distress during delivery, or when the baby is not in the headfirst position.

Although modern medical techniques have made childbirth a great deal safer than it was in the past, some medical personnel claim that many of these technologies are used more often than they should be (Martin, 1998). The use of cesarean deliveries is one prominent example. The number of cesarean sections performed in the United States began to increase significantly during the 1970s. By 1997, 21 out of every 100 births in the United States were by cesarean section (Centers for Disease Control and Prevention, 1999), and by 2002 this rate had increased to 24 out of 100 births (Martin et al., 2002). Critics argue that many of the cesarean operations performed in the United States not only are unnecessary but raise the cost of childbirth, expose the mother to the risk of postoperative infection, and cause mothers to be separated from their infants while they heal from surgery. They may also be detrimental to the babies' well-being. For example, Herbert Renz-Polster and his colleagues report increased susceptibility of children delivered by cesarean section to hay fever and asthma (Renz-Polster & Buist, 2002), while others report increased chances of maternal death (Kusiako, Ronsmans & Van der Paal, 2000).

Concerns about unnecessary medical intervention also extend to other procedures, such as induced labor, which has doubled during the past decade, and electronic monitoring of the vital signs of the fetus during labor, which has been associated with the increase in cesarean sections (Martin, 1998). In part because of such concerns, there has been increased interest in alternative ways of giving birth that range from birthing at home with the assistance of a midwife to the use of special birthing centers where family members can also be present. Such centers are often located in or near a hospital in case serious complications arise. Alternative measures are especially popular when prenatal examinations find no indications that the birth will be especially complicated. A study carried out in Washington State found that in low-risk pregnancies, certified nurse-midwives were less likely to use fetal monitoring and had lower rates of induced labor than physicians. Their patients also

(a)

Jules Perrier/Corbis

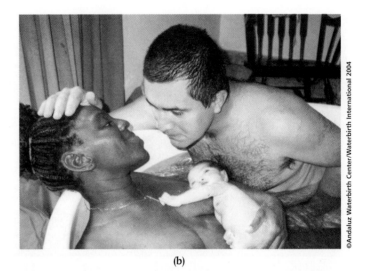

(b)

©Andaluz Waterbirth Center/Waterbirth International 2004

Examples of three different cultural contexts in which the process of birth takes place. (a) The baby is born in a modern hospital and is delivered by an obstetrician. (b) Water births have become popular in some cultures. (c) The entire family is present in the living room of their apartment while a midwife attends to the birth of a baby.

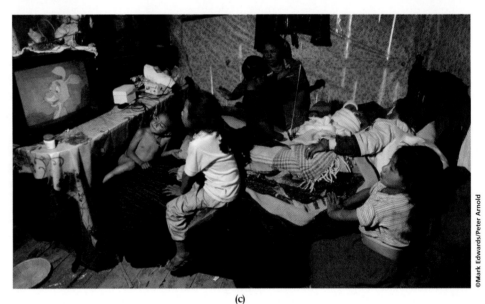

(c)

©Mark Edwards/Peter Arnold

were less likely to have a spinal injection of anesthesia and cesarean sections than the patients of both family physicians and obstetricians (Rosenblatt et al., 1997).

Unfortunately, the reduction in death rates has not been evenly spread through all segments of the population. While the mortality rate has declined significantly for both African American and white infants, African American infants are still almost twice as likely to die during the first year of life as other infants. Moreover, African American mothers are three times as likely to die in childbirth as other mothers (Centers for Disease Control and Prevention, 2000).

The Baby's Experience of Birth

There is no doubt that the process of being born is stressful for babies, even if all proceeds normally. The baby must squeeze through a very narrow opening which places a great deal of pressure on the head, and the umbilical cord may be constricted reducing the supply of oxygen. Research on the experience of birth, which has focused on the biological mechanisms that equip the baby to cope with the stresses involved, has suggested that as the birth process begins, a surge in the fetus's production of adrenaline and other "stress" hormones protects it from the adverse conditions. They go on to suggest that the stress hormones are of vital importance because these hormones prepare the infant to survive outside the womb (Lager-crantz & Slotkin, 1986).

In support of their hypothesis, Lagercrantz and Slotkin point out that infants delivered by cesarean section often have difficulty breathing. They believe that the cesarean procedure deprives babies of the experiences that produce high levels of adrenaline and other hormones in the hours before birth, hormones that facilitate the absorption of liquid from the lungs and the production of surfactin, which allow the lungs to function well. In addition, the hormones appear to produce an increase in the newborn's metabolic rate, which mobilizes readily usable fuel to nourish cells.

Lagercrantz and Slotkin also believe that the stress hormones are instrumental in increasing blood flow to such vital organs as the heart, lungs, and brain and thus increase the chances of survival of a baby who is experiencing breathing difficulties. Furthermore, these researchers speculate that the hormonal surge during the birth process puts the newborn in a state of alertness. Immediately following birth, most normal newborns have a prolonged period of quiet alertness, lasting as long as 40 minutes, during which their eyes are open in a wide-eyed gaze (Klaus et al., 1995).

The Newborn's Condition

To first-time parents, especially those who imagine that newborns look like the infants pictured on jars of baby food, the real neonate's appearance may cause alarm and disappointment. The baby's head is overly large in proportion to the rest of the body, and the limbs are relatively small and tightly flexed. Unless the baby has been delivered by cesarean section, the head may look misshapen after its tight squeeze through the birth canal. (The head usually regains its symmetry by the end of the first week after birth.) The baby's skin may be covered with *vernix caseosa,* a white, cheesy substance that protects it against bacterial infections, and it may be spotted with blood.

In the United States, neonates weigh an average of 7 to $7^1/_2$ pounds, although babies weighing anywhere from $5^1/_2$ to 10 pounds are within the normal range. During their first days of life, most babies lose about 7 percent of their initial weight, primarily because of loss of fluid. They usually gain the weight back by the time they are 10 days old.

The average neonate is 20 inches long. To a large extent, the length of the newborn is determined by the size of the mother's uterus. It does not reflect the baby's genetic inheritance, because the genes that control height do not begin to express themselves until shortly after birth (Tanner, 1990).

Assessing the Baby's Viability

In medically assisted births, medical personnel check the neonate for indications of danger so that immediate action can be taken if something is wrong. They take note of the baby's size, check vital signs, and look for evidence of normal capacities. A variety of scales and tests are used to assess the neonate's physical state and behavioral condition (Singer & Zeskind, 2001).

Physical Condition

In the 1950s Virginia Apgar (1953), an anesthesiologist who worked in the delivery room of a large metropolitan hospital, developed a quick and simple method of determining if a baby requires emergency care. The **Apgar Scale,** which is now widely employed throughout the United States, is used to rate babies 1 minute after birth and again 5 minutes later using five vital signs: heart rate, respiratory effort,

Apgar Scale A quick, simple test used to diagnose the physical state of newborn infants.

table 3.4

The Apgar Scoring System			
	Rating		
Vital Sign	**0**	**1**	**2**
Heart rate	Absent	Slow (below 100)	Over 100
Respiratory effort	Absent	Slow, irregular	Good, crying
Muscle tone	Flaccid	Some flexion of extremities	Active motion
Reflex responsivity	No response	Grimace	Vigorous cry
Color	Blue, pale	Body pink, extremities blue	Completely pink

Source: Apgar, 1953.

muscle tone, reflex responsivity, and color. Table 3.4 shows the criteria for scoring each of the signs. The individual scores are totaled to give a measure of the baby's overall physical condition. A baby with a score of less than 4 is considered to be in poor condition and to require immediate medical attention.

Behavioral Condition

During the past half century, many scales have been constructed to assess the more subtle behavioral aspects of the newborn's condition (Singer & Zeskind, 2001). One of the most widely used is the **Brazelton Neonatal Assessment Scale,** developed by the pediatrician T. Berry Brazelton and his colleagues in the late 1970s (Brazelton, 1984). A major purpose of this scale is to assess the neurological condition of newborns who are suspected of being at risk for developmental difficulties. It is also used to assess the developmental progress of infants, to compare the functioning of newborns of different cultures, and to evaluate the effectiveness of interventions designed to alleviate developmental difficulties (Lundqvist & Sabel, 2000).

The Brazelton scale includes tests of infants' reflexes, motor capacities, muscle tone, capacity for responding to objects and people, and capacity to control their own behavior (such as turning away when overstimulated) and attention. When scoring a newborn on such tests, the examiner must take note of the degree of the infant's alertness and, if necessary, repeat the tests when the baby is wide awake and calm. Here are some typical items on the Brazelton scale:

- *Orientation to animate objects—visual and auditory.* The examiner calls the baby's name repeatedly in a high-pitched voice while moving his head up and down and from side to side in front of the baby. Does the baby focus on the examiner? Does she follow the examiner with her eyes smoothly?

- *Pull-to-sit.* The examiner puts a forefinger in each of the infant's palms and pulls him to a sitting position. Does the baby try to right his head when he is in a seated position? How well is he able to do so?

- *Cuddliness.* The examiner holds the baby against her chest or up against her shoulder. How does the baby respond? Does she resist being held? Is she passive, or does she cuddle up to the examiner?

- *Defensive movements.* The examiner places a cloth over the baby's face and holds it there. Does the baby try to remove the cloth from his face either by turning his head away or by swiping at it?

- *Self-quieting activity.* The examiner notes what the baby does to quiet herself when she is fussy. Does she suck her thumb, look around?

Brazelton Neonatal Assessment Scale A scale used to assess the newborn's neurological condition.

gestational age The time that has passed between conception and birth. The normal gestational age is between 37 and 43 weeks.

preterm The term for babies born before the thirty-seventh week of pregnancy.

In addition to their primary goal of screening for infants at risk, neonatal assessment scales are also used to predict aspects of newborns' future development such as their temperaments or typical learning rates. Research over the past decade with neonates thought to be at risk shows that these scales are, in fact, satisfactory guides for determining when medical intervention is necessary, and that they are also fairly good at characterizing whether the baby is developing normally in the period following birth (Hart et al., 1999; Schuler & Nair, 1999). They are less useful when it comes to predicting later intelligence or personality, however.

Problems and Complications

Though most babies are born without any serious problems, some are in such poor physical condition that they soon die. Others are at risk for later developmental problems. Newborns are considered to be at risk if they suffer from any of a variety of problems, including asphyxiation (life-threatening loss of oxygen) or head injury during delivery (either of which may result in brain damage), acute difficulty breathing after birth, or difficulty digesting food owing to an immature digestive system (Korner & Constantinou, 2001). These are the kinds of problems that are likely to result in low scores on the Apgar Scale. Most of the newborns who are at risk are premature, abnormally underweight, or both (Singer & Zeskind, 2001).

Prematurity

Prematurity is measured in terms of **gestational age,** the time that has passed between conception and birth. The normal gestational age is 37 to 43 weeks. Babies born before the thirty-seventh week are considered to be **preterm,** or premature. In the United States, approximately 10 percent of all births are preterm (Cunningham et al., 2001). Disorders related to premature birth are the fourth leading cause of infant mortality. With the expert care and technology now available in modern hospitals (see Figure 3.15), mortality rates for premature infants are declining in the United States.

The leading cause of death among preterm infants is immaturity of the lungs (Arias-Camison et al., 1999). The other main obstacle to the survival of preterm infants is immaturity of their digestive and immune systems. Even babies of normal gestational age sometimes have difficulty coordinating sucking, swallowing, and breathing in the first few days after birth. These difficulties are likely to be more serious for preterm infants (see Figure 3.16, p. 102). Their coordination may be so poor that they cannot be fed directly from breast or bottle, so special equipment must be used to feed them. Moreover, their immature digestive systems often cannot handle normal baby formulas, so they must be fed special formulas.

There are many potential contributors to prematurity, some of them known. Twins are likely to be born about 3 weeks early, triplets and quadruplets even earlier. Very young women whose reproductive systems are immature and women who have had many pregnancies close together are more likely to have premature babies. So are women who smoke, who are in poor health, or who have infections of the uterus. The chances of giving birth to a premature infant also vary with socioeconomic status (Witter & Keith, 1993). Poor women are

Figure 3.15 Technological improvements in recent years have greatly increased the chances for survival for the 10 percent of U.S. babies who are born premature.

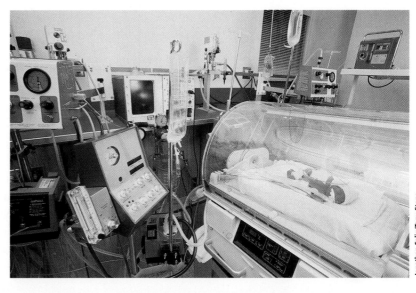

Jonathan Selig/Tony Stone

Figure 3.16 Evidence that premature infants experience difficulty breathing led Evelyn Thoman and her colleagues to create a "breathing teddy bear" attached to an air pump outside the crib. The rhythmic stimulation provided by the bear helps establish a regular breathing pattern in the infant, as well as improve the infant's quality of sleep and reduce crying and other expressions of negative emotions. (Thoman & Ingersoll, 1993; Thoman et al., 1995.)

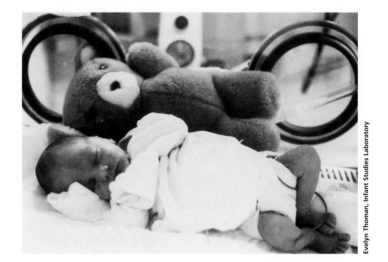

Evelyn Thoman, Infant Studies Laboratory

twice as likely as more affluent women to give birth to small or preterm infants. This disparity can be explained by the fact that poor women are more likely to be undernourished or chronically ill, to have inadequate health care before and during pregnancy, to suffer from infections, and to experience complications during pregnancy. Cultural factors such as the use of fertility drugs and fasting can also play a role (see Figure 3.17, which shows the increased risk of giving birth prematurely owing to fasting).

Many other causes of prematurity are still not well understood. At least half of all premature births are not associated with any of the identified risk factors and occur after otherwise normal pregnancies to healthy women who are in their prime childbearing years and have had good medical care.

Figure 3.17 A sudden drop in maternal food intake leads to hormonal changes that cause some women to go into labor prematurely. This graph shows a doubling of the birth rate among Jewish women on the day following the 24-hour total food and water fast of Yom Kippur. (Adapted from Kaplan et al., 1983.)

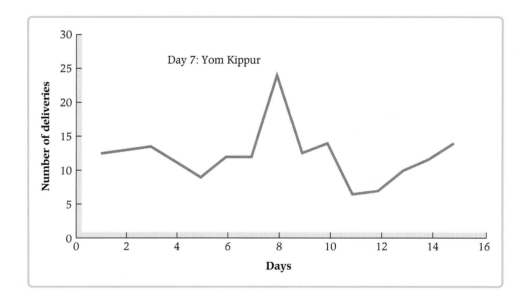

Low Birth Weight

Newborns whose birth weights fall in the lowest 10 percent for their gestational age are said to suffer from **fetal growth retardation;** in other words, they have not grown at the normal rate. Multiple births, intrauterine infections, chromosomal abnormalities, maternal smoking or use of narcotics, maternal malnutrition, and abnormalities of the placenta or umbilical cord have all been identified as probable causes of fetal growth retardation (Meara, 2001).

fetal growth retardation The term for newborns who are especially small for their gestational age.

Developmental Consequences

Intensive research has been conducted on the developmental consequences of prematurity and low birth weight, which often occur together. Babies who fall into either category are at risk for later developmental problems, but they differ in the probable course of their development (Cunningham et al., 2001).

Low-birth-weight infants are at increased risk for developmental difficulty whether they are premature or full-term. Two-thirds of the deaths that occur in the period immediately following birth are among low-birth-weight infants. In addition, low-birth-weight infants are three times more likely to have neurologically based developmental handicaps than are other babies, and the smaller the baby, the greater the risk (Holcroft, Blakemore, Allen, & Graham, 2001).

Common outcomes for low-birth-weight babies are a decrease in coordination and intellectual capacities. For example, one study that compared 7- to 11-year-olds who had a very low birth weight with children born at a normal weight found that the low-birth-weight children performed more poorly on tests of motor coordination, intelligence, and arithmetic (Holsti, Grunau & Whitfield, 2002).

Several factors appear to be important in determining the long-term outcome of prematurity. For example, premature babies who are of normal size for their gestational age stand a good chance of catching up with full-term babies (Lorenz, 2001). However, there is some evidence that even in the absence of any clinically detectable disability, when compared to full-term children, children born prematurely have problems with maintaining attention and with visual–motor coordination when they are school-age (Foreman et al., 1997). Those babies who are premature, are low in birth weight, and have medical complications are more likely to have future developmental difficulties.

The importance of a supportive environment in overcoming the potential risks of prematurity and low birth weight is underscored by research on the social ecology of the families of premature and low-birth-weight infants. Babies who are raised in comfortable socioeconomic circumstances with an intact family and a mother who has had a good education are less likely to suffer negative effects from their condition at birth than are children who are raised without these benefits (Liaw, Meisels & Brooks-Gunn, 1995). Low-birth-weight or premature babies who live in impoverished homes or have neglectful parents are more likely to suffer serious developmental problems in later years (Strathearn, Gray, O'Callaghan & Wood, 2001).

Beginning the Parent–Child Relationship

Because human infants are dependent on the active support and protection of their caretakers for their very survival, the development of a close relationship between infants and their parents is crucial to infants' well-being. However, love and caring between parent and child is neither inevitable nor automatic. The large numbers of infants who are neglected, abused, abandoned, or murdered the world over each year should convince even the most sentimental and optimistic observer of this harsh fact. How, then, is the bond between parent and child formed? And when no strong attachment develops, what has gone wrong? These are broad questions that you will encounter again and again in subsequent chapters, because a close parent–child relationship is not formed in an instant; it develops over many years (see the box "The Controversy over Mother–Newborn Bonding," p. 104). Here we will examine the factors that come into play immediately after birth and that many people believe set the stage for the future: the initial reactions of the parents to their baby's appearance, and the expectations parents have for their babies.

The Controversy over Mother–Newborn Bonding

It has often been claimed that the initial contacts between newborns of many species and their parents, particularly their mothers, produce a special bond that has a profound effect on their future relationship. As recently as a decade ago, this belief was so prevalent that stories urging parents to "discover the magic and mystery of bonding with your baby" were common at local supermarket magazine stands (Baker, 1993). Despite its popularity, this belief has proved very controversial.

The origins of the idea that mother–infant bonding at birth is important to later development arose in research with nonhuman animals several decades ago. For example, if a baby goat is removed from its mother immediately after birth and returned, say, 2 hours later, the mother will attack it. But if the baby goat is allowed to stay with its mother for as little as 5 minutes after its birth before it is removed for a few hours, the mother will welcome its return (Klopfer et al., 1964).

Not long after Klopfer and his colleagues reported these results, Marshall Klaus, John Kennell, and their co-workers began research on mothers whose premature babies were being kept in incubators. Until the babies were considered mature enough to be held, the mothers had little contact with them. Some of these mothers appeared to lose interest in their babies, and the researchers speculated that the early sensitive period for mother–infant bonding among goats had its parallel in a similar sensitive period for the bonding of human mothers and their babies (Klaus et al., 1970).

In a widely publicized study, Klaus and Kennell divided 28 first-time mothers into an experimental and a control group. The mothers in the control group had the amount of contact with their newborn infants that was traditional in many hospitals in the late 1960s: a glimpse of the baby shortly after its birth, brief contact with the baby between 6 and 12 hours later, and then 20- to 30-minute visits for bottle feedings every 4 hours. In between these periods, the baby remained in the nursery. The mothers in the experimental group, however, were given their babies to hold for 1 hour within the first 3 hours after delivery. The babies were dressed only in diapers so that their mothers could have skin-to-skin contact with them. In addition, the mother and child spent 5 hours together each afternoon for the 3 days after delivery. Many of the mothers reported that, although they were already excited by being able to fondle their infants immediately after birth, their excitement rose

higher when they succeeded in achieving eye contact with them.

When the mothers and babies in both groups returned to the hospital 1 month later, the mothers in the experimental group were more reluctant to leave their infants with other caretakers. They also seemed more interested in the examination of their infants, were better at soothing them, and seemed to gaze at and fondle their babies more than did the mothers in the control group. Eleven months later, the extended-contact mothers still seemed to be more attentive to their babies and more responsive to their cries than were the mothers in the control group (Kennell et al., 1974). Drawing an analogy with animal behavior, Klaus and Kennell (1976) suggested that if a mother and child are allowed to be in close physical contact immediately after birth, "complex interactions between mother and infant help to lock them together" (p. 51). The publication of these findings coincided with a broad popular movement to reform hospital childbirth practices to allow mothers and fathers to have prolonged contact with their newborn babies. Pediatricians, nurses, and parents who supported these reforms found in Klaus and Kennell's work a strong rationale for the changes they wanted to make.

However, belief in the importance of early mother–infant contact to promote bonding also provoked criticism (Eyer, 1992). It was pointed out that the experimental and control groups in Klaus and Kennell's study were quite small and unrepresentative of the population at large (there were only 14 women in each group, all poor African Americans). Fur-

thermore, the mothers in the experimental group were probably aware of the special treatment they received. This awareness, rather than the extended contact with their babies, may have been the source of their behavior. In the years since the initial studies were conducted, other researchers have often failed to discover any long-lasting differences associated with early bonding experience, casting further doubt on the phenomenon (Eyer, 1992). Michael Rutter (1995), an influential British physician, summarized professional opinion in the mid-1990s when he declared, "The simplistic superglue notion of maternal bonding has fortunately passed into oblivion" (p. 564).

Developmentalists now believe that instant mother–newborn contact is not essential to establish healthy, long-term, positive emotional relationships. However, the benefits of early and enduring parent–infant contact, especially in the case of infants who are at risk because they were born prematurely, have also come to be accepted quite broadly (Kirsten et al., 2001). Research on the positive benefits of kangaroo care (see Chapter 1, pp. 18–19), an extended form of continuous mother–infant interaction, has substantiated Klaus and Kennell's early speculations that skin-to-skin contact with newborns results in increased nutritional benefits to the child as well as greater parental caring and attention (Furman & Kennell, 2000; Tessier et al., 1998). It seems safe to conclude that the sooner and more firmly parents make their children a central concern in their lives, the sooner a supportive developmental niche is created.

The Baby's Appearance

In their search for the sources of attachment between mother and infant, some developmentalists have turned to *ethology*—the study of animal behavior and its evolutionary bases. These developmentalists believe that examination of what causes nonhuman mothers to protect or reject their young can shed light on the factors that influence human mothers. One important factor that seems to influence animals' responses to their young is their offsprings' appearance. Konrad Lorenz (1943), a German ethologist, noted that the newborns of many animal species have physical characteristics that distinguish them from the mature animal: a head that is large in relation to the body, a prominent forehead, large eyes that are positioned below the horizontal midline of the face, and round, full cheeks (see Figure 3.18). This combination of features, which Lorenz called "babyness," seems to appeal to adults and, more significantly, to evoke caregiving behaviors in them.

Evidence in support of the idea that babyness evokes positive adult responses comes from a study by William Fullard and Ann Reiling (1976). These researchers asked people ranging in age from 7 years to young adulthood which of matched pairs of pictures—one depicting an adult and the other depicting an infant—they preferred. Some of the pictures were of human beings; others were of animals. They found that adults, especially women, were most likely to choose the pictures of infants. Children between the ages of 7 and 12 preferred the pictures of adults. Between the ages of 12 and 14, the preference of girls shifted quite markedly from adults to infants. A similar shift was found among boys when they were between 14 and 16. These shifts in preference coincide with the average ages at which girls and boys undergo the physiological changes that make them capable of reproducing.

Adult responses to the appearance of infants may explain why mothers find it difficult to care for malformed offspring (Weiss, 1997). Mothers of dogs, cats, guinea pigs, and some other species will kill malformed offspring. Though human parents usually do not kill their malformed babies, they do interact less frequently and less lovingly with infants they consider unattractive than with those they consider attractive. They also attribute less competence to unattractive babies (Langlois et al., 2000). This pattern is particularly noticeable for baby girls. While still in the hospital with their newborn girls, mothers of less attractive babies directed their attention to people other than their babies more often than did mothers of attractive babies (Langlois et al., 1995).

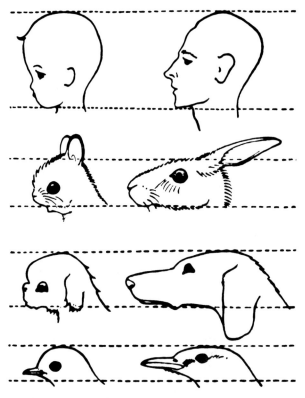

Figure 3.18 Side-by-side sketches of the heads of infants and adults of four species make clear the distinguishing features of "babyness." (From Lorenz, 1943.)

Social Expectations

During pregnancy, most parents-to-be develop specific expectations about what their babies will be like, and no sooner does a baby emerge from the womb than the parents begin to examine the neonate's looks and behaviors for hints of his or her future. Will she have her grandmother's high, round forehead? Does his lusty cry mean that he will have his father's quick temper?

Naturally, the baby will differ in some respects from the one the parents have been imagining. Usually, though, the parents begin to accommodate themselves to the reality of their child at the moment of birth. One of the adjustments parents frequently have to make is to the actual sex of the child when the other sex was wanted (MacFarlane, 1977).

Whether the baby is a boy or a girl, the parents' beliefs and expectations begin to shape their responses to the baby even before the child displays any truly distinctive features. One study found that parents who saw an ultrasound picture of their baby-to-be while it was still in the womb rated female fetuses as softer, littler, cuddlier, calmer, weaker, more delicate, and more beautiful than male fetuses (Sweeney & Bradbard, 1988). In another study, first-time mothers and fathers were asked to choose words that described their newborn babies within 24 hours after their birth (Rubin et al., 1974). The male and female babies did not differ in length or weight or in their scores on the Apgar Scale. Nevertheless, the parents described their daughters as "little," "beautiful," "pretty," or "cute" and as resembling their mothers, whereas they described their sons as "big" and as resembling their fathers. Fathers, the researchers found, were more likely than mothers to sex-type their babies.

There is every reason for their baby's sex to be important to the parents. Children's sex determines what they are named, how they are dressed, how they are treated, and what will be expected of them in later life. There is a disconcerting side to this process, however. We like to think of ourselves as individuals, and we want to be treated with an awareness of who we are, not of what others expect us to be. It therefore comes as something of a shock to realize that so many important aspects of our future may be shaped at the outset by our parents' expectations. For example, when a mother says, upon seeing that her newborn baby is a girl, "She's never going to be a rugby player," and the baby's father comments, "I shall be worried to death about her when she turns 18," these are more than idle comments. They shape the way that the parents treat the child right from the start, even though there is nothing in the child's current makeup to warrant any differential treatment at all (MacFarlane, 1977).

Unless parental expectations are held so rigidly that they become destructive, they do not represent a failing on the parents' part. Rather, parents' responses to their newborns reflect the fact that human infants are not just biological organisms but cultural entities as well. For their parents and for other members of the community, infants have special meanings that are shaped by the culture's ideas about the experiences that infants are likely to encounter as they grow to adulthood. These meanings in turn shape the ways adults construct the environmental contexts within which children develop. When differences are found in the ways boys and girls are treated, they occur not just because parents think that infant boys and girls are different to begin with but, perhaps more significantly, because they believe that men and women have different roles to play (Fagot, 1995).

This orientation to the future is expressed in clear symbolic form by the Zincantecos of south-central Mexico (Greenfield et al., 1989). When a son is born, he is given a digging stick, an ax, and a strip of palm used in weaving mats, in expectation of his adult role. When a daughter is born, she is given a weaving stick. Such future orientation is not only present in ritual; it is coded in a Zincantecan saying: "For in the newborn baby is the future of our world."

Organization of the present in terms of the future is a fundamental cultural source of developmental change and a powerful environmental source of developmental continuity. As the anthropologist Leslie White (1949) wrote, only among humans does the world of ideas come "to have a continuity and permanence that the external world of the senses can never have. It is not made up of the present only, but of a past and a future as well" (p. 372).

Just as infants are born with a set of genetically built-in capacities to learn about and to act upon the world, parents come to this moment with their own tendencies to respond in certain ways that have developed through their experience as members of their culture. The relationship between child and parents that begins at birth is an essential part of the foundation on which later development builds.

S U M M A R Y

The Periods of Prenatal Development

- Many developmental theorists look upon the prenatal period as a model for all periods of development from conception to death.

- Prenatal development is often divided into three broad periods:

  1. The germinal period begins at conception and lasts until the zygote enters the uterus and becomes implanted there about 8 to 10 days later.

     - As the organism grows from a single cell and encounters new environments within the mother's uterus, not only does the organism grow larger but new forms of cells and organs emerge.

     - According to the epigenetic hypothesis, interactions between the cells and their environment generate the new forms.

  2. The embryonic period begins with implantation and ends with the first signs of ossification at the end of the eighth week.

     - At implantation, the organism becomes directly dependent on the mother's body for sustenance.

     - A two-way exchange of nutrients and waste products begins between mother and embryo.

     - During the embryonic period the basic organs are formed and sexual differentiation takes place.

  3. The fetal period begins in the ninth week and continues until birth; during this period the brain grows extensively and the separate organ systems become integrated.

     - The fetus is subject to environmental influences originating from outside as well as inside the mother. The fetus sometimes experiences outside influences directly through its own sensory mechanisms, but often such influences work indirectly, through their effects on the mother.

     - Basic sensory capacities (sensing motion, light, sound) develop during this period.

     - By 15 weeks the fetus exhibits all movements observable at birth.

     - Fetal activity plays an important role in establishing the essential neuronal configurations the baby will need at birth.

     - The fetus is capable of learning from events taking place in the mother's environment while still in the womb.

Maternal Conditions and Prenatal Development

- The mother's reactions to her environment—her feelings and attitudes—are associated with the fetus's well-being.

- Children born to mothers who do not want them or who are under stress are subject to developmental risk.

- Mothers who want their babies but live in stressful circumstances create hormones that negatively influence their children's later development and increase the risk of premature delivery and low birth weight

- The nutritional status of the mother is an important factor in fetal development. Extreme malnutrition in the mother has a devastating effect on her ability to produce a normal child. Lesser degrees of malnourishment associated with other forms of environmental deprivation also increase the risks to fetal and postnatal development.

Teratogens: Environmental Sources of Birth Defects

- Teratogens (environmental agents that can cause deviations from normal fetal development) take many forms. Several basic principles apply to the effects of teratogens:

  1. The susceptibility of the organism depends on the stage of its development.

  2. A teratogen's effects are likely to be specific to a particular organ.

  3. Individual organisms vary in their susceptibility to teratogens.

  4. The physiological state of the mother influences the impact of a teratogen.

  5. The greater the concentration of a teratogenic agent, the greater the risk.

  6. Teratogens that adversely affect the developing organism may affect the mother little or not at all.

- Drugs, infections, radiation, and pollution all act as teratogens that pose threats to the developing organism.

Reconsidering Prenatal Development

- Several basic principles of development are seen in the prenatal period:

  1. Sequence is fundamental.

  2. Timing is important.

  3. Development consists of differentiation and integration.

  4. Development is characterized by stagelike changes.

  5. Development proceeds unevenly.

  6. Development is punctuated by periods of apparent regression.

  7. Development is still a mystery.

Birth: The First Bio-Social-Behavioral Shift

● Birth is the first bio-social-behavioral shift in postnatal development.

● The process of birth begins approximately 266 days after conception, when changes in the mother's body force the fetus through the birth canal.

● Labor proceeds through three stages. It begins with the first regular, intense contractions of the uterus, and it ends when the baby is born, the umbilical cord is severed, and the afterbirth is delivered.

● Although the biological process of labor is roughly the same everywhere, there are marked cultural variations in the organization of childbearing.

● Drugs given to the mother to reduce pain may have negative effects on the neonate.

● Medical interventions including induction of labor and cesarean section are widely used in the United States, but their use has encountered resistance, leading to the organization of a variety of alternative birthing practices.

● Birth is a stressful experience for the baby, but it is believed that hormones induced by the stress help babies both to cope with the birth process and to be in a state of heightened awareness when they emerge from the womb.

The Newborn's Condition

● The infant's physical state at birth is usually assessed by the Apgar Scale, which rates the infant's heart rate, respiratory effort, reflex responsivity, muscle tone, and color. Babies with low Apgar scores require immediate medical attention if they are to survive.

● Scales have been developed to assess the neonate's behavioral capacities. These scales are satisfactory for identifying neonates who require medical intervention; they appear to be modestly useful, at best, for predicting later patterns of development.

● Many premature babies who are of normal size for their gestational age can catch up with full-term infants if they are well cared for. Those who have low birth weights and small heads are especially at risk for long-term developmental problems.

● Prematurity—birth before the thirty-seventh week after gestation—poses a number of health risks to the newborn.

● Low birth weight, which often accompanies prematurity, is an additional risk factor threatening the newborn's health.

● The combined effects of low birth weight and prematurity pose long-term threats to the baby's development.

Beginning the Parent–Child Relationship

● A newborn's appearance plays a significant role in the parents' responses to the baby.

● The parents' expectations, patterned by the culture's belief system, influence the child's environment in ways that shape the child's development and promote the continuation of cultural traits from one generation to another.

Key Terms

Thought Questions

1. Give examples of quantitative and qualitative changes that take place during prenatal development. What are the important differences between the two kinds of changes?

2. What makes transitions from one stage of prenatal development to the next risky for the organism?

3. What is the role of activity in fetal development?

4. Skim back through the chapter to list as many examples as you can of instances where the environment plays a significant role in prenatal development. Do you think that the role of the environment changes after birth? How?

5. Parents have well-formed expectations about the future behaviors of their newborn babies. How might these expectations shape the child's development?

part II Infancy

Bio-Social-Behavioral Shifts

Biological Domain
- Growth of muscles and hardening of bones
- Myelination of motor neurons to lower trunk, legs, and hands
- Myelination of cerebellum, hippocampus, and frontal lobes
- New forms of EEG activity in cortex

Social Domain
- Wariness of strangers
- New emotional response to caregiver (attachment)
- Social referencing
- Secondary intersubjectivity

Behavioral Domain
- Onset of crawling
- Fear of heights
- Coordinated reaching and grasping
- Action sequences coordinated to achieve goals
- Object permanence displayed in actions
- Recall memory
- Wariness in response to novelty
- Babbling

All cultures recognize infancy as a distinct period of life. Its starting point is clear; it begins when the umbilical cord is severed and the child starts to breathe. The end of infancy is not so easily defined. According to the ancient Romans, an infant is "one who does not speak," and the ability to speak a language is still considered an important indicator that infancy has come to an end. It is not a sufficient marker by itself, however. Modern developmentalists look for converging changes in several spheres of children's functioning to determine when one stage has ended and another has begun. These changes include not only infants' acquisition of language but changes in their biological makeup, physical capacities, modes of thought, and social relations as well. It is this ensemble of changes that marks the transformation of babies from helpless infants into young children who, though still dependent upon adults, are on their way to independence.

The chapters in Part II are organized to highlight the important sequences of changes in each sphere of development and the interconnections among them during infancy. Chapter 4 begins with a description of infants' earliest capacities for perceiving and acting on the world. It then traces events in infant development from birth to about $2\frac{1}{2}$ to 3 months of age. The most obvious requirement of this earliest postnatal period is that infants and their caretakers become sufficiently coordinated in their interactions so that adults can provide infants with enough nourishment and protection

to support their continued growth. This requirement is met through a wide variety of cultural systems of infant care that call upon and promote infants' basic capacities to learn from experience. If all goes well, by the end of this period, the development of crucial brain structures will have enhanced infants' abilities to experience the world, resulting in a reordering of the social and emotional interactions between infants and their caretakers. This ensemble of changes is the first postnatal bio-social-behavioral shift.

Between $2\frac{1}{2}$ to 3 months and 12 months of age, the period covered in Chapter 5, infants' capacities in all spheres of development change markedly. Increases in size and strength are accompanied by increases in coordination and mobility: the ability to sit independently appears at about 5 or 6 months; crawling at about 7 or 8 months; and walking at about 1 year. Both memory and problem-solving abilities improve, providing infants with a finer sense of their environment and how to act upon it.

Sometime between 7 and 9 months, infants' increased physical ability and intellectual power bring about additional changes in their emotions and social relations. They are likely to become wary of strangers; they become upset when left alone; and they begin to express strong emotional attachments to their caretakers. They also begin to make their first speech-like sounds. These changes mark what appears to be a second bio-social-behavioral shift during infancy.

Chapter 6 describes the changes that occur between 12 months and $2\frac{1}{2}$ years, culminating in the bio-social-behavioral shift that signals the end of infancy. Rapid growth in the baby's ability to use language is accompanied by the emergence of pretend play and more sophisticated forms of problem solving. Toward the end of infancy, children begin to show a concern for adult standards, and they attempt to meet those standards. Caretakers, for their part, view these changes as a sign that children are no longer "babies." They begin to reason with their children, to explain things to them, and to make demands upon them.

The coverage of infancy ends with Chapter 7, which takes up an enduring question: Does the pattern of development that is established during infancy persist into later years, fixed and unchangeable, or can it be significantly altered by the maturational changes and experiences that will occur during childhood and adolescence? This scientific question has a practical counterpart: Should society intervene in the lives of at-risk infants to prevent later problems, or should it wait until there are actual problems? As we shall see, opinions about these matters are sharply divided. Nevertheless, the efforts of developmentalists to study them underscore how important it is to consider the whole child in the context of both family and community if we are to gain a scientific understanding of development and make informed decisions about social policies that affect children.

Infant Capacities and the Process of Change

"*Babies control and bring up their families as much as they are controlled by them; in fact, we may say that the family brings up a baby by being brought up by him. Whatever reaction patterns are given biologically and whatever schedule is predetermined developmentally must be considered to be a series of potentialities for changing patterns of mutual regulation.*"

—Erik Erikson, *Childhood and Society*

The enormous changes that occur over the first 90 days of postnatal life are vividly reflected in the ways that mothers respond to their infants. Pediatricians Kenneth Robson and Howard Moss asked new mothers to describe their feelings during the first several weeks after they brought their babies home from the hospital. One mother expressed her feelings this way:

> In the beginning when they are so young and can't be appeased you just don't know what to do for them, that is the frightening part . . . and I think that realizing you are dealing with an infant mind is such a shock— that this is a mind that just doesn't know from anything else. Go reason with it, talk to yourself, cry; nothing you are going to do is going to help. (Robson & Moss, 1970, pp. 979)

Then, around 2$\frac{1}{2}$ months of age, the quality of mother–child interaction changes in a manner that is caught beautifully by Daniel Stern, a specialist in early mother–infant interaction:

> His eyes locked on to hers, and together they held motionless. . . . This silent and almost motionless instant continued to hang until the mother suddenly shattered it by saying "Hey!" and simultaneously opening her eyes wider, raising her eyebrows further, and throwing her head up and toward the infant. Almost simultaneously the baby's eyes widened. His head tilted up . . . his smile broadened. . . . Now she said, "Well hello! . . . hello . . . heeelloooo!," so that her pitch rose and the "hellos" became longer and more stressed on each successive repetition. With each phrase the baby expressed more pleasure, and his body resonated almost like a balloon being pumped up. (Stern, 1977, p. 3)

Clearly babies undergo tremendous changes in the first months after birth—changes that transform the seemingly unresponsive newborn into a highly interactive infant. What new capacities do infants acquire during this period of transformation?

Of course, the newborn mind is not as formless as the first quotation suggests. Despite parents' uncertainty about what their newborns are seeing and feeling, the evidence concerning prenatal development clearly shows that babies arrive in the world with at least elementary abilities to see and hear their environment, to move, to learn, and to remember. In this sense, they are ready to be born. But compared with many animals that are able to negotiate their environments at birth almost as well as their parents, human beings are born in a state of marked immaturity. The ability to suck, for example, is of no help in obtaining food unless the infant's mouth is in touch with a source of milk, and newborns cannot yet bring the nipple to their mouths by themselves. They must be physically supported to accomplish even such an elementary function as feeding.

Developmentalists who have studied the evolution of childhood believe that human infants, even those who spend a full 9 months in their mothers' wombs, are born "prematurely" as an adaptation to the unusual circumstance that their ancient, prehistorical ancestors began to walk on two feet. Upright walking, the argument goes, required a change in the size of the pelvis, making the birth canal relatively narrow. If fetuses grew too large, they would be unable to make their way through the birth canal, resulting in their death, as well as the death of their mothers (Bogin, 2001).

The relative helplessness of human babies at birth has two obvious consequences. First, for many years, human offspring must depend on the efforts of their parents and other adults for their survival. Second, in order to survive on their own and eventually reproduce, humans must acquire a vast repertoire of knowledge and skills that they do not possess at birth.

This chapter describes the capacities and characteristics of children at birth and the processes of developmental change that occur in the initial period of infancy, a period beginning immediately after birth and ending some $2^1/_2$ months later. During this time, significant changes take place in several essential biological, behavioral, and social processes. There is a rapid increase in the number and complexity of the neurons in infants' brains and other parts of their central nervous systems, and their vision and movements improve markedly, allowing them to become more responsive to the people and objects around them. These changes converge about $2^1/_2$ to 3 months after birth to enable new kinds of behavior that in turn make it possible for a distinctively new kind of social and emotional relationship to develop between infants and their caregivers. This convergence of changes in different domains is the kind of qualitative reorganization in the child's functioning that we have referred to as a bio-social-behavioral shift.

Development of the Brain

Changes in the brain are responsible for many of the developmental changes you will encounter in this chapter. As you saw in Chapter 3 (pp. 79–82), well before full-term babies are born, their brains and central nervous systems support elementary sensory and motor functions: fetuses respond to distinct sounds, for example, and they move spontaneously. These basic capacities are sufficient for them to learn to recognize the sound of their mothers' voices and the language spoken around them and form the basis for newborns' earliest adaptations to their new environment.

In an authoritative study, W. M. Cowan (1979) found that during the period of maximum prenatal brain development, which occurs between 10 and 26 weeks after conception, the brain grows at a rate of as many as 250,000 brain cells per minute. It is estimated that the cerebral cortex, the area of the brain that most distinctively distinguishes human beings from other animals, contains more than 10 *billion* nerve cells. Each of these nerve cells makes multiple connections with other nerve cells.

At birth the brain contains the vast majority of all the cells it will ever have, yet it will become four times larger by the time the baby reaches adulthood. To understand how such growth comes about, we need to look more closely at the basic operative unit of brain activity—the nerve cell referred to as the **neuron**—and the brain structures into which neurons are organized.

Neurons and Networks of Neurons

Neurons transmit information to other neurons or to muscle or gland cells. This function causes neurons to differ from other body cells in several respects. Most body cells look smooth and regular, more or less in the shape of a sphere or a disk. By contrast, neurons have highly irregular shapes, with many spiky areas sticking up from their surfaces (see Figure 4.1). Every neuron has one main protruding branch, called an **axon,** along which it sends information to other cells in the form of small electrical impulses. If a neuron needs to communicate with more than one other nerve cell, its axon forms branches (referred to as *axon terminals*) at its tip to make the necessary connections. The parts of the neuron that protrude from its surface are called **dendrites.** The dendrites, as well as other parts of the cell body, receive messages from the axons of other cells.

The actual site at which one neuron is linked to another is a tiny gap between axons and dendrites called the **synapse.** When an impulse from the axon arrives at the synapse, the sending cell secretes a chemical, called a **neurotransmitter,** that carries the impulse across the synaptic gap, setting off a reaction in the receiving cell.

The combination of a sending and a receiving neuron creates an elementary neuronal circuit. As a rule, neurons transmit and receive impulses from only a few other neurons. However, in some cases, one axon branches to come in contact with many diverging neuronal networks; in other cases, many axons converge on a receptor neuron. The results of such multiple forms of connectivity, combined with the fact that there are billions of neurons, make possible a virtually infinite variety of patterns of brain activity and behavior.

The basic architecture of neurons and neuronal circuits suggests two of the reasons for the fourfold growth in brain size that occurs by adulthood. First, there is an increase in the size and complexity of the dendrites that protrude from every neuron. The increased complexity means that many new synapses are being formed, a process referred to as **synaptogenesis** (the technical term for synapse formation). Synaptogenesis is especially prominent in prenatal development and infancy, and then again during adolescence. Second, there is an increase in the number of branches that axons form as they create connections to multiple receiving neurons. These two sources of growth combine to increase the number of synapses and to form more complex neural circuits (see Figure 4.2, p. 116).

Another source of increased brain size and complexity of brain functions is *myelination,* the process by which axons become covered by **myelin,** a sheath of fatty cells that insulates them and speeds transmission of nerve impulses from one neuron to the next. Myelinated axons transmit signals anywhere from 10 to 100 times faster than unmyelinated axons, making possible more effective interconnections between parts of the brain and more complicated forms of thought and action (Nelson, 2001).

neuron A nerve cell.

axon The main protruding branch of a neuron that carries messages to other cells in the form of electrical impulses.

dendrite The protruding part of a neuron that receives messages from the axons of other cells.

synapse The tiny gap between axons and dendrites.

neurotransmitter A chemical secreted by a cell sending a message that carries the impulse across the synaptic gap to the receiving cell.

synaptogenesis The process of synapse formation.

myelin A sheath of fatty cells that insulates axons and speeds transmission of nerve impulses from one neuron to the next.

Figure 4.1
The neuron receives information from other neurons through its dendrites and feeds that information to other neurons through its axon. The photograph shows a neuron in the cerebellum.

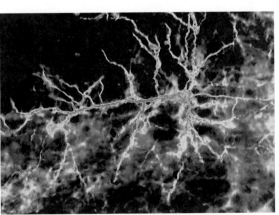

©BSIP/Phototake

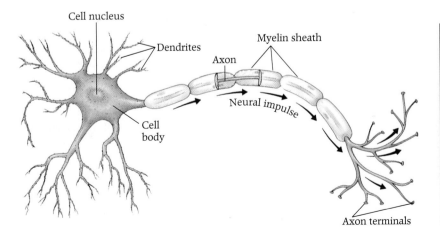

Figure 4.2
These drawings from photomicrographs of infant brain tissue show the marked increases in the size and number of cerebral neurons during the first 15 months of postnatal life. (From Conel, 1939/1963.)

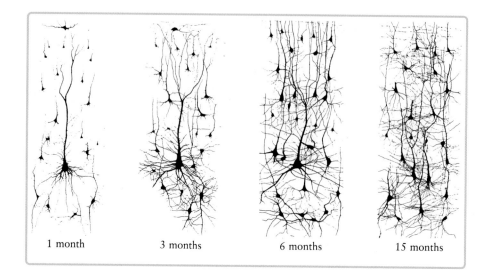

1 month   3 months   6 months   15 months

Experience and Development of the Brain

The principle that development emerges from dynamic interaction between the organism and the environment applies no less to the development of the brain than to the development of behavior. Developmentalists distinguish two major classes of brain development, which they refer to as experience-expectant and experience-dependent (Breuer & Greenough, 2001).

The prenatal brain growth described in Table 3.1 (p. 77) provides the prototype for **experience-expectant** processes of brain development. During formation of the central nervous system, the basic circuitry of the brain develops under genetic control independent of experience, stimulation, or activity. One result of this spontaneous process is rapid increase in synaptogenesis, resulting in the production of more synapses than will be useful when the growing embryo begins to encounter new experiences. This early oversupply of synapses provides the raw material for experience-expectant development. As in the case of movement in chick embryos (Chapter 3, p. 80), a selection process begins that determines which synapses of this oversupply will survive and which will die (Webb, Monk & Nelson, 2001). This process of selective dying off of non-functional synapses is referred to as **synaptic pruning,** which is seen again during infancy, middle childhood, and adolescence (Giedd et al., 1999) (see Figure 4.3).

In **experience-dependent** brain development, synapses are not created in advance of experience; instead they are generated in *response to* experience. It is this experience-dependent brain–environment relationship that allows humans to learn from experience.

An example of experience-dependent brain development comes from pioneering studies by Mark Rosenzweig and his colleagues (Rosenzweig, 1984), in which groups of young male laboratory rats from the same litter were raised in three different environments. Rats in the first group were housed individually in standard laboratory cages. Members of the second group were

Figure 4.3
The number of synapses in the human visual cortex as a function of age. The first spurt of synaptogenesis peaks at about 1 year of age; through the process of synaptic pruning, the number then declines until about 10 years of age, at which time the number levels off until early adulthood. (From Huttenlocher, 1994.)

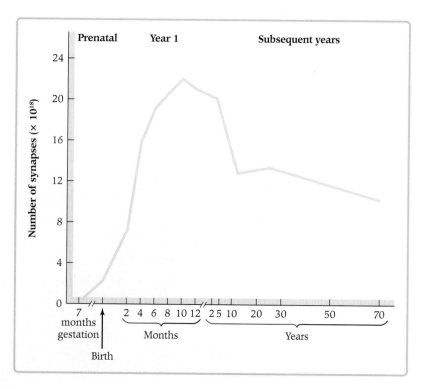

housed together in standard laboratory cages. Those in the third group were provided with enriched conditions. These rats were housed in a large cage that was furnished with a variety of playthings. A new set of playthings, drawn from a pool of 25 objects, was placed in the cage every day. Often the animals in this group were given formal training in running a maze or were exposed to a toy-filled open field.

At the end of the experimental period, which lasted anywhere from a few weeks to several months, behavioral tests and examinations of the animals' brains revealed differences that favored the animals raised in enriched conditions. These rats demonstrated:

- Increased rates of learning in standard laboratory tasks, such as learning a maze

- Increased overall weight of the *cerebral cortex* (the part of the brain that integrates sensory information)

- Increased amounts of acetylcholinesterase, a brain enzyme that enhances learning

- Larger neuronal cell bodies and glial cells (which provide insulation, support, and nutrients to neuronal cells)

- More synaptic connections

These findings have been replicated and extended numerous times in recent decades (Nelson & Bloom, 1997).

Interaction with the environment is a crucial factor in the production of these changes. In one study, rats were raised within an enriched environment but were housed singly in small cages so that they could do no more than observe what was going on around them. The learning capacity of these rats differed in no way from that of the animals that were housed in individual cages away from the enriched environment (Forgays & Forgays, 1952).

Although these results were obtained with nonhuman animal species, they are consistent with what is known about the importance of active involvement with the environment for human development. They show that behavioral changes should not be thought of as secondary consequences of changes that occur in the brain. Behavioral changes induced by culturally organized environmental stimulation (early support for walking, for example) can themselves lead to changes in the brain that then support more complex forms of behavior (Greenfield, 2002).

The Central Nervous System and the Brain

The central nervous system is conventionally divided into three major sections—the spinal cord, the brain stem, and the cerebral cortex. The **spinal cord** is encased in the spinal bones that extend from below the waist to the base of the brain. The nerves that lie within the spinal cord carry messages back and forth from the brain to the spinal nerves along the spinal tract. The spinal nerves that branch out from the spinal cord communicate with specific areas of the body. Some of these neurons carry messages to the brain from the skin and other body parts and organs; others carry messages from the brain to the various body parts to initiate actions such as muscle movement.

The brain itself grows out of the top of the spinal cord (see Figure 4.4, p. 118). At its base is the **brain stem,** which controls such elementary reactions as blinking and sucking, in addition to such vital functions as breathing and sleeping. All of these capacities can be found in at least rudimentary form during the later stages of prenatal development. At birth the brain stem is one of the most highly developed areas of the central nervous system.

experience-expectant Development of neural connections under genetic controls that occurs in any normal environment.

synaptic pruning The process of selective dying off of nonfunctional synapses.

experience-dependent Development of neural connections that is initiated in response to experience.

spinal cord The part of the central nervous system that extends from below the waist to the base of the brain.

brain stem The base of the brain, which controls such elementary reactions as blinking and sucking, as well as such vital functions as breathing and sleeping.

Figure 4.4
A schematic view of the brain, showing the major lobes or divisions of the cerebral cortex (including the areas where some functions are localized), the brain stem, the cerebellum, and the spinal cord. (Adapted from Tanner, 1978.)

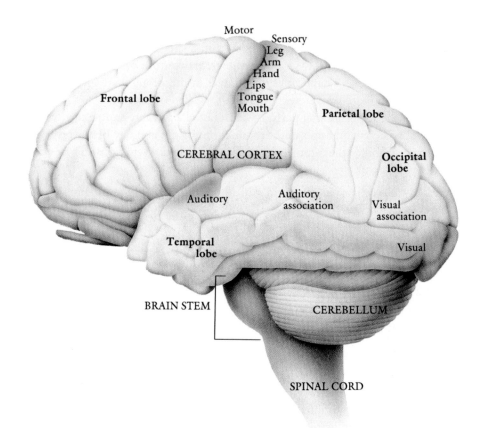

cerebral cortex The brain's outermost layer. The networks of neurons in the cerebral cortex integrate information from several sensory sources with memories of past experiences, processing them in a way that results in human forms of thought and action.

primary motor area The area of the brain responsible for nonreflexive, or voluntary, movement.

primary sensory areas The areas of the cerebral cortex responsible for the initial analysis of sensory information.

The neurons of the brain stem do not respond to specific forms of sensory input in a precise, one-to-one manner, with different sensory inputs arriving at the brain as isolated signals. Instead, the brain stem contains neural pathways that mix various sources of sensory input with impulses from other regions of the brain and the body. Stimulation that reaches the brain stem from the sensory receptors is modulated and reorganized within these pathways, increasing the complexity of behaviors that it can support.

Structures in the brain stem connect to the **cerebral cortex,** the brain's outermost layer. The cerebral cortex is divided into two hemispheres, each of which is divided into four sections, or lobes, separated by deep grooves. Under ordinary conditions of development, the *occipital lobes* are specialized for vision; the *temporal lobes,* for hearing and speech; the *parietal lobes,* for spatial perception; and the *frontal lobes,* for control and coordination of the other cortical areas to enable complex forms of behavior and thought.

It has been estimated that an average cerebral cortex is capable of a million billion connections, creating a biological organ of incredible complexity (Edelman, 1992). Once stimulation from the environment reaches the cerebral cortex, it travels through networks of interacting neurons so complex that scientists have thus far found it impossible to trace completely the fate of a single stimulus event, such as a touch on the cheek. The networks of neurons in the cerebral cortex integrate information from several sensory sources with memories of past experiences, processing them in a way that results in distinctively human forms of thought and action.

Although various areas of the brain are named according to the functions that they will later carry out, for many functions there is considerable interplay among areas. In addition, the human cortex, unlike that of other animals, has large areas that are not "prewired" to respond directly to external stimulation in any discernible way (see Figure 4.5). These "uncommitted" areas provide infants with the capacity to develop brain circuits that grow and change depending upon the experiences they encounter as they develop. This is the property of development we referred to in

Chapter 1 (p. 11) as *plasticity,* which, as you can now appreciate, depends heavily on environment-dependent changes in brain structure.

In general, the lower-lying areas of the central nervous system, the spinal cord and the brain stem, mature (that is, grow more dendritic trees, have more myelin, increase the complexity of their neural circuitry) earlier than the cerebral cortex. At birth the circuitry of the cerebral cortex is both relatively immature and poorly connected to the lower-lying parts of the nervous system that receive stimulation from the environment. Because of their relative maturity, the spinal cord and brain stem enable movement, responses to visual stimuli, and even elementary forms of learning without cortical involvement (Woodruff-Pak et al., 1990). As the nerve fibers connecting the cortex with the brain stem and spinal cord become myelinated, the infant's abilities expand.

Different parts of the cerebral cortex continue to develop at different times throughout infancy and well into childhood and adolescence (Johnson, 2001). Using criteria such as the size and complexity of neurons, their degree of myelination, and the complexity of their connections, scientists estimate that the first area of the cerebral cortex to undergo important developmental change is the **primary motor area,** which is the area responsible for nonreflexive, or voluntary, movement (Kolb & Whishaw, 2001). Within the primary motor area, the first cells to become functional are those that control the arms and the trunk. By about 1 month of age, the neurons in this area are becoming myelinated, so they can now conduct neural impulses more efficiently. The region of the primary motor area that governs leg movements is the last to mature; it is not fully developed until sometime in the second year.

As a result of this sequence of biological changes, the development of voluntary movement in the arms and legs follows the cephalocaudal (from-the-head-down) pattern, introduced as a general principle of developmental change in Chapter 3 (p. 77). At the end of the first month, many infants can raise their heads while lying on their stomachs. At 3 months of age, they have more voluntary control of the muscles that move the upper trunk, shoulders, arms, and forearms. A few months later, they begin to gain voluntary control of leg movements.

The **primary sensory areas** of the cortex—those areas that are responsible for the initial analysis of sensory information—also continue to mature in the months after birth. The nerve fibers responsible for touch are the first to mature, followed by those in the primary visual area and then those in the primary auditory area. By 3 months of age, all the primary sensory areas are relatively mature (Sinclair & Dangerfield, 1998).

The *frontal cortex,* which is essential in a wide variety of voluntary behaviors, including behaviors that require planning, is quite immature at birth. It gradually begins to function in infancy and continues to develop throughout childhood (Johnson, 2001). The development of the frontal lobes makes possible the complex forms of behavior and thought associated with specifically human psychological processes.

Figure 4.5
In these six mammalian species, the proportions of the brain mass that are devoted to different functions vary widely. The areas designated "uncommitted cortex" are not dedicated to any particular sensory or motor functions and are available for integrating information of many kinds. (Adapted from Fishbein, 1976.)

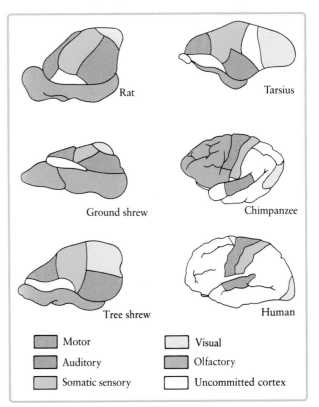

Sensing and Responding to the Environment

Scholars interested in development have always had a special fascination with the question of newborn babies' initial capacities to perceive, to act upon, and perhaps even to think about the world into which they are born. A century ago there was broad agreement with William James's belief that infants' perceptual world is a "blooming, buzzing confusion" (1890, p. 488). By the 1990s, scientific opinion had swung strongly in the opposite direction, to the belief that children are born with greater capacities for perceiving and acting in the world than their normally observed behavior reveals, a belief summed up by the term "the precocious infant" (Haith & Benson, 1998). At present developmentalists are sharply divided on the issue (Baillargeon, 2000; Cohen, 2002).

This difference of opinion about the "starting points" of development strongly influences the kind of theory needed to explain subsequent processes of developmental change. The idea of a precocious infant points to biology and processes of maturation as the essential driving force of development, while the idea of an infant initially confronting total confusion suggests that development depends almost entirely upon information from the environment. As you'll see, most developmentalists adopt an intermediate position in which initial capacities are innately specified but only to a degree sufficient to guide how experience shapes later development.

You don't have to spend much time with a newborn infant to understand the difficulties of arriving at a definitive conclusion of infants' initial capacities. Babies sleep a lot, and when they are awake they may be drowsy or upset. Even when they appear to be alert, they often seem to be simply "taking in the scene" and not paying special attention to anything in particular. From time to time it appears that something catches the baby's attention, but such moments are fleeting. These constant fluctuations in the state of the newborn make it difficult for developmentalists to repeat each other's experiments in order to provide reliable and replicable evidence on the state of particular capacities.

Sensory Processes

Organisms receive information from the environment through their sensory systems. Normal full-term newborns enter the world with all sensory systems functioning, but not all of these systems have developed to the same level. For example, their sense of touch is considerably more advanced than their visual acuity. This unevenness illustrates the general rule of development (heterochrony) that we remarked on with respect to the fetal period: Various organ systems develop at different rates throughout childhood.

The basic method developmentalists use to evaluate infants' sensory capacities is to present them with a stimulus and observe how their overt behaviors or physiological processes are affected by it. There are several ways in which this general strategy can be implemented. For example, an investigator might sound a tone or flash a light and watch for an indication that the newborn has sensed it, such as a turn of the head, a variation in brain waves, or a change in the rate at which the baby sucks on a nipple. Another widely used technique is to present two stimuli at once to determine if the baby will display a preference by looking at one longer than the other. If so, the baby must be able to tell the stimuli apart.

Yet another technique for assessing sensory capacities is to present a stimulus to which the infant clearly attends and continue presenting it until the infant gets bored and stops paying attention. The process in which attention to a novel stimulus decreases following repeated exposure is called **habituation.** The next step is to make a change in some aspect of the stimulus: the frequency of a musical tone or the arrangement of syllables in a spoken nonsense word, for example. If the infants show renewed interest after the change in the stimulus, they are said to exhibit **dishabituation,** and the investigator can conclude that they perceived the change. The use of such subtle indicators of infant's attention to sensory stimuli provides developmentalists with essential tools for understanding human development while the infants are still too immature to make their experiences known through coordinated movement or speech.

habituation The process in which attention to novelty decreases with repeated exposure.

dishabituation The term used to describe the situation in which an infant's interest is renewed after a change in the stimulus.

phonemes The smallest sound categories in human speech that distinguish meanings. Phonemes vary from language to language.

Hearing

Since even fetuses respond to sounds outside the mother's womb, it is no surprise that in their first hours after birth newborns also respond to sound. Make a loud noise and infants only minutes old will startle and may even cry. They will also turn their heads toward the source of the noise, an indication that they perceive sound as roughly localized in space (Morrongiello et al., 1994). Yet newborns' hearing is not so acute for some parts of the sound spectrum as it will be when they are older (Fernald, 2001). Sensitivity to sound improves dramatically in infancy and then more slowly until the age of 10, when it reaches adult levels. Newborns are especially attuned to the sounds of language. They can distinguish the sound of the human voice from other kinds of sounds, and they seem to prefer it. Newborns all over the world are particularly interested in speech directed to them that is spoken with the high pitch and slow, exaggerated pronunciation known as "baby talk" or "motherese" (Kitamura, Thanavishuth, Luksaneeyanawin & Burnham, 2002). This preference for motherese even appears when the speaker is speaking a foreign language (Werker, Pegg & McLeod, 1994). By the time they are 2 days old, however, babies would rather hear the language that has been spoken around them than a foreign language (Moon et al., 1993).

One of the most striking discoveries about the hearing of very young infants is that they are particularly sensitive to the smallest sound categories in human speech that distinguish meanings. These basic language sounds are called **phonemes.** (Linguists denote phonemes and other language sounds by enclosing them in slashes, as we do below.)

Phonemes vary from language to language. In Spanish, for example, /r/ and /rr/ are two phonemes; "pero" and "perro" sound different ("perro" has a rolling *r*) and have different meanings. In English, however, there is no such distinction. Similarly, /r/ and /l/ are different phonemes in English but not in Japanese.

In a pioneering study, Peter Eimas and his colleagues demonstrated that even 2-month-olds can distinguish among a variety of phonemes (Eimas, 1985). The researchers began by having the infants suck on a nipple attached to a recording device in a special apparatus (see Figure 4.6). After establishing a baseline rate of sucking for

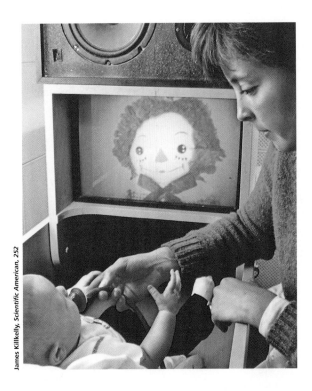

James Killkelly, *Scientific American, 252*

Figure 4.6
Apparatus for presenting artificially manipulated speech sounds to young infants. The baby sucks on a pacifier connected to recording instruments as speechlike sounds are presented from a loudspeaker just above the Raggedy Ann doll.

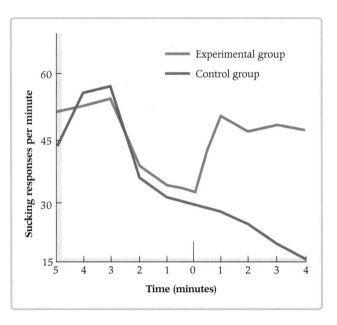

Figure 4.7
When two groups of infants were repeatedly presented with a single consonant over a 5-minute period, their rates of sucking decreased to just over 30 sucks per minute. For half of the infants (the experimental group) the consonant was changed at the time marked 0. Note that their rate of sucking increased sharply. For the remaining infants (the control group), who continued to hear the same consonant, the rate of sucking continued to decrease. (Adapted from Eimas, 1985.)

each baby, they presented the speech sound /pa/ to the babies each time they sucked. At first the babies' rate of sucking increased as if they were excited by each presentation of the sound, but after a while they settled back to their baseline rates of sucking. When the infants had become thoroughly habituated to the sound of /pa/, some of them heard a new sound, /ba/, which differed from the original sound only in its initial phoneme—/b/ versus /p/. Others were presented with a sound that differed an equal amount from the original sound but remained within the /pa/ phoneme category. The babies began sucking rapidly again *only* when they heard a phoneme of a different category, an indication that they were especially sensitive to the difference between the /b/ and /p/ sounds (see Figure 4.7).

Follow-up studies have shown that very young infants are able to perceive all the categorical sound distinctions used in all the world's various languages. Japanese babies, for example, can perceive the difference between /r/ and /l/, even though adult speakers of Japanese cannot (Aslin, Jusczyk & Pisoni, 1998). The ability to make phonemic distinctions apparently begins to narrow to just those distinctions that are present in one's native language at about 6 to 8 months of age, the same age at which the baby's first halting articulations of languagelike sounds are likely to begin (see Figure 4.8).

These data make it tempting to conclude that human infants are born with special perceptual skills that are pretuned to the properties of human speech, but stud-

Figure 4.8
Infants can distinguish among language sounds that do not occur in their native language, but this capacity diminishes during the first year of life. Note the decrease in the proportion of infants from an English-speaking background who respond to consonants in Hindi and Salish (a North American Indian language). In contrast, at 1 year Hindi and Salish infants retain the capacity to distinguish sounds in their native languages. (Adapted from Eimas, 1985.)

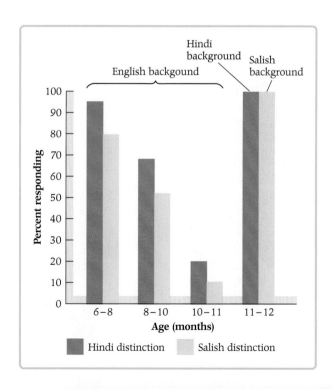

ies have long indicated that other species can make similar distinctions (Aslin et al., 1998). The difference is that humans use this ability as a stepping-stone to the mastery of language, an achievement that is beyond the capacities of other animals.

Vision

The basic anatomical elements of the visual system are present at birth, but they are neither fully developed nor well coordinated. The lens of the eye and the cells of the retina are somewhat immature. In addition, the movements of the baby's eyes are not coordinated well enough to align the images on the two retinas to form a clear composite image. The result is that the baby's vision is blurry. The immaturity of some of the neural pathways that relay information from the retina to the brain further limits the newborn's visual capacities (Atkinson, 1998). Numerous studies have been conducted to determine exactly what, and how well, infants can see.

Color Perception Newborns seem to possess all, or nearly all, of the physiological prerequisites for seeing color in a rudimentary form. When two colors are equally bright, however, they do not discriminate the difference between them. By 2 months of age, infants' ability to perceive different colors appears to approach adult levels (Kellman & Banks, 1998).

Visual Acuity A basic question about infants' vision is how nearsighted they are. To determine newborns' visual acuity, Robert Fantz and his colleagues (Fantz et al., 1962) developed a test based on the fact that when a striped visual field moves in front of the eyes, the eyes start to move in the same direction as the pattern. If the gaps between the stripes are so small that they cannot be perceived, the eyes do not move. By varying the width of the gaps and comparing the results obtained from newborns with those obtained from adults, these researchers were able to estimate that neonates have 20/300 vision—that is, they can see at 20 feet what an adult with normal vision can see at 300 feet. The exact estimate of newborn acuity differs somewhat according to the particular measures used, but all suggest that the newborn is very nearsighted (Martin, 1998). (See Figure 4.9, which indicates what infants can see at different ages.)

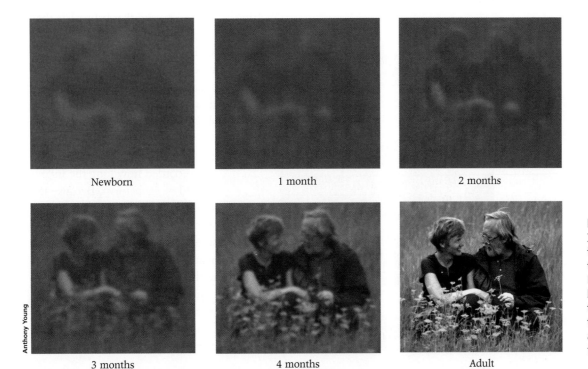

Newborn

1 month

2 months

3 months

4 months

Adult

Anthony Young

Figure 4.9
Infants' visual capacity increases dramatically over the first few months of life. By the age of four months, a baby can see nearly as distinctly as an adult, as seen in this artist's conception of the appearance of a visual scene for infants of different ages.

Poor visual acuity is probably less troublesome to newborns than to older children and adults. After all, newborns are unable to move around unless someone carries them, and they cannot hold their heads erect without support. Still, their visual system is tuned well enough to allow newborns to see objects about a foot away—roughly the distance of the mother's face when they are nursing. This level of acuity allows them to make eye contact, which is important in establishing the social relationship between mother and child (Stern, 2002). Between 2 and 3 months of age, infants can coordinate the vision of both their eyes (Atkinson, 1998). By 7 or 8 months of age, when infants are able to crawl, their visual acuity is close to the adult level.

Visual Scanning Despite their nearsightedness and their difficulty in focusing, newborns actively scan their surroundings from the earliest days of life (Bronson, 1997). Marshall Haith and his colleagues developed recording techniques that allowed them to determine precisely where infants were looking and to monitor their eye movements in both light and dark rooms. They discovered that neonates scan with short eye movements even in a completely darkened room. Since no light is entering their eyes, this kind of scanning cannot be caused by the visual environment. It must therefore be *endogenous,* originating in the neural activity of the central nervous system. Endogenous eye movements seem to be an initial, primitive basis for looking behavior (Haith, 1980).

Haith's studies also revealed that neonates exhibit an early form of *exogenous* looking, that is, looking that is stimulated by the external environment. When the lights are turned on after infants have been in the dark, they pause in their scanning when their gaze encounters an object or some change of brightness in the visual field. This very early sensitivity to changes in illumination, which is usually associated with the edges and angles of objects, appears to be an important component of the baby's developing ability to perceive visual forms (Haith, 1980).

Perception of Patterns and Objects What do babies see when their eyes encounter an object? Are they able to see objects much as adults do?

Until the early 1960s it was widely believed that neonates perceived only a formless play of light. Robert Fantz (1961, 1963) dealt a severe blow to this assumption by demonstrating that babies less than 2 days old can distinguish among visual forms. The technique he used was very simple. Babies were placed on their backs in a specially designed "looking chamber" and shown various forms (see Figure 4.10). An observer looked down through the top of the chamber and recorded how long the infants looked at each form. Because the infants spent more time looking at some forms than at others, presumably they could tell the forms apart and preferred the ones they looked at the longest. Fantz found that neonates would rather look at patterned figures, such as faces and concentric circles, than at plain ones (see Figure 4.11).

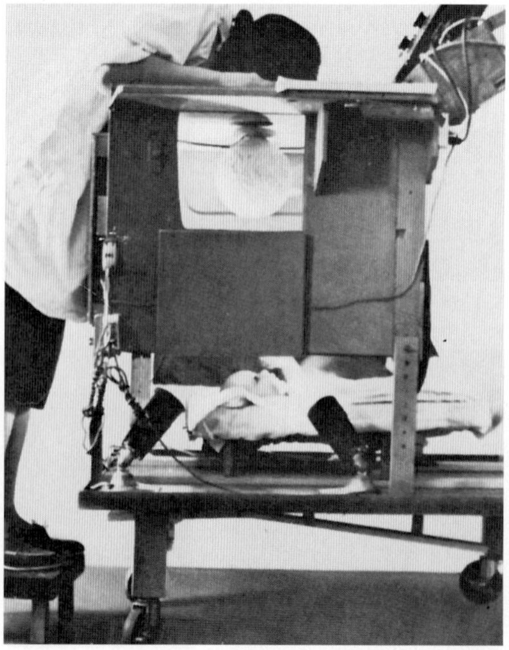

Figure 4.10
The "looking chamber" that Robert Fantz used to test newborns' visual interests. The infant lies in a crib in the chamber, looking up at the stimuli attached to the ceiling. The observer, watching through a peephole, determines how long the infant looks at each stimulus.

David Linton, *Scientific American, 204*

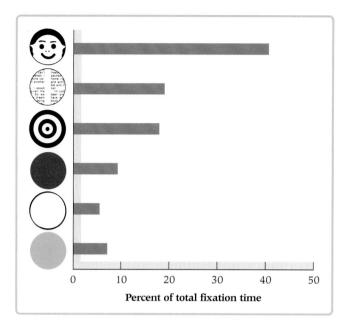

Figure 4.11
Infants tested during the first weeks of life show a preference for patterned stimuli over plain stimuli. The length of each bar indicates the relative amount of time the babies spent looking at the corresponding stimulus. (Adapted from Fantz, 1961.)

Fantz's findings set off a search to determine the extent of newborns' capacity to perceive objects and the reasons they prefer some forms over others. That research has confirmed that infants visually perceive the world as more than random confusion, but it has also provided evidence that infants do not enter the world prepared to see it in the same way adults do. Their ability to perceive objects emerges over the first several months following birth (Johnson et al., 2003).

Within a few months, infants begin to show evidence that in some circumstances they see the boundaries between objects and recognize that objects are three-dimensional (Arterberry & Yonas, 2000). These abilities are by no means as elementary as they may seem to an adult. How, for example, does a newborn who is staring at a cat on a chair know that the cat is not part of the chair? The most obvious clue to the fact that they are separate objects comes when the cat jumps off the chair and walks away.

The role of movement in helping babies segment objects that are in close proximity was convincingly demonstrated in a classic experiment by Philip Kellman and Elizabeth Spelke (1983). The infants were shown a display like that in Figure 4.12a, which adults perceive as a single rod moving back and forth behind a block. After habituating to the display so that they lost interest in it, the infants were shown the two displays of rods in Figure 4.12b. Kellman and Spelke thought that if the infants assumed, as adults do, that there is a single rod behind the block, they would look longer at the two rod segments because they would be novel—and that is exactly what the babies did.

The key to explaining why the babies perceived the two rod segments as a single object was that they moved together at the same speed and in the same direction. If the infants were shown a display just like the one in 4.12a, except that the rod was stationary, they looked at the two displays in 4.12b for equal amounts of time because the situation was ambiguous when there was no common movement and they could not tell if it was one object or two. As children mature and have more experience, their ability to perceive the boundaries between objects continues to increase.

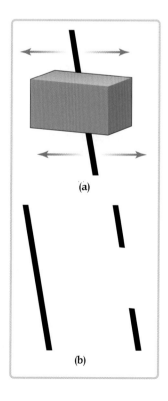

(a)

(b)

Figure 4.12
Movement seems to play a crucial role in allowing young infants to perceive that two objects placed one on top of or one behind another are, in fact, separate. In this experiment, the infants were shown a rod moving behind a block (a). Next they were shown a single rod and two rod segments (b). They looked longer at the two rod segments suggesting that they were surprised because what they thought was a single object appeared as two separate objects. However, when the experiment was conducted without moving the rod, the infants looked equally long at the single rod and the two rod segments, indicating their uncertainty about whether the rod and blocks were separate or not. (From Kellman and Spelke, 1983.)

Figure 4.13
Visual scanning of a triangle by young infants. The triangle was mounted on a wall. A video camera was mounted just beneath it, positioned to record the eye movements of infants as they gazed at the triangle. Note that the 2-week-olds concentrated their gaze on only one part of the figure, whereas the 12-week-olds visually explored the figure more fully. Large dots indicate long fixation times; small dots represent short ones. (Adapted from Bronson, 1991.)

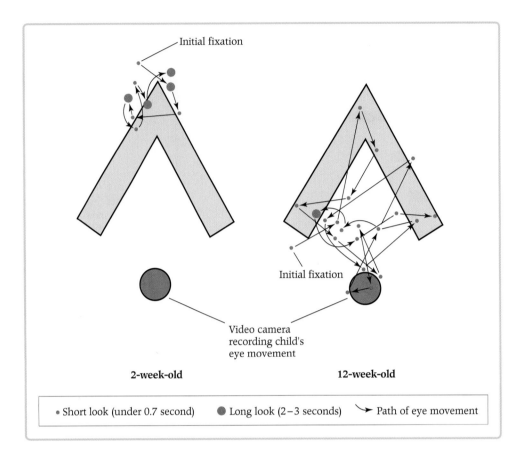

A number of studies have shown that the vision of young infants is best under conditions of high contrast, such as when a visual field is divided clearly into parts that are black and parts that are white (Kellman & Banks, 1998). Gordon Bronson (1991, 1994, 1997) used this property of newborn vision to study the way 2-week-old and 12-week-old babies scan outline drawings of simple figures, such as a cross or a v, on a lighted visual field. When adults are shown such figures, they scan the entire boundary. Two-week-old babies appear to focus only on areas of high contrast, such as black lines and angles on a white background (see Figure 4.13). This kind of looking behavior is clearly not random; it shows that infants are born with the ability to perceive basic patterns. At 12 weeks of age, as Figure 4.13 indicates, infants scan more of the figure than at 2 weeks, although their scanning movements are sometimes off the mark and may still be arrested by areas of high contrast. In one of his studies, Bronson (1994) found that 13-week-old infants scanned more rapidly and extensively than infants 10 weeks and under. The developmental change was so marked that Bronson concluded that "by 3 months of age [the] infants appear[ed] to be quite different organisms, at least with respect to their scanning characteristics" (p. 1260). He suggests that as the nervous system matures, it becomes more sophisticated and can begin to control visual scanning.

Perception of Faces In Fantz's early studies, one of the complex forms presented to the babies was a diagram of a human face (Fantz, 1961, 1963). When Fantz presented newborn infants with this schematic face and a form in which facial elements had been scrambled, he found that the infants could distinguish the schematic face from the jumbled face (see Figure 4.14). Although the preference for the schematic face over the scrambled face was small, the possibility that newborns have an unlearned preference for a biologically significant form naturally attracted great interest.

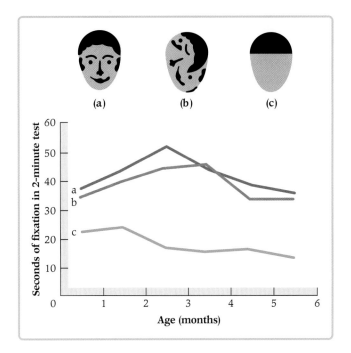

Figure 4.14
Visual preferences of infants for (a) a schematic face, (b) a scrambled schematic face, and (c) a nonfacelike figure, all having equal amounts of light and dark area. The infants preferred both facelike forms over the nonfacelike form, and they accorded the "real" face slightly more attention than the scrambled face. (Adapted from Fantz, 1961.)

More recent work has shown that a crucial element in newborns' preference for faces is the presence of more elements in the upper part of the configuration than in the bottom half. This imbalance corresponds to the fact that there are more visual elements in the top half of actual faces, and babies show they are sensitive to this imbalance. Even a facelike stimulus is not preferred over a scrambled stimulus unless it has more visual elements in the upper half (Turati, Simion, Milani & Umilta, 2002)

A key finding in recent research on face perception has been that, as in the case of partially hidden objects, motion critically influences newborns' perception. In Fantz's studies and earlier replications, researchers used only stationary schematic representations of faces. The newer studies have shown that babies as young as 9 *minutes* old will turn their heads to gaze at a schematic face if it moves in front of them and will look at it longer than at a moving scrambled face (Mondloch et al., 1999). In real life, people move both their heads and the features of their faces, such as their eyes and the shape of their mouths. Under these naturalistic conditions, newborns only 2 to 7 hours old recognize their mother's face when it is contrasted with that of a stranger, even after a delay as long as 15 minutes between the time that the infant last saw the mother's face and the time that testing commenced (Bushnell, 2001).

Taste and Smell

Neonates have a well-developed sense of both taste and smell (Crook, 1987). They react very differently to sweet and sour tastes, slowing down to savor the taste of sugar-infused water but turning away or spitting out vinegary water. The characteristic facial expressions they make in response to various tastes look remarkably like those adults make when they encounter the same tastes, evidence that these expressions are innate (Rosenstein & Oster, 1988) (see Figure 4.15).

Figure 4.15
Facial expressions evoked by various tastes in an infant and an adult: (a) a neutral expression follows the presentation of distilled water; (b) a hint of a smile follows the presentation of a sweet stimulus; (c) the pucker comes in response to a sour stimulus; (d) a bitter stimulus evokes a distinctive grimace. (Adapted from Steiner, 1979.)

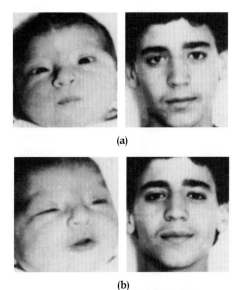

(a)

(b)

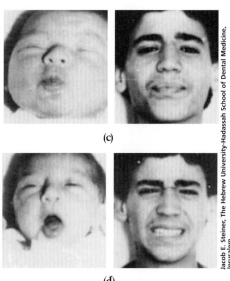

(c)

(d)

Jacob E. Steiner, The Hebrew University-Hadassah School of Dental Medicine, Jerusalem

reflex A specific, well-integrated, automatic (involuntary) response to a specific type of stimulation.

To test for reactions to different smells, experimenters held either an odorless cotton swab or a swab soaked in one of various aromatic solutions under the newborns' noses. The infants reacted strongly to unpleasant odors, such as garlic or vinegar, by pursing their lips or wrinkling their noses, while they smiled when they smelled something sugary. Their responses indicate not only that newborns are sensitive to odors but that they can tell one odor from another. Only a few hours after birth, newborns turn toward the smell of their mother's body or milk and turn away from the smell of the amniotic fluid of another mother (Marlier, Schaal & Soussignan, 1998; Soussignan, Schaal, Marlier & Jian, 1997).

Other Senses

The abilities to detect a touch to the skin, changes in temperature, and changes in physical position develop very early in the prenatal period. Although these sensory capacities have not received as much attention as vision and hearing, they are no less important to the baby's survival, as the research on kangaroo care discussed in Chapter 1 (pp. 18–19) clearly indicates.

Overall, there is extensive evidence that babies come into the world with sensory capacities in good working order and far more structured than were once thought. (Infants' sensory capacities are summarized in Table 4.1.) The question then arises: What capacities do infants have for acting on the world? By combining the ability of infants to take in information from the environment with their abilities to act on that information, it becomes possible to begin to characterize the starting point of postnatal psychological development.

Response Processes

As the previous examples indicate, infants are born with a variety of ways of perceiving the world. In this section we will focus on the repertoire of responses initially at their disposal before turning in the next section to the remarkable ways in which sensory experiences and infants' actions either are coupled at birth or become coordinated through learning early in infancy.

Reflexes

Newborn babies come equipped with a variety of **reflexes**—specific, well-integrated, automatic (involuntary) responses to specific types of stimulation. Some of the reflexes with which infants are born are described in Table 4.2. Virtually all developmentalists agree that reflexes are important building blocks out of which various complex behavioral capacities of later life are constructed.

table 4.1

Early Sensory Capacities	
Sense	**Capacity**
Hearing	Ability to distinguish phonemes
	Preference for native language
Vision	Slightly blurred, slightly double vision at birth
	Color vision by 2 months of age
	Ability to distinguish patterned stimuli from plain
	Preference for moving, facelike stimuli
Smell	Ability to differentiate odors well at birth
Taste	Ability to differentiate tastes well at birth
Touch	Responsive to touch at birth
Temperature	Sensitivity to changes in temperature at birth
Position	Sensitivity to changes in position at birth

table 4.2

Reflexes Present at Birth

Reflex	Description	Developmental Course	Significance
Babinski	When the bottom of the baby's foot is stroked, the toes fan out and then curl	Disappears in 8 to 12 months	Presence at birth and normal course of decline are a basic index of normal neurological condition
Crawling	When the baby is placed on his stomach and pressure is applied to the soles of his feet, his arms and legs move rhythmically	Disappears after 3 to 4 months; possible reappearance at 6 to 7 months as a component of voluntary crawling	Uncertain
Eyeblink	Rapid closing of eyes	Permanent	Protection against aversive stimuli such as bright lights and foreign objects
Grasping	When a finger or some other object is pressed against the baby's palm, her fingers close around it	Disappears in 3 to 4 months; replaced by voluntary grasping	Presence at birth and later disappearance is a basic sign of normal neurological development
Moro	If the baby is allowed to drop unexpectedly while being held or if there is a loud noise, she will throw her arms outward while arching her back and then bring her arms together as if grasping something	Disappears in 6 to 7 months (although startle to loud noises is permanent)	Disputed; its presence at birth and later disappearance are a basic sign of normal neurological development
Rooting	The baby turns his head and opens his mouth when he is touched on the cheek	Disappears between 3 and 6 months	Component of nursing
Stepping	When the baby is held upright over a flat surface, he makes rhythmic leg movements	Disappears in first 2 months but can be reinstated in special contexts	Disputed; it may be only a kicking motion, or it may be a component of later voluntary walking
Sucking	The baby sucks when something is put into her mouth	Disappears and is replaced by voluntary sucking	Fundamental component of nursing

They disagree, however, about the nature of the initial reflexes and how they contribute to the development of more complex capacities.

Some reflexes are clearly part of the baby's elementary survival kit. The *eyeblink reflex,* for example, has a clear function: it protects the eye from overly bright lights and foreign objects that might damage it. The *respiratory occlusion reflex,* which sometimes interferes with nursing (see Table 4.5, p. 151), ensures that children turn their heads vigorously if their breathing is blocked. The *sucking* and *swallowing reflexes* are essential to feeding. The purpose of some other reflexes, such as the *grasping reflex* (closing fingers around an object that is pressed against the palm) (see Figure 4.16) or the *Moro reflex* (grasping with the arms when hearing a loud noise or when suddenly experiencing a feeling of being dropped), is not as clear. Some developmentalists believe that these reflexes currently serve no purpose but were functional during earlier evolutionary stages, allowing infants to cling to their mothers in threatening situations, as do infants of most primate species (Jolly, 1999). Others believe that such presumably useless reflexes may still be functional because they promote a close relationship between mother and infant (Bowlby, 1973; Prechtl, 1977).

Within a few months after birth, several of the reflexes with which infants are born disappear, never to return. Others disappear for a while and then seem to reappear as part of a more mature behavior. Still others are transformed into more complex behaviors without first disappearing. Many researchers see these changes in the structure of early reflexes as important evidence about the way the maturation of higher brain centers changes behavior (Fox & Bell, 1990).

Figure 4.16

The grasping reflex is an important component of normal neurological development in newborns

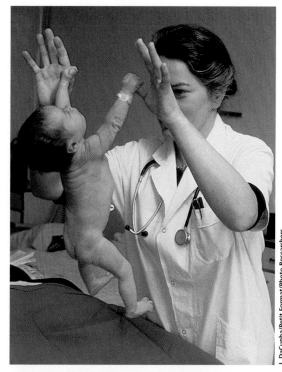

J. DaCunha/Petit Format/Photo Researchers

Figure 4.17
Babies held upright with their feet touching a flat surface move their legs in a fashion that resembles walking. Experts have debated the origins and developmental history of this form of behavior, called the stepping reflex.

Elizabeth Crews

For example, when newborn babies are held in an upright position with their feet touching a flat surface, they make rhythmic leg movements as if they were walking, a form of behavior often referred to as a "stepping reflex" (see Figure 4.17). But they stop doing so at around 3 months of age. Around 1 year of age, babies use similar motions as a component of walking, a voluntary activity that is acquired with practice.

There are competing explanations for the developmental changes in these rhythmic leg movements. According to Philip Zelazo (1983), the newborn's movements are a genuine reflex, and their disappearance is an instance of the suppression of a lower reflex by the maturation of higher cortical functions. He maintains that the old reflex reappears in a new form as a component of voluntary walking after a period of brain reorganization.

Esther Thelen and her colleagues reject this explanation, believing instead that the stepping reflex is really a form of kicking (Thelen, 1995). According to these researchers, early upright kicking behavior disappears because of changes in the baby's muscle mass and weight that make kicking difficult, not because of changes in the cortex. In support of their view, Thelen and her colleagues hypothesized that if infants were partially submerged in water and supported to stand, the behavior described as the stepping reflex would reappear. They reasoned that the buoyancy of the water would counterbalance the infant's increased weight and relative lack of leg strength. They were correct: when they held infants who had stopped exhibiting the stepping reflex upright in water up to their waists, the kicking behavior reappeared.

For Thelen and her colleagues, the changes associated with the stepping reflex are but one example of a general principle of developmental change: Developing human beings take an active role in organizing their own behavior. The patterns of change found in their development arise from the interaction of *all* the complex systems in which they find themselves (Thelen, 2002). With respect to stepping, the dynamic relations between newborn infants and the physical characteristics of their context interact to create what appears to us as a stepping reflex. As they become heavier and their body mass changes, infants' dynamic relations to the environment change, and the prior behavior (stepping) is not seen unless the context is changed to include water of just the right depth and support of just the right kind, in which case it appears again (Thelen & Smith, 1998).

In addition to their role as starting points from which more mature, deliberate behavior may develop, reflexes are also used to diagnose the functioning of the central nervous system. For example, the absence of a neonatal reflex, such as sucking, often indicates that the infant suffers some form of brain damage. Brain damage is also indicated when a reflex persists beyond the age at which it should have disappeared. For example, the Moro reflex typically disappears in the months after birth. It is seen again only in the event of injury to the central nervous system (Zafeiriou, Tsikoulas, Kremenopoulos & Kontopoulos, 1999).

Although the "stepping reflex" seems to disappear around 3 months of age, Esther Thelen and her colleagues demonstrated that it would reappear if babies were given proper support. Here, a baby who no longer exhibits a stepping reflex under normal conditions makes the same stepping motions when partially submerged in water.

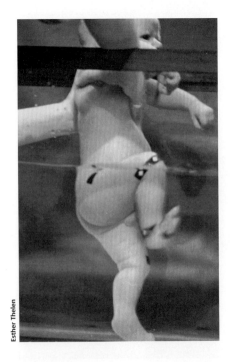

Esther Thelen

Imitation

The ability to imitate, which is widely believed to be present at birth, provides another way to learn during infancy and later life. Despite newborns' limited visual capacities and poorly coordinated movements, several studies have reported that babies are capable of rudimentary forms of imitation (Heimann, 2002; Meltzoff & Prinz, 2002). These studies have generated intense interest among developmentalists because it had long been believed that imitation does not become possible until several months after birth (Piaget, 1962).

In earlier research conducted by Andrew Meltzoff and Keith Moore (1977, 1994), an adult stood over alert newborn babies and made distinctive facial expressions, such as opening his mouth very wide and sticking out his tongue. Meltzoff and Moore reported that the infants often imitated the facial expression of the adult.

Meltzoff and Moore's research has promoted many follow-up studies (Meltzoff & Prinz, 2002). Tiffany Field and her colleagues found support for Meltzoff and Moore's conclusions when they used somewhat different procedures and responses (Field et al., 1982). They arranged for an adult to model three facial expressions—happy, sad, and surprised—for babies who were an average of 36 hours old. The babies showed that they could distinguish among the model's facial expressions by the fact that they habituated to the repeated presentation of a single expression but then began to pay close attention again when the model presented them with a different facial expression. Most important, the babies appeared to imitate these new expressions. An observer who could not see the model and who did not know what expressions were being presented to the babies was able, on a statistically reliable basis, to determine the facial expression of the model from the facial movements of the babies. These results are difficult to explain without assuming that the infants somehow matched what they did with what they saw the model doing. Precisely how infants accomplished this matching remains uncertain.

However, in most studies, imitation is observed only part of the time, is restricted to elementary movements of the face, and is present more often in some babies than in others (Heimann, 2002). This variability has led some researchers to doubt if the babies were actually imitating what they saw. These researchers suggest either that there was some peculiarity in Meltzoff and Moore's procedures or that the behavior they observed is a very special form of imitation (Anisfeld et al., 2001). Meltzoff and Moore disagree, arguing that newborn imitation provides an important mechanism of development from birth. Meltzoff and Moore propose that infant imitation is an important precursor of the development of empathy toward others and the ability to understand other people's thoughts.

Whether or not imitation is present at birth, it develops markedly over the first year of life (Meltzoff, 2002). If present, newborns' imitations are restricted to movements of the face and head, while older babies imitate sounds and a wide variety of movements. In addition, while very early imitation is slow and inconsistent, the imitation of a 9-month-old is rapid and consistent, suggesting that a different mechanism is at work.

Demonstration from one of Andrew Meltzoff and Keith Moore's studies that some newborns can imitate adult facial expressions.

Reaching

Even from the earliest days of postnatal life, babies' arms are often moving, sometimes allowing them to bring their fingers to their mouths to initiate sucking, and sometimes bringing their hands in contact with objects in the world around

The appearance of a brightly colored, slow-moving object may cause newborns to reach out and make grasping motions. Such "pre-reaching" is unsuccessful, however, as young infants cannot yet coordinate these motions.

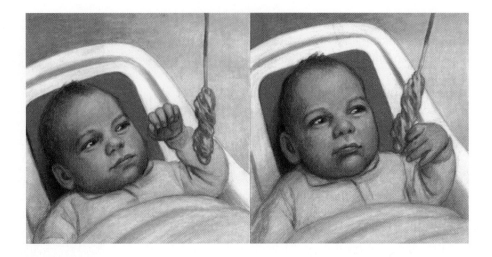

them. At first, contact with objects other than their mouths appears to be totally accidental, but research initiated by Claus von Hofsten (1982, 1984) identified an early form of movement that he referred to as *pre-reaching* (von Hofsten, 1984). He elicited this form of movement in the period shortly after birth by showing babies a large, colorful, slow-moving object such as a ball of yarn. As the bright ball of yarn passed in front of them, newborns reached toward it. However, they were unable to grasp an object even after repeated attempts, because newborn's reaching and grasping movements are coupled such that as the arm extends, the fingers of the hand extend too. Over the next several weeks, this pattern changes and the infants make a fist when they reach for the object.

At about 3 months of age, and coincidental with maturational changes in the visual and motor areas of the cerebral cortex, such visually *initiated* reaching is transformed into visually *guided* reaching. Now, once infants locate an object by either seeing or hearing it, they can use feedback from their own movements to adjust the trajectory of their reach and get their hands close to the object. They are also able to open their fingers in anticipation of grasping the object. Remarkably, they can do this even when a bright object is presented in a darkened room so that they cannot see their own arms, clear evidence that it is feedback from their movement relative to the object that is controlling their reaching and grasping (McCarty, Clifton, Ashmead, Lee & Goubet, 2001). A short time thereafter, infants begin to open their hands as soon as they start to reach for an object and begin to close their hands a brief interval before they touch it, clear evidence that they have begun to coordinate reaching and grasping (von Hofsten, 1984, 2001).

In an ingenious experiment, Amy Needham and her colleagues demonstrated that the process of engaging objects can be accelerated if infants are provided with support for actually grasping an object (Needham, Barrett & Peterman, 2002). They provided half of a group of 3-month-old infants with specially designed Velcro-covered mittens and attached Velcro to objects that were within their reach. Compared to a control group of infants who did not have such mittens, the assisted infants showed markedly increased interest in objects as well as greater skill in grasping objects when they were later tested with no special mittens to help them.

Integration of Sensory and Response Processes

An important point made in recent research is that the development of sensory processes and behaviors appears to be coupled in various ways beginning at birth. That is, infants may be born prepared to see certain stimuli as inherently connected to each other.

That a certain object or event can be simultaneously perceived by more than one sensory system (such as touch, sound, and vision) is known as **intermodal perception** (Gibson & Pick, 2000). For example, a standard item on many tests of newborns' neural and behavioral development is their ability to turn their heads toward a sound located on their right or their left, indicating a built-in connection between what they hear and how they perceive the location of their bodies in space.

A convincing demonstration that babies only a few hours old also expect sights and sounds to be connected with each other comes from a study by Barbara Morrongiello and her colleagues (1998). These investigators paired the sight of a small Sesame Street Muppet with the sound of popcorn rattling (the sounds were tape-recorded and played through a small speaker attached to the back of the Muppet). The babies were held upright in front of a long, black puppet stage, which provided a uniform backdrop for presentation of the Muppet. Half the time the rattling Muppet was presented to the babies on their left side and half the time on their right side. These presentations of the rattling Muppet continued until the babies indicated that they had lost interest by reducing the time they stared at the Muppet by 50 percent.

After the babies had habituated to the rattling Muppet, the Muppet and the sounds were decoupled for two successive trials. The Muppet was presented on one side of the babies' bodies while the sound came from the opposite side. The babies stared at this new event just as long as they had the first time they encountered the Muppet–sound combination. The experimenters obtained the same results if they changed the Muppet instead of decoupling the familiar Muppet from its sound. These results show that even newborn babies link the sights and sounds they encounter and expect the sight and sound of novel objects to remain coupled regardless of the object's location.

An important implication of newborn babies' abilities to integrate information from different sensory modalities is that this starts them on the path to developing a sense of themselves as distinct beings. Evidence that even newborns discriminate between information coming from their own actions and information coming from the world around them was obtained by Susan Hespos and Phillipe Rochat (1997). These researchers found that infants exhibited a rooting reflex three times more frequently when an experimenter touched the corner of their mouths than when the infants touched the same spot themselves, indicating that as early as 24 hours after birth, self-stimulation and environmental stimulation are psychologically different for the infants.

Taken together, evidence about newborns' sensory capacities and their ability to act on the world indicates that their experience of the world is far more systematic than previously believed. However, this does not mean that intermodal perception occurs with equal ease regardless of the age of the infant or the particular sensory qualities being combined. Daphne Maurer and her colleagues sought to replicate earlier findings that 1-month-old infants would visually identify smooth and bumpy pacifiers that they had been allowed to explore orally, but these researchers failed to find evidence of intermodal perception (Maurer, Stager & Mondloch, 1999). However, there is no doubt that the ability to integrate information from different sensory modalities is an important source of information from early infancy onward.

> **intermodal perception** The understanding that a certain object or event can be simultaneously perceived by more than one sensory system.

The Qualities of Infant Experience and Behavior

Thus far we have focused on the *quantitative* features of newborns' psychological characteristics: What kinds of stimuli are infants able to perceive? What kinds attract the most attention? What sorts of actions are they capable of, and what circumstances evoke what kinds of actions? In this section we shift our focus to the *quality* of infants' psychological life. What sort of emotions do infants experience? What sort of characteristic qualities do they display when responding to the many new events they experience?

Emotion

When we talk about emotions in everyday conversation, we are usually referring to the feelings aroused by an experience. If we unexpectedly win a prize, we feel happy and excited. When we say good-bye to a loved one whom we will not see for some time, we feel sad. If someone prevents us from achieving a goal, we become angry.

Emotions as Complex Systems

Developmentalists believe that the feelings aroused by such experiences are only one aspect of emotions. In addition to feelings, emotions include the following features (Saarni, 1998):

- A *physiological aspect*. Emotions are accompanied by identifiable physiological reactions such as changes in heart rate, breathing, and hormonal functioning.

- A *communicative function*. Emotions communicate our internal feeling states to others through facial expressions and distinctive forms of behavior.

- A *cognitive aspect*. The emotions we feel depend upon how we appraise what is happening to us.

- An *action aspect*. How we act depends jointly on how we evaluate what is happening to us, the physiological states that accompany our experiences, and the feelings that result. When something causes us to be suddenly joyful, for example, we laugh or cry or do both at once. Sometimes we jump up and hug the nearest person.

Technically speaking, then, **emotion** can be defined as a feeling state produced by the distinctive physiological responses and cognitive evaluations that motivate action (Witherington, Campos & Hertenstein, 2002). The intimate ties between feelings and thought are clearly revealed by our habit of equating the two in everyday speech. For example, we routinely use "I think you are wrong" and "I feel you are wrong" as substitutes for each other. Emotions simultaneously communicate *to* others and regulate interactions *with* others. They are complex processes that emerge from many elements.

The Origins of Emotion

Developmentalists have long been divided on the question of which emotions are present at birth. At present many favor the view that emotions develop from two primitive states, contentment and distress, that are the extremes of a fluctuating state of excitement. According to this view, additional emotions arise by splitting off, or *differentiating* themselves, from these original two states as the baby develops: joy becomes differentiated from contentment at about 3 months; anger and fear differentiate from discontent at about 4 months and 6 months, respectively (Lewis 1998).

Developmentalists who believe that a set of core, primary emotions is present at birth have relied heavily on the assumption that facial expressions are reliable indicators of one's emotional state (Ekman, 1999). Specifically, they believe that certain facial expressions universally communicate a basic set of emotional states and that

emotion A feeling state produced by the distinctive physiological responses and cognitive evaluations that motivate action.

the facial expressions of very young infants signal the presence of the corresponding basic emotion. On the basis of their babies' facial expressions and vocalizations, for example, the mothers interviewed in one study reported that their infants were expressing several emotions by the age of 1 month, including joy, fear, anger, surprise, sadness, and interest (Johnson et al., 1982).

Mothers' reports about their babies are notoriously biased. Recognizing this problem, Carroll Izard and his colleagues videotaped infants' responses to a variety of emotion-arousing events such as having an inoculation or the approach of a smiling mother (Izard, 1994). He showed the videotapes, or stills from them, to college students and nurses, who agreed fairly consistently about which facial expressions communicated interest, joy, surprise, and sadness (see Figure 4.18). To a somewhat lesser extent, they also agreed on which expressions showed anger, disgust, and contempt.

Additional support for the idea that there is a universal set of basic emotions and corresponding facial expressions comes from the cross-cultural research of Paul Ekman and his associates (Ekman, 1999). The researchers asked people in widely different cultures to pose expressions appropriate to such events as the death of a loved one or being reunited with a close friend. Adults from both literate and nonliterate societies configured their faces in the same way to express each emotion. When shown photographs of actors posing the different expressions, the adults from different cultures also agreed on the photographs that represented happiness, sadness, anger, and disgust. Nonetheless, culture-specific experience must play some role in judging emotional expressions because people are more accurate in judging emotions displayed by members of their own culture group (Elfenbein & Ambady, 2003).

Despite this evidence, many believe that judgments about emotions cannot depend solely on facial expressions. Not only facial expressions but voice quality, gestures, actions, and physiological indicators must also be taken into account. Because emotions arise from a relationship between what people are trying to do and what actually happens, judgments based only on facial expressions, with no information about the context, are unlikely to be valid indicators of the same emotional states across all contexts and ages (Witherington et al., 2002).

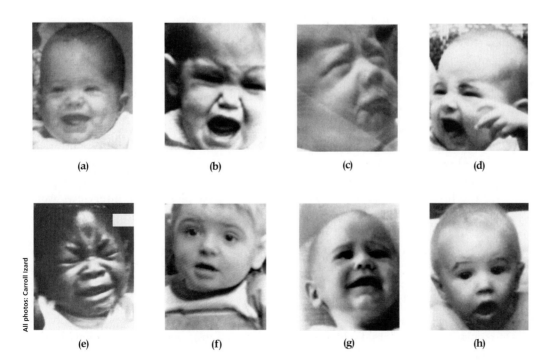

(a)   (b)   (c)   (d)

(e)   (f)   (g)   (h)

All photos: Carroll Izard

Figure 4.18
Images from a videotaped recording of infants' facial expressions used by Carroll Izard and his colleagues to assess the possible universal relation between emotion and facial expression. What emotion do you think each facial expression represents? The responses most of Izard's adult subjects gave are printed upside down below. (Izard et al., 1980.)

(a) joy; (b) anger; (c) sadness; (d) disgust; (e) distress/pain; (f) interest; (g) fear; (h) surprise.

In particular, critics argue, it is a mistake to attribute adult emotions to newborns on the basis of facial expressions. Newborns may cry because they are hungry. In this case, their facial expressions and associated emotion are responses to their immediate physical discomfort. Adults may cry, however, because they feel guilty, ashamed, sad, or chagrined. Their tears are the result of complex evaluations of their actions and circumstances and depend upon the development of cognitive abilities that involve interaction among the higher brain centers. None of these aspects of emotion are present at birth. Consequently, some of the psychological and biological processes that link facial expressions of newborns to emotions may differ from those reflected by the same facial expressions in older infants, children, and adults.

Whatever their views about the initial repertoire of emotions present at birth, developmentalists agree that the feeling states associated with emotions and modes of emotional expression develop throughout the course of childhood. As infants grow older, their initial repertoire of emotions (whether two, or four, or a few more) becomes entwined with their developing intellectual capacities and the new kinds of social relations into which they enter. New emotions, such as pride, shame, and guilt, emerge as infants act, think, communicate, and relate to others in new ways. Thus, in the chapters ahead, we will frequently find ourselves considering the development of emotions in connection with the intellectual, social, and physical aspects of development.

Temperament

A commonly held intuition about human nature is that people are born differing from one another in their characteristic predispositions to respond to the world. Mike and Sheila's daughter, for example, has a tendency to approach life with boundless energy and an optimistic demeanor. Confronted with barriers, she rarely gives up, but finds some way to surmount them or to go around them. Her brother, by contrast, is a dreamier person. He is more likely to intellectualize a problem and more likely to vent his frustration. **Temperament** is the name given to these individual modes of responding to the environment that appear to be consistent across situations and stable over time (Kagan, 2001).

Pioneering studies of temperament and its role in development were conducted by Alexander Thomas, Stella Chess, and their colleagues (Chess & Thomas, 1996). They began their research in the late 1950s with a group of 141 middle- and upper-class children in the United States. Later they broadened their longitudinal study to include 95 working-class Puerto Rican children and several groups of children suffering from diseases, neurological impairments, and mental retardation. Chess and Thomas began conducting structured clinical interviews of the children's parents shortly after the birth of their child and continued with follow-up interviews over several decades. Included were questions about such matters as how the child reacted to the first bath, to wet diapers, and to the first taste of solid food. As the children grew older, these interviews were supplemented by interviews with teachers and by tests of the children themselves. This work has had a great deal of influence over the years not only because of its broad scope but also because Thomas and Chess's methods served as a starting point for later studies of temperament using a variety of techniques (Wachs & Bates, 2001).

Chess and Thomas identified nine behavioral traits that contributed to their overall description of temperament: activity level, rhythmicity (the regularity or irregularity of the child's basic biological functions), approach–withdrawal (the child's response to novelty), adaptability, the minimum intensity of stimulation re-

temperament The term for the individual modes of responding to the environment that appear to be consistent across situations and stable over time. Typically included under the rubric of temperament are such characteristics as children's activity level, their intensity of reaction, the ease with which they become upset, their characteristic responses to novelty, and their sociability.

quired to evoke a response (referred to as the threshold of responsiveness), intensity of reaction, quality of mood (negative or positive), distractibility, and attention span or persistence (see Table 4.3). After scoring the children on each of these nine traits, they found that most of the children could be classified in one of three broad temperament categories from the time they were infants:

- *Easy babies* are playful, are regular in their biological functions, and adapt readily to new circumstances.

- *Difficult babies* are irregular in their biological functions, are irritable, and often respond intensely and negatively to new situations or try to withdraw from them.

- *Slow-to-warm-up* babies are low in activity level, and their responses are typically mild. They tend to withdraw from new situations, but in a mild way, and require more time than easy babies to adapt to change.

Table 4.3

Basic Indicators of Temperament According to Chess and Thomas		
Trait	**Definition**	**Example**
Activity level	The level of movement typical of a given child's actions and the relative amount of time spent in action and inaction	Even in the uterus some babies kick and move around a lot, while others are relatively still; similar differences are seen in the level and frequency of arm waving and kicking in early infancy and in the tendency of some young children to spend most of their waking hours in rapid motion
Rhythmicity	The degree of regularity and predictability of basic biological functions	Beginning shortly after birth, marked individual differences can be seen in the ease with which babies adapt to regular feeding and sleeping schedules and to bodily functions such as defecation
Approach–withdrawal	The nature of the baby's initial response to something new	Novel experiences such as the first substitution of a bottle for the breast, meeting a strange person, or the sudden appearance of a jack-in-the-box cause some children to be fearful and withdraw, while others actively explore and seek further stimulation
Adaptability	The ease with which a baby's initial responses to a situation are modified	Whether they initially withdraw from or take to a new experience, babies differ in how rapidly the novelty wears off and how easily they adjust to new circumstances, such as being given solid food in place of milk or being left with a baby-sitter
Threshold of responsiveness	The intensity level required in order for a stimulus to evoke a response	It takes very little noise to make some babies awaken from a nap or very little moisture in their diapers to make them cry, whereas others appear to react only when the stimulation becomes relatively intense
Intensity of reaction	The energy level of a response	It seems that whatever the circumstances, whether pleasant or unpleasant, some babies remain relatively placid in their responses, cooing when pleased and frowning when upset, whereas others laugh heartily and cry vigorously
Quality of mood	The amount of joyful, pleasant, and friendly behaviors in comparison to unpleasant and unfriendly behaviors	Some babies laugh frequently and tend to smile at the world, whereas others seem to be unhappy much of the time
Distractibility	The extent to which novel stimuli disrupt or alter ongoing behaviors	Parents often seek to distract a crying baby by offering a pacifier or teddy bear, but such tactics work best with distractible babies
Attention span/persistence	The extent to which an activity, once undertaken, is maintained	Some babies will stare at a mobile or play happily with a favorite toy for a long time, whereas others quickly lose interest and move frequently from one activity to another

Source: Chess & Thomas, 1982.

Although these three categories of temperament are widely used by developmentalists, a number of efforts have been made to create a more refined set of temperament types. For example, analyzing data from a large sample of New Zealand children whose health and development were studied systematically over many years, Denise Newman and her colleagues distinguished five different clusters of temperamental characteristics: well-adjusted, lacking in self-control, reserved, confident, and inhibited (Newman et al., 1997). In another approach, Mary Rothbart and her colleagues in the United States created a child behavior questionnaire that provided scores on 195 questions divided into 15 different scales. Parents were asked to decide how well each item applied to their child in the past half year. Statistical analysis of these results suggested three dimensions of temperamental variation, providing a unique profile of children's temperamental proclivities (Rothbart, Ahadi & Evans, 2000):

- *Reactivity*—the characteristic level of arousal, or activeness
- *Affect*—the dominant emotional tone, gloomy or cheerful
- *Self-regulation*—control over what one attends to and reacts to

The fact that different researchers come up with slightly different basic dimensions of temperament suggests that their results depend on the specific methods used and how people interpret them (Rothbart, Chew & Gartsetin, 2001). However, statistical analyses have shown that there is a large degree of overlap among the different scales currently in use. Consequently, results from studies using slightly different scales can be combined, although caution is needed when drawing conclusions about specific outcomes (Wachs & Bates, 2001).

Temperament scales have been used to assess ethnic and national differences in the basic dimensions of temperament. Comparing large groups of children from the People's Republic of China and the United States, Mary Rothbart and her colleagues found that their three basic dimensions emerged from the data within *both* countries, suggesting that dimensions of temperament are found in all cultures (Ahadi et al., 1993). However, when they made between-country comparisons, they found differences. For example, they found that the Chinese children were less active than the American children, a fact they attributed to Chinese child-rearing practices. Chinese parents place a high value on interdependence, and this leads them to discourage high levels of activity and impulsiveness.

Although the last finding suggests that there can be an environmental, cultural component to temperament, there is widespread agreement that genetic factors provide the foundation for temperamental differences. In fact, many developmentalists incorporate the idea that temperamental characteristics are innate biological predispositions as part of their definition of development (Emde & Hewitt, 2001). Direct evidence for such a position comes from the work of Stephen Suomi (2000). Working with monkeys, he found that an allele on a specific gene is associated with a highly reactive temperament while a different allele is associated with a calmer temperament.

This evidence for a genetic basis to temperamental traits implies that one should expect to find relatively stable biological "biases" in the way individuals respond to their environment and thus that it should be possible to predict the characteristic style with which individuals will behave at later stages of development. Evidence for the stability of temperamental characteristics comes from a variety of studies conducted in several different societies. On the basis of data from temperament questionnaires filled out by parents beginning when their children were infants and continuing periodically through childhood and adolescence, a number of researchers have reported stability in traits including irritability, persistence, and flexibility (Emde & Hewitt, 2001).

It needs to be emphasized that even when statistical evidence indicates that temperamental traits remain somewhat stable as children develop, most studies find that the degree of stability is modest, indicating that many factors contribute to temperament (Wachs, 2000).

Becoming Coordinated with the Social World

While infant survival depends upon the basic "tool kit" of capacities with which babies are born, these characteristics by themselves are insufficient. Babies' survival and continued development also depend crucially on their ability to coordinate with the activities of their caregivers.

Caregivers cannot always be hovering over their baby, anticipating every need before it is expressed. They must find a way to meet their infant's needs within the confines of their own rhythms of life and work. Whether parents work the land and must be up with the sun or work in an office where they are expected to appear at 9 A.M. sharp, they need to sleep at night. This need is often in direct conflict with their infant's sleep and hunger patterns, a conflict that for many caregivers means getting up several times a night. Such circumstances cause parents to attempt to modify their babies' patterns of eating and sleeping so that they will fit into the life patterns of the household and the community (see the box "Sleeping Arrangements" on page 141).

In the United States such attempts to modify an infant's initial pattern of sleeping and eating behavior are often referred to as "getting the baby on a schedule." Getting the baby on a schedule is more than a convenience. By coordinating with each others' activities, babies and parents create a system of mutual expectations that serves as an essential foundation for later developmental change.

Parents' efforts to achieve a common schedule with their baby focus on the infant's sleeping and eating. Crying is the baby's earliest means of signaling when these efforts fall short.

Sleeping

As with adults, the extent of newborns' arousal varies from deep sleep to frantic activity. The patterns of their rest and activity are quite different from those of adults, however, particularly in the first weeks after birth. To find out about the range and cycles of

newborns' arousal patterns, developmentalists use a variety of methods, ranging from observation to video recordings to the use of sophisticated electronic monitoring devices (Salzarulo & Ficca, 2002). In a classic study in which babies' eye movements and muscle activity were observed over the first several weeks following birth, Peter Wolff (1966) was able to distinguish seven states of arousal. (They are described in Table 4.4, p. 140.)

Additional research has shown that a distinctive pattern of brain activity is associated with each state of arousal (Estevez et al., 2002). In this kind of research, measurements are carried out simultaneously using an *electroencephalograph (EEG)* to record tiny electrical currents generated by the brain's cells, eye movements, and the movement of muscles in the arms and legs.

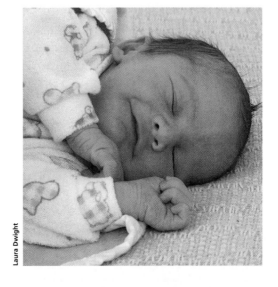

Laura Dwight

This newborn is smiling during REM sleep.

table 4.4

States of Arousal in Infants	
State	**Characteristics**
Non-rapid-eye-movement (NREM) sleep	Full rest; low muscle tone and motor activity; eyelids closed and eyes still; regular breathing (about 36 times per minute)
Rapid-eye-movement (REM) sleep	Increased muscle tone and motor activity; facial grimaces and smiles; occasional eye movements; irregular breathing (about 48 times per minute)
Periodic sleep	Intermediate between REM and NREM sleep—bursts of deep, slow breathing alternating with bouts of rapid, shallow breathing
Drowsiness	More active than NREM sleep but less active than REM or periodic sleep; eyes open and close; eyes glazed when open; breathing variable but more rapid than in NREM sleep
Alert inactivity	Slight activity; face relaxed; eyes open and bright; breathing regular and more rapid than in NREM sleep
Active alert	Frequent diffuse motor activity; vocalizations; skin flushed; irregular breathing
Distress	Vigorous diffuse motor activity; facial grimaces; red skin; crying

Source: Wolff, 1966.

EEG recordings of infants' brain waves shortly after birth distinguish two kinds of sleep that are the precursors of adult sleeping patterns: (1) an active pattern, called *rapid-eye-movement (REM) sleep,* which is characterized by uneven breathing, rapid but low-level brain-wave activity, and a good deal of eye and limb movement; and (2) a quiet pattern, called *non-rapid-eye-movement (NREM) sleep,* in which breathing is regular, brain waves are larger and slower, and the baby barely moves (see Figure 4.19) (McNamara, Lijowska & Thach, 2002). During the first 2 to 3 months of life, infants begin their sleep with active (REM) sleep and only gradually fall into quiet (NREM) sleep. After the first 2 or 3 months, the sequence reverses, and NREM sleep precedes REM sleep. Although this reversal is of little significance to parents, who are most concerned with the child's overall pattern of sleeping and waking, it is an important sign of developmental change because it shows a shift toward the adult pattern. The failure of such a shift to take place is considered a sign that the infant is not developing normally (Rao, Lutchmansingh & Poland, 2000).

Neonates spend most of their time asleep, although the amount of sleep they need gradually decreases. Several studies have shown that babies sleep about $16\frac{1}{2}$ hours a day during the first week of life. By the end of 4 weeks, they sleep a little more than 15 hours a day; and by the end of 4 months, they sleep a little less than 14 hours a day (Thoman & Whitney, 1989).

Figure 4.19
The contrast between quiet and active sleep patterns in newborns is seen in the patterns of respiration, eye movements, and brain activity (EEG). Active sleep is characterized by irregular breathing, frequent eye movements, and continuous low-voltage brain activity. (Adapted from Parmelee et al., 1968.)

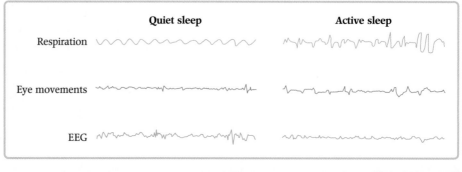

Sleeping Arrangements

One of the benefits of comparisons across cultures is that they make us aware of practices that are so common in our own culture that we assume they are the only way things can possibly be done. The ability of cross-cultural research to teach us about ourselves is nicely illustrated by studies conducted to determine where and with whom young infants sleep.

In a study of 120 societies around the world, 64 percent of the mothers surveyed reported that their infants sleep in the same bed with them (a practice referred to as *co-sleeping*). Societies where co-sleeping is widely practiced include highly technological countries, such as Japan and Italy, as well as rural communities in many countries, including Mexico and China. The United States was the only country surveyed where it is common to have young babies sleep in their own beds in their own rooms and where they are expected to sleep through the night at an early age (Wolf et al., 1996). The practice of having infants sleep separately is particularly common among college-educated, middle-class American families and is less widely practiced by other social groups in the United States and in certain regions of the country. Among a group of newborns in eastern Kentucky, for example, 36 percent shared their parents' beds and 48 percent shared their parents' rooms. Space did not seem to be the issue (Abbott, 1992). African American babies are more likely than Caucasian children to have a caregiver present when they fall asleep, to sleep in their parents' rooms, and to spend at least part of the night in their parents' beds (Wolf et al., 1996).

Sleeping practices are related to broad cultural themes regarding the organization of interpersonal relations and the moral ideals of the community (Shweder et al., 1995). Whereas middle-class American mothers emphasize the values of independence and self-reliance, mothers in societies where co-sleeping is the norm emphasize the need for babies to learn to be interdependent and to be able to get along with and be sensitive to the needs of others (Shweder et al., 1998). These underlying values are reflected in a study by Gilda

Henning Christoph/DAS FOTOARCHIVE

This Mongolian baby is being comforted in two popular ways — by being swaddled in blankets and by sucking on a pacifier.

Morelli and her colleagues, who interviewed rural Mayan peasants in Guatemala and middle-class American mothers about their infants' sleeping arrangements (Morelli et al., 1992). None of the American parents in the study allowed their infants to sleep with them. Many parents kept the sleeping child in a nearby crib for the first few months but soon moved the baby to a separate room. They gave such reasons for their arrangements as "I think he would be more dependent . . . if he was constantly with us like that," and "I think it would have made any separation harder if he wasn't even separated from us at night."

In contrast, the Mayan mothers always had each new child sleep in the same bed with them until the next baby was born. They insisted that this was the only right thing to do. When they were told about the typical U.S. practice, they expressed shock and disapproval at the parents' behavior and pity for the children. They seemed to think the American mothers were neglecting their children. Similar sentiments have been voiced by mothers from other societies where co-sleeping is a common practice.

An emphasis on independence versus interdependence is not the only cultural value reflected in sleeping arrangements. For example, Richard Shweder and his colleagues found that in Orissa, India, such moral values as female chastity, respect for hierarchy, and protection of the vulnerable exerted strong influences on specific choices of who slept with whom (Shweder et al.,

1995). The people of Orissa are more likely than Americans to arrange for the father and mother to sleep apart, and to avoid having children of very different ages sleeping in the same room.

For some, the object of such comparisons is to show that one arrangement is better or worse for infants. For example, Melissa Hunsley and Evelyn Thoman (2002) report that co-sleeping is stressful because infants spend more of their time in quiet sleep, which has been associated with slower development. In contrast, James McKenna (1996) reports no ill effects and concludes on the basis of cross-cultural evidence that "infant–parent co-sleeping is biologically, psychologically, and socially the most appropriate context for the development of healthy infant sleep physiology." On balance, it appears that except in rare cases, whether the infant sleeps in a bed alone or with its mother does not seem to make a great deal of difference. All cultural systems are relatively successful in seeing that infants get enough sleep and grow up normally.

However, while co-sleeping or solitary sleeping may not make a big difference at the time, describing cultural differences in family sleeping arrangements highlights the fact that all such arrangements are organized with a view toward ways in which children will be expected to act at a later time. This is another case where cultural beliefs organize the current environment to accord with people's expectations for the future.

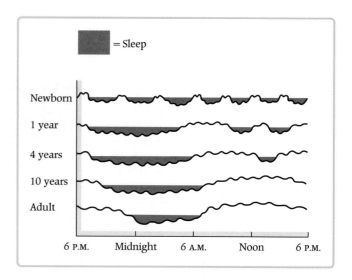

Figure 4.20
The pattern of sleep/wake cycles among babies in the United States changes rapidly during infancy. A long period of sleep comes to replace many brief periods of alternating sleep and wakefulness. (From Kleitman, 1963.)

If babies sleep most of the time, why do parents lose so much sleep? The reason is that newborns tend to sleep in snatches that last anywhere from a few minutes to a few hours. Thus they may be awake at any time of the day or night. As babies grow older, their sleeping and waking periods lengthen and coincide more and more with the night/day schedule common among adults (Salzarulo & Ficca, 2002) (see Figure 4.20).

A marked shift toward the adult night/day cycle occurs in the first weeks after birth among many American babies: by the end of the second week, their combined periods of sleep average $8\frac{1}{2}$ hours between 7 P.M. and 7 A.M. (Kleitman, 1963). But their sleep pattern still results in some loss of sleep for their parents because the longest sleep period may be only 3 or 4 hours.

Although babies' adoption of the night/day sleep cycle seems natural to people who live in industrialized countries and urban settings, studies of infants raised in other cultures suggest that it is at least partly a function of cultural influences on the infant (Fitzgerald et al., 1999). In a widely cited example of the role of social pressure in rearranging newborns' sleep, the development of the sleep/wake behavior of U.S. infants was compared with that of Kipsigis babies in rural Kenya. In the United States, parents typically put their infants to bed at certain hours—often in a separate room—and try not to pick them up when they wake up crying at night, lest they become accustomed to someone running in whenever they make a fuss. In rural Kenya, infants are almost always with their mothers. During the day they sleep when they can, often while being carried on their mothers' backs as the mothers go about their daily round of farming, household chores, and social activities. During the night they sleep with their mothers and are permitted to nurse whenever they wake up. Among Kipsigis infants, the longest period of sleep reported at 1 month is only about 3 hours; many shorter periods of sleep are sprinkled throughout the day and night. Eventually Kipsigis infants begin to sleep through the night, but not until many months after American infants have done so. Even as adults, the Kipsigis are more flexible than Americans in their sleeping hours (Super & Harkness, 1972).

In the United States, the length of the longest sleep period is often used as an index of the infant's maturation. Charles Super and Sara Harkness (1972) suggest that parents' efforts to get babies to sleep for long periods of time during the early weeks of life may be pushing the limits to which young infants can adapt. They believe that the many changes that occur in a newborn's state of arousal in every 24-hour period reflect the immaturity of the infant's brain, which sets a limit on how quickly the child can conform to an adult routine. This may be the explanation for the failure of some infants in industrialized countries to adopt a night/day pattern of sleeping and waking as quickly and easily as their parents would like them to. (See the box "Sudden Infant Death Syndrome.")

Sudden Infant Death Syndrome

Among infants 1 to 6 months of age, *sudden infant death syndrome*, often referred to as *SIDS*, is the most common cause of death in the United States as well as a major cause of death in many other countries in the world (Nagler, 2002). SIDS is the sudden death of an apparently healthy infant that is seemingly inexplicable based on the infant's prior health conditions, the family and its medical history, and the circumstances of death.

SIDS is usually discovered when parents check on their supposedly sleeping infant only to find that he or she has died. The infant may be found with clenched fists, discharge from the nose or mouth, and mottled skin.

The earliest medical report about SIDS was published more than 50 years ago (Garrow & Werne, 1953); since that time there has been an increasingly intense research program to discover its causes and ways to prevent it. Early research suggested that some infants are prone to a condition referred to as *sleep apnea*—irregular breathing because of a failure of the brain to signal the muscles controlling the lungs to breath. According to this diagnosis, the most effective prevention is provided by an electronic monitoring device that sounds an alarm whenever an infant experiences an episode of apnea, so that an adult can come and revive the baby in time.

Subsequent research has shown that young infants do, indeed, experience episodes of apnea during sleep. Postmortem studies of infant brains have shown that insufficient development of a key area in the brain stem called the *arcuate nucleus* is associated with increased rates of SIDS (Matturri et al., 2002). However, even apparently normal infants still have immature brain structures, and while they may experience episodes of sleep apnea, they are generally startled awake by such incidents, which cause no lasting harm.

Consequently, researchers began to look at other potential causes, such as accidental smothering when a baby's nose is obstructed by a soft pillow, blankets, or a stuffed animal or accidental suffocation when a baby is sleeping in bed with an adult. Lewis Lipsitt (2003) noted that most deaths from SIDS occur when babies are 2 to 5 months of age. Babies this age are especially vulnerable, he suggested, because they have lost the reflex that causes them to turn their heads when they cannot breathe (which disappears prior to $2^1/_2$ months) but have not yet developed firm voluntary control of their head movements.

An important turning point in the quest to eliminate SIDS came in 1994 when the American Academy of Pediatrics, in conjunction with the National Institutes of Health and other organizations, began informing parents about SIDS through a campaign called the "Back to Sleep" movement. This clever phrase identified the major strategy upon which the campaign was based: placing babies on their backs to sleep, instead of having them sleep on their stomachs, which greatly increased the chances of accidentally obstructing their breathing. In the past decade the rate of SIDS in the United States has been cut in half, from 1.5 per 1000 births to approximately 0.7 per 1000 births. There have been similar reductions in other countries where awareness of the back-to-sleep practice has been increased. Nonetheless, SIDS clearly remains a serious threat, so current research is seeking to discover what additional factors might, either singly or in combination, increase infants' risk. A number of such factors have been found, some of which apply before the baby is born, some after (Hauck et al., 2003).

Among the leading prenatal risk factors for SIDS are:
- Maternal malnutrition and smoking, which increase prematurity (Immaturity of the brain stem is almost certainly involved in apnea episodes.)
- Teratogenic agents (discussed at length in Chapter 3)

Among the leading risk factors for SIDS after birth are:
- Secondary tobacco smoke—the greater the exposure to tobacco smoke, the greater the risk of SIDS
- Formula-feeding of babies, which results in a higher SIDS rate than does breast-feeding
- Placing infants to sleep on their stomachs, on a soft mattress with stuffed animals or other toys in the crib

A great many studies have shown differences between ethnic groups in the incidence of SIDS (Pollack & Frohna, 2002). For example, Native Americans have a higher rate of SIDS than European Americans, while Latinos have a lower rate. There are also wide variations in the incidence of SIDS in different countries (Fitzgerald, 2002). Current research strongly suggests that these variations result from cultural differences in eating habits, alcohol and cigarette consumption, and sleeping patterns, not from any population differences in genetic predisposition for SIDS. Consequently, preventive measures focus on informing local populations of the factors they can change to ensure that their babies will not become victims of SIDS.

Feeding

Besides attempting to regulate their babies' sleeping patterns, parents encourage their infants to adjust to a regular pattern of feeding. Pediatricians' recommendations as to when babies should be fed have changed significantly over the years. Today, pediatricians often tell parents to feed their newborn baby whenever they think the baby is hungry, perhaps as often as every 2 to 3 hours. But from the early 1920s through the 1940s, mothers were advised to feed their babies only every 4 hours, even if the babies showed signs of hunger long before the prescribed time had elapsed. As one pediatrician expressed the wisdom of the time:

Feed him at exactly the same hours every day.
Do not feed him just because he cries.
Let him wait until the right time.
If you make him wait, his stomach will learn to wait.
(Weill, 1930)

For a very small infant, 4 hours can be a long time to go without food, as was demonstrated by a study of mothers and infants in Cambridge, England. The mothers were asked to keep records of their babies' behaviors and their own caregiving activities, including when they fed their babies and the time their babies spent crying. All the mothers were advised to feed their babies on a strict 4-hour schedule, but not all followed the advice. The less experienced mothers tended to stick to the schedule, but the more experienced mothers sometimes fed their babies as soon as 1 hour after a scheduled feeding. Not surprisingly, the reports of the less experienced mothers showed that their babies cried the most (Bernal, 1972).

What happens if babies are fed "on demand"? In one study, the majority of newborn babies allowed to feed on demand preferred a 3-hour schedule (Aldrich & Hewitt, 1947). The interval gradually increased as the babies grew older. At $2\frac{1}{2}$ months, most of the infants were feeding on a 4-hour schedule. By 7 or 8 months, the majority had come to approximate the normal adult schedule and were choosing to feed about four times a day. (Some parents reported the four feedings as "three meals and a snack.") A more recent study found no difference in growth rate between babies fed on demand and those fed on a strict schedule (Saxon, Gollapalli, Mitchell & Stanko, 2002).

Crying

One of the most difficult problems parents face in establishing a pattern of care for their babies is how to interpret their infants' needs. Infants obviously cannot articulate their needs or feelings, but they do have one important way of signaling that something is wrong—they can cry.

Crying is a complex behavior that involves the coordination of breathing and movements of the vocal tract. Initially it is coordinated by structures in the brain stem, but within a few months following birth the cerebral cortex becomes involved, enabling babies to cry voluntarily (Zeskind & Lester, 2001). This change in the neural organization of crying is accompanied by physical changes in the vocal tract that lower the pitch of infants' cries. At this point, parents in the United States begin to report that their infants are "crying on purpose," either to get attention or because they are bored (Lester et al., 1992).

Developmentalists concerned with the evolution of human behavior believe, on the basis of observations not only of human babies but of infants from other mammalian species, that human crying evolved as a signal to promote caregiving (Zeifman, 2001). Babies' cries have a powerful effect on those who hear them. Targeted areas in the brains of experienced parents and childless adults alike respond to infants' cries, producing increases in heart rate and blood pressure, both of which are physiological signs of arousal and anxiety (Loerberman et al., 2002). When nursing mothers hear babies' cries, even on recordings, their milk may start to flow (Newton & Newton, 1972).

Presumably newborns cry because something is causing them discomfort. The problem for the anxious parent is to figure out what that something might be. Both parents and those who are not regularly in contact with newborn babies can distinguish among infants' cries (Zeskind et al., 1992). According to Phillip Zeskind and his colleagues, the higher pitched the cries and the shorter the pauses between them, the more urgent and unpleasant adults perceive them to be. In addition, listeners in a variety of cultures can distinguish the higher-pitched cries of normal infants from the cries of low-birth-weight babies and babies who have been exposed prenatally to alcohol or the chemicals from cigarette smoke (Worchel & Allen, 1997). This finding provides additional evidence that crying developed during earlier stages of human evolution as a means of eliciting care taking.

This infant's cries are likely to be taken as a peremptory command for someone to do something quickly.

Elizabeth Crews

Parents throughout the world employ different methods in their attempt to comfort their babies when whey are distressed.

In spite of their ability to distinguish between types of crying, even experienced parents rarely can tell precisely why their baby is distressed from the cry sounds alone. One reason is that prolonged crying of all kinds eventually slips into the rhythmic pattern of the hunger cry. In many instances, then, only the intensity of the distress is evident. Hunger is, of course, a common reason for a newborn baby to cry. Studies of crying before and after feedings have confirmed that babies cry less after they are fed (Wolff, 1969).

It is widely believed that some children suffer from a medical condition called *colic,* which causes them to cry excessively. However, while there are marked individual differences in the amounts that infants cry, the cries of babies thought to suffer from colic are not distinguishable from those of others who cry frequently. Such results have led Ian St. James-Roberts and his colleagues to conclude that the specific sounds of crying may be less important in parental reactions than "its unpredictable, prolonged, hard to soothe, and unexplained nature" (St. James-Roberts et al., 1996, p. 375).

These uncertainties make it difficult for parents to know what to do when their baby cries, especially when the cry does not signal acute pain. One natural response is to seek to comfort the infant. When parents are under stress or the crying is persistent, the uncertainty about how to comfort the child and the negative emotions that crying evokes in adults are sometimes too much to bear, and some parents respond by physically abusing their infants (Hobbes et al., 2000).

Caregivers' efforts to get babies on a schedule and to comfort them when they are distressed continue as the months go by. These parenting activities are so commonplace that it is easy to overlook their significance, but they are the foundation for the more dramatic changes of the first months of life.

Mechanisms of Developmental Change

Almost immediately after birth, the behavioral repertoire of neonates begins to expand, enabling them to interact ever more effectively with the world around them. The changes in behavior that occur during the first months of life are partly a matter of perfecting capacities that already exist. As infants become able to suck more effectively, for example, they obtain more food, so they can go longer between feedings without distress. The perfecting of existing behaviors does not, however, explain how new behaviors arise. By the age of $2^{1}/_{2}$ months, infants raise their heads to look around, smile in response to the smiles of others, and shake rattles put into their hands. A major goal of the developmental sciences is to explain how these new forms of behavior arise. We will address this issue by first focusing on a crucial new behavior that emerges in early infancy—nursing. Then we will consider how the four major theoretical approaches explain the development of this new behavior.

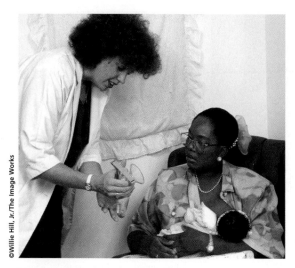

Figure 4.21
Nursing is a complex behavior that often requires practice. Here, a lactation consultant works with a new mother to help her learn the best techniques for nursing her new baby.

From Sucking to Nursing

One new behavior that appears in early infancy is nursing. When we compare the way newborn infants feed with the nursing behavior of 6-week-old infants, a striking contrast is evident. As noted earlier, newborns possess several reflexes that are relevant to feeding: rooting (turning the head in the direction of a touch on the cheek), sucking, swallowing, and breathing. These component behaviors are not well integrated, however, so babies' early feeding experiences are likely to be uncoordinated affairs.

When newborns are first held to the breast, a touch to the cheek will make them turn their heads and open their mouths, but they root around in a disorganized way. When they do find the nipple, they may lose it again almost immediately, or the act of sucking may cause the upper lip to fold back and block the nostrils, eliciting a sharp head-withdrawal reflex. Furthermore, breathing and sucking are not well coordinated at first, so newborns are likely to have to stop sucking to come up for air. Nursing is clearly a learned behavior in which both the mother and the infant participate (see Figure 4.21).

By the time infants are 6 weeks old, a qualitative change is evident in their feeding behavior, a change that is more than just a perfection of the sucking reflex. For one thing, infants anticipate being fed when they are picked up and can prepare themselves to feed. More significant, they have worked out the coordination of all the component behaviors of feeding—sucking, swallowing, and breathing—so they can perform them in a smooth, integrated sequence (Meyers, 2001). In short, feeding has become nursing. In fact, babies become so efficient at nursing that they can accomplish in less than 10 minutes what originally took them as long as an hour.

Although the acquisition of nursing is commonplace, it raises the question of how developmental change comes about. Nursing is clearly not a reflex. It is a new form of behavior that develops through the reorganization of the various reflexes with which infants are born. Each of the four broad theoretical frameworks—the biological-maturation perspective, the environmental-learning perspective, the constructivist perspective, and the cultural-context perspective—emphasizes different factors in its efforts to explain development (see Chapter 1, pp. 30–37). By examining the seemingly simple behavior of nursing from each perspective you will gain a sense of how each perspective contributes to our understanding of the development of other behaviors during infancy and beyond.

The Biological-Maturation Perspective

To explain the development of nursing and other new behaviors after birth, biologically oriented developmental theorists invoke precisely the same mechanism that they use to explain all aspects of prenatal development—maturation. New behaviors, they say, arise from old behaviors as a result of distinct maturational changes in the physical structures and physiological processes of the organism. In their view, the role of the organism's genetic inheritance is considered to be of paramount importance, and the role of the environment in development is considered to be minimal, just as during the prenatal period.

According to the biological-maturation perspective, the infant's increasing success at nursing, like the gradual lengthening of the intervals between feedings and between periods of sleep, appears to depend at least in part on the maturation of underlying brain structures. One compelling piece of evidence for this view comes from studies of a rare abnormality in which infants are born with an intact brain stem but little or no cerebral cortex. Such babies may have normal reflexes at birth—sucking, yawning, stretching, and crying (see Figure 4.22). They also exhibit

Figure 4.22
Even babies like this one, born with little or no cerebral cortex, display basic reflexes such as sucking.

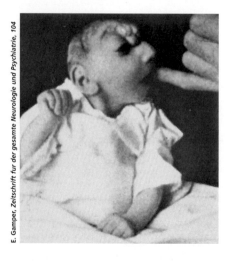

habituation (see Figure 4.23). Such responses suggest that newborns' initial reflexes are controlled by the brain stem and do not require input from the cerebral cortex (Gamper 1926/1959; Graham et al., 1978; Kolb & Whishaw, 1996).

Babies born without a cerebral cortex do not live long, however. Those that do live more than a few days fail to develop the complex, well-coordinated behaviors, including nursing, seen in normal babies. In contrast, if a baby's brain and central nervous system are developing normally, both the number and the efficiency of connections between the brain stem and the cerebral cortex begin to increase dramatically following birth.

Although no one has yet identified the cortical areas responsible for such new behaviors as nursing, it seems safe to say that the maturation of the baby's cortical structures (along with development of the baby's muscles) must be an important factor in the development of this new form of behavior. At the same time, it is not clear that all the brain connections associated with nursing develop before the baby begins to nurse or that they develop independent of environmental influence, as some biological maturationists seem to imply. Rather, some of these brain developments are brought about by infants' interactions with their environment.

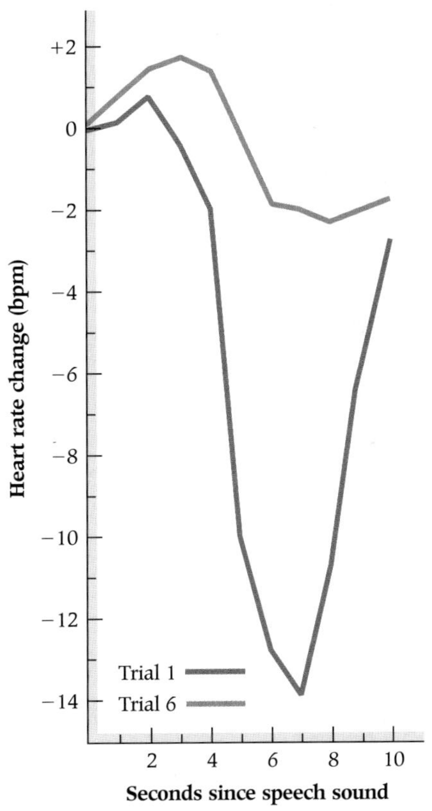

Figure 4.23
Evidence of habituation in a 1-month-old baby born with no cerebral cortex. On the first exposure to the sound of human speech, there is a marked decrease in heart rate, indicating attention. After five additional presentations of the sound, the infant's heart rate no longer changes dramatically, indicating habituation. (Adapted from Graham et al., 1978.)

The Environmental-Learning Perspective

Whatever biology may contribute to an infant's development of nursing behavior, some form of input from the environment is also clearly necessary. Otherwise, a mother would have to continue to present her breast in precisely the position required to elicit the sucking reflex throughout her child's infancy. In fact, babies quickly become accustomed to nursing in any number of positions, adjusting to the specifics of each occasion for maximum comfort and efficiency.

How do a baby's innate reflexes become coordinated with one another and with appropriate stimuli in the environment to transform reflex sucking into nursing? Environmental-learning theorists argue that such coordination requires **learning,** a relatively permanent change in behavior brought about by the experience of events in the environment. Several types of learning are believed to operate throughout development, including habituation and imitation (described on p. 120 and 131), as well as two processes referred to as *classical conditioning* and *operant conditioning.*

Classical Conditioning

Classical conditioning is learning in which previously existing behaviors come to be elicited by new stimuli. The existence of this very basic learning mechanism was demonstrated at the turn of the century by the Russian physiologist Ivan Pavlov (1849–1936). Pavlov (1927) showed that after several experiences of hearing a tone just before food was placed in its mouth, a dog would begin to

learning A relatively permanent change in behavior brought about by experience of events in the environment.

classical conditioning Learning in which previously existing behaviors come to be elicited by new stimuli.

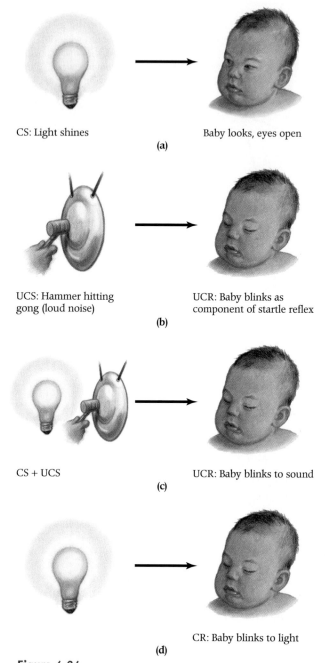

CS: Light shines

Baby looks, eyes open

(a)

UCS: Hammer hitting
gong (loud noise)

UCR: Baby blinks as
component of startle reflex

(b)

CS + UCS

UCR: Baby blinks to sound

(c)

CR: Baby blinks to light

(d)

Figure 4.24
Classical conditioning. In the top panel
(a) the sight of a light (CS) elicits no particular response. In (b) the loud sound of
a gong (UCS) causes the baby to blink
(UCR). In (c) the sight of the light (CS) is
paired with the sound of the gong (UCS),
which evokes an eyeblink (UCR). Finally
(d), the sight of the light (CS) is sufficient to cause the baby to blink (CR),
demonstrating that learning has occurred.

salivate in response to the tone before it received any food. In
everyday language, the dog began to expect food when it heard
the tone, and its mouth watered as a result.

In the terminology of environmental-learning theories,
Pavlov paired a **conditional stimulus (CS)**—a tone—with an
unconditional stimulus (UCS)—food in the mouth. The food is
called an unconditional stimulus because it "unconditionally" causes
salivation, salivation being a reflex response to food in the mouth.
Salivation, in turn, is called an **unconditional response (UCR)**
because it is automatically and unconditionally elicited by food in
the mouth. The tone is called a conditional stimulus because the behavior it elicits depends on (is conditional on) the way it has been
paired with the unconditional stimulus. When the unconditional response (salivation in response to food in the mouth) occurs in response to the CS (the tone), it is called a **conditional response
(CR)** because it depends on the pairing of the CS (the tone) and
the UCS (the food). The key indicator that learning has occurred is
that the CS (tone) elicits the CR (salivation) before the presentation
of the UCS (food) (see Figure 4.24).

A number of developmentalists seized on Pavlov's demonstrations
as a possible model for the way infants learn about their environments. One of Pavlov's co-workers demonstrated conditioned feeding
responses in a 14-month-old infant based on the principle of classical
conditioning (Krasnogorski, 1907/1967). The baby opened his mouth
and made sucking motions (CRs) at the sight of a glass of milk (CS).
When a bell (a new CS) was sounded on several occasions just before
the glass of milk was presented, the baby began to open his mouth
and suck at the sound of the bell, an indication that classical conditioning built expectations in the infant by a process of association. The
crucial point of these observations is that there is no biological connection between the sound of a bell and the mouth-opening and
sucking responses it elicited. Rather, the fact that the new stimuli
elicited these responses shows that learning has occurred.

In recent decades, intensive research has demonstrated that classical conditioning can occur within hours of birth if infants are presented with stimuli that are biologically significant to them and if
they are alert. A clear example of classical conditioning in young infants was demonstrated by Lewis Lipsitt and his colleagues, who
showed that neonates will form a conditioned reflex to a puff of air to the eye. Infants 10, 20, and 30 days of age learned to shut their eyes in anticipation of an air
puff that came $1\frac{1}{2}$ to 2 seconds after a tone sounded. The youngest infants did not
seem to retain what they had learned, but those 20 and 30 days old showed indications of remembering the experience 10 days later (Lipsitt, 1990).

Operant Conditioning

Classical conditioning explains how infants begin to build up expectations about the
connections between events in their environment, but it does little to explain how
even the simplest new behaviors come into being. The kind of conditioning that
gives rise to new and more complex behaviors is called **operant conditioning,** in
which behaviors are shaped by their consequences. The basic idea of operant conditioning is that organisms will tend to repeat behaviors that lead to rewards and will
tend to give up behaviors that fail to produce rewards or that lead to punishment

(Skinner, 1938). A consequence (such as receiving a reward) that increases the likelihood that a behavior will be repeated is called a positive **reinforcement.** According to an operant explanation of the development of nursing, such behaviors as turning the head away from the bottle or burying the nose in the mother's breast will become less frequent because they do not lead to milk and may make it difficult for infants to breathe—results infants find unsatisfying. At the same time, such behaviors as well-coordinated breathing, sucking, and swallowing will become more frequent because they are likely to be rewarded with milk.

Operant conditioning in young infants has been experimentally demonstrated with a variety of reinforcers, such as milk, sweet substances, the appearance of an interesting visual display, the opportunity to suck on a pacifier, and the sound of a heartbeat or the mother's voice (Rovee-Collier & Barr, 2001). In an early study of operant conditioning, Einar Siqueland (1968) demonstrated that neonates can learn to turn their heads in order to suck on a pacifier. The key requirement of operant learning is that some sort of behavior has to occur before it can be reinforced. Head turning is ideal in this respect because it is something even the youngest neonates do. While the babies lay in laboratory cribs, Siqueland placed a band around their heads that was connected to a device for recording the degree their heads moved to either side (see Figure 4.25). Siqueland first recorded how often the babies naturally turned their heads. Once this baseline rate was established, he set his apparatus to signal when the babies had turned their heads at least 10 degrees to either side. As soon as they did, they were given a pacifier to suck on. After only 25 occasions on which the head turning was reinforced with the pacifier, most of the babies had tripled the rate at which they turned their heads. To make certain that the increase in babies' head turning was not due to the excitement of being placed in the crib, Siqueland included another group of infants in his experiment who were rewarded with a pacifier for holding their heads still. These infants learned to keep their heads still during the course of the experiment.

Support for the argument that learning is an important contributor to behavioral development comes from studies that show that even very young infants are capable of remembering what they have learned from one testing session to the next (Rovee-Collier & Barr, 2001). These studies demonstrate that memory for newly learned behaviors improves markedly during the first several months of life, a finding to which we will return at the end of this chapter and again in Chapter 5 (pp. 192–193). In addition, they provide important evidence that infants are not only learning but accumulating knowledge from the earliest days of life.

In addition to focusing on the role of learning in development, the environmental-learning approach differs from the biological-maturation perspective by emphasizing continuity in developmental processes as children grow older; the processes of classical and operant conditioning appear to be in place at birth and remain present throughout development. However, whether attempting to explain the transformation of the sucking reflex into nursing or to explain any other aspect of developmental change, the environmental-learning approach has difficulty accounting for individual differences in behavior. According to this perspective, such variations can be accounted for only by variations in the experiences of individuals; the effects of genetic variation are discounted. Contemporary research on individual differences, such as the evidence concerning different patterns of temperament in different newborns, has made this extreme view difficult to justify.

conditional stimulus (CS) In classical conditioning, a stimulus that elicits a behavior that is dependent on the way it is paired with the unconditional stimulus (UCS).

unconditional stimulus (UCS) In classical conditioning, the stimulus, such as food in the mouth, that invariably causes the unconditional response (UCR).

unconditional response (UCR) In classical conditioning, the response, such as salivation, that is invariably elicited by the unconditional stimulus (UCS).

conditional response (CR) In classical conditioning, a response to the conditional stimulus (CS).

operant conditioning Learning in which changes in behavior are shaped by the consequences of that behavior, thereby giving rise to new and more complete behaviors.

reinforcement A consequence, such as a reward, that increases the likelihood that a behavior will be repeated.

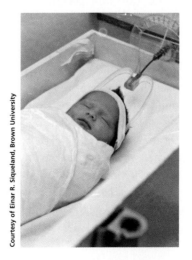

Courtesy of Einar R. Siqueland, Brown University

Figure 4.25
A newborn with a specially designed headpiece that records head turning. In Siqueland's operant-conditioning experiment, head turns of more than 10 degrees were reinforced by the opportunity to suck on a pacifier. (Siqueland, 1968.)

The Constructivist Perspective: Piaget

Jean Piaget (1896–1980) is widely considered the most prominent developmental psychologist of the twentieth century. His special interest was how children acquire knowledge, particularly knowledge controlled by logical thought processes. He objected to both the biological-maturation and the environmental-learning theories of his day. He criticized biological explanations for their failure to take into account important ways in which the environment of human infants interacts with their biological capacities to produce developmental change (Piaget & Inhelder, 1969). At the same time, he was critical of environmental-learning explanations because they assumed that the environment is the originator of developmental change, failing to take into account the central role of children's own actions in producing development. He also was a firm believer in the idea that developmental change occurs as a series of qualitative, stagelike changes as children construct more and more complex understandings of the world around them.

Piaget's Theory of Developmental Change

In Piaget's view, infants' knowledge is acquired (in his words, "constructed") through action. Consequently, to understand development, one must begin at the beginning with the most elementary potentials for action present at birth, reflexes.

In Piaget's theoretical framework, a reflex is a primitive *schema,* which he considered the most basic unit of psychological functioning. A **schema** is a mental structure that provides a model for action in similar or analogous circumstances (Piaget & Inhelder, 1969). During the first month of life, the "reflex schemas" babies are born with provide them with a kind of skeleton for action that is gradually fleshed out by experience. Eventually these initial schemas are either strengthened or transformed into new schemas through **adaptation,** a twofold process involving what Piaget termed *assimilation* and *accommodation.*

During the phase of change called **assimilation,** various experiences are mentally taken in by children and incorporated into their existing schemas, strengthening those schemas and helping them work more efficiently. For example, in Piaget's view, the primitive schema of reflex sucking is initially so closely tied to a small group of eliciting stimuli, such as a nipple placed in the mouth, that newborns are actually unable to distinguish between their own sucking and the object sucked upon. But sucking does not remain strictly bound to particular eliciting objects for long. Soon babies are likely to find, say, a pacifier instead of a nipple touching their lips and start sucking on it. Since a pacifier is designed to be similar to a nipple, the infants can suck on it in much the same way they suck on the nipple. In other words, they *assimilate* the pacifier, a new object, into their existing sucking schema. But not all pacifiers are alike, and pacifiers are not the only objects beside nipples that infants are likely to encounter. As a consequence, not every object babies encounter can be assimilated into an existing schema. If infants encounter a blanket, for instance, they may try to suck on it. However, because the qualities of the blanket—the satin binding, perhaps, or the fuzzy, flat center of the blanket—are so unlike the qualities of a nipple or a pacifier, they are unable to assimilate the blanket as an object to suck on. They therefore must make some **accommodation** to this new object; that is, they must modify the way they suck, perhaps by choosing a corner of the blanket and sucking on that, using approximately but not exactly the same schema they had used to suck on a nipple.

Once it has undergone changes as a result of the attempts at assimilation and accommodation, the sucking schema can now be applied to new environmental experiences. But if a baby encounters a toy truck and tries to suck on it, accommodation

schema In Piagetian terms, a mental structure that provides an organism with a model for action in similar or analogous circumstances.

adaptation Piaget's term for the twofold process involving assimilation and accommodation.

assimilation Piaget's term for the process by which various experiences are mentally taken in by the organism and incorporated into existing schemas.

accommodation In Piagetian terms, a modification of a previous schema so that it can be applied to both old and new experiences.

equilibration The Piagetian term for the back-and-forth process of the child's seeking a fit between existing schemas and new environmental experiences.

is unlikely to occur because the toy is so difficult to suck on; in this case, the baby's sucking schema will be unmodified.

One way to summarize Piaget's theory is to view development as a constant tug-of-war between assimilation and accommodation as the infant acts on the world. Piaget believed that this back-and-forth process of the child's search for a fit between existing schemas and new environmental experiences creates a new balance between child and environment, which he referred to as **equilibration.** This process of achieving equilibrium between the developing infant's present understanding of the world and the infant's new experiences of it creates a more inclusive, more complicated form of knowledge, bringing the child to a new stage of development. Of course, this balance can't last for long because the process of biological maturation and the accumulation of experience/knowledge leads to new imbalances, initiating a new tug-of-war between assimilation and accommodation in the search for a new equilibrium and a still higher, more inclusive level of adaptation.

Piaget identified four major developmental stages, corresponding to infancy, early childhood, middle childhood, and adolescence.

Table 4.5 provides a summary of the four stages of development described by Piaget. The *sensorimotor stage,* which occurs during infancy, is discussed below and in Chapters 5 and 6. We will examine the *preoperational, concrete operational,* and *formal operational* stages in Chapters 9, 12, and 16, respectively.

table 4.5

Piaget's Stages of Cognitive Development and the Sensorimotor Substages			
Age (years)	**Stage**	**Description**	**Characteristics of Sensorimotor Substages**
Birth to 2	Sensorimotor	Infants' achievements consist largely of coordinating their sensory perceptions and simple motor behaviors. As they move through the six substages of this period, infants come to recognize the existence of a world outside themselves and begin to interact with it in deliberate ways.	**Substage 1 (0–1$\frac{1}{2}$ months)** *Reflex schemas exercised:* involuntary rooting, sucking, grasping, looking **Substage 2 (1$\frac{1}{2}$–4 months)** *Primary circular reactions:* repetition of actions that are pleasurable in themselves
2 to 6	Preoperational	Young children can represent reality to themselves through the use of symbols, including mental images, words, and gestures. Still, children often fail to distinguish their point of view from that of others, become easily captured by surface appearances, and are often confused about causal relations.	**Substage 3 (4–8 months)** *Secondary circular reactions:* dawning awareness of the effects of one's own actions on the environment; extended actions that produce interesting change in the environment
6 to 12	Concrete Operational	As they enter middle childhood, children become capable of mental operations, internalized actions that fit into a logical system. Operational thinking allows children mentally to combine, separate, order, and transform objects and actions. Such operations are considered concrete because they are carried out in the presence of the objects and events being thought about.	**Substage 4 (8–12 months)** *Coordination of secondary circular reactions:* combining schemas to achieve a desired effect; earliest form of problem solving **Substage 5 (12–18 months)** *Tertiary circular reactions:* deliberate variation of problem-solving means; experimentation to see what the consequences will be
12 to 19	Formal Operational	In adolescence the developing person acquires the ability to think systematically about all logical relations within a problem. Adolescents display keen interest in abstract ideas and in the process of thinking itself.	**Substage 6 (18–24 months)** *Beginnings of symbolic representation:* images and words come to stand for familiar objects; invention of new means of problem solving through symbolic combinations

Laura Dwight

Blowing bubbles is an early instance of a primary circular reaction in which an accidental aspect of sucking is prolonged for the pleasure of continuing the sensation.

The Sensorimotor Stage

Piaget referred to infancy as the **sensorimotor stage** because during this period the process of adaptation consists largely of coordinating sensory perceptions and simple motor responses to gain knowledge of the world. During the first few months of life, infants are said to progress through two sensorimotor substages, exercising reflex schemas and primary circular reactions.

Substage 1: Exercising Reflex Schemas Piaget believed that from birth to approximately 1 to $1^1/_2$ months infants learn to control and coordinate the reflexes present at birth, which provide them with their initial connection to their environments. However, these initial reflexes add nothing new to development because they undergo very little accommodation. In this sense, they seem to accomplish little more than solidifying the "preestablished boundaries of the hereditary apparatus" (Piaget & Inhelder, 1969).

Nevertheless, Piaget argued that the initial reflexes do provide the conditions for new development, because they *produce* stimulation at the same time that they are responses to stimuli. When infants suck, for example, they experience tactile pressure on the roof of the mouth, which stimulates further sucking, which produces more tactile pressure, and so on. This stimulus-producing aspect of basic reflexes is the key to the development of the second sensorimotor substage because it results in the earliest extensions of the reflexes with which babies are born.

Substage 2: Primary Circular Reactions This substage is said to last from about 1 to 4 months. The first hints of new forms of behavior are that existing reflexes are extended in time (as when infants suck between feedings) or are extended to new objects (as when infants suck their thumbs). Piaget noted that babies may suck their thumbs accidentally as early as the first day of life. (We now know they may do so even before birth.) He believed, however, that the thumb-sucking seen during substage 2 reflects a qualitatively new form of behavior.

In substage 1, infants suck their thumbs only when they accidentally touch their mouths with their hands. During substage 2, in contrast, if a baby's thumb falls from her mouth, the baby is likely to bring the thumb back to her mouth so that she can suck it some more. In other words, infants in this substage repeat pleasurable actions for their own sake. Piaget used the term **primary circular reaction** to characterize such behavior. Behaviors of this type are considered *primary* because the objects toward which they are directed are parts of the baby's own body; they are called *circular* because they lead only back to themselves.

Piaget's evidence for many of his ideas about the earliest substages of the sensorimotor period can be seen in the notes he kept about his own children's behavior. In the excerpt below, note how new behaviors arise in the process of attempting to repeat something just for the pleasure of it:

> After having learned to suck his thumb, Laurent continues to play with his tongue and to suck, but intermittently. On the other hand, his skill increases. Thus at 1 month, 20 days I notice he grimaces while placing his tongue between gums and lips and in bulging his lips, as well as making a clapping sound when quickly closing the mouth after these exercises. (Piaget, 1952b, p. 65)

Piaget believed that such primary circular reactions are important because they offer the first evidence of cognitive development. "The basic law of dawning psychological

sensorimotor stage Piaget's term for the stage of infancy during which the process of adaptation consists largely of coordinating sensory perceptions and simple motor behaviors to acquire knowledge of the world.

primary circular reaction The term Piaget used to describe the infant's tendency to repeat pleasurable bodily actions for their own sake.

activity," he wrote, "could be said to be the search for the maintenance or repetition of interesting states of consciousness" (Piaget, 1977, p. 202).

Over the first few months of life, these circular reactions undergo both *differentiation*—infants learn to use different grasps for different objects and learn not to suck on toy trucks—and *integration*—infants can grasp their mothers' arms with one hand while sucking on a bottle in a newly coordinated way. All the while, infants' experiences are providing more nourishment for their existing schemas and are forcing them to modify those schemas, permitting them to master more of the world.

In contrast to the infants portrayed by biological-maturation and environmental-learning approaches, Piagetian infants are active problem-solving beings who are busy acting on the environment in the process of adapting to it right from birth. All three perspectives discussed thus far designate inborn reflexes as the starting point for development, but they view the significance of these reflexes in different ways. Because Piaget saw reflexes as schemas for action, he downplayed the role of the environment in evoking or reinforcing particular behaviors or maturational processes in the brain and instead emphasized the role of infants' constructive activity in shaping the way the environment will exert its effects.

The Cultural-Context Perspective

As we indicated in Chapter 1 (pp. 36–37), the cultural-context perspective shares Piaget's beliefs that (1) development occurs as individuals act on their environment and (2) biology and experience play equal and reciprocal roles in the development of a human being. However, cultural-context theorists also consider two additional sources of developmental change: (1) the active contribution of other people in the child's community and (2) the cultural "designs for living" accumulated over the history of the larger social group. Such designs for living are present in all human societies, and in this sense they are universal. But their particular shape varies from one society to the next, giving rise to culturally specific modes of interaction. These culture-specific variations encourage development along certain lines while discouraging it along others, thereby producing distinctive patterns of change (Shweder et al., 1998).

Let us look once again at the process through which sucking develops into organized feeding, this time to highlight how the universal factors of maturation and learning and infants' active strivings vary culturally in ways that shape infants' behavior in the present and give hints of further changes to come.

The Mother's Contribution

A close look at the acquisition of new forms of behavior during the first $2^1/_2$ months of life reveals that changes in a baby's behavior are intimately related to reciprocal changes in the social world. In particular, the mother's behavior appears to be just as essential to the infant's development as are the changes that occur in the infant's biological maturation.

In the beginning, the mother's nursing behavior may not be much more coordinated than her baby's (Page-Goertz, McCamman & Westdahl, 2001). She must learn how to hold the baby and adjust herself so that the nipple is placed at exactly the right spot against the baby's mouth to elicit the sucking reflex. She must also learn not to press the baby so tightly to her breast that the infant's breathing is disrupted, triggering the head-withdrawal reflex.

When the mother breast-feeds, the baby's (reflex) sucking initiates reflex responses in her that combine with her voluntary efforts to maximize the amount of milk the baby receives. This system of mutually facilitating reflexes in infant and

Figure 4.26
The reflexes that establish a reciprocal relationship between the infant being fed and the mother. The infant's sucking stimulates the release of hormones that increase milk production and help trigger the ejection of milk from the mammary glands. (Adapted from Cairns, 1979.)

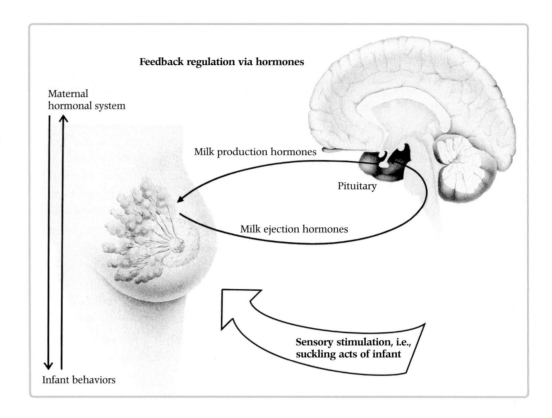

mother changes the consequences of reflex sucking, as shown in Figure 4.26. The infant's sucking not only transports milk from nipple to mouth but also stimulates the production of more milk, thereby increasing the adaptive value of the sucking reflex.

A different type of mutual facilitation arises from the physical movements mothers make while they are feeding their infants by either breast or bottle. Kenneth Kaye (1982) and his colleagues found that even during the very first feeding, mothers occasionally jiggle the baby or the bottle. These jiggles come not at random intervals but during the pauses between the infant's bursts of sucking. The jiggles increase the probability of sucking and prolong the feeding session, thereby increasing the amount of milk the neonate receives.

Sucking in response to jiggling is not a reflex in the sense that rooting is a reflex. Rooting is an automatic, involuntary response to being touched on the side of the mouth. There are no known neural connections that make sucking an inevitable response to the mother's jiggle. Yet sucking in response to jiggling happens, is to some extent automatic, and has clear adaptive value. Scholars do not know for sure where such adaptive patterns come from. Kaye calls them "preadapted responses," implying that they may have arisen in the course of human evolution.

Kaye speculates that the mother's jiggle between her infant's bursts of sucking is her way of intuitively "conversing" with her baby by filling in her "turn" during the pauses in the baby's rhythmic sucking. Mothers' reports support Kaye's view. Although they are not aware that they are jiggling their babies in a systematic way, mothers report that they actively try to help their babies nurse. They notice the pauses between bursts of sucking. When mothers are asked about their jiggling behavior, a typical response is that the baby "gets lazy, or dozes off, so I jiggle her to get her going again."

Jiggling during feeding is just one of myriad ways in which mothers actively interpret the meaning of their babies' behavior in terms of their cultural categories (such as the attribution of "laziness" to a 2-day-old child). This culturally shaped interpretation then shapes how mothers structure their babies' experience—just one small example of how maternal beliefs influence mothers to become "co-constructors" of their children's development.

Cultural Variations

In their discussion of culture and development, Margaret Mead and Frances Macgregor (1951) noted that cultures "differ from each other in the way in which the growth process is interwoven with learning" (p. 26). This principle, they went on to explain, first operates in the various ways adults of different cultures respond to such basic neonatal capacities as the sucking reflex and to the fact that the mother's milk does not begin to flow until a day or two after she has given birth:

> The existence of the sucking reflex at birth . . . will be taken advantage of in some cultures by putting the baby at once to the mother's breast, so that the infant's sucking is used to stimulate the flow of the mother's milk while the infant itself remains hungry, or the infant may be put at the breast of a wet nurse with a well-established flow of milk, in which case the infant's sucking behavior is reinforced but the mother is left without the stimulation that it would have provided. As another alternative, the infant may be starved until the mother has milk, and as still another, the infant may be given a bottle with a different kind of nipple. (p. 26)

Despite such differences, the infant feeding practices of all cultures are equivalent in that they are all ways in which parents arrange for infants' innate sucking reflexes to become part of nursing. In this respect, nursing is both universal *and* culturally organized.

According to the cultural-context perspective, cultural variations in the way nursing is handled have both a *direct* effect on the infant's early experience and an *indirect* effect on later experiences. To continue with the example provided by Mead and Macgregor, if a baby is bottle-fed until the mother's milk begins to flow, changes in the baby's sucking that are adaptive to bottle-feeding may interfere with subsequent breast-feeding. If the interference is great, breast-feeding may be given up altogether. This outcome will have a direct effect on both the kind of nutrition that the infant receives and the forms of social interaction between infant and mother that are a part of feeding.

However, such differences in cultural practices also have an indirect effect on the baby. Because specific cultural practices such as breast-feeding, bottle-feeding, or the use of a wet nurse are linked to larger patterns of social life that will shape the child's future experiences, the child's later development is affected by which method of feeding is decided upon. For example, if a mother who stays at home gives her baby a bottle because she believes that bottled milk is more nutritious than her own, the use of a bottle rather than breast-feeding may have no differential impact on the development of social relations between the mother and the child. However, if an employed mother takes her baby to a daycare center, bottle-feeding is likely to become part of patterns of social interaction that include peers and a succession of nonmaternal caregivers.

In many parts of the world, such as sub-Saharan Africa, where artificial means of birth control are unavailable, breast-feeding babies for 2 or more years is an essential birth control strategy (LeVine et al., 1994). The Sukuma of Tanzania, for example, try to space pregnancies by 24 to 30 months and describe someone who does not breast-feed for this length of time as a woman who "gives birth like a chicken." The Baganda of Uganda tradi-

Although babies are nursed in all cultures, there are wide variations in the way babies' nursing behavior is organized.

©Phil Schermeister/Corbis

tionally forbade sexual activity by a new mother because if a new baby followed too closely after the birth of a child, the first child would be in danger of contracting kwashiorkor, an often-fatal form of protein-calorie malnutrition. Breast-feeding not only provides babies with protein but also suppresses menstruation for up to 2 years, increasing the intervals between the birth of children. This delay allows the mother to pay more attention to and better feed her youngest and most vulnerable offspring.

In summary, different cultural patterns lead to different child-rearing practices that have different effects on further development, as we will see in later chapters. For this reason it is essential to keep cultural factors in mind when we consider the mechanisms of developmental change (Greenfield, Keller, Fugigni & Maynard, 2003).

Integrating the Separate Threads of Development

The complexities involved in accounting for the way nursing develops during the first months of life provide some hint of the enormous difficulties involved in attempting to account for human development as a whole. Even for a behavior as seemingly simple as nursing, the contributions of biological and environmental factors, including cultural influences and the specific circumstances in which infants find themselves, must all be considered. And the difficulties do not end there. A child's various behaviors develop not in isolation but as parts of an integrated system of developing behaviors. Thus developmentalists must also study the parts of the system in relation to one another. Nursing, for instance, must be understood as but one element in a system of developing behaviors that includes increasingly longer sleeping and waking periods and the buildup of elementary expectations about the environment.

To meet the requirement that developing behaviors be considered individually and as parts of a larger whole, we have found the analytical strategy developed by Robert Emde and his associates to be especially useful (Emde et al., 1976). As we mentioned in Chapter 1 (pp. 37–39), this strategy involves tracing developments in the biological, behavioral, and social domains as they relate to one another. It allows the identification of bio-social-behavioral shifts, those periods when changes in the separate domains converge to create the kind of qualitative reorganization in the overall pattern of behaviors that signals the onset of a new stage of development. You can see the usefulness of this approach by examining the first postnatal bio-social-behavioral shift after birth, which occurs when a full-term baby is about $2^1/_2$ months old.

The First Postnatal Bio-Social-Behavioral Shift

At present, a great many developmentalists agree that during the third month the "modes and mechanisms" of infant behavior undergo a rather abrupt shift (Emde et al., 1976; Lavelli & Fogel, 2002). This shift arises from the convergence of developmental changes that previously had proceeded in relative isolation. Table 4.6 lists in capsule form representative changes in the separate domains that converge to create the first postnatal bio-social-behavioral shift. To appreciate the far-reaching significance of this and subsequent bio-social-behavioral shifts, we must visualize what it means for all the changes listed in Table 4.6 to occur at about the same time. Following the lead of Emde and his colleagues, we will illustrate the meaning of a bio-social-behavioral shift by tracing how changes in infants' smiling are related to other aspects of their development.

table 4.6

Elements of the First Postnatal Bio-Social-Behavioral Shift (2½ Months)	
Biological domain	**Central nervous system:** • **Myelination of cortical and subcortical neural pathways** • **Myelination of primary neural pathways in some sensory systems** • **Increased cortical control of subcortical activity** • **Increases in the number and diversity of brain cells** **Psychophysiology:** • **Increases in amount of wakefulness** • **Decreases in active (REM) sleep as a proportion of total sleep time** • **Shift in pattern of sleep; quiet (NREM) sleep begins to come first**
Behavioral domain	**Learning is retained better between episodes** **Increases in visual acuity** **More complete visual scanning of objects** **Onset of social smiling** **Decreases in generalized fussiness and crying** **Visually initiated reaching becomes visually guided reaching**
Social domain	**New quality of coordination and emotional contact between infants and caretakers** **Beginning of "crying on purpose"**

The Emergence of Social Smiling

During the first week of life, the corners of a baby's mouth often curl up in a facial expression that looks for all the world like a smile. Most experienced mothers do not pay much attention to such smiles, however, because the smiles are most likely to come when the infant is asleep or very drowsy. During the second week, smiles begin to appear when the infants are awake, but they do not correlate with any particular events in the environment. Between the ages of 1 month and 2½ months, infants begin to smile indiscriminately at almost any form of external stimulation. Thus this earliest form of smiling is not really social, even when it is stimulated from the outside.

To become truly social, babies' smiles must be reciprocally related to the smiles of others; that is, the baby must both smile in response to the smiles of other people and elicit others' smiles. This is precisely what begins to happen for the first time around the age of 2½ to 3 months.

The changes in infants' behavior that accompany the social smile are not lost on their parents. Quite the opposite; parents report a new emotional quality in their relationship with their child. The remarks made by a mother concerning her feelings about her baby before the shift and the description of a mother's interactions with her baby after the shift provided at the beginning of this chapter give an excellent idea of the social and emotional implications of the new kind of smiling. In the earliest week of postnatal life, mothers are acutely aware of the limited interpersonal contact they have achieved, and they respond in quite

Pascal Maitre Cosmos/Matrix

This father and son from Kaokoland, Namibia, are sharing an important sense of connectedness.

tangible ways when they experience the shift in connectedness that accompanies the shift in infant capacities.

Scottish psychologist Colwyn Trevarthan (1998) refers to the new quality of emotional relationship that accompanies well-organized, reciprocal smiling as **primary intersubjectivity.** The coordination of movement and mood that mothers and infants display indicates that the infants are able to recognize and share the mental state of their mothers with whom they are in direct interaction. This new form of interaction is taken as additional evidence that very early in infancy, infants are able to coordinate a rudimentary sense of themselves with an equally rudimentary, but developing, sense of other people in their immediate environment.

The significance of the emergence of the social smile as a marker of a new level of development is not an exclusively European American phenomenon. It is clearly reflected in a special ritual traditionally practiced by the Navajo:

> When visitors come to the hogan [house] it is polite to inquire: "Has the baby laughed yet?" When it does so, this is an occasion for rejoicing and for a little ceremony. The baby's hands are held out straight by the mother, and some member of the family (usually a brother or a sister) puts a pinch of salt with bread and meat upon them. . . . The person who sees the baby smile first should give a present (with salt) to all members of the family. The father or mother will kill a sheep and distribute this among relatives along with a bit of salt for each piece. (Leighton & Kluckhohn, 1947/1969, p. 29)

Biological Contributions to Social Smiling

Several lines of evidence point to important biological changes as part of the emergence of social smiling. In their pioneering studies, Emde and his colleagues recorded the brain waves of babies when they were and were not smiling. They found that in the early days after birth babies' smiles came primarily during REM sleep and were accompanied by bursts of brain-wave activity originating in the brain stem. Emde and Jean Robinson (1979) call these endogenous smiles *REM smiles.* They found that even when the infants were awake, their smiles were accompanied by the pattern of brain waves characteristic of drowsiness and REM sleep. The frequency of REM smiles decreased rapidly during the next several weeks, to be replaced at about $2^{1}/_{2}$ months by smiles that were no longer associated with brain waves characteristic of REM sleep.

Subsequent research has shown that the visual system, including parts of the cerebral cortex that underpin vision, also undergoes important maturational changes between $2^{1}/_{2}$ and 3 months (Nelson, 2001). Some of these changes were mentioned in earlier sections of this chapter, such as the increased visual acuity associated with maturation of the eye. In addition, research has shown that during the second and third months of postnatal life there is a marked increase in the activity of the occipital and parietal lobes of the brain, both of which are involved in processing visual information. The improved visual capacity resulting from these biological changes permits babies to focus their eyes, and thus their smiles, on people, allowing earlier forms of smiling stimulated by the environment to become truly reciprocal, social smiling.

Social Contributions to Social Smiling

The importance of social feedback and reciprocity to the achievement of bio-social-behavioral shifts is dramatically demonstrated in research conducted on the development of congenitally blind infants. Like sighted infants, blind babies exhibit REM smiles. But unlike sighted infants, they may not exhibit the same shift to social smiling at $2^{1}/_{2}$ months. Since, under normal conditions of growth, the social

primary intersubjectivity The emotional sharing that occurs between very young infants and their caregivers. It is restricted to face-to-face communication.

smile depends both on increased visual capacity and on visual feedback from people who smile back, it seems that blind infants lack the feedback loop they need in order to develop social smiling. The frequent failure of blind infants to make the expected shift toward social smiling also means that their sighted parents cannot use their babies' facial expressions to gauge how their infants respond to them.

However, the absence of vision does not mean that blind infants cannot receive social feedback or that they cannot acquire social smiling. After all, for the most part, their brains are maturing like those of sighted children. The problem is that they cannot express their increased capacities in visually related ways. In the absence of this major channel for social feedback, parents must find alternative ways to interact with their blind children.

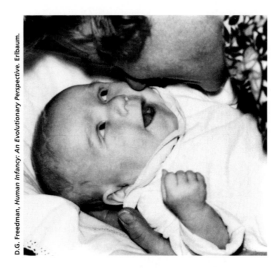

D.G. Freedman, *Human Infancy: An Evolutionary Perspective*. Erlbaum.

Blind infants and their parents interact in different ways, relying on sound and touch to communicate. Here, a blind infant's smile is prompted by the sound of her mother's voice in much the same way sighted infants might respond to the appearance of their parent's face.

The intuitive solution that some parents of blind children work out is to establish communication through touch. In her work with blind children, Selma Fraiberg (1974) noticed that many of these parents bounce, nudge, and tickle their children far more than the parents of sighted children. At first all this manipulation struck Fraiberg as socially abnormal, but then she noticed that the touching made the children smile and realized that tactile stimulation was a good substitute for the smiling face that elicits the smiles of sighted babies. Through touch the parents had found a way to get the feedback they needed from their infants—and to provide feedback the infants needed from them. Fraiberg used this observation to design a training program to help blind infants and their parents. Parents were taught to attend carefully to the way their children used their hands to signal their intentions and reactions. They were also taught to play with their babies' fingers and to provide rattles and other toys that would allow them and their babies to play together. Once the parents were able to provide the babies with appropriate feedback, the babies began to smile socially.

The success of Fraiberg's training program indicates that social smiling does not arise simply from the fact that an infant's brain has matured to the point where social smiling is possible. For social smiling to emerge, appropriate interaction with others is necessary; when this new behavior does emerge, a new emotional quality is able to develop between infants and their parents. As we will see in other periods of a child's life, development results from a complex interaction of biological, social, and behavioral changes. The notion of bio-social-behavioral shifts helps us to keep this important principle in mind.

Summing Up the First 2$^1/_2$ Months

Looking back over the first 2$^1/_2$ months or so of postnatal life, you can see a remarkable set of changes in infants' behaviors. Babies are born with a rudimentary ability to interact with their new environment. They have reflexes that enable them to take in oxygen and nutrients and expel waste products. They are able to perceive objects, including people, although they tend to focus on only a part of the entire stimulus. They are sensitive to the sounds of human language, and they quickly develop a preference for the sound of their mothers' voices. Although they sleep most of the time, they are occasionally quite alert.

The moment parents and their babies make eye contact is pleasurable for both parties.

From the moment of birth, infants interact with and are supported by their parents or other caregivers, who come equipped with the biological and cultural resources necessary to see that their babies receive food and protection. Despite these resources, the first interactions of babies and their caregivers are tentative and somewhat uncoordinated. Within a matter of days, however, a process of mutual adjustment has begun that will provide an essential framework for later development.

The developmental changes that characterize the first 10 to 12 weeks have clear origins in biology and in both the physical and the sociocultural environments. In the domain of biology, there is rapid maturation of the central nervous system, particularly in the connections between the brain stem and the cerebral cortex. As a consequence of frequent feeding, the baby grows bigger and stronger. As a consequence of practice at feeding, the elementary reflex of sucking becomes efficient nursing, an accomplishment that owes a good deal to the complementary efforts of the baby's caregivers, primarily the mother.

Between the ages of $2^1/_2$ and 3 months, several lines of development that have been proceeding more or less independently now converge. The consequences are qualitatively different forms of behavior and a new type of social relationship between babies and their caregivers. The story of the development of the seemingly simple behavior of social smiling illustrates the intricate way in which these different lines of development must relate to one another for a transition to a qualitatively new level of development to occur:

1. Maturation of the visual system enables a new level of visual acuity and a new ability to analyze the visual field.

2. As a consequence, smiling, a seemingly unrelated behavior, may be transformed.

3. With the advent of social smiling, parents report that they experience a new sense of connectedness with their babies, and babies begin to express a new emotion, joy.

This transformation will take place only if proper feedback is provided by the social world. Without appropriate feedback, as in the case of some blind children, social smiling does not develop. And if social smiling does not develop, the development of social interactions may be disrupted.

In later chapters you will see versions of this pattern repeated again and again. For a stretch of time the child's overall level of development remains stable while various systems undergo changes in relative isolation. Then there is a brief period during which these separate lines of development converge, resulting in a new level of organization with regard to the child's behaviors, the social reciprocity between child and caregiver, and the range of emotions that the child expresses. Later in life it will not always be possible with equal certainty and rigor to identify the specific biological, social, and behavioral factors that contribute to the emergence of new stages of development. But as a means of keeping the whole child in mind, it is always useful to consider the various domains that enter into the process of developmental change.

S U M M A R Y

Development of the Brain

- At birth the brain contains most of the cells (neurons) it will ever have, but it will become four times larger by adulthood.

- Increased size results primarily from an increase in the connections among neurons and increased myelination, which insulates axons and speeds transmission of impulses.

- Different parts of the brain develop at different rates throughout childhood. The brain stem, which initially controls most reflexes, is relatively mature at birth. Areas of the cortex that mature most rapidly following birth are the primary motor and sensory areas.

Sensing and Responding to the Environment

- Infants are born with remarkable sensory and behavioral capacities with which to experience and respond to their postnatal circumstances.

  1. Neonates are not able to hear sounds in the range of frequencies that are audible to older children and adults, but they display a special sensitivity to the basic sound categories of human language.

  2. Although infants are nearsighted, they systematically scan their surroundings and are sensitive to areas of high contrast between light and dark. They will track moving facelike forms at birth, and within a few days they seem to be able to distinguish their mothers' faces from those of others.

  3. Neonates can distinguish various tastes and smells. They prefer sweet tastes, and their sense of smell is sufficiently acute that they can distinguish the smell of their mothers' milk from that of other women.

  4. The senses of touch, temperature, and position are relatively mature at birth.

- A variety of response mechanisms are present at birth, including reflexes, imitation, and visually initiated reaching.

- Several sensory and response processes appear to be coordinated at or near birth.

The Qualities of Infant Experience and Behavior

- At birth infants display at least two primary emotional states: contentment and distress. Many developmentalists believe that they also experience several basic emotions—joy, fear, anger, surprise, sadness, and interest—although there is some doubt about whether or not such emotions have the same quality as do those experienced by older children and adults.

- Individual variations in temperament—in style of response and dominant mood—are present at birth. Temperamental characteristics include activity level, irritability, intensity of reaction, response to novelty, and sociability. Individual differences in certain aspects of temperament may be relatively stable and thus may constitute an important source of developmental continuity.

Becoming Coordinated with the Social World

- The basic behavioral capacities with which infants are born are sufficient for their survival only if they are coordinated with adult caregiving activities.

- "Getting the baby on a schedule" is more than a convenience. By coordinating schedules, babies and their parents create a system of mutual expectations that supports further development.

- Newborn babies sleep approximately two-thirds of the time, but their periods of sleep are relatively brief and are distributed across all 24 hours of the day. When babies finally begin to sleep through the night depends in part on the sleep patterns of the adults who care for them, and those patterns vary from culture to culture.

- Newborn babies tend to eat about every 3 hours if they are given constant access to food. Babies fed only every 4 hours may have trouble adjusting to such a schedule, although most infants adopt a 4-hour schedule spontaneously by the time they reach $2^1/_2$ months of age.

- Infants' crying is a primitive means of communication that evokes a strong emotional response in adults and alerts them that something may be wrong. Certain distinctive patterns of early cries may indicate difficulties.

Mechanisms of Developmental Change

- In the beginning, feeding is based on primitive reflex mechanisms that are not well coordinated. Within several weeks, this form of behavior is reorganized and becomes voluntary; the various constituent reflexes become integrated with one another, and the baby becomes well coordinated with the mother.

- The four basic perspectives on development can all be applied to the earliest forms of infant development; each emphasizes a different way in which biological and environmental factors contribute to early developmental change.

- According to the biological-maturation perspective, postnatal development follows the same principles as prenatal development. New structures are said to arise from endogenous (inherited) capabilities that unfold as the baby matures. Changes in nursing as well as in other behaviors, according to this view, result from such factors as the increased myelination of neurons and the growth of muscles.

● The maturation of brain structures contributes to the reorganization of early reflexes. Some of these early reflexes disappear completely within a few months of birth. Others may disappear and then reappear later as an element in a new form of activity. Still others remain and are transformed into voluntary behaviors under the control of the cerebral cortex.

● Environmental-learning theories assign the environment a leading role in the creation of new forms of behavior through the mechanism of learning.

● Infants' ability to learn from experience is present from the earliest days of life. Classical conditioning permits infants to form expectations about the connections between events in their environment. Operant conditioning provides a mechanism for the emergence of new behaviors as a consequence of the positive or negative events behaviors produce. Some evidence indicates that young infants can exhibit some kinds of imitation, but it seems unlikely that imitation is an important mechanism of learning in the first months of life.

● Constructivist theories assign equal weight to biological and environmental factors in development. Reflexes, in this view, are coordinated patterns of action (schemas) that have differentiated from the more primitive state of global activity characteristic of the prenatal period.

● In the view of Jean Piaget, the leading constructivist of the twentieth century, developmental change is constructed through the interplay of assimilation (modification of the input to fit existing schemas) and accommodation (modification of existing schemas to fit the input). The interplay of assimilation and accommodation continues until a new form of equilibrium between the two processes is reached. New forms of equilibrium constitute qualitatively new forms of behavior; they are new stages of development.

● According to Piaget, infancy is characterized by sensorimotor ways of knowing. He divides the sensorimotor period into six substages, the first two of which occur during the first 10 to 12 weeks of postnatal life:

  1. Substage 1 is characterized by the exercise of basic reflexes.

  2. Substage 2 is characterized by the beginning of accommodation and the prolongation of pleasant sensations arising from reflex actions.

● Cultural-context theories of development emphasize the active roles of both the child and the people around the child, as well as the historically accumulated "designs for living," as contributors to the process of developmental change.

● Significant and pervasive cultural variations in parents' everyday activities and their interactions with their newborn children influence both short-term and long-term development.

Integrating the Separate Threads of Development

● In order to explain development, it is necessary to understand how different parts of the process change with respect to one another, as parts of an integrated bio-social-behavioral system in its cultural context.

The First Postnatal Bio-Social-Behavioral Shift

● At approximately $2\frac{1}{2}$ months of age a bio-social-behavioral shift occurs in the overall organization of infants' behavior. Changes in brain function owing to maturation are accompanied by increased visual acuity and the ability to perceive the forms of objects and people, increased wakefulness, and social smiling. Caregivers respond with new feelings of connectedness to the infant.

Key Terms

accommodation, p. 150

adaptation, p. 150

assimilation, p. 150

axon, p. 115

brain stem, p. 117

cerebral cortex, p. 118

classical conditioning, p. 147

conditional response (CR), p. 148

conditional stimulus (CS), p. 148

dendrite, p. 115

dishabituation, p 120

emotion, p. 134

equilibration, p. 151

experience-dependent, p. 116

experience-expectant, p. 116

habituation, p. 120

intermodal perception, p. 133

learning, p. 147

myelin, p. 115

neuron, p. 114

neurotransmitter, p. 115

operant conditioning, p. 148

phonemes, p. 121

primary circular reaction, p. 152

primary intersubjectivity, p. 158

primary motor area, p. 119

primary sensory areas, p. 119

reflex, p. 128

reinforcement, p. 149

schema, p. 150

sensorimotor stage, p. 152

spinal cord, p. 117

synapse, p. 115

synaptic pruning, p. 116

synaptogenesis, p. 115

temperament, p. 136

unconditional response (UCR), p. 148

unconditional stimulus (UCS), p. 148

Thought Questions

1. In the quote at the chapter's opening, Erik Erikson writes, "Babies control and bring up their families as much as they are controlled by them." Explain this statement.

2. Many years ago William James characterized infants' perceptual world as a "buzzing, blooming confusion." How does this description fare in light of recent research on the perceptual world of the young infant?

3. What is the developmental significance of "getting on a schedule"?

4. List the ways in which neonatal development is continuous with development before birth. List the ways in which it is discontinuous.

5. Explain the development of social smiling at $2\frac{1}{2}$ to 3 months of age. Why is this development a good example of a bio-social-behavioral shift?

The Achievements of the First Year

> "The question . . . is not where or when mind begins. Mind in some . . . form is there from the start, wherever 'there' may be."
>
> —Jerome Bruner, In Search of Mind

Two neighbors—Jake, who is about to celebrate his first birthday, and his mother, Barbara—have been out for a walk and have stopped by the Coles's house. Sheila is in the kitchen preparing dinner. Jake is sitting on his mother's lap at the kitchen table, drinking apple juice from a plastic cup while the two women chat. Jake finishes his juice, some of which has dribbled onto his shirt, and puts the cup down on the table with a satisfied bang. He squirms around in his mother's lap so that he is facing her. He tries to get her attention by pulling at her face. When Barbara ignores him, Jake wriggles out of her lap to the floor, where he notices the dog.

"Wuff wuff," he says excitedly, pointing at the dog.

"Doggie," Barbara says. "What does the doggie say, Jake?"

"Wuff wuff," Jake repeats, still staring at the dog.

Following his pointing finger, Jake toddles toward the dog. His walk has a drunken, side-to-side quality, and he has a hard time bringing himself to a stop. Barbara grabs hold of Jake's extended hand, redirecting it from the dog's eyes.

"Pat the doggie, Jake."

Jake pats the dog's head.

The dog does not like the attention and escapes into the living room. Jake toddles after her like a pull toy on an invisible string. The dog leads him back into the kitchen, where Jake bumps into Sheila's legs and falls to a sitting position.

"Well, hello, Jake," Sheila says, as she bends over and picks him up. "Did you fall down? Go boom?"

Jake, who until now hasn't taken his eyes off the dog, turns, looks at Sheila with a smile, and points at the dog. "Wuff wuff," he repeats.

Then Jake's body suddenly stiffens. He stares searchingly at Sheila's face for an instant and then turns his head away and holds his arms out to his mother.

Sheila hands Jake to Barbara, who says, "Did you get scared? It's only Sheila."

But Jake eyes Sheila warily and hides in his mother's arms for several minutes.

At almost 1 year of age, Jake behaves far differently than a newborn. At that earlier age, Jake's main activities were eating, sleeping, and gazing around the room. He could hold his head up and turn it from side to side, but he could not readily reach out and grasp objects or move around on his own. He took an interest in mobiles and other objects when they were immediately in front of him, but he quickly lost interest in them when they were removed from his view. Although he seemed most comfortable with his mother, he did not seem particularly unhappy when he was cared for by someone else. His communications were restricted to cries, frowns, and smiles.

The contrast between Jake's behavior then and his behavior at 1 year gives you a picture of some of the amazing changes that occur in the first year of infancy and presents a challenge to the developmentalists who seek to explain them. Perhaps

Penny Tweedie/Tony Stone Worldwide

Figure 5.1 The differences in size, strength, shape, and motor control between small infants and babies in their second year are evident in the contrast between the infant supported in this mother's arms and the older infant beginning to use a mortar and pestle.

most obvious are the outwardly visible biological changes (see Figure 5.1). Infants are markedly larger and stronger at 12 months than at $2^1/_2$ months. Invisible but essential maturation has also taken place in the central nervous system, particularly the cerebral cortex and other parts of the brain.

Largely as a result of these changes, infants become more coordinated and better able to move about. At 3 months infants are just beginning to be able to roll over. Their parents know that they will remain more or less wherever they are put down. At about 7 to 8 months they begin to crawl, and at about 1 year they begin to walk. All during this period, infants also become much more adept at reaching for objects and grasping them. They prod, bang, squeeze, push, and pull almost anything they can get their hands on, and they often put objects into their mouths to learn about them. As infants' mobility and curiosity about the world increase, their parents must constantly watch to keep them out of harm's way.

Important changes have also occurred in their cognitive abilities. Older babies learn more rapidly and remember what they have learned for longer periods of time. They have expanded the rudimentary categories they use to interpret their experiences to an astonishing degree. They anticipate the course of simple, familiar behavioral routines, and they act surprised if their expectations are violated. This new understanding of events makes it possible for them to play simple games such as peekaboo.

Finally, the social and emotional relationship between infants and their caregivers changes in significant ways toward the end of the first year. Infants become upset when they are separated from their caregivers, and sometimes they are wary of strangers, as Jake was when he noticed Sheila. They also begin to check their caregivers' facial expressions for indications of how to behave in uncertain situations, and they can understand a few words, which increases their ability to coordinate with their caregivers.

As you shall see, these changes in biological makeup, motor behavior, cognitive capacities, range of emotions, and forms of social relationship come together to produce another bio-social-behavioral shift in development as babies approach their first birthdays. The new qualities that emerge from this reorganization of developmental processes set the conditions for further changes that will bring children to the end of infancy.

Biological Growth

The extensive changes that occur in babies' motor behavior and cognitive abilities between the ages of $2^1/_2$ months and 1 year depend on changes in their body proportions, muscles, bones, and brains. These changes are connected both with each other and with the development of the new behavioral capacities babies display. For example, their greater weight requires larger and stronger bones to support them and strong muscles to enable movement. Their developing cognitive capacities make them want to explore new aspects of the world, but to do so requires that they coordinate their constantly changing size and strength in new ways.

Size and Shape

During their first year, most healthy babies triple in weight and grow approximately 10 inches, with the typical 1-year-old in the United States weighing about 20 pounds and standing 28 to 30 inches tall. As Figure 5.2 shows, the rate of physical growth is greatest in the first months after birth; it then gradually tapers off through the rest of infancy and childhood until adolescence, when there is a noticeable growth spurt.

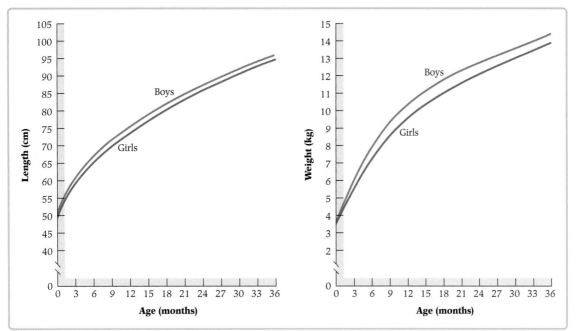

Figure 5.2 U.S. babies' lengths roughly double and their weights increase by five or six times during the first 3 years of life. Note that at this stage, boys tend, on average, to be heavier and taller than girls. (Adapted from the Centers for Disease Control, 2000.)

While it is possible to create norms for children's growth, such as those depicted in Figure 5.2, by using large samples of children, individual children normally grow at widely varying rates (Tanner, 1998). Many factors contribute to the variations in size and shape, including children's diet, genetic constitution, and socioeconomic status (Ruel & Menon, 2002) (see Figure 5.3).

Increases in babies' height and weight are accompanied by changes in their body proportions (see Figure 5.4, p. 168). At birth the baby's head is 70 percent of its adult size and accounts for about 25 percent of the baby's total length. At 1 year of age the head will account for 20 percent of body length, and by adulthood, 12 percent. Infants' legs at birth are not much longer than their heads; by adulthood the legs account for about half of a person's total height. By 12 months the changes in body proportions have led to a lower center of gravity, making it easier for the child to balance on two legs and begin to walk (Thelen, 2002).

Figure 5.3 Environmental conditions play an important role in infant growth. Babies born in Malawi, a country in southeast Africa, face conditions such as widespread malnutrition, chronic poverty, disease, and a rising HIV/AIDS infection rate. As a result of this complicated array of factors, Malawian infants grow at a slower rate than their American counterparts. These graphs show height and weight curves for the 50th percentile of Malawian and American children. Compared to their American counterparts, the Malawian children were on average 2.5 cm (1 inch) shorter and 510 g (1.12 pounds) lighter. (Adapted from Maleta, 2003.)

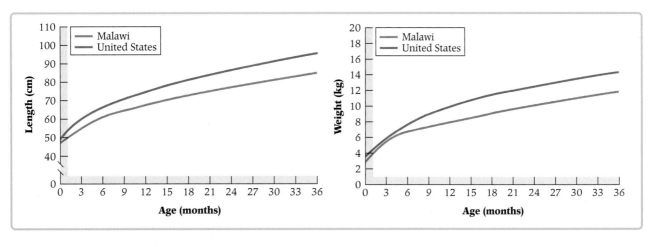

Figure 5.4 The proportions of body length accounted for by the head, trunk, and legs at different stages of development. During the fetal period, the head accounts for as much as 50 percent of body length The head decreases from 25 percent of body length at birth to 12 percent in adulthood. (From Robbins et al., 1929.)

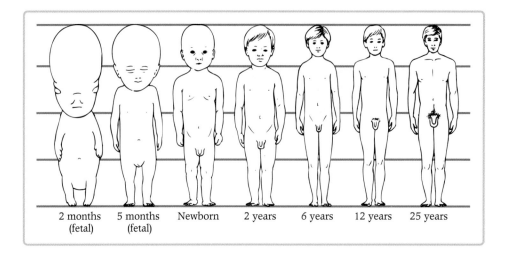

| 2 months (fetal) | 5 months (fetal) | Newborn | 2 years | 6 years | 12 years | 25 years |

Muscle and Bone

As babies grow, the bones and muscles needed to support their increasing bulk and mobility undergo corresponding growth. Most of a newborn's bones are relatively soft, and they harden (ossify) only gradually as minerals are deposited in them in the months after birth. The bones in the hand and wrist are among the first to ossify. They harden by the end of the first year, making it easier for a baby to grasp objects, pick them up, and play with them.

At the same time, infants' muscles increase in length and thickness, a process that will continue throughout childhood and into late adolescence. In infancy, increases in muscle mass are closely associated with the development of the baby's ability to crawl, stand alone, and walk.

Sex Differences in Rates of Growth

Although, as Figure 5.2 clearly indicates, boys are generally larger than girls, research supports the common wisdom that girls mature faster than boys. In fact, sex differences in growth rate are apparent even before birth. Halfway through the prenatal period, the skeletons of female fetuses are some 3 weeks more advanced in development than those of male fetuses. At birth, X rays of the growth centers *(epiphyses)* at the ends of bones show that the female's skeleton is 4 to 6 weeks more mature than the male's, and by puberty it is 2 years more advanced. Girls are more advanced in the development of other organ systems as well. They get their permanent teeth, go through puberty, and reach their full body size earlier than boys (Bogin, 1999).

The Brain

The entire nervous system continues to grow in size and complexity between the ages of 3 and 12 months. Especially noteworthy is an increase in the number of synapses, which reach a level of density roughly double what it will be by early adolescence. This growth in synaptic density is so rapid and extensive that it has been given a special name, **exuberant synaptogenesis** (Huttenlocher & Dabholkar, 1997). Developmentalists believe that the brain massively overproduces synapses and that, over time, these synapses are either selectively reinforced or eliminated, depending on the individual's experience. This idea fits closely with the Darwinian idea that evolution proceeds by a process of random reproduction and subsequent natural selection. As a result of the early overproduction of synapses, infants are prepared to establish neural connections for virtually any kind of experience they may have. Over time, the environment makes its contribution: synapses

exuberant synaptogenesis The rapid growth in synaptic density that occurs between 3 and 12 months of age.

that are regularly used flourish and are strengthened, while those that go unused are gradually "pruned away"—that is, they atrophy and die off.

Each region of the brain develops at a different rate (another example of developmental *heterochrony*). As you read in Chapter 4, at $2\frac{1}{2}$ to 4 months of age the visual cortex undergoes an explosive surge in the creation of new synapses, which appears to be crucial to the changes associated with the first bio-social-behavioral shift at $2\frac{1}{2}$ to 3 months of age (see Chapter 4, p. 157). Changes in the auditory cortex follow a similar pattern (Johnson, 2001). This pattern occurs somewhat later in other areas of the brain. The motor cortex undergoes exuberant synaptogenesis around 6 months of age, followed by the prefrontal and frontal cortexes at about 9 months of age. The prefrontal and frontal cortexes continue to develop at least well into adolescence (Bell, 2001; Huttenlocher, 2002).

The prefrontal area of the cortex plays a particularly important role in the development of voluntary behavior. When this area begins to function in a new way sometime between 7 and 9 months, infants' ability to regulate themselves increases and they can, for example, stop themselves from grabbing the first attractive thing they see. With the emerging ability to inhibit action, they can also better control what they attend to. In effect, they begin to be able to stop and think (Diamond, 2000; Stevens, Quittner, Zuckerman & Moore, 2002).

Perception and Movement

One of the most dramatic developments following the bio-social-behavioral shift between 2 and 3 months is the enormous increase in infants' ability to explore their environment by looking, moving around, listening, and manipulating. As we emphasized in Chapter 4 (p. 128), changes in perceiving and acting are intimately connected. For example, it would be nearly impossible for babies to move from one place to another if their coordinated motor actions were not constantly modified in light of perceptual information about the layout of the environment and their current spatial position. Infants, no less than adults, perceive in order to obtain information about how to act and then act in order to perceive (Gibson & Pick, 2000).

Figure 5.5 In the first months after birth, eye–hand coordination takes effort. (*top*) Here, a $2\frac{1}{2}$-month-old reaches out and tries unsuccessfully to grasp a pacifier. (*bottom*) A 9-month-old baby reaches and successfully grasps an object.

Reaching and Grasping

Remember from Chapter 4 (p. 132) that shortly after birth infants begin reaching for an object moving in front of them, a reflexlike motion we referred to as visually *initiated* reaching. At this initial stage, the perceptions and actions involved in reaching and grasping are not yet coordinated. Infants may reach for an object but fail to close their hands around it, usually because they close their hands too soon. Then, as a part of the bio-social-behavioral shift at about $2\frac{1}{2}$ months, babies begin to gain voluntary control over their movements, so reaching and grasping occur in the proper sequence. At first, their reaching and grasping is pretty much a hit-and-miss affair (von Hofsten, 2001). With practice, their perceptual–motor coordination gradually improves, although there are marked individual differences in the rapidity and vigor of their reaching movements (see Figure 5.5). At about 5 months of age, infants can gauge when an object is beyond their reach, and they no longer attempt to reach for it. By the time they are 9 months old, most babies can guide their movements with a single glance, and the movements they use to reach for and grasp objects look as well integrated and automatic as a reflex (Smitsman, 2001). This is the time when caretakers need to "babyproof" their homes by putting dangerous or fragile objects out of the infant's reach. They also have to watch out for the sudden appearance of unexpected items in the grocery cart if the baby is along for the ride.

Laura Dwight/Omni-Photo Communications, Inc.

Elizabeth Crews/The Image Works

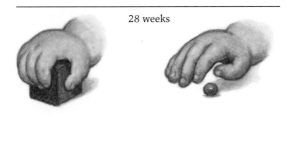

28 weeks

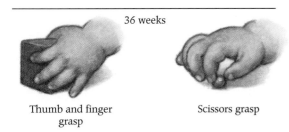

36 weeks

Thumb and finger grasp

Scissors grasp

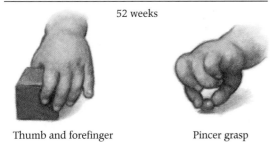

52 weeks

Thumb and forefinger grasp

Pincer grasp

Figure 5.6 Babies find ways to grasp objects from an early age, but good coordination of the thumb and forefinger requires at least a year to achieve. (Adapted from Halverson, 1931.)

In the period between 7 and 12 months of age, fine motor movements of the hands and fingers become better coordinated. As shown in Figure 5.6, 7-month-olds are still unable to use their thumbs in opposition to their fingers to pick up objects, but by 12 months babies are able to move their thumbs and other fingers into positions appropriate to the size of the object they are trying to grasp. As their reaching and grasping become better coordinated and more precise, babies' explorations of objects become more refined. They are increasingly able to do such things as drink from a cup, eat with a spoon, and pick raisins out of a box (Connolly & Dalgleish, 1989).

Rachel Karniol (1989) found a regular sequence in the way babies manipulate objects as their fine motor skills increase during the first 9 months of life. They begin by simply rotating an object and then progress to moving it, shaking it, and holding it with one and then two hands, until they can use it as part of a sequence of actions to achieve a goal such as placing a block into a hole in a box. Such sequences lend support to theories that view development as a series of qualitative changes in the organization of the biology and behavior of the child.

With respect to the exploratory behaviors themselves, Eleanor Gibson (1988) points out that as babies gain control over their hands, different objects invite them to explore in different ways: "Things can be displaced, banged, shaken, squeezed, and thrown—actions that have informative consequences about an object's properties" (p. 20). Rattles, for example, lend themselves to making noises, while soft dolls lend themselves to pleasurable touching. Studies of the development of reaching and grasping leave little doubt that babies learn about the different properties of the objects in their environment as their ability to grip and manipulate them improves (Bushnell & Boudreau, 1991). Perceptual–motor exploration is an all-important way to find out about the environment and to gain control over it (see Figure 5.7).

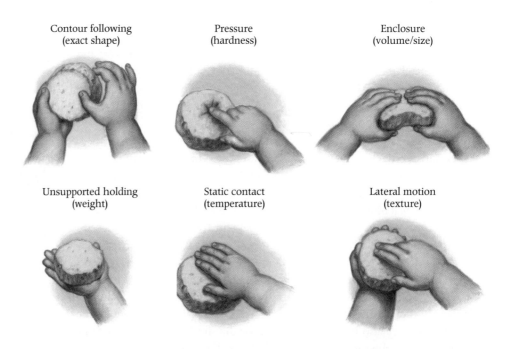

Contour following (exact shape)

Pressure (hardness)

Enclosure (volume/size)

Unsupported holding (weight)

Static contact (temperature)

Lateral motion (texture)

Figure 5.7 The objects that children explore differ from each other in many ways. As they begin to move about and explore the world, children must learn a large variety of hand movements and shapes in order to explore their worlds effectively. (Adapted from Bushnell & Boudreau, 1991.)

Locomotion

Progress in **locomotion,** the ability to move around on one's own, is central to the pattern of developmental changes that occur toward the end of the first year of postnatal life. The ability to get around on their own separates infants from their caregivers in a distinctive way that changes the basic conditions for their further development. Locomotion also provides babies with a wider field for exploration of the objects in their environment. They can now approach, crawl away from, reach for, manipulate, or push away things that interest or frighten them.

locomotion The ability to move around on one's own.

Before infants can move around the environment effectively, however, they must be able to integrate the movements of many parts of their bodies. Motor control of the body begins at the head and neck and then proceeds gradually to the trunk and legs (the *cephalocaudal* pattern of development). An important milestone enabling increased exploration of the environment between 3 and 12 months of age is the ability to sit up unaided (see Table 5.1). Independent sitting frees the hands to carry out the kinds of manipulations depicted in Figures 5.6 and 5.7.

During the first month of life, when movements appear to be controlled primarily by subcortical areas of the brain, infants may occasionally creep short distances, propelled by the rhythmic pushing movements of their toes or knees (see Figure 5.8, p.172). At about 2 months of age this reflexive pushing disappears, and it will be another 5 or 6 months before babies can crawl about on their hands and knees (Adolph et al., 1998).

Most infants can crawl on regular surfaces with some skill by the time they are 8 to 9 months of age, when the various components of crawling are knitted into the well-coordinated action of the whole body. The onset of crawling has a wide range of effects on infants and their families, to which we will return at the end of this chapter (pp. 196–197). For the present, consider how crawling allows babies to explore their environment in a new way, acquiring new information about the world and changing how they respond to it.

One manifestation of infants' new ability to explore and respond to the environment is their wariness of heights, which typically appears between 7 and 9 months of age among American children (Scarr & Salapatek, 1970). This wariness is demonstrated by means of a "visual cliff," a transparent platform that gives the

table 5.1

Age (in Months) at Which Infants Reach Milestones in Motor Development

Note the wide variations in the ages at which normal children are able to perform the various behaviors. Although 50 percent of the babies studied could sit without support by the time they were just over 5.5 months old, for example, some 8 percent were not able to sit unaided until more than 2 months later.

Motor Milestone	Percentage That Have Reached Milestone			
	25%	50%	75%	90%
Lifts head up	1.3	2.2	2.6	3.2
Rolls over	2.3	2.8	3.8	4.7
Sits without support	4.8	5.5	6.5	7.8
Pulls self to stand	6.0	7.6	9.5	10.0
Walks holding on to furniture	7.3	9.2	10.2	12.7
Walks well	11.3	12.1	13.3	14.3
Walks up steps	14.0	17.0	21.0	22.0
Kicks ball forward	15.0	20.0	22.3	24.0

Source: Frankenburg et al., 1981.

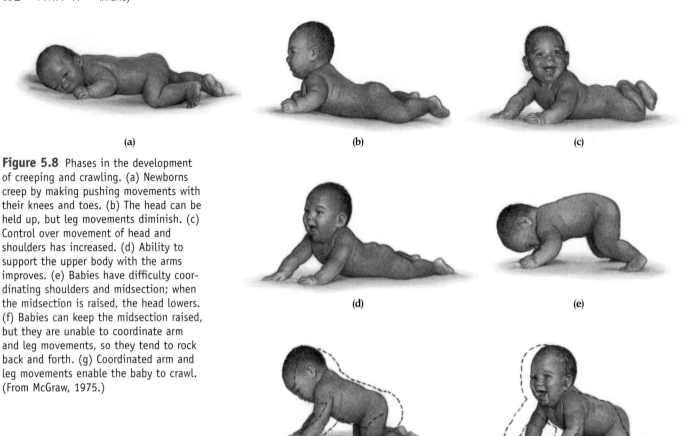

(a) (b) (c)

(d) (e)

(f) (g)

Figure 5.8 Phases in the development of creeping and crawling. (a) Newborns creep by making pushing movements with their knees and toes. (b) The head can be held up, but leg movements diminish. (c) Control over movement of head and shoulders has increased. (d) Ability to support the upper body with the arms improves. (e) Babies have difficulty coordinating shoulders and midsection; when the midsection is raised, the head lowers. (f) Babies can keep the midsection raised, but they are unable to coordinate arm and leg movements, so they tend to rock back and forth. (g) Coordinated arm and leg movements enable the baby to crawl. (From McGraw, 1975.)

illusion of a sharp drop in elevation (see Figure 5.9). Typically, on the first few trials all infants crawl across the cliff, without hesitation. On subsequent trials over the next several weeks, however, the infants become increasingly reluctant to cross over the visual cliff, even though nothing bad has happened when they crossed over it before. Something seemed to be building up in the infants' minds as they gained experience. But what was building up, and what experience was causing it?

Joseph Campos and his colleagues noted that 7 to 9 months is also the typical time when babies begin to crawl. They hypothesized that the experience of moving around made possible by crawling is an important reason that babies begin to show wariness about heights. To confirm their hypothesis, Campos and his colleagues conducted a number of experiments to see if locomotion really influenced wariness of heights. For an early experiment, the researchers located 92 infants who were near the age at which they might be expected to start crawling and begin showing a fear of heights (Campos et al., 1992). The infants were then divided into experimental and control groups. Over several days the infants in the experimental group were given

Figure 5.9 A baby hesitates at the edge of a visual cliff, a transparent platform that makes it appear to the baby that there is a sharp drop just ahead.

more than 40 hours of experience moving about in baby walkers before they learned to crawl (see Figure 5.10). The children in the control group were provided with no special experience in locomoting.

Forty hours of careening around a room in a walker may not seem like a lot of experience, but it apparently made a big difference in the way the infants in the experimental group responded to the visual cliff. Although responses varied somewhat, in general the infants in the experimental group showed fear on their first exposure to the visual cliff, whereas the infants in the control group did not, supporting the researchers' hypothesis that movement like that associated with crawling may affect other areas of infant behavior, such as fear of heights.

Campos and his colleagues have confirmed the central role of locomotion for psychological development using a variety of techniques, including observational studies of American children in their homes, the study of children growing up in China in tiny apartments where they had no space to crawl, and the study of children who suffer from central nervous system damage that restricts their movement (this research is summarized in Campos et al., 2000). We will return to discuss the implications of this research later in this chapter (pp. 196–197).

The Role of Practice in Motor Development

Studies of motor development were among developmentalists' earliest strategies for discovering the relative roles of nature and nurture. During the 1930s and 1940s it was commonly believed that learning and experience played little or no role in the development of such motor milestones as sitting and walking. One of the studies cited to support this view was conducted by Wayne and Margaret Dennis among Hopi families in the southwestern United States (Dennis & Dennis, 1940).

In traditional Hopi families, babies are wrapped up tightly and strapped to a flat cradle board for the first several months of life. They are unwrapped only once or twice a day so that they can be washed and their clothes can be changed. The wrapping permits very little movement of the arms and legs and no practice in such complex movements as rolling over. The Dennises compared the motor development of traditionally raised Hopi babies with that of the babies of less traditional parents who did not use cradle boards. The two groups of babies did not differ in the age at which they began to walk by themselves, which is consistent with the notion that this basic motor skill does not depend on practice for its development.

Observations of babies from other cultural settings, however, provide evidence that practice can have an effect on the age at which babies reach motor milestones and that it may even alter the sequence of changes. Charles Super (1976) reported that among the Kipsigis people of rural Kenya, parents begin to teach their babies to sit up, stand, and walk shortly after birth. In teaching their children to sit up, for example, Kipsigis parents seat their babies in shallow holes in the ground that they have dug to support the infants' backs, or they nestle blankets around them to hold them upright. They repeat such procedures daily until the babies can sit up quite well by themselves. Training in walking begins in the eighth week. The babies are held under the arms with their feet touching the ground and are gradually propelled forward. Kipsigis babies reach the developmental milestones of sitting 5 weeks earlier and walking 3 weeks earlier, on the average, than babies in the United States. At the same time they are not advanced in skills they have not been taught or have not practiced. They learn to roll over or crawl no faster than American children, and they lag behind American children in their ability to negotiate stairs. Similar results have been reported among West Indian and Camaroonian children, whose mothers put them

Figure 5.10 A walker exposes infants to the experience of locomotion before they learn to walk or crawl. How does using a walker influence performance on the visual cliff?

Martha Cooper

Library of Congress

Babies who are just beginning to stand up find other people and furniture to be handy aids. (*left*) The Filipino baby who lives in a house on stilts is being trained at an early age in the essential skill of climbing a ladder. (*right*) Here a Balinese child is holding on to the anthropologist Margaret Mead.

through a culturally prescribed sequence of motor exercises during the early months of infancy (Hopkins & Westen, 1988; Keller, 2003).

Further evidence for the impact that practice—or lack of it—can have on early motor development comes from the Ache, a nomadic people living in the rain forest of eastern Paraguay. Hilliard Kaplan and Heather Dove (1987) reported that Ache children under 3 years of age spend 80 to 100 percent of their time in direct physical contact with their mothers and are almost never seen more than 3 feet away from them. A major reason is that Ache hunter-gatherer groups do not create clearings in the forest when they stop to make camp. Rather, they remove just enough ground cover to make room to sit down, leaving roots, trees, and bushes more or less where they found them. For safety's sake, mothers either carry their infants or keep them within arm's reach.

Ache infants perform at North American norms on various tests of social ability, but they are markedly slower to acquire gross motor skills such as walking. They begin walking, on the average, at about 23 months of age, almost a full year later than children in the United States. At about the age of 5, however, when Ache children are deemed old enough to be allowed to move around on their own, they begin to spend many hours in complex play activities that serve to increase their motor skills. Within a few years they are skilled at climbing tall trees and at cutting vines and branches while they balance high above the ground in a manner that bespeaks normal, perhaps even exceptional, perceptual–motor skills.

The recent cultural change in the United States associated with the movement to eradicate SIDS (Chapter 4, p. 143) has had the unexpected effect of delaying the onset of crawling in North American babies by as much as 2 months or so (Davis, Moon, Sachs & Ottolini, 1998). Since time spent in the prone position (face down) provides babies with their earliest experiences of bearing their body weight with their arms, shifting their weight to reach for a toy, and trying out coordinated movements of their arms and legs, children who spend their waking as well as sleeping hours on their backs miss out on developmentally appropriate experience. As a consequence, pediatricians in the United States are urging parents to provide their young infants with "tummy time to play" so that they can practice pushing themselves up as a precursor to crawling (Pontius et al., 2001).

Cognitive Changes

From the studies of fetal development and the behavior of newborn infants reviewed in Chapters 3 and 4, it is clear that human babies, while helpless in many ways, are born with an impressive array of abilities for learning about the world they are entering. For example, they display a special sensitivity to human language and distinguish the particular language that surrounds them at birth from others; they immediately show a preference for human faces, the sources of that language; they need no special training to expect the sound and location of objects to coincide; and they arrive in the world equipped to coordinate with, and receive life-giving support from, their caretakers.

There is now massive evidence demonstrating that infants' **cognitive processes**—psychological processes through which humans acquire, retain, and use knowledge about the world—develop rapidly between 3 and 12 months of age. However, developmentalists are less certain about when particular cognitive milestones are achieved, and they are deeply divided about how the milestones are reached. Intensive research and debate concerning the development of 3- to 12-month-olds has centered on the following issues:

- When do young infants begin to understand that objects may exist even if they are out of sight, and what does this understanding tell us about the way they think?

- What other knowledge do young infants acquire very early in life, and what knowledge must they learn about through extensive experience?

- When and how do young infants become sensitive to the fact that different objects and events are members of different categories, and what kinds of categories do they recognize?

- How does infant knowledge of the world accumulate?

Underlying developmentalists' disagreements about these issues is uncertainty about the best methods for assessing cognitive changes in infants: How can you know what babies know and how they think if they cannot tell you?

Constructing a Stable World

Recall from Chapter 4 (pp. 152–153) that Piaget referred to infancy as the stage of *sensorimotor* development because of his belief that at this early age, infants acquire knowledge exclusively through motor actions that are directed at their immediate environment and guided by their sensory organs. He combined the terms "sensory" and "motor" to emphasize the intimate relationship between sensing the world and acting upon it. Each influences the other: what we perceive depends on what we are doing, and what we do depends on what we perceive (Piaget, 1973).

In order to understand Piaget's description of development, keep in mind his central idea that the endpoint of all cognitive stages is the emergence of a qualitatively new way of knowing. In the case of the stage of sensorimotor development this qualitative change comes to an end with the emergence of a new ability to picture the world mentally and think about an object or event *before* acting. He called this new way of thinking **representation.** Piaget believed that babies begin to represent objects mentally to themselves at about 8 months of age but that the representational ability does not become fully developed until they are 18 to 24 months of age.

As you saw in Chapter 4 (p. 150), it appeared to Piaget that infants have little or no understanding that objects even exist—all they know about is their own

cognitive processes Psychological processes through which children acquire, store, and use knowledge about the world.

representation The ability to picture the world mentally and think about an object or event in its absence

table 5.2

Sensorimotor Substages and the Development of Object Permanence			
Substage	**Age (months)**	**Characteristics of Sensorimotor Substage**	**Developments in Object Permanence**
1	0–1$\frac{1}{2}$	*Reflex schemas exercised:* involuntary rooting, sucking, grasping, looking	Infant does not search for objects that have been removed from sight.
2	1$\frac{1}{2}$–4	*Primary circular reactions:* repetition of actions that are pleasurable in themselves	Infant orients to place where objects have been removed from sight.
3	4–8	*Secondary circular reactions:* dawning awareness of relation of own actions to environment; extended actions that produce interesting changes in the environment	Infant will reach for a partially hidden object but stops if it disappears.
4	8–12	*Coordination of secondary circular reactions:* combining schemas to achieve a desired effect; earliest form of problem solving	Infant will search for a completely hidden object; keeps searching the original location of the object even if it is moved to another location in full view of the infant.
5	12–18	*Tertiary circular reactions:* deliberate variation of problem-solving means; experimentation to see what the consequences will be	Infant will search for an object after seeing it moved but not if it is moved in secret.
6	18–24	*Beginning of symbolic representation:* images and words come to stand for familiar objects; invention of new means of problem solving through symbolic combinations	Infant will search for a hidden object, certain that it exists somewhere.

actions. He believed that it is between the ages of 4 to 5 months and 12 months that infants start to form an idea of objects as part of an external reality. This cognitive growth occurs as they complete substages 3 and 4 of sensorimotor development (see Table 5.2). (You will read about substages 5 and 6 in Chapter 6.)

Substage 3: Secondary Circular Reactions (4 to 8 months)

In substage 3, 4- to 8-month-old infants begin to direct their attention to the external world—to objects and outcomes. This new interest in external things gives rise to a characteristic behavior observed in infants during this substage—the repetition of actions that produce interesting changes in the environment. Piaget termed these new actions **secondary circular reactions** because the focus of infants' actions is on objects external to themselves. When babies in this substage accidentally discover that a particular action, like squeezing a rubber toy, produces an interesting effect, such as squeaking, they repeat the action again and again to produce the effect. Similarly, when babies vocalize by cooing or gurgling and a caregiver responds, they repeat the sound they made. In each case, the reaction is not only "secondary" (it applies to something outside of itself) but "circular" (it produces its own feedback). This circularity remains a central characteristic of all interactions between children and their environments from this time on.

The change from primary circular reactions to secondary circular reactions indicated to Piaget that infants are beginning to realize that objects are more than an extension of their own actions. In this substage, however, babies still have only a rudimentary grasp of objects and space, and their discoveries about the world seem to have an accidental quality.

Substage 4: Coordination of Secondary Circular Reactions (8 to 12 months)

The hallmark of the fourth sensorimotor substage is the emergence of the ability to engage in behaviors directed toward achieving a goal, which Piaget called **intentionality.** He believed such behavior to be the earliest form of true problem solving.

Piaget's son, Laurent, provided a demonstration of intentional problem solving of this kind when he was 10 months old. Piaget had given him a small tin container, which Laurent dropped and picked up repeatedly (a secondary circular reaction characteristic of behavior in substage 3). Piaget then placed a washbasin a short distance from Laurent and struck it with the tin box, producing an interesting sound. From earlier observations, Piaget knew that Laurent would repeatedly bang on the basin to make the interesting sound occur (another typical secondary circular reaction). This time Piaget wanted to see if Laurent would combine the newly acquired "dropping the tin box" schema with the previously acquired "make an interesting sound" schema. Here is his report of Laurent's behavior:

> Now, at once, Laurent takes possession of the tin, holds out his arm and drops it over the basin. I moved the latter as a check. He nevertheless succeeded, several times in succession, in making the object fall on the basin. Hence this is a fine example of the coordination of two schemas of which the first serves as a "means" whereas the second assigns an end to the action. (Piaget, 1952b, p. 255)

In Piaget's view, it is as a result of traversing substages 3 and 4 of sensorimotor intelligence that infants become capable of intentional action directed at objects and people around them. However, these abilities come fully into play only when the objects and people in question are present to their senses.

The Emergence of Object Permanence

Piaget (1954) maintained that until substage 4 of sensorimotor development, infants live in a world in which objects come and go from their line of sight, each "a mere image which reenters the void as soon as it vanishes, and emerges from it for no apparent reason" (p. 11). If we interpret him literally, Piaget believed that for young babies, out of sight is literally out of mind.

Evidence that infants cannot keep absent objects in mind comes from observations of 5- and 6-month-old babies, as the following cases illustrate:

- *Observation 1.* A baby seated at a table is offered a soft toy. He grasps it. While he is still engrossed in the toy, the experimenter takes it from him and places it on the table behind a screen. The baby may begin to reach for the toy, but as soon as it disappears from sight he stops short, stares for a moment, and then looks away without attempting to move the screen (see Figure 5.11) (Piaget, 1954).

- *Observation 2.* A baby is placed in an infant seat in a bare laboratory room. Her mother, who has been playing with her, disappears for a moment. When the mother reappears, the baby sees three of her, an illusion the experimenter has created through the use of carefully arranged mirrors. The baby displays no surprise as she babbles happily to her multiple mother (Bower, 1982).

secondary circular reactions The behavior characteristic of the third substage of Piaget's sensorimotor stage, in which babies repeat actions to produce interesting changes in their environment.

intentionality The ability to engage in behaviors directed toward achieving a goal.

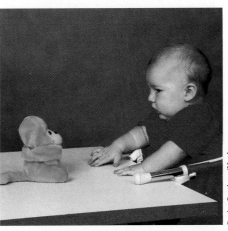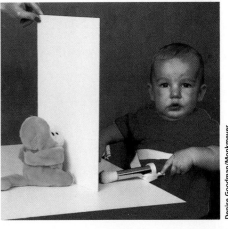

Figure 5.11 Instead of searching behind the screen when his toy disappears, this infant looks dumbfounded. This kind of behavior led Piaget to conclude that objects no longer in view cease to exist for infants younger than 8 months of age.

Denise Goodman/Monkmeyer

object permanence The understanding that objects have substance, maintain their identities when they change location, and ordinarily continue to exist when out of sight.

• *Observation 3.* From the comfort of his mother's lap, a baby follows a toy train with his eyes as it chugs along a track (see Figure 5.12). When the train disappears into a tunnel, the child's eyes remain fixed on the tunnel's entrance rather than following the train's expected progress through the tunnel. When the train reappears at the other end of the tunnel, it takes the child a few seconds to catch up with it visually, and the child shows no surprise when the train that comes out of the tunnel is a different color or shape (Bower, 1982).

Piaget maintained that infants respond in this manner because they cannot represent the object to themselves when it is out of sight. He believed that the ability to understand that objects continue to exist when they are out of sight **(object permanence)** is demonstrated only after infants begin actively to search for the absent object, as when—in a classic Piagetian test—they uncover a toy they have just seen the experimenter hide under a cloth or behind a barrier. According to Piaget, this ability first appears at around 8 months of age.

Initially, however, infants' mastery of object permanence is incomplete. In searching for objects that have disappeared from view, babies between 8 and 12 months tend to make a characteristic mistake: if, after they have successfully searched for an object hidden in one location, the object is then hidden in a new location right before their eyes, they will still search for the object where they previously found it.

Suppose, for example, an object is hidden under cover A and the baby is allowed to retrieve it. Then, in full view of the baby, the object is placed under cover B.

Figure 5.12 Infants who have yet to gain a firm understanding of object permanence, according to Piaget's criteria, fail to track the motion of a toy train when it enters a tunnel. (From Bower 1979.)

Infant watches train approach tunnel.

Infant watches train enter tunnel.

Infant's eyes remain fixed on tunnel's entrance.

Infant notices train moving away from tunnel.

All photos: Adele Diamond

Figure 5.13 In this movie sequence, an object is placed in the circle on the left (position B), and then both circles (positions A and B) are covered with a cloth while the baby watches. In a previous trial, the object had been placed in the right-hand circle (position A), and the baby had correctly retrieved it. This time, while remaining oriented toward the hidden object at position B, the baby nonetheless picks up the cloth at position A, where the object was hidden before. (Courtesy of A. Diamond.)

When allowed to retrieve the object a second time, the baby will typically look under cover A, where the object was found before, rather than under cover B, where the baby has just seen it placed (Piaget, 1954) (see Figure 5.13). Piaget interpreted this pattern of responding (referred to as "the A-not-B error") as evidence that the child remembers the existence of the object but cannot reason systematically about it. He believed that true representation requires the ability both to keep in mind the existence of an absent object *and* to reason about that absent object mentally, an achievement he did not think occurs until late in the second year.

Challenges to Piaget's Theory

There is little disagreement about Piaget's descriptions of the sequence of behavioral changes as children progress through the early stages of dealing with objects. His observations have been widely replicated, not only in Europe and the United States but in traditional societies as well. For example, Baule infants living in rural areas of the west African country of Ivory Coast have been found to proceed through the same sequence of object-related behaviors on almost exactly the same timetable as European children, despite vast differences in their cultural environments (Dasen, 1973). In fact, the sequence and timing of sensorimotor stages occurs so reliably that Piaget's procedures were long ago standardized for assessing the development of children who are at risk because of disease, physical impairment, or extreme environmental deprivation (Uzgiris & Hunt, 1975).

However, in the past two decades there have been challenges both to Piaget's theory and to his methods. Some of these challenges attack the idea that infants are unable to represent objects they cannot see. Others attack Piaget's reliance on overt action as the *essential* measure of, as well as the central condition for, infants' increased understanding. These critics argue that a variety of other factors such as memory, motor skill, and attention may be involved.

perseveration Young infants' tendency to repeat a movement rather than shift movements to fit events.

Other Sources of Infant Difficulty

In an influential series of studies, Adele Diamond (1991) suggested that young infants face several difficulties in searching for hidden objects that make it hard to determine what they do and do not understand about absent objects. She focused her attention on babies' limited ability to remember and on their innate tendency to repeat actions they have just made.

To demonstrate the role of memory limitations, Diamond varied the time between the moment of switching an object from location A to location B and the moment when children were allowed to reach for the hidden object (Diamond, 1991, 2000). She found that if they were allowed to respond *immediately,* $7\frac{1}{2}$-month-old babies correctly located the object at position B, but a delay as short as 2 seconds led to the reappearance of the A-not-B error. By 9 months, infants could withstand a delay of 5 seconds before beginning to make mistakes; at 12 months they were correct up to a delay of 10 seconds. According to these results, young infants *are* capable of representing objects they cannot see, but they quickly forget and become confused (the baby in Figure 5.11 is displaying this form of behavior).

Diamond also believed that young infants' tendency to repeat a movement rather than shift movements to fit events, a phenomenon known as **perseveration,** is an important source of errors that obscures infants' knowledge of the existence of the hidden object. She noted that some infants who make the A-not-B error look at (the correct!) location B but reach toward (the now incorrect) location A out of habit.

Esther Thelen and her colleagues propose a different view of the way that motor habits influence infant responding in the object permanence task (Thelen, Schoener, Scheier & Smith, 2001). They conducted an experiment in which no objects were hidden, but the basic sequence of events in the classic Piagetian experiment was preserved. An attractive object was presented in position A, infants' attention was drawn to it, and they were allowed to play with it for a while. After several such experiences, a new object was placed in position B, and infants' attention was attracted to the new object in the new position. Even though nothing was hidden, the infants still reached toward position A. Such evidence supports Diamond's contention that infants' difficulty with the A-not-B task may arise from their tendency to repeat movements rather than a failure to understand object permanence.

A New Test of Object Permanence: Violation of Expectations

Evidence that young infants' ability to display what they understand about objects is obscured by their limited memories and motor capacities has prompted several experimenters to design new tests of Piaget's theory. If infants were not required to demonstrate their understanding by reaching and manipulating things, these researchers reasoned, it might be possible to show that infants are capable of representational thought at or near birth.

To challenge Piaget's theory of how representation develops (see Chapter 4, p. 151), Renée Baillargeon and her colleagues exploited the well-known tendency of infants to stare at novel events. They arranged for young infants to watch a screen as it slowly rotated forward and backward through a 180-degree arc on a hinge attached to the floor of the viewing surface (Baillargeon, 1998; Baillargeon et al., 1985). The screen could rotate toward the babies until it was lying flat and away from them until it was again lying flat. In its upright position, the screen was like a fence behind which an object might be hidden from view (see Figure 5.14a).

When $3\frac{1}{2}$- and 6-month-old infants were first shown the rotating screen, it was a novel event and they stared at it for almost a full minute. However, after several trials they gradually lost interest (became *habituated* to this event) and stared for only about 10 seconds. Once the infants had become habituated, the experimenters placed a box behind the screen so that the infants could see it when the screen lay flat but not when the screen moved into its perpendicular position.

In the crucial part of the experiment, they arranged for the screen to move in one of two ways. For half of the infants in each age group the screen rotated until it reached the point where it should have bumped up against the box (see Figure 5.14b) and then returned to its flat starting position. For the other half of the infants at each age, they secretly lowered the box through the floor of the apparatus as soon as the screen had hidden it from the babies' view; then the screen rotated through its full 180-degree arc, as if it were moving right through the "hidden" box (see Figure 5.14c).

The researchers reasoned that if the infants thought the box still existed even when it was hidden by the screen, they would stare longer (dishabituate) when the screen behaved in a physically impossible manner by moving through the space where the box was supposed to be than they would when the screen seemed to bump into the box (the physically expectable event) before returning to its starting point. Alternatively, if "out of sight" was really "out of mind" for the infants (or in Piaget's terms, if they failed to represent the box when it was blocked by the screen), they should stare longer when the screen stopped after it had rotated only part of the way before returning to its starting position, because this was a novel event they had never seen before.

Baillargeon and her colleagues reported that the infants showed no special interest when the screen rotated only partway, seemed to bump into the box, and returned to its starting point. Instead, even the $3^1/_2$-month-olds stared longer (dishabituated) when the screen passed right through the place where the box had been located *even though this was the event to which they had previously habituated.*

The infants' seeming lack of interest when the screen bumped into the hidden object and their increased interest when the screen continued to rotate "through the hidden object," even though this was the habitual pattern of events, implied that the infants (1) expected the object to continue to exist behind the screen and (2) believed that it is impossible for screens to move through solid objects. In Baillargeon's terms, they stared longer at an "impossible event" than at a possible one because their expectations were violated. These results led Baillargeon (1993) to conclude that "contrary to what Piaget claimed, infants as young as 3.5 months of age represent the existence of occluded [hidden] objects" (p. 272).

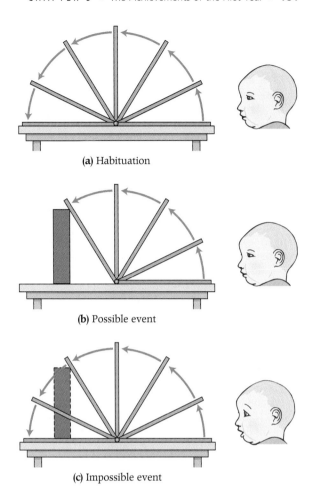

(a) Habituation

(b) Possible event

(c) Impossible event

Figure 5.14 The habituation and test events arranged for babies by Renée Baillargeon and her colleagues. In the habituation event (a), the screen is unimpeded and rotates 180 degrees. In the possible event (b), a box stands in the way of the screen and stops it from rotating the full distance. In the impossible event (c), a box stands in the way of the rotating screen but the screen appears to pass right through it. (From Baillargeon, 1987.)

Evaluating Piaget's Critics

Experiments such as Baillargeon's, which rely on violation of expectation and measure differential looking times to assess claims about what infants do and do not understand, have had a major impact upon developmentalists' view of cognitive development during infancy and beyond (Bremner & Fogel, 2001; Lacerda, von Hofsten & Heimann, 2001). It is now widely believed that infants develop at least rudimentary forms of many basic cognitive capacities, including object permanence, far earlier than anyone had suspected. (See the box "Bringing Up Brainy Babies" on p. 182 for a description of how the belief in infant precocity has given rise to a market for infant development products.) Understandably, since some of these capacities appear to develop before the infant has had any significant experience in the world, biological-maturational theories of development have increased greatly in popularity. But the shift toward a belief in infant precocity and the biological-maturation theory of development that it suggests is by no means universally accepted (Bremner, 2001).

Bringing Up Brainy Babies

Parents in many parts of the world believe that just as nature takes its course, children will develop at their own pace. There is no need for them to force nature's hand (Rogoff, 2003). But American parents have a seemingly unstoppable desire to speed up their offspring's rate of development. Piaget referred to this parental desire as "the American problem."

One by-product of current research on infant development is a major growth industry in toys, books, and videotapes designed to speed up some aspect of young infants' development in the belief that such acceleration will give them an advantage over their peers in later life. Some of these products (such as attractive mobiles hung over the baby's crib) have a solid foundation in research; others do not (Jones & Zigler, 2002). The range and ingenuity of the products that have been created to speed infant growth is matched only by the enormous amounts of money that have poured into the new "growth industry." At present, the market for development-enhancing products for infants and small children is estimated to be at least $1 billion (della Cava, 2002).

Although the idea that environmental stimulation can enhance young infants' cognitive and social competence has been around since the middle of the twentieth century, the current craze in providing special stimulation for very young infants received a significant boost from various lines of research conducted in the 1980s. First, there were studies showing that newborns learned from the environment outside of their mother's womb (such as the preference for listening to *The Cat in the Hat*) (see Chapter 3, p. 81). Second, research began to appear on experience-dependent brain growth, showing that animals raised in enriched environments produced increased brain cells and had improved problem-solving abilities (see Chapter 4, pp. 116–117). Third, data appeared (such as those by Rovee-Collier in this chapter, p. 190) showing that young infants learned to categorize alphabet letters and that this learning was retained for sometimes surprisingly long intervals.

With all of this scientific attention focused on the early capacities of young infants, it should come as no surprise that articles began to appear in both professional journals and the press promoting the idea that even fetuses were capable of learning that extended into their later lives.

Then, in 1993, Frances Rauscher and her colleagues published an article in the prestigious scientific journal *Nature* in which they reported that listening to a Mozart sonata enhanced IQ by an average of 8 to 9 points (Rauscher et al., 1993). This report attracted extensive attention and was followed in 1997 by a book, written by a former choral conductor, entitled *The Mozart Effect* (Campbell, 1997). The book was a best-seller and was convincing enough for the then-governor of Georgia to propose giving every newborn in the state a classical music CD to enhance the baby's cognitive development. The "brainy baby" movement was well on its way.

Subsequent scientific research has not been kind to the "Mozart effect." When positive effects on intelligence are reported, they are generally short-lived (on the order of a dozen minutes or so), and the number of failures to obtain any effect at all have led many to conclude that it's "curtains for the Mozart effect" (McKelvie & Low, 2002). It is too early to tell whether or not these negative findings will slow the brainy baby movement.

One reason to suspect that scientific efforts to promote infant development will continue to resonate with parents is that some of this research has much stronger evidence to back it up than does the Mozart effect. For example, Susan Goodwyn and her colleagues sought to accelerate infants' language development by teaching them symbolic gestures such as sniffing to represent "a flower," tapping index fingers together to stand for "more," and moving thumb to mouth to stand for "bottle" (Goodwyn, Acredolo & Brown, 2000). Their findings indicated that the ability to produce and understand signed words before they were able to understand and use spoken words does accelerate oral language development and may have long-term positive effects on children's cognitive development.

At present it appears clear that environmental stimulation can speed up certain aspects of children's development. But whether or not it provides any lasting benefits for children depends strongly on the nature of the extra stimulation and the cultural context of the infants' later lives.

For example, Cara Cashon and Leslie Cohen (2000) have argued that the results of studies using differential looking to reveal infant understanding about objects have misled researchers into attributing too much knowledge to young infants. They repeated Baillargeon's "impossible-event" experiment with 8-month-old infants. Like Baillargeon, they found that the infants stared longer at the screen that rotated 180 degrees, the so-called impossible event. However, Cashon and Cohen suspected that something else might be responsible for the infants' responses, so they also tested other patterns of screen movement with and without the block "behind it." For example, they included a procedure in which the infants were habituated to the event in which there was no block and the screen continued to rotate 180 degrees. Although the latter event was perfectly possible, and although the babies had been habituated to a screen that moved 180 degrees, they now stared more than twice as long at this possible event as they had at the impossible event to which they had been habituated. When Cohen and Cashon combined the results from all the trials using different combinations of degrees of screen rotation and presence or absence of a block, they obtained the results depicted in Figure 5.15.

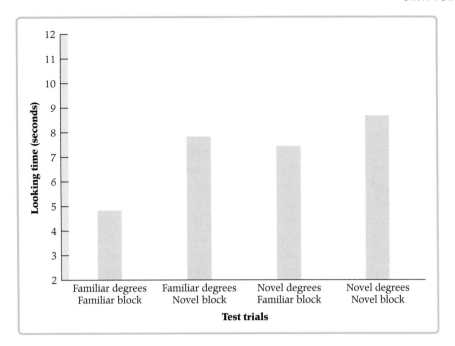

Figure 5.15 When 8-month-old infants were habituated to "possible" and "impossible" movements of a screen and subsequently shown either familiar or novel events, they looked longer at the novel events, whether possible or impossible. (From Cashon & Cohen, 2000.)

As the figure indicates, the critical variable accounting for how long the infants looked was the similarity of the testing conditions to the habituation conditions. When screens moved farther in the testing conditions than in the habituation conditions, or some novel object was introduced into the testing conditions, it was novelty and amount of screen movement that counted: the babies' attention was unaffected by whether the events were possible or impossible. Similar results have been obtained by other researchers (Bogartz, Shinskey & Schilling, 2000).

Students who read about this research can be forgiven for asking why so much attention should be paid to so seemingly trivial a question as why 9- to 12-month-old infants search in the wrong place for objects. After all, before long, they will be able to reason more logically and consistently, whatever developmentalists claim about the specifics of this one case. The answer, we believe, is that this case shows with special clarity the close link between the methods that developmentalists use to tease out the processes that underlie behavioral changes and the kinds of theoretical explanations that they arrive at. You will encounter many examples of the ways in which theoretical explanations and methods of research are interconnected, but none more clear-cut than those in the study of object permanence.

Additional Forms of Object Knowledge

The possibility that infants understand far more about object permanence than was previously assumed possible has generated investigations of a wide variety of other aspects of infant knowledge. Three areas of research have attracted special attention because, like the research on object permanence, they challenge long-standing assumptions about infant knowledge concerning objects: intermodal perception, understanding of physical laws and how objects influence each other (causation), and early knowledge about quantity.

Intermodal Perception

As we noted in Chapter 4, young infants have surprised developmentalists by their ability to associate objects' various sensory aspects with each other without any special experience. For example (p. 133), you saw that even newborn infants coupled the sight and sound of a Muppet, an ability we referred to as *intermodal perception*.

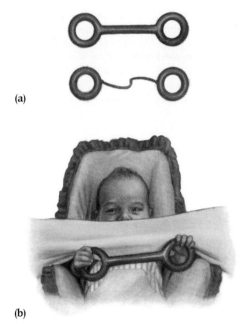

(a)

(b)

Figure 5.16 Objects (a) and apparatus (b) for experiments on the way infants use information gained in one sensory modality to recognize the same object in another. (a) Rings connected by a rigid bar or flexible cord, one of which is presented until the baby habituates. (b) This infant is feeling the rigid rings hidden from sight and later will be able to distinguish them by sight from the flexible ones. (From Streri & Spelke, 1988.)

Figure 5.17 Infants display their understanding that objects do not pass through solid objects by showing surprise when an object that is dropped behind a barrier is found under a shelf rather than on the shelf.

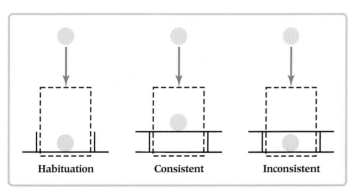

With the increased motor capacities shown in the latter half of the first year of life, evidence for intermodal perception has been extended beyond sights and sounds to the important property of the way objects feel.

For example, Arlette Streri and Elizabeth Spelke (1988) showed that how things look and how things feel are closely linked in 4-month-olds' perceptions of objects. In this case the researchers arranged for the infants to hold two rings, one in each hand, under a cloth that prevented them from seeing the rings or their own bodies (see Figure 5.16). For some infants the rings were connected by a rigid bar and therefore moved together. For others the rings were connected by a flexible cord and therefore moved independently. All the infants were allowed to hold and feel just one or the other type of rings until they had largely lost interest (habituated). They were then shown both types of rings. The babies looked longer at the rings that were different from those they had been exploring with their hands. That is, babies who had been handling the independently moving rings looked longer at the rigid ones, while babies who had been holding the rigidly connected rings looked longer at the flexibly connected ones.

These and other data on intermodal perception confirm that infants do *not* have to construct the understanding that sights, sounds, feel, and other basic properties of objects are related to each other. Rather, they seem to assume this is true even without an extended process of learning (Bahrick 2002; Rochat, 2000).

Understanding Additional Physical Laws

Using the violation-of-expectancies method, investigators have found that between 3 and 9 months of age, and sometimes earlier, infants appear to have at least an initial grasp of a wide variety of physical laws concerning the behavior of objects. For example, Elizabeth Spelke and her colleagues demonstrated that by 4 months of age, infants appear to believe that objects cannot move through a solid physical obstruction (Spelke, Breinlinger, Macomber & Jacobson, 1992).

At the start of the experiment, 4-month-olds were habituated to a display in which a ball was dropped behind a screen (see Figure 5.17). Initially the infants were shown the background wall and floor, then a screen was lowered, after which a hand holding a ball appeared and dropped the ball behind the screen. The screen was then removed to reveal the ball on the floor of the display. After the infants viewed this event several times until they habituated, a shelf was placed on the display some distance from the floor and the screen was again lowered.

Now the critical test trials were presented. Again the hand appeared and dropped the ball behind the screen. But half of the time, when the screen was removed, the ball was resting on the floor of the display *below the shelf,* while the other half of the time it was resting on the shelf. The infants stared longer at the case where the ball rested on the floor of the display, even though this was the event they had been habituated to. The fact that they stared less at the novel event of the ball lying on the shelf implied that they expected the ball to fall until it hit a solid barrier, consistent with the laws of physics.

Renée Baillargeon and her colleagues also carried out a number of experiments to assess infants' initial expectations concerning a variety of physical events (Baillargeon, 2001). An early experiment in this series investigated the idea that if an object is suspended in midair, unsupported, even 4-month-olds will expect it to fall (Needham & Baillargeon, 1993). The experimenters repeatedly presented $4\frac{1}{2}$-month-old infants with the event shown at the top of Figure 5.18, in which a hand reaches out and places one block on another

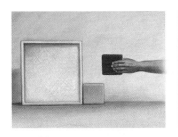
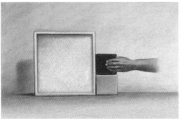
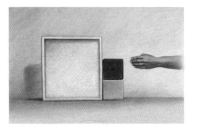

Possible event

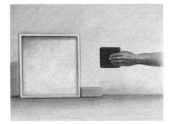
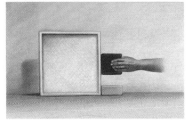

Impossible event

Figure 5.18 Evidence that very young infants have some appreciation of the laws of gravity is demonstrated by the fact that they stare longer at impossible events, such as a block remaining suspended in air, than possible events, such as a hand holding an object above the table top.

before withdrawing. Then they presented either an event that defies the law of gravity, in which the block is left dangling in midair as the hand withdraws, or a control event, in which the hand withdraws partway and continues holding the block unsupported by the bottom block. Infants stared longer only in the case where the block appeared to be suspended in midair without any visible support, a response that indicated to the researchers that the babies expected the block to fall.

Understanding Causation

Piaget believed that young infants have only a dim awareness that their own actions can cause an effect. For example, at 10 months of age, his daughter took his hand and pressed his fingers in order to make him squeeze a doll to make it sing. But, he believed, it is not until around their first birthdays that infants gain a firm understanding of causal relations external to themselves.

Using the violation-of-expectancy method, Alan Leslie and his colleagues have argued that Piaget and other developmentalists seriously misunderstood the development of causal thinking. In Leslie's view, primitive knowledge about physical causality is innate—it does not require prior experience of the world to develop (Leslie, 1994, 2002). Leslie and his colleagues presented 6-month-old children (the youngest they could test reliably) with a computer display in which one small square seemed to bump into a second and the second square moved. In one case, the second square moved immediately, an event that adults perceive as the result of the first square *causing* the second one to move. In the other case, there was a delay in the movement of the second square, suggesting an absence of causation. The researchers showed the infants the causal event several times in a row and then showed them either a different causal event or the "noncausal" event. The infants stared longer at the noncausal event, thus supporting Leslie's contention that they were sensitive to causality as it is manifested in these simplified circumstances, even though the events they witnessed were not connected in any way to their own actions.

Other researchers have replicated Leslie's results but added observations that undercut his claim that this development is controlled by maturation alone. For example, Lisa Oakes and Leslie Cohen (1990) found that when they replaced Leslie's simple squares with realistic objects in the experiment, 6-month-old infants became overloaded and no longer could respond on the basis of causality. Such results support the idea that the infants are learning to infer causality and will display such knowledge only under properly arranged circumstances (Cohen et al., 2002).

Understanding Quantity

An important part of Piaget's theory about knowledge of objects is that even after children begin to be aware that objects exist when they do not see them, they cannot reason about those unseen objects. This belief was put to the test by Karen Wynn (1992) using the evidence of differential looking that occurs when infant expectations are violated. Wynn showed 4-month-old infants the events depicted in Figure 5.19. First, a mouse doll was placed on an empty stage while the baby watched. Then a screen was raised to hide the doll from the baby's view. Next, the baby saw a hand holding an identical doll go behind the screen and then come out without the doll. The screen was then lowered so that any hidden dolls would be visible. In half the cases there were two dolls behind the screen (the expected outcome); in the other half there was only one doll (the unexpected outcome). The infants looked longer when there was only one doll, which suggests that they had mentally calculated the number of dolls that ought to be behind the screen. Similarly, when the experiment began with two dolls on the stage and the infants observed the hand remove one doll from behind the screen, they seemed to be surprised when the screen was lowered to reveal two dolls. Such experiments appear to demonstrate that infants are capable of making simple arithmetical calculations in their heads far ahead of Piaget's timetable.

However, as in other cases of apparently precocious infant abilities, Wynn's research has not gone unchallenged. For example, Ann Wakely and her colleagues, among others, attempted to replicate Wynn's findings and were unable to do so (Wakely et al., 2000). Leslie Cohen and Kathryn Marks (2002) were able to repeat Wynn's findings using her procedures. But they also found that the infants looked longer the more objects there were, and they looked more at a familiar display, no matter how many items were in it. When these factors were controlled for in their experiments, the infants behaved as if they were adding or subtracting, even when no addition or subtraction problems were involved. At present, there is no definitive evidence to show whether young infants have developed fragile abilities to add and subtract, or whether they are responding to subtle aspects of the displays that the experimenters have not successfully controlled.

Figure 5.19 After 4-month-olds observe the sequence of events at the top of the figure, they show surprise when the screen is removed and only one mouse remains. Apparently the babies not only remember the presence of the first mouse hidden behind the screen but mentally add the second mouse and expect to see it. (After Wynn, 1992.)

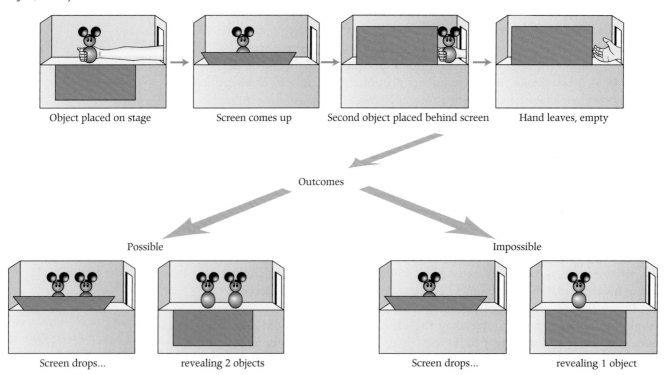

Object placed on stage → Screen comes up → Second object placed behind screen → Hand leaves, empty

Outcomes

Possible

Screen drops... revealing 2 objects

Impossible

Screen drops... revealing 1 object

Who Has the Right Answer?

At present there is no consensus on how much innate knowledge about objects to attribute to infants. Those who take a Piagetian position are inclined to see differential-looking experiments as susceptible to many subtle procedural errors. They interpret findings that fail to support the existence of innate knowledge as justification for their skepticism about the idea of infant precocity. Some see justification for Piaget's constructivist theory in these failures (Rivera et al., 1999). From this perspective, action remains central to the development of understanding (see the box "Action and Understanding," p. 189).

Biological-maturation theorists acknowledge the weaknesses in some of the experimental evidence for innate knowledge, but they argue that failures to replicate their results have not undermined their experiments. They maintain their basic conclusion that infants are born with a good deal more knowledge than Piaget gave them credit for. From their perspective, there is no need for babies to go through the long process of construction Piaget claims they do (Baillargeon, 2000).

Environmental-learning theorists view the evidence against precocious knowledge as support for their view that the only innate capacities young infants have are such general abilities as to be able to pay attention to primitive perceptual features of the environment, such as novelty and intensity, complemented by the ability to learn from experience. They believe that knowledge of physical principles such as causality or object permanence is acquired through learning, both from simply observing the world and through acting on it (Cohen & Marks, 2002).

Between these well-established positions there is also a middle ground which Rochel Gelman and Joan Lucariello refer to as "skeletal principles." These innate basic cognitive principles are important for directing babies' attention to the cues they need in order to acquire knowledge rapidly. Skeletal principles get a cognitive process started and provide some initial direction, but babies need repeated opportunities to learn in order to "flesh out" the skeletal knowledge that they are born with (Gelman & Lucariello, 2002). We return to this important idea in Chapter 9.

Categorizing: Knowledge about Kinds of Things

Categorizing is the process of responding to different objects or events as equivalent because of a similarity between them (Rakison & Oakes, 2003). Categorization is essential to the process of human cognitive development for many reasons. It allows infants to treat objects, sounds, animals, and events they have never seen before as if they are somehow "the same as" ones they have previously experienced. To the extent that infants can categorize their experience, they are able to make correct inferences about novel events, so it is not necessary to learn about them all over again. For example, infants who have encountered a cat and learned that it purrs when you pet it do not have to learn this information about cats again whenever they see a new cat.

Infants display an ability to form categories very early in life. For example, Peter Eimas and Paul Quinn demonstrated that 3-month-old infants quickly learn to categorize different kinds of animals. They showed the infants a series of pictures of cats, two at a time. The cats shown in each pair were different, so the babies never saw the same cat twice. After the babies had seen pictures of several pairs of cats, they were shown a new pair of pictures, but this time a new picture of a cat was paired with a picture of a dog. The infants looked longer at the picture of the dog than they did at the picture of the new cat even though the two pictures were both shown for the first time. This preferential looking indicated that the infants had formed a category for cats that excluded dogs (see Figure 5.20, p.188) (Quinn et al., 1993; Quinn & Eimas, 1996).

categorizing The process of responding to different things as equivalent because of a similarity between them.

Figure 5.20 Three-month-old babies shown a sequence of pictures of cats are surprised when they see a picture of a dog, indicating that they are sensitive to the category of cats.

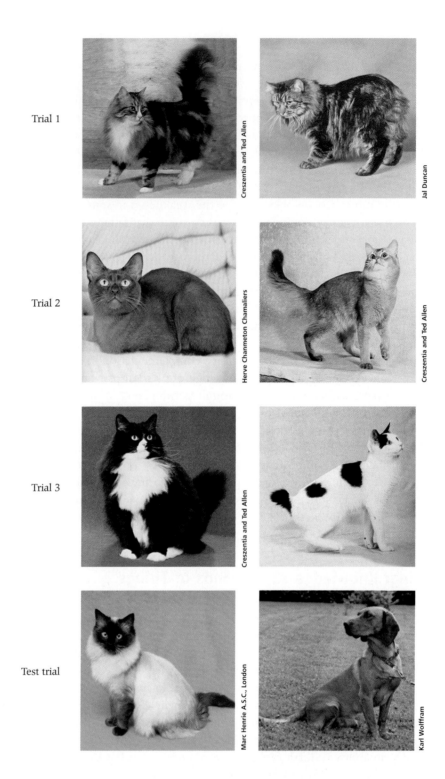

Trial 1

Trial 2

Trial 3

Test trial

Young infants also form more inclusive categories. In one of many demonstrations of this ability, 3- to 4-month-olds were familiarized with pictures of eight different kinds of mammals (cats, dogs, tigers, and so on). Then they were shown one of three new pictures: a mammal they had not been shown before; an animal that is not a mammal (for example, a bird or a fish); or a piece of furniture, such as a table or chair. The infants looked longer at nonmammals and the pieces of furniture than at the new mammal, a result indicating that they had formed a category for mammals (Behl-Chadha, 1996).

Action and Understanding

Piaget's hypothesis that children's own activities are the driving force of their development has led many psychologists to study the developmental consequences of restricted or enhanced movement early in life. A basic intuition guiding such research is the idea that locomotion not only allows babies to learn how to move their bodies in space but also provides them with a new understanding of the objects, including other people and themselves, that fill space. As Selma Fraiberg (1959) has noted:

> Travel changes one's perspective. A chair, for example, is an object of one dimension when viewed by a six-month-old baby propped up on the sofa, or by an eight-month-old baby doing push-ups on a rug. It's even very likely that the child of this age confronted at various times with different perspectives of the same chair would see not one chair, but several chairs, corresponding to each perspective. It's when you start to get around under your own steam that you discover what a chair really is. (p. 52)

A classic study demonstrating a close link between motor experience and the understanding of spatial relations was carried out by Richard Held and Alan Hein (1963) with kittens who were raised from birth in total darkness. When the kittens were old enough to walk, they were placed two at a time in an apparatus called a "kitten carousel." One kitten, harnessed to pull the carousel, controlled the movements of the carousel, so what it saw depended upon how it moved. The other kitten was carried in the gondola of the carousel and except for head movements, its movements did not control what it saw. Instead, the visual experiences of the passive kitten were controlled largely by the actions of the kitten pulling the carousel. Each pair of kittens was given 3 hours of visual experience in the carousel every day for 42 days. Between these sessions, they were returned to the dark. Thus the only visual experience the kittens had, and hence the only opportunity they had to learn to coordinate vision and movement, was the time they spent in the carousel.

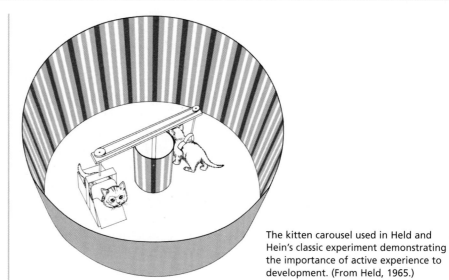

The kitten carousel used in Held and Hein's classic experiment demonstrating the importance of active experience to development. (From Held, 1965.)

The influence of active versus passive movement on the kittens' responses to their environment became strikingly apparent when Held and Hein lowered them onto the surface of a visual cliff similar to the one shown in Figure 5.9 (p. 172). This apparatus had stripes painted on it like the stripes around the sides of the kitten carousel, except that they were painted to look as if one side of the apparatus were far below the other. The kittens that had been active in the carousel shied away from the deep side of the visual cliff and appropriately stretched out their legs to land on it. The passive kittens did not try to avoid the deep side of the cliff, nor did they make appropriate adjustments in the positions of their legs in anticipation of landing on it.

This finding fits well with the results of the visual cliff experiment by Joseph Campos and his co-workers, described in this chapter (pp. 172–173), that confirmed the importance of movement in human cognitive development (Bertenthal et al., 1984).

Campos and his co-workers have also shown that locomotion enhances the development of infants' understanding of object permanence. Babies who had extensive experience in moving around in baby walkers before they could move about on their own were more adept at locating hidden objects in standard object permanence tests than were children of the same age who had no such experience (Campos et al., 1986,

2000). Martha Ann Bell and Nathan Fox (1997) report that the onset of locomotion is accompanied by changes in the activity of the frontal lobes, which, in turn, are associated with more successful performance on object permanence tasks. (Parents of infants should take note, however, that some children have been injured as a result of using walkers; this raises the question of whether the benefits of using a walker outweigh the risks [Atkinson, 1997].)

A very different kind of evidence for the close connection between locomotion and development at the level of behavior is provided by a study of the development of infants who suffered from a neural-tube defect, or failure of myelin to develop properly in the motor cortex, impeding locomotion (Telzrow, Campos, Kermoian & Bertenthal, 1999). Such children were found to be delayed 5 to 6 months in the development of object permanence. They began to search for hidden objects correctly only after they had begun to move voluntarily.

The results of these experiments suggest that active engagement with the world does make a fundamental contribution to development at every level: biological changes in the brain and body; psychological changes in problem solving, classification, and memory; and interpersonal changes in emotional attachment and interpersonal understandings.

Courtesy of Carolyn Rovee-Collier, Rutgers University

A 3-month-old baby viewing a mobile with blocks inscribed with an *A* that moves when the baby kicks. After three 15-minute sessions, each with a different-color *A*, the baby will kick a mobile with yet a fourth color. But if a new shape is inscribed on the blocks used in the fourth session (for example, a *B*), the baby will not kick. This indicates that the baby has formed a category and remembered prior experience.

Infants also form categories on the basis of how objects relate to their own actions. Carolyn Rovee-Collier and her colleagues demonstrated this ability in many experiments using a procedure that demands more active responding on the infants' part than does differential looking (Hayne & Rovee-Collier, 1995). First the babies learned to kick to make a mobile move. Then they were shown a mobile made of unfamiliar figures. Ordinarily they would not kick because the mobile looked different. But in this case the experimenter made the new mobile move while the infants watched it (the infants were not attached to the mobile, so their actions did not affect its movement). Even though they had never before seen the novel mobile, they began kicking as if they had. According to Rovee-Collier and her colleagues, the new mobile had entered the category of "familiar mobiles" not because of how it looked but because of how it functioned.

It appears that as they reach 8 to 9 months of age, infants begin to form new kinds of categories (Quinn, Slater, Brown & Hayes, 2001). While the initial categories they form tend to be quite general, later categories are somewhat narrower. In an early demonstration of this developmental change, Jean Mandler and Laraine McDonough (1993) showed that 7-month-old babies responded to toy birds and toy airplanes as if they were members of the same category. By contrast, 9- to 11-month-olds treated toy airplanes and birds as members of different categories even though they looked very much alike: the toy birds all had outstretched wings and looked like the airplanes (see Figure 5.21). There is still uncertainty among developmentalists about the basis for this change and the subtlety of categories babies are able to form. Some researchers believe that *perceptual* similarity—similarities in how things look, feel, or sound—is fundamental to category formation; thus the older children, whose sensory systems are more developed and who have greater experience, are sensitive to more subtle cues (Quinn, 2002). Others believe that before the end of the first year, infants become capable of forming genuine *conceptual* categories—categories based on such features as what things do and how they come to be the way they are—in addition to perceptual categories.

What makes the idea that 9- to 11-month-olds have formed a conceptual distinction between birds and airplanes so interesting is that the apparent shift from perceptual to conceptual categorizing could not have resulted from actual experience with the objects involved. Infants between 9 and 11 months old have little or no direct experience with birds, let alone airplanes. So what might bring about a

Figure 5.21 Seven-month-old babies treat plastic toy birds or airplanes, which are perceptually similar, as if they are members of the same category. Babies 9 to 11 months old treat them as members of different categories, despite their perceptual similarity.

Jean Mandler and Laraine McDonough

change from perceptual to conceptual categorizing in infants so young? Jean Mandler (2000) argues that there is actually a qualitative change in the way infants categorize as they reach the end of the first year of life. She believes that around 3 to 4 months of age, infants begin to think actively about the objects they see. She refers to this form of thinking as "perceptual analysis" and believes that it transforms the purely perceptual information infants receive into primitive conceptual categories. According to Mandler, this process of perceptual analysis makes possible conceptual categorization because when babies "begin to encounter animals, vehicles, furniture, utensils and so forth, they must form some idea of the meaning of . . . the roles they play in events" (p. 8).

In support of this view, McDonough and Mandler (1998) tested the tendency of 9- and 11-month-olds to imitate actions involving either animals or vehicles. Animal examples mimicked actions that animals do—such as a dog drinking from a bowl—while vehicle examples performed actions such as inserting a key to make a vehicle move. Infants imitated appropriately: they did not imitate a key turning on a dog or a truck sleeping, but they did imitate actions appropriate to the category of objects they were shown, even if they had not seen that exact example. The strongest evidence in favor of Mandler's idea of perceptual analysis is that the infants' imitations in this study could not be based on physical similarity alone.

Animate versus Inanimate Objects

A categorical distinction of special interest to developmentalists is that between animate and inanimate objects. This distinction is essential for understanding how and why objects behave the way they do.

Intense research in the past decade has brought about wide agreement that infants are especially sensitive to the different forms of motion of animate and inanimate objects (Gergely, 2002). Unlike inanimate objects, animate objects:

1. Engage in *self-motion,* that is, begin to move without any other object acting on them and may stop moving for no apparent reason

2. Do not necessarily move in a straight line and may change direction without any obvious force acting on them

3. May influence the movement of other animate objects without acting directly on them; that is, they are able to cause action at a distance

There is still no agreement on exactly how early infants become sensitive to the distinction between animate and inanimate objects, but it is certain that the understanding of the basis of animacy continues to develop well beyond infancy. There does seem to be agreement that acquisition of this distinction in regard to objects appears by 9 months of age. In regard to human beings, the ability to distinguish animacy may appear even earlier (Mandler, 2000).

Intentional versus Nonintentional Actions

Developmentalists believe that one of the keys to infants' acquisition of the distinction between animate and inanimate objects is that they begin to distinguish goal-directed behavior from behavior that has no obvious goal (intentional versus nonintentional actions; Woodward, 1998). There is as yet no agreed-upon explanation for how this change comes about. Some believe that the key ingredient to understanding that an animate being is intentionally acting is that the movement is self-propelled. A block does not move unless an external object bumps into it, but a cat may move when there is no external object pushing it (Gelman & Lucariello, 2002). Others argue that to be considered intentional behavior, the action must, in some sense, be rational (Csibra & Gergely, 1998; Gergely, 2002). So, for example, if

Figure 5.22 In this experiment, infants were shown a small circle repeatedly jumping over a barrier to get to another circle (a). After they had habituated to this event, the obstacle was removed. In subsequent tests, the infants looked longer if the circle repeated its familiar jumping action (b) (which was not a reasonable behavior since the barrier was no longer there) than if it took a novel, but more efficient, straight-line route (c).

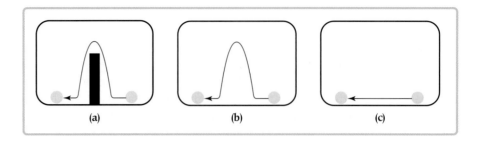

one animated object is shown "jumping over" a barrier to be with another object, the jumping action is rational in the sense that it is the only way for the objects to come in contact with each other. But if there is no barrier, and the object still jumps in order to reach another object for no apparent reason, the jumping doesn't fit the constraints of physical reality and in this sense is not rational. At 9 months, infants react with surprise when they observe "irrational" behavior of this kind (see Figure 5.22).

Humans: A Special Category

From evidence presented in Chapter 4 (p. 126) it is clear that some form of categorization associated with human beings is present at birth. Newborns respond to the sounds of human language as distinct from other sounds and produce different actions in the presence of people and objects (von Hofsten & Ronnquist, 1993). At 2 to 3 months of age, infants may imitate tongue protrusion and mouth opening if it is modeled by an adult but not if it is "modeled" by a mechanical object (Legerstee, 2001).

A clear demonstration of the way infants show they have acquired categories of people and objects associated with their behavior was provided by Maria Legerstee (1991). In her experiment 6-month-old infants were first exposed to an adult who either talked to or made a swiping gesture at something hidden behind a curtain. Then they were shown either a person or an object (such as a broom) behind the curtain. The infants who had seen the adult talk and then saw a person behind the curtain showed no surprise and did not stare as much as infants who had seen the adult talk to what turned out to be a broom. Similarly, infants who had seen the adult make a swiping movement with her hand were surprised and stared longer when a person appeared behind the curtain than when a broom appeared.

These data provide one more indication that something special is beginning to happen to the process of cognitive development at approximately 6 months of age. Before examining the pattern provided by the many different threads we have discussed thus far, we must consider a final important domain of cognitive development: remembering, the process by which past experiences accumulate.

The Growth of Memory

You have seen ample evidence that infants steadily acquire skills and knowledge over the course of the first year of postnatal life. But thus far we have not paused to examine the question of how they retain this skill and knowledge over time—how they remember. Memory, like other cognitive functions, undergoes developmental changes in early infancy.

Studies of the development of memory for past events have repeatedly found that young animals of many species, including human beings, forget rapidly (Delacour, 1999). However, Carolyn Rovee-Collier and her colleagues have demonstrated that remembering in humans increases rapidly during the first year of life (Rovee-Collier et al., 2001). Adapting the procedure in which babies make a mobile move by kicking, the researchers removed babies of various ages from the test setting when they had learned to kick vigorously as soon as one of their legs was attached to the mobile. They brought the babies back after different waiting periods to assess what they remembered from their earlier experience. They found that 2-month-olds started kicking immediately following a 24-hour delay, a finding indicating that the infants remembered the initial experience. But after 3 days, 2-month-olds seemed to forget their training; they took just as long to start kicking as they had taken when they were first trained to do so. Three-month-olds could remember their training for 8 days but not for 13. Six-month-olds showed almost perfect recall at 14 days but none at 21 days. An extension of this research in which infants up to 18 months of age learned to press a lever to make a train move showed a steady increase in the number of days that infants could remember their prior experiences (Hartshorn et al., 1998) (see Figure 5.23).

Additional studies have shown that if infants are given a brief visual reminder, they can remember their earlier training much longer. In one such study, Rovee-Collier and her colleagues trained a group of 3-month-olds and a group of 6-month-olds to activate a mobile by kicking. They then tested the infants' memories after intervals that ranged from 1 week to 6 months and varied the duration of the visual reminders from only $7^1/_2$ seconds to 120 seconds. They found that after 1 week the 3-month-olds needed to view the reminder for 120 seconds in order for it to be effective while $7^1/_2$ seconds was sufficient for the 6-month-olds (Joh, Sweeney & Rovee-Collier, 2002; Rovee-Collier et al., 1999).

Recall and Wariness

In the previous sections we discussed the development of categorization and the development of memory as if they were separate phenomena. In fact, however, the way that infants remember experiences depends, at least in part, on how those experiences have been categorized. And how infants categorize current experiences depends, in part, on how they categorized, and thus remember, prior experiences.

Interconnections between Changes in Memory and Categorization

Rovee-Collier and her colleagues believe that the improvement in infant memory over the course of the first year of life is a continuous process that does not involve any new principles of learning or remembering (Joh et al., 2002; Rovee-Collier, 1997). This conclusion parallels the view discussed above (p. 190) that the development of categorization is also a gradual process of change, based on perceptual processes, that does not involve the emergence of qualitatively new abilities during the first year (Quinn, 2002).

However, just as there are developmentalists who believe that categorization shifts from perceptual to conceptual categories sometime between 6 and 9 months of age, there are those who believe that a qualitative shift in memory occurs at the same time. According to the latter view, young infants move from relying on **implicit memory,** which allows them to recognize what they have experienced before, to acquiring the ability to engage in **explicit memory,** which allows them to recall ("call to mind") absent objects and events without any clear reminder (Bauer et al., 2003; Mandler, 1998). Explicit, or recall, memory is considered an especially important cognitive achievement because it seems to require the conscious generation of a mental representation for something that is not present to the senses—the same criterion that is used by those who believe that conceptual categorization begins to supplement perceptual categorization during the same period. However, as was true when trying to

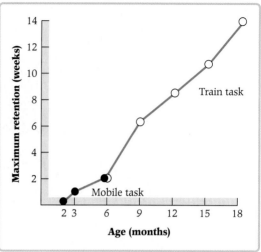

FIGURE 5.23 Results of memory retention studies on babies 2 to 18 months. The 2-, 3-, and 6-month-olds were tested with a mobile moved by kicking. The 6- to 18-month-olds were tested by having them move a lever which set a train in motion. Note that 6-month-olds were tested in both the mobile and the train tasks. (Data for mobile task are from Vander Linde et al., 1985 [2-month-olds]; Greco et al., 1986 [3-month-olds]; and Hill et al., 1988 [6-month-olds]. Data for train task are from Hartshorn & Rovee-Collier, 1997.)

implicit memory The ability to recognize objects and events that have been previously experienced.

explicit memory The ability to recall absent objects and events without any clear reminder.

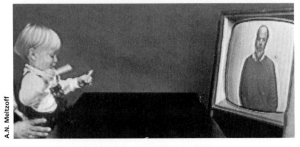

A.N. Meltzoff

Figure 5.24 Studies by Andrew Meltzoff (1988a) have shown that young infants imitate live models and will also imitate actions they have seen on television. This child observes a televised adult model manipulate blocks, and then immediately the child imitates the adult's actions. Meltzoff also demonstrated that infants who watch a televised model on one day will reproduce the model's behavior 24 hours later. (Courtesy of A. Meltzoff.)

deferred imitation The ability to imitate an action observed in the past.

make a firm distinction between perceptual and conceptual categories in young infants, the task of distinguishing between implicit remembering and explicit remembering is a tricky one.

One technique used to study the early origin of explicit memory is to test children's ability to engage in delayed or **deferred imitation,** that is, imitation of a new behavior the infant witnessed at a previous time. In one such test, Andrew Meltzoff (1988b) demonstrated three simple actions to 9-month-old infants seated on their parents' laps. First he took a small board attached in an upright position to a base by a hinge and pushed it until it lay flat on its base; then he pushed a black button that sounded a beeper; and then he rattled an orange plastic egg with nuts and bolts in it. After watching him do these things, the babies were taken home. The next day they were brought back to the laboratory and allowed to play with a few small toys. Then the board, the buzzer, and the plastic egg were brought out. Although the babies had never themselves done such things, most of them imitated one or more of the actions they had seen Meltzoff perform with these objects the day before (see Figure 5.24). According to Meltzoff, they had recognized the items (implicit memory), and they had recalled his use of them (explicit memory).

Later studies by Harlene Hayne and her colleagues, using similar procedures, showed that even 6-month-olds imitated at least one of the actions they had seen 24 hours earlier (Hayne, Boniface & Barr, 2000). However, their memory was disrupted if the experimenter changed the objects used in the demonstration session (in this case, different puppets). By contrast, 12-month-olds continued to imitate what they had seen even after the change; this indicates that their explicit, recall memory was based on an ability to categorize different puppets as "the same thing," a result that supports the important links between categorization and memory. These data clearly demonstrate that by their first birthdays, infants are capable of recalling past events for considerable periods of time even without reminders.

Memory, Categorization, and the Onset of Wariness

The question of how changes in memory are related to changes in categorization takes on added importance because at some time between the ages of 6 and 9 months, babies begin to be overtly wary and even afraid whenever something out of the ordinary happens (see Figure 5.25) (Rothbart, 1988). Some researchers believe that such wariness would not be possible if infants had not first developed the ability to recall earlier events. To demonstrate the onset of wariness, Rudolph Schaffer (1977) repeatedly presented babies between the ages of 4 and 9 months of age with a strange object until they became habituated to it. He then presented them with a new strange object, a plastic model of an ice-cream sundae. Most 4-month-olds strained toward the sundae immediately, without any hesitation. Most 6-month-olds hesitated for a second or two, showing that they noticed the change, and then reached for the sundae impulsively, often bringing it to their mouths. Nine-month-olds tended to hesitate longer, and some of them even turned away or started to cry. Alan Sroufe (1979) reported that such wariness is "rare in the first 6 months of life, common by 8 or 9 months, and increasingly frequent throughout the first year" (p. 24).

It seems plausible that the increased wariness displayed between 8 and 9 months is caused by a newly acquired ability to compare current events with remembered past events in a systematic way that fits well with the definition of recall. Thus 9-month-olds not only note that strange new objects (like ice-cream sundaes) are unfamiliar but search their memories to determine if such an object corresponds to any category of things they have seen before, and they become upset if it does not.

The question of when explicit, recall memory first appears and how it is related to changes in categorization is by no means settled. On the basis of their experiments in eliciting infants' imitation of facial expressions (see Chapter 4, p. 131), Andrew Meltzoff and Keith Moore (1994) argue that explicit memory (in the form of deferred imitation of tongue protrusion) may appear as early as 6 weeks! They found that 6-week-old infants not only imitate a person who sticks out his tongue as soon as they see him do it but repeat that movement when they see the same person 24 hours later. Meltzoff and Moore suggest that perhaps what is special about memory late in the first year of life is that it can operate on objects as well as people. Other investigators believe that early forms of imitation such as tongue protrusion are specialized, restricted responses that newborns are unconscious of making; these researchers want to credit infants with recall only when they must deliberately bring prior information to mind (Mandler, 2000). Whether the form of memory in these experiments is explicit or implicit may be difficult to decide. But what is clear is that developments in memory, categorization, and infant responses to strange events become intertwined in a new way toward the end of the first year of life.

Figure 5.25 Infants who are exposed to something new—even a spoonful of cereal from a stranger—display the wariness characteristic of the bio-social-behavioral shift that occurs at 6 to 9 months.

New Social Relationships

Jake's wariness of Sheila at 12 months, described at the start of this chapter, belongs to a new pattern of social behaviors that first appears around 7 months of age. When Jake was 2 months old, he did not show any overt sign of distress when Sheila cared for him. This does not necessarily mean that he did not notice the difference between Sheila and his mother. Keiko Mizukami and her colleagues have shown that when 2- to 4-month-olds see their mothers leave the room and a stranger appears over their cribs, their skin temperature drops—a physiological indicator that they are concerned. But such early indicators are not yet apparent in behavior (Mizukami et al., 1990). At 1 year of age, however, Jake was not only surprised when he looked up and saw Sheila where he expected his mother to be; he was also distressed, and he showed it by turning away and reaching for his mother.

Many developmental psychologists agree that in the second half of the first year, babies' fear of an unfamiliar adult and their distress when their primary caregiver disappears are closely connected to their increasing ability to move around, to categorize, and to remember (Campos et al., 2000). Their increased mobility also brings about changes in infant–caregiver emotional relationships and patterns of communication.

The Role of Uncertainty in Wariness

When we try to discover why the combination of infants' beginning to locomote, increased understanding of the nature of objects, and improved memory should be associated with overt wariness and fear, we have to remember the predicament young infants are in. They are constantly encountering new situations and new objects, but they have little experience to guide their actions and little physical strength or coordination to respond if the situation turns out to be threatening. They cannot eat, dress, or take off an uncomfortable diaper by themselves. What's more, they have no reliable system of communication. Therefore, to get through each day reasonably well fed and comfortable, they must depend on adults and older siblings to know what needs to be done and how to do it, as the following case illustrates:

> Amy, almost 4 months old, sat in her father's lap in a booth at the coffee shop. He was talking to a friend. Amy was teething on a hard rubber ring he had brought along for her. Her father supported Amy's back with his left arm, keeping his hand free. Twice he used that hand to catch the ring when it fell to her lap or his own lap. When Amy dropped the ring for the third time, he interrupted his conversation, said "Klutz," picked it up, and put it on the table. She leaned toward it, awkwardly reached out and touched it, but was not able to grasp it well enough to pick it up. Her father had returned to his conversation, and this time without interrupting it (though he was glancing back and forth between Amy's hand and his friend) he tilted the ring upward toward Amy so that she could get her thumb under it. She grasped the ring and pulled it away from him. Absorbed in chewing on the toy, Amy did not look at him. He went on talking and drinking his coffee, paying no further attention to her until he felt the toy drop into his lap once again. (Kaye, 1982, pp. 1–2)

Here you see a few of the ways in which adults act for and with infants so that they can function effectively despite their relative ineptness. The adult's actions must be finely coordinated with the baby's abilities and needs, or else the baby will experience some form of difficulty.

The kind of finely tuned adult support that assists children in accomplishing actions that they will later come to accomplish independently creates what Lev Vygotsky (1978) called a **zone of proximal development.** Vygotsky attributed great significance to such child–adult interactions throughout development. The zone he referred to is the gap between what children can accomplish independently and what they can accomplish when they are interacting with others who are more competent. The term "proximal" (nearby) indicates that the assistance provided goes just slightly beyond the child's current competence, complementing and building on the child's existing abilities instead of directly teaching the child new behaviors. Notice, for example, that Amy's father did not put the teething ring in Amy's hand, nor did he hold it up to her mouth for her to teethe on. Instead, he tilted it upward so that she could grasp it herself, and he did so almost automatically while doing something else. To coordinate behaviors in this way, the adult must know what the child is trying to do and be sensitive to the child's abilities and signals.

These findings provide an important clue to the sources of infants' wariness of strangers. The adults with whom young infants interact each day provide a predictable and generally supportive environment for them at a time when their communicative abilities are restricted. There are only a few people young infants can count on to arrange the environment in accordance with their expectations. Before babies reach the age of 7 months, their capacity to classify people as "those who can be trusted to help" versus "unpredictable strangers," and to remember the likely implications for them of each category of person, is at best limited.

Once infants can firmly form such categories, however, and use them to compare a current situation with past ones, there is a qualitative change in the way they respond to strangers. Babies realize that strangers do not have routines for interacting with them and cannot be depended upon to notice and understand their signals or to do what they need them to do.

The Infant–Caregiver Emotional Relationship

All the developments we have discussed in this chapter converge late in the first year of life with a change in the emotional relationships between parents and their infants. According to Joseph Campos and his colleagues, locomotion is a critical factor in these changes (Campos et al., 2000). As a way of getting empirical evidence about the role of locomotion in orchestrating the psychological changes that

zone of proximal development The gap between what children can accomplish independently and what they can accomplish when they are interacting with others who are more competent.

attachment An enduring emotional bond between babies and specific people.

secondary intersubjectivity The sharing between infants and their caregivers of understandings and emotions that refer beyond themselves to objects and other people.

begin between 7 and 9 months, Campos and his colleagues interviewed parents of 8-month-old infants, some of whom had begun to crawl and some of whom had not. Parents of children who had begun to crawl had more intense positive and negative feelings about their infants than did parents whose infants had not yet begun to crawl. The parents of children who were crawling said that they now gave their children tighter hugs, roughhoused with them more, and talked to them more affectionately. They also reported that they became angry at their babies and increased their attempts to control them with angry remarks.

Infants' expressions of emotion also seem to change in conjunction with locomotion. The parents of babies who had begun to crawl reported that their babies now became angry more frequently and more intensely when their efforts to achieve a goal were frustrated. The babies who crawled also seemed to become more upset when their parents left their sides. One mother reported:

> If I leave [the room] she gets upset unless she's busy and doesn't see it. But as soon as she notices, she starts hollering. I don't think it mattered the first four months. When she started doing more, sitting up, crawling, that's when she'd get upset when I would leave. (Campos et al., 1992, p. 33)

Many developmental psychologists believe that these new forms of expression signal a new, emotionally charged bond, which they call **attachment** (Cassidy & Shaver, 1999; Steele, 2003). Eleanor Maccoby (1980) lists four signs of attachment in babies and young children:

1. They seek to be near their primary caregivers. Before the age of 7 to 8 months, few babies plan and make organized attempts to achieve contact with their caregivers; after this age, babies often follow their caregivers closely, for example.

2. They show distress if separated from their caregivers. Before attachment begins, infants show little disturbance when their caregivers walk out of the room.

3. They are happy when they are reunited with the person they are attached to.

4. They orient their actions to the caregiver, even when he or she is absent. Babies listen for the caregiver's voice and watch the caregiver while they play.

The special relationship with their primary caregivers that babies begin to display between 7 and 9 months of age undergoes significant changes during the remainder of infancy and beyond.

The pleasure this child and mother take in their interaction using a fork is an example of the kind of emotional sharing referred to as secondary intersubjectivity.

The Changing Nature of Communication

As you saw in Chapter 4 (pp. 157–159), by 3 months of age infants and their caregivers are jointly experiencing pleasure in simple interactions. This early form of communication, which we referred to as *primary intersubjectivity,* is restricted to direct face-to-face interactions and still depends for most of its support on the efforts of the adult participant.

Between 9 and 12 months of age (depending upon the exact circumstances) babies begin to interact with others in a new and more complex way. This new form of connection between babies and their caretakers is referred to as **secondary intersubjectivity.** In Chapter 4 (p. 158), you encountered the phenomenon of primary intersubjectivity, which occurs when infants are able to recognize and share the mental state of the

©Rick Gomez/Masterfile

This newcomer to the world of upright posture is looking back to see what his mother thinks of his exploits. His inquiring gaze is an example of social referencing.

mother with whom they are in direct interaction. This form of psychological sharing is called secondary intersubjectivity because now the infant and the mother share feelings about a third object, such as their pleasure in seeing a passing puppy dog.

Social Referencing

An obvious form of secondary intersubjectivity is the form of behavior called **social referencing**—babies' tendency to look to their caregivers for some indication of how they should feel and act when they encounter some unfamiliar object or event in the presence of their caretakers. Social referencing becomes a common means of communication as soon as babies begin to move about on their own (Campos et al., 2000). When babies notice that the caregiver is looking at the same unfamiliar thing they are looking at and appears to be concerned, they hesitate and become wary. If, instead, the caregiver smiles and looks pleased, they relax. As they grow more experienced, babies become increasingly sensitive to where the caregiver is looking and will even check back to see how the caregiver responds to an object after they have made their own appraisal of it (Rosen, Adamson & Bakeman, 1992; Striano & Rochat, 2000).

Researchers in the United States have found a difference in the ways baby boys and baby girls respond to their caregivers' worried looks. Baby girls are more likely than baby boys to move away from an object their caregivers observe with fear. Perhaps as a result, caregivers find it necessary to use more intensely fearful facial expressions when communicating worried concern to boys (Rosen et al., 1992).

Between approximately 9 and 12 months of age, infants become able to share attention to objects and evaluations of events with their caregivers in more sophisticated ways. For example, Tricia Striano and Phillipe Rochat (2000) compared the way 7- and 10-month-old infants reacted to the appearance of a remote-controlled toy dog that barked intermittently. An experimenter in the room with the infant was instructed either to look at the infant when the dog barked or to look away. The 7-month-olds kept checking with the adult even if the adult ignored them, while the 10-month-olds immediately stopped checking with the adult unless the adult looked at them when the dog barked. Striano and Rochat believe that the 10-month-olds were beginning to engage in "*selective* social referencing" because the infants knew they could obtain information from the adult only if the adult was attending to them.

Gaze Following and Pointing

Another way in which infants can communicate with their caretakers once they start moving about is by following the caretaker's gaze to see what the caretaker is looking at and to look at what the caretaker is pointing at. If a mother and her 5-month-old baby are looking at each other and the mother suddenly looks to one side, the infant will not follow the mother's gaze. And if the mother points at some object in the room, the baby is more likely to stare at the end of the mother's finger than to look in the direction the mother is pointing. But if the mother suddenly gazes to one side when the infant is 6 or 7 months of age, and the circumstances are made very simple and clear, the infant will follow her gaze to see what she is looking at (Butterworth, 2001).

Pointing and gaze following, like social referencing, become stronger and more reliable means of communication after their initial appearance between 7 and 9 months (Carpenter, Nagell & Tomasello, 1998). A baby's ability to look in the direction a caretaker points increases rapidly between 10 and 12 months, while the more subtle form of communication involved in following another's gaze continues to improve well into the second year; the ability to use pointing as a means of controlling others' attention will not appear yet for several months.

Smiles, other facial expressions, and pointing are only rudimentary means of communication. As babies become more mobile and more likely to wander out of their caregivers' sight and reach, facial expressions become less available as a source of information. A new means of interaction, one that will allow babies and caregivers to communicate at a distance, now becomes an urgent necessity. We refer, of course, to language.

The Beginnings of Language Comprehension and Speech

Infants are able to recognize their own names and distinguish them from names with similar stress patterns, such as "Amy" versus "Suzie," as early as 4 months of age (Jusczyk, 1997). By 6 months of age they begin to show the first signs of comprehending words for highly familiar objects such as "mommy" or "daddy," and by the time they are 8 to 9 months of age they begin to identify phrases as they listen to streams of speech (Jusczyk, 2001; Nazzi, Kemler Nelson, Jusczyk & Jusczyk, 2000). These abilities function as "perceptual scaffolding" on which language-learning capacities can be built.

At about 9 months of age, children begin to understand some common expressions such as "Do you want your bottle?" "Wave bye-bye," and "Cookie?" when they are used in highly specific, often routine, situations. One little girl observed by Elizabeth Bates and her colleagues touched her head when asked, "Where are your little thoughts?" Another would bring her favorite doll when she was asked to "bring a dolly," but she did not understand the word "doll" as referring to any doll but her own (Bates et al., 1979).

The ability to produce language can be traced back to the cooing and gurgling noises babies begin to make at 10 to 12 weeks of age (Butterworth & Morisette, 1996). Soon thereafter, babies with normal hearing not only initiate cooing sounds but also begin to respond with gurgles and coos to the voices of others. When their cooing is imitated, they will answer with more coos, thereby engaging in a "conversation" in which turns are taken at vocalizing. They are most likely to vocalize with their caregivers and other familiar people.

Babbling, a form of vocalizing that combines a consonant and vowel sound, such as "dadadadadadada" or "babababababa," begins around 7 months of age (Adamson, 1995). Recent research indicates that babbling is controlled by the left hemisphere of the brain; this shows that even at this early age before recognizable language has begun, the brain areas that will support language are already active and behaving in language-specific ways (Holowaka & Petitto, 2002). At first babbling amounts to no more than vocal play, as babies discover the wealth of sounds they can make with tongue, teeth, palate, and vocal cords. They practice making these sound combinations endlessly, much as they practice grasping objects or rolling over. Early babbling is the same the world over, no matter what language the baby's family speaks, and babies even produce syllables they have never heard before and will not use when they learn to speak (Blake & de Boysson-Bardies, 1992). At about 9 months of age, however, babies begin to narrow their babbling to the sounds produced in the language that they hear every day (Davis, MacNeilage, Matyear & Powell, 2000). Since babies often babble when they play alone, early babbling does not seem to be an attempt to communicate. It is almost as if children are singing to themselves using repeatable parts of their language.

Toward the end of the first year, babies begin to babble with the intonation and stress of actual utterances in the language they will eventually speak. Such vocalizations are called **jargoning.** At this point, as Lauren Adamson (1995) describes it, "a

social referencing Babies' tendency to look at their caregivers for some indication of how they should feel and act when they encounter something unfamiliar.

babbling A form of vocalizing by babies that includes consonant and vowel sounds like those in speech.

jargoning Babbling with the stress and intonation of actual utterances in the language that the baby will eventually speak.

stream of babbling often flows like speech, following its distinctive intonational patterns of declarations, commands, and questions" (p. 163). At about the same time, babies start to repeat particular short utterances in particular situations, as if their utterances have some meaning.

When Jake was about 10 months old, for example, if he wanted the juice bottle in the bag hanging on the back of his stroller, he would turn around in his seat, say, "Dah, dah," and reach toward the bag while looking up at his mother in appeal. She immediately knew what he wanted and gave it to him.

By about 12 months of age, infants are able to comprehend about a dozen common phrases, such as "Give me a hug," "Stop it!" and "Let's go bye-bye." During the same period, the first distinguishable words make their appearance, although their use is restricted to only a few contexts or objects (Fenson et al., 1994).

The course of vocalizing by deaf children provides an instructive contrast to that of hearing children. It used to be thought that deaf children began to babble at the same age as hearing children (Lenneberg et al., 1965). Research has shown, however, that the vocalizations of deaf and hearing infants differ markedly in ways that indicate that only deaf children with residual hearing actually babble (Koopmans-van Beinum, Clement & van den Dikkenberg-Pot, 2001). By 1 year of age or so, totally deaf children rarely vocalize. However, if their caregivers communicate with each other in sign language, these infants "babble" with their hands, making the movements that will become the elements of sign language (Cormier, Mauk & Repp, 1998).

These budding linguistic abilities, which we discuss in more detail in Chapters 6 and 8, are part and parcel of the reorganization of babies' perceptual–motor, cognitive, and social capacities that signals the advent of a new bio-social-behavioral shift.

A New Bio-Social-Behavioral Shift

Table 5.3 summarizes prominent changes that converge to create a bio-social-behavioral shift in infants' development that begins between 7 and 9 months of age and continues at least to the end of the first year (Campos et al., 2000; Emde et al., 1976; Rochat, 2000). Whereas the crucial biological events at the $2^1/_2$-month bio-social-behavioral shift involved changes in the connections between the sensory cortex of the brain and the brain stem, the shift that begins at 7 to 9 months involves changes in the frontal lobes of the cerebral cortex, which are essential for planning and executing deliberate action. Equally significant are increases in the strength of muscles and bones, which are necessary to support locomotion.

As we noted earlier, locomotion appears to orchestrate the reorganization of many other functions that have been developing in parallel with it during infancy. For one thing, the acquisition of new motor skills leads infants to discover many properties of objects in their immediate environment. They become capable of reaching for objects efficiently and picking them up, feeling them, tasting them, moving around them, and using them for various purposes of their own. As babies learn that some of the "objects" out there move and respond in coordination with them, their interactions with people take on a whole new dimension. They begin to recognize that sympathetic adults buffer them against discomfort and danger. These adults can be counted on to understand their signals, to complete their actions for them, and to arrange things so that they can act more effectively for themselves.

These experiences would not amount to much, however, if memories of them did not accumulate adequately in infants' minds. Once babies are able to move away from the immediate presence of watchful adults, they can no longer rely on the

table 5.3

Elements of the Bio-Social-Behavioral Shift at 7 to 9 Months	
Biological domain	Growth of muscles and hardening of bones
	Myelination of motor neurons to lower trunk, legs, and hands
	Myelination of cerebellum, hippocampus, and frontal lobes
	New forms of EEG activity in cortex
Social domain	Wariness of strangers
	New emotional response to caregiver (attachment)
	Social referencing
	Secondary intersubjectivity
Behavioral domain	Onset of crawling
	Fear of heights
	Coordinated reaching and grasping
	Action sequences coordinated to achieve goals
	Object permanence displayed in actions
	Recall memory
	Wariness in response to novelty
	Babbling

adults' assistance and protection as they did before. It is not enough to recognize that one has seen an object before or to respond with curiosity if it is new. Babies must be able to recall ("bring to mind") their earlier experiences with objects, including people, so that they can anticipate how to behave effectively.

Both the baby and the caregiver must accommodate themselves to the uncertainties of their increasing separation as babies begin to move about on their own. Babies begin to exhibit emotions, such as anger when their efforts to reach a goal are frustrated, fear when confronted by strangers, and wariness when encountering something unexpected, as well as strong feelings of attachment for their caregivers. Caregivers arrange the environment so that the babies are likely to come to no harm, and they keep a watchful eye (or ear) open for anything amiss. Babies, for their part, are more skilled at getting help from their caregivers and can better understand what caretakers are trying to do.

As their first birthdays approach, many babies have progressed from crawling to walking upright. Walking increases both their independence and the importance of using all their accumulating cognitive and communicative abilities to coordinate their actions with those of their caregivers.

Sophisticated as 1-year-olds may be in comparison with babies of $2\frac{1}{2}$ months, the pattern of adaptation that they have achieved is destined to change. The factor that seems to play a pivotal role during the next period of development is a new level of symbolic capacity, that is, an enhanced capacity to represent the world to oneself and to use tools and symbols.

S U M M A R Y

Biological Growth

- Although there is great individual variation, most healthy babies triple in weight during the first year of life. Changes in size are accompanied by changes in overall body proportions that are important for the eventual achievement of balanced walking.

- Hardening of the bones and increases in muscle mass contribute to the development of crawling, walking, and coordinated movements of the arms and hands.

- There is massive overproduction of synapses between the ages of 3 and 12 months that are then reduced in number as a result of experience.

- Development in the prefrontal cortex makes possible the voluntary control and planning that begin to emerge between 3 and 12 months of age.

Perception and Movement

- The initial stage of poorly coordinated reaching and grasping is followed by a stage of visually guided reaching and grasping, which gives way to swift and accurate voluntary movements after several months of practice.

- Increasing skill in grasping objects with the hands makes possible the discovery of many new properties of objects.

- Locomotion, which begins during the second half of the first year of life, brings about a fundamental change in infants' relationships with their environments. Motor control of the body begins at the head and neck and proceeds gradually to the trunk and legs. At 7 to 8 months, infants begin to crawl or creep, using a combination of leg and arm movements. Walking is achieved a few months later, around the first birthday.

- Motor development can be speeded up by extensive practice or slowed when adults seek to protect the child against danger, depending upon the cultural circumstances.

Cognitive Changes

- Four questions dominate the study of cognitive development late during the first year of life:

  1. When do young infants begin to understand that objects may exist even if they are out of sight, and what does this understanding tell us about the way they think?

  2. What other knowledge do young infants acquire very early in life, and what knowledge must they learn about through extensive experience?

  3. When and how do young infants become sensitive to the fact that different objects and events are members of different categories, and what kinds of categories do they recognize?

  4. How does infant knowledge of the world accumulate?

- According to Piaget, infants do not acquire the idea that objects exist when they are out of sight until they are between 8 and 12 months of age; even then, the understanding is fragile and easily disrupted.

- The sequence of changes that occur in infants' ability to keep absent objects in mind goes through several stages:

  1. For the first 3 months of life, infants appear to forget objects not present to their senses.

  2. There is uncertainty about what infants between 4 and 8 months old understand about objects that are out of sight. Some experiments indicate that infants understand that objects exist even when they cannot see them but they are incapable of acting on this knowledge. Other experiments indicate that infants this young fail to understand the continuing existence of objects that are out of sight.

  3. At about 8 months of age, infants begin to search for hidden objects but quickly become confused or forget their location.

- Several studies that assess infant understanding of object permanence and do not require active reaching have indicated that primitive forms of this understanding may be present many months before infants can actively search for unseen objects.

- The belief that infants are born with rudimentary knowledge of such concepts as object permanence has led to the idea of the "precocious infant."

- The existence of such precocious knowledge (including the ability to add and subtract and to interpret causal relations) is hotly contested, but it is fairly certain that by 3 to 4 months of age infants are able to perceive the correspondence between such varied properties of objects as the way they look and how they feel. It is not known how early such understandings develop or what aspects of them are present at birth.

- The ability to perceive a wide variety of objects as being members of a single category appears as early as 3 months of age. There is uncertainty about the course of early categorization abilities. Some believe that early categories are based on similarity of perceptual features and that categories based on conceptual features do not begin to appear until the end of the first year. Others believe that conceptual categories are present as early as they can be tested for.

- Categorization behavior as specifically human is present in some forms from birth and appear to undergo an important change around 9 months of age, when infants begin to treat other humans as intentional agents.

- Between the ages of $2^1/_2$ and 12 months, memory increases steadily. When provided with a specific reminder of training received a month earlier, infants as young as 3 months of age remember how to make a mobile move.

- About the same time that babies begin to crawl, they show signs of being able to recall objects and people that are not present and activities they have not practiced.

- The development of memory and categorizing abilities combine to make infants wary when they encounter unfamiliar events.

New Social Relationships

- Changes in social and emotional behavior accompany changes in motor skills and cognition. Infants become wary of strangers and upset when they are separated from their primary caregivers, with whom they have formed an emotional bond called attachment.

- Increased locomotion is accompanied by a new form of communicative activity. Babies begin to monitor the expression on the caregiver's face to determine the caregiver's reaction to an object or event they are both attending to. Such social referencing helps babies to evaluate their environment.

- Infants begin to comprehend and produce aspects of the language in their environment.

A New Bio-Social-Behavioral Shift

- Events in the major developmental domains converge between the ages of 7 and 9 months to initiate a new bio-social-behavioral shift that ushers in a qualitatively new stage of development.

Key Terms

attachment, p. 197
babbling, p. 199
categorizing, p. 187
cognitive processes, p. 175
deferred imitation, p. 194
explicit memory p. 193

exuberant synaptogenesis, p. 168
implicit memory p. 193
intentionality, p. 177
jargoning, p. 199
locomotion, p. 171
object permanence, p. 178

perseveration, p. 180
representation, p. 175
secondary circular reactions, p. 176
secondary intersubjectivity, p. 197
social referencing, p. 198
zone of proximal development, p. 196

Thought Questions

1. List some of the physical and intellectual abilities a baby needs in order to eat a cookie without help from anyone else.

2. Why is it so difficult to determine how precocious infants really are? In other words, why is it so difficult to determine what knowledge is innate and what knowledge is acquired as a result of experience? (Base your answer on evidence from this chapter.)

3. How does the way infants search for hidden objects cast light on their mental abilities for thinking about the world?

4. What sorts of links are believed to connect wariness of strangers to changes in memory and categorizing ability late in the first year of life?

5. What are the major elements of the bio-social-behavioral shift that occurs between 7 and 9 months of age?

The End of Infancy

> "*The self and its boundaries are at the heart of philosophical speculation on human nature, and the sense of self and its counterpart, the sense of other, are universal phenomena that profoundly influence all our social experiences.*"
> —Daniel Stern, *The Interpersonal World of the Infant*

Just before Jake's second birthday, his mother, Barbara, and his father and sisters went to Switzerland for a few weeks, leaving Jake in the care of his Aunt Retta. Before the trip, Jake's mother arranged to spend a week at Retta's with Jake so that he would have a chance to become familiar with the household.

At first Jake ignored everyone at his aunt's house except his mother and his 4-year-old cousin, Linda. The first afternoon in the sandbox with Linda, he sat and watched with fascination as she conducted a tea party for her teddy bear and bunny rabbit. After a while he placed several small containers in a row on the edge of the sandbox, filled a large container with sand, and then poured its contents into the smaller ones in perfect imitation of his cousin. Then Linda caught his eye. Calling, "Beep-beep! Get out of my way!" she took a toy truck and ran it along the edge of the sandbox, knocking over the teacups and stuffed animals. In an instant Jake was yelling, "Beep-beep!" and knocking over his containers with a toy car. Linda laughed wildly. Jake laughed too and chased her truck around the edge of the sandbox with his car.

From then on Jake followed Linda around the house. If she asked her mother for something to eat or drink, he was right behind her, waiting for his share. Jake did not talk to his aunt directly, and he would not permit her to change his diaper or help him. A lot of the time he refused help from anyone, but if he really couldn't manage, he said, "Mommy do it." Jake knew that Barbara was leaving. "You goin', Mommy?" he asked her several times during that week.

At the airport Jake held Linda's hand and watched bravely as his mother disappeared into the plane. But that afternoon he cried. Linda tried to distract him, but he would not join her in play. Finally she brought him his favorite pillow, which he carried around for the next few days. Then he seemed to adjust to his mother's absence so well that he began to call his aunt "Mommy."

When Jake's family returned 20 days later, there was much excitement at the airport. No one paid any attention when Jake sat on his aunt's lap on the ride back to her house.

That afternoon Jake fell and scraped his knee while he was kicking a ball. He ran crying to his father. His father, who was busy at that moment, suggested that he ask his mother to put a Band-Aid on his scrape. Jake ran into the kitchen where his aunt and his mother were sitting. "Mommy fix it," he said, showing his injured knee to his aunt and ignoring his mother. When Barbara offered to help, Jake refused.

Later, in the swimming pool, Jake was showing his father all the new things he had learned to do. "Show Mommy," his father said, suspecting something. His suspicions were confirmed when Jake turned and tried to get his aunt's attention.

Jake had called his uncle "Daddy" throughout his stay, but as soon as his father was on the scene again, his uncle became "Uncle Len" and his father became "Daddy." No such switch occurred for "Mommy." For the 3 days that Jake's family remained at his aunt and uncle's house, Jake ignored Barbara and refused to allow her to do anything for him. When they were preparing to return to their own home, however, Jake looked up at his aunt and said, "Bye, Auntie Retta." Then, turning to Barbara, he addressed her directly for the first time since she had returned. "Let's go, Mom," he said, raising his arms as a signal for her to pick him up.

The changes that have occurred in Jake's behavior since his first birthday reveal a lot about the developmental phenomena that mark the second year of life. On his first birthday, Jake was just beginning to walk; approaching his second, he runs and climbs with ease. He is also far more skilled in manipulating small objects. At 12 months of age his active vocabulary consisted primarily of single words and a few set phrases—"juice," "woof," "Mommy," "all gone"; now Jake's language skills enable him to communicate more effectively and to participate in imaginative play with another child. Jake is still wary of strange people and places, and he is still so strongly attached to his parents that it was difficult for him to adapt to being left at his aunt's home. Cognitively, he is sufficiently sophisticated to "punish" his mother for her absence by treating his aunt as his mother right up to the moment of getting in the car to go home.

Jake's behavior provides excellent examples of the kinds of changes that infants undergo as they complete the period of infancy. As a result of changes in brain, body, and experience, children's reasoning about, and interactions with, the world of objects and people become increasingly sophisticated. In their second year, children acquire the ability to, among other things, imitate complex sequences of actions, engage in pretend play, communicate using language, experience new kinds of emotions, and participate in social relationships with other children and their caregivers in a new way.

Each of these facets of development is interesting in its own right, a single thread in a tapestry. What is most important, however, is the way in which these separate aspects of development converge to create a new bio-social-behavioral shift marking the end of infancy and the beginning of a new, broad stage of development.

Biological Maturation

During the second year of life, children's bodies continue to grow rapidly, but the rate of their growth is much slower than it was in the first year (Bogin, 2001). Among children raised in the United States today, average height increases from 30 to 34 inches and weight increases from 22 to 27 pounds. Almost all, if not all, of their teeth will appear. However, there is considerable variation from one child to the next in each of these developmental domains. As their bodies stretch out, most will lose the potbellied look so characteristic of younger infants; they begin to look more like children than infants. Their appetites lessen, and they may be particular about food. But they are still growing fairly rapidly.

There are several changes in brain structures during the second year that developmentalists believe are linked to the emergence of infants' new psychological capacities (Bruer & Greenough, 2001; Nelson & Luciana, 2001). For example, myelination accelerates both for neurons that connect different parts of the cerebral cortex and for neurons that link the brain stem and lower-lying areas of the central nervous system with the cerebral cortex. Both of these changes increase coordination between different parts of the child's brain, and between the child and the world.

This myelination improves several kinds of functioning by increasing the overall complexity and efficiency of the central nervous system. For example, myelination of the neurons that link the prefrontal cortex and frontal lobes to the brain stem, where emotional responses are partially generated, creates new potential patterns of interaction between thinking and emotion. Myelination of neurons linking the various areas of the cortex provides for analogous increases in the way sensory processes enter into thinking. These various centers now begin to work in greater synchrony, which appears vital to the emergence of psychological functions that define late infancy, including a new and more complex form of self-awareness,

This child's first steps display the posture and uncertainty characteristic of toddlers just learning to walk.

more systematic problem solving, the voluntary control of behavior, and the acquisition of language (Thatcher, 1997).

There is also evidence that toward the end of infancy the length and the degree of branching of the neurons in the cerebral cortex approach adult magnitudes: each neuron now has multiple connections with others, usually numbering in the thousands (see Figure 4.2, p. 116). At this time, the various areas of the brain, which have been maturing at very different rates, reach similar levels of development (Nelson, 2001). By the end of the second year, most of the brain structures that eventually will support adult behavior are present. After infancy the brain generally develops at a more modest pace punctuated by bursts of growth.

Gaining Coordination and Control

As a result of the biological maturation that occurs during the second year, children gain increased control of arm, hand, bladder, bowel, and leg muscles, as well as improved coordination of their perceptions and movements.

Locomotion

As infants approach their first birthdays, many become able to stand up and walk, which allows them to cover more distance and frees their hands for exploring and manipulating objects. At first they need assistance of some kind in order to walk. This assistance can come in several forms. Many babies pull themselves into a standing position by grasping a chair leg or reaching up to hold on to the seat of a couch or the railing on a porch (Berger & Adolph, 2003). Seeing such attempts, caretakers often help by holding both the baby's arms to support the initial hesitant steps.

In a series of studies, Esther Thelen and her colleagues traced how a number of separately developing skills converge to enable the child to walk (Thelen, 2002; Thelen & Ulrich, 1991). One crucial element in this process is the ability to coordinate leg movements with shifts of body weight from one foot to the other as each foot steps forward in its turn. The researchers found, for example, that if infants are placed on a treadmill and given the needed support, they execute the pattern of leg movements needed for walking as early as 7 months of age. They also begin to make walking movements when placed in water deep enough to support their bodies (see Chapter 4, p. 130). But babies this age cannot yet walk on a stationary surface without support that enables them to shift their weight, keep their balance, and coordinate their arm and leg movements.

No one factor can be considered the key to walking; rather, walking becomes possible only when all the component motor skills (upright posture, leg alternation, muscle strength, weight shifting, sense of balance) have developed sufficiently and when the child has been able to practice combining them (Thelen, Fisher & Ridley-Johnson, 2002). These new motor skills must then be combined with an increased sensitivity to perceptual input from the environment. Walking ability, changing size, and the ability to perceive the conditions of the environment develop together (Adolph & Eppler, 2002).

Karen Adolph and her colleagues demonstrated the confluence of these developments by arranging for infants to move up and down ramps of varying steepness (Adolph, 1997; Adolph et al., 1993). The children were studied from before they were able to crawl until after they had been walking for a few months (for this group of children, crawling began on average at about $8\frac{1}{2}$ months, while walking began between 12 and 13 months). The researchers wanted to know if all the infants would perceive the degree of slope and adjust their movements accordingly so as not to fall and whether the ability to crawl up and down slopes carried over to walking (see Figure 6.1).

When these children first began to crawl, they demonstrated that they perceived how steep the ramp was—they spent more time exploring the surface of the steeper ramps and exhibited increased caution. But when they did try to crawl down a steep ramp, they had difficulty adjusting their movements appropriately. Many tumbled down the ramps into their mothers' waiting arms. With experience crawling, infants worked out efficient ways to crawl down the slope, such as inching down backward, and they learned not to attempt ramps that were too steep for them.

Experience crawling up and down slopes did not seem to carry over to walking. Infants who were just beginning to walk had to learn all over again how to gauge a ramp's slope relative to their abilities from an upright position. Beginning walkers experienced great difficulty with even a gently sloping ramp. By contrast, when more experienced walkers encountered a gentle slope, they climbed it without hesitation. But when it was steeper, or when they were outfitted with special weights that change the conditions of locomotion, they hesitated and tried various alternative methods of getting down (Adolph & Eppler, 2002). Often they would sit and slide down the slope or revert to crawling, backing down slowly on their hands and knees. The work of Adolph and her colleagues provides excellent illustrations of how the maturation of motor and perceptual skills combine with experience to create flexible new systems of behaviors as the conditions of development change.

When they take their first steps on their own, babies become "toddlers," so named for the characteristic way they spread their legs and toddle from side to side. Most 1-year-olds are unbalanced and fall often, but falling does not stop them. The fall is a short one after all, and walking is too exciting to give up on, so they simply get up and rush ahead to the next tumble. Within a few months of their first steps, infants are usually walking in a coordinated fashion (see Figure 6.2).

Walking brings even more changes to babies' lives than crawling did. As Selma Fraiberg (1959) so eloquently put it, walking represents "a cutting of the moorings to the mother's body. . . . To the child who takes his first steps and finds himself walking alone, this moment must bring the first sharp sense of uniqueness and separateness of his body and his person, the discovery of the solitary self" (p. 61).

Figure 6.1 Between the ages of 8 and 14 months, the transition from crawling to walking changes the way these two babies approach the task of going down a ramp. (*left*) The 8½-month-old sees that there is a slope but plunges down it just the same. (*right*) The toddler hesitates and feels the incline of the ramp with his foot before attempting to descend it.

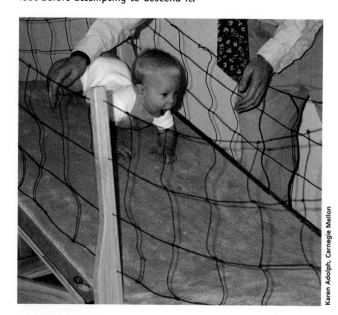

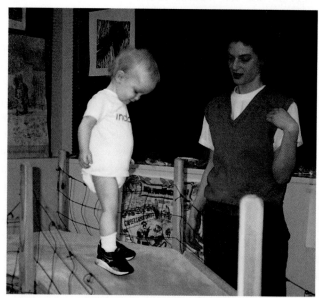

Karen Adolph, Carnegie Mellon

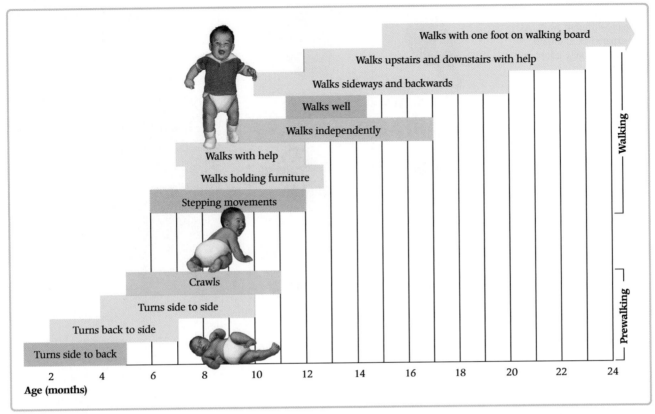

Figure 6.2 The progression from creeping to crawling to walking follows a classic developmental sequence. Each new stage in locomotion allows children to move more rapidly and involves a qualitative change in the pattern of their behavior.

Manual Dexterity

An infant's exploration of the world is aided not only by improved locomotion but also by improved abilities to pick up, explore, and manipulate objects. Coordination of fine hand movements increases significantly between 12 and 30 months. Infants 1 year old can only roll a ball or fling it awkwardly; by the time they are $2\frac{1}{2}$ they are more likely to throw it. They can also turn the pages of a book without tearing or creasing them; they are learning to snip paper with scissors, string beads with a needle and thread (although the hole might need to be pretty big!), build a tower six blocks high with considerable ease, hold a cup of milk or a spoon of applesauce without spilling it, and dress themselves (as long as there are no buttons or shoelaces) (Bayley, 1993). Each of these accomplishments may seem minor in itself, but each skill requires a good deal of practice to master, and each increases infants' overall competence.

Even an act as elementary as using a spoon requires incredibly precise coordination (Connolly & Dalgleish, 1989). Figure 6.3 (p. 210) depicts the variety of ways in which infants between 10 and 23 months of age attempt to hold a spoon. After the spoon is dipped into the food, it must be held level so that nothing spills while it is raised to the lips. Then its contents must be emptied into the mouth. At 10 to 12 months of age, babies can do only simple things with a spoon, such as banging it on the table or dipping it repeatedly into the bowl. Slightly older children can coordinate the actions of opening the mouth and bringing the spoon to it, but as often as not, the spoon is empty when it arrives. This problem is the next one to be solved, as infants learn to get food onto the spoon, carry it to the mouth without spilling it, and put the food in the mouth. Once this elementary sequence of actions is achieved, it is then adjusted until it is smooth and automatic.

Figure 6.3 Grip patterns. Babies initially grip a spoon in many different ways. As they accumulate experience and gain motor control, they eventually adopt an adult grip.

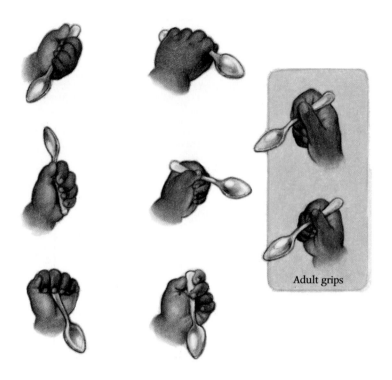

Adult grips

The ability to handle the pieces of puzzles and board games is evidence of toddlers' increasing manual dexterity.

Recent research by Michael McCarty and his colleagues (McCarty, Clifton & Collard, 1999; McCarty, Clifton & Collard, 2001) has shown that between 9 and 19 months of age, infants also become more sophisticated in their ability to choose the most effective way to grasp a tool. They presented infants with a variety of potential tools such as spoons, hairbrushes, and toy hammers. Two interesting changes were observed in the ways that infants grasped and used the tools. First, only the 19-month-olds would adjust the orientation of the object so that they could then grasp it efficiently with the dominant hand. Second, from 14 months on, infants were more likely to use proper grips when they used the object on themselves (fed themselves with a spoon versus fed a doll, or brushed their hair versus a doll's). These age-related differences in sophistication of tool use become an important element in infant problem-solving behavior, as you shall see below (p. 215).

Control of Elimination

Another important element in the growing ability of children to act on their own is the acquisition of voluntary control over the muscles that govern elimination. In the early months of life, elimination is an involuntary act. When the baby's bladder or bowels are full, they stimulate the appropriate sphincter muscles, which open automatically, causing elimination. Before a baby can control these muscles voluntarily, the sensory pathways from the bladder and bowels must be mature enough to transmit signals to the brain. Children must then learn to associate these signals with the need to eliminate. They must also learn to tighten their sphincters to prevent elimination and to loosen them to permit it.

Until the 1950s, toilet training in many countries was begun as early as possible, not only for convenience in an era before there were washing machines and

The presence of friends no doubt encourages these young children in their attempts to learn to use the potty.

disposable diapers but also because it was believed that early training would ensure bowel regularity, which was considered important for good health. (The first edition of *Infant Care,* a magazine for parents published by the U.S. Children's Bureau in 1914, advised mothers to begin bowel training by the third month or even earlier [Wolfenstein, 1953]). Then, with the advent of washing machines and disposable diapers, parental practices began to change. For example, Remo Largo and his colleagues found that in the 1950s, Swiss parents strongly believed that early toilet training was desirable: 96 percent of Swiss parents began toilet training before their infants were 12 months old. By the mid-1970s, parental beliefs and practices had changed radically, with the vast majority of Swiss parents not beginning toilet training until 36 months of age. The toilet training of the earlier generation succeeded in the limited sense that young infants learned to eliminate when placed on the potty. But there was no change at all in the ages at which children gained sufficient control over their bladder and bowel functions to stay dry at night (Largo et al., 1996). Similar trends were found in a study conducted in Belgium (Bakker & Wyndaele, 2000). These results provide strong evidence that the processes of gaining voluntary control over bowel and bladder are under maturational control.

By the time they are 2 years old, some children are able to remain dry during the day, owing in large measure to the watchfulness of adults who place them on the potty when they show signs of needing it. Many children in the United States and Europe today, however, do not achieve this milestone until sometime later, and most do not manage to stay dry while they are asleep until they are $3\frac{1}{2}$ to 4 years old (Schum, Kolb, McAuliffe, Simms, Underhill & Marla, 2002). The successful completion of toilet training is an important milestone because it allows children a noticeably greater degree of independence.

New Modes of Thought

During the second year of life, as toddlers are perfecting their ability to get around on their own two legs, to eat with utensils, and to control their body functions, they also begin to engage in more sophisticated ways of thinking. Although there is disagreement concerning just how firm such abilities are, the evidence presented in Chapter 5 indicates that by their first birthdays infants have achieved at least rudimentary control over a wide range of cognitive abilities that will form the foundation for cognitive advances to come. These include:

1. Goal-directed problem solving

2. The ability to keep nonpresent objects in mind, if only for a short time

3. The knowledge that aspects of objects are inherently connected to each other, such as the sight and feel of an object

4. Core knowledge about several basic physical laws

5. Some understanding of causal relations

6. The ability to form categories based on conceptual as well as perceptual relations

7. The distinction between animate and inanimate entities and between intentional and unintentional behavior

8. The first signs that they are beginning to understand language and taking the first, halting, steps to use language themselves

Between their first and second birthdays, infants build upon and expand these accomplishments. The sum total of these achievements, in combination with the biological and socioemotional changes with which they are interwoven, will result in a new ensemble of behaviors that signal the new bio-social-behavioral shift that brings infancy to a close.

Completing the Sensorimotor Substages

Recall that for Piaget, the qualitative transformation that occurs between 18 and 24 months of age results from the emergence of *representation*—that is, the ability to mentally have one thing stand for, or represent, another (see Table 6.1). In Piaget's view, the pathway to representational thought leads through sensorimotor substage 5, which is traversed between 12 and 18 months of age, and substage 6, which is completed by about the age of 2.

Substage 5: Tertiary Circular Reactions (12–18 Months)

As you will recall, in substage 4 infants develop the ability to combine simple actions to achieve a simple goal. The fifth substage of the sensorimotor period is characterized by an ability to vary the actions of substage 4 systematically and flexibly. Piaget referred to this as the substage of **tertiary circular reactions.** Whereas *primary* circular reactions are centered on the child's body and *secondary* circular reactions are focused on objects, *tertiary* circular reactions are focused on the relationship between the two. Now, in addition to making interesting events continue by using already established secondary circular reactions, infants become capable of deliberately varying their action sequences, thereby making their explorations of the world more complex. Piaget (1952b) referred to tertiary circular reactions as "experiments in order to see," because children seem to be experimenting in order to find out about the nature of objects and events (p. 272). Piaget observed this kind of behavior in his son Laurent, then age 10 months and 11 days. Laurent is lying in his crib:

> He grasps in succession a celluloid swan, a box, etc., stretches out his arm and lets them fall. He distinctly varies the positions of the fall. . . . Sometimes he stretches out his arm vertically, sometimes he holds it obliquely, in front of or behind his eyes, etc. When the object falls in a new position (for example, on his pillow), he lets it fall two or three times more on the same place, as though to study the spatial relations; then he modifies the situation. (p. 269)

tertiary circular reactions The fifth stage of the sensorimotor period, which is characterized by the deliberate variation of action sequences to solve problems and explore the world.

table 6.1

Substage	Age Range (months)	Characteristics of Sensorimotor Substage	Development of Object Permanence
1	0–1½	*Reflex schemas exercised:* involuntary rooting, sucking, grasping, looking	Infant does not search for objects that have been removed from sight.
2	1½–4	*Primary circular reactions:* repetition of actions that are pleasurable in themselves	Infant orients to place where objects have been removed from sight.
3	4–8	*Secondary circular reactions:* dawning awareness of relation of own actions to environment; extension of actions that produce interesting changes in the environment	Infant will reach for a partially hidden object but stops if it disappears.
4	8–12	*Coordination of secondary circular reactions:* combining schemas to achieve a desired effect; earliest form of problem solving	Infant will search for a completely hidden object; keeps searching the original location of the object even if it is moved to another location in full view of the infant.
5	12–18	*Tertiary circular reactions:* deliberate variation of problem-solving means; experiments to see what the consequences will be	Infant will search for an object after seeing it moved but not if it is moved in secret.
6	18–24	*Beginnings of symbolic representation:* images and words come to stand for familiar objects; invention of new means of problem solving through symbolic combinations	Infant will search for a hidden object, certain that it exists somewhere.

According to Piaget's observations, although infants in substage 5 can manipulate objects in their immediate physical environment in various ways, they still do not seem to be able to reason systematically about actions and their probable consequences ahead of time. Theirs is still very much a "here-and-now" world.

Substage 6: Representation (18–24 Months)

According to Piaget, the hallmark of substage 6, the final stage of the sensorimotor period, is that babies begin to base their actions on internal, mental symbols, or *representations,* of experience. When they can re-present the world to themselves—that is, when they can present it to themselves over again, mentally—they can be said to be engaging in true mental actions.

Piaget cited several new behaviors as evidence of the emergence of symbolic representational thought, and other developmentalists have added interesting examples of their own. This broad agreement allows us to put aside the question of the precise time at which representational thought makes its first appearance and instead highlight the way in which infancy comes to an end and a new stage of development emerges. The phenomena we have selected to highlight are:

- the systematic search for hidden objects
- a new level of systematic problem solving
- the emergence of pretend play
- the ability to imitate novel events well after they have occurred
- the ability to understand visual representations and models

Object Permanence

As you will recall from Chapter 5, when substage 4 infants find an object hidden in one location and then observe it being hidden in a second location, they will search for the object in its original hiding place. In substage 5, infants are markedly less likely to become confused by the switching of hiding places while they are watching and will now search for the object in its new location. However, substage 5 babies are still likely to become confused and stop searching if an object's location is changed without their seeing it moved. For example, if you pretend to hide an object in your hand while you really hide it behind your back, a substage 5 baby will continue to search for it in your hand, failing to reason that it must be somewhere else nearby. A version of this procedure that is used in many studies is shown in Figure 6.4.

The key change that occurs in substage 6 of the sensorimotor stage is that infants no longer act confused when the object is not where they expected it to be. They seem to reason, "Well, the toy wasn't where I expected, but it must be here somewhere," so they systematically check other possible locations.

Figure 6.4 Children in stage 5 of the development of object permanence cannot maintain a firm idea of the permanence of an object when its location is changed without their knowledge. (From Bower, 1982.)

(a) Infant sees apple

(b) Researcher hides apple as infant watches

(c) Researcher distracts infant and moves apple

(d) Infant is confused

(e) Infant searches for apple under wrong cloth

Whether Piaget was correct about the underlying mechanism of change or whether the change actually reflects increased memory, the ability to inhibit actions, or some other mechanism, once they begin to engage in systematic searching for a hidden object, infants are thinking in a new way. They are reasoning logically about something they cannot see. One manifestation of this ability is that they anticipate the trajectory of a moving object that has disappeared behind a barrier and predict where it will reappear. When a ball rolls under a couch, for example, a 2-year-old will go around to the other side of the couch to look for it instead of looking under the couch.

Problem Solving

The ability to reason about the locations of unseen objects is only one manifestation of infants' increased ability to solve a variety of problems through the manipulation of mental representations. Piaget's observations of his daughters nicely illustrate how this ability permits older infants to solve problems systematically instead of by trial and error. Both girls were confronted by the same problem—how to pull a stick through the bars of their playpen (see Figure 6.5)—but they solved the problem in significantly different ways because one, Jacqueline, was in substage 5 and the other, Lucienne, was in substage 6. Jacqueline, age 15 months, is seated in her playpen:

> Outside is a stick 20 centimeters long, the distance of about three spaces between the bars. At first Jacqueline tries to pull the stick into her playpen horizontally, but it will not go through the bars. The second time, she accidentally tilts the stick a little in raising it. She perceives this and reaches through the bars and tilts the stick until it is sufficiently vertical to pass through the bars. But several subsequent attempts make it clear that this is an accidental success; she does not yet understand the principle involved. On the next several tries she grasps the stick by the middle and pulls it horizontally, against the bars. Unable to get it in that way, she then tilts it up. It is not until the seventeenth try that she tilts the stick up before it touches the bars, and not until the twentieth that she does so systematically. (Adapted from Piaget, 1952b, p. 305)

Jacqueline seemed to have a clear goal in mind because she was certainly persistent. She continued to work at the problem until it was solved. But her efforts were rather hit-or-miss. When she succeeded, she did not understand why. She grasped the solution only after many trials and many errors. This experience is typical of substage 5 of the sensorimotor period.

Although Lucienne was 2 months younger than Jacqueline was when she was presented with this problem, Lucienne's problem solving was more sophisticated, a reminder that age norms associated with Piagetian stages, like other developmental norms, are only approximate.

George S. Zimbal/Monkmeyer

Figure 6.5 This child in substage 5 of the sensorimotor period carries out deliberate problem solving but still relies on trial and error.

symbolic play (pretend, fantasy play)
Play in which one object stands for, or represents, another.

Lucienne grasps the stick in the middle and pulls it horizontally. Noticing her failure, she withdraws the stick, tilts it up, and brings it through easily. When the stick is again placed on the floor, she grasps it by the middle and tilts it up before she pulls it through, or she grasps it by one end and brings it through easily. She does this with longer sticks and on successive days. Unlike her sister Jacqueline, who had to grope her way toward a solution, Lucienne profits from her failure at once. (Adapted from Piaget, 1952b, p. 336)

In Lucienne's actions we see the essence of substage 6 sensorimotor behavior: she seems to be using information that is not immediately available to her senses to solve the problem. Instead of going through the slow process of trial and error, as her sister did, Lucienne seems to have pictured a series of events in her mind before she acted. She imagined what would happen if she pulled the stick horizontally. She then inferred that if she turned the stick so that it was vertical and parallel to the bars, it would fit between them.

Play

Many developmentalists see the forms of children's play as a clear manifestation of their current stage of cognitive development. The early origins of play can be seen when infants kick their feet while being bathed for the sheer pleasure of the feel and sight of splashing water. Later sensorimotor play goes beyond the baby's own body to incorporate objects and relations between objects and to involve other people, as in peekaboo.

During the period from 12 to 30 months of age, new forms of play arise that appear to reflect representational mental abilities (Lillard, 2002). At 12 to 13 months, babies use objects in play much as adults would use them in earnest; that is, they put spoons in their mouths and bang pegs with hammers. However, at about 18 months babies begin to treat one thing as if it were another. They stir their "coffee" with a twig and comb the doll's hair with a toy rake or, as Jake and his cousin did, act as if the edge of a sandbox were a roadway and the sand were food or water. This kind of behavior is called **symbolic play** (also **pretend** or **fantasy play**): it is play in which one object stands for *(represents)* another, as the rake stands for a comb.

Studies have shown that symbolic play becomes increasingly complex after it makes its appearance during the second year. Two-year-olds not only engage in pretend play themselves but are skillful at interpreting and responding to the pretend actions of others (Walker-Andrews & Kahana-Kahana, 1999). In the simplest case, children direct their play actions at themselves (for example, an infant pretends to feed herself with a spoon). In the most complicated cases, which are not usually seen until about 30 months of age, children can make a toy (in developmental parlance, an "agent") perform actions fitting a social role (for example, the infant makes a mother doll feed her baby doll) (see Table 6.2).

Many developmentalists believe that children's play not only is an index of their cognitive development but also serves important functions for cognitive and social growth. Piaget (1962) believed that play during infancy consolidates newly acquired sensorimotor schemas. Anthony Pellegrini (2002) suggests that rough-and-tumble play, aside from any positive influence it might have on physical development, may also provide experience of dominant and submissive social relations.

This child, who is "giving Godzilla a drink," is engaging in the kind of complicated symbolic play that appears to emerge between the ages of 18 and 24 months.

Laura Dwight

table 6.2

Four Steps in the Development of Agent Use in Pretending	
Type of Agent Use	**Example**
Self as agent	The infant puts his or her head on a pillow to pretend to go to sleep
Passive other agent	The infant puts a doll on a pillow to pretend that it goes to sleep
Passive substitute agent	The infant puts a block on a pillow to pretend that it goes to sleep
Active other agent	The infant has a doll place a block on the pillow to go to sleep, as if the doll were actually "putting the block to bed"

Source: Adapted from Watson & Fischer, 1980.

Many developmentalists believe that early forms of play provide opportunities to acquire abilities that will become important later, just as the seemingly aimless movements of the embryo are a vital part of the process of fetal development (Göncü, 1999). As we will discuss in more detail in Chapter 10 (p. 378), according to this interpretation, the "as-if" nature of pretend play allows children to perform actions that are developmentally more advanced than those they can perform on their own. Thus a child can "pour tea" in a make-believe game in which the demands for precision are far more lenient than they would be if the child were to try to pour a glass of milk at the breakfast table.

Also, as the cultural-context approach would predict, the amount, kind, and sophistication of infants' social play depends on the social context in which it occurs. For example, Mayan parents do not place a high value on children's pretend play, and such play is relatively rare among their children (Gaskins, 2000). By contrast, Japanese mothers do place a lot of emphasis on pretend play, and the sophistication of the play of Japanese infants is more advanced than that of their American counterparts (Tamis-LeMonda, Bornstein, Cyphers, Toda & Ogino, 1992). Interestingly, toddlers' play is often more advanced when they play frequently with older siblings than it is when they play with their mothers, probably because the siblings are better able to enter into the fantasy than the adults (Farver & Wimbarti, 1995; Zukow-Goldring, 1995).

Imitation

Within Piaget's theoretical framework, the ability to imitate an action observed in the past (deferred imitation) provides one of the key lines of evidence that children have acquired the capacity to represent experience mentally. The following example, taken from Piaget's work (1962), illustrates both deferred imitation and the importance that Piaget attributed to deferred imitation as evidence that children are beginning to think in a new, more representational way. Jacqueline, now 16 months old, was astonished by the temper tantrum of an 18-month-old boy:

> He screamed as he tried to get out of his playpen and pushed it backwards, stamping his feet. J. stood watching him in amazement, never having witnessed such a scene before. The next day, she herself screamed in her playpen and tried to move it, stamping her foot lightly several times in succession. The imitation of the whole scene was most striking. Had it been immediate, [the imitation] would naturally not have involved representation, but coming as it did after an interval of more than twelve hours, it must have involved some representative or pre-representative element. (p. 63)

Piaget's example of deferred imitation does, indeed, offer a clear instance of representation. However, as you saw in our discussion of the development of memory in Chapter 5 (p. 195), deferred imitation of actions directed toward objects makes its first appearance as part of the bio-social-behavioral shift that occurs between 6 and 9 months of age, well before Piaget thought it possible. Recall also Andrew Meltzoff's demonstration that infants this age would imitate actions they had seen him perform 24 hours earlier, such as rotating a board, pushing a button to make a noise, and rattling bolts in a plastic cup (Chapter 5, p. 195).

Meltzoff and Elizabeth Hanna used a somewhat different imitation task to show that children can learn from one another by imitation by the age of 14 months (Hanna & Meltzoff, 1993). To demonstrate this kind of learning, the researchers selected outgoing and sociable infants at a day-care center to model several novel actions, such as poking a finger into a small black box to make a buzzer sound, pulling a triangular block across a table by a string, or picking up a string of pink beads and putting them into a cup. The infants modeled these actions at the table where all the children ordinarily engaged in group activities. Two days later an adult observer brought the objects used in the demonstration to the homes of the children who had watched it and presented them one at a time to the children. Even after a 2-day delay and a marked change in context, the children imitated approximately three of the actions they had seen at the day-care center.

An intriguing experiment by Meltzoff indicates that a new, more complex ability to represent nonvisible actions *does* arise at about 18 months, as Piaget assumed. At this age, infants "imitate" actions that people intend but do not actually complete (Meltzoff, 1995). To demonstrate this ability, Meltzoff arranged for 18-month-old infants to observe an adult repeatedly trying to pull the ends off a wooden dumbbell or trying to hang a bead necklace over a wooden cylinder. With half the children, the adult succeeded in those tasks; with the other half, the adult did not complete the actions. The adult then gave the objects to the infants to see if they would imitate the actions they had just observed. The babies who had seen the adult try repeatedly, but fail, to complete the action nevertheless "imitated" and completed the action just as frequently as those babies who had observed the actions being completed. Since the first group had not seen the complete action they themselves produced, Meltzoff reasoned that they must have understood, and imitated, the adult's intentions.

To see if children attribute intentions exclusively to people, Meltzoff conducted a second study in which he substituted a mechanical device for the human model (see Figure 6.6). Of the infants who observed the mechanical device as it either "tried and failed" or succeeded in removing the two end blocks from a wooden dumbbell, only 1 in 10 imitated the machine. Meltzoff argues that such behavior is evidence that babies attribute intentions to other human beings but not to machines, an indication that they have acquired the ability to represent the mental

Figure 6.6 Procedure used by Andrew Meltzoff to determine if infants imitate intended actions, even if they are not completed. (a) An adult tries to pull the ends off the dumbbell. (b) The analogous actions being modeled by a mechanical device.

(a)

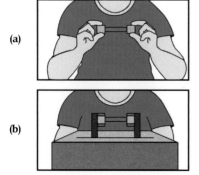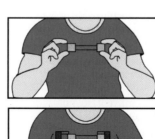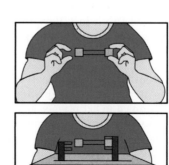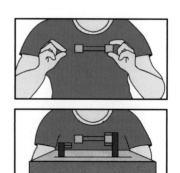

(b)

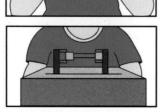

states of other people, which, of course, are not visible. Judging from the evidence presented at the end of Chapter 5 (p. 191), this ability begins to emerge around 9 months of age and becomes more solidified in the following months.

New Categorizing Abilities

As you saw in Chapter 5 (pp. 187–191), even very young infants display an ability to recognize a variety of categories. For example, they respond differently to what they experience depending on whether it appears to be animate and intentional or inanimate. They distinguish between actions carried out by people and actions performed by mechanical devices (Figure 6.6). Note, however, that young infants primarily contrast "natural" categories (such as animals and people) with each other or with "unnatural" artifacts (such as vehicles and airplanes). These forms of category contrasts involve, in Rochel Gelman's terms, "core domains" toward which infants are innately predisposed—domains that organize the acquisition of knowledge in fundamental domains such as rudimentary biology, physics, and psychology (Gelman & Lucariello, 2002).

However, much of the categorizing that we do does not involve such species-wide, easily acquired core domains. Rather, it involves artifacts, things produced by people, which are part of the cultural environment. The world of objects made by human beings is often categorized in a bewildering variety of ways in different cultures (Gelman, 1998). According to Gelman, in contrast with learning that involves core domains and can therefore build on the skeletal knowledge that is present in early infancy, learning that involves artificial categories has to be "learned from scratch." One illustration of the development of this capacity that arises during infancy is the ability to categorize what appears to be a jumble of artificial objects according to multiple features.

This ability was clearly demonstrated by Susan Sugarman (1983). She presented 12- to 30-month-old babies with a haphazard array of eight objects that could be classified according to such features as shape and color. (Figure 6.7 shows one such set of objects, composed of blue and red boats and blue and red dolls.) To determine what kinds of groupings they would create, Sugarman urged the toddlers, who were sitting on their mothers' laps, to "fix up" the random array of objects. If this suggestion failed to produce results, she showed them ways to group the objects and then urged them to continue grouping the objects themselves. Sugarman noted four stages in the progression of categorizing behavior:

1. One-year-olds would pick up one of the toys, look it over, and then touch it to the other toys one at a time. The only indication that they noticed the similarities between individual objects was that they were most likely to touch the toy they picked up to other toys that had the same shape.

2. The 18-month-olds would create a little work space in front of them and put two or three objects of the same kind in it.

3. The 24-month-old toddlers divided the objects into two distinct categories, working on one category at a time. For example, they would select all the boats first and then all the dolls. If Sugarman offered a boat to children who were collecting dolls, they immediately set the boat aside and kept working on the dolls.

Figure 6.7 How many ways can you see to organize these objects? The ability to categorize boats of one color and dolls of another and to subcategorize them according to color and form emerges during late infancy. (From Sugarman, 1983.)

4. The 30-month-old children simultaneously coordinated their work on the two major categories and created subcategories in which the objects were grouped according to color as well. They began by making a work space in front of them and then created two categories within it. They filled the categories by picking up whatever toy was nearest at hand and adding it to the appropriate group. If these children were handed a doll right after they had placed a boat in its group, they put it with the other dolls.

It appears, then, that one of the key cognitive changes associated with the end of infancy is the ability to go beyond recognition of conceptual relationships to active use of these relationships. Children can now construct categories according to conceptual differences and correspondences in a more flexible and systematic way.

Understanding Visual Representations and Models

Another cognitive change that begins to emerge at the end of infancy is the ability to understand that pictures and models are representations of objects, not the objects themselves, and to use this information effectively. Judy DeLoache and her colleagues (summarized in DeLoache, 2002) emphasize that the key element in using pictures, models, and other such symbolic representations is the ability to engage in what she refers to as **dual representation**. By dual representation, DeLoache means that the child must be able to mentally represent *both* the symbol (a picture, for example) *and* its relationship to the thing it depicts. At 2 years of age, children are incapable of this form of thought. At 3 they are proficient at it. It seems that $2^1/_2$ years, just the time when infancy is coming to a close, is a key transition point following which dual representation becomes possible.

This conclusion is illustrated in a series of studies focused on children's ability to use pictures as a source of information to find objects. In the first of these studies, 9- and 19-month-olds were shown realistic photos of various objects. The 9-month-olds explored the pictures with their fingers and even tried to grasp the objects in them, indicating that the babies were confusing the pictures with the objects they represented. This kind of confusion was rarely observed in the 19-month-olds (Pierroutsakos & DeLoache, 2003).

However, even 2-year-olds cannot use the information in pictures to draw inferences, for example, about the location of a hidden object. To test for this ability, the researchers showed children pictures of rooms and indicated where a toy was hidden in the picture. Then they took the children to the actual room shown in the picture and asked them to find the toy. Two-year-olds rarely could make use of the pictorial information. However, by the time they were $2^1/_2$ years old, these children were usually successful in finding the hidden toy (DeLoache & Burns, 1994).

A second series of studies focused on infants' ability to use models to guide their actions. In the first of these studies, DeLoache asked $2^1/_2$- and 3-year-olds to watch while she hid an attractive toy within a scale model of the room they were in. Then the children were asked to find an analogous toy that had been hidden in the corresponding place in the room itself. The $2^1/_2$-year-olds could not use the model as a guide and were confused by the task, but the 3-year-olds completed the task rather easily (Figure 6.8).

In a follow-up study, DeLoache and her colleagues arranged to convince half of a group of $2^1/_2$-year-olds that it is possible (with a special machine) to shrink an actual tent into a small model replica or to expand the model into the real tent (DeLoache, 1995). When the children believed that the model and tent were the same thing made large or small by the machine, the $2^1/_2$-year-olds successfully used the model to find objects in the tent. But the $2^1/_2$-year-olds who were told that the model was a toy version of the tent could not use information about an object's

dual representation The mental representation of both a symbol and its relationship to the thing it depicts.

(a)

(b)

All photos courtesy of Judy DeLoache

(c)

Figure 6.8 The ability to guide one's behavior using a model emerges at the end of infancy. (a) The experimenter (Judy DeLoache) hides a small toy troll in a scale model as a 3-year-old watches. (b) The child retrieves a larger toy troll that was hidden in the corresponding place in the room. (c) The child retrieves the small toy that she originally observed being hidden in the model.

location in one to help them locate a corresponding object in the other. This result supports DeLoache's belief that the key difficulty facing the $2^1/_2$-year-olds is that they cannot keep in mind the dual nature of the model: it is an interesting object in and of itself, and it stands for the thing it models. When they interpret the model as a shrunken version of the original, it does not function for them psychologically as a symbol, so the complicating aspect of the task has been removed. Three-year-olds are able to see the model as both a symbol and an object, so they effectively use the model to find objects in the normal-size space and do not need to have the problem simplified for them. Further support for this view comes from a recent study in which the model was placed behind a glass window in order to reduce its physical salience. This simple manipulation made it possible for the $2^1/_2$-year-olds to use the model as a symbol, a result showing that $2^1/_2$ years is a pivotal time for the development of this essential human ability (DeLoache, 2000).

Relating Words, Thoughts, and Actions

Longitudinal studies indicate that during the second year of life there is a steady increase in the number of words and phrases that infants can understand and use properly (Bloom & Tinker, 2001; Fenson et al., 1994). Infants as young as 14 to 16 months understand an average of approximately 150 words such as "doggie," "head," "drink," and "stop," as well as a number of common phrases such as "more milk" or "Mommy is going bye-bye." By 21 months of age, toddlers are able to follow relatively complex verbal instructions. When told to "put the block under the doll's chair," for example, they can place the block correctly. Their ability to create multiword sentences also increases, making possible the expression of more complex ideas.

The use of words that stand for people, objects, and events is sufficient by itself to show that children have begun to engage in mental representation. But what especially intrigues developmentalists are the connections between children's use of representational words and the development of the other forms of mental representation such as symbolic play, searching for hidden objects, deferred imitation, and the ability to form categories (Bloom, 2001; Gopnik & Meltzoff, 1997; Waxman, 2002).

The link between deferred imitation and word acquisition is perhaps the most obvious, since to a great extent children's early use of words is closely tied to words they have heard adults speak. "More," for example, was one of the first words used by Mike and Sheila's daughter Jenny. Earlier, whenever she finished drinking a cup of milk or juice, Jenny would bang the empty cup on the tray of her highchair. Her parents would then ask her, "Do you want some more?" Shortly before her first birthday, she began to hold up her cup and say "More" before anyone asked her if that was what she wanted.

Likewise, there is a clear association between language and symbolic play, both of which involve the representation of absent persons, objects, or actions. In symbolic play, arbitrary objects are used to stand for other objects—a banana is treated as a telephone, for example, or a sandbox edge becomes a highway. In language, sounds are the substitutes for objects and events. Initially, children's fantasy play is restricted to single actions, and their utterances are restricted to single words. But at about 18 months of age, when children begin to combine two actions in play, they also begin to create two-word sentences (Bloom & Tinker, 2001; Gopnik & Meltzoff, 1997). So, for example, about the same time that children begin to say "All gone milk," they also begin to pretend that they are pouring water into a cup and helping a baby drink it.

Karen Lifter and Lois Bloom demonstrated close relationships between the early acquisition of vocabulary and the sophistication with which infants search for hidden objects and play with objects (Lifter & Bloom, 1989). They found that children began to speak their first words at about the same time that they first began to search for hidden objects, and that they underwent a spurt in the rate of acquiring new words at approximately the same time that they began to exhibit logical search patterns. The same sort of linkages appeared when Lifter and Bloom looked at the sophistication of play: children who had not begun to talk moved toys around but did not combine their actions, as they do when they use a toy teapot to pour pretend water into a cup and then pretend to drink it. Play involving such combinations of actions appeared with children's first words, and more complex constructions appeared in conjunction with a spurt in vocabulary. Alison Gopnik and Andrew Meltzoff also found that a spurt in vocabulary occurs at approximately the same time as do several cognitive shifts, including the ability to classify objects into two groups, sophisticated behaviors in searching for objects, and insightful problem solving (Gopnik & Meltzoff, 1997).

Infants' acquisition of new words is clearly related to what they are attempting to do and their interest in the events they experience. For example, Gopnik and Meltzoff report that between 12 and 24 months, when infants show an intense interest in the appearance and disappearance of objects, they are also likely to say "gone" every time something disappears. In fact, research in several cultures has shown that a term equivalent to "gone" or "all gone" is one of the most frequent words in children's vocabularies at 18 months (Fenson et al., 1994; Gopnik & Choi, 1990). Gopnik describes one 18-month-old who liked to hide a ring under a pillow. On one occasion the child hid the ring 13 times in a row, each time saying "gone" as he did so.

The Development of Child–Caregiver Relations

During the second year of life, children find novelty and excitement everywhere. A walk to the corner drugstore with a $1\frac{1}{2}$-year-old can take forever. Each step presents new and interesting sights to explore: a bottle cap lying by the edge of the sidewalk requires close examination; a pigeon waddling across a neighbor's lawn invites a detour; even the cracks in the sidewalk may prompt sitting down to take a closer look.

As you saw in Chapter 5, however, things that attract babies may also cause them to be wary. Whizzing cars, strange people, and novel objects are often frightening to toddlers as well as fascinating. There needs to be a balance between interest and fear as infants continue to explore and learn about the world. They cannot spend their entire lives in close proximity to their parents, but they cannot survive for long if they wander off on their own too soon.

Research with both monkey and human mothers and babies indicates how the balance between exploration and safety is created and maintained in ways that allow development to continue. A key element in this process is the emotional bond called *attachment* that develops between children and their caregivers sometime between the ages of 7 and 9 months, which we briefly described at the end of Chapter 5 (p. 197). Explaining how this attachment comes about and how it influences later development has proved to be a major challenge to developmentalists.

Courtesy of Sheila Cole

Many small children become strongly attached to a teddy bear, a blanket, or some other object. The British psychiatrist D. W. Winnicott (1971) has called such objects "transitional objects." They support children in their attempts to understand and deal with the reality that exists beyond their own bodies. The strong attachment this little girl feels for her teddy bear is written all over her smiling embrace.

Explanations of Attachment

The fact that 7- to 9-month-old children everywhere begin to become upset when they are separated from their primary caregivers suggests that attachment is a universal feature of development (Simpson, 2001). This possibility has led to a lively debate about the evolutionary reasons for attachment, the causes of changes in attachment behaviors as children grow older, and the influence of the quality of attachment on children's later development. Three major explanations of the basis of attachment have dominated this debate: Sigmund Freud's suggestion that infants become attached to the people who satisfy their need for food; Erik Erikson's idea that infants become attached to those they can trust to help them; and John Bowlby's somewhat similar hypothesis that infants become attached to those who give them care and protection, which provides them with a firm foundation for exploring the world.

Sigmund Freud's Drive-Reduction Explanation

The process of attachment plays an important role in Sigmund Freud's theory of development. Freud held that the early interactions between children and their social environment, particularly the people who care for them, set the pattern for later personality and social development. In adulthood, Freud wrote, the relationship with the mother becomes "the prototype for all . . . love relations for both sexes" (1940/1964, p. 188).

While Freud's emphasis on the importance of attachment for development is widely shared, his explanation for the causes of attachment is not (Fonagy, 2001). He believed that human beings, like other organisms, are motivated in large part by **biological drives**—states of arousal, such as hunger or thirst, that urge the organism to obtain the basic prerequisites for its survival. When a drive is aroused, the organism seeks to satisfy the need that gives rise to it. Pleasure is felt when the need is satisfied, reducing the drive, and the organism returns to a more comfortable biological equilibrium. In this sense pleasure-seeking is a basic principle of existence. With respect to attachment in particular, Freud asserted that "love has its origin in attachment to the satisfied need for nourishment" (1940/1964, p. 188). Thus, the first person infants become attached to is expected to be the mother, who is the

biological drives States of arousal, such as hunger or thirst, that urge the organism to obtain the basic prerequisites for its survival.

one most likely to nourish them. The major problem with this explanation is that research has not substantiated Freud's notion that attachment is caused by the reduction of the hunger drive, as you will see below.

Erik Erikson's Psychosocial Explanation

A more promising explanation of attachment than Freud's was proposed by Erik Erikson (1963), one of Freud's most influential students. Erikson, whose theory of development will figure in many discussions throughout the remainder of this book, believed that there are eight stages in the human life cycle, each characterized by a distinctive conflict that the individual must resolve. (These stages are laid out in full in the box "Psychodynamic Theory: Freud and Erikson" on pp. 32–33.)

The conflicts characteristic of the first two stages that Erikson proposes provide an explanation for the increase in children's anxiety when they are separated from their mothers late in the first year of life and its decline during the second year. According to Erikson's scheme, during the first stage of development, which lasts from birth to roughly 1 year of age, the issue that infants deal with is trust. Babies either learn to trust others who care for them or they learn to mistrust them. In Erikson's view, children become attached to the people who reliably minister to their needs and who otherwise foster a sense of trust. Once babies gain faith in their caregivers, usually during the second year, they cease to be distressed during brief separations because they trust their caregiver to come back. This understanding prepares them for the second stage of development, which lasts until about the age of 3. During this stage, infants must deal with the issue of autonomy. They must learn to exert their will and to control themselves; failure to do so leads to doubt that they can do things by themselves.

John Bowlby's Ethological Explanation

John Bowlby's theory of attachment arose from his study of the mental health problems of British children who had been separated from their families during World War II and were cared for in institutions (Bowlby, 1969, 1973, 1980). Bowlby reviewed observations of children in hospitals, nurseries, and orphanages who had either lost their parents or been separated from them for long periods of time. He also looked at reports of clinical interviews with psychologically troubled or delinquent adolescents and adults. He found a similar sequence of behaviors described in these various sources. When children are first separated from their mothers, they become frantic with fear. They cry, throw tantrums, and try to escape their surroundings. Then they go through a stage of despair and depression. If the separation continues and no new stable relationship is formed, these children seem to become indifferent to other people. Bowlby called this state of indifference **detachment.**

In his attempt to explain the distress of young children when they are separated from their parents, Bowlby was particularly influenced by the work of the ethologists, who emphasize a broad, evolutionary approach to understanding human behavior (see Chapter 1, p. 16). Ethological studies of monkeys and apes revealed that infants of these species spend their initial weeks and months of postnatal life in almost continuous, direct, physical contact with their biological mothers. Bowlby noted that these primate infants consistently display several apparently instinctual responses that are essential to human attachment: clinging, sucking, crying, and separation protest. After a few weeks or months (depending on the species of primate), infants begin to venture away from their mothers to explore their immediate physical and social environments, but they scurry back to the mother at the first signs of something unusual and potentially dangerous (Suomi, 1995). These

detachment The state of indifference to others that children manifest when there is a continuing separation from their caregivers.

primate behaviors, Bowlby hypothesized, are the evolutionary basis for the development of attachment in human babies as well.

Bowlby conceived of the process of attachment formation by analogy to a thermostat. Just as a thermostat switches a furnace on or off when the temperature falls or rises past a set point, attachment functions to provide a balance between infants' need for safety and their need for varied learning experiences. Bowlby (1969) believed that attachment normally develops through four broad phases during the first 2 years of life, eventually producing a "dynamic equilibrium between the mother–child pair" (p. 236):

1. *The preattachment phase* (birth to 6 weeks). In the first few weeks of life, while infants and caregivers are working out the initial systems of coordination (see Chapter 4, p. 139), infants remain in close contact with their caregivers, from whom they receive food and comfort. They do not seem to get upset when left alone with an unfamiliar caregiver.

2. *The "attachment-in-the-making" phase* (6 weeks to 6–8 months). Infants begin to respond differently to familiar and unfamiliar people, and by the time they are 6 or 7 months old they start to show signs of wariness when confronted with unfamiliar objects and people (as discussed in Chapter 5, pp. 195–196).

3. *The "clear-cut attachment" phase* (6–8 months to 18–24 months). During this period children display full-blown **separation anxiety,** becoming visibly upset when the mother or another caregiver leaves the room. Once this phase of attachment is reached, it regulates the physical and emotional relationship between children and those to whom they are attached. Whenever the distance between attachment figures and the child becomes too great, one or the other is likely to become upset and act to reduce that distance: just as babies become upset if their mothers leave them, mothers become upset if their babies wander out of sight. Attachment provides the child with a feeling of security. The mother becomes a **secure base** from which babies make exploratory excursions and to which they come back every so often to renew contact before returning to their explorations. During the early months of the attachment phase, the mother bears the greater responsibility for maintaining the equilibrium of the attachment system, because the infant's capacities to act and interact are quite restricted.

4. *The reciprocal relationship phase* (18–24 months and later). As the child becomes more mobile and spends increasingly greater amounts of time away from the mother, the pair enter a reciprocal state in which they share responsibility for maintaining the equilibrium of the system. Every so often, either the mother or the child will interrupt what she or the child is doing to renew contact with one another. Among humans, this transitional phase lasts several years.

Once achieved, a firm, reciprocal emotional relationship between infants and caregivers helps children to retain feelings of security during the increasingly frequent and lengthy periods of separation from their caregivers. It is noteworthy that this phase develops at the same time that symbolic representation is becoming a dominant element in children's thought processes. Bowlby believed that as a consequence of infants' growing symbolic capacities, parent–child attachment begins to serve as an **internal working model,** a mental model that children construct as a result of their experiences and that they use to guide their interactions with caregivers and others.

separation anxiety The distress that babies show when the person to whom they are attached leaves.

secure base Bowlby's term for the people whose presence provides the child with the security that allows him or her to make exploratory excursions.

internal working model A mental model that children construct as a result of their experiences with their caregivers and that they use to guide their interactions with their caregivers and others.

Figure 6.9 This baby monkey spent most of its time clinging to the terry cloth substitute mother even when its nursing bottle was attached to a wire substitute mother nearby. This preference indicates that bodily contact and the comfort it gives are important in the formation of the infant's attachment to its mother.

Martin Rogers/Tony Stone

Evidence from Animal Experiments

Ethical considerations make it difficult, if not impossible, to conduct experiments to determine the sources of human attachment. When Harry Harlow and his co-workers wished to test ideas about attachment, they carried out a series of experiments with rhesus monkeys. They began by testing the drive-reduction theory of attachment (Harlow, 1959). In one of these studies, the researchers separated eight baby monkeys from their mothers a few hours after birth and placed them in individual cages with two inanimate substitute mothers—one made of wire, the other of terry cloth (see Figure 6.9). Four of the infant monkeys received milk from the wire mothers, four from the terry cloth mothers. The two types of substitute mothers were equally effective as sources of nutrition: all eight babies drank the same amount and gained weight at the same rate. Only the feel of bodily contact with the substitute mothers differed.

Over the 165-day period that they lived with the substitute mothers, the baby monkeys showed a distinct preference for the cloth mothers. Even if they obtained all of their food from a wire mother, the babies would go to it only to feed and would then go back to cling to the terry cloth mother. From the perspective of drive-reduction theory, it made no sense at all for the four infant monkeys who received their food from a wire mother to prefer to spend their time with a terry cloth mother that might feel good but satisfied no apparent biological drive, such as hunger or thirst. Harlow (1959) concluded, "These results attest to the importance—possibly the overwhelming importance—of bodily contact and the immediate comfort it supplies in forming the infant's attachment to its mother" (p. 70).

In later investigations, Harlow and his colleagues sought to determine whether attachment to their substitute mothers had any effect on the infants' explorations, a crucial test of Bowlby's evolutionary theory (Harlow & Harlow, 1969). Knowing that normal human and monkey babies run to their mothers for comfort when faced with an unfamiliar and frightening situation, the researchers created such a situation for the monkeys who had received milk from the wire substitute mothers. They placed a mechanical teddy bear that marched forward while beating a drum in the monkeys' cages. The terrified babies fled to the terry cloth mothers, not to the wire ones (see Figure 6.10). Once the babies had overcome their fear by rubbing their bodies against the cloth mother, however, they turned to look at the bear with curiosity. Some even left the protection of the terry cloth mother to approach the object that had so terrified them only moments before.

The infant monkeys demonstrated their attachment to the terry cloth mothers after separations of up to a year. The researchers would place the monkeys in an apparatus in which, by pressing on one of three levers, they could choose to look at the terry cloth mother, the wire mother, or an empty box. The monkeys who had been raised with a wire mother that provided milk and a milkless terry cloth mother spent more time pressing the lever that gave them a glimpse of the terry cloth mother than the lever that allowed them to see the wire mother. They were no more interested in the wire mother than in the empty box. Even monkeys who had been raised with only a wire mother showed no signs of attachment when they were given a chance to view it (Harlow & Zimmerman, 1959).

Harlow concluded that soothing tactile sensations provide the baby with a sense of security that is more important to the formation of attachment than food. This finding undermines the drive-reduction hypothesis that infants become attached to the people who feed them. At first glance it may also seem to undermine Bowlby's idea of the reciprocal nature of attachment, since the terry cloth mothers did nothing for the infant monkeys except provide soothing physical contact. However, as Harlow's team discovered, although soothing tactile sensations appear to be necessary for healthy development, they are not sufficient. As these monkeys grew older, they showed signs of impaired development: they were either indifferent or abusive to other monkeys, and none of them could copulate normally. The researchers concluded that the nourishment and physical comfort provided by the cloth-covered mother that supplied milk in the monkey's infancy does not produce a normal adolescent or adult. "The [substitute] cannot cradle the baby or communicate monkey sounds and gestures. It cannot punish for misbehavior or attempt to break the infant's bodily attachment before it becomes a fixation." (Harlow & Harlow, 1962, p. 142)

Harlow Primate Laboratory, University of Wisconsin

Figure 6.10 (*top*) This baby monkey clings to its terry cloth substitute mother and hides its eyes when it is frightened by the approach of a mechanical teddy bear. (*bottom*) After gaining reassurance, the baby monkey looks at the strange intruder. The terry cloth mother, which does not provide nourishment, acts as a secure base, whereas the wire mother, which does provide nourishment, does not. This contradicts drive-reduction theories of attachment.

The later social behavior of these monkeys supports Bowlby's belief that attachment is a highly evolved system of regulation between the mother and the infant. Such regulation is a two-sided process that requires social interaction for healthy emotional development. The infant monkeys clearly turned to the terry cloth mothers for security, but in the absence of a live mother, all the adjusting was left to the baby, and a proper regulatory system did not form.

Patterns of Attachment

The maladaptive social behavior of monkeys raised with inanimate substitute mothers poses a question: What kinds of interactions between mother and child provide the most effective basis for the development of healthy human social relations?

Because no two mother–infant pairs are alike and because the environmental conditions into which human babies are born vary enormously, we should not expect to find one right pattern of attachment that meets the basic requirements for social development in all cases. Many investigators believe, however, that it is possible to identify general patterns of mother–child interaction that are most conducive to development.

Research on such patterns of mother–child interaction has been greatly influenced by the work of Mary Ainsworth. On the basis of observations of mother–infant pairs in Africa and the United States, she concluded that there are consistent, qualitatively distinct patterns in the ways mothers and infants relate to each other during the second and third years of infancy (Ainsworth, 1967, 1982). Most of the mother–infant pairs she observed seemed to have worked out a comfortable, secure relationship by the third year, but some of the relationships were characterized by persistent tension and difficulties in regulating joint activities.

To test the security of the mother–child relationship, Ainsworth designed a procedure called the **strange situation.** The basic purpose of this procedure is to observe how babies make use of the mother as a secure base from which to explore, to respond to separation, and to respond to a stranger. Different patterns of reactions, she reasoned, would reflect different kinds of relationships. The following case study, summarized from research reported by Mary Ainsworth and Barbara Wittig, illustrates the strange-situation procedure and how a typical 12-month-old middle-class North American child behaved in it (Ainsworth & Wittig, 1969, pp. 116–118).

[An observer shows a mother and her baby into an experimental room that has toys scattered on the floor.] *Brian had one arm hooked over his mother's shoulder as they came into the room. . . . He looked around soberly, but with interest, at the toys and at the observer.*

[The observer leaves the room.] *After being put down, Brian immediately crept towards the toys and began to explore them* [Figure 6.11a]. *He was very active. . . . Although his attention was fixed on the playthings, he glanced up at his mother six times.*

[After 3 minutes the stranger enters, greets the mother, and sits down quietly in a chair.] *Brian turned to look at the stranger . . . with a pleasant expression on his face. He played with the tube again, vocalized, smiled, and turned to glance at his mother. . . . When the stranger and his mother began to converse, he continued to explore actively. . . . When the stranger began her approach by leaning forward to offer him a toy, he smiled, crept towards her, and reached for it* [Figure 6.11b].

[The mother leaves the room, leaving her purse on the chair, while the stranger distracts Brian's attention.] *He did not notice his mother leave. He continued to watch the stranger and the toys. . . . Suddenly, he crept to his mother's chair, pulled himself up into a standing position, and looked at the stranger. She tried to distract him with a pull-toy . . . but he glanced again at his mother's empty chair. He was less active than he had been when alone with his mother, and after two minutes his activity ceased. He sat chewing the string of the pull-toy and glancing from the stranger to his mother's chair. He made an unhappy noise, then a cry-face, and then he cried. The stranger tried to distract him by offering him a block; he took it but then threw it away.*

[Brian's mother returns to the room.] *Brian looked at her immediately and vocalized loudly . . . then he crept to her quickly and pulled himself up, with her help, to hold on to her knees. Then she picked him up, and he immediately put his arms around her neck, his face against her shoulder, and hugged her hard* [Figure 6.11c]. *. . . He resisted being put down; he tried to cling to her and protested loudly. Once on the floor, he threw himself down, hid his face in the rug, and cried angrily* [Figure 6.11d]. *His mother knelt beside him and tried to interest him in the toys again. He stopped crying and watched. After a moment she disengaged herself and got up to sit on her chair. He immediately threw himself down and cried again.*

[Brian's mother gets up and leaves the room again.] *As she said "bye-bye" and waved, Brian looked up with a little smile, but he shifted into a cry before she had quite closed the door. He sat crying, rocking himself back and forth* [Figure 6.11e].

[The stranger, who had earlier left the room, reenters.] *Brian lulled slightly when he saw the stranger enter, but he continued to cry. She first tried to distract him, then offered her arms to him. Brian responded by raising his arms; she picked him up, and he stopped crying immediately. . . . Occasionally he gave a little sob, but for the most part he did not cry. But when she put him down, he screamed. She picked him up again, and he lulled.*

At the moment that his mother returned Brian was crying listlessly. He did not notice his mother. The stranger half-turned and pointed her out. Brian looked towards her, still crying, and then turned away. But he soon "did a double take." He looked back and vocalized a little protest. His mother offered her arms to him. He reached towards her, smiling, and leaned way out of the stranger's arms and his mother took him.

strange situation A procedure designed to assess children's attachment on the basis of their responses to a stranger when they are with their mothers, when they are left alone, and when they are reunited with their mothers.

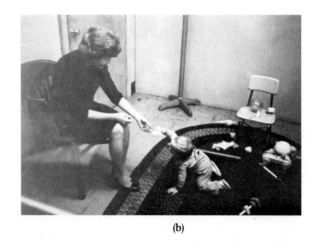

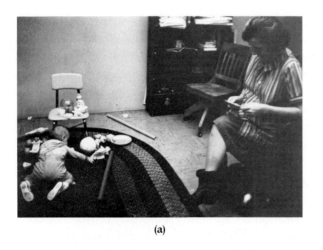

(a)

(b)

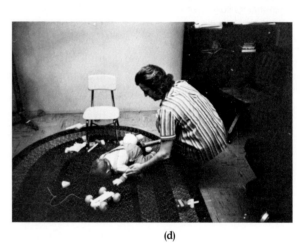

(c)

(d)

(e)

All photos: Mary D. Ainsworth

Figure 6.11 Brian in the strange situation. (a) Brian explores the toys. (b) Brian responds to the stranger. (c) Brian hugs his mother when she returns to the room after a brief absence. (d) Brian throws himself on the floor when his mother puts him down. (e) Brian cries and rocks back and forth when he is left alone again.

To permit systematic comparisons between children, Ainsworth and her colleagues worked out a method of categorizing infants' responses in the strange situation (Ainsworth et al., 1971; Ainsworth et al., 1978). The categories are based on the child's behaviors when the child and mother are alone in the playroom together, when the mother leaves the room, when a strange woman offers comfort, and when the mother returns. The researchers found that the way the child reacts to the return of the mother is the key indicator of attachment and that the responses fall into three categories: *secure attachment* and two types of *insecure* attachment, *anxious/avoidant* and *anxious/resistant*.

secure attachment A pattern of attachment in which children play comfortably and react positively to a stranger as long as their mothers are present. They become upset when their mothers leave and are unlikely to be consoled by a stranger, but they calm down as soon as their mothers reappear.

anxious/avoidant attachment The attachment pattern in which infants are indifferent to where their mothers are sitting, may or may not cry when their mothers leave, are as likely to be comforted by strangers as by their mothers, and are indifferent when their mothers return to the room.

anxious/resistant attachment The attachment pattern in which infants stay close to their mothers and appear anxious even when their mothers are near. They become very upset when their mothers leave but are not comforted by their return. They simultaneously seek renewed contact with their mothers and resist their mothers' efforts to comfort them.

- **Secure attachment.** Brian is a classic example of secure attachment. As long as the mother is present, securely attached children play comfortably with the toys in the playroom and react positively to the stranger. These children become visibly and vocally upset when their mothers leave, and they are unlikely to be consoled by a stranger. However, when the mother reappears and they can climb into her arms, they quickly calm down and soon resume playing. This pattern of attachment is shown by about 65 percent of U.S. middle-class children. They demonstrate a healthy balance between attachment and exploratory behaviors.

- **Anxious/avoidant attachment.** During the time the mother and child are left alone together in the playroom, anxious/avoidant infants are more or less indifferent to where their mothers are sitting. They may or may not cry when their mothers leave the room. If they do become distressed, strangers are likely to be as effective at comforting them as their mothers. When the mother returns, these children may turn or look away from her instead of going to her to seek closeness and comfort. About 23 percent of U.S. middle-class children show this pattern of attachment. Their exploratory behaviors dominate at the expense of attachment behaviors.

- **Anxious/resistant attachment.** Anxious/resistant children have trouble from the start in the strange situation. They stay close to their mothers and appear anxious even when they are near. They become very upset when the mother leaves, but they are not comforted by her return. Instead, they simultaneously seek renewed contact with the mother and resist her efforts to comfort them. They may cry angrily to be picked up with their arms outstretched, but then arch away and struggle to climb down once the mother starts to pick them up. These children do not readily resume playing after the mother returns. Instead, they keep a wary eye on her. About 12 percent of U.S. middle-class children show this pattern of attachment. Their attachment behaviors dominate at the expense of exploratory behaviors.

As experience using the strange situation accumulated, researchers noted that some children were difficult to classify in terms of one of the three main categories. After reviewing videotapes of over 200 cases that seemed not to fit easily in the established categories, Mary Main and her colleagues suggested a fourth category, which they labeled *disorganized* (Main & Solomon, 1990). Children who fit this category seemed to lack any coherent, organized method for dealing with the stress they experienced. This disorganization expressed itself in a variety of ways. Some children cried loudly while trying to climb onto the mother's lap; others approached her while refusing to look at her; still others stood at the door and screamed while she was gone but moved away from her silently when she returned. In some extreme cases, the children seemed to be in a dazed state and refused to move while in their mothers' presence.

Attachment between mother and child can be observed in the emotions they express when reunited after a period of separation.

Over the past three decades, developmentalists have conducted a good deal of research trying to understand the causes of these basic patterns of attachment behavior (summarized in Cassidy & Shaver, 2001, and Waters & Cummings, 2001). Most of this research has focused on the mother–infant relationship, although other attachments that are important in children's lives have also been studied (see the box "Attachment to Fathers and Others").

Attachment to Fathers and Others

Discussions of infant attachment have tended to focus almost entirely on the role of mothers to the exclusion of fathers and other caretakers. There are several reasons for this one-sided treatment of babies' social relationships.

Perhaps the most legitimate reason for focusing on the mother's role is that in most of the world's societies the mother spends far more time with her infant than any other adult (Parke, 1995). In the United States, for example, Michael Lamb and his colleagues reported that in two-parent families in which the mother does not work outside the home, fathers spend only 25 to 30 percent as much time in one-to-one interaction with their infants as mothers do. Perhaps more significant, even when these fathers are with their children, they assume little or no responsibility for their day-to-day care or rearing (Lamb et al., 1987). Similar patterns of interaction are found in many societies but by no means all (Roopnarine & Carter, 1992; Sun & Roopnarine, 1996). While there is evidence that this pattern is changing, and paternal involvement with children is increasing, the mother continues to play the dominant role in rearing the family's children (Pleck & Masciadrelli, 2003).

However, many other patterns of family life that support infants' development exist, and contemporary students of attachment recognize that it is important to consider the entire caregiving system in its cultural context when seeking to understand the conditions that promote secure attachment or put it at risk (George & Solomon, 1999). Even in her early reports about attachment based on her observations among Ganda infants in East Africa, Mary Ainsworth noted that almost all the babies who became attached to their mothers while she was studying them also became attached to other familiar people—fathers, grandparents, an older sibling, or another older adult living in the household (Ainsworth, 1967).

Research focused on fathers in societies where they spend relatively little time caring for their infants found that they are by no means indifferent or lacking in caregiving ability. When fathers spend time with their children, they are most likely to play with them, but increasingly they play a direct role in routine caretaking as well (Grossmann

Among the Aka of the Ituri forests, men play a major role in the care of their young children, promoting close emotional bonds.

et al., 2002; Pleck & Masciadrelli, 2003). When fathers in the United States have been observed feeding their infants, for example, they respond sensitively to their babies' feeding rhythms and engage their babies in social episodes just as often as mothers. Moreover, the infants of fathers who are judged to be sensitive caregivers are likely to be as securely attached to them as they are to their mothers (Howes, 1999).

The specifics of family relationships play an important role in determining infant–father attachments. In nontraditional American families in which fathers have the role of primary caregiver, babies turn to their fathers, not their mothers, for comfort when they are under stress (Geiger, 1996). This same result has been observed among Aka pygmies, a hunter-gatherer group who live in central Africa. Aka men, women, and children generally hunt together, and Aka adult couples spend more time together than do couples in any other documented social group (Morelli et al., 1999). Hewlett (1992) reports that "Aka fathers are within an arms reach of their infants 47% of the day and are more likely than mothers to hug or soothe their infants while holding them than are

mothers" (p. 238). In contrast with families in the United States and many other countries, Aka fathers are more likely than their wives to pick up infants who crawl over to them and request to be held. Hewlett concludes, on the basis of his findings, that when cultural patterns lead fathers to be closely involved in their children's upbringing, attachment to the two parents occurs in the same way.

Of course, mothers and fathers are not the only people with whom infants form attachments. Babies also form attachments with peers, siblings, nonfamily caretakers, teachers, and grandparents (Howes, 1999). Studies that compare children's social relationships with day-care providers and with parents show that while most children developed positive relationships with their care providers, they were less likely to be securely attached to nonparental care providers than to their parents. Secure attachments between children and child-care workers were more likely when the adult–child ratios were low and the children were younger, female, and from higher socioeconomic backgrounds (Ahnert, Pinquart & Lamb, 2003).

Many families in the United States, particularly families living close to, or below, the poverty line, have historically created caregiving systems that include networks of adults, such as grandparents and other kin, to whom children become attached (we will return to this topic in Chapter 11). And in some societies, such as that of the !Kung of the Kalahari Desert, babies are cared for in groups of children beginning around the age of 1 year so that their mothers can resume their work as the society's food gatherers (Konner, 1977). Under such circumstances, babies form strong attachments to many older children in the group in addition to adults.

The critical feature that seems to determine to whom infants become attached is whether the caregiving provided plays a positive supporting role in the child's development—a safe base from which to explore the world and a source of comfort. To the extent that such caregiving is restricted to the mother, she is the natural object of attachment. But when caregiving is distributed to include fathers and others, they also become effective attachment figures.

Ituri Forest Peoples Fund

Two major questions have dominated the study of attachment patterns. First, what are the causes of variations in the patterns of attachment? Second, do these variations have important consequences for later development? We will concentrate on the first question here and address the consequences of different patterns of attachment in Chapter 7.

The Causes of Variations in Patterns of Attachment

Research on what leads to variations in patterns of attachment has focused on four likely factors: the behavior of the caretaker toward the child, the capacities and temperamental disposition of the child, stresses within the family, and the child-rearing patterns of the cultural group to which the mother and child belong.

Parental Behaviors

In an early study of the antecedents of attachment, Mary Ainsworth and Silvia Bell hypothesized that different patterns of attachment were the result of differences in mothers' sensitivity to their infants' signals of need (Ainsworth & Bell, 1969). They found that 3-month-olds whose mothers responded quickly and appropriately to their cries and were sensitive to their signals of need were likely to be evaluated as securely attached at 12 months.

Over the past several decades many additional studies have examined the relationship of parental sensitivity to measures of attachment. Michael Lamb and his colleagues reported that parents of securely attached infants are generally more involved with their infants, more in synchrony with them, and more appropriate in their responsiveness (Lamb et al., 1999). As might be expected, children raised by extremely insensitive or abusive caregivers are especially likely to be rated as insecurely attached or disorganized (Thompson, 1998). Although such studies support Ainsworth and Bell's basic findings, some researchers have failed to find the expected relationship between sensitivity and attachment. An analysis of 65 studies conducted in many parts of the world revealed only a modest correlation between measures of sensitivity and secure attachment, indicating that many factors linking parental behaviors to attachment are still not well understood (DeWolff & van IJzendoorn, 1997).

Characteristics of the Child

Close observation of the interactions between parents and their children reveals that interactional synchrony is a joint accomplishment: just as infants need responsive parents to develop secure attachments, parents need a responsive infant in order to achieve their full potential as caregivers. To test the idea that infants' behaviors contribute to attachment relations, Michael Lewis and Candice Feiring observed 174 infant–mother pairs at home when the infants were 3 months old, noting in particular the relative rates at which the infants engaged in object play or interacted with their mothers (Lewis & Feiring, 1989). They then evaluated the infants' reactions in a version of the strange situation 9 months later. They found that infants who had spent more time playing with objects than interacting sociably with their mothers during the home observations were more likely to display signs of insecure attachment later on.

Such observations have led a number of researchers to focus on the role of the infant's temperament in the development of attachment. It seems intuitively reasonable, for example, that mothers would find it more difficult to establish interactional synchrony with infants who are fearful or who easily become upset than with infants who are temperamentally easy. However, studies that compare attachment behaviors of children displaying different temperamental characteristics have, like those that focused on the relationship of sensitivity to attachment, yielded small effects. Some studies have found that infants judged to have difficult temperaments are more likely to be evaluated as insecurely attached at 1 year of age, while other studies have not (Vaughn & Bost, 1999).

Family Influences

A variety of factors that contribute to stress on parents have been found to reduce the probability that infants will display secure attachment. Maternal depression has been consistently linked to reductions in secure attachment behaviors (Diener, Nievar & Wright, 2003). Maternal depression is, in turn, related to another factor that reduces secure attachment—low socioeconomic status: children living in poverty are less likely than children who live in better economic circumstances to exhibit secure attachment behaviors (Lyons-Ruth & Jacobvitz, 1999). Another factor is marital discord: couples who are experiencing problems in their marriage are more likely to have insecure children (Belsky, 1999). Researchers believe that these stressors are related to insecure attachment in two ways. First, difficult conditions within the family are likely to increase maternal depression and lower parental sensitivity, which in turn decreases the likelihood of a secure attachment relationship forming. Second, witnessing angry or violent interactions between adult caretakers or experiencing unpredictable changes in caregiving arrangements is likely to make children feel that the adults involved are not reliable sources of comfort and safety.

Cultural Influences

At present there is sharp disagreement among developmentalists concerning the extent to which the process of attachment is influenced by cultural variations. Some have argued that there are important cultural variations in attachment and that the very notion of what constitutes a secure human relationship, which is a part of the concept of attachment, is culturally specific (Rothbaum, Weisz, Pott & Morelli, 2000).

Others have argued that attachment is a universal feature of human development (see van IJzendoorn & Sagi, 2001, for a review of conflicting evidence). Several studies demonstrate cultural differences using the strange situation as a means to assess attachment.

For example, several decades ago, children who grew up on some Israeli kibbutzim (collective farms) were raised communally from an early age. Although they saw their parents daily, the adults who looked after them were usually not family members. When at the age of 11 to 14 months such communally raised children were placed in the strange situation with either a parent or a caregiver, only 56% were classified as securely attached, and 37% were classified as anxious/resistant (Sagi et al., 1985).

Abraham Sagi and his colleagues suspected that the high rate of insecure attachment among these children was caused by the fact that the communal caregivers could not respond promptly to the individual children in their care and by staffing rotations that did not allow the adults to provide the children in their care with individualized attention. To test this hypothesis, these researchers compared the attachment behaviors of children raised in traditional kibbutzim, where they slept in a communal dormitory at night, with those of children raised in kibbutzim from which they returned to sleep in their parents' home at night (Sagi et al., 1995). Once again, using the strange situation, they found a low level of secure attachments among the children who slept in communal dormitories. Those who slept at home displayed a significantly higher level of secure attachments, supporting the idea that cultural differences in the opportunities for sensitive caregiving accounted for cultural differences in attachment quality.

This child is clearly distressed at separating from Mom while she goes to work and at being left with a caregiver.

Ron Chapple/Getty Images

A number of other studies have also suggested that cultural factors sometimes influence behavior in the strange situation (Grossmann et al., 1985; Miyake et al., 1985). The evidence of cultural variation, however, is balanced by evidence that there is a general tendency in all societies for children to become attached to their caregivers. Differences appear to be concentrated on what form the disturbed attachment takes in different societies, but these variations are at present not well understood.

An influential review of research on attachment spanning many cultures, conducted by Marinus van IJzendoorn and Abraham Sagi, reported that while the proportion of children displaying one or another pattern of attachment behaviors may vary in a small number of cases, the overall pattern of results is remarkably consistent with Ainsworth's initial findings and Bowlby's theory. Moreover, these researchers argue that the possible universality of attachment does not exclude the possibility that attachment behaviors develop in specific ways that depend on the cultural niche in which the child has to survive (van IJzendoorn & Sagi, 2001). The challenge to contemporary developmentalists who focus on attachment is to provide a more finely tuned account of when and where cultural variations are likely to be important within the overall common human heritage of social relations (see Figure 6.12).

Figure 6.12 Secure attachments predominate across culture, but the percentage of different forms of insecure attachments varies. (Adapted from van IJzendorn & Sagi, 2001.)

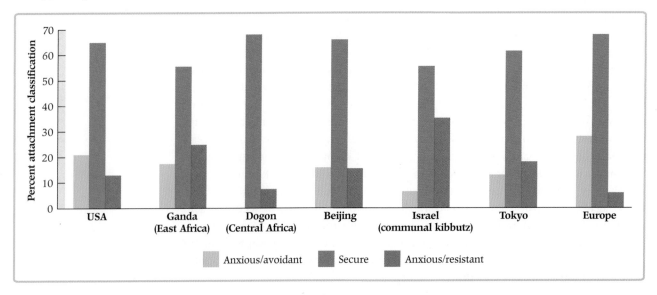

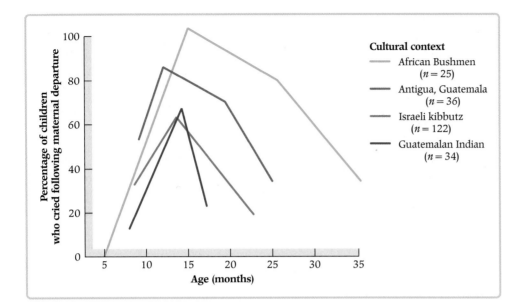

The Developmental Course of Attachment

No single factor seems to account for any one pattern of attachment. Rather, there are many pathways to secure or insecure attachment relationships. The complicated interrelationships among the caregivers' behaviors, the temperamental characteristics of the children, stresses on the family, and the cultural context, as well as many other aspects of children's life circumstances, create these different developmental pathways.

As we noted, there are marked individual and cultural differences in the precise patterns of behavior that infants display in the strange situation. Interpretations of those differences are equally varied and a matter of debate among developmental psychologists. The bottom line, however, is that infants all over the world, in every cultural setting, appear to show great consistency in the age at which they first express distress on being separated from their mothers. As Figure 6.13 indicates, 5-month-old babies do not appear to be distressed when their mothers leave. It is not until they are about 7 months old that babies begin to show distress. After that age, the proportion of children who are upset when the mother leaves the room increases until children are about 15 months old and then begins to wane. This changing pattern of distress indicates that the developmental course of attachment is a general characteristic of human infants and that, as time passes, the attachment relations established earlier in life become integrated into a new psychological system.

A New Sense of Self

By the time they are 6 months old, infants have acquired a great deal of experience interacting with objects and other people and have developed an intuitive sense of themselves as a result (Rochat, 2000). The ability to locomote provides them with still further experience of their separateness from their caregivers and promotes new forms of social relations. Infants at that age begin to learn that they can share experiences and compare reactions, especially through their emerging use of language (Trevarthen, 1998). As infancy comes to an end, at around $2^{1}/_{2}$ to 3 years of age, the process of developing a distinctive sense of self undergoes yet another transformation, one that is recognized by parents the world over.

On the South Pacific island of Fiji, parents say that children gain *vakayalo*— sense—around the second birthday; they can be held responsible for their actions because they are supposed to be able to tell right from wrong. Similarly, the Utku of the Hudson Bay area say that the 2-year-old has gained *ihuma,* or reason. Parents in the United States acknowledge the end of infancy from a different perspective: they tend to focus on their infants' newly acquired independence and the dwindling of their own control over them, labeling the change as the onset of the "terrible twos."

However parents describe it, the distinctive pattern of infants' behavior at around the age of 2 signals to adults that a new stage of development has been entered. This new stage seems to comprise several interconnected elements: children's increasing self-awareness, including the ability to recognize themselves in a mirror; their growing sensitivity to adults' standards of what is good and bad; their new awareness of their own ability to live up to those standards; an ability to create plans of their own that they then judge against adult standards; and a strong desire to see that their plans are not thwarted by adults (Harter, 1998; Kagan, 2000). As a result of all of these elements taken together, children begin to experience new emotions appropriate to their more active and complicated participation in the events of everyday life (Lewis, 2001). Their increasing competence provides the basis for the growing sense of autonomy that Erikson (1963) says normally characterizes this time of life.

Self-Recognition

Consciousness of self is among the major characteristics said to distinguish human beings from other species and 2-year-olds from younger children. This is an interesting idea, but finding a way to demonstrate it convincingly has been a problem.

Several decades ago, Gordon Gallup (1970) reported an ingenious series of experiments using mirrors with chimpanzees that has since been repeated with children. Gallup showed adolescent wild-born chimpanzees their images in a full-length mirror. At first the chimps acted as if another animal were in the room: they threatened, vocalized, and made conciliatory gestures to the "intruder." After a few days, however, they began to use the mirror to explore themselves; for example, they picked bits of food from their faces, which they could see only in the mirror.

To make certain of the meaning of these reactions, Gallup anesthetized several chimps and painted a bright, odorless dye above one eye and on the ear on the opposite side of the head. When they woke up and looked in the mirror, the chimps immediately began to explore the marked spots with their hands. Gallup concluded that they had learned to recognize themselves in the mirror.

This kind of self-recognition is by no means universal among monkey species. Gallup gave a wild-born macaque monkey over 2400 hours of exposure to a mirror over more than 5 months, but it never showed any sign of self-recognition. The problem was not simply dealing with the mirror image, because the monkey quickly learned to find food that it could see only in the mirror. The monkey simply could not recognize itself.

Gallup's procedure has been replicated with chimpanzees and, in modified form, used with human infants between the ages of 3 and 24 months (Inoue-Nakamura,

Children's ability to recognize themselves in a mirror attests to the emergence of a new sense of self at the end of infancy.

Laura Dwight

2001). The results fit nicely with the evidence that there are several stages in learning to recognize oneself in a mirror (Bigelow, 1998). Before the age of 3 months, children held up to a mirror show little interest in their own images or in the image of anyone else. At about 4 months, if a toy or another person is reflected in the mirror, babies will reach out and touch the mirror image. At this stage, they clearly don't understand that they are seeing a reflection. Ten-month-olds will reach behind them if a toy is slowly lowered behind their back while they are looking in the mirror, but they will not try to rub off a red spot that has been surreptitiously applied to their nose. Not until children are 18 months old will they reach for their own nose when they see the red spot. Some try to rub the spot off; others ask, "What's that?" Within a few months, whenever someone points to the child's mirror image and asks, "Who's that?" the child will be able to answer unhesitatingly, "Me" (Rochat, 2000).

The Self as Actor

When speech first emerges, most of children's one-word utterances name objects they are looking at. Children point at or pick up an object and say its name. These first descriptions include no explicit reference to the self. Between the ages of 18 and 24 months, about the same time that children begin to use two-word utterances, they also begin to describe their own actions. A child completing a jigsaw puzzle exclaims, "Did it!" or "Becky finished." When a tower of blocks falls down, a child exclaims, "Uh-oh. I fix." In these utterances we see not only children's ability to refer to themselves explicitly but also their ability to represent in words their recognition of adult standards of behavior and their desire to meet them.

A Sense of Standards

As you have seen repeatedly, infants are sensitive to perceptual events that violate their expectations. Around the age of 2 years, children also become emotionally sensitive to events that violate the way things are "supposed to be." Children at this age become upset if the plastic eye of their teddy bear is missing or if there is mud on the hem of a new dress. When 14-month-olds are brought to a playroom where some of the toys are damaged, they seem to be unaware of the flaws and play as if nothing were wrong. But 19-month-olds say disdainfully, "Yucky" or "Fix it" (Kagan, 1981, p. 47). Apparently their emerging ability to classify objects extends to an ability to classify events as proper and improper according to adult standards.

Children also express sensitivity to adult standards when they feel that they are supposed to imitate an adult. In several studies, Jerome Kagan (1981) had an adult perform various activities in front of children in a play setting. The adult might make one toy monkey hug another monkey, or build a stack of blocks, or enact a small drama using toy blocks as animals. Many of the acts were too complex for 2-year-olds to imitate. Starting around 18 months of age, the children in Kagan's study seemed to feel that they were expected to do what the adult had done even when they couldn't. As a result, many of them started to fret, stopped playing, and clung to their mothers. Kagan concluded that their distress signaled a new ability to recognize adult standards and an associated sense of responsibility to live up to them.

Further evidence that toddlers develop a sense of standards comes from situations in which children set themselves a goal or adults set goals for children. It is not at all unusual, for example, to encounter $2\frac{1}{2}$-year-olds struggling to achieve the self-imposed goal of using all the available blocks to build a tower or to fit every available doll into a single toy baby carriage so that all the babies can go on a trip.

Tony Freeman/Photo Edit

Figure 6.14 A mastery smile signals infants' growing focus on social standards. When you reach the pinnacle of achievement, there is the double pleasure of pleasing yourself and knowing that you are pleasing others at the same time.

secondary emotions Emotions such as embarrassment, pride, shame, guilt, and envy that depend on children's ability to recognize, talk about, and think about themselves in relation to others.

In a study designed to trace children's ability to adhere to task standards set by adults, Merry Bullock and Paul Lütkenhaus showed infants how to carry out such tasks as building a tower of blocks, dressing a doll, and washing a blackboard and then asked the infants to perform these tasks (Bullock & Lütkenhaus, 1989). At 17 months, the children performed the activity that was requested, but few of them could keep the desired goal in mind and frequently needed to be reminded. At 20 months, they started out to do the tasks according to adult standards but became distracted by the materials and ended up playing according to their own whims. It was only at 26 months that they first showed that they could stick to the task until they met adult standards. However, it was not until they approached their third birthdays that this kind of self-control became the rule rather than the exception. These findings led the researchers to conclude that children's problem solving is easily sidetracked until they are able to think of themselves in relation to a future goal.

Accompanying the emergence of children's ability to set goals for themselves is the appearance of a new kind of smile. As the topmost block is placed on the stack or the last doll is stuffed into the carriage, the child smiles with self-satisfaction. Kagan (1981) refers to this kind of smile as a *mastery smile* (see Figure 6.14).

Once children can set goals for themselves and realize that there are standards of performance that they must meet, they begin to interact with their parents in a new way: they actively seek their parents' help in reaching the goals and meeting the standards—though not always directly. When confronted with a task that appeared too difficult, one child is reported to have said, while clinging to his mother, "It's Mommy's turn to play" (Kagan, 1981, p. 49).

The Emergence of Secondary Emotions

Whether they believe emotions are present at birth or develop in the months after birth, developmentalists agree that babies experience and communicate six primary emotions by the time they reach their first birthdays—joy, fear, anger, surprise, sadness, and disgust (see Chapter 4, p. 135). They also agree that sometime between the ages of 18 and 24 months, babies begin to experience new emotions, including embarrassment, pride, shame, guilt, and envy. These new emotions are referred to as **secondary emotions** because they depend on babies' newly acquired abilities to recognize, talk about, and think about themselves in relation to other people. Primary emotions bear a simple and direct relation to the events that elicit them. Distress, for example, is a direct response to pain; disgust is a direct response to something that tastes or smells terrible; fear is a direct response to a visible threat. Secondary emotions, by contrast, are reflective and indirect. Jake, for example, felt upset and betrayed by his mother, but instead of lashing out at her directly, he responded indirectly. Such complex combinations of cognition and emotion do not appear until children are able to think about and evaluate themselves in relation to other people and the goals they desire. In this sense, secondary emotions can be considered social emotions (Barrett, 1995). Because they also involve either injury to or enhancement of the child's sense of self, Michael Lewis (2001) refers to secondary emotions as "self-conscious" emotions.

Take pride, for example. To feel pride, toddlers must be able to judge their own behavior as proper and admirable in the eyes of other people. Until they are about 18 months old, babies have no basis for feeling pride because they are incapable of thinking about other people's standards and their own behavior at the same time (Tomasello, 1999). But 2-year-olds can measure their behavior against the expectations of others. Pride can be observed in a toddler's self-satisfied smile when placing the last block on a still-standing stack or when putting on socks without assistance. Shame or embarrassment can be seen when toddlers lower their eyes, hang their heads, cover their faces with their hands, or hide after doing something they know is "bad."

Adults and other members of the child's community play an important role in the development of secondary emotions. They provide the standards of behavior against which toddlers learn to measure themselves. By observing and learning from others, toddlers discover when it is appropriate to feel guilt, shame, pride, and other secondary emotions.

Secondary emotions play an important role in children's social development. Pride and shame, for example, enter into children's feelings about others as well as about themselves. Guilt functions to motivate children to make amends. Interpreted in this way, the development of secondary emotions can be seen as part of a larger ensemble of changes that mark the beginning of a new stage in the process of growing up.

The End of Infancy: A New Bio-Social-Behavioral Shift

Sometime between their second and third birthdays, several changes combine to produce a stagelike transition in overall behavior that we have identified as a bio-social-behavioral shift. Table 6.3 summarizes these changes, including children's ability to think using symbolic representations, their increased autonomy, and their more differentiated self-concepts that emerge between the ages of 18 and 30 months. This table provides a reminder that the social, emotional, and cognitive changes that have figured so prominently in this chapter not only are part and parcel of others but arise in conjunction with seemingly more mundane behavioral changes, such as coordinated walking and bladder control, that depend on the physical development of the body.

The new configuration of characteristics that emerges in the third year does not, of course, permit children to survive on their own. Far from it. But the qualitatively new form of psychological processes they display does set the stage for a new type of interdependence and a new system of interaction between children and their environments. If all goes well, the individual aspects of this new, distinctive stage of development will give way to the next: early childhood.

table 6.3

The Bio-Social-Behavioral Shift at the End of Infancy	
Biological domain	Myelination of connections among brain areas
	Leveling off of brain growth
	Maturation of brain areas in roughly equal degrees
Social domain	Decline of distress at separation
	Distinctive sense of self
	Acceptance of adult standards
	Emergence of secondary emotions
Behavioral domain	Walking becomes well coordinated
	Manual dexterity becomes adequate to pick up small objects
	Control over bladder and bowels
	Planful problem solving
	Symbolic play
	Conceptual representations
	Elementary vocabulary and beginning of word combinations
	Smile accompanying mastery

S U M M A R Y

- Sometime between their second and third birthdays, children complete the period of development called infancy. The end of infancy is marked by changes in biological processes, by expanding physical and mental abilities, and by the appearance of a new relationship with oneself and the social world.

Biological Maturation

- Important connections in the cerebral cortex and between the cortex and the brain stem become myelinated, and the cortical centers work in greater synchrony. Neurons in the brain begin to achieve adult length and density, and the rate of overall brain growth slows.

Gaining Coordination and Control

- Children gain increasing control over several muscle systems, which makes it possible for them to walk upright and, several months later, to run and jump.

- Increased manual dexterity makes it possible for infants to execute such movements as eating with a spoon and picking up small objects.

- Voluntary control over elimination becomes possible, making children more independent, although total control is not achieved for some time.

New Modes of Thought

- A new configuration of cognitive abilities is manifested in many domains: problem solving, play, imitation, categorization of objects, the ability to interpret visual representations and models, and communication.

- According to Piaget's theory, toddlers' completion of the sensorimotor stage of development is marked by several achievements:

  1. Systematic problem solving to achieve goals makes its appearance.

  2. Children search systematically for hidden objects.

  3. Solutions to problems are achieved without extensive overt trial and error.

- Play evolves from variations in patterns of movements to the pretend use of objects in imaginary situations.

- Pretend play itself evolves. Children 1 to 1½ years old can use themselves as agents to carry out a single pretend act at a time. By the time they are 2 years old, children can carry out a sequence of pretend actions in which objects such as dolls are used as the agents.

- Current evidence indicates that deferred imitation can occur several months earlier than Piaget anticipated, but by 14–18 months children learn from each other by imitation and imitate what models intend to do even if the model fails.

- Presented with a collection of artificial objects to group, toddlers create a separate work space and categorize objects in accordance with adult criteria.

- Toddlers' vocabularies grow rapidly at the same time that the children begin to solve problems insightfully and to search logically for hidden objects, all of which bespeak the presence of the capacity of mental representation.

- The ability to combine words to make elementary two-word sentences coincides with the ability to combine objects in pretend play.

The Development of Child–Caregiver Relations

- Developmentalists interpret infants' distress when they are separated from their mothers as an indicator of feelings of attachment. This distress increases steadily until sometime in the second year and then declines.

- A variety of theories offer competing explanations for the onset of attachment:

  1. Freud believed that attachment has its roots in the reduction of biological drives such as hunger.

  2. Erikson explained attachment as the establishment of a trusting relationship between parent and child.

  3. Bowlby hypothesized that attachment serves to reduce fear by establishing a secure base of support from which children can explore their environments.

- Research with monkeys has disproved the drive-reduction theory by showing that infant monkeys can become attached to inanimate substitute mothers that provide soothing tactile sensations but no food.

- The social incapacity of monkeys raised with inanimate substitute mothers has focused research on the role of maternal responsiveness in the development of normal social interactions.

- The "strange situation" has been widely used to assess distinctive patterns of infants' attachment to their primary caregivers. Research has focused on the causes and consequences of three broad patterns of attachment: secure, anxious/avoidant, and anxious/resistant.

- Patterns of attachment can be affected by a variety of factors:

  1. The best predictor of secure attachment is attentive, sensitive caregiving. Abusive, neglectful, or inconsistent caregiving is likely to lead to insecure attachment.

  2. Children's own characteristics may contribute to the quality of their attachments. Children who are easily upset or who display less interest in people than in objects may be more difficult for adults to coordinate with, a situation impeding the development of a secure attachment.

3. Attachment status can be affected by the presence or absence of such family stressors as low socioeconomic status and marital discord.

4. Attachment appears to be a universal feature of human interactions that follows a similar course in all cultures. Where cultural variations occur, they appear primarily in the particular ways in which failures to achieve attachment express themselves

A New Sense of Self

● A new sense of self appears around the time of a child's second birthday. It is manifested in:

1. Immediate recognition of one's image in the mirror and the emergence of self-reference in language

2. A growing sensitivity to adult standards, a concern about living up to those standards, and a new ability to set one's own goals and standards

3. The appearance of secondary emotions as the child assesses the self and others in relation to a set of social standards

The End of Infancy: A New Bio-Social-Behavioral Shift

● The convergence of biological, perceptual–motor, cognitive, emotional, and social changes in the months following a child's second birthday produces a new bio-social-behavioral shift and the beginning of a new stage of development.

Key Terms

anxious/avoidant attachment, p. 230
anxious/resistant attachment, p. 230
biological drives, p. 223
detachment, p. 224
dual representation, p. 220

internal working model, p. 225
secondary emotions, p. 238
secure attachment, p. 230
secure base, p. 225

separation anxiety, p. 225
strange situation, p. 228
symbolic play (pretend, fantasy play), p. 216
tertiary circular reactions, p. 212

Thought Questions

1. How do changes associated with the development of upright walking illustrate the close connection between changes in perceptual and motor abilities?

2. What common new ability appears to underlie the cognitive changes associated with the end of infancy?

3. What are some of the strengths and weaknesses of the "strange situation" as a way to investigate changing social and emotional relationships between infants and their caretakers in the second year of life?

4. Argue for and against the view that play promotes cognitive development.

5. What kinds of cognitive changes appear to be linked to the appearance of secondary emotions?

Early Experience and Later Life

> " *"Children need people in order to become human beings."*
> —Uri Bronfenbrenner

In a creaky bus bumping along the back roads of Changsha, China, Jeff and Christene take in the passing scenes of marshy rice paddies and smokestacks. They want to remember this landscape so that they can describe it some day to their 2-year-old daughter, Jin Yu, whom they are about to meet for the first time. They arrive at a hotel with 25 other new parents from America, waiting in turn to receive their children. One by one the children are handed over. And one by one they wail in protest. But not Jin Yu. And this disturbs Jeff and Christene. In preparing for this life-altering moment, they learned that such tears are a sign that the child has formed attachments to her orphanage caregivers, and is therefore able to form new attachments to her adoptive parents. Jeff and Christene take Jin Yu to their hotel room where she sits silently on the bed, lethargic and unmoving save for a vague shrugging of her shoulders. While trying to assure her that all is well, Jeff and Christene discover a ragged scar running across her head. They are frightened—for Jin Yu and for themselves. But she is their daughter now, and committed to this fact, they brace themselves for the unknowable. Back in the United States, doctors relieve their fears; the scar was probably just a scratch that became infected. Most reassuring, however, is Jin Yu's own rapid development. In 6 months, she grows 5 inches, gains 5 pounds, and takes an avid interest in her environment—the click of the refrigerator door, the disappearing ink of her Etch A Sketch. And she hums little melodies to herself. Jeff and Christene take great comfort in knowing that someone took time to sing to their baby. Perhaps a caregiver that they would never know gave them and Jin Yu the foundation for building loving relationships in their new life together.

—Adapted from J. Gammage, "Bringing Jin Yu Home"

Jeff and Christene's questions and concerns about their daughter's development are shared by other adoptive parents. They are also of importance to developmentalists, who seek to determine how, and to what extent, an infant's experiences shape the course of the child's later development. What are the social and emotional needs of infants? What happens when their needs are not met? Can the negative effects of early deprivation be overcome? These are just some of the questions discussed in this chapter.

The Primacy of Infancy

The idea that early experiences can significantly shape later development is called **primacy.** We can find the concept in our proverbs— "As the twig is bent, so grows the tree"—and in our heritage from the Greeks. Plato (428–348 B.C.) expressed this view when he wrote:

> And the beginning, as you know, is always the most important part, especially in dealing with anything young and tender. That is the time when the character is being molded and easily takes any impress one may wish to stamp on it. (1945, p. 68)

primacy The idea that early experiences can significantly shape later development.

During the twentieth century, primacy has come to be associated with the idea that children's experiences during infancy do not merely influence, but *determine* their future development (Brazelton & Greenspan, 2000). This line of thought was greatly influenced by Freud's claim that psychological illness in adulthood can be traced back to unresolved conflicts in the first years of life (Freud, 1940/1964). It is by no means restricted to Freudian theorists, however. In summarizing his research on intellectual development, the psychologist Burton White argued that *"to begin to look at a child's educational development when he is two years of age is already much too late,* particularly in the area of social skills and attitudes" (White, 1975, p. 4; italics added). Similarly, Alan Sroufe and his colleagues maintain that the nature of children's first attachments greatly influences the way they form subsequent relationships (Sroufe et al., 1999b).

In this chapter we focus on the question of whether, and, if so, to what extent, the experiences of infancy exert more influence than later experiences on the course of development. The answer to this question is central to such issues as how society and parents can best provide for infants to ensure their optimal development and what can be done to improve the lives of children who have suffered deprivation early in life. As you will see, there is no doubt that infants' experiences *can* have a significant effect on their later development. But whether they *will* have long-lasting effects depends heavily on the extent to which subsequent experiences act to reinforce or counteract the patterns set up in infancy. Consequently, while focusing on infancy, our discussion will examine the lives of older children as well. Consideration of later experience is essential to understanding the extent to which early experiences are or are not especially important.

You will also discover that the effects of early experience are sometimes unexpected. For example, you might expect developmental abnormalities from a child who has been isolated from other people, terribly mistreated, or exposed to the terrors of war. Indeed, many children made to suffer in these ways show gross deficits in their development. Others, however, grow up into relatively normal adults. Developmentalists are interested in knowing what contributes to children's resilience in the face of significant risks.

A few words of caution are in order about the nature of the research featured in this chapter. In many of the studies we discuss, the data involve children who have suffered some kind of unusual deprivation that is not under the investigators' control: they have been raised in an orphanage, or in poverty, or by parents who are mentally unstable. In such studies, the basic principle of a true psychological experiment is violated; the subjects are not assigned at random to experimental and control conditions. As a consequence, it is not possible to conclude with certainty that any differences between these and other groups of children in later life are caused by the particular form of deprivation that the children experienced during infancy and early childhood; it is possible that some covarying factor is the real cause of the observed differences. (Review the box "Correlation in Causation" in Chapter 1, pp. 20–21.) For example, any differences found between children growing up in orphanages and in homes might actually reflect the fact that children in orphanages generally come from poorer families or were born in a time of war, where multiple physical and psychosocial risk factors are more frequently encountered.

One way that developmentalists attempt to cope with the lack of control inherent in these studies is to conduct research with nonhuman animals, particularly nonhuman primates. As you will see below, in many studies of nonhuman animals the researchers control a variety of environmental and biological risk factors. For example, they can randomly assign animals to environments that contain different levels of stress or social isolation. In some cases, researchers can also control the breeding history of the animals, or otherwise manipulate key genetic factors such as temperament or aggressivity. Although this sort of work permits insight into causal relationships, developmentalists must still be careful about comparing across species.

Modifying the Impact of Early Experience

When children must live through extremely undesirable life circumstances beginning in infancy, especially circumstances that are abnormal for the society in which they live, it should be expected that their negative experiences will have detectable effects on their later development. As you will see, even the children who make remarkable recoveries show some residual signs of their past deprivation.

Two factors appear to be able to modify the impact of early experiences on the later development of human lives. The first is changes in the environment. Whether these changes are positive (such as a supportive school environment or a community-based support network) or negative (such as the outbreak of war or the death of a parent), they may create discontinuities in children's experiences that will set them on a new path into the future.

The second factor that may act to modify the long-term effects of experience is the bio-social-behavioral shifts that reorganize physical and psychological functions into qualitatively new patterns that change the way children experience their environment. Such factors as the acquisition of language, new cognitive capacities, and a new relationship with the social world that emerge at the end of infancy, for example, result in a new way of experiencing and dealing with the world. A 12-month-old who is easily frustrated when she cannot get her own way may become a placid preschooler once she has learned to speak and can better coordinate with her surroundings on her own terms. Alternatively, a placid baby who seems to take little interest in the world around him may suddenly display enormous curiosity and energy once he begins to walk. Such observations have led Jerome Kagan to argue that "each life phase makes special demands, and so each phase is accompanied by a special set of qualities" (Kagan, 1984, p. 91). Kagan believes that discontinuities between succeeding life phases are so marked that some of one's past history is actually "inhibited or discarded." This strong view of developmental discontinuities implies that the problems of infancy do not inevitably lead to later developmental problems; in effect, each new stage presents its own opportunities.

Transactional Models

Many contemporary developmentalists take the position that the effects of early experience ultimately depend on relationships between children and their environments. Such approaches to children's development are called **transactional.** Transactional models trace the ways in which the characteristics of the child and the characteristics of the child's environment interact across time ("transact") to determine developmental outcomesm (Sameroff & Mackenzie, 2003).

As you will learn in this chapter, transactional models are important for understanding how children from similar environments can have radically different developmental outcomes. For example, in extremely impoverished communities across the world, many children die from malnutrition. One important child characteristic that seems to help some children survive is temperament. You will learn in this chapter that children with "difficult" temperaments, that is, those who are fussy and demanding, have higher survival rates compared with children with "easy," more quiet dispositions.

transactional models Models of development that trace the ways in which the characteristics of the child and the characteristics of the child's environment interact across time ("transact") to determine developmental outcomes.

Because they emphasize changing child—environment relationships over time, transactional models also help us to understand how experience at one point in time may have a dramatically different effect than the same experience at another point in time. This, of course, is the whole idea behind primacy—that experience during infancy is particularly crucial to development. But the concept of the timing of experience also applies in a more specific sense. As you recall from the discussion of *plasticity* in Chapter 1, there are certain moments when the developing system is especially sensitive to the effects of the environment—when stimulation, or lack thereof, exerts a pronounced and lasting effect on development. In this chapter, you will learn how the timing of changes in the child's environment can promote or defeat developmental progress.

Transactional models have been particularly useful for understanding the development of attachment, the changing emotional relationship between children and their caregivers.

Developing Attachment

Many developmentalists argue that the development of a secure attachment relationship is crucial to infant mental health as well as to the quality of the child's future relationships (Osofsky & Fitzgerald, 2000; Zeanah, 2000). In Chapter 6 we identified three main patterns of attachment—secure, anxious/avoidant, and anxious/resistant—as well as several causes of variations in these patterns. Now we turn to the consequences of these patterns of attachment: how does a child's early attachment status correspond to his or her later behavior? Studies of the long-term consequences of the various patterns of attachment assess children's attachment just before their first birthday and then again after several years (Bretherton & Waters, 1985). Such studies have yielded mixed results concerning later developmental outcomes of particular attachment patterns.

Developmentalists who emphasize *continuity* in attachment believe that early interactions between children and their caregivers provide a foundation for later relationships.

©Rolf Bruderer/Masterfile

Continuity and Discontinuity

Given the complicated interplay of the child's developing capacities, the changes these capacities bring about in the way the child experiences the environment, and changes in the environment itself, developmentalists have focused on uncovering patterns of continuity and discontinuity between attachment during infancy and later life.

Alan Sroufe and his colleagues have reported that when children who are judged to be securely attached at 12 months of age are assessed at $3\frac{1}{2}$, they are more curious, play more effectively with their agemates, and have better relationships with their teachers than do children who were insecurely attached as infants (Erikson et al., 1985; Frankel & Bates, 1990; Sroufe & Fleeson, 1986). In follow-up observations conducted when the children were 10, and then again when they were 15, researchers found that those who had been assessed as securely attached in infancy were more skillful socially, formed more friendships, displayed more self-confidence, and were more open in expressing their feelings. (For a recent summary, see Sroufe et al., 1999.)

More recent longitudinal studies bear out the general conclusion reached by Sroufe and his colleagues regarding the *continuity* of attachment from infancy to adulthood. For example, a 20-year longitudinal study conducted by Everett Waters and his colleagues indicated that 72 percent of the sample received the same attachment classification (secure or insecure, as assessed through interviews) as adults that they had received as infants (Waters et al., 2000a; Waters et al., 2000b).

Researchers who see patterns of attachment as tending to remain consistent throughout development emphasize that such continuity depends on one key fact. In their view, children's attachment to their primary caregiver serves as the model for all later relationships (Bretherton & Munholland, 1999). Drawing on a formulation by John Bowlby (1969), Inge Bretherton (1985) proposed that on the basis of their interactions with their primary caregiver, infants build up an *internal working model* of the way to behave toward other people and then use the model to figure out what to do each time they enter a new situation. As long as their working model allows them to interact effectively with the people they encounter, children will continue to use it in all of their relationships. But if their application of the working model leads to difficulties, they may change or replace it. In short, continuity and discontinuity depend on the cumulative outcomes of everyday transactions between children and their environments.

Although research findings generally support the idea that attachment patterns are relatively stable over the lifespan, they also indicate that these patterns can adapt to changes in the child's experiences. Waters's research, cited above, found a minority of the individuals in the 20-year study did not demonstrate continuity of attachment over time. Interviews conducted with the children's mothers indicated that negative life events may have contributed to these discontinuities. Nearly half of the mothers whose children changed classifications reported the occurrence of at least one of the following experiences:

- loss of a parent
- parental divorce
- life-threatening illness of parent or child
- parental psychiatric disorder
- physical or sexual abuse by a family member

These and other traumatic events, such as isolation and deprivation, can have a lasting impact on a child's attachment status. (We will address some of these cases later in the chapter.)

The degree of developmental continuity is also influenced by more common experiences. To understand the role of children's transactions in this process, consider the finding that anxious/resistant children tend to cling to their mothers (Chapter 6, p. 230). Suppose that we observe such a child in a preschool setting. If she is using her internal working model, which is based on her prior interactions to guide her behavior, this little girl can be expected to try to stay close to the teacher. The consequences of her use of this internal working model at school will depend on how it is interpreted. If the teacher sees such behavior as politeness, cooperation, and eagerness to learn, the child will be likely to find this internal working model effective. Thus the same pattern of interaction will probably continue and may even be reinforced by the teacher. But suppose the teacher interprets the little girl's behavior as overly dependent. She may arrange for the girl to help younger, shyer children, thereby providing her with the experience of a new form of social interaction. As a result, the child's internal working model may change and her subsequent interactions with others may diverge from the earlier pattern.

Here you see, on the one hand, how internal working models of relationships can produce continuity in social interactions over time and, on the other hand, why it may be difficult to predict whether infants' patterns of interaction will be maintained in later life. The degree of continuity will depend on the nature of the initial

Stephanie Maze/Woodfin Camp & Associates/R. Hutchings/Photo Edit

Families throughout the world use out-of-home care with increasing frequency. Although the distress shown by this French child is a common response to separation from the parent, the long-term developmental consequences of such separations remain controversial.

internal working model and the extent to which it proves to be adaptive in children's transactions in the many contexts they encounter later in life.

Application of a transactional approach to understanding attachment relationships also helps to account for cases in which infant attachment status fails to predict later attachment behaviors (Thompson, 1998). For example, in a longitudinal study of 100 children, Michael Lewis (1997) assessed the children's attachment to their mother when they were 1 year old and then interviewed the children when they were 18 years old to assess their current attachment to their parents and their memory of social and emotional relationships when they were children. He also asked the 18-year-olds and their teachers to fill out a questionnaire that was designed to measure their emotional development.

Lewis's findings cast doubt on the idea that attachment relationships in infancy set the pattern for later socioemotional relationships. First, he found that the "young adults' current attachments bore absolutely no relation to what they actually were like at one year of age, neither for the entire group of children nor even for those children who were insecurely attached earlier" (Lewis, 1997, p. 62). Second, the 18-year-olds' current mental health status, whether based on what the teenagers or their teachers reported, bore no relationship to their attachment status in infancy. According to Lewis, these data support the view that attachment relations early in life do not provide a working model, or template, that lasts into adulthood and causes a particular pattern of attachment relations to persist.

At present it appears that, under some circumstances, there can be measurable long-term consequences of early attachment status, but there are many exceptions to this generalization. One conclusion is clear, however. Infants are highly sensitive to the relational contexts of their environments; their early relationships with others are dynamic and malleable, changing as their life circumstances are revised.

Out-of-Home Care: A Threat to Attachment?

In the United States today, one of the most common features affecting young children's developing network of relationships, certainly one that has raised the most attention from developmentalists, is children's placement in nonparental child care (Greenspan, 2003). (We will return to the subject of child care in Chapter 11, where we discuss its various forms and impact on slightly older children.) The increasingly common practice of placing infants in some form of out-of-home care during the first year of life is related to two trends in North American society: (1) the growing number of single-parent households, and (2) the increasing economic need for both parents to work full-time. At present, women constitute the fastest-growing segment of the workforce, and a majority of women who work and become mothers return to their jobs before their infants are 1 year old. More than half of all infants and toddlers in the United States spend some time in the care of people other than their parents during the first year of life (see Figure 7.1) (Casper, 1996).

The issue of out-of-home care for infants has been the subject of controversy among developmentalists for several decades (Lamb, 1998). Prominent among those who questioned the effect of out-of-home care during the first year of life was Jay Belsky (Belsky, 1986, 1990; Belsky et al., 1996). His concern was aroused by evidence that children who had experienced extensive nonmaternal care (more than

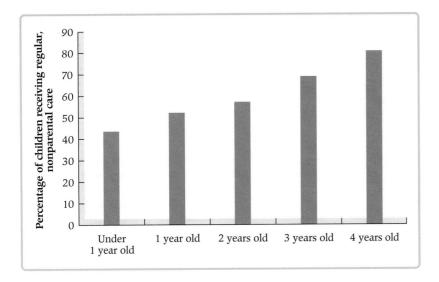

Figure 7.1 By the time they are 4 years of age, nearly all children in the United States are in nonparental care on a regular basis. In fact, nearly half of all infants are regularly cared for by someone other than their mothers and fathers. Developmentalists, as well as parents, are anxious to know whether such care has adverse effects on children's development. (From National Research Council, 2000, p. 298.)

20 hours a week) during the first year of life were more likely to exhibit insecure patterns of attachment in the strange situation, were less compliant in meeting adults' demands, and were more aggressive in interactions with peers. Belsky's concerns were supported by studies that found that firstborn children who had been placed in child-care arrangements before their first birthday were significantly more likely to display insecure forms of attachment when they were 12 to 13 months old than were children who stayed at home with their mothers (Bargelow et al., 1987).

These findings prompted the U.S. government to initiate a massive study, called the National Institute of Child Health and Human Development Early Child Care Research Network. Its ongoing mission is to determine the influence that various kinds of child care during infancy and early childhood have on later development. The study is carried out by a network of leading researchers from centers in ten different geographical locales. Data are collected on characteristics of the children's families, including their educational and income levels, ethnicity, and size. The quality of the care provided is judged using measures of the general setting, such as the ratio of adults to children, group sizes, quality of facilities, as well as the quality of

The effect of child care quality on children's development is an international issue. Whereas some developmentalists believe that any form of child care during the early years of life is detrimental to development, others maintain that children are able to form warm, close attachments with paid caregivers when their families have access to affordable, high-quality care, such as that provided in this Japanese center.

table 7.1

Indicators of Day-Care Quality	
Qualitative Ratings	**Definition**
Sensitivity/responsiveness to nondistressed communication	Caregiver responds to infant's social gestures and is attuned to infant's needs and moods
Detachment/disengagement	Caregiver is emotionally uninvolved, disengaged, and unaware of infant's needs
Intrusiveness	Caregiver is highly controlling and adult-centered in interactions with infant
Stimulation of cognitive development	Caregiver engages in activities that can facilitate infant's learning, such as talking to infant or demonstrating a toy
Positive regard	Caregiver expresses positive feelings in interaction with infant
Sensitivity/responsiveness to infant distress	Caregiver responds to the infant's distress signals consistently, promptly, and appropriately

Source: NICHD Early Child Care Research Network, 1996.

caregiving the children received (see Table 7.1). To assess the effects of the care on the children, data are collected on the children's emotional attachment, self-control, compliance with adult demands, mental development, and language development.

As you will see in Chapter 11 when we discuss the effects of child care in more detail, the results of these studies indicate that the amount of time that young children spend in child care has slight negative effects on their attachment relationships, as well as their social behaviors and intellectual development. Much stronger effects are found for "insensitive mothering" and the socioeconomic status of the family (NICHD, 2003).

The stakes in assessing the effects of child care are very high. On the one hand, everyone is aware that it is in the interests not only of the children in question but of society as a whole to ensure that children grow up to be emotionally stable and socially competent adults. On the other hand, economic and social pressures are bringing many mothers into the workforce and keeping fathers there. The problem is how best to deal with these conflicting realities to maximize children's life chances, particularly for low-income families who are often unable to afford high-quality care. Belsky suggests that this goal could best be achieved if parents received a subsidy for staying home with their infants during their first year of life. Others argue that what is called for instead is better and more available child care. Proponents of this latter view suggest that responsive, stable, and loving environments can be provided outside the home and point to a number of recent studies indicating that infants and children establish warm, close relationships with a large variety of nonparental figures, including other family members and friends, as well as paid child-care providers (Shonkoff & Phillips, 2000; see "Attachment to Fathers and Others," in Chapter 6, p. 231).

Effects of Deprivation

Questions about how certain experiences and relationships during infancy can affect the course of a life become particularly important in situations of early deprivation. For a variety of reasons, many infants and young children throughout the world are deprived of basic levels of stimulation and care. Some endure horrific conditions over extended periods of time. Genie, whose case is discussed on page 257, spent 11 years in deplorable conditions that resulted in permanent disabilities in virtually every aspect of her development. Other children, those raised in orphanages, for example, may suffer less severe conditions and even be rescued early in their development through adoption into loving families. In the following discussion, we will consider babies who have experienced one or an other of a wide range of deprivation, from residence in an orphanage to extreme cases of isolation.

Children Reared in Orphanages

Jeff and Christene's concerns about Jin Yu's development are common among adoptive parents. Likewise, developmentalists have sought to understand how children raised in orphanages or other suboptimal environments are affected by their early experiences. Under what circumstances does early deprivation result in permanent damage? Under what conditions is there hope for recovery? We will explore these questions of *plasticity* in the context of understanding the effects of early deprivation.

Children who spend their early lives in orphanages because their parents have died or are unable to care for them may experience significant levels of deprivation. As you will see, the effects on children of living in institutions can vary dramatically depending on such factors as:

- the nature of the depriving conditions (that is, whether they are physical, social, cognitive)
- the intensity or severity of the conditions
- the length of time that the child remained in the orphanage
- the quality of the child's environment after leaving the orphanage

Researchers have always been interested in the development of orphans. From the perspective of *basic science* (see Chapter 1), the orphanage provides a natural laboratory in which to study important theoretical topics, including the relationship between biology (nature) and the environment (nurture). From an *applied* perspective, research on orphaned children can suggest ways in which to help them recover from the effects of their experiences.

A classic long-range study of orphanage-raised children was carried out by Wayne Dennis (1973) and his colleagues in an orphanage in Lebanon. The children were brought to the orphanage shortly after birth. Once there, they received little attention: there was only one caregiver for every ten children. These caregivers had themselves been brought up in the orphanage until the age of 6, when they were transferred to another institution. According to Dennis, the caregivers showed little regard for the children's individual needs or temperaments. They rarely talked to the children, did not respond to their infrequent vocalizations, and seldom played with them while bathing, dressing, changing, or feeding them. Instead, they left the babies to lie on their backs in their cribs all day and the toddlers to sit in small playpens with only a ball to play with.

The harmful effects of this low level of stimulation and human contact were evident within a year. Although the children were normal at 2 months, as measured by an infant scale, Dennis found that they had developed intellectually at only half the normal rate when he tested them at the end of the first year. The later developmental fates of these children depended on their subsequent care. Those who were adopted into families made a remarkable recovery. The children who were adopted before they were 2 years old were functioning normally when they were tested 2 to 3 years after their adoption, and those who were adopted between 2 and 6 years of age were only slightly retarded in their intellectual functioning.

The children who remained institutionalized fared less well. At the age of 6, the girls were sent to one institution and the boys to another. The girls' institution, like the orphanage, provided few stimulating experiences and virtually no personal attention. When these girls were tested at 12 to 16 years of age, they were found to

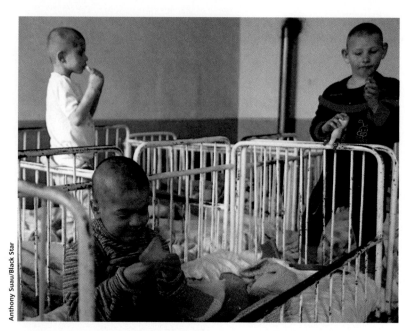

The conditions in orphanages such as this one in Romania provide insufficient stimulation for normal mental development.

be so retarded intellectually that they would be unable to function in modern society. They could barely read, they could not tell time, and they were not able to dial a seven-digit telephone number or count out change in a store.

The outcome for the boys was quite different. The institution to which they were transferred provided far more intellectual stimulation and more varied experiences than did the orphanage. What is more, the boys had frequent contact with the workers at the institution, who came from the surrounding communities. As a result, when the boys were tested at 10 to 14 years of age, they showed a substantial recovery from their initial intellectual lag. Although their performance on standardized tests was below the norm and below the performance of the children who had been adopted, it was within the range that would allow them to function in society.

In recent years the plight of orphans has again captured the attention of the research community as well as the general public. This interest was prompted by the wave of Romanian orphans adopted into families in Western Europe and North America during the early 1990s (Rutter and the English and Romanian Adoptees [ERA] Study Team, 1998; Shonkoff & Phillips, 2000). Altogether, the numerous studies of Romanian orphans tell a heart-wrenching story about the conditions that these babies endured, and the severe developmental effects of this early care. In these institutional settings, infants and young children were warehoused with little social and intellectual stimulation, and few opportunities to develop close relationships. At 4 and 5 years of age, the orphans were able to communicate only with simple gestures, such as reaching toward food to indicate their hunger. When distressed, they often frantically banged or even bit their own arms (Brazelton & Greenspan, 2000). Surprisingly, despite such deficits, some of these children showed a remarkable recovery when rescued from their depriving environment. For example, based on their study of severely deprived Romanian orphans who were adopted into British families before the age of $3\frac{1}{2}$, Michael Rutter and Thomas O'Connor concluded that despite evidence of brain damage, many of these children functioned normally by the time they reached their sixth birthdays. It appears that even biological damage does not inevitably determine poor developmental outcomes.

Kim Chisholm (1998) followed the development of a group of infants and young children who were adopted into Canadian homes from orphanages in Romania. Chisholm found that those Romanian children who were adopted before they were 4 months of age were indistinguishable from native-born Canadian children who lived in the homes of their biological parents. However, children who had spent 8 months or more in an orphanage showed residual effects of their earlier experiences. Although a special attachment interview indicated that they all had formed emotional attachments to their adoptive parents, they tended to display more evidence of insecure attachment in the strange situation (see Chapter 6, pp. 228–230) than the children adopted before the age of 4 months. They also tended to be overly friendly to strangers, which seems to indicate that they were hungry for attention.

Chisholm is cautious in attempting to account for the residual effects of their early experiences on these later-adopted children. They had spent, on average, more than a year in the orphanage, while the children who had been adopted before they were 4 months old had spent an average of only a month in institutional care. Perhaps the children who were not adopted as young infants suffered from genetic defects or poorer prenatal care that resulted in conditions that made them less "attractive" to prospective parents. Or perhaps the differences in the age at which they were adopted or the length of time they spent in institutional care was a critical factor. Complicating the picture further is the fact that the amount of time spent in an orphanage is associated with increased illness, malnourishment, maltreatment, and ongoing changes in caregivers (Shonkoff & Phillips, 2000). Alone or in combination, any of these factors may be key to poor developmental outcomes, making it difficult to place all the blame on the length of time spent in the orphanage.

Yet another factor that affects recovery is the nature of the adoptive family. Chisholm noted that children who displayed evidence of insecure attachment were most likely to have been placed with economically less well-off Canadian families, and he suggested that perhaps the extra burden these families experienced with children who came to them in a state of medical and psychological distress made it difficult for them to create optimal conditions for helping the children recover. This is also suggested by the finding that children's problems are more persistent when a family adopts two or more simultaneously from the same orphanage (Ames, 1997).

The results of Chisholm's study are difficult to interpret precisely because there are so many potential factors involved. However, more recent research on Romanian adoptees has attempted to be more systematic. These studies indicate that even when levels of malnutrition and birth impairments are taken into account, children who live in institutions longer show poorer outcomes compared with earlier-adopted children (O'Connor et al., 2000; Rutter and the English and Romanian Adoptees Study Team, 1998). The conclusion that institutional rearing itself is to blame is further supported by another study that compared Romanian children reared from infancy in individual foster homes with those reared in group institutions (Roy et al., 2000). All of the children came from very high-risk environments and their biological parents had severe mental disorders. Nevertheless, only the children living in group institutions showed high levels of hyperactivity and attentional deficits.

In general, hyperactivity and attentional deficits are associated with problems in neurological functioning. Naturally, a serious concern is whether early deprivation has caused damage to the child's developing brain. Indeed, brain scans of a group of children who had been adopted out of Romanian orphanages showed significant deficits in the functioning of certain areas in the limbic system (Chugani et al., 2001). Interestingly, work with rats and other animals indicates that the specific areas affected are especially responsive to stress, particularly when it is experienced early in development.

Most of the research on orphans' recovery from deprivation shows remarkable "catch-up" effects in the areas of language and cognitive development once the children are placed into stable and loving families. However, the picture is more clouded in the case of social and emotional development, even when the orphanage is judged to be of good quality. Barbara Tizard and Jill Hodges studied 65 English children of working-class backgrounds who were raised in residential nurseries of high quality from just after birth until they were at least 2 years old (Hodges & Tizard, 1989a, 1989b; Tizard & Hodges, 1978; Tizard & Rees, 1975). The children were fed well, the staff was trained, and toys and books were plentiful. The turnover and scheduling of staff members, however, discouraged the formation of close personal relationships between adults and children. Tizard and Hodges estimated that some 24 nurses had cared for each child by the time the children were 2 years old. By the age of $4^{1}/_{2}$, each child had been cared for by as many as 50 nurses. This situation certainly appears to preclude the kind of intimate knowledge and caring that presumably underlie sensitive caregiving.

Research on the large numbers of Romanian orphans who were adopted into Canadian and U.S. families indicates that the ability of children to recover from their early deprivation depends at least in part on the stable, sensitive, and loving care that they receive in their new homes. Adopted from a Romanian orphanage, the younger boy in this photo is well on his way to developing a close relationship with his new older brother.

AP Photo/Vadim Ghirda

Tizard and her colleagues evaluated the developmental status of the children when they were $4\frac{1}{2}$ years old and 8 years old, and again when they were 16 years old. They grouped the children into three categories:

1. Children who had returned to their families after the age of 2

2. Children who were adopted between the ages of 2 and 8 years

3. Children who remained in the institutions

The researchers also evaluated a control group consisting of children with a similar working-class background who had always lived at home.

They found that leaving institutional care had a positive effect on the children, as the studies we have described would lead us to expect. But how much difference it made depended on what kind of environment they entered and what aspect of psychological functioning was studied. One of the surprising findings was that the children who were restored to their biological families did not fare as well as the children who were adopted, a pattern that persisted even at the follow-up study conducted when the children were 16 years old. The adopted children scored higher on standardized tests of intellectual achievement and they were able to read at a more advanced level. In addition, almost all the children who were adopted formed mutual attachments with their adoptive parents, no matter how old they were when they were adopted. This was not the case for the children who returned to their biological parents. The older they were when they left the orphanages, the less likely it was that mutual attachment developed.

One reason the adoptive homes may have produced better outcomes than the biological homes was that many of the families who took back their children were not altogether happy to have them. Many of the mothers expressed misgivings, but they accepted the responsibility because the children were their own. Often the children returned to homes in which there were other children who required their mother's attention or a stepfather who was not interested in them. Most of the adoptive parents, by contrast, were older, childless couples who wanted the children and gave them a good deal of attention. Also, most of the adoptive families were financially better off than the children's biological families had been (Tizard & Hodges, 1978).

The improvements seen in most children who leave institutional care speak against the theory that children can form emotional attachments only during a critical period in early infancy (Ames & Chisholm, 2001). Although the environment in orphanages usually prevents children from forming emotional attachments with their caregivers, most children who were adopted into new families formed attachments with their adoptive parents, even the children who were past their second birthday when they left the orphanage (Thompson, 2001). The research by Tizard and her colleagues confirms the idea that characteristics of children's environments during later periods of their life are influential in determining whether or not the lack of early attachments will prove to be an enduring problem.

Some of the work described above was inspired by a desire to understand and meet the developmental needs of the Romanian orphans adopted during the 1990s. More recently, there has been a new surge of public concern driven by statistics on the millions of children worldwide who are orphaned because of the HIV-AIDS epidemic. In sub-Saharan Africa alone, there are estimated to be more than 12 million children living as orphans because their parents have died from AIDS (Christian Aid, 2001; Liddell, 2002) (see Figure 7.2). In African culture, orphaned children traditionally would be cared for by extended

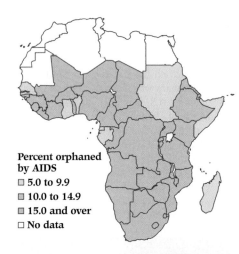

Figure 7.2 In some areas of sub-Saharan Africa, more than 15% of all children have been orphaned because of AIDS. The crisis has put terrible pressure on the African extended family system which has traditionally been a refuge for family members in need. The woman in this photograph is the grandmother and now the primary caregiver and provider for six grandchildren whose parents died from the disease. (From USAID et al., 2002.)

Percent orphaned
by AIDS
☐ 5.0 to 9.9
☐ 10.0 to 14.9
☐ 15.0 and over
☐ No data

UNICEF/HQ93-2043/Cindy Andrew

Children suffering from AIDS face a host of medical problems that are made worse by malnutrition. This boy stands before a vast crop failure caused by another serious plague affecting Africa—drought.

Brent Stirton/Getty Images

family. However, the vast and exponentially growing number of parents killed by AIDS has overburdened the extended family system. While orphanages are rarely seen in most Western nations, in Africa the need for such facilities is quickly outpacing the supply (Liddell, 2002). As you might expect, many AIDS orphans suffer the same effects of institutional care that have been documented in past studies of orphaned children.

Isolated Children

The most extreme cases of deprivation on record are those of children who have been separated from human contact altogether. During the past 200 years several of these so-called feral children have been discovered, the most famous being the Wild Boy of Aveyron, Victor, discussed in Chapter 1. Such children never fail to excite public interest because the idea of little children fending for themselves in nature is so dramatic. The circumstances leading to such children's isolation and their condition before they became isolated are usually unknown. As a result, it is rarely possible to draw firm conclusions about the effects of their experiences during their isolation.

There are, however, a few well-documented modern cases of children who have been isolated early in life by sociopathic parents. Because public officials now keep good birth records and other health records, enough is known about the early lives of these children to permit more solidly based conclusions about the developmental impact of their bizarre circumstances. Studies of isolated children leave little doubt that severe isolation can profoundly disrupt normal development, but they also show that early deprivation of caregiving and of normal interaction with the environment is not necessarily devastating to later development (Skuse, 1984).

Jarmila Koluchova (1972, 1976) studied one of these cases, which involved identical twin boys born in Czechoslovakia in 1960 to a mother of normal intelligence. The mother died shortly after the twins' birth and, when the boys were about $1^1/_2$ years old, their father married a woman who took an active dislike to the babies. At her insistence, the twins were forced to live in a small, bare closet without adequate food, exercise, or sunshine. They were not allowed to enter the parts of the house where other family members lived, and they were rarely visited.

The boys came to the attention of the authorities when they were 6 years old. They were abnormally small and suffered from rickets, a disease caused by a vitamin deficiency that leaves bones soft and bent. They could barely talk, they did not recognize common objects in photographs, and they were terrified of the new sights and sounds around them. The twins were taken to a children's home where they

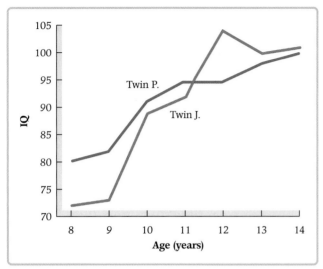

Figure 7.3 After the twins studied by Koluchova were released from isolation, their intellectual abilities showed gradual recovery and eventually became normal. (Adapted from Koluchova, 1976.)

were well cared for and housed with children younger than themselves in a nonthreatening environment.

In these new circumstances, the twins soon began to gain weight, take an active interest in their surroundings, and learn to speak. When they were first tested at the age of 8 years, the boys' intelligence measured well below normal. But year by year their performance improved until, at the age of 14, both of them manifested perfectly normal intelligence (see Figure 7.3).

An even more severely neglected child was Genie, who was kept locked in a room by herself, beginning sometime before her second birthday (Curtiss, 1979). For more than 11 years, Genie spent her days chained to a potty and her nights tied up in a sleeping bag. No one spoke to her. When her father came to tie her in for the night or to bring her food, he growled at her like a beast and scratched her with his fingernails.

Genie was a pitiful creature when she was liberated from these horrible circumstances. Although she was 13 years old, she weighed only 59 pounds and was only 4 feet, 6 inches tall. She did not make intelligible sounds and was not toilet-trained. She could not walk normally; instead, she shuffled her feet and swayed from side to side. Remarkably, a battery of psychological tests revealed that Genie had an amazing ability to perceive and think about spatial relationships even though she had little to look at in her room.

Genie learned to control her bowels and to walk normally, but she never developed normal language. When first found, she showed no emotion at all when people left her; eventually, though, she became attached to other people who lived in her hospital rehabilitation unit. She developed ways to make her visitors stay longer and became upset when they finally did leave. However, her social behavior never improved to the point where she could live without special care. (For more about Genie's treatment, see the box "Genie and the Question of Ethics Revisited.")

Fortunately, such cases are extremely rare. However, because they are, it is still not known how long and how severe a child's isolation has to be before the damage it causes is irreversible. The infrequency of such cases also makes it difficult to assess the impact of isolation on individual aspects of development. Emotional, intellectual, and physical development may all be affected by isolation, but probably not all are affected in the same way (Clarke & Clarke, 1986).

An important question raised, but not answered, by the studies of extreme isolation is, How do environmental conditions during and following isolation interact with each other? Is it important, for example, that the twins described by Koluchova had each other for company when they were isolated? Was Genie's aptitude for spatial thinking a special intellectual ability that would have shown up regardless of her isolation, or did it develop as a consequence of her immobility and her social isolation? The answers to such questions would contribute to an understanding of both the developmental risks faced by children raised in less extreme but still adverse circumstances and the factors that might enable them to recover despite these circumstances.

prevention science An area of research that examines the biological and social processes that lead to maladjustment as well as those that are associated with healthy development.

risk factors Personal characteristics or environmental circumstances that increase the probability of negative outcomes for children. Risk is a statistic that applies to groups, not individuals.

Vulnerability and Resilience

Questions about the impact of different care environments are motivated by a desire to protect children from harm and promote their health and well-being. In recent years a new area of research called **prevention science** has emerged, which examines the biological and social processes that lead to maladjustment as well as those that are associated with healthy development (Wandersman & Florin, 2003).

Genie and the Question of Ethics Revisited

Research done with Genie, the girl who was kept locked up for over 11 years by her abusive father, strikingly demonstrates how scientific and ethical issues can conflict, even when everyone involved in a research program has good intentions. The ethical controversy surrounding Genie focuses on whether the scientists who studied her development after she escaped from her confinement did all they could to ensure her recovery, or whether their desire to solve a scientific puzzle led them to subordinate Genie's well-being to the goal of scientific progress.

Russ Rymer (1993), who wrote a book about the case, argues that Genie's well-being was indeed sacrificed in the name of scientific inquiry. The scientists in charge of Genie's care deny any wrongdoing; they contend that Genie was treated as well as possible given the very unusual and difficult circumstances of her history and condition.

When Genie was first liberated, she was placed in Los Angeles Children's Hospital. Because her case was one of the most severe cases of child isolation on record it quickly drew scientific interest. According to David Rigler, then chief psychiatrist at the hospital and the man who eventually became Genie's principal investigator, human values and science alike called for a systematic study of Genie's development:

> Theories of child development hold that there are essential experiences for achievement of normal psychological and physical growth. If this child can be assisted to develop in cognitive, linguistic and social, and other areas, this provides useful information regarding the critical role of early experience which is of potential benefit to other deprived children. The research interest inherently rests upon successful achievement of rehabilitative efforts. The research goals thus coincide with (Genie's) own welfare and happiness. (Rymer, 1993, p. 58)

Unfortunately for Genie, this is not how things worked out. For the first several months after her liberation, Genie lived at Children's Hospital. David Rigler obtained a research grant to bring consultants together to decide what approach to take with Genie. Some saw Genie as a scientific opportunity to answer questions about the development of language and thought. Inspired in part by the questions left unanswered by the case of Victor, the Wild Boy of Aveyron, they wanted to use Genie to test the hypothesis that there is a critical period—up until puberty—after which language cannot be acquired. They proposed a program of intensive training to see if she could still develop language.

Others argued that therapy for Genie should come first and that everything else should be a secondary consideration. The psychologist David Elkind, one of the consultants, wrote, "Too much emphasis on language could be detrimental if the child came to feel that love, attention, and acceptance were primarily dependent upon her speech" (Rymer, 1993, p. 59).

Those pushing for a scientific investigation prevailed, and the researchers obtained a grant that focused on Genie's acquisition of language—not so much teaching Genie language as watching how she learned it. Shortly after this decision was made, Genie was taken into the home of Jean Butler, her teacher at Children's Hospital. In the next 2 months, Genie made enormous strides in acquiring vocabulary. But Jean Butler strongly objected to the intrusiveness of the scientists who were studying Genie. She said that their training procedures were disrupting the girl's life and impeding her recovery. A battle for Genie's custody ensued. Butler applied to the Department of Public Social Services to become Genie's foster parent, but her request was denied in favor of Rigler and his wife.

Genie lived in the Rigler household for 4 years. During that time she was treated as much as possible like a member of the family. She was taught how to chew solid food, to behave properly at the table, to express her emotions and indicate her desires appropriately, and to stop masturbating, which she had been doing whenever and wherever she felt the urge to. But she was also being constantly observed and tested by linguists and psychologists.

Within a short time after her move to the Riglers' home, Genie's progress in language learning slowed to a standstill. Her speech resembled the language used in telegrams. She never learned to ask a real question or to form a proper negative sentence. Nor did she learn to behave normally in social situations. Scientists at the National Institutes of Mental Health, which sponsored the research on Genie, became dissatisfied with the project. Largely because it was a single case study based on anecdotal evidence and no controls were possible, they denied further funding for her study.

When the project ended, Genie was returned to her mother's custody. Her mother could not cope with Genie's disabilities and placed her in foster care. She is now residing in a home for mentally retarded adults in Southern California. Overall, her behavior has significantly regressed. She is stooped and rarely makes eye contact. She cannot talk normally and continues to engage in inappropriate social behaviors.

Rigler and his colleagues chose to focus on Genie's language deprivation rather than on any of the other major domains of development. What if they had instead followed the lead of research on recovery from severe isolation? Would Genie have recovered more fully if they had provided her with social therapy emphasizing attachment and loving relations with others? There is no way to know. Russ Rymer titled his book *Genie: A Scientific Tragedy*. It tells the unfortunate sequel to the personal tragedy of a parent's inhuman treatment of a helpless child.

Developmentalists working within this field are particularly interested in identifying **risk factors,** personal characteristics or environmental circumstances that increase the probability of negative outcomes for children. Risk is a statistic that applies to groups, not individuals. One can say, for example, that children who have depressed parents are more likely than the general population to become depressed themselves, but one cannot say that a particular child whose father or mother is depressed will inevitably become depressed. Most risk factors are not the direct cause of the developmental problems or disorders with which they are associated, but

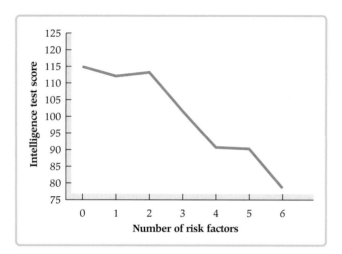

Figure 7.4 The average IQ scores for 13-year-olds decrease markedly when their development is affected by more than two risk factors. (From Sameroff et al., 1993.)

interact in complex ways with other factors (Roosa, 2000). For example, having a poorly educated mother is a risk factor for school failure, but a mother's lack of education does not cause her children to fail in school. However, because of her lack of education and familiarity with the demands of school, her children may have more difficulty succeeding academically than children whose parents are educated.

Many studies have demonstrated that a combination of biological, social, and environmental risk factors interacting over a considerable period of time is associated with most serious developmental problems (Cicchetti & Toth, 1998; Lunthar et al., 2000; Sameroff et al., 1998; Shaw et al., 1998) (see Figure 7.4). At the same time, all these studies find marked individual differences in outcome among children who live in highly stressful circumstances. Many children who grow up in the face of adversity—who are raised by alcoholic parents, attend substandard schools, have siblings who belong to gangs, experience dislocation due to war, or homelessness due to poverty—are able to rise above their circumstances and lead healthy, productive lives. That is, they seem to be **resilient**—to have the ability to recover quickly from the adverse effects of early experience or to persevere in the face of stress with no apparent negative psychological consequences. Such observations have led psychologists to search for the sources of children's resilience, referred to as **protective factors** (Lunthar et al., 2000; Robinson, 2000).

Table 7.2 summarizes the risk and protective factors associated with early childhood behavior problems, which are grouped according to the levels of the

Now living in Jordan, this refugee family fled Iraq to escape poverty and hardship. The father, an amputee injured in the Iran-Iraq wars, was unable to accompany them. Despite this sad history, and the difficulty making ends meet with a low-paying job in their new community, this photograph captures a loving moment suggesting the family's resilience to difficult circumstances.

table 7.2

Examples of Risk and Protective Factors Associated with Childhood Problems

Risk Factors	Protective Factors
Child Characteristics	
Difficult infant temperament	Easy infant temperament
Limited cognitive abilities	High intelligence
Insecure attachments	Secure attachments
Low self-esteem	High self-esteem
Poor peer relations	Positive peer relations
School difficulties	Positive adaptation to school
Psychopathology	Good mental health
Microsystem	
Domestic violence	Good marital relations
Financial hardship	Consistent employment
Hostile family environment	Positive family relations
Parental psychopathology	Good parental mental health
Maladaptive child-rearing skills	Positive child-rearing skills
Exosystem	
Community violence	Supportive social network
Crime in neighborhood	Good community resources
Social isolation	Supportive church
Impoverished community	Gaining community resources
Lack of community services	Accessing social support networks
Macrosystem	
Violent culture	National support for education
Parenting customs	Belief in children's rights
Racism	National commitment to rehabilitating substance abusers
Social acceptance of violence	Lower unemployment rate
Recession	Elected officials committed to improving plight of disadvantaged

Source: Adapted from Cicchetti et al., 2000.

ecological system model of development discussed in Chapter 1 (p. 17). We will examine the sources of risk and protective factors within each level: the child, the family (the microsystem), the community (the exosystem), and the culture (the macrosystem).

Characteristics of the Child

Research on how characteristics of the child relate to developmental risk suggest that different temperamental characteristics are likely to put children at risk, but somewhat differently, depending on the child's age (Carey & McDevitt, 1995). In infancy and early childhood, U.S. and British children who are difficult—that is, who display irregularity of biological functions, negative responses to new situations and people, and frequent negative mood—and who have a high activity level are at greater risk than placid, easy children. In middle childhood, children who are easily distracted, who have a short attention span, and who have a hard time adjusting to new circumstances are at greater risk.

resilience The ability to recover quickly from the adverse effects of early experience or persevere in the face of stress with no apparent special negative psychological consequences.

protective factors Environmental and personal factors that are the source of children's resilience in the face of hardship.

Children with difficult temperaments can be taxing to those who care for them, parents in particular. Infants who are irritable, difficult, and fussy can set in motion a chain of reactions from others that puts them at risk for developing psychological and behavioral problems (Collins et al., 2000). Difficult infants tend to evoke hostility, avoidance, coercive discipline, and a lack of playfulness in mothers. These parenting responses, in turn, correlate with insecure attachments. A longitudinal study of adopted children provides further supporting evidence (O'Connor et al., 1998). In particular, the researchers discovered that children who were at genetic risk for behavior problems received more negative parenting from their adoptive parents than did children who were not at risk.

It should be noted that whether or not a particular temperament represents a risk factor can depend on cultural circumstances. Research by Marten De Vries (1994) provides dramatic evidence that temperamental traits considered "difficult" in the United States can be crucial to development in another cultural setting. In one study, De Vries developed a temperament questionnaire based on Chess and Thomas's classifications (see Chapter 4, p. 137) and administered it to mothers of 48 4- to 5-month-old Masai children in East Africa (De Vries, 1987). At the time this research was conducted, a severe drought was plaguing Masai country and many people were moving out of their villages in search of food. When De Vries returned several months later to conduct follow-up tests with the 10 most difficult and 10 least difficult infants identified by the earlier questionnaires, he could locate only 13 families, 7 from the "easy child" group and 6 from the "difficult child" group. De Vries found that 5 of the 7 "easy" children had died, while only 1 of the 6 "difficult" children had died. Coupled with the work of Scheper-Hughes in Brazil discussed on page 273, this study suggests that in chronically deprived circumstances, being demanding (which children with difficult temperaments tend to be) may actually help the child to survive.

Emmie Werner and Ruth Smith (1992) offer additional evidence that personal characteristics can help the child to survive difficult circumstances. On the basis of records provided by health, mental health, and social service agencies and educational institutions, as well as personal interviews and personality tests, they report that the children who were able to cope best with their life circumstances during their first two decades were those whom their mothers described as "very active" and "socially responsive" when they were infants. The mothers' reports were verified by independent observers, who noted that these children displayed "pronounced autonomy" and a "positive social orientation." When they were examined during their second year of life, these children scored especially well on a variety of tests, including measures of motor and language development.

Characteristics of the Family

The family is the main support system for the child. You would expect, then, that variations in the kinds of support that families provide for children should be associated with children's ability to withstand threats to their development. This idea is borne out by a variety of research (Prevatt, 2003). Many of the ways in which family characteristics influence risk factors and resilience can be seen in the results of an ambitious longitudinal study of a multiracial group of 689 children born on the Hawaiian island of Kauai in 1955 (Werner & Smith, 1982). Of these children, 201 were considered especially likely to suffer developmental problems because they experienced four or more risk factors by the time they were 2 years old. The risk factors included being a member of a low-income family, being born prematurely or suffering from stress during the birth process, having a mother whose educational level was low, and having a parent who had some form of psychopathology (see the box "Maternal Depression as a Risk Factor," p. 262).

The ways that families cope with misfortune can dramatically affect their children's risk for developmental problems. If the children living in this railroad car are cared for as well as their beautiful garden suggests, they may escape many of the usual consequences of poverty.

The researchers found that the following family circumstances gave these children some protection against developmental difficulties:

- The family had no more than four children.
- More than 2 years separated the child studied and the next younger or older sibling.
- Alternative caregivers were available to the mother within the household (father, grandparents, or older siblings).
- The work load of the mother, even when she was employed outside the home, was not excessive
- The child had a substantial amount of attention by caregivers during infancy.
- A sibling was available as a caregiver or confidant during childhood.
- The family provided structure and rules during the child's adolescence.
- The family was cohesive.
- The child had an informal, multigenerational network of kin and friends during adolescence.
- The cumulative number of chronic stressful life events experienced during childhood and adolescence was not great.

Other evidence that the family can buffer the child's risk for developmental problems comes from a Finnish study that compared two groups of adopted children (Tienari et al., 1994). In one group, the biological parents had been diagnosed with schizophrenia. In the other, there was no known parental psychopathology. It was found that children in the first group were more likely to develop psychiatric disorders than were children in the second group, but only if they had been adopted into dysfunctional families. When the genetically at-risk children were placed into well-functioning families, they developed in ways similar to the children who had no family history of schizophrenia. It seems that a dysfunctional family environment may trigger the expression, or *phenotype,* of the biological predisposition, or *genotype* (Collins et al., 2000; see Chapter 2 for a discussion of phenotype–genotype relations).

Maternal Depression as a Risk Factor

Extensive research over the past decade has shown that chronic maternal depression (depression that lasts for 6 months or more) is a risk factor in children's development (Brennan et al., 2000, Hammen, 1999). Such prolonged depression, which extends well beyond the "baby blues" that many mothers experience following the birth of a child, interferes with mothers' daily functioning and is related to a variety of negative developmental outcomes for their babies.

As we have seen in a variety of examples presented in earlier chapters, normal social interchanges between mothers and their infants are jointly regulated. The baby smiles and the mother smiles back at her baby in response; the baby vocalizes and the mother answers with a vocalization. This kind of responsive turn-taking is what developmentalists are talking about when they refer to sensitive mothering that facilitates the infant's goal of communicating and acting on the world.

In cases of chronic maternal depression, by contrast, mothers are less responsive and sensitive to their babies' signals and they have difficulty providing an adequate level of social stimulation for their babies (Weinberg & Tronick, 1997). Depressed mothers don't touch their babies as often as other mothers do and they engage them in fewer activities and games. Compared with nondepressed mothers, depressed mothers speak to their babies less often and are less sensitive to their babies' vocalizations. Instead of responding to their babies' smiles with answering smiles, depressed mothers are more likely to look sad and anxious when interacting with their infants.

Correspondingly, the babies of depressed mothers tend to have lower activity levels, smile less, and frown more than babies of nondepressed mothers. They do not vocalize or play as much as other babies, and they tend to be more fussy and tense. They are also less likely to be securely attached to their mothers (Teti et al., 1995). The negative style of these babies' interactions with their mothers even carries over to their interactions with strangers who are not suffering from depression (Field, 1995).

Psychologists and psychiatrists who work with the children of depressed mothers are well aware of these facts but cannot be certain how to interpret them. The depressed behavior of some of these babies is similar enough to that of their mothers to suggest that they became depressed either in imitation of their mothers' negative style of responsiveness or in reaction to their mothers' depressed behavior. There is some evidence, however, that at least some babies who behave this way are depressive from birth, suggesting that genetic or prenatal factors may cause their depression (Field et al., 2001; Murray & Cooper, 1997). For example, Tiffany Field and her colleagues studied a group of women who were diagnosed as suffering from depression while they were still pregnant. When their babies were assessed shortly after birth, they were found to be more irritable, to have less developed motor tone and depressed activity levels, and to show limited responses to social stimulation (Field et al., 2001).

The effects of early infant depression, whether the result of the mother's behavior or inherited factors, continue if the mother's depression continues. Older children of mothers who were depressed when they were infants and remain depressed over time are not only at risk for depression but also have been found to perform more poorly than other children on measures of cognitive, linguistic, and social functioning at 3 years of age (NICHD Early Child Care Research Network, 1998a, 1998b). School-aged children of chronically depressed mothers have been found to get in trouble in school because their attention wanders, they fidget in class, and they fight with other children on the playground (Dodge, 1990; Hammen, 1991). A rare, longitudinal study of nearly 5,000 mothers and their children found that higher levels of depression in mothers were associated with higher levels of behavioral and cognitive problems in their 5-year-old children (Brennan et al., 2000).

However, if the mother recovers from her depression, it is possible for the child to begin to function more normally. It is when the mother's depression is persistent, or comes and goes in cycles, that makes children especially at risk for long-term developmental problems. In these cases, the presence of supportive adults other than the depressed mother is very important (Carro et al., 1993).

To help prevent depression in infants of depressed mothers, developmentalists have been creating therapeutic techniques geared to modifying the mother's behavior (Field, 1997). Some of the most effective interventions include teaching the depressed mother to imitate her baby's positive social behaviors, to communicate clearly when she talks to her baby, and to play games with her baby that are appropriate to the baby's developmental level. Babies whose mothers are given this kind of "interaction coaching" show increased eye contact and fewer expressions of distress (Field, 1997), creating more favorable conditions for their future development.

Characteristics of the Community

The characteristics of the communities in which children live also seem to affect the likelihood that children will develop problems. In general, children in impoverished communities are more likely to suffer from developmental difficulties than are children in less economically depressed communities (Harrison et al., 2004). In addition, those who live in poor inner-city neighborhoods have a significantly higher risk of developing a psychological disorder than do those who live in poor small towns or rural areas (Richters & Martinez, 1993).

One factor found to protect children against the impact of negative community characteristics is the strength of the social support networks provided by kin, neighbors, and social service agencies (Cochran & Niego, 1995). For example, Patricia Hashima and Paul Amato (1994) found that parents living in poverty who had friends and neighbors they could turn to for advice and call on in an emergency were significantly less likely to yell at their children or hit them than were those who lacked such support. Similarly, Susan Crockenberg (1987) found that teenaged mothers in England who received the community-based social support services for parents provided by the National Health Service showed significant increases in the amount and quality of their interactions with their infants.

Another factor outside the home that helps to buffer children from stressful and depriving life circumstances is the school. Children in disadvantaged and discordant homes are less likely to develop psychological problems if they attend schools that have attentive personnel and good academic programs (Rutter, 1987).

Other community influences on children's development and well-being, including violence and poverty, will be addressed in detail in Chapter 11.

In addition to their importance to education, schools help to buffer children from stressful circumstances. Although the school in this war-torn community in Angola provides these children with much-needed stability, it is nonetheless difficult to escape the reminders of violence and destruction, as demonstrated by the classroom's blown-out window and shot-up walls.

Characteristics of the Culture

As suggested in the discussion above regarding risk and temperament, there are wide cultural differences in how risks are identified, interpreted, and managed. In her analysis of risk in African childhood, Christine Liddell (2002) argues that Western assumptions regarding risk, resilience, and recovery need to be considered very cautiously when examining risk in non-Western cultures. A case in point is the Western assumption that continuity in early relationships, that is, stable, dependable caregivers, is essential to the development of secure attachments. Multiple disruptions and separations from primary caregivers are assumed to contribute to poor outcomes for children. Many African children, however, experience routine disruptions and separations from their parents due to the traditional cultural practice of **cross-fostering.** Cross-fostering is an elaborate system of child exchange within families. Children are fostered for a variety of reasons, and for varying amounts of time. A child may be given to an aunt who is unable to bear her own children, or who needs additional help because her husband has died prematurely. Economic circumstances may also motivate cross-fostering. An older child may be fostered for a few months in order to help relatives harvest a crop, or prepare their goods for market. A very young child may be fostered for several years to allow the mother to return to work, and then returned to the birth home when he or she requires less supervision and can contribute to the household. A child in a rural area may be fostered by relatives living in a city in order to attend school or learn a trade. It has been estimated that about one-third of South African children live in families that include at least one fostered child (Kaufman, Maharaj, & Richter, 1998).

To a Western eye, the routine movement of children between households may seem to place them at risk for developing insecure attachments. However, within African culture, the kinship network that develops through cross-fostering ensures reciprocity and care, protecting children from a variety of risks common to their particular cultural environments, including death of a parent from AIDS or displacement due to war (Becker, 2000) (see the box "Children and War," p. 264).

cross-fostering A system of child exchange within families; it is a traditional practice in many African societies.

Children and War

Political violence has been identified as a major risk that threatens the lives and well-being of children across the globe (Kaslow, 2001). A United Nations (1996) report catalogs a horrifying list of traumas and rights violations suffered by children and their families. Children are recruited as soldiers and made to commit murder and other atrocities; they are exposed to disease and malnutrition when they are forced to flee their homes or while living in refugee camps; their access to education and health care is severely curtailed due to relocation, or because their schools and hospitals have been destroyed; children are injured, permanently disabled, or killed in conflict, often intentionally, sometimes by stumbling on unexploded land mines; they are raped and otherwise exploited sexually; they witness the murder of family members and neighbors; and they are orphaned (see table).

The traumas of war are multifaceted (Cairns, 1996; Dybdahl, 2001). Some of the consequences are direct, relating to children's personal experiences of war: hearing and seeing explosions; witnessing people and animals being hurt; or being hurt themselves. Other consequences are indirect, involving the loss of family, exposure to disease and poverty, and dislocation. Children exposed to war often show symptoms of traumatic stress, including irritability, sleep difficulties, separation anxiety, and nightmares (Dybdahl, 2001). However, studies on the long-term effects of war on children present a complex picture. While some children suffer greatly, become depressed and develop psychosocial problems, the majority appear to be relatively resilient (Cairns & Dawes, 1996). It is important to understand that children's relative resilience does not mean that they are without distress, only that they are coping and functioning reasonably well in everyday life.

An important protective factor in children's resilience to the effects of war is parenting (Miller, 1996). We know from studies in other areas of children's behavior that the family can be either a risk factor or a protective factor in the development of problems

UNICEF/HQ92-0587/I Dream of Peace

Children who experience the horrors of war firsthand often show psychological and emotional symptoms that are similar to those associated with post-traumatic stress syndrome. This child's drawing illustrates the frightening effects of war on home and village life.

(see p. 259). Because political violence places families under significant stress, parenting may deteriorate. In the face of the pressures of war, parents often become more authoritarian and less emotionally positive in their interactions. They also tend to provide their children with less supervision.

The United Nations has called for the development of international strategies to help children and families cope in the face of political violence. A number of nutritional and health intervention programs have been instituted, but because the need for action has been so great, there have been relatively few controlled studies of intervention programs. One exception to this is a study conducted by Ragnhild Dybdahl on mothers and children who became refugees due to the war in Bosnia and Herzegovina.

Mothers and their children were randomly assigned to either an experimental group or a control group. Participants in both groups were provided with free basic health care. In addition, those in the experimental group

UNICEF/HQ94-0911/Roger Lemoyne

In addition to its harmful psychological and emotional effects, war also impacts children's education. In many war-torn areas, schools are closed because it is too dangerous for children to travel.

The more distributed attachment system encouraged by cross-fostering is apparent in the earliest interactions between infants and caregivers. Many studies of African infant–mother interactions indicate that mothers talk less to their babies and are less likely to seek eye contact compared with Western mothers. For some years, the African pattern was assumed to be less optimal for infants' social and emotional development. However, a cultural-context framework emphasizes the

participated in an intervention program that focused on sensitizing mothers to the importance of emotionally responsive communications with their children and providing an emotionally warm and supportive environment. The mothers also participated in therapeutic discussion groups with other women who experienced war trauma.

Compared with the control group, mothers in the experimental group showed a reduction in trauma symptoms and increased life satisfaction. They also reported that their children appeared less anxious and sad, and had fewer nightmares compared with reports by mothers in the control group. Their children also benefited. In particular, children in the experimental group gained more weight, showed higher levels of improvement on tests of cognitive reasoning, and perceived their mothers as more emotionally supportive compared with children in the control group. Dybdahl believes that the children benefited because their mother's symptoms were reduced, allowing them to be more attentive to their children's needs.

Children's cultural traditions can also be a significant protective factor against the trauma of war. An example of this is provided in studies of child soldiers (Honwana, 2000; Summerfield, 1999). In many war-torn African nations, including Zimbabwe, Mozambique, Angola, and Ethiopia, young boys are recruited to fight. Part of the process of recovering from war involves participating in ritualized cleansing ceremonies. When young soldiers return home, they are symbolically cleansed of the contaminating ancestral spirits of their victims, which would otherwise spread from the soldiers to the entire social body (Honwana, 2000). The children are forbidden to speak of their war experiences, as this would "open a door" for the harmful spirits to infect the community. In contrast to Western traditions that view trauma as a personal problem, African traditions view it as a potential threat to the larger social group. It is therefore not only the individual who undergoes a process of recovery, but the entire community.

War Experiences of Children and Families		
Type of Event	**n**	**%**
Had to flee from my home	76	100
Thought I would die	70	92
Experienced war activities	68	90
Been shot at	64	84
Separated from close family	57	75
Family members missing	50	66
Family members wounded	49	65
Serious food deprivation	48	63
Seen dead bodies of victims	46	61
Family members killed	44	58
Witnessed home destroyed	23	30
Wounded	16	21
Forced to do things against own will	22	17
Witnessed torture	17	13
Abused, tortured	9	12
Been in concentration camp	6	8

Data were collected during the war in Bosnia and Herzegovia (1992–1995); *n* = 76.
Source: Dybdahl, 2001, p. 1221.

EPA/Stephen Morrison/AP Wide World

One of the most disturbing ways that children become victims of war is by being recruited as armed combatants into armies and other militant groups.

importance of considering the broader social contexts of infants' environments. In contrast to children raised in middle-class America, African babies experience substantial shared caregiving by multiple family and community members, particularly older sisters (Whaley et al., 2002). When developmentalists broaden the scope of their study to include other caregivers in addition to mothers, they find, between cultures, comparable levels of verbal interaction and mutual gaze.

Recovery from Deprivation

You have seen that studies predict a greater likelihood of long-term developmental damage when children are exposed to negative risk factors during infancy. But these risk factors do not condemn children to poor outcomes. On the contrary, research with both humans and nonhumans suggests that later life experiences and specially designed therapeutic interventions can mitigate the effects of early misfortune.

The Impact of Later Circumstances

It is important to remember that risk factors do not occur in isolation; they interact and influence each other. It is also important to recognize that the impact of these factors can be moderated by later circumstances. This fact is highlighted by transactional models (pp. 245–246) that suggest how risk factors enter into the general process of development (Clarke & Clarke, 1986; Sameroff & Mackenzie, 2003).

Thomas and Chess (1984) used a transactional model to show how later circumstances and parents' changing interpretations of the child's personality and behavior can interact with a child's temperamental traits to influence the child's mental health. The girl they describe, starting in her preschool years, exhibited a difficult, demanding, and volatile personality.

> [Her] father responded with rigid demands for quick, positive adaptation and hostile criticisms and punishment when the girl could not meet his expectations. The mother was intimidated by both her husband and daughter and was vacillating and anxious in her handling of the child. With this extremely negative parent–child interaction, the girl's symptoms grew worse. Psychotherapy was instituted, with only modest improvement. But when she was 9–10 years of age, the girl blossomed forth with musical and dramatic talent, which brought her favorable attention and praise from teachers and other parents. This talent also ranked high in her parents' own hierarchy of desirable attributes. Her father now began to see his daughter's intense and explosive personality not as a sign of a "rotten kid," his previous label for her, but as evidence of a budding artist. He began to make allowances for her "artistic temperament," and with this the mother was able to relax and relate positively to her daughter. The girl was allowed to adapt at her own pace, and by adolescence all evidence of her neurotic symptoms and functioning had disappeared. (Thomas & Chess, 1984, p. 7)

As this description suggests, transactional histories are characterized by complex interactions between a changing environmental context and the particular characteristics of the child that are highlighted in each new situation.

Transactional analysis is applied to groups of people as well as to individuals. Michael Rutter and his colleagues used a transactional model to explain the later life adjustments of young Londoners who had spent significant parts of their infancy and childhood in child-care facilities (Quinton & Rutter, 1985; Rutter et al., 1990). These children had been placed in institutions not because of any behavioral problems but because their parents could not cope with child rearing. Many of them remained in institutions throughout their infancy and early childhood. At 21 to 27 years old, they were compared with another group of the same age from the same part of London who had been raised by their parents without interruption.

Focusing first on "ex-care" (formerly institutionalized) women, Rutter and his colleagues found that these young adults had experienced difficulties that the women in the comparison group had not. To begin with, 42 percent had become pregnant before the age of 19, and 39 percent of them were no longer living with the fathers of their children. One-third had experienced a relatively serious breakdown in caring for their children. By contrast, only 5 percent of the women in the comparison group had become pregnant by the age of 19, all were living with the fathers of their children, and none had experienced a serious breakdown in the care of their children. When the women's current parenting practices were studied, the "ex-care" women were far more likely to receive poor ratings than were the women in the comparison group (see Table 7.3).

At first these findings may appear to be straightforward evidence of the long-term effects of early misfortune. But when they are viewed from the perspective of a transactional model, it becomes clear that the early misfortune set in motion a series of events that tended to perpetuate the difficulty. Institutional care led first to a lack of strong attachments during infancy and childhood and difficulties in forming good relationships with peers. These problems increased the likelihood of teenage pregnancy. The early pregnancy reduced the likelihood of further education or job training. The ensuing economic pressures created a disadvantaged environment, which in turn created the stresses that were the immediate cause of poor parenting.

Early institutionalization did not necessarily lead to continual misfortune, however. Those women raised in institutions who had supportive husbands were found to be just as effective at parenting as the women in the comparison group. These positive results led the researchers to conclude that institutionalization during infancy and childhood and the lack of strong personal attachments that goes with it do not necessarily doom women to become poor mothers. If the usual chain of consequences can be broken and favorable transactions established, normal behavior is likely to follow.

The profiles of the young men who had spent time in child-care institutions showed that positive later-life experiences decreased their risk of long-term difficulties as well. One particularly interesting gender difference was that men were more likely than women to find a supportive spouse and to raise their children in an intact family, thus blocking the transmission of their own negative early experiences to the next generation (Rutter et al., 1990).

The mounting evidence that the long-term consequences of misfortune depend to a significant degree on later circumstances has spurred a search for principles of successful intervention. A key element in any effort to repair developmental damage is removal from the damaging environment, but such a change alone is not sufficient for recovery. When the Lebanese children were moved from the orphanage to other institutions, they did not reach normal levels of development, nor did Genie ever show sufficient recovery to become normal for her age. Could the Lebanese children or Genie have fared better? What conditions are necessary to foster more complete recovery from early deprivation? Is it possible that some as yet undiscovered environmental conditions might have allowed them to regain normal functioning? Or did their deprivation start too early and last too long to permit them ever to recover completely?

Such questions are impossible to answer in full because human babies cannot deliberately be assigned to live in potentially damaging circumstances to satisfy the quest for scientific knowledge. Research with monkeys, however, combined with scattered studies of human subjects, suggests what some of the aids to recovery might be.

table 7.3

Child-Care Behaviors in Two Groups of Mothers		
Child-care difficulty	**Mothers Raised in Institutions** (*n* = 40)	**Comparison Group** (*n* = 43)
Lack of expression of warmth to children	45%	19%
Insensitivity	65%	28%
Lack of play with children	33%	16%
At least two of the above	59%	23%

Source: Quinton & Rutter, 1985.

Harlow's Monkeys Revisited

In Chapter 6 (pp. 226–227) we examined Harry Harlow's studies of infant monkeys raised in isolation with inanimate substitute mothers. One of Harlow's important findings was that infant monkeys had difficulty developing normal social relations after they were introduced into cages with their peers. This was the case even with the monkeys who had become attached to substitute terry cloth mothers, although the severity of the behavioral disruption varied with the length of the isolation and the age of the monkey when the isolation began (Suomi & Harlow, 1972). Monkeys who were totally isolated for only the first 3 months of life, for example, did not seem to be permanently affected by the experience. When they were moved to a group cage, they were overwhelmed by the more complex environment at first, but within a month they had become accepted members of the social group.

Monkeys who were totally isolated for their first 6 months of life, in contrast, rocked, bit, or scratched themselves compulsively when they were placed in a cage with other monkeys. Monkeys who had been isolated during the second 6 months of life (but not the first) became aggressive and fearful when they were put back with other monkeys.

The long-term behavior of these groups of monkeys also differed. Those whose isolation began after 6 months of social interaction in the colony recovered quickly and were able to mate normally when they came of age. But those whose 6-month isolation started at birth recovered only partially. At 3 years of age, when they should have been able to mate, they proved to be incapable of normal sexual behavior.

Total isolation for the entire first year of life produced full-fledged social misfits who showed no propensities for social play or social interchange with monkeys the same age (Harlow & Novak, 1973). When they were placed in a group cage, these monkeys were often the targets of their peers' aggression. As time passed, they showed no signs of spontaneous recovery.

Recovery from Isolation

After their initial experiments, Harlow and his associates thought that the period from birth to 6 months of age might be critical for social development in these monkeys. If this were the case, recovery would be impossible for monkeys isolated throughout the 6-month period, regardless of any subsequent changes in their environment. The researchers tried various ways of aiding the adaptation of such monkeys to their new social world. One technique they used was to punish the monkeys for inappropriate behaviors by administering a mildly painful shock. Another approach was to introduce them to the new environment slowly, on the assumption that an abrupt change from total isolation to the busy activity of the group cage induced an "emergence trauma" that blocked recovery. The ineffectiveness of all these efforts seemed to support the idea that there was a critical period for social development. As it turned out, such was not the case at all.

The first hint that there might be an effective therapy for these monkeys came from observations of the maternal behaviors of the females, who had been artificially inseminated (Suomi et al., 1972). Many of them beat their newborns and sat on them, and few of the babies survived. If a baby did live, however, the mother began to recover. As the researchers watched these babies with their mothers, they began to suspect how this change came about. If the baby monkeys could manage to cling to their mother's chest, as newborn infant monkeys normally do, they survived. While clinging, they not only had access to life-sustaining milk but also could usually escape their mothers' attempts to harm them. The longer they held on and the stronger they grew, the more time their mothers spent behaving in ways that were approximately normal, if not loving. By the end of the usual period of nursing, the mothers were no longer abusive and interacted more or less normally with

This mature female monkey, who was isolated for the first 6 months of life, finds it difficult to react to the baby monkey. But if the baby is sufficiently persistent in its attempts to interact with her, the older monkey may eventually learn to interact more or less normally with it.

Harlow Primate Laboratory, University of Wisconsin

their babies. Even more striking was the caregiving behavior of these mothers when they had a second baby. It was indistinguishable from that of their nondeprived peers. They had recovered normal social functioning.

The recovery of these mothers led Harlow and his colleagues to speculate that it might be possible to reverse the social pathologies of previously isolated monkeys by introducing them into a mother–infant type of relationship with a younger monkey (Harlow & Novak, 1973; Suomi & Harlow, 1972). The researchers introduced normal 2- to 3-month-old monkeys, who were strong enough to survive the abuse they were likely to receive, into a cage with monkeys who had been isolated for 12 months. The playful, love-seeking babies provided an environment that allowed the older monkeys to learn appropriate social behaviors. Over a period of 18 weeks, the former isolates gradually stopped rocking and clasping themselves and they stopped abusing the baby monkeys. They began to move around more, to explore their environments, and to engage in social play. In the end, all of the former isolates became so well adjusted that even experienced researchers could seldom tell them from monkeys who had been raised normally.

This baby monkey is "providing therapy" to an older monkey raised in isolation.

Implications for Human Recovery

Harlow's research with monkeys suggests that placing previously isolated children in an environment in which they can interact with younger children may be therapeutic. This idea seems to be supported by the limited information available about the recovery of human children from extreme social deprivation. When the twins Koluchova (1972, 1976) studied were removed from their isolation, for example, they were at first placed in a special environment in which they lived with younger children. The twins recovered normal functioning despite their years of isolation.

A more formal test of the therapeutic potential of having socially isolated children interact with younger children was conducted by Wyndol Furman, Donald Rahe, and Willard Hartup (1979). Through observations in day-care centers, the researchers identified 24 children between the ages of $2\frac{1}{2}$ and 5 years who interacted so little with their peers that they were judged to be "socially isolated." These children were randomly assigned to three groups of eight children each. The children in the first group participated in one-on-one play sessions with a child 1 to $1\frac{1}{2}$ years younger than they were. The children in the second group participated in one-on-one play sessions with a child their own age. The final group served as a control and received no special treatment. Each child in the first two groups had 10 of these play sessions of 20 minutes each over a 6-week period. During each session, the two children were placed together in a room in which there were blocks, puppets, clothes to dress up in, and other toys that might promote positive social interaction. An observer sitting in the corner of the room took notes but otherwise tried not to interfere with the children.

After the last play session, the social interactions of all the children in the day-care classrooms were rated by observers who did not know which children had participated in the study. Their reports showed that the rate of peer interaction had almost doubled for the socially isolated children who had played with a younger child. Right from the start they provided help to, and shared with, the younger child. The children who had played with an agemate showed some improvement, but they did not differ statistically from the control group. These results show that interactions with younger children, even for a relatively brief period, can reduce the effects of social isolation. Furman and his colleagues (1979) suggested that the key benefit for the socially isolated children in having younger and less capable playmates was that it gave them the opportunity to initiate and direct social activity.

Such evidence of successful therapeutic intervention suggests the intriguing possibility that a given child's failure to recover from isolation or other forms of social deprivation may actually result from a failure to arrange the proper therapeutic environment, not from some irreversible damage done to the child. Obviously, the best environment for a formerly deprived or isolated child is not necessarily one that is common or easy to create. Practitioners ordinarily have limited time to spend with children, and they may not instinctively provide the special forms of attention and playfulness that will help deprived children to reorganize their patterns of social interaction. Nevertheless, cases of significant recovery both in young animals and in children who have experienced extreme isolation or deprivation show that practitioners should not write such children off; rather, a concerted effort should be made to give them as therapeutic an environment as possible.

Shaping Developmental Pathways

In addition to learning how profoundly children's development can be shaped by their early experiences, particularly those of extreme deprivation, you have gained an understanding of how their developmental pathways can be reshaped by improving their environments. Most of the studies described above involve children and nonhuman primates who have been exposed to highly unusual conditions of isolation and deprivation. Recently, developmentalists have begun to examine variations within a normal range of rearing conditions, parenting practices and behavior in particular, using nonhuman animal species.

An interesting example of how differences in "normal" parenting behavior can shape developmental pathways is found in studies of the "mothering" of rats. Normal rat mothers vary widely in the amount of time they spend licking and grooming their young (Caldji et al., 1998). Researchers find that such maternal differences have a significant impact on the development of offspring. In particular, rat pups that are licked and groomed extensively are less afraid to leave their home cages to explore new environments. As adults, they produce smaller amounts of stress-related hormones when placed in anxiety-provoking situations.

Another example of how the behavior of parents affects the course of development is Suomi's (1997) study of young rhesus monkeys. Like humans and many other species, monkeys are born with different genetically based temperamental characteristics (Suomi, 2001). One such characteristic observed by Suomi is the "emotional reactivity" of different monkey babies. He found that more reactive monkeys are hesitant about exploring new environments and become extremely anxious when separated from their mothers. In contrast, other monkeys are more at ease. Because of the genetic component of this particular temperamental characteristic, highly reactive mothers typically produce highly reactive offspring. However, when highly reactive rhesus babies were placed with (fostered out to) calm mothers for the first 6 months of life, they became adept at avoiding stressful situations and in enlisting the support of other monkeys to help them cope with the stress. These babies were also likely to become competent parents (Collins et al., 2000). In contrast, anxious babies that were reared by anxious mothers tended to be socially incompetent, more vulnerable to stress, and eventually, poor parents.

Optimal Conditions for Infant Development

If developmental pathways are influenced both positively and negatively by a child's normal environment, how can caregivers best foster babies' initial growth and development? Terry Brazelton and Stanley Greenspan, developmental pediatricians who have extensive experience working with and studying children from a variety of backgrounds, urge everyone concerned with the well-being of children—

parents, educators, counselors, and policy makers—to work toward meeting the following "irreducible needs of children":

- the need for ongoing nurturing relationships
- the need for physical protection, safety, and regulation
- the need for experiences tailored to individual differences
- the need for developmentally appropriate experiences
- the need for limit setting, structure, and expectations
- the need for stable, supportive communities and cultural continuity

That infants and young children everywhere share fundamental developmental needs is reflected in a document drafted by the General Assembly of the United Nations in 1959, called "The Rights of the Child" (see Table 7.4). For the first time in history, governments recognized the importance of protecting and nurturing the world's children (Colon & Colon, 2001). At this writing it has been ratified by all countries except two—Somalia and the United States.

Ideas about the nature of optimal development depend, of course, on cultural values, but in Western societies it is commonly held that the ideal conditions are those that provide for a rich variety of educational experiences and that allow as many doors as possible to remain open for a child's future.

In such societies, it is often suggested that development is best fostered when the mother, or whoever else cares for the baby, is sensitive and responsive to the baby's signals and states (Thompson, 1998). We encountered this idea in Chapter 6 (p. 232), in research on the conditions that promote secure attachment. A particularly powerful vision of the sensitive mother is provided by the nineteenth-century Danish philosopher Søren Kierkegaard:

> The loving mother teaches her child to walk alone. She is far enough from him so that she cannot actually support him, but she holds out her arms to him. She imitates his movements, and if he totters, she swiftly bends as if to seize him, so that the child might believe that he is not walking alone. . . . And yet, she does more. Her face beckons like a reward, an encouragement. Thus, the child walks alone with eyes fixed on his mother's face, not on the difficulties in his way. He supports himself by arms that do not hold him and constantly strives towards the refuge in his mother's embrace, little suspecting that in the very same moment he is emphasizing his need for her, he is proving that he can do without her, because he is walking alone. (Quoted in Sroufe, 1979, p. 462)

Kierkegaard's "loving mother" is so finely attuned to her child's needs that she creates the illusion of physical support where none exists. This illusion provides the child with a sense of capability and self-confidence that encourages maximum effort and courage. These character traits are widely admired in Western European and North American cultures. Consequently, the child-rearing behaviors that foster them, particularly sensitive and responsive mothering, are often considered the optimal conditions for development.

But what is the "right" kind of responsiveness? How much support is too much, and how much is not enough? Will the same kind of responsiveness that prepares children to succeed in school also prepare them as adults to cope with frustration, inadequate housing, discrimination, or extended periods of unemployment?

As we indicated earlier, answers to questions about what constitutes adequate preparation for later life depend on the historical and cultural circumstances into which a child is born. Japanese mothers, for example, like mothers in the United States, aspire to have their children develop into effective adults. But when viewed through an American cultural lens, Japanese mothers seem excessively responsive to their children, to the point of encouraging considerable emotional dependence (Miyaki et al., 1986). Japanese mothers' high level of responsiveness, however, does not mean that they provide inappropriate environments for their children's development. In contrast to American society, which values self-determination and

table 7.4

United Nations Declaration of the Rights of the Child

Proclaimed by General Assembly Resolution 1386(XIV) of 20 November 1959

Principle 1

The child shall enjoy all the rights set forth in this Declaration. Every child, without any exception whatsoever, shall be entitled to these rights, without distinction or discrimination on account of race, color, sex, language, religion, political or other opinion, national or social origin, property, birth or other status, whether of himself or of his family.

Principle 2

The child shall enjoy special protection, and shall be given opportunities and facilities, by law and by other means, to enable him to develop physically, mentally, morally, spiritually and socially in a healthy and normal manner and in conditions of freedom and dignity. In the enactment of laws for this purpose, the best interests of the child shall be the paramount consideration.

Principle 3

The child shall be entitled from his birth to a name and a nationality.

Principle 4

The child shall enjoy the benefits of social security. He shall be entitled to grow and develop in health; to this end, special care and protection shall be provided both to him and to his mother, including adequate pre-natal and post-natal care. The child shall have the right to adequate nutrition, housing, recreation and medical services.

Principle 5

The child who is physically, mentally or socially handicapped shall be given the special treatment, education and care required by his particular condition.

Principle 6

The child, for the full and harmonious development of his personality, needs love and understanding. He shall, wherever possible, grow up in the care and under the responsibility of his parents, and, in any case, in an atmosphere of affection and of moral and material security; a child of tender years shall not, save in exceptional circumstances, be separated from his mother. Society and the public authorities shall have the duty to extend particular care to children without a family and to those without adequate means of support. Payment of State and other assistance towards the maintenance of children of large families is desirable.

Principle 7

The child is entitled to receive education, which shall be free and compulsory, at least in the elementary stages. He shall be given an education which will promote his general culture and enable him, on a basis of equal opportunity, to develop his abilities, his individual judgement, and his sense of moral and social responsibility, and to become a useful member of society. The best interests of the child shall be the guiding principle of those responsible for his education and guidance; that responsibility lies in the first place with his parents.

The child shall have full opportunity for play and recreation, which should be directed to the same purposes as education; society and the public authorities shall endeavor to promote the enjoyment of this right.

Principle 8

The child shall in all circumstances be among the first to receive protection and relief.

Principle 9

The child shall be protected against all forms of neglect, cruelty and exploitation. He shall not be the subject of traffic, in any form.

The child shall not be admitted to employment before an appropriate minimum age; he shall in no case be caused or permitted to engage in any occupation or employment which would prejudice his health or education, or interfere with his physical, mental or moral development.

Principle 10

The child shall be protected from practices which may foster racial, religious and any other form of discrimination. He shall be brought up in a spirit of understanding, tolerance, friendship among peoples, peace and universal brotherhood, and in full consciousness that his energy and talents should be devoted to the service of his fellow men.

independence, Japanese society values interdependence and cooperation. Accordingly, Japanese mothers strive to foster a different overall pattern of adult characteristics in their children than American mothers do (Lebra, 1994). It makes sense that their strategies for achieving their "optimal" pattern should differ as well.

A quite different set of circumstances prevails in the poverty-stricken areas of northeastern Brazil (Scheper-Hughes, 1992). The environment into which babies are born there is extremely hostile to survival: the drinking water is contaminated, there is little food to eat, there are no sanitary facilities, and there is little medical care. Almost 50 percent of the children born in these communities die before the age of 5 years. For those who survive, success in later life is rarely influenced by academic ability, since little schooling is available. Most of these children can look forward to labor as unskilled farm workers, which affords no hope of economic advancement or even of a comfortable living.

In response to these conditions, according to Nancy Scheper-Hughes (1992), the mothers in this region have developed beliefs and behaviors about child rearing that seem harsh and uncaring by the standards of middle-class families in either the United States or Japan. They are fatalistic about their infants' well-being. They view children who are developmentally delayed or who have a passive, quiet temperament as inherently weak and unlikely to survive. Consequently, they may neglect these children or simply leave them to die if they become sick. In such circumstances, where weakness means death and resources are few, the favored children are those who are precocious, active, and demanding, because they are judged to be the ones who will survive. Further, mothers expect children who have lived to the age of 5 or 6 years to start contributing to the family's livelihood. The boys are allowed to roam the streets, searching for food and stealing if necessary. The girls are required to pick sugarcane or do housework.

From the perspective of financially secure families in the United States, the form of mothering observed among impoverished Brazilian families may appear abusive. But as the report by Scheper-Hughes makes evident, these mothers are doing the best they can to prepare their children to survive in an environment where weakness almost certainly leads to death. Cross-cultural research of this kind shows us that judgments about the optimal conditions for development must take into account the actual conditions in which children and their families live.

The Unpredictability of Development

While factors ranging from parental responsiveness to cultural context influence a child's development, ultimately, there is no set of conditions that guarantee a particular developmental outcome. Although recent research points to significant continuities between infancy and later developmental periods, it falls well short of implying that any trait is always continuous and predictable. As noted, the correlations between behaviors in infancy and later behaviors are generally very modest. Consequently, data showing marked recovery from early traumatic conditions (which suggest that psychological functioning can change markedly after infancy) and data showing a moderate correlation in individual behavioral traits over time (which imply continuity of functioning) should not be seen as contradictory. Together they provide evidence that a child's development is simultaneously continuous and discontinuous.

Many years ago Freud (1920/1924) pointed out that whether development seems continuous and predictable or discontinuous and uncertain depends to a certain extent on one's vantage point:

> So long as we trace the development [of a psychological process] from its final stage backwards, the connection appears continuous, and we feel we have gained an insight which is completely satisfactory or even exhaustive. But if we proceed the reverse way,

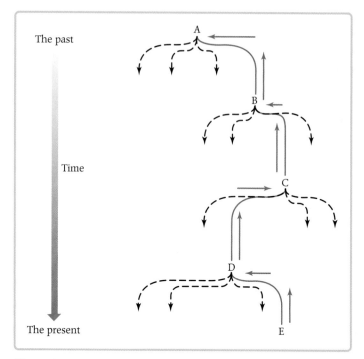

Figure 7.5 It is relatively easy to trace development backward to its origins (red arrows). But the many decision points with uncertain outcomes (A, B, C, D) that confront the individual during the life span defeat efforts to predict his or her future. (Adapted from Emde et al., 1976.)

if we start from the premises inferred from the analysis and try to follow these up to the final result, then we no longer get the impression of an inevitable sequence of events which could not be otherwise determined. We notice at once that there might have been another result. (p. 226)

Figure 7.5 is a schematic representation of Freud's insight regarding retrospective analysis. If we start at some point in later life, E, and trace a person's history back to its beginnings, A, we can build a convincing case for why that precise life history proceeded as it did; the developmental state at time E resulted from events at time D, which resulted from events at time C, and so on. At each decision point, we believe we can distinguish the various contributing factors and discern which had the most influence. Only one route leads into the past at each point. But standing at the beginning, A, and looking ahead to the future, we cannot foresee the choices that will be made at points B, C, and D.

For parents, the unpredictability of the outcome of their caregiving efforts is a natural source of anxiety. Research on primacy, however, shows us that this uncertainty has its good side. A perfectly predictable future holds no possibility of choice. Without the uncertainties that arise from changes in the environment and the changes in the child that accompany development, parents could not dream about influencing the course of their baby's future. It would be immutable. With these uncertainties come the possibility and the challenge of taking advantage of those changes to promote the child's welfare.

SUMMARY

The Primacy of Infancy

- Many people believe that experiences in infancy are the most significant forces in the shaping of later behavior.

- Three factors appear to modify the impact of early experiences: changes in the environment, bio-social-behavioral shifts, and the way children experience their environments as a result of their increased capacities.

- Many contemporary developmentalists adopt transactional models to explain how characteristics of the child and the characteristics of the child's environment interact across time to determine developmental outcomes.

Developing Attachment

- Many developmentalists argue that the development of a secure attachment relationship is crucial to infant mental health as well as to the quality of the child's future relationships; however, studies have yielded mixed results concerning later developmental outcomes of particular attachment patterns.

- Research shows both continuity—attachment patterns tend to remain stable over time—and discontinuity—patterns can change in response to changes in the child's environment

- Experts dispute the consequences of short daily separations resulting from out-of-home care during the first year of life.

Effects of Deprivation

- Extended residence in a poorly staffed orphanage retards both mental and social development. Residence in a well-staffed orphanage produces less-pronounced developmental difficulties. The degree to which children recover from such experiences depends on their subsequent environments and the age at which they leave the institution.

- Total isolation leads to severe mental and social retardation. If children are moved to a supportive environment before they are 6 or 7 years old, recovery is sometimes possible. If their circumstances are not changed until adolescence, full recovery appears to be impossible.

Vulnerability and Resilience

- Personal characteristics or environmental circumstances that increase the probability of negative outcomes for children are called risk factors. Risk factors are cumulative in nature.

- Protective factors buffer children against risk.

- Children's vulnerability to stressful circumstances depends on several factors, including:

  1. Characteristics of the child, such as variations in temperament

  2. Characteristics of the family, such as the number of siblings, the mother's work load, and the presence of a network of kin and friends

  3. Characteristics of the community, such as whether the neighborhood is in an urban slum or a rural area and the quality of the local school

  4. Characteristics of the culture, such as traditional practices that structure child–caregiver relations.

- The processes that lead to various developmental outcomes can be thought of as transactions between child and environment over an extended period of time.

Recovery from Deprivation

- Transactional models emphasize that later experiences can either moderate or enhance the effects of risk factors

- Studies of monkeys suggest that recovery from early isolation can be achieved later than was once thought possible if an adequate therapeutic environment can be arranged.

- Research has shown that similar principles can be applied to socially isolated children.

Shaping Developmental Pathways

- Research with animals has shown how differences in "normal" parenting behavior can shape developmental outcomes.

- To foster optimal development, the caregiver must be sensitive and responsive to the infant's needs and signals. The kinds of sensitivity and responsiveness that are considered optimal in child rearing, and the way they are expressed, depend on the historical and cultural circumstances into which the child is born.

- Three factors limit the degree to which the psychological characteristics of infants can predict later development.

  1. Changes in the child's environment

  2. The bio-social-behavioral shifts that qualitatively reorganize the child's physical and psychological characteristics

  3. An increase in the child's capacity to cope with the environment

---

Key Terms

cross-fostering, p. 263
prevention science, p. 256
primacy, p. 243

protective factors, p. 258
resilience, p. 258

risk factors, p. 257
transactional models, p. 245

Thought Questions

1. Imagine that you are the director of an orphanage. In view of the information provided in Chapters 4 through 7, what are some of the practices you would promote to provide the best possible development for the children in your institution?

2. Imagine that you are the director of a community program to improve the early experiences of children living in a poor community. What sorts of programs would you try to promote? Give a research-based rationale for your suggestions.

3. How does a transactional approach to developmental change relate to the adage "As the twig is bent, so grows the tree"?

4. How does the African practice of cross-fostering challenge developmentalists to think more broadly about the development of attachment and how to define "family"?

5. Why are retrospective explanations of development problematic?

part III Early Childhood

Bio-Social-Behavioral Shifts

Biological Domain
- Myelination of connections among brain areas
- Leveling off of brain growth
- Maturation of brain areas in roughly equal degrees

Social Domain
- Decline of distress at separation
- Distinctive sense of self
- Acceptance of adult standards
- Emergence of secondary emotions

Behavioral Domain
- Walking becomes well coordinated
- Manual dexterity becomes adequate to pick up small objects
- Control over bladder and bowels
- Planful problem solving
- Symbolic play
- Conceptual representations
- Elementary vocabulary and beginning of word combinations
- Smile accompanying mastery

By the age of $2\frac{1}{2}$ or 3, children are clearly infants no longer. As they enter early childhood—the period between ages $2\frac{1}{2}$ and 6—they lose their baby fat, their legs grow longer and thinner, and they move around the world with a great deal more confidence than they did only 6 months earlier. Within a short time, they can usually ride a tricycle, control their bowels, and put on their own clothes. They can get out of bed quietly on Sunday morning and turn on the TV to amuse themselves while their parents still sleep. They can help their mothers bake cookies and take the role of flower girl or ring bearer at an aunt's wedding. Most 3-year-olds can talk an adult's ears off, even if their train of thought is difficult to follow, and they provide an avid audience for an interesting story. They can be bribed with promises of a later treat, but they won't necessarily accept the terms that are offered, and they may try to negotiate for a treat now as well as later. They develop theories about everything from where babies come from to why the moon disappears from the sky, and they constantly test their theories against the realities around them.

Despite their developing independence, 3-year-olds need assistance from adults and older siblings in many areas. They cannot hold a pencil properly, cross a busy road safely by themselves, or tie their shoes. They do not yet have the ability to concentrate for long without a great deal of guidance. As a result, they often go off on tangents in their games, drawings, and conversations. One minute a 3-year-old may be

Mommy in a game of house, the next minute Cinderella, and the next a little girl in a hurry to go to the toilet.

In early childhood, children still understand relatively little about the world in which they live and have little control over it. Thus they are prey to fears of monsters, the dark, dogs, and other apparent threats. They combat their awareness of being small and powerless by wishful, magical thinking that turns a little boy afraid of dogs into a big, brave, cowboy who dominates the block.

Although developmentalists have studied early childhood for decades, considerable uncertainty remains about how best to characterize this period of life. In some respects, it appears to be a distinctive stage with its own special modes of thinking, feeling, and acting. In other respects, it appears to be simply the beginning of a long period of gradual change that extends throughout childhood.

Our discussion of early childhood development covers four chapters. Chapter 8 focuses on the nature of language and its development. By definition, acquisition of language is the human characteristic that signals the end of infancy. Language is the medium through which children learn about their roles in the world, acceptable behavior, and their culture's assumptions about how the world works. Simultaneously, language enables children to ask questions, to explain their thoughts and desires, and to make more effective demands on the people around them.

Chapter 9 examines thinking during early childhood. The major challenge faced by developmentalists is to explain how children can behave competently with logical self-possession at one moment only to become fanciful, emotionally overwrought, and dependent the next. The chapter considers whether their apparently illogical behavior is the result of their lack of experience or is governed by its own special logic.

Chapter 10 shifts attention to young children's social development and personality formation, their growing sense of a distinct identity, their ability to control their actions and feelings, the ways they think about rules of proper behavior, and their relations with the people around them. The chapter focuses on the acquisition of a distinct sense of culturally acceptable sex roles and on children's changing ability to get along with each other, particularly as they learn to balance their own desires with the demands of their social group.

With these general characteristics of early childhood as background, Chapter 11 addresses the influence of various contexts on young children's development: first, the family, where children come to learn about who they are and what adults expect of them; then, their seemingly endless fascination with pretend play as it is organized in a variety of community settings, including day-care centers and preschools; and finally the media, which link their experiences in different settings and have important socializing effects on young children.

Language Acquisition

> **Girl (on toy telephone):** David!
> **Boy (not picking up second phone):** I'm not home.
> **Girl:** When you'll be back?
> **Boy:** I'm not here already.
> **Girl:** But when will you be back?
> **Boy:** Don't you know if I'm gone already, I went before so I can't talk to you!
>
> —George Miller, Language and Speech

Comparing the following two monologues of a little girl named Emily will give you an idea of the incredible speed with which language development occurs in young children. Emily's parents recorded her speech as she talked to herself in her crib before going to sleep at night. Here is a fragment of her first recorded monologue when she was 21 months old ("baby" is her name for her doll):

> baby no eat dinner
> broccoli, soup carrots cause rice
> baby eat *that*
> baby no in night
> broccoli broccoli soup carrots cabbage
> no baby sleeping
> then baby get sick
> Emmy no eat dinner
> broccoli soup cause
> no baby sleeping
> baby sleeping all night

One year later, Emily's monologue sounds like this:

> actually it's Stephen's koala bear . . .
> when Stephen wakes up I'll have to throw his koala bear in his room
> cause *it's* really Stephen's
> as a matter of fact Stephen's
> as a matter of fact *it's* sleeping with me now
>
> (Levy, 1989, pp. 158 and 169)

As you can see, the first fragment is barely interpretable, with one statement following another, but the meaning of the whole is difficult to figure out. The phrases are brief and relatively simple, and their order often seems capricious. The word "cause" appears in both fragments, but we have difficulty figuring out what "broccoli, carrots soup cause rice" means, and in fact, only a culturally shared notion that broccoli is somehow not a favorite food seems like a clue to what Emily is saying.

By contrast, the second fragment not only has longer phrases, but also expresses temporal and possessive relationships and more clearly conveys Emily's meaning. Her language is not yet fully developed by any means, but it is significantly more adult-like and easy to interpret. The progress Emily has made in her ability to use language during the intervening year is amazing but by no means exceptional; similar increases in language-using ability will continue to occur for several years to come.

In the period between 2 and 6 years of age, children's mental and social lives are totally transformed by an explosive growth in the ability to comprehend and use language. Children are estimated to learn several words a day during this period, and by the time they are 6 years old, their vocabularies have grown to anywhere between 8,000 and 14,000 words (Anglin, 1993; Biemiller & Slonim, 2001). They can understand verbal instructions ("Go wash your face—and don't come back until it's clean"), chatter excitedly about the tiger they saw at the zoo, or insult their sisters and brothers. Although they will continue to acquire linguistic nuances and a more extensive vocabulary, 6-year-old children are competent language users. Without this achievement, they could not carry out the new cognitive tasks and social responsibilities that their society will now assign them.

We begin this chapter by reviewing and elaborating on the early foundations of linguistic communication that we discussed in earlier chapters. Next, we identify and discuss the two basic puzzles confronting language-acquisition scholars. First, how do children acquire the ability to refer to objects and events using words? Second, how do they acquire grammar? To understand these problems, we then trace the course of children's mastery of the four basic subsystems that constitute language: the sound system, the words, the grammar, and the uses to which language is put. With the facts of language development in hand, we turn to competing theories about the processes that underlie this unique and fundamental human capacity. Finally, we examine what is known about the necessary prerequisites for acquiring human language.

Prelinguistic Communication

The evidence presented in previous chapters leaves little doubt that children are born predisposed to attend to language and to communicate with the people around them. At birth they show a preference for speech over other kinds of sounds and are capable of differentiating the basic sound categories, or *phonemes,* characteristic of all the world's languages. Within a few days after birth they can distinguish the sounds of their native language from those of a foreign language. Well before they are able to speak intelligibly, the range of sound distinctions they recognize becomes narrowed to the sound categories of the languages they hear around them (p. 199).

Newborns' abilities to communicate are initially limited to a small set of facial expressions and crying. Though variations in cry patterns are not particularly informative, they do provide caregivers with rudimentary information about the severity of the distress. At about $2\frac{1}{2}$ months, babies' communicative abilities are enhanced by social smiles. Soon their sound repertoire expands to include *cooing,* which in turn is supplanted by *babbling* and then *jargoning* (see Chapter 5, p. 199); each change brings the baby closer to producing recognizable words. From at least 7 months of age, well before they can speak, infants become increasingly familiar with the sound patterns of the language that envelops them, learning to pick out typical sequences and sound patterns (Thiessen & Saffran, 2003).

At the same time that babies' capacity to distinguish and produce linguistic signals increases, they are also becoming more adept at interacting with the people and objects around them. At birth their weak muscles and restricted vision make it difficult for them to carry out the most elementary functions, such as nursing or examining an object in a coordinated way. Within a few weeks, with a good deal of support from their caregivers, these functions become part of a daily routine that gives structure to babies' limited experiences. *Primary intersubjectivity,* the ability to match one's behavior to that of another person and to share experiences in direct face-to-face interaction, emerges at about 3 months of age (Chapter 4, p. 158). This ability is evident in the rounds of greeting noises and smiling in which caregivers and babies engage, to their mutual delight.

Between 9 months and a year, babies acquire *secondary intersubjectivity,* the ability to share mental states with another person and to understand what they are intending to do (Chapter 5, p. 197). The close link between secondary intersubjectivity and communication is evident in the form of behavior called *social referencing,* the process through which babies check their caregiver's reactions to an uncertain event or an unfamiliar person as a guide to their own behavior. Secondary intersubjectivity is a crucial precursor to language acquisition because babies and their caregivers are sharing knowledge about the objects and events that are the focus of their joint attention.

Secondary intersubjectivity is also apparent when babies begin to point at objects (Butterworth, 2003). Pointing is clearly a communicative act intended to create a joint focus of attention, but it is a primitive one. When 12-month-olds see a remote-controlled car roll past them, first they point at it and then they look to see how their caregivers react to it (social referencing). At 18 months of age, the function of pointing becomes communicative in a more complex way. Now children are more likely first to look at their caregivers to see if they are looking at the car and then to point to it. If babies this age are alone in the room when the electric car appears, they do not point until the caretaker walks back into the room, clearly demonstrating that their pointing has a purpose and is meant to communicate to another person (Butterworth, 2003).

As you will see, during the second year of life, children's repertoire of words grows considerably, slowly at first and then at an increasing rate. As this is happening, children's ability to produce and understand the word ordering that makes up sentences increases.

In sum, when we look at development from birth to the start of the third year of life, we can see that the capacity for communication has already developed to a remarkable degree well before the child can actually hold a conversation (see Table 8.1). The question that intrigues developmental scientists is how this capacity arises.

table 8.1

The Progress of Language Development	
Approximate Age	**Typical Behavior**
Birth	Phoneme perception
	Discrimination of language from nonlanguage sounds
	Crying
3 months	Cooing
6 months	Babbling
	Loss of ability to discriminate between nonnative phonemes
9 months	First words
	Holophrases
12 months	Use of words to attract adults' attention
18 months	Vocabulary spurt
	First two-word sentences (telegraphic speech)
24 months	Correct responses to indirect requests ("Is the door shut?")
30 months	Creation of indirect requests ("You're standing on my blocks!")
	Modification of speech to take listener into account
	Early awareness of grammatical categories

The Puzzle of Language Development

Although language is one of the most distinctive characteristics of our species, its development in the individual is still very poorly understood. Two basic questions have proved especially difficult to answer. The first involves the problem of reference: How do children discover what words mean? The second involves the problem of grammar: How do children learn to arrange words and parts of words in a sequence that has meaning to others?

The Problem of Reference

Perhaps the most basic intuition that we have about language is that each word refers to something: words name real or imagined objects and relationships in the world. This idea seems so commonsensical that it is difficult to grasp the mystery it conceals, a mystery that no philosopher, linguist, or psychologist has ever adequately explained: How, among all the many things or relations to which any word or phrase may refer, do we ever learn to pick out its intended referent—the object or relation to which it refers?

To get an intuitive feel for just how puzzling the problem of reference is, examine Figure 8.1. Imagine that you are the child in the picture, and try to decide what the Russian father is saying. It's a puzzle, isn't it? At first you may wish to argue that the example is unfair because the utterance is in a foreign language. A little more reflection reveals that the example may be fair after all: in the beginning, all languages are foreign to newborn babies, who must somehow figure out that the sounds they hear are in fact meant to refer to something in the ongoing flow of experience—to indicate an actual object, event, or feeling.

To make the difficulty clearer, suppose you know all the words that the father says except one: "Look, son, there sits a *ptitsa*." Even this additional information does not tell you which of the objects in the scene is a *ptitsa*. The cat sitting on the wall? The helicopter sitting on the roof? Or the bird sitting in the tree? If you know Russian, you know that the father is pointing at the bird. But the language-learning child, even the *Russian* language-learning child, is not born knowing the meaning

Figure 8.1 For children just beginning to acquire language, the problem of learning what words refer to is particularly acute. What is this father referring to?

"Vot, sinochik, tam sidit ptitsa."

"That's Harvey."

"That's a rabbit."

"That's an ear."

"That's the Easter Bunny."

"That's a picture."

"That's white."

"That's an animal."

Figure 8.2 An adult can point to the animal in this picture or to many parts of the animal and apply the same kind of declaratory statement: "That's a _____." How do children know what is being referred to? (From Miller, 1991.)

of the sound package, *ptitsa*. Somehow the child must learn that when the father says *ptitsa* he is talking about the winged creature in the tree and not about any of the other objects.

The problem of how children come to know what words refer to is complicated by the fact that a single object or event has many parts and features that can be referred to in a great many ways. George Miller (1991) illustrates this problem with the example in Figure 8.2. If an adult points to the object in Figure 8.2 and refers to it in the various ways indicated, how is the child to avoid the conclusion that "rabbit," "ear," "white," and "Harvey" are synonyms? Yet somehow, despite all the apparently confusing ways in which objects and actions are referred to, children learn the meanings associated with all of the different kinds of references.

The Problem of Grammar

For words to be combined into a comprehensible sentence, they must be related not only to objects and events but to one another. That is, they must be governed by **grammar,** the rules for sequencing words in a sentence and the ordering of parts of words for a particular language.

Recent evidence using the habituation technique discussed in Chapter 4 (p. 120) indicates that by the time they are 7 months old, infants are not only sensitive to the ordering of words in simple sentences presented to them but can extract abstract patterns of word usage from such sentences (Jusczyk, 2002; Marcus et al., 1999). This ability comes into play several months later as children begin to create their own multiword utterances and is instrumental in their subsequent acquisition of grammatical rules.

One indicator that children who are beginning to produce multiword utterances have some grasp of grammatical rules comes from the errors they make when they string words together. When we hear a child make such statements as "My doggy runned away" or "Mommy, Johnny camed late," we know immediately that the child has confused one grammatical form with another. Such errors are so common that it is easy to overlook their significance. Children cannot have been taught to say such things, nor could they have learned them by simple imitation, because they virtually never hear such incorrect sentences uttered. Where could these sentences come from?

grammar The rules of a given language for the sequencing of words in a sentence and the ordering of parts of words.

recursion The embedding of sentences within each other.

No less puzzling is the appearance in children's language of **recursion,** the embedding of sentences within each other (Hauser & Chomsky, 2002). Recursion provides language with great economy and flexibility of expression. For example, the three sentences "The boy went to the beach," "He saw some fish," and "The boy got sunburned" can easily be combined to create "The boy who went to the beach saw some fish and got a sunburn": three sentences for the price of one. There is no evidence that recursion is ever consciously taught to young children. How, then, do they develop it?

The problems of reference and grammar illustrate the central puzzle of language acquisition. On the one hand, almost all children, even many who have severe cognitive impairments, acquire the ability to communicate with words, so language appears to be a fundamental capacity that is easy for humans to acquire, like learning to walk. On the other hand, the complexities and subtleties of language are so great that it is difficult to understand how word meanings or grammatical rules could ever be acquired.

Somehow, in the space of a very few years, children accomplish something denied all other species. What is it they do, and how do they manage to do it?

Four Subsystems of Language

Language, according to *Webster's Eleventh New Collegiate Dictionary,* is "the words, their pronunciation, and the methods of combining them used and understood by a community." This definition identifies four central aspects of language: sounds, words, methods of combining words, and the communal uses that language serves. For the sake of clarity we will describe the development of each of these aspects separately, but it is important to keep in mind that language is a system: each of its aspects is connected to all of the others as well as the social world of which it is an essential part.

Sounds

In the change from babbling to pronouncing words that occurs late in the first year, children give up their indiscriminate freedom to play with sounds and begin to vocalize the particular sounds and sound sequences that make up the words in the particular language of their community (Kuhl, 2001).

It takes children several years to master the pronunciation of the separate words of their native language. Their first efforts may be no more than crude stabs at the right sound pattern that frequently leave out parts of words (resulting in "ca" instead of "cat," for example). Multisyllable words are often turned into a repeating pattern. For example, a child may use the sound pattern "bubba" to say "button," "bubble," "butter" and "baby." A long word, such as "motorcycle," can come out sounding like almost anything: "momo, "motokaka," or even "lomacity" (Preisser et al., 1988).

Children's command of their native sound system develops unevenly. Sometimes children will find a particular sound especially difficult to master, even after they understand many words that employ that sound. At the age of $2\frac{1}{2}$ for example, Mike and Sheila's son, Alexander, could not say /l/ sounds at the beginning of words, so he could not pronounce the name of his friend's dog, Lucky. Instead, he called the dog "Yucky," much to everyone's amusement.

Learning to make language sounds properly takes time and practice.

Neil Smith (1973) showed that such substitutions do not arise because children are incapable of pronouncing certain sounds. When he asked one young child to say the word "puddle," the child responded with "puzzle," and when he asked for "puzzle," the response was "puggle." This example suggests that the basic sounds of a language are learned as parts of overall sound patterns, rather than as isolated sounds.

As you learned in Chapter 4 (p. 122), even newborn children can perceive the differences between the basic sounds of their language, but this does not mean that the ability to hear and produce phonemes is "just there" at birth. When, for example, a child learns to employ the English phoneme /l/, more is involved than learning to reproduce a particular sound wave by creating a particular mouth shape. In reality, /l/ is a phoneme of English because in our language it contrasts with other phonemes, such as /y/, as part of meaningful words. We hear /l/ and /y/ as different sounds only because they can create different meanings: English speakers must learn that "lap" and "yap" or "lard" and "yard" are not simply variations in the pronunciation of a single word, as they could be in another language. Children's attention to the differences between sounds is not simply a mechanical skill but develops along with their growing understanding of the meanings of words.

The close connection between phonemes and meanings becomes clear when one is attempting to learn a foreign language. Some native speakers of Spanish, for whom /b/ and /v/ sound much the same, find it difficult to produce or to hear any difference between them. To native English speakers, "boat" and "vote" sound quite different; to Spanish speakers, these two words sound much the same. Likewise, the English speaker frequently has difficulty hearing and producing the difference between the French *u* and *ou*, because that difference does not exist in English.

Although it is often convenient to think of words as the basic units of meaning in language, many words contain more than one meaning-bearing part, or **morpheme.** A morpheme may be a whole word or only a part of one. The word "transplanted," for example, is made up of three morphemes. The root of the word is *plant,* which means "to fix in place." The morpheme *trans* means "across, over, beyond," and the morpheme *ed* is a marker of past tense. We do not stop to ponder all of these relations when we say a sentence with the word "transplanted" in it. In fact, until the rules are pointed out, we rarely stop to think about the parts of words or the way we compose them. Yet every child must acquire the ability to decipher and reproduce just such intricate interweaving of sound and meaning. By the time they are 8 or 9 years old, children can use knowledge about morphemes to figure out the meanings of made-up words such as "treelet" (Anglin, 1993).

Words

Precisely when a given child utters his or her first real words is often difficult to determine. Parents may be so eager to claim their child can speak that they discover "words" in early cooing and babbling. However, as Erica Hoff points out, words are more than a set of sounds that communicate. Rather, words are *symbols*—they stand for something beyond themselves (Hoff, 2001). Genuine words appear only late in the first year, after children have been babbling for some time and after the contours of their sounds—or of their hand movements, if they are learning a sign language— have gradually become more speechlike (as you saw in Chapter 5, p. 199).

It is useful to think of the process of word formation as a special sort of joint effort. Neither the adult nor the child really knows what the other is saying. Each tries to gather in a little meaning by supposing that the other's utterance fits a particular sound pattern that corresponds to a particular meaning. This joint effort may eventually result in something common, a word that both can understand. This process may also fail. As the following examples make clear, the process of word

morpheme The smallest unit of meaning in the words of a language.

formation can proceed in a variety of ways, depending on how the parent interprets the relation between the child's sounds and actions.

At 8 months of age, Pablo began to say "dahdee." Although this "first" word sounds like "daddy," Pablo used "dahdee" for commands and requests when his father was nowhere to be seen, so it must have had some other meaning for him. Adults interpreted "dahdee" to mean either "Take it from me" (when Pablo said it while he offered something to someone) or "Give it to me"; they ignored the fact that Pablo's first word sounded like "daddy." At about the age of 12 months, "dahdee" disappeared from Pablo's vocabulary (Shopen, 1980).

A different fate befell Brenan's first word, "whey." Around 1 year of age, Brenan began to say "whey" after one of his parents had spoken. In this case, "whey" not only sounded something like "why" but also came at a position in normal conversational turn-taking where "why" would be a possible (if not always appropriate) thing to say. Brenan's parents therefore responded to "whey" as if Brenan had asked a question and rephrased what they had said in order to "answer his question," expanding on their original utterance. Over time, Brenan pronounced and used "whey" more and more like a true "why" until it became a genuine "why" in the English language (Griffin, 1983).

In both of these examples, the child uses a sound that adults might interpret because of its similarity to a word with which they are familiar. But in Pablo's case, the use of "dahdee" did not fit the patterns of usage for its soundalike, "daddy," so his parents simply ignored it. Brenan's use of "whey" both sounded like "why" *and* was used in his utterances in a way consistent with their guess that he meant "why" so they provided the feedback necessary for Brenan to adjust his pronunciation to fit adult norms. Each illustrates the general point that adults collude with each other and their children to create word meanings.

The Earliest Vocabulary

Developmentalists who study language have gathered much of their evidence concerning children's earliest words by having parents keep records of their children's vocabulary development or by making recordings of children's speech in their homes or in organized play facilities (Dromi, 1999). A number of studies have shown that children typically begin to produce their first comprehensible words around their first birthday and continue to utter single words for several months or more. Infants, on average, acquire the ability to use approximately 10 words by 13 to 14 months of age, 50 words by the time they are 17 to 18 months old, and approximately 300 words by the time they reach their second birthday. Their receptive vocabulary—that is, the vocabulary they understand—is considerably larger. For example, when they can produce 10 words, they can understand over 100 (Fenson et al., 1994). However, there is a great deal of variation in the ages at which children reach particular levels of language production (see Figure 8.3).

One of the most common findings in research among children in the United States is that nouns referring to objects make up a large proportion of the early vocabularies of young children and that most of the first words children acquire are closely linked to actions that they can accomplish with the things named (Dromi, 1999). "Hat" and "sock" are common in the initial vocabularies of American children, but "sweater" and "diapers" are not, presumably because little children can put on and take off hats and socks more or less effectively, but cannot

For infants, pointing is a precursor to linguistic communication.

Pamela Duffy

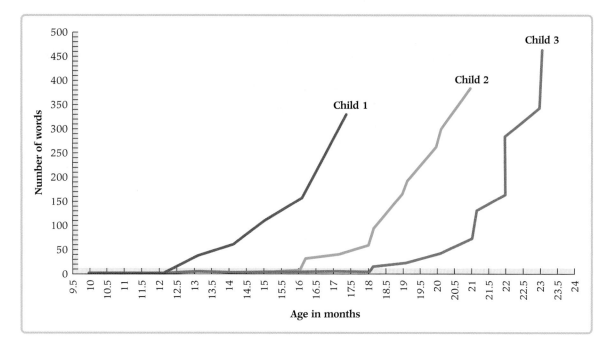

Figure 8.3 There are commonly wide variations in the rates at which young children acquire new words. Each of the curves in this figure indicates the number of words that the designated child spoke during the time when they were in the "one-word phase." Note that despite the variability, each child shows a growth spurt in vocabulary size of the sort that accompanies the onset of elementary two-word and then multiword utterances. (After Dromi, 1999, p. 104.)

do the same with sweaters and diapers. In addition, objects that can change and move and thus capture children's attention (such as cars and animals) are likely to be named, whereas large, immobile objects such as trees and houses are "just there" and are not likely to be named. Although nouns used to label objects dominate the first 100 or so words that English-speaking children learn, as their vocabularies grow, more verbs and adjectives appear; by the time they are 2 years old, nouns usually account for less than half of their vocabularies. In some languages, such as Mandarin Chinese and Korean, verbs may outnumber nouns in children's early vocabularies, although the precise balance between nouns and verbs depends upon the particular activity in which children are engaged (Choi & Gopnik, 1995; Tardif et al., 1999). For example, they use more verbs when playing with a toy than when they are read to by a caregiver.

Toddlers' growing vocabularies also include a variety of relational words that are used to communicate about changes in the state or location of an object (Gopnick & Meltzoff, 1997). "Gone" may be said when an object disappears, and "here" may announce its appearance. One of the most useful relational words in children's early vocabularies is "no," which can fulfill such important communicative functions as rejection, protest, and denial. "No" can also be used to comment on unfulfilled expectations and on an object's absence. Given these multiple functions, it is little wonder that "no" is among the earliest and most frequently used words in a child's early vocabulary (Bloom, 1973).

Allison Gopnick and Andrew Meltzoff (1997) identify an additional class of words that children begin using around the age of 2 years to comment on their successes ("There!" "Hooray!") and failures ("Uh-oh"). The appearance of these words seems to support the idea that children this age become sensitive to social expectations and begin to set standards for themselves (see Chapter 6, p. 237).

Confronting Problems of Reference

Children confront a number of ambiguities that complicate their task as they learn their first words. One major problem is that words do not have unique or fixed meanings. "Table," for example, can refer to an article of furniture, or an arrangement of data in rows and columns, or the action of putting off a topic for discussion

table 8.2

Typical Overextensions in the Speech of Young Children			
Child's Word	**First Referent**	**Extensions**	**Possible Common Property**
Dog	Dogs	Dogs, lambs, cats, wolves, cows	Four-legged animal
" 'peca"	Wound	Cuts, wounds, Scotch tape, spots on fabric, balloons	Uncertain, partially defect or injury of some kind
Kick	Kicking ball	Cartoon turtles doing cancan, pushing chest against mirror, watching a butterfly	Common movement pattern
"Tik"	Handbag	Folders, nylon bags, plastic sacks, box, hat upside down, pockets	Containing object

Source: Dromi, 1999.

(as in "let's table the motion"). The ambiguity inherent in words can never be completely eradicated. But as children gain familiarity with the ways people around them use words, their own language conforms more and more closely to the general uses in their cultural group. They achieve this feat by narrowing the range of objects and events to which they apply a particular label, by broadening the range of application of other labels, and by learning to use words at an appropriate level of abstraction (Waxman, 2002).

Overextension It is common for young children to use a single label in circumstances in which adults use many, a process referred to as **overextension.** Adults are amused, for example, when a 2-year-old wanders into a room full of adults and proceeds to call each of the men there "daddy." This form of mislabeling, in which many members of a category are referred to by a single term that is conventionally used to label only one of them, is called an overextension (Dromi, 1999).

Children's early overextensions appear to be strongly influenced by perceptual features of the items named as well as by the way children perceive the functioning of the named items. A word such as "kitty" may be extended to cover a wide variety of small four-legged animals because of their common shape, or it may cover a variety of soft, furry objects because of their similar texture, or it may even refer to other small animals such as rabbits that people keep as pets. (See Table 8.2.)

Underextension Children also use words in a narrower way than adults do, a process called **underextension** (Barrett, 1995). It is common, in fact, for children's early words to have a unique reference that is closely associated with a particular context (Golinkoff et al., 1994). For example, 1½-year-old Emmy used "bottle" only for the plastic bottle she drank from, not for other kinds of bottles. Young children may hotly deny that a lizard, a fish, or a mommy is an animal. They may also believe that "cat" applies only to their family's cat, not to cats in the neighborhood or on television.

Levels of Abstraction In choosing how to refer to something, children must learn to deal with the fact that several words can be used to refer to the same object. In speaking of someone she sees at the supermarket, a child may point and say, "Mommy, look at Sally," or "Mommy, look at that girl," or "Mommy, look at her," or "Mommy, look at that person." All these forms of referring to the girl are equally accurate, but they are not equally appropriate in all circumstances. If the girl being

---

overextension A term for the error of applying verbal labels too broadly.

underextension A term used for applying verbal labels in a narrower way than adults do.

talked about is well known to the mother and daughter, it would be inappropriate to refer to her as "that person" or "that girl." It might be appropriate under some circumstances to refer to the girl as "her" instead of "Sally," but to do so would change the meaning of the utterance. It requires time and experience for children to choose words that are at the appropriate level of abstraction.

An interesting characteristic of the level of abstraction of children's early words is that they tend to refer to objects at a basic level of abstraction (Golinkoff et al., 1995). Words at the basic level refer to objects that look alike, provide similar kinds of interactions, and have many component parts in common (Poulin-Dubois, 1995). To illustrate young children's use of basic category labels, Jeremy Anglin (1977) showed children posters that contained four pictures of objects that could be related at some level of abstraction and asked them for a label that applied to the whole set (see Figure 8.4). One poster might have four pictures of roses, which could be labeled by the relatively specific category "roses"; another might have a rose, a daisy, a carnation, and a pansy, which could be labeled at the basic level of abstraction as "flowers"; a third might have an elm, a rose, a rubber plant, and a cactus, which could be labeled at a higher level of abstraction as "plants." Anglin found that adults were able to vary the level of generality of their labels appropriately, whereas children between the ages of 2 and 4 tended to label all the sets at the same, basic, level of generality. They not only called the set containing the daisy, rose, carnation, and pansy "flowers," but also called all four roses "flowers," and were unable to provide a single label for the four plants. Most 4- and 5-year-olds were able both to name specific flowers and to use the general term "plants," but they too tended to use the basic-level term "flowers" far more than the adults did. These same results were obtained with many other category hierarchies, such as "animals, dogs, collies."

Children's limitations in labeling specific objects and general categories do not mean that they fail to understand differences between objects. Even children who labeled all pictures of dogs and cats as "cat" could still pick out the picture of the proper animal when they were asked to do so (Naigles & Gelman, 1995). Moreover, as we noted in Chapter 5 (p. 190) children under 2 years of age display knowledge of higher-level categories (vehicles) as well as basic-level categories (truck, train, airplane) through the way they play with objects.

Figure 8.4 Young children fail to differentiate levels of abstractness in the way they label sets of objects, using an intermediate level more frequently than adults do. (Adapted from Anglin, 1977.)

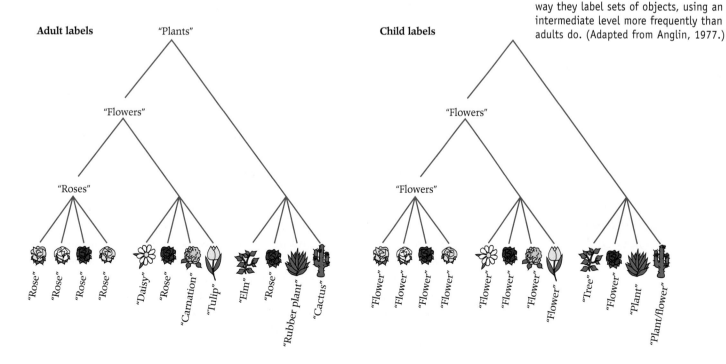

The Changing Structure of Children's Vocabularies

Clearly, the growth of children's vocabularies involves more than a simple increase in the number of individual words they know and more than a simple improvement in the accuracy with which they apply labels to objects. As we have just seen, vocabulary growth is accompanied by fundamental changes in the ways children relate words to one another to create more extensive and more complex categories in which individual words vary in their generality.

A different way in which the structure of children's word meanings changes can be seen by tracing the developmental course of children's use of a single word such as "dog." The first words and phrases children use are likely to represent the specific circumstances of the first time they associate the sound and its referent with their feelings playing as important a role as their thoughts. "Dog" may mean something terrible if the child has just been bitten; the same word may mean something wonderful if the dog lies on the rug and allows the child to burrow in its fur.

As children gain experience with dogs, the word "dog" begins to evoke a range of situations in which "dog" is only one element. The structure of the vocabulary at this stage is dominated by the pattern shown in Figure 8.5a. There "dog" is a unifying element in several situations: dog growls, dog barks, dog is petted, dog runs away, dog fights. Each situation is connected to "dog" in a specific way as part of a specific kind of action.

Further experience reveals that dogs are not the only creatures that bite. Cats bite too, and so do babies. At the same time, it becomes clear that cats do not bark (seals do) and they rarely take walks (but mommies do). Some of the things you can say about dogs you can just as easily say about cats (or seals or mommies), but some you cannot. When children are familiar with a large number of concrete situations in which the same word is used, words begin to acquire conceptual meanings that do not depend on any one context, or even on a real-world context. This aspect of language development is depicted in Figure 8.5b.

Once a word's meaning is influenced by the categories of the language, the word "dog" evokes more than the single emotion of fear or the single concrete image of Fido begging at the table. It has become part of an abstract system of word meanings independent of any particular situation. "Dog" becomes an instance of the category "domestic animal," or the more general category "animal," or the still more general category "living thing."

One of the simplest ways to assess the changing structure of children's vocabularies is to ask children of different ages to say the first word that comes to mind each time they hear a word. Early in their language development, children respond to "dog" with a word related to specific actions they associate with dogs, such as "bites" or "barks"; later they respond to "dog" with a general category word, such as "cat" or "animal" (Nelson, 1977). Very similar results are obtained when children are asked, "Tell me all you can about _____ s" or "What kind of a thing is a _____ ?" (Anglin, 1985).

Although new forms of word meaning reshape the child's vocabulary, old forms do not disappear. Adults, no less than children, respond with fear, love, or some other emotion to "dog." And much of adults' use of language depends on a fine-tuned appreciation of the way words relate to each other in particular contexts. What distinguishes the adult's vocabulary from the child's, other than its greater size, is the presence of several alternative forms of meaning for each word, which provide a richer arsenal of linguistic tools for reasoning about dogs, cats, and everything else, and for talking about these things with other people.

Figure 8.5 (a) For a young child, word meanings are dominated by the contexts of action in which the words have played a role. (b) As children acquire the formal conceptual categories of their language, the structure of word meanings changes accordingly. (Adapted from Luria, 1981.)

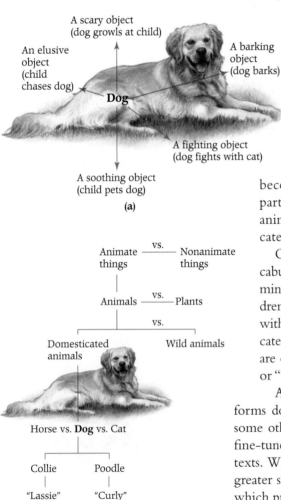

A scary object
(dog growls at child)

An elusive object (child chases dog)

A barking object (dog barks)

Dog

A fighting object (dog fights with cat)

A soothing object (child pets dog)

(a)

Animate things —vs.— Nonanimate things

Animals —vs.— Plants

vs.

Domesticated animals   Wild animals

Horse vs. **Dog** vs. Cat

Collie   Poodle

"Lassie"   "Curly"

(b)   **(b)**

Words as Mediators

From birth onward, infants' cries and coos express their emotional states. At some point, usually around 11 to 12 months of age, babies discover that the sound sequences they make can recruit adults' attention and help. What began as a process of making sounds that merely expressed emotion becomes a process of producing sounds that also anticipate, guide, and stimulate their own and others' action and feeling. With the emergence of the capacity to use words, children acquire the ability to express themselves and organize their activity in a new way.

This ability is illustrated in observations that Elizabeth Bates (1976, p. 55) made of a 13-month-old girl:

> C. is seated in a corridor in front of the kitchen door. She looks toward her mother and calls with an acute sound *ha*. Mother comes over to her, and C. looks toward the kitchen, twisting her shoulders and upper body to do so. Mother carries her to the kitchen, and C. points toward the sink. Mother gives her a glass of water, and C. drinks it eagerly.

In this interaction we also see two key features of the process of early word use. First, it is an excellent example of secondary intersubjectivity in verbal communication; initially the linguistic object, *ha*, and then its referent, the glass of water, are jointly attended to by mother and child. Second, the episode illustrates clearly that it is the relation of the sound to action (C.'s looking toward the kitchen, and then pointing to the sink), and not just some property of the sound itself, that gives the sound its meaning. Of course, in this case *ha*, the "word" in question, functions in a very small community, that is, the mother and child. Nonetheless, the child's use of *ha* displays an important new ability. Instead of trying to act *directly* on the object (by, for example, attempting to toddle over to the sink), the child operates *indirectly* through an idiosyncratic sound that evokes the desired action from another person.

In this and the remaining chapters of this book, we will refer to the property of language illustrated in Bates's example as the *mediated* character of language. Until children acquire the ability to use and understand words, they are restricted to immediate, or direct, actions. But with the advent of language, they can also deliberately act indirectly, using words to mediate their actions. They can make something happen without doing the thing themselves. The same principle applies to the way children can be influenced by others; once they start to understand words, children can be influenced by others both directly, via nonverbal actions, and indirectly, through the mediating power of words and the culturally organized knowledge that words embody (Vygotsky, 1978) (see Figure 8.3, p. 287).

Alexander Luria (1981, p. 35) beautifully summarized the new intellectual power that human beings obtain when their behavior begins to be mediated by words:

> In the absence of words, humans would have to deal only with those things which they could perceive and manipulate directly. With the help of language, they can deal with things which they have not perceived even indirectly and with things which were part of the experience of earlier generations. Thus, the word adds another dimension to the world of humans. . . . Animals have only one world, the world of objects and situations which can be perceived by the senses. Humans have a double world.

This child is making clear the close connection between words, meanings, and gestures.

Joel Gordon

Sentences

As you saw in Chapter 6, a watershed of language development is reached toward the end of infancy, when children begin to produce utterances consisting of two or more words. But at what point do such multiple word utterances become sentences? The change is more difficult to specify than one would suspect.

holophrase A term for babies' simple-word utterances that some believe stand for entire phrases or sentences.

Are Early Words Sentences?

A number of developmentalists believe that even when children can utter only single words, they are communicating in simple sentences called **holophrases.** According to this view, the use of words like "up" or "bottle" may represent whole sentences to the child (McNeill, 1970). But Patricia Greenfield and Joshua Smith (1976) offer a different interpretation. They believe that the single-word utterance stands for only one element of the situation the child wants to talk about, not the whole idea. Greenfield and Smith point out that children's single words are almost always accompanied by nonverbal elements, such as gestures and distinctive facial expressions. The single word *in conjunction with the gestures and facial expressions* is the equivalent of the whole sentence. By this account, the single word is not a holophrase, but one element in a complex of communication that includes nonverbal actions.

It is difficult to decide between competing theories of children's linguistic understanding at the stage of single-word utterances because too little information is available. Certainly, adults respond as if the child's single-word utterances are meaningful. A child says "shoe," for example, and the father responds by saying, "Oh, you want Daddy to tie your shoelace." But it is impossible to say how much of this meaning is the child's and how much of it is the adult's interpretation of the utterance based on information gleaned from the context in which the child speaks. Although this problem of interpretation never completely disappears, it becomes less vexing when the child begins to string words together.

Beginning to Combine Words

Even two-word utterances carry more than twice as much information as a single word alone because of the meaning conveyed by the relationship between the two words. With as few as two words children can indicate possession ("Daddy chair"), nonexistence ("All-gone cookie"), and a variety of other meanings. They can vary the order of the words to create different meanings ("Chase Daddy" and "Daddy chase"). This new potential for creating meaning by varying the arrangement of linguistic elements marks the birth of grammar. (See Table 8.3 for a sample of two-word utterances.)

However, sentences restricted to two words often remain ambiguous. This shortcoming of two-word utterances is illustrated in an amusing way by a series of incidents in *Higglety, Pigglety, Pop,* Maurice Sendak's tale of an adventurous dog who accepts a job as nanny for Baby, a child caught in the grip of the terrible twos. At first the dog attempts to get the baby to eat, and the baby says, "No eat!" When the dog decides to eat the food himself, the baby again says, "No eat!" Finally the baby and dog find themselves confronted by a lion, and the baby says for the third time, "No eat!"

Aware of the context in which each utterance occurs we have no difficulty understanding what the child means. Devoid of context, these two-word utterances provide no clue in themselves to the meaning intended. Similarly, the ambiguity of many young children's two-word utterances is likely to restrict effective communication to occasions when listeners can reliably interpret the child's context.

Increasing Complexity

At the same time that children begin to string more and more words together to form complete sentences, they increase the complexity and the variety of words and grammatical devices they use. These changes are illustrated by the following prodigious sentence spoken by an excited 2-year-old girl: "You can't pick up a big kitty 'cos a big kitty might bite!" (De Villiers & De Villiers, 1978, p. 59).

table 8.3

Sample Two-Word Utterances	
See boy	Mail come
See sock	Mama come
Night night office	Bunny do
Night night boat	Want do
More care	Boat off
More sing	Water off

Source: Braine, 1963.

This sentence is by no means typical of 2-year-olds, but it provides a good opportunity to assess how more complex utterances communicate more explicitly. The sentence communicates not only that the little girl doesn't want to pick up a big cat but also that no one should pick up a big cat; it also conveys her understanding that big cats sometimes bite but do not invariably do so. Such complex sentences communicate shades of meaning that help adults to respond sensitively to children's experiences.

As Figure 8.6 indicates, the length of 2-year-olds' utterances grows explosively, along with their vocabularies and grammatical abilities (Brown, 1973; Fenson et al., 1994). Note that the growth in the length of utter-

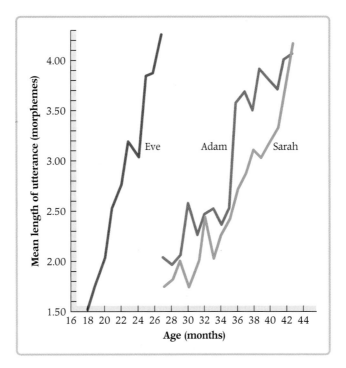

Figure 8.6 This graph shows the rapid increase in the mean length of utterances made by three children during the first four years of life. (From Brown, 1973.)

ances (or the "mean length of utterance"), is indicated by the average number of morphemes per utterance rather than by the average number of words. The phrase "That big bad boy plays ball," for example, contains six words and seven morphemes, whereas the phrase "Boys aren't playing" contains only three words but six morphemes (*boy, s, are, [not], play, ing*). Assessing linguistic complexity by counting morphemes rather than words provides an index of a child's total potential for making meaning in a particular utterance.

Grammatical Morphemes The complexity of the little girl's long sentence about picking up cats is attributable in large measure to just those little words and word parts that are systematically absent in two-word utterances. The article "a" ("a big kitty") indicates that it is big cats in general, not just this particular big cat, that are worrisome. The word "'cos" connects two propositions and indicates the causal relationship between them. The contraction "can't" specifies a particular relationship of negation. These elements are called **grammatical morphemes** because they are units that create meaning by showing the relations between other elements within the sentence. Whether the rate of language acquisition is fast or slow, grammatical morphemes appear in roughly the same sequence in the speech of all children (at least those who acquire English as a first language).

As Table 8.4 (p. 294) indicates, the grammatical morpheme likely to appear first in children's language production is *ing,* indicating the present progressive verb tense. This verb form allows children to describe their ongoing activity. Morphemes indicating location, number, and possession make their appearance next. Morphemes that mark complex relations, such as in "I'm going" (which codes a relation between the subject of the action and the time of the action), are generally slower to emerge.

The appearance of grammatical morphemes is a strong indicator that children are implicitly beginning to distinguish nouns and verbs, because their speech conforms to adult rules that specify which morphemes should be attached to which words in a sentence. Children demonstrate their intuitive grasp of the rules for using grammatical morphemes by the fact that they do not apply a past-tense morpheme to a noun ("girled"); nor do they place articles before verbs ("a walked").

grammatical morphemes Words and parts of words that create meaning by showing the relations between other elements within the sentence.

table 8.4

Usual Order of Acquiring Grammatical Morphemes		
Morpheme	**Meaning**	**Example**
Present progressive	Temporary duration	I walk*ing*
In	Containment	*In* basket
On	Support	*On* floor
Plural	Number	Two ball*s*
Past irregular	Prior occurrence	It *broke*
Possessive inflection	Possession	Adam*'s* ball
To be without contraction	Number; prior occurrence	There it *is*
Articles	Specific/nonspecific	That *a* book
		That *the* dog
Past regular	Prior occurrence	Adam walk*ed*
Third person regular	Number; prior occurrence	He walk*s*
Third person irregular	Number; prior occurrence	He *does*
		She *has*
Uncontractible progressive auxiliary	Temporary duration; number; prior occurrence	This *is going*
Contraction of *to be*	Number; prior occurrence	That*'s* a book
Contractible progressive auxiliary	Temporary duration; prior occurrence	I*'m* walking

Source: Brown, 1973.

Evidence collected by a number of language-development researchers shows that although children begin to produce grammatical morphemes relatively late in the language acquisition process, they are sensitive to the existence of grammatical morphemes in the language they hear at least by the time they are starting to produce their first multiword utterances (Golinkoff et al., 1999).

Complex Constructions Between the ages of 2 and 6, children begin to use a great many new constructions that conform to the "grammatical rules" that bedevil students in language classes throughout their schooldays. Some of these grammatical constructions obey rules of such subtlety that, although we follow them intuitively in our speech, we can't say why we use them as we do.

Consider a common grammatical form known as the tag question (Dennis et al., 1982)—words added to the end of a declarative sentence to turn it into a question. "They won the prize, didn't they?" and "You will come, won't you?" are typical tag questions. It's no easy matter to provide a rule specifying how such questions are formed, is it?

A somewhat more complicated demonstration of the gap between our ability to use language and our ability to understand the principles that underlie our talk is provided by the following sentences:

1. John is easy to please.

2. John is willing to please.

Both sentences seem to follow the same ordering principle. But these sentences, despite their surface similarity, differ grammatically. We can clarify the difference by adding a single word to the end of each sentence while still preserving the order of elements. Compare the two new sentences:

3. John is willing to please Bill.

4. John is easy to please Bill.

Sentence 3 is just as acceptable in the English language as sentences 1 and 2, but even though the surface ordering is unchanged, sentence 4 is not grammatically acceptable, and we cannot interpret it. Such examples suggest that acquiring the grammar of a language involves mastery of highly abstract rules that even adult speakers of a language cannot explain (unless they are linguists!). Yet such rules appear to be acquired by all normal children, regardless of the language they speak.

Figurative speech A variety of evidence suggests that not long after children begin to name objects, they begin to use figurative speech, specifically, *metaphors*. A metaphor is a figure of speech containing an implied comparison in which a word or a phrase ordinarily used to name one thing is used for another. For example, a $2^1/_2$ year-old may point at his yellow plastic baseball bat and say with delight, "Corn!"

The use of metaphors provides evidence that language production is a creative process, not simply an imitative one. In the eyes of many developmentalists, metaphors are essential tools of human thought (Ortony, 1993). To generate a metaphor, children must recognize a similarity between two things and express that similarity in a way that they have never heard before (Dent-Read, 1997; Winner, 1988).

Although children between the ages of 2 and 6 years use many metaphors, they often fail to understand the figurative meaning of adult speech that does not refer to simple actions or to an object's perceptual characteristics. Kornei Chukovsky (1968, pp. 12–13), a Russian linguist, translator, and children's poet, offers this example:

> Four-year-old Olya, who came with her mother to visit a Moscow aunt, looked closely at this aunt and her husband as they were all having tea, and soon remarked with obvious disappointment: "Mama! You said that Uncle always sits on Aunt Aniuta's neck [a Russian expression for being bossy and controlling] but he has been sitting on a chair all the time that we've been here."

The ability to understand and use metaphors develops throughout childhood. During middle childhood, children have difficulty understanding metaphors that link physical terms to people. Such metaphors ("That kid is a bulldozer") require the child to compare human personality traits to perceptual characteristics of the object world. This kind of comparison appears difficult because young children still lack knowledge about personality traits, so they find it difficult to understand what aspect of similarity underlies the metaphor. Not until they enter adolescence will children be able to create metaphors based on many kinds of similarity (Pan & Snow, 1999).

The Uses of Language

In order to communicate effectively, children must master more than the grammatical rules of their language and the meanings of its words. Such knowledge would be of little use if they did not simultaneously master the **pragmatic uses of language**—that is, the ability to select words and word orderings that are appropriate to their actions in particular contexts.

Conversational Acts

One way of describing how language is used for pragmatic purposes is to think of utterances as **conversational acts,** actions that achieve goals through language. According to Elizabeth Bates and her colleagues (Bates et al., 1975), children's earliest conversational acts fall into two categories, protoimperatives and protodeclaratives. *Protoimperatives* are early ways of engaging another person to achieve a desired object. When Mike and Sheila's daughter, Jenny, first began holding up her cup and saying "More," she was using a protoimperative.

pragmatic uses of language The ability to select words and word orderings that are appropriate to their actions in particular contexts.

conversational acts Actions that achieve goals through language.

Young children around the world take great delight in their ability to communicate by using their rapidly developing linguistic skills.

Myrleen Ferguson/PhotoEdit

Protodeclaratives are important because they allow young children both to initiate and maintain dialogues with adults. Perhaps the earliest form of a protodeclarative is the act of pointing discussed in Chapter 5 (p. 198). This form of referring is often accompanied by words, as when a baby points to a dog and says "Doggie." Another early form of protodeclarative conversation is giving. As babies master this form, they may be seen bringing all their toys, one after another, to lay at a visitor's feet if each gift is acknowledged by a smile or a comment (Bates et al., 1987).

In the process of acquiring the pragmatic uses of language, children also come to understand that a single sequence of words may accomplish several alternative goals. For example, the sentence "Is the door shut?" has the grammatical form of a request for information. But it may also be a request for action or a criticism because it is pragmatically equivalent to "Please shut the door" or "You have forgotten to shut the door again."

As children's vocabularies grow and their command of grammar improves, the range of actions they can be verbally induced to perform expands. Marilyn Shatz (1978) found that children as young as 2 years old responded correctly to their mother's indirect commands, such as "Is the door shut?" Instead of responding to the surface grammatical form and answering "Yes" or "No," Shatz's toddlers went to shut the door. At the same time, children's ability to control others verbally increases. A 3-year-old observed by John Dore (1979) used three different grammatical forms to achieve a single goal: "Get off the blocks!" "Why don't you stay away from my blocks?" and "You're standing on my blocks."

In the hope of getting a proper overall picture of language development, a number of scholars have attempted to catalog the full set of language functions that children have to master (Dore et al., 1979). This task has proved to be formidable because there is so much variety in the uses of speech, even by 3-year-olds. The 3- and 4-year-olds these researchers studied have come a long way from mere pointing or the use of idiosyncratic "words" such as "dahdee." They can solicit information ("What happened?") or action ("Put the toy down!"). They can assert facts and rules ("We have a boat"), utter warnings ("Watch out!"), and clarify earlier statements.

Conversational Conventions

As part of the task of learning how to achieve their goals through talking, children must come to appreciate basic rules that apply in any conversation. Their failure to understand such rules is a common source of misunderstanding when they are talking to adults.

According to the philosopher H. P. Grice (1975, p. 45), the master rule of ordinary conversation is the **cooperative principle:** make your contributions to conversation at the required time and for the accepted purpose of the talk exchange. Grice lists four maxims that must be honored if the cooperative principle is to operate effectively:

1. *The maxim of quantity:* Speak neither more nor less than is required.

2. *The maxim of quality:* Speak the truth and avoid falsehood.

3. *The maxim of relevance:* Speak in a relevant and informative way.

4. *The maxim of clarity:* Speak so as to avoid obscurity and ambiguity.

In conversation among adults, everyone understands that these rules are often violated to make deliberately nonconventional statements. The act of encouraging a child, for example, may evoke an exaggerated statement such as "You can do it, Suzie. You're a big girl now, and you know that big girls try hard. They don't give up. I'm sure you can do it." This kind of talk might violate the maxim of quantity (the speaker is saying more than is required) except for the fact that it is acceptable for the special task of providing encouragement.

Some figurative uses of language (such as irony, in which someone means the opposite of what he or she says) depend on deliberate violation of a conversational maxim. For example, if a friend has just spilled her ice cream cone in your lap while you are trying to tie her shoe lace and you respond by saying (ironically), "That was a *big* help, Suzie," you are violating the maxim that assumes you are telling the truth because you really mean "that was very unhelpful." Learning the circumstances in which the basic speech-act conventions do and do not apply requires years of additional experience (Clark, 1995).

Children must also acquire knowledge of the social conventions that regulate what is to be said and how to say it (Ninio & Snow, 1999). These conventions may vary markedly from one culture to another. In the United States, children are expected to say "please" when they request something and "thank you" when they are given something. But in certain Colombian communities such verbal formulas are frowned upon in the belief that "please" and "thank you" signal the speaker's inferiority; obedience, not formulaic politeness, is what these adults expect of their children (Reichel-Dolmatoff & Reichel-Dolmatoff, 1961).

cooperative principle The conversational principle to make your contributions to conversation at the required time and for the accepted purpose of the talk exchange.

Even 4-year-olds adapt their language when they speak to younger children.

©Tom Nebbia/Corbis

Explanations of Language Acquisition

During much of the twentieth century, two widely divergent theories dominated a great deal of the research on language acquisition. These theories correspond roughly to the polar positions on the sources of human development—nature versus nurture. The environmental-learning approach attributes language to nurture, especially to the language environment and teaching activities provided by adults. The biological-maturation perspective, among language theorists called the *nativist* approach, attributes language acquisition largely to nature. It assumes that as children mature, their language-using capacity appears naturally, with only minimum input from the environment and without any need for special training.

In recent decades both theoretical positions have been modified. There has been a growing consensus that an environmental-learning approach that depends *entirely* on such mechanisms as learning by association, classical and operant conditioning, and imitation is insufficient to solve either of the two basic puzzles of language—how children learn what words refer to and how they master grammar. At the same time, even language acquisition theorists who identify themselves as nativists agree that it is important to specify how the environment, however minimally, contributes to language acquisition. As a result of these changes, the two broad categories of language-acquisition theories are now considered to be nativisim and interactionism, each of which consists of a body of related theories (Hoff, 2001).

The Nativist Explanation

For half a century, the nativist view of language acquisition has been dominated by the work of the linguist Noam Chomsky (Chomsky 1999; Hauser & Chomsky, 2002). According to Chomsky, the fact that children acquire language quickly and effortlessly without any direct instruction and that they produce a vast array of sentences that they have never before heard makes it impossible to claim that language could be acquired primarily through learning mechanisms. Rather, language is innate and develops through a universal process of maturation. Chomsky (1988, p.134) phrased this idea as follows:

> Language learning is not really something that the child does; it is something that happens to the child placed in an appropriate environment, much as the child's body grows and matures in a predetermined way when provided with the appropriate nutrition and environmental stimulation.

In likening the acquisition of language to the maturation of the body, Chomsky also emphasized that language is a special psychological mechanism, which he referred to as a "mental organ" by analogy with such bodily organs as the heart or the liver. Just as the functions of a physical organ such as the liver are specific, so are the functions of the "mental organ" of language (Chomsky, 1980, p. 52). This view is echoed by psycholinguist Steven Pinker in a book pointedly titled *The Language Instinct*. In Pinker's words, language is a "distinct piece of the biological makeup of our brains . . . distinct from more general abilities to process information or behave intelligently" (1994, p. 18). The fact that Chomsky describes language as a distinct process that matures does not mean that he denies its connection to other psychological processes or to the environment. In a recently published interview, he states quite clearly that while he believes there are properties of language that are unique, language is not completely isolated from other functions (Maratsos, 1999). He acknowledges that "children acquire a good deal of their verbal and non-verbal behavior by casual observation and imitation of adults and other children" (Chomsky, 1959, p. 49). But such factors, he argued, cannot fully account for language acquisition.

Chomsky's strategy for discovering the nature of the "language organ" and the conditions for its acquisition is to determine the linguistic structures and principles that are common to a variety of sentences despite variability from one utterance to the next. He refers to the actual sentences that people produce as the **surface structure** of the language. At the level of surface structure, there is great variability in the grammatical rules of different languages. However, according to Chomsky, there exists a basic set of rules shared by all languages. This basic set of rules from which the surface structures of different languages can be derived is called the **deep structure** of the linguistic system.

Chomsky suggested that the ability to use language arises from a mechanism he dubbed the **language acquisition device (LAD).** The LAD is like a genetic code for the acquisition of language, programmed to recognize the universal rules for the deep structures that underlie any particular language that a child might hear. At birth the child's language acquisition device is presumed to be still in an

surface structure In Chomskian terms, the actual sentences that people produce.

deep structure In Chomskian terms, the basic set of rules of a language from which the actual sentences that people produce are derived.

language acquisition device (LAD) Chomsky's term for an innate language-processing capacity that is programmed to recognize the universal rules that underlie any particular language that a child might hear.

embryonic state. Chomsky theorizes that as children mature and interact with the environment, maturation of the LAD enables them to use increasingly complex language forms. The eventual result of this process is the adult capacity to use language.

Those who, like Chomsky, believe that language development is a maturational process argue that the language children hear around them and the feedback they get on their early utterances provide insufficient information for them to induce the rules of grammar. Hence, nativist theorists conclude, there must be some preexisting linguistic structure that functions to guide children's language learning (Pinker, 2002). One strategy for evaluating this argument is to document how much feedback children actually receive about their use of language. The answer, based on several decades or research, is "very little" (Valian, 1999). Furthermore, even when parents do attempt to correct erroneous grammar, the effort is likely to fail, as shown in a classic exchange reported by David McNeill (1966, pp. 106–107):

"No, Timmy, not 'I sawed the chair.' It's 'I saw the chair' or 'I have seen the chair.'"

Child: Nobody don't like me.
Mother: No, say "nobody likes me."
Child: Nobody don't like me.

[*This interchange is repeated several times. Then:*]

Mother: No, now listen carefully; say "nobody likes me."
Child: Oh! Nobody don't likes me.

Extreme resistance to such corrections, even when the child is obviously trying to cooperate, seriously undermines the idea that specific teaching is important to language acquisition and bolsters the nativist position that language acquisition depends only minimally on the environment.

In summary, nativists contend that the essential structures that make language acquisition possible—the universals of grammar—operate on different principles than other psychological processes and are determined far more by the evolutionary history of our species than by the experiential history of particular children. Experience does of course determine which of the many possible human languages a child actually acquires. Children who never hear Chinese spoken will not grow up speaking Chinese, even though they are genetically capable of learning that language. According to Chomsky's theory, however, the experience of hearing a particular language does not modify the LAD; it only triggers the innate mechanisms designed for language acquisition and implements the particular language features it encounters.

Interactionist Explanations

Interactionist theorists concur with nativist theorists that innate features of the human brain play an important role in the acquisition of language. However, instead of focusing on what is innate, they attempt to link language development either to (1) the development of general cognitive processes such as remembering, categorizing, and attending; or (2) social organization of the environment (Elman et al., 1996; Karmiloff & Karmiloff-Smith, 2001; Tomasello, 2000). Those who take the first approach sometimes

A great deal of language learning takes place in casual interactions among family members. In this Asian American family, foreign words are likely to be mixed with the children's English vocabulary.

draw upon ideas associated with Piaget's constructivism, which emphasizes the way cognitive development sets the stage for and constructs language development. Those who take the second approach, which is associated with the cultural-context perspective, emphasize the way the sociocultural environment enters into partnership with the child. Adherents of this approach focus on the ways that children participate in a broad range of cultural practices that allow them to achieve language, culture, and individual development simultaneously.

Emphasizing Cognition

Alison Gopnik and Andrew Meltzoff (1997) suggest that changes in the way children use words at around 18 months arise as a consequence of the kind of cognitive changes described by Piaget. As you have seen, 18 months is the age at which infants begin to reason systematically about hidden objects, deliberately vary their actions to achieve a goal, and display increasing awareness of social standards (see Table 4.5, p. 151). Correspondingly, before 18 months of age, children are restricted to words that reflect what they are experiencing at the moment, "social words" such as "Bye-bye" and "Hereyare" (a mother leaving for work or discovering a searched-for toy). After the age of 18 months, however, they can articulate knowledge of absent objects ("gone"), describe their own activities ("Done it"), and comment on their perceived failure to meet social expectations ("Uh-oh").

Because they deny that the ability to acquire grammar is primarily innate, a major challenge for interactionists is to explain how children acquire grammar, since grammatical structures appear to be well beyond the ability of young children (and many adults) to understand. One approach to this challenge has been proposed by Elizabeth Bates and her colleagues, who have been central to promoting an interactionist approach to language development. In their view, the mastery of grammatical structures is a by-product of the growth of vocabulary and of children's attempts to express increasingly complex thoughts (Elman et al., 1996).

To illustrate how complex grammatical structures may arise from everyday verbal interactions, Elizabeth Bates (1999) points to the way a complex beehive is formed as a byproduct of the process by which bees collect and store honey. To make a structure to store the honey, bees secrete wax from their abdomens and, with their heads, push their load up against the wax deposited by other bees. This process creates a honeycomb labyrinth made up of hexagonal cells. Certainly, bees inherit genes that influence the development of their round heads, but it is implausible to conclude that bees inherit a gene to make hexagons. Instead, as Bates points out, hexagons are inevitably created whenever circles or spheres are packed together in as small a space as possible. Bates applies this same logic to linguistic structures, arguing that grammars emerge from packing words together as "solutions to the problem of mapping a rich set of meanings onto a limited speech channel, heavily constrained by the limits of memory, perception, and motor planning" (1999, p. 3).

Evidence for this view comes from research demonstrating a correlation between the size of children's vocabularies and the degree of complexity of the grammatical utterances they can make (Bates & Goodman, 1999). As we saw earlier (Figure 8.4, p. 289), individual children vary greatly in the rates at which they acquire vocabulary. The same is true for their acquisition of grammar (Fenson et al., 1994). However, when grammatical complexity is related directly to the number of words that children know, there is an almost perfect relationship between vocabulary size and grammatical complexity, regardless of how old the children are. Bates and her colleagues argue that such data clearly demonstrate how grammar develops to deal with a growing vocabulary (see Figure 8.7).

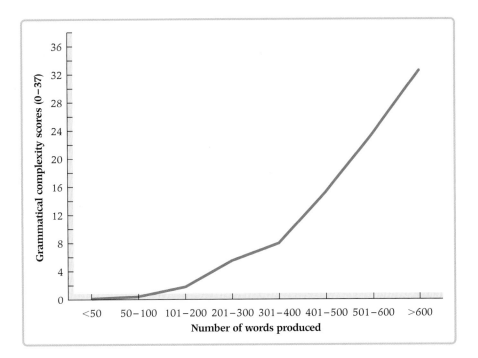

Figure 8.7 When the size of children's vocabulary is plotted against the degree of grammatical complexity of their utterance, there is a clear, positive relationship. These data are used by Elizabeth Bates and her colleagues to argue that grammar emerges from the need to use many words to convey complex messages. Note that there is an acceleration of grammatical complexity that begins when children's vocabularies reach approximately 400 words. (From Bates, 1999.)

Emphasizing Cultural Context and Social Interaction

Interactionists who emphasize the role of cultural context in the development of language focus on the fact that the acquisition of language is necessarily a social process (Vygotsky, 1978). Cultural-context theorists point out that the social environment is highly organized to incorporate the child as a member of an already existing language-using group (Ochs & Schieffelin, 1995; Tomasello, 2000). In an early and influential statement of this position Jerome Bruner (1982) argued that the earliest social structures for language development involve what he calls **formats**—recurrent socially patterned activities in which adult and child do things together. Simple formatted activities include such games as peekaboo and the routines surrounding bathing, bedtime, and meals, which provide a structure for communication between babies and caregivers even before babies have learned any language. In this way, formats serve as "crucial vehicles in the passage from communication to language" (Bruner, 1982, p. 8).

Bruner nicely summarized the cultural-context view of language development:

> Language acquisition cannot be reduced to either the virtuoso cracking of a linguistic code, or the spinoff of ordinary cognitive development, or the gradual takeover of adults' speech by the child through some impossible inductive tour de force. It is, rather, a subtle process by which adults artificially arrange the world so that the child can succeed culturally by doing what comes naturally, and with others similarly inclined. (1982, p. 15)

Bruner argued that, as an ensemble, the formatted events within which children acquire language constitute **a language acquisition support system (LASS),** which is the environmental complement to the innate, biologically constituted LAD emphasized by nativists.

Whether they point inward toward the development of general cognitive capacities that enable the acquisition of language, or outward at the way in which the culturally organized environment structures children's experience of language, interactionists deny that language is simply triggered by children's exposure to it. Rather, it emerges from the many different contributing factors we have identified in the preceding pages of this chapter. (For a discussion of another debate surrounding language acquisition, see the box "Bilingual Language Acquisition," p. 302.)

format Recurrent socially patterned activities in which adult and child do things together.

language acquisition support system (LASS) Bruner's term for the parental behaviors and formatted events within which children acquire language. It is the environmental complement to the innate, biologically constituted LAD.

Bilingual Language Acquisition

Although approximately 75 percent of the world's countries have only one official language, well over 50 percent of the world's people are bilingual—they speak two or more languages (Tucker, 1999). Moreover, there is ample evidence that young children can acquire two or more languages effortlessly (Bialystok, 2001). At the same time, it is widely believed among North American parents that early exposure to two languages might actually harm children because they would become confused, either delaying the normal process of language acquisition or leading to a situation where they are only partially competent in any language. As a result of these concerns, many bilingual parents deliberately choose to withhold knowledge of one family language from their children until it is "safe" to add a second language to their repertoire (Petitto et al., 2001).

Psycholinguists who study early bilingualism have been divided in their interpretation of whether, and to what extent, acquiring two languages at the same time differs from acquiring one language and then another. Some adhere to the *unitary language hypothesis*. They believe that children exposed to two languages from birth interpret the two languages as part of a single, fused, system. In support of this view, they point to cases where infants in the one-word stage acquire words in one language, but not the other (for example, if a child knows the word *dog* in one language, she will not know the corresponding word in the other language), suggesting that they have not differentiated their two native vocabularies. Supporters of this view also point to cases where a child is exposed to two languages, such as English and German, and says things like "Lots of *Möwen* [seagulls] Granddad" even though he knew the English word. Sometimes this same child would use both the German and English words, such as hot/*heiss* to refer to fire, as if uncertain of which term was appropriate under the circumstances. According to this view, children do not differentiate the two languages until they are about 3 years old. The unitary language hypothesis supports those who recommend delaying exposure to a second language in order to avoid confusion and possible language delay.

Those who support the *differentiated language hypothesis* accept the evidence that children mix two languages, but emphasize that their speech exhibits regular grammatical patterns that are appropriate to both languages they speak. In addition, the language they use is sensitive to the language used by the adults around them.

A remarkable study comparing language acquisitions among hearing children of deaf parents (who acquired the sign language of Quebec, Canada, and French) and hearing children who were acquiring spoken French and English showed that there was no evidence of language delay for either group of children. Whether the combination of languages was sign–French or French–English, children reached the key milestones of acquiring their first word, their first two-word combination, and their first 50 words at almost precisely the same age as the established norms for monolingual children (Petitto et al., 2001).

In a second analysis, Petitto and her colleagues showed that the children clearly differentiated synonyms in the two languages they were acquiring in the one-word stage. The researchers created conditions where the child was speaking with a person who knew only one of the relevant languages (French, English, or sign). The children almost always used the language that the adult knew. This evidence shows that even very young bilinguals differentiate their two languages from the very first words they use.

Nor was there any evidence that as their grammatical competence increased, the children began to confuse their two languages.

Rather, the degree to which they mixed the two languages matched closely the degree to which their parents mixed languages in their everyday home life with the children.

Taken as a whole, these data appear to lay to rest the idea that there is anything harmful about children acquiring two languages simultaneously from the beginning. There is even a good deal of evidence to indicate that under most circumstances, children who acquire a second language early in life benefit from the extra knowledge. They not only acquire the ability to communicate with a wider variety of people, but increase their ability to analyze language to solve a variety of intellectual tasks (Bialystok, 2001).

In addition, there is very convincing evidence to show that the older people are when they begin to acquire a second language, the less proficient, on the average, they will be (Hakuta, Bialystok, & Wiley, 2003). In a massive study of more than 2 million Spanish-speaking and more than 300,000 speakers of Chinese who emigrated to the United States, the linguist Kenji Hakuta and his colleagues showed a steady decrease in English proficiency from childhood through adulthood in both languages. While the precise level of proficiency in English depended upon a variety of factors, clearly getting an early start on second language acquisition and being given opportunities to develop proficiency through practice are important to achieving the benefits of bilingualism.

In today's world, the ability to not only speak, but also read and write in foreign languages is becoming an increasingly important part of every child's development.

Essential Ingredients of Language Acquisition

Regardless of theoretical preferences, developmentalists agree that the ability to use language is especially highly developed in, if not unique to, our species. In this sense language is innate. They also agree that actual participation in a language-using community is essential for its development. Alternative approaches help to explain one or more of the many elements of the overall phenomenon. But none of the theories so far advanced provides a complete explanation of all the processes at work in the development of language. To shed further light on the nature and nurture of language, we can pose two questions:

1. What biological properties must an organism have to be able to acquire human language?

2. What aspects of the environment are crucial to the development of language among human beings, and how do they operate?

The Biological Prerequisites for Language

Developmentalists have tackled the question of biological contributions to language acquisition in two fundamentally different ways. The first is to inquire whether other species are capable of producing and comprehending language. If they are not, then membership in the human species is a biological prerequisite for language development. The second is to investigate children with marked biological deficits to see if and how those deficits affect their acquisition of language.

Is Language Uniquely Human?

For most of human history it has seemed obvious that the basic requirement for acquiring language is that the learner be a human being. Many other species make a variety of communicative sounds and gestures, but none has evolved a system of communication as powerful and flexible as human language (Hauser & Chomsky, 2002). At this very basic level of analysis, virtually all developmentalists agree that the process of language development has a significant genetic basis.

However, current research with chimpanzees is challenging the assumption that only human beings can acquire language. One strategy in this research has been to raise chimpanzees in the home as though they were human children, hoping that these near phylogenetic neighbors would acquire oral language if they were treated just like humans. Early research with chimpanzees raised at home demonstrated that chimpanzees can, in fact, learn to comprehend dozens of spoken words and phrases (Hayes & Hayes, 1951; Kellogg & Kellogg, 1933). But the chimps never themselves produced language. Subsequent research that relied on manual signs instead of spoken words produced clear evidence that chimps can learn to use signs to request and to refer to things. However, the evidence that they can acquire language is still disputed (Savage-Rumbaugh et al., 1998; Tomasello, 2000).

Current enthusiasm for the idea that chimpanzees have the capacity to understand and produce language has been inspired by the work of Sue Savage-Rumbaugh and Duane Rumbaugh (Rumbaugh et al., 1994). The Rumbaughs combined several strategies that had been developed by others and added some of their own. They provided their chimpanzees with a "lexical keyboard" whose keys bore symbols that stood for words, and they used standard reinforcement

Kanzi uses a specially designed keyboard composed of lexical symbols to communicate.

Courtesy of Iowa Primate Learning Sanctuary

learning techniques to teach the chimpanzees the basic vocabulary symbols ("banana," "give," and so on). In addition, the people who worked with the chimpanzees used natural language in everyday, routine activities such as feeding.

The Rumbaughs' most successful student has been Kanzi, a bonobo ape who initially learned to use the lexical keyboard by being present when his mother was being trained to use it. Kanzi is able to use the keyboard to ask for things and he can comprehend the meanings of lexical symbols created by others. He has also learned to understand some spoken English words and phrases (Rumbaugh & Washburn, 2003).

Kanzi correctly acted out the spoken request to "feed your ball some tomato" (he picked up a tomato and placed it in the mouth of a soft sponge ball with a face embedded in it). He also responded correctly when asked to "give the shot [syringe] to Liz" and then to "give Liz a shot": in the first instance, he handed the syringe to the girl, and in the second, he touched the syringe to the girl's arm.

Kanzi's ability to produce language is not as impressive as his comprehension, however. Most of his "utterances" on the lexical keyboard are single words that are closely linked to his current actions. Most of them are requests. He also uses two-word utterances in a wide variety of combinations, however, and occasionally makes observations. For example, he produced the request "car trailer" on one occasion when he was in the car and wanted (or so his caretakers believed) to be taken to the trailer rather than to walk there. He has created such requests as "play yard Austin" when he wanted to visit a chimpanzee named Austin in the play yard. When a researcher put oil on him while he was eating a potato, he commented, "potato oil."

Bonobos and chimpanzees can produce language roughly at the level of a 2-year-old child using the lexical keyboard. In their productions, they form telegraphic utterances that encode the same semantic relations as children (for example, a two-symbol combination relating an agent to its action—"Kanzi eat") (Lyn & Greenfield, 2004). These telegraphic utterances can either combine visual symbols or combine gesture with symbol. Bonobos are also capable of comprehending English speech at roughly the level of a 2-year-old child (Savage-Rumbaugh, 1993).

How Is Language Affected by Biological Impairment?

While researchers have studied primates to discover biological prerequisites for language, studies of humans are necessary to identify how the human brain supports the development of language. One of the most effective strategies for learning about the brain's language functions is to study cases in which it malfunctions, either because of damage to the brain from a blow to the head or a stroke, or because of a genetic impairment.

Language and Brain Damage Scientists have long been aware that the left side of the brain plays a dominant role in language ability. But it was not until the middle of the nineteenth century that the brain bases of language became an active area of research in medicine and psychology. In particular, it was the work of two physicians, each studying a different form of a speech disorder called *aphasia,* which led to the discovery of language areas of the brain (Luria, 1973).

In 1861 French surgeon Paul Broca treated a man who was unable to speak. When his patient died, Broca studied his brain and found damage on the outside surface of the left frontal lobe in an area that came to be known as *Broca's area.* Patients with damage to this area of the brain suffer from what is called *Broca's aphasia,* a condition in which normal speech is either absent or severely disrupted.

A few years later, German physician Carl Wernicke discovered that damage to an area slightly to the rear of Broca's area results in an inability to *comprehend* language. People with damage to this area, now called *Wernicke's area,* are often capable of grammatical speech, although much of what is said is confused and makes little sense (a condition known as *Wernicke's aphasia).*

Contemporary studies of the brain and language have shown that injuries to the left hemisphere in either Broca's or Wernicke's areas among adults are overwhelmingly more likely to cause aphasia than injuries to the corresponding parts of the right hemisphere (see Figure 8.8). This evidence appears to confirm the idea that there is indeed a part of the brain that is genetically programmed to produce language, consistent with the nativist view of language.

However, recent research with children strongly suggests that it is possible to develop normal, or near-normal language even if Broca and Wernicke's areas are damaged, as long as that damage occurs early in life (Bates & Roe, 2001). Data in

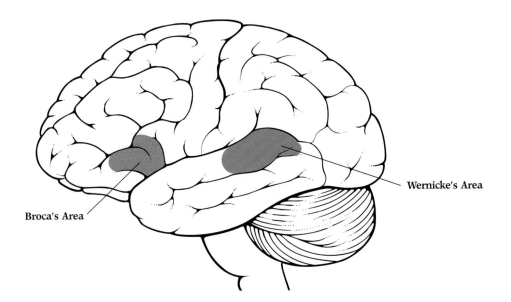

Wernicke's Area

Broca's Area

Figure 8.8 A view of the left hemisphere of the brain that highlights two key areas for normal language processing in adults. Wernicke's area is central to processing sounds and comprehension. Damage to this area results in an inability to comprehend language. Broca's area is central to motor control and language production. For patients with damage to this area of the brain, normal speech is either absent or severely disrupted. (From http://faculty.washington.edu/chudler/lang.html.)

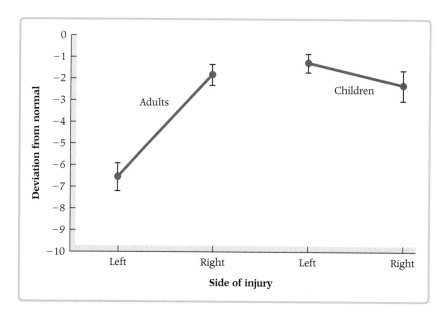

Figure 8.9 The figure shows the difference in the impact of brain injury to right and left hemispheres for both children and adults. When presented with novel phrases, the performance of adults with left hemisphere damage was far worse than the performance of those with right hemisphere damage. There was no significant difference in performance between children with left hemisphere damage and those with right hemisphere damage. This result shows the plasticity of the brain in early development. (After Bates & Roe, 2001.)

support of this conclusion come largely from studies of children who suffered strokes just before, during, or after birth that cut off the blood supply to the left or right hemisphere of the brain. Such strokes are caused by inherited blood abnormalities that make infants more likely to have a blood clot or congenital heart disease that disrupts blood flow to the brain. When young children suffer strokes in the cerebral cortex of the brain, they are still able to acquire language abilities, although their performance may be at the lower end of the normal range. Most importantly, however, children who suffer damage only to the left hemisphere, where language appears to be localized in adults, show *no* deficits in language development! Instead, parts of the right hemisphere become the brain center for their language (see Figure 8.9).

Bates and her colleagues interpret these and similar results to indicate that, in the absence of any interfering factors, the infant brain is *predisposed* to ensure the eventual emergence of an area in the left hemisphere of the brain that is specialized to process language. But this outcome is not *predetermined*. If, owing to a traumatic event such as a stroke, young children lose left hemispheric function, their brains are still plastic enough for the right hemisphere to take over the function processing of language. This evidence of plasticity suggests that the brain mechanisms of language are not fixed at birth, as nativists would argue. Rather, "learning itself plays a major role in organizing the brain for efficient language use" (Bates & Roe, 2001, p. 305).

Language and Cognitive Impairments Children are also capable of developing some degree of language competence even in the face of intellectual impairment. In Chapter 2 (pp. 62–63) we briefly described Down syndrome, a genetic disease that produces moderate to severe mental retardation. Although children with Down syndrome are able to hold a conversation, their vocabulary is relatively restricted and their talk is grammatically simple. When tested for the ability to produce and comprehend complex linguistic constructions, they fail. Such results suggest that normal language development requires normal cognitive functioning.

This broad conclusion is brought into question, however, by research on children who suffer from a rare genetic disorder called Williams syndrome. Children afflicted with Williams syndrome are also mentally retarded, yet their language is not as impaired as that of Down syndrome children. Although initial language acquisition is often delayed, many of Williams syndrome children eventually produce sentences that are grammatical, clearly pronounced, and understandable. They are also able to tell stories that are meaningful and display considerable subtlety in their portrayal of human feelings (Bellugi et al., 1999; Karmiloff & Karmiloff-Smith, 2001).

Overall, data on children who suffer some form of genetic disease indicate that at least some aspects of language develop independently of general cognitive functioning. However, some minimal level of biological maturation and inherited capacity are necessary for a child to develop normal linguistic functioning.

The Environment of Language Development

Evidence of the limitations of nonhuman primates' abilities to communicate demonstrates that one absolute biological precondition for full language acquisition is to be a human being. Evidence discussed below, as well as evidence from cases such as that of Genie, the girl who grew up in total isolation from normal human interaction and language (described in Chapter 7), indicates the corresponding precondition on the environmental side: one must grow up among humans who provide a language-acquisition support system. Beyond the specification of these two minimum requirements, however, important questions remain: Which aspects of the environment are necessary to trigger language? How are they arranged? What is the optimal support system for ensuring that the language capacity will be fully developed?

A variety of evidence shows that in order to acquire language, children must be included in normal human activities with others who have already acquired a language. The crucial role of active participation in human activity mediated by language is demonstrated by research on children who grow up in an environment without direct exposure to language but with normal human interaction in a language-mediated environment. One such situation occurs in the case of deaf

Children with hearing impairments acquire language at a comparable rate to hearing children, especially when they receive support from the environment. Here, deaf Palestinian children learn sign language in a special school in the Gaza Strip.

children whose hearing parents do not know sign language and discourage its use (Feldman et al., 1978; Goldin-Meadow, 2003).

We know that the biological condition of deafness need not be an impediment to normal language acquisition: deaf children born to deaf parents who communicate in sign language acquire language at least as rapidly and fully as hearing children born into hearing households (Morgan & Woll, 2002). Thus, any delays or difficulties in deaf children's language development must result from the way the environment is organized.

In studies of deaf children conducted by Susan Goldin-Meadow and her colleagues, the parents of the children did not know sign language and refused to learn it because they believed that their children could and should learn to read lips and to vocalize sounds. As a consequence, at an age when other children are hearing (or seeing) language, these children received extremely restricted language input in their home surroundings. However, they did participate in everyday, formatted, routine activities coordinated through the language and cultural system of the adults.

Earlier studies had shown that many deaf children raised under these circumstances spontaneously begin to gesture in "home sign," a kind of communication through pantomime (Fant, 1972). Goldin-Meadow and her colleagues wanted to find out if the home-sign systems developed by the deaf children displayed the characteristic features of language. They discovered that the gestures these children developed did indeed have certain characteristics of language, even though the children had no one to show them the signs.

Home sign begins as pointing. The children gesture one sign at a time—at the same age when hearing children develop single-word utterances. Home-sign gestures seem to refer to the same kinds of objects, and to fulfill the same functions, as the early words of hearing children or of deaf children with signing parents. Remarkably, home-signing children go on to make patterns of two, and sometimes three or more, signs around their second birthday, about the same time that hearing children utter multiword sentences.

Analysis of these multipart signs reveals ordering principles much like those seen at the two word stage in hearing children. In addition, Goldin-Meadow reports that these deaf children were embedding sign sentences within each other ("You/Susan give me/Abe cookie that is round"). This is the property of recursion, which, as we pointed out at the beginning of this chapter, is characteristic of all human languages and absent from the communicative system of chimpanzees and other creatures even after long training. Goldin-Meadow and Susan Mylander observed home sign among the deaf children of Mandarin-speaking parents living in Taiwan, where child-rearing practices and the use of gesture to accompany speech are quite different from those in the United States (Goldin-Meadow & Mylander, 1998). There they found the same patterns of spontaneous home-sign production, despite differences in the cultural environments of the children, suggesting that universal, biological processes of language creation are at work. (See the box "Children Creating a Language.")

However, once these children are able to make two- to three-word "utterances" in their home sign and begin to embed sign sentences within each other, their language development appears to come to an end. They fail to master complex grammatical distinctions. Thus it seems that the mere fact of being raised in an environment where the actions of all the other participants are organized by human language and culture is sufficient to allow the child to acquire the rudiments of linguistic structure, but that without access to the additional information provided by the sights (or sounds) of language in the environment, the child has no opportunity to discover its more subtle features. Confirmation of this

Children Creating a Language

From research on deaf children, such as those raised by hearing parents who do not know sign language, we know that children can generate signed utterances of greater complexity than anything they have encountered in the gestures of those around them, but their language development stops well short of full-fledged language. An intriguing suggestion of the linguistic environment necessary for children to acquire a full-fledged language comes from the study of Nicaraguan children who began life among adults who could not sign, but had the opportunity to live among other signing children (Helmuth, 2001; Senghas & Coppola, 2001).

Before the 1970s there was no national education system for deaf Nicaraguans. They were socially isolated and marginalized in Nicaraguan society. But in 1977 a school for 25 deaf children was built in the capital city, Managua. Two years later the school was expanded to 100 children and a year later a vocational school was opened for deaf adolescents. These schools served more than 400 students. Within a few years, a community of deaf people ranging in age from childhood to adulthood developed.

The initial instruction in this school focused on teaching the children to lipread or fingerspell in Spanish, but with little success. Because there was no organized deaf community, there was no Nicaraguan sign language; but on the playgrounds at the school and on the school bus, the children began to communicate with one another using the home signs that they had invented before coming to school. Adults noticed that independently of anything they were teaching, a language community of deaf children emerged. The number and variety of signs that children used began to increase dramatically. Most importantly, the complexity of their utterances increased in a manner that had been seen before when people who spoke no common language were brought together and had to find a way to communicate, such as occurred in Haiti and Hawaii a few hundred years ago.

At the start of the second and third school years, new groups of children arrived at the school; with no deliberate instruction, the home signs were conventionalized and combined in simple phrases known as a *pidgin* language, where two words for very common and basic needs might be used in combination such as "no money" or "want food." Pidgins have no formal grammar and are often referred to as "proto-" languages. Within a very few years children arriving at school were encountering a pidgin language in place of home signs. They further elaborated on and enriched the pidgin language they encountered. Over time, their signs became less like home signs, more arbitrary, and more stylized. The signing of younger students was also more rapid and compact. Perhaps most important, the younger children introduced new grammatical forms that were not present in the signing of the older students. They also began to use the spatial arrangements of signs to make grammatical distinctions. In short, they began to communicate with each other in a language that exhibits the same structure as any other natural human language. Nicaraguan sign language was born, and with it the conditions for deaf children to become fluent speakers of a unique, native language (Schaller, 1991).

conclusion comes from the case of a hearing child raised by deaf parents (Sachs et al., 1981). This child's parents exposed him to neither conventional oral nor conventional manual language input. He heard English only on TV and during a brief time spent in nursery school. The course of development for this child was precisely the same as for the deaf children of nonsigning, hearing parents: he developed the basic features of grammar but not the more complex ones. Once he was introduced to normal American sign language, at the age of 3 years and 9 months, he quickly acquired normal language ability.

Taken together, such studies narrow the search for the critical environmental ingredients of language development. The beginnings of language may appear during the second year of life even in the absence of direct experience of language, as long as children participate in the everyday life of their family. However, the kind of language that appears under such linguistically impoverished conditions resembles the language behavior of children at the two-word phase. Apparently, participation in culturally organized activity, while necessary, is not always sufficient to allow the child to fully acquire language (Schaller, 1991).

Interaction and Fast Mapping

On the basis of the evidence just presented, it seems clear that in order for children to acquire more than the rudiments of language, they must not only participate in family or community activity but must also hear (or see) language as they mature. When children are included in the everyday activities of the language-speaking

fast mapping The way in which children quickly form an idea of the meaning of an unfamiliar word they hear in a familiar and highly structured social interaction.

members of their community, they acquire words quickly and with little apparent effort. What makes this rapid acquisition possible?

Elsa Bartlett and Susan Carey made use of the normal routine of a preschool to find out what happens when a totally new word is introduced into conversation with children (Bartlett, 1977; Carey, 1978). They chose to study the acquisition of color terms. None of the 14 children in the classroom knew the name of the color that adults call olive; some children called it brown, others called it green, and some didn't refer to the color by name at all. Bartlett and Carey decided to give it an implausible name, chromium, just in case some children had partial knowledge of the real name that they had not revealed.

After the children had been tested to determine that they did not know the name of the color olive, one cup and one tray in the classroom were painted "chromium" (olive). While preparing for snack time, the teacher found an opportunity to ask each child, "Please bring me the chromium cup; not the red one, the chromium one," or "Bring me the chromium tray; not the blue one, the chromium one."

This procedure worked. All of the children succeeded in picking the correct cup or tray, although they were likely to ask for confirmation ("You mean this one?"). Some of the children could be seen repeating the unfamiliar word to themselves.

One week after this single experience with the new word, the children were given a color-naming test with color chips. Two-thirds of the children showed that they had learned something about this odd term and its referents; when asked for chromium, they chose either the olive chip or a green one. Six weeks later many of the children still showed the influence of this single experience.

Such findings contradict both the idea that children acquire language because adults explicitly reward their efforts and the idea that children learn by the simple process of imitation. Rather, when children hear an unfamiliar word in a familiar, structured, and meaningful social interaction, they seem to form a quick, "first-pass" idea of the word's meaning (Clark & Wong, 2002). This is why developmentalists refer to this form of rapid word acquisition as **fast mapping.** Fast mapping has been observed in children as young as 15 months of age in controlled experiments (Schafer & Plunkett, 1998). The challenge is to explain how participation in normal activities makes fast mapping possible.

The Child's Contribution

Developmentalists have proposed three cognitive principles that young children could be using to narrow their guesses quickly about what words mean, making fast mapping possible (Woodward & Markman, 1998):

- *The whole-object principle.* When children hear a new word in connection with some object, they assume that the word applies to the whole object. Young children appear to assume, for example, that when the word "cup" is used in conjunction with the thing that holds their juice, the new word applies to the entire object, not just the handle.

- *The mutual-exclusivity principle.* Children assume that an object can have only one name. As a consequence, if they already know a label for dog, they will think that a new label they hear while they are looking at a group of animals that includes dogs, such as "giraffe," does not apply to dogs.

- *The categorizing principle.* Children appear to assume that object labels extend to classes of similar objects. For example, toddlers use the word "dog" to refer not only to the family dog but to other dogs as well.

A study by Sandra Waxman and Rochel Gelman shows how very young children use the categorizing principle to help them figure out word meanings (Waxman & Gelman, 1986). These researchers asked 3-year-olds to interact with three "very picky" puppets, each of which liked only one of three kinds of things—animals, clothing, or food. Children were offered a set of objects to give to the puppets in one of three ways. One third of the children were instructed that "this puppet likes animals" (for example) and were asked to give the puppet several objects from an array that contained all three kinds of objects. A second group was shown several instances from a category (for example, animals) and told that "this puppet likes dogs, horses, and ducks" without mentioning the word "animal." The children were then asked to give the puppet several objects from the same array. A third group of children was also shown three examples of what the puppet liked and in addition was encouraged to consider the objects as a group by such comments as "Look, those make a really good group. They really go together well, don't they?" But neither the word "animal" nor the specific animal was mentioned.

The researchers found that unless the 3-year-olds were directly introduced to a group label such as "animal," they ignored the categories and gave the "picky puppets" objects from all three categories. Showing examples, even with broad hints to consider them as a category, was not effective.

In a follow-up study, the researchers substituted an unfamiliar (Japanese) word for the correct label. Even though the children could not know what the word actually referred to, the mere fact that the adults applied a verbal label to a group of objects was enough to induce the 3-year-olds to use the category information effectively.

Although the various principles offered to explain fast mapping differ in their details, they all suggest that the process of acquiring new words involves the child's making certain simplifying assumptions (new words apply to whole objects and categories) and comparing his or her existing knowledge of word meanings with new words. These strategies permit new meanings to be incorporated into the child's preexisting system of meanings. Over time, this set of meanings provides a richer and richer foundation for rapidly acquiring still more vocabulary.

Contributions from the Social Context

The child's social context is one obvious source beyond the individual child of constraints that might help children to solve the puzzle of word reference. As demonstrated by the study in which children were asked to fetch a "chromium" tray, fast mapping occurs when social interaction introduces new words into the normal flow of events at precisely the right moment so that everything but the new word is treated routinely.

The crucial role of finely tuned and well-timed interaction in supporting word learning is seen in a series of studies by Michael Tomasello and his colleagues (summarized in Tomasello, 2000). These researchers videotaped mothers interacting with their young children in order to identify the precise moment at which the mothers referred to objects in the immediate environment. They found that the mothers talked mostly about objects that were already a part of the child's current actions and the focus of the child's and mother's joint attention, thus greatly reducing the child's problem in figuring out the referents of the mother's words. In a related study, these investigators deliberately taught new words to the children in one of two ways: with half the children, an experimenter named an object that was not the focus of the child's attention in an effort to direct the child's attention to

Language is acquired in the context of ongoing activity. This mother interacts with her daughter, who is trying to carry her purse.

Stephanie Rausser/Getty Images

it; with the other half, the experimenter named an object after the child had focused on it. The strategy of naming an object after the child was already attending to it proved more effective than trying to get the child to attend to a new object and a new word at the same time.

The social conditions that enable rapid acquisition of vocabulary clearly correspond well to the kinds of adult-guided constructive processes emphasized by cultural-context theorists (Ochs & Schieffelin, 1995; Rogoff, 2003). As cultural-context theorists see it, explicit rewards for learning language are unnecessary. The reinforcement comes from children's increased success at communicating and their enhanced participation with others in valued activities.

Is There a Role for Deliberate Instruction?

As we have described it thus far, deliberate instruction ("This is an apple," "This is a truck") or the use of explicit rewards for learning appear to play no role in language acquisition. Are efforts to foster language development by teaching about language at all effective?

Adults in many cultures certainly seem to think so, and believe that it is important to actively teach their children how to talk (Ochs & Schieffelin, 1995). The Kaluli of New Guinea, for example, believe that children must be explicitly taught language just as they must be taught other culturally valued forms of behavior. The Kaluli make no effort to start teaching language until they believe the child is ready, which they judge to be as soon as the child's first words are spoken. Then the parents begin to engage their babies in a form of speech activity called *elema:* the mother provides the utterance she wants the child to repeat followed by the command "Elema" ("Say like this"). Eleanor Ochs (1982) described similar practices among Samoans, and Peggy Miller (1982) reported that working-class mothers in Baltimore, Maryland, follow a similar strategy with respect to teaching vocabulary.

motherese Speech directed to young children that is characterized by a special high-pitched voice, an emphasis on the boundaries between idea-bearing clauses and a simplified vocabulary.

Even in societies in which adults do not engage in deliberate teaching strategies, many investigators have noted that when speaking to young children, adults are likely to use a special speech register dubbed *child-directed speech,* or more popularly, **motherese.** This speech is characterized by a special high-pitched voice, an emphasis on the boundaries between clauses that are especially significant for what the adult wants to communicate, and a simplified vocabulary (Fernald, 1991; Kitamura et al., 2002). Such modifications to normal speech are believed to provide a variety of clues that children can use in segmenting the flow of speech to identify words.

As Table 8.5 indicates, middle-class parents in the United States simplify virtually every aspect of their language when they speak to their children. In addition, several studies have shown that the complexity of adults' speech to children is graded to the level of the complexity of the child's speech (Hoff, 2001; Snow, 1995).

Catherine Snow (1972) showed how such tailoring processes can work in the case of a mother directing a child to put away toys: "Put the red truck in the box now . . . The red truck . . . No, the red truck . . . In the box . . . The red truck in the box." Note the sequence of the mother's directions. Snow argues that this kind of grading of language, in which statements are gradually simplified and their meaning highlighted, isolates constituent phrases at the same time that it models the whole correct grammatical structure.

In their efforts to aid children's comprehension (and perhaps their discovery of how to use language), American adults not only simplify what they say to children; they also expand upon and reformulate what children say. In a classic study, Roger

table 8.5

Simplifications Used by Middle-Class U.S. Adults Speaking to Small Children
Phonological Simplifications
Higher pitch and exaggerated intonation
Clear pronunciation
Slower speech
Distinct pauses between utterances
Syntactic Differences
Shorter and less varied utterance length
Almost all sentences well formed
Many partial or complete repetitions of child's utterances, sometimes with expansion
Fewer broken sentences
Less grammatical complexity
Semantic Differences
More limited vocabulary
Many special words and diminutives
Reference to concrete circumstances of here and now
Middle level of generality in naming objects
Pragmatic Differences
More directives, imperatives, and questions
More utterances designed to draw attention to aspects of objects

Source: De Villiers & De Villiers, 1978.

Brown and Ursula Bellugi (1964) studied adult expansions and reformulations because they seemed to transform the child's utterance into a grammatically correct adult version. A mother whose child says "Mommy wash," for example, might respond with "Yes, Mommy is washing her face"; and to the declaration "Daddy sleep," she might respond "Yes, Daddy is sleeping. Don't wake him up."

Recently developmental psycholinguist Eve Clark and her colleagues focused on adult reformulations of young children's utterances and confirmed that this practice is widespread, providing novice language learners essential feedback about the grammar of their language (Chouinard & Clark, 2003).

Despite widespread belief that adult teaching, simplifying, and highlighting behaviors help children to master language, the necessity of such practices has been the subject of longstanding disagreement among scholars who study language acquisition. When Courtney Cazden (1965) attempted to "force-feed" children with a heavy diet of feedback by expanding and correcting their incorrect sentences, she found no special effect on language development. Subsequent studies have sometimes found effects of parental expansions or corrections (Saxton, 1997), but failures to find such effects are at least as numerous (Valian, 1999). Consequently, no firm conclusions about the influence of deliberate parental feedback are yet possible.

Nevertheless, the sheer amount of language that children hear does have a strong influence on the development of vocabulary (Hart & Risley, 1999). Betty Hart and Todd Risley recorded the language spoken in the homes of welfare families, working-class families, and professional families. The differences were quite marked: the 1- to 3-year-old children in welfare homes heard only 33 percent as much language as the children in working-class families, and only 20 percent as much language as children from professional families. The rate at which children acquired vocabulary closely tracked the amount of language they heard.

Perhaps the most important conclusion to come out of several decades of work on the relation between special adult behaviors and children's acquisition of language, over and above the sheer amount of talk children hear, is that the differences in the everyday, intuitive practices of adults throughout the world make relatively little difference in the rate at which children acquire language: all normally developing children become competent language users. All cultural groups take into account the fact that small children do not understand language and make some provision for seeing that they have the opportunity to acquire it. However, it has not been possible to prove that a particular practice that might be called "teaching the child to speak" has an important impact on language acquisition or that one method of structuring children's language experience is universally essential.

Reconsidering the Basic Puzzles of Language Acquisition

At the beginning of this chapter we introduced two basic questions about the way children acquire language: How do they come to understand what words mean and how do they acquire the ability to arrange words in acceptable sequences to express and understand the complex meanings needed to interact successfully with other people?

The information we have presented in this chapter does not definitively answer these questions, because neither language nor the way children acquire it is fully understood. But research discussed in this chapter has at least narrowed the scope of the quest.

Consider the problem posed in Figure 8.1, in which the father and son are gazing out of a window and the father tells the boy to look at the *ptitsa* (bird). What this picture leaves out is a history of interaction between parent and child, in the course of which they have developed many routines for understanding each other. It also leaves out any indication of what they were in the midst of doing when the father said, "Look, son, there sits a *ptitsa*." Perhaps they had been playing naming games, or perhaps they had been feeding their pet bird. A full account would also include the other words the child already knew, because, as we learned from the data on fast mapping, children use the words they already know to help them figure out what new words mean. Knowing these things would certainly reduce the mystery of how the child might come to understand the father but would not eliminate it entirely.

The puzzle of grammar remains especially mysterious. Perhaps, as nativist theorists claim, linguistic competence is achieved through an innate language-acquisition device. Or perhaps, as Elizabeth Bates and her colleagues argue, grammar emerges as a by-product of vocabulary growth. But it is still unclear what minimal environmental conditions are needed to permit this device to function properly. Goldin-Meadow's work with deaf children in hearing households suggests that participation in normal cultural routines can be sufficient for the rudiments of language to appear. And evidence collected in both the United States and other societies indicates that children acquire normal linguistic competence without special instruction if they can have access to language (either oral or sign) and if they participate in routine, culturally organized activity, which serves as a language-acquisition support system. As Jerome Bruner whimsically suggested, language is born from the union of the LAD and the LASS.

Although children 2½ to 3 years of age can properly be considered language-using human beings, their language development is obviously incomplete. All aspects of language continue to develop during childhood, and in some cases into adulthood (Clark, 1995). Moreover, as children begin to acquire the specialized skills they will need to cope with adult life in their culture, deliberate teaching may begin to play a conspicuous role in language development. Such specialized activities as reciting nursery rhymes, acting in a play, and writing an essay are all forms of language activity that require practice and instruction. We shall return to examine some of the more specialized language developments associated with middle childhood in Chapter 13.

SUMMARY

Prelinguistic Communication

• Linguistic communication builds on an extensive foundation of prelinguistic communicative achievements, including babbling, turn-taking, and the ability to focus one's attention on objects and activities in concert with other people.

The Puzzle of Language Development

• Despite intensive investigation, scientists' understanding of language acquisition remains incomplete. No theory is able to explain satisfactorily how children come to understand either the meanings of words or the rules that govern their arrangement (grammar).

Four Subsystems of Language

• In the transition from babbling to talking, children begin to conform to the restricted set of sounds of the language their parents speak. The basic sounds of a language (phonemes) are those that distinguish one word from another.

• Early words for objects are associated with actions and with changes in an object's state or location.

• Early words indicate children's emerging ability to operate on the world indirectly (in a mediated way) as well as directly.

• Early word meanings often correspond to an intermediate level of abstraction. As a consequence, words may be used too broadly (overextension) or too narrowly (underextension) to conform to adult definitions.

• As children's vocabularies expand, their understanding of word meanings changes fundamentally; meanings embedded in particular contexts of action are supplemented by meanings dominated by logical categories.

• Children's first words are often nonconventional; interpretation depends to a great extent on the listener's knowledge of the context in which they are used.

• Two-word utterances allow children to take advantage of the relationships of words within utterances to convey meaning, marking the birth of grammar. As the length of utterances increases, so does the complexity of the grammatical rules governing the arrangement of words within sentences and of elements (morphemes) within words.

• The growth of children's vocabularies and their increased ability to use complex grammatical constructions are accompanied by a corresponding growth in their ability to engage in conversational acts that achieve a variety of goals.

• Central to the successful use of language is the ability to say things in a way that is understandable to one's partner in conversation. Children reveal at an early age their ability to tailor their language to their listeners' needs.

Explanations of Language Acquisition

• Two classes of theories have come to dominate current explanations of language acquisition.

1. Nativist theories claim that children are born with a language acquisition device (LAD) that is automatically activated by the environment when the child has matured sufficiently.

2. Interactionist theories emphasize the cognitive preconditions for language acquisition and the role of the social environment in providing a language acquisition support system (LASS).

Essential Ingredients of Language Acquisition

• Language is a particularly human communicative ability, but aspects of language-like communication can be found among chimpanzees and other primates.

• Children acquire the basic elements of language with no special assistance from adults if they are raised in normal speaking or signing homes where communication is appropriate to the hearing ability of the child. Development of the full range of language abilities, however, requires both participation in human activity and exposure to language as part of that activity.

Reconsidering the Basic Puzzles of Language Acquisition

• Developmentalists seek answers to the problem of word reference by

1. Seeking specialized principles that children appear to use to constrain their inferences about what words might mean.

2. Identifying general cognitive abilities that help children to infer word meanings.

3. Identifying sociocultural constraints that limit the range of possibilities of a word's meaning.

• Answers to the question of how grammar is acquired have proved especially difficult to achieve. There appear to be special biological prerequisites that are unique to being a human being, but participation in culturally organized activities also appears essential.

Key Terms

conversational acts, p. 295

cooperative principle, p. 297

deep structure, p. 298

fast mapping, p. 310

format, p. 301

grammar, p. 283

grammatical morphemes, p. 293

holophrase, p. 292

language acquisition device (LAD), p. 298

language acquisition support system (LASS), p. 301

morpheme, p. 285

motherese, p. 313

overextension, p. 288

pragmatic uses of language, p. 295

recursion, p. 284

surface structure, p. 298

underextension, p. 288

Thought Questions

1. George Miller said that both the environmental-learning and nativist approaches to the acquisition of language were unsatisfactory, the first because it was impossible and the other because it was miraculous. What did he mean? Was this a fair statement of the problem?

2. Jerome Bruner characterized language acquisition as "a subtle process by which adults artificially arrange the world so that the child can succeed culturally by doing what comes naturally." What sorts of subtle arranging appear necessary for language acquisition to occur?

3. Once children move beyond the single-word stage of language development, how does their ability to combine two words to form a sentence affect their ability to create meaning?

4. What makes the cartoon on p. 299 both humorous and relevant to theories of language acquisition?

5. Some developmental psycholinguists now claim that non-human primates can be trained to acquire a protolanguage that makes their communicative ability equivalent to that of a 2- to 2$\frac{1}{2}$ year-old child. How do the communicative capacities of such animals help us to gain a better understanding of the development of human language?

Early Childhood Thought: Islands of Competence

"*In every sentence, . . . in every childish act [of the 2- to 5-year-old] is revealed complete ignorance of the simplest things. Of course, I cite these expressions not to scorn childish absurdities. On the contrary, they inspire me with respect because they are evidence of the gigantic work that goes on in the child's mind which, by the age of 7, results in the conquest of this mental chaos.*"

—Kornei Chukovsky, From Two to Five

A group of 5-year-old children have been listening to "Stone Soup," a folktale retold by Marcia Brown. "Stone Soup" is about three hungry soldiers who trick some peasants into feeding them by pretending to make soup out of stones. "Do stones melt?" asks Rose, one of the children. Master Teacher Vivian Paley reports the conversation that followed this question:

> "Do you think they melt, Rose?"
> "Yes."
> "Does anyone agree with Rose?"
> "They will melt if you cook them," said Lisa.
> "If you boil them," Eddie added.

No one doubted that the stones in the story had melted and that ours, too, would melt.

> "We can cook them and find out," I said. "How will we be able to tell if they've melted?"
> "They'll be smaller," said Deana.

The stones are placed in boiling water for an hour and then put on the table for inspection.

> **Ellen:** They're much smaller.
> **Fred:** Much, much. Almost melted.
> **Rose:** I can't eat melted stones.
> **Teacher:** Don't worry, Rose. You won't. But I'm not convinced they've melted. Can we prove it?

Ms. Paley suggests weighing the stones to see if they will lose weight as they boil. The children find that they weigh two pounds at the start. After they have been boiled again, the following conversation ensues:

> **Eddie:** Still two [pounds]. But they are smaller.
> **Wally:** Much smaller.
> **Teacher:** They weigh the same. Two pounds before and two pounds now. That means they didn't lose weight.
> **Eddie:** They only got a little bit smaller.
> **Wally:** The scale can't see the stones. Hey, once in Michigan there were three stones in a fire and they melted away. They were gone. We saw it.
> **Deana:** Maybe the stones in the story are magic.
> **Wally:** But not these.

(Adapted from Paley, 1981, pp. 16–18)

Fables and magical stories are an endless source of fascination for young children, who are still struggling to separate fact from fiction, cause from effect, and real from imaginary.

This discussion among a group of preschool children and their teacher illustrates both the fascination felt by, and the frustrations confronting developmentalists who focus on cognitive changes that happen in the first few years following infancy.

On the one hand, you can see that when Ms. Paley entices the children into reconciling the world of the story and the world of their senses, the children exhibit a pattern of thinking that is typical of young children—a mixture of sound logic and magical thinking. The children correctly believe that when things are "cooked down," they grow smaller, and that small stones should be lighter than big ones. At the same time, they are willing to believe that there really are such things as magical stones that melt, and so they miss the point of "Stone Soup." Their way of thinking appears to wobble back and forth between logic and magic, insight and ignorance, the reasoned and the unreasonable.

A similar mixture of competence and incompetence can be found in the youngsters' ability to remember objects and events. It is quite common for young children to recall the names and descriptions of their favorite dinosaurs, details of trips to the doctor's office, or the location of their favorite toy with an accuracy that can astound their parents (Nelson & Fivush, 2000). At the same time, if an adult asks them to remember a set of words or toy objects they find it difficult to do so, even just a few minutes later—a task that would be easy for older children and adults (Tulving & Craik, 2000).

Young children's intellectual performances highlight in a special way the unevenness of development, one of the key principles discussed in Chapter 3 (see p. 93 for the list of principles). At the same time, it raises important questions about the nature of development. Should early childhood be considered a distinct stage of development? If so, what explains the uneven and variable quality of thought during the years between $2\frac{1}{2}$ and 6?

As you can probably anticipate from your reading thus far, there is no general consensus about *the* correct answer to these questions. Rather, different theorists emphasize one or more factors that appear to play a leading role in the developmental changes of early childhood. Some focus primarily on general processes of change to account for the special characteristics of this age period, and treat the unevenness of children's performance as a secondary phenomenon. For stage theorists, the development of an entirely new and pervasive set of logical abilities arises from physical maturation and aspects of the environment that are found everywhere—the presence of other people, a variety of objects, the laws of gravity—while uneveness is largely attributable to variations in the familiarity of problem content or the specific ways in which the problems are posed to children. Those who view development as a process of incremental change, while not denying that physical maturation and universal aspects of the environment play a role, argue that mental development results from changes in many, relatively isolated, psychological abilities simultaneously.

Whatever the specific mechanism they propose, advocates of the view that development reflects improvement in general psychological processes face the challenge of explaining the obvious unevenness and variability observed in young children's behavior, while those who believe that processes of development are first and foremost domain specific face the opposite problem. Even if a developmental change occurs first in a particular cognitive domain or cultural context, it cannot remain totally encapsulated or every new context would have to be encountered as totally novel and knowledge could not accumulate. In addition, these theorists must explain why grownups in many societies around the world see enough generality in young children's thinking to treat the years from roughly $2^1/_2$ to 6 years of age as a special developmental stage.

Bio-Behavioral Foundations of Early Childhood Thinking

During the period beginning at about $2^1/_2$ to 3 years of age, there is little question that children undergo marked physical changes that change the ways in which they can act on and experience the world.

Physiological Growth and Behavior

As children move beyond their third birthdays, their rate of growth slows to about $2^1/_2$ to 3 inches per year and will remain more or less constant until a new growth spurt takes place at the onset of puberty (see Ch. 15, p. 583). They are no longer toddlers, holding their arms and hands out to help them balance themselves as they walk as if they were sailors home from a long voyage just getting used to walking on land. Instead, their walking is distinctly adultlike with their hands at their sides. They hurry up and down stairs, careen around corners, nimbly climb on jungle gyms, and ride the cleverly designed animal sculptures on springs that inhabit their local parks.

Their fine-motor skills have improved to the point where they can unbutton a jacket without popping the buttons, they are more agile in controlling their eating utensils, they can pour water more or less reliably, and their control of crayons is much improved. There is plenty of room for further improvement, of course. They cannot button their jacket or tie their shoes, but these accomplishments will gradually be achieved during the next few years. These increased physical capacities markedly increase their abilities to explore their environments and add significantly to the variety of experiences they can have, providing ample occasions for the development of new ways to think and act.

Maturation of the Brain

At the start of early childhood, the brain has attained about 50 percent of its adult weight. By the time children are 6, it has grown to 90 percent of its full weight (Huttenlocher, 1994). Much of this overall enlargement results from the continuing process of myelination, which speeds the transmission of neural impulses within and among different areas of the brain (Sampaio & Truwitt, 2001). During early childhood, myelination is most prominent in the association areas, which are important for planning and executive control functions (Paus et al., 1999). Consistent with the evidence on the rate of myelination, studies of changes in the brain's electrical activity show a rapid increase during early childhood in the overall frequency and size of brain waves when children are engaging in cognitive tasks (Fischer & Rose, 1996; Thatcher, 1997). The fastest growth rates during early childhood occur in myelination and organized electrical activity in the frontal cortex networks that regulate planning of new actions (Paus et al., 2001).

It is not difficult to see how the relative immaturity of the brain could explain general limitations on children's problem solving. For example, low levels of myelination in the hippocampus and frontal cortex, which support short-term and working memory, may account for the restricted working memories of young children, and hence their difficulties in tasks that require them to keep several things in mind at once. Similarly, immaturity of the frontal cortex, or of connections between the frontal cortex and association areas, could explain failures to consider someone else's point of view or to think through the consequences of one's actions. Because these general biological limitations have different psychological consequences, depending upon the particular cognitive demands of the tasks that young children are asked to confront, they provide one way of understanding the unevenness of development during this age period.

An additional source of unevenness in cognitive development is that such processes as dendrite formation and myelination do not occur at an even rate throughout the nervous system. When one part of the brain develops more rapidly than others, or when the neural pathways connecting a particular combination of cortical areas undergo a spurt in myelination, the psychological processes supported by those brain systems can be expected to undergo rapid change as well. High levels of performance are expected to occur when a given task calls upon brain systems that are highly developed, and, correspondingly, low levels of performance are expected to occur when a given task calls upon brain systems that are not yet mature.

The cultural context also plays a role in this process because different culturally organized activities will promote *experience-dependent* proliferation in those areas of the brain that are most important for the activity in question. For example, if the young child lives in a culture that emphasizes hunting or weaving, both of which require orienting in space and mental processing of spatial relations, it can be expected that there will be increased growth of cells in the parietal cortex. By contrast, if the child's culture places a heavy emphasis on verbal games, proliferation of activity in the language centers of the brain is most likely to undergo additional development.

Focusing on General Processes of Cognitive Change

As noted above, a variety of developmentalists focus on general processes of change in their accounts of cognitive development during early childhood, even though they disagree about the specific mechanisms involved. Piaget is perhaps the best known advocate of this approach, but he is not alone in his emphasis on general mechanisms of change.

Sociodramatic play—"let's pretend"—is a leading activity for children from the ages of 2½ to 6.

While current research makes it appear that young children are more competent than Piaget believed, sharp disagreements remain about whether this appearance of greater competence is real or illusory and how best to explain the process of developmental change.

Piaget's Account of Early Childhood Thinking

Once again we begin by outlining Piaget's account of cognitive development. As was the case in theories of infancy, Piaget's influence has been so great that whether specialists agree or disagree with his theories, they use his work as the starting point for their own efforts to explain early childhood (Beilin & Fireman, 2000).

table 9.1

Piaget's Stages of Cognitive Development: Preoperational			
Age (years)	**Stage**	**Description**	**Characteristics and Examples**
Birth to 2	Sensorimotor	Infants' achievements consist largely of coordinating their sensory perceptions and simple motor behaviors. As they move through the 6 substages of this period, infants come to recognize the existence of a world outside of themselves and begin to interact with it in deliberate ways.	Centration, the tendency to focus (center) on the most salient aspect of whatever one is trying to think about. A major manifestation of this is egocentrism, or considering the world entirely in terms of one's own point of view. • Children engage in collective monologues, rather than dialogues, in each other's company.
2 to 6	Preoperational	Young children can represent reality to themselves through the use of symbols, including mental images, words, and gestures. Objects and events no longer have to be present to be thought about, but children often fail to distinguish their point of view from that of others, become easily captured by surface appearances, and are often confused about causal relations.	• Children have difficulty taking a listener's knowledge into account in order to communicate effectively. • Children fail to consider both the height and width of containers in order to compare their volumes. • Children confuse classes with subclasses. They cannot reliably say whether there are more wooden beads or more brown beads in a set of all wooden beads.
6 to 12	Concrete Operational	As they enter middle childhood, children become capable of mental operations, internalized actions that fit into a logical system. Operational thinking allows children mentally to combine, separate, order, and transform objects and actions. Such operations are considered concrete because they are carried out in the presence of the objects and events being thought about.	Confusion of appearance and reality. • Children act as if a Halloween mask actually changes the identity of the person wearing it. • Children may believe that a straight stick partially submerged in water actually does become bent. Precausal reasoning, characterized by illogical thinking and an indifference to cause-and-effect relations.
12 to 19	Formal Operational	In adolescence the developing person acquires the ability to think systematically about all logical relations within a problem. Adolescents display keen interest in abstract ideals and in the process of thinking itself.	• A child may think a graveyard is a cause of death because dead people are buried there. A form of moral reasoning that sees morality as being imposed from the outside and that does not take intentions into account.

In Piaget's theoretical framework, early childhood is a time of transition between infancy and middle childhood (Piaget & Inhelder, 1969). When, as a combination of biological maturation and active explorations of the world, children complete the final sensorimotor substage (described in Chapter 6), they are able to think symbolically, using one thing to stand for ("re-present") another. This is the fundamental capacity upon which their newfound ability to use language is based.

Piaget believed that as a result of continued development, around the age of 7 or 8, children become capable of **mental operations,** mental "actions" in which they combine, separate, and transform information in a logical manner. This new form of mental action makes it possible for them to arrange their stamp collections according to country of origin and estimated value, for example, or to assemble a complex new toy right out of the box. They are better able to formulate explicit strategies because they can think through alternative actions and modify them mentally before they actually act. Piaget believed that until children are able to engage in mental operations, their thinking is subject to fluctuations of the kind that were evident when Ms. Paley's class tried to answer her questions about "Stone Soup."

Piaget's belief that young children are often led into error and confusion because they are still unable to engage in true mental operations is captured in the name that he gave to this period of development, the **preoperational stage.** This designation indicates that the thinking of 3-, 4-, and 5-year-olds *is not yet fully operational,* so he viewed cognitive development during early childhood as a process of overcoming the limitations that stand in the way of operational thinking (see Table 9.1).

mental operations In Piaget's theory, the mental process of combining, separating, or transforming information in a logical manner.

preoperational stage According to Piaget, the stage of thinking between infancy and middle childhood in which children are unable to decenter their thinking or to think through the consequences of an action.

As you have seen in Chapters 5 and 6, infants already possess a great deal of knowledge about the objects that surround them. They know that objects exist even if they are out of their sight. They are also capable of discriminating between different kinds of objects by identifying their essential properties. For example, they are aware that animals can have intentions whereas inanimate things like cars and chairs cannot. They are also aware that objects are subject to different laws and serve different functions.

Despite these important achievements, Piaget still considered young children's thinking to be limited because of its "one-sidedness." The young children that Piaget studied appeared to focus their attention on (or "center on," as Piaget called it) no more than one salient aspect of whatever they were trying to think about. Only after overcoming this one-sidedness, Piaget believed, do children make the transition to the stage of operational thinking, in which they are able to coordinate two perspectives simultaneously. A classic example of centering comes from one of his key demonstrations of the difference between preoperational thinking and the concrete operational thinking of middle childhood (by which time children can mentally combine and manipulate information about concrete objects and events). The child is presented with two identical beakers, each filled with exactly the same amount of water. While the child watches, the water in one of the beakers is poured into a third, narrower and taller beaker, with the result that the level of the water in the new beaker is higher than that of the water in the original beaker. Witnessing this event, 3- and 4-year-olds ordinarily conclude that the amount of water in the new beaker has somehow increased.

Piaget maintained that young children make this error because they center on only a single dimension of the problem—in this case, the height of the water in the beakers. They are unable to consider the height and width of the beakers simultaneously. Once they are capable of mental operations, however, children firmly deny that the amount of water has changed, presumably because they can coordinate the relative effects of changes in width and height mentally. They are also able to imagine the reversal of the process they have witnessed and thus to think through what would happen if the water were poured back into its original beaker. (We will return in Chapter 12 to research based on these examples because it also plays a central role in disputes about the nature of mental development in middle childhood.)

Piaget considered young children's inability to keep two aspects of a problem in mind to be at the heart of what he saw as the three salient characteristics of thinking during early childhood: (1) egocentrism, (2) the confusion of appearance and reality, and (3) nonlogical, or *precausal,* reasoning. In the sections to follow we will first summarize the evidence that led Piaget to these conclusions; then present findings that challenge his interpretations; and finally, examine alternative approaches to explaining the unevenness of early childhood thought.

Egocentrism

Egocentrism has a narrower meaning in Piaget's theory than in everyday speech. It does not mean selfish or arrogant. Rather, egocentrism refers to the tendency to "center on oneself," or, in other words, to consider the world entirely from one's own point of view. According to Piaget, young children are trapped in their own point of view; they cannot decenter.

The cognitive limitations that correspond to egocentrism were documented by Piaget and many later researchers who have been inspired by his work. The particular limitations one sees depend on the specific task at hand. We will examine two tasks: spatial perspective taking and conversing with playmates.

egocentrism In Piaget's terms, to "center on oneself," to consider the world entirely in terms of one's own point of view.

Lack of Spatial Perspective Taking The classic example of egocentrism as a failure to take another person's perspective is called "the three-mountain problem." In this procedure, young children were shown a large diorama containing models of three mountains that were distinctively different in size, shape, and landmarks (Piaget & Inhelder, 1956) (see Figure 9.1). First, the children were asked to walk around the diorama and become familiar with the landscape from all sides. Once the children had done this, they were seated on one side of the diorama. Next, a doll was placed on the opposite side of the diorama so that it had a "different view" of the landscape. The children were then shown pictures of the diorama from several perspectives and were asked to identify the picture that corresponded to the doll's point of view. Even though they had seen the diorama from the location the doll was in, the children almost always chose the picture corresponding to their own point of view, not the doll's.

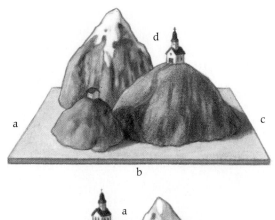

Egocentric Speech The egocentric quality of children's thought also appears in their speech. Consider the following example of two young American children holding a conversation:

> **Jenny:** They wiggle sideways when they kiss.
> **Chris:** (vaguely) What?
> **Jenny:** My bunny slippers. They are brown and red and sort of yellow and white. And they have eyes and ears and these noses that wiggle sideways when they kiss.
> **Chris:** I have a piece of sugar in a red piece of paper. I'm gonna eat it but maybe it's for a horse.
> **Jenny:** We bought them. My mommy did. We couldn't find the old ones. These are like the old ones. They were not in the trunk.
> **Chris:** Can't eat the piece of sugar, not unless you take the paper off.
> **Jenny:** And we found Mother Lamb. Oh, she was in Poughkeepsie in the trunk in the house in the woods where Mrs. Tiddywinkle lives.
> **Chris:** Do I like sugar? I do, and so do horses.
> **Jenny:** I play with my bunnies. They are real. We play in the woods. They have eyes. We all go in the woods. My teddy bear and the bunnies and the duck, to visit Mrs. Tiddywinkle. We play and play.
> **Chris:** I guess I'll eat my sugar at lunch time. I can get more for the horses. Besides, I don't have no horses now. (Stone & Church, 1957, pp. 146–147)

Figure 9.1 Preschool children shown this diorama of three mountains with a distinctive landmark on each mountain were unable to say how the scene might look from perspectives other than the one they had at the moment. (From Piaget & Inhelder, 1956.)

The children seem perfectly content playing together and they take conversational turns appropriately, but they do not appear to be engaging in a real conversation, leading Piaget to characterize such interactions as "collective monologues" rather than true dialogues. He believed that these young children, owing to their inability to decenter, are not yet even trying to communicate.

Confusing Appearance and Reality

As we noted above, Piaget believed that young children tend to focus exclusively on surface appearances—a tendency that would make it difficult for them to distinguish between the way things seem to be and the way they are. We consider here two kinds of confusion between appearance and reality: cases that involve objects and cases that involve events.

Distinguishing Real from Fake Objects Difficulty distinguishing between appearance and reality would explain why $2\frac{1}{2}$-year-olds often become frightened when an older child puts on a mask at Halloween, as if the mask had actually changed the other child into a witch or a dragon. In a classic study of this form of behavior, Rheta De Vries (1969) studied the development of the appearance–reality distinction with

Peter Huizdak/The Image Works

When this little girl's daddy put on a Halloween mask, she became frightened even though she had seen him put it on.

the help of Maynard, an unusually well-behaved black cat. At the start of the experiment all the children said that Maynard was a cat. After they played with Maynard for a short while, De Vries hid Maynard's front half behind a screen while she strapped a realistic mask of a ferocious dog onto his head (see Figure 9.2a). As she removed the screen, De Vries asked a set of questions to assess the children's ability to distinguish between the animal's real identity and its appearance: "What kind of animal is it now?" "Is it really a dog?" "Can it bark?"

By and large, the 3-year-olds focused almost entirely on Maynard's appearance (see Figure 9.2b). They said he had actually become a ferocious dog, and some of them were afraid he would bite them. Most of the 6-year-olds scoffed at this idea, understanding that the cat only looked like a dog. The 4- and 5-year-olds showed considerable confusion. They didn't believe that a cat could become a dog, but they did not always answer De Vries's questions correctly.

Similar confusions between appearance and reality have been reported by John Flavell and his colleagues, who showed young children various objects that appeared to be one thing but were really another: a sponge that appeared to be a rock; a stone that appeared to be an egg; and a small piece of white paper placed behind a transparent piece of pink plastic so that the paper appeared to be pink. The children were shown the objects and asked, "What does that look like?" (the appearance question) and "What is it really?" (the reality question) (Flavell et al., 1986; Melot & Houde, 1998).

Flavell and his colleagues found that 3-year-olds are likely to answer appearance–reality questions incorrectly. For example, it is to be expected that the children would initially think that the sponge "rock" was a rock because it was realistic enough to fool adults. But once they discover by touching it that the "rock" really is a sponge, they begin to insist that it not only feels like a sponge but also looks like a sponge! Four-year-olds seem to be in a transition state; they sometimes answer correctly, sometimes incorrectly. Five-year-olds have a much

Figure 9.2 (a) Maynard the cat, without and with a dog mask. (b) A chart plotting the age-related increase of children's ability to understand that Maynard remains a cat even when his appearance is changed so that he looks like a dog. (Adapted from De Vries, 1969.)

(a)

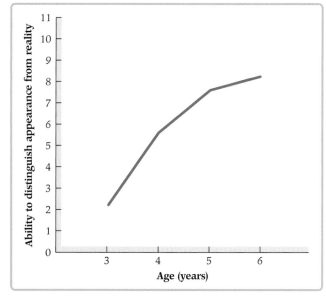

(b)

firmer grip on the appearance–reality distinction in these circumstances and usually answer the experimenters' questions in an adultlike manner.

The failure of children under 4 years of age to distinguish appearance from reality using the procedures developed by Flavell and his colleagues, has been replicated in several countries including China, Germany, and France (Huelsken et al., 2001; Melot & Houde, 1998).

Distinguishing Real from Pretend Events An entirely different line of evidence that children acquire the ability to distinguish between appearance and reality comes from an extensive literature on pretending, which, as we saw in Chapter 6 (p. 216), makes its appearance during the second year of life. When children "ride" a broomstick and pretend that it is a pony, there is little doubt that they can distinguish between ponies and broomsticks (that is, they can distinguish between reality and representations of reality), but choose to combine them for the purposes at hand.

Despite the early appearance of behaviors indicating that children can distinguish between real and pretend events, children often become easily confused about what is real and what is pretend well into middle childhood (Bourchier & Davis, 2002). For example, Catherine Garvey and Rita Berndt (1977, p. 107) report the following dialogue between two 5-year-olds:

> Pretend there's a monster coming, okay?
> No. Let's don't pretend that.
> Okay. Why?
> 'Cause it's too scary, that's why.

Similarly, even 8-year-old children playing a computer game with unrealistic graphics of a mysterious house where someone has been murdered may become genuinely caught up in the game and hide under the table (Cole & Subbotsky, 1993).

There is agreement that pretense requires a distinction between reality and appearance. And there is agreement that even at the start of early childhood some forms of pretense are present (Davis, Wooley, & Bruell, 2002). But as yet there is no explanation of why young children sometimes confuse appearance and reality when they are engaged in pretend play.

Precausal Reasoning

Nothing is more characteristic of 4- to 5-year old children than their love for asking questions. "Why is the sky blue?" "What makes clouds?" "Where do babies come from?" Clearly, children are interested in the causes of things. Despite this interest, Piaget believed that because young children are not yet capable of true mental operations, they cannot engage in genuine cause-and-effect reasoning. He claimed that instead of reasoning from general premises to particular cases (deduction) or from specific cases to general ones (induction), young children think *transductively,* from one particular to another. As an example, he described how his young daughter missed her customary nap one afternoon and remarked, "I haven't had a nap, so it isn't afternoon." As a consequence of such reasoning, young children are likely to confuse cause and effect. Because he believed that transductive reasoning precedes true causal reasoning, Piaget referred to this aspect of young children's thinking as **precausal thinking** (Piaget, 1930).

Mike and Sheila's daughter gave a splendid demonstration of how transductive reasoning can lead a young child to confuse cause and effect. At the age of $3\frac{1}{2}$, Jenny happened to walk with them through an old graveyard. Listening to Mike read the inscriptions on the gravestones, she realized that somehow the old moss-covered stones represented people. "Where is she now?" she asked when he finished reading the inscription on one stone.

precausal thinking Piaget's description of the reasoning of young children that does not follow the procedures of either deductive or inductive reasoning.

Young Children as Witnesses

The nature of young children's thought processes becomes an important social issue when they are called upon to give testimony in a court of law, either as witnesses to a crime or as crime victims. Adults have long been reluctant to believe the word of young children. Psychologists have traditionally viewed children as suggestible (Stern, 1910), unable to distinguish fantasy from reality (Piaget, 1926), and prone to fantasize sexual events (Freud, 1905/1953a). Judges, lawyers, and prosecutors have also expressed reservations about children's reliability as witnesses (Bottoms, Goodman, Schwartz-Kenney & Thomas, 2002; Goodman et al., 1998). Legal rulings on the admissibility of children's testimony continue to reflect these longstanding doubts. In many states, for example, it is left up to the judge to determine whether a child below a certain age is competent to testify.

Owing to a growing concern about the prevalence of sexual and physical abuse of children in recent years, the legal community has reexamined the reliability of children's testimony. At the same time, psychologists are trying to determine when and under what conditions young children can testify reliably about past events (Ceci & Bruck, 1998; Wright & Loftus, 1998). At the heart of the current discussion of child testimony are two questions: How good are children's memories for unusual events at various ages? How susceptible are young children to suggestions that might change their memories?

Reason for concern is provided by children's behavior both in actual criminal trials and in experimental studies conducted by psychologists. When researchers ask young children about events that have personal significance for them, such as whether or not they were given an injection when they went to the doctor's office, they are likely to provide correct answers (Goodman et al., 1990). However, a series of studies in which children ranging in age from 3 to 7 were interviewed immediately after a visit to the doctor and then again at intervals from 1 to 12 weeks later found that, as time passed, the youngest children were increasingly likely to become inaccurate in their answers (Ornstein et al., 1997). This finding is important for legal proceedings in which children are likely to be interviewed about the same event repeatedly over a period of several months, if not years.

An additional problem highlighted in these studies is that the youngest children often provide little information in response to the open-ended question "Can you tell me what happened when you went to the doctor?" (Ornstein et al., 1997). So, naturally, lawyers ask more detailed, probing, questions. But in their attempts to probe children's memory more fully, the interviewers often ask the children several strange and even silly questions, such as "Did the doctor cut off your hair?" or "Did the nurse lick your knee?" The youngest children were much more likely than the older children to say that these things happened even though they didn't.

Stephen Ceci and Maggie Bruck (1998) suggest that one reason the older children are more consistent in their responses to strange questions than the younger ones is that they have better knowledge of the scripts for doctor's visits and do not need to check their memories before they answer. They know already that "things like that" don't happen at the doctor's office.

Another problem arises because in actual criminal proceedings, children are often asked to tell and retell their stories to several people, who question them and sometimes, in an attempt to probe their recall of events more deeply and build a case, ask suggestive questions based on erroneous assumptions. For example, when an interviewer, probing a child's testimony, makes an erroneous suggestion about what happened, the suggestion tends to become blended with the child's original memory to produce a new, hybrid "memory." This hybrid memory can block the original memory, preventing the child from accurately recalling the actual events. It is also possible that the child remembers both what the adult suggested happened and what really happened but can no longer tell which version is authentic (Ceci & Bruck, 1993).

Children are by no means the only ones whose memories are vulnerable to the suggestions of the people who question them. Adults, too, can be led astray in such situations (Loftus, 1996; Massoni et al., 1999). Young children are considered to be especially susceptible, however, because of their limited ability to remember, their lack of experience with legal proceedings, and their tendency to try to please adults.

The following transcript from an actual

"She's dead," Mike told her.

"But where is she?"

Mike tried to explain that when people die, they are buried in the ground, in cemeteries. After that, Jenny steadfastly refused to go into cemeteries and would become upset when she was near one. At bedtime every evening, she repeatedly asked about death, burial, and graveyards. Sheila answered her questions as best she could, yet she kept repeating the same questions and was obviously upset by the topic. The reason for her fear became clear when the Cole family was moving to New York City. "Are there any graveyards in New York City?" she asked anxiously. Exhausted by her insistent questions, Sheila's belief that they should be honest was crumbling.

"No," Sheila lied. "There are no graveyards in New York City." At this response, Jenny visibly relaxed.

"Then people don't die in New York," she added a couple of minutes later.

Jenny had reasoned that since graveyards are places where dead people are found,

Three-year-old Amanda Conklin looks out at a crowded Van Nuys, California, courtroom as the judge questions her during the trial of her father for the murder of her mother.

interview in the case of Kelly Michaels, a New Jersey nursery school teacher who was convicted and jailed for sexually abusing children in her school, provides an example of how such suggestions might be made:

Interviewer: Well, what about the cat game?

Child: Cat game?

Interviewer: Where everybody went like this, "Meow, meow."

Child: I don't think I was there that day.

Despite the fact the child denied knowing about a cat game when she was interviewed, later, at the trial, she described a cat game in which all the children were naked and licking each other (from Ceci & Bruck, 1998).

Although we do not know why this child testified the way she did after telling the interviewer she didn't think she was present at the game, we can speculate that she may have genuinely come to recall such a cat game after being told of one by the interviewer. Her answer may also have reflected the fact that young children are likely to believe that adults know more than they do. When they are being questioned in a legal proceeding, as this child was, they may incorporate the adult's suggestions in their answers to please the adult, even when they know the adult's suggestions are wrong. Asked the same questions more than once, they change their answers because they

assume that something was wrong with their first answer (Siegal, 1991b).

The problem of using results of experimental studies to decide about the reliability of child witnesses is that in experimental studies children are asked to testify about relatively mundane events and/or to conceal relatively trivial information. In real life, children do not come to a courtroom to testify about breaking a Barbie doll, but about more intense emotional events, such as being sexually abused or witnessing a murder. The great emotional significance of such events can impact the reliability of children's reports in many different ways and makes it hard to determine whether or not a specific child can provide reliable testimony.

Another problem in obtaining a reliable eyewitness report from children is their tendency to conceal their own or other people's misdeeds because they are afraid of punishment, because of their desire to protect loved ones, or their tendency to obey an authority figure (Bottoms et al., 2002). Perpetrators of a crime may also put pressure on children to "keep their secret." Although even 4-year-olds are capable of keeping secrets, an experimental study by Bette Bottoms and her colleagues (2002) clearly indicates a developmental change. They found that 5- to 6-year-olds who were instructed to keep a secret withheld more information than did the children who were not instructed to keep secrecy. Overall, these complexities make it very difficult to evaluate the truthfulness of young children's testimony.

graveyards must be the cause of death. This reasoning led her to the comforting but incorrect conclusion that if you can stay away from graveyards, you are not in danger of dying.

The Problem of Uneven Levels of Performance

The examples we have provided thus far (summarized in Table 9.1 on page 323) are only a sample of the phenomena supporting the idea that there is a distinctive mode of thought associated with early childhood. But they are sufficient to give the flavor of the sorts of evidence collected by Piaget and others to argue that an inability to decenter one's thought pervades the preoperational stage of cognitive development, making it difficult for young children to consider multiple aspects of a situation simultaneously or to think through a problem systematically (for an example of the real-world challenges presented by young children's cognitive limitations, see the box "Young Children as Witnesses").

A variety of studies seem to show that Piaget's reliance on verbal interviews and the specific tasks he used as key sources of data led him to misjudge young children's cognitive abilities. Much of this new evidence indicates that early childhood cognitive development is a good deal more uneven than Piaget's depiction of it suggests. Under some circumstances, children show evidence of cognitive abilities well before Piaget believed possible (Goswami, 2002; Inagaki & Hatano, 2002; Rosengren & Brasswell, 2001).

Nonegocentric Behavior

Examples of new experimental methods for assessing children's thought processes that have led to questions about Piaget's assessments are his perspective-taking and speech tasks. In each case, this evidence points strongly to young children's potentials to engage in the existence of a nonegocentric form of reasoning.

Reasoning about Spatial Perspectives In one often-cited test of Piaget's ideas about spatial egocentrism, Helen Borke (1975) replicated Piaget and Inhelder's three-mountain experiment (see Figure 9.1 on p. 325) with children between 3 and 4 years of age. She also presented the children with an alternative form of the problem, a farm scene that included such landmarks as a small lake with a boat on it, a horse and a cow, ducks, people, trees, and a building (Figure 9.3). In this alternative version, Grover, a character from *Sesame Street,* drives around the landscape in a car. From time to time he stops and takes a look at the view. The child's task is to indicate what that view looks like from Grover's perspective.

Children as young as 3 years old performed well on this perspective-taking problem, whereas their performance on the three-mountain version of the problem was poor, just as Piaget and Inhelder's experimental results would have predicted. These contrasting levels of performance between the two forms of a logically identical problem led Borke to conclude that when perspective-taking tasks involve familiar, easily differentiated objects and when care is taken to make it easy for young children to express their understanding, young children demonstrate that they are able to take spatial perspectives other than their own.

Nonegocentric speech Several decades ago it was established that children as young as $2\frac{1}{2}$ years of age show that they are able to take the listener into account by modifying what they say to include information important to the listener (Wellman & Lempers, 1977). By the time they are $3\frac{1}{2}$ years old they are sufficiently mindful of what another person needs to know that, when they try to communicate their choice of a toy from an array, they provide more information to someone who is blindfolded than to someone who is not (Maratsos, 1973). They also use simpler language when they talk to younger children than when they talk to adults, an indication that in some way they know the younger child's language ability is more primitive than their own (Tomasello & Mannle, 1985).

This ability to modify speech so that younger children can easily understand it does not

Figure 9.3 Borke's modification of Piaget's three-mountain perspective-taking task. When a diorama contains familiar objects, preschoolers are more likely to be able to say how it looks from a point of view other than their own.

depend on experience in talking to younger children. Only children are just as likely to simplify their speech as children with little brothers and sisters. Interestingly, small children make the same kinds of simplifications in their speech when they play with a baby doll, but not when they play with a grown-up doll (Sachs & Devin, 1973).

Distinguishing Appearance from Reality

According to the data we presented earlier (pp. 325–327), children do not begin to distinguish between appearance and reality consistently until somewhere between the ages of 4 and 6 years. However, additional research using somewhat different methods suggests that the difficulties experienced by the youngest children depend in part on the special features of the experimental procedures being used (Deak et al., 2003).

In an interesting modification of the experiment that turned Maynard, the cat, into a ferocious dog, Carl Huelsksen and his colleagues in Germany demonstrated that young children can make appearance–reality distinctions if an adult dresses up in a costume (Huelsken et al., 2001). In 4 out of 5 cases, 3- to 4-year olds indicated that they knew the person in the costume was the same as the person in his or her regular clothing, although a majority had difficulty providing an explicit verbal distinction between appearance and reality. Felicity Sapp and her colleagues also found that the main difficulty experienced by 3-year-olds is to formulate the appearance–reality distinction in words (Sapp, Lee, & Muir, 2000). These findings illustrate just how careful experimenters must be to create appropriate versions of their tasks so that they are meaningful for young children and the children are given ample opportunity to reveal what they know.

The same kind of result has been obtained for trick objects like sponge "rocks." Catherine Rice and her colleagues (1997) repeated and extended the studies of 3- to 4-year-olds' ability to judge the reality of sponge "rocks" and other such misleading objects by using a procedure that engaged the children as coconspirators in a deception. The experimenter began by asking the child to help trick another adult with a fake object such as a sponge rock. While the second adult was conveniently out of the room, the experimenter and child placed the trick object on the table in place of the original. While waiting for the second adult to return, the experimenter asked the child several questions: What is the object, really; what does it appear to be, and what will the absent adult think it is? In this playlike context, the children were able to say that the object was a sponge but that it looked like a rock—and that the adult would think it was a rock. Thus, they were clearly able to distinguish reality from appearance.

Effective Causal Reasoning

Merry Bullock and Rochel Gelman demonstrated the ability of 3- to 5-year-olds to understand the basic principle that causes come before effects, using the apparatus shown in Figure 9.4 (Bullock, 1984; Bullock & Gelman, 1979). Children observed two sequences of events. In the first, a steel marble was dropped into one of two slots in a box, both of which were visible through the side of the box. Two seconds after the marble disappeared at the bottom of the slot, a Snoopy doll popped out of the hole in the apparatus's middle. At that moment, a second ball was dropped into the other slot. It too disappeared, with no further result. The children were then asked to say which of the balls had made Snoopy jump up, and to provide an explanation.

Figure 9.4 The apparatus used by Bullock and Gelman to test preschoolers' understanding that cause precedes effect. (a) A marble was dropped into one of the slots. (b) Two seconds after the marble disappeared, a Snoopy doll popped out of the hole in the middle of the apparatus. At the same moment, a second marble was dropped into the other slot, where it disappeared, with no further result. Preschoolers are generally able to indicate which marble caused Snoopy to jump up. (Based on Bullock & Gelman, 1979.)

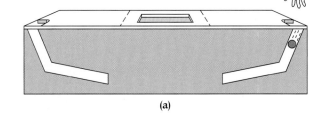

(a)

(b)

Even children as young as 3 years old usually said that the first ball had caused Snoopy to jump up. The 5-year-olds had no difficulty with the task at all. However, there was a marked difference between the age groups in their ability to explain what had happened. Many of the 3-year-olds could give no explanation or said something completely irrelevant ("It's got big teeth"). Almost all the 5-year-olds could provide at least a partial explanation of the principle that causes precede effects. Subsequent research has shown that if the problem is slightly complicated, 3-year-olds become confused and can neither solve nor explain what appear to be relatively simple mechanical cause–effect relationships (Frye, 2000).

Piagetian Explanations for Unevenness

As was true of the research on infant precocity you encountered in Chapters 5 and 6, many developmentalists continue to argue that Piaget remains correct in his insistence that knowledge must be constructed through action, even if some of his particular conclusions need modification (Beilin & Fireman, 2000). From this perspective, apparently contradictory evidence such as that we have summarized in the previous pages results either from faulty experimentation that oversimplifies the task or from a failure to understand Piaget's theory. Orlando Lourenço and Armando Machado, for example, argue that most of the studies that have challenged Piaget's results are based on "methodological errors and conceptual confusions" (Lourenço & Machado, 1996, p. 146).

Piaget himself was well aware that a child's performance could vary somewhat from one version of a problem to another, even though the problems seemed to require the same logical operations. He believed that subtle differences in the logical requirements of the different versions of a task are an important source of variations in children's performance in what appear to be logically identical cognitive tasks. He was also aware that the interview technique, from which much of his data derived, might itself obscure the thought process being studied, producing an apparent unevenness in performance, especially in young children who were still novices in the use of language (Piaget, 1929/1979). However, his own work convinced him both that he had overcome the problems of interviewing young children and that his research accurately demonstrated that preoperational children consistently fail to distinguish their point of view from that of someone else, become easily captured by surface appearances, and are often confused about causal relations.

However, at present there appears to be a growing consensus that the problems with Piaget's approach are sufficiently acute to require serious revision or outright rejection. These alternatives take a variety of paths but share the twin goals of understanding the sources of unevenness in children's performance and the conditions under which developmental change appears to be general and stagelike, or piecemeal and gradual (Case, 1998; Fischer & Pare-Blagoev, 2000; Goswami, 1999). Information processing approaches propose general psychological mechanisms such as increases in short term memory capacity and knowledge to account for both the process of cognitive change and the unevenness of young children's cognitive performances. A competing set of theories relegates general mechanisms to a secondary role and focuses on the ways in which cognitive development builds upon domain-specific psychological processes.

Information-Processing Approaches to Cognitive Change

During the 1960s, when Piaget's ideas were becoming popular among developmentalists, a different view of cognitive functioning was also gaining attention: the **information-processing approach.** Information-processing theorists, like Piaget, believe that mental development can be explained by the application of general principles, and that nature and nurture play an equal role as sources of development.

information-processing approach A strategy for explaining cognitive development based on an analogy with the workings of a digital computer.

The emergence of the information-processing approach was largely motivated by a dissatisfaction with what they considered the vagueness of Piaget's ideas concerning the process of developmental change. This dissatisfaction was described by David Klahr, a leading proponent of the information-processing perspective. Klahr referred to the Piagetian concepts of assimilation and accommodation as "mysterious and shadowy forces . . . the Batman and Robin of developmental processes" (1982, p. 80). "How do they operate?" he asked. "We know no more about them than when they first sprang upon the scene."

As a means of repairing this perceived shortcoming of Piaget's approach, information-processing theorists proposed that cognitive development can usefully be studied as a complex system that regulates the flow of information it receives from internal and external sources. Cognitive development, from this perspective, arises from a combination of improvements in biological capacities and psychological factors. Each contributes to increasing knowledge and the ability to deploy effective strategies (Chen & Siegler, 2000).

Information-processing models of development are often understood by analogy with the workings of a digital computer, and success in writing a computer program that realistically models changes in children's learning and problem solving is often used as key evidence to support this theoretical approach (Siegler, 2000). Investigators who employ the analogy of child-as-information-processor generally conceive of biological changes as changes in children's neural "hardware," such as increased myelination of a particular brain region, while the acquisition of a new strategy for remembering would be seen as reflecting changes in children's cognitive "software." The use of the computer analogy encourages developmentalists, in their attempts to explain developmental change, to focus on an array of psychological *processes* that work in concert with longer-term, psychological *structures*.

An overview of the essential components of this view of the mind is illustrated in Figure 9.5. There are three boxes labeled sensory register, short-term storage, and long-term storage. This represents the basic system for attending to, interpreting, and storing information. No matter what, part of the great welter of experience should be registered, compared with past information, and acted upon. At the top

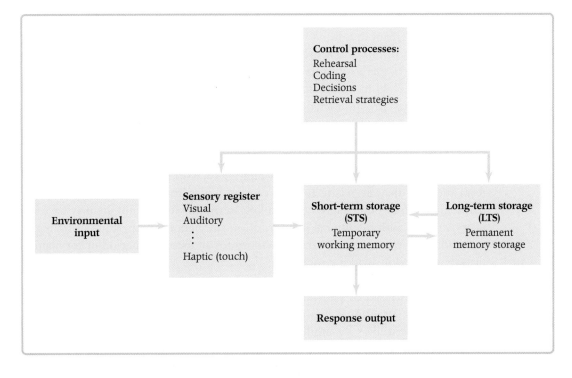

Figure 9.5 The major components of an information-processing model of mental actions. (Adapted from Atkinson & Shiffrin, 1968.)

sensory register That part of the information-processing system that stores incoming information for a fraction of a second before it is selectively processed.

short-term (working) memory That part of the information-processing system that holds incoming sensory information until it is taken up into long-term memory or forgotten.

long-term memory Memory that is retained over a long period of time.

of the figure is a box that, in effect, monitors and modifies the results of this ongoing process of comparing new and old information for its significance.

You can follow the potential flow of information by starting at the left of the figure. The presumed starting point of any problem-solving process is the **sensory register,** which stores incoming information for a fraction of a second before it is attended to and selectively processed. Stimulation from the environment ("input," in the language of computer programming) is detected by the sensory organs and is passed on to the sensory register. If the input is not attended to, it will disappear almost immediately. If it is attended to, it may be "read into" **short-term (working) memory,** where it can be retained for several seconds. Working memory is the part of the information-processing system where active thinking takes place. Working memory combines incoming information from the sensory register with memory of past experiences, or **long-term memory,** changing the information into new forms. If the information in working memory is not combined with information in long-term memory, it is easily forgotten.

Figure 9.5 also shows the way in which the flow of information between sensory register, working memory, and long-term memory is coordinated by control processes. These control processes determine how the information temporarily held in working memory is applied to the problem at hand. Important control processes include attention, rehearsal, and decision making. The "software" that implements the control processes determines the particular information that must be attended to, whether long-term memory must be searched more thoroughly, or whether a particular problem-solving strategy should be used. Control processes also determine whether a piece of information in short-term memory needs to be retained or can be forgotten.

You can get an overall idea of the information-processing approach by considering what occurs when a mother tries to teach her 4-year-old daughter to remember the family phone number. The mother sits with the child at the phone and shows her the sequence of buttons to push, say, 543-1234. The child watches what the mother does and hears what her mother is saying. First the set of numbers enters the child's sensory register as a sequence of sounds and is transferred to short-term memory. Next, meanings corresponding to those sounds are retrieved from long-term memory and matched with the sounds in short-term, working, memory. The child recognizes each number and applies control processes in order to "try to remember," perhaps by using the strategy of repeating each item to herself. Remembering occurs when the information concerning the numerical sequence enters long-term memory so that it is retrievable at a later time.

The young child in our example may experience difficulty at any phase of this process. She may pay insufficient attention to what her mother is saying, in which case the information will not enter her sensory register. Being young, she has a small (immature) working-memory capacity and may not be able to hold all the numbers in working memory as she tries to remember them. The speed with which she can transfer information from the sensory register to working memory and to long-term memory may be relatively slow, causing her to forget some of the numbers before they can be enduringly stored in long-term memory. Lastly, she may have little experience with intentional memorization and hence no repertoire of strategies for holding information in working memory for an extended period or for manipulating numbers in working memory.

In sum, from an information-processing perspective, young children's cognitive difficulties are caused by general cognitive factors including limitations in knowledge, memory, attentional control, and the speed with which they can process information, as well as by limited strategies for acquiring and using information (Siegler, 2000). Children's performance improves as they grow older because these limitations are gradually reduced through maturation of their brains ("hardware"),

(a)

(b)

(c)

(d)

All drawings courtesy of Carrie Hogan

Figure 9.6 A sequence of drawings by an American child indicates how increasing information processing and motor skills influence children's ability to represent the world on paper. When she was very small, all Carrie could draw were lines of different colors, but at $3\frac{1}{2}$ (a), she was able to draw global representations of a person; at 5 years (b) she added a body and legs to the creatures she drew, and set her main figure in a scene. Motion, rhythm and greater realism are evident in the drawings she produced at $7\frac{1}{2}$ years (c). At 12 years (d), she was able to draw a cartoon of a realistic scene.

the development of more effective information-processing strategies ("software"), and a greater store of knowledge ("long-term memory storage"), each of which reduces the overall load on the information-processing system. An interesting way in which increasing information processing capacities are manifested in children's behavior is illustrated in Figure 9.6.

By this same logic, if conditions arise where information-processing limitations are reduced or absent, even very young children should display noticeably higher levels of performance. A convincing demonstration of such an island of competence was provided by Michelline Chi and Randi Koeske (1983). These investigators focused on a 4-year-old boy's knowledge of a relatively obscure topic, dinosaurs. Chi and Koeske (1983) first elicited the names of all the dinosaurs the child knew by questioning him on several occasions. These elicitations produced a total of 46 different dinosaur names for this unusually well-versed child! Next they drew up two lists consisting of the 20 dinosaurs he mentioned most frequently and the 20 he mentioned least frequently. In order to study how the child's comparative knowledge influenced his memory and reasoning about each group, Chi and Koeske then read the two lists of dinosaurs to the child three times each and at each reading asked him to memorize as much of the list as he could. He recalled twice as many items from the list of dinosaurs he knew more about than from the list with which he was less familiar (an average of 9.7 dinosaurs versus 5.0

The extensive knowledge that young children acquire when they become engrossed in subjects like dinosaurs may only be a passing phase. But children's expertise about such matters is scientifically important because it shows that even young children, when they accumulate an extensive knowledge base in a specific domain, will display cognitive abilities more like those of adults.

dinosaurs). The researchers concluded that the more extensive a child's knowledge about a topic, the easier it is to recall items that pertain to it. Since young children have relatively little knowledge about many topics familiar to adults, they will appear to have weaker memories than older children and adults, but the real difference is their relative lack of knowledge, not their ability to remember.

A follow-up study showed that extensive knowledge about a topic also affects reasoning about it: the more you know, the more powerful your ability to reason will be. Chi and her colleagues (1989) found that young dinosaur "experts" organize their knowledge about dinosaurs in more integrated and coherent ways than do novices. For example, they mentally group dinosaurs according to common behaviors ("meat eaters" versus "plant eaters") as well as the common attributes that go with these classes ("has sharp teeth" versus "has a duckbill"). By contrast, those who know less about dinosaurs mentally group them according to less significant features, such as size. The shift from novice to expert is often slow and appears to be continuous. But if they do develop a sufficiently rich knowledge base, children become experts and appear to engage the task in qualitatively new ways. Insofar as the novice-to-expert change represents a change in the child's stage of development for the specific topic in question, the information-processing approach reveals the importance of learning from the environment in accounting for islands of competence.

Such results, which have been replicated for many kinds of cognitive problems, have led Siegler to emphasize that all during childhood and beyond, human cognition *at any age* is characterized most prominently by its *variability.* In his words,

> At any given time, several ways of thinking [which Siegler refers to as "strategies"] are present in a child's thinking. These strategies compete with each other, and with experience, some become more frequent, some become less frequent and some become more frequent and later less frequent. Further, new strategies are introduced and other old strategies stop being useful. This overlapping waves model seems more in accord with what is known about cognitive development than do depictions that show children suddenly moving from one approach to another. (Siegler, 1998, p. 92)

Siegler's notion of cognitive development as a sequence of overlapping waves, each representing a particular information-processing strategy such as how to add one-digit numbers, is depicted in Figure 9.7. Different cognitive strategies are constantly appearing and competing with each other in a never-ending "survival of the fittest." Many factors enter into the appearance and disappearance of a particular strategy, including the maturation of brain functions to support it, how easily and quickly it achieves its goal, and the range of available strategies with which it is in competition.

Figure 9.7 Siegler's "overlapping wave" model of developmental change (a) shows changes as slow and uneven, depending upon the strategies used by the child. Stage models, in contrast, see development as divided into discontinuous stages (b).

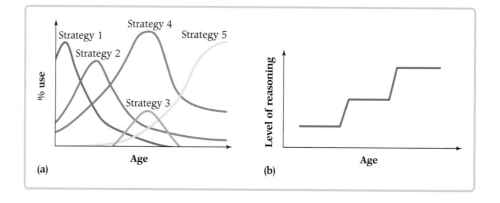

As Siegler points out, his overlapping wave model of development directly contradicts Piaget's notion that cognitive change is a stagelike process. When performance is averaged across all of the different strategies, what emerges is a gradual shift toward more effective problem solving, not a leap in the overall logic of behavior.

An information-processing approach, then, provides a theory based on psychological principles that apply to every domain of cognitive functioning, and also accounts for the unevenness of development. Further illustrations of this approach will be provided in Chapter 12, where our focus shifts to cognition in middle childhood. When developmentalists are able to compare the same kind of information processing in both early and middle childhood, they obtain a clearer picture of how cognitive limitations are gradually overcome, ushering in developmental change.

Focusing on Domain-Specific Approaches to Cognitive Change

Early in his career, when Piaget conducted research on young children's explanations of how the world works in many different knowledge domains, he concluded that 3- to 6-year-olds suffer the same general kinds of logical confusions regardless of whether the knowledge domain in question involved clouds, dreams, rocks, trees, and so on. They would attribute life to nonliving things such as clouds or rocks and would claim that natural objects like mountains are made by human beings. The fact that young children made the same kinds of logical mistakes regardless of the specific content of the questions confirmed Piaget's view that cognitive change results from *general* rather than *specific* processes. And, as we have just seen, using a quite different approach, information-processing theorists also focus on general rather than specific processes to account for change.

But in line with current research on infancy, modern developmentalists have invented some clever ways to assess 3- to 6-year-old children's ways of thinking that have led them to conclude that in early childhood, as in infancy, the content of what children are asked to remember or think about *does* matter—they can be shown to reason differently, for example, about rocks and about people. This evidence focuses developmentalists' attention on the content- and context-specificity of cognitive development, leading some to conclude that mental development results from changes in many, relatively isolated, domains simultaneously. In the sections that follow we will summarize evidence supporting this domain-specific view of children's reasoning and different approaches to explaining how domain-specific knowledge develops.

Privileged Domains

A major challenge confronting those who believe that cognitive development is closely linked to the content and contexts that children encounter is to be clear and consistent about what is meant when referring to a "domain," be it a domain of knowledge or a domain of activity (Gelman & Lucariello, 2002). For example, as you read in Chapter 5 (p. 184), Elizabeth Spelke and her colleagues believe that there is a domain of knowledge about inanimate physical objects because young infants appear to assume that their environment is three-dimensional, made up of things that occupy space, that move as units, and that move only when acted upon.

It is possible to allow young children to reveal what they consider to be a domain by recording their conversations in everyday situations. This approach was used by Anne Hickling and Henry Wellman (2001), who obtained their data from

privileged domains Cognitive domains that call upon specialized kinds of information, require specifically designated forms of reasoning, and appear to be of evolutionary importance to the human species.

a giant computer database of children's conversations made available to researchers interested in language and development (MacWhinney, 2000). Hickling and Wellman analyzed conversations of four native English-speaking children who were about 2 years old at the start of the recordings, which continued until they reached the age of 5. The researchers focused on utterances that sought explanations for a wide variety of events the children encountered in their daily lives.

Hickling and Wellman identified four frequently referenced cognitive domains based upon four modes of explanation the children offered for different kinds of things: (1) physical explanations typically applied to objects and were used to explain things in terms of mechanical force where one object came in contact with another (e.g., "The teddy's arm fell off, because you twisted it too far"); (2) psychological explanations in which events were explained in terms of actors' mental states, such as beliefs, intentions, and desires ("I talking very quiet because I don't want somebody to wake me up"); (3) biological explanations that referred to phenomena such as growth, nutrition, reproduction, or illness ("He needs more meat because he is growing long arms"); and (4) social explanations referring to interpersonal rules or cultural conventions and traditions ("I got this candy because it is a prize").

Overall, Hickling and Wellman concluded that children frequently produced causal utterances, both by asking causal questions ("Why do the scissors have to be clean?") and even more often by offering explanations such as those illustrated in the previous paragraph. Evidence for the reality of these domains was the fact that the children successfully matched modes of explanation (e.g., "psychological," "physical," "biological") to appropriate entities (persons, objects, animals). Their adherence to the adult rules for each domain suggests that young children really do interpret these phenomena in domain-specific ways.

Because these domains call upon specialized kinds of information, require specifically designated forms of reasoning, and appear to be of evolutionary importance to the human species, Zhe Chen and Robert Siegler (2000) use the term **privileged domains** to identify cognitive domains identified by Hickling and Wellman. In the sections that follow we summarize the data supporting the domain-specific view of children's cognitive development. We then consider how to reconcile the extremes of totally general and totally specific mechanisms of thought, and the question of the uniqueness of early childhood as a stage of development.

The Domain of Physics

Developmentalists refer to an early understanding of mechanical and material phenomena—such as motion, the consequences of objects colliding, gravity, or changes of material state such as water turning into ice—as *naïve physics* (Baillargeon, 2002; Wellman & Gelman, 1998). As you saw in Chapter 5, it appears that within months after birth children have some grasp of at least a few very basic physical principles, including expectations that two objects cannot occupy the same location at the same time and that an object cannot pass through physical obstructions. You also encountered evidence in Chapters 5 and 6 that infants appear to reason differently about mechanical causation (objects influence each other only when they touch, such as when one ball bumps into another) than they do about human causation (one person can influence another at a distance, for example, by chasing him or her).

When Vivian Paley's children argued that stones melt when they are heated, they seemed to demonstrate an intuitive understanding that physical materials will melt if they are heated sufficiently. Of course, for stones to melt one needs much greater heat than the temperature provided by a stove. Moreover, by the time the stones would start to melt, there would not be any water or pot left. Children's reasoning about melting stones is consistent with scientific theory and raises an interesting question as to how children acquire this understanding.

A frequently studied phenomenon in the domain of naïve physics is children's understanding of the impact of gravity and inertia on the motion of objects. For example, Kyong Kim and Elizabeth Spelke conducted a series of several experiments with children varying in age from 7 months to 6 years, as well as with adults, and found that understanding of the physical principles of gravity and inertia undergo a long and uneven course of development (Kim & Spelke, 1999). They showed infants and young children videotaped sequences in which a ball moved along a surface that ended abruptly. The ball then either kept moving in a straight line at the same speed (defying the laws of gravity and inertia), plummeted straight down (following the law of gravity but not inertia), or fell in a gradual arch according to the physical laws of inertia and gravity (see Figure 9.8).

In these experiments, the 7-month-olds showed no understanding of gravity or inertia. They stared with equal interest at a ball moving straight ahead through space, falling straight down, or following a curved descent to the floor. The results for the 2-year-olds were mixed. Sometimes they seemed indifferent to whether a ball kept moving in a straight line or fell in a (natural) curve to the ground. But in other conditions they stared longer at the ball that violated the law of inertia by falling precipitously at the edge of the board along which it had been traveling when compared with the ball that fell in a natural curving motion, indicating that they were beginning to have some understanding of inertia. When 6-year-olds were tested on their understanding of inertia and gravity, they displayed sensitivity to both, but were not entirely consistent, indicating that both concepts had continued to develop from whatever core physical concepts that were present in early infancy but were still not fully mastered (Spelke, 2000).

Terry Au (1994) demonstrated that young children also have a pretty good grasp of the physical makeup of objects. She showed middle- and working-class children as young as 3 years of age various natural and artificial substances, including wood and play dough, which she then transformed in three ways while they watched. In some cases large chunks were broken into smaller chunks; in other cases chunks were turned into powder; and in the remaining cases, the powder was dissolved in water! Even when confronted with the most drastic transformation—dissolving a physical substance in water—the 3-year-olds were correct in arguing that the substance had not changed, despite changes in such features as smell and wetness. As Wellman and Gelman (1998, p. 534) point out, "These data show that even quite young children know that larger objects are composed of smaller pieces and these pieces, even if invisible, have enduring physical existence and properties."

There is a great deal more to be learned about physical laws, as everyone who has taken an introduction to physics knows. But by the age of 5 to 6 years, children have developed a serviceable set of ideas about the physical world that appear to be shared by people all over the world.

Figure 9.8 Test used by Kim and Spelke to test children's knowledge of the physical principles of gravity and inertia. All the children saw the ball roll across a smooth surface (a), and then were tested with events such as those in b–d, to see which of these test events violated their expectations and thus revealed awareness of the relevant physical laws. (Adapted from Kim & Spelke, 1999.)

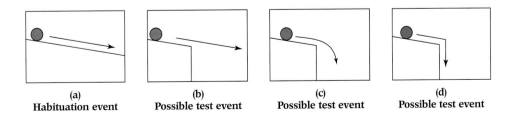

(a)	(b)	(c)	(d)
Habituation event	**Possible test event**	**Possible test event**	**Possible test event**

The Domain of Psychology

For present purposes, we shall use the term *naïve psychology* to designate a domain-specific tendency for children to understand the actions of other people in terms of those people's mental states (Wellman & Gelman, 1998). No one is precisely certain when children develop a naïve psychology, but in Chapter 4 you learned that newborns prefer visual and auditory stimuli that bear distinctive human characteristics (e.g., voices, faces), and in Chapter 5 you learned that by the end of the first year, infants possess at least an intuitive understanding that other people's actions are caused by their goals and intentions. Certainly, by the time they are 3 years old, children generally distinguish mental and physical states. For example, if 3-year-olds are told about a child who has a dog and another child who is simply thinking about a dog, they have no difficulty telling an adult which dog can actually be seen, touched, or petted (Harris, Brown, Marriot, Whittall, & Harmer, 1991; Wellman & Estes, 1986). But their grasp of the distinction between imagined and real entities is still not adultlike. As we noted earlier, they continue, in some circumstances, to confuse "pretend" and "real" objects and become afraid of a "real" monster in the closet even though the monster started out as a pretend entity (Bourchier & Davis, 2002).

In the transition from infancy to early childhood, and all during early childhood, children gain a more comprehensive idea about how other peoples' desires and beliefs are related to how they act in the world. Even at the age of 2, children are able to distinguish between their own desires and those of others. From studies of children's spontaneous speech in a wide variety of settings, developmentalists have established that by the age of 2 years, children are already capable of using terms such as "want" and "like" correctly (Wellman & Woolley, 1990; Wellman, Phillips, & Rodriguez, 2000).

If the child herself likes strawberry ice cream, but a character in a story prefers chocolate ice cream, the child will predict that the storybook character will choose chocolate ice cream. Three-year-olds, but not 2-year-olds, also seem to recognize that when someone desires something, the desire is specific to the objects of desire. Three-year-olds are also able to mentally separate desires from actions and outcomes. For example, a boy this age may desire to get his teddy bear, but go and sit on his father's lap while his grandmother patches its tattered paw (Wellman & Wooley, 1990). Three-year-olds can reason about others' desires, but they still have difficulty reasoning about others' beliefs.

Developmentalists use two techniques to determine when children develop a full theory of how people's beliefs and desires combine to shape their actions. In the first method, children are presented with a brief story and asked to predict how one of the characters in the story will behave. The story and the prediction question are designed to reveal the child's ability to think about what goes on in another person's mind. Here is a typical story and follow-up question:

> **Story:** Once there was a little boy who liked candy. One day he put a chocolate bar in a drawer and went out to play for a while. While he was gone, his mother came. She took the candy out of the drawer and put it in the kitchen. When the little boy came back he was hungry and went to get his candy.
>
> **Question:** Where do you think the little boy will look for his candy?

When 3-year-olds are asked this question, they say that the boy will look in the kitchen where *they* know the candy to be and not in the drawer where *the boy in the story* left it. In short, they respond as if the boy who left the room had the same information that they do. Five-year-olds are far more likely to say that the little boy will look in the drawer, presumably because they understand that the child who left the room has a false belief about the location of the candy.

In the second method, children themselves experience a false belief. In this version of the task, children are shown a box covered with pictures of candy, such as M&Ms, and are asked what they think is in the box. All, of course, answer, "Candy." Then they are shown that they are wrong—the box actually contains something else, such as a pencil. Next the children are asked what a friend who has not yet seen inside the box would think it contains. Even though they have just gone through the process of being deceived themselves, most 3-year-olds say that the friend will think the box contains a pencil despite the fact that it has pictures of candy on it. Five-year-olds respond correctly (Astington, 1993).

In addition, 3-year-olds will often deny that they themselves have held a false belief just minutes earlier. If asked what they first thought was in the box (candy) and are then shown that it is really pencils, they will declare that they had known there were pencils there all along (Wimmer & Hartl, 1991). This kind of result supports the idea that young children still experience difficulty thinking of things separately from the way they have represented them mentally.

However, just as evidence of the ways that young children's performance on Piagetian tasks differs according to how the problem is posed for them, there is also evidence that in some circumstances 3-year-olds can appreciate the false-belief states of others (Carpenter, Call, & Tomasello, 2002). One way to induce such young children to solve false-belief tasks is to change the social role they play in the experiment. Using a variation of the pencil-in-the-candy-box task, Kate Sullivan and Ellen Winner (1993) arranged for an adult accomplice to be present together with the child while the experiment was in progress. In their procedure, the experimenter first pulls the standard candy-box trick (described above) on the child and adult and then leaves the room. Next the adult companion suggests that she and the child play a trick on the experimenter just like the trick that the experimenter has played on them. Making a great display of being a coconspirator in the plot to fool the experimenter, the adult takes a crayon box out of her purse and helps the child remove the crayons and replace them with something unexpected. Finally, while the experimenter is still out of the room, the adult, in a hushed, conspiratorial tone, asks the child what the experimenter will think is in the crayon box when she returns. In this gamelike situation, 75 percent of 3-year-olds predicted that the experimenter would mistakenly expect crayons. This result indicates that the children were, at least in these circumstances, able to think about the thought processes of others. By comparison, only 25 percent were correct in the standard false-belief task, a rate that was in line with the typically reported results. The researchers suggest that their version of the task engaged the children in the familiar scripted activity of fooling someone else, which primed the children to think about other people's mental states.

This and a variety of corroborating evidence from false-belief tasks conducted in industrialized countries indicates that the ability to think about other people's mental states, often referred to as a **theory of mind,** is in a transition around 3 years of age and becomes more-or-less solidified when children are 4 or 5 years old (Frye, 2000; Wellman, Cross, & Watson, 2001). However, as in the case of naïve physics, children do not acquire understandings of mental states all at once, but gradually (see Table 9.2, p. 342). For example, children younger than 5 who appear to understand others' beliefs in a simple case may incorrectly evaluate others' desires when there is a conflict of desires, such as in competitive games (Moore, 1996).

The Domain of Biology

Young infants have direct experience of their physical world and other people, but their experience of other living things is generally more restricted, even if their family owns a pet, or they live on a farm or in the forest. Thus, it seems only

theory of mind The ability to think about other people's mental states and form theories of how they think.

table 9.2

Development of Theory of Mind	
Age	**Evidence for Developing Theory of Mind**
Birth	Children prefer visual and auditory stimuli that bear distinctive human characteristics (e.g., voices, faces); they selectively imitate some human actions.
4 months	Children and caretakers achieve primary intersubjectivity; they attend to each other and share simple emotions, such as happiness.
6 months	Children distinguish between different emotional expressions.
9 months	Children and caretakers achieve secondary intersubjectivity, the ability to share attention to and evaluate a common object separate from either.
10 months	Children display social referencing, sensitivity to caretaker evaluation of unusual event.
End of first year	Children possess at least an intuitive understanding that other people's actions are caused by their goals and intentions.
18–24 months	Children engage in pretend play, indicating onset of symbolic capacity needed to understand mental states of others.
3 years	Children generally distinguish mental and physical states, perceptions and desires.
4–5 years	Children are able to think about the relation between their own beliefs and those of others.

natural that knowledge in the domain of biology would develop later than knowledge about physical and psychological phenomena. At a minimum, they must come to realize that there are living things that do not have goals or intentions, and do not move spontaneously, such as plants. However, plants and animals share with humans the ability to reproduce and the need for food, among other things. To complicate matters further, sometimes there are nonliving objects, like robots, that appear to move on their own.

As in the case of naïve psychology, an important starting point for developing biological understandings is the distinction between animate and inanimate things. For example, Christine Massey and Rochel Gelman (1988) demonstrated that 3- to 4-year-olds make correct generalizations concerning living creatures based on the distinction between self-initiated and externally initiated movements. They showed the children photographs of unfamiliar objects and asked them if each of the objects could walk uphill "all by itself" (see Figure 9.9). The photographs included unfamiliar animate creatures (for example, marmoset, tarantula) and artifacts (statues of animals; objects with wheels, such as a golf caddy; and complex, rigid objects such as a camera).

Many of the 3-year-olds and most all of the 4-year-olds knew that only the live animals and not the artifacts could move uphill on their own. Even though the animals were not seen in motion, the children's comments often focused on feet and "little legs" (Gelman, 1990). This is especially interesting because as you can see from Figure 9.9, no "little legs" are visible for the animal (an echidna), yet the children said that it could walk uphill, while the statue of the four-footed animal could not.

Young children also know that living objects grow and change their appearance, in contrast to artifacts, which may be scuffed up or broken but do not grow.

Drawings by Mary McManus, images courtesy of Dr. Rochel Gelman, Rutgers.

Figure 9.9 Pictures of unfamilar creatures and artifacts used by Massey and Gelman to determine if young children distinguish between animate things (which move on their own) and inanimate things (which do not). Children judged that the clay figure on the left would not move on its own, but the echidna on the right would even though its legs are hidden.

Moreover, as illustrated by the following interview with Japanese children, they also recognize that if neglected, living things may die:

> **A boy (3 years old)** [sees sweet potatoes drooping]: "Poor thing! Are you thirsty? I give lots of water (to you). So, cheer up."

> **A girl (5 years, 5 months old)** [when asked what would happen to a tulip if it was not watered for a whole day]: "The tulip will wither. 'Cause if the tulip doesn't drink water, it won't become very lively." (Quoted in Inagaki & Hatano, 2002, p. 19)

At present, developmentalists who support the idea of a privileged domain of *naïve biology* are uncertain about the earliest origins of this domain of thinking. Some believe that it slowly differentiates itself from naïve psychology, as little children gain greater experience with living things. Others believe that as children come into contact with different kinds of living creatures, they draw analogies between themselves and other living creatures to reason about the biological world. This tendency is clearly shown in the response of an almost 6-year-old Japanese boy interviewed by Kayoko Inagaki and Giyoo Hatano. Asked if it was inevitable that a baby rabbit would grow, the child replied, "We can't keep it [the rabbit] forever the same size. Because, like me, if I were a rabbit, I would be 5 years old and become bigger and bigger" (Inagaki & Hatano, 2002, p. 51).

The Social Domain

The fourth domain identified by Hickling and Wellman applies to children's knowledge about the rules of interpersonal interaction and the social conventions that govern behavior in everyday events. Rochel Gelman and Joan Lucariello (2002) point out that in the social domain, objects (that is, people) move without being directly acted upon by others and the behavior of one person depends upon the behavior of other(s). Another major characteristic of the domain is the importance of *temporal sequence:* the order in which actions follow each other. As we noted in Chapter 8, young children acquire language in the course of routine events that have such a predictable structure to them that the events provide a *format* that supports language development. Knowledge about the rules and conventions that are expected in different events have the same character. Children acquire knowledge of appropriate social behavior simply from participating.

Judy Dunn reported that when 3-year-old English children and their mothers have a disagreement, about one-third of their disagreements are about social conventions such as the following, where a mother and her two children are in the kitchen and the mother is organizing the children to do some cooking:

Mother: Would you two like to go and wash your hands? . . . Go and wash your hands please.
Child: Why don't you wash *your* hands?
Mother: Well, it's you two that are doing the cooking. (Dunn, 1988, p. 35)

Hickling and Wellman found many examples of explanations focused on social conventional reasoning when young children are talking to each other—statements such as "[I won't chew any more gum] because my Daddy says I shouldn't" or "I have to go like that because it's a game" (Hickling & Wellman, 2001, p. 678). Such explanations as well as the mother's explanation of why her children should wash their hands clearly distinguish the social domain of reasoning from the others we have discussed previously.

Several additional examples of reasoning in the social domain will appear in Chapter 10. Social reasoning is part and parcel of the development of children's understandings of social groups and their place within them.

Explaining Domain-Specific Cognitive Development

Claims for the existence of privileged domains still do not account for the acquisition of this knowledge. There are three major approaches to explaining this knowledge acquisition. The first, referred to as *modularity theory,* relies heavily on a form of domain-specific maturation associated with innate mental faculties; the second approach combines *skeletal* principles, a weaker form of domain-specific maturational mechanisms, with the idea that children continually construct their knowledge in much the same way that scientists construct new theories; while the third approach incorporates the *culturally organized environment* as a major source of change that weaves together the contributions of biological and general cognitive factors.

Knowledge Acquisition as a Modular Process

The important role that preprogrammed brain development appears to have in cognitive growth has led some theorists to conceive of cognitive development in terms of **mental modules,** innate mental faculties that receive inputs from particular classes of objects in the environment and produce as output corresponding domain-specific information about the world (Atran, 1998; Fodor, 1983). Recognition of faces, particular patterns of motion relating objects to each other, and elementary perception of causality—all abilities present from infancy (see Chapters 4 and 5)—provide popular examples of mental modules (Pinker, 2002; Wellman & Gelman, 1998). The term *mental module* comes from the work of Noam Chomsky and his followers (see Chapter 8, pp. 298–299), who argued that many cognitive processes are like language in that they "consist of separate systems with their own properties" (Chomsky, 1988, p. 161). Such psychological processes do not need special tutoring in order to develop. They are present "at the beginning" in the normal human genome. This line of thinking is known as modularity theory.

The way in which modularity theory carries Chomsky's ideas into cognitive development more generally is revealed by the key assumptions that cognitive modularity theory shares with Chomsky's concept of the language faculty and the process of language acquisition.

1. Psychological operations are presumed to be domain specific. For each domain, the essential psychological processes apply to different objects, follow different principles, and organize human experience in a distinctive way. The mental operations required to perceive and create language are

mental modules Innate mental faculties that receive inputs from particular classes of objects and produce corresponding information about the world.

autism A mental condition defined primarily by an inability to relate normally to other people and low scores on intelligence tests.

different from those required to recognize a face; and the operations of both processes differ from those required to think about physical causation.

2. The psychological principles that organize the operation of each mental module are assumed to be *experience expectant;* that is, they are coded in the genes and need no special instruction to develop. They depend upon a fixed neural structure, they operate automatically, and they need only be "triggered" by the environment.

3. It is assumed that modules do not interact directly. Instead, they are only loosely connected to each other through a "central processor" that assembles the information from the separate modules.

In effect, there is no development at all in the sense of a series of qualitative changes in cognitive processes over time. All the essentials are a part of the module from the beginning, although they may become more complex through further maturation of their parts.

To take an example from the domain of naïve psychology, an intriguing line of evidence used by modularity theorists comes from research on a genetically induced disease called **autism.** Autism is a poorly understood condition that is defined primarily by an inability to relate normally to other people (Frith, 2003). Many autistic children score poorly on tests of intelligence (Baron-Cohen et al., 2002; Serra et al., 2002). Young autistic children rarely use language to communicate; do not engage in symbolic, pretend play; and engage in unusually repetitive movements such as rocking, spinning, or flapping their hands.

What makes autism so interesting for modularity theorists is that autistic children routinely score poorly on false-belief tasks, such as the one described earlier in this chapter. For example, children are told a story about a mother who moves a candy bar from one place to another while her child is absent (pp. 340–341). They are then asked to say where the child will look for the candy when he returns and how he will feel when he looks there. Autistic children of various ages perform like typical 3-year-olds, failing to realize that the absent child has a false belief about the location of the candy and will be disappointed when he looks in the wrong location. At the same time they may be very clever at solving mechanical puzzles such as putting together blocks to make a racing car.

In an early study to demonstrate the domain-specific nature of autism, Simon Baron-Cohen and his colleagues (1986) asked groups of young children to arrange sequences of four picture cards into a story. There were three types of stories on the cards:

Mechanical sequences depicting physical interactions between people and objects: a man kicks a rock, which rolls down a hill, then splashes in the water (Figure 9.10a, p. 346).

Behavioral sequences depicting interactions among people: one child takes an ice cream cone from another and eats it (Figure 9.10b).

Mentalistic sequences depicting stories that involve mental events: a girl puts a toy down behind her while she picks a flower. Another person comes up behind her and takes the toy; the girl looks surprised when she turns around and finds the toy gone (Figure 9.10c).

Nadia, an autistic preschooler with only minimal exposure to models, displayed an uncanny ability to capture form and movement in her drawings. This drawing is her copy of a picture of a horse.

Figure 9.10 Stimuli used to assess autistic children's ability to think about mental states. At the top of the figure is a mechanical sequence (a) showing a man kicking a rock, which rolls down a hill; the middle behavioral sequence (b) shows a girl taking an ice cream cone from a boy; the bottom mentalistic sequence (c) shows a boy taking a girl's teddy bear when her back is turned.

Figure 9.11 The level of performance achieved by normal, mentally retarded, and autistic children when asked to create meaningful mechanical, behavioral, and mentalistic sequences. Note that the autistic children are especially good at creating mechanical sequences but have even greater difficulty than retarded children when asked to create mentalistic sequences.

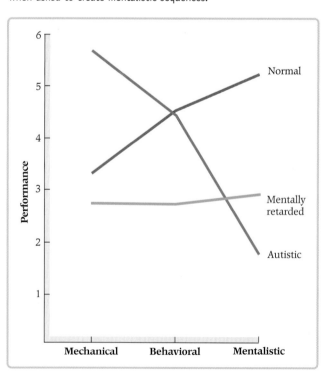

Of the 4-years-olds studied, some were autistic, some were not autistic but were mentally retarded, and some were normal. The autistic children outperformed the normal children when asked to create mechanical sequences. They are just as proficient as normal children when thinking about a behavioral sequence where the emotions of the participants are obvious. But they were unable to create meaningful mentalistic sequences (see Figure 9.11). They did not attribute the mental state of surprise to the girl whose toy disappears while her back is turned (Figure 9.10c). This evidence suggesting a domain-specific cognitive defect, coupled with the evidence of specific neurological abnormalities associated with autism, provides compelling support for the existence of a theory-of-mind module (Serra et al., 2002).

Skeletal Principles and Theory Testing

As you might anticipate from disagreements about an innate language acquisition device (Chapter 8, pp. 298–299), widespread acceptance of the biological basis for autism does not mean that all developmentalists agree that there is a theory-of-mind module that is present at birth and is uniquely associated with the affliction (Tager-Flusberg, 2001). Like all theories that propose innate mechanisms, modularity theories have difficulty explaining change by any mechanism other than maturation; they do little to specify how the environment and the child's own actions influence development. In the case of autistic children, many display marked changes when they are engaged in intensive therapeutic programs. They learn to interact with other children, to carry out simple household routines, and some are eventually able to hold jobs (Scheuermann, 2002). Such facts naturally raise the question: How does experience influence domain-specific development?

An influential approach that acknowledges the importance of biological factors in acquiring domain-specific knowledge yet includes an important role for the active, constructive efforts of the child is referred to by developmentalists as the *theory theory*. According to this approach, young children, from birth or shortly thereafter, have theories of how the world works and seek to test those theories in much the same way as do scientists (Gopnik & Wellman, 1994; Gopnik, Meltzoff, & Kuhl, 1999).

Instead of modules that provide children with "ready-made" cognitive processes, "theory theorists" assume that children are born with **skeletal principles,** innate basic cognitive principles specific to domains that have been important in evolution (Gelman & Lucariello, 2002). These domain-specific skeletal principles are important for directing infants' attention to relevant features of the environment so that they are biased to pay attention to the right cues; but active theory testing is required for development to occur.

Children's thinking within privileged domains (sometimes referred to as *core domains*)—such as physics or psychology—is like scientific theorizing in several senses. First, children's knowledge is accompanied by causal explanations. If asked why a little girl who climbs a tree and hangs from a branch soon falls to the ground, they provide a reasonable biological explanation: she is not strong enough so her arms get tired and she eventually has to let go. If asked why a little boy who declares that he is going to step off a stool and float in the air actually falls to the ground, they provide explanations such as "he is too heavy to float in the air," or "gravity brings him down." Second, their knowledge generates reasonable predictions, as a theory should. They will predict that the little boy who fails to float will be disappointed and that the little girl who drops from the tree will hurt herself if the branch is high off the ground. Although 3-year-olds may sometimes confuse biological and psychological explanations, by the time they are 4 years old, American children invoke the right kinds of theory to fit what it is that needs explaining. If the situation calls for the use of psychological explanation (where will the child look for the candy) they give a psychological explanation and if it calls for a physical explanation (why did the boy fall to the ground after stepping off a stool) they invoke a physical theory (Wellman, Hickling, & Schult, 1997).

The factors that come to bear on children's theory development are apparent in recorded conversations of Mexican-American parents and their children at specially organized science exhibitions focused on agricultural phenomena. This environment prompted children to ask questions that fall within the domain of biology. The researchers found that the parents offered domain-appropriate causal explanations. For example, when one child asked, "Why can't I water the plants too much?" his mother answered, "Because they are going to drown; they don't need that much water." Another parent used an analogy to provide a basis for the child's theory development. When asked "Why do insects eat each other?" the mother answered, "Because insects are food for other animals just like other animals are food for us." (Tenenbaum, Callanan, Alba-Speyer, & Sandoval, 2002). Sometimes parents spontaneously offered up explanations of puzzling phenomena, providing a rich source of information that confirmed or denied children's initial theories. This study highlights the important role of parents in the process of theory testing; teachers, peers, and personal experience also contribute to children's construction of their knowledge base.

The Role of Cultural Context

From a cultural context perspective, the cultural contexts that children inhabit (their developmental niches) are the places where they have the experiences that flesh out the skeletal principles that are part of their genetic endowment.

skeletal principles Domain-specific principles that get particular cognitive processes started and provide some initial direction, but require subsequent experience in order to realize their potential.

As we noted earlier, in terms of mental development, both the way children are included in ongoing activities and the ways that parents and other family members talk about the world while they are engaged with their children appear essential to the development of the privileged domains you have just been reading about.

The Mental Representation of Contexts A major task of all theories of cognitive development is to explain how children convert the world external to their bodies into mental structures that organize their thinking during the course of development. As we have seen, Piaget held that in the course of their activity, children construct schemas, organized patterns of knowledge, that represent objects and their interrelationships. Privileged-domain theorists also believe that children acquire schemas but contend that they are not as general as those proposed by Piaget.

Schemas are also important in cultural-context explanations of development, but they are conceived of somewhat differently than from any of the perspectives you have encountered so far. Katherine Nelson (1996) suggested that as a result of their participation in routine, culturally organized events, children acquire a category of schemas she refers to as *generalized event representations,* or **scripts.** Scripts are schemas that specify who participates in an event, what social roles they play, what objects they are to use during the event, and the sequence of actions that make up the event. Scripts exist both as external, cultural artifacts—the words, the customary procedures, the customs and routines that punctuate daily experience—and as internal representations of those artifacts. Scripts are, in both their internal and external aspects, tools of thought.

Initially, scripts are a good deal more external than internal. Anyone who has made the attempt knows that "taking a bath" is something an adult does *to* a 2-month-old infant. An adult fills a sink or appropriate basin with warm water, lays out a towel, a clean diaper, and clothing, then slips the infant into the water, while holding the infant tightly to keep the head above water. The infant's contribution consists of squirming around. Gradually, however, as they become stronger and more familiar with the script of bath taking (and their caregivers perfect their role as bath givers), babies acquire more competence in parts of the activity and assume a greater role in the process.

By the age of 2 years, most children have "taken" many baths. Each time, roughly the same sequence is followed, the same kinds of objects are used, the same cast

"Taking a bath" as done to an infant.

Courtesy of Sheila Cole

of characters participates, and the same kinds of talk accompany the necessary actions. Water is poured into a tub, clothes are taken off, the child gets into the water, soap is applied and rinsed off, the child gets out of the water, dries off, and gets dressed. There may be variations—a visiting friend may take a bath with the child or the child may be allowed to play with her water toys after washing—but the basic sequence has a clear pattern to it.

During early childhood, adults still play the important role of "bath giver" in the scripted routine called "taking a bath." Adults initiate children's baths, scrub their ears, wash their hair, or help them dry off. Not until adulthood will the child be responsible for the entire event, including scouring the tub and worrying about clean towels, hot water, and the money to pay for them.

Nelson points out that, as in the "taking a bath" script, children grow up inside other people's scripts. As a consequence, human beings rarely, if ever, experience the natural environment "raw." Rather, they experience the world, including such simple activities as taking a bath and eating a meal, in a way that has been prepared (cooked up!) according to the scripts prescribed by their culture.

Nelson and her colleagues have studied the growth of scripted knowledge by interviewing children and by recording the conversations of children playing together. When Nelson asked children to tell her about "going to a restaurant," for example, she obtained reports like the following:

> **Boy aged 3 years, 1 month:** "Well, you eat and then go somewhere."
> **Girl aged 4 years, 10 months:** "Okay. Now, first we go to restaurants at night-time and we, um, we, and we go and wait for a while, and then the waiter comes and gives us the little stuff with the dinners on it, and then we wait for a little bit, a half an hour or a few minutes or something, and, um, then our pizza comes or anything, and um, then when we're finished eating the salad that we order we get to eat our pizza when it's done, because we get the salad before the pizza's ready. So then when we're finished with all the pizza and all our salad, we just leave." (Nelson, 1981, p. 103)

Even these simple reports demonstrate that scripts represent *generalized* knowledge. For one thing, the children are describing general content: they are clearly referring to more than a single, unique meal. The 3-year-old uses the generalized form "you eat" rather than a specific reference to a particular time when he ate. The little girl's introduction ("First we go to restaurants at nighttime") indicates that she, too, is speaking of restaurant visits in general.

Besides containing general content, children's scripts are organized into a general structure, similar to that of adult scripts. Even very young children know that the events involved in "eating at a restaurant" do not take place haphazardly. Instead they describe a sequence: "First we do this, then we do that." Children evidently abstract the content of a script and its structure from many events and then use that knowledge to organize their behavior.

The Functions of Scripts Scripts are guides to action. They are mental representations that children and adults use to figure out what is likely to happen next in familiar circumstances. Until children have acquired a large repertoire of scripted knowledge, they must use a lot of mental effort to construct scripts as they participate in unfamiliar events. When they lack scripted knowledge, they must pay attention to the details of each new activity. As a consequence, they may be less likely to distinguish between the essential and the superficial features of a novel context. The little girl interviewed by Nelson, for example, seemed to think that eating pizza is a basic part of the "going to a restaurant" script, whereas paying for the meal was entirely absent. However, because the little girl has grasped a small part of the restaurant script, and going to restaurants is a routine activity in her family, she will be free to attend to new aspects of the setting the next time she encounters it. Over time, she will gain a deeper understanding of the events she participates in and the contexts of which they are a part.

A second function of scripts is to allow people within a given social group to coordinate their actions with each other. This function of scripts becomes possible because, according to the cultural-contextualist perspective, script knowledge is knowledge generally held in common, including its embodiment in a common language. "Without shared scripts," Nelson says, "every social act would need to be negotiated afresh." In this sense, "the acquisition of scripts is

scripts Event schemas that specify who participates in an event, what social roles they play, what objects they are to use during the event, and the sequence of actions that make up the event.

Participation in scripted activities, such as Caterina's birthday party in the Tuscany region of Italy, provide a context within which children can develop more complex understandings of their culture's basic concepts and ways of doing things.

central to the acquisition of culture" (Nelson, 1981, pp. 109, 110). When children go to the average restaurant in the United States, they learn that first you ask the host or hostess for a table and are assigned a seat. A somewhat different script applies to fast-food restaurants. Discoordination can result if the script is violated (for example, if the child were to enter a restaurant and sit down at a table where an elderly stranger was midway through a meal).

A third function of scripts is to provide a means by which abstract concepts that apply to many kinds of events can be acquired and organized. When, for example, children acquire scripts for having a meal at home, having a meal at their grand-parents' house, and having a meal at a restaurant, they are accumulating specific examples of "having a meal" that they can then subsume in a general category.

The Special Role of Language Central to the cultural-context view of cognitive development is the special role that language plays in the process of children's participation in culturally organized activities (Nelson, 2003; Rogoff, 2003). As Barabara Rogoff emphasizes, language bridges gaps in understanding between

Cultural variations in the developmental niches that children occupy have a strong influence on the skills they learn and the values they will adopt in later life.

people, and allows them to coordinate in shared activities. The words of a language, and the ways in which these words are used in everyday contexts, provide children with ready-made templates for the meanings and distinctions that are important in their community.

Considerations of language are important for thinking about the nature of privileged domains because cultures vary widely in how they talk about them. For example, there is ample evidence from cultures around the world that there is enormous variety in the extent and ways that mental states and actions are conceived (Lillard, 1998; Vinden, 2002). In terms of sheer number, English is at one extreme of the continuum, possessing more than 5000 words for emotions alone. By contrast, the Chewong people of Malaysia are reported to have only five terms to cover the entire range of mental processes, translated as *want, want very much, know, forget, miss* or *remember* (Howell, 1984).

At present, evidence from cultures where mental terminology is sparse does not give a clear picture of whether the lack of mental terms in a language slows down, or even eliminates altogether, the development of the kind of naïve psychology found in the United States, Europe, and other industrialized countries where such language is prevalent. In some cases, there appears to be no lag in performance, for example, on standard false belief tasks (Avis & Harris, 1991). In other cases, there does seem to be a significant delay and in still other cases it appears that the sort of theory of mind assumed to be universal by privileged domain theorists does not appear at all (Vinden, 1999, 2002).

Within countries where talk about minds and mental processes is prevalent, it remains the case that children who grow up in households where the parents engage in more conversation about mental processes in the course of their daily interactions acquire competence in the standardized tests for theory of mind more rapidly (Nelson et al., 2003).

The influence of language and cultural variation on presumably privileged domains is not restricted to the domain of naïve psychology. Reporting on work among the Tainae of Papua New Guinea, Penelope Vinden found that people believe that certain among them can literally transform themselves from humans into pigs or other animals, and that such a pig can (and does) physically assault young children. Such beliefs defy the distinction we ordinarily make between human beings, animals, and inanimate natural objects, calling into question the universality of naïve biology distinct from a naïve psychology. Nor are such beliefs rare among human societies, including our own, where, for example, surveys show that a majority of the adult population believes in the existence of angels who can take the form of human beings and cause changes in the events of everyday life, defying the distinction between a naïve psychology and biology. (See the box "Believing the Imaginable: 'Stone Soup' Revisited," p. 352.)

Reviewing the literature on the development of privileged domains, Giyoo Hatano argued that because innately specified knowledge is still *skeletal* it is essential to study the ways in which cultural groups organize children's experience to enhance, and perhaps in some cases, to modify the knowledge endowed by evolution (Hatano & Inagaki, 2002). For example, young children arrive at preschool with skeletal knowledge about fish and animals, but experience is needed to flesh out that knowledge. Keiko Inagaki (1990) arranged for some 5-year-olds to raise goldfish at home while a comparison group had no such experience. The goldfish raisers soon displayed far richer knowledge about the development of fish than their counterparts who had not raised fish. They could even apply what they learned about fish to frogs. If asked, for example, "Can you keep the frog in its bowl forever?" they answered, "No, we can't because goldfish grow bigger. My goldfish were small before, but now they are big" (quoted in Hatano & Inagaki, 2000, p. 272).

Believing the Imaginable: "Stone Soup" Revisited

Despite many differences among them, theories of cognitive development share one characteristic that is particularly obvious when talking about early childhood: they assume that cognitive development moves in the direction of more rational, logical, and effective ways of thinking and away from magical thinking. Thus, for Piaget, the development of thought is the development of ever-more powerful and inclusive forms of logic. "Theory theorists" believe that from a very early age, if not from birth, children are developing ever-more powerful theories in the manner of scientists (Gopnik et al., 1999). As Carol Nemeroff and Paul Rozin (2000, p. 2) put it, "Magic is seen as false or failed science, and its primary flaw is its assumption that the world of reality functions according to the same principles as our thoughts."

In recent years, however, a number of psychologists have argued that this view of cognitive development is misguided. Instead, rational thinking does not erase magical thinking. Rather, magical thinking is seen as a natural and intuitive way of thinking that continues to exist alongside rational thinking in a "fight for dominance" all during life (Subbotsky, 2001). There is a growing body of evidence to support the belief that even highly educated adults, for whom scientific logic is very important, retain magical thinking as an important part of their modes of thinking. In early 2002, for example, a survey conducted by the Scripps School of Journalism and Ohio University revealed that substantial numbers of Americans believe in supernatural entities that visit earth. The survey asked 1127 adults about their attitudes concerning angels. Approximately 80 percent of those who had attended some college said they believed that angels come to earth and enter into human affairs, and 20 percent claimed to have had personal interactions with angels (Scripps Howard News Service, 2002). Just a few years earlier, anthropologist Tanya Luhrmann (1989) conducted a study among highly educated people working in technical fields who believed in witchcraft and professed to employ magic in their lives.

Studying developmental changes in the magical thinking of British children, Eugene Subbotsky demonstrated that while magical thinking about physical causality appears to decrease all during childhood, older children or adults will revert to such thinking when confronted with physical phenomena they cannot understand and that carry some potential danger for them—even if they deny that magic is possible (Subbotsky, 2001). To make this point, Subbotsky created a special box with hidden spaces in it so that he could make objects mysteriously disappear or transform. For example, he would open the box, show that it was empty, and then place a stamp in the box. After saying a few "magical words" the child or adult was asked to open the box to find that the stamp was cut in half. Under these circumstances, children 9 years old and adults rejected magical explanations, although they could not explain what happened and when allowed to search the box as thoroughly as they liked.

However, when Subbotsky asked people to put something they highly valued, such as their drivers' licenses, in the box and asked them if it would be all right to say the "magic words," many adults refused to allow him to do so. Although they rejected magical explanations in a hypothetical, verbal situation, they were not willing to take the chance of ruling out magic altogether.

In many parts of the world belief in magic is more pervasive than it is in industrialized societies. When Subbotsky and his colleague repeated this experiment in rural Mexico, they did not need to put valuable possessions at risk. Adults readily accepted the idea that the experimenters could, indeed, perform magical acts. In fact, villagers feared them because of their presumed powers. (Subbotsky & Quinteros, 2002).

According to the view of those currently studying the development of magical thinking, it exists because of its local, real-world value, not because of its rational failure. Nemeroff and Rozin suggest two major functions that make magical thinking attractive to adults as well as children. First, it provides a sense of understanding and control. No one understands all the events they witness or participate in. Facing the unknown and unexplained can be frightening; the belief in magic provides the self-confidence not to give in to feelings of helplessness. Second, it provides a feeling of connection, and meaning for what otherwise would seem like meaningless events—the sudden loss of a loved one, an unexplained illness, or the sudden good fortune of a neighbor (Nemeroff & Rozin, 2000).

Existing evidence confirms the critical role of participation in everyday activities for the development of young children's thinking in privileged domains. Together, the combination of privileged domains and activities that elaborate on them provide a plausible account of young children's cognitive development.

Cultural Context and the Unevenness of Development

Once children leave the confines of their cribs and their caregivers' arms, they begin to experience a great variety of contexts that compel them to acquire a variety of new scripts, even as they refine their knowledge of the scripts with which they are already familiar. Thus it is natural, according to the cultural-context approach, that development during early childhood should appear to be so uneven. The content and structure of the new events in which young children participate will depend crucially on the activities provided by their culture and on the roles they are expected to play within those activities. In familiar contexts, where they know the expected sequence of actions and can properly interpret the requirements of the situation, young children are most likely to behave in a logical way and adhere to adult standards of thought. But when the contexts are unfamiliar, they may apply inappropriate scripts and resort to magical or illogical thinking.

Overall, cultures influence the unevenness of children's development in several basic ways (Laboratory of Comparative Human Cognition, 1983; Rogoff, 2003; Super & Harkness, 2002):

1. *By arranging the occurrence and nonoccurrence of specific activities:* One cannot learn about something without observing or hearing about it. A 4-year-old growing up among the !Kung of the Kalahari Desert is unlikely to learn about taking baths in bathtubs or pouring water from one glass to another. Children growing up in Seattle are unlikely to be skilled at finding water-bearing roots in a desert.

2. *By determining the frequency of basic activities:* Dancing is an activity found in all societies, but all societies do not focus equally on dancing. Owing to the importance placed on traditional dancing in Balinese culture, many children growing up in Bali become skilled dancers by the age of 4 (McPhee, 1970), while Norwegian children are more likely to become good skiers and skaters.

3. *By how they relate different activities:* If pottery making is a valued activity, children are not only likely to become skilled pottery makers but to learn a variety of related skills as well. When molding clay is associated with making pottery, it is experienced in the company of a whole host of related activities: digging from a quarry, firing clay, glazing clay, painting designs, and selling the products. Molding clay as part of a nursery school curriculum will be associated with a distinctively different pattern of experiences, skills, and knowledge.

4. *By regulating the child's role in the activity:* Children enter most activities as novices who bear little responsibility for the outcome. As their roles and responsibilities change, so do the specialized abilities they develop.

Reconciling Alternative Approaches

By this point, you should be convinced that the exceedingly uneven and complex picture that emerges from studies of childhood thought in the first few years following infancy cannot be explained by any single approach. Although a strong case can be made for domain-specific knowledge acquisition, clearly development and developmental change are not *entirely* domain specific. If they were, children would not be able to generalize what they know from one domain to another; their "islands of competence" would be *completely* isolated. Young children's behavioral competence is uneven, but it is not incoherent and chaotic. General and domain-specific aspects of behavior live side by side in the same child. Young children's abilities sometimes appear to change rapidly in a stagelike sequence; but at other times it appears that variability and gradual change are the rules.

In recognition of these circumstances, there have been a number of attempts at formulating more inclusive theories that are capable of accounting for *both* the generality and the domain-specificity of young children's development *and* its multiple sources *and* the fact that it sometimes appears to occur in discontinuous leaps and at other times as a process of gradual change.

One influential attempt at synthesis of rival perspectives was proposed by developmental psychologist Robbie Case (Case & Okamoto, 1996). Case and his colleagues included maturational, biological factors, particularly growth of the brain, as central to cognitive change. Like Piaget and those who view the child as a scientist testing theories, they retain the idea that the child actively constructs knowledge. From the information-processing approaches they adopt the idea that increases in basic, general cognitive abilities such as memory capacity strongly influence both the process of change and the level of performance. From the domain-specific approach they emphasize that stagelike changes are most likely to be seen in specific domains and even then, only under specially crafted circumstances. And from the cultural-context theorists they adopt the idea that different cultures will provide different amounts of experience in different domains.

Robert Siegler's "wave theory" of cognitive change represents another attempt at synthesis, but from a different point of view (see Figure 9.7, p. 336). Siegler seeks to unify different theories around the idea that developmental change arises from a multitude of processes that operate universally. Because of the way these processes are combined, in particular circumstances, what appears to be a stage is simply the result of a sufficiently fine-grained analysis of the multiple processes of change operating simultaneously. This view has gained many adherents in recent years as developmentalists have come to realize the tremendous variability in human development, depending, as it does, on so many factors converging to shape behavior at any given moment. These include the nature of the task, the level of maturation of relevant brain functions, the familiarity of the task, the availability of appropriate tools, and the presence or absence of supporting others, to name just a few of the many factors you have encountered in this chapter.

Developmentalist Kurt Fischer has proposed a synthesis in which Siegler's notion of development as the gradual replacement of one dominant strategy by another is *not* incompatible with the idea of stagelike change. Fischer has shown that whether change appears continuous and gradual, or abrupt and stagelike, depends crucially upon the relationship between the specific cognitive process being investigated and the context in which it occurs. Fischer has demonstrated that under conditions of optimal support from the context, increases in the level of children's performance go through a series of stagelike changes. But when support is low (and a child has many distracting problems to deal with simultaneously) change is continuous (see Figure 9.12).

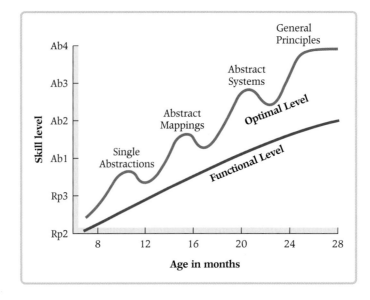

Figure 9.12 A representation of Fischer's solution to the problem of whether developmental change is stagelike or gradual. The curve marked "optimal level" depicts Fischer's findings that when children are given maximally supportive conditions, change in their cognitive abilities (here indicated as levels of abstraction) is abrupt and stagelike, while under less optimal conditions change is gradual. (From Fischer & Yan, 2002.)

On the basis of such results, Fischer argues that "context affects the developmental level or stage of a person's competence even when the effects of experience and domain are controlled for" (Fischer, Bullock, Rotenberg, & Raya, 1993). Consequently, children cannot be characterized by a single developmental level reflecting their personal competence, even when assessment is restricted to a single domain. The culturally organized context of which the performance is an element must always be taken into account.

You are now in a better position to appreciate why there could be continuing doubts about the reality of a developmental period dubbed "early childhood." If one considers the criteria for distinguishing a developmental stage presented in Chapter 1 (pp. 9–10) each is brought into question by the data on early childhood: it is difficult to identify a unique quality that defines it as a stage; change is slow and uneven, not rapid and pervasive; and no single, coherent pattern of changes across domains is evident. In fact, early childhood, with its uneven development and slow, piecemeal changes, seems almost to represent an "anti-stage." No wonder, then, that Piaget and Inhelder, in a popularized summary of his theory, referred to the years from 2 to 6 as a "time of organization and preparation" for the full-blown appearance of operational thinking, and not a distinctive stage of its own (Piaget & Inhelder, 1969, p. 96).

S U M M A R Y

- Young children's thought processes are characterized by great unevenness; islands of competence exist in a sea of uncertainty and naïveté.

Bio-Behavioral Foundations of Early Childhood Thinking

- Between their third and sixth birthdays, increased size, dexterity, and language ability contribute to young children's greater behavioral capacities and enhanced abilities to broaden their range of experiences.

- The brain, which is approximately 50 percent of its mature size at the start of early childhood, will achieve 90 percent of adult size over the next three years.

Focusing on General Processes of Cognitive Change

- Many developmentalists focus on general processes of change to account for the special characteristics of early childhood, although they differ in their specific accounts.

- Piaget's explanation of thought during early childhood stresses its one-sided nature: the inability to think simultaneously about two aspects of a problem in relation to each other causes children to "center" on the most salient feature of the problem.

- Cognitive limitations that Piaget associated with egocentric thought include the inability to take the perspective of another person, to understand other people's thought processes, to distinguish appearance from reality, and to reason about cause and effect.

- Many believe that the unevenness of children's thought is greater than Piaget realized, calling into question his explanation of the preoperational stage.

- Using natural observations and experimental methods that used toys as props and often engaged children in gamelike situations revealed that under a variety of circumstances, children appear to display the cognitive abilities that Piaget thought lacking.

- Contemporary Piagetians seek to refine his theory and to demonstrate the inadequacy of apparent demonstrations that he underestimated the abilities of young children.

- According to the information-processing view, Piaget's account of development is too vague and his emphasis on stagelike change is incorrect.

- Information-processing theorists conceive of cognitive development as a process of expanding the young child's limited attentional, memory, and problem-solving capacities.

- Information-processing theorists conceive of thought processes using the analogy of a digital computer.

- The unevenness of young children's thought is explained by differences in children's knowledge base and the demands made by the various tasks used to evaluate their thinking.

Focusing on Domain-Specific Approaches to Cognitive Change

- A number of developmentalists have come to the conclusion that cognitive development is first and foremost organized around basic conceptual domains of evolutionary importance such as physics, psychology, and biology.

- Studies of 2- to 3-year-olds' language use in everyday settings provide evidence that these domains, as well as the domain of social interaction and social conventions, are prevalent in young children's speech.

- A wide variety of experimental studies support the notion that these domains are present in skeletal form early in children's development and develop further during early childhood.

- Domain-specificity theorists differ in how they conceive of these domains and the mechanisms of change.

  1. According to some, the brain is organized into mental modules that are domain specific, innately structured, and relatively isolated from one another. Physics, psychology, and biology are a subset of these domains. The mental capacities of autistic children, who are unable to think about the mental processes of others but may have precocious mechanical abilities, are used to support this hypothesis.

  2. According to others, innate organization of the brain is restricted to skeletal principles that must be fleshed out by active theory testing on the part of the child, which operates according to the same mechanisms of theory testing used by adult scientists. From this perspective, both differential development of different brain structures and differential experience account for the unevenness of young children's cognitive development.

  3. In the cultural-context view, the mental aspects of everyday events are generalized event representations, or scripts, which adults and children use to organize their joint activity. Evidence of cultural variation in vocabulary as well as performance on a variety of experimental tasks point to the role of culture and language in shaping mental connections between domains.

Reconciling Alternative Approaches

- Various attempts are under way to reconcile competing perspectives.
- One strategy, focused on conceptual structures, has combined Piagetian ideas about children's active construction of knowledge, information-processing theorists' ideas about mechanisms of change, domain-specificity theorists' ideas about specific knowledge domains, and cultural-context theorists' emphasis on the way cultures emphasize different domains in their everyday practices.

- Alternative approaches seek to reconcile the evidence of gradual change with stagelike change.
- Researchers systematically vary the amount of support given for performing an unfamiliar cognitive task to show that development appears stagelike when support is present and continuous when it is not.
- The various theories of early childhood development are best treated as complementary perspectives, rather than as competing explanations.

Key Terms

autism, p. 345

egocentrism, p. 324

information-processing approach, p. 332

long-term memory, p. 334

mental modules, p. 344

mental operations, p. 323

precausal thinking, p. 327

preoperational stage, p. 323

privileged domains, p. 338

scripts, p. 348

sensory register, p. 334

short-term (working) memory, p. 334

skeletal principles, p. 347

theory of mind, p. 341

Thought Questions

1. Suppose you were Piaget and you were confronted with evidence that even young infants appear to be surprised when the events they observe contradict laws of physical location. How might you interpret the data to fit your theory that young children are precausal thinkers?

2. In what ways is the biologically inspired concept of a mental module similar to the constructivist concept of a skeletal principle? In what ways do the two approaches differ?

3. Give an example of magical thinking you have observed among fellow college students. Why does this form of thinking persist into adulthood?

4. What is the strongest evidence for the idea of privileged knowledge domains? What evidence most strongly calls this idea into question?

5. How is it possible to reconcile the view that early childhood represents a stage of cognitive development with evidence that cognitive change follows the same course of change throughout childhood?

Social Development in Early Childhood

> "*The incorporation of the individual as a member of a community, or his adaptation to it, seems like an almost unavoidable condition which has to be filled before he can attain the objective of happiness. . . . Individual development seems to us a product of the interplay of two trends, the striving for happiness, generally called 'egoistic,' and the impulse towards merging with others in the community, which we call 'altruistic.'*"
>
> —Sigmund Freud, Civilization and Its Discontents

There is a dark point in many children's lives when they realize that everyone else in the house stays up beyond the time that they are put to bed. In the case of one little girl, the realization brought with it a good deal of curiosity about what went on after her bedroom light went out—as well as a creeping sense of injustice. She imagined, her mother told us, that her family watched cartoons, ate ice cream, and had their friends over to play. The mother remembers one discussion on the subject particularly well. Like many similar conversations, it began with the little girl asking, as she was settled into bed, "What are you gonna do now?"

"Well," her mother replied, "maybe read a little or watch some TV."

"I want to do that, too," said the little girl.

"No, you need to go to bed."

"Why don't you go to bed?"

"I'm not sleepy yet."

"Well, I'm not sleepy, too."

"That may be," her mother conceded, "but you are a little girl, and little girls need lots of sleep so they can grow up big and strong like their mommies."

The mother believed her logic was unassailable. After all, mothers have been making exactly this argument for generations. The little girl, however, was unmoved. She looked at her mother and declared, matter-of-factly, "I am not a little girl anymore." Naturally, the mother was charmed to think that at the tender age of three her daughter had become, in her own eyes at least, a big girl.

"Oh?" said the mother, playing along, "So you're not a little girl anymore? Well then, what are you?"

And with the sobriety of none but a three-year old, the little girl replied, "I am a possum."

She was quite serious in her declaration, and even went on to remind her mother of the nocturnal habits of the species, this being their main attraction at the moment. It was around this time, too, that she became engaged to Chester, her cat. It was a drawn-out affair that she finally broke off in kindergarten when she met and fell head over heels in love with a classmate named Christine.

There is only a small window of time in children's development when they take their own identity as a simple matter of expedience that allows them to become a possum, for example, if it serves their purpose, and when there are no obstacles to true love and marriage. Over the course of early childhood, as you will discover in this chapter, children develop a relatively stable sense of their identities as boys or

In addition to fulfilling a traditional role in a wedding ceremony, these little flower girls are learning about many important aspects of the social roles and behaviors expected of them when they grow up.

girls, as members of particular ethnic or racial groups, and as distinct individuals in their own right. This chapter will explore how children develop a sense of themselves in relation to the societies in which they live, a process known as *social development.*

Social development is a two-sided process in which children simultaneously become integrated into the larger social community and differentiated as distinctive individuals. One side of social development is **socialization,** the process by which children acquire the standards, values, and knowledge of their society. The other side of social development is **personality formation,** the process through which children develop their own unique patterns of feeling, thinking, and behaving in a wide variety of circumstances.

As you shall see in this and later chapters, societies around the world differ markedly in the ways that their members conceive of the relationship between individuals and their communities. Of special interest has been the extent to which the dominant values of a society place greater emphasis on the independence of individuals or on their interdependence with other members of their social group (Greenfield, 2002). Since the very meaning of the term "social development" depends on the relationship between the individual and the community, it should be no surprise that cultural variations in social development are an especially active area of contemporary research (Rubin et al., 1998; Turiel, 2002).

The process of socialization begins as soon as a child is born and her father says, for example, "She could be a concert pianist with these long fingers," or her mother remarks, "Or a basketball player." Such predictions are not just idle talk. The beliefs that give rise to such statements lead parents to shape their child's experience in ways they deem appropriate. Socialization continues as an aspect of every encounter children have with other members of their society, as they learn to eat and sleep on a schedule, to prefer clothes appropriate to their gender, to be polite to their elders, to take their vitamins, and to love their siblings.

Both adults and children play active roles in social development. Adults communicate to children how they should behave; display pleasure or disapproval with the way they do behave; and reward, ignore, or punish them accordingly. Adults also select the neighborhoods their children live in, the day-care centers or preschools they attend, and other contexts in which they become conversant with their culture's funds of knowledge and rules of behavior. But children do not automatically or passively absorb the lessons adults intend. They interpret and select from the many socializing messages they receive. For example, if 4-year-old Mark admires his older cousin Eric and wants to be like him, will he imitate Eric's socially appropriate style of dress, his socially inappropriate use of slang, or both? In addition, children have goals of their own—staying up past the usual bedtime, for example. As a consequence, conflict is as much a part of socialization as nurturing and caring.

Part of this important process involves the ability to think about **social roles,** categories that reflect social expectations about the child's rights, duties, and obligations, as well as appropriate forms of behavior. In the passage above, the mother refers to such social roles—"you are a little girl"; little girls grow up to be "like their mommies." It is not sufficient for children simply to learn what adults mean by words such as "little girl" and "mommies"; it is also necessary for them to learn to fill these social roles in ways that correspond to adults' expectations and values. The little girl exhibits budding awareness that certain categories correspond to specific behaviors—she claimed to be a possum in order to stay up late. The mother, however, redirects the girl toward culturally meaningful categories and labels. She identifies the social role ("little girl") and specifies behaviors appropriate to the label, including getting plenty of sleep. It is not surprising that adults take the necessity of socializing their children for granted. What is remarkable is that most children come to accept the socially prescribed roles and rules as reasonable and even necessary.

The second side of social development, **personality,** is the unique pattern of temperament, emotions, interests, and intellectual abilities that a child develops as the child's innate propensities and capacities are shaped by his or her social interactions with kin and community. Since no two people have precisely the same experiences, no two people ever have precisely the same personality, not even identical twins.

The early origins of personality are no less visible at birth than the presence of socializing influences. As we saw in Chapter 4 (p. 136), neonates display individual differences in characteristic levels of activity, responses to frustration, and readiness to engage in novel experiences. We referred to these patterns of responsivity and associated emotional states as *temperamental traits* and noted that temperament is moderately stable over time: children who draw back from novel experiences in infancy, for example, are more likely to behave shyly when they first enter a nursery school.

Although temperamental traits provide a foundation for personality, by the time children reach the age of 3 or 4, there is more to their personalities than temperament (Thomas & Chess, 1989). We cannot say that a child is honest or compulsive at birth, because there is no temperamental characteristic corresponding to honesty or compulsiveness, or to a host of other personality characteristics. Those characteristics are gradually acquired as children's initial temperamental styles of interacting with their environments are integrated with their developing cognitive understanding, emotional responses, and habits (Sanson et al., 2002).

An important aspect of personality is the way in which children come to conceive of themselves in relation to other people — their **self-concept.** Self-concept provides a double-sided link between personality and social development that was described at the turn of the century by one of the founders of developmental psychology, James Mark Baldwin (1902):

> The development of the child's personality could not go on at all without the constant modification of his sense of himself by suggestions from others. So he himself, at every stage, is really in part someone else, even in his own thought of himself. (p. 23)

Personality formation and socialization are in constant tension as children discover the dilemma that their individual desires and ideas often conflict with their culture's norms and the desires of others. A 5-year-old boy who sucks his thumb may be discouraged from doing so by his parents and teased by his peers. A child who is jealous of the attention her baby brother receives must learn that she cannot get what she wants by pinching him and that she must find some socially acceptable way to gain her mother's attention and to deal with her socially unacceptable feelings.

During early childhood, children learn a great deal about the roles they are expected to play, how to behave in accordance with social standards, how to control aggressive feelings, and how to respect the rights of others. But these are difficult lessons and not every child is able to, or cares to, comply with adult expectations. With increasing age, children learn not only how to be "good" but also how to manipulate situations in order to upset those around them (Turiel, 2002).

As they gain experience interacting with a variety of people, young children develop a more explicit sense of themselves, their abilities, and the ways in which they can use to their own advantage the rules and tools that society is attempting to press upon them. The resulting changes in social development do not, of course, occur independently of the biological and cognitive changes discussed in Chapter 9. Socialization, personality formation, biological maturation, and cognitive development occur simultaneously.

social development A two-sided process in which children simultaneously become integrated into the larger social community and differentiated as distinctive individuals.

socialization The process by which children acquire the standards, values, and knowledge of their society.

personality formation The process through which children develop their own unique patterns of feeling, thinking, and behaving in a wide variety of circumstances.

social roles Categories that reflect adult expectations about the child's rights, duties, and obligations, as well as appropriate forms of behavior.

personality The unique pattern of temperament, emotions, interests, and intellectual abilities that a child develops as the child's innate propensities and capacities are shaped by his or her social interactions with kin and community.

self-concept The way in which children come to conceive of themselves in relation to other people.

Acquiring a Social and Personal Identity

Developmentalists agree that one factor essential to the process of socialization is **identification,** a psychological process in which children try to look, act, feel, and be like significant people in their social environment. They disagree, however, about the mechanisms by which identification is achieved.

The development of identification can be studied with respect to almost any social category—a family, a religious group, a neighborhood clique, or a nationality. The overwhelming majority of studies on identification in early childhood, however, focus on the acquisition of sex roles. Consequently, we will devote the lion's share of our attention to this social category before turning to ethnic identity, an especially important social category in today's world and one that has been the object of increased research by developmentalists.

Sex-Role Identity

If an infant wearing nothing but a bright-eyed smile and a diaper was placed in your arms, you would probably have a hard time determining the baby's sex. Not so for the 3-year old! In the short span of three years, children come to behave in ways that give clear signals about whether they are boys or girls (Golombok & Hines, 2002). By the time they enter preschool, boys and girls differ in both *what* they play and *how* they play. They have distinctly different toy preferences, and boys are more active and rough-and-tumble, whereas girls tend to be more verbal and nurturing. Even their selection of playmates becomes gender-typed. By age 3, girls prefer to play with other girls, and boys prefer other boys, a phenomenon observed throughout the world and known as **gender segregation.**

Because sex-role identity is so central to adult experience, the question of how children acquire a personal sense of their sex-role identity and how they interpret that sex role* is of great interest to developmental psychologists (Eckes & Trautner, 2000). Here we will explore three major views of sex-role identity development: psychodynamic, environmental-learning, and cognitive.

The Psychodynamic View: Identification through Differentiation and Affiliation

By far, the best-known account of sexual identity formation is that of Sigmund Freud (1921/1949, 1933/1964). Although many of Freud's specific hypotheses about development have not been substantiated, he remains an influential theorist. Certainly, many parents can tell stories of "Freudian moments" when their own young children began to test the boundaries between their personal desires and culturally accepted behavior, as reflected in the following conversations:

> "When I grow up," says [4-year-old] Jimmy at the dinner table, "I'm gonna marry Mama."
> "Jimmy's nuts," says the sensible voice of 8-year-old Jane. "You can't marry Mama and anyway, what would happen to Daddy?" . . .
> "He'll be old," says [Jimmy], through a mouthful of string beans. "And he'll be dead."
> Then, awed by the enormity of his words, [Jimmy] adds hastily, "But he might not be dead, and maybe I'll marry Marcia instead." (Fraiberg, 1959, pp. 202–203)

---

* Some psychologists recommend the use of the word "gender" instead of "sex" when this topic is discussed because they believe that the term "sex" implies that all sex-typed behavior is ultimately determined by biology. Others argue against the term "gender," which they think implies that sex-linked behavior is ultimately determined by the environment. We will use both "sex" and "gender" in contexts where they appear most appropriate, without implying either that sex/gender roles are basically biological or that they are basically environmental.

The next conversation took place when Mike and Sheila's daughter, Jenny, was 4 years old. She was lying on her mother's side of her parents' bed, watching her mother comb her hair:

Jenny: You know, Mommy, when you die I am going to marry Daddy.
Sheila: I don't think so.
Jenny: *(nodding her head gravely)* I am, too.
Sheila: You can't. It's against the laws of God and man.
Jenny: *(close to tears)* But I want to.
Sheila: *(going to comfort her)* You'll have your own husband when you grow up.
Jenny: No, I won't! I want Daddy. I don't like you, Mommy.

The 4-year-olds' thinking in these conversations is easy to understand. Both children have had several years to observe the family life around them. Jimmy knows that he is a boy, and Jenny knows that she is a girl. Although neither has a deep understanding of what these labels imply, they know that they want the things that big boys and big girls have. The "big girl" in Jenny's household has a special relationship with Daddy. The "big boy" in Jimmy's household has a special relationship with Mommy. At this early stage of sex-role identification, the best way children can think of to get what they want is literally to take the place of the person they want to be like, to "stand in the person's shoes" (or sleep on that person's side of the bed).

Boys and girls in early childhood tend to choose same-sex parents as models to identify with. Yet the developmental paths that bring the two sexes to their respective identities differ in at least one respect. Although family configurations vary widely both within and among societies, the person who usually looms largest in the lives of both boys and girls during the first 2 years of life is the mother. She is likely to be the single greatest source of physical comfort, food, and attention for the very young child, whether a boy or a girl. She is, in Freud's terms, the "first love object." But while little girls soon begin to identify with their mothers, little boys generally do not.

As children enter their third year, their demonstrations of strong and obvious attachment to their mothers diminish (see Chapter 6, p. 235). During this period of early childhood, the feeling of "wanting to be near" that is dominant in infancy is supplanted by "wanting to be like."

For boys, becoming like their father requires that they become different from the person with whom they have had the closest relationship: their mother. Girls, on the other hand, seek to become like the person with whom they have had the closest relationship. Disagreements about the implications of this sex-linked difference in developmental goals have sparked intense debate about the process by which children acquire the sex-role identification they will have as adults. Indeed, Freud proposed that boys and girls go through two, quite different, processes of identity formation.

By Freud's account, when Jimmy says that he wants to "marry Mama," he is playing out the universal male predicament of boys around the age of 3 or 4, the dilemma of the **phallic stage** of development, which follows the oral and anal stages in Freud's theory of development. It is in this period that children begin to regard their own genitals as a major source of pleasure. Here's how Freud (1940/1964) saw the conflict that this new pleasure evokes:

> In a word, his early awakened masculinity seeks to take his father's place with [his mother]; his father has hitherto in any case been an envied model to the boy, owing to the physical strength he perceives in him and the authority with which he finds him clothed. His father now becomes a rival who stands in his way and whom he would like to get rid of. (p. 189)

identification A psychological process in which children try to look, act, feel, and be like significant people in their social environment.

gender segregation The term for the preference of girls to play with other girls, and boys to play with other boys.

phallic stage In Freudian theory, the period around the fourth year when children begin to regard their own genitals as a major source of pleasure.

Many young boys are fascinated by their father's act of shaving, just as many young girls are fascinated by their mother's act of applying makeup. Seldom, however, do children become fascinated with the cosmetic rituals of the other-sex parent. Why this is the case would be explained differently by each of the major theoretical perspectives.

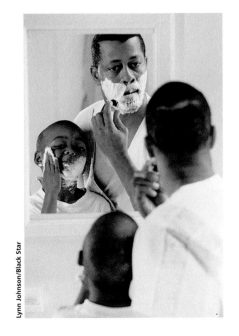

Lynn Johnson/Black Star

Oedipus complex In Freudian theory, the fear, guilt, and conflict evoked by a little boy's desire to get rid of his father and take the father's place in his mother's affections.

These feelings cause Jimmy a lot of mental anguish. He is old enough to know that feelings like wanting your father to die are bad, and he is young enough to believe that his parents, who are powerful figures in his life, are always aware of what he is thinking. So he lives in fear of being punished and feels guilty about his bad thoughts.

Freud called this predicament the **Oedipus complex,** referring to the ancient Greek tragedy in which Oedipus, king of Thebes, unknowingly kills his father and marries his mother. Little boys do not, of course, literally repeat this tragedy. Rather, according to Freud, as they leave infancy and enter childhood, boys must mentally reorder their emotional attachments by distancing themselves from their mothers and becoming closer to their fathers. In other words, they must *differentiate* themselves from their mothers and *affiliate* with their fathers. This process is driven by complex social emotions such as guilt and envy.

The key event in the development of a girl's sex-role identity, according to Freud, is her discovery that she does not have a penis: the girl is "mortified by the comparison with boys' far superior equipment" (Freud, 1933/1964, p. 126). She blames her mother for this "deficiency" and transfers her love to her father. Then she competes with her mother for her father's affection.

As is the case with boys, the wish to replace the same-sex parent results in guilt. The girl is afraid that her mother knows what she is thinking and that she will be punished by loss of her mother's love. She overcomes her fear and guilt by repressing her feelings for her father and intensifying her identification with her mother. Freud believed that this pattern of identity formation, in which women affiliate with their mothers, renders women "underdeveloped" versions of men because their attempts to differentiate themselves from their mothers were short-circuited. He concluded that women show less sense of justice than men, that they are less ready to submit to the great challenges of life, and that their judgments are more often colored by their emotions (Freud, 1925/1961, pp. 257–258).

Not surprisingly, Freud's argument has been strongly attacked. First, critics reject Freud's belief that female development is somehow secondary to male development. If any priority is to be given to one sex or the other, it is more likely to be given to the female. As we saw in Chapter 3 (p. 78), the sex organs and the brain of all human embryos initially follow a female path of development; these organs become male only if they are modified through the action of male hormones. Second, modern research indicates that there is more to children's achievement of sex-role identities than resolving the Oedipus complex, because aspects of identity

Caring for others is an important component of socialization. Here a little girl willingly learns about infant care by imitating her mommy.

Courtesy of Jennifer Cole

formation can be discerned well before the age at which Freud assumed it to occur (Ruble & Martin, 1998). Third, researchers now consider adults in the child's family, not the child, to be the primary carriers of sexual fantasies. Disturbances in identity formation currently are thought to result from psychological traumas caused by parents who are sexually abusive or seductive and not from children's inability to resolve infantile sexual desires (Coates & Wolf, 1997).

Freud's ideas, however criticized, continue to influence both popular and scholarly thinking about the acquisition of sex roles. The challenge facing those who dispute his theories is to provide a better account of the processes at work.

An Environmental-Learning View: Identification through Observation and Imitation

Freudian theories of identification assume that young children are caught in hidden conflicts between their fears and their desires. Identification with the same-sex parent is their way of resolving those conflicts. As you will see below, the environmental-learning view differs from this in several important ways. First, social-learning theories emphasize entirely different developmental processes. Second, they assume that parents are not the only ones responsible for the child's sex-role development (Eagly et al., 2000).

As far as developmental processes are concerned, environmental-learning theorists assume that sex-role identity is not driven by inner conflict, as Freud supposed, but is a matter of two key processes: **modeling,** in which children observe and imitate individuals of the same sex as themselves, and **differential reinforcement,** in which girls and boys are differently rewarded for engaging in gender-appropriate behavior (Rust et al., 2000). According to this view, children observe that male behavior and female behavior differ. From this observation, they develop hypotheses about appropriate male and female behaviors. Further, children learn that adults reward boys and girls for different kinds of behavior, so they choose to engage in sex-appropriate behaviors that will lead to rewards.

In addition to having a different view on the processes of sex-role development, environmental-learning theorists believe that it is too simplistic to think that children acquire gender-role identity primarily by imitating their same-sex parents. Instead, in coming to understand their gender role, children rely on peers, siblings, other adults in their lives, and gender stereotypes communicated in their cultures (Sadovsky & Troseth, 2000).

Siblings, for example, are known to be important resources in the child's construction of gender roles. In a major longitudinal study, John Rust and his colleagues (2000) examined the gender development of more than 5000 preschoolers. Some of the preschoolers had an older sister, some had an older brother, and some were only children. They found that boys with older brothers and girls with older sisters showed the greatest amount of sex-typed behavior. In contrast, boys with older sisters, and girls with older brothers were the least sex-typed. Those without siblings were somewhere in the middle. Clearly, older siblings exert significant influence on the gender-role development of their little brothers and sisters.

There is abundant evidence that children model the gender-type behaviors of others, and are rewarded for doing so. It is equally clear that children spend time in specific contexts that vary widely in how gender is emphasized. One preschool teacher may greet her class with an enthusiastic, "Good morning, boys and girls!" During circle time, she may say, "All the boys with blue socks stand up! Now, all the girls wearing sweaters stand up!" Later, when it's time to go outside, she may say, "Okay, let's line up boy-girl-boy-girl." In her classroom, gender categories organize activities, and

modeling The process by which children observe and imitate individuals of the same sex as themselves.

differential reinforcement The process by which girls and boys are differently rewarded for engaging in gender-appropriate behavior.

This Tarahumara Indian man and his son are hoeing a field of vegetables in a remote canyon in Mexico. The process of acquiring an identity is facilitated by participating in important tasks.

©Phil Schermeister/Corbis

gender-type language is used frequently. Children who spend time in preschool classrooms that emphasize gender in this way have higher levels of gender stereotyping compared with children in preschools that are more gender neutral (Biggler, 1995).

In addition to their sensitivity to gendered language and activities, very young children are highly sensitive to the effects of gender stereotypes (Ruble & Martin, 2002). For the most part, the stereotype of the male is defined more clearly—and more rigidly—compared with the stereotype of the female. Likewise, our culture is relatively permissive when girls engage in typically malelike behaviors and correspondingly intolerant when boys engage in typically feminine behavior. One young mother told us of a time when her $2\frac{1}{2}$-year-old son snuggled up to her on the sofa while she was painting her fingernails. He put his hand out and said, "Me, too, Mommy." The mother took great pride in her efforts to raise a son who would be as affectionate and gentle as he was assertive and independent, and made sure that he had dolls as well as trucks with which to play. She painted one stubby fingernail a pearly pink. And then she stopped, unable to finish her task.

It seems that crossing from male into female territory is difficult even for those who are trying hard to break down gender stereotypes. It is no surprise that while girls and women will admit to being "tomboys," very few boys and men will confess to being "sissies." Interestingly, the way that cultures tolerate (or fail to tolerate) cross-gendered behavior may influence children's developing knowledge about gender. For example, a study by Marion O'Brien and her colleagues (2000) found that preschool-age boys and girls are equally knowledgeable about male stereotypes, but girls are considerably more knowledgeable than boys about female stereotypes. It may be that the male stereotype, being more rigid than the female stereotype, is easier for boys and girls to learn. It is also possible that girls know both stereotypes well because they are allowed to experiment with both, whereas boys are confined to behaviors that are consistent with what society defines as the "male domain."

The environmental-learning view has done much to help us understand how children's environments contribute to the development of sex-role identity. The third and final view that we explore focuses on how children's cognitive development contributes to the process.

A Cognitive View: Identity Formation as Conceptual Development

The belief that a child's own conceptions are central to the formation of sex-role identity is implied by Piaget's theory of cognitive development, and is the cornerstone of the *cognitive-developmental approach* to sex-role acquisition proposed by Lawrence Kohlberg (1966). In contrast to the social-learning theorists' assumption that children passively absorb the gender-relevant information around them, Kohlberg argues that "the child's sex-role concepts are the result of the child's active structuring of his own experience; they are not passive products of social training" (p. 85). In contrast to Freud, Kohlberg claimed that the "process of forming a constant sexual identity depends less on guilt and fear than on the general process of conceptual development" (p. 85).

Kohlberg believed that sex-role development goes through three stages:

1. Basic sex-role *identity*. By the time children are 3 years old, they are able to label themselves as boys or girls.

2. Sex-role *stability*. During early childhood, children begin to understand that sex roles are stable over time—boys grow up to be men and girls grow up to be women.

3. Sex-role *constancy*. Young children may believe that their sex may be changed by altering their outward appearance in some way. Their sex-role development is completed when they understand that their sex remains the same no matter what the situation. They know that even if they dress up as a member of the opposite sex for Halloween, they won't turn into a member of the opposite sex.

Figure 10.1 These South African girls have just won awards at a beauty pageant. They are learning that physical appearance in girls is valued and rewarded in their community.

©David Turnley/Corbis

Whereas the environmental-learning theorists assume that the thought sequence of male children is "I want rewards, I am rewarded for doing boy things, therefore I want to be a boy," Kohlberg (1966) proposed the following sequence: "I am a boy; therefore I want to do boy things; therefore the opportunity to do boy things (and to gain approval for doing them) is rewarding" (p. 89).

There is a good deal of evidence that the development of sex-role identity goes through the general sequence proposed by Kohlberg (Szkrybalo & Ruble, 1999). However, psychologists remain divided about the processes that produce the sequence. Kohlberg himself believed that sex-role identity begins to guide thoughts and actions only after children attain sex-role constancy, because only then are they "categorically certain" that their sex is unchangeable (Kohlberg, 1966, p. 95). Current data, however, do not support Kohlberg's strict idea of sex-role constancy as the critical turning point in the development of sex-role identity. For example, well before they attain sex-role constancy as defined by Kohlberg's criteria, children prefer the same toys as other members of their sex and imitate the behavior predominantly of same-sex models (see Figure 10.1) (Maccoby, 2003).

A Combined Approach: Gender Schema Theory

To many psychologists it appears that an adequate explanation of how children's sex-role identity develops must include features of both social-learning and cognitive-developmental theories. One such approach is *gender schema theory.*

Gender schema theory is similar in some respects to Kohlberg's cognitive-developmental theory. Adherents of both approaches believe that the environment affects the child's understanding indirectly, through a *schema,* or cognitive structure. Once formed, this schema guides the way the child selects and remembers information from the environment. It also provides a model for action. A **gender schema,** then, can be considered a mental model containing information about males and females that is used to process gender-relevant information (Liben & Bigler, 2002).

Gary Levy and Robin Fivush (1993) point out that children form gender schemas not only for objects and people but for familiar events as well. Accordingly, at the same time that they are discovering how to classify people and objects in terms of their gender, gender information is becoming a part of the scripts that boys and girls

gender schema A mental model containing information about males and females that is used to process gender-relevant information.

Figure 10.2 The process of identity formation is clearly visible in the ways that young children imitate parents of the same sex.

Figure 10.3 An example of an information-processing sequence associated with gender schema formation. In this case, the child is a girl who has been offered four objects to play with. (Adapted from Martin & Halverson, 1981.)

are expected to draw upon and apply in different circumstances (a barbecuing script or a grocery shopping script, for example) (see Figure 10.2).

Gender schema theorists depart from Kohlberg's cognitive-developmental theory in two ways. First, they believe that, even prior to the onset of Kohlberg's stages, children's developing schematic knowledge motivates and guides their gender-linked interests and behavior. Second, these theorists often employ an information-processing, rather than stage, approach to describe how the cognitive and learning elements of the system work together.

Carol Martin and Charles Halverson (1987) conceive gender schema theory in terms of the diagram in Figure 10.3. A little girl who can say that she is a girl and that her brother is a boy is presented with four objects with which to play. Two of the objects are gender-neutral—an orange and an artichoke—and two are stereotypically male or female—a truck and a doll. When the girl is presented with the doll, she must first decide if it is specifically relevant to her. She decides that "dolls are for girls" and that "I am a girl," so "dolls are relevant to me." As a result of this decision, write Martin and Halverson (1981), "she will approach the doll, explore it, ask questions about it, and play with it to obtain further information about it" (p. 1121). This sequence is depicted by the yellow line in the diagram.

When the little girl is presented with a truck, by contrast, she will think, "trucks are for boys" and "I am a girl." This reasoning will lead her to decide that "trucks are not relevant to me." As a result, she will avoid the truck and not be interested in knowing anything else about it. Asked about these toys later on, she will remember more about the doll than about the truck.

At this time no single theory appears to be able to encompass all the data concerning children's acquisition of sex-role identity (see Table 10.1). Recent cognitive approaches have confirmed the importance of such signposts as the ability to label one's own sex and the realization that one's sex remains constant over time and in different contexts. Cognitive theory does not, however, explain the fact that young children's toy preferences and behaviors become gender-appropriate even before they can label their own sex. It seems plausible that this intuitive knowledge comes from the fact that everyone around them is treating them either as little boys or little girls and is praising or criticizing them according to their sex-role categorization. That is, social learning is a part of the process from the very beginning. Biological factors, such as sex differences in levels of activity and play style, are also important. The continuing challenge facing researchers who study gender and personality formation is to document the complex interplay between developing cognitive understandings and behavior in the overall process of social development.

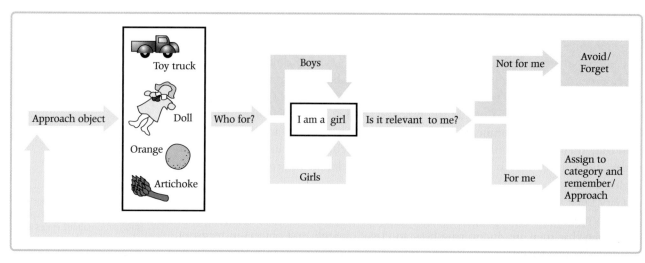

table 10.1

Paths to Sex-Role Identity	
Process	**Hypotheses/Variations**
Differentiation and integration	Boys differentiate from their mothers and identify with their fathers through resolution of the Oedipus complex; girls identify with their mothers after resolving their anger over the lack of a penis.
	A girl's path to identity formation is through affiliation, thus providing a basis for development of intimacy. A boy's path is through differentiation; as a consequence, boys tend to reject intimacy.
Observation and imitation	Boys observe and imitate masculine behavior because they are rewarded for doing so, while girls are rewarded for feminine behavior. This ultimately produces observed gender differences.
Cognition	Children first form a permanent schema of their gender and then define what is rewarding in terms of that schema.
Combined mechanisms (gender schema theory)	Sexual identity emerges from a combination of observation, imitation, and schema formation. The development of gender knowledge both depends on and is changed by the development of more sophisticated gender schemas.

A shortcoming shared by all these approaches is that they do not account for the role of such emotions as guilt, fear, and envy in shaping sex-role identity formation. As a consequence, many of the emotional phenomena that inspired the explanations of Freud and his followers remain to be incorporated into a comprehensive account of how sex-role identities are formed.

Ethnic Identity

In a society populated by many ethnic groups and races*, children's developing sense of their own ethnic identity is an important social issue. As a consequence, researchers have studied how children acquire the ethnic categories prevalent in their community, identify their own ethnic group, and form stable attitudes toward their own and other groups (Cross & Phagen-Smith, 1996; Jackson et al., 1997).

Jean Phinney (2001) defines *ethnic identity* as "a subjective sense of belonging to an ethnic group and the feelings and attitudes that accompany this sense of group membership" (p. 136). Perhaps the most famous research on the development of ethnic identity was carried out by Kenneth and Mamie Clark (1939, 1950), who asked African American children and European American children to make preferential choices between pairs of dolls. The children, who were 3 years old and older, were presented with pairs of dolls representing the two ethnic groups and were asked to choose "which boy [doll] you would like to play with" or "which girl you don't like." The Clarks reported that most of the youngest children could distinguish between the categories of dolls and, more important, that African American children of all ages seemed to prefer the white dolls, a phenomenon that has come to be called "the white bias" (Justice et al., 1999). On the basis of this research, many psychologists concluded that African American children define themselves entirely in terms of the majority group, thereby denying the importance of their own families and

---

* The terms "race" and "ethnicity" have different meanings that are easily confused. "Race" generally refers to one's genetic background, and is often reflected in the color of one's skin. In contrast, "ethnicity" typically refers to a cultural background of shared customs, language, and history—such as Haitian and Irish. Although race and ethnicity tend to go together, sometimes they do not. Both Haitian Americans and African Americans have black skin and a common racial background, but their ethnic backgrounds differ significantly. Recognizing that race and ethnicity are often difficult to separate in developmental research, we have chosen to use the term "ethnicity".

communities in shaping their identities (Jackson et al., 1997). Plaintiffs in the case of *Brown* v. *Board of Education of Topeka* (1954) used the Clarks' evidence in their argument that racial segregation in the schools leads to a negative sense of self among African American children. On the basis of this and other evidence, the U.S. Supreme Court ruled that racial segregation in the public schools is unconstitutional.

Studies conducted since the 1950s have confirmed the Clarks' findings (Justice et al., 1999; Spencer & Markstom-Adams, 1990) and extended them to other groups, including Native Americans (Annis & Corenblum, 1987) and Bantu children in South Africa (Gregor & McPherson, 1966). However, these studies have also cast doubt on the notion that minority-group children acquire a generalized negative ethnic self-concept. Margaret Spencer (1988), for example, showed that while many of the 4- to 6-year-old African American children she interviewed said that they would prefer to play with a white doll, 80 percent of these children displayed positive self-esteem. Several other studies confirm that the "white bias" is not connected to the way that children think about and evaluate themselves (Justice et al., 1999). Ann Beuf (1977) reported incident after incident in which Native American children who chose white dolls made evident their understanding of the economic and social circumstances that make their lives difficult in contrast to the lives of white people. In one study, 5-year-old Dom was given several dolls representing Caucasians and Native Americans (whose skins were depicted as brown) to put into a toy classroom:

> **Dom:** *(holding up a white doll)* The children's all here and now the teacher's coming in.
> **Interviewer:** Is that the teacher?
> **Dom:** Yeah.
> **Interviewer:** *(holding up a brown doll)* Can she be the teacher?
> **Dom:** No way! Her's just an aide.
>
> (Beuf, 1977, p. 80)

In Beuf's view, the children's choices are less a reflection of their sense of personal self-worth than of their desire for the power and wealth of the white people with whom they had come in contact. Her views are echoed by James Jackson and his colleagues (Jackson et al., 1997), whose review of existing data provided little support for the idea that minority-group children's recognition that they are members of a relatively powerless group translates into a negative personal sense of themselves.

Other studies have shown that young children's expressed ethnic or racial preferences vary with the circumstances. Focusing on the interview situation itself, one

Despite an early awareness that white Americans are more likely than black Americans to have wealth and power, African American children generally display positive self-esteem. These young girls are participating in an International Parade in Florida that celebrates their African heritage, which may contribute to their sense of ethnic pride.

©Jeff Greenberg/The Image Works

study reported that Native American children show a greater preference for dolls representing their own group when they are tested in their native language (Annis & Corenblum, 1987). Harriette McAdoo (1985) reports that African American preschoolers' professed preference for white dolls has declined since the 1950s. She does not speculate on the reasons for this trend, but the end of racial segregation and several decades of political and cultural activism in the African American community are likely candidates. This conclusion is supported by Beuf's (1977) finding that young children of parents who were active in promoting Native American cultural awareness and social rights more often chose dolls representing Native Americans than did children whose parents took little interest in Native American affairs.

Developmentalists have become increasingly interested in how parents communicate with their children about issues of race and ethnicity. **Racial socialization** refers to the race-related messages communicated to children by their parents. Several categories of messages have been identified, including (Hughes & Chen, 1999, p. 473):

1. *Cultural socialization,* which emphasizes racial heritage and pride

2. *Preparation for bias,* which stresses racial discrimination and prejudice

3. *Promotion of racial mistrust,* which encourages mistrust of the majority race

4. *Egalitarianism,* which emphasizes the equality of members of all races

In a study of African American preschoolers, Margaret Caughy and her colleagues (2002) discovered that the vast majority of parents in their sample routinely incorporated a variety of racial socialization messages when interacting with their young children. Nearly all of the parents (88 percent) communicated messages that emphasized cultural heritage and pride; the majority also had Afrocentric items in their homes. In contrast, messages promoting mistrust were less frequent, communicated by 65 percent of the parents. The greater emphasis placed on socializing ethnic pride over mistrust and bias has also been found in studies of Puerto Rican and Dominican parents (Hughes, 2003).

As discovered by Caughy and her colleagues, differences in the form of racial socialization bear importantly on children's cognitive abilities and behavioral adjustment. In their study, parents who promoted racial pride and provided a home that was rich in African American culture had children with stronger cognitive abilities and problem-solving skills, and fewer behavior problems compared with children whose parents provided other forms of racial socialization. Although similar findings have been reported in older school-age children (Johnson, 2001), Caughy's study indicates that the process of forming an ethnic identity is well underway very early.

Personal Identity

> I'm 3 years old and I live in a big house with my mother and father and my brother, Jason, and my sister, Lisa. I have blue eyes and a kitty that is orange and a television in my own room. I know all my ABC's, listen: A, B, C, D, E, F, G, H, L, K, O, M, P, Q, X, Z. I can run real fast. I like pizza and I have a nice teacher at preschool. I can count up to 100, want to hear me? I love my dog Skipper. I can climb to the top of the jungle gym, I'm not scared! I'm never scared! I'm always happy. I have brown hair and I go to preschool. I am really strong. I can lift this chair, watch me! (Harter, 1999, p. 37)

Developing a sex role and ethnic identity are just two aspects of children's increasingly complex sense of self that develops during early childhood. Traditionally, psychologists like James Mark Baldwin (quoted on p. 359) view the self as double-sided (Baldwin, 1902; James, 1890). One side, the subjective side, or the "I," is the person looking out at the world. This side includes the sense of oneself as a person

racial socialization The race-related messages communicated to children by their parents.

who exists over time and who acts and experiences the world in a particular way: "I like pizza. I'm never scared! I'm always happy." The other side of the self is the objective side, the side looking from the outside, or the "me." This side includes the characteristics that others see, such as our physical appearance, abilities, and personality traits: "I live in a big house. I have blue eyes and a kitty." The "I" and the "me" are two sides of the same coin; they shape each other continuously over the course of development. We saw this double-sided process at work with the emergence of the distinctive sense of self and the advent of conversational uses of language at the end of infancy (p. 238); children who exhibit a need to live up to adult standards are likely to say "I want to do it myself" when confronted with a new and challenging task.

Once children are old enough, developmentalists often assess their self-knowledge by asking them to describe themselves, either in face-to-face interviews or through questionnaires. This research has revealed a predictable pattern: young children's self-descriptions are typically no more than a long list of concrete and loosely connected behaviors, abilities, and preferences ("I can count; I have a brother; I am strong; I like pizza"). Children tend to focus on specific characteristics rather than combining them into generalized traits such as "being shy" or "being smart." For this reason, the self-attributes of the very young child are not well integrated into a personality structure. Instead, they tend to be disjointed, fluid, and shifting. The integration of the self system is a gradual process that continues throughout childhood and adolescence (see Chaper 16, p. 636).

Young children's self-evaluations also tend to be unrealistically positive because they have difficulty distinguishing between what they want to do and what they are able to do. For example, a child will say, "I know all my ABCs," or "I can swim the whole way across the pool," when he or she can do neither of these things. By the time children are 4 or 5 years old, they are able to group some of their attributes into categories. A child might say, for example, "I am good at running, jumping, and climbing." While children know that "good" is the opposite of "bad," their cognitive limitations typically prevent them from acknowledging their negative characteristics. As a result they continue to describe themselves only in positive terms (Harter, 1999). As you will see in Chapter 14, not until middle childhood can children reliably distinguish between a "real" and an "ideal" self.

The continuing process of developing personal identity is greatly influenced in early childhood by children's increasingly sophisticated use of language. Recall from Chapter 8 (p. 300) that language is acquired in routine, scripted activities during which young children interact with their caregivers. The same routine activities in family settings are crucial contexts for further development of the self. Not only do caregivers tell children that they are good or bad, boys or girls, black or white, Japanese or Irish, but they also help them acquire an enduring sense of themselves by helping them to create a personal narrative about themselves. This personal narrative is referred to as **autobiographical memory.**

Autobiographical memory is usually created in situations in which adults help children recall and interpret events in which they have participated (Fivush, 1998). A father might ask his little boy, "Do you remember when we stopped at the light and the man in the ape suit waved?" The child nods his head silently, or says, "I was scared." Initially, the father carries the burden of remembering and structuring the conversation. Gradually, with increasing age and growing facility with language, the child assumes a more active role, as Mike and Sheila's daughter, Jenny, did when she was about $2\frac{1}{2}$ years old. "Tell me what Jenny did," she would say every night at bedtime, and her parents would oblige her by recounting the events of the day in a schematic way that highlighted events that were particularly interesting or

autobiographical memory A personal narrative that helps children acquire an enduring sense of themselves.

worrisome to her. These conversations would go like this: "Do you remember this morning, when we went to pick up Michael, and Mandy (the dog) came running out?" and Jenny would say, "Doggie go wuff, wuff, wuff." "And what did Mandy do?" Mike and Sheila would prompt. "Wagged her tail," Jenny would respond. "And what else did Mandy do?" they would ask, and she would laugh remembering, "She kissed me!" Although Mike and Sheila continued to guide the narrative, as Jenny grew older, she increasingly corrected them and added details of her own until she stopped asking them to tell her what happened and started telling them the events of her day (or refusing to tell, as she often did).

Like all parents in such interactions, Mike and Sheila were not simply mirrors reflecting Jenny's experiences. As participants in creating the stories that became part of her autobiographical memory, her parents strongly influenced what events she remembered and how she remembered them, and in doing this, they were influenced by the larger culture and by their personal histories, values, and interests. What is more, in telling Jenny these stories about herself, Mike and Sheila did not try to be objective. Rather, they liked to embellish and exaggerate to heighten the stories and make them more exciting. They tended to play down Jenny's incompetence and some of her fears and exaggerate her capabilities and bravery. Other parents might stay closer to the objective facts in recounting the events in their children's lives, or they might structure the stories of prior events so that they teach moral lessons. There are great variations among individuals in what events they remember and how such personal narratives are structured (Nelson, 2003). Despite this variation, by the time most children are 4 years old they have internalized the narrative structures appropriate to their culture and can recount their personal experiences by themselves.

A New Moral World

Beyond the fundamental changes in identity, early childhood is a time of remarkable transitions in children's understanding of the moral world, and their ability to align and evaluate their behavior according to the moral standards of their communities. As you learned in Chapter 6, the beginnings of these changes become apparent at the end of infancy.

Learning about Right and Wrong

Children develop their first, primitive ideas of what is good and bad from the ways in which the significant people in their lives respond to their behavior. The following discussion with several 5-year-olds clearly shows that adult evaluations about right and wrong form the basis for children's self-evaluations:

> **Eddie:** Sometimes I hate myself.
> **Teacher:** When?
> **Eddie:** When I'm naughty.
> **Teacher:** What do you do that's naughty?
> **Eddie:** You know, naughty words. Like "shit." That one.
> **Teacher:** That makes you hate yourself?
> **Eddie:** Yeah, when my dad washes my mouth with soap.
> **Teacher:** What if he doesn't hear you?
> **Eddie:** Then I get away with it. Then I don't hate myself.
>
> (Paley, 1981, p. 54)

As Vivian Paley (1981) comments, "Bad and good depended on the adult response. . . . An angry parent denoted a naughty child" (p. 55).

social domain theory The moral domain, the social conventional domain, and the personal domain have distinct rules that vary in how broadly the rules apply, and what happens when they are broken.

Paley is echoing the opinion of Jean Piaget (1932/1965), who called this pattern of thinking the "morality of constraint," or *heteronomous* morality (morality subject to externally imposed controls). Piaget proposed that children's beliefs grow out of their experience of the restrictions placed on them by powerful elders. It has always been the child's experience that older people announce the rules, compel conformity, and decide what is right and wrong.

According to Piaget, as children enter middle childhood and begin to interact increasingly with their peers outside of situations directly controlled by adults, heteronomous morality gives way to a more autonomous morality. This new form of moral thinking is based on an understanding of rules as arbitrary agreements that can be challenged and even changed if the people who are governed by them agree. (This idea will be discussed further in Chapter 14.)

Contemporary studies of young children's moral development emphasize that the various rules they must learn are not all of the same kind. According to **social domain theory**, three major domains or categories of social rules can be distinguished from one another: moral rules, social conventions, and the personal sphere (Nucci, 1996; Turiel, 2002) (see Table 10.2). At the most general level are moral rules, social regulations based on principles of justice and the welfare of others. Moral rules are often believed to derive from a divine source; they are obligations that cannot be transgressed. Such rules are found in some form in all societies.

At the next level of generality are social conventions—rules that are important for social coordination in a given society. Social conventions are important aspects of the cultural scripts that young children are acquiring. They include prescriptions about the kinds of behavior that are appropriate for males and females or the kind of clothes people should wear in public, as well as rules about who has authority over other people, how authority is exercised, and how it is acknowledged. Social conventions vary tremendously, not only among societies but also among various subcultural groups within a society. Consequently, it may be difficult, at least from the child's perspective, to tell whether one has broken a moral rule or a social convention. Among Samoans, when a young child says

table 10.2

Events and Infractions of Moral Rules, Social Conventions, and Personal Rules	
Sample Event Types	**Sample Infractions**
Moral Rules	
Physical harm	Hitting, pushing
Psychological harm	Hurting feelings, ridiculing
Fairness and rights	Refusing to take turns
Prosocial behaviors	Laughing when another child is crying
Social Conventions	
School rules	Chewing gum in class, talking back to the teacher
Forms of address	Calling a physician "Mr." when he is working
Attire and appearance	Wearing pajamas to school
Sex Roles	Boy wears barrette to keep hair out of eyes while playing football
Personal Sphere	
Personal Rules	Swearing, making loud noises while eating
Hygiene	Not brushing teeth
Social	Forgetting to thank someone for a gift, forgetting best friend's birthday

Source: After Turiel et al., 1987.

"shit," the act is treated as a violation of a social convention; but when Eddie says "shit" and his mouth is washed out with soap, he might well believe that he has broken a moral rule!

At the most specific level are the rules that govern the *personal sphere,* in which children can make decisions on the basis of their personal preferences. They are allowed to choose which game they want to play after dinner and with whom, among the children they know, they want to be friends. Rules in the personal sphere govern particular events, such as "I sleep with the light on because I am afraid of the dark" or "I always eat the cake part first and save the icing for last." It is in the personal sphere that children are able to develop what is unique about the way they deal with the world (Nucci, 1996; Turiel et al., 1987).

Several studies have found that children as young as 3 or 4 years old from a variety of cultures can distinguish among moral, social, and personal rules. For example, they respond quite differently to moral rule violations, such as hurting another child or taking another's favorite toy, than they do to violations of a social convention, such as throwing trash out the car window (Turiel, 1998).

Just as there are cultural variations in the boundaries between the moral and social conventional spheres, there are differences within a culture regarding what is considered conventional behavior and what is a matter of personal choice. Parents, for example, may treat wearing a bathing suit at the beach as a matter of social convention; it is something everybody does. Their little children, however, may treat wearing a bathing suit as a matter of personal choice, so they take it off to play naked in the water. The borders between the three levels of rules are not easy to keep straight. It takes children many years to acquire their culture's normative separations, and even then, deciding which rules should be applied in which situations requires a good deal of negotiation (Nucci, 1996; Smetana, 2000).

The Role of Internalization

Internalization is the process by which external, culturally organized experience becomes transformed into internal psychological processes that, in turn, organize how people behave. Internalization appears to be essential if socialization is to be successful (that is, for the child to grow into an accepted member of the community). Children must have both the ability and the desire to behave in ways that others find acceptable (Kochanska, 2002a,b). As with self-identity, the study of internalization has been influenced by the work of Sigmund Freud.

According to Freud, internalization is responsible for the creation of a new mental structure. He identified three mental structures that develop from early childhood. The **id,** which is present at birth, is unconscious, impulsive, and concerned with the immediate satisfaction of bodily drives (Freud, 1933/1964). The first phase of self-regulation emerges with the development of the second mental structure, the **ego,** the intermediary between the demands of the id and the demands of the social world, which are often at odds with each other. By about age 5, children's internalization of adult standards, rules, and admonitions results in the formation of the **superego.** In Freud's words, the superego "continues to carry on the functions which have hitherto been performed by the [parents]: it observes the ego, gives it orders, judges it and threatens it with punishments, exactly like the parents whose place it has [partially] taken. We call this agency the superego and are aware of it in its judicial functions as our conscience" (Freud, 1940/1964, p. 205). It is, finally, the emergence of the conscience, and all its associated emotions of shame and guilt, that contributes to children's abilities to regulate their behaviors according to their new sense of right and wrong (we will address the implications of this development for moral reasoning in Chapter 14).

internalization The process by which external, culturally organized experience becomes transformed into internal psychological processes that, in turn, organize how people behave.

id In Freudian theory, the mental structure present at birth that is the main source of psychological energy. It is unconscious and pleasure-seeking and demands that bodily drives be satisfied.

ego In Freudian theory, this is the mental structure that develops out of the id as the infant is forced by reality to cope with the social world. The ego's primary task is self-preservation, which it accomplishes through voluntary movement, perception, logical thought, adaptation, and problem solving.

superego In Freudian terms, the conscience. It represents the authority of the social group and sits in stern judgment of the ego's efforts to hold the id in check. It becomes a major force in the personality in middle childhood.

Developing Self-Regulation

In the process of learning about basic social roles, their niche in society, and their sense of identity, children are also learning to act in accordance with the expectations of their caregivers, even when they do not want to and are not being directly monitored. The ability to control one's emotions, behaviors, and mental states, referred to as *self-regulation,* spans a multitude of developmental tasks and stages, and involves a variety of developmental domains. Early in development, infants acquire the physiological capacity to maintain a constant body temperature once they leave the womb, and later, to regulate their sleep/wake cycles and their crying. With increasing age, children are able to tune out distractions in order to complete a task; they can put aside hurt feelings in order to patch up a friendship; they can keep secrets.

Infants and young children require a great deal of assistance with regulation. They are soothed by caregivers when they cry; their interpersonal relationships are often orchestrated by others ("tell him you're sorry and make up"); and their emotional expressions are monitored and managed ("no hitting!"; "use your words!"). Even the large and simple figures contained in young children's coloring books reflect the culture's response to children's need for assistance in regulating their attention and behavior (in this case, their fine motor behavior).

Because the ability to regulate one's own emotions, behaviors, and attentional states is such an important part of what it means to function independently, many developmentalists consider self-regulation to be the cornerstone of children's development (Ruff & Capozzoli, 2003; Shonkoff & Phillips, 2000).

Regulating Thought and Action

To intentionally focus one's attention, or remember to do something, or map out a plan to solve a problem involves the regulation of cognitive processes. Consider the preschooler who is stringing beads (after Shonkoff & Phillips, 2000, p. 116). In order to accomplish this task, she must:

- Generate and maintain a mental representation that directs her behavior: "I need to hold up the string and put the end through the hole in the bead."

- Monitor her own progress: "I got one on; now I'll try another."

- Modify her problem-solving strategies: "This bead won't go on; I need one with a bigger hole."

The ability to regulate one's attention is essential to staying focused on the task at hand.

Ellen Senisi/The Image Works

The simple act of stringing beads calls on a host of skills that require the child to select certain actions (holding the bead to the string), eliminate others that don't fit the goal (throwing the bead), and inhibit actions as the task requires (stop trying the bead with the too-small hole). The inhibition of an action that is already underway, also called **effortful control,** can be particularly difficult for young children, as anyone knows who has observed a game of Red-Light Green-Light or Simon Says (Shonkoff & Phillips, 2000). Once a behavior has been initiated, especially in a highly exciting situation, it can be difficult to stop.

The challenge of mastering these self-regulatory skills becomes particularly apparent in preschool settings. Here, new demands for problem-solving—both cognitive and social—require children to develop new self-regulatory resources. Children meet these challenges differently due to normal variations in the pace of development, individual differences in temperament, and, sometimes, due to more serious issues, such as attention deficit hyperactivity disorder (Barkeley, 1997). Sorting out those children who are in need of special assistance from those who are impulsive, fidgety, and inattentive simply because they are "normal" preschoolers has become a major challenge for child and school psychologists (Rutter & Sroufe, 2001).

In addition to exploring how children come to regulate thought and action in the service of solving problems, developmentalists have asked how children regulate themselves in order to achieve social goals such as pleasing a parent or teacher. The most common way of studying this form of self-regulation is to examine children's ability to resist temptation and comply with adult norms. For example, Lisa Bridges and Wendy Grolnick (1995) arranged for 3- and 4-year-olds to visit a room in which they were shown an attractive toy but were told not to play with it. One of the strategies the children used to control their interest in the forbidden toy was to reorient their attention to other toys and play with them in a focused way. This strategy, which the researchers called *active engagement,* was rarely used by children before they were 2 years old. Between the ages of 2 and 5, however, children become better able to control themselves and follow the directions.

In a similar study, Grazyna Kochanska and Nazan Aksan (1995) videotaped and analyzed the behavior of more than 100 children between the ages of 2 and 5. The children were studied while they interacted with their mothers in two situations. In the first, the mother and child were given a large number of attractive toys to play with in their own home. After the children played with the toys for a while, their mothers asked them to put them away. Only 10 percent of the children overtly disobeyed. Some exhibited what the researchers called "committed compliance," that is, the children wholeheartedly embraced their mothers' agenda. Most, however, engaged in "situational compliance," meaning that they had to be continually prompted by their mothers to do as they were told. Consistent with what we know about effortful control, the children clearly found it difficult to put away the attractive toys with which they were still playing.

In the second situation, which took place in a laboratory, the mothers were instructed to tell their children not to touch a set of especially attractive toys on a shelf. After the children had been playing for a while, the researchers asked each mother to come to an adjoining room to see if her child would continue to obey her even when she was not watching. The injunction not to touch the forbidden toys turned out to be easier to obey than the command to put the toys away, which required effortful control. That is, most of the children complied

Giving away a brand-new toy is serious business for most 3-year-olds. This young boy's father helps him learn the common cultural practice of giving a birthday present to a friend.

effortful control The inhibition of an action that is already underway.

wholeheartedly. Some of the children were heard to talk to themselves, saying such things as "We don't touch these." Their use of the word "we" in such circumstances is a clear sign that they identified with their mothers and accepted their mothers' rules.

You have probably recognized that children's ability to control themselves in this manner is an example of internalization. In addition to being a key component of Freud's theory of moral development, internalization is also central to the developmental theory of Lev Vygotsky. But unlike Freud, Vygotsky had a broader, more benevolent view of the process. For Freud, internalization is a response to an ongoing battle against parental authority—a battle that the child will ultimately lose. Vygotsky, on the other hand, believed that internalization is the process through which social regulations, organized in the zone of proximal development (see Chapter 5), are transferred to the child's psychological system. Once the social regulations are internalized, the child is capable of self-regulation without the assistance of others.

You know from Chapter 5 that Vygotsky believed that the zone of proximal development is constructed as the child interacts with a more capable partner. Consider, for example, how young Simone learns to wave "bye-bye." Perched on her mother's hip as the guests depart, her hand is flapped up and down with enthusiasm by her mother, who repeats several times, "Wave bye-bye, Simone. Say bye-bye." Very likely, the guests will also take part, with exaggerated waving and musical "bye-byes." With time, Simone will need less and less prompting until, finally, she is able to complete the ritual on her own.

Although gaining control of one's own behavior by interacting with "experts" is a crucial type of development, Vygotsky believed that children can create their own zones of proximal development in the absence of experts. They accomplish this through play (Vygotsky, 1933/1978).

Self-Regulation and Play

Play occupies a conspicuous role in young children's cognitive development, as well as in their physical and social development. According to Vygotksy and his adherents, it also plays a key role in self-regulation (Elias & Berk, 2002). Vygotksy's argument concerns children's ability to separate the object of their play from their thoughts about it. Remember that early in development children have difficulty separating their thoughts and actions from the objects and situations that they

In addition to describing how the zone of proximal development is created in instructional settings with the aid of adults and other more capable partners, Vygotsky argued that children create their own zones of proximal development in play, which he believed to be an essential ingredient of cognitive development.

©Elizabeth Crews/The Image Works

Play provides an important opportunity for acquiring self-control. These young Tanzanian girls are regulating their behavior so that it is coordinated with that of their playmates.

think about and act upon. For example, and as you recall from Chapter 6 (p. 216), prior to the age of 2, a child can pretend to talk on a telephone only if the toy is a pretend telephone, complete with buttons to push and a handle to hold up to the mouth and ear. Not until the age of 2 can the child let one object substitute for another, for example, play "telephone" with a block. The ability to detach the idea of the telephone from the object itself continues through the next year, and by the age of 3, the attributes of the play symbol can be entirely independent of the object that it represents. So, for example, the child can play "telephone" with a baby doll or a Tinker Toy or any other object. The ability to separate thought—which carries the *idea* or *meaning* of the object—from the object that is thought about, means that the child is regulating her thoughts and actions. She is making herself imagine that the baby doll is a telephone, and she is making herself act on it accordingly. Vygotsky believed that the child's greatest self-control occurs in this type of imaginary play.

A particularly important and complex type of imaginary play is **sociodramatic play**—make-believe play in which two or more participants enact a variety of related social roles. Sociodramatic play requires a shared understanding of what the play situation involves, which often must be negotiated as part of the play. This kind of play is illustrated by the following scene involving several children in preschool. As we enter the scene, the girls in the group have agreed upon the roles they will play: mother, sister, baby, and maid.

> **Karen:** I'm hungry. Wa-a-ah!
> **Charlotte:** Lie down, baby.
> **Karen:** I'm a baby that sits up.
> **Charlotte:** First you lie down and sister covers you and then I make your cereal and then you sit up.
> **Karen:** Okay.
> **Karen:** *(to Teddy, who has been observing)* You can be the father.
> **Charlotte:** Are you the father?
> **Teddy:** Yes.
> **Charlotte:** Put on a red tie.
> **Janie:** *(in the "maid's" falsetto voice)* I'll get it for you, honey. Now don't that baby look pretty? This is your daddy, baby.
>
> (Adapted from Paley, 1984, p. 1)

sociodramatic play Make-believe play in which two or more participants enact a variety of related social roles.

Coping with Chronic Illness through Play

The sight of a child unable to breathe carries unspeakable anxiety. Life begins with the first breath and ends when breathing does. Children's connection to life is only as reliable as inhaling and exhaling. Against this fact of life, asthma stalks, specterlike.

—Cindy Clark, 2003, p. 89

A parent's letter to Mr. Rogers:

Our five and a half year old daughter has an inoperable brain tumor. Our only hope to remove the tumor is radiation. On the first day of her radiation treatment, she screamed and cried when she found out that she would have to be in the room all by herself. . . . We kept saying that it would only take a minute . . . Finally, she asked me, "What is a minute?" . . . I looked at my watch and started singing, "It's a beautiful day in this neighborhood, a beautiful day for a neighbor," and before I could finish the song I said "oops, the minute it's up. I can't even finish Mr. Rogers' song." Then Michelle said, "Is that a minute? I can do that." And she did. She laid perfectly still for the entire treatment; but there was a catch to it. I have to sing your song every time over the intercom.

From an interview with a child living with chronic asthma:

If I had a magic wand, all asthma medicine would taste good, not like the yucky stuff. And my inhaler and breathing machine would work as fast as I can snap my fingers, so I could start breathing and go play. My breathing machine takes ten thousand years. That's how slow it seems to me. Sometimes, I play games with myself when I do my breathing machine. I pretend I have a friend who is a dragon, and the dragon breathes smoke. You know the steam coming from the machine? That's dragon smoke. Another game is, I have a toy airplane. I fly my airplane through the steam. I pretend to fly away, to a place away from this. That's really fun to pretend, getting up and away.

Children afflicted with serious illness and disease face a number of challenges. The disease itself can be painful and physically exhausting—and terribly frightening. It can also be socially isolating, as when children need to stay home or in hospitals, away from their friends and schoolmates.

Beyond the physical, psychological, and social costs of the disease itself, chronically ill children pay a heavy toll as a consequence of the medical procedures required to heal them. As expressed in the stories above, the procedures can be scary and seem to make time stand still. Medical procedures can also unnerve the very people on whom sick children count for support, friendship, and comfort. That is, children with chronic illness are often shunned inadvertently by peers, and even family members, who may be squeamish in the face of the diabetic child's insulin shots and blood tests, the hair loss that typically accompanies chemotherapy, or the disfigurement of surgery.

How do children cope with chronic illness? According to Cindy Clark's (2003) intensive study, they cope surprisingly well, particularly when they are allowed to play. In her interviews with children living with chronic severe asthma or diabetes, Clark found that play is an important means of altering the meanings of medical procedures and devices, and symbolically recasting what it means to be ill.

Play provides children with a sense of control and empowerment over conditions and circumstances that are otherwise forced upon them by doctors and parents, and the medical regimes that keep them alive.

Thus, Clark found that parents and children often develop games and playful routines that transform unpleasant medical experiences into something fun, or at least endurable. The examples above of singing Mr. Rogers's song or imagining smoke-breathing dragons are cases in point. Parents of children with asthma described a variety of playful ways of counting to ten while their children used their inhalers (inhalers are devices, also known as puffers, that deliver medicine; see figure)—they counted in French, in Pig Latin, in the voice of the Count from *Sesame Street*. Sometimes, the medical devices themselves were transformed into toys. Certain types of inhalers make a whistling sound to signal the patient that they are inhaling too quickly. As you might imagine, a lot of asthmatic children get the giggles by using their inhalers (improperly) as musical instruments. One mother reported that she needs to monitor her 8-year-old son's use of his inhaler because, "If he's in the kitchen doing it, he tries to get the dog in the face with it as it blows out. Sometimes I yell at him." Another mother recounted how her daughter played with a breathing mask used with the nebulizer (a breathing machine that delivers medicine, often to children too young to manipulate the more complicated puffer). The mother had intentionally acquired the second mask, thinking that using it in the

---

This transcript illustrates several features of young American children's sociodramatic play. The children are enacting social roles and using scripts that they have encountered numerous times in their daily lives, on television, or in stories. Babies make stereotypic baby noises, maids get things for people, and fathers wear ties. At the same time that they are playing their roles in the pretend world, the children are also outside it, giving stage directions to one another and commenting on the action. The "baby" who sits up has to be talked into lying down, and the boy is told what role he can play. The children here are clearly acting against immediate impulse and regulating their thoughts and behaviors according to the imaginary situation as it evolves in the course of interacting with their playmates.

Recently, developmentalists have sought empirical evidence for the link between sociodramatic play and the more general ability of children to regulate their actions. An example is a study conducted by Cynthia Elias and Laura Berk (2002). They observed fifty-one 3- and 4-year-olds in their preschool classrooms, and

William Clark

Traditional devices that deliver asthma-relief medication are made for function, not fun. However, the new "playful" device, called a "Puffapal," may help young children cope better with their medical treatments.

fear, pain, embarrassment, and confusion are ordered and controlled through song, jokes, art, pranks, and funny stories. From a Vygotskian perspective, the blending of fantasy play and medical treatment creates a zone of proximal development through which the child gains a sense of control over the uncontrollable and frightening. Much of the play is spontaneously generated by children. However, some is encouraged by adults—parents in particular—who are sensitive to how children can regulate their thoughts and feelings in the context of play.

Increasingly, the therapeutic value of play is recognized by the medical community. At one hospital, the pediatric blood-testing machine is named "Herbie"; his most distinctive characteristic is his inclination to "suck your blood." One of Herbie's child "victims" claimed that his encounter with blood-sucking Herbie was the best part of his hospital stay, and that Herbie made the procedure seem like it didn't hurt quite so much. Other hospitals have systematically incorporated play into children's treatment regimes. Many now employ *child life specialists* whose primary duties involve familiarizing children with treatment and facilitating their coping and adjustment through the use of play and games.

Currently, developmentalists like Clark are seeking new ways of using the functions of play to help children deal with debilitating diseases and medical procedures. Clark is now engaged in a study that incorporates inhalers shaped like toys (see figure). And you can bet that if they whistle, it's not when they are being used improperly.

context of play might facilitate her daughter's coping with asthma. Sure enough, the girl "played asthma" with her little friends, placing the mask on their faces, instructing them to sit quietly, and promising that mommy would read stories to pass the time.

At an "illness camp" for children with diabetes, syringes and paint are used to create art; at an asthma camp, some of the children put on a skit of "The Three Little Pigs," in which the big, bad wolf was unable to blow

the houses down because he had life-threatening asthma. He was taken to the hospital, received a lung transplant, and was thereafter able to blow down just about anything. The audience laughed and laughed.

In her child-centered approach to understanding chronic illness, Clark attempts to reveal how children attach meaning to their illness, and the medical procedures and devices that they endure and use on a daily basis. What she found is a child's world in which

recorded the complexity of their sociodramatic play. To assess the level of the children's self-regulation, they observed how well the children participated in cleanup and how attentive they were when they gathered in a circle to listen to the teacher. They used a short-term longitudinal design, assessing both play and self-regulation in the fall, and assessing self-regulation again several months later.

The findings support Vygotsky's main idea regarding the role of play in facilitating self-regulation (see the box "Coping with Chronic Illness through Play"). In particular, children who engaged in a lot of sociodramatic play in the fall also showed high levels of self-regulation several months later, even though there was no correlation between the two variables at the time of the first assessment. Interestingly, the correlation was especially strong for the most impulsive children, indicating that they benefited more than their less impulsive peers from opportunities to engage in sociodramatic play. Based on their findings, as well as what is known about the social and academic difficulties that go along with poor self-regulation skills (a matter that will be addressed below), Elias and Berk argued that sociodramatic play deserves an important place in preschool curricula and may be an important form of early intervention for highly impulsive children.

Both theory and research support the notion that sociodramatic play provides an important context for the development of self-regulation. It is, however, but one of many contexts through which children come to master themselves. Children encounter a vast array of social norms, parenting practices, school curricula, and work demands, which vary according to the child's culture and gender. All provide possible contexts for the construction of zones of proximal development in support of the child's journey toward independence in thought and action.

Regulating Emotions

To be competent members of society, children must learn how to control their emotions in addition to controlling their thoughts and actions. As we noted in Chapter 6 (p. 238), the development of qualitatively new, secondary emotions is one of the key changes associated with the transition from infancy to early childhood. Pride, shame, and embarrassment—the self-conscious, social emotions—now join with anger, joy, and the other primary emotions to enable participation in new and more complex social relationships (Mascolo et al., 2003). Children must learn to interpret the emotional states of others, manage their own emotions, and mask their true feelings when necessary.

Controlling Feelings

Most of us know what it feels like to carry a chip on one's shoulder, stew over a negative experience, or react explosively to a frustrating situation. Such feelings present special challenges to children's developing self-regulation abilities. Even very young babies are capable of modulating their emotions by sucking on their fingers or a pacifier and by rocking themselves; the ability to control feelings develops dramatically during early childhood.

In the years from 2 to 6, children continue to use these strategies and develop others to help them keep their emotions under control (Grolnick et al., 1999; Saarni, 1999; Thompson, 1998). They avoid or reduce emotionally charged information by closing their eyes, turning away, and putting their hands over their ears. They use their budding language and cognitive skills to help them reinterpret events to create a more acceptable version of what is occurring ("I didn't want to play with her anyway; she's mean"), to reassure themselves ("Mommy said she'll be right back"), and to encourage themselves ("I'm a big girl; big girls can do it"). At the age of 3, Mike and Sheila's daughter, Jenny, displayed a useful strategy for regulating her fright when hearing Maurice Sendak's story *Where the Wild Things Are:* she hid the book so her parents couldn't read it to her.

The emerging ability to control emotions helps the preschool-age child deal with the disappointments, frustrations, and injured feelings that are so common at this stage. In addition, emotional regulation affects children's social behavior. For example, when children observe a playmate falling down and getting hurt, they will likely feel anxious themselves. Those children who are better able to moderate their personal distress are more likely to show sympathy toward the playmate compared with those children who cannot manage their own vicarious emotional reactions (Eisenberg et al., 2003). Indeed, in order to sustain play, children must create and maintain a delicate balance of emotional expression and regulation (Halberstadt et al., 2001). As you will see, the skills associated with this balance are significantly related to children's altruistic, or *prosocial,* behaviors.

Controlling the Expression of Emotion

Young children must learn not only to control their feelings, but also to express these feelings in a socially appropriate way. Young infants display no such ability. They communicate their emotions directly, regardless of the circumstances. A 2-month-old who becomes upset during a wedding because he is hungry is not going to stop crying until he is fed. It takes several years for children to learn to control the emotions they display.

In the United States, for example, it is considered socially inappropriate to act disappointed when someone gives you a present. You are expected to thank the giver and to say something nice about the present, whether or not you like it. Several researchers have studied the ability of children to understand the need to mask their real emotions and their ability to do so (Cole, 1986). In some studies, children were asked to interpret stories about a child who expects an exciting present and gets something undesirable instead. In other studies, the children themselves are put in situations where they expect a desirable object and experience disappointment (as when, for example, they are led to expect a toy car as a prize for playing a game but get a picture book instead).

Several general results come from this type of research (summaries are provided in Saarni, 1999, and Thompson, 1998). First, during early childhood, children around the world appear to gain the ability to recognize when someone is masking his or her feelings. Second, girls are generally able to recognize, and display, masked emotion better than boys are. Third, there are wide cultural variations in the age at which children learn about masking emotion and the conditions under which it is expected. For example, one study found that young English children acquired rules for masking negative emotions earlier than young Italian children did (Manstead, 1995), while 4-year-old girls from India were more sensitive to the need to conceal negative emotions than were their English counterparts (Joshi & MacLean, 1994).

Children's increasing ability to read the emotions of others and to control their own emotional expression is measured in terms of **socioemotional competence,** the ability to behave appropriately in social situations that evoke strong emotions. Carolyn Saarni (2000) proposed that socioemotional competence involves a variety of skills, most of which are acquired in early childhood. The skills include an awareness of one's own emotional state and the emotional states of others, the capacity for empathy and sympathy, and the realization that outward expressions do not necessarily reflect inner emotions. It should come as no surprise that preschool children who display the characteristics of socioemotional competence are better liked by both their peers and their teachers (Eisenberg et al., 2003; Saarni, 1999).

In recent years psychologists have developed methods for categorizing and comparing children in terms of their level of socioemotional competence and for investigating the factors that promote it. These methods have led to the creation of experimental social programs for improving the competence of children who are having difficulty learning to behave in a socially acceptable manner. In these programs, children are explicitly taught methods for responding to aggression in acceptable ways, for empathizing with others, and for maintaining positive group interaction (Goldstein et al., 1998).

Cultural Regulation of Emotion

As you know from the previous section on regulating thought and action, the developmental task of self-regulation is not a solitary accomplishment. The child receives a great deal of social and cultural assistance. Developmentalists are just beginning to explore how a culture's values, meanings, and belief systems can shape children's emotions and self-regulation.

socioemotional competence The ability to behave appropriately in social situations that evoke strong emotions.

Consistent with the philosophy of Confucianism, Chinese parents commonly play down their children's successes and use "shaming techniques" when their children perform poorly.

©Yang Liu/Corbis

For example, Michael Mascolo, Kurt Fischer, and Jin Li (2003) have explored differences in the emotional development of children growing up in China and the United States. The two cultures embrace vastly different values and beliefs. In the United States, great emphasis is placed on individuality and personal achievement. Children are socialized to express themselves and take pleasure in their own accomplishments: "Good girl! You did it all by yourself!" Accordingly, American parents act to bolster their children's self-esteem and protect them from feelings of shame and failure. In contrast, the Chinese embrace the philosophy of Confucianism, which emphasizes harmony with others as a principal goal. When a child succeeds at a task, the culturally appropriate response is not self-celebration, but modesty and praise for the other: "You did all right, but now you need more practice. Play down your success." When a child fails, Chinese parents often utilize a variety of "shaming techniques." Mascolo and his colleagues report that if a child does poorly in school, a parent might say, "Shame on you!", "You didn't practice hard enough!", "Everyone will laugh at you!" You learned in Chapter 6 that shame, for American children, is a secondary emotion that doesn't emerge until the transition to early childhood, well past the time when children express the primary emotions of happiness, sadness, and fear. For Chinese children, however, Mascolo and his colleagues argue that shame is one of the first emotion labels used. As shown in Figure 10.4, children's emotional responses to their accomplishments follow radically different pathways as a consequence of their cultural traditions.

Figure 10.4 While children in the United States are socialized to strive for and take pleasure in personal accomplishments, children in China are encouraged to downplay personal accomplishments and feel honor in meeting their social obligations.

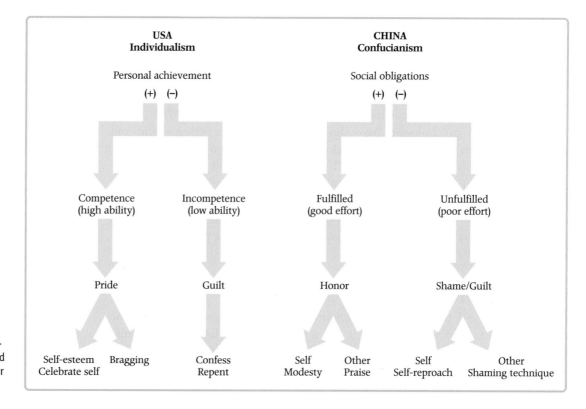

Understanding Aggression

Our discussion thus far makes it clear that self-regulation takes shape in culturally organized social contexts. However, we have focused mainly on situations in which young children are interacting with authority figures, usually their parents. An equally important aspect of social development is the emerging ability of young children to behave themselves when they are interacting with other children their own age. In order to be accepted as members of their social group, young children must learn to regulate their anger when their goals are thwarted and to subordinate their personal desires to the good of the group when the situation demands it. Learning to control aggression is one of the most basic tasks of young children's social development. Indeed, researchers have argued that early childhood holds the key to understanding both the origins of aggressive behavior and how to control it (Tremblay, 2000).

Because children have difficulty regulating their emotions, playful interactions sometimes turn into aggressive exchanges.

The Development of Aggression

Aggression is difficult to define. At the core of its meaning is the idea of a person committing an act intended to hurt another (Coie & Dodge, 1998). According to this definition, aggression can begin only after children understand that they can be the cause of another person's distress. This understanding seems to take shape very early, especially within the family.

As children mature, two forms of aggression enter their behavioral repertoire (Berkowitz, 2003). **Instrumental aggression** is directed at obtaining something—for example, threatening or hitting another child in order to obtain a toy or to gain peer approval. **Hostile aggression** is intended to injure the victim, regardless of what other goals might be achieved.

Judy Dunn (1988), who observed young English children and their siblings in their homes, found that children between the ages of 1 and 2 showed a rapid increase in instrumental aggression toward their siblings (see Figure 10.5, p. 386). One of the causes of increased instrumental aggressiveness is that as children approach the age of 2 (just when a new and distinctive sense of self seems to emerge, as we saw in Chapter 6, p. 235), they begin to worry about "ownership rights." At this point, having one's toys commandeered becomes a serious affair.

One of Dunn's most interesting findings is that until the age of about 18 months, teasing and physical aggression occur with equal frequency. But as children approach their second birthdays, they are much more likely to tease their siblings than to hurt them physically. Teasing is a subtle form of aggression requiring the ability to understand the specific characteristics of another child. Dunn reports, for example, that 16- to 18-month-olds already know so well what will upset their siblings that they may break off a fight with a brother or sister in order to do something to "get" the child indirectly, like destroying his or her favorite toy.

Many studies of childhood aggression from around the world have reported that boys are more aggressive than girls in a wide variety of circumstances (Segall et al., 1999). Boys are more likely than girls to hit, push, hurl insults, and threaten to beat up other children (Coie & Dodge, 1998; Loeber & Hay, 1993). When asked to pretend about situations that might happen to them in preschool (e.g., a peer knocks over a block tower or refuses to share a toy), boys are more likely than girls to offer aggressive rather than positive solutions (Walker et al., 2002). This difference seems to emerge during the second and third years of life (Underwood, 2002). As you can

aggression The committing of an act intended to hurt another.

instrumental aggression Aggression that is directed at obtaining something.

hostile aggression Aggression that is aimed at hurting another person as a way of establishing dominance, which may gain the aggressor advantages in the long run.

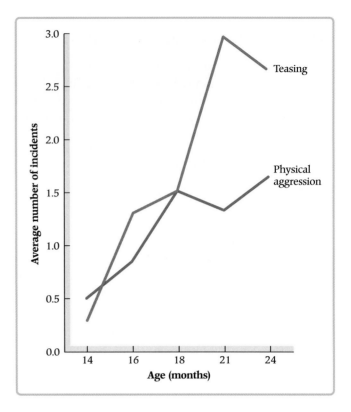

Figure 10.5 Early in the second year of life, siblings are as likely to hurt each other physically as to tease each other; but as they approach their second birthdays, teasing becomes much more frequent than physical aggression. (Adapted from Dunn, 1988.)

see in Figure 10.6, which plots the frequency of overtly aggressive acts among young children, overt aggression by girls drops markedly as they approach their second birthdays, while boys become slightly more likely to exhibit overt aggression.

This does not mean that girls are not aggressive. Qualitative analysis of boys' and girls' social interactions has shown that both sexes engage in aggressive behavior but the forms of their aggression differ. Rather than engaging in overt aggression, girls tend to exhibit more indirect forms, such as being disobedient (Wood et al., 2002). And, as we will discuss in more detail in Chapter 14, girls are more likely to harm another child's friendships or exclude that child from the group (Crick et al., 1997; Hennington et al., 1998). This form of aggression, called *relational aggression,* can be heard in such statements as "We don't want to play with you," "I won't be your friend if you play with her," and "Emily says she doesn't like you anymore." As anyone who has been on the receiving end of such statements knows, they can hurt as much as a punch on the arm or a kick to the shin.

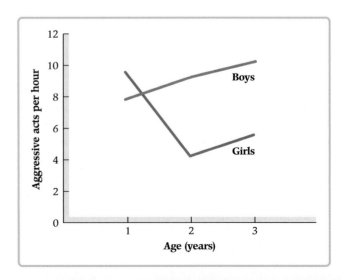

Figure 10.6 As children in a nursery school approach their second birthdays, acts of aggression decline significantly among girls but increase slightly among boys. (After Legault & Strayer, 1990.)

What Causes and Controls Aggression?

More people have died in wars during the twentieth century than in all earlier centuries combined. Every day our newspapers carry stories of people killing other people for money, to avenge a perceived wrong, or for no apparent reason at all. Among all the questions that can be asked about human social relations, none are more fraught with concern and uncertainty than questions about the causes of aggression and the means of controlling it.

Patterns of aggressive behavior often emerge during early childhood as personality becomes more defined. There is substantial evidence that 3-year-old children who behave defiantly and disobediently with adults, are aggressive toward their peers, and are impulsive and hyperactive are likely to still have these problems during middle childhood and adolescence (Coie & Dodge, 1998). A number of longitudinal studies have found that, for boys in particular, the earlier age at which children begin to exhibit such problem behaviors, the greater the likelihood that they will continue to behave in those ways later in life (Patterson et al., 1998). But what initiates these behaviors in young children? And how can such aggression be controlled? In studying aggression, developmentalists have generally focused on one of three factors: biological contributions, social and cultural influences, or cognitive responses.

Biological Contributions

Those who emphasize the role of biology in the development of aggression base their arguments on evolutionary and physiological factors (Bjorklund & Pelligrini, 2002). Noting that no group in the animal kingdom is free of aggression, many students of animal behavior have proposed that aggression is an important force in animal evolution (Lorenz, 1966). According to Darwin (1859/1958), a species gradually comes to assume the characteristics of its most successful individuals. Darwin defined as "successful" those individuals who manage to pass on their genetic characteristics to the next generation. Because each individual is, in some sense, competing with every other individual for the resources necessary for survival and reproduction, evolution would seem to favor competitive and selfish behaviors. Such animal behaviors as defense of a territory, which ensures that a mating pair will have access to food, have been interpreted as survival-oriented competition (Wilson, 1975). According to this interpretation of evolution, aggression is natural and necessary; its appearance automatically accompanies the biological maturation of the young.

While aggression is widespread among animal species, so are mechanisms that limit it. The aggressive behavior in litters of puppies, for example, changes in accordance with a maturational timetable (James, 1951). At about 3 weeks, puppies begin to engage in rough-and-tumble play, mouthing and nipping one another. A week later the play has become rougher; the puppies growl and snarl when they bite, and the victims may yelp in pain. Once injurious attacks become really serious, however, a hierarchical social structure emerges, with some animals dominant and others subordinate (see Figure 10.7). After such a *dominance hierarchy* is formed, the dominant puppy needs only to threaten in order to get its way; it has no need to attack. At this point, the frequency of fighting diminishes (Cairns, 1979). Throughout the animal kingdom one finds such hierarchies, which regulate interactions among members of the same species.

Figure 10.7 Many species of animals have innate mechanisms for signaling defeat to allow the establishment of a social dominance hierarchy without bloodshed.

Michael H. Francis

The developmental history of aggression and its control among puppies is similar in some interesting ways to development in human children. F. F. Strayer (1991) and his colleagues observed a close connection between aggression and the formation of dominance hierarchies among 3- and 4-year-olds in a nursery school. They identified a specific pattern of hostile interactions among children: when one child would aggress, the other child would almost always submit by crying, running away, flinching, or seeking help from an adult. These dominance encounters led to an orderly pattern of social relationships within the group. Once children know their position in such a hierarchy, they challenge only those whom it is safe for them to challenge. They leave others alone, thereby reducing the amount of aggression within the group. As you will see in Chapter 14, a similar argument has been used to explain the increase in bullying that is associated with children's transitions into the new social environments of middle school.

Physiological factors also play an important role in the development of human aggression. Studies both of twins and children who have been adopted indicate that genes play a role in aggressive behavior (Eley et al., 1999). This does not mean that there are genes for aggressive behavior. Rather, genetic influences on aggression come about indirectly through their effects on physiologically based characteristics, which in turn influence behavior.

One such physiologically based characteristic that has often been cited as an explanation for the difference in the levels of aggression between boys and girls is the hormone testosterone. There is a correlation between circulating testosterone levels and aggression in both boys and girls during childhood (Dobbs, 1992). However, this correlation does not mean that testosterone directly causes aggressive behavior. Studies with both animals and humans have found that increased levels of testosterone can be the result of dominance over others or success in conflict. In other words, testosterone both influences and is influenced by aggressiveness (Mazur & Booth, 1998).

Researchers currently believe that testosterone affects behavior indirectly by affecting a child's activity level. As we have seen, in general, boys have higher activity levels than girls, which, in turn, lead them to exhibit play preferences different from those of girls. Boys are often involved in more physical games than girls typically engage in, and they tend to play in larger groups than girls do. These differences might make physical aggression more functional for boys than for girls (Boulton, 1996; Coie & Dodge, 1998). The sex differences in levels of aggression interact with individual differences in children's temperaments to determine whether particular children are more likely than their peers to behave aggressively.

Other physiological processes that seem indirectly to make one child more aggressive than another include differences in levels of neurotransmitters and differences in nervous system activity. Difficult temperaments and certain types of brain damage have also been linked to aggression (Coie & Dodge, 1998).

Social and Cultural Influences

A second explanation for the causes and controls of aggression refers to social and cultural influences. That is, people learn to behave aggressively because aggression is sanctioned in their cultures. Children learn aggression by imitating the aggressive behaviors of others or because they are rewarded for behaving aggressively (Patterson & Crosby, 1992; Segall et al., 1999). For example, G. R. Patterson and his colleagues (Patterson et al., 1967) spent many hours watching the aggressive behavior of nursery school children. Whenever they observed an incident of aggression, they identified the aggressor, the victim, and the consequences. In well over three-quarters of the cases, aggressive acts were followed by positive consequences for the aggressor: the victim either gave in or retreated. Each victory increased the probability that the aggressor would repeat the attack.

The Spanking Controversy

"This is gonna hurt me more than it hurts you."

—Prelude to a whuppin'.

At 2½ years old, Mairin is starting to get the upper hand in her house—but not the kind of upper hand she had in mind. She throws her food across the kitchen, pitches tantrums when anyone touches "her" television, and recently got up and marched out the door when asked to sit still at the dinner table. So how's her mother responding? With a firm swat on the backside. "I know some people think it's awful," says her mother, "But how many of them have a two-year-old?" (as reported by Costello, 2000).

Studies estimate that between 70 percent and 90 percent of parents in the United States spank their children at least occasionally. Punitive forms of discipline are more often associated with poverty. Surprisingly, as many as 75 percent of college-educated mothers spank their toddlers an average of 2.5 times per week (American Academy of Pediatrics, 1998). Recently, several states have passed laws explicitly granting parents the right to spank their children. The right to spank, moreover, extends well beyond the homefront. Currently, 23 states currently permit the practice in public schools. A few years ago, a department-store Santa Claus was arrested in Boston for spanking a child who kept yanking his beard (Costello, 2000). He was quickly released to return to his duties and the admiring cheers of supporters who lined the streets to greet him.

In addition to being one of the more common forms of discipline in the United States, spanking is also one of the most controversial. Most parents do not like to hit their children and resort to spanking only after other tactics, such as reasoning and time-out, fail to produce the desired results. However, the argument made by those who oppose spanking is that it can damage children psychologically and emotionally. In fact, the practice has been outlawed in many European countries where public opinion takes a much dimmer view of its effectiveness. In Sweden, for example, only 11 percent of adults believe that spanking is an appropriate method of discipline, whereas the vast majority of American parents endorse the practice (Day et al., 1998).

In the United States, most spanking is done by mothers, largely because they spend more time with their children compared with fathers (Dietz, 2000). Not surprisingly, individuals who were spanked as children are more likely to spank as parents (Rodriguez & Sutherland, 1999). In fact, the acceptability of spanking varies not only between families, but between geographic regions. In the United States, for example, spanking is more common and acceptable in the South compared with other regions (Straus & Stewart, 1999).

Spanking is also more common in African American families, perhaps because of the unfair stigma attached to active African American children, particularly boys. According to Howard Stevenson and his colleagues (2001), African American parents may feel pressure to limit the mobility of their children because it causes tension and anxiety in authority figures. There is added concern that if the African American child is not controlled at home, he or she will receive harsher discipline not only from the law but also from other authority figures who don't understand black culture and life experiences.

Is spanking an effective form of discipline? This question is at the heart of developmental research on the effects of spanking, as well as the advice given to parents by pediatricians and other child-care experts. In general, developmentalists discourage the practice. A host of studies link physical discipline to increased aggression and low self-esteem in children and adolescents. Vonnie McLoyd and Julia Smith (2002), for example, followed more than 2000 children from three different racial–ethnic groups over a period of 6 years, and found that spanking predicted an increase in children's problem behaviors over time. In addition, abusive parents are known to spank their children more than nonabusive parents, prompting speculation that relying on spanking may increase parents' risk for using more severe forms of punishment (Walsh, 2002).

On the other hand, some studies suggest that physical discipline does not inevitably place children at risk for later problems. The consequences of spanking seem to depend on other dimensions of parenting that tend to be associated with spanking. For example, many parents who spank are also more emotionally rejecting and less involved with their children. In the study described above, McLoyd and Smith (2002) found that the negative effects of spanking are particularly pronounced when parents provide low levels of emotional support. However, when parents provide high levels of warmth and emotional support, the negative effects typically associated with spanking disappear. Nevertheless, the bulk of research, as well as professional opinion, urges parents to seek alternatives to spanking. After many years of relative silence on the subject, the American Academy of Pediatrics has recently issued a statement indicating that the practice is harmful to both children and parents.

These researchers also found that parents of aggressive children often reinforce their children's aggressive behaviors (Patterson & Crosby, 1992). In some cases, they provide positive reinforcement by paying more attention, laughing, or signaling approval when their children are aggressive. In other cases, children are "rewarded" for their aggression because their actions are successful in halting parental coercion. Patterson and his colleagues suggest that in coercive households aggressive behavior in a child is functional because it makes it possible for the child to survive in punishing social circumstances (see the box "The Spanking Controversy").

Since young children sometimes become aggressive in order to gain attention, a recommended strategy for reducing aggression has been to ignore it and to pay attention to children only when they are engaged in cooperative behavior. One way for adults to employ this strategy is to step in between the children involved in an altercation and to pay attention only to the victim, ignoring the aggressor (Allen et al., 1970). The adult may comfort the injured child, give the child something interesting to do, or suggest nonaggressive ways in which the victim might handle future attacks. Children are taught to say, for example, "no hitting" or "I'm playing with this now." When teachers use this selective-attention technique, aggression in their classroom declines significantly (Brown & Elliot, 1965).

Such selective-attention procedures may work to reduce aggression in several ways. First and foremost, the aggressor is rewarded neither by the adult's attention nor by the victim's submission. In addition, because the victim is taught how to deal with such attacks without becoming an aggressor, the aggression is kept from escalating. Moreover, other children who may have observed the scene are shown that it is appropriate to be sympathetic to the victim of aggression and that nonviolent assertion in the face of aggression can be effective.

A second line of research that focuses on social and cultural contributions to the development and control of aggression comes from cross-cultural evidence that children model the aggressive behavior of adults (Segall et al., 1997). This work shows that societies differ markedly in the levels of interpersonal violence they consider normal. For example, Douglas Fry (1988) compared the levels of aggression of young children in two Zapotec Indian towns in central Mexico. On the basis of anthropological reports, Fry chose one town that was notable for the degree to which violence was controlled and a second town that was notable for the fact that people often fought at public gatherings, husbands beat their wives, and adults punished children by beating them with sticks.

Fry and his wife established residences in both towns so that they could get to know the people and develop enough rapport to be able to make their observations unobtrusively. They then collected several hours of observations of 12 children in each town as they played in their houses and around the neighborhood. When the researchers compared the aggressive acts of the children in the two towns, they found that those in the town with a reputation for violent behavior performed twice as many violent acts as the children in the other town.

Because these data were collected in naturally occurring interactions, it is not possible to assert that observational learning was the only factor in the levels of aggression displayed by the children. Fry reports, for example, that adults in the more violence-prone town sometimes directly encouraged their sons and daughters to be aggressive and did not always break up fights between their children. The differences he observed, however, could not plausibly be explained by reference to biological dispositions, so the results fit most comfortably within an environmental-learning or cultural-context approach. At the same time, it should not be overlooked that even in the town that discouraged aggression, the children sometimes acted aggressively, a fact that is difficult to explain purely in terms of social-learning mechanisms.

Emotional and Cognitive Influences

Another way to explore the development of aggression is to focus more particularly on how children feel and think about social situations that might provoke aggressive responses. It is known, for example, that aggressive children often misinterpret social interactions in negative ways that evoke aggressive responses in inappropriate contexts (Coie & Dodge, 1998). Children's emotional reactions to events, and their ability to regulate their emotional reactions, depends importantly on how they interpret social contexts, and their ability to understand the emotions and intentions of others.

According to one view, aggression results from the negative feelings that arise in frustrating situations (Berkowitz, 2003). According to Len Berkowitz, when a child fails to achieve a goal, or win a parent's approval, or is rejected by a peer, negative emotions arise that initiate a fight-or-flight process. As shown in Figure 10.8, the initial tendencies to withdraw or to be aggressive are associated with rudimentary emotions of fear or anger, respectively. These initial feelings, however, can be significantly modified by cognitive processes, including the child's anticipation of consequences, or what he or she understands to be acceptable behavior. For example, suppose that a child is playing with a toy and a playmate takes it away. According to the model, the child will experience negative feelings, and, depending on his temperament and past social experiences, he may be inclined to act aggressively. However, having internalized the "no hitting" rule of the classroom, and knowing that violating the rule carries the consequence of time-out, instead of furiously pushing his playmate in order to retrieve the toy, he becomes annoyed and enlists the help of his teacher.

Developmentalists are building a strong case for the role of thought processes in children's aggressive behavior. A major influence on young children's aggressive tendencies is their understanding of their own and others' emotions, goals, and behaviors, and how they are all linked together (Halberstadt et al., 2001).

One line of research focuses on children's knowledge about emotions (Lemerise & Arsenio, 2000). The general argument is that children who have a more

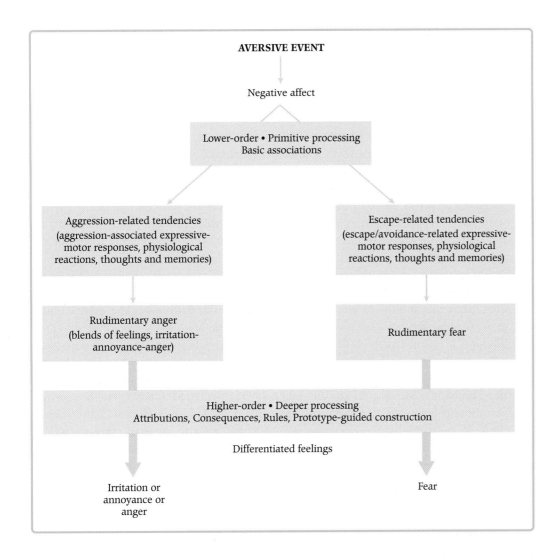

Figure 10.8 According to Len Berkowitz's model, initial emotional reactions to an event are significantly modified by cognitive processes.

advanced understanding of emotions, including what causes them and how they are expressed, will be less likely to behave aggressively.

Susanne Denham and her colleagues (Denham et al., 2002) tested this argument in a longitudinal study that followed 127 children between preschool and kindergarten. The researchers used puppets to assess children's emotional knowledge. The procedure involved asking children questions about the puppet's emotions in different situations—its basic emotions (What does she look like when she's sad?), its emotions in particular situations (What does she look like when she's had a nightmare?), and its emotions in social situations that require masking emotions (What does she look like if she's getting teased, but if she shows she's upset, she'll get teased even more?). The children responded by choosing and attaching a face to the puppet. Children's anger and antisocial behaviors were assessed through both naturalistic observation of their play and through teacher reports. In general, the researchers found that both boys and girls who had less advanced knowledge of emotions and their expression in preschool were more likely to behave aggressively toward their peers in kindergarten.

Another study examined preschoolers' beliefs about aggression as an enduring trait of individuals rather than a changeable behavior (Giles & Heyman, 2003). Jessica Giles and Gail Heyman argued that children who take an *essentialist* view of aggression, that is, believe that individuals who are aggressive in one situation will very likely be aggressive in the future, may be more likely to jump to conclusions about the hostile intention of a peer who behaves aggressively, and therefore be more likely to endorse the use of aggressive solutions.

To test preschoolers' essentialist beliefs about aggression, Giles and Heyman presented a group of 100 children of mixed racial backgrounds with brief scenarios such as, "Imagine there is a new girl in your class. She steals things from people, calls people mean names, and trips kids at recess. Do you think this new girl will always act this way?" Some children tended to believe that aggressiveness would endure over time, whereas others rejected the notion of essentialism.

The children's endorsement of aggressive solutions was tested by presenting scenarios such as, "Renee scribbled all over Belinda's art project. So Belinda hit Renee. What else could Belinda have done to solve the problem?" Some children said things such as, "Well, she could kick her instead"; others, however, provided more prosocial solutions such as, "She could tell the teacher." Consistent with their hypothesis, Giles and Heyman found that children who believed in the stability of aggressiveness as an enduring trait were more likely to endorse aggressive solutions.

Using testing methods such as those described above, developmentalists are amassing significant evidence that aggression must be understood in light of children's thoughts and beliefs about the emotional lives of themselves and others. This general idea suggests the possibility of controlling aggression by using reason. Though it is sometimes difficult to hold a rational discussion with a 4-year-old who has just grabbed a toy away from a playmate, such discussions have been found to reduce aggression even at this early age. In one demonstration of this tactic, Shoshana Zahavi and Steven Asher (1978) arranged for the teacher in a preschool program to take the most aggressive boys aside, one by one, and engage them in a 10-minute conversation aimed at teaching them that: (1) aggression hurts another person and makes that person unhappy; (2) aggression does not solve problems and only causes resentment in the other child; and (3) children can often resolve conflicts by sharing, taking turns, and playing together. The teacher taught each concept by asking the child leading questions and encouraging the desired response. After these conversations, the boys' aggressive behavior decreased dramatically and their positive behavior increased.

Children rely on adults to help them regulate the expression of emotions.

An important component of this technique was that the children were made aware of the feelings of those they aggressed against. Indeed, all the successful techniques for teaching children to control their aggression go beyond the mere suppression of aggressive impulses. Instead, aggression is controlled by encouraging children to stop their direct attacks and to consider another way to behave.

In contrast to employing cognitive strategies to help children select nonaggressive solutions, many people believe that aggression can best be controlled by providing children with harmless ways to be aggressive. This belief is based on the assumption that unless aggressive urges are "vented" in a safe way, they build up until they explode violently. Psychologists refer to this process of "blowing off steam" as **catharsis,** a general term for the release of fear, tension, or other intense negative emotions. According to this theory, the way to control aggression is to arrange for it to be vented before trouble erupts (Bemak & Young, 1998).

Despite the popularity of this hypothesis in folk belief and clinical practice, there is little convincing evidence to support catharsis as a means of controlling aggression. Nonetheless, the idea that catharsis releases negative emotions continues to be widely applied in psychotherapy with young, troubled children.

Developing Prosocial Behaviors

David: I'm a missile robot who can shoot missiles out of my fingers. I can shoot them out of everywhere—even out of my legs. I'm a missile robot.
Josh: *(tauntingly)* No, you're a fart robot.
David: *(protestingly)* No, I'm a missile robot.
Josh: No, you're a fart robot.
David: *(hurt, almost in tears)* No, Josh!
Josh: *(recognizing that David is upset)* And I'm a poo-poo robot.
David: *(in good spirits again)* I'm a pee-pee robot.

(from Rubin, 1980, p. 55)

As suggested in the dialogue above, young children can be remarkably sensitive to the emotional needs of their playmates. Josh not only recognized his friend's distress at being teased, but was able to remedy the situation by making similar deprecating remarks about himself. Such diplomacy becomes relatively common during early childhood as children acquire a number of sophisticated *prosocial* skills.

catharsis A general term for the release of fear, tension, or other intense negative emotions.

Children can be remarkably sensitive to the emotional distress of others. These two Yugoslavian brothers have fled their war-torn home in Kosovo, leaving their father behind. Whatever his own fears and anxieties, the older brother attempts to comfort his younger sibling.

AP Photo/David Brauchli

Prosocial behavior is defined as voluntary action intended to benefit others (Grusec et al., 2002). Sharing, helping, caregiving, and showing compassion are all examples of prosocial behaviors. The psychological state that corresponds to prosocial behavior in the way that anger corresponds to aggression is *empathy,* the sharing of another person's emotions and feelings. However, in order to feel empathic toward another, it is first necessary to identify what the other is feeling.

Understanding Others' Emotions

As you learned in Chapter 9, research on theories of mind indicates that early childhood is a time during which children expand their understanding of how other people think. Likewise, to behave properly in the many new social situations they encounter in early childhood, children must expand their understanding of other people's emotions. Recall that by the time they are 6 or 7 months old, babies can "read" their mothers' faces as a guide to how they are expected to feel about a situation. By the time they are 2 years old, they know that other people feel bad when you hit them and that giving them something nice makes them feel good. At this early age, such statements as "Katie had tears. I pushed Katie out of the chair. I'm sorry" and "Daddy angry, I cry in crib" show that young children have some understanding of how others feel (Bretherton et al., 1986).

To track the development of children's ability to assess other people's emotions and the causes of those emotions, Richard Fabes and his colleagues (1991) observed a large number of 3- to 6-year-old children in a day-care center as they interacted over the course of the day. When the observers noted overt signs of emotion and its probable cause (Jennifer laughed because Suzy was tickling her), they approached one of the nearby children and asked, "How does Jennifer feel?" and "Why does Jennifer feel that way?" Even 3-year-olds could usually interpret other children's emotions correctly; and more than 80 percent of the time the 5- to 6-year-olds agreed with the adults' assessment of other children's emotional states and the events likely to have caused them.

A similar developmental pattern in the ability to assess others' emotions has been found in interview studies in which children are asked to interpret how other children would feel in hypothetical circumstances (Saarni, 1999). For

prosocial behavior Behavior such as sharing, helping, caregiving, and showing compassion.

(a) Felicia has a birthday party

(b) Felicia's mother has pink hair

(c) Felicia's dog runs away

(d) Felicia's food tastes awful

(e) Her sister knocks over Felicia's tower of blocks

(f) Felicia gets lost in the supermarket

Figure 10.9 As children's understanding of social events increases, so does their ability to predict Felicia's feelings in these scenes. (From Michalson & Lewis, 1985.)

example, Linda Michalson and Michael Lewis (1985) presented the pictures shown in Figure 10.9 to children between the ages of 2 and 5. Each picture was accompanied by a story about a little girl called Felicia. In Figure 10.9a, for example, Felicia is having a birthday party, and the children were asked to say how Felicia feels. At 2 years of age the children could say that Felicia was happy about the birthday party. But they could not say that Felicia was afraid when she was lost in the supermarket (Figure 10.9f) or sad when her dog ran away (Figure 10.9c). The older children were much better at assessing the negative emotions. Here again we can see a clear tie to cognitive changes that we discussed in Chapter 9. The younger children are less knowledgeable about emotional-display rules and more prone to egocentric interpretations of events. They "bias" their interpretation of pictured events to fit the way they wish things were.

Empathy

Empathy is widely believed to provide the essential foundations for prosocial behavior (Eisenberg et al., 2003). According to Martin Hoffman, a child can feel empathy for another person at any age. As children develop, however, their ability to empathize broadens and they become better able to interpret and respond appropriately to the distress of others.

Children as young as 3 or 4 display empathy and concern for the happiness of their peers.

Laura Dwight

Hoffman has proposed four stages in the development of empathy that are significantly linked to stages in the child's self-development. The first stage occurs during the first year of life. As we noted earlier, babies as young as 2 days become stressed and cry at the sound of another infant's cries (Dondi et al., 1999). Hoffman calls this phenomenon *global empathy*. These early cries are akin to innate reflexes, since babies obviously can have no understanding of the feelings of others. Yet they respond as if they were having those feelings themselves.

During the second year of life, as children develop a sense of themselves as distinct individuals, their responses to others' distress change, and *egocentric empathy* emerges. Now when babies are confronted by someone who is distressed, they are capable of understanding that it is the other person who is upset. This realization allows children to turn their attention from concern for their own comfort to comforting others. Since they have difficulty keeping other people's points of view in mind, however, some of their attempts to help may be inappropriate and egocentric, such as giving a security blanket to an adult who looks upset.

The third stage in the development of empathy, corresponding roughly to early childhood, is brought on by the child's increasing role-taking skills. Being able to keep straight one's own emotional needs as distinct from those of another allows the child to respond more sensitively, rather than egocentrically. In addition, the increasing command of language and other symbols during early childhood vastly increases the contexts in which children can behave empathically. Language allows children to empathize with people who are expressing their feelings verbally, without visible emotions, as well as with people who are not present. Information gained indirectly through stories, pictures, or television permits children to empathize with people whom they have never met.

Note that Hoffman's theory of empathy is linked to Piaget's theory of cognitive development. Each new stage of empathy corresponds to a new stage of cognitive ability that allows children to understand themselves better in relation to others.

Perhaps because it is linked so closely to what children understand, Hoffman's explanation of the development of empathy tends to leave out how they feel. It is tacitly assumed that the more children understand, the more intensely they adopt the feelings of the person in distress. The catch, as Judy Dunn (1988) points out, is that children may understand perfectly well why another child is in distress and feel glad as a result.

Evidence of the Development of Prosocial Behaviors

Other researchers have been more attentive to the emotional component of empathy, particularly regarding its role in prosocial behaviors. One of the best examples is the work of Nancy Eisenberg and her colleagues (Eisenberg et al., 2003). Similarly to Hoffman, she argues that empathy results as an emotional reaction akin to what is experienced by another. But in contrast to Hoffman's theory, Eisenberg proposes that empathy often turns into sympathy and/or personal distress. *Sympathy* involves feelings of sorrow or concern for another person. A child who is being sympathetic is not feeling the same emotion as the other person. Instead, he or she feels "other-oriented concern." In contrast, *personal distress* is a self-focused emotional reaction in the face of another's distress.

Eisenberg argues that it is important to distinguish between sympathy and personal distress because they have entirely different consequences for prosocial behavior. For example, when shown films that depict characters who are distressed, children who exhibit concern or sadness are more likely to engage in prosocial behaviors than are children who exhibit personal distress (Eisenberg & Fabes, 1998).

Personal distress, according to Eisenberg, stems from empathic overarousal in response to the negative emotions of another (Eisenberg & Fabes, 1992). When another person's distress generates too much negative emotion in the child, the result is a focus on the self, rather than the other-directed focus that underlies sympathy. Not surprisingly, personal distress is associated with poor social skills.

A deciding factor in whether the child's initial empathic response becomes a matter of personal distress or of sympathy is the child's capacity to regulate his or her emotions. The relationship between emotional regulation and sympathy was illustrated in a series of studies involving 6- to 8-year olds. The studies focused on three variables: (1) *general emotional intensity,* the children's personal tendencies to respond to another's distress with strong feelings; (2) *emotional regulation,* the ability to modulate their negative feelings; and (3) *sympathy,* the expression of concern for the other. The first study found that children who were rated low in regulation were also low in sympathy, regardless of their general emotional intensity (Eisenberg et al., 1996). However, for those children who could regulate their emotions, greater emotional intensity was associated with greater levels of sympathy.

The second study went one step further and examined how attention focusing—another form of self-regulation—might enter into the picture (Eisenberg et al., 1998). The researchers argued that children who are more capable of focusing their attention may take in more information about other people and their circumstances, leading to increased perspective taking and, by extension, greater sympathy. They found that children who were low in emotional intensity and attention focusing were also low in sympathy. However, children who were low in emotional intensity but high in attention focusing were relatively high in sympathy.

All of this suggests that sympathy results from an optimal level of emotional arousal, but that an optimal level can be achieved by different routes. Children who are inclined to extreme emotional reactions need to be able to regulate their emotions in order to be sympathetic. For children who are not as emotional, the ability to focus attention on others may enhance their understanding of others' needs.

Promoting Prosocial Behaviors

Adults are, of course, eager to encourage children's prosocial behavior. One common strategy that adults use in this endeavor is to reward children for prosocial behaviors. However, when Joan Grusec (1991) observed children in their homes, she

explicit modeling The kind of modeling in which adults behave in ways they desire the child to imitate.

induction A means of promoting children's prosocial behavior in which adults give explanations of what needs to be done and why children should behave in a prosocial manner.

found that rewards were not effective in increasing 4-year-olds' prosocial behavior. The children who were most inclined to act prosocially were those who received no recognition for their prosocial acts. These results contrast markedly with the effects of socially rewarding aggression.

As a consequence of such findings, developmentalists suggest two less direct means of promoting prosocial behavior. One such method is **explicit modeling,** in which adults behave in ways they desire the child to imitate. The other method is **induction,** in which adults give explanations of what needs to be done or why children should behave in a prosocial manner that appeal to their pride, their desire to be grown-up, and their concern for others (Eisenberg & Fabes, 1998).

Most studies of explicit modeling contrast the behavior of two groups of schoolchildren. In the "modeling" group, teachers are told to stage periodic training sessions in which they demonstrate sharing and helping behaviors: they share candies among the children with explicit fairness, read stories about helping a child who is feeling sad or who is being teased, and so on. In the "nonmodeling" group, no special arrangements are made for teachers to model prosocial behaviors such as helping and sharing. These studies clearly show that the modeling techniques used do, in fact, increase prosocial behavior among children.

Since induction strategies involve explanation and reasoning, studies of their efficacy have usually been carried out with older children. For example, Julia Krevans and John Gibbs (1996) found that when parents used inductive discipline strategies, their 12- to 14-year-old children displayed higher levels of empathy and prosocial behavior. A study of early prosocial behaviors in the home found that younger children, too, performed more prosocial acts when their mothers attempted to induce prosocial behavior (Zahn-Waxler et al., 1979). Reason by itself, however, was not the crucial factor; the most effective mothers combined reason with loving concern and high expectations for prosocial behavior.

It is worth remembering that in real life, outside of research settings, the strategies to increase prosocial behavior do not occur in isolation from efforts to decrease aggressive behavior. Rather, a great variety of techniques are likely to be brought into play, interacting with and reinforcing one another to create overall patterns of socialization. (This patterning of socialization is discussed further in Chapter 11.)

Taking One's Place in the Social Group

The kindergartners in Vivian Paley's classroom are discussing the story of Tico, a wingless bird who is cared for by his black-winged friends.

In the story, the wishingbird visits Tico one night and grants him a wish. Tico wishes for golden wings. When his friends see his golden wings in the morning, they are angry. They abandon him because he wants to be better than they are. Tico is upset by his friends' rejection and wants to gain readmission to the group. He discovers that he can exchange his golden feathers for black ones by performing good deeds. When at last he has replaced all the golden feathers with black ones, he is granted readmission by the flock, whose members comment, "Now you are just like us" (Leoni, 1964).

> **Teacher:** I don't think it's fair that Tico has to give up his golden wings.
> **Lisa:** It is fair. See, he was nicer when he didn't have any wings. They didn't like him when he had gold.
> **Wally:** He thinks he's better if he has golden wings.
> **Eddie:** He is better.

Jill: But he's not supposed to be better. The wishingbird was wrong to give him those wings.
Deana: She has to give him his wish. He's the one who shouldn't have asked for golden wings.
Wally: He could put black wings on top of the golden wings and try to trick them.
Deana: They'd sneak up and see the gold. He should just give every bird one golden feather and keep one for himself.
Teacher: Why can't he decide for himself what kind of wings he wants?
Wally: He has to decide to have black wings.

(Paley, 1981, pp. 25–26)

This conversation shows that the children understand that by wishing for golden wings, Tico has wished himself a vision of perfection. Each child has done the same thing countless times: "I'm the beautiful princess"; "I'm Superman; I'll save the world." For the blissful, magic moments when the world of play holds sway, perfection is attainable, even by a lowly bird or a preschool child. Wally and his friends also appreciate the dilemmas of perfection. In their eyes, Tico not only thinks he is better but *is* better—yet he is not supposed to be. Try as they may to conceive of a way for Tico to retain his prized possessions, the children realize that conformity is unavoidable. Wally's summary is difficult to improve upon: Tico has to choose to conform.

The children's discussion of Tico and his community of birds reveals more than an appreciation of the heavy hand of society as it is experienced by children everywhere. It also shows the children's awareness that individuals have a responsibility for regulating social relations. They understand that it is the wishingbird's job to grant wishes, therefore it is not the wishingbird's fault that Tico wished himself to be better than the others. Tico should have been able to control himself and make a reasonable wish.

This story returns us to the theme with which this chapter began—that social development and personality development are two aspects of a single process. When children engage in acts of sharing and comforting, they reveal their ability to know another person's mental state. At the same time, they are displaying their own ways of thinking and feeling—in other words, their personalities. As part of the process of personality formation within the social group, individual strengths and weaknesses, interests, and opportunities will lead to increasing differentiation between the self and others.

As they approach their sixth birthdays, children have by no means completed the socialization process; but they have come a long way from infancy, when their sense of themselves and the social world was general and undifferentiated.

Before we turn in Part IV to the wide range of new roles and rules that children encounter in middle childhood and the corresponding changes that take place in their sense of themselves, we need to round out the discussion of early childhood by investigating the range of contexts and social influences that make up the world of the young child. As we shall see in Chapter 11, even young children are exposed to a great variety of social influences and cultural prescriptions. It is in the course of dealing with the variety of concrete circumstances that structure their everyday experiences that children create the synthesis of cognition and emotion called personality and acquire their social identities.

SUMMARY

Acquiring a Social and Personal Identity

- Social development is the two-sided process by which children become integrated into their community while differentiating themselves as distinct individuals.

- One side of social development is socialization, the process by which children acquire the standards, values, and knowledge of their society.

- The other side of social development is personality formation, the process by which children come to have distinctive and consistent ways of feeling and behaving in a wide variety of situations.

- Identification, the process of molding one's behavior to that of a person one admires, contributes to children's distinctive sense of themselves at the same time that it places each of them in a salient social category, such as male or female.

- Competing theories of identification emphasize four mechanisms:

  1. Identification as a process of differentiating oneself from others.

  2. Identification as a process of affiliation—empathy with and attachment to others.

  3. Identification resulting from observation and imitation of powerful others and from the rewards gained by appropriate behavior.

  4. Identification resulting from the cognitive capacity to recognize oneself as a member of a social category and the desire to be like other members of that category.

- Sex-role identity goes through a sequence of cognitive milestones that begin with the early ability to identify oneself as a boy or girl, followed by the understanding that one's sex does not change over time, and finally a full understanding that one's sex is a permanent characteristic.

- Current evidence indicates that both conceptual change and learning of appropriate behaviors contribute to the development of sex-role identity, but the precise relationship between these processes is not well understood.

- Children acquire a sense of ethnic identity around the age of 4. Their attitudes toward their race or ethnicity are heavily influenced by how their social group is perceived in the society as a whole. Ethnic identity is also a product of racial socialization, the race-related messages communicated to children by their parents

- By the age of 4, children have acquired a sense of personal identity that includes a narrative about their own lives. However, their self-evaluation remains unrealistically positive.

A New Moral World

- Young children distinguish three categories of social rules: moral rules, social conventions, and rules in the personal sphere. Children as young as 3 or 4 can distinguish between these types of rules; the actual boundaries between them will vary according to culture.

- Internalization is the process by which external culturally organized experience becomes transformed into internal psychological processes that, in turn, organize how people behave.

- According to Freud, internalization is responsible for the creation of a new mental structure, the superego, or conscience.

Developing Self-Regulation

- Children learn to act in accordance with adult expectations, and modify their behaviors accordingly.

- Self-regulation requires a host of skills, the most difficult of which is effortful control, the ability to stop an action that is already underway.

- Early forms of self-control are situational. They require adult supervision. As children internalize adult standards, situational compliance is augmented by committed compliance.

- Sociodramatic play has been linked to children's increasing abilities to regulate themselves—children must learn not only to regulate their behavior, but their emotions as well. They must also be able to interpret others' emotional states. This ability is referred to as socioemotional competence.

- Children's emotional responses are also shaped by their cultural environments.

Understanding Aggression

- Aggression, the committing of an act that is intended to hurt others, does not appear until the second year of life.

- Instrumental aggression is directed at obtaining desirable resources. Hostile aggression may also gain resources, but it is more directly aimed at causing pain to another person.

- Boys' and girls' aggressive behaviors often differ. Whereas boys tend to use instrumental aggression to cause physical pain, girls more often use relational aggression to create psychological pain.

- There are three major factors to human aggression:

  1. Aggression is a result of our evolutionary past. Aggression is observed among animals of many species. From an evolutionary perspective, aggression is seen as a natural consequence of competition for resources.

2. Aggressive behavior is a result of social and cultural influences. It may increase among children because they are directly rewarded for it or because they imitate the aggressive behavior of others. The influence of learning on aggression may be seen in wide cultural variations in the amount of aggression.

3. Aggression is a cognitive response. Children's behavior is determined by how they regulate their emotional response to certain events. Children's choice to adopt (or not adopt) aggressive solutions is also linked to their knowledge of others' emotional states and the nature of aggression itself.

- There are large and stable individual differences in the levels of aggression among individuals arising from the interweaving of biological, social, and cultural factors.

- Several mechanisms have been suggested as means of controlling aggression:

    1. The development of aggression is accompanied by the development of social dominance hierarchies, which control aggression.

    2. Among humans, additional effective means for controlling aggression are rewards for nonaggressive behaviors

and cognitive training that induces children to consider the negative consequences of aggressive behaviors.

- Physical punishment, which is widely used to deal with aggression, is generally ineffective because it often engenders more aggression.

Developing Prosocial Behaviors

- Prosocial behavior, voluntary action intended to benefit others, corresponds to the emergence of empathy. Children's ability to understand others' emotional state is a necessary precursor to empathy.

- Prosocial behavior can be promoted by explicit modeling, in which adults behave in ways they desire the child to imitate, or by induction, in which adults give explanations that appeal to children's pride, their desire to be grown-up, and their concern for others.

Taking One's Place in the Social Group

- Social development and personality development are two aspects of a single process. As children are socialized to understand others and regulate themselves, they also learn to differentiate increasingly between the self and others.

Key Terms

aggression, p. 385
autobiographical memory, p. 372
catharsis, p. 393
differential reinforcement, p. 365
effortful control, p. 377
ego, p. 375
explicit modeling, p. 398
gender schema, p. 367
gender segregation, p. 362
hostile aggression, p. 385

id, p. 375
identification, p. 362
induction, p. 398
instrumental aggression, p. 385
internalization, p. 375
modeling, p. 365
Oedipus complex, p. 364
personality, p. 361
personality formation, p. 360
phallic stage, p. 363

prosocial behavior, p. 394
racial socialization, p. 371
self-concept, p. 361
social development, p. 360
social domain theory, p. 374
social roles, p. 360
socialization, p. 360
sociodramatic play, p. 379
socioemotional competence, p. 383
superego, p. 375

Thought Questions

1. Thinking about the four types of racial socialization messages identified by Hughes and Chen (p. 371), how might preschool teachers organize their classrooms to encourage ethnic pride? How might this affect the white children in their classrooms as well as the ethnic-minority children?

2. In Kochanska and Aksan's study of compliance (pp. 377–378), the children found it easier to adhere to the "don't touch" instructions than to the "cleanup" instructions. Propose an explanation for this finding, and design a study to test your ideas.

3. What basic cognitive abilities must children acquire before they will be able to tease a sibling?

4. Give examples of how 5-year-olds might demonstrate each of the components of socioemotional competence proposed by Saarni (p. 383).

5. Give examples of how adults might help children control their aggression by influencing their behavior, their cognitive development, and their emotional development.

The Contexts of Early Childhood

> "*A new level of organization is in fact nothing more than a new relevant context.*"
>
> —C. H. Waddington, *Organizers and Genes*

Maung Thura lives in Myanmar (formerly Burma), a country in southeast Asia known for its natural beauty, its poverty, and its violent, dictatorial government. When he was 3 months old, Maung Thura's grandmother took him in because his father had been killed and his mother arrested and jailed. Like many caregivers from poverty-stricken countries who focus on their children's physical survival, the grandmother knew little about the intellectual, social, and emotional needs of young children. In addition, because she worked and had no access to child care, she often left Maung Thura home alone. When he was brought at the age of 2 to an early-childhood care center sponsored by UNICEF, he showed signs of acute malnutrition, including an enlarged head and a shrunken lower body. He was unable to stand, walk, or talk. At the center, he was fed nutritious food and provided with basic health-care services. Caregivers trained in early childhood development, as well as a group of rambunctious toddlers, provided Maung Thura with an intellectually and socially enriched environment, and he quickly began to show signs of recovery. Recently, his mother was released from jail. She now participates in a support group organized by the center, and is learning how to promote Maung Thura's ongoing development at home by using proper sanitation techniques and engaging her son in play.

Families, neighborhoods, schools, governments, the media—these and other settings constitute the contexts of children's development. Thus far we have treated these settings primarily as a background; in this chapter we alter our focus to highlight the role that children's contexts and activities play in their cognitive, physical, and social development.

As we shift our attention to the contexts of early childhood, it is helpful to refer once again to Urie Bronfenbrenner's idea that the environments of development should be thought of as the nested arrangement of ecosystems that are represented in Figure 1.5 (p. 17). The innermost system in this diagram, the *microsystem,* includes such contexts as the home, the church, the local park, and the preschool. Maung Thura's microsystem included his grandmother's home and, later, the child-care center and the home of his mother. Also important are the contexts of the *exosystem,* such as the parents' workplaces, government agencies, and the mass media, which influence children either directly, as television does, or indirectly, through their impact on parents and other family members. The work of Maung Thura's grandmother clearly influenced his care. So, too, did the dictatorial government that broke up his family, and the international organization, UNICEF, that rescued him from circumstances that might otherwise have resulted in permanent disability or death.

Viviane Moos/Corbis

Across the globe, patterns of family life show interesting diversity as well as remarkable similarity. Developmentalists study how family differences and similarities impact children's development.

Each level of context in Bronfenbrenner's ecological model is reciprocally related to the other levels. Children are directly influenced by what occurs in their homes, but what occurs in their homes indirectly influences their experience at school, on the playground, and in other settings. Parents' behavior at home is influenced by the experiences they have at work and in their communities, while the society of which the community is a part both shapes and is shaped by its members.

The context that most directly influences young children's development is the family. Parents influence their children's development in two complementary ways. First, they shape their children's cognitive skills and personalities by the tasks they pose for them, the ways they respond to their particular behaviors, the values they promote, both explicitly and implicitly, and the patterns of behavior they model. But that is only part of the story. Parents also influence their children's development by selecting many of the other contexts to which children are exposed, including the places they visit, the means by which they entertain themselves, and the other children with whom they play.

From the very beginning, of course, the shaping influence of parent–child interaction goes both ways, for children also shape their parents' behavior (Valsiner, 2000). Each child's distinctive interests, temperament, appearance, verbal ability, and other characteristics all play roles in the process of social development by influencing how the parents interact with the child. Likewise, children do not passively soak up the contexts in which they live, but actively modify them and shape them to their own designs (Rogoff, 2003).

We begin our discussion of the early contexts of development by comparing family configurations and personality development in two markedly different societies. This cross-national comparison is followed by an examination of the major varieties of family configuration and child-rearing patterns in North America. Next, we discuss the socializing effects of two social institutions designed specifically to serve young children and their families in modern industrialized societies: child care, which substitutes for parental care at home; and preschools, which go beyond minding children to fostering their cognitive and social development. Finally, we examine the influence of books, television, and interactive media, three communications media that link the family to the larger society.

The Family as a Context for Development

A classic study by Beatrice and John Whiting (1975) nicely illustrates how differences in family life shape the development of children. The Whitings organized teams of anthropologists to observe child rearing in six communities from vastly different cultures. A comparison of two of the groups, the Gusii of Nyansongo, Kenya, and Americans in a small New England town, demonstrates how cultural belief systems, practices, and economics are expressed in family contexts, affecting the way parents treat and socialize their children.

At the time of the Whitings' work in the 1950s, the Gusii were agriculturalists living in the fertile highlands of western Kenya. The basic family unit was large, including several generations headed by a grandfather. Polygyny was the traditional marriage form, with several wives living in a single compound that contained one house for the husband. Women, who did most of the farmwork, often left their infants and toddlers in the care of older siblings and elderly family members. As is typical of agrarian societies, children's labor was valued for the production of food and the care of younger children. Beginning at the age of 3 or 4, Gusii children were expected to start helping their mothers with simple household tasks. By the age of 7, their economic contributions to the family were indispensable.

New England's "Orchard Town" represented the opposite extreme in family organization and social complexity. Most of the men of Orchard Town were wage earners who lived with their wives and children in single-family dwellings. A few of the mothers had part-time jobs, but most spent their time caring for their children, their husbands, and their homes. The children of Orchard Town divided their time between playing at home (rarely were they asked to do chores) and attending adult-structured and supervised schools.

When the Whitings observed children's behavior patterns in these cultures, they found notable overall differences. The Gusii children, for example, were more likely to offer help and support and make responsible suggestions to others. At the same time, they were more likely to reprimand and assault other children. Both of these tendencies are consistent with their child-tending duties: they needed to be nurturing and responsible, but also to exert high levels of control both for safety's sake and to communicate the cultural value of respecting one's elders.

Orchard Town children, in contrast, were more often observed seeking, rather than giving, help and attention, and were more often observed in sociable horseplay, touching others, and joining groups in an amiable way. According to the Whitings, children of industrialized societies, such as those in Orchard Town, are less nurturing and responsible because they do not contribute economically to the family, and because they spend most days in school competing with other children rather than helping them. On the other hand, the higher level of intimacy shown by the Orchard Town children is likely a reflection of the close bonds that develop between individuals living in **nuclear families,** that is, families consisting of a husband, a wife, and their immediate offspring. The Gusii, in contrast, socialize attachments to the broader group, consistent with their **extended family** living pattern. Extended families (which we will discuss in detail below) include parents and their children as well as other kin, including grandparents, cousins, aunts and uncles, and others.

Cultural comparisons such as the one conducted by the Whitings show us that families can differ in many ways that impact children's lives and development. Comparisons of modern American families with those of the 1950s also illustrate how the family system changes in response to broader ecological changes. The Orchard Town family pattern is no longer the status quo for the United States. For example, changing economic trends and new ideas about the social roles of women are associated with a rise in **single-parent families,** those that are headed by one parent, usually the mother. More recently, changing beliefs and government policies regarding gays and lesbians has created another layer of diversity in American family types. And throughout the world, for many different reasons, families are leaving their homes of origin to chart new lives in the United States, and adjusting their traditional parenting strategies as a result.

A culture's changing economy, values and beliefs, and governmental policies can all affect how families are organized as well as how family members interact and communicate with each other. At the same time, families, like children, are not static entities that respond blindly or uniformly to the social, economic, and political forces around them. Rather, they are active agents that interpret, adapt to, and even resist the broader systems and institutions with which they interact.

nuclear family A family consisting of a husband, a wife, and their children.

extended family A family in which not only parents and their children but other kin — grandparents, cousins, nephews, or more distant family relations — share a household.

single-parent family A family that is headed by one parent, usually the mother.

In many cultures, children care for younger children. This responsibility requires both nurturance and control.

Sean Sprague/Stock Boston

family A group of people traditionally defined by *shared ancestry* (blood relations), *shared residence,* and/or *marital ties.*

family structures Refers to how the family unit is socially organized

family dynamics Refers to how families function, specifically, patterns of interaction and communication among members

Family Structures and Dynamics

The study of families presents a major challenge to developmentalists. Typically, **family** is defined by *shared ancestry* (blood relations), *shared residence,* and/or *marital ties.* However, this definition leaves much to interpretation. Is a live-in housekeeper "family"? What about a father who left and has virtually no contact with his wife and children? Latina mothers often have *comadrazgo* (comothers) who provide extensive care and support; are they "family"? Is it appropriate to call a young single mother and her child a "single-parent family" if they live with the grandparents? As you can see, it is often difficult to draw boundaries around a family.

In addition to having fluid boundaries, families experience significant transitions throughout their own "life courses." They gain and lose members through births, marriages, remarriages, and deaths. Children go off to school, and often return again, sometimes with spouses or children of their own. And, naturally, family members themselves undergo personal developments that affect family life. Parents age, retire, change jobs or spouses. Children's development precipitates changes in patterns of communication, dependency, and control; and they may bring literacy or new technologies into their homes. The major challenge facing family researchers, therefore, is to understand the complex interplay among these factors (Hareven, 2000).

In discussing the role of families, developmentalists utilize two terms. The first, **family structures,** refers to how the family unit is socially organized. You are familiar already with three family structures—the nuclear family, the extended family, and the single-parent family. The second term, **family dynamics,** refers to how families function, specifically the patterns of interaction and communication among members. In the following sections we examine several different family structures present in contemporary American society. Then we will turn our focus to a specific area of family dynamics—parenting practices.

The Nuclear Family

The effects of ecological change on the family are particularly evident in the history of nuclear families. At the time the Whitings conducted their famous study, families like those observed in Orchard Town were the norm and were also popularly believed to be superior to other family structures.

A major source for understanding nuclear families is the historical work of Philippe Ariès. According to Ariès, the nuclear family is a newly arrived and highly private structure unique to modern societies. Many historians suggest that large migrations of individuals from rural areas into newly industrialized cities contributed to a shift from extended-family farm life to nuclear family patterns. In the relative isolation of nuclear families, close relationships between parents and children take on greater importance "than the honor of a line, the integrity of an inheritance, or the age and permanence of a name" (Ariès, 1962, p. 393). Ariès compares the private, nuclear family to the more sociable families of premodern times when "people lived on top of one another, masters and servants, children and adults, in houses open at all hours" (p. 406). Children reared in these conditions were exposed to an enormous diversity of roles, relationships, styles and patterns of interacting—experiences lost to children of nuclear families.

Ariès initiated a great debate regarding which family type—private and nuclear or extended and sociable—is best suited to preparing children for their futures. However, some researchers have called his work into question. First, there is evidence that the nuclear family pattern is much older than once believed, dating back as far as medieval times, and therefore not simply a response to industrialization (Herlihy, 1985). In fact, studies indicate that when new migrants moved into the cities, they often moved in with family members who had migrated previously and established residences. Thus, extended families tended to increase, not decrease after industrialization (Laslett, 1972).

In addition to questioning the relationship between family structure and industrialization, developmentalists have expressed doubt about the conclusion that nuclear families are relatively more private and socially isolated compared to extended families. In particular, researchers suggest that many nuclear families, past and present, are embedded in kinship ties that extend beyond the confines of their homes. Tamara Hareven's study of nineteenth- and twentieth-century urban families revealed the central role of extended kin in organizing migration back and forth between rural and urban areas. In describing her study, Hareven writes that, "following 'chain migration' routes, villagers who went to work in urban factories spearheaded migration for other relatives by locating housing and jobs. Those who remained in the communities of origin often took care of aging parents and other relatives who stayed behind" (2000, p. 109).

While the merits of nuclear families continue to be debated, the proportion of such families has been steadily declining in the United States in recent decades. Correspondingly, the extended family has assumed a more prominent role in American life.

Extended Families

Extended families have always played an important role in contemporary American society, although it is uncertain just how widespread the phenomenon has become in recent decades. According to the most recent U.S. Census report, extended families account for nearly 4 percent of all family types. However, there are indications that the figure may be much higher in areas with high concentrations of immigrants, where family budgets have difficulty meeting the local housing costs, and when the mothers are young and single (U.S. Bureau of the Census, 2001).

Scholars identify two major sources for the formation of an extended family: cultural traditions and economic hardship. Extended family arrangements of various kinds were the norm among the African peoples brought to the Americas and sold into slavery. These strong family affiliations persisted during slavery, despite attempts to destroy them (Genovese, 1976). Richard Griswold del Castillo (1984) offers a similar explanation of the high incidence of extended families among Hispanic Americans. He traces the contemporary Hispanic American family back to the period before the Spanish conquest, when extended kin relations were a central feature of the cultures of these people's Amerindian ancestors.

Many scholars see the extended family as a natural strategy for dealing with the combined handicaps of low income and low social standing (McLoyd, 1998a). Young, economically disadvantaged minority children in particular draw on the problem-solving and stress-reducing resources of the extended family (Smith, 2002). Extended families also appear to play an especially important role in providing support for children born to young, single mothers (Chase-Lansdale, Brooks-Gunn, & Zamsky, 1994). They provide income, child care, and help in maintaining the household, as well as less tangible assistance, such as emotional support and counseling (Jarrett, 2000). In some circumstances, grandmothers provide care that is more responsive and less punitive than that of their teenage daughters (Chase-Lansdale et al., 1994). Furthermore, the presence of other adults in the house makes it possible for the children's mothers to obtain additional education, which in turn improves the family's economic circumstances.

The evidence that extended family relations help to buffer children against the harmful effects of poverty has led psychologists to emphasize the importance of social networks in shaping parental behaviors toward their children (Manns, 1997).

When poor families are isolated from their communities, and especially when single young women attempt to raise their children without a social support system, the children are particularly at risk (Ceballo & McLoyd, 2002). By contrast, young mothers who belong to a social network that allows them to interact regularly with friends and neighbors, and to engage in such activities as attending church and participating in community events, raise their children in a more nurturant and sensitive way (McLoyd, 1998a, 1998b).

Single-Parent Families

It is estimated that half of all children born in the United States today will spend at least some portion of their childhood in a single-parent home. According to U.S. Census data, in the past 40 years there has been a 280 percent increase among European Americans and a 543 percent increase among African Americans in single-parent families (Kesner & McKenry, 2001). In 1999, female-headed households accounted for 14 percent of European American families, 23 percent of Latino families, and 45 percent of African American families (U.S. Bureau of the Census, 2002).

In stark contrast to research on extended families that finds benefits for children, studies of children from single-parent families report a number of behavioral, social, and academic problems. A variety of explanations have been offered to explain why children from single-parent families fare less well than those from two-parent or extended families. One explanation is that with only one parent available to work, take care of the children, and see to household chores, parental contact and supervision are reduced, giving children more unregulated time. According to this explanation, the very structure of the family places children at risk.

Other researchers argue that having only one parent is not itself a problem; rather, other factors that often correlate strongly with single-parenthood are to blame. For example, with only one wage earner, single-parent families have fewer material resources and experience greater financial stress compared to two-parent families. According to this view, having one parent or two is not the issue; exposure to poverty is what matters.

Yet another explanation associates the problems of children from single-parent families with the traumatic effects of divorce (you will learn more about the effects of divorce and poverty later in this chapter). From this perspective as well, single-parent families are not a problem in and of themselves. Rather, the crisis of divorce generates behavioral, social, and academic problems for children, problems that are expected to decline over time as the family learns to cope with the transition.

In an effort to untangle these competing explanations, Gunilla Weitoft and her colleagues (2003) launched a nationwide study comparing health outcomes for children in single-parent and two-parent families in Sweden. They identified almost one million children who were living with the same single adult or the same two, opposite-sex, adults in both 1991 and 1999. Using national records of child deaths, social welfare benefits, and hospital discharges, they found that socioeconomic status was the most important factor in accounting for differences between the two groups. However, even when income level was taken into account, children in single-parent families were at greater risk for psychiatric disorders, suicide, injury, and addiction.

Although the results of such large-scale studies can provide important information about populations of individuals in general, as Weitoft and her colleagues suggest, they reveal little about family dynamics, communication patterns, child-rearing practices, the origin of single-

Although the rise in single-parent families is often associated with changing economic trends and new ideas about the social roles of women, the number of single-parent fathers has also risen dramatically.

©Will Hart/Photo Edit

parenthood, relationships with other kin, and other factors that may influence the well-being of children in single-parent families. Another weakness is that most studies on children from single-parent households are conducted primarily with Caucasian families, raising the question of whether the results apply as well to ethnic-minority families.

In an attempt to answer this question, John Kesner and Patrick McKenry (2001) studied 68 preschool children and their parents living in a large city in the southeastern United States. Most of the families were African American (66 percent) and Hispanic (10 percent). Sixty-six percent of the children lived with both parents, and 34 percent lived with their mothers who had never been married. There were no differences between the single- and two-parent families in terms of ethnicity or socioeconomic level.

Kesner and McKenry examined the children's social skills and conflict-management styles and found no differences between children from single- and those from two-parent families. In discussing their results, the researchers note that compared to European Americans, African Americans are more supportive of single-parent families and attach less stigma to them. In addition, the extended-family pattern characteristic of the African American cultural tradition (described earlier) suggests that children may have a network of kin that provides additional support. Finally, Kesner and McKenry point out that because the single mothers in their study had never been married, their families were not exposed to the sudden emotional and financial changes typically experienced by divorced families. Furthermore, they may have stronger commitments to their nonconventional family structure compared with mothers who may have been divorced against their choice.

Parenting Styles and Family Dynamics

As suggested in the preceding discussion, families differ not only in how they are structured and organized, but in how members interact and communicate with each other. Of particular interest to developmentalists are the strategies and practices that parents use to raise their children.

On the basis of his study of child-rearing practices in diverse cultures, the anthropologist Robert LeVine (1988) has proposed that three major goals are shared by parents the world over:

1. The *survival goal:* to ensure that their children survive, by providing for their health and safety.

2. The *economic goal:* to ensure that their children acquire the skills and other resources needed to be economically productive adults.

3. The *cultural goal:* to ensure that their children acquire the basic cultural values of the group.

These goals form a hierarchy. The most urgent goal for parents is their children's physical survival. It is not until the safety and health of their children appear secure that parents can focus on the other two goals, passing on the economically important skills and cultural values the children will need as adults to ensure the continued existence of their family and community.

LeVine found that the way parents raise their children reflects the extent to which any of these goals is threatened by the local ecology. For example, child-care practices in places with high infant mortality rates, as is the case in Maung Thura's country, look fairly uniform throughout the world, despite vast differences in geographic location, language, and cultural and spiritual beliefs. In places as different as Indonesia, Africa, and South America, when a general threat exists to the goal of physical survival, parents tend to keep their infants on their bodies at all times, respond quickly to infant cries, nurse their babies often, and show little concern for the infant's emotional and behavioral developments. Rarely do these parents attempt to elicit smiles from their babies, or engage them in vocal play.

LeVine argued that parents are not necessarily aware of the strategies that they are employing. That is, they do not make conscious decisions to carry their babies about, nurse them frequently, and so on, for the explicit purpose of ensuring their physical survival. How, then, are such parenting practices transmitted? According to LeVine, two related factors operate to foster their transmission. One is biological. Parents who engage in successful practices will have more surviving offspring and, therefore, more children to pass their strategies on to. The second factor is associated with observational learning. Parents with more surviving offspring become magnets of attention in communities plagued by infant mortality, and their parenting ways are likely to be modeled by others.

Parenting Styles and Their Effects

Research in the United States has shown that, while child-rearing practices vary widely, they can be analyzed using measures of parental warmth and control. This research addresses the question: What mix of control, autonomy, and expression of affection contributes most to healthy development?

In the early 1970s, Diana Baumrind (1971, 1980) launched one of the best-known research programs on the developmental consequences of parenting styles. On the basis of interviews and observations of predominantly white, middle-class preschoolers and their parents, Baumrind and her colleagues found that parenting behaviors in 77 percent of their families fit one of three patterns (see Table 11.1):

- **Authoritarian parenting pattern:** Parents who follow an authoritarian parenting pattern try to shape, control, and evaluate the behavior and attitudes of their children according to a set traditional standard. They stress the importance of obedience to authority and discourage verbal give-and-take between themselves and their children. They favor punitive measures to curb their children's willfulness—whenever their children's behavior conflicts with what they believe to be correct.

- **Authoritative parenting pattern:** Parents who demonstrate an authoritative pattern take it for granted that although they have more knowledge and skill, control more resources, and have more physical power than their children, the children also have rights. Authoritative parents are less likely than authoritarian parents to use physical punishment and less likely to stress obedience to authority as a virtue in itself. Instead, these parents attempt to control their children by explaining their rules or decisions and by reasoning with them. They are willing to consider the child's point of view, even if they do not always accept it. Authoritative parents set high standards for their children's behavior and encourage the children to be independent.

- **Permissive parenting pattern:** Parents who exhibit a permissive pattern exercise less explicit control over their children's behavior than do both authoritarian and authoritative parents, either because they believe children must learn how to behave through their own experience (permissive parenting) or because they do not take the trouble to provide discipline (neglectful parenting). They give their children a lot of leeway to determine their own schedules and activities, and often consult them about family policies. They do not demand the same levels of achievement and mature behavior that authoritative and authoritarian parents do.

Baumrind found that, on the average, each style of parenting was associated with a different pattern of children's behavior in the preschool:

- **Children of authoritarian parents** tended to lack social competence in dealing with other children. They frequently withdrew from social contact and rarely took the initiative. In situations of moral conflict, they tended to look to outside authority to decide what was right. These children were often characterized as lacking spontaneity and intellectual curiosity.

- **Children of authoritative parents** appeared more self-reliant, self-controlled, and willing to explore, as well as more content than those raised by permissive or authoritarian parents. Baumrind believes that this difference is a result of the fact that while authoritative parents set high standards for their children, they explain to them why they are being rewarded and punished. Such explanations improve children's understanding and acceptance of the social rules.

- **Children of permissive parents** tended to be relatively immature; they had difficulty controlling their impulses, accepting responsibility for social actions, and acting independently.

Verbal discipline coupled with explanation is characteristic of the authoritative pattern of parenting.

Baumrind's pioneering work inspired hundreds of studies on how parenting practices affect children's development. In more recent research, developmentalists have extended their focus in several ways. First, they have attempted to view the family from a more transactional perspective (see Chapter 7) that takes into account how parents affect children, children affect parents, and how parenting styles and practices change over time (Collins et al., 2000; Maccoby, 2000). For example, Avshalom Caspi (1998) has summarized a variety of research suggesting that it is just as likely that

table 11.1

Baumrind's Parenting Styles		
Parenting Style	**Description**	**Typical Children's Characteristics**
Authoritative	• Demanding but reciprocal relationship • Favor reasoning over physical punishment • Encourage independence	• Self-reliant • Self-controlled • Display curiosity • Content
Authoritarian	• Demanding and controlling • Favor punitive methods over reasoning • Stress obedience over independence	• Other-directed • Lack social competence • Lack curiosity • Withdrawn
Permissive	• Undemanding and little control exercised • Allow children to learn through experience as a result of indulgence or neglect • Neither independence nor obedience stressed	• Dependent on others • Poor impulse control • Relative immaturity

Authoritarian parents often stress the importance of obedience to authority and use punitive measures to control their children's behavior.

Photomondo/Getty Images

parenting style is influenced by the child's characteristics as it is that the child is shaped by a particular style of parenting. A particularly active and easily frustrated child, for example, may elicit authoritarian parenting, whereas from the same parents, an easygoing or timid child might elicit an authoritative style.

An examination of parenting styles provides one way to assess family dynamics; a second line of research looks beyond the parent–child relationship to the role of other family members in children's socialization.

The Role of Siblings

Studies show that although parents are of primary importance in children's socialization (see the box "Fathers"), siblings also play significant roles (Dunn, 2002). The roles of siblings are most obvious in agricultural societies, like the Gusii discussed in this chapter, where much of the child care is performed by older siblings. It is through these child caretakers, who are sometimes no more than 4 years older than their charges, that many of the behaviors and beliefs of the social group are passed on (Zukow-Goldring, 1995). However, in many industrialized societies, including the United States, increasing numbers of working parents have led to corresponding increases in the number of children who are called upon to provide care for their younger siblings (McHale & Crouter, 1996). Within African American families, reliance on siblings for child care and socialization is commonplace and believed to reflect African family traditions (Brody & Murry, 2001).

There is ample evidence that young children learn a lot from their older siblings (as you also saw in our discussions of identity formation in Chapter 10). Margarita Azmitia and Joanne Hesser (1993) arranged for young children to play with building blocks while their older sibling and an older friend (who were approximately 9 years old) played with blocks nearby. The younger children spent more time imitating and consulting with their sibling than with the friend. Their older sibling, in turn, offered more spontaneous help than did the friend. When the two older children were asked to help a younger child build a copy of a model out of blocks, the sibling again provided more explanations and encouragement.

Older siblings may not always play the role of tutor, however. Other research has shown that until about the age of 7 or 8, older siblings may simply take over and do such tasks for their younger brothers or sisters rather than explaining or helping them to do it themselves (Perez-Granados & Callanan, 1997).

Fathers

In "Father of Mine," Everclear sings of desertion, when the whole world disappeared because "Father of mine...gave me a name...then walked away." In "Dance with My Father," Luther Vandross describes a different childhood, one colored by an image of his father lifting him high, dancing with him and his mother, spinning him around until he fell asleep: "Then up the stairs he would carry me; and I knew for sure I was loved."

Whether of loss and pain, or love and security, the lyrics by Everclear and Vandross capture the importance of fathers in the lives of their children. Nonetheless, research on fathers and fathering is just beginning to make a significant mark in the developmental sciences (Marsiglio et al., 2000). Part of the recent interest in fathers may be due to evidence suggesting that they are more involved than ever in bringing up their children. In the past 30 years, for example, fathers have provided increasing amounts of child care while their wives work. There has also been a rise in the numbers of single fathers raising children—nearly 510 percent between 1970 and 2000, compared with the 330 percent increase in single mothers raising children (U.S. Bureau of the Census, 2002). Furthermore, it seems that today's fathers may be interacting differently with their children compared with fathers of the past. Rather than being regarded primarily in the economic role of "breadwinner," the "new father" is expected to provide daily physical care, be emotionally connected to his children, and more attuned to their experiences and concerns (Yeung et al., 2001).

Indeed, one of the most significant new developments in research on fathers is an expanded notion of paternal involvement. Instead of focusing simply on the amount of time that dads spend with their children, contemporary researchers are looking in detail at the different types of activities that they engage in. It seems, in fact, that the sheer amount of time that fathers devote to their children is less important to children's well-being than how that time is spent. For example, going out together to dinner or to the movies is unrelated to children's levels of life satisfaction, whereas talking over problems and sharing and encouraging accomplishments are associated with high levels of satisfaction (Young et al., 1995). In general, fathering practices typically associated with authoritative parenting—providing emotional support, monitoring children's behaviors, and noncoercive discipline—seem to be most beneficial to children (Marsiglio et al., 2000).

Other research demonstrates that the influence of fathers extends well beyond the quality of their interactions with children. Fathers who know their children's friends, who maintain contact with teachers and coaches, and who are generally connected to other individuals and institutions in the community, help their children develop and maintain important social networks. Fathers, in other words, can play a decisive role in developing their children's social ecologies (Furstenberg, 1998).

Interestingly, at the same time that fathers are gaining more attention, studies suggest that increasingly fewer men are experiencing fatherhood (Eggebeen, 2002). In the mid-1960s, nearly 60 percent of men were living with children, compared with only 45 percent today. Developmentalists are beginning to ask questions regarding men's images of fathering, and what it means to them to be fathers. Probing the identity issues surrounding the role of father, and the emotional and subjective experiences of fathering, may shed additional light on how much, and how well, fathers parent their children.

Sibling relationships are often ambivalent, sometimes loving and caring, and sometimes hostile and full of rancor. When conflict in sibling relationships escalates, brothers and sisters may avoid each other, spend little time in activities that involve caregiving and teaching, and socialize maladaptive patterns of behavior in the younger sibling (Garcia et al., 2000). One factor that reliably affects the siblings' relationship is the emotional climate of their family (Brody, 1998; Erel et al., 1998). Siblings are more likely to fight when their parents are not getting along well together, when their parents divorce, and when a stepfather enters the family, especially if one or both of the siblings are boys (Hetherington, 1988).

While the studies described previously have examined siblings' influence on each other's competence, the effect of parental behavior on the quality of their relationships, and the influence of the family's cultural and ethnic background, very few studies have attempted to examine these factors simultaneously. One exception is Gene Brody and Velma Murry's study (2001) of sibling socialization in single-parent African American families. Noting that research on African American families has focused disproportionately on negative issues, Brody and Murry asked about the interplay among parenting practices, sibling relationships, and levels of cognitive and social competence in African American children living in rural areas.

The researchers expected that the level of competence in younger siblings would be influenced by the level of competence of their older brothers and sisters, as well as by the quality of their relationship. However, the level of competence in the older children was anticipated to reflect the mother's parenting style, which was in turn

A positive relationship between siblings fosters social and cognitive competence.

©William Waldron/The Image Works

expected to be influenced by her level of education. The logic of their hypothesis is shown in Figure 11.1.

Brody and Murry studied 152 African American single-mother-headed families living in a rural area of the South. In addition to assessing the level of the mothers' education, they assessed the mothers' use of *no-nonsense parenting*, a style that includes a mixture of high levels of vigilant control with high levels of support. Children's competence was assessed through teacher ratings of cognitive competence, social competence, and self-regulation. Finally, the researchers measured the quality of the sibling relationship by asking the oldest sibling to complete a questionnaire about the amount of antagonism, quarrelling, and competition they experienced with their young brothers and sisters.

Consistent with their predictions, Brody and Murry found that maternal education was linked to no-nonsense parenting, no-nonsense parenting was linked to older siblings' competence, and older siblings' competence was linked to younger siblings' competence, *when the siblings enjoyed a positive relationship.* Clearly, then, parenting styles and sibling relationships combine to exert a unique influence on children's development.

Figure 11.1 Studies of single-parent African American families suggest that a mother's level of education affects her parenting style, which, in turn, affects her children's level of competence. (Adapted from Brody & Murry, 2001.)

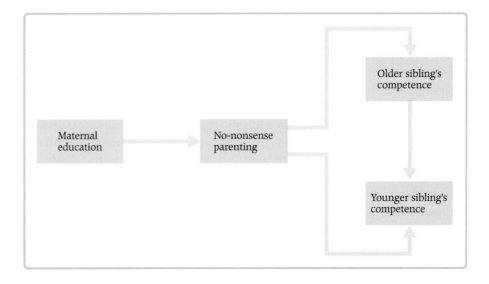

Family Diversity

Changes in values, politics, economies, and transportation technologies have altered the face of "family" in many parts of the globe. Contemporary families in many communities represent diverse ethnic backgrounds, cultural heritages, and lifestyles. Here we will examine two patterns of diversity in American families: the rising number of immigrant families, and families with gay and lesbian parents.

Immigrant Families

Ethnic diversity has been present in the United States throughout its history as a result of the colonization of Native Americans, the arrival of slaves from Africa, and a continuous stream of immigrants. However, in the past few decades the United States has witnessed an enormous influx of families from other parts of the globe. Currently, one in five children in the United States has immigrant parents. These changing family patterns are also typical of Canada, Australia, Germany, and several other European countries (United Nations Commission on Population and Development, 1996). As shown in Figure 11.2, more than 50 percent of U.S. immigrants come from Latin America, 25 percent from Asia, and 15 percent from Europe or elsewhere.

One of the most common ways of exploring diversity in families is to examine differences in parenting styles. For example, research indicates that African American parents are more likely to use authoritarian strategies, compared with parents of European descent. Although Baumrind's original work included white, middle-class families, and found that authoritarian practices are associated with less-positive outcomes for children, more recent research has found that African American teenagers whose parents adopted an authoritarian style were more likely to succeed in school than were students whose parents adopted an authoritative style (Lamborn et al., 1996). Clearly, it is essential to understand parenting styles within the broader contexts of families' lives. Indeed, the very categories and language that we use to describe differences in styles may be culturally specific (Parke & Buriel, 1998).

For example, in a study comparing Chinese American and European American families and their children, researchers encountered a major obstacle when they attempted to apply such categories as "authoritarian" and "authoritative": these words do not have the same meanings for both groups (Chao, 1994). In describing this study, Ruth Chao wrote that the English word "authoritarian" carries with it many negative connotations—such as hostility, aggressiveness, mistrust, dominance—that are not applicable to the core methods of socialization in the Chinese family. While it is true that Chinese place high value on obedience and parental control, the preferred Chinese pattern of socialization is closer to the American notion of "training." Chao maintains that Chinese parents exercise control over their children and demand their obedience "in the context of a supportive, highly involved, and physically close mother–child relationship" (p. 112).

Chao (1996) tested her idea that Baumrind's parenting categories do not apply well to Chinese parenting patterns by administering a questionnaire to 50 Chinese American and 50 European American mothers. The questionnaire included standard items such as those used by Baumrind, plus a set of questions that related specifically to Chinese notions of training young children for life (the mothers were asked, for example, to indicate their level of agreement with the statement "Mothers must train their children to work very hard and to be disciplined"). As others had done before her, Chao found that the Chinese American mothers scored higher on the standard measures of control and authoritarianism. But even after she controlled for their scores on control and authoritarianism, the Chinese American mothers were

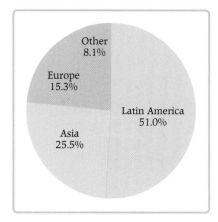

Figure 11.2 The wave of immigrants to the United States has led to sweeping changes in the racial and ethnic diversity of the country. Today, one in five children has immigrant parents. (Adapted from Suarez-Orozco, 2001.) This chart shows the percentage of immigrants to the United States from various parts of the globe.

distinguished from the European American mothers on the measure of training, indicating a culturally distinctive pattern of parenting was at work.

Just as parenting styles vary across cultures, so do the values that parents seek to instill in their children. Many recent immigrants to the United States come from countries that place great value on education as a means to achieving a successful life. Indeed, immigrant parents tend to place greater weight on the importance of education than do native-born Americans. In his ethnographic case study of an Hispanic immigrant family, Gerardo Lopez (2001) reported that the parents would often take their children with them as they worked in the fields in order to underscore important "life lessons" about how hard they work and how poorly they are compensated. The most important lesson, however, is that education is the key to a better life.

What accounts for this difference in the valuing of education? Many developmentalists have pointed to the "ideologies of opportunity" and "cultures of optimism" that motivate families to migrate in the first place (Suarez-Orozco, 2001). In short, parents believe that life in the new country will provide increased opportunities for their children. Sadly, and perhaps counterintuitively, research indicates that length of residence in the United States is associated with declining health, school achievement, and aspirations among immigrant Asian and Latino children alike (Portes & Rumbaut, 2001; Steinberg, 1996; Waters, 1999). Carola Suarez-Orozco (2000) suggests that the "Americanization" of foreign-born children often includes exposure to persistent forms of racism, as well as peer influence that together undermine their initial sense of optimism and regard for education.

Gay and Lesbian Parents

Another significant change in the nature of families is the increasing number of gay and lesbian parents. Because many gay and lesbian parents choose to hide their sexual orientation out of fear of discrimination, it is difficult to get an accurate count, but national estimates range from 2 to 8 million families raising 3 to 14 million children (Lowry, 1999).

The families of gay and lesbian couples are diverse in size, ethnicity, religion, and socioeconomic status.

AP Photo/Eric Risberg

Like families in general, those with gay and lesbian parents are diverse in size and structure, ethnicity, religion, and socioeconomic class. Some gay and lesbian coparents came out after having their children in a heterosexual relationship. More recently, openly gay and lesbian couples and individuals are choosing to raise children that they have adopted or conceived by means of insemination or surrogacy (Ariel & McPherson, 2000). In the United States, adoption is often a difficult procedure for gay and lesbian couples because traditional family law does not recognize such couples as constituting a legal marriage (Dalton & Bielby, 2000). Thus, coparents who wish to adopt their partners' legal or biological children often must convince judges to reinterpret adoption statutes in ways that are inclusive of gay and lesbian unions (Ryan, 2000).

A number of studies have sought to determine whether children raised in gay and lesbian households are different from children raised in heterosexual families. In their comprehensive review of these studies, Jane Ariel and Dan McPherson (2000) conclude that such children are just as healthy as those raised by heterosexual parents on measures of gender identity, sexual orientation, intelligence, moral reasoning, behavior problems, personality, and locus of control.

If family diversity has become increasingly visible due to globalization and changing cultural values, so, too, have the risks and stressors faced by many families.

Distressed Families

Developmentalists studying families at risk have identified several factors that can seriously impede children's intellectual, social, and emotional developments. The most pernicious factor of all is poverty.

Families and Poverty

One of the most reliable findings in research on families is the relationship between economic hardship and children's well-being. Poverty touches all aspects of family life: the quality of housing and health care, access to education and recreational facilities, and even one's safety as one walks along the street (Duncan & Brooks-Gunn, 1997; McLoyd, 1998a, 1998b). Interest in the influence of poverty on children's development has increased in recent years owing, in part, to the rising rates of poor children in the United States. According to data compiled by the United Nations Children's Fund (cited in Kaul, 2002), nearly one in four children in the United States is currently living in poverty (see Figure 11.3).

Contrary to popular belief, only half of all poor children and families are chronically and persistently poor. In a nationwide study, Duncan and his colleagues found that family income fluctuates significantly across the family's life cycle and tends to increase as children age (Duncan & Raudenbush, 1999). However, they also found that being poor during early childhood presents a greater challenge to children's well-being, particularly their academic achievement, than being poor during later stages of development. Considering that the family's socioeconomic status is the most powerful predictor of cognitive skills when children enter school, and that early school success forecasts lifelong achievement and adjustment, the effects of poverty are particularly serious (Stipek, 2001).

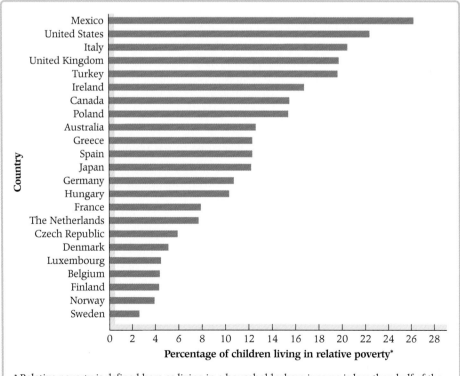

Figure 11.3 In the United States, nearly one in four children lives in poverty, and is consequently at risk for a variety of illnesses, mental health problems, and school difficulties. (Adapted from UNICEF, 2000.)

* Relative poverty is defined here as living in a household where income is less than half of the national median.

Children growing up in poverty are also at greater risk for later mental and health problems. Recent research indicates that poverty in early childhood places individuals at risk for major depression in adulthood, regardless of adult socioeconomic status (Gilman et al., 2003). However, poverty-stricken children's mental health problems can be significantly reduced if their family's income rises above the poverty level. This was demonstrated in an eight-year study by Jane Costello and her colleagues (2003) of Native American children growing up on an Indian reservation. Some of the children lived in poverty; others did not. Halfway through the eight-year study, a casino opened on the reservation, moving many (but not all) of the poor families out of poverty. Children whose families moved out of poverty due to the income provided by the casino showed a significant decrease in mental health disorders. In contrast, there was no change in the mental health of children whose families remained below the poverty level.

In addition to mental health problems, poverty is also associated with intellectual and physical problems. Environmentally induced illnesses such as tuberculosis, lead poisoning and asthma are all observed at higher rates in poor children compared with nonpoor children (Books, 2000; Shonkoff & Phillips, 2000). Poverty also appears to affect parents' approach to child rearing. Studies in many parts of the world have found that in families living close to the subsistence level, parents are likely to adopt child-rearing practices that are controlling, in a manner akin to the authoritarian pattern described by Baumrind. According to Robert LeVine (1974), parents who know what it means to eke out a living "see obedience as the means by which their children will be able to make their way in the world and establish themselves economically in young adulthood when the basis must be laid for the economic security of their nascent families" (p. 63).

An emphasis on obedience is also frequently encountered in poor families in the United States, in part for the economically based reason cited by LeVine. In addition, some researchers have suggested that poor minority mothers in the United States demand unquestioning obedience and discourage their children's curiosity because the dangerous circumstances of their daily life make independence on the part of their children too risky (McLoyd, 1998b).

Another important way in which poverty influences parenting is by raising the level of parents' stress. Low-income parents have higher rates of depression, negative feelings of self-worth, and negative beliefs about control (summarized in Shonkoff & Phillips, 2000). Parents who are under stress are less nurturant, more likely to resort to physical punishment, and less consistent when they interact with their children (Sameroff et al., 1998).

The studies reviewed here indicate that poverty has ubiquitous and long-lasting effects on children's development. Poverty, however, is associated with other risk factors. One of the most common associations is the age of the parent.

Teen Mothers

Many women who are raising children are still teenagers. As Figure 11.4 indicates, despite a decline in the 1990s, the number of single teenage mothers in the United States remains high. This situation is of great concern because research has shown that children of unmarried teenage mothers are at a developmental disadvantage. Preschool children of single teenage mothers have been found to be more aggressive, less self-controlled, and less cognitively advanced than the children of older, married mothers (Coley & Chase-Lansdale, 1998; Dunn et al., 1998). In a study of one hundred twenty-one 3-year-olds born to adolescent mothers, the researchers found that less than one-third scored within normal ranges on tests of intelligence, language, and socioemotional functioning (Sommer et al., 2000).

Frank Furstenberg and his colleagues (1992) believe that two factors contribute to the negative developmental effect of being raised by a young unmarried mother. First, young mothers are often less prepared to bring up children and have little interest in doing so. As a consequence, they tend to vocalize less with their babies than older mothers do. A lack of verbal communication seems to lead in turn to lowered cognitive ability in preschool and elementary school. Second, young mothers, especially those without husbands, are likely to have very limited financial resources. As a consequence, they are likely to be poorly educated, live in disadvantaged neighborhoods, lack quality health care, and be socially isolated. Often these factors are so closely intertwined that it is difficult to specify how much each contributes to the developmental problems of children raised by young unmarried mothers (Duncan & Brooks-Gunn, 1997).

However, it is important to recognize that not all children born to teenage mothers have equally grim outcomes. Tom Luster and his colleagues (2000) compared "more successful" and "less successful" preschool-age children of adolescent mothers. Children who were most successful, as measured by a standardized test of intellectual and language functioning, were more likely to live in intellectually stimulating and less stressful environments compared with their less successful peers. In addition, the mothers of the most successful children had received more years of education, were more likely to be employed, had fewer children, lived in more desirable neighborhoods, and lived with a male partner. Likewise, a study of adolescent mothers' participation in welfare-reform programs indicates that highly involved mothers—those who take advantage of center-based child care, educational opportunities, and job training programs—have children with more advanced cognitive ability than children whose mothers are less involved (Yoshikaw et al., 2001).

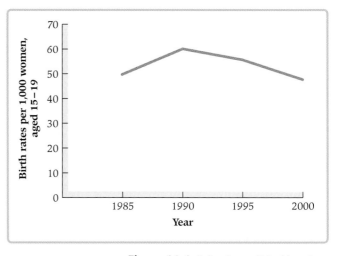

Figure 11.4 Following a disturbing rise during the 1970s and 1980s, the number of babies born to teenage mothers declined significantly between 1990 and 2000. (Alan Guttmacher Institute, 2004.)

Divorce

Approximately half of all marriages in the United States end in divorce, affecting more than one million children annually (U.S. Bureau of the Census, 1998, Table 157). While the divorce rate in the United States is by far the highest in the world, the rate of divorce in Canada and Europe is rising rapidly.

Children whose parents have divorced are twice as likely as children whose parents are still together to have problems in school, to act out, to be depressed and unhappy, to have lower self-esteem, and to be less socially responsible and competent (Amato, 2000; Sun & Li, 2002).

Divorce leads to several changes in children's life experiences that might be expected to contribute to these negative outcomes. Many of the problems associated with divorce are of the same kind as those faced by unmarried single women. First, the average income of single-parent families created by divorce or separation falls by 37 percent within 4 months of the breakup (U.S. Bureau of the Census, 1991). Only 73 percent of the custodial parents who are due child support receive any money at all from their former spouses, and most receive only a portion of what is owed to them (U.S. Bureau of the Census, 1999). As a consequence, about 30 percent of all custodial parents find themselves living below the poverty threshold. (In 1999, the Census Bureau defined a family of four as poor if its annual income fell below $15,150.) These changes in economic status often mean that after their parents divorce, children have to move away from their friends and neighbors to poorer neighborhoods with different schools and lower-quality child care. These changes are difficult for children to deal with. According to Mavis Hetherington and her colleagues, even when economic status is not changed by divorce, negative consequences of divorce often remain (Hetherington et al., 1998).

Second, parents raising children alone are trying to accomplish by themselves what is usually a demanding job for two adults. Both fathers and mothers who have sole custody of their children complain that they are overburdened by the necessity of juggling child care and household and financial responsibilities by themselves (Amato, 2000). Divorce forces many mothers to enter the workforce at the same time that they and their children are adapting to a new family configuration. Seventy-eight percent of divorced mothers are in the labor force; most of them work full-time (U.S. Bureau of the Census, 1995). Because of the many demands on their mothers' time, children of divorce not only receive less guidance and assistance but tend to lose out on important kinds of social and intellectual stimulation (Hetherington et al., 1999).

In studying the consequences of divorce, developmentalists have employed a *crisis model* in which divorce was viewed as a specific disturbance to which parents and children adjusted over time. More recently, however, developmentalists have created a *chronic strain model* that recognizes ongoing hardships, including financial insecurity and continuing conflict between parents, that may affect children's lives and adjustments for many years to come. Paul Amato (2000) has attempted to represent both the short-term trauma associated with divorce as well as its long-term effects with the *divorce-stress-adjustment perspective,* shown in Figure 11.5. This more inclusive model views marital dissolution not as a discrete event, but as a complex process that varies depending on the specific stressors and protective factors influencing the family as a whole and its individual members.

Although it makes intuitive sense that the losses associated with the breakup of a family are the cause of the various behavioral and social problems experienced by children of divorce, a number of studies that collected data about children *before* their parents divorced have cast doubt on this idea.

An alternative to the divorce-stress-adjustment perspective, in which child problems begin with the divorce itself, is the *selection perspective.* According to this model, most of the negative effects of family disruption may be accounted for by problems

Figure 11.5 Children's adjustment to divorce depends on both risk and protective factors. (Amato, 2000.)

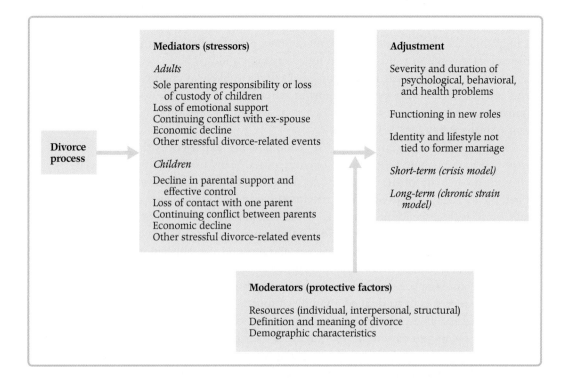

that predate the divorce (Sun, 2001). Several large longitudinal studies indicate that long-standing dysfunctional family patterns and inherent characteristics of parents, such as antisocial personality traits, create unhealthy environments for children, thereby contributing to their adjustment problems (Hetherington, 1999; Sun, 2001).

Interestingly, the similarity in divorce rates among twin pairs is higher for monozygotic twins than for dizygotic twins, suggesting that a genetic component may be at work (Jockin et al., 1996). That is, children from divorced families might be more troubled than those from intact families because they have inherited pre-dispositions from their troubled parents that place them at greater risk for a variety of problems, including divorce (Vangelisti, Reis, & Fitzpatrick, 2002). According to these studies, the divorce itself has negligible effects on children's adjustments.

There is, of course, a range of individual differences in how children adjust to divorce. In his comprehensive review of research in the area, Paul Amato (2000) identified the following factors that have been found to facilitate positive adjustment: active coping skills such as seeking social support; support from peers; and access to therapeutic interventions, including school-based support programs. Factors that impede adjustment include avoidant coping mechanisms, a tendency toward self-blame, and feelings of lack of control.

Amato, among others, realizes that research on the consequences of divorce fuels a contentious debate. Some see divorce as a source of a variety of social ills and child problems. Others, however, see it as a benign force that allows parents to seek happiness in new relationships and provides an escape for children otherwise trapped in dysfunctional families. On the strength of several decades of research, Amato concludes that "divorce benefits some individuals, leads others to experience temporary decrements in well-being that improve over time, and forces others on a downward cycle from which they might never fully recover" (Amato, 2000, p. 1285). Given the rising divorce rates in the United States and other countries, continued research on the consequences of divorce remains a high priority.

Abusive Families

In recent decades the public has become increasingly aware that many children in the United States are mistreated by members of their own families. Scarcely a day goes by without a story in the media about a child who has been neglected, mal-treated, or even murdered by a parent or other relative. Currently, about 13 in every 1000 children are abused (National Child Abuse and Neglect Data System, 2002). Although there has been a slight improvement during the past decade, it is clear that child maltreatment in the United States remains a serious problem.

More than half of all the reported cases of child abuse are for neglect of the physical well-being of the child, which includes inadequate provision of food and clothing, as well as a lack of supervision. Physical abuse, such as beating, burning, kicking, or hitting a child with an object, accounts for about a quarter of the reported cases, while sexual abuse accounts for 13 percent of the cases. Emotional maltreatment was reported in 5 percent of the cases, and medical neglect (failing to take a child who is ill or injured to a doctor) was reported in 3 percent of the cases (NCCAN, 1997). Often children who are exposed to one kind of abuse are also exposed to others (Edwards et al., 2003). Many experts consider all types of abuse and neglect to be greatly underreported. The only certainty is that each year large numbers of children are abused or neglected (Finkelhor & Dziuba-Leatherman, 1995).

With the exception of extreme maltreatment and sexual abuse, judgments about the applicability of these categories are likely to be difficult because what is deemed appropriate and inappropriate treatment of children, including the frequency and severity of physical punishment, varies dramatically from one family and community to the next (Holden, 2002). According to a variety of surveys, for example, over 90 percent of all parents in the United States have spanked their children—a practice, as you saw in Chapter 10, that is viewed as unacceptable in countries such as Sweden. Clearly the borders between culturally acceptable physical punishment and physical punishment that is defined as maltreatment depend very much on parents' beliefs about children and the modes of interaction sanctioned in the children's families and communities.

Why do parents abuse their own children? It is generally believed that parents who were physically abused by their parents are more likely to abuse their own children than are parents who were not themselves abused (Ammerman et al., 1999). However, only 30 percent of those who were abused become child abusers themselves; 70 percent do not (Kaufman & Zigler, 1989). Hence, a history of abuse may be considered a risk factor in later abuse but cannot be considered a simple cause. Rather, a complex interplay of multiple risk factors seems to set the stage for maltreatment (Barnett et al., 1997).

There is a good deal of evidence that one risk factor is stress on the family. The stresses can be of many kinds, several of which you have already encountered in this chapter: chronic poverty, recent job loss, marital discord, and social isolation have all been linked to increases in the incidence of child abuse (Gordon et al., 2003). The likelihood of abuse is also higher when the mother is very young, is poorly educated, abuses drugs or alcohol, or receives little financial support from the father (Goodman et al., 1998; Gordon et al., 2003).

Any child may be neglected or abused, but some children seem to be at greater risk than others. Age is one factor: children 7 years old and younger represent half the cases of child maltreatment. Of the children who died as a result of abuse in the United States in 1995, 77 percent were under 3 years of age, and almost half were under the age of 1. Gender is a second factor: boys are far more likely than girls to be the target of physical abuse, while girls are twice as likely as boys to be the victims of sexual abuse. Race is a third factor: in 55 percent of the cases of child maltreatment reported in 1997, the children were white; in 27 percent, they were African American; in 10 percent, Hispanic; and in 2 percent, Native American (NCCAN, 1999). Socioeconomic class is a fourth factor: children living in poverty are more likely than middle-class children to be abused (Barnett et al., 1993; Barth, 1998; Wilson & Saft, 1993).

Studies that compare the intellectual, social, and emotional consequences of child abuse attest to its negative effects (Cicchetti & Toth, 2003). Many maltreated infants are sad, fearful, and frequently angry. They rarely initiate social contact, and their attachment behavior in the strange situation is likely to be classified as insecure or avoidant (Kim & Cicchetti, 2003). In preschool, physically abused children find it difficult to get along with other children and are less well liked than their peers (Haskett & Kistner, 1991). Their popularity remains low in middle childhood because their peers and teachers see them as more aggressive and less cooperative than other children (Salzinger et al., 1993). They are reported to be more afraid than other children of angry interactions between adults (Hennessy et al., 1994). A review of school and social service records found that maltreated children had poorer grades than their peers, performed poorly on standardized tests, and were more likely to have to repeat a grade (Eckenrode et al., 1993).

Studies of abusive families suggest that they show less positive and more negative emotions toward their children compared with nonabusive families. Recent work by Seth Pollack and his colleagues indicates that the emotional home environment of abused and neglected children seriously impinges on their ability to understand emotions in others (Pollack et al., 2000). They studied three groups of preschool-aged children (3- to 5-year-olds). One group had a history of physical neglect; another of physical abuse; the third group came from nonmaltreating families. The children were told short stories depicting different emotions and were asked to point to a photograph that showed how the protagonist in the story felt. Here are a few examples:

Happy: Johnny/Susie wanted his/her friends to come over to play. So he/she asked them, and they came to play with him/her at his/her house (the gender of the protagonist was made to match the gender of the child).
Sad: Johnny/Susie was the only one in class not to get any Valentines on Valentine's Day.
Disgusted: Someone threw up on Johnny/Susie during lunch at school.
Afraid: Johnny/Susie was dreaming about a monster in his/her nightmare.
Angry: Johnny's/Susie's little brother broke his/her favorite toy on purpose.

After hearing each story, the child was asked to chose which of three photographs showed how Johnny/Susie felt. The researchers found that neglected children were less accurate in identifying the emotion of the story protagonist compared with children in the other two groups, suggesting that they had more difficulty discriminating between emotional expressions. Physically abused children, on the other hand, had more difficulty recognizing sadness and disgust, but recognized anger as accurately as nonmaltreated children. In general, neglected children showed a "bias" toward selecting sad expressions, whereas abused children tended to chose angry expressions. No such biases were observed in the nonmaltreated control group. The researchers concluded that the history of children's emotional experiences in the family has a significant bearing on their interpretation and understanding of the emotional lives of others. It is interesting to consider how maltreated children's diminished ability to interpret emotional expressions bears on their day-to-day social interaction and the development of interpersonal relationships.

Many scholars who have studied the physical abuse of children in the United States see it as a social disease that accompanies the acceptance of violence in families, local communities, and society at large. Two kinds of evidence support this position: first, most child abuse occurs when parents set out to discipline their children by punishing them physically and then end up hurting them (Zigler & Hall, 1989). Second, countries in which the physical punishment of children is frowned upon, such as Sweden and Japan, have very low rates of physical abuse of children (Belsky, 1993; Cicchetti & Toth, 1993). The multiple cultural, family, parent, and child risk factors that operate together in cases of child maltreatment suggest that broad-based, systematic intervention campaigns would offer the best hope for reducing the problem in the long run (Hughes et al., 2001).

Affluent Families

It is no surprise that children are at risk when their families are poverty-stricken, headed by teen parents, torn apart by divorce, or are abusive. However, there is evidence to suggest that children from wealthy families are also at risk for behavioral and emotional problems. Suniya Luthar and Bronwyn Becker (2002) studied middle-school students living in one of the most affluent suburban communities in the United States. Their results showed high levels of depression, particularly among girls, as well as high levels of substance abuse. What is the cause of their distress? According to the results, children of wealth feel themselves to be under a great deal of pressure to achieve—in school, in sports, socially, and financially. They also tend to be isolated from adults and feel emotionally distant from their mothers.

home care Child care provided in the child's own home, primarily by the father or a grandmother, while the mother is at work.

family care Child care provided in someone else's home, that of either a relative or a stranger.

child-care center An organized child-care facility supervised by licensed professionals.

Luthar and Becker's study supports recent concerns voiced in the popular press that wealthy families have become overly invested in performance and achievement issues, and that their children are suffering as a consequence. Their children's time is over-scheduled, and often spent in the company of peers, many of whom endorse substance abuse as a means of "letting off steam." The study stands as a cautionary note against the assumption that children of means lack for nothing.

Early Contexts of Care

Child care is a fact of life for nearly all children in the United States. By the time they reach 3 years of age, more than 90 percent will experience regular nonparental care and more than 50 percent will be spending more than 30 hours per week in care (NICHD, 2001b). In the United States and other industrialized countries, one of the most important tasks many parents face is selecting the child-care facility or preschool that will provide the upbringing of their children during those hours.

Varieties of Child Care

One of the most popular arrangements for children younger than 5 is **home care**—care provided in the children's own homes, primarily by their grandmothers or other relatives—while their mothers are at work. Children cared for at home experience the least change from normal routine: they eat food provided by their parents and take naps in their own beds. They also come in contact with relatively few children their own age (Clarke-Stewart, 1993).

Child care provided in someone else's home, that of either a relative or a stranger, is called **family care** (U.S. Bureau of the Census, 1998). Family child care often exposes children not only to caretakers from outside the family circle but also to new settings and to children of other families. The children in a family child-care setting may range widely in age, forming a more diverse social group than is likely to exist at home. The routine of activities in family child care, however, is usually very similar to the routine at home (Clarke-Stewart, 1993).

Child care offers children a variety of educational and social experiences.

Bob Daemmrich/The Image Works

table 11.2

Determining Quality of Child-Care Centers

Questions about the program:

- Is the program licensed by the state or local government?
- Is the program accredited by the National Association for the Education of Young Children or the National Association of Family Child Care?
- Does the program offer staff medical benefits and leave; does it support caregivers' continuing education through tuition reimbursement programs and/or sponsoring attendance at professional conferences and workshops?
- Does the staff-to-child ratio conform to state-regulated guidelines for the age group?
- Does the program encourage parent involvement through volunteering in the classroom, or participating on the Board of Directors or other committees?

Questions about the environment:

- Is the environment safe and sanitary?
- Is the place appealing, with comfortable lighting and an acceptable noise level?
- Does the environment accommodate the child who may have special needs?
- Are toys and materials well organized so children can choose what interests them?

Questions about the caregivers:

- Are the caregivers certified by the Council for Early Childhood Professional Recognition with a Child Development Associates degree credential for infant/toddler caregivers or an equivalent credential that addresses comparable competencies (such as an A.A./A.S./ B.A./B.S.)?
- Are the caregivers responsive, that is:
  - Playful partners who introduce new ideas and games
  - Supportive of children in their social contacts with other children and adults
  - Respectful of the child's individual development, rhythms, style, strengths and limitations
  - Respectful of the child's native culture or ethnicity

Source: Adapted from *Zero to Three*, 2003.

Child-care centers—organized child-care facilities supervised by licensed professionals—have attracted the most public attention. They have also been the focus of the most extensive study by developmentalists.

Child-Care Centers

Licensed child-care centers generally offer a wider variety of formal learning experiences than family or home child care and are likely to employ at least one trained caretaker (see Table 11.2 for important questions that parents are urged to ask regarding the quality of child care). Waiting lists for places in child-care centers tend to be long because the demand far exceeds the available openings.

The programs available vary in style and philosophy. Some offer an academic curriculum, emphasize discipline, and have a school-like atmosphere. Others emphasize social development and allow children to exercise more initiative in their activities. Because licensed child-care centers often receive public financing, they have been more accessible to researchers, who have studied both their characteristics and the way these characteristics affect children's development.

Preschool provides an important context for developing "children's culture." Hand-clapping games, like the one shown in this Malaysian preschool, are but one example of the many games and rituals that children learn from other children.

Paul Chesley/Getty Images

Developmental Effects of Child Care

As you saw in Chapter 7 (p. 248), the effects of child care during the first 2 years of life depend primarily on the quality of the care provided and not on the mere fact of parent–child separation during the day. Nevertheless, concerns about the effects of child care in later years continue to be raised, primarily regarding children's intellectual development, social development, and emotional well-being.

Physical and Intellectual Effects

When children enter care outside the home, they enter a whole new world. There are new routines and expectations, new toys and children to play with, new adults who will provide care and comfort, and, as any parent will tell you—new *germs.* In fact, children under 3 years of age in care arrangements with more than 6 other children are at increased risk for upper respiratory infections, gastrointestinal illnesses, and ear infections (NICHD, 2003). Although cold and flu bugs make regular rounds in child-care facilities, and often follow children home to their families, there is no evidence that increased illness takes a toll on children's overall development or school readiness (NICHD, 2003).

Stress is another physical consequence of time spent in child care. Sarah Watamura and her colleagues (2003) measured levels of salivary cortisol (a steroid used as an indicator of general stress) in groups of infants and toddlers who received care either in their homes or in child-care centers. Of those in child care, 35 percent of the infants and 71 percent of the toddlers showed a rise in cortisol across the day. Of those receiving care in their homes, however, 71 percent of the infants and 64 percent of the toddlers showed *decreases* in cortisol levels. As you learned in Chapter 7 (p. 270), animal studies indicate that the quality of "mothering" can have lasting effects on the stress levels of offspring and the way they respond to new and challenging environments (Brotman et al., 2003; Meaney, 2001).

Despite the evidence that children in care may experience more illnesses and stress, research conducted in Europe as well as the United States indicates that intellectual development of children in high-quality child-care centers is at least as good as that of children raised at home by their parents (Campbell et al., 2001) (see Figure 11.6). Of special importance is the level of training received by the caregivers and appropriate child-to-staff ratios (NICHD, 2002). In some cases experience in high-quality child-care programs lessens or prevents the decline in intellectual performance that sometimes occurs in children of low socioeconomic backgrounds who remain at home with poorly educated parents after the age of 2 (NICHD, 2003b).

Impact on Social and Emotional Development

Children who attend child-care centers in the United States tend to be more self-sufficient and more independent of parents and teachers, more verbally expressive, more knowledgeable about the social world, and more comfortable in new situations than children who do not attend child-care centers. Compared with children with no child-care experience, they are also happier and more enthusiastic about sharing toys and participating in fantasy play. However, the development of social competence is not simply a matter of learning how to get along by interacting with a variety of playmates. Caregivers play a crucial role. Children's social play and peer interactions become more com-

Figure 11.6 Performance on tests of intellectual development by children cared for in day-care centers and by those cared for at home. The tests were specially constructed to assess children's ability to use language, form concepts, and remember information. (From Clarke-Stewart, 1984.)

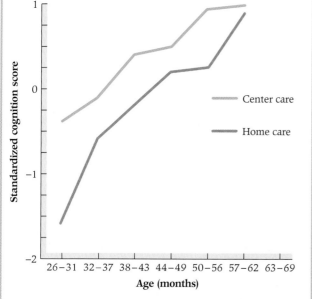

plex and skilled when they are monitored and facilitated by warm, responsive care-givers (NICHD, 2001b).

On the other hand, children who attend child-care centers also tend to be less polite, less agreeable, less compliant with adults, and more aggressive than those who do not. These effects seem to be related to the number of years a child spends in full-time nonparental care, with more extensive time being associated with more aggressive behavior and a greater likelihood of behavior problems in kindergarten (NICHD Early Child Care Research Network, 2003). These negative behavioral effects, however, tend to be mild, particularly when compared with the effects of other factors such as the mother's sensitivity and the family's socioeconomic level.

Taken together, the research would seem to suggest that child care may adverse-ly affect children's social behavior and emotional well-being. However, many devel-opmentalists take issue with this conclusion. Some have argued that the quality, not the quantity, of out-of-home-care exerts the biggest influence on children's adjust-ment. For example, an experimental study by John Love and his colleagues (2003) of children from low-income families (who would be expected to be at special risk for behavioral problems) found that those who received high-quality child care benefited in many ways and had less aggressive behavior problems than similar chil-dren who did not receive child care.

Others have argued that children's home life, including their preexisting rela-tionship with parents, is more important in determining adjustment to child care. A study of middle-class German children in child care found that their mothers compensated for being away during the day with intense bouts of inter-action and intimacy during the early morning and evening hours (Ahnert & Lamb, 2000). Likewise, Lieselottte Ahnert and Michael Lamb (2003) argue that one reason children in child care have trouble is because their working mothers are stressed, and have little time and energy to engage their young children in high-quality interactions.

Research that looks at factors of income, children's relationships with parents, and amount of parental stress goes well beyond the typical focus on how parental versus nonparental care affects children's development. In particular, this research alerts us to how other features of the ecology contribute to how children experi-ence and adapt to different contexts of care.

An Ecological Approach to Child Care

An ecological approach to child care is particularly important for understanding the child-care contexts of ethnic-minority and immigrant children. Deborah Johnson and her colleagues have pointed out that much of the research on child care does not include children of color, and when it does, it tends to ignore important vari-ables such as family structure and values, segregation and racism, and issues of cultural identity that affect children's access to care, the type of care they receive, and how they respond to such care (Johnson et al., 2003). For example, the very distinc-tion between maternal and nonmaternal care is complicated in the more open and fluid structures characteristic of many African American and Latino families who believe that parenting is a duty that extends throughout a system of extended kin.

Figure 11.7 (p. 428) shows an ecological model for studying the contexts of care and development in minority children. Following Bronfenbrenner's general approach, the model includes interacting components of the *macrosystem* (Boxes 1–2: dominant beliefs and ideologies related to racism and oppression), *exosystem* (Box 3: institutions supporting segregation), *mesosystem* (Boxes 4–5: schools, neigh-borhoods, and networks of care), and *microsystem* (Boxes 6–8: immediate contexts of development associated with the individual child and family).

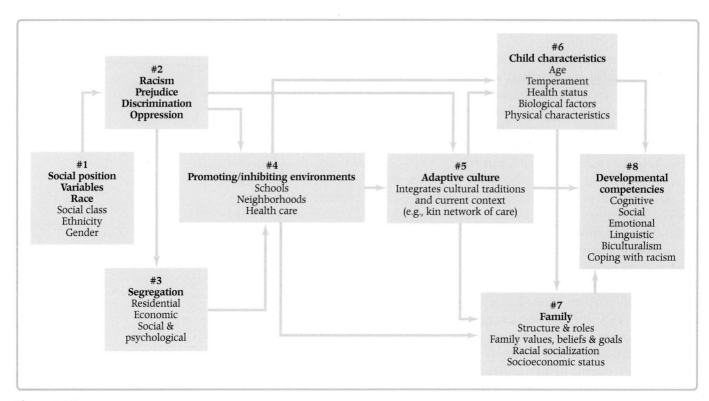

Figure 11.7 An ecological approach to child care and development in minority children explores the interacting components of the macrosystem, exosystem, mesosystem, and microsystem. (Adapted from Johnson et al., 2003.)

The model allows researchers to investigate the substantial racial and ethnic differences in the type of care that families need, prefer, and have access to. Racism and segregation, for example, have contributed to women of color being overrepresented in jobs that involve shift work, long hours, and work disruption due to layoffs. The child-care needs and resources of these women are very different from those who work traditional, office-based, 9-to-5 jobs. Likewise, the value systems of some families may lead them to seek child care that promotes positive racial or ethnic identity. Such "promoting environments" that are sensitive to children's native culture and language may enhance children's comfort and learning experiences. The bottom line for Johnson and her colleagues (2003) is that, "who cares for our children, how they are cared for, and the consequences of that care must be addressed in the appropriate ecological contexts, bringing to center the issues most relevant to the populations under study" (p. 1240).

Preschool

Child care originated in response to the needs of adults who wanted their children supervised while they themselves worked or went to school. By contrast, the purpose of preschool (which used to be called nursery school) is primarily educational. Preschools came into being early in the twentieth century, initiated by educators' and physicians' concern that the complexities of urban life were overwhelming children and stunting their development. The preschool was conceived as "a protected environment scaled to [children's] developmental level and designed to promote experiences of mastery within a child-sized manageable world" (Prescott & Jones, 1971, p. 54).

A typical preschool's layout and schedule reveal prevalent ideas of how best to foster development from the age of 2½ to 6. There are likely to be several kinds of play areas: a sandbox, a water-play table, a doll corner, a block area, a large area with a rug where children can gather to listen to stories or sing songs, a cluster of low tables used

Entering the play of other children may be a challenge, but it is by no means impossible, especially if you have control of an attractive plaything.

for arts-and-crafts projects and for snacks, and an outdoor area with jungle gyms, slides, and swings. Each area provides an environment for developing a different aspect of children's overall potential: their ability to understand physical transformations in play materials; to control their own bodies; to create in language, music, clay, and paint; to adopt various social roles; and to get along with other children.

During the 2½ to 3 hours a day that children may spend in a preschool, they are guided from one activity area to another. The developmental spirit of preschools is reflected in their lack of pressure on children to perform correctly on preassigned tasks and in their emphasis on exploration.

Preschools and Social Reform

In the 1960s a variety of scientific and social factors combined to create great interest in preschools' potential to increase the educational chances of the poor. On the scientific side was a growing belief that environmental influence during the first few years of life is crucial to all later abilities, especially intellectual ones (recall our discussion of primacy in Chapter 7). This belief coincided with broader historical pressures to improve the status of ethnic and racial minorities and with widespread political concern that social barriers between the rich and the poor and between whites and blacks were creating a dangerous situation in the United States. In his 1963 book, Michael Harrington warned that the United States was creating "an enormous concentration of young people who, if they do not receive immediate help, may well be the source of a kind of hereditary poverty new to American society" (p. 188). Commentators on the lives of poor young children issue the same warning today (Mason et al., 1998).

This combination of social, political, and scientific factors led the U.S. Congress to declare a "war on poverty" in 1964. One of the key programs in this "war" was Project Head Start. Its purpose was to intervene in the cycle of poverty at a crucial time in children's lives by providing them with important learning experiences that

By attending Head Start, these preschoolers from low-income families acquire learning skills and attitudes designed to help them succeed in school in the years ahead.

Laura Dwight

they might otherwise miss. Federal support enabled Head Start programs to offer these experiences at no charge to low-income families.

This strategy of social reform through early childhood education rested on three crucial assumptions:

1. The environmental conditions of poverty-level homes are insufficient to prepare children to succeed in school.

2. Schooling is the social mechanism that permits children to succeed in our society.

3. Poor children could succeed in school, and thereby overcome their poverty, if they were given extra assistance during the preschool years.

Originally conceived as a summer program, Head Start soon began to operate year-round, serving approximately 200,000 preschool children at a time (Consortium for Longitudinal Studies, 1983). More than three decades later, Head Start programs have expanded to provide services for more than 750,000 children. Despite its phenomenal growth, the program serves only 38 percent of the children who are eligible to participate (Devaney et al., 1997).

What Difference Does Head Start Make?

Because Head Start preschools have gained considerable social acceptance since the 1960s, it might be assumed that the preschool experience proved to have positive benefits for children. The data are not so clear-cut.

The first reports were promising. Children who attended a single summer program showed marked gains in standardized test scores. In addition, hundreds of thousands of parents were involved in their children's school lives for the first time, whether as members of Head Start planning boards, as participants in special training programs for parents, or as classroom helpers. For a great many children, Head Start also meant better nutrition and health care.

In recent decades a large number of studies have evaluated preschool programs for poor children, including Head Start and a variety of similar efforts (summarized in Lamb, 1998; Zigler & Finn-Stevenson, 1999). Some of the studies have been able to do follow-up evaluations of children as they reached their early twenties and to include broader developmental indicators such as crime rates and earned income in the assessment. These broad evaluations revealed a variety of positive findings, although success has not been uniform. On the positive side, children who attend regular Head Start or special, model programs show meaningful gains in intellectual performance and socioemotional development. Children who attend Head Start are also less likely to be assigned to remedial special-education classes when they attend school. As is the case with child-care programs, however, the success of Head Start programs depends upon the quality of the classroom experience; and, unfortunately, while most classrooms have been rated as adequate in quality, very few are considered of high quality.

Nonetheless, the success of well-run programs is now broadly accepted (Lamb, 1998; Zigler & Finn-Stevenson, 1999). In one of the best and most heavily studied cases, the Perry Preschool Program in Ypsilanti, Michigan, it has been possible to follow up the progress of experimental and control children for more than 35 years. The children in the experimental group had higher achievement scores than those in the control group at the ages of 9 and 14. They were more likely to graduate from high school, more likely to be employed at the age of 19, less likely to have run afoul of the law by the age of 28, and less likely to have gone on welfare. W. Steven Barnett (1996), who conducted a study of the costs and benefits of the expenditures of the Perry preschool intervention, calculated that for every dollar spent on the program, the public saved $7 in decreased costs for later welfare and incarceration.

The preschool experience is an opportunity to make friends with children one's own age at the same time that children are acquiring culturally valued skills.

Media Linking Home and Community

As suggested by an ecological approach, the family and other contexts of care are influenced by components of the broader ecosystem. A major avenue of influence is media, including letters, books, magazines, newspapers, radio, television, videotape, CDs, and the Internet.

The sheer magnitude of children's immersion in modern communications media makes it important to understand the role that experience with these media plays in their development. Yet the issue has long been, and remains, a contentious one.

The Lessons of History

Given the current social approval of reading as "good for children," it might come as a surprise that when literacy was first introduced into Greek society around the fourth century B.C., it was met with suspicion by the philosopher Plato. In one of his famous dialogues, the *Phaedrus*, he argued that contrary to popular opinion, learning to read and write would lead to a weakening of memory, eroding the basis for obtaining wisdom. The true path to knowledge, he believed, was face-to-face dialogue that followed the rules of logic.

The echoes of Plato's arguments can be found in discussions of media effects today, but now literacy is an "old" medium and, despite some concerns, is thought to enhance development. It is the new electronic media of our times that raise the most severe doubts. This is particularly apparent in concerns that children's frequency of television viewing and computer use cuts into time that they might otherwise spend reading books (Desmond, 2001; Roberts et al., 1999).

Two questions dominate modern research on the developmental impact of various media: (1) How does the physical form of the medium contribute to its effects on development? and (2) What role does the content of the medium play in shaping any observed effects? In Chapter 13 we will consider these issues in the context of schooling. Here we consider them as they influence young children who are in the earliest stages of being socialized by books, television, and interactive media.

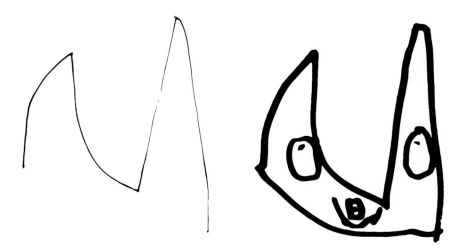

Figure 11.8 Left: "An M. . . . What does that spell? It spells M for Molly." Right: "And it could be a rabbit. See, it's got big ears." Here 3½-year-old Molly uses the letter M in two different ways as she begins to get the idea of writing. For her, it is difficult to differentiate between the letter and the drawing. (From Gardner et al., 1982.)

Books

In the United States, young children of every social class are exposed to print in some form almost every day, even if only for a few minutes (Purcell-Gates, 1996). Such experiences teach them that the letter symbols on billboards, in picture books, and on the milk cartons at the breakfast table somehow convey information. This form of knowledge about reading and writing is referred to as "emergent literacy" (Cassell, 2004) (see Figure 11.8).

Early Literacy Experiences

An important class of experiences that contributes to emergent literacy is being read to. Evidence indicates that young children who are often read to at home acquire an appreciation of the use of print to make meaning, and that this appreciation helps them when they start school (Reese & Cox, 1999). Often a child's introduction to print begins with the reader's directing the child's attention to the illustrations that accompany a story. As the child's knowledge increases, adults supply less help. This kind of tailored support keeps changing to fit children's growing competence in a manner that creates a zone of proximal development (Vygotsky's concept introduced in Chapter 5, p. 196). Zones of proximal development allow children to participate in a full activity (in this case, reading a book) before they are fully competent (Cassell, 2004).

Being read to contributes to emergent literacy in young children.

SW Productions/Getty Images

Courtesy of Sheila Cole

Learning to read involves understanding how to hold a book and turn pages, and what to look for on the page.

Appropriate Content

Despite the generally positive orientation that adults have toward books and reading, books that have traditionally been read to children sometimes come under fire. Most fairy tales and myths were created in the centuries before childhood was considered a special "innocent" period of life and before any literature had been specifically devised for children (Sale, 1978). Adults have occasionally argued that fairy tales should not be read to children because they are cruel, brutal, and frightening, or because they are not realistic portrayals of the world. One irate reader condemned Kornei Chukovsky, a famous Russian author of children's poems, as follows:

> [You are] filling the heads of our children with all kinds of nonsense, such as that trees grow shoes. I have read with indignation in one of your books such fantastic lines as:
> Frogs fly in the sky,
> Fish sit in fishermen's laps,
> Mice catch cats
> And lock them up in
> Mousetraps.
> Why do you distort realistic facts? Children need socially useful information and not fantastic stories about white bears who cry cock-a-doodle-doo. (Chukovsky, 1968, p. 11)

But the presence of fantastic, and even violent, content in fairy tales has its defenders, such as the psychoanalyst Bruno Bettelheim (1977), who insisted that children need fairy tales: "Like all great art, fairy tales both delight and instruct; their special genius is that they do so in terms which speak directly to children" (p. 56). Bettelheim believed that the very unreality of such stories allows children to use them to find solutions to their own inner conflicts; it is certainly less threatening to think about Cinderella's evil stepmother than to think consciously about real negative feelings toward one's own mother or father.

Another frequent complaint about many children's books is that they ignore or misrepresent certain ethnic and racial groups, women, and working-class and poor people. These concerns are well grounded in surveys of the contents of children's books (Gooden & Gooden, 2001; Pescosolido et al., 1997).

When we turn from books and reading to television viewing, concerns about the content and form of children's experiences are similar in some respects but different in others. Generally, television's role in development is viewed with greater concern.

Television

It is estimated that a TV set is on for 6 or more hours each day in the average American home and that young children are in front of it for 2 or more of those hours (Huston & Wright, 1996). Television viewing during childhood is so pervasive that Dorothy and Jerome Singer argue that "no other extraparental influence has penetrated the lives of children as television has" (Singer & Singer, 1990, p. 177).

The evidence that the behavior of young children and even infants can be influenced when they watch TV is irrefutable. In Chapter 5 (p. 194) we saw that 14-month-olds imitate actions they see on a TV screen (Meltzoff, 1988a). Infants and young children also imitate the language they hear on TV. Dafna Lemish and Mabel Rice (1986) report that one 2-year-old they observed at home approached her father, pointed at the bottle of beer in his hand, and declared, "Diet Pepsi, one less calorie." Further, young children identify with superheroes and mythical creatures they see on television. The pervasive influence of such identification can be seen in everything from their fantasy play and the toys they play with to the cereals they insist on having—clear evidence that what children learn from television influences their everyday behavior (Dyson, 2003).

What Is Real?

A special concern about television viewing is that young children easily confuse TV make-believe and reality. Research summarized in Chapter 9 (pp. 325–327) indicated that young children sometimes have trouble distinguishing between reality and appearance. It seems reasonable to assume that their confusion is compounded when they watch television entertainment programs in which believable people are shown engaging in behavior and events that could actually be happening. A child in a TV program who runs away from home is a real child filmed on a set that looks like a real home. The question for researchers has been at what age children watching such programs would know whether they are looking at a window on reality or a fantasy on film.

Research concerning the appearance–reality distinction shows that at the end of infancy children have little understanding of the boundary between what they see on television and the rest of their perceptual environment (Troseth, 2003). They are likely to think that a bowl of popcorn shown on TV would spill if the TV set were turned upside down (Flavell et al., 1990b). Even 4- and 5-year-olds may display such difficulty, believing, for example, that Sesame Street is a real place or that television characters can see and hear the people who are watching them on TV (Nikken & Peters, 1988).

By the time they are approaching the age of 6, children in the United States have a good feel for the various categories of programming they watch, such as news programs, dramas, educational programming, and cartoons, and they understand that news programs are more likely to be about real events than cartoons or entertainment programs. They generally understand that the objects seen on the screen are not literally inside the TV set, and they can identify a wide variety of fanciful events as "not real" (Davies, 1997). They are still susceptible to confusion, however. Aimee Dorr (1983) reports that children under the age of 7 may have difficulty understanding that when a bad guy is shot on television, the actor isn't really dead, or that when a husband beats his wife, the actress isn't really hurt. Even 7- and 8-year-olds will claim that actors and actresses who play married couples must be friends, and they do not realize that fictional programs are rehearsed (Wright et al., 1994).

Confusion about the reality of television is not restricted to children. From time to time one reads of an irate adult assaulting an actor who portrays an evil character in a soap opera. But the problem is more acute for young children because they have little independent knowledge of the world with which to compare what they see on television.

Television Form

Another set of concerns arises from difficulties that young children have in understanding the techniques employed in television programs. One of the major goals of educational programming is to understand how young children attend to, process, and comprehend the material presented in their programs (Bickham et al., 2001). Aware that the viewer's attention is attracted by movement and change, television directors use quick cuts from one scene or one camera angle to another. The popular children's program *Sesame Street,* for example, was deliberately designed to have a new cut on the average of every 30 seconds as a means of maintaining the attention of young children (Lesser, 1974). Other techniques are used to focus viewers' attention and highlight the central message: close-up shots pick out essential details; camera placement gives hints about point of view; flashbacks fill in earlier parts of the story (Schmitt et al., 1999). These thought-shaping techniques are a great resource for conveying meaning, at least for older viewers, but for young children, they have their negative side as well (Huston & Wright, 1996). Unless the subject matter is familiar, young children have difficulty interpreting sequences of quick scene changes without transitions. Juxtapositions of images intended to convey the relation of one action to another may also give them difficulty (see Figure 11.9).

As a consequence of the limitations in their understanding of the conventions of television forms, young children often fail to comprehend a good deal of what they watch, although they do better when the program has been designed to take their special interpretive needs into account (Lorch, 1994). Comprehension improves markedly during middle childhood, but even 9- and 10-year-olds have difficulty understanding fast-paced programs that do not clearly show the continuity of action from one sequence to the next (Huston & Wright, 1996).

Another effect blamed on the fast pacing of television programming is that it makes it difficult for children to stop and ponder what is being presented. As a consequence, according to some psychologists, children acquire a kind of mental laziness that makes it difficult for them to do the mental work required to learn from written texts (Salomon, 1984). However, research over the past two decades has failed to support the idea that television viewing induces any generalized mental laziness (Huston & Wright, 1996).

Figure 11.9 An item from a test that assesses children's ability to re-create an entire setting on the basis of partial glimpses. Each card corresponds to a camera angle used in films and television programs. Children are asked to put the four cards together to make a meaningful scene. (From Greenfield, 1984.)

Television Content

Television exposes children to a great range of content. The Count teaches counting; Mr. Rogers counsels on the importance of caring for others; cartoon characters meet violent ends, sometimes more than once; prime-time dramas, as well as the evening news, depict violence and aggression, but also empathy and tenderness. For decades, developmentalists have been deeply interested in how television content affects children's behavior, attitudes, and development—both positively and negatively.

Media Stereotypes Throughout the history of television in North America, the people who populated the television screen have not been representative of the population of viewers. Most of the major characters on commercial television are European American men. Even in children's commercial programming, men significantly outnumber women; and, with some exceptions, the situation is not much better on educational programming directed at children (Comstock & Scharrer, 1999). In light of the changing demographics of American society, developmentalists are rightly concerned about television's role in the multicultural awareness of children (Berry & Asamen, 2001).

Surveys of program content conducted in the 1970s and 1980s routinely reported significant differences in the portrayals of men and women. Men were presented as being in control—in relationships, in the workplace, indeed, everywhere. Women, by contrast, were presented as submissive, passive, physically attractive, and sensual. If the women were shown working at all, they were more likely to be nurses or secretaries than doctors and CEOs (Comstock & Scharrer, 1999). Today more programs feature realistic portrayals of women, and more women are appearing as anchors on local TV shows. However, while gender stereotypes are less dominant than they once were, many still remain.

The misrepresentation of ethnic minorities and foreigners is an equally significant problem, although there has been improvement for some groups. Most promising are the changing depictions of African Americans. In the early days of television, African Americans did not appear on the screen often, and when they did appear, they were presented primarily as servants and criminals (Barcus, 1986). In contrast, today African Americans are likely to be portrayed more positively than European Americans are, including engaging in proportionately less violent or criminal behavior. Other ethnic groups have not fared as well, however. Hispanic Americans, for example, are even less visible than they were in the 1950s, and they are disproportionately portrayed in criminal roles (Lichter et al., 1997).

That children are keenly aware of these stereotypes is apparent in a study conducted with 1200 children (300 African Americans, 300 European Americans, 300 Latinos, and 300 Asian Americans) between 10 and 17 years of age (Children Now, 1998; reported in Cortés, 2000, p. 126). Some of the major findings include the following:

1. Asian American children believed the news media provided fairer coverage of Asian Americans than did the entertainment media, whereas the opposite was true for African Americans.

2. Asian American, Latino, and African American children all favored black television figures, whereas European American children preferred white figures. No Latino or Asian American figures were selected as favorites.

3. Only about one-fifth felt that there were enough Latino or Asian American main characters. A majority of each ethnic group believed it is important for young people to see those of their own racial or ethnic background on television.

4. Despite the recent changes in how black and white characters are depicted, the vast majority of each group believed that white characters were portrayed most positively: wealthy, well-educated, and in positions of leadership. Likewise, nearly 60 percent believed that black actors are most likely to be cast as criminals.

Stereotyping on television is of concern because (1) it may create or maintain negative intergroup attitudes, and (2) it may influence young children's attitudes toward their place in society. Bradley Greenberg and Jeffrey Brand (1994) report that when asked about their favorite programs and favorite characters, children identify with the protagonists who are members of their own ethnic group, when they are available. Thus, the absence of positive role models for certain groups is another source of concern.

Violence No one living in the contemporary United States can escape the widespread and continuing debate about the potential role of television violence as a contributing factor in the epidemic of killings that plagued U.S. schools in the 1990s. In fact, the high level of violence on television has been a social concern for many years. In 1972 the surgeon general of the United States issued a report arguing that television violence increases aggressiveness among viewers, an opinion that has been frequently repeated by congressional committees in the intervening decades.

Fully 80 percent of the television programs that young Americans watch include at least one violent event, and many contain more (Lichter et al., 1997). Researchers estimate that by the age of 18, children have witnessed 200,000 acts of television violence and 16,000 television murders. To be sure, a large portion of these images are in the form of cartoons, in which the likes of Roadrunner and the Coyote commit mayhem on each other, only to recover miraculously to fight another day. But there is a great deal of graphic and realistic violence as well.

To the public at large, it seems obvious that a constant diet of violent behavior on television, even cartoon violence, fosters the attitude that violence is an acceptable way to settle disputes. To the frustration of many, psychological research assessing the relationship between televised violence and aggressive behavior remains shrouded in controversy. Experimental studies, which in principle should be able to show causal relations between televised violence and aggressive behavior do, in fact, show that after children watch a violent program, they act more aggressively in a laboratory playroom than children who have watched more benign programs. However, critics have claimed that the artificial circumstances of these studies are so different from the way children view television at home that it is impossible to generalize the results to real-life circumstances.

Many studies that attempt to relate children's levels of viewing violence on television to aggressive behavior also find that more aggressive children watch more violent programming (Comstock & Scharrer, 1999; Huston & Wright, 1996). However, since all this research is correlational, it cannot confirm whether a higher level of watching TV violence is a cause of greater aggressiveness or the consequence of a greater predisposition to aggression.

Some of the most convincing evidence that watching TV violence increases children's aggressive behavior comes from "natural experiments" on children in communities that have gained access to television for the first time. Tannis Williams (1986) conducted one such study in three small communities in Canada in the 1980s. One community had never had TV before, one had a single channel, and one had several available channels. Williams found that in the previously isolated community, elementary school children's behavior on the playground became more aggressive during the two years after the introduction of TV. The level of children's aggressiveness did not change in the two communities that already had television, an indication that the introduction of television was the causal factor underlying the increased aggression in the first case. Similar studies carried out in other countries (reviewed by Huston & Wright, 1996) produce similar findings. However, because these were natural experiments, the possibility remains that some change in the affected communities other than the introduction of television could have caused the increase in the children's aggressive behavior.

Despite the technical difficulties of proving a causal link between viewing violence on television and behaving aggressively, the current consensus among psychologists is that watching violence on television does in fact increase aggressive behavior by creating a cultural climate in which aggression and even violence are seen as an acceptable ways to settle disputes. Even so, scholars who specialize in the study of television and its effects are careful to acknowledge the ambiguities that necessarily accompany correlational data (Comstock & Scharrer, 1999; Huston & Wright, 1996).

Educational Programs Of course, not all of the television content that children view is negative. Children's educational programming, in particular, is specifically designed to generate consequences that help children in school, in peer relationships and, most recently, in moral reasoning (Rosenkoetter, 2001). However, studying the effects of children's educational programming suffers from many of the same problems as research on the effects of viewing violent programs. That is, most studies are correlational, making it difficult to separate out all of the factors that might predispose young children to watch educational programs in the first place. For example, parents who encourage their children to watch something like *Sesame Street* are probably more likely to encourage other school-readiness activities. Such parents also are probably more highly educated and have higher incomes compared with parents who are less inclined to push their children toward educational programs (Bickham et al., 2001).

One recent effort to tease apart these factors is found in a longitudinal study conducted by John Wright, Aletha Huston, and their colleagues (2002). They assessed the association between television viewing patterns and academic skills, school readiness, and school adjustment in relatively low-income children over a 3-year period. They found, overall, that children who watched more educational programming at ages 2 and 3 scored higher at age 5 on measures of language, math, and school readiness. However, the relationship did not hold for children who were "heavy watchers" at age 4, suggesting that the impact of educational programming may be greatest for younger children. On the other hand, viewing general audience (adult) entertainment and cartoons was associated with lower academic scores.

The effects of educational programming seem to be long-lasting. A "recontact study" of teenagers between 15 and 19 years of age who had participated in a study of television viewing when they were 5 years old showed continued positive associations between preschool educational viewing and a test of creativity, especially for fans of the show *Mr. Rogers' Neighborhood*. High levels of educational viewing also predicted higher high school grades in English, science, and math, particularly for boys. Likewise, negative associations persisted between general audience viewing and grades, especially for girls.

What to make of the gender effects? The researchers suggest that when viewing patterns reinforce gender-specific tendencies, they have less of an impact. For example, boys are typically less prepared than girls for kindergarten. On a steady diet of cartoons, they are only somewhat less prepared than they would be otherwise. A diet of educational programming, however, can really make a difference for them. The same logic applies to girls. Because they are typically more prepared for school,

The Muppet Kami is a newcomer to the cast of *Sesame Street* in South Africa. She likes nature, collecting stuff, and telling stories. She is also HIV positive.

AP Photo

they are only somewhat better off as a consequence of viewing educational programming. Heavy viewing of cartoons, on the other hand, can do much to undermine the school readiness of girls.

Family Influences

Concerns about the possible negative effects of television viewing on children have led to repeated suggestions that parents take an active role in supervising their children's experiences with television (American Academy of Child and Adolescent Psychiatry, 2000). In North America, at least, parents generally do not impose severe restrictions on how much TV children watch. However, they do try to restrict children's access to programs that contain graphic violence, sexuality, or frightening content. They also encourage their children to watch educational programs or programs that they believe provide appropriate entertainment for children (Huston & Wright, 1996).

Research summarized by Aletha Huston and John Wright (1996) indicates that when parents and children watch television together, the viewing experience can be more worthwhile. Adult explanations of the plots, motivations of characters, and events in dramatic programs increase children's understanding of the content. Such conversations also provide ready-made occasions for parents to discuss questions of social values and moral issues.

Unfortunately, while joint television viewing can have positive developmental effects, current evidence indicates that parents generally spend little time watching and discussing TV with young children. Moreover, when they do watch television with their children, the programs are more likely to be ones that the parents want to watch, not programming directed at children (Van Evra & Page, 1998). It appears that adult entertainment, not children's education, provides the major motive for parents and their children to watch television together.

In light of data indicating the positive benefits of parental involvement in their young children's television watching, and the deep concerns about the way that television enters into so many aspects of the growing child's "ecological niche," some developmentalists have created special interventions to help parents overcome what they see as the harmful effects of the medium (Thoman, 1999). The goal of these interventions is to maximize the educational potential that television can provide

When families watch TV together, adults have the opportunity to clarify children's misunderstandings and to discuss events that are frightening or disturbing.

John Maier, Jr./The Image Works

while minimizing the potential harm from viewing violent and frightening events (Cantor, 1998; Jason & Hanaway, 1997).

Based on several decades of research on children's television viewing, it would appear that television is a powerful medium that can have significant and long-lasting effects—both positive and negative—on children's development. As you will see in the following section, similar claims of benefit and harm are currently being made in regard to new interactive media.

Interactive Media

During the past decade there has been an explosion of new media in the lives of children in modern, industrialized societies—the digital media, which are bringing together the "old" media of telephone and television and the "new" media of computers and the Internet. While the television set continues to attract the lion's share of children's leisure time, the computer is closing in quickly. In fact, computers now outrank televisions as the "favorite medium" of boys and girls from 8 to 18 years of age (Roberts et al., 1999). Some adults, including the grandfather quoted below, see this as a change for the better (in Subrahmanyam et al., 2001):

> It's taking them away from TV actually, which they had a problem with. With TV, they would be glued to the screen, especially the seven year old, she was almost mesmerized. You couldn't even communicate with her, she would just sit there with that blank stare on her face and just watch, I still don't believe she had a clue as to what was going on. It was just emotion. So now she's onto the computer and she stays away from the [TV]. So it's helped keeping them away from the TV (p. 91).

Whether or to what degree computer use is preferable to TV viewing is still a matter of debate. The popularity of the new media, however, is undisputed.

Form

The new media are attractive to many young children, owing to both their form and their content. In the form of computer games, their capacity for graphic and auditory representation makes it possible to present children with attractive cartoonlike scenarios of the kind seen on Saturday morning television. But unlike television, the new media allow children to interact with the pictures and stories they see, controlling the movements of characters and engaging in active problem solving at the same time that they are being entertained. Other programs allow children to create sequences of pictures to develop their own stories and even to program their own games using attractive, easily understood symbols. In general, computer games call upon a number of cognitive skills, including divided attention, spatial imagery, and representation (Subrahmanyam et al., 2001).

In addition to stimulating cognitive and intellectual processes, interactive media can stimulate emotional responses in children. A recent example is *Tamagotchi,* a game toy created in Japan. The *Tamagotchi* is an artificial life form that communicates its needs for food, sleep, or play by beeping its owner. The goal of the game is to keep the *Tamagotchi* alive as long as possible, which requires the child's constant attention. As you can imagine, *Tamagotchis* are dropping like flies; there are even virtual Internet "cemeteries" available in which to "bury" them. One researcher observed a young girl in a restaurant burst into tears when her own *Tamagotchi* bit the dust (Richards, 1998; reported in Subrahmanyam et al., 2001). The appearance–reality phenomenon associated with children's interpretation of television is clearly just as operative in the case of interactive media.

Beyond their potential as toys and a new mode of expression, digital media are increasingly being used in preschools as a means for teaching basic literacy and math skills. In these settings, the interactive game-playing capacity of computers is combined with such tasks as identifying letters of the alphabet, matching colors and shapes, or making elementary arithmetic calculations. Controlled experiments indicate that young children not only acquire vocabulary and a variety of academic skills in such gamelike activities but also learn to carry out a variety of computer operations that many adults are unsure about (Klein & Starkey, 2000).

One concern about computer use, particularly game playing, is that it tends to be a solitary activity. Spending time with a machine, however interactive, may interfere with children's peer relationships. However, research does not support this concern. Indeed, one study found that boys who play computer games often spend *more* time with their friends outside of school compared with boys who are infrequent users (Colwell et al., 1995).

A related concern is how computer use affects family relationships. An early study found that new computer games brought families together for shared play and interaction (Michell, 1985). However, now that games and computers are more common, and children are often more knowledgeable than their parents about how to operate them, such sharing may be less frequent (Subrahmanyam et al., 2001). Indeed, most parents are fairly ignorant of the interactive games that appeal to their children. One survey found that only 1 of 50 parents had ever heard of *Duke Nukem,* a violent, M(mature)-rated game known to 8 of every 10 junior high school students (Oldberg, 1998).

Content

Inspired by work on children's television viewing, developmentalists and the general public have been concerned about the violent content of many interactive games. In their review of experimental studies, Kaveri Subrahmanyam and her colleagues (2001) conclude that there are at least short-term effects of game playing on children's aggressive behavior. That is, after playing a violent game, children are likely to include aggressive content in their free play, or react with hostility to nonthreatening events. However, studies that attempt to relate the amount of game playing with children's aggressiveness have not resolved the question of whether game playing causes aggressiveness, or more aggressive children (particularly boys) find such games appealing and thus spend more time playing them.

Interactive computer games have introduced entirely new ways of playing ball.

HEART OF THE CITY   *BY MARK TATULLI*

An interesting issue for developmentalists, and a challenge for marketers of children's games, concerns the gender difference in game use. By huge margins, boys are more likely than girls to play and own interactive games. In fact, girls lag behind boys in the use of computers in the classroom (Cassell & Jenkins, 1998).

Early on, it was believed that girls were put off by the violence and the lack of female characters. In response, the software industry created several "girl games," such as *Let's Talk About Me* and *Barbie Print and Play*. They did not go over well. However, *Barbie Fashion Designer* generated some enthusiasm among girls. Developmentalists have speculated that *Barbie Fashion Designer* owes its marketing success to the nurturing and creative themes that are involved (Subrahmanyam & Greenfield, 1998).

All told, research on the effects of media on children's development paints a consistent, if complex picture. Children are immersed in media, and media can have pronounced effects on how and what children think and feel. At the same time, children are active agents in the process; their individual differences and preferences shape how they are affected.

On the Threshold

This chapter has by no means surveyed all the contexts that significantly influence early childhood development: young children also learn from trips to the beach, outings in the park, attendance at houses of worship, visits to the doctor's office, and trips to the market. Each new context brings with it new social and intellectual challenges as the children gradually piece together a deeper understanding of their world and their place in it.

Recognizing the influence of context on early childhood development helps us make sense of the variable picture each young child presents to the world. In familiar contexts, where children know the appropriate scripts and their own roles in them, they may display mature reasoning and surprising competence. But often they find themselves novices in strange settings where they do not know the appropriate scripts, where they are expected to work out social relationships with strangers, and where they are set new tasks that require them to master new concepts. In these circumstances, their powers of self-expression and self-control are put under great strain, and their thought processes may be inadequate for the heavy demands placed on them.

The problem of being a novice is by no means unique to young children; people face it throughout their lives. But the difficulties are particularly acute at the beginning of early childhood because young children know so little about how their culture works. Consequently, children of this age need almost constant supervision. When they play together, they need some powerful organizing activity, such as pretend play, to support their fragile ability to coordinate with one another.

By the end of early childhood, children's vocabularies and command of grammatical forms have grown immensely. They have greater knowledge about a wide variety of contexts and a more sophisticated sense of themselves; and they are vastly more competent to think about the world, to control themselves, and to deal with other children. In these and many other ways they indicate a readiness to venture into new settings, to take on new social roles, and to accept the additional responsibilities that await them as they enter middle childhood.

S U M M A R Y

The Family as a Context for Development

- The factors that influence children's lives can be usefully thought of as a nested set of contexts, or ecosystems, that influence one another.

- The family influences children's development in two ways: by shaping their behavior within the family and by selecting other contexts for them to inhabit.

- The term *family* is often difficult to define precisely because of a family's fluid boundaries and the transitions that occur throughout the life course of its members.

- Nuclear families, long the dominant structure in North American society, have been declining in number. The origin, nature, and value of this family structure is also being debated by developmentalists.

- Extended families play an especially important role among certain ethnic groups, for whom this structure is part of their cultural heritage, and among families experiencing economic hardship

- The number of single-parent families has grown dramatically in recent years. Although children from such families are often at a developmental disadvantage, developmentalists are questioning whether it is the structure of the family, or other factors, that lead to these negative outcomes.

- Although parenting styles vary, parenting everywhere has three goals: to ensure that the child

  1. survives into adulthood.

  2. acquires the skills and resources needed for economic self-sufficiency.

  3. acquires the cultural values of the group.

- Cross-cultural comparisons of family life reveal that children's social behavior and personalities develop to fit the overall demands of economic activity and community life in their society.

- Family socialization patterns vary within societies, depending on such factors as the family configuration and the values, beliefs, education, income, and personalities of the family members.

- Patterns of socialization can be grouped for purposes of comparison. Child-rearing practices in the United States in most cases follow one of three patterns:

  1. Authoritarian families use set standards and emphasize conformity.

  2. Authoritative families emphasize control through reasoning and discussion.

  3. Permissive families avoid overt control and believe that children should make their own decisions.

- Among white middle-class two-parent families, authoritative child-rearing practices are associated with children who are more self-reliant, self-controlled, and willing to explore than those raised by permissive or authoritarian parents.

- Siblings also play an important role in children's socialization. Their influence is related to the quality of the sibling relationship as well as the emotional climate of the family.

- The composition of "traditional" families has altered due to changes in values, politics, economics and transportation technologies. Two examples are the rising prevalence of immigrant families, and gay and lesbian families.

- Children from distressed families often experience a cascade of risk factors.

- Poverty affects family life in many ways, increasing the stress on parents at the same time that it reduces their resources for dealing with it. Stress, in turn, is associated with authoritarian parenting styles. Poverty plays an especially deleterious role in children's development, affecting their cognitive abilities, mental and physical health, and family dynamics.

- A significant number of U.S. children grow up in single-parent families headed by a young unwed mother. These children tend to be more aggressive, less self-controlled, and less cognitively advanced than the children of older, married couples. These effects can be mediated by income level, mothers' education, and a more positive home environment.

- Children whose parents have divorced may display a variety of negative reactions, including sleep disturbances, irritability, and aggressiveness. The severity and duration of the dislocation resulting from divorce depend on a variety of factors, including the family income and the configuration of the new family that results if the custodial parent remarries. Recent research has sparked debate about whether factors other than the divorce itself might be linked to negative outcomes for children.

- Child abuse continues to be a serious problem in the United States. Children from abusive families suffer intellectual, social, and emotional effects. Such abuse may be in part a result of a societal disease that accepts violence within families.

- Children of affluent families may be exposed to pressure to achieve, which increases the likelihood of their risk for problems such as depression and substance abuse.

Early Contexts of Care

- Once children begin to spend time outside the home, their experience changes in fundamental ways.

- Child care in the United States can vary widely in social setting, philosophy, and physical facilities. The most common forms are family care, home care, and child-care centers.

- The size of the group is of special importance to the quality of child care in the United States: the smaller the group, the higher the quality. Other factors that contribute to the quality of care are the stability, commitment, and training of the staff.

- Child care in the United States affects children in several ways. Physical consequences include increased illnesses and stress. Intellectual development of children in high-quality day care is at least as good as that for children raised at home. Social and emotional effects include:

  1. Increased self-sufficiency and decreased compliance with adults' wishes.

  5. Increased ability to engage in peer-led group activity.

- An ecological approach to studying child care is particularly important when studying ethnic-minority and immigrant children, whose environments often vary greatly from those of their peers.

- Preschools evolved during the twentieth century as a means of promoting the development of children who had to cope with the complexities of urban life.

- Since the early 1960s, preschool education has been promoted as a means of combating school failure among people living in poverty.

Media Linking Home and Community

- Influences from the community enter the family through such media as books, newspapers, radio, television, and the Internet. Each medium of communication is assumed to influence children's development in specific ways.

- In evaluating the role of media in the development of children, two basic questions need to be addressed: (1) Are there formal features of the medium that shape the experiences children are a part of? and (2) How does the content of media influence development?

- Young children usually encounter books in the form of activity called "being read to."

- Being read to furnishes young children with an early model of activities that will be important in school.

- Parents have considerable control over both the form and the content of the reading experience of their young children.

- Children learn from television and act upon what they have learned from a very young age.

- Television's potential for realism makes it difficult for children to distinguish reality from fiction in television content; and their understanding of the content is confused by such cinematic techniques as rapid cuts and zoom shots.

- Television content influences people's basic beliefs about the world. Insofar as reality is distorted by television, children who watch television acquire false beliefs about the world.

- Misrepresentation of ethnic groups and foreigners is a significant problem because it may create or maintain negative intergroup attitudes, and it may influence young children's attitudes toward their place in society.

- A variety of evidence indicates a correlation between watching violent programming and engaging in violent behavior. However, there remains uncertainty about whether and how violent programming causes aggressiveness in children.

- Viewing educational programming can have mixed effects, depending on the age and gender of the child watching, and the number of hours viewed.

- Parents can influence television's impact on their children by controlling what their children watch and by watching with them and talking about what is happening on the screen.

Interactive Media

- Interactive media, such as the Internet and video games, are gaining in popularity among children. As with television, however, similar questions about the effects of the media's form and content persist.

- While interative media have been utilized successfully as learning tools, they also present young children with appearance–reality problems; the increased use of video games may also affect family relationships.

- Questions about interactive media include issues of violent content in video games and gender differenes in computer use.

On the Threshold

- The fact that children begin to spend extended time in unfamiliar contexts is a key feature of development in early childhood.

- Exposure to a variety of new contexts stimulates the social and intellectual development of young children.

- The fact that young children are novices in the new contexts they inhabit is one of the reasons for the unevenness that is characteristic of their thought and action.

Key Terms

child-care centers, p. 425

extended family, p. 405

family, p. 406

family care, p. 424

family dynamics, p. 406

family structures, p. 406

home care, p. 424

nuclear family, p. 405

single-parent family, p. 405

Thought Questions

1. A basic assumption of Bronfenbrenner's cultural-context approach is that contexts are reciprocally related. Give some examples from this chapter in which experiences in one context influence behavior in another.

2. Suggest a research design for isolating the causes and effects of different parenting styles (as a follow-up to Diana Baumrind's research program). What obstacles do you anticipate in carrying out your proposed study?

3. Consider the two models of divorce described on p. 420. What are your expectations for the child's adjustment to divorce according to each model? As a family therapist, how would each model influence the issues that you would want to address in your efforts to help the child's adjustment?

4. Compare and contrast television with the new, interactive media regarding their effects on children's cognitive development.

part IV Middle Childhood

Bio-Social-Behavioral Shifts

Biological Domain
- Loss of baby teeth and gain of permanent teeth
- Growth spurt in frontal lobes and in overall brain size
- Sharp increase in EEG coherence

Social Domain
- Peer-group participation
- Rule-based games without direct adult supervision
- Deliberate instruction
- Golden Rule morality
- Coregulation of behavior between parent and child
- Social comparison

Behavioral Domain
- Increased memory capacity; strategic remembering
- Concrete operations
- Logical classification
- Decreased egocentrism and improved perspective taking

Anthropological descriptions of a wide variety of cultures indicate that as children reach the age of 5 to 7 years, they are no longer restricted to the home or to settings where they are carefully watched by adults. Instead, they become responsible for behaving themselves in a variety of new contexts. The new activities they encounter in these contexts vary from one society to the next. Among some of the Mayan people in the highlands of Guatemala, for example, boys go out to gather wood, a solitary activity that takes them well beyond the range of watchful adults, while girls spend more time at home doing domestic work in the company of their mothers and the older women of the village (Rogoff, 2003). In the United States, by contrast, boys and girls alike spend long hours in school, with their peers, receiving formal education.

In spite of such differences, however, the cross-cultural regularities of the changes that occur between the ages of 5 and 7 are so impressive that this period seems to signal the emergence of a new stage of development (Sameroff & Haith, 1996). At first glance, time spent in solitary activity or with peers when no adults are present may appear less important to development than time spent in educational settings. However, solitary activities, such as gathering wood or chasing birds and small animals away from a growing rice crop, and peer interaction—playing games, gossiping, or simply "hanging out"—are more significant for development than they might initially seem. Being in charge of the family cornfield or a younger sibling or engaging in informal interaction with peers provides children with important opportunities to learn what it means to take responsibility, to explore social relationships, and to develop moral understanding and personal identity.

Key to their ability to manage in the new contexts of middle childhood are children's acquisition of the biological and cognitive capacities needed to support their newly granted autonomy and responsibility. As you shall see, evidence from experiments, naturalistic observations, and clinical interviews makes it clear that during middle childhood children are increasingly able to think more deeply and logically, to follow through on a task once it is undertaken, and to keep track of several aspects of a situation at one time.

Our discussion of middle childhood is divided into three chapters. Chapter 12 focuses on the changes in children's biological and cognitive capacities between the ages of 6 and 12 that support the new freedoms and responsibilities that adults place upon them. The next two chapters examine children's behavior in two social contexts that are central to development in middle childhood in many countries: school and peer groups. Chapter 13 examines the influence of schooling on development, with particular attention to the organization of school activities and to the intellectual capacities that schooling both demands and fosters. Chapter 14 focuses on the developmental significance of the new social relations that emerge during middle childhood, particularly among peers. The influence of biological, cognitive, and social factors, as they are woven together in different cultural contexts, creates the particular tapestry of middle childhood as it is encountered around the world.

Cognitive and Biological Attainments of Middle Childhood

chapter 12

"

"Walking was my project before reading. The text I read was the town; the book I made up was a map. . . . I pushed at my map's edges. Alone at night I added newly memorized streets and blocks to old streets and blocks, and imagined connecting them on foot. . . . I felt that my life depended on keeping it all straight—remembering where on earth I lived, that is, in relation to where I walked. It was dead reckoning. On darkened evenings I came home exultant, secretive, often from some exotic leafy curb a mile beyond what I had known at lunch, where I had peered up at the street sign, hugging the cold pole, and fixed the intersection in my mind. What joy, what relief, eased me as I pushed open the heavy front door!—joy and relief because, from the very trackless waste, I had located home, family, and the dinner table once again.

An infant watches her hands and feels them move.

Gradually she fixes her own boundaries at the complex incurved rim of skin. Later she touches one palm to another and tries for a game to distinguish each hand's sensations of feeling and being felt. What is a house but a bigger skin, and a neighborhood map but the world's skin ever expanding?"

—Annie Dillard, *An American Childhood*

One of the best ways to gain a sense of the new freedoms and responsibilities that adults expect as their children enter middle childhood is to observe how and where they spend their time, a topic that has received increasing attention worldwide (Ben-Arieh & Ofir, 2002) In perhaps the most detailed and exhaustive studies of this kind, Roger Barker and Herbert Wright (1951) arranged for observers to follow children living in a small community in the United States through every minute of one day. The resulting portrait of 7-year-old Raymond Birch, titled *One Boy's Day,* is a classic in the literature of child development. The following excerpt provides insight into the activities, behaviors, and contexts of middle childhood.

Raymond gets up, dresses himself (although his clothes have been laid out for him by his mother), and takes care of his own grooming. He eats breakfast with his mother and father. Then he helps his father to clear the dishes. He negotiates with his mother about the need to wear a jacket to school and grudgingly accepts her judgment that a jacket is in order. He decides on his own not to take his bike to school because it might rain.

After spending a few minutes casting a fishing rod with his father in the backyard (he is the only one who caught fish on their last outing), he accompanies his mother to the courthouse where she works. At the courthouse he greets adults politely, and holds the door open for a man who is going out at the same time he is. He plays by himself outside while his mother works. When it is time for him to go to school, he walks the few blocks by himself, crossing the street cautiously. On the playground, he and the other children are unsupervised. A few minutes before 9 A.M. he enters his classroom, which the second-graders share with the first grade. While waiting for school to begin, he draws on the board, looks at a book with a friend, and chats quietly with other children. When the teacher comes into the room promptly at

9 A.M., he turns in his seat (all the seats are arranged in rows, facing front). While the teacher readies the first-graders to go to music, Raymond, who has become worried that he left his coat on the playground, asks permission to search for it. He has forgotten that he has hung it in the cloakroom. When he discovers this, he comes back and makes May baskets out of paper strips with the rest of the second-graders. He goes to music, listens to other children's stories, and goes outside for recess.

In the afternoon he does poorly on the spelling test. When another boy asks, "What did you get on your spelling?" he blushes and looks down at his desk. In a swift hoarse whisper he tells the boy that his grades are his own business. He seems embarrassed when he speaks. Close to dismissal time, the class searches for the money another boy has reported lost. When it turns out to have been in his desk all the time, Raymond smiles companionably at him and leans back to pat his hand. Then the boy pats Raymond's hand. They pat harder and harder, grinning broadly, until the teacher intervenes with a directive for the entire class.

While his mother is preparing dinner after work, Raymond pushes the lawn mower for a minute. He then joins his 11-year-old neighbor Stewart Evarts and Stewart's 3-year-old nephew Clifford in the vacant lot across the street. Playing with their trucks in a pit that was once the basement of a house, Raymond discovers a dilapidated wooden crate about 5 feet long buried in the weeds. He drags the crate out, and the boys devise several ways to play with it, despite its unwieldy size. They lift it out of the pit and send it crashing back in, get in the crate and pretend it is a cage and that they are monkeys, and hang on with their hands and feet as it rocks and tumbles over and over. At the same time, the older boys are careful that Clifford is not harmed by their games.

This condensed fragment illustrates several kinds of behavior indicating that this 7-year-old is able to behave responsibly, keep track of his belongings, and monitor where he needs to be next in a manner that meets the requirements of the situation and adult expectations:

- He dresses himself and decides on his own that it looks like rain, so he will not take his bicycle to school.
- Without being told to do so, he follows social conventions of politeness by holding open the door of the courthouse for an adult.
- When it is time to go to school he shows due caution in crossing streets.
- Although he is mistaken as to its whereabouts, he is aware that he is missing his coat and takes initiative in finding it.
- He is aware of expected standards of performance and is embarrassed when he performs poorly.
- He keeps a wary eye out for the 3-year-old while playing, unsupervised, in the lot across from his house

Although the specific events of Raymond's day depend upon the time and place in which he grew up, research conducted in many societies shows that adults begin to

The transition to middle childhood is often marked by new responsibilities, privileges, and rituals. Here, young girls participate in the Dasai Festival in Darjeeling, India.

Earl & Nazima Kowall/Corbis

have new expectations when their children approach 6 years of age (see the box "Out and About on Your Own," p. 452). Among the Ngoni of Malawi, in central Africa, for example, adults believe that the loss of milk teeth and the emergence of second teeth (which begins around the age of 6) signal that children should begin to act more independently. They are supposed to stop playing childish games and start learning skills that will be essential when they grow up. They are also expected to understand their place and are held accountable for being discourteous. The boys leave the protection and control of women and move into dormitories, where they must adapt to a system of male dominance and male life. Margaret Read (1983) describes the difficulties that this transition to a new stage of life causes for Ngoni boys:

> There was no doubt that this abrupt transition, like the sudden weaning [several years earlier], was a shock for many boys between six-and-a-half and seven-and-a-half. From having been impudent, well fed, self-confident, and spoiled youngsters among the women many of them quickly became skinny, scruffy, subdued, and had a hunted expression. (p. 49)

Observations of life among the Ifaluk of Micronesia provide a similar picture. The Ifaluk believe that at the age of 6 years, children acquire "social intelligence," which includes the acquisition of important cultural knowledge and skills, as well as the ability to work, to adhere to social norms, and to demonstrate compassion for others—all valued adult behaviors (Lutz, 1987). In Western Europe and the United States, this same transition has long been considered the advent of the "age of reason" (White, 1996).

Adults' expectations that their children will begin to behave more maturely at around the age of 6 or 7 arise from a combination of ecological circumstances, cultural traditions, and their observations of how well their children now cope with new demands (see Figure 12.1) (Sameroff & Haith, 1996). At the age of 6, children are strong and agile enough to catch a runaway goat or to carry their little sisters on their hips. They know not to let a baby crawl near an open fire. They can wait for the school bus without wandering off. They can, sometimes under duress, sit still for several hours at a time while adults attempt to instruct them, and they are beginning to be able to carry out their chores in an acceptable manner. In short, they can perform tasks independently, formulate goals, and resist the temptation to abandon them.

It takes patience and self control to sit through the long communion service and then walk in a dignified line following the ceremony, as these young girls are doing on the Caribbean island of St. Lucia.

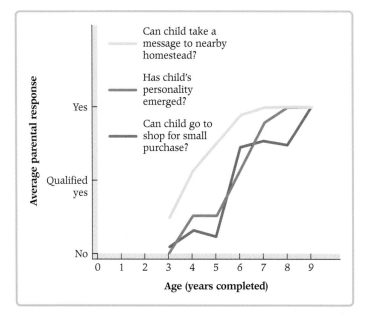

Figure 12.1 The ages at which Kipsigis mothers in Kokwet, Kenya, believe their children undergo basic developmental changes. Note the sharp discontinuity in this culture's estimates of personality development and the ability to carry out an errand involving money. But according to this culture, there is continuity in the development of memory needed to convey a message. (From Harkness & Super, 1983.)

Out and About on Your Own

Middle childhood is a time when children's activities take them farther and farther from home. It is the age at which children typically begin to walk by themselves to various places in their neighborhoods, including their friends' houses, the store, the library, the playground, and, of course, school.

Navigating new streets and new places and returning home safely requires several cognitive skills, collectively referred to as *way-finding* (Golledge, 1999). Successful way-finding requires that children pay attention to where they are going and to such dangers as passing cars. They have to remember important landmarks, and they have to recognize these landmarks from a different perspective when they return.

The experience of walking to school illustrates the kinds of cognitive challenges that way-finding poses for children once they are allowed to go about their neighborhoods on their own. Kate Simon, who immigrated to the United States from Poland as a young girl, vividly recalls the strategies she used to ensure that she and her little brother got to and from school safely:

My family arrived [in the Bronx] the summer before I was six and ready to be enrolled in the first grade, my brother in kindergarten. As I had learned to do in European trains and stations, in inns, on the vastness of the ship *Susquehanna* when I was an immigrant four-year-old, I studied every landmark, every turning of our new surroundings.

On the day we registered for school, P.S. 58 on Washington Avenue at 176th Street, my mother pointed out each turn, the number of blocks to the left or right and here we were at the big red building, the school, across from the little white building, the library. On the first day of school we went unaccompanied—hold his hand, don't talk to strange men. He complained that I was squeezing his hand and I probably was, tense and worried, avidly searching for the places I had marked out on our route; first to Tremont Avenue and right to the cake store, cross Third Avenue under the El, pass the butcher's with the pigs' feet in the window, cross Tremont at the bicycle shop to the barber's pole, continue on to the white library, and cross Washington Avenue to the school. It was a long walk, and I reached the school confused and exhausted, with just enough presence of mind to thrust the papers my mother had given me at the first teacher I saw, who led us to our respective rooms. We made the trip three more times that day, home for lunch and back and home again at three, and I was so bloated with triumph on the last journey that I varied the turns and crossings while my brother pulled in the directions he had memorized, as frightened as I had been that morning. With no memory of the feeling and no sympathy, I pulled him along, calling him a crybaby. (Kate Simon, *Bronx Primitive*, 1982, pp. 7–8.)

How do children develop the way-finding skills necessary to walk to school? To trace age-related increases in way-finding ability, Edward Cornell and his colleagues (1992) tested the abilities of 6- and 12-year-old children to find their way back across a university campus, and then compared the children's performances with those of 22-year-old college students. As might be expected, given their more limited cognitive abilities and way-finding experience, the 6-year-olds performed less well than the 12- and 22-year-olds, whose performance was virtually flawless. Children's abilities to find their way can be improved somewhat by calling their attention to stable, memorable landmarks and if they are told to glance back at their path as they go (Cornell et al., 1989). This result complements findings that the distance from home that a parent permits a child to venture independently (referred to as the *home range*) expands rapidly during the early elementary school years and remains stable after 10 or 12 years of age (Moore & Young, 1978).

Despite possessing the necessary way-finding abilities, only about 10 percent of children nationwide walk to school regularly. Even among those children living within a mile of their school, only 25 percent walk regularly (www.walktoschool.org). There are a number of potential reasons why parents might be concerned about having their children walk to school—the availability of school and public transport, increased reliance on automobiles, and fears about allowing their children to walk unattended, either because they are afraid they may be hit by a car or molested by a sexual predator. Nonetheless, there are compelling reasons to have children walk to school—not the least of which is that it is one proven way to combat the alarming rise in obesity rates in children in the United States (see the box "Obesity: A Childhood Epidemic," p. 455). The physical activity of walking to school provides one means of combating this problem.

As they begin to navigate away from home on their own, another kind of way-finding becomes even more important for many children than retracing their path: the ability to find their way safely across busy streets. Some 25,000 child pedestrians are injured by motor vehicles each year. A study of children's ability to find safe ways to cross the road found that only 10 percent of the 5-year-olds and 21 percent of the 7-year olds chose a safe route (Ampofo-Boateng et al., 1993). The children's performance could be improved, however, by a special safety course that emphasized the importance of visibility and choosing the shortest possible route whenever possible. Other specific suggestions for improving children's safety when walking include:

- providing safe, well-maintained walkways separate from vehicles;
- teaching children to cross streets at marked crossings, and providing ample, well-designed, accessible, and, when necessary, monitored crosswalks;
- slowing traffic in neighborhoods and near schools

In this chapter we focus on the biological changes and improved cognitive abilities that might justify adults' new demands and expectations. The physical changes of middle childhood—continued growth, improved motor skills, and increased brain activity—are readily observable. Children's cognitive functioning, however, is more difficult to measure and, as you might expect, has been the subject of competing theories.

Biological Developments

An obvious reason that children can do more on their own is that they are bigger, stronger, and have more endurance than they had when they were younger. Their size and strength increase significantly during middle childhood, although more slowly than in earlier years. Motor development shows marked improvement as children perfect the skills needed for running, throwing, catching, and turning somersaults. Perhaps the most important biological changes, however, occur in the brain, where continued growth and development provide the foundation for the cognitive changes we will discuss in this chapter.

Patterns of Growth

Average 4-year-olds in the United States are about 39 inches tall and weigh about 36 pounds; by the time they are 6 years old they are about 45 inches tall and weigh about 45 pounds. At the start of adolescence, 6 or 7 years later, their average height will have increased to almost 5 feet and their weight to approximately 90 pounds (Cameron, 2002). Like all aspects of development, children's growth during middle childhood continues to depend on the interaction of environmental and genetic factors.

Height

A child's height is clearly influenced by genetic factors. Tall parents tend to have tall children. Monozygotic twins reared together are very similar in their patterns of growth, and those reared apart still tend to resemble each other more than do dizygotic twins, who share only 50 percent of their genes. Yet environmental conditions also play a significant role, as attested to by the existence of many cases in which one monozygotic twin is significantly smaller than the other because of the effects of illness or a poor environment (see Chapter 2, p. 50).

The environmental contribution to size can also be seen in the variations in the height and rate of growth typical of different populations that undergo changes in living conditions. From the late 1970s to the early 1990s Mayan families from Guatemala migrated to the United States in record numbers (Bogin et al., 2002). Births to Mayan immigrant women created a sizable number of Mayan American children. Barry Bogin and his colleagues measured the height of more than four hundred 5- to 12-year-old Mayan American children in 1999 and 2000. These data were compared with a sample of more than 1000 Mayan children living in Guatemala at the time. The Mayan American children were about $4\frac{1}{2}$ inches taller, on average, than Mayan children living in Guatemala. These results add support to the hypothesis that the heights of human populations are sensitive indicators of the quality of the environment for growth.

One of the key environmental factors that moderate genetic growth potential is nutrition. Poor children, who have less access to nutritious food and good health care, are usually smaller than children of the same age in well-off families. For example, Bogin reports more than a 2-inch superiority in height when comparing high- and low-socioeconomic-class children aged 7 to 13 years in Guatemala (Bogin, 1999). In many industrialized countries, where the population on the whole is better off than the population in countries like Guatemala, the gap in size between the children of the poor and those born into well-off families is much smaller.

As indicated, health also plays a role in a child's growth. Growth slows during illnesses, even mild illnesses. When children are adequately nourished, this slowdown is usually followed by a period of rapid "catch-up growth," which quickly restores them to their genetically normative path of growth (Georgieff & Raghavendra, 2001). When nutritional intake is inadequate, however, the children never do catch up, and their growth is stunted.

Weight

Body weight, like height, is influenced by genetic factors. A study of 540 Danish adoptees found a strong correlation between the adoptees' weight as adults and the weight of their biological parents, especially their mothers (Stunkard et al., 1986). Yet environmental factors—including the quantity and quality of food available—play a significant role in determining weight (Whitaker et al., 1997). For example, the number of calories consumed in an average day can have long-term effects for a child's growth. The consumption of as little as 50 extra calories a day can lead to an excess weight gain of 5 pounds over a course of a year (Kolata, 1986).

In recent years, increased attention has been focused on the issue of children's weight, and the factors that contribute to it, in light of the rising rates of obesity among American children. (See the box "Obesity: A Childhood Epidemic.") While obesity is commonly measured by weight, many researchers have argued that it can be diagnosed earlier and more accurately by measuring *body mass index* (BMI), the ratio of weight to height (American Academy of Pediatrics, 2003). BMI can be calculated by dividing a person's height in inches by the square of their weight in pounds, then multiplying this result by 703. The average BMI for a 5-year-old girl is 15.2; for an average 5-year-old boy it is 15.4 (Centers for Disease Control, 2000). Children whose BMI falls between the 85th and 95th percentile are considered at risk for obesity—roughly 15 percent of 6- to 11-year-olds now fit in this category (American Academy of Pediatrics, 2003).

Motor Development

Walking along the beach one day, Sheila and Mike saw a girl about 7 years old and her little brother, who was about 4 years old, following their father and older brother, who was 10 or 11 years old. The father and older brother were tossing a ball back and forth as they walked. The girl was hopping along the sand on one foot, while her younger brother scrambled to keep up with her. Suddenly the little girl threw her arms up in the air, leaned over, threw her feet up, and did a cartwheel. She then did another cartwheel. Her younger brother stopped to watch her. Then he tried one. He fell in a heap in the sand, while she continued doing one perfect cartwheel after another. He picked himself up and ran ahead so that he was now between his father and his older brother. His father tossed the ball to him. He missed it, and when he picked it up and tried to throw it back, it flew off to the side. His older brother retrieved it and made a perfect throw.

In such everyday scenes you can see the increases in motor development that occur over the course of middle childhood (see Figure 12.2, p. 456). Children become stronger and more agile, and their balance improves. They run faster; throw balls farther, with greater efficiency, and are more likely to catch them. They also jump farther and higher than they did when they were younger, and learn to skate, ride bikes, sail boats, dance, swim, and climb trees as well as acquire a host of other physical skills during this period. Nonetheless, studies indicate that about 10 percent of 9-year-olds fail to develop skills like kicking and throwing, indicating that such achievements require practice, and do not develop purely as a result of maturation (Haywood & Getchell, 2001).

As a general rule, boys and girls differ in their physical skills. By the time they are 5 years old, boys, on average, can jump a little farther, run a bit faster, and throw a ball about 5 feet farther than the average girl. Boys also tend to be better at batting, kicking, dribbling, and catching balls than most girls. Girls, on the other hand, tend to be more agile than boys. Over the course of middle childhood, these sex

Obesity: A Childhood Epidemic

Despite the high value placed on thinness in the United States, there has been an epidemic of obesity among children in this country. Since 1970 the incidence of childhood obesity has increased more than 50 percent among children between the ages of 6 and 11 years and nearly as much among adolescents age 12 to 17 (Houpt, 2003).

The consequences of becoming obese during childhood and adolescence are severe. Obese children are often rejected by their peers, causing many of them to become withdrawn and suffer from a loss of self-esteem. When these children become adolescents and young adults, they are frequently discriminated against in ways that have serious consequences for their education and their future as wage earners. A study that followed a large group of randomly selected adolescents and young adults for 7 years found that females who were overweight at the beginning of the study completed less school, were less likely to marry, and had lower household incomes—with an almost doubled risk of living in poverty—than those whose weight was normal at the beginning of the study (Gortmaker et al., 1993).

At least as serious as their social and psychological problems, obese children are more vulnerable to a variety of serious health problems. Obese children have been shown to be at increased risk for asthma, heart disease, diabetes, respiratory disease, and orthopedic disorders (Strauss, 1999). In recent years, there has been an alarming increase among obese minority children in the incidence of Type II diabetes, a serious condition that can lead to kidney disease, eye disorders, and nervous system problems as well as heart disease and stroke.

There appear to be three important periods during which there is an increased risk for developing obesity that persists into adulthood (Strauss, 1999). The first is the prenatal period, during which, it is believed, either maternal overnutrition or maternal undernutrition can cause metabolic changes in the fetus that permanently alter the child's appetite regulation. The second important period is related to what is known as the adiposity rebound period, during which children's body fat begins to increase again after a period of decreasing. Normally, the adiposity rebound period occurs at around age 6. Longitudinal studies have found that children whose body fat increases before the age of 5½ are significantly more likely than other children to become and remain obese. One reason for the early weight gain of these children may be that they are maturing early, and early maturation is associated with obesity. Another possible explanation is that children who go through the period of adiposity rebound early may have been exposed to maternal diabetes during the gestational period, which altered their metabolism. The third important period for the development of persistent obesity is adolescence, when there are changes in the quantity and location of body fat. This period is especially critical for girls. In boys the quantity of body fat normally decreases by about 40 percent, whereas in girls the quantity of body fat increases by about 40 percent, putting girls at elevated risk for becoming and staying obese.

What is causing the increase in obesity among children? Dietary fat is one of the prime suspects. The diets of obese children have been found to have a higher percentage of calories from fats than the diets of other children (St-Onge et al., 2003). Another suspected culprit is a reduction in activity levels over time. Obese children tend to be less active than children of normal weight. As part of their inactivity, they also tend to watch more television than their normal-weight peers, and television watching in itself has been found to dramatically lower children's metabolic rates—reducing the rate at which children burn calories (Dietz & Gortmaker, 1985; Gortmaker et al., 1996). Decreases in fat intake and increases in physical activity are associated with decreases in children's weight gain, so a combination of these approaches would seem an obvious remedy (Klesges et al., 1995).

Unfortunately, exercising is generally difficult for obese children, and losing weight becomes increasingly difficult once obesity develops because a subsequent loss in weight tends to trigger increased appetite and lowered metabolic rates, driving the person's weight back to its preexisting level (Strauss, 1999). As many as 80 percent of the obese children who do lose weight gain it back (Epstein et al., 1993).

The prevalence of obesity among children and the difficulty of designing effective therapeutic programs have inspired a good deal of research. Because children's food preferences and eating habits are influenced by those of their parents, most successful weight-loss programs for children target not only the obese children but also their parents, who are likely to be obese as well (Golan et al., 1998). The most effective programs also combine clear-cut procedures for identifying high-fat foods with carefully designed exercise programs that specify how many calories are burned up by each form of exercise. In a 5-year follow-up study of one such exemplary therapeutic effort, Leonard Epstein and his colleagues found that the children in the sample had sustained an average weight loss of 12 percent (Epstein et al., 1990).

Another promising avenue for combating obesity is to change the food available to children when they are away from home. Sugary drinks and fast foods are readily available to children in restaurants and schools (Prentice & Jebb, 2003). Food is also a heavily promoted commercial product and children are often the targets. It is estimated that children are exposed to 10,000 advertisements for food each year, 95 percent of which are for candy, soft drinks, sugared cereals, and fast foods (Horgen, 2001). Consequently, to combat childhood obesity effectively, public attitudes must change to shift responsibility from individuals to the social institutions that currently create a demand for unhealthy foods (Schwartz & Puhl, 2003).

differences in motor skills become more pronounced (Malina, 1998). On average, boys tend to be slightly advanced in motor abilities that require power and force, while girls often excel in fine motor skills, such as drawing and writing, or in gross motor skills that combine balance and foot movement, such as skipping and hopping and the skills needed in gymnastics (Cameron, 2002).

(a)

(b)

Figure 12.2 The physical changes of childhood make possible a range of new activities. The ability to kick a ball, for example, improves dramatically. A young child learning to kick will simply push the leg forward (a), while an older child will step forward, cock the leg, and take a limited swing at the ball (b). By the end of middle childhood, the child is able to take a full swing at the ball while simultaneously moving arms and trunk to provide support and balance (c). (From Haywood & Getchell, 2000.)

(c)

Boys tend to have slightly greater muscle mass than most girls and are slightly bigger—until about the age of $10\frac{1}{2}$, when girls spurt ahead in height for a few years—but these sex-related physical differences are not large enough in themselves to account for the superiority of boys in many motor skills during middle childhood. Cultural conceptions of the activities appropriate to boys and to girls also play a large role in shaping these differences in behavior. For example, being able to throw, catch, and hit a baseball is a valued set of skills for boys in American culture. American parents usually encourage their sons, much more than their daughters, to develop these skills by buying them balls and bats, taking them to ballgames, talking about baseball with them, playing with them, and enrolling them in Little League. And in all cultures, it is also much truer for boys than for girls that those who are considered to be good athletes are more popular with their peers than those who show no athletic ability. While the participation of girls in such sports as baseball, soccer, and tennis has increased significantly in a number of countries in recent decades, girls are still not given the amount of encouragement and coaching that boys receive in these sports, nor are they rewarded to the extent boys are for having the abilities these sports require (Horn, 2002).

Brain Development

The years between ages 6 and 8 witness the continued growth of the brain and the development of specific kinds of brain functioning that are believed to underlie changes in cognitive skills:

1. Myelination, particularly in the frontal cortex, continues up to adulthood (Janowsky & Carper, 1996; Sowell et al., 2002). (Recall from Chapter 4 that myelination provides the axon of cortical neurons with an insulating sheath of tissue that speeds transmission of nerve impulses.)

EEG coherence The synchronization of electrical activity in different areas of the brain.

2. Synaptic pruning, the process by which nonfunctional synapses die off, continues for late-maturing areas of the brain (the frontal and prefrontal cortices), reducing the density of synapses among neurons. At the same time, more stable connections are found among remaining neurons (Sowell et al., 2002).

3. Brain activity patterns as measured by an EEG (electro-encephalogram) undergo a dramatic change (see Figure 12.3). Until the age of 5, EEGs recorded when children are awake display more theta activity (characteristic of adult sleep states) than alpha activity (characteristic of engaged attention). Between 5 and 7 years of age, the amounts of theta and alpha activity are about equal, but thereafter alpha activity (engaged attention) dominates (Corbin & Bickford, 1955).

4. The synchronization of electrical activity in different areas of the brain, called **EEG coherence,** increases significantly, reflecting the fact that different parts of the brain function more effectively as coordinated systems (see Figure 12.4). Particularly important, according to Robert Thatcher (1994), is evidence of increased coordination between the electrical activity of the frontal lobes and the electrical activity in other parts of the brain.

This pattern of changes in brain structure and function—particularly in the frontal lobes and their connections to other parts of the brain—suggests that maturation of the brain plays an important role in the development of thinking during middle childhood, as in earlier periods.

The pattern of brain changes following the onset of middle childhood permits the frontal lobes to coordinate the activities of other brain centers in a qualitatively more complex way, enabling children to better control their attention, to form explicit plans, and to engage in self-reflection, all behaviors that appear to undergo significant development in the transition to middle childhood (see Figure 12.5, p. 458). The importance of the frontal lobes in these developments is supported by the fact that when the frontal lobes are damaged in humans and in other animals, individuals are unable to maintain goals, their actions become fragmentary and uncontrolled, they respond to irrelevant stimuli, and they are easily thrown off track by interruptions and pauses.

One of the most convincing demonstrations that changes in brain functioning lead to changes in problem-solving processes comes from a study of changes in the brain activity of 5-year-old children being tested on a standard Piagetian task (conservation of quantity, which we will discuss later). The children wore caps that contained recording electrodes, allowing the researchers to track the changes in brain activity that accompanied their problem-solving endeavors. The children were tested three times, one year apart, first at the age of 5, then 6, and then 7. Initially the children did not succeed in solving the problem, but as they grew older, those who did succeed had a pattern of brain activity different from that of the children who failed at the task (Stauder et al., 1999), while the brain patterns of those who failed were similar to those observed among young children (see Chapter 9). These findings seem to support the idea that the increasing role of the frontal lobes in overall brain organization is related to the behavioral changes of middle childhood.

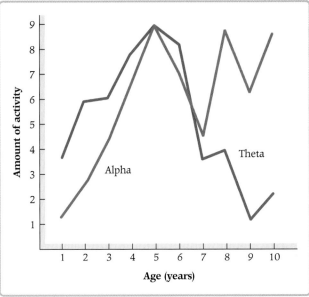

Figure 12.3 Changes in the amount of theta (sleeplike) and alpha (alert) EEG activity during development. Note that alpha waves come to predominate over theta waves around the age of 7. (From Corbin & Bickford, 1955.)

Figure 12.4 Changes in EEG coherence in the transition from early to middle childhood. (From Thatcher, 1991.)

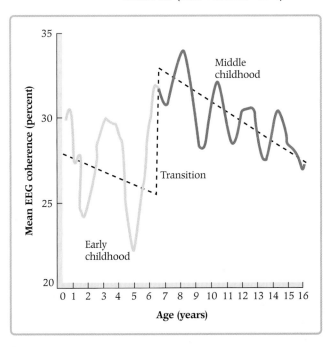

Figure 12.5 The rate of increase in the area of the frontal lobes and in the maturation of nerve cells during development. (From Luria, 1973.)

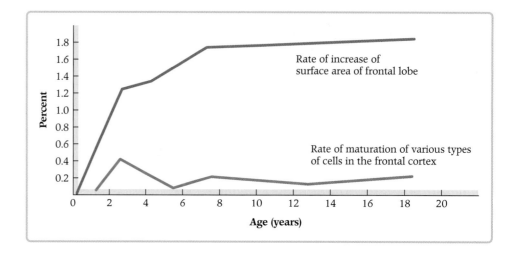

Despite this evidence, we must be cautious about inferring direct causal links between particular changes in the brain and specific changes in behavior. The evidence we have cited is correlational: as children grow older, we observe changes in their brains and changes in their behavior, but the direction of causation remains uncertain. As explained in Chapter 5 ("Action and Understanding," p. 189), the development and strengthening of neural pathways in the brain both affects, and is affected by, the individual's experience.

All of the biological changes of middle childhood—increased growth, improved motor skills, and continued brain development—enable children to meet the new expectations placed on them by adults. At the same time, these changes are joined by cognitive achievements, which help children cope with their increased freedom and responsibility.

Cognitive Developments: Bridging the Islands of Competence

In early childhood, one finds islands of competence that become apparent in situations in which children can draw upon knowledge from core domains and familiar cultural scripts to guide their thinking and where the environment supports young children's efforts (Chapter 9). When we turn to middle childhood, the question naturally arises, What new cognitive developments appear that link up those islands of competence? What new processes enable children to participate in the new and more complex cognitive tasks that they encounter in the ever widening variety of settings they inhabit?

Although the mechanisms proposed for bridging between domain-specific abilities differ in their specifics, they all suggest that in middle childhood, children can hold more characteristics of a situation in mind while thinking about it. This finding has led many to conclude that children's improved working memory in a broad variety of contexts is an important factor in encouraging parents to make new demands on their children and to give them greater freedom.

Piaget's Bridge: A Change in Logical Thinking

As you should anticipate on the basis of the discussion of cognitive development to this point, Piaget conceives of this new ability in terms of the logic of action. Piaget called the new form of thought he saw emerging in middle childhood **concrete operations,** coordinated mental actions that fit into a logical system in a way that

concrete operations Coordinated mental actions that fit into a logical system in a way that creates greater unity of thinking.

creates greater unity of thinking. (See Table 12.1 for a summary of concrete operations in relation to other Piagetian stages.) These mental operations are concrete in the sense that they depend upon support from concrete objects in everyday activities. At the same time, concrete operations are distinguished from preoperations because they are double-sided: they include two aspects of a problem in a single logical system simultaneously.

According to Piaget, in the transition from early to middle childhood, the advent of concrete operations transforms all aspects of psychological functioning. The physical world becomes more predictable because children come to understand that certain physical aspects of objects, such as size, density, length, and number, remain the same even when other aspects of the object's appearances have changed. Children's thinking also becomes more organized and flexible. They can think about alternatives and reverse their thinking when they try to solve problems.

table 12.1

Piaget's Stages of Cognitive Development: Concrete Operational

Age (years)	Stage	Description	Characteristics and Examples of Concrete Operations
Birth to 2	Sensorimotor	Infants' achievements consist largely of coordinating their sensory perceptions and simple motor behaviors. As they move through the 6 substages of this period, infants come to recognize the existence of a world outside of themselves and begin to interact with it in deliberate ways.	**New features of thinking** • **Decentration:** Children can notice and consider more than one attribute of an object at a time and form categories according to multiple criteria. • **Conservation:** Children understand that certain properties of an object will remain the same even when other, superficial ones are altered. They know that when a tall, thin glass is emptied into a short, fat one, the amount of liquid remains the same.
2 to 6	Preoperational	Young children can represent reality to themselves through the use of symbols, including mental images, words, and gestures. Objects and events no longer have to be present to be thought about, but children often fail to distinguish their point of view from that of others, become easily captured by surface appearances, and are often confused about causal relations.	• **Logical necessity:** Children have acquired the conviction that it is logically necessary for certain qualities to be conserved despite changes in appearance. • **Identity:** Children realize that if nothing has been added or subtracted, the amount must remain the same. • **Compensation:** Children can mentally compare changes in two aspects of a problem and see how one compensates for the other. • **Reversibility:** Children realize that certain operations can negate, or reverse, the effects of others.
6 to 12	Concrete operational	As they enter middle childhood, children become capable of mental operations, internalized actions that fit into a logical system. Operational thinking allows children mentally to combine, separate, order, and transform objects and actions. Such operations are considered concrete because they are carried out in the presence of the objects and events being thought about.	**Declining egocentrism** • Children can communicate more effectively about objects a listener cannot see. • Children can think about how others perceive them. • Children understand that a person can feel one way and act another. **Changes in social relations** • Children can regulate their interactions with each other through rules and begin to play rule-based games.
12 to 19	Formal operational	In adolescence the developing person acquires the ability to think systematically about all logical relations within a problem. Adolescents display keen interest in abstract ideas and in the process of thinking itself.	• Children take intentions into account in judging behavior and believe the punishment must fit the crime.

Figure 12.6 The procedure Piaget used to test for the conservation of quantity. First, present two beakers of equal size with equal amounts of liquid. Second, present a taller, thinner beaker and pour contents of one of the other beakers into it. Third, ask, "Which beaker has more liquid, or do they contain the same amount?" Did this girl display conservation?

Piaget invented a number of problem-solving tasks to enable him to diagnose the presence or absence of concrete-operational thinking. We present two of many possible examples of this key Piagetian concept, which demonstrate with special clarity why he believed that preoperational and concrete-operational thinking are characteristic of qualitatively different stages (Piaget & Inhelder, 1973).

Conservation of Quantity

Conservation is Piaget's term for the understanding that some properties of an object or substance remain the same even when its appearance is altered in some superficial way. As we mentioned in Chapter 9 (p. 324), one of the most famous versions of his conservation task involves presenting children with two identical glass beakers containing the same amounts of liquid, to see if they understand conservation of quantity (see Figure 12.6). The experimenter begins by pouring the contents of one of the beakers into a third beaker that is taller and narrower. Naturally, the liquid rises higher in the new beaker. The experimenter then asks the child, "Does the new beaker contain more liquid than the old beaker, does it contain the same amount, or does it contain less?"

Ordinarily, 3- to 4-year-old children say that the taller beaker has more. When asked why, they explain, "There's more because it's higher," or "There's more because it's bigger," or even "There's more because you poured it." They appear to focus their attention on a single aspect of the new beaker—its height. (Focusing on a single attribute of an object is the phenomenon of "centering," introduced in Chapter 9, p. 324). Even when the experimenter points out that no liquid was added or subtracted, and even after the liquid is poured back into the original beaker to demonstrate that the amount has not changed, 3- and 4-year-olds generally claim that there is more liquid in the taller, narrower beaker.

Piaget found that around the age of 5 or 6 years, children's understanding of conservation goes through a transitional stage. At this point children seem to realize that it is necessary to consider both the height and the circumference of the beakers, but they have difficulty keeping both in mind simultaneously and coordinating the changes so that they can properly compare them.

According to Piaget, children fully master the principle of conservation around the age of 8, when they understand not only that the new beaker is both taller and narrower but that a change in one dimension of the beaker (increasing height) is offset by a change in the other (decreasing circumference). Children who have acquired the concept of conservation of continuous quantity recognize the *logical necessity* that the amount of liquid remain the same despite the change in appearance. When asked the reasons for their judgment, they offer arguments such as the following, showing that they understand the logical relationships involved:

- "They were equal to start with and nothing was added, so they're the same." This mental operation is called **identity;** the child realizes that a change limited to outward appearance does not change the actual amounts involved.

- "The liquid is higher, but the glass is thinner." This mental operation is called **compensation;** changes in one aspect of a problem are mentally compared with and compensated for by changes in another.

conservation Piaget's term for the understanding that some properties of an object or substance remain the same even when its appearance is altered in some superficial way.

identity A mental operation in which the child realizes that a change limited to outward appearance does not change the substances involved.

compensation A mental operation in which the child realizes that changes in one aspect of a problem are compared with and compensated for by changes in another aspect.

- "If you pour it back, you'll see that it's the same." This mental operation is called *negation* or **reversibility;** the child realizes that one operation can be negated, or reversed, by the effects of another.

In each case, conservation of continuous quantity includes two aspects of the problem that need to be considered, and the child is led to the logical conclusion that the visual change does not change the underlying logical relationship.

reversibility A mental operation in which the child realizes that one operation can be negated, or reversed, by the effects of another.

Conservation of Number

Children's developing understanding of conservation of number provides another example of the changes that occur when children acquire concrete operations. By "conservation of number" Piaget meant the ability to recognize the one-to-one correspondence between two sets of objects of equal number, despite a difference in the sizes of the objects or in their spatial positions (Piaget, 1952a).

The basic procedure for testing the ability of children to conserve number is to present them with two rows of objects such as those shown in Figure 12.7a. Both the numbers of objects and the lengths of the two lines are equal, and children are asked to affirm that they are. Then one of the rows is either spread out or compressed (see Figure 12.7b), and the children are asked if the numbers of objects in the two rows are still equal. Children below the age of 6 or 7 rarely display conservation of number unless the total number of objects is very small, saying, for example, that the elongated row has more. In contrast, older children realize that on the grounds of *logic alone* the number must remain the same. Applying concrete operations to the number conservation task, they are able to say to themselves, in effect, "There must be the same number of cards, because if the experimenter moved the cards in his row back to where they were at the beginning, nothing would have changed." This understanding of logical necessity—that "it *has* to be that way"—is Piaget's key criterion of a stagelike change in thinking. (See the box "What's So Funny?" on p. 462 for how changing reasoning changes the kinds of jokes that children find funny.)

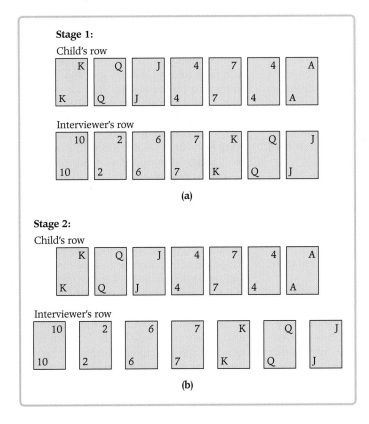

Figure 12.7 The procedure used to test for the conservation of number. (a) In stage 1, the child's and the interviewer's seven cards are arrayed at equal intervals. (b) In stage 2, the interviewer spreads out his cards and asks the child if she and the interviewer still have the same number of cards. (From Ginsburg, 1977.)

What's So Funny? Humor as a Window on Cognitive Development

"**K**nock, knock."
"Who's there?"
"Bugspray."
"Bugspray who?"
"Bugs pray that snakes won't eat them."

To a 5-year-old, this and a hundred other "knock-knock jokes" can be so funny that they tell them over and over again. As an adult, you might at first find the joke mildly amusing, but less so as your niece or friend's child continues to repeat it. The only "humor" you might see in this situation is the sight of the child rolling in laughter the tenth time the joke comes around.

Developmentalists are interested in humor for many reasons. Freud believed that humor is a mechanism for coping with sources of anxiety, such as repressed sexual desires (Freud, 1963). Others have emphasized the role of jokes in establishing positive social relations with one's own group and negative relations with people considered outsiders (Martineau, 1972). But for our purposes in this chapter, humor is of special interest because it is an excellent indicator of the level of children's cognitive development.

Developmentalists are uncertain of when children first display a sense of humor and precisely where to draw the line between humor and other forms of activity that make us laugh (McGhee, 1979; Ruch, 1998). Perhaps the most widely agreed-upon early form of humor is the game of peek-a-boo, which appears sometime toward the end of the first year of life. The question is, what makes this game funny? According to developmentalists, the humor arises from the key feature of *incongruity,* events that violate our expectations. Incongruity forms the basis for many jokes that young children find funny. In late infancy, when children are busily focused on language learning, they laugh when a ball is called an apple or a pumpkin; even older children who no longer find such mislabeling funny will laugh if shown a picture of a ball that has a nose and ears.

Although children continue to find incongruous events and statements funny, the types of incongruity they find amusing change as they age. The "childish" sense of humor exemplified by love of knock-knock jokes is beneath the dignity of an 8- or 9-year old, because they understand the word meanings and events that present such intriguing incongruities to younger children. At the same time, they are unable to appreciate jokes that adolescents find funny (see figure).

Doris Bergen (1998) asked a large group of parents from many parts of the United States

to record examples of their children exhibiting appreciation of humor by recording each example on a specially designed form. The form included the kind of humor (a joke, word play, slapstick, etc.), the age of the child, and the circumstances in which the incident occurred. The children ranged in age from early childhood to 7 years old. The youngest children were most likely to find humor in play with words. One child created his own joke by changing the lyrics of a song from "peanut butter" (in the original) to "tuna butter." Young children also laughed at slapstick events (all the doors fall off a house in a TV cartoon). Older children also found word play humorous but favored riddles and practical jokes. For example, one 6½-year-old, riding in the car with his family, asked his uncle and father, "Why was 6 afraid of 7? Because 7, 8, 9."

Evidence of a shift between 4 to 5 and 6 to 7 years of age in sources of incongruity that make a joke funny comes from studies that present riddles in two forms, one of which involves an incongruity, the other of which does not. For example:

Question: "Why did the farmer name his hog Ink?"
Answer 1: "Because he kept running out of the pen."
Answer 2: "Because he kept getting away." The first alternative answer requires appreciation of the double meaning of "pen" and its relationship to "ink" while the second alternative answer does not (from Shultz, 1972). Shultz found the 4- to 6-year-olds thought the

second alternative was as funny as the second, while older children clearly preferred the first answer.

The fact that preferences for different kinds of jokes, and the ability to understand them, show a marked shift around the age of 6 to 7 years made it natural for developmentalists to explain the age-related change in Piagetian terms. Younger children presumably focus on superficial aspects of events they are asked to interpret and have difficulty thinking through a problem systematically, so they miss the "hidden" foundation of the joke. Older children, who have achieved the ability to engage in concrete operations do not suffer these limitations, so they get the joke more quickly.

Of course, older children have more developed vocabularies than younger children and know more about what to expect in a variety of situations simply by virtue of their greater experience. When the content and vocabulary of riddles is made simple enough, even 4- to 5-year-olds will often find them funny (Pien & Rothbard, 1976). This result is consistent with the extensive research showing that "preoperational" children will display more sophisticated modes of thought when experimenters use familiar content and well-known routines.

Overall, research on the development of a sense of humor supports the idea that incongruity is central to what makes a joke a joke, while what makes an event incongruous or mundane depends crucially upon the knowledge of the teller and the listener, which in turn is bound up with their level of cognitive development.

Information-Processing Bridges Between Islands of Competence

Although most developmentalists agree with Piaget's *description* of the two-sidedness of children's thinking during middle childhood, many find his *explanation* of how this change comes about unsatisfactory. Instead, they prefer explanations that appeal to an array of psychological processes that are most closely associated with the information approaches to cognitive development, including increased memory capacity, more rapid and efficient mental operations, and the acquisition of a variety of mental strategies.

The Role of Memory

According to many developmentalists dissatisfied with Piaget's explanation of cognitive change in middle childhood and beyond, children's increased memory abilities play a central role in allowing them to hold two or more aspects of a problem in mind while they are thinking. For example, a young soccer player racing for the goal can keep in mind the positions of her teammates, the goalie's well-known difficulty blocking low shots, and the special maneuver her coach taught her in practice. Younger players may have a difficult time simply remembering they are in a soccer game and may run after the ball only when it passes in front of them. Four factors, taken together, appear to bring about the memory changes characteristic of this period (Schneider & Bjorklund, 1998):

1. brain-related increases in the speed of memory processing and memory capacity

2. an increase in knowledge about the things one is trying to remember

3. the acquisition of more effective strategies for remembering

4. an improved ability to think about one's own memory processes

Increased Speed and Capacity On pp. 456–457 we summarized evidence of increased brain development located primarily in the frontal and prefrontal areas of the brain. Although there are only a few studies linking brain development to increases in memory *capacity*, the speed with which children's brains can respond to complex stimuli has been shown to increase gradually during middle childhood by placing electrodes over different parts of the brain (Travis, 1998). Indicators of brain maturation have also been directly linked to memory performance in children aged 7 to 16 years (Sowell et al., 2001).

A common behavioral method of measuring the changing capacity of working memory is to assess children's **memory span,** the number of randomly presented items of information children can repeat immediately after the items are presented. Most 4- and 5-year-olds can recall four digits presented one after another; most 9- and 10-year-olds can remember about six; most adults can remember about seven (Schneider & Pressley, 1997).

In order to store into working memory several numbers presented at random, children must somehow represent each number to themselves, perhaps by silently repeating "ten, six, eight, two." Young children take longer than older children simply to repeat a number such as 10 or 2. Because it takes them longer to say the numbers, memory for the numbers already presented is more likely to decay and be lost. Older children name individual numbers quite quickly, reducing the time interval between numbers and thereby increasing the likelihood of retaining the numbers in memory (see Figure 12.8) (Case et al., 1982).

memory span The number of randomly presented items of information that can be repeated immediately after they are presented.

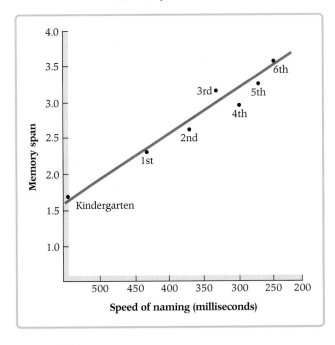

Figure 12.8 Relationship between memory span and speed of naming. Note that as children grow older in grades kindergarten through 6, their counting span increases accordingly. (From Case et al., 1982.)

Cross-cultural research enriches these conclusions. When Chuansheng Chen and Harold Stevenson (1988) compared the memory spans of U.S. and Chinese children age 4 to 6 years, they found that the Chinese children were able to recall more digits at each of the ages tested. At first, this finding might seem to suggest that the working memory of Chinese children was larger than that of the American children. However, as Chen and Stevenson pointed out, the Chinese words for the digits are shorter than the English words. Thus the task was easier for the Chinese children for the same reason that it was easier for the older North American children: there was a shorter interval between repeated items. This hypothesis was supported by a study in which Stevenson and his colleagues used lists of objects whose names were equal in length in English and Chinese. When these words were presented for remembering, Chinese and American children were found to have equal memory capacities (Stevenson et al., 1985).

Robert Kail and his colleagues have shown that the speed with which children can retrieve information *already* stored in long-term memory also increases from early childhood well into adulthood (Kail, 2000). They report that 11-year-old children retrieved information from long-term memory approximately six times faster than 4- and 5-year-olds but still significantly slower than adults. As a consequence of this increase in mental processing speed, older children and adults can be expected to execute more cognitive operations in a given time span than younger children and, therefore, to demonstrate increased intellectual effectiveness.

Expanded Knowledge Base The second factor that contributes to improved memory during childhood is the greater knowledge that older children are likely to have about any given topic simply because they have accumulated more experience in the world than younger children have. This experience provides older children with a richer knowledge base, or store of information, on which to draw in a new situation. As a consequence, when asked to remember new information, they have more prior information to which to relate it.

Skill at cards requires the ability to remember the cards that have been previously dealt and the relative values of different hands, as well as the ability to use strategies to defeat your opponent.

As we saw in Chapter 9 (p. 335), the positive effect that a large knowledge base has on memory development is demonstrated by studies in which younger subjects who have a rich knowledge base in a given area remember more new information related to that area than older subjects whose knowledge base is not as rich. The same is true in middle childhood and throughout life. In one such experiment, Michelene Chi (1978) compared memory for the arrangement of chess pieces among 10-year-old chess buffs with the memory abilities of college-age chess amateurs. The 10-year-olds recalled the chess arrangements that occurred in the course of a game better than the college students, but when the two groups were compared on their ability to recall a random series of numbers, the college students' performances were far superior. A replication of this study by German researchers confirmed the basic results and extended them by showing that when subjects were asked to remember random arrangements of chess pieces, rather than meaningful arrangements that might plausibly occur during a game (thereby removing the importance of knowledge of chess), the advantage of the chess experts was greatly reduced (Schneider et al., 1993).

Improved Memory Strategies A **strategy** is a deliberate, controllable cognitive operation performed for the purpose of attaining a particular goal (Bjorklund & Miller, 1997). All strategies are "two-sided" in the sense that they require children to think simultaneously about a goal and about a way to achieve that goal. When we say that children use memory strategies, we mean that they engage in deliberate actions in order to enhance remembering.

A large number of studies have shown that children's spontaneous use of strategies for remembering undergoes a marked increase between early and middle childhood (Schneider & Bjorklund, 1998). Three memory strategies whose development has been intensively studied are rehearsal, organization, and elaboration.

Rehearsal is the process of repeating to oneself the material that one is trying to memorize, such as a word list, a song, or a phone number. It is not an easy task to observe young children rehearsing things that they want to remember, because their repetition is often not visible. In a classic study of the development of rehearsal strategies in children, John Flavell and his colleagues (Keeney et al., 1967) presented 5- and 10-year-olds with seven pictures of objects to remember. The children were asked to wear a "space helmet" with a visor that was pulled down over their eyes during the 15-second interval between the presentation of the pictures and the test for recall. The visor prevented the children from seeing the pictures and allowed the experimenter to watch their lips to see if they repeated to themselves what they had seen. Few of the 5-year-olds were observed to rehearse, but almost all the 10-year-olds did. Within each age group, children who rehearsed the pictures recalled more than children who did not. When those who had not rehearsed were later taught to do so, they did as well on the memory task as those who had rehearsed on their own.

In a more recent study, children who were trying to remember lists of three and five single-digit numbers were videotaped so that the researchers could look for more subtle indicators of rehearsal (McGilly & Siegler, 1989). The researchers found that even kindergarten children are capable of rehearsing the things they want to remember. According to the investigators, this finding suggests that increases that occur in children's short-term memory in middle childhood result from increasingly effective use of strategies and not from the sudden appearance of the ability to use a new strategy.

Marked changes are also found in **memory organization**, a strategy in which children mentally group the materials to be remembered in meaningful clusters of closely associated items so that they have to remember only one part of a cluster to gain access to the rest. The use of organizational strategies is often studied by means of a procedure called *free recall*. In a free-recall task, children are shown a large number of objects or read a list of words one at a time and then asked to remember them. This kind of memory is called "free" recall because the children are free to recall the items in any order they choose.

Research has demonstrated that 7- and 8-year-olds are more likely than younger children to group the items they have to remember into easy-to-remember categories (Schneider & Bjorklund, 1998). The kinds of groupings that children impose on lists of things to be remembered also change with age. Younger children often use sound features, such as rhyme ("cat," "sat"), or situational associations ("cereal," "bowl") to group words they are trying to remember. In middle childhood, children are more likely to link words according to categories such as animals ("cat," "dog," "horse"), foods ("cereal," "milk," "bananas"), or geometric figures ("triangle," "square," "circle"). The consequence of these changes is an enhanced ability to store and retrieve information deliberately and systematically.

©LWA-Dann Tardif/Corbis

Chess provides children with many opportunities to hone their skill in using strategies effectively.

strategy A deliberate, controllable cognitive operation performed for the purpose of attaining a particular goal.

rehearsal The process of repeating to oneself the material that one is trying to memorize.

memory organization A memory strategy in which children mentally group the materials to be remembered in meaningful clusters of closely associated items.

elaboration A memory strategy in which children identify or make up connections between two or more things they have to remember.

metamemory The ability to think about one's memory processes.

Although children from traditional agricultural societies sometimes perform poorly on psychological tests, their cognitive abilities are often manifested in other ways. This Ugandan boy has constructed his toy car out of bits of wire and some wooden wheels.

Kirk McRoy/Material World

Children who do not spontaneously use rehearsal and organizing strategies can be taught to do so (Moely et al., 1995). The effectiveness of this training indicates that there is no unbridgeable gap between the memory performance of 4- to 5-year-olds and that of 7- to 8-year-olds or between children who use strategies spontaneously and those who do not. Over the course of middle childhood, children become increasingly better at using various strategies to help them remember better.

A third kind of strategy, **elaboration,** is a process in which children identify or make up connections between two or more things they have to remember. Elaboration strategies have usually been studied in cases where children are presented with two words and asked to remember the second one when they hear the first. For example, they might be asked to remember the word "street" after hearing the word "tomato." An elaboration strategy for this word pair could be to think of a tomato squashed in the middle of a street.

Research with adults shows that elaboration strategies are effective when they are used (Schneider & Bjorklund, 1998). However, it is only during middle childhood that children begin to use elaboration strategies spontaneously, and skill in the use of this kind of strategy continues to increase with age (Miller, 1990).

Thinking about Memory

Most 7- and 8-year-olds not only know more about the world in general than do 3- to 5-year-olds, but also are likely to know more about memory itself (knowledge referred to as **metamemory**). Even 5-year-olds have some understanding of how memory works. In a study that has stimulated a great deal of the subsequent research on memory development, 5-year-olds said they knew that it was easier to remember a short list of words than a long one, to relearn something you once knew than to learn it from scratch, and to remember something that happened yesterday than something that happened last month (Kreutzer et al., 1975).

Nevertheless, most 8-year-olds have a better understanding of the limitations of their own memories than most 5-year-olds do. When shown a set of ten pictures and asked if they could remember them all (something most children at these ages generally cannot do), most of the 5-year-olds—but only a few of the 8-year-olds—claimed that they could. The 5-year-olds also failed to evaluate correctly how much effort they would need to remember the pictures. Given unlimited time to master the set of pictures, the 5-year-olds announced that they were ready right away, even though they succeeded in remembering only a few of the items. The 8-year-olds, by contrast, knew enough to study the materials and to test themselves on their ability to remember (Flavell et al., 1970).

Even when children know that metamemory knowledge can enhance remembering, they often do not use their knowledge, just as they don't always use the rehearsal and organizational strategies they know (Schneider, 1999). In one memory study, William Fabricius and John Hagen (1984) created a situation in which 6- and 7-year-olds used an organizational strategy on some trials and not on others. When the children used the organizational strategy, they almost always remembered better. These researchers asked the children to tell them what they thought accounted for their better remembering efforts. Some of the children did not notice that the organizing strategy was helpful, even though they had just used it successfully. They attributed their better recall to slowing down and being more careful or to paying more attention to the stimuli. Other children attributed their better recall to the deliberate use of the organizing strategy. When the children were brought back for a second session, in which their ability to remember was tested in a slightly different situation, 99 percent of those who had understood the helpfulness of the organizing strategy in the first session used the same strategy the second time around. By contrast, only 32 percent of the children who attributed their better remembering efforts to some other factor used the organizing strategy. These and similar results indicate that children must acquire the ability to use metamemory knowledge in addition to acquiring useful strategies.

Combining Memory Development and Logical Stages

Thus far we have offered two explanations for children's increased mental abilities in middle childhood: a stagelike change in their ability to think through problems and the consequences of their actions logically, and increased memory capacities. Instead of pitting one explanation against the other, it seems more productive to many developmentalists to determine how these two sources of mental capacity might work together. This is the route taken by Robbie Case and his colleague whose efforts at synthesizing rival theories was introduced in Chapter 9 (p. 354). These developmentalists argued that it is the increase in the capacity of working memory that allows children to think more logically (Case, 1998; Okamoto & Case, 1996). They carried out a series of studies designed to probe the ability of 6-, 8-, and 10-year-olds in the domains of number, storytelling, and drawing. The specifics of their procedures naturally differed according to the domain in question, but all the problems they presented to the children required them to mentally manipulate information in working memory in increasingly complex ways.

The researchers' data on the development of 6- to 10-year-old children's understanding in the domain of number provides a good example of their overall approach and complements their research among younger children discussed in Chapter 9 (p. 354). Case and his colleagues hypothesized that the *mental number line* provides a common conceptual tool (which they refer to as a "central conceptual structure") for the domain of number. The problems presented to the children were classified into four categories of difficulty, based on how many number lines the children had to keep in mind and mentally manipulate to come up with the answer:

The kinds of work that children are assigned afford different kinds of learning opportunities. Young street vendors acquire a variety of arithmetic skills that sometimes surpass those of children of the same age who attend school.

- *Category 1:* Problems required judgments only about whether specified numbers were more or less than other numbers.

- *Category 2:* Problems required calculations on a single number line. In typical problems children were asked questions like "What number comes after 7?" or were shown a card with several numbers printed on it (for example, 8, 5, 2, 6) and were asked, "Which number comes first when you are counting?"

- *Category 3:* Problems required coordinating two number lines to answer the questions. Typical problems were of the following kind: "How many numbers are in between 3 and 9?" To answer this question, the child had to be able to deal with one mental number line to represent the position of the two numbers and a second mental number line to calculate the difference between them.

- *Category 4:* Problems required that children compare the results of two problems like those in category 3 and calculate the difference. A typical problem was of the following kind: "Which difference is bigger, the difference between 6 and 9 or the difference between 8 and 3?"

table 12.2

Percentage of Correct Responses as a Function of Age and Problem Complexity			
	6-Year-Olds	**8-Year-Olds**	**10-Year-Olds**
Category 1	100	100	100
Category 2	89	97	99
Category 3	28	66	86
Category 4	4	24	49

Source: Okamoto & Case, 1996.

The study focused on 6-, 8-, and 10-year-olds because prior research had shown that while 4-year-olds can count and can make judgments about whether a given set of objects is "a lot" or "a little," they are unable to integrate these two mental operations into a single system or to answer such questions as "Which is more, 4 or 5?"

The children were presented with several problems from each category. The scores of each age group of children were averaged together for each category of problems. As shown in Table 12.2, when the problems were simple and only required the children to use one number line ("What number comes after 7?") there was little difference in the performance among the age groups. But the performance of 6-year-olds deteriorated markedly when they had to coordinate two number lines to answer such questions as "How many numbers are in between 2 and 7?" The 8-year-olds had less trouble with such problems, but they ran into serious difficulty when solving category 4 problems that required them to hold in mind two number lines as well as the results of their calculations on each and then to compare the two. The 10-year-olds had some difficulty when they were asked to solve category 4 problems, but they were successful half the time.

This pattern of results illustrates the researchers' claims of a close relationship between problem-solving ability and the capacity of working memory. Each time the demands on working memory were increased, fewer children at a given age level could manage the task.

Recently Andreas Demetriou and his colleagues extended Case's analysis to link speed of processing to working memory, and logical problem solving (Demetriou et al., 2002). They found these three aspects of cognition build upon each other. Increased speed of processing leads to increases in working memory, which in turn lead to increases in the effectiveness of problem solving. This kind of analysis provides compelling evidence of a close link between stages of development within specific cognitive domains and the growth of more general capacities (such as speed of processing and working memory) which facilitate bridging between domains.

Cognitive Development as the Evolution of Strategies

Common to both Piaget and to those who seek to show how changes in memory might contribute to changes in logical thinking is the assumption that developmental change is *discontinuous,* passing through a series of stages. Case nicely illustrated the spirit of this approach by titling one of his books *The Mind's Staircase.* But as we noted in Chapter 9, a different approach is taken by Robert Siegler, who argues that children will use different strategies at different times to solve the same problem. He proposed that instead of seeking stagelike changes, it

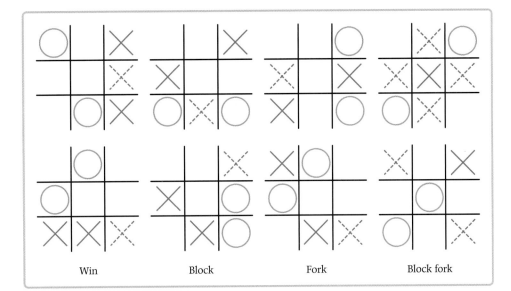

Figure 12.9 Eight game configurations presented to children to see what strategies they would use. The solid X's and O's are already in place. The dashed X's represent the possible correct moves the child could make. (From Crowley & Siegler, 1993.)

Win Block Fork Block fork

was more productive to view cognitive development as the *gradual* replacement of less successful strategies by more effective ones (Siegler, 1996). Over time, children's use of more effective strategies to solve a particular problem will increase, while their use of less effective ones will become rare or disappear, creating the wavelike progression shown in Figure 9.7 (p. 336).

To illustrate how problem solving develops through strategy development, growth, and selection during middle childhood, Siegler and his colleague, Kevin Crowley, traced strategy development in the game of tic-tac-toe (Crowley & Siegler, 1993). Working with 6-, 7-, and 9-year-olds, they began by describing the strategies that were appropriate to the game (see Figure 12.9). The simplest strategy was to focus entirely on winning by getting three X's or O's in a single row. The next most complex strategy was to block an opponent from winning in order to gain a tie. A still more complicated strategy was to "fork" by choosing a move that made it possible to win along either of two rows.

As they anticipated, Crowley and Siegler found that children entertained several strategies at once. What changed with age was the mixture of strategies they used to win. Most of the 6-year-olds used a simple win strategy and tried to get three X's or O's in a row. Almost half of the 6-year-old children could also use a second strategy, blocking their opponent when needed. The 7-year-olds all could use the win strategy, almost all used blocking strategies, and a few set up forks. The 9-year-olds used all strategies under the appropriate circumstances, but not the most sophisticated "block-fork" strategy (see Table 12.3).

table 12.3

Six Types of Change That Contribute to the Development of Strategic Thinking
1. The acquisition of new strategies.
2. Changes in the frequencies with which existing strategies are used.
3. Changes in the speed of executing strategies.
4. Changes in the accuracy with which strategies are carried out.
5. Changes in the degree to which strategies are used automatically.
6. Changes in the range of situations in which each strategy can be applied.

Source: From Lemaire & Siegler, 1995.

table 12.4

Strategy Use by 6-, 7-, and 9-Year-Olds				
	Type of Game			
	Win	**Block**	**Fork**	**Block Fork**
Kindergartners	95	45	0	0
1st graders	100	80	10	0
3rd graders	100	100	65	0

Numbers give the percentage of subjects of each age who made at least one correct move and provided a consistent explanation for each tic-tac-toe rule.
Source: From Crowley & Siegler, 1993.

Siegler provides a marked alternative to Piaget's ideas about the stagelike nature of cognitive development. (See Table 12.4 for a summary of changes that Siegler believes contribute to the development of strategic thinking.) In one important respect, however, he agrees with those who favor the idea of stagelike changes: the advanced strategies in every case involve the same two-sidedness that other developmentalists have claimed to be characteristic of middle childhood.

Additional Cognitive Bridging Mechanisms

While being able to remember more as well as to think more logically, strategically, and systematically are important to bridging islands of competence during middle childhood, they are insufficient by themselves to explain the increased scope and reliability of children's thinking. To carry out even simple everyday activities—getting along with other children on the playground, doing their schoolwork, running errands for their parents, finding their way to a friend's house and back, or playing soccer—children also have to be able to pay attention to the task at hand without being distracted, make plans for handling the task, and know something about their own thinking processes. At the same time, their increasing experience is being coded in language, providing them with a large store of organized, retrievable knowledge with which to meet the demands of daily life. As you will now see, each of these processes provides additional bridges between the islands of competence seen in early childhood.

Attention

From the earliest days of life, children attend to unusual events in their environment that "capture" their interest. In earlier chapters, you saw that infants attend more to some objects or events than others and then gradually stop attending (or habituate) to them as they become used to them.

After infancy there is a steady increase in both the quality of attention and the length of time children pay attention to objects that interest them. A number of studies have shown that the ability to sustain attention to items that do not particularly interest them grows steadily throughout middle childhood.

A classic study by Elaine Vurpillot (1968) illustrates the kinds of changes observed by many researchers. She recorded the eye movements of children age 3 to 10 while the children examined pairs of line drawings of houses such as those shown in Figure 12.10. In some trials, children were shown identical houses; in others, the houses differed in one or more relatively subtle ways. The children were asked to say whether or not the houses were identical.

Vurpillot found that all the children responded correctly when the houses were identical but that the younger children were more likely to make mistakes when the

plan Cognitive representations of the actions needed to achieve a specific goal.

Figure 12.10 Stimuli used by Vurpillot to assess the development of visual search strategies. It is not until middle childhood that children pay attention to each of the four houses in a systematic way to discover the subtle differences between them. (From Vurpillot, 1968.)

houses differed, especially if the houses differed in only one way. Her recordings of eye movements pinpointed the difficulty. Rather than systematically paying attention to each of the houses to see how they differed from one another, the younger children scanned the houses in a haphazard order. By contrast, the older children paid attention to each of the houses in the picture, scanning, and sometimes rescanning, row by row or column by column until they had checked almost all of them. It seems from this that older children have a greater ability to select and execute an effective attentional strategy.

The ability to attend to the most important features of a situation is not the only aspect of children's attention that develops during early and middle childhood. More recent studies show that children also acquire the ability to ignore distractions and gain voluntary control over what they choose to pay attention to in order to obtain information more efficiently (Dossett & Burns, 2000; Huang-Pollack et al., 2002).

Planning Being able to develop a plan for achieving goals is a key new aspect of children's thinking during middle childhood. Preschoolers can be heard saying things to one another like, "When you come over, we'll play house and have a party," but they have no plans to achieve their goal aside from informing their mothers that they want to play with the other child. During middle childhood, children begin to **plan** in the sense that they form cognitive representations of the actions needed to achieve a specific goal. To make a plan, they have to keep in mind what is presently happening, what they want to happen in the future, and what they need to do in order to get from the present to the future. They must also have enough self-control to keep their attention on achieving the goal.

Research has demonstrated that increased use of planning in a variety of situations is one of the changes that make children more reliable without direct adult control. Take, for example, the kind of planning that is required in choosing a route to a destination. William Gardner and Barbara Rogoff (1990) asked groups of 4- to 6-year-olds and 7- to 10-year-olds to solve mazes such as the one shown in Figure 12.11. A glance at this maze quickly reveals that a child who simply begins to trace a path from the nearest opening, without first scanning the maze to see what barriers lie ahead, is certain to fail. To see how children's ability to plan a solution to the maze developed, Gardner and Rogoff gave different instructions to half the children in each age group. One subgroup was told that they should plan ahead from the start because it was most important to avoid making wrong turns. The

Figure 12.11 A maze of the kind used by Gardner and Rogoff (1990) to assess children's ability to plan ahead. Trace the route from start to finish to get a feel for how planning is needed to avoid encountering a dead end.

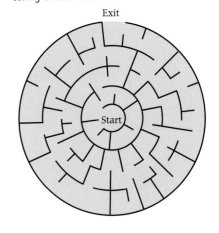

other children were told the same thing but were also told that they had to go through the maze as quickly as possible.

When both speed and accuracy mattered, the children in both age groups planned out part of their route ahead of time and then planned only when they came to uncertain choice points. When accuracy in navigating the maze was the only factor that counted, many of the older children realized that a better strategy was to plan their entire set of moves before they began. In contrast, 4- to 6-year-olds did not change their planning when speed didn't matter, either because they did not understand that they would make fewer errors if they planned ahead more systematically or because they could not keep this possibility in mind when they tackled a difficult maze.

Planning is also important in reasoning tasks. Games that require children to solve logical problems, like checkers or Mastermind, become popular in middle childhood. To play these games skillfully, children have to analyze both the goals and the means of attaining them. A good example of such a game is the Tower of Hanoi, the goal of which is to move a set of size-graded objects from one location to another. There are two rules: (1) only one object can be moved at a time; and (2) a larger object must go on top of a smaller one.

In an experimental form of this game (see Figure 12.12), the child is presented with three cans, the smallest on the bottom, the largest on the top, and is asked to move the cans to the peg opposite the experimenter's model. The problem depicted in Figure 12.12 requires a logical minimum of seven moves.

A variety of research (summarized in Siegler, 1998) shows that between the ages of 6 and 7 years, children become better at playing the game. This trend is not surprising, since, according to the evidence, older children are increasingly able to keep in mind both their current circumstances and the circumstances they want to create. What makes the pattern of data especially interesting is its similarity to Gardner and Rogoff's findings with respect to negotiating a maze. Three-year-olds could not keep the rules in mind at all. Six-year-olds began to form subgoals that would take them part of the way to a solution, but they could not think the problem all the way through, and they still found it difficult to assemble their subgoals into an overall plan. If the problems require too many moves, even 9- and 10-year-olds fail to plan their solutions to problems of this kind all the way through (Spitz et al., 1985).

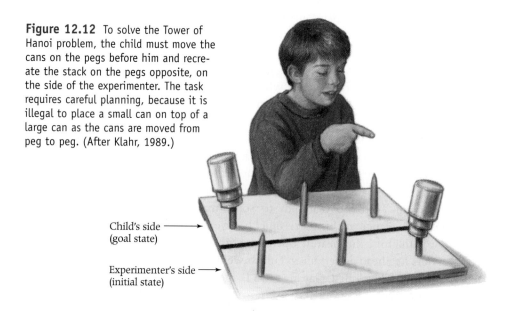

Figure 12.12 To solve the Tower of Hanoi problem, the child must move the cans on the pegs before him and recreate the stack on the pegs opposite, on the side of the experimenter. The task requires careful planning, because it is illegal to place a small can on top of a large can as the cans are moved from peg to peg. (After Klahr, 1989.)

Child's side (goal state)

Experimenter's side (initial state)

Metacognition

Another important bridging mechanism is the ability to think about one's own thoughts, called **metacognition.** The term "metacognition" applies to all forms of human cognitive activity (metamemory is one kind of metacognitive process). Metacognition allows one to assess how difficult a problem is likely to be and to choose strategies to solve it in a flexible way.

The general pattern of the development of metamemory abilities described in the earlier section on p. 466 appears to apply to the development of a wide variety of metacognitive processes (Estes, 1998; Flavell et al., 1995). By the age of 4 or 5, children begin to be able to explain what they are doing when they solve such mental puzzles as determining whether a pair of two-dimensional figures are different figures or the same figure in different orientations (Estes, 1998). But in situations where they are not actively engaged in a challenging problem-solving task, they are less likely to realize that they have been thinking about something, even if it is an unusual event.

A series of studies by John Flavell and his colleagues nicely illustrates how children's ability to think about their own thought processes improves as they grow older (Flavell et al., 1995). The basic strategy they used was to create a situation that would be expected to cause children to think about something in particular and then to question them to see if they did. For example, in one study, a group of 5-year-olds and a group of 7- to 8-year-olds were shown a magic trick, such as a scarf that changes colors when pulled through the experimenter's hand, or a puzzling object, such as a large pear inside a bottle with a narrow neck. After the children were shown such things, they followed the experimenter to a nearby location. When they arrived at the new location, the experimenter asked them what they had been thinking about on the way. About two out of three 5-year-olds said they weren't thinking about anything at all, and most of the remainder said that they were thinking about something that had nothing to do with the puzzling event they had just witnessed. About two out of three 7- to 8-year-olds said they were thinking about the puzzling experiences they had just witnessed, thus indicating to the researchers that they had greater awareness of their own thought processes. Nonetheless, the ability of the 7- to 8-year-olds to continue thinking about the puzzling event was far from perfect, leaving considerable room for improvement.

The growth of metacognitive skills provides children with important cognitive resources. As metacognitive skills increase, children are better able to keep track of how successfully they are accomplishing their goals, and this allows them to modify their strategies so that they are more successful. Such metacognitive skills are especially important for thinking about how one kind of cognitive task relates to another, providing another bridging mechanism.

Language and Classification

Essential to bridging the islands of cognitive competence that were characteristic of early childhood is the continued, rapid development of various language capacities during middle childhood. Changes in the sphere of language take many forms (Garton & Pratt, 1998). Here, we will focus on children's expanding vocabularies, utilization of more sophisticated categories, and enhanced conversational abilities.

First, the sheer size of children's vocabularies, and hence the range of topics they can understand, increases markedly. Although precise estimates vary, 6- to 7-year-olds understand perhaps 10,000 words. Two years later, the number has doubled; and by the time they are 10 to 11 years old, they possess vocabularies of approximately 40,000 words (Anglin, 1993). Children's expanding vocabulary knowledge,

metacognition The ability to think about one's own thought processes.

combined with their growing abilities to understand and produce complex sentences, increases the complexity of the events they can think about and communicate about effectively.

As you have seen in earlier chapters, even before they are 7 or 8 years old, children have a large fund of organized conceptual knowledge to draw upon in their thinking about the world, especially in core domains, such as "living things," that apply to the natural world. As their knowledge of the categories to which objects belong is incorporated into their active vocabularies, children can make reasonable inferences about a wide range of events, even ones they have never before seen. Suppose, for example, that a child is invited over to her friend's house to see her new komondor. If the child has never heard the word "komondor" before, she won't know what to expect. But if she asks, "What's a komondor?" and learns that it is a dog breed, she will immediately know that the thing she is going to see is likely to run around, wag its tail, bark, soil the rug until it is trained, and so on.

Middle childhood is a time during which children are exposed to, and become familiar with, the immense variety of artificial objects that are central to culturally organized activities in every society. This dramatic growth in the quantity of cultural knowledge provides children with their culture's ideas about how human life should be organized as well as experience in using their culture's storehouse of such knowledge.

Whether derived from the natural world or the world of artificial objects, children's accumulating knowledge of their language and culture is organized into increasingly complex systems of categories. One significant change in the organization of knowledge is the ability to understand the hierarchical structure of categories, as you saw in Chapter 6 (p. 219). Another is to understand the logical relation of inclusion that holds between a superordinate class and its subclasses (for example, the subclass of cats is included in the superordinate class of mammals).

When 4- to 6-year-old children are shown a set of brown wooden beads and white wooden beads and asked, "Are there more brown beads or more beads?" they are likely to say there are more brown beads than beads. According to Piaget, they answer this way because they cannot attend to the subclass (brown beads) and the superordinate class (beads) at the same time. Instead, they compare one subclass (brown beads) with another subclass (white beads). In middle childhood, subordinate–superordinate

Systematic cataloging of a card collection requires the ability to classify according to multiple criteria.

relations become more stable so the children realize that brown beads are a subset of the overall set of beads, and answer correctly.

Another important change in the organization of categorized knowledge is the ability to categorize objects according to multiple criteria. This kind of logical classification can be seen when children begin to collect stamps or baseball cards. Stamp collections can be organized according to multiple criteria. Stamps come from different countries. They are issued in different denominations and in different years. There are stamps depicting insects, animals, sports heroes, rock stars, and space exploration. Children who organize their stamps according to type of animal and country of origin (so that, for example, within their collection of stamps from France, all the birds are together, all the rabbits are together, and so on) are creating a multiple classification for their collections. Similarly, the child who groups baseball cards according to league, team, and position creates a multiple classification. The result is a marked increase in the number of relations among objects and events that children can think about and increased flexibility in the particular relations they choose to use under particular circumstances.

Increases in children's linguistically coded knowledge are accompanied by a general increase in a variety of other language-related abilities that have a direct bearing on the increased power and reliability of thought during middle childhood (Warren & McCloskey, 1997). As you saw in earlier chapters (Chapter 8, p. 297, and Chapter 9, p. 330), while young children can sometimes modify what they say to take into account the knowledge or perspective of their conversational partner, their modifications are not always successful and they often fail to recognize when they have strayed from the topic. Older children are better at making sure that they and their conversational partners understand each other and have a greater ability to maintain coherence in a conversation over longer periods of time. The older children's ability to maintain more complex, organized conversations appears to depend upon a mix of factors that include better listening skills, improved memory abilities, and the use of special linguistic markers to signal transitions in topics or to tie what is being said at the moment to something said earlier, such as "Getting back to . . . " or "As I was saying . . . " Older children also provide ongoing feedback to their conversational partners by nodding or saying "Uh hum" to let them know that they are tracking the conversation (Dorval, 1990).

The Role of Social and Cultural Contexts

Thus far we have treated cognitive changes between early and middle childhood as if they were entirely determined by development of the brain and the specific internal, mental processes brought to bear on the task at hand. But as Usha Goswami cautions us, "The functioning of even these relatively specific developmental mechanisms . . . turns out to be influenced by the social . . . and cultural context in which learning takes place" (Goswami, 2002, p. 227). Cross-cultural research on developmental changes in cognitive ability underlines this point.

Is the Acquisition of Conservation Universal?

It was Piaget's (1966/1974) belief that the development of conservation is a universal achievement of human beings, regardless of the cultural circumstances in which they live. The only cultural variation he expected in the acquisition of conservation was that children in some cultures might acquire this form of reasoning earlier than others, because their culture provided them with more extensive relevant experiences.

However, cross-cultural research on the acquisition of conservation has provoked a great deal of controversy regarding its presumed universality. Using Piaget's own conservation tasks, several researchers found that children in traditional, nonindustrial societies who have not attended school lag a year or more behind the norms established by Piaget. In addition, in some cases such children appear not to acquire this basic form of reasoning at all, even as adults. Reviewing the evidence available in the early 1970s, Pierre Dasen (1972) wrote, "It can no longer be assumed that adults of all societies reach the concrete operational stage" (p. 31).

This conclusion was quickly challenged because of its wide-reaching implication that traditional, nonliterate adults think like the preschool children of industrialized countries. For example, Gustav Jahoda (1980), a leading cross-cultural psychologist, rejected outright the possibility that in some cultures people never achieve the ability to think operationally. Jahoda pointed out that it is difficult to see how a society could survive if its members were indifferent to causal relations, incapable of thinking through the implications of their actions, or unable to adopt other people's points of view. He concluded that "no society could function at the preoperational stage, and to suggest that a majority of any people are at that level is nonsense almost by definition" (Jahoda, 1980, p. 116).

To resolve this issue, developmentalists who questioned nonschooled children's apparent failure to understand conservation designed new tests. They sought to demonstrate that Piaget's research methods somehow misrepresented such children's mental capacities, either because they were unfamiliar with the test situation or because the experimenters, working in an unfamiliar culture and language, did not make their intentions clear. (This is the same line of reasoning used to challenge Piaget's views on the thought processes of preschool-age children [see Chapter 9]).

Dasen and his colleagues tackled the problem by training children to solve conservation tasks. They reasoned that if the children in traditional cultures did not seem to understand conservation because they were unfamiliar with the procedures, training on similar tasks should be sufficient to overcome their difficulties.

In a series of studies, these researchers demonstrated that by the end of middle childhood, relatively brief training in procedures similar to those used in the standard conservation task was sufficient to change the pattern of performance on the conservation task itself. One such result is shown in Figure 12.13, which compares the performance of children in the Australian city of Canberra with Inuit children living in the remote area of Cape Dorset in northern Canada. Without training, half the Inuit children seemed to fail to acquire the concept of conservation of quantity altogether. But when they were trained in the procedures used, their test results showed that they did understand the basic concept of conservation of quantity. Even with training however, the Inuit children lagged behind the Canberra children by approximately 3 years, a situation suggesting that their nomadic, hunter-gatherer form of life does not provide the kinds of experiences that make for easier acquisition of this concept (Dasen et al., 1979).

A number of developmentalists subsequently suggested that if researchers know the local language and culture well so that children are able to follow the flexible questioning procedures that are the hallmark of Piaget's clinical interviews, the children will demonstrate conservation without any lags. Raphael Nyiti (1982), for example, compared the conservation performances of 10- and 11-year-old children of two cultural groups, both living on Cape Breton, Nova Scotia. Some of the children were of English-speaking European backgrounds, and some were of the Micmac Indian tribe. The Micmac children all spoke

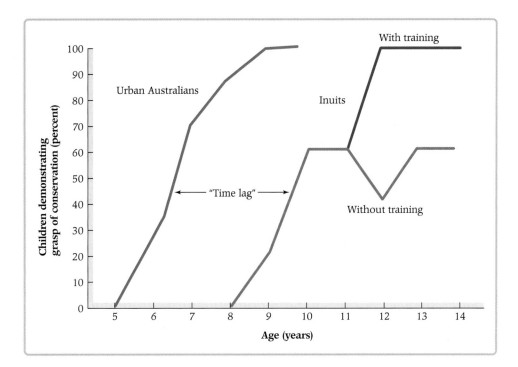

Figure 12.13 Curves representing the actual percentages of Australian and Inuit children who demonstrated a grasp of the concept of conservation. Inuit children lagged behind urban Australian children with European backgrounds. Without training, 50 percent of Inuit children as old as 14 years failed to demonstrate an understanding of the concept of conservation. With training, all accomplished the task. (From Dasen et al., 1979.)

Micmac at home, but they had spoken English in school since the first grade. The children of European backgrounds were all interviewed in English by an English speaker of European background. The Micmac children were interviewed once in English and once in Micmac.

Nyiti found that when the children were interviewed on the conservation tasks in their native languages, there was no difference in the performances of the two cultural groups. But when the Micmac children were interviewed in English, only half as many seemed to understand the concept of conservation. Nyiti (1976) obtained similar results in a study of children in his native Tanzania, as did other researchers in the West African country of Sierra Leone (Kamara & Easley, 1977).

Taken as a whole, these studies, along with others, demonstrate that when Piaget's clinical procedures are applied appropriately, using contents with which people have extensive experience, conservation of liquid quantity (and by extension, concrete operations) is a universal cognitive achievement of middle childhood, just as Piaget assumed it was (Segall et al., 1999). However, the evidence also shows that there are quite dramatic cultural variations in children's familiarity with the contents and procedures used in standard Piagetian tests of conservation and these variations clearly influence children's performances on the tests.

Cultural Variations in the Use of Memory Strategies

Cross-cultural research has revealed striking variations in the use of organizational strategies in free-recall studies, but these results must be interpreted with great caution. For example, Michael Cole and his colleagues studied the development of memory among people living in rural Liberia (summarized in Cole, 1996). In one set of studies they presented groups of children of different ages with a set of 20 common objects that were selected to be members of familiar and salient categories, such as food, clothing, and tools. Half the children at each age were attending school, while half were not because there were no schools located in their villages.

The researchers found that children who had never gone to school improved their performance on these tasks very little after the age of 9 or 10. These children remembered approximately 10 items on the first trial, and managed to recall only 2 more items after 15 practice trials on the full set of 20 items. The Liberian children who were attending school, by contrast, learned the materials rapidly, much the way schoolchildren of the same age do in the United States.

Failure to use organizational strategies seemed to be the cause of the poor performance of the children who had not attended school. Schoolchildren in Liberia and the United States used categorical similarities among the items to aid their recall. After the first trial, they clustered their responses, recalling first, say, the items of clothing, then the items of food, and so on. The Liberians who had never attended school did very little clustering, an indication that they were not using the categorical relationships among the items to help them remember.

To track down the source of this difference, the researchers varied aspects of the task. They found that if, instead of presenting a series of objects in random order, they presented the same objects in a meaningful way as part of a story, their non-schooled Liberian subjects recalled them easily, clustering the objects according to the roles they played in the story. When memory for traditional children's stories was tested, cultural differences were also absent (Mandler et al., 1980). Similar results on tests of children's memorization skills have been obtained in research among Mayan people of rural Guatemala (Rogoff & Waddell, 1982).

The implication of these cross-cultural memory studies differs from that of the cross-cultural studies of concrete-operational thinking. The latter studies probed basic mental operations presumed by Piaget and his followers to reflect the logic underlying everyday actions and reasoning in any culture. The ability to remember is also a universal intellectual requirement, but specific strategies for remembering are not universal. Indeed, many of them—the ones most often studied by psychologists—are associated with formal schooling.

As you will see in the next chapter, schooling presents children with specialized information-processing tasks—committing large amounts of information to memory in a short time, learning to manipulate abstract symbols in one's head and on paper, using logic to conduct experiments, and performing many more tasks that have few if any analogies in societies without formal schooling. The free-recall, random-order task that Cole and his colleagues initially used to assess memory among Liberian tribal people has no precise analogy in traditional Liberian cultures, so it is not surprising that subjects who had not attended school failed to show skill at such tasks.

Cultural Variations in Planning

A cross-cultural study by Shari Ellis and Bonnie Schneiders (reported in Ellis & Siegler, 1997) shows how differences in cultural values can shape the likelihood that children will plan ahead in the manner demonstrated by Ellis and Gauvain (see Figure 12.14). Using a schematic drawing of a maze representing a rural scene, Ellis and Schneiders studied the way that Navajo and European American children planned their routes to and from different parts of the maze. They were interested in contrasting these two groups because the two cultures place different values on doing things speedily. The Navajo emphasize doing things thoughtfully rather than quickly (John, 1972). By contrast, speed of mental performance is often treated as an index of intelligence among Americans of European background (Sternberg, 1990). This cultural difference in values was expressed in the children's behavior as they planned their routes through the maze. The Navajo children spent almost ten times as long planning their movements as the European-American children did—and as a result, they made significantly fewer errors.

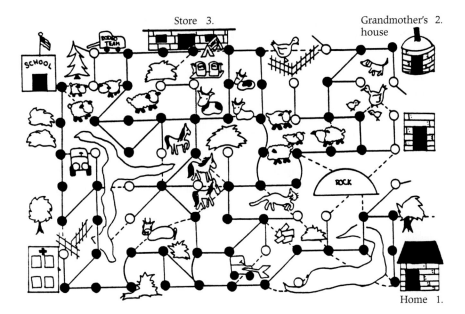

Store 3.

Grandmother's 2. house

Home 1.

Figure 12.14 Schematic drawing of the maze used in Ellis and Schneiders, 1989. Children were asked to find the shortest obstacle-free path from home to Grandmother's house, where they would pick up some money and then go to the store. The dotted lines and open circles on this diagram indicate incorrect routes; solid lines and solid dots are acceptable routes. (From Ellis & Gauvain, 1992. Copyright 1992 by Lawrence Erlbaum Associates.)

Reconsidering the Cognitive Changes in Middle Childhood

Taken one at a time, the changes in children's biological and cognitive abilities between early and middle childhood point to specific features of children's physical abilities and thought processes that are becoming more systematic and can be applied across a broader variety of settings. When we consider these changes as part of an ensemble, rather than as isolated achievements, we start to get a better idea of the reasons why adults can begin to treat children in a different manner during middle childhood.

However, the scant cross-cultural work available reminds us that we have not yet taken a direct look at the contexts where experience of the culturally organized environment exerts its effects. Consequently, we need to withhold judgment about whether the new behaviors seen in middle childhood should be considered to signal a general stagelike shift in development. To address the question properly, we first need to reach beyond the relatively narrow range of tasks that has been featured in psychologists' studies of cognitive development and investigate the changes that children display in a variety of social contexts, especially in classrooms and peer groups, where children in middle childhood begin to spend so much of their time. Many developmentalists believe that experiences in both of these contexts are crucial to the cognitive changes associated with middle childhood. Once we have a more well-rounded picture of children's experiences, we can return to examine the central issue of the distinctiveness of middle childhood and the forms of thought that are said to characterize it.

S U M M A R Y

- The onset of middle childhood is recognized in cultures around the world. When children reach the age of about 6, adults begin to hold them responsible for their own actions and sometimes assign them tasks that take them away from adult supervision. This reorientation in adult behavior implies an increase in children's physical capacities, in their ability to follow instructions, and in their ability to keep track of what they are doing.

Biological Developments

- Size and strength increase significantly in the years from 6 to 12, but more slowly than during early childhood.

- There is a significant genetic contribution to growth; nutrition and general health factors are two important environmental contributors.

- Agility, balance, and coordination improve markedly during this period. Boys, on average, tend to excel at motor abilities that emphasize power and force, while girls most often excel in fine-motor coordination and agility.

- Several significant developments in brain structure and function occur between the ages of 5 and 7:
  1. Myelination continues to increase, particularly in the frontal cortex.
  2. Synaptic pruning continues, resulting in fewer, more stable connections between neurons. During this period, it is especially prominent in higher brain centers.
  3. Alpha activity comes to dominate theta activity.
  4. The synchronization of electrical activity in different parts of the brain increases significantly, producing marked coordination between the frontal lobes and other areas.

Cognitive Developments: Bridging the Islands of Competence

- In middle childhood, the islands of competence seen in earlier years become better connected. The challenge is to explain how this bridging occurs.

- There is general agreement that in middle childhood, children's thinking becomes more "two-sided." Disagreements center on what brings about this change.

- Piaget believed that around the age of 7, children become capable of concrete mental operations; they can now combine, separate, reorder, and transform objects mentally. New,

previously isolated knowledge can be systematically thought about.

- Dissatisfaction with Piaget's explanation for how cognitive development occurs has led to proposals for alternative bridging mechanisms and processes of change.

- According to many developmentalists, increases in memory provide a crucial bridging mechanism because changes in memory ability are associated with
  1. The capacity to hold several items of information in mind at one time.
  2. Increased knowledge relevant to the information to be remembered.
  3. The use of memory strategies, such as organization and rehearsal.
  4. The ability to think about one's own memory processes.

- Some information-processing theorists have proposed that changes in memory capacity are combined with changes in the logic of thought, making possible the stagelike changes in the logic of thought studied by Piaget.

- Other scholars argue that children's problem-solving tasks reveal the presence of more than one strategy at any given time. From this perspective, development consists of the discovery of new strategies and changes in the frequency, spontaneity, and accuracy with which more effective strategies are used.

- A number of additional processes that help to bridge islands of competence contribute to improved cognitive performance during middle childhood:
  1. The ability to control attention and not be distracted.
  2. The ability to plan systematically before acting.
  3. The ability to think about and control one's own thought processes.
  4. Increased linguistic abilities and associated classification skills.

- Cross-cultural variations in logical reasoning, memory, and planning indicate that the social and cultural context play a significant role in the overall pattern of cognitive development in a variety of ways.

- When changes in specific cognitive processes are considered as an ensemble, they help explain why adults can begin to give children greater responsibilities as they move into middle childhood.

Key Terms

compensation, p. 460

concrete operations, p. 458

conservation, p. 460

EEG coherence, p. 457

elaboration, p. 466

identity, p. 460

memory organization, p. 465

memory span, p. 463

metacognition, p. 473

metamemory, p. 466

plan, p. 471

rehearsal, p. 465

reversibility, p. 461

strategy, p. 464

Thought Questions

1. In what significant ways have you observed middle childhood in your community to resemble and to differ from that of Raymond Birch?

2. What is the major evidence to support the view that in middle childhood thought processes are generally more "two-sided" than was true in early childhood?

3. Give specific examples of how various memory strategies might be used to learn the information presented in this chapter.

4. How are biological and cultural factors interconnected in the behavioral and cognitive changes observed in middle childhood?

5. What are some of your everyday nonacademic tasks that require planning? What role does metacognition play in your planning behaviors?

> "To learn is to change. Education is a process that changes the learner."
> —George B. Leonard, Education and Ecstasy.

Laurie Lee grew up in a small village in central England in the 1920s. The village school was a small stone barn divided into two rooms, one for the younger children and one for the older ones. There was one teacher who was sometimes assisted by a teenaged girl. All the children in the valley attended the school, starting at about the age of 4 and continuing until they were 14 years old, when, as a rule, they went to work full-time in the fields or in nearby factories.

Although the school was different from modern schools in many ways, anyone who has attended school will recognize part of their own past experience in Lee's account of his early schooling:

> I spent that first day picking holes in paper, then went home in a smoldering temper.
> "What's the matter, Love? Didn't he like it at school, then?"
> "They never gave me the present."
> "Present? What present?"
> "They said they'd give me a present."
> "Well, now, I'm sure they didn't."
> "They did! They said: You're Laurie Lee, aren't you? Well you just sit there for the present. I sat there all day but I never got it. I ain't going back there again." (Lee, 1965, p. 51)

When Lee graduated to the room for big kids, he found the teacher "about as physically soothing as a rake." Each morning began with the children standing at attention. "Miss B walked in, whacked the walls with a ruler, and fixed us with her squinting eye. "Good a-morning, children!" "Good morning, Teacher!" (p. 57). After reciting the Lord's prayer, the lessons began.

> Through the dead hours of the morning, through the long afternoons, we chanted away at our tables. . . . "Twelve-inches-one-foot. Three-feet-make-a-yard. . . . " We absorbed these figures as primal truths declared by some ultimate power. Unhearing, unquestioning, we rocked to our chanting, hammering the gold nails home. "Twice-two-are-four. One-God-is-Love. One-Lord-is-King. One-King-is-George. . . . " So it was always; had been, would be forever. We asked no questions; we didn't hear what we said; yet neither did we ever forget it. (p. 62)

Like Laurie Lee, children in many parts of the modern world are required to attend school from the ages of about 6 to 16. For 9 or more months of the year, 5 or 6 days a week, they spend 5 to 7 hours listening to teachers, answering questions, reading books, writing essays, solving arithmetic problems in workbooks, taking tests, and generally "being educated." Before they take their places as adult workers, most young Americans will have spent more than 15,000 hours in classrooms, and in some countries, the amount of time children spend in school is even greater (Kaul, 2002). It is no surprise, then, that in many societies formal schooling plays a central role in defining children's characteristics during middle childhood and beyond.

To determine the specific influences that schooling has on children's development, we need to address a series of questions:

Figure 13.1 The relationship between years of education and expected income in the United States. The marked increases in income associated with increased levels of education underscore the importance of educational achievement to later life success. (U.S. Census Bureau, 2000.)

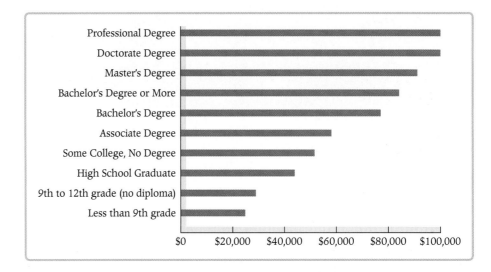

- What is the nature of school as a context for children's development, and under what historical conditions do schools arise?
- How does learning in school differ from learning in other contexts?
- How does schooling influence cognitive development?
- What special abilities does schooling require, and what factors account for success in school?
- How do the communities where the school is located shape what happens in school and its effects on children?

Answers to these questions have far-reaching significance in modern societies. Children who fail to thrive in school or who drop out may be confined as adults to less interesting, less secure, and lower-paying jobs than children who meet society's expectations by completing high school and higher levels of education (U.S. Bureau of the Census, 2000) (see Figure 13.1). Despite the emphasis society places on education, many millions of young people in the United States do not thrive in school. In the opinion of policy makers, resulting low levels of literacy and mathematical skills jeopardize the country's ability to compete effectively in the international arena (Serwach, 2003). As a consequence, educational policies have routinely played a major role in presidential politics for many years. At the same time, these concerns have made the study of learning and development in the schools one of the most active areas of research in developmental psychology.

The Contexts of Learning

In Chapter 10 we examined socialization, concentrating on the ways in which young children are raised within the context of the family to acquire the basic knowledge, skills, and beliefs that are essential in their society. Socialization is a universal human process that has always been a part of human experience. In addition to the socialization that occurs within the family, as we discussed in Chapter 12, sometime around the sixth or seventh year of life, all societies begin to socialize children into new tasks that are designed to provide them with the skills necessary for adult life. What is not universal is the specific content of the new tasks, or the ways these new activities are socially organized.

One way to arrange for children to acquire adult skills and knowledge is through education. **Education** is a form of socialization in which adults engage in *deliberate*

education A form of socialization in which adults engage in deliberate teaching of the young to ensure that they acquire specialized knowledge and skills.

apprenticeship A form of activity combining instruction and productive labor that is intermediate between the implicit socialization of family and community life and the explicit instruction of formal education.

teaching of the young to ensure their acquisition of specialized knowledge and skills. It is not known if education existed among the hunter-gatherer peoples who roamed the earth hundreds of thousands of years ago, but deliberate teaching is not a conspicuous part of socialization in contemporary hunter-gatherer societies (Rogoff, 2003). Among the !Kung of Africa's Kalahari Desert, for example, basic training in the skills expected of adults is embedded in everyday activities. The basic means by which adults ensure that children acquire culturally valued skills and knowledge is to include children in adult activities.

> There is . . . very little explicit teaching. . . . What the child knows, he learns from direct interaction with the adult community, whether it is learning to tell the age of the spoor left by a poisoned kudu buck, to straighten the shaft of an arrow, to build a fire, or to dig a spring hare out of its burrow. . . . It is all implicit. (Bruner, 1966, p. 59)

Apprenticeship arrangements in which children learn by observing adults and working alongside them are still an important form of education despite the spread of formal schools.

When societies achieve a certain degree of complexity and specialization in the roles people play, the tools they use, and the ways they secure food and housing, preparation for some occupations is likely to take the form of **apprenticeship,** a form of activity intermediate between the implicit socialization of family and community life and the explicit instruction of formal education. A young apprentice learns a craft or a skill by spending an extended period of time working for an adult master (Smits & Stromback, 2001). The settings in which apprentices learn are not organized solely for the purpose of teaching. Rather, instruction and productive labor are combined; from the beginning, apprentices contribute to the work process.

Researchers have found that novice apprentices receive relatively little explicit instruction in their craft (Rogoff, 2003). Instead, they are given ample opportunity to observe skilled workers and to practice specific tasks. In many societies, the apprentice's relationship with the master is part of a larger web of family relationships. Often the apprentice lives with the master and does farm or household chores to help pay for his upkeep. In this way the tasks of education and community building are woven together (Vickerstaff, 2003).

The earliest forms of formal schooling have been traced back to around 4000 B.C. in the Middle East, when changes in technology made it possible for one sector of a population to grow enough food to support a large number of people besides themselves. This shift made possible a substantial division of labor and the development of city-states. It also created a need for systems of writing and arithmetic (Damerow, 1998). The places where young people were brought together to learn to read and write were the earliest schools (see Figure 13.2).

Figure 13.2 The earliest writings, which date back to around 4000 B.C., were in the form of clay tablets etched with cuneiform symbols. This type of writing originated from pictograms, basic outline drawings of the objects being referred to. Over time and use, the pictograms became simplified and rendered as wedge-shaped (cuneiform) symbols that could convey sounds and abstract concepts, as well as objects. The tablet shown here, from Tello in ancient southern Mesopotamia, is a tallying of sheep and goats.

As it has since developed, schooling differs from informal instruction in the family and from apprenticeship training in four main ways (Lave & Wenger, 1991; Singleton, 1998):

1. *Motivation.* Apprentices get to practice their craft from the beginning and see the fruits of their labor. Students in schools must work for years to perfect their skills before they can put their knowledge to use in adult work. In the meantime, they are asked to engage in tasks they often find boring.

2. *Social relations.* Unlike masters of apprentices, schoolteachers are rarely either kin or friends of the family, and may not even live in the same community as their students.

3. *Social organization.* Apprentices are most likely to learn in a work setting among people of diverse ages and skill levels, so they have more than one person to turn to for assistance. At school, children have traditionally found themselves in a large room in the company of other children of about their age and only one adult. As a rule, they are expected to work individually; asking for assistance from their peers is likely to be considered cheating.

4. *Medium of instruction.* Apprenticeship instruction is usually conducted orally in the context of production. Speech is also important to formal schooling, but it is often speech of a special kind that requires children to acquire skills and knowledge through manipulation of written symbols.

Taken together, these differences create **schooling** as a special cultural context, one that can have profound implications for children's development.

Literacy and Schooling in Modern Times

Formal schooling for purposes of teaching numeracy, literacy, and a wide range of curricular topics has become a routine part of children's everyday lives during different historical eras in different parts of the world. Even today, however, there are societies where schooling is far from universal (UNESCO, 2003).

In Western Europe and the United States it was not until the nineteenth century, in response to the Industrial Revolution and the movement of people from their farms into large urban areas, that these societies began to institute mandatory schooling and strive for widespread literacy. When mandatory school attendance was in its infancy, there were two kinds of education. *Mass education* was aimed at the great majority of working-class children. It enabled them to recite from a religious text such as the Bible or the Koran, to write for simple purposes, and to calculate small sums. This instruction was obviously not intended to give children a general education as we understand that term today. It stressed "mastery of the basics" because no one expected working-class children to use literacy or numeracy for complex purposes when they grew up. Teachers in the mass education system were typically confronted by many students. They based their instruction largely on drill, practice, and group recitation, and often employed harsh disciplinary measures (see Figure 13.3) (Gallego & Cole, 2000).

By contrast, children of the political and economic elite and a growing number of children among the rapidly rising professional classes were provided a *liberal education,* in which they were taught individually by a tutor or in small groups. These children were expected to go beyond "the basics" to the mastery of more complex subjects, including history, the arts, and the sciences. President Woodrow Wilson articulated the different purposes of the two forms of education in 1910 when he wrote: "We want one class of persons to have a liberal education and we want another class of persons, a very much larger class, to forgo the privilege of a liberal

schooling A form of education that is characterized by special forms of motivation, social relations, social organization, and communication using written language.

1839

Bettmann/Corbis

Figure 13.3 This picture of hundreds of children sitting in a large, barnlike structure, illustrates a method of schooling called the "Lancaster Method," in which young children sat at long tables monitored by older children who were themselves supervised by adults. Named after Joseph Lancaster, an English educator, this method used a strict system of rewards and punishments to control children's behaviors. The large objects hanging from the ceiling are toys which were lowered when the children were good and raised when they were bad. This method was later replaced by the lecture method, which remains in force in most classrooms the world over.

education and fit themselves to perform specific, difficult manual tasks" (quoted in Lucas, 1972, p. 42).

During the eighteenth and nineteenth centuries, the Western powers colonized a sizeable part of the rest of the world, bringing with them new forms of economic activity, especially the widespread use of money as a means of exchanging goods, their religion, and their forms of education (Rogoff, 2003). These new modes of life were often profoundly disruptive of the lives of the people upon whom they were visited. In many countries, marital relations changed because husbands often left home for long periods to engage in wage labor in order to pay taxes while wives experienced increased work loads in order to make up for the lack of male help. At the same time, women's social status decreased because they were not wage earners. Family authority relations were also disrupted because the children learned European languages, customs, and values.

Because of their different historical experiences of schooling, the impact of schooling on children's lives has by no means been uniform across cultures. However, the forms of activity in classrooms have been more or less similar, permitting developmentalists to make some generalizations that apply across time and cultural boundaries.

A prominent feature of current education in most industrialized nations is that everyone is expected to have the "liberal education" that was once restricted to the upper classes. As a recent report from the National Research Council put it, "To be employable in the modern economy, high school graduates need to be more than merely literate. They must be able to read challenging material, to perform sophisticated calculations, and to solve problems independently" (Snow et al., 1998, p. 20). In short, contemporary life requires all children to attain a level of education equal to, or surpassing, the levels once reserved for a small group of the elite.

No contemporary society has attained this ideal; many children fail to finish the prescribed number of years of schooling, and many fail to master even the basic skills upon which further learning often depends. School failure is more than a personal problem for children whose development is restricted by poor academic performance. It is also a political and economic problem because of its implications for society as a whole (Lovitt, 2000). One important step in addressing these problems is to understand the processes through which children acquire academic skills in schools.

Learning to read and write are the heart of schooling in all societies.

©Michael S. Yamashita/Corbis

Acquiring Academic Skills

From the earliest schools of the ancient Middle East to neighborhood schools throughout the modern world, instruction in school has focused on two basic symbol systems, written language and mathematics, the basic "tools of the intellect" required for all further education. However, given the fact that many children fail to achieve the levels of literacy and numeracy that society holds out as its standard, there has been ongoing controversy about how to design instruction more effectively. Opinion seems to oscillate back and forth between two extremes.

One school of thought begins with the assumption that instruction should proceed from the simple to the complex: Start with basic skills, and after these are mastered, move on to teaching how the basic skills can be used to solve a variety of more complicated tasks that require higher-order skills. The other school of thought argues that an exclusive focus on the acquisition of basic skills causes children to lose sight of the larger goal—how to use reading, writing, and arithmetic to accomplish interesting and important tasks. The consequence for many children, according to this view, is a loss of motivation and a failure to thrive in school. This fundamental difference of opinion about the appropriate organization of school-based instruction can be clearly seen in the different strategies proposed for teaching reading and numeracy (Bransford et al., 1999).

Learning to Read

There is broad agreement among psychologists and educators that reading is not a unitary skill; it is a complex system of coordinated skills and knowledge (Sweet & Snow, 2003). A good deal is known about how skilled readers translate marks on a page into meaningful messages. But despite intensive research efforts throughout the past century, and especially over the past two decades, the process of learning to read is still not fully understood (Stanovich, 2000).

Prereading The first step that children must take in learning to read is to realize that there is a correspondence between the marks on the printed page and the spoken language. But once they understand that each word is represented by a cluster of graphic signs, they still have to figure out how each graphic sign is related to a linguistic sound, as well as the meaning of the written text.

At first, most children believe that there is one symbol for each word. Then they begin to focus on syllables, minimal clusters of spoken language. Eventually they realize that the letters are supposed to correspond to each of a word's phonemes (Tolchinsky & Teberosky, 1998).

In addition to understanding the basic idea that the letters of the alphabet correspond to the sounds that make up words, children must also learn to "see letters." That is, they must recognize which sounds correspond to which letters or combinations of letters. The process of establishing letter–sound correspondences is referred to as **decoding.** Children must also learn to *comprehend* what they read—to combine their knowledge of letter–sound correspondences with their knowledge of the spoken language and the world to derive meaning from the text as a whole.

Decoding In order to learn the letter–sound correspondences required to read, children need to be skilled at analyzing sounds (Thompson & Nicholson, 1999). That is, they must learn to "hear phonemes" (for example, to recognize that "balloon" begins with a *b*), a process referred to as **phonemic awareness.**

The ability to hear phonemes does not appear to occur without deliberate instruction: nonliterate adults in various parts of the world do not seem to be aware of them (Scholes, 1998). Peter Bryant and his colleagues have conducted a wealth of research demonstrating that children in different countries who find it difficult to

decoding The process of establishing letter–sound correspondences when reading.

phonemic awareness The ability to "hear phonemes" (for example, to recognize that "balloon" begins with a *b*).

break words into their constituent syllables and phonemes in a purely oral task have difficulty linking sounds and letters (Bryant & Nunes, 1998). This research has spawned special educational programs that provide children with enriched experiences in oral language analysis before they are taught to read or when they experience difficulty in reading (Sunseth & Bowers, 2002). The lessons include practice in rhyming, breaking words down into syllables, and special language games such as pig Latin, in which the first phoneme of each word is moved to the end of the word and then followed by an "ay" (as in "igpay atinlay").

The results of such special instruction can be dramatic (for reviews, see Adams et al., 1998, and Snow, Burns, & Griffin, 1998). For example, Benita Blachman (2000) implemented such a program in two inner-city schools during the first and second grades (and in the third grade for children who were still experiencing reading difficulty). Then the children were tested in the fourth grade. Before Blachman's program was introduced, the fourth-grade reading performance in the schools was 7 months behind the national norm. The children in the experimental program, by contrast, scored 7 months *above* the national norm, and the gains were even greater a year later. Such results not only support the theoretical link between language analysis and reading acquisition but also show that the theory can be usefully applied in practice.

Learning which sounds go with which letters is one of the essential tasks facing beginning readers.

Even after they have acquired the ability to segment the spoken language into phonemes, children who are learning to read and write in English face an additional difficulty: there is no one-to-one relationship between letters of the alphabet and the phonemes that make up English words. Instead, the 26 letters of the English alphabet represent 52 basic phonemes. So, for example, a child acquiring literacy in English must grasp the fact that *t* is pronounced differently in the words "tea" and "both," and such seemingly different phonemes as *gh* and *f* can be used to produce a single sound, as in "muff" and "rough." Similar lessons must be mastered for the entire alphabet.*

Another difficulty is that the phonemes in a word cannot be correctly sounded out in isolation, as when *c* in "*cat*" is separated from the *a*, and the *a* from the *t*. Faced with this problem, teachers may resort to a strategy called *blending*. In the case of "cat," they first attempt to pronounce the phoneme that corresponds to each letter ("cuh," "ah," "tuh"). Note that even if children have learned the names of the three letters, "cee," "ay," and "tee," this demonstration may not help much because neither "cuh-ah-tuh" nor "cee-ay-tee" sounds much like "cat." No matter how quickly the children pronounce these letter names in sequence, the result will not blend the sounds to transform *c-a-t* into "cat." This circumstance makes it difficult to teach children who do not spontaneously "get the idea." For example, Marilyn Adams (1990) estimated that approximately 25 percent of children taught to read using a "decoding first" strategy are unsuccessful.

Comprehension: Bottom-Up Versus Top-Down Processing Thus far we have described the process of learning to read as if children come to read words by first decoding the letters that compose the words "from the bottom up" and then figure out their meaning. Proceeding in this way, we could conceive of learning to read as a process in which the child decodes individual letters of a word to get access to its meaning, then puts words together into phrases, then into sentences, in order to comprehend them.

*A famous example of the alphabet's complex relation to spoken English is attributed to the British writer George Bernard Shaw (1963). Shaw suggested that the word "fish should be written 'ghoti'; gh as in 'cough,' o as in 'women,' ti as in 'nation.'"

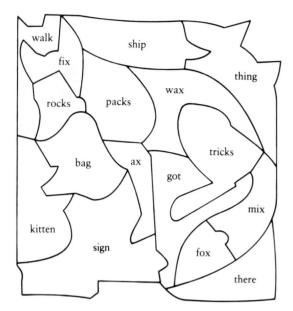

Figure 13.4 A great deal of reading instruction in the elementary grades is carried out in workbook exercises, such as this one for building decoding skills. Find all the words with the same last sound.

Reading in unison is common in classrooms throughout the world.

©Dean Conger/Corbis

Many teachers adhere to some version of this bottom-up approach. In early grades they emphasize "word-attack skills" and use a variety of workbook assignments to foster the ability to decode automatically (see Figure 13.4). The texts used in this approach are especially designed to give intensive practice in phonemic analysis. While they may be quite successful in this respect, they often do not make for very interesting reading. Aesop's tale of the tortoise and the hare, for example, has been presented in word-attack form like this:

> Rabbit said, "I can run. I can run fast. You can't run fast."
> Turtle said, "Look, Rabbit. See the park. You and I will run. We'll run to the park."
> Rabbit said, "I want to stop. I'll stop here. I can run, but Turtle can't. I can get to the park fast."
> Turtle said, "I can't run fast. But I will not stop. Rabbit can't see me. I'll get to the park." (Quoted in Green, 1984, p. 176)

Although reading instruction is frequently carried out in this way, a good deal of research in recent years has demonstrated that such bottom-up decoding processes represent only half the story of learning to read (Hulme & Joshi, 1998). When adults read for meaning, the information supplied by words and phrases must simultaneously be integrated with the relevant knowledge they have already acquired. Interpretation based on prior knowledge is referred to as "top-down" processing because it begins with general knowledge that becomes increasingly focused as the reader combines it with the bottom-up information obtained from letters and words.

A number of alternatives to the bottom-up approach have been proposed in order to take the comprehension half of the learning-to-read process into account. These top-down, or comprehension-first, alternatives are based on the idea that reading is a special case of comprehending the world through symbols, an ability that children acquire when they learn language in the first place. Advocates of a comprehension-first approach argue that reading for comprehension should not be put off until children are fluent decoders. Since children arrive at school eager to "read the world," the main requirement of a good reading curriculum is many rich opportunities to experience written language as a useful tool for exploring and problem solving. Emphasis on correct and automatic decoding is replaced by a belief that children should be encouraged to figure out the overall meaning of what they are reading before they zero in on the details. At first their text interpretation may not be strictly correct according to conventional standards, but that is not a matter for concern. What matters is that the children perceive reading as a good way to achieve important goals; gradual mastery of conventional forms will follow.

Kenneth and Yetta Goodman refer to such comprehension-based alternatives as a *whole-language curriculum,* because reading is not taught in isolated lessons. Instead, literacy is made part of the ongoing intellectual life of the classroom; when children begin to experience reading and writing as useful, these theorists argue, they will naturally incorporate it in their repertoire of cognitive skills (K. Goodman, 1998).

The major issue in organizing the process of learning to read is how to balance top-down and bottom-up processes successfully. (We will return to discuss research on effective instructional approaches to reading after we consider the other basic skill at the core of schooling, namely, mathematics.) As you shall see, the issue of coordinating top-down and bottom-up features arises in math as well as reading, and similar educational strategies are often used in each domain in order to orchestrate optimal conditions for learning.

Learning Mathematics

Learning mathematics requires children to acquire a distinctive set of concepts and to master a special notation system for dealing with quantity and form.

Kinds of Mathematically Relevant Knowledge

Several years ago, Rochel Gelman and her colleagues (Gelman et al., 1986) identified three kinds of knowledge that must be acquired and coordinated for the development of higher-order mathematical skills:

1. **Conceptual knowledge,** the ability to understand the principles that underpin the problem

2. **Procedural knowledge,** the ability to carry out a sequence of actions to solve a problem

3. **Utilization knowledge,** the ability to know when to apply particular procedures

Subsequent research has confirmed the central importance of these kinds of knowledge in mathematical learning (Baroody, 2003).

A good example of the development of *conceptual* knowledge in the domain of arithmetic is provided by Jeffrey Bisanz and Jo-Anne Lefevre's (1990) study of children's understanding of inversion. Inversion is the arithmetic principle that adding and subtracting the same number leaves the original quantity unchanged. Bisanz and Lefevre presented problems of the form $a + b - b$ (for example, $10 + 8 - 8$) to children ranging in age from 6 years to adulthood. They found that calculating became progressively speedier between 6 and 9 years of age, but that some of the children did not seem to grasp inversion. Instead of creating a shortcut based on the inversion principle, they would dutifully add the second number to the first and then subtract the third number from the sum. The larger the second and third numbers, the longer it took them to get an answer (it required more time to figure out the answer to $4 + 9 - 9$, for example, than to solve $4 + 5 - 5$). In contrast, most 11-year-olds and virtually all adults responded very rapidly, no matter how large the second and third numbers were, an indication that they had mastered the inversion principle and were using it to cancel out the second and third numbers.

Using microgenetic designs, investigators have also documented the development of children's *procedural* knowledge during the course of mathematics instruction. Robert Siegler and his colleagues (Siegler & Stern, 1998), for example, applied their theory of "wavelike" strategy development to strategies that are essential to the mastery of procedures for addition, subtraction, and other mathematical operations (see Chapter 9, p. 336). To add a pair of numbers, such as 4 and 3, first- and second-graders may count on their fingers starting with "one" (1-2-3-4 . . . 5-6-7). Eventually they may hit on the strategy of holding up fingers corresponding to the first of the pair and counting up (4 . . . 5-6-7). If asked to add $2 + 9$, first-graders may start with 2 and then use their fingers to add 9 more; a year or so later children are more likely to convert $2 + 9$ into $9 + 2$, a strategy that both simplifies the task and shows their understanding of the principle that order is not important in addition. And, of course, if they think they know the sum "by heart," children will directly recall the answer (or what they believe to be the answer). As children grow older and more knowledgeable, the direct recall strategy comes to dominate addition of small numbers, and a variety of paper-and-pencil procedures replace fingers as strategic tools under most circumstances.

The importance of knowing when to use mathematical knowledge according to the context of the problems encountered (*utilization* knowledge) was

conceptual knowledge The ability to understand the principles that underpin a problem.

procedural knowledge The ability to carry out a sequence of actions to solve a problem.

utilization knowledge The ability to know when to apply particular problem-solving procedures.

Counting on fingers is a universal strategy for children just learning arithmetic.

Elizabeth Crews

made clear by Terezinha Nunes and her colleagues (Nunes et al., 1993). These Brazilian researchers studied mathematical problem solving among schoolchildren working as vendors in the streets and marketplaces in the Brazilian city of Recife. Nunes and her colleagues first posed arithmetic problems to the children "on the job," as part of the process of buying the goods the children were selling. A typical exchange with a 12-year-old child went like this:

> **Interviewer:** How much is one coconut?
> **Child:** 35.
> **Interviewer:** I'd like ten. How much is that?
> **Child:** (Pause) Three will be 105; with three more, that will be 210. (Pause) I need four more. That is . . . (pause) . . . I think it is 350. (Nunes et al., 1993, pp. 18–19)

Under these conditions, the children were correct about 98 percent of the time. The interviewers then gave the children a paper and pencil and asked them to solve identical problems. Again the children were correct 98 percent of the time.

Later, in a follow-up interview, the researchers tested the children on two different sets of math problems, one presented strictly as mathematical operations ("How much is 10 times 35?") and the other presented orally as real-world word problems. In this interview, the children were correct on the orally presented word problems 74 percent of the time but could solve only 37 percent of the problems that required strictly mathematical computation without any real-world connections.

Analysis revealed that in the second, formal interviews, the children failed to use the successful computational strategies they had applied in their selling activity. In the marketplace, for example, one 9-year-old had calculated the price of 12 lemons at 5 cruzeiros each by counting "10, 20, 30, 40, 50, 60" while separating out two lemons at a time. But when she was asked to solve the problem 12 × 5 in the formal interview, she "brought down" first the 2, then the 5, and then the 1 and came up with an answer of 152. She failed to employ a strategy she knew to be effective and produced an answer that, in other circumstances, she would have recognized as ridiculous.

Learning Mathematical Notation Systems

Learning to read and write the numbers in mathematical notation systems is among the basic skills that are taught in middle childhood. One of the first tasks children face when they encounter mathematics at school is to learn to write the first ten digits. Since it is only a cultural convention that the symbol 9 should stand for the spoken word "nine," the first stage of this process requires memorization.

Once children learn the first ten digits, they must learn the conventions for writing larger quantities and the concept of place value that underpins the decimal notation system. The required correspondences are not intuitively obvious. Some first-graders, for example, may write 23 as 203. This representation, although erroneous, follows the conventions of our way of speaking (20-3) and our system for representing spoken language in print ("twenty-three"). Unfortunately, from the child's point of view, conventions for representing place value in arithmetic do not follow the conventions of the spoken language. While numbers such as 203 ("two hundred and three") are, so to speak, pronounced from left to right, they are actually constructed right to left from the decimal point, which is ordinarily written only when some fraction of a whole number is to be indicated. So, for example, "Two hundred and three and forty-five-hundredths" is written 203.45. (See Figure 13.5 for a much different type of notation system.)

It takes most children several years to master these complexities, a fact that influences their ability to carry out such basic operations as addition and subtraction on paper. Common mistakes are to add numbers in the order in which they are said—

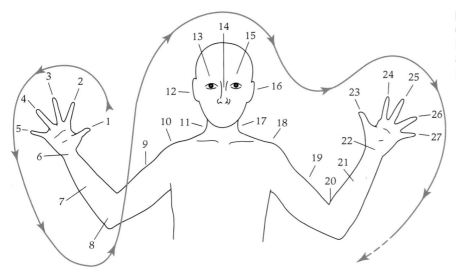

Figure 13.5 The Oksapmin of New Guinea do their arithmetic by using a basic set of 27 numbers corresponding to a conventionalized sequence of body parts. (From Saxe, 2004.)

from left to right—and to line up numbers from the left. Misunderstandings of this kind produce such errors as writing 123 +1 as

$$\begin{array}{r} 123 \\ +1 \\ \hline 223 \end{array}$$

Children who produce such answers are applying previously acquired basic skills inappropriately. Their focus on bottom-up processing produces absurd answers contrary to their own common sense, and they often fail to notice the mistake because they are not attending to the overall meaning of the problem (that is, to engage in top-down processing).

Organizing Instruction

Recommendations for effective teaching of mathematics cluster at two polar extremes, analogous to the dichotomy between the bottom-up (code-first) and the top-down (comprehension-first) approaches to reading instruction. At one end are those teachers who believe that instruction is best carried out through intensive drill and practice on basic building blocks of the overall system. In their view, children need to learn the correct procedures for adding, subtracting, multiplying, and dividing before they can begin to solve the kinds of problems in which they must, for example, calculate where two trains traveling toward each other at different speeds will meet (Stone & Clements, 1998). At the other end are those who believe that learning should begin with problems that draw upon children's real-world experience and that include exposure to mathematical principles necessary for children's continued conceptual growth in the domain of mathematics (Cobb & McClain, 2002). Again, as in the case of learning to read (p. 490), the agreed-upon solution is to ensure that bottom-up, basic processes and top-down, higher-order processes are properly integrated; but achieving the right balance is a difficult challenge (Sfard & Kieran, 2001).

The Social Organization of Classroom Instruction

When we turn our focus from the basic processes of reading and writing to inquire about how best to organize the settings in which those basic skills are taught, we immediately encounter a constraint faced by all educators. The average public school classroom in more prosperous countries is populated by 25 to 40 children

instructional discourse A distinctive way of talking and thinking that is typical in school but rarely encountered in everyday interactions in the community or home.

initiation-reply-feedback sequence An instructional discourse pattern in which the teacher initiates an exchange, usually by asking a question; a student replies; and then the teacher provides feedback.

and one adult. This ratio is often higher, sometimes much higher, in poorer countries. This constraint on social organization results in a set of possibilities for organizing children's experience very different from earlier forms of enculturation and apprenticeship—and it creates an enormous challenge for teachers.

The Standard Classroom Format

Excavations of classrooms in the ancient world, as well as floor plans of American classrooms during the late twentieth century, bear a striking resemblance to the typical classroom found in schools throughout the world. Far and away the most common arrangement is for the teacher to sit at a desk or stand at a blackboard facing the children who sit in parallel rows, facing front (Gallego, Cole & LCHC, 2000). These physical circumstances are combined with the assumption that the teacher is an authority figure who is there to teach and talk, while the children are there to listen and learn. This combination of assumptions routinely gives rise to a unique form of **instructional discourse,** a distinctive way of talking and thinking that is typical in school but rarely encountered in everyday interactions in the community or home. The central goals of instructional discourse are to give children information stipulated by the curriculum and feedback on their efforts to learn it, while providing teachers with information about their students' progress (Wells, 2001).

By far the most common form of instructional discourse encountered in classrooms follows what is commonly referred to as a "recitation script" (Mehan, 1998). A distinctive feature of instructional discourse that follows the recitation script is the **initiation-reply-feedback sequence,** demonstrated in Table 13.1. In this pattern, the teacher initiates an exchange, usually by asking a question; a student replies; and then the teacher provides feedback, in this case, an evaluation. The initiation-reply-feedback sequence uses the "known-answer question"—a form of questioning that is rarely encountered in everyday conversation among adults. When the teacher asks Beth, "What does this word say?" the teacher already knows the answer and is actually seeking information about Beth's progress in learning to read. Learning to respond easily to known-answer questions, in addition to learning the academic content of the curriculum, is an important early lesson of schooling (Mehan, 1979).

The initiation-reply-feedback sequence can be quite flexible. When Ramona hesitates (Table 13.1), the teacher immediately calls on Kim, who provides the answer. This arrangement allows Ramona to learn from Kim's answer and the teacher's response to it at the same time that it allows the teacher to assess Ramona's need for more instruction. On other occasions, the teacher might use the feedback part of the exchange as a means to open up new aspects of the topic at hand or to involve another child in the discussion (Nassaji & Wells, 2000).

Another special facet of instructional discourse is the emphasis placed on the linguistic form of students' replies, shown in the lesson on the use of prepositions in Table 13.2. When you read this exchange, note that the teacher gradually builds an understanding of the linguistic form that she considers appropriate by using the

table 13.1

Initiation-Reply-Feedback Sequence		
Initiation	**Reply**	**Feedback**
T [Teacher]: What does this word say? Beth.	Beth: One.	T: Very good.
T: What does this word say? Jenny.	Jenny: One.	T: Okay.
T: Now look up here. What does this word say? Ramona.	Ramona: Umm.	
T: Kim.	Kim: First.	T: Okay.

Source: Mehan, 1979.

table 13.2

Lesson on Use of Prepositions	
Initiation	**Reply**
T [Teacher]: Make a red flower under the tree. *[pause]* Okay, let's look at the red flower. Can you tell me where the red flower is?	Children: Right here, right here.
T: Dora?	Dora: Under the tree.
T: Tell me in a sentence.	Dora: It's under the tree.
T: What's under the tree, Dora?	Children: The flower.
T: Tell me, the flower . . .	Dora: The flower is under the tree.
T: Where is the red flower, Richard?	Richard: Under the tree.
T: Can you tell me in a sentence?	Richard: The flower is under the tree.
T: Cindy, where is the red flower?	Cindy: The red flower is under the tree.
	Richard: *[noticing that Cindy actually drew the "red" flower with a yellow crayon]:* Hey, that's not red.

Source: Mehan, 1979.

turn-taking rules of the recitation script. Second, note that for the purposes of this lesson, the truth of what the children say is less important than the way they say it. Cindy gave her answer in the form the teacher was looking for, but, as Richard noticed, Cindy had named the wrong color! She was correct in school terms, although she clearly violated norms of everyday language use.

In everyday conversations people usually have ample opportunity to check their interpretations of what is being said against reality. But in the closed world of the classroom, the real-world objects and events that are the content of the conversation are often unavailable to help children interpret what is being said. Consequently, in order to master the specialized knowledge taught in school, children must learn to focus on language itself as the vehicle of instruction.

Despite wide variations among them, each of these settings is immediately recognizable as a school.

Monkmeyer/Forsyth

Betty Press/Woodfin Camp & Associates

Will & Deni McIntyre/Corbis

D. Peter Menzel/Material World

reciprocal teaching A method of teaching reading in which teachers and children take turns reading text in a manner that integrates decoding and comprehension skills.

Alternative Forms of Classroom Instruction

Although use of the recitation script is widespread in classrooms around the world, many developmentalists argue that it is not the best way of organizing instruction. Among other shortcomings, children taught in this manner are placed in the role of passive recipients of predigested information. They gain very little practice formulating problems for themselves. Yet expanding children's knowledge of language functions, including the language of mathematics, is one of the important tasks of schooling (Lampert & Blunk, 1998).

Alternative means of organizing classroom instruction can be located on a continuum. At one end are whole-group recitation-script lessons combined with seat work in which students practice parts of the lesson. At the other end are project-oriented, activity-based classrooms where teachers spend little time talking to the class as a whole and spend most of the school day moving from one small group to another, providing encouragement and intellectual and material resources as they seem needed (Wells, 2001). The effectiveness of the latter approach is illustrated by two programs—one focused on reading, the other on mathematics. (See the box on pages 498–499, "Computers in Schools," for a discussion of yet another form of classroom instruction.)

Reciprocal Teaching **Reciprocal teaching** was designed by Ann Brown and Annemarie Palincsar as a way to integrate decoding skills and comprehension skills. It was targeted at the many children who have learned to read in the sense that they can decode simple texts but have difficulty making sense of what they read (Brown, Palinscar, & Arbruster, 1994).

In the reciprocal-teaching procedure, a teacher and a small group of students read silently through a paragraph of text and then take turns leading a discussion of its meaning. The discussion leader (adult or child) begins by asking a question about the main idea and then summarizes the content in his or her own words. If members of the group disagree with the summary, the group rereads the passage and discusses its contents to clarify what it says. Finally, the leader asks for predictions about what will come in the next paragraph.

Note that each of the key elements in reciprocal teaching—asking questions about content, summarizing, clarifying, and predicting—presupposes that the purpose of the activity is comprehension: figuring out what the text means. And because these strategies involve talking about (and arguing over) the textual meaning, the children are able to see and hear the teacher and other children model metacognitive behaviors that aid comprehension. For example, the teacher might point to relevant information in a prior paragraph that needs to be taken into account, or relate an idea in the text to some common experience that all the children have had, as a way of making sense of what is being read. As Brown (1997) points out, reciprocal teaching is an application of Vygotsky's notion of a "zone of proximal development" (Chapter 5, p. 196), which allows children to participate in the act of reading for meaning even before they have acquired the full set of abilities that independent reading requires.

A number of studies (summarized in Brown, 1997) have found that reciprocal teaching can produce rapid and durable increases in children's reading skills. Figure 13.6 shows the findings of a study in which reciprocal reading was being used in a science class and a social studies class, not as a "reading lesson" but as a way to foster mastery of the course material. Used in this manner, the reciprocal-reading activity goes beyond the teaching of reading for its own sake to reading that increases knowledge of valued subject matter at the same time that it improves reading skills.

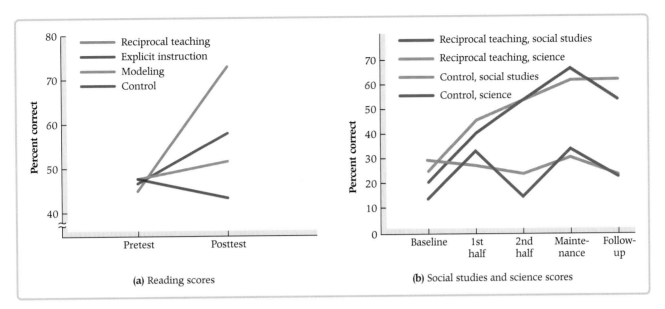

(a) Reading scores

(b) Social studies and science scores

Realistic Mathematics Education Recognizing the limitations of recitation scripts and the bottom-up approach, the National Council of Teachers of Mathematics adopted a set of standards for improving mathematics education that shifts the focus of mathematics instruction from training in basic skills, procedures, and memorization toward conceptual understanding and linkages between mathematics and real-world problems (National Council of Teachers of Mathematics, 2000). An example of a mathematics program that seeks to implement these goals is provided by the work of Paul Cobb and his colleagues, who draw upon a theory of "realistic mathematics education," which is widely used in the Netherlands (Cobb et al., 1997). According to these researchers, realistic mathematics education should:

1. *Use meaningful activities.* For example, a first-grade teacher might introduce counting up to 20 by creating a make-believe situation with a bus conductor on a double-decker bus with 10 seats on each deck who has to keep track of how many people are on the bus. As we have learned from the experimental research on children's problem solving discussed in previous chapters, such pretend stories help to provide a meaningful context for carrying out cognitive operations.

2. *Support basic mathematical skills.* In the case of the double-decker bus, for example, the teacher wanted children to learn how to group numbers for calculation, to realize that there are 8 people on the bus if there are 4 on top and 4 on the bottom, or 6 on the top and 2 on the bottom, or 2 on the top and 6 on the bottom, and so on. Each configuration is a different way of representing a total of 8.

3. *Employ models in educational activity.* Cobb describes a number of studies that use an "arithmetic rack," with two rows containing 10 beads each. For the conductor-on-the-bus context, the arithmetic rack provides a rather precise spatial model with each of its rows corresponding to a deck of the bus. But the beads on the rack can also be used to represent the number of cookies put in or taken out of a cookie jar and a variety of other story contexts that have equivalent mathematical properties.

Over time, children gradually master the conceptual structures that the stories and models initially support, and they can carry out the needed calculations without such aids.

Figure 13.6 Reciprocal teaching (a) not only proved to be more effective than traditional strategies such as explicit instruction or modeling (b) but also produced marked improvement in children's reading success in social studies and science. Both explicit instruction and reciprocal teaching led to improved reading, but reciprocal teaching was by far the more effective procedure. Students given practice in reciprocal reading showed large and sustained improvements in their social studies and science classes, whereas students who received no special reading instruction did quite poorly. (From Brown et al., 1992.)

Computers in Schools

Over the past two decades, the growth of computer use in schools has been phenomenal. In 1983 there was approximately 1 computer for every 168 students in U.S. schools. In 1998 there was 1 computer for every 6 students and the number has continued to increase (see figure). Moreover, the use of more and more powerful computers in schools is expected to accelerate in the decades to come (Anderson & Dexter, 2000).

This growth in the quantity of computers has been accompanied by their falling costs, their vastly increased processing speed and memory capacity, and easier access to the Internet, which have enabled computers to become a powerful medium of communication. These changes in cost, power, and function have allowed computers to have an impact on classrooms all over the industrialized world.

The actual changes that occur in the classroom environment when computers are introduced depend very much on how many there are, how powerful they are, and how they are used. In many classrooms there is still only one computer, which is used to reward well-behaved children with an opportunity to play a computer game; use of the Internet to provide access to motivating, educationally relevant content is minimal or absent. But in some schools, computers have transformed the entire organization of education (Bowman, Pieters, Hembree, & Mellender, 2002; Warschauer, 2003).

Several years ago Charles Crook identified four approaches to the design of computer-based educational activities that continue to provide useful metaphors for relating computers to the teaching process (Crook, 1996).

The Computer as Tutor

The earliest use of computers in education was based on the idea that the computer would play the role of a human teacher. The spirit and hopes for this approach were stated early in the computer revolution by Patrick Suppes, a leader in using digital computers in education:

> In a few more years, millions of school children will have access to what Phillip of Macedonia's son Alexander enjoyed as a royal prerogative: the personal services of a tutor as well-informed and responsive as Aristotle. (Suppes, 1966, p. 207)

The prototypic application used in this approach is CAI—computer-aided instruc-

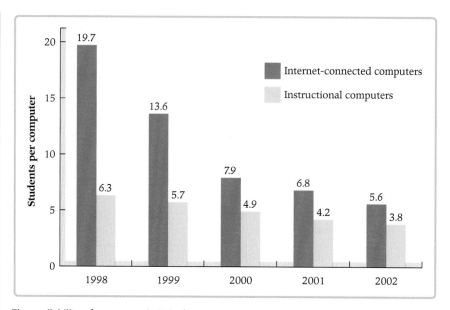

The availability of computers in U.S. classrooms continues to increase. At the same time, ways of using computers as educational resources have changed, with Web access increasing rapidly to the point where if a school has a computer, it is probably connected to the Internet.

tion. The computer begins by presenting the student with the information to be learned, along with questions that test whether learning has occurred. The computer then records the student's answers and gives appropriate feedback. Basic reading and math skills, as well as a variety of subject matters such as geography and history, have been taught in this way (Forbus & Feltovich, 2001).

One advantage that CAI has over traditional drill-and-practice workbooks is the capacity to keep track of the individual child's exact performance and to respond accordingly using sophisticated models of the individual student's learning profile. An algebra tutor designed by Kenneth Koedinger and his colleagues, for example, accumulates a database of users' problem-solving strategies and common errors and then uses these data to present specifically relevant problems that are sensitive to the users' cognitive strengths and weaknesses (Koedinger, 2001). Such individualized instruction is impossible in a classroom with 1 teacher and 30 students sitting at their desks—a major argument for the application of computers to education. This and other "intelligent tutoring" programs have been shown to be effective in a variety of circumstances and are always

being modified and improved (Forbus & Feltovich, 2001) .

However, to date it has not been possible to create a computerized tutor that rivals the flexibility and subtlety of well-qualified human teachers. So far, at least, computer programs have been unable to anticipate what children will have trouble with or to find alternative ways to phrase a problem or entice children's curiosity with situationally appropriate hints.

The Computer as Pupil

The computer-as-tutor approach allows learners little opportunity to guide the course of their own learning; they can only respond to the problems they are given. Influenced by Piaget's theory that to achieve deep understanding, children must construct their understandings through active exploration of their environments, Seymour Papert and his colleagues at MIT's Media Laboratory developed a simplified computer language called LOGO, which has undergone a number of revisions as the power of the computers has increased (Kafai & Resnick, 1996; Papert, 1980, 2002). This resource aims to help educators and their students learn to build their own models.

The use of computers for instruction has become a routine part of education across the industrialized world.

Using the early generations of LOGO, children controlled the movements of a robot turtle that actually moves around the floor of the room following explicit instructions that the child "teaches it" by programming them into the computer's memory. By learning to "teach the turtle" to carry out their instructions, children acquire ideas and procedures that are fundamental not only to computer programming but to mathematics in general. For example, in order to teach the turtle to run around in a circle or build a house, children acquire basic principles of both algebra and geometry. More recently, Papert and his colleagues have extended this simple computer language with programmable objects such as Lego blocks, enabling children to build Lego robots and maneuver them through environments that the children create for them (Resnick, 1998).

Research on the effectiveness of treating computers as pupils has shown that Papert's constructionist approach can produce useful educational activities for children (Kafai & Resnick, 1996). However, research also shows that in order to be effective, LOGO applications need to be a central part of classroom life in which teachers are involved along with the children, providing ongoing support and guidance for the children's learning (Suomala & Alajaaski, 2002).

The Computer as Resource

The third approach to using computers in school emphasizes the fact that whatever may set it apart from other human tech-

nologies, the computer is, at bottom, a tool that can be used to provide a broad range of resources for learners. This idea, which underpins much of the current enthusiasm for the use of computers in the classroom, assumes that if it is possible to provide active learners with abundant information, learning is sure to occur. There is no doubt that computers, with their current multimedia capacities and access to the World Wide Web can provide enormous amounts of information in interesting formats. But as in the case of each of the other uses of computers, there is a tendency for those who champion computers as information resources to lose sight of the fact that these resources are unlikely to be used if the school does not have a social system that encourages and supports children's initiatives. Computers may actually contribute to the performance gap between schools in wealthy and poor neighborhoods (Warschauer, 2003).

The Computer as Transformer

Several developmentalists argue that one of the greatest potentials of classroom computers is to reorganize the entire fabric of the educational experience by changing children's interactions not only with the materials to be learned but also with the teacher and one another, the school as an institution, and the world at large (Kupperman & Fishman, 2002; Milson, 2002). A few examples give the flavor of this approach.

Researchers associated with the Cognition and Technology Group at

Vanderbilt University have taken advantage of the newly emerging combinations of interactive video disks and CD-ROM technology to create a curriculum that begins with a series of televised adventures and mysteries for the children to enter into (Zech et al., 1998). In one such program, "The River Adventure," learners watch a video about a trip on a houseboat in which the protagonists must take into account such factors as the food and gas they will need, the docking facilities they will require, and so on. The children then determine when and why to use various kinds of data to achieve such goals as docking at a particular marina and returning home quickly under various conditions.

Students who engage in this type of multimedia problem solving acquire many kinds of expertise in using computers and a variety of academic skills as well. Just as important, their interest in school and their self-confidence as students have been shown to increase.

Several research groups have used computer networks to forge relationships between schools in different parts of the world, enabling students to engage in joint learning projects in which, for example, they measure and record levels of acid rain or compare the histories of their cultural groups in relation to each other (Riel, 1998). The use of computer networks also allows students to participate in projects they find genuinely interesting. For example, they can interact on-line with scientists engaged in such exciting activities as exploring space, the polar regions, or undersea canyons, and be directly involved in analyzing important data and figuring out what they mean. These projects naturally promote work in small groups, mastery of many aspects of computer use, and the development of multiple academic skills. Teachers find that they do not need to urge children to attend to such studies; instead, it is common for children to ask permission to keep working on their projects during the lunch break and recess.

Numerous studies have shown that computers can make a positive difference in the classroom when properly used. The challenge now is to realize this potential, making effective uses of the new technology a routine part of every child's education.

A common use of computers in the early grades is to provide children more drills and practice in basic skills.

As in the case of reciprocal teaching, the creation of classroom norms that support the mixing of bottom-up knowledge with top-down conceptual and utilization knowledge is key. Teachers work to establish a classroom culture in which children are expected to justify their reasoning when they answer a question. Children are also expected to try to understand the reasoning behind other children's answers. In addition, children are expected to be helpful to the group. When working alone, they are encouraged to solicit help from others and to share what they have learned.

"Problem-oriented" approaches that emphasize the processes of reasoning about mathematical problems have been found successful well beyond the elementary school years (Boaler, 2001; Lampert & Blunk, 1998). Jo Boaler observed students in two secondary school classrooms in England. One class followed a traditional recitation-script approach to learning mathematics, while the other used a small-group, problem-oriented approach. In the traditional classroom, the teacher began lessons by presenting a standard problem and the standard method for solving it ("Here is how to determine the area of a parallelogram"). The students observed the solution method and then practiced using it on their own. The teacher did not explain why the method worked and did not encourage students to invent their own methods. In the activity-centered classroom, the teacher would begin a lesson by presenting a problem to the whole class designed to intrigue the students. In one case, for example, the students were presented with a problem called "36 pieces of fencing." A fence with 36 planks was depicted and the students were asked to figure out all the different shapes they could make from these materials. After the problem was introduced, the students were encouraged to ask questions as a way of orienting themselves to the task. Then they worked in small groups while the teacher moved around the room providing help when it was requested.

The teachers in both classrooms believed strongly that their approaches were superior, and they passed their enthusiasm on to their students. They also reported that discipline problems were virtually nonexistent, but the researchers noted that the project-oriented classroom was somewhat noisier and that the students more often engaged in "off-task" activities such as chatting with their friends.

When the students were tested at the end of the year on both standard tests and tests that assessed their ability to apply mathematics to new problems, there were striking differences between students in the two classrooms. Students who participated in the traditional instructional format scored better on knowledge of prespecified mathematical procedures, but students in the project-based class were significantly better on conceptual questions and on questions that required them to apply their knowledge to a novel problem, such as designing an apartment.

Overall, the evidence indicates that when properly organized, instructional methods that induce students to be active contributors to classroom discourse can be quite effective. But such methods are more complex to organize than the recitation script and are still encountered in only a minority of classrooms.

Studying the Cognitive Consequences of Schooling

The contrasting success of different modes of instruction should make it clear that what children learn in school depends importantly on the kind of instruction they receive. However, as we noted earlier, a very high proportion of schools follow whole-class recitation methods. This allows developmentalists to treat schooling as a uniform kind of experience when they try to assess how learning in schools affects cognitive development. Regardless of instructional approach, schooling expands children's knowledge, gives them massive experience in deliberate remembering, and trains them in systematic problem solving. Recent decades of research demonstrate that these experiences do affect children, but the effects depend on the particular cognitive processes in question (Christian, Bachman, & Morrison, 2001).

There are three major research designs that developmentalists use to assess the cognitive impact of schooling:

1. *The "school-cutoff" strategy* compares 6-year-olds who have experienced formal schooling with children of the same age who have not yet experienced it.

2. *School/nonschool comparisons* take advantage of circumstances where schooling has been introduced unevenly into a society, so that some children are born in towns with schools and some are born in towns without schools, for reasons over which they have no control.

3. *Second-generation studies* also contrast people who have been to school with those who have not, but focus on differences between children whose mothers have or have not attended school.

Each approach has certain strengths and weaknesses, which we consider in the sections following.

Using the School-Cutoff Strategy

In many countries, school boards require that children must be a certain age by a particular date to begin attending school. To enter grade 1 in September of a given year, children in Edmonton, Alberta, Canada, for example, must have passed their sixth birthday by March 1 of that year. Six-year-olds born after that date must attend kindergarten instead, so their formal education is delayed for a year. Such policies allow researchers to assess the impact of early schooling while holding age virtually constant: they simply compare the intellectual performances of children who turn 6 in January or February with those who turn 6 in March or April, testing both groups at the beginning and at the end of the school year. This procedure is known as the **school-cutoff strategy** (Morrison et al., 1995).

Researchers who have used the school-cutoff strategy find that the first year of schooling brings about a marked increase in the sophistication of some cognitive processes but not others. Frederick Morrison and his colleagues (1995), for example, compared the ability of first-graders and kindergartners to recall pictures of nine common objects. The first-graders were, on average, only a month older than the kindergartners. The performances of the two groups were virtually identical at the start of the school year. At the end of the school year, however, the first-graders could remember twice as many pictures as they did at the beginning of the year, whereas the kindergartners showed no improvement in memory at all. Significantly, the first-graders engaged in active rehearsal (a memory strategy you encountered in Chapter 12, p. 465) during the testing, but the kindergartners did not. Clearly, one year of schooling had brought about marked changes in their strategies and performance.

The same pattern of results was obtained for such tasks as recognizing the names of the letters of the alphabet, in standardized reading and mathematics tests, as well as in a variety of deliberate remembering tests. But *no effects* of attending a year of school were found when children were administered a standard Piagetian test of conservation (see Chapter 12, pp. 460–461), or assessed for the coherence of their storytelling or for the number of vocabulary words they understood (Christian et

school-cutoff strategy A means of assessing the impact of education while controlling for age by comparing children who are almost the same age but begin schooling a year apart because of school rules that set a specific cutoff birthday date for starting school.

al., 2001). Performance in these latter tasks improved largely as a consequence of children's age. These findings both confirm the importance of schooling in promoting a variety of relatively specific cognitive abilities and support Piaget's belief that the ability to understand the conservation of quantity develops without any special instruction at some time between the ages of 5 and 7.

Comparing Schooled and Nonschooled Children

Although the school-cutoff strategy provides an excellent way to assess the cognitive consequences of small amounts of schooling, it is, by definition, limited to only the first year. For a longer-range picture of the contribution of formal education to cognitive development, researchers have conducted studies in societies where schooling is available to only a part of the population. We will summarize evidence from three cognitive domains that have figured heavily in our earlier discussions of cognitive development: logical thinking, memory, and metacognitive skills.

Logical Thinking

A large number of cross-cultural studies have been conducted to determine if participation in formal schooling enhances performance on Piagetian conservation tasks and other tasks created to reveal concrete operational thinking (Segall et al., 1999). The results have split more or less evenly between those who find enhanced performance among children who have attended school and those who do not. Consistent with the evidence presented in Chapter 12 (pp. 476–477), when schoolchildren do better than their unschooled peers on the standard Piagetian tests, their greater success appears to have less to do with more rapid achievement of concrete operational thinking than with their greater familiarity with the circumstances of test taking. Such specialized test-taking knowledge includes familiarity with the forms in which questions are asked, greater ease in speaking to unfamiliar adults, and fluency in the language in which the test is given when the testing is not conducted in the child's native language. When these factors are taken into account, the overall pattern of results indicates that the development of concrete operational thinking increases with age and is relatively unaffected by schooling.

Memory

In Chapter 12 (p. 478) you saw that, unlike North American children, children in some cultures do not show an increase in free-recall memory performance as they grow older. Research comparing schooled and nonschooled children in other societies, like the comparative data on first-graders and kindergartners presented previously, has shown that schooling is the crucial experience underlying these cultural differences. When children in other cultures have had an opportunity to go to school, their memory performance is more similar to that of their North American counterparts in the same grade than it is to that of their age-mates in the same village who have not been to school (Rogoff, 2003).

A study by Daniel Wagner (1974) suggests the kind of memory-enhancing information-processing skills that children acquire as a consequence of schooling. Wagner conducted his study among Mayans in Yucatán, Mexico, who had completed different amounts of schooling. He asked 248 people varying in age from 6 years to adulthood to recall the positions of picture cards laid out in a line (see Figure 13.7). (To ensure that the items pictured on the cards would be familiar to all the subjects, the pictures were taken from a local version of bingo called *lotería,* which uses pictures instead of numbers.) On each trial, each of seven cards

(a) Take a good look and turn the page

Figure 13.7 (a) Cards used to test short-term memory. Seven cards are selected and then turned facedown one at a time. The person being tested is then shown a duplicate of one of the cards (see p. 504) and asked to select the card that corresponds to it from the seven that are face down. (b) Which card has a matching picture? (From Wagner, 1978.)

was displayed for 2 seconds and then turned facedown. As soon as all seven cards had been presented, a duplicate of a picture on one of the cards was shown and the subject was asked to point to its twin. By selecting different duplicate pictures, Wagner in effect manipulated the length of time between the presentation of a picture and the moment its location was to be recalled.

As in similar research in the United States, Wagner found that the performance of children who were attending school improved markedly with age (see Figure 13.8). However, older children and adults who did not attend school remembered no better than young children, leading Wagner to conclude that it was schooling that made the difference. Additional analyses of the data revealed that the use of rehearsal by those who attended school was responsible for the improvement in their performance.

Evidence such as this does not mean that memory simply fails to develop among children who have not attended school. The difference between schooled and non-schooled children's performance in cross-cultural memory experiments is most noticeable after several years of schooling and when the materials to be learned are not related to one another according to any everyday script. When the materials to be remembered are part of a meaningful setting, such as the kinds of animals found in a barnyard or the furniture placed in a toy house, the effects of schooling on memory performance disappear (Rogoff & Wadell, 1982). It appears that schooling helps children to develop specialized strategies for remembering and thereby enhances their ability to commit arbitrary material to memory for purposes of later testing. There is no evidence to support the conclusion that schooling increases memory capacity per se.

Metacognitive Skills Schooling appears to influence the ability to reflect on and talk about one's own thought processes (Rogoff, 2003; Tulviste, 1991). When children have been asked to explain how they arrived at the answer to a logical problem or what they did to make themselves remember something, those who have not attended school are likely to say something like "I did what my sense told me" or to offer no explanation at all. Schoolchildren, on the other hand, are likely to talk about the mental activities and logic that underlie their responses. The same results apply to metalinguistic knowledge. Sylvia Scribner and Michael Cole (1981) asked schooled and unschooled Vai people in Liberia to judge the grammatical correctness of several sentences spoken in Vai. Some of the sentences were grammatical, some not. Education had no effect on the interviewees' ability to identify the ungrammatical sentences; but schooled people could generally explain just what it was about a sentence that made it ungrammatical, whereas unschooled people could not.

Figure 13.8 Short-term memory performance as a function of age and number of years of education. In the absence of further education (as among the rural people tested in this study), performance does not improve with age. Thus, schooling appears to be a key factor in one's ability to do well at this task. (Numbers in parentheses represent the average number of years of education for the designated group.) (From Wagner, 1974.)

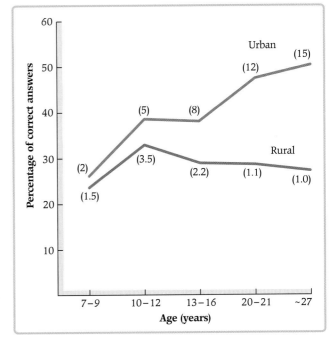

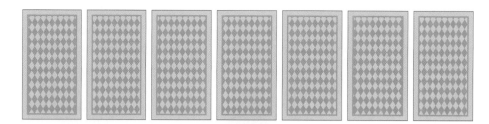

(b) Which card has matching pictures?

The Second-Generation Impact of Schooling

The evidence from both school-cutoff and cross-cultural research supports the conclusion that the cognitive consequences of schooling are quite specific to the particular skill being tested. The clearest evidence for a *general* cognitive impact of schooling comes from studies of the child-rearing practices of mothers who have, or have not, gone to school and the subsequent school achievement of their children.

Based on evidence collected in many countries over several decades, Robert LeVine and his colleagues emphasize three major changes in children's status linked to maternal education that have been widely documented over the last several decades: the children of women who have attended elementary school experience a lower level of infant mortality, better health during childhood, and greater academic achievement (LeVine et al., 2001). These researchers propose a set of habits, preferences, and skills that mothers acquired while they were children in school. This set includes, in addition to rudimentary literacy and numeracy skills:

1. The ability to understand written texts and use oral communication that is directly relevant to the negotiation of interactions in health and educational settings involving their children.

2. Models of teaching and learning based on the scripted activities and authority structures of schooling, which they then employ in the home, talking more to their children and using less directive child-rearing methods.

3. An ability and willingness to acquire and accept information from the mass media, such as following health prescriptions more obediently.

LeVine and his colleagues hypothesized that young women who have been to school retain these habits of mind into adulthood and apply them in the course of raising their own children. The work of these researchers has been supported by direct observations of the teaching styles of Mayan mothers who have, or have not, been to school. Pablo Chavajay and Barbara Rogoff found that mothers who had experienced 12 years of schooling used school-like teaching styles when asked to teach their young children to complete a puzzle; while those with 0 to 2 years of schooling participated *with* their children in completing the puzzle and did not explicitly teach them (Chavajay & Rogoff, 2002). There is nothing inherently wrong with the unschooled mothers' teaching style, but it does not prepare their children well for schools, which rely heavily on the recitation script as the mode of instruction.

When the effects on health-related behaviors, resulting from socialization in the school, are combined with changes in maternal ability to use modern social welfare institutions and to adopt new ways of interacting with their children, the effects of schooling appear to be general in the society.

The Evidence in Overview

Overall, extensive research on the cognitive consequences of schooling has produced a mixed picture. On the one hand, there is only minimal support for the idea that schooling is directly responsible for broad changes in the way the mind works "in general." In some ways, as shown by the evidence from children who focus too narrowly on the mathematical procedures taught in school, schooling can actually have a negative impact on the development of mental abilities. When schooling has been found to improve cognitive performance, the effect appears to work in one of three ways: (1) by increasing children's knowledge base, including ways of using language; (2) by teaching specific information-processing strategies that are relevant primarily to school itself; and (3) by changing children's overall life situations and attitudes, which they pass on to their children in the form of new child-rearing practices that promote school achievement.

Perhaps the most important aspect of schooling for the majority of people is social and not simply cognitive; schooling is a gateway to economic power and social status. As we noted earlier in this chapter (Figure 13.1, p. 484), the associations between years of schooling, income, and job status are strong (U.S. Bureau of the Census, 2000). On the average, the more years of schooling people complete, the higher their incomes are and the more likely they are to obtain white-collar and professional jobs.

Success in school is such an important contributor to children's later economic well-being in literate societies that developmental psychologists and educators are greatly interested in understanding the factors that promote or inhibit it. One commonly held popular belief is that many children who succeed simply have a special "aptitude for schooling" that others lack. But as we shall see, there is more to success in school than academic aptitude. The nature and quality of education as well as the social environment of the school itself also play essential roles in children's school success.

Aptitude for Schooling

Although people need basic literacy and numeracy skills to function well in modern, industrialized societies, many youngsters leave school without having acquired them. It is estimated that as many as 22 percent of adults in the United States read so poorly that they cannot cope adequately with the demands of everyday life (National Center for Educational Statistics, 2003). What gives rise to this high failure rate and what can be done to promote greater success in the kinds of learning that take place in school? Over the past hundred years, answers to such questions have been influenced by the idea that variations in an aptitude called "intelligence" explain differences in school achievement.

The concept of intelligence is very widely accepted. All languages have terms that describe individual differences in people's ability to solve various kinds of problems (Serpell, 2000). But the precise meanings of these terms vary among cultures, and it has proved difficult—some say impossible—to define intelligence so that it can be measured as precisely as weight or height.

For example, Robert Serpell found that the nearest equivalent to "intelligence" among the Chewa of eastern Zambia emphasizes cooperation and obedience. This emphasis on the social dimension of "intelligence" appears quite widespread in more traditional societies, but it is the cognitive dimension that dominates notions of intelligence in Europe and North America.

Both dimensions of the term have been found in recent work by Elena Grigorenko and her colleagues (Grigorenko et al., 2001). These researchers report that among the Luo of rural Kenya, there are four words that people apply to different kinds of problem-solving abilities. One of these words appears to correspond to the notion of cognitive competence, which is at the heart of European and U.S. conceptions of intelligence. The others refer to social qualities such as diligence or obedience, or personal qualities with social implications, such as a willingness to take initiative.

Despite uncertainties about what intelligence "really is," almost all children growing up today in North America can expect to take an intelligence test focused on cognitive competence at some time before they complete their education. Such tests are used to decide the kind of education they will receive and the kind of work they will do, which in turn will influence the lives they will lead as adults. It is thus important to understand the nature of intelligence embodied in these tests, as well as the nature of intelligence testing itself as a factor in children's development.

The Origins of Intelligence Testing

Interest in measuring intelligence became widespread at the beginning of the twentieth century, when mass education was becoming the norm in industrialized countries. Though most children seemed to be able to profit from the instruction they were given, some seemed unable to learn in school. Concerned education officials tried to determine the causes of these difficulties and find remedies for them.

In 1904, the French minister of public instruction named a commission to distinguish between what he termed "defective" children and children who were failing to learn in school for other reasons. The commission asked Alfred Binet, a professor of psychology at the Sorbonne, and Théodore Simon, a physician, to create a means of identifying those children who needed special educational treatment. Binet and Simon set out to construct a psychological examination for diagnosing mental subnormality that would have all the precision and validity of a medical examination. They especially wanted to avoid *incorrectly* diagnosing children as "mentally subnormal" (Binet & Simon, 1916).

The diagnostic strategy adopted by Binet and Simon was to present children of different ages with a series of problems that were considered indicative of intelligence in France at that time. The problems were tailored to differentiate between children at each age, so that children who were far behind could be identified and given special instruction. Binet and Simon (1916) surmised, for example, that one aspect of intelligence is the ability to follow directions on a task while keeping several components of the task in mind at once. To test for this ability, they presented children aged 4 to 6 with tasks such as the following:

> Do you see this key? You are to put it on the chair over there (pointing to the chair); afterwards shut the door; afterwards you will see near the door a box which is on a chair. You will take that box and bring it to me. (p. 206)

At 4 years of age, few children could carry out all parts of this task without help. At 5 years, about half of the children responded adequately, and at 6 years, almost all children completed the task fully. This age-linked pattern of achievement provided Binet and Simon with the test characteristics they needed. A 4-year-old who passed the test was considered precocious while a 6-year-old who failed was considered retarded with respect to this ability.

Other tasks required children to identify the missing parts of a picture, to name colors, to copy geometric figures, to remember strings of random digits, to count backward from 20, to make change for 20 francs, and so on. After extensive pretesting, Binet and Simon tested slightly more than 200 children ranging in age from 3 to 12 years, giving a different set of questions to each age group. As they had hoped, almost precisely 50 percent of these children scored at the expected age level. Of the remainder, 43 percent were within 1 year of expectation and only 7 percent deviated above or below the norm by as much as 2 years.

Binet and Simon concluded that they had succeeded in constructing a scale of intelligence. They called the basic index of intelligence for this scale **mental age (MA).** A child who performed as well on the test as an average 7-year-old was said to have an MA of 7; a child who did as well as an average 9-year-old was said to have an MA of 9; and so on. The MA provided a convenient way to characterize mental subnormality. A "dull" 7-year-old child was one who performed like a normal child one or more years younger.

To verify that their scale reflected more than a lucky selection of test items, Binet and Simon tested their findings against teachers' judgments of the children's intelligence. To a high degree, their scale identified as most and least able the children identified by the teachers.

Turning their attention to the causes for school failure, Binet and Simon (1916) suggested that a child might lack either the "natural intelligence" (the "nature") needed to succeed in school or the cultural background (the "nurture") presupposed by the school:

> A very intelligent child may be deprived of instruction by circumstances foreign to his intelligence. He may have lived far from school; he may have had a long illness . . . or maybe some parents have preferred to keep their children at home, to have them rinse bottles, serve the customers of a shop, care for a sick relative or herd the sheep. In such cases . . . it suffices to pass lightly the results of tests which are of a notably scholastic character, and to attach the greatest importance to those which express the natural intelligence. (pp. 253–254)

This approach may appear intuitively plausible, but it contains a crucial ambiguity: nowhere do Binet and Simon offer a definition of "natural intelligence" that would allow them to separate tests of natural intelligence from tests of a "scholastic character." Instead of defining natural intelligence in a way that distinguishes it from cultural experience (which they refer to as a problem of "fearful complexity"), Binet and Simon (1916) contented themselves with pointing out that whatever natural intelligence is, it is not equivalent to success in school. In their view, not only is there more to intelligence than schooling; there is also more to schooling—and to life—than intelligence:

> Our examination of intelligence cannot take account of all these qualities, attention, will, regularity, continuity, docility, and courage which play so important a part in school work, and also in after-life; for life is not so much a conflict of intelligences as a combat of characters. (p. 256)

The Legacy of Binet and Simon

Many refinements of Binet and Simon's original tests have been made since the early days of intelligence testing, and a number of new tests have been devised. Some follow Binet and Simon's approach by including many different kinds of items in order to sample a broad range of possible abilities. These tests contain "subscales" that ask test takers to give the meaning of words, solve arithmetic word problems, assemble a jigsaw puzzle, complete a series of pictures, indicate which of a series of words doesn't belong with the others, and so on (see Figure 13.9). This broad sampling approach was followed by Lewis Terman, a professor at Stanford University, who modified the original Binet-Simon scales to create the Stanford-Binet Intelligence Scale (Terman, 1925), and David Wechsler, who devised tests for use with both adults and children (Wechsler, 1939). Other tests focus on only a single kind of ability. For example, the Peabody Picture Vocabulary Test seeks to measure vocabulary size by having children name items in pictures, and the Raven's Progressive Matrices are designed to assess reasoning about perceptual patterns (see Figure 13.10).

mental age (MA) The measure of intelligence proposed by Binet and Simon to describe the test performance of an average child of a given age.

Figure 13.9 Simulated items from the Wechsler Intelligence Scale for Children. (© 1948, 1974, 1991 by the Psychological Corporation. Reproduced by permission. All rights reserved.)

Information (30 items)

How many wings does a bird have?

What is steam made of?

Picture Completion (26 items)

What is the missing part of the picture?

Similarities (17 items)

In what way are a lion and a tiger alike?

In what way are an hour and a week alike?

Picture Arrangement (12 items made up of 3 to 5 picture cards each)

(The person is asked to arrange the cards so that the story of the woman weighing herself makes sense)

Comprehension (17 items)

What should you do if you see someone forget his book when he leaves a restaurant?

What is the advantage of keeping money in a bank?

Figure 13.10 A sample item from a widely used intelligence test designed to assess the ability to perceive patterns. Note that though these test items do not require elaborate verbal formulation, they assume that the test taker is familiar with two-dimensional representations of figures, a convention that does not exist in many cultures. (From Raven, 1962. Reprinted with permission of J. C. Raven Limited.)

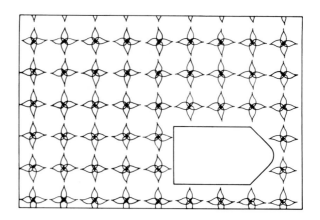

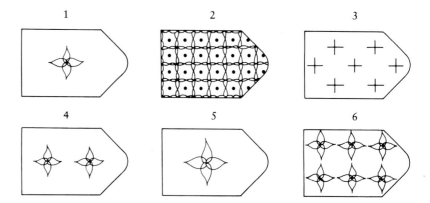

An important refinement in the way intelligence tests were thought about and applied was introduced by William Stern (1912), a German developmental psychologist. He suggested that intelligence levels should be measurable independent of the age of the child. He used the simple strategy of dividing children's mental age by their chronological age (CA) to obtain a measure of their intelligence with age factored out. Thus was born the unit of measurement that we use today, the **intelligence quotient (IQ):**

$$IQ = (MA/CA)100$$

The stratagem of multiplying the relative magnitude of MA/CA by 100 is simply a convenience. Calculation of IQ in this fashion ensures that when children are performing precisely as expected for their age, the resulting score will be 100; thus 100 is an "average IQ" by definition (see Figure 13.10). A 9-year-old child with a mental age of 10, for example, is assigned an IQ of 111 ($10/9 \times 100 = 111$), while a 10-year-old child with a mental age of 10 is assigned an IQ of 100 ($10/10 \times 100 = 100$).

In recent decades the method of calculating IQ has been refined to take into account the fact that mental development is more rapid early in life. Raw IQ scores do not, for example, take into account the fact that the difference between 4- and 5-year-olds' mental functioning is greater than the difference between 14- and 15-year-olds'. To overcome this difficulty, psychologists now use a score referred to as a "deviation IQ" (Wechsler, 1974). Calculation of IQ scores as deviations takes advantage of the statistical fact, illustrated in Figure 13.11, that the raw IQ scores calculated for a large sample form an approximately normal distribution. When psychologists base the IQ scores assigned to children on the differences between their raw scores and the standardized mean of 100, they have a statistical standard that is the same for all children of all ages. In this sense, IQ *cannot* be related to development because age has been standardized out of it.

intelligence quotient (IQ) The ratio of mental age to chronological age, calculated as IQ = (MA/CA)100. Calculation of IQ in this fashion ensures that when children are performing precisely as expected for their age, the resulting score will be 100; thus 100 is an "average IQ" by definition.

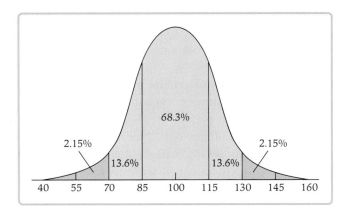

Figure 13.11 An idealized bell-shaped curve of the distribution of IQ scores. A bell-shaped curve is a distribution of scores on a graph in which the most frequent value, the mode, is in the center and the less frequent values are distributed symmetrically on either side. By definition, the modal IQ score is 100.

Despite various revisions, the logic of the procedures devised by Binet and Simon is still the basis of standardized intelligence tests. The key tasks in the creation of an IQ test are as follows:

1. To select a set of items that produces a range of performances among children at the same age level

2. To arrange the items in the order of difficulty, so that as children grow older, they are more likely to answer each successive item correctly

3. To make certain that the items are so designed that performance on the test corresponds to performance in school

Enduring Questions about Intelligence

The adoption and refinement of their testing methods by later generations of developmentalists represent only part of Binet and Simon's legacy. Equally important have been the questions they brought to the fore, three of which have dominated research on intelligence ever since. The first question focuses on the nature of intelligence itself: first, how is intelligence to be defined? Is it a general characteristic of a person's entire mental life, or is it a bundle of relatively specific abilities? Second is the nature–nurture question: What causes variations in intelligence test scores? Third, why do variations in IQ scores predict variations in school performance?

The Nature of Intelligence: General or Specific?

Although Binet and Simon (1916) were skeptical about the possibility of defining intelligence, they attempted to specify the quality of mind they were trying to test for:

> It seems to us that in intelligence there is a fundamental faculty, the alteration or lack of which is of the utmost importance for practical life. This faculty is judgment, otherwise called good sense, practical sense, initiative, the faculty of adapting oneself to circumstances. To judge well, to comprehend well, to reason well, these are the essential activities of intelligence. (p. 43)

By referring to intelligence as "a fundamental faculty" Binet and Simon signaled their belief that intelligence is a basic characteristic. Many others have followed this approach, although their views have varied on the question of exactly what kind of faculty intelligence is (Mackintosh, 1998). For example, Charles Spearman (1927), an English psychologist, demonstrated a significant correlation among individuals' scores on the different subscales and items used by Binet and Simon and by subsequent IQ tests. He argued that the fact that people who score high (or low) on one task tend to score high (or low) on the others indicated the existence of a general faculty, which he called *g*, for "general intelligence." He believed that *g* measures the ability to see relationships among objects, events, and ideas. Arthur Jensen (1999), who reignited interest in intelligence testing in the 1970s, lent support to the idea of *g*, arguing that neural processing speed is the "fundamental faculty" that underpins *g* and results in differences in intelligence.

However, many psychologists reject the idea of general intelligence. Spearman himself noted that although there was a positive correlation among scores on separate test items, the correlation was far from perfect. He suggested that *g* is supplemented by secondary, specific, abilities. L. L. Thurstone (1938), an American psychologist, subsequently argued that there are seven "primary mental abilities." He created a Primary Mental Abilities Test, which contained subscales for verbal ability, inductive reasoning, perceptual speed, facility with numbers, spatial relations, memory, and verbal fluency. Others have since proposed as many as 120 kinds of specific intelligences (Guilford, 1967).

Two approaches that depict intelligence in terms of distinctive capacities have been particularly influential. Howard Gardner (1999) has proposed a theory of *multiple intelligences*, each of which coincides with a different cognitive module and follows its own developmental path (see Table 13.3). For example, musical intelligence often appears at an early age; logical mathematical intelligence seems to peak in late adolescence and early adulthood; and the kind of spatial intelligence on which artists rely may reach its peak much later. Gardner argues that the expression of each kind of intelligence depends upon a combination of three factors: (1) innate biological brain structures; (2) the particular forms of intelligence that a given culture emphasizes; and (3) the extent to which a child is provided deliberate instruction in activities associated with the various forms of intelligence.

Robert Sternberg (1999) has proposed what he calls a "triarchic" theory of intelligence governed by three distinct principles. According to Sternberg, the three kinds of intelligence are:

1. *Analytic,* the abilities we use to analyze, judge, evaluate, compare, and contrast

2. *Creative,* the abilities we use to create, invent, discover, and imagine or suppose

3. *Practical,* the abilities to apply knowledge by putting it into practice

table 13.3

Gardner's Multiple Intelligences	
Kind of Intelligence	**Characteristics**
Linguistic	Special sensitivity to language, which allows one to choose precisely the right word or turn of phrase and to grasp new meanings easily
Musical	Sensitivity to pitch and tone, which allows one to detect and produce musical structure
Logical-mathematical	Ability to engage in abstract reasoning and manipulate symbols
Spatial	Ability to perceive relations among objects, to transform mentally what one sees, and to re-create visual images from memory
Bodily-kinesthetic	Ability to represent ideas in movement; characteristic of great dancers and mimes
Personal	Ability to gain access to one's own feelings and to understand the motivations of others
Social	Ability to understand the motives, feelings, and behaviors of other people

Source: Gardner, 1983.

Sternberg reports that an individual's performance level can vary from one kind of intelligence to another and argues that only analytic intelligence is measured by standard IQ tests.

The distinction between analytic and practical (everyday) intelligence has been made by a number of psychologists who link analytic intelligence with "academic" intelligence (Neisser, 1976; Sternberg et al., 2000). Several characteristics seem to distinguish the analytic problems demanded by schools from problems encountered in everyday settings:

- School problems are formulated for the learner by other people, whereas everyday problems require learners themselves to recognize or formulate problems.

- School problems generally have little or no intrinsic interest to the learners, whereas everyday tasks are intrinsically important to them.

- School problems are clearly defined, whereas everyday problems are generally poorly defined.

- School problems usually have a single correct answer that can be reached by a single method, whereas everyday problems have several acceptable solutions that can be reached by a variety of routes.

- School problems come with all the information needed to deal with them, whereas everyday problems require people to seek new information.

- School problems are detached from ordinary experience, whereas everyday problems are embedded in routine experiences.

What Explains Population Differences?

Along with their disagreements about what intelligence means and whether it is specific or general, developmentalists also disagree about why people's intelligence-test performances vary. The current debate dates back to the beginning of World War I, when Robert Yerkes proposed that all military recruits be given an intelligence test to determine their fitness to serve in military capacities. The testing also generated data about the intelligence of the U.S. male population as a whole (Yerkes, 1921). Approximately 1.75 million men were given IQ tests in groups—written tests for those who could read and write English, a picture-completion test for those who could not (see Figure 13.12). Never before had IQ tests been administered to such large groups of people at one time or to people for whom the language of the tests was not their native language.

Yerkes's research began a controversy that continues to the present time. Two results appeared to be particularly provocative. First, the average mental age of native-born Anglo Americans was assessed to be 13 years. Since, by the standards of the time, a mental age of 8 to 12 years was considered subnormal for an adult, it appeared that a substantial part of the Anglo population consisted of "morons." Second, there was a substantial difference between the scores obtained by recruits of European American and of African American origin. Overall, the average for recruits of European origin was a mental age of 13.7 years, whereas African Americans averaged slightly more than 10 years.

Several of the pioneer testers of intelligence interpreted such differences as the result of innate, immutable differences in natural intelligence ("nature"). According to this **innatist hypothesis of intelligence,** some people are born generally smarter than others, and no amount of training or variation in the environment can alter this fact. The generally lower test scores of members of ethnic minority groups and the poor (who often, but not always, are the same people) were widely interpreted to mean that such groups are innately and irrevocably inferior (Herrnstein & Murray, 1994).

innatist hypothesis of intelligence The hypothesis that some people are born generally smarter than others and no amount of training or variation in the environment can alter this fact.

Figure 13.12 Items from the picture-completion test used by Robert Yerkes and his colleagues to test recruits during World War I. Each picture is incomplete in some way; the task is to identify what is missing. (From Yerkes, 1921.)

During the 1930s and 1940s the general-intelligence, innatist position was balanced by an **environmental hypothesis of intelligence,** which asserted that intelligence is both specific and heavily dependent on experience. It was demonstrated, for example, that after people had moved from rural areas to the city, their intelligence test scores rose (Klineberg, 1935), and that when orphans were removed from very restricted early environments, their intelligence test scores improved markedly (see Chapter 7).

One of the most striking new lines of evidence for the environmental hypothesis of intelligence is the fact that worldwide there has been a steady increase in IQ test performance since testing began roughly 100 years ago (Flynn, 1999). Although the amount of improvement differs somewhat according to the kind of test that is used and the particular country in which it is administered, the general result for the 20 countries where such testing has been widely carried out for many decades indicates that IQ scores have been going up an average of 10 to 20 points for every generation. This means, for example, that the average African American adult in 1990 had a higher IQ than the average European American adult in 1940, and that the average English person in 1900 would score at the level currently considered to indicate mental retardation.

environmental hypothesis of intelligence The hypothesis that intelligence is both specific and heavily dependent on experience.

There is no clear consensus about what environmental factors are causing IQ scores to go up, but it is certain that the change must involve the environment, since rapid change in the genetic constitution of people all over the world has not taken place, but large changes in the environment have (Dickens & Flynn, 2001). As James Flynn points out, it is almost impossible to determine *precisely* how the environment contributes to the development of intelligence because all the possible causal factors are closely connected with each other, and all lead to changes that are in the same direction. The list of the possible causal factors ranges from improved nutrition and increasing years of education to an increase in the complexity of life, and even to the spread of interactive video games. (For extensive discussions of environmental factors that raise IQ scores, see Sternberg & Grigorenko, 2001.)

IQ Performance and School Success

At the present time, no responsible scholar believes that the variation in intelligence-test scores from person to person can be attributed entirely to either environmental or genetic factors. As we noted in Chapter 2, a number of large-scale studies report significant heritability of IQ test performance. At the same time, even those who believe that genetic variation plays a major role in variations in IQ readily acknowledge a significant role for the environment (Mackintosh, 1998).

As we pointed out in Chapter 2, the attempt to tease apart the specific gene–environment interactions that shape human beings is especially difficult in relation to traits like intelligence that are polygenic—that is, traits that are shaped by several or many genes acting in combination in a given set of environmental conditions. Thus, even when it has been possible to estimate the genetic contribution to a trait, little can be said about precisely which genes are interacting with the environment in what way. Efforts to separate the various influences of nature and nurture on the phenotype are further complicated by the fact that parents contribute both to their children's genetic constitution and to the environment in which their children grow up. And then there is the final knot in the parsing of gene–environment interaction: children actively shape their own environments in response to both genetic and environmental influences.

Attempts to understand how genetic and environmental factors combine to create the phenotypic behavior called "intelligence" face another, even greater difficulty. As we noted earlier, psychologists disagree profoundly about what, precisely, they are measuring when they administer an intelligence test. All they can say with any confidence is that these tests predict later school performance to a moderate degree. We can understand this problem better if we compare the gene–environment interactions that might determine intelligence with those that determine height.

To determine how environmental variation influences height, we might study sets of monozygotic (identical) and heterozygotic (fraternal) twins. Suppose that the twins to be studied were all born in Minnesota. Suppose further that some of the twins were separated, with one member of each pair being sent to live among the !Kung of the Kalahari Desert. The environments of Minnesota and the Kalahari Desert do not represent the most extreme variations compatible with human life, but they are sufficiently different in climate, diet, daily activities, and other relevant factors to represent a plausible test of the relative importance of genetic and environmental contributions to height.

If, within this environmental range, genetic factors dominate the expression of the phenotype (measured height), then we would expect two facts to emerge:

- The heights of identical twins should be roughly as much alike when the twins are raised far apart as when they are raised in the same family.

- The similarity between the heights of identical twins should be greater than the similarity between the heights of fraternal twins. In fact, the similarity of the heights of identical twins raised in very different environments might be greater than that of fraternal twins raised in the same environment.

Note that whether the children are in Minnesota or in the Kalahari Desert, we can be pretty confident about our measure of height. Whether we use a yardstick or a metric scale, we have a valid standard for measuring the twins' heights, regardless of the cultural environment in which we use it.

At first glance, IQ tests may appear to be standard measures logically similar to a yardstick. But this appearance is an illusion. Precisely because intelligence tests derive their validity from their correlation with academic achievement, they are rooted in the schooled society in which they are developed and bound to the graphic systems of representation that are central to all schooling. But these modes of representation are generally absent in nonliterate societies. To be administered to a !Kung child, every existing intelligence test would thus require some modification—and not just translation from English to !Kung. If, for example, one of the test questions asks how many fingers are on two hands, the testers might assume that the test could be adapted to !Kung with only minimal modification—but that assumption would be wrong. The number system used by the !Kung is not the same as that used by Minnesotans, and it plays a different role in their lives. In !Kung society, the relative importance of knowing the number of fingers on a hand is less important than knowing how to tie knots with those fingers.

When it comes to the tests that require interpretation of pictures or some form of written answer, even more serious difficulties arise. The !Kung have no tradition of either drawing or writing, and research with nonliterate peoples in several parts of the world and with young children in the United States shows that people without such experience do not automatically interpret two-dimensional pictures of objects as they would the objects themselves (Pick, 1997; Serpell, 2000). For them, interpreting the pictures requires additional mental work. As a result, tests that used pictures or required copying figures graphically would be inappropriate, as would any tests that depended on the ability to read. We thus cannot assume that an IQ test is like a yardstick, yielding equivalent measures in all cultural environments.

Various attempts have been made to create "culture-free" tests, but no generally satisfactory solution has yet been found: all tests of intelligence draw on a background of learning that is culture-specific (Cole, 1999; Serpell, 2000). The fact that intelligence cannot be tested independently of the culture that gives rise to the test greatly limits the conclusions that can be drawn from IQ testing in different social and cultural groups.

A number of studies have used comparisons of identical and fraternal twins to distinguish genetic from environmental contributions to intelligence, but those studies suffer an important limitation. According to the logic of twin studies, the twins' environments must differ enough for it to be possible to detect their differential contributions with the test. But if the environmental variation is very great, as in the case of a child transported from Minnesota to the Kalahari Desert, both twins' intelligence cannot be validly measured by the same test.

Despite these difficulties, a large literature has grown up around studies of twins' IQ test performance, along with studies of children of interracial marriages and of children adopted across racial and ethnic lines (reviewed in Mackintosh, 1998). Controversy continues to surround this work, but the following conclusions appear to be the most defensible.

1. Some part of individual differences in performance on IQ tests is attributable to inheritance. The degree of heritability is in dispute: some investigators claim that it is very high (Herrnstein & Murray, 1994); some claim that

it is very low or indeterminate (Bronfenbrenner & Ceci, 1993). Most researchers in the field estimate that perhaps 50 percent of the variation in test performance within population groups is controlled by genetic factors (Sternberg & Grigorenko, 2001).

2. There are significant differences among ethnic groups in their average IQ scores. Americans of European origin score about 15 points higher than African Americans, while Asian Americans score a few points higher than European Americans. Other ethnic groups in the United States, such as Native Americans and Hispanics, score at some intermediate level between African Americans and European Americans (Mackintosh, 1998).

3. There is no evidence that the average difference in scores among ethnic groups in the United States is the result of inherited differences in intelligence, however defined.

At first glance, the first two facts may appear to conflict with the third: if inheritance is responsible for a part of the differences between individuals in tested intelligence, and if there are differences between groups in tested intelligence, wouldn't it logically follow that the source of the differences among groups is the same as the source of the differences among individuals?

There are two answers to this question, one logical and the other empirical. The logical answer was provided many years ago by Richard Lewontin (1976). It is illustrated by an example from plant genetics (see Figure 13.13). Suppose that a farmer has two fields, one fertile and the other depleted of nutrients. He randomly takes corn seed from a bag containing several genetic varieties and plants it in the two fields. He cares for them equally. When the plants have reached maturity, he will discover that in each field some plants have grown taller than others. Since all the plants within a given field experienced roughly the same environment, their variation can be attributed to genetic factors. But the farmer will also discover variation between the fields: the plants grown in the fertile field will, on average, be taller than the plants grown in the nutrient-poor field. The explanation for this average difference in the heights of the plants lies in their environments, even though the degrees of heritability in the two fields may be equal.

This same argument applies to variations in test performance between ethnic and racial groups. Even though the heritability of intelligence within ethnic or racial groups may be the same, the average difference in performance between groups may still be caused not by their genetic endowment but by differences in the environments in which the children have been raised.

Lewontin's example also illustrates another important point about heritability that applies equally to IQ. As pointed out in Chapter 2, heritability is a *population* statistic: it applies to *groups,* not to individuals. If the heritability statistic for height in a field of corn or a set of IQ scores is .50, it does not mean that 50 percent of the height of each corn plant or each IQ score is determined by genetic factors. It means, rather, that 50 percent of the variation in height in the entire field of corn or of the variation in scores in the entire set of IQ scores can be traced to genetic differences. The other 50 percent of the variation must somehow be explained in terms of environmental factors.

Suggestive evidence concerning environmental factors that account for ethnic, racial, and class differences in tested IQ comes from a study of ethnicity and IQ among a large sample of 5-year-old African American and European American low-birthweight premature children, most of whom were from relatively poor families (Brooks-Gunn et al., 1996). The researchers studied these children from birth. In addition to giving the children IQ tests when they were 5 years old, they collected data on neighborhood and family poverty, the social structure of the families, maternal characteristics such as education and IQ, and the degree of cognitive stimulation in the home

Figure 13.13 The difference in the heights of the plants in each box reflects genetic variations in the seeds planted in it. The difference between the average heights of the plants in the two boxes is best explained by the quality of the soil, an environmental factor. Differences in IQ test scores of human groups are explained by the same principle. (Adapted from Gleitman, 1963.)

Poor soil

Seed

Fertile soil

Between-group differences (cause: the soils in which the plants were grown)

Within-group differences (cause: genetic variation in the seeds)

environment. In line with prior research, the African American children's IQ scores were significantly lower than the scores for the European American children (85 versus 103). When adjustments were made for ethnic-group differences in poverty, however, the difference in IQ score was reduced by over half. When the differences in the cognitive stimulation provided in the home environment were also controlled for statistically, the ethnic differential in IQ was reduced by another 28 percent. As the authors note, these results do not imply that heredity has no role in IQ, because they are not based on twin studies that allow estimates of heritability. They do show clearly, however, that when socioeconomic differences in the lives of African American and European American children are taken into account, IQ differences between the groups are all but eliminated.

Personal and Social Barriers to School Success

Evidence for strong family and community influences on children's school success confirms Binet and Simon's declaration that there is more to school success than can be captured by an intelligence test. In the following sections, we examine different factors related to the lack of school success among children whose tested intellectual aptitude is in the normal range. Some of these factors appear to be clearly related to the propensities of individual children; others implicate social factors.

Specific Learning Disabilities

Specific learning disabilities is a term used to refer to the academic difficulties of children who fare poorly in school despite normal IQ test performance. The U.S. government defines specific learning disabilities as follows:

> Children with special learning disabilities exhibit a disorder in one or more of the basic psychological processes involved in understanding or in using spoken or written language. These may be manifested in disorders of listening, thinking, talking, reading, writing, spelling, or arithmetic. They include conditions which have been referred to as perceptual handicaps, brain injury, minimal brain dysfunction, dyslexia, developmental aphasia, etc. They do not include learning problems which are due primarily to visual, hearing, or motor handicaps, to mental retardation, emotional disturbance, or to environmental disadvantage (U.S. Office of Education, 1977).

Identifying children with learning disabilities presents special challenges to developmentalists. Unlike physical disabilities such as blindness or deafness, specific learning disabilities are rarely apparent until children enter school. Even then, it is sometimes impossible to identify children with specific learning disabilities until they begin to use graphic symbols as a tool of communication.

Even greater difficulties in identifying learning-disabled children are reflected in the official definition of learning disability. There are so many factors included in the list of identifying criteria! What, for example, distinguishes a child who has a disorder of "listening, thinking, talking, reading, writing, spelling, or arithmetic" from a child who is retarded? How do we know if a specific disorder arises from features of the brain or the consequences of living in a "disadvantaged environment"? Disputes over how best to isolate the critical criteria for specific learning disabilities have made it difficult to estimate the number of children who suffer from them (Warner et al., 2002).

Although it has been repeatedly criticized as imprecise, the most widely used method to distinguish children with a specific learning disability from their classmates is to analyze their performance on both an intelligence test and on an academic-achievement test that covers many parts of the curriculum (D'Angiulli & Siegel, 2003). According to this approach, to qualify as specifically learning-disabled (and not retarded), a child should have an overall IQ test score in the normal range but a large

specific learning disabilities A term used to refer to the academic difficulties of children who fare poorly in school despite having normal intelligence.

discrepancy between different parts of the test (for example, a high score on a subtest that taps verbal ability but low scores on subtests that tap quantitative ability). The profile of the child's academic performance should correspond to the pattern in the IQ test. That is, we would expect a child with low verbal ability and high quantitative ability to be able to learn arithmetic normally but to have difficulty learning to read. This pattern of performance, called *dyslexia,* is the most frequent form of specific learning disability. Other children display a pattern of performance called *dyscalculia,* in which verbal IQ is high and quantitative IQ is low. Correspondingly, their ability to read is normal but they have great difficulty learning arithmetic. Yet another pattern characterizes *dysgraphia,* or special difficulties in learning to write, and so on. We focus our discussion on dyslexia, which is the most frequently encountered specific learning disability and the one about which the most is known.

Children who are considered dyslexic may have difficulty reading for several different reasons. Among the primary reasons is difficulty in phonological processing. As we saw earlier, phonological awarenesss—the ability to understand the rules that relate graphic symbols of the writing system (graphemes) to phonemes—is important for learning to read an alphabetic language (pp. 488–489). As might be suspected, severe delays in the development of phonological processing skills are closely associated with indicators of dyslexia (Hulme & Joshi, 1998).

The leading test of phonological processing skills employs *pseudowords,* pronounceable combinations of letters that are not real words but can be read by following the rules for converting graphemes into phonemes. "Shum," "laip," and "cigbet" are all pseudowords. Even though they are not real words (and hence their pronunciation could not have been learned before the experiment), these letter combinations can be read by anyone who knows the rules for decoding English words.

To demonstrate the link between deficient phonological processing and dyslexia, Linda Siegel and her colleagues have studied the ability to read pseudowords in normal and disabled readers (Gottardo et al., 1999; Siegel & Ryan, 1988). By 9 years of age, the normal readers were quite proficient in reading the pseudowords, but 14-year-old disabled readers were able to perform the pseudoword task no better than normal readers who were 7 years old. Even when disabled readers and normal readers were matched for reading level on a standardized test (and hence the disabled readers were considerably older than the normal readers), the disabled readers performed more poorly when asked to read pseudowords.

Current theories about the causes of dyslexia assume that the difficulties arise because of anomalies in brain development, but there is still uncertainty about how to link specific reading difficulties to specific abnormalities in specific areas of the brain. In line with evidence pinpointing difficulties in phonological processing, Paula Tallal and her colleagues report that children diagnosed with dyslexia differed from normal children in the parts of the brain that became active when the children were asked to identify rhyming and nonrhyming letter names (D–B versus M–T for example). These differences appeared in just those areas of the brain known to be specialized for language processing, supporting the idea that the difficulties of the dyslexic children had a specific brain location (see Figure 13.14) (Tallal, 2003).

Figure 13.14 Brain activation of normal and dyslexic readers. The children were given the task of providing a rhyming sound when they heard a letter pronounced. Comparison of the two groups shows significant differences in left-hemisphere activity (brightness of red indicates degree of activation) for normal and dyslexic children.

(a) While the normal children display heightened activity in both the visual cortex and Broca's area (specialized for language) the dyslexic readers do not (b). However, after intense training in discriminating between phonemes, the dyslexic children display activity in the same areas as do the normal children (c).

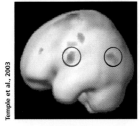

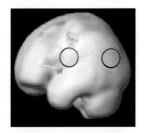

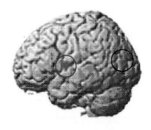

(a) Normal   **(b) Learning disabled**   **(c) Learning disabled; after training**

Temple et al., 2003

academic motivation The ability to try hard and persist at school tasks in the face of difficulties.

Remedial programs have been designed both for dyslexic children who have an oral-language deficit and for those who do not. For children whose language development is delayed, Tallal has created computer games that provide rich practice in making accurate discriminations between very brief, rapidly changing sounds. With as few as 16 hours of such therapy, children learned to recognize brief and rapidly changing speech sounds (Tallal et al., 1998) (Figure 13.14c). Remedial programs for dyslexic children whose oral language is not delayed generally focus on fostering phonemic awareness by using rhyming and word-game techniques, such as those described on p. 489, which have been shown to promote reading acquisition.

Motivation to Learn

As we noted earlier, a distinctive aspect of formal education is that children are expected to pay attention and to try hard even though the material they are asked to learn may be difficult for them to master and hold little interest for them. They must also learn to cope with the fact that they will not always be successful in their schoolwork. In such circumstances, a significant proportion of children lose their **academic motivation**—the ability to try hard and persist at school tasks in the face of difficulties.

Confronted with this problem, developmental researchers have been studying the question of why some children are motivated to try hard in school in the face of difficulties and even failure, while others give up when they encounter difficulties and lose faith in their own abilities (Linnenbrink & Pintrich, 2003; Wigfield & Eccles, 2001).

Researchers who focus on the problem of motivation distinguish between two ways in which children approach school tasks (Anderman, Austin, & Johnson, 2001): *mastery orientation,* in which children are motivated to learn, to try hard, and to improve; and *performance orientation,* in which children are motivated by their level of performance, ability, and incentives for trying.

Mastery and performance orientations have consistently been associated with two different outcomes in terms of children's academic success. Children who adopt a mastery orientation are more likely to succeed in the long run, use more advanced learning strategies, and relate what they are trying to accomplish at the moment to relevant prior knowledge. Even if these children have just done poorly or failed at a task, they remain optimistic and tell themselves, "I can do it if I try harder next time." As a result of this kind of thinking, they tend to persist in the face of difficulties and to look for challenges similar to those they are struggling with. Over time, this kind of motivational pattern allows these children to improve their academic performance. By contrast, children who adopt a *performance orientation* show mixed results. When they fail at a task, they are more likely to tell themselves, "I can't do that," and they may give up trying altogether. When they encounter similar tasks in the future, they tend to avoid them.

It might be thought that more able students would typically display the mastery-oriented pattern and that less able students would be the ones to adopt a performance orientation so that they readily give up in the face of difficulty and avoid challenges. However, the evidence concerning motivational orientation and school achievement is mixed. Carol Dweck and her colleagues report that these two patterns were not related to children's IQ scores or their academic achievement. She reports that many able students give up in the face of difficulty and many weaker students show a mastery orientation (Dweck, 1999). But a large-scale review of many recent studies reports that mastery motivation does promote cognitive development (Jennings & Dietz, 2003).

This student seems to be the personification of academic motivation: if she happens to give an incorrect answer this time, she won't give up and is likely to work harder to get it right the next time.

Mary Kate Denny/Photo Edit/Picture Quest

In an extensive series of studies, Dweck has related these different motivational patterns to children's conceptions of ability (Dweck, 2001). She reports that even $2\frac{1}{2}$ year-olds are sensitive to success or failure in their problem-solving attempts and are vulnerable to becoming discouraged and unmotivated. But it is not until the onset of formal schooling that children are directly compared with one another in a public manner through grading practices. Then the notion of ability becomes a distinctive category that children use to evaluate themselves and their relationship to academic challenges.

Children's conceptions of ability continue to change during the elementary school years. They are less likely to engage in wishful thinking about what problems they can and cannot solve, and increasingly see ability as a fixed characteristic of people.

Around the age of 12, when children make the transition from elementary to middle school, North American children begin to articulate theories about what it means to "be intelligent." Some children adopt an *entity model* of intelligence. They see intelligence as a fixed quality that each person has a certain amount of. Other children, by contrast, have an *incremental model* of intelligence. They see intelligence as something that can grow as one learns and has new experiences.

Middle-school children's theories about intelligence also include ideas about how effort is related to outcome. Some children believe that academic success depends primarily on ability, which they believe to be a fixed category; others believe that academic success depends on effort, and that expending effort can lead to increased intelligence.

Dweck has found that children who adopt an entity model of intelligence are also likely to adopt a performance orientation to problems they encounter. They believe that they fail because they lack ability and that nothing they can do will change this. Because they view intelligence as a fixed entity, they try to avoid situations that put them at risk for failure, and feel hopeless when they are confronted with challenging tasks. Children who develop an incremental pattern adopt precisely the opposite interpretation of challenging situations because they believe that if they apply themselves and try hard enough, they will succeed and become more intelligent. When these children fail, their response is to try harder the next time. As children encounter the more challenging environment of middle school, their particular ways of interpreting and responding to failure cause notable achievement gaps between students who adopt one or other of the basic motivational patterns and beliefs about ability.

Findings such as these challenge developmentalists to devise ways to assist children who develop a helpless motivational pattern. One approach has been to train teachers to provide feedback to students in ways that foster a mastery orientation. Another has been to retrain the children themselves so that they attribute their failures to a lack of effort rather than a lack of ability (Dweck, 1999).

Mismatches between Home and School Cultures

Each of the factors discussed so far applies to the school achievement of children from all family backgrounds. We now shift our focus away from universal psychological processes "in the child" to cultural and economic circumstances that structure children's experience of schooling. A number of general cultural factors have been identified, some focusing on broad cultural patterns, some focused on language, and some focused at the junction between language and culture as they intertwine in everyday interactions. (For a broad cross-national look at schooling, see the box on page 520, "Comparing Mathematics Instruction across Cultures"; for a Web page of a professional organization that focuses on this issue, see http://www. lab.brown.edu/tdl/index.shtml.)

Comparing Mathematics Instruction across Cultures

Typical classrooms and school curricula appear similar in many respects whether they are found in crowded cities such as New York and Tokyo or rural villages in West Africa and Australia. Yet many studies of classroom life and academic performance in different societies reveal that despite surface similarities, both the process and the products of schooling vary markedly from one culture to the next (Serpell & Hatano, 1997).

In the classrooms of rural Liberia, for example, children are taught basic reading, writing, and arithmetic through rote instruction (Cole et al., 1971). A favorite method used by Liberian teachers is to have the entire class recite lessons in unison, with little attention devoted to the meaning of the recitation. When John Gay and Michael Cole (1967) asked a Liberian student questions about arithmetic, he launched into a singsong patter ("La lala lala, la lala lala, la lala lala"). Asked what he was doing, he answered that he was adding numbers, but that so far he had learned only the tune, not the words. Not surprisingly, the academic achievement of the typical Liberian child is low by U.S. standards.

But the achievement of American schoolchildren is itself low in comparison with that of children in many other industrialized societies (Hiebert et al., 2003). The results presented for the performance of eighth-grade students on mathematics tests are representative of the kinds of differences found in this research (see figure).

Findings such as these have spurred attempts to identify the factors responsible for variations in children's achievement from one society to the next. A series of studies initiated by psychologist Harold Stevenson in the 1980s has provided a good deal of insight into the ways in which cultural differences in elementary school education lead to variations in children's performance (Stevenson & Stigler, 1992; Stigler, Gallimore, & Hiebert, 2000). These studies used videotapes of actual classroom lessons in three countries—

Average mathematics scores from 8th graders in seven countries from different parts of the world. (Adapted from National Center for Educational Statistics, 1999.)

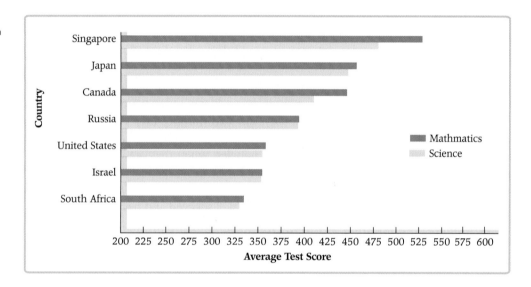

Cultural Styles

A number of scholars have proposed that every culture can be described in terms of its own particular worldview, a dominant way of thinking about and relating to the world that arises from a people's common historical experience. This dominant pattern of interpreting events is called a **cultural style** (Greenfield, Keller, Fuligni, & Maynard, 2003; Kagitçabasi, 1997). Cultural styles can be viewed on a continuum in terms of their emphasis on the importance of the individual versus the group. Some cultures, like the dominant culture in the United States, for example, emphasize independence and the importance of the individual, while others, like traditional Latin American cultures, for example, place more emphasis on interdependence and the importance of the individual's relations to others.

Patricia Greenfield and her colleagues have proposed that the cultural practices of standard American classrooms favor children who come from home cultures that emphasize independence, with the goal of socializing children to become autonomous individuals who enter into social relations by personal choice (an *individualistic* orientation). Correspondingly, they believe that the standard culture of

cultural style A dominant way of thinking about and relating to the world that arises from a people's common historical experience.

the United States, Japan, and Taiwan—to discover how differences in modes of instruction were related to overall test performance (the list of participating countries has now swelled to 38). Several results stood out when comparing the ways classroom behaviors differed among the three countries.

First, the researchers found that the two factors in which American and Asian schooling differed the most were the amount of time spent in the teaching and learning of mathematics and the social organization of classroom interactions. Asian children attended school more days each year than did the American children (240 days versus 180). At the fifth-grade level, Japanese children went to school 44 hours a week; Chinese students, 37 hours a week; and American children, 30 hours a week. On each school day the two Asian groups spent as much time on mathematics as they did on reading and writing, but the American group spent almost three times as much on language arts. As James Stigler and Michelle Perry (1990, p. 336) note, the disparity in the sheer number of hours spent on mathematics lessons was large enough to "go a long way toward explaining the differences in mathematics achievement."

However, the differences in the Asian and American approaches to education are not restricted simply to gross amounts of time spent on mathematics: Asian classrooms are organized quite differently from American classrooms. By and large, classrooms in the two Asian countries are centrally organized, with the teacher instructing the whole class at once. The American classrooms are generally more decentralized; often the teacher devotes attention to one group at a time while the other children work independently at their seats. Two important differences in the quality of teacher–student interactions are correlated with these differences in classroom organization. First, American children spend a good deal of time being instructed by no one. This might not make much difference if the children were absorbed by their workbooks and truly working independently. But here another difference in students' behavior comes into play: American children do not use their independent study time well, spending almost half of it out of their seats or engaged in inappropriate behavior such as gossiping with friends or causing mischief. Asian children spend far more time attending to schoolwork than their American counterparts do.

There are also differences in the content of the lessons. First, the Japanese teachers devote twice as much instruction time to helping children reflect on and analyze mathematics problems as the Chinese and American teachers do. Second, both the Chinese and Japanese teachers are more likely than their American counterparts to have students use concrete manipulable objects in working out math problems and to provide a meaningful context for the mathematics problems they teach. Third, the Asian teachers stress the connections between problems encountered at different points in the lesson, or even between problems in one lesson and another, giving greater coherence to their teaching.

In the most recent studies, with many more countries participating, the picture has become more complex (Stigler & Gallimore, 2000). For example, while eighth-grade students in Hong Kong and Japan received similar overall mathematics scores, they were not taught in the same way. In Hong Kong, students spent 84 percent of their time practicing mathematical procedures and only 13 percent of their time making connections to other mathematical ideas. Japanese teachers focused on making mathematical connections 54 percent of the time, and only 41 percent of their teaching was directed at procedures. Performance at the lower end of the scale, such as that in the Netherlands and the United States, also shows that similar overall scores are achieved by different means. The teachers in the Netherlands were far more likely than their U.S. counterparts to use problems that make connections to everyday experiences of children.

Such results have led Stigler and his colleagues to caution against the notion that there is one right way to organize effective instruction. They argue that classroom learning is a cultural activity in which many different factors are always at work. Following the advice of sociologist Merry White (1987), they remind us that cross-cultural research does not provide a blueprint for improving the education of children. Rather, it provides a mirror that sharpens our awareness of our own cultural practices and provides some hints about how they might be changed to make teaching and learning more effective.

American schools is disadvantageous to children from cultures that emphasize interdependence, with the goal of socializing children to become adults who place a strong value on social networks, especially the family, and who downplay personal achievement (a *collectivist orientation*). (Table 13.4 summarizes the differences between independent and interdependent cultural styles.) To help bridge what they see as a gap between the cultural beliefs of the ordinary American classroom and the beliefs of children from homes that privilege interdependence, Greenfield and her colleagues have conducted special training programs that sensitize teachers to work effectively with children and their families from societies with an interdependent orientation (Turnbull, Rothstein-Fisch, Greenfield, & Quiroz, 2001).

Other researchers have found that even if children come from families that adopt an interdependent cultural model that conflicts with the cultural norms of the classroom, the family can play a strong positive role in the success of their children's schooling. For example, Nathan

These Japanese children are studying for an examination. Their dedication is indicated by the fact that this study session is on New Year's Eve.

©Hashimoto Noboru/Corbis Sygma

table 13.4

Cultural Styles: Independent (Individualist) versus Interdependent (Collectivist)	
Individualist	**Collectivist**
Emotional detachment from in-group	Self-defined in-group terms
Personal goals have primacy over in-group goals	Behavior regulated by in-group norms
Behavior regulated by attitudes and cost-benefit analysis	Hierarchy and harmony within in-group
Confrontation is OK	In-group is seen as homogeneous
Source: Triandis et al., 1990.	Strong in-group–out-group distinctions

Caplan and his colleagues studied the children of refugees who fled to the United States from Vietnam, Cambodia, and Laos during the 1970s and 1980s. These children, whose home cultures are characterized by an interdependent cultural model, have been conspicuously successful in educational pursuits (Caplan, Choy, & Whitmore, 1991). Although they had lost from one to three years of formal education in refugee camps, and most were unable to speak English when they entered school in the United States, eight out of ten students surveyed had a B average or better within 3 to 6 years. Almost half received A's in mathematics. These achievements are all the more noteworthy because they were attained in schools in low-income, inner-city areas traditionally associated with fewer resources and less motivated, more disruptive students.

In trying to account for the spectacular success of these immigrants, Caplan and his colleagues found the parents' involvement with their children to be crucial. Almost half of the parents surveyed said that they read to their children, many in their native language. Apparently, the parents' poor knowledge of English had less effect on their children's school performance than did the positive emotional associations of being read to and the cultural wisdom they shared as they read the stories. The parents demonstrated their commitment to education not only by owning books and reading to their children but also by requiring their children to do extensive homework. Parents reported that their children devoted an average of almost 3 hours of every weekday evening to homework, twice the average for native-born American children.

Independence–interdependence is only one dimension used to define cultural styles. According to Wade Boykin, African American children inherit a rich tradition of using expressive movement as a part of their everyday communicative behavior. Boykin believes that when they arrive in classrooms that emphasize sitting quietly while learning, their cultural heritage has to be suppressed. He conducted experiments with African American children in which some of the children were presented stories to remember and problems to solve under conditions that allowed them to dance, run, and jump, while other children were presented the same problems under conditions where they had to be still or, at most, move in a "school-like" manner. The children allowed to express themselves with high levels of movement significantly outperformed their counterparts, supporting Boykin's idea about the importance of this cultural style for the children's learning (Boykin & Cunningham, 2001).

Taken together, these different studies strongly implicate home cultural values and modes of behavior as important factors in children's school success. But they also indicate that there is no "one right way" to incorporate such differences into classroom practices.

The Structures and Purposes of Language Use

Even when people speak the same language, or a dialect of the same language, it does not mean that they use their language in the same way. Language is used in schools in rather distinctive ways, as we have seen. Many of the ways children experience oral and written language in the home differ not only from language practices at school but from other homes within the same community.

Shirley Heath (1983) conducted an ethnographic study of three populations of children and their families over a period of years in order to gain insight into how oral and written language used in the home differs from language practices associated with school success. The populations she studied, all from the same geographical locale, included the families of a group of European American schoolteachers, a group of European American textile workers, and a group of African Americans engaged in farming and textile jobs.

Conducting observations both in people's homes and in their children's classrooms, Heath found that the families of European American teachers experienced the least mismatch with the school. As we have already seen, "instructional discourse" involving known-answer questions is a prominent feature of classrooms, and Heath found that it also appeared in about half of the conversations she recorded in the teachers' homes. In addition, the teachers involved their children in labeling objects, naming letters, and reading. When reading with their children, they went well beyond the text itself to make clear the relationships between what was in the book and other experiences the child might have had or might have in the future. In a sense, the teachers were being teachers at home as well as at school. As a result, their children did well in school.

The families of European American textile workers, like the teachers, gave their children practice in naming the letters of the alphabet, labeling objects, and learning to answer such questions as "What is that?" They also taught them to listen attentively while a story was being read. But, unlike the teachers, these parents encouraged their children to look for the moral of the stories they were read and they discouraged them from imaginatively linking the stories to life. Children from these working-class European American homes generally did well in the early grades of school when their habits of focusing on the literal meaning of a text fit the task, but in the higher grades, where it becomes necessary to draw novel inferences from complex texts, their performance fell. Overall, these children did not do well in school.

A third pattern of language use was characteristic in the homes of the African American children. These children were rarely asked known-answer questions about some fact ("What color is your jacket?"). Rather, adults most often asked children questions that encouraged them to think about similarities across situations related to the children's own experience ("Do you think you can get along with your cousin on this visit?"). Such questions often served as the pretext for discussing some interesting event and helped children think about their shifting roles and responsibilities in different situations. Heath also documented many inventive uses of language in teasing and storytelling. But the children never heard language used in the ways expected of them at school, and they, too, generally did not perform well. Similar findings have been reported for Latino children (Vasquez, 2002).

These patterns are perfectly understandable in terms of local cultural practices. At the same time, it is the goal of teachers to be successful with all children. So the question becomes one of how to design educational interventions to make it possible for everyone to learn effectively.

Schooling in a Second Language

For some parts of the U.S. population, especially recent immigrants, school-going children may have little or no command of the local language of official life, including the language of the school. Unless something is done quickly to

Research has shown that parents' involvement in their children's education, including reading to them regularly and discussing what is being read, can contribute significantly to their school-children's achievement.

Laura Dwight/Omni-Photo/Communications

solve the problems these children face because they cannot speak English, their life chances are reduced through school failure.

In a landmark decision in 1974, the U.S. Supreme Court recognized the seriousness of this situation by declaring that children who arrive at school unable to speak or understand English must be given special help to deal with the challenges they face. According to the Court's ruling, such special help will be considered adequate only if it prevents children from being foreclosed from meaningful education (*Lau* v. *Nichols,* 1974, p. 26). Since the ruling, local school districts have spent a great deal of money trying to meet its requirements. This effort has been complicated by the fact that the Court did not specify what form the "special help" should take, leaving the matter up to the states and local school districts.

Further complicating efforts to develop English proficiency in non-English-speaking children and promote their scholastic achievement are sharp divisions of opinion regarding how these goals should be achieved (Krashen, 1999; Ovando & McLaren, 2000). On one side of the debate are those who believe that children should be immersed in the English language—hearing and speaking English exclusively—so that they can quickly achieve the competence necessary to participate in all aspects of the curriculum. Educators who favor this view believe that time spent communicating in the child's native language only postpones the day when the child will be fluent in English. On the other side are those who believe that providing the children with a firm grounding in basic literacy and numeracy skills in the child's home language promotes later academic achievement in a broad variety of courses taught in English (see Augusta & Hakuta, 1998).

Research on bilingualism and education is clouded by the difficulty of conducting experiments in which appropriate versions of the competing strategies can be properly pitted against each other. It is simply not possible to set up a true experiment, since that would require controlling the curricula and language policy of a group of schools and randomly assigning children to those schools. No community would permit such procedures. Consequently, to test their hypotheses about the efficacy of bilingual education, researchers have had to make do with "quasi-experiments" that use spontaneously occurring differences in language programs. For example, some school districts have adopted an English-only policy; other districts provide instruction to the children in their home language for 2 or 3 years before moving them to English-based instruction; and still others have made their schools bilingual, with everyone receiving half their instruction in their home language—which is often Spanish—and half their instruction in English (Augusta & Hakuta, 1998; Cloud et al., 2000).

Learning other languages has become an important part of school curricula in many countries.

Comparisons of performance in these schools are open to doubt because they cannot guarantee that the programs being compared differ only in the variable being studied—the use of English-only versus home-language-first instruction, for example. Since the comparisons are often made across different schools in different parts of a town or even in different towns, the schools usually vary on such relevant characteristics as the social class of the students, the training and enthusiasm of the teachers, and the resources available for teaching. Such variations have been shown to have a significant impact on academic achievement no matter what language approach was being used.

As a result of these difficulties in evaluating competing theories of effective bilingual education, controversy remains. Christine Rossell and Keith Baker, for example, published a review of 72 studies comparing English-only programs versus bilingual programs designed to ease children into full English use after 3 or 4 years (Rossell & Baker, 1996). They concluded that there is no evidence that bilingual programs are superior to immersion in English. This conclusion was immediately contested by Stephen Krashen (1996), who argued that when one considered only those studies that had adequate bases for comparison and reliable quantitative data, the evidence showed that bilingual programs are more effective than immersion programs. This same conclusion was reached by a panel of the National Research Council (Augusta & Hakuta, 1998).

Krashen based his conclusion on an extensive review of the literature, which suggested that four features lead to the creation of an effective environment for helping immigrant children to learn English:

1. Easy-to-understand lessons in English, using techniques that have been shown useful in teaching English as a second language

2. Teachers who have command of their subject matter and who can teach in the child's native language when appropriate

3. Literacy development in the child's native language

4. Continued development in the child's native language, for cognitive and economic advantages

As a starting point for effective bilingual education, this approach requires that teachers take seriously children's cultural contexts as they are embodied in the language, values, and practices of their homes.

An important factor not mentioned by Krashen is the need to give the process of acquiring the second language enough time. This point is emphasized by linguist Kenji Hakuta, who reports that although minority-language children generally become reasonably fluent in colloquial English within 2 or 3 years of starting school in the United States, they need as many as 4 to 5 years to master the language skills needed for academic success (Hakuta, 1999).

A major obstacle to applying the lessons from the research on bilingual education successfully is that there are far too few qualified bilingual teachers to teach the many languages represented by the school-aged population of the United States. In California, for example, English was a second language for 37 percent of the children (more than 1.5 million) attending school in 2001–2002; and in the lower grades, the percentage was considerably higher (California Department of Education, 2003). If the current research is valid, such a situation certainly seems to call for bilingual instruction, but that solution is difficult to implement in some areas because the schools have to contend with several of the more than 50 languages spoken by California schoolchildren.

Culturally Responsive Classroom Strategies

The evidence presented in this chapter should leave no doubt that schools can be problematic contexts for children whose home culture differs significantly from that of the school. The emergence of increasingly multicultural schools in the United States has led several developmentalists who focus on education to propose classroom procedures that are responsive to cultural variation as a means of enhancing children's performance (Lee, 2001).

An early and influential example of the culturally responsive approach occurred in a classroom of students from the Odawa Indian tribe in Canada taught by an expert Odawa teacher (Erickson & Mohatt, 1982). On the surface, the teacher appeared to adhere to a recitation-script approach, talking for most of the lessons, asking many known-answer questions, and limiting the students' role to answering her questions. But she did so in a special way consistent with the language use and cultural patterns employed in Odawa homes. When she was giving instruction, she organized students into small groups instead of rows, approximating the way the children interacted in groups at home. She generally addressed the children as a group and did not single out individual children. Instead of saying "good" when she was giving the children feedback on their responses to her questions, she signaled her acceptance of students' answers by moving on to the next question. She never reprimanded students in public, but she did praise them in public, in accordance with Odawa norms against public criticism. This culture-sensitive way of implementing classroom lessons worked well to improve children's academic performance.

Carol Lee drew upon African American high school students' familiarity with, and appreciation of, the linguistic form called *signifying* (Lee, 1995). Within the African American community, to signify means to speak in a manner that uses innuendo and words with double meanings, to play with the sounds and meanings of words, and to be quick-witted and funny, all at the same time.

According to Lee, African American adolescents use signifying for a wide variety of speech functions including:

- To challenge someone in a verbal dual, but remain friendly
- To persuade someone by driving home a message in a distinctive way
- To criticize someone in a way that is difficult to pin down

Lee began by presenting students examples of signifying dialogues of the sort they were familiar with and getting the students to analyze and explain how each example of signifying worked to achieve a specific goal. Then she had them read stories and novels by African American writers that included signifying and asked them to apply the rules, which they knew intuitively, to the interpretation of complex inferential questions from the literary texts.

When Lee compared the performance of students who engaged in this kind of culturally responsive instruction with students who took the regular literature course, they demonstrated a significantly higher level of literary understanding and active engagement with the problem of literary interpretation.

These examples could be multiplied to encompass a wide variety of ethnic and social-class groups—wide enough to make a convincing case that it is possible to organize effective contexts for education by taking into account local variations in

Flag-raising ceremony at a small village school in Papua New Guinea.

Courtesy of Geoffrey Saxe

culture and social class (Tharp & Yamauchi, 2000). At the same time, it needs to be recognized that there is no single "right way" to connect classroom instruction to home culture. Research on this topic makes it clear that a wide variety of specific classroom strategies can successfully engage students from the vast variety of backgrounds characteristic of American society. However, culturally specific strategies are likely to be applicable only when there is a culturally homogeneous classroom (Gallego & Cole, 2000).

Neighborhoods Matter

Given the fact that neighborhoods in most cities around the world are to a greater or lesser degree segregated according to socioeconomic status (as well as ethnicity), it seems only reasonable to expect that the quality of the neighborhood from which children come should affect their academic achievement. Not only do poor neighborhoods make it more likely that children will be exposed to poisons in their environment, which have been shown to harm their cognitive development, but they are also exposed to violence, which increases the likelihood of psychiatric disorders. To make matters more complicated, financing for schools in poor neighborhoods is often inadequate, and such schools are disproportionately assigned inexperienced teachers because experienced teachers find such schools unpleasant to work in (Powers, 2003).

A remarkable study carried out in Chicago demonstrates the impact of changing neighborhoods on children's academic performance. The study was undertaken because a court in Chicago ruled that families living in high-rise housing projects, where poverty and crime are pervasive, should be allowed to move to new, private housing. The tenants in these housing projects were almost all African American. Almost 4000 families volunteered for the program, which permitted them to move either to predominantly working-class European American neighborhoods within urban Chicago or to predominantly middle-class Chicago suburbs. While the families had the choice to move or stay in their current housing, those who moved did not get to choose which of the two alternative kinds of neighborhoods they would move to. They were assigned to city or suburban locations according to which kind of housing became available, producing a "natural experiment" for studying the impact of neighborhoods on academic achievement. The researchers compared the academic performance of the children from the families that had moved to the suburbs with the performance of those who had changed neighborhoods but remained in an urban environment. They found a marked increase in several indicators of academic achievement for the suburban children. Their dropout rates decreased during high school and their college attendance markedly increased (Rubinowitz et al., 2000).

Overall, the evidence supports the gloomy conclusion that children raised in poor neighborhoods face extremely difficult tasks in seeking to get an education that could prepare them for jobs that would allow them to escape the circumstances of their birth. While the provision of excellent schooling can make some difference in helping children to overcome the handicaps of poverty and social exclusion, "equal opportunity" remains an ideal to be struggled for rather than a reality for millions of American children.

Outside the School

As important as schooling is to middle childhood, it is not the only context beyond the family that influences children. Especially important is the time spent in new kinds of activities with friends and one's peer group. On weekday afternoons and evenings, on weekends and holidays, elementary-school-age children are likely to be found among other children their own age, engaged in activities of their own choosing. Some of these settings have an adult or two present, but in many cases, adults are not on the scene.

Participation in these peer groups provides a kind of preparation for adult life that is quite different from that organized by adults in classrooms or at home. At the same time, peer-group experiences influence life at home and in school. Consequently, a full understanding of the nature of middle childhood requires investigation of peer contexts as well, so we turn to this important topic in Chapter 14.

SUMMARY

- School is a specialized socialization environment that is specific to certain societies and historical eras.

The Contexts of Learning

- Traditional hunter-gatherer and agricultural societies achieve the goals of education in the context of everyday activities. As societies become more complex, adults pay increasing attention to instructing children in the skills they will need as adults themselves by organizing apprenticeships.

- Schooling arose coincidentally with the emergence of city-states as a means of training large numbers of scribes to keep the records on which complex societies depend.

- Formal education in schools differs from traditional training, such as apprenticeship, in the motives for learning as well as in the social relations, the social organization, and the medium of instruction.

Literacy and Schooling in Modern Times

- Mastery of two basic symbol systems, written language and mathematics, is essential to the process of schooling.

- When schooling was extended to large segments of the population in industrialized countries in the nineteenth century, most students received "mass education," which focused on the basics of literacy and numeracy, while children of the economic and professional elites received a "liberal education," which included complex uses of literacy and numeracy.

- Reading an alphabetic language is a complex cognitive skill in which information the reader obtains by learning the correspondences between letters and sounds must be coordinated with higher-order information about the content of the text.

- Researchers are divided in their ideas about how reading should be taught.

  1. Those who favor the code-first approach believe that children should first be taught to decode fluently before instruction is concentrated on comprehension.

  2. Those who favor the comprehension-first approach believe that from the outset decoding should be learned in the context of reading for meaning.

- Learning mathematics in school requires students to acquire and coordinate three kinds of knowledge:

  1. Conceptual knowledge, or the understanding of mathematical principles

  2. Procedural knowledge, or the ability to carry out sequences of actions to solve a problem

  3. Utilization knowledge, or the knowledge of when to apply particular procedures

- Theories of how best to teach both reading and mathematics vary between two extremes, one emphasizing the need for drill and practice, the other emphasizing the centrality of conceptual understanding. Most current teaching techniques attempt to balance drill with explanation.

- Classroom instruction occurs in settings characterized by specialized modes of social interaction and a special form of language use called instructional discourse.

  1. Traditional modes of classroom discourse follow a recitation script in which teachers ask known-answer questions and provide direct feedback on the basis of children's answers.

  2. A great emphasis is placed on the use of correct linguistic forms in classroom discourse organized around a recitation script.

  3. Alternative forms of classroom organization emphasize the role of small-group interaction and the use of tasks designed to be meaningful to the children.

Studying the Cognitive Consequences of Schooling

- Research comparing the cognitive performances of schooled and unschooled children reveals that formal schooling in middle childhood enhances the development of certain cognitive skills, including logical problem solving, memory, and metacognition.

- There is no evidence that schooling enhances cognitive development in general.

- General effects of schooling can be seen in subsequent generations. Children whose mothers have been to school are healthier and achieve better in school than peers whose mothers have not attended school.

Aptitude for Schooling

- Tests of aptitude for schooling first appeared when education was extended to the population at large. The earliest tests were designed to identify children who needed special support to succeed in school.

- Binet and Simon's key innovation in constructing their test of school aptitude was to sort test items according to the age at which children could typically cope with them, thus producing a scale of "mental age."

- The aptitude measure called IQ represents a child's mental age (as determined by the age at which average children answer each test item correctly) divided by chronological age, with the result multiplied by 100 (a number arbitrarily chosen to represent the average IQ): $IQ = (MA/CA)100$.

- IQ test scores have been found to be correlated significantly with later school success.

- An important unresolved question about intelligence tests is the degree to which the aptitudes they tap are general across all domains of human activity or are closely related to specialized activities, such as those involved in schooling and music.

- Persistent class, racial, and ethnic differences in IQ test performance have inspired fierce debates about whether such differences are the result of genetic or environmental factors.

- Modern research comparing the IQs of identical and fraternal twins indicates that IQ has a genetic component that accounts for perhaps 50 percent of the variation in test performance within groups.

- Large increases in IQ test scores of children around the world during the twentieth century indicate that average differences in IQ scores among groups are strongly influenced by environmental factors.

Personal and Social Barriers to School Success

- A variety of factors other than IQ have been shown to be related to school success.

  1. Some children who have normal tested intelligence are believed to suffer disabilities in school learning in areas such as reading and arithmetic.

  2. Children develop different responses to failure that help or hinder their learning and performance in school.

  3. Children's school achievement is hindered when patterns of interaction and language use in the family do not match those of the school.

  4. When mismatches are recognized, school curricula can be modified to take advantage of family interaction patterns.

  5. Severe poverty and life in high-crime neighborhoods negatively influence children's preparation for, and ability to succeed at, formal education

Key Terms

academic motivation, p. 518

apprenticeship, p. 485

conceptual knowledge, p. 491

cultural style, p. 520

decoding, p. 488

education, p. 484

environmental hypothesis of intelligence, p. 512

initiation-reply-feedback sequence, p. 494

innatist hypothesis of intelligence, p. 511

instructional discourse, p. 494

intelligence quotient (IQ), p. 508

mental age (MA), p. 507

phonemic awareness, p. 488

procedural knowledge, p. 491

reciprocal teaching, p. 496

schooling, p. 486

school-cutoff strategy, p. 501

specific learning disabilities, p. 516

utilization knowledge, p. 491

Thought Questions

1. When you look back over your own work and school experiences so far, what personal examples can you recall of the differences between learning in other contexts and learning in school?

2. What factors might give rise to the special language of schooling? What might account for the fact that aspects of this way of using language are also found in some homes?

3. Paraphrase Binet and Simon's contention (quoted on p. 507) that "life is not so much a conflict of intelligences as a combat of characters." How does this idea bear on disputes about the significance of IQ testing as a means of assessing cognitive development?

4. Suppose you were assigned the task of creating a culture-free intelligence test. How would you go about it? What major obstacles would you expect to encounter?

5. How might greater knowledge of children's home cultures be helpful in organizing effective classroom instruction?

Social Development in Middle Childhood

> *Cassie and Becca had been best friends since first grade. When the girls were in fifth grade, Kelly moved into town. At first, the three of them were quite close. But something happened a few weeks ago. According to 10-year-old Cassie:*
>
> *Kelly kind of forgot me. They started to get really close and they just forgot me. And then they started ganging up on me and stuff. Like, after lunch we have a place where we meet and stuff. We get in a circle and just talk. And they'd put their shoulders together and they wouldn't let me, you know, in the circle. They would never talk to me, and they would never listen to what I had to say. I don't think I've ever done anything to them. I've always been nice to them. I feel like I don't want to go to school, because I don't know what they'll do every day. I talk to my mom but it kind of makes her mad because she says I should ignore them. But I can't. And I can't concentrate. They're like—they look at me and stuff like that. They stare at me. I can hear them saying stuff and whispering and they look right at me.*
>
> *—Adapted from Simmons, Odd Girl Out*

Between the ages of 6 and 12, U.S. children typically spend more than 40 percent of their waking hours in the company of **peers,** children of their own age and status. This is twice the time they spent with peers during the preschool years, and it is accompanied by a corresponding decrease in time spent with parents (Zarbatany et al., 1990). In some of their peer interactions, children are brought together and supervised by adults—in school, at church, or in organized sports. But sometimes they are together without direct adult oversight, and the opportunity to interact with peers without adult supervision affects children's behavior in two important ways. First, the *content* of peer activity is usually different. When adults preside over children's activities, some form of instruction or work is likely to be going on, whether it involves arithmetic homework, a piano lesson, or sliding into second base. When several children get together with no adults present, they will probably play a game or just sit in a circle and talk, as Cassie describes above.

Second, the *forms of social control* in peer activity are different. When children are under the watchful eyes of adults, either at home or in school, it is the adults who keep the peace and maintain social order. If a child acts selfishly or excludes another from play, an adult is there to invoke society's rules and to settle disputes. But when children are on their own in peer groups, they must establish authority and responsibility themselves. Sometimes the rule of "might makes right" prevails, as when an especially strong child dominates the group. At other times, the complexity of social relationships, including popularity, sets the tone (Thompson et al., 2001).

The increased time that children spend among their peers is both a cause and an effect of their development during middle childhood. Adults begin to allow their children to spend extensive time with friends because they recognize the children's greater ability to think and act for themselves. Thus, Cassie's mother was reluctant to intervene in Cassie's social problems. At the same time, the new

peers Others of one's own age and status.

experiences with peers challenge children to master new cognitive and social skills in order to hold on to their increased freedom of action (Rubin et al., 1998).

Children's sense of themselves and their relations with others also changes in middle childhood. As long as they spend their time primarily among family members, their social roles and sense of self are more or less predefined. Their place in the social world is determined for them. When children spend more time among their peers, the sense of self they acquired in their families no longer suffices, and they must form new identities appropriate to the new contexts they inhabit (Harter, 1999). The child who seems fearless at home and who dominates her younger siblings may find that she needs to be more restrained on the playground with her peers.

Middle childhood also brings changes in the quality of children's relations with their parents. Parents can no longer successfully demand blind obedience from their children, nor can they easily just pick them up and remove them from danger or from situations in which they are behaving badly. Parents can still monitor their children's whereabouts, but they must rely on their children's greater understanding of the consequences of their actions and on their desire to conform to adult standards to keep them out of harm's way and behaving appropriately. As a result, parents' socialization techniques become more indirect, and they increasingly have to rely on discussion and explanation to influence their children's behavior. As you will see in Chapter 15, parents' control over their children's behavior is lessened even further during the adolescent years.

All of these changes are obviously of great interest to developmentalists. Unfortunately, current research methods cannot always do justice to the greatly increased diversity of experience that is so central during middle childhood. This limitation arises largely because, unlike younger children, school-age children are likely to behave differently with their peers when an adult observer appears on the scene than when they are playing on their own. Scientific knowledge about middle childhood is therefore fragmentary in several respects. We have extensive information about how children behave with peers in school and how they respond when researchers ask them to reason about hypothetical moral dilemmas, or to articulate their conceptions of friendship, or to solve a variety of intellectual puzzles. And we have experimental and observational findings on children in small-group interactions. But we have little systematic information about children's behavior in those settings where no adults are present and children are on their own.

To complement our discussion of school contexts in Chapter 13, in this chapter we will examine evidence about the social aspects of middle childhood chiefly

In middle childhood, children are given more freedom to interact with each other without adult supervision.

Frans Lanting/Minden Pictures

through the lens of research on children's interactions in peer groups. Then we return to the question, raised in Chapters 12 and 13, of the ways in which middle childhood does and does not correspond to a distinctive stage of development.

Games and Group Regulation

The increasing prominence of peer groups among 6- to 12-year-olds raises a central question about middle childhood: How do children learn to regulate their social relations when adults are not present? The precise psychological mechanisms have not been identified with certainty, but it appears that one important arena for this development is game playing (Hughes, 1995; Piaget, 1995).

Games and Rules

Like 4- and 5-year-olds, children who have entered middle childhood engage in fantasy role play, with each child taking a part in an imaginary situation: cops chase robbers, shipwrecked families take up residence in tree houses, runaway children hide in secret forts (Singer & Singer, 1990). But in middle childhood, children also engage in a new form of play—games based on rules. This is not to suggest that rules are totally absent from fantasy play in early childhood. When young children perform their fantasy roles, they typically follow implicit social rules. The pretend teacher tells the pretend students to sit quietly; the students do not tell the teacher what to do. In addition, young children use rules to negotiate the roles they adopt and to maintain and manage the make-believe context. In one classroom, in response to students who complained that the play was often too "gross and scary," the students and teacher together devised the following rules for fantasy play with aggressive content (Katch, 2001):

1. No excessive blood.
2. No chopping off of body parts.
3. No guts or other things that belong inside the body can come out.

At about the age of 7 or 8, rules become the essence of many games. The rules determine what roles are to be played and what one can and cannot do in playing those roles. Rules also enter differently into the content of the games of middle childhood. Whereas the rules in preschool fantasy play can change on a whim, the rules in the games characteristic of older children must be agreed upon ahead of time and consistently followed. Anyone who changes the rules without common consent is "cheating."

Piaget conducted some of the most famous and influential studies of the development of games with rules by observing changes in how children play the game of marbles. He found that young children (6–8 years) have a "mystical respect" for the rules of the game. Children believe that rules are "eternal and unchangeable" because they have been handed down by authority figures such as parents, grandparents, or even God (Piaget, 1995, pp. 206–207) (see the box "Children's Ideas about God"). You may recognize this as the *heteronomous morality* discussed in Chapter 10. Older children (10–12 years), in contrast, recognize that the rules have been agreed upon by the players, and can be modified if everyone agrees to it. Consistent with the onset of *autonomous morality*, rules are no longer mystical, but rational.

Children's play changes importantly in middle childhood as fantasy play gives way to games with consistent rules.

Lauren Greenfield/Sygma

Children's Ideas about God

Caren, age 9:

Once upon a time in Heaven.... God woke up from his nap. It was his birthday. But nobody knew it was his birthday but one angel.... And this angel rounds up all these other angels, and when he gets out of the shower, they have a surprise party for him. (Heller, 1986, cited in Barrett, 2001)

God is infinite, pervasive, and man finite and limited to a locality. Man cannot comprehend God as he can other things. God is without limits, without dimensions. (Ullah, 1984, cited in Barrett, 2001)

The quotes above would seem to support the conclusion shared by many developmentalists that children's understanding of God moves from primitive, anthropomorphic conceptions—God has birthdays, naps, and showers—to abstract concepts that refer to God's infinite knowledge and power, formlessness, and existence beyond the realm of physical and natural laws.

This was certainly the view held by both Freud and Piaget, who believed that, early on, children's conceptions of God are similar to their conceptions of parents. Freud, for example, argued that the idea of God is a projection of our need for a protective parent figure. Piaget, as you have come to expect, adopted an approach that links changing conceptions of God to changing cognitive systems. In particular, children initially attribute godlike properties to God and their parents. Once they realize that their parents are, indeed, fallible—vulnerable to errors in judgment and knowledge—they differentiate the divine from the merely human, granting ultimate supremacy to God alone. Not until adolescence and the advent of abstract reasoning do children begin to understand God in terms of "infinite knowledge," and "formlessness."

Children's developing conceptions of God have been studied using a variety of methods. Children have been asked to describe God, or to draw pictures of God, or the house that God lives in. In general, the studies suggest that major cognitive shifts occur across childhood. For example, Dimitris Pnevmatikos (2002) asked first- through fifth-grade Catholic and Greek Orthodox children living in Luxembourg to draw the house where God lives. He found a tendency for first- and second-graders to draw real houses or churches on earth, sometimes next door to their own homes. Many third-graders, however, located the buildings in clouds, suggesting a more heavenly neighborhood. With increasing age, material buildings became less frequent in the drawings, which began to include symbolic elements, including Heaven's gates, angels, and planets. Not until fourth grade did a very few children, perhaps on the threshold of adolescent abstract reasoning, begin to depict God as coexisting with qualities such as goodness, love, peace, and so on, rather than as residing in tangible structures.

On the other hand, some developmentalists have argued that the differences between younger and older children, or between children and adults, are not as robust or dramatic as once believed, and depend greatly on the demands of the task. Some studies have found evidence that under certain circumstances, adults are prone to anthropomorphize God, much as children do. In one such study, adults of several faith traditions in the United States and India were told a story in which a boy was swimming in a swift and rocky river. His leg became caught between two rocks, and he began to struggle and pray. Although God (or Vishnu, Shiva, Brahman, or Krishna, depending on the child's faith) was answering another prayer in another part of the world when the boy started praying, before long God responded by pushing one of the rocks so the boy could get his leg out. The boy then struggled to the riverbank and fell over exhausted (Barrett, 2001).

When asked to interpret the story, most adults reported that God had been busy answering another prayer, and attended to the drowning boy as soon as business allowed. Attributing such qualities as divided or limited attention suggests that adults, like children, are quite capable of anthropomorphizing God. Interestingly, when God was replaced in the story by a space alien named Mog, who had godlike properties, most adults believed that Mog could handle both problems simultaneously. It would seem that adults' conceptions of God are complex, and depend at least in part on the context of reasoning.

Yet another challenge to the idea of a dramatic shift in conceptions of God comes from evidence that very young children, like adults, think of God in abstract terms. Using a version of the "false-belief task" (see Chapter 9, p. 341), Justin Barrett and his colleagues showed 3- to 6-year old children a closed cracker box which, when opened, revealed rocks. The children were asked what their mother, in another room, would

Rule-based games seem to require the same kinds of concrete operational mental abilities that support the performance of the new tasks and responsibilities typically assigned to 6- and 7-year-olds (see Chapter 12). Children must be able to keep in mind the overall set of preestablished task requirements as they pursue the goals of the moment. At the same time, to be successful, they need to engage in social perspective taking, understanding the relation between the thoughts of the other players and their own actions ("If I move my checker to this square, she'll double-jump me"). For Piaget, the advent of games marks a major decrease in egocentrism associated with the onset of concrete operational thought.

Compared with the fantasy play of early childhood, rule-based games expand both the number of children who can play together and the likely duration of their joint activity. Typically, in early fantasy play, only two or three children play together at a time, and their play episodes are likely to last less than 10 minutes

Young children's drawings of the house where God lives often depict real houses, whereas older children's drawings link God's "house" to abstract ideas such as "goodness," "love," and "peace."

"My house"　　　"God's house"

think was in the closed box if she were to come in and see it on the table. Consistent with much of the theories-of-mind research, the youngest children replied "rocks," not appreciating that their mother could have a different point of view, whereas the 5 and 6 year olds replied "crackers." However, when asked what *God* would think was in the box, children of all ages were equally likely to say "rocks." Thus, the 5- and 6-year-olds seemed to understand that a "God's-eye view" is much different, and less limited, than their mother's.

Based on his review of the research described here, Justin Barrett (2001) suggested that conceptions of God, for children and adults, depend importantly on the context,

and may not be as different as once supposed. You may recall, in this context, the studies on adults' beliefs in magic, presented in Chapter 9 ("Believing the Imaginable: Stone Soup Revisited," p. 352). In the same way that rational and magical thinking

seem to continue to develop and interact well into adulthood, it may be that anthropomorphic and abstract conceptions of God are not mutually exclusive, but remain relevant to the ways that individuals try to make sense of the divine.

(Corsaro, 1985). When larger groups gather, it is almost certainly because an adult has deliberately coordinated their activity. School-age children, by contrast, often play games for hours in groups numbering up to 20 (Hartup, 1984). The increased duration and complexity of children's play provide evidence that, at least under some conditions, children who have entered middle childhood are capable of regulating their own behavior according to agreed-upon social rules.

Games and Life

In early childhood, the connections between pretend play and children's everyday lives are fairly obvious because children use adult roles and familiar scripts as the basis of their fantasy. And, as you learned in Chapter 10, sociodramatic play provides an important context for learning self-regulation. At a glance, it may be less obvious how a game of baseball or checkers relates to social behavior in middle childhood and later life. Nonetheless, the idea that rule-based games are preparation for life has widespread appeal. The old adage, "it's not whether you win or lose, but how you play the game," refers mainly to the importance of playing a fair game. Indeed, the relationship between game playing and moral behavior has been explored by a number of developmentalists.

Piaget (1932/1965) believed that games are models of society. First, similar to social institutions, they remain basically the same as they are transmitted from one generation to the next. Thus, like other social institutions—a church service, for example—rule-based games provide an existing structure of rules about how to behave in specific social circumstances. Second, like all social institutions, rule-based games can exist only if people agree to participate in them. There would be no religions if there were no practicing believers; there would be no hopscotch if children stopped playing it. In order to participate in social institutions and games, people must subordinate their immediate desires and behavior to a socially agreed-upon system, be it a religious ceremony or the rules of soccer. Piaget (1932/1965) linked this ability to play within a framework of rules to children's acquisition of respect for rules and a new level of moral understanding.

In Piaget's (1932/1965) view, it is through game playing, that is, through the give-and-take of negotiating plans, settling disagreements, making and enforcing rules, and keeping and breaking promises, that children come to understand that social rules make cooperation with others possible. As a consequence of this understanding, peer groups can be self-governing, and their members capable of autonomous moral thinking.

Piaget took *rules* to be of central importance to children's games and development. Other developmentalists, however, are more interested in other aspects of children's game playing. The questions that motivate their work tend to focus on children's social relationships and the nature of their interactions while playing. Who gets to play? Who plays with whom? How do the players talk and interact with each other?

One of the more fascinating examples of this sort of behind-the-scenes look at children's games and moral behavior is Gary Fine's (1987) classic study of Little League baseball. Adults, as you know, have their own moral agenda for involving their sons in Little League. Parents and coaches focus on developing such character traits as hustle, teamwork, sportsmanship, and responding appropriately in the face of winning and losing. The boys, on the other hand, are working on a moral code of their own, and one which is frequently broken. In the field and in the dugout, the boys struggle with moral themes such as controlling aggression and not breaking the bond of unity. Aggression, for example, is a common theme in the boys' interactions, but typically it takes the form of verbal insults or threat of injury: "Knock him down if he's in the way;" "Smack his head in" (Fine, 1987, pp. 82–83). Verbal aggression is rarely expressed in physical behavior, and when aggressive interactions threaten to become physical, other boys usually step in to "cool their friends off." Interestingly, not just anyone can "get away with" making insulting remarks or threats, even to the opposing team. A lot depends on social structure and power relations. Gary Fine writes that "insults can be directed down or across the status hierarchy, but it is rarer for them to be directed upward" (p. 118). In his field notes, Fine records the consequences to low-status boys who direct their insults upward to boys of higher status:

> Tim, a ten-year-old utility outfielder on the Rangers, calls out to the opposing catcher, a twelve-year-old: "There's a monkey behind the plate." One of his teammates shoots back "He's a better player than you!" Later in the game several of the older Rangers verbally attack Bruce, a low-status eleven-year-old, for criticizing their opponents.

©Marc Vaughn/Masterfile

Baseball and other team sports provide an adult-supervised context in which children learn not only the rules of the game, but other culturally valued lessons such as teamwork and how to control aggression.

Gary Fine sees Little League Baseball as a stage on which preadolescent boys enact the moral and social issues that are most important to them. Whether one is inclined to emphasize the rule structure of games, as Piaget did, or the social structure of the players, as Fine did, games clearly play a role in the moral lives of children.

Reasoning about Social and Moral Issues

One of the most significant changes in social and moral development is the child's ability to *internalize* social and moral rules. Remember from Chapter 10 that internalization occurs when children's reasoning and behaviors become less dependent on external rewards and punishments, and more dependent on an internal, personal sense of right and wrong. According to Freud's psychoanalytic theory (see Chapter 10), this transition occurs with the development of the *superego*. The superego, remember, is the part of the personality that monitors and evaluates whether the individual's actions are morally appropriate. It is the individual's conscience—the *internalization* of society's moral codes. Once the superego has formed, the child is able to draw upon his or her *own, internal* notions of right and wrong in making moral judgments, rather than be driven by hope of reward or fear of reprisal.

Interest in the shift from external to internal control is also apparent in work that follows in Piaget's footsteps. Much of this work has focused on exploring children's reasoning about what is morally right or unjust, and the relationship between moral reasoning and their moral behavior (see Figure 14.1).

Reasoning about Harm and Justice

The most influential attempt to build on Piaget's approach to moral development was carried out by Lawrence Kohlberg. However, whereas Piaget believed that children begin to think in moral terms at relatively young ages when they begin to form respect for adults and have a mystical respect for rules, Kohlberg argued that until 10 years of age, children's moral reasoning is based on considerations of

Figure 14.1 This is an e-mail message from the Cole's 9-year-old granddaughter to her father, Sasha. Leila has many Spanish-speaking kids on her block, and she wanted to make sure they understood her clubhouse rules.

From: Leila Ciszewski
To: Alexander Cole
Subject: The rules in English

The rules:
Respect all people
  1. No fighting
  2. No bullying
  3. Respect club dogs
  4. Follow directions

Respect all things
  1. No littering
  2. No stealing
  3. No breaking things
  4. Do not touch things unless you are told to

Other rules
  1. If you don't follow the rules, leave.

Dear Sasha,
  These are the rules in English. Please send them back to me in Spanish.
  Figure out the code, knwd, xntq cztfgsdq, Kdhkz

rewards and punishments, and that it is not until adolescence that children develop respect for rules and authority (Turiel, 2002). A second important difference between Piaget and Kohlberg concerns the number of stages involved in the development of moral reasoning. In place of the two stages of *heteronomous* and *autonomous* moral reasoning proposed by Piaget, Kohlberg argued for the existence of a sequence of six stages extending from childhood into adolescence and adulthood. These six stages are grouped into three hierarchical levels of moral reasoning: preconventional, conventional, and postconventional (Colby & Kohlberg, 1987; Kohlberg, 1969, 1976, 1984). We will focus here on the application of Kohlberg's ideas to middle childhood and postpone an overall evaluation of his approach until the discussion of adolescent moral development in Chapter 16. (Table 14.1 summarizes the first three stages of Kohlberg's theory.)

table 14.1

Kohlberg's Six Moral Stages

Level and Stage	What Is Right	Reasons for Doing Right	Social Perspective
Level I—Preconventional			
Stage1—Heteronomous morality	• Adherence to rules backed by punishment. • Obedience for its own sake. • Avoidance of physical damage to persons and property.	• Avoidance of punishment. • Superior power of authorities.	Egocentric point of view: doesn't consider the interests of others or recognize that they differ from one's own; doesn't relate two points of view. Actions are considered in physical terms rather than in terms of psychological interests of others. Confusion of authority's perspective with one's own.
Stage 2—Instrumental morality	• Following rules only when doing so is in one's immediate interest. • Acting to meet one's own interests and needs and letting others do the same. • Seeing fairness as an equal exchange.	• To serve one's own needs or interests in a world where other people have their own nterests.	Concrete individualistic perspective: aware that all people have their own interests to pursue and these interests conflict, so that right is relative.
Level II—Conventional			
Stage 3—Good-child morality	• Living up to what is expected by people close to you. • Having good motives, and showing concern about others. • Keeping mutual relationships by such means as trust, loyalty, respect, and gratitude.	• The need to be a good person in one's own eyes and those of others. • Caring for others. • Belief in the Golden Rule. • Desire to maintain rules and authority that support stereotypical good behavior.	Perspective of an individual in relationships with other individuals: aware of shared feelings, agreements, and expectations. Ability to relate points of view through the Golden Rule.
Stage 4—Law-and-order morality	• Upholding the law.	• To keep the institution going as a whole.	Perspective of an individual in relation to the social group.
Level III—Postconventional, or Principled			
Stage 5—Social-contract reasoning	• Being aware that people hold a variety of values and opinions.	• A sense of obligation to law because of one's social contract to act for the welfare of the group.	Prosocial perspective: perspective of a rational individual aware of others' values and rights.
Stage 6—Universal ethical principles	• Following self-chosen ethical principles.	• A belief in the validity of universal moral principles.	Perspective of a moral point of view from which social arrangements derive.

Source: Adapted from Kohlberg, 1976.

Kohlberg's method for studying moral reasoning was to present children with stories about people faced with dilemmas involving the value of human life and property, people's obligations to each other, and the meaning of laws and rules. In the manner of Piaget's clinical interview technique, Kohlberg would read the story, ask the child's opinion about how the protagonist should behave in response to the dilemma, and then probe the child's reasoning behind that opinion. Kohlberg's (1969) most famous story is the "Heinz dilemma":

> In Europe, a woman was near death from cancer. One drug might save her, a form of radium that a druggist in the same town had recently discovered. The druggist was charging $2,000, ten times what the drug cost him to make. The sick woman's husband, Heinz, went to everyone he knew to borrow the money, but he could get together only about half of what it cost. He told the druggist that his wife was dying and asked him to sell it cheaper or let him pay later. But the druggist said no. The husband got desperate and broke into the man's store to steal the drug for his wife. Should the husband have done that? Why? (p. 379)

In Kohlberg's theory of moral development, stage 1 coincides with the end of the preschool period and the beginning of middle childhood. Children at stage 1 adopt an egocentric point of view of right and wrong: they do not recognize the interests of others as distinct from their own. What is right or wrong for them must be right or wrong for others. Moreover, their judgments about the rightness and wrongness of an action are based on its objective outcome, which in this case is how authorities would respond to it. In stage 1, children might assert that Heinz must not steal the medicine because he will be put in jail.

In stage 2, which ordinarily appears around the age of 7 or 8, children continue to adopt a concrete, self-interested (egocentric) perspective but can recognize that other people have different perspectives. Justice is seen as an exchange system: you give as much as you receive. Kohlberg referred to the moral reasoning of children at this stage as *instrumental morality* because it assumes that it is perfectly acceptable to use others for one's own interests. Children at this stage might respond to the Heinz dilemma by saying that Heinz should steal the drug because someday he might have cancer and would want someone to steal it for him.

Stage 2 is the key transition associated with school-age children's ability to get along without adult supervision. Children no longer depend on a strong external source to define right and wrong; instead, their behavior is regulated by reciprocal relations between group members. Sometimes the resulting behaviors are desirable ("I'll help you with your model, if you help me with mine"); other times, they are less so ("I won't tell Mom you went to the arcade, if you don't tell her I got in a fight at school"). In either case, this form of thinking allows children to regulate their actions with each other.

In stage 3, which children begin to achieve around the age of 10 or 11, moral judgments are made on the basis of a social-relational moral perspective. At this stage, children see shared feelings and agreements, especially with people close to them, as more important than individual self-interest. One child quoted by Kohlberg (1984) said, "If I was Heinz, I would have stolen the drug for my wife. You can't put a price on love, no amount of gifts make love. You can't put a price on life either" (p. 629). Stage 3 is often equated with the golden rule (Treat others as you wish to be treated), a moral rule of reciprocity found in scriptures in all major religions.

Kohlberg's theory and interview method have been extremely influential in studies of children's moral development. The lion's share of contemporary research continues to present children with hypothetical stories or dilemmas for the purpose of identifying stagelike changes in different areas of moral reasoning. A good example is found in studies of prosocial moral reasoning.

prosocial moral reasoning The thinking that is involved in deciding whether to share with, help, or take care of other people when doing so may prove costly to oneself.

Prosocial Moral Reasoning

Prosocial moral reasoning refers to the thinking that is involved in deciding whether to share with, help, or take care of other people when doing so may prove costly to oneself (Eisenberg & Fabes, 1998). According to Nancy Eisenberg (1992; Eisenberg & Fabes, 1998), prosocial moral reasoning goes through stagelike developmental changes similar to those proposed by Kohlberg for moral reasoning involving issues of harm and justice.

In her research on prosocial moral reasoning, Eisenberg used story dilemmas that generally included a conflict between immediate self-interest and the interest of others. For example, in one such story, a child is having a good time playing in his yard and sees a bully hurting another child when no adults are around. In another, the child has to choose between going to a birthday party or stopping to help a child who has injured his leg. The contrasts between a 5-year-old and a 10-year-old responding to the latter story illustrate the changes in reasoning typically observed between early and middle childhood:

Age 5 years

Interviewer: What do you think [Eric, the story protagonist] should do?
Child: Go to the party.
Interviewer: Why is that?
Child: Because he doesn't want to be late.
Interviewer: Why doesn't he want to be late?
Child: 'Cause then it'd be over.

Age 10 years

Interviewer: What do you think Eric should do?
Child: Go get the boy's parents.
Interviewer: Why do you think he would want to get his parents for him?
Child: Because he doesn't want him to have a broken leg and he wants him to get to the hospital real fast because he doesn't want him to get a broken leg or anything worse.
(Eisenberg, 1992, p. 29)

Although many factors are involved in determining the sophistication of children's prosocial moral reasoning, reviews of the large literature on this topic show that as children get older, their reasoning reflects the trend in these two examples: young children's reasoning is focused on themselves, and helping others is justified in terms of what is to be gained personally. With increasing age, children express more empathy for the person in difficulty and a greater consideration of social norms.

As children acquire more advanced forms of prosocial reasoning, they show higher levels of prosocial behavior.

Jeff Isaac Greenberg/Photo Researchers

As you recall from our discussion in Chapter 10 regarding the link between empathy and prosocial behavior, developmentalists are interested in understanding the relationship between how children think or feel about others, and how they act toward them. It should come as no surprise that the relationship between prosocial *reasoning* and prosocial *behavior* has been a focus for research in this area. For example, are children who reason at advanced levels about hypothetical stories more likely to exhibit higher levels of morality in their actual behavior? In an extensive survey of studies on children's prosocial reasoning, Nancy Eisenberg and her colleagues (2003) found that higher levels of reasoning are indeed positively related to higher levels of prosocial behavior. Studies of cheating, for example, find that children who score at higher levels on tests of prosocial reasoning are less likely to cheat compared with children who score at lower levels. However, even children with advanced reasoning will succumb to temptation if it seems that they can get away with it (Damon, 1977; Subbotsky, 1993). Apparently, there is no guarantee that a person will engage in high levels of prosocial behavior, even though he or she may have the intellectual means of doing so.

Reasoning about Moral Rules versus Social Conventions

Much of the work discussed in the previous sections suggests that school-age children rely on external consequences and authority for deciding right and wrong. However, there is increasing evidence to suggest that children may demonstrate a relatively strong sense of justice and fairness, as well as an ability to question the legitimacy of authority, at earlier ages than developmentalists once thought (Turiel, 2002). This research often presents children with stories that place authority issues in conflict with issues of justice and harm. For example, children might be told of a situation in which two children are fighting on the school playground. A peer tells the two to stop fighting; however, a teacher says that it's okay for the fight to continue. Researchers find that children as young as 5 or 6 years of age will insist that the peer's position to stop the fight is more legitimate than the teacher's position to allow it to continue (Laupa et al., 1995).

The priority that children give to the morality of the act over the status of the authority figure has been found even in cultures that are assumed to attach great weight to authority, such as Korea (Kim, 1998). This suggests that instead of deferring to rules and authority, children rely on concepts of harm and welfare in judging moral behavior. This fact led Elliot Turiel and his colleagues to conclude that reasoning about moral issues is quite different from reasoning about authority and social conventions. In other words, moral issues and social conventions are separate domains (Turiel, 2002).

Consider the following example, in which children from 5 to 11 years of age are presented with two different stories about school rules (Turiel, 1983, p. 62). In one story, the school allows children to take off their clothes when the weather is hot (a social conventional issue); in the other, the school permits children to hit each other (a moral issue). A child in the study gave this response when asked whether it's appropriate to allow children to remove their clothes:

> Yes, because that is the rule. (*Why can they have that rule?*) If that's what the boss wants to do, he can do that. (*How come?*) Because he's the boss, he is in charge of the school.

On the other hand, the child was much less likely to recognize the principal's authority to dictate whether children can hurt each other:

> No, it is not okay. (*Why not?*) Because that is like making other people unhappy. You can hurt them that way. It hurts other people, hurting is not good.

Over the course of the past 20 years, more than 100 studies have supported the claim that children distinguish between the moral domain and the social conventional domain when they judge how people should and should not behave (reviewed in Killen et al., 2002; Nucci, 2001). Consequently, researchers have begun to look at children's development in the two separate domains. In the moral realm, for example, research indicates that young children's moral judgments are based on concepts of harm or welfare, whereas the judgments of older children and adolescents make use of the more abstract concepts of justice and rights. Children of all ages, however, are unlikely to judge moral transgressions, such as hitting or stealing, according to existing rules, the dictates of authority, or common practices. Hitting, for example, is wrong even if there is no rule against it, even if the school principal says it's okay, and even if hitting is a common behavior in a particular context.

Children's reasoning about social conventional issues also shows significant changes over time. In contrast to judgments in the moral domain, reasoning about social conventions takes into account rules, authority, and custom. In general, young children's reasoning about social conventions tends to emphasize social rules, whereas older children's reasoning tends to emphasize more abstract concepts such as social roles and the social order. For example, a young child might argue that it's wrong to call a teacher by her first name because there is a rule against it, whereas an older child might express concern that the students would begin to treat the teacher as a peer rather than as someone in authority (Turiel, 1983). Over the course of middle childhood, children become increasingly concerned with social group roles and effective group functioning (Killen & Stangor, 2001). As you will discover later in this chapter, changes with age in the social conventional domain impact how children interpret peer rejection and social exclusion.

A current source of controversy among the developmental psychologists who study reasoning about social rules is whether children around the world think about social rules in the same way North American children do. Using culturally appropriate versions of Turiel's stories, researchers have replicated his basic findings in a wide variety of societies (summarized in Turiel, 1998). Others researchers, using slightly different methods to elicit judgments, have concluded that people in at least some cultures are more likely than North Americans to consider breaches of social convention to be moral issues (Shweder et al., 1987). For example, in parts of India it is considered a serious moral infraction for a widow to eat fish two or three days a week, while such behavior would be considered a matter of personal choice in the United States. At present, the issue of cultural variations in thinking about moral rules and social conventions is still in dispute. We will return to discuss this issue again in Chapter 16, because most of the relevant cross-cultural data have been collected from adolescents and adults, making it risky to draw conclusions about the role of cultural differences in such reasoning during middle childhood.

Moral Reasoning and Theories of Mind

Yet another way to look at moral reasoning is to ask how it relates to other areas of development. For example, when judges and juries deliberate a criminal case, a lot of time is devoted to understanding the mental status of the accused: Did he or she intend to commit the crime? Was it premeditated? What was the motive? You learned in Chapter 9 that around 4 to 5 years of age, children develop a *theory of mind,* that is, the ability to think about other people's mental states. Research indicates that the way that children judge someone's moral behavior may depend on their ability to understand the person's subjective mental state. Michael Chandler and his colleagues have explored this in a series of studies that involve a *Punch and Judy* puppet theater.

Courtesy of Dr. Michael J. Chandler

Punch and Judy, a famous slapstick puppet show in which the characters are continually trying to kill each other, provides a context for studying the relationship between developing theories of mind, and how children reason about moral issues.

Punch and Judy is a famous slapstick puppet show that can be found at carnivals, beaches, amusement parks, and other places frequented by children. If you have ever seen it, you probably remember that Punch and Judy are comically and literally at each others throats, each trying unsuccessfully to "off" the other.

Some of the scenarios devised for Chandler's studies unfolded as follows:

Scenario 1: Punch and Judy are on stage with two large boxes. One is orange. The other is some other nonorange color, and Punch and Judy are busily filling it with oranges. At some point Punch is made to leave the stage briefly. In his absence Judy trips and falls into the box containing the oranges. "Help!" she cries, "I have fallen into the orange box!" Punch rushes on stage and, seeing this as his golden opportunity to be rid of Judy forever, pushes the orange colored box — the empty one — off the edge of the stage.

Scenario 2: In another scene, Punch and Judy are again on stage with boxes. One is green. The other is white with a large, green number "1" painted on it. Again Punch leaves briefly, and again, in his absence, Judy accidentally falls into one of the boxes — the green-colored box. Shouting for help, she cries, "Check the green one!" This time Punch really and truly tries to rescue Judy. However, misinterpreting her cry to mean that she is in the box with the green "1", he inadvertently pushes the green box — the one that Judy fell into — off the edge in a frenzied effort to reach her.

When children were asked to rate the "badness" of Punch's behavior in the two scenes, the youngest commonly claim that he behaves most badly in Scenario 2 because it ends with Judy jettisoned off stage. They maintain what Chandler describes as an **objective view of responsibility,** an understanding that responsibility depends on objective consequences alone. Older children and adults, on the other hand, demonstrate a **subjective view of responsibility** in that they considered Punch's considered intentions. The failed attempted murder of the first scenario was therefore rated much more negatively than the accidental manslaughter of scenario 2.

Clearly, moral deliberations are tied importantly to children's developing theories of mind. With increasing age, children become more competent at interpreting a person's objective behavior in light of his or her subjective mental state.

objective view of responsibility An understanding that responsibility depends on objective consequences alone.

subjective view of responsibility An understanding that responsibility depends on both intentions and consequences.

social structure A complex organization of relationships between individuals.

relational aggression Actions that threaten the relationships and social standing of peers.

The Individual's Place in the Group

Once children begin to spend significant amounts of time among their peers, they must learn to create a satisfying place for themselves within the social group. Their greater appreciation of social rules and their increased ability to consider other people's points of view are essential resources for this developmental task. But no matter how sensitive or sophisticated they may be about social relations, there is no guarantee that they will be accepted by other children. In creating a life for themselves among peers, all children must learn to compete for social status, come to terms with the possibility that they may not be liked, and deal with the conflicts that inevitably arise.

Peer Relations and Social Status

Whenever a group of children exists over a period of time, a **social structure** emerges. Social structures are complex organizations of relationships between individuals. Developmentalists describe children's social structures in several ways, one of which focuses on the relative degree of dominance between children. As is true for many other species, dominance hierarchies contribute to the functioning of human social groups, including those of children (see Chapter 10, pp. 387–388). Dominance is usually achieved through a repeated pattern of fighting or arguing and then making up (Pellegrini & Bartini, 2001). Over time, individuals who are skilled at managing the conflict-reconciliation pattern establish dominance status within the group (Hawley et al., 2002). Dominant children are those who control "resources"—toys, play spaces, the determination of group activities, and so forth.

Although dominance hierarchies are evident even in preschool social groups (Hawley & Little, 1999), there are crucial moments in development when children work hard to negotiate their positions with each other. One such moment is the transition between elementary and middle school, when new social groupings are being formed. In a longitudinal study that followed more than 100 students from fifth through seventh grades, Andrew Pellegrini and Jeffrey Long (2002) found that bullying is used by elementary and middle school children to influence the dominance hierarchy. Moreover, the incidence of bullying peaks during the sixth grade, the first year of middle school, when children are working to establish dominance in new social groups, and then diminishes significantly during the seventh grade, once the dominance patterns have been fully formed (see the box "Bullies and Their Victims: The Darker Side of Children's Relationships").

Our usual stereotype about bullies and dominance hierarchies is that they belong entirely to the world of boys. However, recent research calls this bias into question. Whereas boys may tend to engage in direct, physical aggression, girls often practice **relational aggression,** actions that threaten the relationships and social standing of their peers (Simmons, 2002). Common forms of relational aggression include making mean and derogatory comments, spreading rumors, or gossiping in ways intended to tarnish a peer's reputation (Crick et al., 2002). Nikki Crick and her colleagues find that relational aggression, like more familiar forms of bullying, peaks during the sixth and seventh grades. It also seems to be used as a way of raising one's status within the peer system. Thus, girls who are particularly well-practiced in the art of relational aggression tend to be among the most popular. They have been called *alpha-girls* in tribute to their position at the top of the dominance hierarchy. Crick and her colleagues suggest that relational aggression can be at least as damaging as more direct forms of bullying, and should be taken just as seriously (Crick & Rose, 2000).

Bullies and Their Victims: The Darker Side of Children's Relationships

In April of 1999 two teenagers with automatic weapons entered their high school, massacred 15 individuals, and then killed themselves. It was widely speculated that they were social outcasts and may have been teased and taunted by their peers. The tragedy at Columbine turned a national spotlight on school violence. There has since been a flood of research directed toward identifying different forms of aggression, the factors that contribute to schoolchildren's aggressive behaviors, and the social and emotional consequences of being either the agent or the victim of violent acts.

Bullies and their victims have received a great deal of attention from developmentalists as well as the general public (Pellegrini & Long, 2002). Bullies engage in unprovoked aggression intended to harm, intimidate, and/or dominate. Their attacks can be physical—pushing and hitting, for example—or verbal, as in teasing and name-calling. Children's access to communication technologies—cell phones and e-mail, in particular—creates a whole new world for bullies who can now intimidate through text messages, anytime, anywhere. Because bullying is instrumental, that is, a means of controlling other people and getting one's way, developmentalists consider it a form of *proactive aggression*. Proactive aggression is distinguished from *reactive aggression*, which is usually impulsive and displayed in response to a perceived threat or provocation (Coie & Dodge, 1998). Research on aggression in middle childhood finds that proactive aggression may even be valued in some peer groups, and a basis for friendship and group formation among middle school boys (Poulin & Boivin, 2000). In the same vein, some researchers argue that bullies often have quite well-developed social skills (Crick & Dodge, 1999; Sutton et al., 1999), and are sometimes among the boys considered to be most popular by their 11- to 12-year-old classmates (Rodkin et al., 2000).

A nationwide survey of school children conducted by the U.S. Department of Justice (2000) yielded several findings (see figure). As you can see, boys are somewhat more inclined than girls to report bullying; bullying is reported more often by children from rural communities that from urban or suburban communities; and reports of bullying are highest among sixth-graders (the youngest group sampled for this study), and then drop off dramatically between seventh and eighth grade. This last finding is consistent with the results of longitudinal studies showing that bullying reaches a peak during the transition between the elementary and

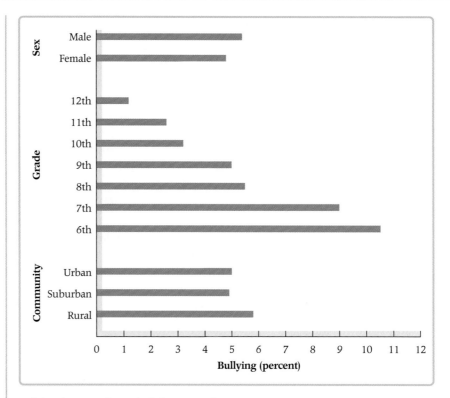

Bullying decreases dramatically between 6th and 12th grade. Boys report being bullied somewhat more often than girls. The highest rates of bullying occur in rural communities. (Adapted from U.S. Department of Justice, 2000.)

middle school years, perhaps due to children's need to establish dominance in their new peer groups (Pellegrini & Long, 2002). Interestingly, in Ireland and England, where children do not change schools at this age, bullying simply declines without interruption (Smith et al., 1999).

Bullies often target the same children in their attacks. In middle childhood, victims of chronic bullying are known by other children as the kids most often teased, bullied, and "picked on" (Goodman et al., 2001). *Peer victimization* is the term used by developmentalists to describe the experiences of children who are chronically harassed, teased, and bullied at school. Studies indicate that boys are more often victimized than girls, probably because they tend to hang out with other boys, and boys are more likely to bully. And while bullies engage in proactive aggression, their victims are most likely to engage in reactive aggression (Boivin & Poulin, 2000; Poulin & Boivin, 2000). Victimized children experience a variety of social difficulties in addition to the mistreatment they receive directly from their peers: in general, they lose their tempers easily, have difficulty regulating their attention, and act in an immature and dependent way

(Craig, 1998; Finnegan et al., 1998; Schwartz et al., 1998). Peer victimization decreases from the middle school years through adolescence, in part because bullying decreases, but also because children learn to ignore, avoid, and/or retaliate against their aggressors (Pellegrini & Long, 2003; Smith et al., 2001).

The longitudinal research on bullies and victims has important implications for the timing and the content of prevention and intervention efforts. It would seem that the early elementary school years are a ripe time to introduce prevention measures that help children to recognize and respond to bullying behaviors. However, intervention efforts may be most effective if applied during that part of middle childhood when children experience the major social transition from primary to secondary schools (Goodman et al., 2001). With the understanding that a major function of bullying is to establish status and relationships in the peer group, some researchers have suggested that schools devise ways to help children foster more varied and closer peer relationships as they move from the socially more intimate context of elementary school to the larger, hard-to-navigate social scene of secondary school.

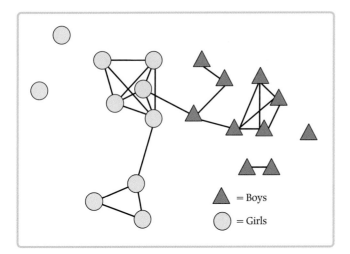

Figure 14.2 A sociogram of the relationships among a group of fifth-grade boys and girls. Note that the one boy who has a friendship with a girl is only marginally related to the two groups of boys. The girl in this friendship, by contrast, is part of a group of girls. Two girls and one boy are social isolates, while a pair of boys have chosen each other in isolation from the group. (Adapted from Gronlund, 1959.)

▲ = Boys

● = Girls

Beyond children's relative position in a dominance hierarchy, another way to describe their social standing is to focus on how the child is perceived by others in the group. Who are the popular children? Who are the outcast or excluded children? In most children's social groups it is possible to identify a few members whom almost all the others like, others who enjoy less popularity, and some who are actively disliked by most of the group. Researchers who study the relative social status of group members usually begin by asking children how they feel about other children in the group. Two techniques are widely used for this purpose: the nomination procedure and the rating scale.

When investigators use a nomination procedure, they ask members of a group to name their friends in the group or the children they would like to sit near, play with, or work with. They may also ask children to name those whom they do not like. Alternatively, researchers may use a rating scale, asking children to rank every child in the group according to a specific criterion, such as popularity, or desirability as a friend or as a teammate in sports. Sometimes researchers use both techniques in the same study to evaluate the validity of the results.

The results from these assessment techniques can be compiled to create a *sociogram,* a graphic representation of how each child feels about every other child (Rubin et al., 1998) (see Figure 14.2). The picture of social relations reflected in the sociogram is then used to investigate how the children's individual characteristics are related to their group status.

Using these techniques, developmentalists have identified social status categories defined by children's position in their social group (Rubin et al., 1999). The following list of categories has been compiled from several sources (Asher & Coie, 1990; Ladd, 1999; Rubin et al., 1998, 1999):

- *Popular* children are those who receive the most positive nominations or highest ratings from their peers.

- *Rejected* children are those who receive few positive nominations and many negative ones from their peers. They are actively disliked.

- *Neglected* children are those who receive few nominations of any kind. These children seem to be ignored by their peers rather than disliked.

- *Controversial* children, as the label suggests, are those who receive both positive and negative nominations.

Factors Relating to Sociometric Status

One of the most pervasive findings of research on social status is that popularity is related to physical attractiveness (Boyatzis et al., 1998). In one study, a group of boys was categorized into five subgroups according to their popularity among their peers. Then adult raters who did not know the boys were asked to judge their attractiveness from photographs (Langlois, 1986). In general, the lower the popularity standing of the boys' subgroup, the lower they were rated in terms of attractiveness. Other research, using similar methods, has shown that attractiveness and popularity are also correlated among girls (Boyatzis et al., 1998). Attractive children also appear to benefit from the stereotypic assumption that attractive individuals are generally superior.

However, there is more to popularity than good looks. Popular children are generally skilled at initiating and maintaining positive relationships. Kenneth Rubin and his colleagues comment that when popular children attempt to enter a group, "it is as if they ask themselves, 'What's going on?' and then, 'How can I fit in?'" They are also good at compromising and negotiating. Overall, their behavior appears to be socially competent (Rubin et al., 1999).

The factors associated with the status of rejected children appear to be more complicated. Studies conducted in the United States and the Netherlands find that some children are rejected because they are shy and withdrawn (Parke et al., 1997). These children value getting along with others as highly as do other children, and they are aware of their social failure (Asher et al., 2001). As a result, their rejection makes these shy children lonelier than other children, more dissatisfied with their social relations at school, and more distressed about them (Crick & Ladd, 1993). However, studies of peer rejection indicate that the most common reason for rejection is that the child is aggressive; children quite naturally do not like to be around others who behave unpleasantly or hurt them (Dodge et al; 2003). Aggressive rejected children overestimate their social skills and competence and underestimate how much their peers dislike them (Bellmore & Cillessen, 2003; Hymel et al., 2002). They are also more likely to misinterpret an accidental injury from another as deliberate, which may contribute to a desire to retaliate. These deficits in social information processing contribute to the frequent conflicts they have with the people around them. Rejection is especially likely to occur when lower levels of sociability and cognitive ability are combined with aggressiveness (Kokko & Pulkkinen, 2000). As you will see in more detail later in this chapter, numerous studies conducted in several countries associate childhood aggression with a variety of negative developmental outcomes, including academic difficulty, poor intellectual achievement, delinquency, health problems, and even long-term unemployment in adulthood (Kokko & Pulkkinen, 2000; Schneider, 2000; see Chapter 10).

Once children are rejected, they may acquire a reputation as such and have a difficult time gaining acceptance by their peer group even if their behavior changes. In a study of first-, third-, and fifth-graders who had been rated either low or high on a questionnaire, researchers focused on children's attempts to gain entry to a group of children who were playing a game in the school playground. They noted little difference in the skill with which low-status and high-status children sought entry to the game, yet the low-status children were more than twice as likely to be ignored as the high-status children were. In the familiar setting of a school playground, apparently, children may be rejected before they utter a word or make a move because the group has already formed a negative opinion of them (Putallaz & Wasserman, 1990).

In addition to being emotionally painful, peer rejection fosters negative opinions about oneself, and can lead to a reputation of being a "loser".

Shelley Hymel and her colleagues found that when negative opinions about a child become general in a group, the child's reputation ("He is always hitting"; "She never gives anyone else a turn") can become self-perpetuating (Hymel et al., 1990). These researchers described a number of cases in which a peer group's expectations caused the members to interpret a child's behavior as aggressive or unfriendly even when, by objective standards, it was not. Such biased interpretations make the rejected child's task of winning acceptance more difficult and may even evoke the very behaviors (grabbing, hitting, tattling, or crying) that led to the child's being rejected in the first place.

Middle childhood may be a particularly vulnerable time for gaining a reputation as rejected or victimized. Research shows that during middle childhood children increasingly compare themselves to their peers, become more concerned about their own social standing, and are more aware of the school experiences of their classmates (Goodman et al., 2001). In addition, teasing escalates at this age as a means of maintaining social status in one's peer group. Matthew Reader Goodman and his colleagues (2001) suggest that the combination of social comparison and teasing behaviors that emerge during this period is key to how children interpret rejection, be it their own or their classmates'.

Overall, the evidence indicates that rejection by one's peers is the result of a bundle of factors, each of which carries the potential to influence a child to interact in socially inappropriate ways. The consequences of this unhappy situation are that the child is socially isolated and lonely, and this only makes a difficult situation worse.

Neglected children, like rejected children, are less sociable than their peers but they are neither aggressive nor overly shy. A study conducted in Holland found that neglected children are more likely than rejected children to improve their social status among their classmates over the course of the school year (Cillessen et al., 1992). Neglected children also perform better academically than rejected children, are more compliant in school, and are better liked by their teachers (Wentzel & Asher, 1995).

Controversial children, who are unusual in that they are both highly accepted and highly rejected, tend to behave even more aggressively than rejected children. However, they compensate for their aggression by joking around about it or by using other social and cognitive skills to keep their social partners from becoming angry enough to break off the relationship (Newcomb et al., 1993).

Controversial and neglected children tend not to be particularly distressed by their relative lack of social success. This may be the case because such children are usually liked by at least one other child, and these friendships may be sufficient to prevent loneliness. Children without best friends, no matter how well they are accepted by their classmates, are lonelier than children with best friends (Parker & Asher, 1993).

In general, developmentalists have identified a number of specific traits or characteristics associated with social success and failure. Of particular importance is children's **social competence,** the set of skills and abilities that collectively contribute to children's social functioning with peers. But beyond this general definition, there is little consensus on what, exactly, defines the socially competent (or incompetent) child. Research conducted over the past 50 years (see Schneider, 2000) has identified a long list of features associated with social competence, including:

- athletic ability

- academic success

- leadership ability; confidence

- cooperativeness; helpfulness

- competence in entering peer activities

social competence The set of skills that collectively result in successful social functioning with peers.

- physical attractiveness

- nonaggressiveness

- happy, positive affect during social interactions

- social skills, including problem solving skills

- social-cognitive skills, including role taking

- competence in understanding nonverbal emotional information

Children differ widely in their social competence and, therefore, their ability to make and manage friendships. What significance do peer relations have for children's development? The current thinking among developmentalists is that children who are successful with peers are on track for success in other areas of development, whereas those who fail in their peer relationships are at risk for maladaptive outcomes (Parker et al., 1995). As you will see in the following section, a great deal of research supports this view.

Peer Relations and Children's Development

Children's peer-group relations in middle childhood are clearly related to their cognitive and social development, their achievement in school, their success in forming good social relations in adolescence, and their own personal sense of well-being (see Figure 14.3). However, the processes that produce these kinds of outcomes are only partially understood (Collins & Laursen, 2004, Collins, 2002).

Researchers have used two methods for tracking this potential cascade effect of peer-group relationships: retrospective and prospective studies. **Retrospective studies** use a "follow-back" method that starts with developmental outcomes in later childhood and beyond and looks back at the individual's early life for predictive signs of those outcomes. For example, a psychologist might examine the records of people who become school dropouts or criminals to see if there are any signs in their early lives that might have predicted these outcomes.

Perhaps the most convincing retrospective evidence for the importance of childhood peer relationships for later development comes from a study by Emory Cowen and his colleagues (Cowen, 1973). These researchers, who initially were interested in the long-term consequences of children's social status, asked third-graders to select classmates they thought would fit certain roles (such as the hero/heroine or the villain) in a hypothetical class play. Over a decade later, a county psychiatric registry was created that contained the names of everyone who had come in contact with a psychiatric facility in that county. The existence of this registry made it possible for Cowen and his colleagues to conduct a retrospective analysis by identifying all the third-graders in their study whose names appeared in the registry and then checking to see what their social status had been. As you might expect, those whose names appeared in the registry were those who were likely to have been chosen by their third-grade classmates for the less desirable roles in the play.

The second method used to trace the outcomes associated with different peer statuses is the **prospective study,** in which children are studied as they grow older. Developmentalists prefer to use this forward-looking, longitudinal approach because they can be sure that the data are gathered with the goal of testing a particular hypothesis about developmental pathways.

retrospective study A follow-back research method that starts with developmental outcomes in later childhood and looks back at the individual's early life for predictive signs of those later outcomes.

prospective study A forward-looking research method in which children are studied as they grow older.

Figure 14.3 A letter from a friendless man giving his account of the importance of childhood friendships for development. (From Hartup, 1978.)

DEAR DR
I read the report in the Oct. 30 issue of _____ about your study of only children. I am an only child, now 57 years old and I want to tell you some things about my life. Not only was I an only child but I grew up in the country where there were no nearby children to play with. My mother did not want children around. She used to say 'I don't want my kid to bother anybody and I don't want nobody's kids bothering me.'

. . . From the first year of school I was teased and made fun of. For example, in about third or fourth grade I dreaded to get on the school bus to go to school because the other children on the bus called me 'Mommy's baby.' In about the second grade I heard the boys use a vulgar word. I asked what it meant and they made fun of me. So I learned a lesson—don't ask questions. This can lead to a lot of confusion to hear talk one doesn't understand and not be able to learn what it means . . .

I never went out with a girl while I was in school—in fact I hardly talked to them. In our school the boys and girls did not play together. Boys were sent to one part of the playground and girls to another. So, I didn't learn anything about girls. When we got into high school and the boys and girls started dating I could only listen to their stories about their experiences.

I could tell you a lot more but the important thing is I have never married or had any children. I have not been very successful in an occupation or vocation. I believe my troubles are not all due to being an only child, but I do believe you are right in recommending playmates for preschool children and I will add playmates for the school agers and not have them strictly supervised by adults. I believe I confirm the experiments with monkeys in being overly timid sometimes and overly aggressive sometimes. Parents of only children should make special efforts to provide playmates for [their children].

Sincerely yours,

The prospective evidence that peer relations affect later life is considerably more detailed than the retrospective evidence, but the major conclusion is the same: peer status and friendship in middle childhood predict a good deal about what kinds of successes and difficulties children will have in later years.

A few studies give a representative sample of these findings. For example, John Coie and his colleagues (Coie et al., 1992) conducted a 3-year prospective study during which children graduated from elementary school and began attending middle school. The junior high teachers of the children who were rejected in elementary school reported that many of these children misbehaved in class, were aggressive and physically uncontrolled, and had short attention spans. The children themselves reported their own sense of being rejected. They were more likely than other children to fail a grade and experienced more difficulties in the transition to middle school. They were also more likely to drop out of school. In another study, 25 percent of rejected children later dropped out of school, compared with 8 percent of children who were not rejected by their peers (Ollendick et al., 1992).

Rejected children experience difficulties that extend beyond the classroom into everyday life. They show higher levels of delinquency, substance abuse, and psychological disturbances than children who are accepted by their peers, and, unsurprisingly, they are almost twice as likely to be arrested as juvenile delinquents (Kupersmidt et al., 2004; Ollendick et al., 1992).

Recall, however, that not all forms of rejection are the same. Across studies, it appears that a combination of aggressiveness and rejection in peer interactions is especially perilous for children. Rejected aggressive children are the ones most likely to come into contact with law enforcement or spend time in a psychiatric ward (Ladd & Troop-Gordon, 2003). A similar fate awaits bullies. One influential study found that bullies were four times as likely as other children to have criminal records as young adults (Olweus, 1993).

Getting Along with Others

The previous discussions have focused mainly on the social competence and social status of individual children. Yet another way to look at social relationships in middle childhood is to ask about factors that influence the formation and functioning of peer groups. The following discussion explores how competition, cooperation, and gender affect children's group relationships.

Competition and Cooperation among Peers

As they begin to spend more time among their peers, children must learn to balance the ways they compete with each other and the need to cooperate in order to get things done. A classic series of studies by Muzafer and Carolyn Sherif (1956) provides the best evidence to date about the conditions that foster cooperation and competition in children's social groups. In the most famous of these studies, 11-year-old boys from similar backgrounds but all strangers to one another, were divided into two groups and brought to two separate summer camps in Robbers Cave State Park in Oklahoma. To ensure that the boys at each encampment formed a cohesive group, the adults arranged for them to encounter problems they could solve only by cooperating. They provided the ingredients for each day's dinner, for example, but left it to the boys themselves to prepare and apportion the food. By the end of the week, friendships had formed and leaders had emerged within each group. Each group had adopted a name: they were the Rattlers and the Eagles.

When it was clear that both the Rattlers and the Eagles had formed a stable pattern of group interactions, the adults let each group know about the other. The two groups soon expressed a keen desire to compete against each other, and the adults arranged for a tournament between the two, with prizes for the winners. On the first day of competition, the Eagles lost a tug-of-war with the Rattlers. Stung by their defeat, they burned a Rattlers' flag that had been left behind. When the Rattlers returned the next morning and discovered the burned flag, they immediately seized the Eagles' flag. Scuffling and name-calling ensued. Over the next 5 days, hostilities escalated. Once the intergroup hostility had reached a high level, the experimenters took steps to reverse it. First, they tried bringing the boys together in a series of pleasant social gatherings—joint meals, attendance at a movie, setting off firecrackers—but these attempts all failed miserably. The boys used these occasions to escalate hostilities by throwing food and calling names.

Next, the experimenters introduced a series of problems that affected the welfare of both groups equally, requiring them to cooperate to reach a solution. The most successful application of this technique occurred during an overnight camping trip. The adults arranged for the truck that was to bring food to get stuck in a position where it could not be pushed. The boys came up with the idea of using their tug-of-war rope to pull the truck out of its predicament. The Sherifs (1956) describe the outcome: "When, after some strenuous efforts, the truck moved and started there was jubilation over the common success" (p. 323).

After this joint achievement, the boys apparently saw no point in preparing separate meals. The two groups cooperated, making dinner without much discussion and with no outbreaks of name-calling or food throwing. The experimenters soon arranged for the truck to get stuck again. This time the boys immediately knew what to do, and the two groups mixed freely as they organized the rope pull.

By the end of the series of joint-activity problems, the boys' opinions of each other had changed significantly. Mutual respect had largely replaced hostility, and several of the boys had formed friendships in the opposite group.

The Sherifs' experiment carries an important lesson. Cooperation and competition are not fixed biological characteristics of individuals or of groups. They are forms of interaction that can be found at some time in all social groups and in all individuals; they can be, and are, heavily influenced by social context.

In addition to being sensitive to changes in the social context, patterns of cooperation and competition are also known to vary according to cultural context, a fact that was neatly illustrated by Millard Madsen and his colleagues (Kagan & Madsen, 1971) in a study of two different groups of Israeli children (Shapira & Madsen, 1969).

One group was composed of children who lived in agricultural communes, or *kibbutzim;* the other group was made up of children from a middle-class urban neighborhood. Middle-class urban Israelis, like their U.S. counterparts, encourage their children to achieve as individuals. Kibbutzim, by contrast, prepare children from an early age to cooperate and work as a group. Kibbutz adults deliberately reward cooperation and punish failure to cooperate (Spiro, 1965). Competition is so discouraged that children may feel ashamed to be at the top of their class (Rabin, 1965).

Six- to ten-year-old children of both communities were brought together, four at a time, to play a game with the apparatus depicted in Figure 14.4. At the start of each round of the game, four children were seated at the corners of the board. In the center of the board was a pen connected to each corner by a string, which each child could pull to move the pen.

Figure 14.4 Diagram of apparatus used to assess children's predispositions to compete or cooperate. The pen at the center of the board must be moved to the target circles, an act that requires changes in the lengths of the strings manipulated by four players. (From Shapira & Madsen, 1969.)

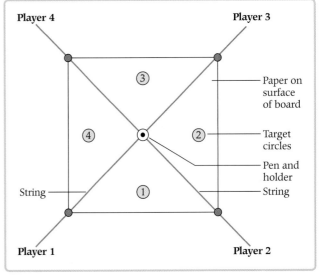

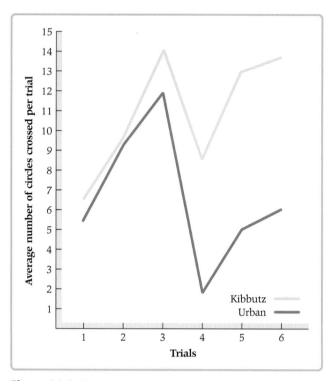

Figure 14.5 The average number of successful attempts to cross a target circle by urban Israeli children and by Israeli children raised on a kibbutz. On the first three trials, children were rewarded for cooperating. On the second three trials, rewards were distributed for individual achievement. Children raised on a kibbutz continued to cooperate and succeed after the first three trials, but urban children began to compete, lowering their success rate. (From Shapira & Madsen, 1969.)

The board itself was covered with a clean piece of paper, on which the pen left a mark as it moved.

The game called for the children to move the pen to specific places on the game board marked by four small circles. To bring the pen to one of these circles, the children had to cooperate in pulling the strings; otherwise, the pen would remain in the center or move erratically.

Each group of children was asked to play the game six times. For the first three trials, Madsen and Ariella Shapira told them that the object of the game was to draw a line over the four circles in 1 minute. If they succeeded, each of them would get a prize. If they covered the four circles twice, they would get two prizes, and so on. But if they covered fewer than four circles, no one would receive a prize. Under these circumstances, children from both kinds of communities responded similarly, in a generally cooperative manner (see Figure 14.5).

After the first three trials, the experimenters changed the conditions for getting a prize. Now, a child received a prize whenever the pen crossed the circle to his or her right. Under these new conditions, a cultural difference quickly became apparent. Among the urban children, each started pulling the pen toward himself or herself. These children persisted in competing even on the fifth trial, by which time they had had ample opportunity to see that they were getting nowhere. In some cases the children would agree to cooperate, but the cooperation would break down as soon as one child pulled a little too hard on the string. As a result, their rate of success was greatly reduced.

In contrast, the children from kibbutzim responded by quickly setting up cooperative rules, saying such things as "Okay, gang, let's take turns." They also directed one another during the game with such suggestions as "We'll start here, then here." The kibbutz children were concerned that no one be rewarded more than the others, and they set up rules to see that they all shared equally in the prizes.

Using this same procedure, Madsen and his colleagues found that urban European American children, especially older ones, were far more competitive than children their own age from rural Mexico (Kagan & Madsen, 1972). When Ariela Friedman and her colleagues replicated this research in Kenya two decades later, they also found that urban children were more competitive than rural children (Friedman et al., 1995).

A similar pattern of results was obtained by George Domino (1992) when he compared the competitive and cooperative tendencies of European American children with those of children from China. In this study, the children were asked to exchange tokens for various prizes. In some cases the token could be obtained by working alone, while in other cases collaboration was required. Most of the U.S. children preferred to work alone so that they could obtain as many tokens as possible for themselves. By contrast, the Chinese children were more likely to favor collaboration with others over individual success.

At present there is no overarching explanation for what cultural factors in particular foster collaboration over competition. One leading possibility is that societies that value interdependence over independence also foster collaboration over competition (Kagitçibasi, 2003). But evidence of urban-rural differences in countries as unlike as the United States, Mexico, and Kenya suggest that relatively local cultural factors may be at work.

Evidence for the impact of local cultural factors comes from studies of cooperative learning environments and their effects on children's academic and social development. As a moment's reflection on your own educational experiences would probably reveal, traditional educational practices in the United States foster interpersonal comparisons and competition among children. When children show themselves better than their peers, they are publicly praised and rewarded. Their papers and tests are showcased on classroom bulletin boards, they make honor roll, their parents display bumper stickers proclaiming their academic excellence. However, a new approach to education has surfaced during the past decade, driven mainly by the understanding that positive peer interactions can facilitate academic and social success. In a review of recent research on cooperative learning, Barry Schneider (2000) found evidence that when children care about each other's learning, they do better in school, engage in more prosocial behavior, and show improved relations with teachers and peers. It has been suggested that cooperative learning is particularly beneficial in classrooms where students have diverse cultural origins or ability levels (Klinger et al., 1998).

Clearly, the types of competitive and cooperative activities that children engage in affect the organization of their social groups. Often times, such activities are influenced by cultural values and practices, or by adults who want to manipulate children's social experiences. However, children's social relationships are also affected by factors that extend well beyond cooperation and competition. For example, children are known to sort into groups based on race, socioeconomic status and, as you will see below, gender.

Relations between Boys and Girls

During middle childhood, children of all cultures spend a great deal of time in sexually segregated groups (Pellegrini & Long, 2003). In nonindustrialized societies, sexual segregation may stem from the kinds of chores that children are assigned by adults. The girls help their mothers around the village by fetching water, doing the wash, sweeping, and helping to prepare food, while the boys watch the herds, hunt, and fish (Edwards & Whiting, 1993). In industrialized societies, children's tendency to gather in same-sex groups appears to depend more on their preferences for different kinds of activities and styles of interaction. Studies in the United States have found that when children are 6 years of age, roughly 68 percent choose a child of the same sex as a "best friend"; by the time children are 12, the figure has grown to about 90 percent (Graham et al., 1998)

Crossing gender boundaries can be risky business, or sometimes just plain disgusting.

When gender boundaries are crossed, children often behave as though they have been contaminated just by being near a member of the other sex, and they engage in elaborate "cleansing rituals" to get rid of the "girl cooties" or the "boy germs." Alan Sroufe and his colleagues (1993) report that a boy at a day camp was seen leaving the girls' tent (where he had gone to retrieve his radio) and was bombarded with taunts from his peers like "Uuh, he's with the girls!" and "Did you kiss anyone, Charlie?" He had to chase and hit each taunter in turn to reestablish his place in the group.

From their own and others' observations of children in a variety of contexts in this same day camp, Sroufe and his co-workers abstracted a number of rules under which school-age children find it permissible to have contact with members of the other sex (see Table 14.2). They then analyzed videotaped samples of the interactions among forty-seven 9- to 11-year-old boys and girls at the camp, looking for violations of those rules. The researchers noted who each child's friends were, had the children rated for social skill by their counselors, and interviewed each child about the popularity of others in the group.

The researchers found that most children observed the rules for cross-sex contact. The children who violated the rules were those who were generally unpopular with the other children. They were also judged by their counselors to be less socially competent than their peers.

table 14.2

Knowing the Rules: Under What Circumstances Is It Permissible to Have Contact with the Other Gender in Middle Childhood?

Rule:	The contact is accidental.
Example:	You're not looking where you are going and you bump into someone.

Rule:	The contact is incidental.
Example:	You go to get some lemonade and wait while two children of the other gender get some. (There should be no conversation.)

Rule:	The contact is in the guise of some clear and necessary purpose.
Example:	You may say, "Pass the lemonade," to persons of the other gender at the next table. No interest in them is expressed.

Rule:	An adult compels you to have contact.
Example:	"Go get that map from X and Y and bring it to me."

Rule:	You are accompanied by someone of your own gender.
Example:	Two girls may talk to two boys, though physical closeness with your own partner must be maintained and intimacy with the others is disallowed.

Rule:	The interaction or contact is accompanied by disavowal.
Example:	You say someone is ugly or hurl some other insult or (more commonly for boys) push or throw something at the person as you pass by.

Source: Sroufe et al., 1993.

These strict gender boundaries are sometimes broken in interesting ways. Often, contact between the two sexes occurs in the form of "raids" into enemy territory. From time to time, the boys will run through an area where the girls are playing and try to get the girls to chase them, or a couple of girls, shrieking with laughter, will threaten to kiss a boy. Calling a boy on the telephone and leaving a pseudoromantic message on the family answering machine is another favorite border-crossing technique. These raids are accompanied by a lot of excitement.

Barrie Thorne and Zella Luria (1986) maintain that brief cross-sex encounters, which they refer to as "border work," are a rehearsal for adult romantic relationships. Cross-cultural researchers seem to agree. For example, when Brian Sutton-Smith and John Roberts (1973) examined ethnographic reports of border work in various societies to see who chased whom, they discovered that in societies where girls marry boys from their own communities, boys and girls chase each other. But in societies where girls marry outside their communities, boys do the chasing, the pattern one would expect when males must go outside their group in pursuit of a wife.

In most cultures, sex segregation is by no means total during middle childhood (Best & Williams, 1997; Rogoff, 2000); its extent depends upon the setting (Archer, 1992). There is more mixing of the two sexes, for example, when children are in their neighborhoods than when they are in their schools (Ellis et al., 1981), when they are visiting an unfamiliar setting such as a museum (Luria & Herzog, 1991), or when the children live in a small village and thus do not have many choices of playmates (Edwards & Whiting, 1993). (See the box "Gender Politics on the Playground.")

Boys' and girls' experiences with peers often differ considerably. Observational studies of children on playgrounds report that girls ordinarily congregate to talk or play in groups of two or three, whereas boys tend to play or run around in "swarms" (Daniels-Bierness, 1989). More recent work has shown that these generalizations apply primarily to the most conspicuous and often most popular children present. There is always a sizable proportion of both boys and girls who are not following the pattern of the dominant social group (Thorne, 1993). Nonetheless, it seems clear that for many children middle childhood is a time when boys and girls do not find each other attractive social partners.

Gender Politics on the Playground: Defining a Moral Order

It is lunchime at an elementary school in Southern California. Children are gulping down their food in order to rush off to play. They understand that whichever group is first to occupy a particular area—the soccer field, the jungle gym, the basketball courts—is the group allowed to use the space. But the competition for space isn't overwhelming; this is no free-for-all. Although girls might argue over who gets the hopscotch area first, and boys might quarrel over the basketball court, there are traditions about which groups gain access to different play areas. In an ethnographic study of gender and interaction, Barrie Thorne (1993) documents how boys and girls occupy different territories on elementary school playgrounds. Boys control large spaces intended for team sports. They occupy the grassy soccer fields, baseball diamonds, and basketball courts. In contrast, the space controlled by girls is only one-tenth of that controlled by boys, and tends to be cemented and closer to the school building.

But today is different. A group of fifth-grade girls who like to play soccer is beginning to challenge the idea that the playing fields are an exclusively male space (Goodwin, 2002). On the day of the encounter described below, the girls have rushed through lunch in order to beat the boys to the soccer field. Once they have secured the space, they begin to organize their teams. Soon, however, two boys arrive, demanding their right to the field.

Amy: We have it today.
Paulo: We play soccer every day, okay?
Mark: It's more boys than girls.
Amy: So? Your point?
Mark: This is *our* field.
Amy: It's *not* your field. Did you pay for it? *No.* Your name is not written on this land.
Kathy: Mine is. K-A-T-H-Y [as she writes her name].

The boys move away, but return moments later with the male playground aide who confronts the girls:

Male Aide: Girls. Go somewhere else!
The boys are coming to play and you took over *their* field.
I think I'm gonna go and tell the vice principal. . . .
When the boys are coming out here to play soccer, okay?
You have *no right* to kick them off the field. Listen, I've seen it happen more than once. . . .
You can go over there and play soccer [pointing to the jungle gym area].
You girls can go *any*where to do what you're doing.

During middle childhood, children of all cultures begin to spend a great deal of time in sexually segregated groups.

Laura: Why can't *they* go anywhere.
Aide: They can't go on the blacktop and play soccer.
Somebody's gonna fall and hurt their knee.
Kathy: Well neither can *we!*

Marjorie Goodwin, an anthropologist who studies conversational patterns in children's interaction, recorded and analyzed the dispute presented above. She argued that in negotiating access to the territory the girls not only resisted and challenged the arguments of the boys ("Your name is not written on this land"), and the arguments of the male aide ("Why can't *they* go anywhere"), but the very social structure of the playground. Historically the field had indeed belonged to boys. In all probability, this had been the case for generations of children attending the school.

True to his word, the aide summoned the vice principal who, after hearing from all parties, formulated the problem in terms of exclusion, asking, "At school do we exclude anyone?" The girls responded with a long list of exclusionary practices typical of the boys' behavior: "they hog the ball"; "boys are always team captains"; "they always pick boys first and then girls last." Apparently taking the girls' complaints to heart, the following year the school administrators instituted a rotating system for using the fields that allowed boys and girls equal access. Yet, despite the changes, "boys continued to favor passing the ball to other boys; when they did pass to girls they did it with such force that girls often stopped playing. In addition,

during the sixth grade girls had to contend with boys grabbing their breasts in the midst of the game." The playground aides responsible for supervising the children's activities often looked on such behavior as part of a natural order. One even suggested that it prepared girls for their "appropriate" and "eventual" adult sex roles as sports spectators rather than participants.

Traditions resist change by definition. However, Goodwin's research indicates that some girls on some playgrounds are staging microrevolutions, challenging the status quo, and working to define a new moral order on their own terms. In addition to inviting us to think about the sources of social and political transformation, Goodwin's research is provocative in another sense. In particular, it challenges current thinking that girls, compared with boys, are less concerned about matters of justice and fairness, and instead tend to be more cooperative and focused on preserving harmony and cohesion (Gilligan, 1982; Maccoby, 1998; see Chapter 16). Goodwin (in press) argues that a narrow view of girls and women as nurturing and noncompetitive prevents us all—developmental scientists included—from seeing and studying girls and women as wielders of power and instruments of change. In contrast, a broader view permits an understanding that "we can not only obtain a better picture of children's worlds but also attempt to implement equity policies which promote children's fundamental democratic rights to be spared oppression and humiliation in school" (Goodwin, in press).

Friendship: A Special Type of Relationship

Most studies of children's peer relationships have been devoted to the consequences of being aggressive, rejected, or withdrawn. However, the ability to have and keep even one close friend has been found to be vital to children's well-being (Schneider, 2000). Harry Stack Sullivan (1953), an American psychiatrist, formulated an influential theory of interpersonal development in which friendship is considered essential to healthy adjustment. He proposed that the formation of close, one-on-one relationships, which he called *chumships,* is key to the development of social skills and competencies during middle childhood.

Expanding on Sullivan's early work, researchers have identified several developmental functions of friendships (Hartup, 1992; Parker & Asher, 1993). These functions include providing children with

1. contexts in which to develop many basic social skills, including communication, cooperation, and the ability to resolve conflicts;

2. information about themselves, others, and the world;

3. companionship and fun that relieve the stress of everyday life; and

4. models of intimate relationships characterized by helping, caring, and trust.

Table 14.3 contains a sample set of items used to assess what children value in their friendships. It is clear from the table that friends make each other feel good about themselves, are easy to get along with, and provide mutual assistance, in addition to simple companionship (Parker & Asher, 1993).

The qualitative uniqueness and intensity of feeling that emerge from the valued characteristics of friendships shown in Table 14.3 were described by Harry Stack Sullivan (1953) in this way:

> If you will look very closely at one of your children when he finally finds a chum . . . you will discover something very different in the relationship—namely, that your child begins to develop a new sensitivity to what matters to another person. And this is not in the sense of "what should I do to get what I want," but instead "what should I do to contribute to the happiness or to support the prestige and feeling of worth-whileness of my chum." So far as I have been ever able to discover, nothing remotely like this appears before the age of, say, $8\frac{1}{2}$, and sometimes it appears decidedly later. (pp. 245–246)

Sullivan believed that children's tendency to pick out one or a few other children with whom they feel this kind of special affinity is the childhood precursor of the need for interpersonal intimacy that will be called love when it is encountered again in adolescence. He further claimed that the failure to form such friendships in childhood creates a social deficit that is difficult to remedy later. His general view of the importance of friendships is widely shared by developmentalists (Ladd, 1999; Rubin et al., 1998, 1999). Among other advantages, having friends and being liked by peers provide a buffer against victimization (Hodges & Perry, 1999; Pellegrini & Bartini, 2001). And, as you will see shortly, the benefits of friendship extend well beyond middle childhood.

Forming Friendships

Before children can become friends, they have to spend time together, so it is no surprise that one of the major determinants of friendship between children is proximity (Meyer et al., 1998). But proximity cannot be the full story, because most children are in the company of other children several hours every day and become friends with only a few of them.

table 14.3

Children's Views of the Values of Friendship

Validation and Caring
Make each other feel important and special.
Sticks up for me if others talk behind my back.

Conflict Resolution
Make up easily when we fight.
Talk about how to get over being mad at each other.

Help and Guidance
Helps me so I can get things done quicker.
Loan each other things all the time.

Companionship and Recreation
Always sit together at lunch.
Go to each other's houses.

Intimate Exchange
Always tell each other our problems.
Tell each other secrets.

Source: Parker & Asher, 1993, p. 615, Table 1.

©Ron Fehling/Masterfile

Children tend to pick friends who are similar to themselves in sex, age, race, and general skill level.

Children tend to pick friends who are similar to themselves in a variety of ways (Rubin et al., 1994). Typically, friends are the same age, the same race, the same sex, and have the same general skill level in various activities. Friends are also likely to feel the same way about school (a child who likes school and gets good grades is likely to have a friend who also likes school and gets good grades) and to like the same sports, music, movies, books, and so on.

To determine how children go about becoming friends, John Gottman (1983) arranged for pairs of children of the same age to meet and play together in one of the children's homes for three sessions within the space of a month. Each session was videotaped. The children, who were strangers to each other at the start of the study, ranged from 3 to 9 years in age. In order to find out if the children became friends during the experiment, Gottman asked the host mothers to fill out a questionnaire that probed the strength and quality of the children's relationship. He then analyzed the tapes of the play sessions, comparing children who became friends with those who did not. Five aspects of the children's social interaction appeared to distinguish pairs who became friendly from those who did not:

1. *Common-ground activity.* The children who became friends were those who quickly found something they could do together. In addition, they explored their similarities and differences.

2. *Clear communication.* Children who became friends were likely to listen to each other, request clarification when they did not understand, and speak in ways that were relevant to the task at hand.

3. *Exchange of information.* Children who became friends both asked their partners for relevant information and provided such information to them.

4. *Resolution of conflicts.* Children who became friends gave good reasons when they disagreed, and they were able to bring conflicts to a quick resolution.

5. *Reciprocity.* Children who became friends were likely to respond to their partners' positive behaviors with an appropriate positive contribution of their own.

In reviewing the tapes of the oldest children, Gottman also found that those who became friends were more attentive, emotionally positive, vocal, active, involved, relaxed, and playful with each other than were acquaintances. They were also more likely to share the same mood. These findings nicely mirror how children themselves talk about what they value in friendships.

Components of Successful Friendships

Given the importance of friendships to children's development, it is no surprise that developmentalists have been interested in learning why some children have an easier time than others in making and keeping their friends. Robert Selman and his colleagues have suggested that social perspective taking—the ability to adopt another's perspective—is a key to successful relationships. Table 14.4 shows how higher levels of perspective taking are associated with more mature ways of understanding friendships.

Extensive studies of children with and without friendship problems have led Selman to propose that friendship involves three general spheres of influence that are affected by the development of perspective taking: friendship understanding, friendship skills, and friendship valuing (1997) (see Figure 14.6).

Friendship understanding refers to the child's developing knowledge of the nature of friendship. Selman describes children as young philosophers who have theories about how to make friends, sustain relationships, and manage conflicts. For example, an immature friendship philosophy, typical of preschoolers, is: "A friend is someone who gives me toys." Somewhat more mature, and typical of the early elementary school years, is the idea that "a friend is someone who always does what you want." With increasing interpersonal understanding and a decrease in egocentrism, children define friendships with reference to balancing and even cherishing different perspectives as a means of ensuring both personal autonomy and intimacy in relationships.

However, understanding friendships is not enough to guarantee the development of healthy friendships. The second sphere of influence in Selman's model, *friendship skills,* refers to the specific action strategies that children use in developing their rela-

table 14.4

How Selman Relates Developmental Levels of Perspective Taking to Developmental Levels of Friendship	
Developmental Level in Coordination of Perspectives	**Stage of Understanding Reflected in Close Friendships**
Level 0 (Approximately Ages 3 to 7) Egocentric or undifferentiated perspective. Children do not distinguish their own perspective from that of others. They do not yet recognize that others may interpret the same social experience or course of action differently from the way they do.	**Stage 0** Momentary playmates. A close friend is someone who lives close by and with whom one is playing.
Level 1 (Approximately Ages 4 to 9) Subjective or differentiated perspectives. The child understands that others' perspectives may differ from her own.	**Stage 1** One-way assistance. A friend does what one wants. A close friend is someone who shares the same dislikes and likes.
Level 2 (Approximately Ages 6 to 12) Self-reflective or reciprocal perspective. The child is now able to view his own thoughts and feelings from another's perspective.	**Stage 2** Fair-weather cooperation. With their new awareness of the reciprocal nature of personal perspectives, children become concerned with coordinating their thoughts and actions, rather than adjusting them to a fixed standard, as they did before. Relationships depend on adjustment and cooperation and fall apart over arguments.
Level 3 (Approximately Ages 9 to 15) Third-person or mutual perspective. The child at this level can step outside of an interaction and take the perspective of a third party.	**Stage 3** Intimate and mutually shared relationships. Friendships are seen as the basic means of developing mutual intimacy and mutual support. At this stage, friendship transcends momentary interactions, including conflicts. The primary limitation of this stage is possessiveness and jealousy.
Level 4 (Approximately Ages 12 to Adulthood) Societal or in-depth perspective. Children at this level are able to take the generalized perspective of society, the law, or morality.	**Stage 4** Autonomous, interdependent friendships. This stage is characterized by an awareness of the interdependence of friends for support and a sense of identity and at the same time an acceptance of the other's need to establish relations with other people.

Source: Adapted from Selman, 1981.

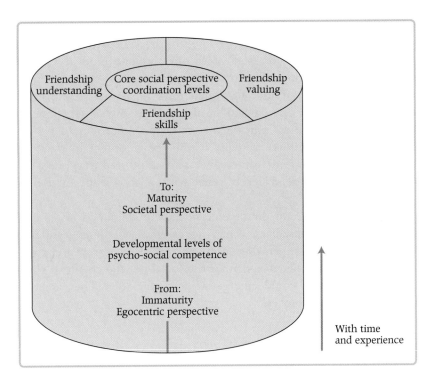

Figure 14.6 The three spheres of influence—friendship understanding, friendship skills, and friendship valuing—develop along separate paths as core social perspective coordination levels increase from the immature egocentric to the mature societal perspective. (Adapted from Selman, 1997.)

tionships. Like friendship understanding, friendship skills also become increasingly sophisticated over time. The action strategies used by preschoolers are often impulsive and focused on getting one's needs met. In a conflict over a toy, for example, there may be grabbing and crying. In just a few years, however, children develop a capacity to take turns. Later, they manage conflicts using complex strategies such as compromise, when each side agrees to give up something in order to achieve a goal.

The final sphere of influence is *friendship valuing.* This relates to the child's personal motivation and emotional involvement in the friendship. As Selman (1997) writes, "to know friendship and practice friendship one must be involved in the process of being a good friend—one must take the risk of investing oneself in meaningful friendship experiences" (p. 44). Consider the girl who breaks a play date with a close friend because a new girl invited her to go to the circus. In the early years of middle childhood, she may defend her decision in a way that is dismissive of the relationship, saying something like, "well, I like elephants." An older child would be more likely to examine her motives and consider them in light of her relationships and the needs of her friend. Selman argues that friendship valuing takes its own developmental path and depends on children's increasing capacity to take responsibility for their own contributions to the friendship, and to see the *personal* consequences of their actions for the relationship.

Overall, it appears that higher levels of social competence provide children with a variety of resources for dealing with their social environment. This is particularly apparent when friends argue and fight. Whereas younger children rely on coercion to resolve their conflicts, as they progress through middle childhood they become aware of several other alternatives. In a major review of research on children's conflict resolutions, Brett Laursen and his colleagues (2001) found that in middle childhood children are more aware of the importance of **social repair mechanisms,** strategies that allow friends to remain friends even when serious differences temporarily drive them apart. Examples of social repair mechanisms include negotiation, disengaging before a disagreement escalates into a fight, staying nearby after a fight to smooth things over,

social repair mechanisms Strategies that allow friends to remain friends even when serious differences temporarily drive them apart.

and minimizing the importance of a conflict once it is over. Each of these strategies increases the likelihood that when the conflict is over, the children will still be friends. However, and consistent with our previous discussion of the difference between friendship knowledge and friendship skills, although children are now aware of the importance of noncoercive repair mechanisms and will even report that they use them when resolving their own disagreements with friends, observational studies indicate that coercion continues to be the most common method that children actually use in their conflict interactions (Laursen et al., 2001). It is not until adolescence and adulthood that one's behavior in conflict encounters more closely reflects one's knowledge of resolution strategies.

Social repair mechanisms take on importance in middle childhood because of children's changed social circumstances. When no caregiver is present, children must settle conflicts on their own. In this confluence of changed social circumstances and increased social competence, neither the social nor the cognitive characteristics of middle childhood could emerge without the other. They are two facets of a single developmental process.

The Influence of Parents

In addition to monumental shifts in the nature and influence of peer relations and friendships, middle childhood is a time of significant change in the relationship between children and their parents. As you will see, the new patterns of interaction that emerge in the family are also felt in other social arenas, including children's peer relationships.

Changing Relations with Parents

As children grow older, the nature of parent–child interactions changes in a number of ways. For one thing, there is an overall decrease in overt affection (Collins et al., 1997). Parents no longer act as if their children are adorable; they expect them to behave themselves and perform appropriately. The children, for their part, are often embarrassed when their parents do show them open affection in public because they don't want to be "treated like a baby." They are also less likely to use such coercive behaviors such as whining, yelling, or hitting; now they argue with their parents and point out their parents' inconsistencies.

Parents are also more severe with older children and are more critical of the mistakes they make (Maccoby, 1984). Two related factors combine to account for this change in parental standards and behavior as children enter middle childhood. First, parents all over the world believe that the children should now be more capable and responsible. Second, the strategies parents adopt to influence their children's good behavior and correct their bad behavior change as children's competence increases (Lamb et al., 1999).

The precise ages at which parents expect children to be able to display behavioral competence in different areas vary across cultures. Jacqueline Goodnow and her colleagues asked Japanese, American, Australian, and Australian Lebanese mothers at what approximate age — before the age of 4 years, between 4 and 6 years, or after 6 years of age — they expected children to be capable of each of 38 kinds of behavior (Goodnow et al., 1984). As Table 14.5 indicates, Japanese mothers expected their children to display emotional maturity, compliance, and ritual forms of politeness at an earlier age than mothers in the other three groups. (Note that the numbers in the table columns represent not ages but the means for three age

table 14.5

Mean Ages at Which Mothers in Four Cultural Groups Expect Their Children to Attain Various Competencies

(1 = 6 years or older; 2 = 4–5 years; 3 = younger than 4 years)

Item	Japan	United States	Australia A*	Bt
Emotional Maturity				
Does not cry easily	2.49	2.08	1.66	1.95
Can get over anger by self	2.67	1.69	1.93	1.38
Stands disappointment without crying	2.34	1.97	1.83	1.65
Does not use baby talk	2.07	1.91	2.66	2.76
Compliance				
Comes or answers when called	2.66	2.21	1.79	1.13
Stops misbehaving when told	2.57	2.33	2.28	1.57
Gives up reading/TV to help mother	1.33	1.54	1.59	1.51
Politeness				
Greets family courteously	2.90	2.22	2.69	2.38
Uses polite forms ("please") to adults	2.08	2.37	2.76	2.73
Independence				
Stays home alone for an hour or so	1.78	1.04	1.10	1.05
Takes care of own clothes	2.17	1.87	1.55	1.35
Makes phone calls without help	1.41	1.21	1.14	1.21
Sits at table and eats without help	2.95	2.76	2.79	2.59
Does regular household tasks	2.03	1.97	2.07	1.32
Can entertain self alone	2.74	2.78	2.72	1.78
Plays outside without supervision	1.98	2.19	2.38	1.40
Social Skills				
Waits for turn in games	2.31	2.12	1.97	1.89
Shares toys with other children	2.62	2.72	2.72	1.73
Sympathetic to feelings of children	1.86	2.13	1.79	1.22
Resolves disagreement without fighting	1.41	1.70	1.45	1.11
Gets own way by persuading friends	1.40	1.94	1.97	1.30
Takes initiative in playing with others	1.59	2.48	2.24	1.73
Verbal Assertiveness				
Answers a question clearly	2.10	1.98	2.14	1.46
States own preference when asked	1.72	2.25	2.00	1.30
Asks for explanation when in doubt	1.71	2.30	2.21	1.38
Can explain why s/he thinks so	1.48	2.09	1.76	1.32
Stands up for own rights with others	1.62	2.27	2.10	1.24
Miscellaneous				
Uses scissors without supervision	2.00	1.54	1.52	1.11
Keeps feet off furniture	2.74	2.30	2.31	2.05
Disagrees without biting or throwing	2.43	2.34	2.38	1.92
Answers phone properly	1.52	1.49	2.10	1.98
Resolves quarrels without adult help	1.52	1.73	1.52	1.46

* Born in Australia.
† Born in Lebanon.

Source: Goodnow et al., 1984.

categories, with 1 representing 6 or older, 2 representing age 4 to 5, and 3 representing under age 4. Thus, the lower the number, the later the children are expected to show competence.) The American and Australian mothers expected their children to develop social skills and the ability to assert themselves verbally relatively early. The Australian Lebanese mothers were distinctive in their willingness to let the children attain the needed competencies in their own good time; their developmental timetables were usually later than those of the other groups. Despite cultural variations in the precise age at which the various competencies were expected to be achieved, all the parents expected their children to master these basic competencies sometime during middle childhood.

Middle childhood is a time when children are expected to master basic competencies that are valued within their particular culture.

Lawrence Migdale/Stock Boston

Related to this change in parents' expectations is a change in the issues that arise between parents and children. According to Eleanor Maccoby (1980), parents of young children are concerned with establishing daily routines and controlling temper tantrums and fights, as well as teaching children to care for, dress, feed, and groom themselves. While some of the issues of early childhood, especially fights among siblings, are still of concern during the years from 6 to 12, a whole new set of issues crop up when children start to take responsibility for chores at home, attend school, work, and spend increasing time away from adult supervision.

In economically developed countries, school is a prominent arena in which children's achievement is judged by parents. Parents worry about how involved they should become in their child's schoolwork, what they should do if a child has academic problems, and how they should deal with school behavior problems. Other matters of concern to parents during middle childhood include the extent to which they should monitor their children's social life and whether they should require their children to do chores around the house and, if so, what standards of performance to expect of them and whether to pay them (Goodnow, 1998). In less developed countries, where a family's survival often depends on putting children to work as early as possible, parents worry about their children's ability to take care of younger kin in the absence of adult supervision and to carry out important economic tasks such as caring for livestock or hoeing weeds (Weisner, 1996).

As children grow older and are increasingly held responsible for themselves, parents attempt to influence their behavior by reasoning with them, appealing to their self-esteem ("You wouldn't do anything that stupid") or to their sense of humor, and arousing their sense of guilt. In many societies, when school-age children break rules, their parents are less likely to spank them than to deprive them of privileges or ground them (Lamb et al., 1999).

In sum, parents increasingly share their control over their children's lives with the children themselves (Collins et al., 1997). Maccoby (1984) terms this sharing of responsibility **coregulation.** Coregulation is built on parent–child cooperation. It requires that parents work out methods of monitoring, guiding, and supporting their children when adults are not present, using the time they are together to reinforce their children's understandings of right and wrong, what is safe and unsafe, and when they need to come to adults for help. For coregulation to succeed, children must be willing to inform their parents of their whereabouts, their activities, and their problems.

coregulation A form of indirect social control in which parents and children cooperate to reinforce the children's understandings of right and wrong, what is safe and unsafe, when they are not under direct adult control.

Parental Influences on Children's Peer Relations

While family life and peer relationships sometimes appear to be two separate social worlds, they are linked in at least two general ways. First, patterns of parent–child interaction, both in early childhood and later, provide working models for how people should interact with each other that carry over to interactions among peers. Second, the way parents keep track of and organize children's interactions with peers has a direct effect on the course of their peer relations (Rubin et al., 2003).

With respect to the idea that early family relationships set the stage for peer relations, there is a considerable body of evidence indicating (as discussed in Chapter 7, p. 246) that secure attachment in infancy enhances development of peer relations in early childhood and leads to better personal relationships later in life (Burgess et al., 2003). Alan Sroufe and his colleagues (Sroufe et al., 1999) call this a "cascade effect, wherein early family relationships provide the necessary support for effectively engaging the world of peers, which, in turn, provides the foundation for deeper and more extensive and complex peer relationships. Each phase supports the unfolding of subsequent capacities" (p. 258). The idea of a cascade effect also applies to negative forms of attachment, which lay the foundation for poor peer relations.

As appealing as the logic of this analysis is, keep in mind the evidence presented in Chapter 7 (p. 248), indicating that early family interactions do not necessarily have discernible long-lasting consequences (Kagan, 1998; Lewis, 1997). Whether or not the developmental cascade that Sroufe describes actually takes place depends critically on the stability of the environmental conditions with which early family interactions are associated. In a controversial book on the influence of parents in children's lives, Judith Harris (1998) cautions researchers against their bias toward the *nurture assumption,* that is, the assumption that children's behavior is caused by how they were raised by their parents. For example, in Chapter 7 you saw that children's temperament affects parents' behavior to a considerable degree, and that a broader, *transactional model* is useful for understanding how characteristics of the child and characteristics of the environment interact to produce developmental outcomes.

There is ample evidence with respect to the idea that current parent–child relations in the family influence peer relations (Rubin et al., 2003). Aggressive behavior is a good case in point. As you saw in Chapter 10, parents may unwittingly encourage their children to behave aggressively when they themselves engage in coercive, power-assertive modes of socialization. Since aggressive behavior in children is associated with rejection by their peers, a number of researchers have focused on coercive family interaction patterns as a possible source of low social status in middle childhood (Granic, Hóllenstein, Dishion, & Patterson, 2003).

In one such study, Thomas Dishion (1990) collected information on the social status of over 200 boys between the ages of 9 and 10 by interviewing their teachers and classmates. Through interviews with the parents and the boys themselves, as well as home observations, he also obtained information about the children's family socialization patterns and their behavior in the family setting. Dishion found that the boys who were exposed to more coercive family experiences at home were the ones most likely to be rejected by their peers at school. These boys not only were more aggressive with their peers but also behaved badly in the classroom. Although boys from lower-income homes were more likely to fall within the rejected category, Dishion's data showed that socioeconomic class was not a direct cause of lower peer status or aggressive behavior. Rather, in accord with findings discussed in Chapter 11 (pp. 417–418), he found that poverty affected ocial status and behavior indirectly by increasing the general level of stress within

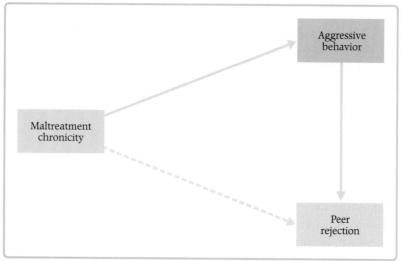

Figure 14.7 Researchers have established that children who are chronically maltreated are often rejected by their peers. In trying to understand why, some have speculated that it is not maltreatment per se that causes peer rejection. Rather, children who are maltreated are more likely to be aggressive, and it is their aggressive behavior that causes their rejection. In testing this hypothesis, researchers found no direct relationship between maltreatment and peer rejection, as indicated by the dotted line in this diagram. However, a significant relationship was found between maltreatment and aggressive behavior, and between aggressive behavior and peer rejection, as indicated by the solid lines—leading the researchers to conclude that maltreatment is an indirect cause of rejection that acts through the influence of aggressive behavior. (Adapted from Bolger & Patterson, 2001.)

the family. When parents coped well enough with the pressures of poverty to treat their children in a noncoercive way, the children were less likely to have low social status among their peers. These results were replicated and supplemented in a study conducted in the People's Republic of China (Chen & Rubin, 1994).

Children who have been maltreated are also at risk for peer rejection (Bolger & Patterson, 2001). In an effort to understand why, Kerry Bolger and Charlotte Patterson (2001) followed two groups of children across the elementary and middle school years. One group included a representative sample of more than 100 maltreated children; the other included an equal number of nonmaltreated children. Bolger and Patterson's results showed that children who are chronically maltreated, through either abuse or neglect, are at greater risk for becoming aggressive. Being aggressive, in turn, places children at risk for peer rejection from childhood to early adolescence. In other words, maltreatment per se does not cause peer rejection. Instead, and as shown in Figure 14.7, children's aggression *mediates* between maltreatment and rejection.

In addition to influencing their children's peer relations indirectly through parent–child interactions, parents can have a direct effect on them in a number of other ways. To begin with, they have considerable power to determine the contexts in which their children spend their time (Whiting, 1980). They choose, for example, the neighborhood in which they live and where their children go to school (and, hence, who their children have as potential playmates and schoolmates). They also provide or deny their children opportunities to interact with other children in specific activities during nonschool hours (Parke & Ladd, 1992). During middle childhood, however, the parents' role in managing their children's social contacts with peers begins to diminish (Schneider, 2000). Studies conducted in Germany and Canada indicate that by middle childhood, parents play a minimal role in facilitating peer contacts (Krappmann, 1989; Schneider et al., 2000). The parents' managerial role also appears to be more pivotal in Western countries as compared with those that view childrearing as the responsibility of the community. For example, in a cross-cultural study, Daniel Hart and his colleagues (Hart et al., 1999) found that although Chinese mothers actively facilitated peer contacts for their 5-year-old children, it was apparently unrelated to their children's competence. In contrast, parental facilitation of peer interaction was positively correlated with children's social competence in Russia.

Another way in which parents directly influence their children's peer relations is by monitoring where their children are, whom they are with, and what they are doing (Pettit et al., 1999). Children whose parents do not know where they are or whom they are with are more likely to engage in antisocial behavior and to face rejection by their peers (see Ladd, 1999, for a review of this evidence).

In conclusion, despite the fact that children between 6 and 12 years of age begin to spend more time with peers, and correspondingly less with parents, a wealth of studies supports the idea that parents continue to exert considerable influence on their children's development and social experiences. At the same time, however, children are gaining a new sense of themselves as individuals who have roles not only within the family, but within a broader social world.

A New Sense of Self

The significant rearrangement of children's social lives that takes place in the transition from early to middle childhood is accompanied by equally striking developments in how children think about themselves, the emergence of a new level of sensitivity to their personal standing among their peers, and their resulting efforts to maintain their self-esteem.

social comparison The process of defining oneself in relation to one's peers.

Changing Conceptions of the Self

A sizeable body of evidence suggests that as children move from early childhood to middle childhood and then to adolescence, their sense of self undergoes marked changes that parallel the changes occurring in their cognitive and social processes (Harter, 2003; Mascolo & Fischer, 1998).

To understand how children's conceptions of themselves change as they grow older, William Damon and Daniel Hart (1988) asked children between 4 and 15 years of age to describe themselves. They found that all the children referred to their appearance, their activities, their relations to others, and their psychological characteristics, but both the importance they attached to these various characteristics and the complexity of their self-concepts changed with age. As the data in Table 14.6 show, children between the ages of 4 and 7 years make categorical statements about aspects of themselves that place them in socially recognized categories ("I'm 6 years old"), but they seldom make comparative judgments. According to these data, comparative judgments relating one's own characteristics to those of others make their appearance sometime between the ages of 8 and 11 years (see Figure 14.8, p. 566, for a self-description from a 7½-year-old girl).

Subsequent research has supported the picture of a general trend from self-concepts based on limited, concrete characteristics to more abstract and stable conceptions arrived at through **social comparison,** the process of defining oneself in relation to one's peers (Pomerantz et al., 1995).

table 14.6

Level of Self-Concept	Area of Evaluation			
	Physical	**Activity-Based**	**Social**	**Psychological**
1. Categorical identification (4–7 years)	I have blue eyes. I'm 6 years old.	I play baseball. I play and read a lot.	I'm Catholic. I'm Sarah's friend.	I get funny ideas sometimes. I'm happy.
2. Comparative assessments (8–11 years)	I'm bigger than most kids. I have really light skin, because I'm Scandinavian.	I'm not very good at school. I'm good at math, but I'm not so good at art.	I like it when my mom and dad watch me play baseball. I do well in school because my parents respect me for it.	I'm not as smart as most kids. I get upset more easily than other kids.
3. Interpersonal implications (12–15 years)	I am a four-eyed person. Everyone makes fun of me. I have blonde hair, which is good because boys like blondes.	I play sports, which is important because all kids like athletes. I treat people well so I'll have friends when I need them.	I am an honest person, so people trust me. I'm very shy, so I don't have many friends.	I understand people, so they come to me with their problems. I'm the kind of person who loves being with my friends; they make me feel good about being me.

Source: After Damon & Hart, 1988.

Figure 14.8 A self-description written by Leila after reading the descriptions of the heroines on the back of the *American Girl* books. She was 7 ½ at the time.

> **All About Me**
>
> Hi, my name is Leila. There are many good things and bad things about me. I'm spunky, mischievous girl. I have brown hair and brown eyes. My eyes are dark and my hair is never the same length for over a year. My hair is sometimes curly, and sometimes straight. I am a Jewish girl.

There is no mystery as to why social comparison begins to play a significant role in children's sense of themselves during middle childhood. The increased time they spend with their peers and their greater ability to understand others' points of view lead children to engage in a new kind of questioning about themselves. Depending on the setting, they must decide on such questions as "Am I good at sports?" "Am I a good friend?" "Do the other kids like me?" "Am I good at math?" Such questions have no absolute answer because there are no absolute criteria of success. Rather, success is measured in relation to the performance of others in the social group. The many comparisons children make in a wide variety of settings provide them with a new overall sense of themselves.

The process of social comparison can be quite complex. When deliberate and pervasive social comparison becomes important at around 8 years of age, children are initially inclined to make overt social comparisons in interaction with their peers, saying such things as "My picture is the best one." But they soon discover that this kind of comparison is perceived as bragging and is likely to evoke negative reactions. As a consequence, they begin to develop more subtle ways of making social comparisons: instead of telling another child that they are faster at doing math or better at a video game, they will ask the other child, "What problem are you on?" or "What was your highest score?" (Pomerantz et al., 1995). Overt expressions of superiority are more likely to be used to intentionally make another child feel bad.

Sometime around the age of 7 or 8, children also begin to describe themselves in terms of more general, stable traits. Instead of saying "I can kick a ball far" or "I know my ABC's," they begin to say "I am a good athlete" or " I am smart." At the same time, they begin to assume more consistently that other people also have stable traits that can be used to anticipate what they will do in a variety of contexts (Ruble & Dweck, 1995). Taken as a whole, studies in this area indicate that children begin to attribute stability to the psychological states of others at about the same time they begin to think about themselves as having stable traits.

Social comparison often takes the form of asking how one's friends are doing on a school assignment.

Elizabeth Crews/The Image Works

Self-Esteem

Erik Erikson (1963) thought of middle childhood as the time when children have to resolve the crisis of industry versus inferiority. If children judge themselves (and are judged by others) as being industrious and meeting the new assignments they are given by adults at work and at school, then they are able to maintain positive **self-esteem,** that is, a positive self-evaluation of one's own worth; but if they fail to demonstrate that they are capable, they feel "inferior" and, as a result, their self-esteem suffers.

Susan Harter, a developmental researcher and clinician, has been intrigued for more than 20 years by the question of children's evaluations of themselves and their development of self-esteem. Her research has shown that self-esteem is an important index of mental health. High self-esteem during childhood has been linked to satisfaction and happiness in later life, while low self-esteem has been linked to depression, anxiety, and maladjustment both in school and in social relations.

To study the basis on which children's evaluations of themselves change in the transition from early to middle childhood, Harter and Robin Pike (1984) presented 4-, 5-, 6-, and 7-year-olds with pairs of pictures and asked them to say whether each picture was a lot or a little like them. Each picture was selected to tap the children's judgments in one of four domains important to self-esteem: cognitive competence, physical competence, peer acceptance, and maternal acceptance. All the items presented to the children were age-appropriate and comparable. For example, an item such as "Knows the alphabet," used to assess cognitive competence in the 4- and 5-year-olds, corresponded to the item "Can read alone" for the 6- and 7-year-olds.

The pattern of children's responses to these self-evaluation tasks revealed that they judged their own worth in terms of two broad categories—competence and acceptance. Statistical analysis revealed that the children lumped cognitive and physical competence together in a single category of competence and combined peer and maternal acceptance in the single category of acceptance. Nevertheless, the scale seemed to tap children's feelings of self-worth in a realistic way. Harter and Pike found, for example, that the picture selections of children who had been held back a grade reflected a self-evaluation of low competence while the picture selections of newcomers to a school reflected a self-evaluation of low acceptance.

In research on somewhat older children (8 to 12 years old), Harter (1982) assessed self-esteem using the written format shown in Figure 14.9. She found that these older children made more differentiated self-evaluations; for example, they distinguished between cognitive, social, and physical competence (Harter, 1987). (Table 14.7 shows the content of sample items in each domain of self-esteem included in Harter's scale for 8- to 12-year-olds.) At the same time that older children's self-evaluations become more differentiated, a new level of integration in the components of self-esteem appears, enabling children to form an overall sense of their general self-worth (Harter, 2003).

Another aspect of children's changing ideas about themselves in middle childhood is that they begin to form representations of the kind of person they would like to be—an "ideal self" against which they measure their "actual self," that is, the person they actually believe they are. The fact that there is likely to be a

self-esteem One's evaluation of one's own self-worth.

Figure 14.9 A sample item from Harter's scale of self-esteem. Choices to the left of center indicate degrees of poor self-esteem. Choices to the right indicate degrees of positive self-esteem. (From Harter, 1982.)

Really true for me	Sort of true for me	Some kids often forget what they learn	but	Other kids can remember things easily	Sort of true for me	Really true for me
☐	☐				☐	☐

table 14.7

Harter Self-Esteem Scale for 8- to 12-Year-Olds	
Area of Self-Evaluation	**Content of Sample Items**
Cognitive competence	Good at schoolwork, can figure out answers, remember easily, remember what is read
Social competence	Have a lot of friends, popular, do things with kids, easy to like
Physical competence	Do well at sports, good at games, chosen first for games
General self-worth	Sure of myself, do things fine, I am a good person, I want to stay the same

Source: Harter, 1982.

discrepancy between children's actual and ideal selves can be either a source of motivation toward self-improvement or a source of distress and discouragement, depending on the perceived degree of discrepancy.

Of course, not all discrepancies between the actual and ideal selves are equally important. If, for example, being athletic is not important to a child, then her self-worth will not be much affected by her feelings that she isn't a good athlete and will never become one. On the other hand, if her athletic ability is a core part of her sense of self, then it can be devastating to know that she will never be much good at sports (Harter, 2003).

Harter and others also report that there is an age-related change in the extent to which children's self-evaluations fit the views of others (Harter, 1999). Younger children's rating of their peers' "smartness" at school generally agrees with teachers' evaluations. Their ratings of their own smartness, however, do not correlate with either their teachers' or their peers' ratings. Around the age of 8, children's self-evaluations begin to fit with the judgments of both their peers and their teachers. This pattern of results fits nicely with the conclusion presented earlier that an overall sense of oneself in relation to others arises around the age of 8.

Foundations of Self-Esteem

Self-esteem has been linked to patterns of child rearing (Coopersmith, 1967; Feiring & Taska, 1996). In an extensive study of 10- to 12-year-old boys, Stanley Coopersmith found that parents of boys with high self-esteem (as determined by their answers to a questionnaire and their teachers' ratings) employed a style of parenting strikingly similar to the "authoritative" pattern described by Diana Baumrind in her study of parenting (see Chapter 11). Recall that authoritative parents are distinguished by their mixture of firm control, promotion of high standards of behavior, encouragement of independence, and willingness to reason with their children. Coopersmith's data suggest that three parental characteristics combine to produce high self-esteem in late middle childhood:

1. *Parents' acceptance of their children.* The mothers of sons with high self-esteem had closer, more affectionate relationships with their children than did mothers of children with low self-esteem. The children seemed to appreciate this approval and to view their mothers as supportive. They also tended to interpret their mothers' interest as an indication of their personal importance, as a consequence of which they came to regard themselves favorably. "This is success in its most personal expression—the concern, attention, and time of significant others" (Coopersmith, 1967, p. 179).

2. *Parents' setting of clearly defined limits.* Parents' imposition and enforcement of strict limits on their children's activities appeared to give the children a sense that norms are real and significant, and contributed to their self-definition.

3. *Parents' respect for individuality.* Within the limits set by the parents' sense of standards and social norms, the children with high self-esteem were allowed a great deal of individual self-expression. Parents showed respect for these children by reasoning with them and considering their points of view.

Taken together, contemporary evidence suggests that the key to high self-esteem is the feeling, transmitted in large part by the family, that one has some ability to control one's own future by controlling both oneself and one's environment (Chirkov & Ryan, 2001; Harter, 2003). This feeling of control is not without bounds. As Coopersmith's data suggest, children who have a positive self-image know their boundaries, but this awareness does not detract from their feeling of effectiveness. Rather, it sets clear limits within which the person feels considerable assurance and freedom.

While several decades of study on the relationship between parenting practices and children's self-esteem provides a fairly consistent picture, most of this work has been conducted on American families of European descent. It has recently been pointed out that other cultures and ethnic groups attach much less weight to the importance of self-esteem in their children's development and are consequently less inclined to organize their parenting practices in ways that explicitly promote it. Peggy Miller and her colleagues (2002) conducted interviews about child rearing with European American and Taiwanese mothers. They discovered that self-esteem plays a prominent role in American mothers' beliefs about child-rearing practices and children's development. The Taiwanese mothers, in contrast, rarely mentioned the role of "self-respect—heart/mind" (the nearest Chinese word to self-esteem). When they did, they expressed concern that it would create psychological vulnerabilities rather than strengths.

Additional support for the idea that self-esteem is a culture-specific concept comes from a comparative study of European American and Mexican American families. In this case, researchers found that the relationship between parenting practices and children's self-esteem was strong in the European American families, but comparatively weak in the Mexican American families (Ruiz et al., 2002).

At the same time that developmentalists are contending with the possibility that "self-esteem" is not a universal feature of children's sense of self but may be specific to particular cultural and ethnic contexts, they are taking a close look at the generality of certain parenting practices. As you saw earlier, the authoritative parenting style in which parents are firm, warm, and willing to negotiate, has been associated with a variety of positive social and intellectual outcomes in European American families. In contrast, a recent study of Korean American families found that only 25 percent could be classified into Baumrind's categories (Kim & Rohner, 2002). Moreover, of those families that could be so classified, children's academic achievement was associated with both authoritative and permissive fathers, suggesting that parental warmth is the critical factor, not firmness or control.

Reconsidering Middle Childhood

With the evidence from this and the preceding two chapters before us, it is appropriate to return to the question of whether the transition from early to middle childhood constitutes a bio-social-behavioral shift. Is middle childhood a stage of development characterized by a common set of features in every culture?

Table 14.8 summarizes the changes that appear to distinguish middle childhood from early childhood. We have placed the social domain at the top because surveys of the world's cultures make it clear that adults everywhere assign 6- and 7-year-olds to a new social category and require that they behave themselves in new (and sometimes stressful) contexts. Whether individual children are fully prepared or not, they must adapt to their new duties and roles or face the displeasure of their parents and the scorn of their peers.

Another universal characteristic of middle childhood is the rise of the peer group as a major context for development. For the first time, children must define their status within a group of relative equals without the intervention of adults. In many cultures, interactions with peers become coordinated, with games governed by rules serving as surrogates for adult control. The experience of negotiating these interactions and comparing themselves with peers contributes to children's mastery of the social conventions and moral rules that regulate their communities. Peer interactions also provide crucial contexts within which children arrive at a new, more complex, and global sense of themselves.

The new cognitive capacities that develop at this time are less obvious than changes in the social domain but are no less important in creating a qualitatively distinct stage of development. As you saw in Chapters 12 and 13, thought processes in middle childhood become more logical, deliberate, and consistent. Children become more capable of thinking through actions and their consequences; they are able to engage in concentrated acts of deliberate learning in the absence of tangible rewards; they keep in mind the points of view of other people in a wider variety of contexts; and they learn to moderate their emotional reactions in order to facilitate smooth relations with their parents and their peers. As we have emphasized several times, these cognitive changes must be considered as both cause and effect of the social changes discussed in this chapter.

Least visible are the biological changes that underpin children's apparent new mental capacities and modes of social interaction. The fact that children are bigger, stronger, and better coordinated is obvious enough. But only recently has modern anatomical and neurophysiological research provided evidence of such subtle changes as the proliferation of brain circuitry, changing relations between different kinds of brain-wave activity, and the greatly expanded influence of the brain's frontal lobes. Without such biological changes,

table 14.8

The Bio-Social-Behavioral Shift That Initiates Middle Childhood	
Biological domain	Loss of baby teeth and gain of permanent teeth Growth spurt in frontal lobes and in overall brain size Sharp increase in EEG coherence
Social domain	Peer-group participation Rule-based games without direct adult supervision Deliberate instruction Golden Rule morality Coregulation of behavior between parent and child Social comparison
Behavioral domain	Increased memory capacity; strategic remembering Concrete operations Logical classification Decreased egocentrism and improved perspective taking

the cognitive and social changes we have reviewed would not be possible. By the same token, when children are severely deprived of experience, such biological changes do not occur normally.

If we were to consider each element in the transition to middle childhood separately, it would be difficult to sustain the argument that it is initiated by a bio-social-behavioral shift and represents a qualitatively stagelike change from earlier periods. After all, preschoolers, in the company of older children, sometimes play without adult supervision; they have been shown to exhibit logical thinking and the use of memory strategies in some contexts; and their play contains elements of rules as well as social roles. But the changes we have documented do not occur separately—they occur in the kind of loosely coordinated ensemble that we have come to expect of a bio-social-behavioral shift. Although the details vary from one culture and one child to the next, the overall pattern is consistent and thus suggests a distinctive stage of life.

The existence of a universal pattern of changes associated with middle childhood in no way contradicts the fact that there are significant variations among cultures in the particular ways they conceive of and organize 6- to 12-year-old children's lives. Societies in which formal schooling is a central arena for children's development are especially likely to encourage uniformity in the age at which children begin to enter into the mode of life typical of middle childhood. Rural agrarian societies, in which the change in children's activities is less extreme, are less precise in the specific age at which a child is accorded the responsibilities and rights of middle childhood. But a few months' variation in the occurrence of various elements in the bio-social-behavioral shift does not substantially change their significance in the overall process of development.

S U M M A R Y

Games and Group Regulation

- Between the ages of 6 and 12, children begin to spend significant amounts of time beyond direct adult control, in the company of children roughly their own age.

- During middle childhood the nature of children's play changes from role-based fantasy to games that require adherence to rules.

- Rule-based games serve as a model of society: they are transmitted from one generation to the next, and they exist only through mutual agreement.

- Piaget saw children's involvement in such games as marking the onset of concrete operational thought. Piaget proposed a two-stage developmental sequence in children's thinking about social rules. Initially, their rules are based on unilateral respect for authority, and then they become based on mutual respect. This change allows children to govern themselves.

Reasoning about Social and Moral Issues

- Piaget's account of the development of thinking about social rules has been challenged in two ways:

  1. His theory has been refined to include more stages of development.

  2. Children's thinking about moral issues has been shown to depend upon the domain of morality involved and the context in which the issues occur.

- Kohlberg has proposed that moral reasoning changes during middle childhood from a belief that right and wrong are based on a powerful outside authority (heteronomous morality) to an instrumental morality based on mutual support and, in some cases, to a belief in reciprocal responsibility (the Golden Rule).

- As children's ability to engage in prosocial moral reasoning increases, their focus changes from personal gain to empathy for others.

- When children first reason about social conventions, they treat conventions as more or less equivalent to natural laws. With increased sophistication they begin to separate empirical associations ("Most nurses are women") from necessity ("A nurse has to be a woman"). Finally, children come to appreciate the usefulness of social conventions in the regulation of social interaction.

- During middle childhood, children become capable of considering people's intentions, as well as the consequences of their actions, in reasoning about moral dilemmas.

The Individual's Place in the Group

- Whenever a peer group forms, a social structure emerges.

- Developmentalists have identified several categories of peer-group status: children who are popular, rejected, neglected, controversial, victimized, and bullies.

- Physical attractiveness is one factor in shaping social status, but relevant social skills—such as making constructive contributions to group activity, adopting the group's frame of reference, and understanding social rules—also play important roles.

- Children's friendships develop from an emphasis on participating in joint activities to an emphasis on sharing interests, building mutual understanding, and creating trust.

- The development of conceptions of friendship is closely associated with an increased ability to adopt other people's points of view and to repair misunderstandings when they arise.

- Participation in peer groups is important to later development. Peer interactions can foster the ability to communicate, to understand others' points of view, and to get along with others. Rejected children are at risk for negative outcomes in later life.

Getting Along with Others

- Patterns of cooperation and competition can be found at certain times in all social groups but are heavily influenced by context and culture.

- Cultures vary in the value they place on cooperation versus competition in peer interactions.

- Middle childhood is a period of relative segregation of the sexes.

- Establishing friendships has been linked to the development of social skills and competencies during middle childhood

- Children become friends for a variety of reasons, including physical proximity, similarity in background, race, views, activities, sex, and skills

- Increased social competence is crucial to the development of successful friendships. Social repair mechanisms take on an increased importance in the absence of adult supervision.

The Influence of Parents

- As children begin to participate in peer groups, their relationship with their parents undergoes significant changes:

  1. Parents become more demanding of their children, with respect to both their domestic duties and their achievement in school.

2. Parents shift from direct to indirect methods of control—to reasoning, humor, appeals to self-esteem, and the arousal of guilt.

• Parents both set the stage for children's peer interactions and influence the quality of their children's peer relations by the way in which they monitor ongoing relationships and activities.

A New Sense of Self

• Children's increased time spent among peers is accompanied by a changing sense of themselves. Initially, children think of themselves in concrete terms associated with distinct areas of activity. With age, their conceptions develop, becoming more inclusive and complex.

• Special challenges to the sense of self arise from the process of social comparison, which occurs when children compete in games and in school.

• During middle childhood children begin to believe that their psychological characteristics and those of other people are stable, so they come to expect consistency in their own and others' behavior in different contexts.

• A strong sense of self-esteem is important to mental health. Family practices that emphasize acceptance of children, clearly defined limits, and respect for individuality are most likely to give rise to a firm sense of self-worth.

Reconsidering Middle Childhood

• Social development is an essential part of the bio-social-behavioral shift that occurs in the years between 5 and 7. Understood as a unique configuration of biological, social, and behavioral characteristics, middle childhood appears to be a universal stage of human development.

Key Terms

coregulation, p. 562
objective view of responsibility, p. 543
peers, p. 531
prosocial moral reasoning, p. 540
prospective study, p. 549

relational aggression, p. 544
retrospective study, p. 549
self-esteem, p. 567
social comparison, p. 565
social competence, p. 548

social repair mechanisms, p. 559
social structure, p. 544
subjective view of responsibility, p. 543

Thought Questions

1. Developmentalists link the emergence of rule-based games in middle childhood to the willingness of adults to allow children to spend time without supervision. What is the psychological connection between these two aspects of development?

2. Piaget asserted that "all morality consists in a system of rules, and the essence of all morality is to be sought for in the respect which the individual acquires for these rules." What are the implications of this view for the relationship between moral and cognitive development?

3. Make up a moral dilemma based on your everyday experience that is logically equivalent to Kohlberg's "Heinz dilemma" (p. 539). Present your version and Kohlberg's to a friend. How is the reasoning produced by the two versions of the dilemma the same, and how does it differ? What gives rise to the differences?

4. Evidence shows that children tend to choose friends who are similar to themselves.

   (a) What might be the psychological basis for this convergence?

   (b) Think of two friends from your own childhood, one who is like you and one who is quite different. What qualities of the two friendships were different? Why?

part V Adolescence

Bio-Social-Behavioral Shifts

Biological Domain
- Capacity for biological reproduction
- Development of secondary sex characteristics
- Attainment of adult size

Social Domain
- Sexual relations
- Shift toward primary responsibility for oneself
- Beginning of responsibility for next generation

Behavioral Domain
- Achievement of formal operations in some areas (systematic thinking)
- Formation of identity

Most of us look back on our adolescence and see it as a special time in our lives. For some of us, it was especially wonderful; for others, it was downright awful. Of course most of us remember something in between—intense friendships, enduring and lost; explosive (often embarrassing) bodily changes; parents who were as supportive as they were maddening; experimentation with everything from sports and drama, to drugs and alcohol; the freedom of driving around in a car with friends. But however we remember it, it is unlikely that any of us feel neutral about that time in our lives that included such significant changes as the onset of sexual maturity, and such momentous events as the first, sexually charged kiss.

Puberty, the cascade of biochemical events that begins around the end of the first decade of life, alters the body's size, shape, and functioning. The most revolutionary of these alterations is the development of an entirely new potential, the ability to engage in biological reproduction. This biological fact has profound interpersonal implications. As their reproductive organs reach maturity, boys and girls begin to engage in new forms of social behavior because of the emergence of sexual attractions.

There is a great deal more to adolescence than a new capacity for biological reproduction, however. Central to the course of human development is the extended process of *cultural* reproduction, in which the "designs for living" evolved by the group are acquired and modified by the next generation.

Much of this cultural reproduction takes place during adolescence. In addition to mastering the skills necessary for economic survival, young people must achieve new and more mature relations with age-mates of both sexes, learn the appropriate social roles associated with adult status, develop emotional independence from parents and other adults, acquire a deeper understanding of their culture's values and ethical system, and learn to behave in a socially responsible manner.

An analysis of information from 175 societies around the world has found that a social stage corresponding to adolescence is widespread, if not universal (Schlegel & Barry, 1991). Wherever it is encountered, adolescence is a time when social relations are in the process of being restructured. The changes in responsibilities and social roles that occur at this time naturally give rise to psychological uncertainties and disruptions as younger and older generations renegotiate their social relations.

The length of adolescence and the degree to which it is associated with social and psychological disruptions vary greatly from one society to the next. In the United States and other industrialized societies, a gap of 7 to 9 years typically separates the biological changes that mark the onset of sexual maturity from the social changes that confer adult status (such as the right to marry without parental consent or to run for elective office). This lengthy period is necessary because it takes young people many years to acquire the knowledge and skills they will need to achieve independence and to contribute to the perpetuation of their society.

By contrast, in some societies there is only a brief delay between the beginning of sexual maturity and the beginning of adulthood (Whiting et al., 1986). These are usually societies in which biological maturity occurs late by Western standards and in which the level of technology is relatively low. By the time biological reproduction becomes possible, at about the age of 15 in many nonindustrial societies, young people already know how to perform the basic tasks of their culture, such as farming, weaving cloth, preparing food, and caring for children.

We will return at the end of Chapter 16 to the question of cultural variations in the length and content of adolescence as a distinctive developmental stage. First, however, in Chapter 15, we examine the advent of biological maturity and its intimate links with changes in social life. These include changes in the nature of interactions with peers, friends, and one's family, as well as with entry into the workforce. Chapter 16 concentrates on what have traditionally been thought of as the psychological characteristics of adolescence: the new modes of thought that are needed to perform the economic tasks and fulfill the social responsibilities of adulthood; the changed sense of personal identity that is occasioned by a transformed physique and altered social relationships; and the new beliefs about morality and the social order that accompany the transition to adulthood.

Biological and Social Foundations of Adolescence

> "*How is it that, in the human body, reproduction is the only function to be performed by an organ of which an individual carries only one half so that he has to spend an enormous amount of time and energy to find another half?*"
> —François Jacob, *The Possible and the Actual*

It was during seventh grade that I became part of a dirty book swap, where girls I knew and I would find books loaded with sexual passages and trade them before volleyball practice. One of my friends had two brothers in college and we found Hustler magazine in their room. The pictures, and more than the pictures, the stories, sexually excited me. It was amazing to see a man's penis. I was very curious. It is amazing to recall that all this sexual turmoil coincided with playing volleyball, singing in the chorus, writing for the newspaper, and getting awards. . . . During seventh grade I said my rosary every night before I went to sleep. I got up every morning to go to mass before school during Lent. I also masturbated at least once a day.

—Anonymous, in A. Garrod et al. (Eds.), *Adolescent Portraits: Identity, Relationships, and Challenges*

Your virginity is what determines whether you're a man or a boy in the eyes of every teenage male. Teenage men see sex as a race: the first one to the finish line wins. In high school, virginity is a self-demeaning label that you want nothing more than to get rid of. . . . It is much tougher for women. . . . A woman who has lots of sex at a young age is considered a slut. Women who don't have sex at all are considered prudes. The double standard is a trap for females.

—Jeff, 16, in W. Pollack, *Real Boys' Voices*

I was truly happy before my mind understood what it was to be sexual at all. My troubles began when my body began changing and when my intellect began understanding those changes and the feelings they caused. Parties were great in middle school until I became sexual. An innocent game of spin-the-bottle among friends was a lot of fun. . . . Things got tougher, however, when one of my oversexed and underexperienced adolescent friends would suggest that we play a game of "French" spin-the-bottle. It sent a shiver up my spine and caused my stomach to contract to the size of a pea. When we entered high school . . . I wasn't comfortable. I just couldn't bring myself to talk about girls and all of the other stuff that high school guys talked about. I did, however, more often than not, awkwardly participate in the talks about girls and sex. However, in the back on my mind was the ever-present feeling that I wasn't normal, and that I must change.

—Anonymous, in A. Garrod et al. (Eds.), *Adolescent Portraits: Identity, Relationships, and Challenges*

These passages reveal many of the biological, social, and behavioral complexities that are often associated with being an adolescent. First, the biological changes of puberty transform the size and shape of young people's bodies and evoke new and initially strange feelings. But while these feelings may be of the most personal and private nature, the journey through adolescence is anything but solitary. Social expectations and cultural values, rituals, and institutions all provide adolescents with maps for their journey toward maturity. For example, just as adolescents observe and react to the radical changes in their own bodies, so do the other people in their lives. Their peers, teachers, siblings, parents—even complete strangers—will interact with them differently now that they show signs of impending sexual maturity. Adolescents will encounter many, sometimes conflicting, expectations about how they should and should not behave in their new bodies, and how they should and should not relate to others. Sexual attractions will trigger changes in peer group activities and friendships. Increasing participation in social systems outside the family will contribute to changes in adolescents' relationships with their parents. In concert with these complex biological and social developments, as you will see in Chapter 16, are major changes in the way young people think about themselves, their relationships, and the communities in which they live. All of these elements converge uniquely in adolescence, defining a new bio-social-behavioral shift.

Developmental researchers face particular difficulty in attempting to gain a comprehensive picture of development during adolescence. Although adolescents are able to talk more reflectively and coherently about their feelings, behaviors, and thought processes than are younger children, they are usually reluctant to talk about many of the topics that preoccupy them, particularly when they are of a sexual nature (Brooks-Gunn & Reiter, 1990; Martin, 1996). In addition, adolescents' behavior is much less accessible to direct observation than younger children's. As a result, the actual facts of adolescents' behavior are difficult to document. Despite this difficulty, developmentalists have long sought to understand the nature of adolescence, both as a transition from middle childhood to adulthood and as a stage of development in its own right.

The "nature of adolescence" is shaped by the views of society (including its interested scholars) at a particular moment in history. Social beliefs about adolescence determine the demands that are made on young people, the rights they are permitted to exercise, and the ways in which their behavior is interpreted. If adolescents live in a society that considers puberty to be the onset of adulthood, they will be expected to

The shopping mall is a perfect environment for adolescents to pursue one of their favorite pastimes–hanging out with friends without the direct supervision of parents and other adults.

maintain themselves economically, to care for others, and to be legally responsible for their actions. Conversely, if they live in a society that considers 15- and 16-year-olds to still be children, they will be cared for by others and will remain free of many of the responsibilities adults must accept. But they will also be expected to conform to adult demands as the price for their continued dependence.

The basic dilemma of adolescence is clear. Because biological maturity fundamentally changes the power relations between children and their parents, adolescence is a transition that we might expect to be difficult. It is especially difficult in societies where the assumption of adult rights and responsibilities is delayed well beyond puberty. Young people must then reconcile the fact that although their bodies allow mature sexual activity, their social circumstances keep them in a state of immaturity and dependence. Parents continue to exert considerable influence over their children, but this influence must be renegotiated because, in a phrase, the children are "too big to be spanked."

In modern industrialized societies such as the United States and Canada, the transition to adulthood is further complicated by two interrelated facts. First, the earlier onset of puberty and the increasingly longer years of education required for economic productivity have combined to lengthen adolescence compared with its duration in earlier eras. Second, the ways in which schooling and work are organized separate adolescents and adults, increasing the influence of peers and dividing generations. Taken together, the biological and social reorganizations that define modern adolescence provide essential conditions for the psychological changes that characterize this developmental period.

Conceptions of Adolescence

You have learned in previous chapters that current trends in research and scientific thought are deeply rooted in history and culture. When we trace the roots of current conceptions of adolescence we find interesting continuities regarding ideas about the special ways that adolescents think and feel about themselves and the world in which they live.

Philosophical Precursors

The idea that a transitional period exists as a bridge between childhood and adulthood is an ancient one. Philosophers have been writing about the special nature and qualities of youth for thousands of years. In fact, the discussions we have today about adolescent behavior and development are strikingly similar to the tendency of ancient philosophical texts to focus on the problems and turmoil of adolescents, and how to keep them out of trouble. Some 300 to 400 years B.C., for example, Plato warned that youth and alcohol were a particularly bad combination, and rallied for a minimum drinking age:

> [B]oys shall not taste wine at all until they are eighteen years of age; . . . fire must not be poured upon fire, whether in the body or in the soul, until they begin to go to work—this is a precaution which has to be taken against the excitableness of youth;—afterwards they may taste wine in moderation up to the age of thirty, but while a man is young he should abstain altogether from intoxication and from excess of wine. (Plato, *Laws, Book 2*)

Plato's student, Aristotle, also wrote about youthful passions and impulses, and the unfortunate consequences to which they could lead. However, he also viewed the period as a particularly fertile one for the development of new powers of thought, and suggested that individuals are not able to profit from "the education of reason" until they reach puberty.

Not surprisingly, interest in youth, and the idea that the period of adolescence is a dangerous one, extended well beyond the gates of philosophy. Literature from the Middle Ages onward is filled with images of young people as passionate, sensual, and impulsive (Kiell, 1959; Violato & Wiley, 1990). In Chaucer's *Canterbury Tales*, for example, young squires are portrayed as seekers of high adventure, willing to take risks in love as well as in battle; likewise, Shakespeare's *Romeo and Juliet* depicts what is probably the most famous literary example of a teenage romance and suicide.

In most of these early accounts, the cause of adolescent trouble and turmoil was thought to be rooted in excessive emotions brought on by puberty. It is against this historical backdrop of philosophical and cultural conceptions that modern scientific accounts have taken shape.

Modern Approaches

Jean-Jacques Rousseau (see Chapter 1, p. 3) was among the first to provide a comprehensive theory that balanced both the promise and the peril of adolescence. Especially influential was his understanding that biological maturation brings about emotional conflict and instability, as well as higher psychological processes, such as self-consciousness and the ability to reason logically (1762/1911).

Then, in the late-eighteenth and early-nineteenth centuries, widespread scientific and public interest in adolescence was sparked and fueled by two related developments. One was increased industrialization; the other was increased education. Child welfare advocates, among others, noted that a great many young people flocked to the cities because industrialization generated wage-paying job opportunities (Addams, 1910; Kett, 1977). However, it quickly became clear that many youths were not just getting jobs—they were also getting into trouble. In response to the rising social problems created by adolescents, efforts were made to provide them with organized services and structured activities that would occupy them during their leisure hours. Jane Addams, a founder of the famous Hull-House of Chicago, initiated several programs designed specifically to deal with problems of youth. Several of them were among the first of their type in

Hull-House of Chicago, founded by Jane Addams, was one of the first in the nation to provide programs for adolescents experiencing a variety of problems.

AP Photo

the nation. The Juvenile Protection Association, for example, was the first juvenile court in the United States (Polikoff, 1999). Addams also spearheaded the creation of the Juvenile Psychopathology Clinic.

Although increased industrialization is thought to have created a context for an increase in youth problems, it also created demands for a more educated citizenry. While many adolescents from less affluent families were leaving their homes eager to seek blue-collar jobs in the cities, those from wealthier families were staying in school longer in preparation for the ever-increasing number of white-collar, professional positions that were available in the new industrial age. As education for adolescents became more extensive, educators were faced with the need to develop new ways of teaching that were appropriate to adolescents' advanced mental capacities. Here we will examine the contributions of two theorists—G. Stanley Hall and Sigmund Freud—to modern understandings of adolescence. Then we will turn our attention to the evolutionary and ethological approaches that they have inspired.

G. Stanley Hall

G. Stanley Hall, the first president of the American Psychological Association and a major figure in the shaping of developmental psychology, was instrumental in promoting the idea that understanding the unique qualities of adolescence was essential to proper education, counseling, and the development of youth programs (Cairns, 1998; Hall, 1904). Two key features of his theory continue to influence modern thinking and research (Arnett, 1999; White, 1991):

1. *Storm and stress:* Like Rousseau, Hall described adolescence as a time of heightened emotionality and oppositions: stratospheric highs and deep depressions, self-confidence and humility, selfishness and generosity. The depiction of adolescence as a period of storm and stress, highs and lows, became central to many theoretical accounts. It has also permeated contemporary cultural conceptions of the adolescent experience.

2. *Recapitulationism:* Consistent with most theorists of his time, Hall held that biological and evolutionary processes governed the unfolding of adolescent development. Specifically, he believed that the development of the child (*ontogeny,* see Chapter 1, p. 9) recapitulates, or summarizes, the evolution of the species (*phylogeny*, see Chapter 1, p. 8). The basic idea is that the developing child passes through stages that correspond to the evolutionary steps of the species, beginning with the primitive, animal-like stage of infancy, and progressing toward the civilized, mature stage of modern adults. According to Hall, middle childhood corresponds to an ancient period of historical development when human reason, morality, feelings of love toward others, and religion were underdeveloped by modern standards. He believed that it is only when they reach adolescence that young people go beyond the biologically predetermined past to create new ways of thinking and feeling. As a consequence, adolescence is more flexible and creative than any other period of development. It is also why Hall believed (as many others do) that adolescents are literally the future of our species.

Sigmund Freud

You may recall from Chapter 1 (p. 32) that Freud's psychoanalytic theory is often best thought of as reflecting a maturational position with respect to the sources of development. In accord with the biological-maturational position, Freud viewed adolescence as a distinctive stage during which human beings can at last fulfill the biological imperative to reproduce themselves. He called adolescence the *genital stage* because this is the period during which sexual intercourse becomes a major motive of behavior.

Like Hall, Freud emphasized both storm and stress and recapitulationism as major features of the stage. In Freud's theory, the emotional storminess associated with adolescence is the culmination of a psychological struggle among the three parts of the personality: the id, the ego, and the superego (see Chapter 10, p. 375). As Freud saw it, the upsurge in sexual excitation that accompanies puberty reawakens primitive instincts, increases the power of the id, and upsets the psychological balance achieved during middle childhood. This imbalance produces psychological conflict and erratic behavior. The main developmental task of adolescence is therefore to reestablish the balance of psychological forces by reintegrating them in a new and more mature way that is compatible with the individual's new sexual capacities.

The theoretical perspectives of Hall and Freud have had a lasting impact on developmental science, particularly on the study of the biological and social foundations of adolescence. Although today there is some dispute regarding the extent of adolescent stress and conflict (McKinney, 1998), it is widely accepted that adolescents are especially prone to argue with their parents, engage in risky behaviors, experience mood fluctuations, and generally think and act in creative, and often rebellious, ways. Likewise, although recapitulationism is no longer accepted as a literal account of ontogenesis, it nevertheless seems that adolescence begins in biology and ends in culture (Conger & Peterson, 1984).

Evolutionary and Ethological Approaches

Modern theorists are attempting to explain how biological, social, behavioral, and cultural factors are interwoven in adolescents' development and experience. The hallmark of biological approaches to adolescence is their emphasis on the idea that development is highly constrained and *canalized* (see Chapter 2, p. 55) by the evolutionary history of our species. A recent trend in the study of adolescence has been a growing interest in applying theories and methods of *ethology* (see Chapter 1, p. 16) and evolutionary biology to the study of human development (Weisfeld, 1999). As you saw in our discussion of social development in early childhood (Chapter 10, pp. 387–388), there are striking similarities between the social interactions of young children and those of several nonhuman species in terms of the development of

In the United States, registering to vote is a "rite of passage" associated with the transition from childhood to adulthood.

©Bob Daemmrich/The Image Works

dominance relations. These similarities in social behaviors between species (chimpanzees and children, for example) provide the foundation for hypothesizing common biological mechanisms underpinning their development (Scott, 1997). Research on the development of social hierarchies and aggressive behavior among teenagers indicates the continued importance of such biologically influential social control mechanisms throughout human development (Weisfeld, 1999).

In his study of the evolution of distinctive periods within the human life cycle, Barry Bogin found that *Homo sapiens* is the only primate that experiences a growth spurt following childhood. This growth spurt is a key indicator of the onset of puberty. Echoing the perspective discussed in the introduction to Part V (p. 575), Bogin (1999) argues that "adolescence became a part of human life history because it conferred significant reproductive advantages to our species, in part, by allowing the adolescent to learn and practice adult economic, social, and sexual behavior before reproducing" (p. 216). Bogin refers to this view as a "biocultural model of adolescence."

puberty The series of biological developments that transforms individuals from a state of physical immaturity into one in which they are biologically mature and capable of sexual reproduction.

gonads The primary sex organs—ovaries in females and testes in males.

Puberty

During the second decade of life, the series of biological developments known as **puberty** transforms young people from a state of physical immaturity to one in which they are biologically mature and capable of sexual reproduction. Puberty begins with a chemical signal from the hypothalamus to the pituitary gland, to increase the production of various growth hormones. The hormones produced by the pituitary gland will stimulate the growth of all body tissue. However, the gonadotrophic ("gonad-seeking") hormones act specifically to stimulate the further development and functioning of the **gonads,** or primary sex organs—ovaries in females and testes in males. The female's ovaries are stimulated to manufacture additional estrogen and progesterone, and to release mature ova (eggs) that eventually allow for reproduction. In males, the testes are stimulated to produce additional testosterone, the hormone that brings about the manufacture of sperm (Bogin, 1999). While estrogen is usually considered to be the female hormone and testosterone the male hormone, both are present in the two sexes, and both are present before the onset of puberty, although in different amounts. During puberty, testosterone in boys increases to 18 times its level in middle childhood, while estrogen undergoes an eightfold increase in girls (Malina & Bouchard, 1991). These hormonal changes are accompanied by other substantial changes in the body, including the growth spurt.

The Growth Spurt

As noted above, one of the first visible signs of puberty is a spurt in the rate of physical growth. Boys and girls grow more quickly now than at any other time since they were babies. During the 2 to 3 years of the growth spurt, a boy may grow as much as 9 inches taller and a girl as much as 6 to 7 inches taller. Although adolescents continue to grow throughout puberty, they reach 98 percent of their ultimate adult height by the end of their growth spurt (Sinclair & Dangerfield, 1998).

The rate of growth during adolescence varies for different parts of the body, prompting James Tanner (1978) to quip, "A boy stops growing out of his trousers (at least in length) a year before he stops growing out of his jackets" (p. 69). As a result of asynchronous growth patterns, many adolescents develop a gangly appearance and become awkward in their movements. Changes in physical size are accompanied by changes in overall shape. Girls develop breasts, and their hips expand. Boys acquire wide shoulders and a muscular neck due to a marked increase in muscle development (Bogin, 1999). Boys also lose fat during adolescence, and so appear more muscular and angular than girls. In fact, near the end of puberty, girls continue to have a higher ratio of fat to muscle, so they have a rounder, softer look.

Most boys not only appear to be stronger than girls after puberty, they are stronger. Before puberty, boys and girls of similar size differ little in strength. But by the end of this period, boys can exercise for longer periods and can exert more force per ounce of muscle than girls of the same size. Boys develop relatively larger hearts and lungs, which give them higher blood pressure when their heart muscles contract, a lower resting heart rate, and a greater capacity for carrying oxygen in the blood, which neutralizes the chemicals that lead to fatigue during physical exercise (Weisfeld, 1999).

The physiological differences between males and females may help to explain why males have traditionally been the warriors, hunters, and heavy laborers throughout human history. They also help to explain why most superior male athletes can outperform superior female athletes. In some important respects, however, females exhibit greater physical prowess than males: they are, on the average, healthier, live longer, and are better able to tolerate long-term stress (Hayflick, 1994). Many differences favoring the strength and health of girls are apparent in infancy (see Chapter 5, p. 168).

Brain Development

Developmentalists believed until fairly recently that most changes in the brain take place well before adolescence. However, new technologies such as magnetic resonance imaging (MRI) provide evidence that the adolescent brain is still a project under construction.

Although the brain attains 90 percent of its adult weight by the age of 5, and grows very little in size during adolescence (Sinclair & Dangerfield, 1998), recent longitudinal studies point to complex changes in its organization and function (Durston et al., 2001; Giedd et al., 1999a; see Figure 15.1). For example, developmentalists have observed significant changes in the frontal lobes. The frontal lobes are associated with a number of advanced behaviors and processes, including memory, decision making, speech, and voluntary movement. As a part of the neocortex, the frontal lobes have developed only recently in evolutionary terms.

Results from MRI studies show two other remarkable changes in the brain during the adolescent years. One concerns the amount of white matter; the other concerns the amount of gray matter. White matter is made up of dense concentrations of myelin, a substance that coats neural sheaths and thereby enhances communication between neurons. Longitudinal studies indicate that white matter increases fairly steadily throughout the brain from childhood to early adulthood (Giedd et al., 1999b). The increase in white matter in the adolescent brain suggests that it is continuing on its course toward greater efficiency.

The story regarding gray matter is a bit more complicated. Unlike white matter, which seems to simply increase throughout adolescence, the amount of gray matter in the brain follows a different pattern: first it goes up; then it goes down. The amount of gray matter is believed to indicate the sheer number of neural connections, or synapses. Changes in gray matter during adolescence therefore suggest a spurt of synapse production in early puberty followed by a decline in late adolescence. This synaptic growth spurt, called *synaptogenesis*, as you may recall from Chapter 4, parallels a similar profusion of synaptic growth that occurs during infancy. Neuroscientists believe that pubertal hormones may trigger the overproduction of synapses in adolescents (Giedd et al., 1999b). They base their speculation on the fact that peak amounts of gray matter occur in boys and girls during early puberty,

Figure 15.1 These images are composites derived from brain scans of normally developing children and adolescents (a) and adolescents and adults (b). The red areas indicate where there is both an increase in the size of the brain and a decrease in gray matter. As you can see, there are substantially more areas of red in the adolescent and adult image, most of which are concentrated in the frontal area of the brain associated with complex cognitive processes. The fact that areas of the brain are growing even though their gray matter is decreasing suggests that the growth is most likely due to an increase in white matter.

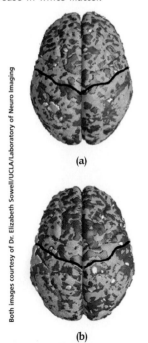

Both images courtesy of Dr. Elizabeth Sowell/UCLA/Laboratory of Neuro Imaging

(a)

(b)

when hormone production is also at its peak. Moreover, gray matter reaches a peak rate of growth in females about one year before it peaks in males, more evidence that the process may be triggered by pubertal hormonal activity.

Developmentalists have known for many years that the synaptogenesis of the infant brain is followed by *synaptic pruning,* a period when the number of synapses actually declines (see Chapter 4, p. 116). However, far from reflecting a less capable brain, synaptic pruning actually improves functioning. The decrease in synapses reflects the consolidation of neural pathways, presumably the result of specific experiences. In fact, there is an ongoing debate about whether synaptogenesis is a sensitive period in infant brain development during which positive or negative experiences can have lasting, developmental effects (Ross & Nelson, 2001).

Similar questions are now being raised about the adolescent brain. That is, with evidence that the adolescent brain undergoes a process of synaptogenesis followed by synaptic pruning, how might its development be affected by particular experiences, including exposure to drugs and alcohol? Researchers speculate that the adolescent brain may be particularly vulnerable to the effects of drugs and alcohol, in much the same way that the fetus's developing systems are vulnerable to the effects of teratogens (see Chapter 3). In the same way that the effects of teratogens vary according to the timing of exposure, the brain may be more susceptible to drugs and alcohol during times of rapid structural and functional developments, during adolescence, for example. And in the same way that the fetus is most vulnerable during the first trimester, when the mother, not yet aware of her pregnancy, may engage in activities that compromise her baby's well-being, the brain is particularly vulnerable at a time when the developing person is particularly prone to experimentation with drugs and alcohol or is showing poor judgment.

Sexual Development

During puberty all the **primary sex organs,** those involved directly in reproduction, enlarge and become functionally mature. In males the testes begin to produce sperm cells, and the prostate begins to produce semen, the fluid that carries the sperm. In females the ovaries begin to release mature ova into the fallopian tubes. When conception does not take place, menstruation occurs.

Secondary sex characteristics, the anatomical and physiological signs that outwardly distinguish males from females, appear at the same time that the primary sex organs are maturing (see Figure 15.2). Secondary sex characteristics play an essential role in communicating to the adolescent, and his or her associates, that sexual maturation is underway. Ethologists have suggested that secondary sex characteristics are "sign stimuli," that is, they signal reproductive development and trigger sexually relevant responses in others—flirting, for example.

The first signs that boys are entering puberty are an enlargement of the testes, a thickening and reddening of the skin of the scrotum, and the appearance of pubic hair. These changes usually occur about 3 years before boys reach the height of their growth spurt. About the time the growth spurt begins, the penis begins to grow, continuing to do so for about 2 years. About a year after the penis begins to grow, boys become able to ejaculate semen. **Semenarche,** the first ejaculation, often occurs spontaneously during sleep and is called a nocturnal emission. For the first year or so after semenarche, the sperm in the semen are less numerous and less fertile than sperm in adult males (Katchadourian, 1977).

Another noticeable change, which can cause embarrassing moments, is the characteristics of the boy's voice. Usually, the boy's voice does not deepen until late in puberty and then does so gradually as the larynx expands and the vocal cords lengthen. During this process, cracks in a boy's voice announce to the world the changes that are taking place in his body.

primary sex organs The organs directly involved in reproduction.

secondary sex characteristics The anatomical and physiological signs that outwardly distinguish males from females.

semenarche The first ejaculation. It often occurs spontaneously during sleep and is called a nocturnal emission.

Figure 15.2 The hormonal changes that accompany puberty cause a wide variety of physical changes in both males and females. (Adapted from Netter, 1965.)

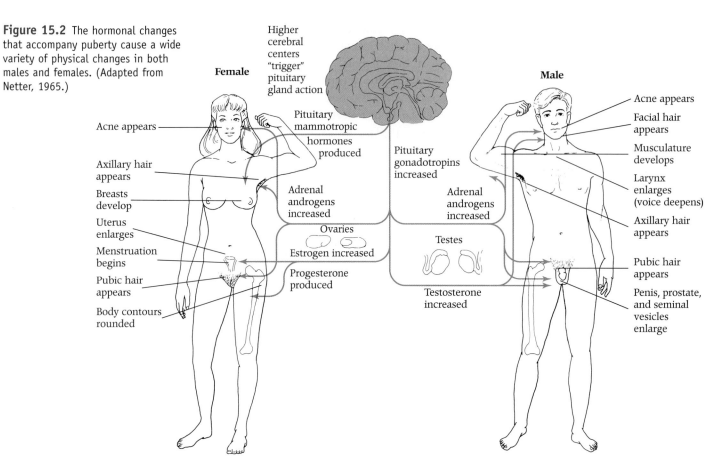

When she reaches puberty, this girl from Kathmandu, Nepal, will face a dramatic change in life. Since she was four, she has been the personification of the goddess Kumari and, except for religious festivals, she has spent her entire childhood secluded in a temple. But as soon as she reaches puberty another four-year-old girl will be chosen and this one will return to her family.

Devendra M. Singh/Agence France Presse

The first visible sign that a girl is beginning to mature sexually is often the appearance of a small rise around the nipples called the breast bud. Pubic hair usually appears a little later, just before the growth spurt begins. About the same time that a girl's outward appearance is beginning to change, her ovaries enlarge, her uterus begins to grow, and her vaginal lining thickens. The pelvic inlet, the bony opening of the birth canal, grows more slowly. It does not reach adult size until girls are about 18 years of age, which makes childbirth more difficult and potentially more dangerous for young adolescents (Bogin, 1999).

Girls' secondary sex characteristics develop throughout puberty. The breasts continue to grow with the development of the mammary glands, which allow for lactation (milk production), and the accumulation of adipose (fatty) tissue, which gives them their adult shape. Usually **menarche**—the first menstrual period—occurs relatively late in puberty, about 18 months after the growth spurt has reached its peak velocity. Early menstrual periods tend to be irregular, and they often occur without ovulation—the release of a mature egg. Ovulation typically begins about 12 to 18 months after menarche (Bogin, 1999).

The Timing of Puberty

A glance around a seventh-grade classroom is sufficient to remind even the most casual observer of the wide variations in the age at which puberty begins. Some of the 12- and 13-year-old boys may look much as they did at the age of 9 or 10, whereas others may have the gangly look that often characterizes the growth spurt. Among the girls, who on average begin to mature sexually somewhat earlier, some may look like mature women with fully developed breasts and rounded hips, some may still have the stature and shape of little girls, and some may be somewhere in between.

Like all significant milestones in development, the timing of puberty depends on complex interactions between genetic and environmental factors. Figure 15.3 displays the average age of menarche for adolescents growing up in urban and rural environments in several different countries. The differences are dramatic, and more so in some countries than in others. Cross-national differences raise several important questions: Why does menarche occur earlier in Finland than in South Africa? Why are the rural/urban differences relatively small in Finland, but quite large in India and South Africa? Identifying the genetic and environmental factors that affect the onset of menstruation would help developmentalists understand these national differences, and might help policy makers identify areas of the world in need of greater levels of health care.

Twin studies have provided an important source of information regarding the influence of biological inheritance. For example, the average difference in the age at which menarche occurs in identical twin sisters is only a few months, whereas the average difference for fraternal twin sisters is closer to a full year (Kaprio et al., 1995; Marshall & Tanner, 1974). Researchers believe that genetic contributions underlie racial differences observed in the United States: African American boys and girls tend to reach puberty at earlier ages compared with boys and girls of European descent (Herman-Giddens et al., 1997; Herman-Giddens et al., 2001).

Several studies have documented the importance of environmental factors in the timing of menarche. One critical factor is caloric intake. The onset of menstruation is associated with increases in body fat, so when calorie intake is insufficient to produce a certain level of body fat, menstruation is delayed or may cease once it has begun. This is why many lean adolescent dancers and girls who participate in a high level of physical exercise reach menarche later than other girls (Calabrese et al., 1983; Warren et al., 1991), and why many overweight girls reach puberty earlier than their average-weight peers (Kaplowitz et al., 2001).

A variety of other environmental factors, such as health, nutrition, stress, and psychological depression, also influence the age of menarche (Romans et al., 2003). One important stress factor is family conflict. Studies in the United States and New Zealand have found that adolescents who experience a high level of family conflict go through menarche earlier than those who live in more harmonious families (Graber et al., 1995; Moffit et al., 1992). There is broad agreement that environmental stress affects children's developing hormonal systems. However, the exact mechanisms of these effects and the significance of their timing remain uncertain.

menarche The first menstrual period.

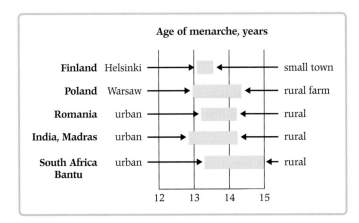

Figure 15.3 Complex interactions between genetic and environmental factors result in large regional differences in the average age of pubertal onset. In general, puberty begins earlier in urban compared with rural areas.

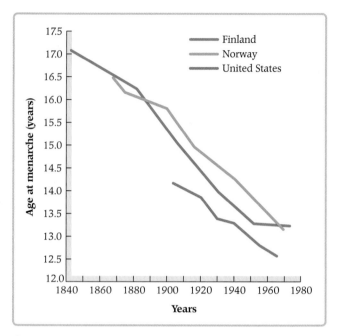

Figure 15.4 The age of menarche has been declining in many countries during the past 150 years. (Adapted from Katchadourian, 1977.)

The age at which menarche is reached has also undergone striking historical changes. In industrialized countries and in some developing countries as well, the age when menstruation begins has been declining among all social groups (Graham et al., 1999) (see Figure 15.4). In the 1840s, the average age of menarche among European women was between 14 and 15 years, whereas today it is between 12 and 13 (Bullough, 1981). Recent studies indicate that, in the United States at least, the average age of pubertal onset has continued to drop for both girls and boys even in the past 20 years. In one large-scale study of 17,000 girls, breast and/or pubic hair development had begun by the age of 8 in nearly half of the African American girls, and in 15 percent of the white girls (Herman-Giddens et al., 1997). A similar trend toward earlier maturation is found for boys. Indicators of pubertal growth in groups of African American, Mexican American, and white boys indicate that they are significantly taller, heavier, and begin genital and pubic hair growth at earlier ages, compared with boys growing up just two decades earlier (Herman-Giddens et al., 2001).

The Developmental Impact of Puberty

In all societies the biological changes associated with puberty have profound social and psychological significance, both to the young people themselves and to their community. Many researchers believe that the impact of puberty is greater than any other developmental period experienced by the child:

> Biologically, the adolescent experiences more change than individuals at any other period of life except infancy. And the biological changes of puberty have a greater effect on the growing adolescent than those of infancy have on the child because of the adolescent's capacity to experience the psychological and social meaning of the changes, as held by oneself and others. (Petersen et al., 1998, p.52)

Adolescents become aware of their development and sexuality in ways that were unavailable to them when they were less psychologically and socially mature. As you will see in Chapter 16, new powers of thought profoundly impact adolescents' understanding of themselves and the meanings of their development. In addition to adolescents' capacity for self-reflection and their ability to consider complex social and interpersonal relationships, the specific ways that puberty is experienced and found meaningful depend also on cultural and social circumstances. Some cultures have elaborate initiation ceremonies in which adolescents are instructed in a variety of "adult" behaviors and provided with specific "adult" knowledge. After participating in the ceremony, the adolescent is considered fully mature. Other cultures have less formal events that are nevertheless celebrated as important milestones of maturity. Some of the more familiar examples include getting a driver's license, registering to vote, and consuming alcoholic beverages. Ceremonial and institutional ways of marking the transition to adulthood are coupled with changing expectations of how adolescents should behave. These expectations are tied to a variety of broader cultural and social beliefs and values, and impact adolescents' experiences of their own development. Gender is a social factor that significantly shapes expectations of adolescents' behaviors, and profoundly affects psychological well-being and the ways that boys and girls respond to pubertal events.

Psychological Responses to Pubertal Events

When boys and girls are asked to report on how they felt about their first ejaculation or menstruation, it is clear that the broader context of their lives plays an important role.

A series of studies conducted by Jeanne Brooks-Gunn and her colleagues demonstrates that girls' perception of menstruation is influenced by the attitudes and beliefs of those around them (summarized in Brooks-Gunn & Reiter, 1990). The researchers found, for example, that physical symptoms during menstruation are often correlated with the expectations girls have before menarche. Girls who reported unpleasant symptoms were more likely to have been unprepared for menarche, to have matured early, and to have been told about menstruation by someone they perceived negatively.

Semenarche has been less thoroughly researched than menarche. However, it does seem that boys' responses to their first ejaculation depend on the broader context. In general, semenarche appears to be a more positive experience compared with girls' reactions to menarche (Martin, 1996). If semenarche occurs during masturbation, the predominant reaction is positive. However, if it occurs as a nocturnal emission ("wet dream"), boys are more likely to feel surprise and confusion. One boy recalled, "It reminded me of peeing in my pants—that was my first reaction even though I'd never done it" (Stein & Reiser, 1994, p. 377).

It is well documented that boys and girls experience puberty in very different ways. Although some amount of anxiety and uncertainty about one's changing body is common for both sexes, puberty seems to be more difficult subjectively for girls than it is for boys. Several studies have examined adolescents' **emotional tone,** that is, the degree to which adolescents experience a sense of well-being versus depression and anxiety (reviewed in Petersen et al., 1998). In general, positive emotional tone increases throughout adolescence for boys, while it plateaus after early adolescence for girls. Similar trends have been found in Mexican adolescents (Benjet & Hernandez-Guzman, 2001). Some developmentalists believe that cultural values and stereotypes contribute to the girls' greater ambivalence toward their changing bodies. In particular, girls' maturing bodies tend to be viewed as sexual objects to a greater extent than boys' bodies, making girls feel more self-conscious (Brooks-Gunn & Warren, 1989; Martin, 1996; Thorne, 1993). It may be that the sexualization

emotional tone The degree to which a person experiences a sense of well-being versus depression and anxiety.

Ed Kashi/IPN/Aurora

Many cultures mark their children's transition to adult status with formal ceremonies and celebrations. In the Hispanic tradition, this girl and her godfather dance at her *quinceanera,* an event that celebrates her fifteenth birthday.

Eating Disorders

Gena was a chubby clarinet player who liked to read and play chess. She was more interested in computers than makeup and preferred stuffed animals to designer clothes. She walked to her first day of junior high with her pencils sharpened and her notebooks neatly labeled. She was ready to learn Spanish and algebra and to audition for the school orchestra.

She came home sullen and shaken. The boy whose locker was next to hers had smashed into her with his locker door and sneered, "Move your fat ass." That night she told her mother, "I hate my looks. I need to go on a diet." Her mother thought, "Is that what this boy saw? When he looked at my musical, idealistic Gena, did he see only her behind?" (adopted from Pipher, 1994, p. 55).

Gena is not the only young adolescent who has decided she hates the way she looks because of a boy's comment. However, boys are by no means the only ones delivering the message that being beautiful in our society means being thin. Images of tall, slim models are ubiquitous in advertisements and fashion magazines. Thin young actresses are the objects of desire in popular movies and television shows. In attempts to achieve this ideal figure, many young women go on fad diets that may cut out entire classes of food, such as fats or carbohydrates; take drugs to suppress their appetites; or induce vomiting and take laxatives to avoid gaining weight (Striegel-Moore & Cachelin, 1999). All these practices endanger their health and, in extreme forms, can lead to psychiatric conditions known as *eating disorders*.

One eating disorder that has received a great deal of attention from the psychiatric community is *anorexia nervosa*, a condition in which girls (and only rarely boys) starve themselves, losing up to 25 percent or more of their body weight. Girls suffering from this condition consider themselves to be fat even when, by objective standards, they are painfully thin. To enhance their weight loss, they may exercise feverishly even when they weigh well under 100 pounds. Anorexia poses numerous health threats, including serious malnutrition, manifested in such symptoms as cessation of menstruation, pale skin, the appearance of fine black hairs on the body, and extreme sensitivity to cold. Anorexia nervosa has one of the highest death rates of all psychiatric disorders (Keel et al., 2003). Anorexia is estimated to afflict approximately 5 in every 100,000 adolescent American girls, but it is much more prevalent among the white middle and upper classes, where the incidence is as high as 1 in every 100 girls (Hendren & Berenson, 1997).

A more common eating disorder is *bulimia nervosa*, which is found in all classes. Estimates are that 5 percent of all girls (and a smaller percentage of boys) are afflicted with this disorder (Keel & Klump, 2003). Girls suffering from bulimia are usually obsessed with their weight. They try to keep it at a suboptimal level by starving themselves, but this effort is broken by periods of "binge eating," during which they eat abnormal amounts. Typically, these binges are followed by self-induced vomiting or the use of heavy doses of laxatives. Bulimia usually begins when a girl is in late adolescence, often when she leaves home for college, and continues into her twenties.

Unlike girls suffering from anorexia, bulimic girls are near normal weight and thus are not in danger of starving themselves to death. However, they are at risk for a variety of health problems, including gastrointestinal damage and heart failure due to electrolyte imbalance. In addition, bulimia has been closely linked with substance abuse (O'Brien & Vincent, 2003). One study of 2016 Canadian high school students found that binge eaters, particularly girls who then compensate for their eating binges by taking laxatives or vomiting, were more likely than their peers to smoke, use marijuana and other illegal drugs, and consume alcohol (Ross & Ivis, 1999).

Several studies have explored the factors that lead to these and other eating problems. Alison Field and her colleagues (1999) conducted a prospective study of nearly 7000 girls. In the course of one year, 74 of the girls developed bulimia. The researchers identified three factors that contribute to the onset of the eating disorder in these girls: the early onset of puberty; the importance of thinness within the girls' peer groups; and the importance that the girls placed on trying to look like models in television, movies, and magazines.

In another longitudinal study, Julia Graber and her colleagues followed 116 adolescent girls from the ages of 14 to 22, the age range during which many girls of normal weight begin to diet (Graber et al., 1994). The girls filled out questionnaires about their attitudes toward food, their satisfaction with the way they looked, and their perception of social pressures to gain or lose weight. The researchers found that several factors were associated with an obsession with weight

of the female body also accounts for the different reactions that parents have to their sons' and daughters' development. In contrast to boys, who report that their parents grant them greater freedom as they become sexually mature, many girls report that their parents become more restrictive (Martin, 1996).

One of the physical changes associated with the growth spurt during puberty, and which carries significant psychological consequences, is an increase in weight. For boys this increase comes largely from an increase in muscle mass. For girls this increase is largely the result of the accumulation of fat. It has been estimated that during adolescence the average girl gains a little over 24 pounds in the form of body fat (Bogin, 1999).

These changes are perfectly normal, but insofar as they result in a body size and shape that deviates from cultural ideals, they can be the source of significant

Although the average developing girl gains as much as ten pounds each year during her puberty, she is surrounded by media messages that glamorize bodies that are grossly underweight.

depression were more likely than their peers to develop an eating disorder.

Recent studies of twins have allowed developmentalists to explore possible genetic contributions to these complex disorders. Several studies have found that both members of identical twin pairs are more likely to develop eating disorders compared with fraternal twin pairs (Bulik et al., 2001; Klump et al., 2003; Wade et al., 2000), a finding that is highly suggestive of a genetic component to the illnesses. Moreover, by identifying identical twin pairs in which one member develops a disorder and the other does not, researchers are able to examine the contributions of specific environmental factors. For example, in one study, twins who developed bulimia were more likely to be anxious and fearful, and demonstrate lower levels of mastery and self-esteem, compared with their unaffected twins (Bulik et al., 2001).

No single treatment has proved to be effective in the case of either of these chronic, frequently relapsing eating disorders (Hendren & Berenson, 1997). Because of the potentially fatal consequences of anorexia nervosa, and because most adolescents suffering from this condition deny that there is anything wrong with them, the first step in treating many victims of anorexia is to hospitalize them in an attempt to restore their body weight to a more normal level. Individual, group, family, and cognitive-behavioral therapies have all been used to help anorexic girls overcome their distorted body image. Most adolescents suffering from bulimia are treated as outpatients with a combination of antidepressant drugs and psychological counseling (Hendren & Berenson, 1997).

and eating, including amount of body fat (heavier girls were most likely to exhibit chronic eating disorders), pubertal timing, body image, and family relationships. Among girls who entered puberty relatively early and who had poor body images, those who were in conflict with their families were at increased risk for chronic eating disorders. Personality factors also played a role: as confirmed in several other studies (Bizeul et al., 2003; Ross & Ivis, 1999), girls who suffered from a higher level of psychological

psychological distress (Polivy & Herman, 2004). In the United States, a thin, prepubertal body shape is taken as the ideal for women, an ideal that is reflected in everything from television, movie, and magazine images to the shapes of dolls given to young girls (Botta, 1999). Reinforcing the ideal is the media's frequent representation of heavy-set people as unhappy, unattractive individuals who lack self-control and are undeserving of respect or admiration. For better or for worse, the thin, prepubertal body shape idealized by the media is unattainable for most females after puberty. As a consequence, many adolescent girls are dissatisfied with their new, more mature bodies. They see themselves as being "overweight" and "ugly" (Rosenblum & Lewis, 1999) (see Figure 15.5, p. 592), and many go to great lengths to lose weight (see the box "Eating Disorders").

Figure 15.5 The relationship of pubertal change to body image. While boys retain a basically positive image of their bodies as they go through puberty, girls' self-image declines dramatically. (From Brooks-Gunn & Petersen, 1983.)

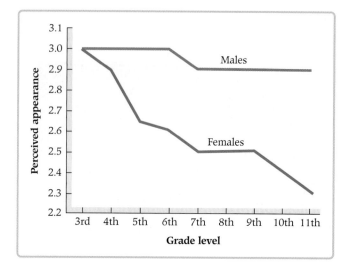

One study found strong correlations between the risk of developing an eating disorder and the extent to which girls reported trying to look like the women they see on television, in movies, or in magazines (Field et al., 1999). The risk for developing an eating disorder was also high for girls who reported that thinness is important to their peers. The study is particularly significant because the scientists used a *prospective study* (see also Chapter 14, p. 549). That is, they gave a questionnaire regarding peer and media influences to nearly seven thousand 9- to 14-year-old girls, and followed up a year later to see which girls developed disorders.

The extent to which girls are satisfied with their bodies is influenced not only by the media but also by how peers and family members respond to their appearance; and these responses, in turn, are influenced by the cultural contexts in which the peers and family members participate (Alsaker, 1996; Jones, 2003). Girls from African American and Mexican American families, for example, are less likely than American girls of European descent to perceive themselves as overweight when their weight is normal, primarily because their cultures value a larger body size (Altabe, 1998; Guinn et al., 1997). African Americans are also less likely than their European American counterparts to define attractiveness exclusively in terms of body size, and to feel less social pressure to be thin (Cross & Gore, 2003).

Early research on eating disorders in central and southeast Asia suggested much lower prevalence rates than those reported in North America. However, this is beginning to change. Recent studies find evidence of body image dissatisfaction and eating disorders among Japanese and Taiwanese adolescent girls, and the incidence seems to be increasing (Nakamura et al., 1999; Wong et al., 2000). Some have argued that cultural biases in diagnosing the disorders led to underreporting prevalence rates early on, while others have argued that increasing rates are due to the increasing influence of Western values throughout Asia (Lake et al., 2000). Either way, understanding eating disorders and, by extension, how to treat them, requires attention to the broader social conditions in which they emerge.

Consequences of Early and Late Maturation

Adolescents' responses to the onset of puberty are also influenced by the age at which they undergo these changes. Research on the effects of early versus late sexual maturation has become an important area for integrating across the biological, social, and behavioral systems of adolescence (Compas, et al., 1995). Several studies have sought to determine how pubertal timing might affect young people's peer relations, personality, and social adjustment. In the case of girls, early development has been identified as a *risk factor* (see Chapter 7, p. 257) that contributes to a variety of problems, including depression (Kaltiala-Heino et al., 2003), eating disorders (Cauffman & Steinberg, 1996), and early drug use and sexual behavior (Mezzich et al., 1997; Stattin & Magnusson, 1990; reviewed in Dick et al., 2000). Late maturation, on the other hand, seems to operate as a *protective factor* (see Chapter 7, p. 258) against some of these negative outcomes.

In elementary school, girls who develop before their peers are often embarrassed about the changes in their bodies and may take to wearing big shirts and slouching to hide their breasts. Later, they are more likely than their late-maturing peers to be dissatisfied with their bodies. This is because early-maturing children tend to weigh more and to be slightly shorter than late-maturing children when they finish puberty, and this difference persists throughout life (Brooks-Gunn & Reiter, 1990). Thus, early-maturing girls are less likely to approximate the ideal body shape promoted in most Western cultures.

For some girls, early maturation brings greater social prestige based on sexual attractiveness. One study found that girls who had reached puberty by the sixth or seventh grade considered themselves more popular with boys and were more likely to be dating than girls who had not yet reached puberty (Simons et al., 1987). But this increased social prestige may carry potential risks. A longitudinal study of Swedish adolescent girls found that early-maturing girls were more likely to be in sexual relationships by mid-adolescence than girls who matured later. They were also more likely to experience a decline in their academic performance and engage in such problem behaviors as truancy, drug and alcohol use, shoplifting, and running away (Stattin & Magnusson, 1990). An interesting study of twin sisters who were highly discordant for pubertal timing (one twin experienced menarche significantly earlier than the other) found that 40 percent of the early maturing sisters began smoking and/or drinking by the age of 13 (Dick et al., 2000). The early onset of tobacco and alcohol use is considered a risk factor for later drug use and addiction (Grant & Dawson, 1997).

One popular explanation for the link between pubertal timing and problem behavior is that early-maturing girls tend to associate with older peers, resulting in experimentation at an earlier age (Stattin & Magnusson, 1990). Other research suggests that associations with boys, in particular, contribute to girls' problem behaviors. For example, Avshalom Caspi and his colleagues compared the behavior of

Although the average age of puberty continues to drop in many developed nations, there continue to be wide individual differences. As shown in this scene, some individuals attain puberty earlier, and some later than average. Developmentalists find that early and late maturation has different psychological consequences for girls and boys.

Girls who are involved in team sports may feel more confidence in themselves, and show higher levels of admiration and respect for each other.

It is likely that these adolescent dancers have a higher sense of well-being, use drugs less, have more positive relationships with their parents, and do better in school compared to their peers who are not involved in sports and dance.

early- and late-maturing girls who attended either an all-girls or a coed secondary school in New Zealand (Caspi, 1995; Caspi et al., 1993). They found that the girls who attended an all-girls school had higher academic performance and lower rates of delinquent behavior than did girls attending a coed school. They attributed the better outcomes at the all-girls school to the absence of boys, because it is boys who most often are the instigators of girls' socially disapproved behavior.

The degree of adult supervision is yet another possible explanation for the relationship between early maturation and problem behavior. Early maturers receive less monitoring by parents and teachers compared to on-time and late maturers (Silbereisen & Kracke, 1997). This finding holds for boys as well as girls, so it is not surprising to learn that adolescent boys who reach puberty at a relatively early age are also more likely to smoke, drink, use drugs, and get in trouble with the law (Duncan et al., 1985). Early sexual maturation is also associated with lower self-control and less emotional stability, as measured by psychological tests (Sussman et al., 1985)

Although *very* early-maturing and late-maturing boys are at risk for depression (Kaltiala-Heino et al., 2003), early-maturing boys seem to have a more favorable attitude toward their bodies. In part, this is because their greater size and strength make them more capable athletes, and athletic prowess brings them social recognition (Graber et al., 1997; Simmons & Blyth, 1987). Physical activity seems to act as a protective factor for many adolescents. Those who engage in physical activity experience greater well-being compared with less physically active adolescents. Studies indicate that high levels of athletic activity are generally associated with less depression, less drug use, better relationships with parents, and higher academic performance, for adolescent girls and boys alike (Field et al., 2001). Karin Martin conducted intensive interviews on issues of sexuality and pubertal development with adolescent girls and boys, and concluded that girls who are involved in sports feel confidence in themselves and their bodies, and show a good deal of admiration and respect for each other (Martin, 1996, p. 109).

It is important to keep in mind that the effects of early and later onset of puberty are not the inevitable outcome of biological processes. Rather, such outcomes are mediated by the social context in which early maturation takes place and by the way others respond to the physical changes young people are experiencing. As you saw in Chapter 7 (p. 245), development is a *transactional* process: whether early or late experience of puberty has lasting effects, and what those effects are, depend on how others respond to the changes when they occur, how the individual reacts to those responses, and the consequences that follow from those interactions.

The Reorganization of Social Life

The dramatic biological changes that young people experience during adolescence are associated with equally dramatic changes in the way they interact with their families and their peers. The nature and influence of different relationships change significantly and become an important ground for testing and experimenting with higher levels of maturity, independence, and responsibility. In this section we will discuss changing patterns of friendship and peer relations, the emergence of sexual relationships, and changing feelings and communication styles between adolescents and their parents.

©Steve Skjold/Photo Edit, Inc.

©Tim Kiusalaas/Masterfile

A New Relationship with Peers

As children enter adolescence, their social relationships with their peers undergo a marked reorganization that involves several major changes (Brown, 1990). First, peer interaction outside school increases to the point where high school students spend twice as much time with their peers as they do with their parents or other adults (Csikszentmihalyi & Larson, 1984; Fuligni & Stevenson, 1995). Moreover, compared with younger children, adolescents are more mobile and better able to avoid the watchful eyes of parents and other authorities. As you will see, not only does the amount of time spent with peers change, but so does the nature of these peer interactions and relationships. Peer groups increase in size and diversity during adolescence, and friendships and other close relationships increase in intensity. Developmentalists have been working to understand the nature of these changes, and the implications they have for other areas of adolescent growth and adjustment.

The social world of adolescents is composed of three primary types of peer relationships, each of which has different functions and fulfills different needs: dyadic friendships, cliques, and crowds. **Dyadic friendships** refer to close relationships between two individuals. Adolescents' close relationships serve two significant developmental functions: intimacy and autonomy, the "yin and yang of social life" (Barr, 1997; Selman et al., 1997). In contrast, cliques (the small, primary peer group of good friends) and crowds (the larger network of friends and acquaintances) are group structures that facilitate the evolution of group norms and values, and the transition to romantic relationships.

Adolescence sets the stage for the emergence of romantic relationships, creating a whole new context for social interactions.

Friendships

You may recall from previous chapters that the friendships of young children are often based on such shifting and transitory factors as being in the same play area together or playing with the same toys. As a preschooler was reported to say about a new companion in his life, "we're friends now because we know each other's names" (Rubin, 1980). Several large-scale studies conducted in the United States and other industrialized countries document the changing basis of friendships as children enter adolescence (Berndt, 1988; Cottrell, 1996; Schneider & Stevenson, 1999). In contrast to the apparently superficial characteristics that bind young children together, adolescent friendships are distinguished by the importance that teenagers place on three fundamental attributes: reciprocity, commitment, and equality (Hartup, 1993; Larsen, 1996). The assumption of reciprocity, the give and take of close relationships, includes emotional sharing as well as the sharing of interests and activities. Commitment refers to the loyalty and trust between friends. Finally, equality refers to the equal distribution of power among friends.

As mentioned previously, adolescent friendships serve at least two significant developmental functions: intimacy and autonomy (Selman et al., 1997). Intimacy, "the gratifying connection between two individuals through some combination of shared feelings, thoughts, and activities," is probably what comes easiest to mind when we reflect on the importance of friendship (Selman et al., 1997, p. 32). However, as Selman and his colleagues have demonstrated in numerous studies of normally developing and psychosocially disturbed children and adolescents, in healthy relationships intimacy is balanced with autonomy—the ability to assert one's own needs. Indeed, unhealthy friendships can place a child at significant risk, depending on whether the scales tip more toward intimacy or autonomy. Selman and his colleagues point out that the inability to assert one's needs without jeopardizing the relationship may contribute to a child's willingness to bow to peer pressure. On the other hand, an excess of assertiveness can become coercive bullying that leads one's peers into risky behaviors.

dyadic friendships Close relationships between two individuals.

The friendship circles of adolescent boys are generally larger and less intimate than those of adolescent girls. Male friends are much more likely to discuss their thoughts about sports, cars, and girls than they are to reveal their self-doubts and anxieties.

Eastcott/The Image Works

While friends are important to both boys and girls during adolescence, there are differences in the quality of their friendships. In particular, research finds that girls' friendships are more intense than friendships among boys (Brown et al., 1999). In middle adolescence, girls' friendships tend to have a feverish, jealous quality about them. At this stage, girls who are close friends often watch each other's every move, calling each other on the telephone several times a day to report to each other and check up on one another. They also copy each other's behavior. If one girl has a boyfriend, her best friend will try to acquire a boyfriend, too. This intense, competitive aspect of girls' friendships tends to wane by late adolescence, perhaps because, as Elizabeth Douvan and Joseph Adelson (1966) suggest, girls are "less haunted by fears of being abandoned and betrayed" (p. 192).

In contrast, boys between the ages of 14 and 16 years report that their friendships are less close, and more numerous, than those of girls. Several explanations have been offered to account for the apparent gender differences in intimacy. Thomas Berndt and Lonna Murphy (2002), for example, suggest that male adolescent friendships are less intimate because teenage boys are less trusting of their friends compared with teenage girls. Duane Buhrmester and Wyndol Furman (1987), on the other hand, suggest that the differences are more a matter of style than of substance. They have found that boys form friendships "in which sensitivity to needs and validation of worth are achieved through actions and deeds, rather than through interpersonal disclosure of personal thoughts and feelings" (pp. 111–112). Yet another argument is that homophobia—an exaggerated fear of homosexuality—prevents adolescent males from demonstrating or admitting to strong feelings of intimacy toward their male friends (Raymond, 1994).

For both boys and girls, adolescent friendships play a developmental role similar in certain respects to the role of attachment in infancy. As you saw in Chapters 5 and 6, during infancy babies engage in "social referencing"—continually looking to their caregivers to see how they evaluate what is going on—and they use their caregivers as a "secure base" to which they can retreat when they feel threatened as they explore their environment. During adolescence, friends look to each other for help in confronting and making sense of uncertain and often anxiety-provoking situations. The first time a boy calls up a girl for a date, his best friend may well be standing at his elbow providing support and maybe some coaching. And no sooner has the girl hung up than she is likely to call her best friend to tell her about the conversation and get her opinion. The two pairs of friends will decide together if the call was a success or a failure and will lay plans for the next move. For both the infant and the adolescent, the attachment bond is gradually modified by successful interaction with the outside world. Eventually, just as the baby relies less on the mother, the adolescent will begin to depend less on the best friend.

Evidence from a number of studies (Eccles et al., 2003) indicates that close friendships have a positive influence on adolescents' social and personality development. Adolescents who perceive their friends as supportive report fewer school-related and psychological problems, greater confidence in their social acceptance by peers, and less loneliness. Difficulty in making friends during adolescence is part of a broader syndrome of poor social adjustment.

The intimacy and autonomy of close relationships are the "yin and yang" of adolescent social life.

Most research on adolescent friendships has included mainly middle-class, European American teenagers. When the relationships of ethnic minority and low-income adolescents are explored, a somewhat different view comes into focus (Way & Pahl, 2001). In particular, researchers have suggested that because interdependence and loyalty may be more highly prized among certain ethnic groups and in particular communities, adolescents' relationships may be correspondingly more intimate, and gender differences may be less apparent. A survey of low-income African American, Latino, and Asian American adolescents indicates that African American and Latino teenagers report more positive and satisfying friendships compared with their Asian American counterparts, perhaps because Asian American parents impose strict rules regarding their adolescents' peer interactions and relationships (Way & Chen, 2000). Moreover, gender differences in adolescents' perceptions of the quality of their relationships were discerned only among the Latinos. Understanding the complex interplay between ethnicity, family values, gender, and socioeconomic status presents a major challenge to developmentalists interested in adolescents' friendships.

Cliques and Crowds

A friendship is the smallest unit of peer interaction, a group of two. As children in some industrialized countries move into adolescence, two additional, more inclusive kinds of peer groups become prominent—cliques and crowds. A **clique** is a group of several young people that remains small enough to enable its members to be in regular interaction with one another and to serve as the primary peer group (Brown & Klute, 2003). Members of cliques are often friends of the same sex who dress alike and share similar interests (Cottrell, 1996). According to John Cottrell (1996), "Cliques are the building blocks of peer society, the anchor of social activities, and the access route for making new friends" (p. 24).

Dexter Dunphy (1963), one of the first researchers to study cliques, noted that they are about the size of a family, and that they serve a similar emotional function as an "alternative center of security" (p. 233). They have an internal structure that usually includes a leader, who tends to be more mature, more socially connected, and is looked to for advice and counsel, particularly with respect to romantic relationships. Most adolescents belong to several different cliques that are organized at different times of the day, or in different settings. For example, an adolescent may be a member of one clique in science class, another during gymnastics practice, and still another in the neighborhood on the weekends. In this respect, cliques differ from friendships, which are not restricted to a particular setting (Cottrell, 1996).

clique A group of several young people that remains small enough to enable its members to be in regular interaction with one another and to serve as the primary peer group.

(a) An adolescent's primary peer group is usually similar in size to a family, and serves similar emotional functions. (b) This crowd of Oxide and Nutrino fans probably includes a number of cliques—smaller groups of good friends who came to the concert together, and will depart together. According to Dunphy, the crowd serves the important function of providing opportunities for adolescents to meet new people and develop new relationships.

The second type of peer-group structure is the **crowd.** According to Dunphy's original work, the crowd is a large, mixed-gender network that emerges when cliques interact. Imagine a big party or get-together. Beforehand, many of the adolescents will assemble in their cliques and travel together to the event. Once they arrive, they will likely intermingle with teenagers from other cliques. When it's time to go home, however, the original cliques will reconstitute. The primary function of the crowd, according to Dunphy's analysis, is to provide adolescents with opportunities to meet new people and develop new relationships. The primary function of the clique is to provide access to a crowd.

Recently, developmentalists have focused on the patterns of behavior, shared interests, beliefs, and values that provide a basis for a crowd's reputation (Brown, 1999). Stereotyped labels such as jocks, brains, loners, druggies, nerds, and so on, are repeatedly encountered in the descriptions adolescents use to differentiate among reputation-based crowds (Brown & Huang, 1995; Eckert, 1995). In schools with a diverse ethnic population, ethnic labels (African Americans, Latinos, Asians, etc.) are also common (Brown & Huang, 1995). As names such as "jocks," "druggies," "brains" indicate, crowds vary in the extent to which their norms and values fit with those of the adult community. These differences are seen clearly in Table 15.1, which summarizes differences among high school crowds studied by Brad Brown and Bih-Hu Huang (1995) with respect to four characteristics: grades, the importance attached to schooling, drug use, and delinquency. Other names—"normal," "outcast"—indicate how the crowd's norms and values adhere to those of the adolescent community. In general, crowds and the way they are categorized help adolescents learn about the alternative social identities that are available to them, and strongly influence whom they are likely to meet and spend time with (Brown et al., 1994).

table 15.1

Crowd Differences in Mean Scores on Outcome Measures								
Outcome	**Total**	**Jock**	**Popular**	**Druggie**	**Outcast**	**Brain**	**Normal**	**Floater**	**Outsider**
GPA	3.06	3.26	3.18	2.82	2.87	3.61	3.19	3.13	2.65
Importance of schooling	3.86	4.22	3.95	3.34	3.84	4.23	4.10	4.02	3.42
Drug use	1.33	1.43	2.61	1.28	1.11	1.27	1.34	2.02	1.62
Minor delinquency	1.41	1.33	1.34	1.77	1.31	1.15	1.21	1.29	1.64

Note. Values are adjusted for the effects of gender and grade level. Higher scores indicate higher levels of the construct described by the scale.
Source: Brown & Huang, 1995.

In addition, being identified as a member of a particular crowd has a significant impact on an adolescent's social status. In a classic study of the relationship between individual status and crowd association, James S. Coleman (1962) analyzed questionnaires distributed to thousands of U.S. students at ten high schools in small towns, small cities, large cities, and suburbs. In every school he studied, Coleman found that students could identify a "leading crowd" against which they evaluated themselves.

The popularity derived from being associated with groups other than the leading crowd seems to vary. For example, as a rule, "brains" occupy a status somewhere between the elite groups and groups that are disparaged. However, in some groups, poor academic achievement is associated with high levels of popularity (Rodkin et al., 2000). This is the case in certain peer groups where aggressive, low achieving individuals are highly popular among their friends (Estell et al., 2002). Likewise, in some working-class African American communities, being labeled as a "brain" can lead to being ostracized, and academically able young people try to mask their abilities in order to avoid this fate (Ogbu, 1997).

Homophily and Conformity

An aspect of adolescent social relationships that has been extensively examined is **homophily.** Homophily refers to the degree to which friends are similar to each other (Kandel, 1978; Patrick et al., 2002). Although adolescents in the United States are more mobile than younger children, attend larger schools, and have more opportunities to meet peers of other social classes and ethnic backgrounds, their close friends tend to be even more similar to them than they were in elementary school, a trend that continues throughout adolescence (Berndt & Keefe, 1995). High school friends tend to be similar in their views of school, their academic achievement, and their dating and other leisure-time activities (Berndt & Murphy, 2002; Patrick et al., 2002). They also tend to feel the same way about drug use, drinking, and delinquency (Akers et al., 1998; Tani et al., 2001; Urberg et al., 1998).

A seminal study by Denise Kandel and her colleagues (1978) focused on the developmental processes through which homophily is established. In a year-long, longitudinal study of drug use, educational goals, and delinquency, she determined that two processes are involved: selection and socialization. In the process of **selection** adolescents seek out other teenagers who seem similar to themselves in important traits and behaviors, especially those that are relevant to the adolescent's social reputation (Bagwell et al., 2000). Hockey players are more likely to break the ice with other hockey players; delinquents seek out other delinquents; and so on. Through selection, adolescents target certain others as potential friends. Once selection has done its job, the second process of *socialization* is engaged. Through socialization, socially significant behaviors are modeled and reinforced in the course of ongoing interactions. Socialization accounts for the tendency of individuals to become increasingly more alike—to show higher levels of behavioral agreement—as their relationships develop over time. For example, recent studies have found that children who are at risk for antisocial behavior and who become friendly with delinquent peers are likely to become delinquent themselves (Rodkin et al., 2000).

For many decades developmentalists have worried that it may be unhealthy for adolescents to spend excessive time with their peers, beyond the observation and control of adults. Frederic Thrasher (1927) argued as much in his classic study of more than 1300 Chicago gangs in existence during the early years of the 1900s. The problem, he argued, was not due to the nature of the boys who joined the gangs, many of which began as neighborhood play groups. Gangs only became problematic when they functioned without supervision and opportunities to participate in more socially acceptable activity. More recently, Urie Bronfenbrenner (1970) made

crowd A large, reputation-based and mixed-gender social network observed when cliques interact.

homophily The degree to which friends are similar to each other.

selection The process by which adolescents seek out other teenagers who seem similar to themselves in important traits and behaviors, most generally those that are relevant to the adolescent's social reputation.

Risk Taking and Social Deviance during Adolescence

While the extent of psychological storm and stress during adolescence continues to be debated, there is little doubt that in modern industrial societies, adolescents engage in an exceptional level of socially disapproved behaviors that pose risks to their long-term well-being (Arnett, 1999; Centers for Disease Control and Prevention, 1998):

- One in four sexually active U.S. adolescents will contract a sexually transmitted disease; this level is twice that of people in their twenties.

- One in five adolescents reports having seriously considered committing suicide in the past year.

- Driving under the influence of alcohol is reported by 17 percent of high school students, and one in three reports participating in "binge drinking" (having five or more drinks on a single occasion) within the prior month.

- Adolescents commit a disproportionate number of petty crimes.

These statistics, coupled with the fact that the levels of such behaviors seem to have risen sharply in recent years, have spurred efforts to determine the causes of adolescent risk taking and social deviance (Call et al., 2002).

One insight into the problem comes from cross-cultural evidence, which indi-cates that high levels of risk taking and antisocial behavior are not a universal outcome of the transition to adulthood (Schlegel & Barry, 1991). Two features distinguish societies where antisocial behavior is common from those where it is not. First, antisocial behavior is comparatively low in societies where adolescent boys spend most of their time with adult men at work. In contrast, antisocial behavior is high in societies where boys spend most of their time in peer groups. Second, the nature of the interactions in a given peer group makes a difference. When peer groups are organized for competition and given special names, antisocial behavior is significantly higher than it is when peer relations are less formally organized and are non-competitive. These results immediately indicate why high levels of antisocial behavior could be expected in industrialized societies such as Canada and the United States, where adolescents spend a great deal of time in peer groups that are often highly organized and competitive, with schools, gangs, and sports teams being prominent examples. Pierre Dasen (1999) points out that in rapidly changing societies in Africa, where traditional authority structures are eroding and adolescent males no longer spend their days with older men, the kinds of problematic risk-taking behaviors that present a significant social problem in the industrialized world are beginning to emerge.

Lauren Greenfield

These girls were photographed inhaling air freshener in the bathroom of their high school. Inexpensive and readily available, inhalants are an increasingly popular avenue to drug abuse among adolescents.

Cross-cultural comparisons identify the social conditions that promote adolescent risk taking, but they do not explain what it is that actually precipitates risk taking in those conditions. One frequently offered explana-

the point that "if children have contact only with their own age-mates, there is no possibility for learning culturally-established patterns of cooperation and mutual concern" (p. 121). In short, the belief was that, left to themselves, adolescents are likely to engage in antisocial behavior.

There is a lot of evidence to support the belief that adolescents are inherently prone to misbehaving. For example, Thomas Berndt and Keunho Keefe (1995) asked a large group of seventh- and eighth-graders to fill out a questionnaire about their involvement in school and any disruptive behaviors they engaged in. They were also asked to identify their friends. Their teachers were asked to fill out a questionnaire about each participant to check on the validity of the self-reports. The questionnaires were given both in the fall and in the spring of the school year.

As one might expect, Berndt and Keefe found that boys and girls whose friends engaged in a high level of disruptive behavior in the fall reported an increase in the level of their own disruptive behavior in the spring, with the girls being more susceptible to such influence. Other studies show that if an adolescent's close friends smoke cigarettes, drink alcohol, use illegal drugs, are sexually active, or break the law, sooner or later the adolescent is likely to do these

tion is that adolescents ignore or greatly underestimate the risks they are taking and don't believe that anything bad can happen to them. To evaluate this possibility, researchers have compared the risk evaluations of adolescents and adults. In general, researchers have found that adolescents are likely to think that they are at less risk than other people for experiencing such events as an automobile accident, an unplanned pregnancy, and alcohol dependency; however, adults are also vulnerable to these types of errors (Quadrel et al., 1993).

Other evidence suggests that an important psychological characteristic underpinning adolescent risk taking is sensation seeking, a personality trait defined by the extent of a person's desire for novelty and intense sensory stimulation (Arnett, 1999). Jeffrey Arnett (1996) and others have repeatedly found significant correlations between measures of sensation seeking and a variety of risk behaviors, including promiscuous sexual activity, drinking, drug use, and antisocial behavior.

While the sensation-seeking hypothesis may apply to some kinds of adolescent risk taking in some contexts, it does not seem applicable to many others. Richard Jessor (1992) levels this criticism:

> Playing the game of "Chicken" on the highway, taking chances on avoiding detection during certain delinquent acts, or pursuing activities like rock climbing may be exemplars [of sensation-seeking behaviors]. But the larger class of adolescent risk behavior does not lend itself to that kind of analysis. Few adolescents continue cigarette smoking for the thrill of seeing whether or not they can avoid pulmonary disease; few engage in unprotected sexual intercourse for the thrill of beating the odds of contracting a sexually transmitted disease or becoming pregnant. Indeed a key concern of health educators is to make adolescents aware that there are risks associated with many of the behaviors they engage in. (p. 379)

Against the prevailing negative view of adolescent risk taking, Cynthia Lightfoot (2004) maintains that some risk taking in adolescence is natural and necessary for normal development. On the basis of interviews with 41 teenagers, 15 to 17 years old, she concluded that risk taking is often a mode of play that helps to create bonds between friends, to test the limits of adult authority, and to test oneself. For example, one 17-year-old answered her question about the attractions of taking risks this way:

> What's appealing? I think growth—inner growth. And a feeling of independence and maturity in trying something new. Even if I fail, I still kind of pat myself on the back and say, "Hey, you tried it, and no one can blame you for sitting back and not participating." I want to be a participant. (Lightfoot, 1997, p. 97)

Robert Selman and his colleagues have also explored the relationship between risk-taking behavior and normal developmental processes. Adopting a perspective that emphasizes the importance of how adolescents interpret their own risk-taking behavior, Robert Selman and Sigrun Adalbjarnardottir (2000) conducted an in-depth analysis of Icelandic boys' alcohol consumption. They proposed that adolescents' understanding of their own drinking behavior depends on their cognitive developmental ability to coordinate individual, peer, and cultural perspectives. For example, one boy said that he began experimenting with alcohol "in order to fit in," reflecting his concern with the peer perspective of social expectations. However, another boy interpreted his drinking in light of broad, Icelandic cultural practices that promote drinking, especially in males: "It was part of my culture. My friends and family like to drink when they are together" (p. 56).

At present, developmentalists have no fully satisfactory explanation or solution for difficulties caused by adolescent risk taking. While it is clear that the social and cultural organization of modern life greatly increases adolescent risk taking and antisocial behavior, the complex ways in which these contextual factors contribute to risk taking make it a very difficult pattern of behavior to explain or to deal with.

things, too (see "Risk-taking and Social Deviance during Adolescence") (Cairns & Cairns, 1994; Reed & Roundtree, 1997).

Dishion and his colleagues have suggested that **deviancy training** contributes to adolescents' antisocial behavior. Deviancy training was defined as the development of positive reactions to discussions of rule breaking. In a series of longitudinal studies, boys and their friends were videotaped as they engaged in problem-solving discussions. As shown in Figure 15.6, deviancy training in the discussion groups at age 13 or 14 predicted the initiation of tobacco, alcohol, and marijuana use by age 15 or 16 (Dishion et al., 1995).

Peer processes similar to deviancy training have been blamed for the surprising finding that group counseling and therapy for delinquent adolescents may actually do more harm than good (Dishion et al., 1999). In fact, recent findings from two experimentally controlled intervention studies indicate that peer-group interventions actually increase adolescents' problem behaviors (Dishion et al., 1999). This is a good lesson in the importance of scientific research in planning and understanding counseling and intervention practices. It also underscores the importance of designing and using developmentally appropriate therapies. Therapeutic strategies that are effective with adults may backfire when used with adolescents.

deviancy training Positive reactions to discussions of rule breaking.

Figure 15.6 Deviancy training occurs when adolescents participate in discussions that portray rule breaking in a positive light. Dishion found that adolescents involved in deviancy training between the ages of 13 and 14 were more likely to exhibit delinquent behavior when they were 15 or 16 years of age.

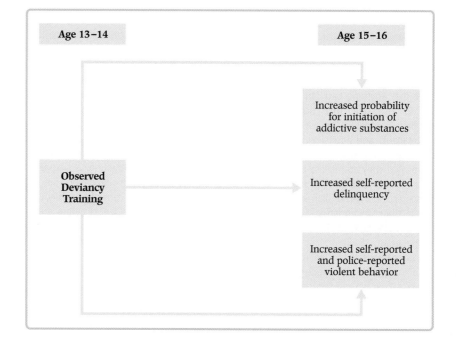

Adolescent gangs have been studied since the early 1900s. Modern developmentalists have focused on understanding the risk factors associated with gang involvement, as well as the social processes involved in deviant behavior.

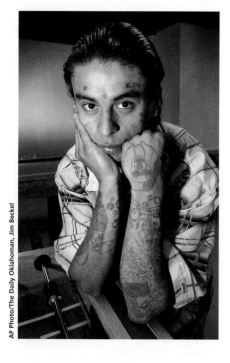

AP Photo/The Daily Oklahoman, Jim Beckel

Although research on deviancy training highlights how adolescents influence each other, it is likely that peer influence is but one of several factors that operate singly or together in influencing deviant behavior. At least three additional factors that have been examined include age, tolerance of deviance, and the desire to act "grown-up." Regarding the influence of age on deviant behavior, Thomas Berndt (1979) found that the level of conformity to peer pressure increased between the third and ninth grades (roughly between the ages of 9 and 15) and then decreased, a pattern that has been confirmed in other studies (Brown et al., 1986). To assess tolerance of deviance, Berndt asked his subjects to evaluate the seriousness of various kinds of antisocial behaviors, such as stealing candy from a store. He found that the adolescents evaluated antisocial behaviors as being less bad than third-graders did. Third-graders were likely to say that stealing candy from a store is very bad, whereas ninth-graders did not seem to think it was particularly bad at all.

Even with evidence showing that older adolescents are increasingly likely to drink alcoholic beverages, smoke cigarettes, and become sexually active if their friends do, it is not clear if such increases are the result of peer pressure or simply a part of the reorientation associated with becoming an adult. Adults disapprove of such activities for young people, though they think nothing of drinking or having sexual relations themselves. This situation has led some developmentalists to argue that age-related increases in drinking and other "grown-up" activities that some people consider risky should be viewed not as social deviance or susceptibility to peer pressure but as an attempt to model accepted adult behavior (Jessor, 1998).

The Transition to Sexual Relationships

In many cultures a key function of the peer group is to provide a context for the transition to romantic and sexual relationships (Connolly et al., 2000; Feiring, 1996; Furman, 1999). Consider the following description, synthesized from observations made by John Cottrell and his students in Australian shopping malls (Cottrell, 1996).

On a weekend evening, groups of five to ten teenagers can be observed "hanging out" at the shopping mall. The cliques of girls are window shopping; the cliques of boys position themselves to watch the cliques of girls. Within each clique there is a continual stream of loud talking and joking as the members covertly look over those in the other cliques around them. Often they seem to be acting up in ways calculated to get the attention of another clique. As the evening progresses, the cliques start to make direct contact with each other, interacting in a nonchalant manner that contrasts with the attention-getting behavior they had engaged in earlier. Cottrell likens the interaction among cliques of 13- to 14-year-old adolescents to a "marshaling area" in which several cliques eventually merge into a single crowd before the entire group goes off to watch a movie or go dancing at a disco.

The initial behavior of the 15- to 16-year-olds is similar, but instead of simply merging into a crowd, male and female cliques begin to interact with each other. As Cottrell puts it, what begins as apparently casual glances between members of two cliques is supplemented by body language that "becomes intense." At some point, one of the boys, usually someone who enjoys high status within his clique, walks over to the girls and begins talking to them. The two cliques remain where they met, and later in the evening, instead of going to some larger public event, they become organized into smaller subgroups composed of members of both sexes.

Dexter Dunphy's earlier study (1963) yielded a similar pattern of behavior. In particular, he documented a transition from the small, same-sex cliques of early adolescence, to the larger, mixed-sex crowds of mid-adolescence, which gradually disintegrate as members mature and begin to take on adult roles. Contemporary work generally supports the sequence of change that he reported, and also marks mid-adolescence as a major turning point during which nearly 50 percent of adolescents report involvement in relatively intense romantic relationships (Feiring, 1996).

Although the general pattern of changes reported in these studies provides convincing evidence of cultural continuity over time, there are important cultural and historical variations in adolescent social relationships (Berndt & Savin-Williams, 1993; Brown et al., 1994). On the basis of the data he collected in the late 1950s, Dunphy reported that the crowd disintegrated into groups of couples who were going steady or were engaged to get married. Fifty years later this pattern may continue in some parts of the world, but it does not appear to be generally characteristic of contemporary industrialized societies. Instead, marriage is often postponed until several years after the initiation of sexual activity (see Figure 15.7). Similarly, romantic relationships may evolve differently within different cultural

Figure 15.7 The length of time between puberty, initiation of sexual activity, and marriage in the United States, 1890 and 1988. (Reproduced with the permission of The Alan Guttmacher Institute from *Sex and America's Teenagers*, 1994, The Alan Guttmacher Institute, New York.)

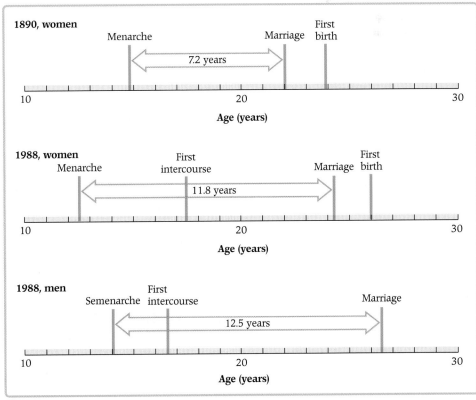

subgroups. For example, Anderson (1990) presented evidence indicating that male gangs in economically depressed neighborhoods actively discourage and even ridicule their members for involvement in significant relationships. And, given that most adolescent peer groups generally disapprove of homosexual relationships, as we will discuss in Chapter 16, it is likely that peer influences are quite different in the formation of gay and lesbian relationships.

Sexual Activity

According to the most recent data available, most U.S. adolescents 15 and under have not had sexual intercourse. The likelihood of teenagers having sexual intercourse increases steadily with age. Over half of 17-year-olds have had intercourse (see Figure 15.8) (The Alan Guttmacher Institute, 1999).

Adolescent sexual activity varies according to contextual factors, including the prevailing behavioral patterns in the culture and historical times in question. For example, in a survey of 114 societies, it was found that among girls, adolescent sexual activity was universal in 49 percent of the societies, common in 17 percent, occasional in 14 percent, and uncommon in 20 percent (Broude & Greene, 1976). The variability among societies in regard to adolescent sexual activity ranges from the customs of many Middle Eastern cultures that prohibit girls from having any contact with males outside their families after they reach puberty, to the expectation among certain groups in the Philippines that sexual activity will naturally occur. The situation in the contemporary United States is contradictory. A great deal of official public rhetoric discourages teenage sexual activity at the same time that the mass media often make it appear desirable and common. (See the box "Teenage Pregnancy," p. 606.)

In addition to differences in the age of onset, the form of sexual activity also varies culturally and historically. For example, oral sex is relatively common among college-educated European Americans, but rare among Hispanic Americans, African Americans, and older Americans (Michael, 1994). Because cultural and historical conditions dictate what constitutes appropriate sexual

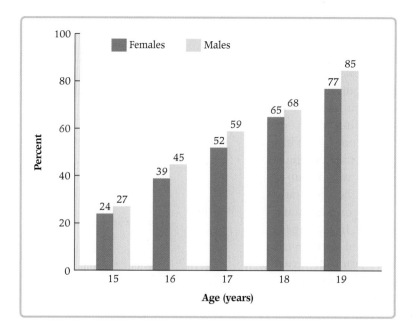

Figure 15.8 Percentage of teenagers who had sexual intercourse at different ages, 1995. (From The Alan Guttmacher Institute, 1999.)

behavior, it is not surprising that sex is not a simple biological act, but a complex process influenced by a variety of social factors and cultural meanings (Michael, 1994; Peplau et al., 1999).

In some cultures, including the Kaguru of Tanzania, knowledge of sexual behavior is communicated in the course of elaborate initiation ceremonies (Beidelman, 1997). Beidelman's extensive ethnographic studies indicate that direct communication between Kaguru parents and their children about sexual matters is strictly forbidden. However, the stories, riddles, and songs that young children are taught are very often colored with allusions to sex and sexuality, and most of the songs taught to pubescent boys and girls at initiation involve instruction about sexual organs and sexual relations, communicated mainly through metaphor. Here are two examples (from Beidelman, 1997, p. 198):

Although the awakening of sexual desire in adolescence is universal, cultures vary widely in how they permit it to be expressed.

©Susan Van Etten/Photo Edit, Inc.

> *Chimudodo chilimo, chidodo cilenga dilenga chitunge ne dikami.*
> *Translation:* The small, small mouth makes milk and water.
> *Explanation:* This song explains that the penis is capable of both urinating and ejaculating semen. Kaguru sometimes describe semen as a kind of nurturant milk. Semen not only produces children but is thought to foster the maturation of girls, who should have frequent intercourse if they want to develop a full, feminine figure.

> *Mang'ina sena mahusi-husi, galonda mbolo gabaka mafuta.*
> *Translation:* Your mothers are conniving to take a penis and anoint it with oil.
> *Explanation:* Women are said to lubricate men's penises with oil before intercourse. Some Kaguru say that a woman should pass down her oil container to her daughter. It is as much a material embodiment of her personhood as a bow and arrow or a shotgun is for a man. Castor oil facilitates the receptivity of women. It is also a means of blessing a person, as in bestowing a name. Any part of the body that is well oiled is thought to be more sexually attractive. At dances women often oil much of their bodies so that they glisten alluringly.

Communication about sexuality and other sexual matters varies dramatically among cultures, ethnic groups, and families. Studies of how mothers communicate with their adolescent children about sexuality and AIDS, for example, find significant differences that impact adolescents' knowledge of sexual matters. In one study it was found that mothers who dominated conversations about AIDS had adolescents who, two years later, were less knowledgeable about AIDS compared with adolescents whose mothers had been more interactive in their conversations (Boone et al., 2003).

Research has also uncovered interesting ethnic differences in communication patterns about sexual matters. For example, Lefkowitz and her colleagues (Lefkowitz et al., 2000) discovered that Latino American mothers tended to dominate conversations about sexuality and AIDS, compared with European American mothers, who demonstrated greater responsiveness in their conversations. The dominating conversational structure of Latino families is consistent with cultural expectations that children will be respectful and obedient toward their parents (Fuligni, 1998).

Teenage Pregnancy

About seven percent of all American teenagers become pregnant each year, giving the United States the highest teenage pregnancy rate among developed countries (National Center for Health Statistics, 2003). U.S. teenagers are no more sexually active than those in the other countries surveyed, so it seems clear that American adolescents use contraception far less often than do adolescents in other developed countries (The Alan Guttmacher Institute, 1999). One reason for the difference in the use of contraceptives may be that adults in many other industrialized countries have a more realistic view of the likelihood of teenage sexual activity and thus better prepare their adolescent children for dealing with their sexuality. In the United States, by contrast, sex education is still controversial in many communities and contraceptive use by teenagers is sporadic (Moran, 2000).

Researchers have identified a number of risk factors that increase the probability of teen pregnancy, including living in a disorganized or dangerous neighborhood or in a lower, socioeconomic-status family (Miller et al., 2001). Risk is diminished when parents provide higher levels of supervision and maintain values opposed to teen intercourse (or unprotected intercourse). Biological factors, including timing of pubertal development and hormone levels, also increase teen pregnancy risk, mainly because of their association with adolescent sexual intercourse.

Of the million teenage pregnancies that occur in the United States each year, the vast majority are unintended, and nearly one-third end in voluntary abortions (National Center for Health Statistics, 2003). However, researchers point out that "unintended" can have different levels of meaning. For teenage girls who are mired in poverty, grow up in communities in which teen pregnancy is common, and see few opportunities to advance themselves in other ways, pregnancy may be a means of establishing a role for themselves. As one teen mother reported, "Most of my friends do have their babies. It seems like most of them are lost and that seems like the only thing—they feel needed, and I figure that is why they get pregnant, because they want to be needed" (Moran, 2000, p. 225).

Race, social class, education, and the strength of religious beliefs all affect a teenager's decision about whether or not to have and keep her child (Coley & Chase-Lansdale, 1998). African American teenagers are more likely than European American teenagers to become single mothers. According to government statistics, 83 percent of the teenagers who give birth come from poor or low-income families (National Center for Health Statistics, 2003). The more education a pregnant teenager's mother has (which is an indirect measure of her social class) and the better the teenager is doing in school, the more likely she is to decide to terminate the pregnancy. On the other hand, teenagers with strong religious convictions are likely to have and keep their babies, no matter what their race or social class (Eisen et al., 1983).

While many of the negative outcomes that follow from teenage pregnancy, such as poverty and low educational achievement, also precede pregnancy (as many as one-third of all teen mothers drop out of school *before* they become pregnant; Aber et al., 1995), teenage childbearing serves to further limit the futures of girls who are already disadvantaged. Compared with women who delay their childbearing, women who give birth while in their teens are, on the average, more likely to drop out of school, to divorce, to continue to have children outside of marriage, to change jobs more frequently, to be on welfare, and to have health problems (Coley & Chase-Lansdale, 1998). They are also more likely to have low-birth-weight babies who are susceptible to illness and infant mortality.

Despite these grim findings, not every girl who bears a child while still in her teens ends up quitting school or living in poverty. Longitudinal studies of mothers who became pregnant as teenagers have found that some of these women eventually complete high school and become economically self-sufficient. Long-term success for these women was predicted by their being at grade level when they become pregnant, coming from smaller families that were not on welfare, and having families that had high expectations for their future and communicated those expectations to them (Furstenberg et al., 1992).

The limited information about teenage boys who become fathers indicates that, like the girls who become mothers, they are often from poor families who live in low-income communities and have low educational

Sex as a Scripted Activity

Researchers who study the development of sexual activity use the concept of *scripts* (see Chapter 9, p. 348) to describe the sequence of behaviors that precedes first intercourse (Michael, 1994). In recent years in the United States and Australia (two countries for which data are available), the typical pattern of discrete "steps" that precedes the initiation of first intercourse proceeds from lip kissing to tongue kissing to caressing breasts through clothing to fondling breasts under the clothing to touching the genitals through clothing to touching genitals directly, and finally to genital contact. Oral sex, if it is a part of this sequence, may or may not precede coitus (Rosenthal & Feldman, 1999). This scripted sequence is also culturally variable. It describes the behavior of European American adolescents but not that of African American teenagers, who are likely to move toward intercourse earlier and with fewer intervening steps (Smith & Udry, 1985).

Among the Kikuyu people of central Kenya at the turn of the twentieth century, approved sexual relations between the young men and women followed a script that

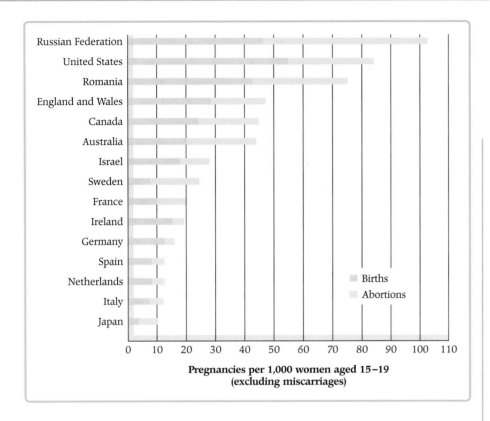

Pregnancies per 1,000 women aged 15–19
(excluding miscarriages)

Despite its steady decline in recent years, the adolescent pregnancy rate in the United States continues to be among the highest in the industrialized world.

at early ages are marrying.

There have been a number of efforts to reduce the probability of teenage pregnancy. Responding to the disproportionately high rates of teen pregnancy among economically disadvantaged African Americans, several Afrocentric educational programs have been developed. The aim of these programs is to instill pride and a sense of self-determination in girls of African descent. One such program, A Journey Toward Womanhood, encourages African American teenagers to explore different cultures and the role of women in history; critique media messages; and develop interpersonal communication skills, job skills, self-confidence, and self-respect. Teens who participated in the program were more likely than nonparticipants to delay the onset of sexual behavior, and to use contraception (Dixon et al., 2000). Research on the effectiveness of these programs indicates that a focus on reproductive education alone is insufficient to affect adolescents' behaviors. To be effective, programs must examine the meaning of sexual behavior and pregnancy within broader social and economic contexts of adolescents' lives.

achievement (Coley & Chase-Lansdale, 1998). However, it has been estimated that boys under the age of 19 account for only about 15 percent of all teenage pregnancies. In general, less than 5 percent of teen pregnancies involve fathers and mothers who are both under the age of 18 (Moran, 2000). The fact that more than half of all teenage mothers are 18 or 19 years of age, and that most of the fathers are in their twenties has prompted some researcher to argue that the "epidemic" of teen pregnancy is not about increasing reproduction rates in the age group per se. Rather, the epidemic is one of nonmarriage; in contrast to their counterparts from the 1950s, fewer young women who become pregnant

differed in many ways from the scripts typically followed by teenagers in the United States (Worthman & Whiting, 1987). For example, Kikuyu maidens were expected to strengthen the social cohesion of the group by entertaining the bachelor friends of their older brothers. The entertainment included not only dancing and feasting but a kind of lovemaking called *ngweko*. Jomo Kenyatta (1938), the first president after Kenya won its independence in 1962, described *ngweko* in the following manner:

The girls visit their boy-friends at a special hut, *thingira,* used as a rendezvous by the young men and women. . . .

Girls may visit the *thingira* at any time, day or night. After eating, while engaged in conversation with the boys, one of the boys turns the talk dramatically to the subject of *ngweko.* If there are more boys than girls, the girls are asked to select whom they want as their companion. The selection is done in the most liberal way. . . . In such a case it is not necessary for girls to select their most intimate friends, as this would be considered selfish and unsociable. . . . After the partners have been arranged, one of the boys gets up, saying "*ndathie kwenogora*" (I am going to stretch myself). His girl partner follows him to the bed. The boy removes all his clothing. The girl removes her upper garment . . . and retains her skirt, *motheru,* and her soft leather apron, *mwengo,* which she pulls back between her legs and tucks in together with her leather skirt, *motheru.* The two V-shaped tails of her *motheru* are pulled forward between her legs from behind and fastened to the waist, thus keeping the *mwengo* in position and forming an effective protection of her private parts. In this position, the lovers lie together facing each other, with their legs interwoven to prevent any movement of their hips. They begin to fondle each other, rubbing their breasts together, whilst at the same time engaged in lovemaking conversation until they gradually fall asleep. (pp. 157–158)

Sexual intercourse was explicitly forbidden as a part of this premarital sexual activity. In fact, both the boys and the girls were taught that if either of them directly touched the genitals of the other, they would become polluted and have to undergo an expensive purification rite. Boys who did not adhere to this restriction were ostracized by their peers. Not until marriage was sexual intercourse sanctioned.

In Chapter 9 you saw that the concept of scripts is important for understanding the mental development of preschool children. Scripts allow small children, who do not understand fully what is expected of them, to participate with adults in such activities as eating in a restaurant, attending a birthday party, and drawing a picture. A similar use of scripts is evident among adolescent boys and girls who are engaging in sexual activity for the first time. Their peer-group experiences, their observations of adults, and their general cultural knowledge provide them with a rough idea of the scripts they are supposed to follow and the roles they are supposed to play. It has been suggested that the absence of a script may contribute to the emotional distress experienced by many gay and lesbian adolescents (Martin, 1996).

A script also gives sexual meaning to individual acts that may have no such meaning in other contexts. Hand holding, kissing, and unzipping one's pants are not inherently sexual acts; each occurs often in nonsexual contexts. It is only within the context of the larger script of dating or of coitus that these acts take on sexual meanings and give rise to sexual excitement.

Motives for Initiating Sexual Activity

Evidence from a wide variety of sources indicates that males and females initiate sexual activity for different reasons (Beal, 1994). To begin with, biological differences between the two sexes set the stage for males and females to have divergent experiences with the erotic potential of their own bodies.

Sexual arousal is more obvious in males than in females because of its expression in clearly visible penile erection. In addition, most males experience orgasm within a few years of the onset of puberty, usually through masturbation (Graber et al., 1998). Not only is sexual arousal more ambiguous in females than in males, but females usually experience their first orgasm much later than males do. Part of the reason is that the clitoris, the center of female sexual pleasure, is small and hidden within the vulva, so girls are less likely to discover its erotic possibilities. Robert Michael and his colleagues report that adolescent girls masturbate considerably less frequently than do boys. Many women begin to masturbate only after they have begun having sexual intercourse (Michael, 1994).

According to John Gagnon and William Simon (1973), differences in the masturbatory behavior of boys and girls have consequences for later sexual behavior. First, masturbating to orgasm reinforces males' commitment to sexual behavior early in adolescence. Second, experience with masturbation tends to focus the male's feelings of sexual desire on the penis, whereas most females, lacking such experiences, do not localize their erotic responses in their genitals until much later, and then primarily as a result of sexual contacts with males.

This conclusion is bolstered by the fact that most teenage boys say that their first experience of sexual intercourse was motivated primarily by curiosity and only secondarily by affection for their partners. Girls, by contrast, rank affection for their partners as the major reason for engaging in sexual intercourse and curiosity as secondary. This difference in orientation between boys and girls led Gagnon and Simon (1973) to comment, "Dating and courtship may well be considered processes in which persons train members of the opposite sex in the meaning and content of their respective commitments" (p. 74).

In general, boys respond more positively than girls to their first experience of intercourse. In one survey, very few boys said they were sorry about having had intercourse, but the girls were more likely to say that they experienced pain and to express ambivalence about the event (Michael, 1994). Many girls are less positive about their initial experience of intercourse for a good reason: they were coerced into having sex. About 60 percent of the girls who had sex before they were 15 years old say that they did so involuntarily (The Alan Guttmacher Institute, 1999).

Changing Parent–Child Relations

The increasing time that adolescents spend with their peers and romantic partners, and the importance they place on these relationships, inevitably change the relationships between parents and their children. In fact, the amount of time that adolescents spend with their families drops by approximately 50 percent between the fifth and ninth grades (Larson & Richards, 1991). At the most general level, adolescents become more distant from their parents and are more likely to turn to their peers than to their parents for advice on a variety of questions about how to conduct themselves in a wide variety of contexts (Paikoff & Brooks-Gunn, 1991; Steinberg & Silk, 2002). At the same time, parents of adolescents are likely to be undergoing significant life changes of their own. They are reaching an age where they probably have increased responsibilities at work; their own parents are aging and may need special care; and their physical powers are beginning to decline. Given the stress that both parents and their adolescent children feel, it is not surprising that conflicts arise between them (Steinberg & Duncan, 2002). However, extensive research shows that the ways in which parent–child relationships change depend on a host of factors.

Adolescent–Parent Conflicts

When developmentalists describe adolescence as a period of "storm and stress," they are usually thinking about the conflicts between adolescents and their parents. Indeed, the parent–adolescent relationship is thought by many to reflect the basic dilemma of adolescence. Teenagers are caught between two worlds, one of dependence, the other of responsibility.

On the basis of a review of a large number of studies carried out over the past several decades, Brett Laursen and his colleagues found that patterns of conflict between families and their children do indeed change over the course of adolescence (Laursen et al., 1998). In particular, they found that both the frequency and the intensity of conflict between adolescents and their parents are highest early in adolescence and then decrease. The decline in conflict coincides with the period when adolescents are spending less and less time at home interacting with their parents, and are shifting their emotional attachments to their peers and romantic partners.

When conflicts do arise, they can evoke strong feelings. In a well-known study, Mihaly Csikszentmihalyi and Reed Larson (1984) asked adolescents to carry a beeper with them for a week, from the time they got up in the morning until they went to sleep at night. At a randomly chosen moment every 2 hours or so, the subjects were "beeped," at which point they filled out a standard report about what they were doing and experiencing. Adolescents' thoughts and feelings about their parents can be extremely negative. Very often, virulent comments are inspired by seemingly trivial events—a parent's insisting the adolescent's room be kept neat, or grounding the adolescent for missing a curfew, or questioning the value of some activity the adolescent is engaged in. Several studies have examined the content of parent–adolescent conflict. In general, adolescents report that most of their arguments with their parents were over such matters as household responsibilities and privileges, dating, involvement in athletics, and financial independence. Arguments over religion and politics were less common (Holmbeck, 1996).

Related to these findings is research suggesting that conflicts emerge when parents and adolescents differ in their understanding of what constitutes "personal space" (Nucci, 1996; Turiel, 1998). As you remember from the discussion of social domain theory in Chapter 10, parents and younger children distinguish among three domains—the moral, the social conventional, and the personal. Each domain provides guidelines for how to act.

Research on social domain theory indicates that parents and children can have conflicts in how they distinguish between the social conventional domain and the personal domain. A parent who insists that a child dress in a socially appropriate way, and a child who insists that dress is a matter of personal choice, are disputing the boundaries of the social conventional and the personal. For example, Larry Nucci and his colleagues (Nucci, 1996; Smetana, 1999) have discovered that parents in Brazil and the United States recognize the importance of providing children with a personal sphere in which to exercise personal freedom and develop independence and autonomy. Nevertheless, conflicts arise regarding exactly what qualifies as "personal," as the following interview excerpt indicates:

> Even now, like at Easter, when I went to Church, my Mom was real concerned with what I was going to wear. And I finally just said, "Look, I'm going to wear what I am going to wear, Mom." I didn't wear anything outrageous, just a skirt and a blouse. But here I am 20 years old, and it was such a concern about what I was going to wear. (Nucci, 1996, p. 51)

Research on parent–adolescent relationships in different ethnic groups shows broad cultural differences in how parents and teenagers define the personal domain (Smetana, 2000). Judith Smetana has found, for example, that middle-class African American families have relatively restricted definitions of what constitutes the adolescent's personal jurisdiction compared with European American families. Even so, negotiating the boundary of authority is still a significant source of parent–adolescent conflict for African American families. It seems that conflicts over "little things" represent deeper disagreements about the major issues of growing up—the power to decide for oneself and to take responsibility for oneself.

Smetana argues that African American families' parenting practices can be better described in terms of social domain theory than by such global terms as authoritarian or parent centered. According to social domain theory, parents' expectations for obedience will vary from one domain of action to the next. This also suggests that parent–adolescent conflict need not characterize the entire relationship; rather, it is confined to certain areas where the authority to have one's way in the face of contentious issues is in dispute. Few adolescents take issue with parents' authority in the domain of moral action, but will challenge it when it is applied to how they dress or color their hair.

Continuing Parental Influences

Although conflicts between parents and their adolescent children may be stormy, they rarely lead to a serious breakdown in relations (Schneider & Stevenson, 1999). It seems clear that parents continue to play a very important role in their children's lives. This continuing influence extends well beyond providing shelter, food, and advice. For example, a major study of more than 600 German adolescents and their parents indicated that adolescents whose parents demonstrate warmth, engage in discussions concerning academic and intellectual matters, and have high expectations for academic performance, do better in school compared with their peers whose parents are less warm and involved (Juang & Silbereisen, 2002). Parents also influence with whom their adolescent children interact and to some extent the timing and content of those interactions, including the kinds of crowds with which their children are likely to become associated (Brown & Huang, 1995; Holmbeck et al., 1995). A study of parent and adolescent occupational aspirations indicated that positive identification with parents was strongly related to adolescents' values, especially in the area of academics, for both African American and European American samples (Jodl et al., 2001).

In a study of sixth- and seventh-graders, Andrew Fuligni and Jacqueline Eccles (1993) asked young adolescents to answer a questionnaire about their parents' strictness, their opportunities to make decisions on their own, and the extent to which their parents monitored their behavior (see Table 15.2). The questionnaire also included questions about the extent to which the adolescents turned to peers rather than to their parents for support, as well as their adjustment to junior high school.

Fuligni and Eccles found that the extent to which the adolescents spent time with their peers and turned to them for advice depended on how their parents' behavior changed in response to their growing up. When children perceived their parents as becoming stricter as they progressed into adolescence, they turned to their peers. When they felt their parents included them in family decisions and encouraged them to express their ideas, they did not orient as much to their peers. At the same time, children whose parents set a curfew for them and asked them to call if they were going to be late coming home were less peer-oriented than those whose parents did not monitor their behavior.

Studies of family communication patterns tell a similar story. In intensive clinical studies into the family dynamics of both normally developing and troubled adolescents, Hausser and colleagues (1991) identified two patterns of family interactions. **Constraining interactions** limit and restrict communication through detachment, lack of curiosity, and other forms of discouragement. On the other hand, **enabling interactions** facilitate and enhance communication through

table 15.2

Sample Items Measuring Relationships between 6th- and 7th-Graders and Their Parents
How does each of the following questions and statements apply to your situation?
Parental Strictness
My parents want me to follow their directions even if I disagree with them.
I have to ask my parents' permission to do most things.
My parents worry that I am up to something they won't like.
Decision-Making Opportunities
How often do you take part in family decisions concerning yourself?
My parents encourage me to give my ideas and opinions even if we might disagree.
Parental Monitoring
When you go out at night, do you have a curfew?
When you are late getting home, do you have to call home?
Do your parents warn you it is dangerous to go out alone?

Source: Fuligni & Eccles, 1993.

constraining interactions Those that limit and restrict communication through detachment, lack of curiosity, and other forms of discouragement.

enabling interactions Those that facilitate and enhance communication through explaining, empathizing, expressing curiosity, and encouraging mutual problem solving.

explaining, empathizing, expressing curiosity, and encouraging mutual problem solving. The researchers argue that parents who promote enabling interactions enhance healthy psychological and identity development in their adolescents by "making the family environment safe for the adolescent to risk 'trying out' new ideas and perspectives, or expressing new feelings" (p. 27).

In a comprehensive review of research on the influence of parenting styles on adolescent behavior, Grayson Holmbeck and his colleagues (Holmbeck et al., 1995) report that the developmental outcomes for adolescents are most favorable when parents:

1. Set clear standards for behavior.
2. Enforce rules in ways that are firm but not coercive.
3. Discipline their children in a consistent way.
4. Explain the basis for their decisions.
5. Permit real discussion of contentious issues.
6. Monitor their adolescents' whereabouts without being overprotective.
7. Foster a warm family environment.
8. Provide information and help their adolescents develop social skills.
9. Respond flexibly to their children as they develop.

This analysis parallels the findings of other studies showing that adolescent children of authoritative parents are more competent in school and less likely to get into trouble than are their peers from authoritarian or rejecting-neglecting families (Steinberg, 2001). Moreover, these positive effects of authoritative parenting apply across different kinds of peer groups, whether the adolescents in question are classified as "jocks," "druggies," "nerds," or "brains" (Brown & Huang, 1995). These effects even extend to the adolescents' friends, who are likely to experience improved school performance and behavior as an indirect result of the effective parenting of their friends' parents (Fletcher et al., 1995).

On the whole, current evidence strongly supports the notion that adolescents' conflicts with their parents increase relative to middle childhood, while their feelings of family solidarity and warmth decrease (Conger & Ge, 1999; Laursen et al., 1998). Some adolescents really do break away and establish relationships outside the family that remove them from their parents both physically and emotionally; but the more common pattern is for adolescents and their parents to negotiate a new form of interdependence that grants the adolescent increasingly equal rights and more nearly equal responsibilities.

Work and Leisure

In addition to changing relationships with parents and peers, adolescents' social lives are transformed though participation in a variety of new work and leisure activities. In many countries, including the United States, access to adult jobs and adult status comes only after a long period of preparation during which young people learn how to work in general and then acquire the skills that particular jobs require. American children's first work experience often consists of doing household chores, such as setting the table, washing dishes, and caring for pets. Around the age of 12 years, many children begin to work at odd jobs around the neighborhood—baby-sitting, delivering newspapers or groceries, mowing lawns. Usually the money they earn from these jobs is theirs to spend with less parental supervision than they would encounter if they were receiving an allowance (Manning, 1990). By the age of 15, many adolescents have progressed from working at casual jobs to regular part-time employment (Finch et al., 1997).

Part-time jobs do not usually provide young people with on-the-job training that will prove useful in adulthood, but they do provide young people with spending money and a sense of accomplishment.

According to official counts, more than one-third of all 16- to 19-year-old students work at least part-time (National Center for Health Statistics, 2000), although the proportion varies considerably by race. For example, the National Center for Health Statistics reported that in April 1999, 45 percent of white 17-year-olds were employed, compared with 30 percent of Hispanic, and 18 percent of African American 17-year-olds. We can speculate that a variety of factors may contribute to these striking racial differences, including racist hiring practices, responsibilities in the home including child care, as well as the economic disadvantage that plagues many communities in which ethnic minority adolescents live.

Racial comparisons of employment can illuminate significant differences in how the social lives of American adolescents are organized. Likewise, cross-national comparisons can reflect how different societies structure their adolescents' experiences. One such cross-national study was conducted by August Flammer and his colleagues (1999). Consistent with other cross-national work, they found that U.S. adolescents work more than adolescents from any another country. As you can see in Figure 15.9, the differences are dramatic.

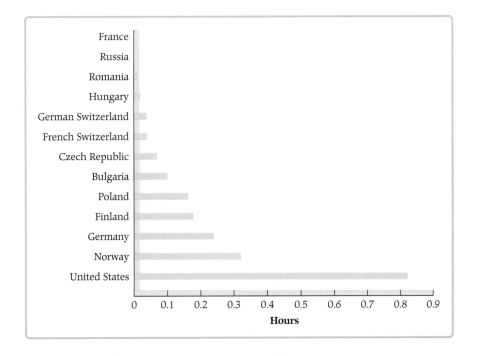

Figure 15.9 Adolescents in the United States spend significantly more time working at paid jobs compared with their peers in other countries. Research suggests that extensive employment is associated with poor school performance and higher rates of delinquency.

While U.S. adolescents are radically different from their European peers in hours spent working, it is interesting to note that Norwegian and German adolescents take second and third place—all three countries have among the shortest school days. Another provocative piece to this story is the finding that time working correlates negatively with time spent on homework. Is it the case that working adolescents don't have time for homework? Or are adolescents assigned less homework in societies that have short school days and permit their youth to work longer hours? The answers aren't clear, but studies of American adolescents indicate that those who work are generally less involved in school than their classmates (D'Amico, 1984; Mortimer & Johnson, 1998). Some developmentalists argue that it isn't work per se that causes school trouble, but working long hours (Bachman & Schulenberg, 1993; Finch et al., 1997; Steinberg et al., 1993). On the other hand, Jeylan Mortimer and her associates found in a longitudinal study that many of the students who work long hours and do poorly in school were less committed to academic work even before they began working (Mortimer & Johnson, 1998).

Developmentalists once widely believed that extensive work experience during adolescence is all to teenagers' benefit, but research on the relationship between work and school achievement casts doubt on this. Also on the negative side, and contrary to the beliefs of many advocates of adolescent work experience, is the fact that part-time jobs do not typically provide students with on-the-job training that will prove useful in adulthood, nor do they usually bring adolescents into contact with many adults (Schneider & Stevenson, 1999). It is also clear that most adolescents are not saving their earnings for education, or applying them to car or family expenses. The University of Michigan's Institute for Social Research (1996) finds that most American adolescents, regardless of gender or race, spend most of their earnings on "personal items." A number of studies have found, furthermore, that extensive part-time employment is associated with higher rates of alcohol use, illegal drug use, psychological distress, and health problems, as well as more frequent delinquency (Mortimer et al., 1996; Steinberg et al., 1993). So it would seem that working doesn't necessarily keep adolescents out of trouble, either.

In addition to examining the time that adolescents in different countries spend working, Flammer and his associates also compared adolescents on a number of leisure activities. Some of their results are shown in Table 15.3. On average, adolescents in Europe and the United States spent a bit more than 4 hours on a weekday engaged in leisure activities. Across all 13 national samples, watching television accounted for more than a third of adolescents' leisure time. The second and third most common activities, on average, were hanging out with friends (17 percent) and playing sports (16 percent).

As you may recall from the famous study of Raymond presented in Chapter 12, detailed knowledge about how children and adolescents spend their time can provide invaluable information about their experiences and life circumstances, including socialization practices and priorities, cultural and individual values and, in some measure, their prospects and opportunities for the future. For example, studies suggest that adolescents view their leisure activities as central to self-definition, suggesting that such activities may be relevant to personal and social development (Flammer et al., 1999). Adolescents also become more deliberate and reflective on the way they spend their time, as increasing cognitive skills permit them to take on a larger, more active role in the organization of their own activities and experiences. These are the types of issues that we will explore in the next chapter. In Chapter 16, we will first examine the special qualities of mind that

table 15.3

Average Daily Hours Spent on Activities (Self-reported)						
Country	**Playing music**	**Leisure reading**	**Doing sports**	**Watching television**	**Hanging around with friends**	**Dating**	**Total leisure activities**
Bulgaria	0.10	0.55	0.35	2.37	1.23	0.39	4.99
Czech Republic	0.10	0.53	0.90	2.20	0.81	0.22	4.79
Finland	0.19	0.64	0.52	1.83	1.63	0.54	5.35
France	0.11	0.27	0.38	1.31	0.54	0.12	2.73
Germany	0.27	0.54	0.87	1.92	0.22	1.23	5.05
Hungary	0.10	0.51	0.82	1.46	0.64	0.35	3.88
Norway	0.25	0.44	1.43	1.60	1.47	0.18	5.37
Poland	0.11	0.44	0.66	1.46	0.77	0.41	3.85
Romania	0.03	0.86	0.38	2.13	0.40	0.22	4.02
Russia	0.17	0.83	0.32	1.49	0.70	0.44	3.95
F–CH	0.25	0.47	0.79	1.66	0.19	0.33	3.69
G–CH	0.34	0.68	0.62	1.46	0.33	0.33	3.76
United States	0.09	0.18	1.18	1.78	0.85	0.53	4.61
Average	0.16	0.53	0.71	1.74	0.75	0.41	4.30

Source: Adapted from Tanner, 1962.
Note. F–CH = French-speaking Switzerland; G–CH = German-speaking Switzerland.

develop as young people struggle to understand their new circumstances and to master the complex systems of technical knowledge that will structure their adult work lives. Then we will consider all three domains of developmental change— the biological, the social, and the psychological—simultaneously as an interacting system of influences in a cultural context.

S U M M A R Y

- The bio-social-behavior shift to adulthood is complicated by the fact that sexual maturity does not necessarily coincide with adult status. The resulting conflict between biological and social forces gives this transition its unique psychological characteristics.

Conceptions of Adolescence

- For the past 300 years, three key issues have preoccupied those who theorize about adolescence:

  1. The degree to which rapid biological changes increase psychological instability.

  2. The possibility that development in adolescence recapitulates earlier stages in achieving an integration appropriate to adulthood.

  3. The relation of biological and social changes to cognitive changes.

- Common to all theories of adolescence is recognition of the child's need to integrate new biological capacities with new forms of social relations.

  1. G. Stanley Hall emphasized the storm and stress of adolescence and the importance of recapitulationism.

  2. Sigmund Freud attributed the characteristics of adolescence (which he referred to as the genital stage) to increases in sexual excitation that upset the psychological balance among the id, the ego, and the superego established during middle childhood.

  3. Ethologists and evolutionary biologists maintain that adolescence arose among human beings because it confers a reproductive advantage over other species.

Puberty

- Puberty, the sum of the biological changes that lead to sexual maturity, is accompanied by a growth spurt during which boys and girls attain approximately 98 percent of their adult size. During puberty the bodies of males and females take on their distinctive shapes.

- Adolescence is also a period of rapid brain development; the amount of white matter (measured in terms of myelination) increases; the amount of gray matter (measured in terms of number of synapses) increases, then decreases. Developmentalists are studying whether these changes constitute a critical period for development and make the brain particularly vulnerable to the effects of drugs and alcohol.

- Menarche, the first menstrual period, usually occurs late in a girl's puberty, after her growth spurt has reached its peak. Among males, semenarche, the ability to ejaculate semen, signals the maturation of the primary sex organs.

- Both genetic and environmental factors affect the onset of puberty. For example, high levels of physical exercise delay the onset of menarche, while family stress is associated with early menarche.

- Changes in body weight during this period affect adolescents' self-image. Girls in particular are susceptible to dissatisfaction with their changing bodies, and may as a result develop eating disorders.

- The age at which biological maturation occurs influences a child's social standing with peers and adults.

- In general, the impact of early sexual maturation is negative for girls and positive for boys, although the impact varies with cultural and personal circumstances.

The Reorganization of Social Life

- Four major changes occur as part of the reorganization of social life during adolescence:

  1. A great deal more time is spent with peers.

  2. Adult guidance is reduced and becomes more indirect.

  3. Cross-sex interactions increase markedly.

  4. Participation in large social groups becomes important.

- The dominant mode of peer relations at the start of adolescence is same-sex friendship focused on shared activities. As adolescence proceeds, same-sex friendship is increasingly characterized by an emphasis on trust, loyalty, and mutual understanding.

- Adolescent friendships serve two fundamental functions: intimacy and automony.

- Three forms of peer groups come to prominence in adolescence: dyadic friendships, cliques, and crowds. Two kinds of crowds are developmentally significant: activity-based crowds, which are associated with the transition to sexual activity; and reputation-based crowds, which are focused on social identity.

- Social status within one's peer group depends on social factors, such as membership in the leading crowd, and personal factors, such as girls' physical attractiveness and boys' athletic ability.

- Developmentalists have extensively studied the establishment of homophily, the degree of similarity between friends. Adolescents tend to seek out friends who are similar to themselves, and the corresponding friendships model and reinforce socially significant behaviors.

- Special susceptibility to peer pressure, especially antisocial peer pressure, is commonly believed to characterize adolescent behavior. Evidence for this concern is mixed.

- Sensitivity to peer pressure seems to peak around the age of 15.

- Most adolescents report that they are more likely to go along with peer pressure that is prosocial than with pressure to misbehave. The more pressure adolescents feel to engage in antisocial behavior, however, the more likely they are to do so.

- The transition to two-person heterosexual relations goes through a number of stages. It begins with membership in small same-sex cliques and participation with the other members in social events that draw heterosexual activity-based crowds. Within these crowds, heterosexual cliques are formed, and couples begin the process of pairing off. As adult sexual relationships emerge, crowds become less prominent in adolescents' social lives.

- Sexual behavior requires the learning of culturally specified scripts and forms of behavior as well as biological maturation.

- The transition to heterosexual relations proceeds in opposite directions for males and females in our culture because of differences in their histories. Males begin with the highly developed goal of sexual satisfaction and only gradually learn to include a deeper social and emotional commitment in their heterosexual relations. Females begin with the highly developed goal of social and emotional affiliation and only gradually acquire the goal of sexual satisfaction.

- Biological maturation and the increasing time spent with peers alter parent–child relations. Parents' authority decreases in relation to the influence of peers, and they must now exercise their authority even more through persuasion than they did earlier.

- Contrary to the hypothesis of a separate youth culture, most adolescents share their parents' values. Dialogue, rather than outright conflict or rejection, is the major method of resolving disagreements between adolescents and their parents.

- Parents continue to exert an important influence on their children's development throughout adolescence. As in earlier years, authoritative parents have children who are more competent in school and less likely to engage in antisocial behavior.

- Conflicts with parents during adolescence seem to center on matters of taste, though often they are actually about larger issues of control.

- Evidence concerning the developmental impact of work experience in the United States is mixed. Moderate amounts of work enhance feelings of independence and efficacy, but too much work is associated with reduced achievement in school.

Key Terms

clique, p. 597
constraining interactions, p. 611
crowd, p. 598
deviancy training, p. 601
dyadic friendships, p. 595

emotional tone, p. 589
enabling interactions, p. 611
gonads, p. 583
homiphily, p. 599
menarche, p. 586

primary sex organs, p. 585
puberty, p. 583
secondary sex characteristics, p. 585
selection, p. 599
semenarche, p. 585

Thought Questions

1. It is clear from the preceding material that there is more to human reproduction than sex. What more is there, and what significance does your answer have for how you think about adolescence as a stage of development?

2. François Jacob calls reproduction the only bodily function for which the individual possesses only one-half of the necessary bodily organs. What might the consequences of this unique situation be?

3. According to the idea of a bio-social-behavioral shift, the biological changes associated with puberty, such as the

growth spurt and the appearance of secondary sexual characteristics, are simultaneously relevant to social and behavioral change. Argue for or against this idea.

4. Provide several reasons for questioning the literature on peer influence during adolescence. What kind of research strategies would you propose to overcome these doubts?

5. Argue for or against the following proposition: for adolescents to complete childhood development effectively, conflict between them and their parents is essential.

The Cognitive and Psychological Achievements of Adolescence

> *"Adolescents are the bearers of cultural renewal, those cycles of generation and regeneration that link our limited individual destinies with the destiny of the species."*
>
> —Louise Kaplan

"When I was seventeen, life changed to a different world. The school's vice principal had a talk with me after his talks with many others. He told me that he wanted to remind me that I was a student leader, a model to the graduates. The policy was there, as strict as math equations. He told me that I belonged to one category. The category of becoming a peasant. He said it was an unalterable decision. The policy from Beijing was a holy instruction. It was universally accepted. It was incumbent upon me to obey. He said he had sent four of his own children to work in the countryside. He was very proud of them. He said that twenty million Chinese worked on these farms. He said many more words. Words of abstractions. Words like songs. He said when one challenges heaven, it brings pleasure; when one challenges the earth, it brings pleasure; when one challenges one's own kind, it brings the biggest pleasure. He was reciting the poem by Mao. He said a true Communist would love to take challenges. She would take it with dignity. I was seventeen. I was inspired. I was eager to devote myself. I was looking forward to hardship."

　　—Anchee Min, *Red Azalea*

"I feel that the impact of school on my sense of identity was strongest in high school, where I embraced the messages the school threw at us. I believed that being anything less than a superwoman would be compromising my potential. By the time cliques had disappeared during junior year, I was respected by peers and teachers as a student, an athlete, and an active member of the student community. My school was the perfect environment in which to fight against my father's views. It gave me a chance to develop into an independent, capable woman who did not need to answer to anyone but herself."

　　—Anonymous in A. Garrod et al., *Adolescent Portraits: Identity, Relationships, and Challenges*

These are the reflections of two individuals who experienced their adolescence in vastly different sociopolitical and historical contexts. Anchee Min, born in 1957, provides an account of the powerful feelings of being caught up in the final years of China's Cultural Revolution. The second reflection, in contrast, is more contemporary and closer to home. But despite the span of years and cultures, both adolescents express a concern with how to define a future self in relation to society; and both make reference to issues of identity, challenge, and commitment that self-definition is assumed to entail.

As we commented in the introduction to our discussion of adolescence, no developmental transition after birth is so well marked as the end of middle childhood. Profound changes in the size and shape of children's bodies are unmistakable signs that they are "ripening." The capacity for biological reproduction, as you learned in Chapter 15, is associated with changes in social relations that propel young people into a new social status, with new rights and responsibilities. Moreover, as you will discover in this chapter, the new bio-social-behavioral shift is distinguished by the development of a new quality of mind, characterized by the ability to think systematically, logically, and hypothetically (see Table 16.1). These changes make it both possible and necessary for adolescents to engage in the complex forms of economic and sociopolitical activity on which the welfare of the community depends.

One manifestation of this new mode of thinking is adolescents' tendency to become critical of received wisdom and even more critical of the discrepancies between the ideals adults espouse and the behaviors in which they actually engage. Arnold Gesell and Frances Ilg (1943) suggest that in response to this disillusionment with adult behavior, the adolescent seeks out adult role models:

> He also seeks out heroes of history and of biography. . . . Literature, art, religion take on new meanings and may create new confusions in his thinking. He has a strangely novel interest in abstract ideas. He pursues them in order to find himself. (p. 256)

In the end, young people must reconcile their own emerging ideals with the world as it actually is. They must also reconcile their view of who they want to be with who they are and have been. In the process, they arrive at their own personal sense of self and identity. Viewed in this way, adolescents' thinking is, on the one hand, their most important psychological means of coming to grips with the tasks of adult life and, on the other, a result of their struggles to reconcile competing social and psychological demands of adult life.

We begin this chapter by examining the experimental evidence for the idea that young people's thought processes become more systematic and logical as they begin the transition to adulthood. This evidence raises a number of questions: No one is systematically logical all the time, so under what circumstances do adolescents engage in systematic, logical thinking? How does the quality of adolescents' thinking depend upon the content of what is being thought? Is the quality of adolescents' thinking the same when they are analyzing the results of a scientific experiment, debating laws that govern society, confronting moral dilemmas, or trying to arrive at their own personal sense of identity? And finally, when the entire pattern of biological, social, and cognitive changes is examined in different cultural contexts, does it support the idea that adolescence is a universal stage of development?

table 16.1

The Bio-Social-Behavioral Shift: Transition to Adulthood	
Biological Domain	Capacity for biological reproduction
	Development of secondary sex characteristics
	Attainment of adult size
Social Domain	Sexual relations
	Shift toward primary responsibility for oneself
	Beginning of responsibility for next generation
Behavioral Domain	Achievement of formal operations in some areas (systematic thinking)
	Formation of identity

Research on Adolescent Thought

Developmentalists who focus on adolescent thought processes emphasize four characteristics that distinguish adolescent thinking from the thinking that is typical of middle childhood (Keating, 1990; Moshman, 1998):

1. *Reasoning hypothetically* Adolescents are more likely than younger children to engage in thinking that requires them to generate and mentally test hypotheses and to think about situations that are contrary to fact. In thinking about going to a beach party with a boy she does not know well, a teenage girl may reason, "What if they get drunk and rowdy? What will I do? I guess if things get too wild, I can always ask someone for a ride. But then they'll think I'm no fun." In an analogous situation, a younger child would make a decision without first contemplating the wide range of possible scenarios.

2. *Thinking about thinking* During adolescence, thinking about one's own thought processes—the *metacognition* we described in Chapter 12— becomes increasingly complex. At the same time, adolescents' more sophisticated *theory of mind* (see Chapter 9) allows them to think more systematically than younger children about other people's points of view, a development that is reflected in the changing nature of adolescent friendships (see Chapter 15, p. 595).

3. *Planning ahead* Adolescence is a time when young people start thinking about what they will do when they grow up. Adolescents by no means always plan ahead, but they do so more often and more systematically than younger children. Contemplating the upcoming summer holiday, an adolescent might think, "Well, I could relax and just goof around with my friends, or I could work on raising that D in algebra, which isn't going to look too good when I apply to college." A younger child would be more likely to focus only on having a good time and forget other responsibilities.

4. *Thinking beyond conventional limits* Adolescents use their more sophisticated cognitive abilities to rethink fundamental issues of social relations, morality, politics, and religion—issues that have perplexed human beings since the dawn of history. Now acutely aware of the disparities between the ideals of their community and the behavior of individual adults around them, adolescents are highly motivated to figure out how to "do it right." Arnold Gesell and Frances Ilg, as quoted earlier, link this aspect of adolescent thought to youth's idealism and search for heroes.

©Michael Newman/Photo Edit, Inc.

According to Piaget's theory, formal operational reasoning is the foundation of scientific thinking. This girl is presenting her work on tornados at a science fair.

One can certainly find adolescents around the world who display these characteristic cognitive abilities. However, as you have seen in previous chapters, the quality of a person's thinking can vary depending on its specific content and the context in which it occurs. As David Moshman notes, it appears that "qualitatively distinct forms of thought and knowledge routinely coexist in the same mind" (1998, p. 950).

Extensive evidence indicates that such variation is characteristic of adolescent thinking, raising basic questions about both the distinctiveness and the universality of cognitive development during adolescence. Many developmentalists continue to believe that adolescent thought processes can be characterized by a small set of general properties such as those listed above. But the fact that the quality of adolescent thinking is variable according to content and contexts has led others to doubt that the transition from middle childhood to adolescence brings about stagelike changes in cognition.

The difficulty of deciding how best to characterize changes in cognition associated with adolescence is nowhere more apparent than in current research on formal operational thinking.

Formal Operations

It was Piaget's contention that changes in the way adolescents think about themselves, their personal relationships, and the nature of their society have a common source: the development of a new logical structure that he called **formal operations** (see Table 16.2). As you will recall, an "operation" in Piaget's terminology is a mental action that

table 16.2

Piaget's Stages of Cognitive Development: Formal Operational			
Age (years)	**Stage**	**Description**	**Characteristics of Formal Operational Thinking**
Birth to 2	Sensorimotor	Infants' achievements consist largely of coordinating their sensory perceptions and simple motor behaviors. As they move through the 6 substages of this period, infants come to recognize the existence of a world outside themselves and begin to interact with it in deliberate ways.	Formal operational reasoning, in which each partial link in a chain of reasoning is related to the problem as a whole • Young people solve the combination-of-chemicals problem by systematically testing all possible combinations. • In forming a personal identity, young people take into account how they judge others, how others judge them, how they judge the judgment process of others, and how all this corresponds to social categories available in the culture.
2 to 6	Preoperational	Young children can represent reality to themselves through the use of symbols, including mental images, words, and gestures. Objects and events no longer have to be present to be thought about, but children often fail to distinguish their point of view from that of others' become easily captured by surface appearances, and are often confused about causal relations.	
6 to 12	Concrete operational	As they enter middle childhood, children become capable of mental operations, internalized actions that fit into a logical system. Operational thinking allows children mentally to combine, separate, order, and transform objects and actions. Such operations are considered concrete because they are carried out in the presence of the objects and events being thought about.	Application of formal operational thinking to a wide variety of life's problems • Young people think about politics and law in terms of abstract principles and are capable of seeing the beneficial, rather than just the punitive, side of laws. • Young people are interested in universal ethical principles and critical of adults' hypocrisies.
12 to 19	Formal operational	In adolescence the developing person acquires the ability to think systematically about all logical relations within a problem. Adolescents display keen interest in abstract ideas and in the process of thinking itself.	

fits into a logical system. Examples of *concrete operations,* typically achieved in middle childhood, include the mathematical operations of adding and subtracting, as well as other logical operations such as placing items in a serial order—say, from shortest to tallest. The concrete operational child is able to apply operations to the real world. The formal operational adolescent, however, is able to apply operations to operations. For this reason, formal operations are also called **second-order operations.** David Moshman provides the following illustration (Moshman, 1999, p. 13):

> Consider the following proportion:
>
> $10/5 = 4/2$
>
> To comprehend the logic of this proportion it must be understood that the relation of 10 to 5 (first number twice as great as the second) is equal to the relation of 4 to 2 (again, first number twice as great as second). The focus is on a relation (of equality, in this case) between two relations. A proportion, in other words, is a relation between two relations, a second-order relation.

Formal operational thinking is the kind of thinking needed by anyone who has to solve problems systematically. This new ability is needed by the owner of a gasoline station who, in order to make a profit, has to take into account the price he or she pays for gasoline, the kinds of customers who pass by the station, the kinds of services the station needs to offer, the hours it needs to stay open, and the cost of labor, supplies, rent, and utilities. Formal operational thinking is also needed by lawyers when they consider a wide variety of alternative strategies, legal precedents, and possible consequences in deciding how best to present a case and counter the arguments of the attorney on the opposing side.

Reasoning by Manipulating Variables

Inhelder and Piaget's studies of formal operational thinking focused on very basic versions of the kinds of problems encountered in scientific laboratories. Typically, these problems require subjects to hold one variable of a complex system constant while systematically searching mentally through all the other variables.

Perhaps the most widely cited example of a Piagetian problem designed to illustrate the nature of formal operations is the combination-of-chemicals problem, which requires the ability both to combine variables and to create in one's mind a "structured, psychological whole," the key characteristics of formal operational thinking. At the start of the task, four large bottles, one indicator bottle, and two beakers are arrayed on a table in front of the child, as in Figure 16.1 (p. 624). Each bottle contains a clear liquid. The liquids are such that when the liquids from bottles 1 and 3 are combined in a beaker and then a drop of the chemical from the indicator bottle (g) is added, the mixture turns yellow. If the chemical in bottle 2 is added to a beaker containing liquid from both 1 and 3, the mixture remains yellow, but if the liquid in bottle 4 is then added, the mixture turns clear again.

The experimenter begins with two beakers already full of liquid. One contains liquid from bottles 1 and 3, the other, liquid from bottle 2. The experimenter puts a drop from bottle g in each beaker, demonstrating that it produces a yellow color in one case but not in the other. Now the child is invited to try out various combinations in an attempt to determine which combination of chemicals will transform the color of the liquid.

Interviews with two of Inhelder and Piaget's subjects, 7- and 14-year-old boys, are shown at the bottom of Figure 16.1. The 7-year-old does not have the kind of overall conceptual grasp of the problem that indicates the presence of a structured whole, that is, a system of relationships that can be logically described and thought about; the 14-year-old does. The younger child is unsystematic in his sampling of possible combinations, even with hints from the experimenter. The adolescent sets about his

formal operations In Piaget's terms, a kind of mental operation in which all possible combinations are considered in solving a problem. Consequently, each partial link is grouped in relation to the whole; in other words, reasoning moves continually as a function of a structured whole.

second-order operations Another term for formal operations, since children at this stage can apply operations to operations.

Full set of chemicals to be combined

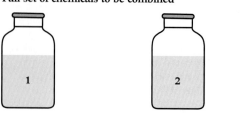  

Experimenter's demonstration

  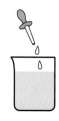 

[Ren (7.1 years old) tries 4 × g, then 2 × g, and 3 × g.]

Ren: I think I did everything. I tried them all.

Exp [Experimenter]: What else could you have done?

Ren: I don't know. *[He is given the glasses again. He repeats 1 × g, etc.]*

Exp: You took each bottle separately. What else could you have done?

Ren: Take two bottles at a time? *[He tries 1 × 4 × g, then 2 × 3 × g, thus failing to cross over between the two sets of bottles. When we suggest that he add others, he puts 1 × g in the glass already containing 2 × 3, which results in the appearance of the color.]*

Exp: Try to make the color again.

Ren: Do I put two or three? *[He tries 2 × 4 × g, then adds 3, then tries it with 1 × 4 × 2 × g.]*

Ren: No, I don't remember anymore.

Figure 16.1 A 7-year-old and an adolescent tackle the combination-of-chemicals task. Note that the 7-year-old starts by testing only one chemical at a time. When it is suggested that he try working with two chemicals at a time, he becomes confused. The 14-year-old also starts with one chemical at a time but quickly realizes that he must create more complicated combinations, which he does in a systematic way until he arrives at the solution to the problem. (From Inhelder & Piaget, 1958.)

[Eng (14.6 years old) begins with 2 × g, 1 × g, 3 × g, and 4 × g.]

Eng: No, it doesn't turn yellow. So you have to mix them. *[He goes on to the six two–by–two combinations and at last hits 1 × 3 × g.]*

Eng: This time I think it works.

Exp: Why?

Eng: It's 1 and 3 and some water.

Exp: You think it's water?

Eng: Yes, no difference in odor. I think that it's water.

Exp: Can you show me? *[He replaces g with some water: 1 × 3 × water.]*

Eng: No, it's not water. It's a chemical product: it combines with 1 and 3 and then it turns into a yellow liquid. *[He goes on to three–by–three combinations beginning with the replacement of g by 2 and by 4–i.e., 1 × 3 × 2 and 1 × 3 × 4.]*

Eng: No, these two products aren't the same as the drops: they can't produce color with 1 and 3. *[Then he tries 1 × 3 × g × 4.]*

Eng: It turns white again: 4 is the opposite of g because 4 makes the color go away while g makes it appear.

task systematically. He starts with the simplest possibility (that one of the chemicals, when combined with g, turns yellow), then proceeds to the next level of complexity—the possibility that two, and later three, chemicals must be combined. When he combines pairs, he discovers that when g is added to a mixture of 1 and 3, the yellow color appears, but because he is methodical in exploring all the logical possibilities, he also discovers that 4 counteracts g, thereby arriving at a systematic understanding of the miniature chemical system that Inhelder and Piaget had arranged for him. The adolescent is exhibiting formal operational thinking par excellence.

Reasoning by Logical Necessity

According to Piaget (1987), one of the consequences of acquiring formal operational thinking is the ability to construct logical proofs in which conclusions follow from **logical necessity,** an understanding that an argument can be logically correct, even if it is not true. The essence of logical necessity is nowhere better described than in Gilbert Keith Chesterton's amusing essay on the relationship between the "science of mental relations" and the "logic of Elfland":

There are certain sequences or developments, which are, in the true sense of the word reasonable. They are, in the true sense of the word, necessary. Such are mathematical and merely logical sequences. We in fairyland (who are the most reasonable of all creatures) admit that reason and that necessity. For example, if the Ugly Sisters are older than Cinderella, it is (in an iron and awful sense) *necessary* that Cinderella is younger than the Ugly Sisters. There is no getting out of it. . . . If Jack is the son of a miller, a miller is the father of Jack. Cold reason decrees it from her awful throne: and we in fairyland submit. If the three brothers all ride horses, there are six animals and eighteen legs involved: that is true rationalism, and fairyland is full of it. . . . We believe in bodily miracles, but not in mental impossibilities. We believe that a Bean-stalk climbed up to heaven; but that does not at all confuse our convictions on the philosophical question of how many beans make five. (Chesterton, 1908/1957, p. 79)

Logical necessity underlies **hypothetical-deductive reasoning,** one of the central processes in scientific thinking. The simplest form of deductive reasoning begins with the statement of a hypothetical premise followed by the statement of a particular specific premise and then by a conclusion. The task of the thinker is to determine whether or not the conclusion follows logically from the premises. Consider, for example, the following arguments (adapted from Moshman, 1999):

Argument 1
General premise: Elephants are bigger than mice.
Specific premise: Dogs are bigger than mice.
Conclusion: Therefore, elephants are bigger than dogs.

Argument 2
General premise: Mice are bigger than dogs.
Specific premise: Dogs are bigger than elephants.
Conclusion: Therefore, mice are bigger than elephants.

Because all of the statements in the first argument are true, the concrete operational child will judge it to be more logical than the second argument, for which all of the statements are false. The formal operational individual, on the other hand, will understand that the second argument is logical—that is, the conclusion follows from the premises—whereas the first argument is not. Correctly solving this task demonstrates the ability of formal thinkers to distinguish between truth and logic, an ability of vital importance in thinking beyond the actual to consider and evaluate the possible. As Piaget wrote, "To be formal, deduction must detach itself from reality and take up its stand upon the plane of the purely possible" (cited in Moshman, 1999, p. 7).

In general, research (summarized by Müller et al., 1999) finds a steady increase in logical reasoning between the fourth and twelfth grades (roughly, between 10 and 18 years of age). In fact, formal deductive reasoning is very rare before the sixth grade (11 to 12 years of age).

Promoting Formal Thinking through Sociocognitive Conflict Given the strong evidence that formal operations flourish better in some contexts than in others, developmentalists have worked to understand the nature of experience that promotes their development. Recall that according to Piaget's theory, developmental change takes place because of a tug of war between *assimilation* and *accommodation,* two processes that work to establish *equilibration*—a balance between the individual's current understanding of the world, and his or her new environmental experiences (Chapter 4, p. 151). Basically, a lack of balance is experienced as a type of mental or cognitive conflict. The conflict is overcome, and the individual returns to a state of equilibration, when he or she moves to a higher, more inclusive level of understanding.

Piaget argued that social interaction is an important source of cognitive conflict (Piaget, 1928, 1995). This is because in social interactions children are exposed to points of view and ways of understanding the world that are different from their

logical necessity When the conclusions of reasoning are set entirely by the rules of logic; example: if the cow jumped over the moon, then we *must conclude* (it is logically necessary) that the moon was under the cow.

hypothetical-deductive reasoning The ability to formulate and evaluate the logical implications of a set of premises, even if it is imaginary or contradicts the real world.

sociocognitive conflict Cognitive conflict that is rooted in social experience.

own, upsetting the balance between their current levels of understanding and new ideas encountered in their interactions. **Sociocognitive conflict** is the term used by developmentalits to describe cognitive conflict that is rooted in social experience.

Insight into the nature of sociocognitive conflict is provided in a study of changes in how college students solve formal operational tasks. Rose Dimant and David Bearison (1991) had college students work through six sessions of increasingly difficult problems that were similar to the combinations-of-liquids task. In some cases the students worked alone. In other cases they worked with another student. Analysis of videotapes of the sessions in which two students worked together revealed that the quality of the students' conversation about the problems was the key to developing formal operational abilities on this task. Students who actively engaged in the task and worked cooperatively showed significantly greater gains when retested than did students who worked alone or students who worked in pairs but did not engage in collaborative problem-solving actions. Interactions that included disagreements, contradictions, and alternative solutions were the most effective in promoting higher levels of functioning. Bearison and Dimant called these types of interactions "theoretically relevant" because of their potential to trigger sociocognitive conflict.

Overall, the evidence suggests that the development of formal operations is not acquired universally, but requires an environment that provides opportunities for individuals to grapple actively with ideas that challenge and contradict their usual ways of understanding and solving problems.

Alternative Approaches to Explaining Adolescent Thought

Investigators who question Piaget's account of adolescent cognition, like those who questioned his account of cognition at early ages, have sought alternative explanations for the kinds of results presented in the preceding sections. In contrast to Piaget's emphasis on solving scientific tasks, these investigators are working to understand how higher-level thinking is used to solve everyday tasks and make decisions in nonscientific contexts. In general, information-processing theorists tend to focus on the way that changing memory capacities and expanding knowledge bases permit the development of more complex "central conceptual structures," more effective problem-solving strategies, and increased metacognitive understanding. Those who emphasize the importance of cultural context have pursued the path that Piaget himself suggested, concentrating on the way specialized practice in particular domains of experience gives rise to the kind of systematic thought that appears to underlie the new quality of adolescent cognition.

Information-Processing Approaches

In the view of information-processing theorists, adolescents' ability to think systematically arises from their larger working memory and ability to apply more powerful problem-solving strategies (Case, 1998; Markovits & Barrouillet, 2002). In problem solving, increased memory capacity makes it possible for older adolescents to coordinate several different factors at once, keep intermediate results in mind, and come up with a solution that is comprehensive and consistent. In contrast to Piaget and Inhelder's view that adolescent thought is due to global, qualitative change, information-processing theorists believe that adolescents' improved skills are better explained as the result of a gradual acquisition and implementation of more powerful rules or strategies that can then be applied to particular problem-solving situations with increasing reliability. Research into adolescent decision making provides an example of how to explore problem solving as a set of component skills.

Adolescent Decision Making The ways that adolescents think about the world have obvious implications for the decisions they make about their own behavior. Adolescent decision making is an area of special interest to developmentalists because it has far-reaching consequences for adolescents' health and well-being. For example, adolescent risk-taking behavior clearly involves decision making. Knowledge of how adolescents go about evaluating risk may help educators, policy makers, and child advocates stem the tide of juvenile crime, suicide, pregnancy, and HIV infection (Miller & Byrnes, 2001). Likewise, the complexity of adolescent thinking is relevant to important legal issues. It is, for example, at the heart of debates about whether adolescents who commit crimes should be tried as adults (Grisso et al., 2003). Likewise, the complexity of adolescent decision making is relevant to questions about whether adolescents should be allowed to undergo medical procedures, including abortions, without the consent of a parent, or whether they are capable of giving *informed consent* (see Chapter 1, p. 28) to participate in research projects (Halpern-Felsher & Cauffman, 2001).

In their review of research on the subject, Bonnie Halpern-Felsher and Elizabeth Cauffman identified five steps that are commonly associated with effective decision making (adapted from Halpern-Felsher & Cauffman, 2001, p. 258):

1. Identify possible decision options

2. Identify possible risks and benefits associated with each option

3. Evaluate the desirability of each consequence

4. Assess the likelihood of each consequence

5. Decide on the best course of action by combining the information obtained in the previous steps according to a decision rule

These students were arrested on suspicion of planning an attack on their school. Despite evidence that teenagers lack adult decision-making and reasoning skills, they are often tried as adults in U. S. courts of law.

In an effort to examine how individuals think about important issues that they might encounter in their daily lives, Halpern-Felsher and Cauffman presented sixth- to twelfth-grade adolescents and young adults with decision-making scenarios in which they were asked to help a peer solve a problem. The problems included whether the peer should undergo a medical procedure (medical domain), should participate in a research project (informed consent domain), or should live with the mother or father after a divorce (family domain). For example, the following dilemma was presented for the medical domain: "I've been thinking about having this operation. It won't make me healthier or anything, but I'd like to have it because it would make me look better since I've always had this ugly thing like a bump on my cheek. I could have an operation to remove it. I'm trying to decide whether to have the operation, and I can't decide. Do you think I should have the operation?" (p. 262).

The participants were played a tape of the dilemmas and instructed to respond out loud with their advice. The researchers then coded their responses, looking for whether or not the participants mentioned options (e.g., "Are there treatments other than surgery?"), risks (e.g., "You could be scarred by the operation"), benefits (e.g., "You could be happy with the results of the surgery"), long-term consequences (e.g., "In the long run, you might feel better about yourself"), or advice seeking ("Have you gotten a second opinion?").

Overall, the researchers found that adults demonstrate significantly higher levels of decision-making competence compared with adolescents. Adults were more likely than adolescents, especially sixth- and eighth-graders, to consider options, risks, long-term consequences, benefits, and advice from others. Despite these age differences, the researchers cautioned against making hard-and-fast legal or social policies based solely on age or (in)competence. Noting that many adolescents in the study displayed high levels of competence, the researchers argued that wide variability in the onset and the use of complex decision-making processes makes it difficult to identify an age boundary between immature and mature individuals. Moreover, it is difficult to justify withholding certain medical treatments (for HIV infection, for example) because adolescents do not fully understand the implications of the treatment. "In such cases," the authors believe, "the benefits of extending health care access may outweigh the risks" (Halpern-Felsher & Cauffman, 2001, p. 272).

The Cultural-Context Perspective

As suggested in the work on decision making, there is a great deal of variability in adolescent reasoning. Indeed, to a much greater extent than the developmental stages that precede it, formal operations show a high degree of variability both within individuals and across groups. Studies find that as few as 30 to 40 percent of well-educated Americans in their late teens and early twenties are able to solve the combination-of-chemicals and other formal operational problems (Moshman, 1998). Moreover, many individuals who are capable of formal thought do not employ formal operational strategies in all situations (Markovits & Barrouillet, 2002). A car mechanic, for example, may use formal thought to troubleshoot an engine problem, but use concrete operational thinking in most other domains of life. Even experts solve problems in ways that suggest that unscientific reasoning is common (Daley, 1999). Expert chess players, for example, do not usually run through all possible combinations of moves, preferring instead to match the overall board pattern to a successful pattern they recall from past experience (Chase & Simon, 1988). Similarly, scientists follow their intuitions and take shortcuts that clearly violate the canons of scientific reasoning (Latour, 1987).

Like the information-processing theorists described previously, developmentalists who examine adolescent thinking from a cultural-context perspective focus mainly on thinking in everyday contexts. The cultural-context approach to adolescent thought begins with an observation similar to Inhelder and Piaget's: new modes of thought become prominent as teenagers prepare to adopt adult roles. Both approaches start by analyzing the structure of adult activity. However, whereas Piaget sought a single new logic underlying all adult thought, cultural-context theorists emphasize the heterogeneity of adult thought processes that arises from variation in the contexts of adult activity. As in earlier periods of development, these theorists believe that in order to understand adolescent thought processes, it is necessary to analyze the structure of activity and the scripts encountered in the various kinds of settings that adolescents are called upon to reason about.

Evidence that formal thought is linked to aspects of the culture is found in studies showing that gender differences in formal reasoning have declined over the past 20 years and are now negligible (Linn & Hyde, 1991; Moshman, 1998). Presumably, as girls and women have been increasingly encouraged to participate in the once male-dominated areas of math and science, they have developed the cognitive abilities necessary for formal thought.

Cultural differences in formal reasoning provide further evidence for the cultural-context approach and offer a greater challenge to the idea that Piaget's stages of cognitive development are universal. Unless they are among the relatively small part of the population who have attended high school or college, people in small, technologically unsophisticated societies rarely seem to use formal operations when they are tested with Piagetian methods (Hollos & Richards, 1993; Segall et al., 1999). This would suggest that a particular type of experience—that offered in formal educational settings, for example—is a necessary precondition for the development of formal thought.

Overall, the evidence from the information-processing and cultural-context perspectives regarding the variability of performance on formal operations tasks would seem to weaken the idea, central to traditional Piagetian theory, of a sharp discontinuity in cognitive development between middle childhood and adolescence. According to these perspectives, the improvements in cognitive ability during this transition may appear either continuous or discontinuous, depending on the depth of the young person's knowledge about a particular context or problem. Only if a qualitatively new mode of thinking appears across a broad range of contexts is it legitimate to conclude that a stagelike change has taken place. Consequently, to resolve the question of whether thinking undergoes a stagelike change in adolescence, we turn now to assess the extent to which adolescent thinking is more systematic than younger children's thinking in a variety of social contexts and content areas.

Adolescent Thinking about Moral Issues

Regardless of their theoretical orientation, developmentalists agree that adolescence is a time during which questions of moral behavior take on special importance for young people: What is right? What is wrong? What principles should I base my behavior on and use to judge the behavior of others? Evidence suggests that the processes used to think about such questions, like those used to think about science problems and politics, undergo important changes between the ages of 12 and 19 years (Moshman, 1999; Turiel, 2002).

Kohlberg's Theory of Moral Reasoning

As we noted in Chapter 14 (pp. 537–539), the study of moral development during middle childhood and adolescence has been greatly influenced by Lawrence Kohlberg, who suggested that moral reasoning progresses through three broad levels during childhood and adolescence, each consisting of two stages (Table 16.3 summarizes these levels and stages). As they develop from one stage to the next, children make more complex analyses of both the moral obligations that prevail among individuals and the obligations that exist between individuals and their social groups.

According to Kohlberg, moral reasoning at the start of middle childhood is at the preconventional level; that is, it is not based on social conventions or laws. Rather, in stages 1 and 2, children judge actions in the light of their own wants and fears and do not yet take into account the fact that social life requires shared standards of behavior. Toward the end of middle childhood, children attain the second level—the conventional level—in which they begin to take social conventions into account and recognize the existence of shared standards of right and wrong. Kohlberg called stage 3 reasoning (the first stage at this level) "good-child morality," because he believed that for the child in stage 3, being moral means living up to the expectations of one's family, teachers, and other significant people in one's life.

Moral reasoning at stage 4 is like that at stage 3 except that its focus shifts from relations between individuals to relations between the individual and the group. People who reason at stage 4 believe that society has legitimate authority over individuals, and they feel an obligation to accept its laws, customs, and standards of decent behavior. Moral behavior from this point of view is behavior that maintains

Their increased understanding of the social order motivates adolescents to question authority and challenge the status quo. This Turkish student is being arrested for protesting against a political council that strictly controls Turkish universities.

Tarik Tinazay/AFP/Getty Images

table 16.3

Kohlberg's Six Moral Stages			
Level and Stage	**What Is Right**	**Reasons for Doing Right**	**Social Perspective**
Level I—Preconventional			
Stage 1—Heteronomous morality	• Adherence to rules backed by punishment; obedience for its own sake.	• Avoidance of punishment.	Egocentric point of view.
Stage 2—Instrumental morality	• Acting to meet one's own interests and needs and letting others do the same.	• To serve one's own needs or interests.	Concrete individualistic perspective: right is relative, an equal exchange, a deal, an agreement.
Level II—Conventional			
Stage 3—Good-child morality	• Living up to what others expect.	• The need to be a good person in one's own eyes and those of others.	Perspective of the individual sharing feelings, agreements, and expectations with others.
Stage 4—Law-and-order morality	• Fulfilling the actual duties to which one has agreed. • Upholding laws except in extreme cases when they conflict with other fixed social duties • Contributing to society, group, or institution.	• To keep the institution going as a whole. • What would happen "if everyone did it"? • The imperative of conscience to meet one's defined obligations (easily confused with stage 3 belief in rules and authority).	Perspective of an individual in relation to the social group: takes the point of view of the system that defines roles and rules.
Level III—Postconventional, or Principled			
Stage 5—Social-contract reasoning	• Being aware that people hold a variety of values and opinions, most of which are relative to the group that holds them. • Upholding rules in the interest of impartiality and because they are the social contract. • Universal values and rights, such as life and liberty, must be upheld in any society, regardless of majority opinion.	• A sense of obligation to law because of one's social contract to make and abide by laws for the welfare of all and for the protection of all people's rights. • A feeling of contractual commitment, freely entered upon, to family, friendship, trust, and work obligations. • Concern that laws and duties be based on rational calculation of overall utility, "the greatest good for the greatest number."	Prior-to-society perspective: perspective of a rational individual aware of values and rights prior to social attachments and contracts. Integrates perspectives by mechanisms of agreement, formal contract, objective impartiality, and due process. Considers moral and legal points of view; recognizes that they sometimes conflict and finds it difficult to integrate them.
Stage 6—Universal ethical principles	• Following self-chosen ethical principles because they are universal principles of justice: the equality of human rights and respect for the dignity of human beings as individual persons. • Judging laws or social agreements by the extent to which they rest on such principles. • When laws violate principles, acting in accordance with the principle.	• A belief in the validity of universal moral principles. • A sense of personal commitment to those principles.	Perspective of a moral point of view from which social arrangements derive: perspective is that of any rational individual recognizing the nature of morality or the fact that persons are ends in themselves and must be treated as such.

Source: Adapted from Kohlberg, 1976.

the social order. For this reason, stage 4 is sometimes referred to as the "law-and-order stage" (Brown & Herrnstein, 1975, p. 289). Stage 4 reasoning begins to appear during adolescence, but stage 3 is still the dominant mode of reasoning about moral questions until people reach their mid-twenties (see Figure 16.2) (Colby et al., 1983).

Kohlberg believed that moral thinking at stages 3 and 4 depends on a partial ability to engage in formal operational reasoning—specifically, the ability to consider simultaneously the various existing factors relevant to moral choices (Kohlberg, 1984). People who are reasoning at stages 3 and 4, however, are still reasoning concretely insofar as they do not yet simultaneously consider all possible relevant factors or form abstract hypotheses about what is moral.

With the transition from stage 4 to stage 5 comes another basic shift in the level of moral judgment. Reasoning at stage 5 requires people to go beyond existing social conventions to consider more abstract principles of right and wrong. This perspective, which Kohlberg called *postconventional,* requires moral reasoning to be based on the idea of a society as bound by a social contract. People still accept and value the social system, but instead of insisting on maintaining society as it is, they are open to democratic processes of change and to continual exploration of possibilities for improving on the existing social order. Recognizing that laws are sometimes in conflict with moral principles, they become creators as well as maintainers of laws. Kohlberg found that stage 5 moral reasoning does not appear until early adulthood, and then only rarely.

People reach stage 6 in Kohlberg's system when they make moral judgments in accordance with ethical principles that they believe transcend the rules of individual societies. Kohlberg and his colleagues failed to observe stage 6 reasoning in their research on moral dilemmas, and Kohlberg eventually concluded that this stage is more usefully thought of as a philosophical ideal than as a psychological reality. Nonetheless, under extraordinary circumstances, otherwise ordinary people have put their lives at risk because of moral beliefs guided by stage 6 reasoning. Such was the case during World War II, when many European gentiles rescued Jews destined for extermination. According to Samuel and Pearl Oliner (1988), most of them were motivated by ethical principles that they believed apply to all of humanity, the hallmark of stage 6 moral reasoning.

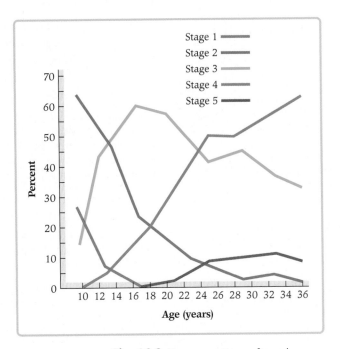

Fig. 16.2 Mean percentage of moral reasoning of U.S. citizens at each of Kohlberg's stages, by age group. (Adapted from Colby et al., 1983.)

Evaluating Kohlberg's Theory of Moral Reasoning

By and large, researchers who have used Kohlberg's methods and criteria for assigning people to different stages of moral reasoning have confirmed that children progress through the sequence proposed by Kohlberg in the predicted order (Rest et al., 1999). However, Kohlberg's approach is not without its difficulties (Moshman, 1999; Turiel, 2002).

One common criticism is that Kohlberg underestimated the age at which children are able to understand the difference between social conventions and moral issues. As you recall from the discussion of *social exclusion* in Chapter 14 (see p. 542), Melanie Killen and her colleagues have argued that social reasoning involves both *moral beliefs* about fairness, equal treatment, and right and wrong, as well as *social-conventional beliefs* about group functioning and group identity. Rather than viewing social-conventional beliefs as a stepping-stone to a higher stage of moral beliefs, Killen thinks that both are integral to children's reasoning about moral issues. In fact, understanding the nuances of social conventions increases throughout middle childhood and adolescence in ways that are highly relevant to social judgments and understanding.

morality of justice A morality that emphasizes issues of rightness, fairness, and equality

morality of care A morality that stresses relationships, compassion, and social obligations.

In one study, first-graders, fourth-graders, and seventh-graders judged whether it was wrong to exclude a peer from a group on the basis of gender or race. Whereas all the children insisted that such exclusion was wrong, and appealed to fairness, rights, and equal treatment, the older children were much more likely to qualify their judgments in the event that inclusion posed a significant threat to group functioning (Killen & Stangor, 2001). A strictly Kohlbergian perspective would predict just the opposite: the younger children would be expected to follow social conventions, while the adolescents would be focused more on the moral issues of fairness and equal treatment.

Kohlberg's theory has also been criticized as having an overly narrow conception of the nature of morality. Carol Gilligan and her colleagues (1982), for example, asserted that Kohlberg's approach reflects a **morality of justice,** that is, a morality that emphasizes issues of rightness, fairness, and equality. However, Gilligan argues that this treatment of the moral domain neglects a key dimension of moral thinking that focuses on issues of responsibility to others. This other dimension, the **morality of care,** stresses relationships, compassion, and social obligations. The morality of justice is associated with abstract principles and conjures up an image of an unbiased judge whose deliberations are unaffected by stereotypes and conventions. The morality of care, in contrast, is concerned with the concrete and often changing dynamics of contexts, relationships, and roles.

Gilligan's work inspired a great deal of debate, not because of her conception of a morality of care, but because of her claim, based on largely anecdotal evidence, that girls and women are oriented to the morality of care, whereas boys and men are oriented toward the morality of justice (Moshman, 1999). More systematic research has found few gender differences in levels of moral reasoning in predominantly white or African American adolescents (Turiel, 1998; Walker et al., 1995; Weisz & Black, 2003). Gender differences, when they are found, seem to depend on a variety of factors, including whether the subjects respond to hypothetical dilemmas or real-life dilemmas, and where they grew up (for example, gender differences are more apparent in North American compared with Norwegian adolescents; Skoe, 1999).

Despite the lack of evidence for strong gender differences, Gilligan's conception of a morality of care provides a broader, more inclusive view of moral reasoning than Kohlberg's original formulation, and has helped to orient researchers to the broader contexts of moral development and judgment.

Cultural Variations in Moral Reasoning

Standard studies of cross-cultural variability in moral reasoning using Kohlbergian dilemmas (such as those presented in Chapter 14, p. 539), like the cross-cultural variability of formal operational reasoning, reveal greater differences between cultural groups than between the two sexes (Kohlberg, 1969; Turiel, 1998). Although there are some exceptions (Shweder et al., 1987), most studies show that people who live in relatively small, face-to-face communities in technologically unsophisticated societies, and who have not received high levels of schooling that take them outside of the traditional way of life, rarely reason beyond stage 3 on Kohlberg's scale (see Figure 16.3). Most often they justify their moral decisions at the level of stage 1 or 2, although people in roles of special responsibility may reason at stage 3 (Snarey, 1995).

Kohlberg suggested that cultural differences in social stimulation produce differences in moral reasoning. However, several developmentalists have argued that culture-specific value judgments are built directly into Kohlberg's stage sequence. In particular, the higher stages seem consistent with the values of Western culture and democracy, whereas the lower stages seem consistent with the values of traditional societies. Are we to believe, such critics ask, that people who grow up in a

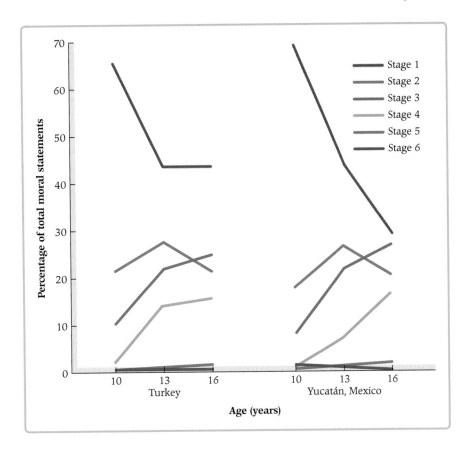

Fig. 16.3 Age trends in the moral judgments of boys in small, isolated villages in two nations. Note the continuing high incidence of stage 1 responses even by 16-year-olds. (From Kohlberg, 1969.)

traditional Third World village are less moral than the residents of a city in an industrially advanced country (Shweder et al., 2002)?

Kohlberg (1984) denied that bias in his scales fosters the conclusion that some societies, the United States among them, are more moral than others. He echoed the classical position of modern anthropology, that cultures should be thought of as unique configurations of beliefs and institutions that help the social group adapt to both local conditions and universal aspects of life on earth (Boas, 1911; Geertz, 1984). In this view, a culture in which stage 3 was the height of moral reasoning would be considered "morally equivalent" to a culture dominated by stage 5 or 6 reasoning, even though the specific reasoning practices could be scored as less "developed" according to Kohlberg's universal criteria.

Nevertheless, other approaches to moral reasoning have produced results that depart markedly from those obtained using Kohlberg's methods. Cross-cultural studies have reported that by adulthood, a shift from conventional to postconventional moral reasoning is quite widespread if not universal (Gielen & Markoulis, 2001). In cases in which differences appear between countries, the level of education provided to the populations in question appears to be the critical factor.

Similarly, Elliot Turiel and his colleagues, in accordance with their *social domain theory*, which emphasizes the need to separate moral issues from issues involving social convention and personal choice (see Chapter 14, p. 541), provide evidence that the pattern of development for moral reasoning is universal. When cultural differences do appear, these researchers contend, the differences are related to issues concerning social conventions and personal choice, the importance of obedience to authority, and the nature of interpersonal relations (Turiel, 2002; Wainryb, 1995). In one extensive study, Cecilia Wainryb compared judgments about social conflicts given by a large sample of Israeli 9- to 17-year-olds. Half the participants were Jews from a secular, Westernized part of the Israeli population. The other half were from

table 16.4

Questions Pitting One Kind of Social Conflict against Another

Justice versus Authority (J–A)
Hannan and his father were shopping and they saw that a young boy inadvertently dropped a 10 shekel bill.
J Hannan told his father that they should return the money to the boy.
A His father told him to keep it.

Justice versus Interpersonal (J–I)
On a field trip, Kobby realized that the school did not provide enough soft drinks for all the children.
I Kobby had to choose between taking two drinks for his two younger brothers who were very thirsty or
J Alerting the teachers so that the drinks could be distributed equally among all children.

Personal versus Interpersonal (P–I)
P Dalya was invited to a party.
She was looking forward to going there with her friends.
I Her young sister sprained her ankle and asked Dalya to stay home with her and keep her company.

Personal versus Authority (P–A)
Anat loves music.
P She wants to participate in an after-school music class.
A Her father does not like music; he tells her not to participate in the music class and take another class instead.

Source: Wainryb, 1995.

Druze Arabic villages, where the cultural norms emphasize hierarchical family structures, fixed social roles, and severe punishment for violating traditional duties and customs. The study pitted questions about justice and personal choice against questions about authority and interpersonal considerations (see Table 16.4).

Wainryb found that, in response to questions involving justice, there were no cultural or age differences. For example, an overwhelming percentage of participants at all ages said that a boy who saw someone lose money should return it, even though the boy's father said to keep the money. Jewish children were slightly more likely than Druze children to choose personal considerations over interpersonal considerations, but the variability within each cultural group was far larger than the variation between them. The only really significant cultural difference was that Jewish children were much more likely to assert personal rights over authority than the Druze children. This result was in line with the hierarchical family structure in Druze culture, in which obedience to authority is a central value.

In a similar vein, Joan Miller and her colleagues found that while people from India and the United States may differ in where they draw the line between moral infractions and personal conventions, members of both groups make this distinction (Miller & Schaberg, 2003). For example, both Indians and Americans judged the violation of dress codes in terms of social conventions, not moral issues; and members of both societies judged theft to be a moral issue, not a matter of social convention. These studies suggest that by dividing up questions of morality into separate domains, it is possible to obtain a more subtle picture of cultural influences on moral reasoning in which there are both universal and culture-specific elements.

The Relation between Moral Reasoning and Moral Action

As you saw in Chapter 14 (p. 541), children may say they would behave one way in a hypothetical moral situation but actually behave in quite a different way. Although the correspondence between moral reasoning and moral behavior continues to be far from perfect in adolescence, there is evidence of a generally positive, if modest, relationship between the two: the higher the individual's score on tests of moral reasoning, the more likely he or she is to behave in a morally appropriate way. It has been found, for example, that adolescents who score at higher levels of moral reasoning are less likely to cheat in school or come in contact with the law, and are more likely to engage in prosocial acts such as helping someone in distress or defending victims of oppression (Blasi, 1994).

Often, however, the links between moral judgments and moral action are not particularly close (Nucci, 2004). In some cases, societal standards and expectations contribute to variability in moral behavior. For example, studies of academic dishonesty among high school students generally find that cheating is widespread, and heavily influenced by school norms and the attitudes of teachers and friends (McCabe, 1999). High school students seem to be less guilt-stricken than college students, and more apt to blame others—schools, teachers, and society—for their dishonesty (Anderman et al., 1998). As one participant in Donald McCabe's study explained, one reason that cheating is universal is because there is no threat of being caught: "I don't know if it's just our school, but like everybody cheats. Everyone looks at everyone else's paper. And the teachers don't care; they let it happen. . . . The students keep on doing it because they don't get in trouble" (p. 683). However, even in the absence of an obvious deterrent, some students expressed ambivalence about their behavior: "I guess the first time you do it, you feel really bad, but then you get used to it. You keep telling yourself you're not doing anything wrong. . . . Maybe you might know in your heart that it's wrong, but it gets easier after a while to handle it" (p. 682). Over time, cheating takes its toll in ways that can be easily discerned by students: "I'm at the point now where I don't know nothing. . . . If I don't cheat, I just fail" (p. 682).

As a consequence of the competing factors that enter into moral choices, there is often a gap between people's moral judgments and their actions. At the same time, the ability to reason about moral issues provides the minimal level of understanding required for moral action. Another factor that helps adolescents to act morally is their increasing ability to understand the plight of others and to reason prosocially (Carpendale, 2000). Indeed, studies of Brazilian and North American adolescents show strong correlations between sympathy, perspective-taking skills, and prosocial reasoning (Eisenberg et al., 2001). As we discuss in the sections following, adolescents are increasingly focused on their sense of identity and more mindful of the need to be true to others as well as to themselves.

Yet another way to examine the relationship between moral reasoning and behavior is to approach it from the perspective of social domain theory. In the same way that the theory has proved useful in accounts of cross-cultural variability in moral reasoning (discussed previously) and parent-adolescent conflict (Chapter 15, p. 610), it provides insight into the relationship between adolescents' moral reasoning and their behaviors. As you recall from the discussion in Chapter 15, much of the strife between parents and their adolescent children results from disagreements about what is and is not within the adolescent's personal domain. It seems that adolescents and parents may also disagree about the boundary and content of the moral domain. In particular, what parents and researchers count as moral issues may be personal issues from the perspective of adolescents. An example comes from a study of the relationship between moral reasoning and risky behavior. Tara Kuther and Ann Higgins-D'Alessandro (2000) found that adolescents who report higher levels of drug and alcohol use are more likely to see their risky behaviors as personal decisions, rather than as moral or conventional decisions. The researchers suggested that directors of drug and alcohol intervention programs take heed, and encourage youth to explore their views of the personal, conventional, and moral realms.

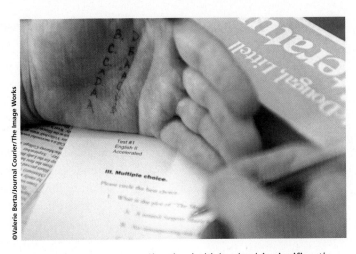

©Valerie Berta/Journal Courier/The Image Works

Cheating in high school is significantly influenced by school norms, attitudes of teachers and students, and the threat of being caught.

Parent and Peer Contributions to Moral Development

Kohlberg argued that parents have a minimal role in the moral development of their children, whereas peer interactions are essential to promoting moral growth (Walker et al., 2000). This is due, he argued, to the differences in power inherent in the two types of relationships. Parents, because of their position of unilateral authority, are less effective than peers in promoting moral development because children are not inclined to interact with them cooperatively and take seriously their contrasting points of view. As you know from the previous discussion of sociocognitive conflict, intense engagement with alternative points of view can be a strong impetus to attaining higher levels of reasoning. Kohlberg believed that the more mutual and cooperative nature of peer relationships would provide a more fertile context for moral development. Indeed, research indicates that both the quantity and quality of peer relationships, including the number of close friendships, amount of participation in social activities, and leadership status, are significantly related to moral reasoning in adolescence (Schonert-Reichl, 1999). Be that as it may, developmentalists have challenged Kohlberg's idea that parents have little impact in the moral realm (Pratt et al., 1999; Walker et al., 2000). Research finds in general that authoritative, democratic, responsive parenting is associated with higher levels of moral maturity (Hart et al., 1999). Lawrence Walker and his colleagues conducted a rare, longitudinal study comparing both parent and peer contexts (2000). Compared with peers, parents provided a higher level of cognitive functioning in discussions of moral issues and, when a "gentle Socratic method" was employed, children's moral maturity was advanced. In contrast, and consistent with the notion of sociocognitive conflict, peer interactions that were more turbulent and conflict-ridden were associated with the development of higher moral levels. The upshot is that both parent and peer relationships were highly influential in moral development, but each type of relationship contributed in distinctive ways.

Concern with personal appearance is part of the formation of identity and self-esteem typical of the adolescent years.

Integration of the Self

One of the most widely held ideas about adolescence is that this is the period during which the individual forges the basis for a stable adult personality. You know from discussions in Chapter 14 that self-conceptions undergo major change during middle childhood. At about the age of 6, when American children enter school, they begin to think of themselves in comparative terms: instead of saying (for example), "I am a girl who likes to skate," they begin to provide such self-descriptions as "I am a better skater than most of the kids in my class." A little later they begin explicitly to include the interpersonal consequences of their attributes: "I am a good skater, so lots of kids like to skate with me" (see Table 14.6, p. 565). During adolescence, a new kind of self-description makes its appearance, in which personal identity is expressed in terms of general beliefs, values, and life plans. Self-descriptions shift from relatively concrete attributes (for instance, "I'm a good listener" or "I am easygoing") to more inclusive, higher-order concepts ("I am tolerant").

However, an identity involves considerably more than a list of self-descriptions (Moshman, 2004). Erik Erikson, probably the most influential modern identity theorist, defines *identity formation* as "a process located in the core of the individual and yet also in the core of his communal culture, a process which establishes, in fact, the identity of those two identities" (Erikson, 1959, p, 48). In other words, one's developing understanding of self is importantly tied to one's developing relationship to community and culture. Adolescents' ability to take several factors into account at the same time when they think about a problem, their broader and deeper knowledge of their society's norms and moral codes, and their increasing awareness that adulthood is approaching all contribute to the establishment of an integrated sense of self and identity.

The Puzzle of Identity

Efforts to understand the nature of self have preoccupied scholars for generations. It is generally agreed that one's identity is an answer to the question "Who am I?" It is also generally agreed that identity is uniquely puzzling. One puzzle, identified by William James (1842–1910), an American psychologist and philosopher, is that the self is *recursive;* that is, it bends back on itself in the process thinking about itself. James's major goal was to understand how the self manages the heady gymnastic of taking itself as an object of reflection. How does the self, in other words, get outside of itself in order to know, judge, disdain, or take pride in its very own actions and being? James's solution to this particular identity puzzle was to define two components of the self—the *me* and the *I*. For James, the **me-self** is the object-self, and includes all of the things that people know about themselves—their social roles and relationships ("I am a student"; "I am Tenisha's fiancé"), material possessions ("I drive a late model Chevy"), traits ("I am ambitious"), and other things that can be objectively known (age, family, school, religion, and so forth). The **I-self** is the subject-self, the part of the system that reflects on, guides, and directs the self. The I-self includes (Harter, 1999, p. 6):

- Self-*awareness,* an appreciation of one's internal states, needs, thoughts, and emotions;
- Self-*agency,* the sense of authorship over one's thoughts and actions;
- Self-*continuity,* the sense that one remains the same person over time;
- Self-*coherence,* a stable sense of the self as a single, coherent, bounded entity.

Many contemporary developmentalists maintain that the self is a story about who one is. If so, then the *me-self* is the character in that story, and the *I-self* is the author and the storyteller.

Although James's distinction between the *me* and the *I* appears to solve the problem of recursion, his theory raises additional puzzles that preoccupy modern developmentalists. Certain aspects of the *I-self,* particularly the aspects of self-continuity and self-coherence, have inspired fascinating debate about the nature of self in the modern world. For example, Kenneth Gergen has suggested that self-coherence is difficult to achieve in technologically advanced societies in which mass communications dramatically accelerate our relations to each other and to our communities. According to Gergen, modern society has resulted in a **saturated self,** that is, a self full to the brim with multiple "me's" that have emerged as a consequence of needing to conform to a dizzying swirl of social roles and relationships that demand different, and sometimes contradictory, selves. The appearance of "multiple selves" in the self-descriptions of adolescents makes it necessary for them to deal with the fact that they are, in some sense, different people in different contexts. It is at this point that the question of personal authenticity—"Who is the *real* me?"—becomes particularly compelling.

me-self (object-self) Includes all of the things that people know about themselves.

I-self (subject-self) The part of the system that reflects on, guides, and directs the self.

saturated self A self full to the brim with multiple "me's" that have emerged as a consequence of needing to conform to social roles and relationships that demand different, and sometimes contradictory, selves.

Adolescents often seek out heroes to adulate and imitate. In the United States, many identify with popular musicians. These young people are waiting outside a funeral home to pay tribute to the platinum-selling rapper known as Big Pun.

Mark Lennihan/AP Photo

In addition to the puzzle of self-coherence is the puzzle of self-continuity. Michael Chandler and his colleagues claim that a major task of adolescence is to be able to understand self-continuity, that is, that selves persist in time even though they change in obvious ways, as do the environments in which they live and to which they adjust (Chandler et al., 2003). As you will see, the task of coming to grips with self-continuity in the face of inevitable personal and cultural change is particularly problematic for adolescents who are developing in conditions of dramatic social upheaval. In such contexts of rapid social change, the path of identity formation can be fraught with difficulty and peril.

Resolving the Identity Crisis

The fact that adolescents are troubled by the feeling of multiple selves makes the search for one's "true self" one of the dominant developmental tasks of adolescents (Meeus & Porton, 1998). According to Erikson (1968a), the need to create a unified sense of identity is the final developmental crisis before adulthood; adolescents must either resolve the crisis by achieving a secure sense of personal identity or confront a variety of psychological problems in later life.

As we noted earlier, Erikson saw the process of identity formation as involving the integration of more than the individual's personality. In order to forge a secure sense of self, adolescents must resolve their identities in both the individual and the social spheres, or, as Erikson put it, establish "the identity of those two identities."

The popularity of Erikson's ideas created a demand for an assessment method that could both depict an identity in the process of being formed and provide quantitative measures of the different states of identity formation (Grotevant, 1998; Grotevant & Cooper, 1998; Marcia, 2002) (for a description of another assessment method, see the box "From Diaries to Blogs: Personal Documents in Developmental Research"). In an early and influential effort at such an assessment method, James Marcia (1966) focused on two factors identified by Erikson as essential to achieving a mature identity: *crisis/exploration* and *commitment*. Crisis/exploration refers to the process through which adolescents actively examine their future opportunities in life, reexamine the choices their parents have made, and begin to search for alternatives that they find personally satisfying. Commitment refers to individuals' personal involvement in, and allegiance to, the goals, values, beliefs, and future occupation that they have adopted for themselves. You read an example of such commitment at the beginning of this chapter: Anchee Min described her adolescence as a time of inspiration and eagerness to devote herself to the political ideology of the Chinese Cultural Revolution.

Marcia interviewed male college students about two life domains that play a central role in identity formation according to Erikson: their choice of occupation and their commitment to beliefs about religion and politics. His questions were designed to elicit information on the degree to which individuals have adopted and fully committed themselves to a point of view.

Marcia (1966, 2002) identified four patterns of coping with the task of identity formation that arise from four possible patterns of crisis/exploration and commitment (see Figure 16.4):

1. *Identity achievement* Adolescents who display this pattern have gone through a period of decision making about their choice of occupation, for example, or their political or religious commitment. They are now actively pursuing their own goals. When people in this group were asked about their political beliefs, they responded with such answers as "I've thought it over, and I've decided to be a _____. Their program is the most sensible one for the country to be following."

2. *Foreclosure* Young people who display this pattern are also committed to occupational and ideological positions, but they show no signs of having gone through an identity crisis. In a sense they never really undergo a personality reorganization. Instead, they just take over patterns of identity from their parents. They respond to questions about their political beliefs with such answers as "I really never gave politics much thought. Our family always votes _____, so that's how I vote."

3. *Moratorium* This pattern is displayed by adolescents currently in an identity crisis. They are likely to answer a question about their political beliefs by saying, "I'm not sure. Both parties have their good points, but neither one seems to offer a better chance for my economic future."

4. *Identity diffusion* Adolescents who manifest this pattern have tried out several identities without being able to settle on one. They are likely to take a cynical attitude toward the issues confronting them, so they may answer questions about political commitment by declaring, "I stopped thinking about politics ages ago. There are no parties worth supporting."

Fig. 16.4 When the combinations of Erikson's two processes of identity formation—crisis/exploration and commitment—are considered together, the result is the four states of adolescent identity formation proposed by Marcia.

Other researchers have extended Marcia's methods to incorporate additional domains of experience, including family life, friendships, dating, and sex roles (Goosens, 2001; Grotevant, 1998). By and large these studies have shown that the proportion of identity achievers increases steadily from the years before high school to the late college years, while the proportion of young people manifesting identity diffusion decreases (Grotevant & Cooper, 1998; Kroger, 2003; Moshman, 1998). (See Table 16.5 for typical results showing how identity status grows in the occupational category.)

Given the emphasis placed on exploration as a precursor to healthy identity formation, it is no surprise that developmentalists have sought evidence of the link between patterns of exploration and subsequent identity statuses. One such study found that childhood exploration, as indicated by participation in various technical and cultural activities, predicted adolescent exploration, which, in turn, predicted identity achievement (Schmitt-Rodermund & Vondracek, 1999). Another study determined that identity exploration was positively correlated to the number of selves that adolescents imagine (Dunkel & Anthis, 2001).

However, while exploration appears essential to healthy identity formation, commitment seems to contribute to adolescents' feelings of satisfaction with themselves and their lives. In a study of more than 1500 Dutch adolescents, Meeus and his colleagues determined that both foreclosure and achievement were associated with a sense of well-being (Meeus et al., 2002).

table 16.5

Percentage of Students Manifesting Four Identity Statuses in the Domain of Vocational Choice, by Age Group				
Age Group	**Identity Achievement, %**	**Moratorium, %**	**Foreclosure, %**	**Identity Diffusion, %**
Pre–high school years	5.2	11.7	36.6	46.4
High school underclass years	9.0	14.6	37.1	39.3
High school upperclass years	21.3	13.5	36.0	29.2
College underclass years	22.8	28.3	25.7	23.2
College upperclass years	39.7	15.5	31.3	13.5

Source: Waterman, 1985.

From Diaries to Blogs: Personal Documents in Developmental Research

Researchers have found that diaries, letters, and other personal documents can provide unique and important insight into major developmental issues and questions. In general, personal documents have been used in two ways. In one, scientists have themselves kept diaries in which they record observations of their own children. In this instance, the diary entries are usually guided by the scientific purpose of the writer, and can be quite specific and focused. The most famous historical example is Darwin's daily record of the early development of his eldest son. By documenting his son's development and determining what characteristics he shared with other species at different ages, Darwin hoped to find support for his thesis of human evolution. Jean Piaget (1952b, 1954) also kept a diary of the development of his children that served as the foundation of his influential theory of cognitive development.

The second way that scientists use personal documents to explore issues of human development is to examine the diaries and letters written by others. The motives of the writers of such documents may be quite diverse. But while a diary might lack specific focus, it often provides rich detail about the person, and his or her life and times. Adolescents' diaries provide a way for researchers to "witness" emotions and issues of a personal nature that adolescents seldom reveal to adults. You have probably heard about or read the diary kept by the Jewish girl, Anne Frank, during World War II. She and her family hid away for several years in a small attic while Holland was occupied by the Nazi army. In the diary, Anne describes her puberty, her sexual awakening, and her changing relationships with family and peers. Viewed though the lens of developmental

theory, the diary provides a record of Anne's cognitive and emotional growth (Haviland & Kramer, 1991; Magai & Haviland-Jones, 2002).

Other developmentalists have taken a different approach to adolescents' diaries. For example, rather than being viewed as a record of experience and development, diary writing can be viewed as an experience in its own right—one that may be helpful in dealing with the identity issues and complex feelings that accompany adolescence. Would Anne have kept such a detailed account of her most personal thoughts and feelings if she had had easy access to friends with whom she could easily talk and share secrets? Did her regular retreat into the privacy of her diary provide her with much-needed personal "space" in the cramped quarters that she shared with members of her own and another family? Barbara Crowther (1999) has analyzed diaries written between the late 1950s and early 1970s by 10- to 14-year-old girls. She suggests, on the basis of her analysis, that writing in a private diary can make a very public statement about independence and individuality. She noted, for example, that writing a diary is rarely kept secret, and that girls will often make a big deal about it, posting "Keep Out!" signs on their doors, or writing warnings such as "Strictly Private—No Entry" on the diary covers. And while all of this appears to be about insuring privacy, it is also a declaration: "I have ideas, feelings, opinions that are *my own*." Writing a diary, from Crowther's perspective, can be a way of establishing a sense of personal autonomy.

It is likely that developmentalists will continue to keep their own diaries for scientific purposes, as well as find scientific value in personal documents written by others. It is

Electronic communications, including on-line diaries, permit the expression of many facets of the self.

interesting to speculate about how the study of personal documents will change as a consequence of technological advances. The Internet has already enabled the construction of entirely new types of personal documents: the personal Web page, and its most recent offspring—the blog. The blog is an on-line journal. Unlike diaries, which can be intensely private, blogs are radically public and interactive, accessible to literally billions of people, any of whom may comment on the diary entries. And whereas diaries are evolving records that preserve past entries, contributing to, or at least reflecting, a *continuous self,* Web pages may reflect something closer to Gergen's *saturated self*. That is, personal Web pages can be entirely

Because identity achievement is considered so important to normal adolescent development, researchers have given special effort to identifying factors that facilitate or retard identity formation and to determining how the process might differ for boys and for girls.

The Role of Family and Friends in Identity Formation

In the opening vignette of this chapter, you read an adolescent's account of how school provided a "perfect environment in which to fight against my father's views," and "gave me a chance to develop into an independent, capable woman who did not need to answer to anyone but herself." Focusing on the contexts of

rewritten to present an entirely different self—or selves—to the world.

It is estimated that there will be 10 million blogs by the end of 2004, more than half of them generated by adolescents (Nussbaum, 2004). Given the explosion of blogging, we might reasonably ask what purpose it serves. According to Emily Nussbaum's interviews with adolescent bloggers, interactive on-line diaries provide a means of self-expression, as well as a sense of community with other teens. The postings of bloggers chronicle their authors' loneliness and insecurities; and they seek and offer advice on everything from finding a mate, to getting rid of a mate, to surviving inept and unreasonable parents. "I need your help," one poster wrote. "Yes,

your help. You, the one reading this . . . what am i supposed to do when the dynamic of a once-romantic relationship sort of changes but sort of doesn't, and the next week i continually try to get in touch with the girl but she is either not there or can't talk very long, and before this change in the dynamic she was always available?" A string of responses suggested a variety of options, including "don't call her so much" and "confront her . . . what she's doing isn't fair to you" (Nussbaum, 2004, p. 35). Although most comments tend to be sympathetic one-liners or wisecracks, some are hurtful and hostile, placing the blogger in a peculiar position relative to the audience of on-line onlookers. As noted by one of the

bloggers interviewed by Nussbaum, "If I get a really mean comment and I go back and look at it again, and again, it starts to bother me. But then I think, if I delete it, everyone will know this bothers me. But if I respond, it'll mean I need to fight back. So it turns into a conflict, but it's fun. It's like a soap opera, kind of" (p. 35).

In addition to the drama, such public displays clearly encourage a high degree of self-reflection that developmentalists consider the hallmark of the I-self. Unfortunately, these new electronic diary forms are ephemeral, making it difficult for developmentalists to find and analyze them after they have served their authors' adolescent purposes.

DOONSBURY by Gary Trudeau

identity formation, Harke Bosma and Saskia Kunnen (2001) have suggested that conflicts arising in the course of adolescents' social relationships trigger higher levels of self-development. They suggest, moreover, that the most fertile contexts for identity development are those that enhance openness to change and provide a high level of support. Research has shown that both the immediate family and the adolescent's peer relations influence the process of identity formation (Sartor & Youniss, 2002). Futhermore, the two contexts of family and peer relationships influence each other.

Harold Grotevant and Catherine Cooper conducted several studies focused on the special role that social relationships within families play in shaping the process of identity formation (Grotevant & Cooper, 1998). They constructed a "family interaction task" to evaluate the way that patterns of family interaction influence the process of identity exploration (Grotevant & Cooper, 1985). In this task, a mother, a father, and their adolescent are asked to make plans for a 2-week vacation together. They have 20 minutes to arrive at a day-by-day plan that covers both the location and the activity for each day. The discussions are scored according to the way the family members express their individuality (for example, by stating their own point of view or by disagreeing with another family member) and their connectedness (as displayed by their responsiveness and sensitivity to others' points of view).

Grotevant and Cooper also interviewed the adolescents in these families to find out how thoroughly they had explored a variety of options for their futures. They hypothesized that identity exploration would be related to individuality (the adolescent had to learn how to develop a distinctive point of view) and connectedness (the family had to provide a secure base from which the adolescent could explore).

In this and subsequent studies, Grotevant and Cooper found that adolescents who scored higher on measures of identity exploration lived in families that supported their right to express their own points of view (Grotevant, 1998). They also found that the role of family relationship patterns in identity formation differed for sons and for daughters. For sons, greater identity exploration was associated with their father's willingness to allow disagreement, to compromise, and to modify his own suggestions in light of theirs—in short, to engage in genuine give-and-take. For daughters, a higher degree of identity exploration was associated with assertiveness, as manifested in their expressions of disagreement with their parents and the assertiveness with which they made suggestions. Despite these somewhat different patterns for boys and girls, it appears safe to say that the family systems that are most effective in promoting identity achievement are those that offer adolescents support and security while encouraging them to create a distinct identity. This is also suggested in recent work showing that secure attachment is positively related to identity achievement, whereas insecure attachment correlates with identity diffusion (Zimmermann & Becker-Stoll, 2002).

Friendships play a complementary role in the process of identity formation, as shown by Wim Meeus and Maja Deković, who conducted a study of almost 3000 Dutch subjects between the ages of 12 and 24. In addition to collecting data about levels of identity achievement, these researchers asked their subjects to indicate the extent to which they felt supported by key people in their lives—father, mother, siblings, friends, and classmates—in their social relations, school, and work. They found that the support of classmates and friends was rated as more important than the support of family members in promoting identity achievement (Meeus & Deković, 1995).

Gender Differences in Identity Formation

Erikson sparked debate on the question of possible gender differences in identity formation by proposing that women cannot complete their identity formation process until they have married and become mothers (Erikson, 1968b). That conclusion may have had some validity for the cultural conditions in which Erikson himself grew up, but it was highly debatable for many young women in the 1960s and is certainly of dubious validity in most Western cultures today.

Recent studies using identity-status interviews like that developed by Marcia have found little evidence of general gender differences in identity formation. However, some gender differences have been found in particular domains. Meeus and Deković (1995), for example, reported that adolescent girls score at higher levels of identity achievement than boys in the domain of friendship. Several theorists have suggested that personal relationships may play a greater role in self-definition for females than for males. In this view, females' first priority in achieving identity is to establish and maintain their close relationships. To explore this issue, Arlene Lacombe and Judith Gay (1998) asked 15- to 16-year-old students to respond to dilemmas involving issues of identity where the quality of the education they would receive was pitted against the value they placed on an intimate relationship. The students were asked to respond to the following dilemma:

> Allison has been accepted at a very prestigious college with a reputation for a high-quality English Department. She knows she wants to major in English. The main drawback is that the college is a six-hour drive from her boyfriend. She also has been accepted to a college an hour from her boyfriend, which has an average English Department. She is unsure of which to choose.
>
> How much consideration should she give to each of the following issues in resolving the dilemma?
> (a) the quality of the program
> (b) the distance from her boyfriend
> Why?

More than 50 percent of the time, both boys and girls chose responses that favored educational identity over those that involved intimacy, and, contrary to expectations, boys chose more intimacy resolutions than girls did. However, girls' explanations of their choices were more likely than boys' to combine concerns with educational identity and intimacy (Lacombe & Gay, 1998).

Although the data on gender differences in the process of identity formation are not entirely consistent, the bulk of the evidence indicates that adolescent girls, like adolescent boys, go through psychologically similar processes, despite some variations in the domains that are most important to them (Moshman, 1999). This is not inconsistent with Erikson's belief that social and historical contexts play a formative role in the development of personal identity.

The Formation of a Sexual Identity

If the formation of identity can be considered an answer to the question "Who am I?" the formation of a sexual identity can be viewed as an answer to "Who am I as a sexual being"? In certain respects, the formation of a sexual identity is similar to the formation of personal identity as just discussed. That is, like the domains of occupation, politics, dating, and sex roles that have been studied by researchers following in the tradition of Erikson and Marcia, the domain of sexual identity may involve exploration and commitment, and may be associated with such concepts as self-continuity, self-coherence, and authenticity. Likewise, in much the same fashion that personal identity development is shaped by social habits and expectations, sexual identity development takes place against a backdrop of sociopolitical and historical traditions, power relations, and stereotypes.

On the other hand, as a domain of identity formation, sexuality is importantly unique. Unlike occupation, politics, and dating, it is not a frequent topic of conversation between adolescents and their parents, peers, or school guidance counselors. As a society, we do not go out of our way to provide adolescents with opportunities to explore their sexualities. And, as you recall from Chapter 15, much of the information that adolescents do receive regarding sexual behavior is delivered in the form of warnings about unwanted pregnancy and STDs. Martha Nussbaum (2001) argues that Western culture, including its scholars, associates strong feelings of shame with the body and its sexual behaviors and desires, and is therefore reluctant to address sexuality in an open manner. The state of affairs that Nussbaum describes — the inherent conflict between the sexual appetites of the body and society's sanctions against their expression — inspired Sigmund Freud's theory of sexuality development, to which you were introduced initially in Chapter 10 (see pp. 362–365).

The Legacy of Sigmund Freud

The work of Sigmund Freud has had an enduring influence on psychologists' thinking about the process of sexual identity formation. As we noted in Chapter 15 (p. 581), Freudian psychologists view adolescence as a period during which children reexperience the conflicts of earlier stages in new guises (Blos, 1972). Central among the early developmental problems that must be reworked, according to Freud, is the child's primitive desire to possess the parent of the other sex, coupled with terror of the possible reprisal of the same-sex parent, who is viewed as a powerful competitor. The way young children resolve this conflict, which Freud called the *Oedipus conflict,* is to repress illicit desire by identifying with the same-sex parent. Freud maintained that this infantile resolution is essential to proper sex-role identification (see Chapter 10, p. 364). These early Oedipal feelings are encountered again in adolescence, but repression and identification with members of the same sex are no longer the adaptive responses that they were at the end of infancy. Puberty, Freud argued, reawakens sexual desire at a time when adolescents are fully capable both of carrying out the forbidden acts and of understanding the incest taboo that denies them the parent as a sexual partner.

Freud held that the combination of awakened desire and social constraint leads the adolescent to search for people outside the family to love. However, the shift in the object of affection from a parent to a peer requires parent–adolescent power struggles and eventual emotional disengagement from the family, which has been the bedrock of emotional security since birth. Recognizing the difficulty of this task, Freud (1905/1953a) referred to the adolescent's reorientation of affection as "one of the most painful psychical achievements of the pubertal period" (p. 227).

Modern Approaches to Sexual Identity Development

Central to Freud's theory was the notion that power relations among the developing child, parents, and society, are inherent in the formation of a sexual identity. Indeed, an emphasis on power and control is present in much of the modern work on sexual identity development. One stream of research has focused primarily on the sexual identity of girls, and how it develops in patriarchal societies such as our own. The second stream focuses on sexual minority youths, and the ways that their development is similar to, and departs from the development of their sexual majority peers.

The Sexual Identity of Girls In our society, girls develop a sexual identity in a cultural context of obvious gender differences. Despite changes indicating that the gender gap is narrowing economically, socially, and politically, women in our society continue to face limitations such as economic dependence, gender inequality, sexism, and expectations to behave in a nurturing way and to work hard at one's personal appearance (Azmitia, 2002). Developmentalists have explored how the "patriarchal belief system" is expressed in the sexual identity development of adolescent girls.

For example, Erica Van Roosmalen (2000) analyzed 875 letters written between 1996 and 1997 to the advice column of *Teen Magazine,* a national publication targeted to adolescent girls. Here are some typical letters:

- I'm just entering junior high school and all around me there are couples kissing, holding hands, and hugging. . . . It really hurts to see everyone with a boyfriend and then me just all alone. (signed) Heartbroken

- My boyfriend is really treating me badly lately, but I don't want to get mad at him because I don't want to lose him. What should I do? (signed) Hurt

- It seems like everyone I go out with wants to have sex with me. I've never done it before, and I'm scared of doing it wrong. I don't "give them some," as they say it. Now no one wants to go out with me unless I have sex with them. (signed) What should I do?

- I think this guy at church might be sexually harassing me. . . . He constantly hugs me and teasingly slaps my butt. It makes me really uncomfortable. When I told my friend about it, she told me to tell my mom or confront him. But what if he is trying to be friendly and I just misunderstood his actions? (signed) Confused

Van Roosmalen's analysis indicates that male dominance and gender-based stereotypes were core issues for girls seeking advice. The fear of being without a boyfriend was a major theme, as was managing boys' sexual advances without either being "dumped" or jeopardizing one's reputation. Popular culture and peer expectations dictate that girls should be "boy crazy" as well as sexual gatekeepers (that is, primarily responsible for fending off the sexual advances of boys). Van Roosmalen argues that charting a course between these two conflicting extremes is a major challenge for adolescent girls because it forces them to be "a tease."

The basic conflicts identified in the letters to *Teen Magazine* are played out in fascinating ways in other cultural contexts. Meenakshi Thapan (2001) has interviewed middle-class adolescent girls growing up in India. Contemporary Indian society is undergoing dramatic social and cultural change. Though India is traditionally patriarchal, with women's roles defined largely by family life and responsibilities, recent economic changes have led to a flood of Western influence through an influx of material goods, as well as the symbols, images, and ideas carried in Western movies and television.

One area of social life particularly affected is the perception of women and their role in family and society. In contemporary India, a more "liberal" and "Westernized" conception of women's roles has become popular, in radical opposition to traditional values. Thapan describes the new view of Indian womanhood as one that defines women as being "of substance," with a more visible role in the workplace. Not only are women taking up new, publicly influential positions as journalists and social activists, they are breaking into traditionally male jobs as police officers, bankers, and soldiers. How does all of this affect the sexual identity of adolescent girls? Thapan found that many spoke of the conflict between traditional and modern expectations. The girls expressed a desire to embrace new educational and professional opportunities, but expected and indeed wanted to put the obligations of family before their own personal dreams and aspirations.

Multicultural influences are pervasive in many parts of the world, creating a special challenge for adolescents who may feel the tug of both traditional and modern beliefs, values, and expectations of behavior.

©B.S.P.I./Corbis

sexual orientation The sex toward which one has erotic feelings.

The influence of Western culture was also apparent in the Indian girls' concerns about their appearance and weight—concerns that, until recently, have been associated with growing up in North America and Europe (see Chapter 15, p. 592). Here are some of the Indian girls' responses to a question regarding their feelings about their appearance:

- I am not happy with the way I look. My hair is too frizzy and I'm way too short.

- Chubby, breasts on the small size, sexy legs, smooth delicate collarbones, very woman. Over all if I was slimmer I'd be pretty nice figured. Hips good for childbearing and shoulders good for working and fighting.

- [I am] fat, ugly and stupid. (I'm a neurotic—just kidding!!). No sometimes I develop a FAT-O-PHOBIA (a word I have made up myself) although I'm underweight at the minute. I like my hair ('coz I bleached it). . . . That's about it!!! . . . Sometimes I exercise a lot also I'm not way overweight but I would like to be thinner. . . .

- In all the schools I've been to, boys seem to give the most importance to the way a girl looks, not just a pretty face but also what she wears. They also give importance to the feminty [sic] of a girl. Studies or a sense of humour doesn't seem too important. Its more the physical outlook.

Thapan argues that the diverse and conflicting set of expectations facing young women in contemporary India create a dilemma about how to define their identities in relation to family, society, and peers. In some ways, the issues they face are unique to their coming of age in a traditional, patriarchal society undergoing rapid social change. But in other ways, their challenges are global and familiar.

Sexual Minority Youth Most adolescents will achieve a sexual identity that is centered on a sexual preference for members of the other sex. However, a sizable number of people exhibit homosexual preferences—that is, a preference for members of their own sex as sexual partners. **Sexual orientation** refers to the sex toward which one has erotic feelings. Estimates vary, but in a representative sample of American adults, between 7 percent and 8 percent reported that they felt a same-sex desire for someone at least once (Laumann et al., 1995). Sexual orientation, however, is not sexual identity, which is influenced by the categories of sexuality present in the culture and the culture's attitudes toward individuals who fit into or claim membership in those categories. In the same national sample, far fewer individuals—between $1\frac{1}{2}$ and 3 percent—*identified* themselves as gay, lesbian, or bisexual.

Developmentalists have attempted to describe stages in the process of sexual identity development for sexual minority youth (Ferrer-Wreder et al., 2002; Troiden, 1993). Richard Troiden has offered a stage model of identity formation that fits the experience of many North American gay men in recent decades. As you read through the stage descriptions, notice how the questions of personal authenticity, self-continuity, and self-coherence that are typical of other identity domains, are complicated for minority youths:

Stage 1: Sensitization; feeling different In retrospective reports, men with a homosexual orientation often say that during middle childhood they had social experiences that made them feel different from other children. Typical comments are: "I couldn't stand sports, so naturally that made me different. A ball thrown at me was like a bomb" (Bell et al., 1981, p. 74).

Stage 2: Self-recognition; identity confusion When such boys enter puberty, they realize that they are attracted to members of the same sex and begin to label such feelings as homosexual. This recognition is the source of considerable inner turmoil and identity confusion:

> You are confused about what sort of person you are and where your life is going. You ask yourself the questions, "Who am I? Am I a homosexual? Am I really a heterosexual?" (Cass, p. 1984, p. 156)

By middle or late adolescence they begin to believe that they are probably homosexual because they are uninterested in the heterosexual activities of their peers. Many homosexual adults recall adolescence as a time when they were loners and social outcasts.

Stage 3: Identity assumption Some young people who have had homosexual experiences and who recognize that they prefer sexual relations with members of their own sex do not act on their preference. Many others, however, move from private acknowledgment of their homosexual preference to admitting it openly, at least to other homosexuals.

Young people who have achieved this level of homosexual identity deal with it in a variety of ways. Some try to avoid homosexual contacts and attempt to pass as heterosexual because they are afraid of being stigmatized. Others begin to align themselves with the homosexual community.

Stage 4: Commitment; identity integration This final level is reached by those who have come to terms with their homosexuality and are "out" in their communities. Identity integration is indicated by a fusion of one's sexuality and emotional commitments, by expressions of satisfaction with one's orientation, and by public disclosure of one's homosexual identity.

Because of homophobic attitudes in many segments of the U.S. population, the decision to "come out" is often agonizing and sometimes dangerous. However, some communities and schools are more sensitive to the social and developmental needs of homosexual adolescents, and will sponsor gay proms, like the one this couple is attending.

Troiden notes that commitment to a homosexual identity may vary from weak to strong, depending on such factors as the individual's success in forging satisfying personal relationships, being accepted by his family, and functioning well at work or in a career. Indeed, the social stigma and oppression facing sexual minority youth, and their fear of being rejected by parents, makes the public disclosure of their sexual identity, or *coming out*, a major challenge (Heights, 1999). Retrospective accounts of gay men indicate that "living a lie," "alienation and isolation," and "telling others" were significant issues in their adolescent experiences (Flowers & Buston, 2002). Table 16.6 illustrates the average age of first disclosure in a sample of 117 young adults who were approximately 20 years of age at the time of the study, and who self-identified as gay, lesbian, bisexual, or queer (Maguen et al., 2002). The data represented in Table 16.6 are noteworthy in several respects. First, the average age of disclosure is similar across the subgroups, despite group differences in the age at which individuals became aware

table 16.6

Milestones of Sexual Orientation								
	Gay		**Lesbian**		**Bisexual**		**Queer***	
Milestone	**Mean**	**n**	**Mean**	**n**	**Mean**	**n**	**Mean**	**n**
Became aware	9.6	53	10.9	34	13.2	25	13.3	3
Sexual contact	14.7	51	14.3	31	14.9	22	11.3	4
Same-sex contact	14.9	49	16.4	30	16.7	20	11.5	4
Disclosure	16.8	53	16.0	34	16.8	22	18.5	4

*Adolescents who identify themselves as "queer" tend to be more public about their identity, and more informed about gay and lesbian issues.

N = 116 (one participant did not report sexual identity).

Source: Maguen et al., 2002.

of same-sex attractions and/or acted on their attractions. This finding prompted the researchers to suggest that public disclosure of sexual orientation is a way of solidifying a public identity, but that it occurs only after the individual is able to "formulate a personal understanding of being different from others and how this difference relates to sexual orientation identity" (p. 229).

Another noteworthy finding concerns the distinct patterns of experience found for the different subgroups. For example, lesbians are more likely than gay men to report sexual contacts with both males and females; moreover, they are more likely than gay men to have had their first sexual contact with a person of the opposite sex. The distinctive pattern that characterizes lesbians is consistent with arguments that women's sexuality is generally more fluid compared with that of men (Ellis et al., 2002). It needs to be emphasized in this context that a sequence of changes in sexual identity like the one described by Troiden should not be considered universal. In some societies, and at other times in history, adolescent same-sex sexual behavior has not been viewed as an expression of a lifelong sexual identity. Rather, it has been variously interpreted as a necessary response to a culture's practice of sex segregation, as a way to learn about sex, as part of the ritual of becoming an adult, or as a playful acting out of the sex drive by young people who have excess sexual energy (Gonsiorek, 1996; Herdt, 2001; Savin-Williams, 2003).

In a critique of research on sexual minority youths, Ritch Savin-Williams (2001) pointed out that in most respects, youths with same-sex attractions are similar to all youths: "regardless of sexual orientation youths need the love and respect of their parents, must negotiate their on-going relationships as they move toward adulthood, are concerned with peer status, desire love and sex, and wonder about their future" (p. 6). Likewise, there is a good deal of diversity within sexual minority youths, just as there is with heterosexual youths. As an example, Savin-Williams points to gender diversity. In terms of their desires for romance and their use of sexual behaviors, adolescent girls with same-sex attractions are more similar to sexual majority girls than to boys with same-sex attractions (Savin-Williams & Diamond, 2001).

Most contemporary scholars believe that sexual orientation, sexual behavior, and sexual identity, like most human behaviors, are the result of a complex interaction of biology and environmental influences. In general, given the enormous diversity among sexual minority youths, it is reasonable to assume that the origin and development of sexual orientation and identity vary widely from one person to the next (Bohan, 1996; Ellis, 1996a). For some sexual minority youths, biology may play a major role; for others, learning, or the social milieu they find themselves in at a particular time in their lives, may be the key factor.

Identity Formation in Ethnic Minority and Immigrant Youths

The process of identity formation is particularly complicated among ethnic minority and immigrant children in the United States for several reasons (Phinney & Haas, 2003). First, in cases in which the values, beliefs, and customs of the minority group differ from those of the majority population, minority-group youth face the task of reconciling two different identities, one based on their own cultural heritage, the other on the cultural heritage of the majority group. In effect, they have at least twice as much psychological work to do. Second, these young people often face prejudice, discrimination, and accompanying barriers to economic opportunity, all of which further complicate their task. Moreover, multiracial births in the United States currently are increasing at a faster rate than monoracial births, raising the question of how multiracial children establish an ethnic identity (Spencer et al., 2000).

As you saw in Chapter 10 (p. 369), ethnic minority-group children entering middle childhood have acquired an awareness of their ethnic identity in the sense that they know the labels and attributes that apply to their own ethnic group and have developed basic attitudes concerning their ethnicity. During middle childhood and adolescence, children in ethnic minority groups undergo three additional stages of ethnic identity formation (Cross, 2003; Phinney & Haas, 2003). Although researchers apply different labels to these stages, they agree on the basic content of each stage and the general kinds of experiences associated with movement from one stage to the next. In this discussion, we have adopted the labels suggested by Jean Phinney because she explicitly links the stages to those used by Marcia, whose methods (described on pp. 638–639) have been widely generalized to the study of ethnic identity.

Unexamined Ethnic Identity

In this initial stage, children still accept and show a preference for the cultural values of the majority culture in which they find themselves. This acceptance may include a negative evaluation of their own group (see Chapter 10, p. 369). In some cases, this initial stage appears to correspond to Marcia's category of foreclosure, because the person refuses to consider the relevant issues and adopts the views of others unquestioningly. One Mexican American male told Phinney, "I don't go looking for my culture. I just go by what my parents say and do, and what they tell me to do, the way they are" (p. 68). In other cases, the failure to examine questions of ethnic identity is more similar to identify diffusion. An example is provided by a young African American female who responded, "Why do I need to learn about who was the first black woman to do this or that? I'm just not too interested" (p. 68).

Faced with a rising multiethnic population, schools and communities provide opportunities to celebrate the cultural heritage of young people. This girl is demonstrating Korean drumming at her school's "International Day."

Ethnic Identity Search

Movement beyond stage 1 is often initiated by a shocking experience in which the young person is rejected or humiliated because of his or her ethnic background. The specifics of such encounters are quite varied (Cross, 2003; Fordham & Ogbu, 1986). A minority student may be accused of cheating when he or she does outstanding work, simply because the teacher assumes that members of the student's ethnic group are incapable of such work; or a boy and girl who have been friends for years may be forbidden to socialize with each other romantically because they have different skin colors, ethnic backgrounds, or religious affiliations. However, a shocking encounter is not necessary for young people to begin pondering their ethnic identity; for some, a growing awareness that the values of the dominant group are not beneficial to ethnic minorities is sufficient to move them into stage 2.

In stage 2, young people show an intense concern for the personal implications of their ethnicity. They often engage in an active search for information about their own group. They are likely to become involved in social and political movements in which ethnicity is a core issue. They may also experience intense anger at the majority group and glorify their own heritage.

Signithia Fordham and John Ogbu (1986) describe several cases in which African American adolescents go through a process of **oppositional identity formation,** rejecting the patterns of dress, speech, mannerisms, and attitudes associated with European American society and adopting an identity that opposes them. These researchers believe that the process of oppositional identity formation provides one of the major explanations for the school failure of African American children. For many of these young people, who feel automatically shut out of the economic

oppositional identity formation The process of rejecting the patterns of dress, speech, mannerisms, and attitudes associated with one's society, and adopting an identity that opposes them.

Suicide among Native American Adolescents

Native American adolescents are at greater risk for killing themselves than any other group in the world (Kermayer, 1994). Michael Chandler and his colleagues are working to understand why (Chandler et al., 2003). Their efforts have led them to evaluate suicide risk in light of the complex relationship between identity development and cultural change.

Simply being an adolescent places an individual at increased risk for suicide and suicidal behaviors. From this sad fact follow several important questions: Why, at a time in life when the future holds such promise, would a young person take his or her own life? What is unique about the period of adolescence that allows the individual to look on death as a resolution to her or his situation? Chandler believes that at least part of an answer is to be found in normative identity issues that adolescents everywhere must resolve.

One such identity issue that all adolescents must face is the problem of self-continuity. *Self-continuity* is understanding oneself as the same person throughout time, despite obvious internal or external changes. For example, we would be very different persons, and perhaps not persons at all, if we thought we were brand-new individuals each time our bodies changed, our boyfriends changed, we had a new idea, or we woke up in a different bed. Without some way to understand that a self will continue in time regardless of change, it's difficult for adolescents to imagine themselves in the future, and to work toward or be invested in their own future selves.

Lorraine Ball and Michael Chandler speculate that suicide risk is particularly high for adolescents who have not solved the problem of self-continuity. They argue that a disruption in self-continuity results in an absence of connection with the future, making suicide seem a more reasonable course of action than it would be otherwise. They tested their

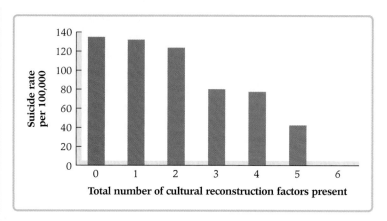

The effects of cultural reconstruction efforts are cumulative; as the number of reconstruction factors rise, so does adolescents' protection from suicide risk.

idea with a group of adolescents who had been admitted to a psychiatric hospital for various psychological disorders, including suicidal thoughts and behaviors. The adolescents were presented with and asked to interpret short stories such as Charles Dickens's *A Christmas Carol,* in which Scrooge was made to see his life course through several radical transitions. The subjects were also asked about their own sense of self-continuity despite dramatic change. Ball and Chandler analyzed the responses of several hundred adolescents who were either suicidal, nonsuicidal but psychologically troubled, or nonhospitalized controls. They determined that the suicidal adolescents were distinct from the other two groups in the extent to which they were unable to provide reasonable accounts of self-continuity.

How is this played out in the case of Native American adolescents? Interviews like those developed with the hospitalized adolescents were conducted with adolescents of western European and of Native American descent in

Children who grow up in tribes that preserve their cultural ceremonies and practices may be less vulnerable to suicide risk in adolescence.

opportunities of the majority culture, successful identity formation requires that they find school and the academic activities that go on there to be irrelevant to their lives. Evidence suggests that similar identity processes are at work in the development of adolescents of many minority groups (Phinney & Haas, 2003).

Ethnic Identity Achievement

Individuals who achieve a mature ethnic identity have resolved the conflicts characteristic of the prior stage and now accept their own ethnicity and have a positive self-concept. At this stage, the tension and defensiveness characteristic of an individual at stage 2 is replaced by a secure self-confidence in their ethnicity (Cross, 2003).

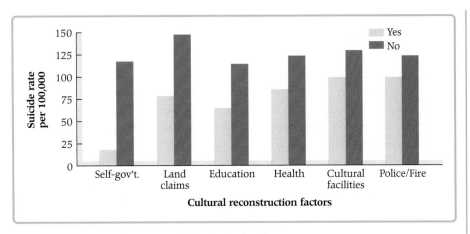

Native American tribes that engage in forms of cultural reconstruction and efforts to be self-determining have lower adolescent suicide rates compared with tribes whose cultural traditions have been eroded or lost.

the Canadian Pacific Northwest. In the course of this work, Chandler and his colleagues identified cultural differences in the ways that adolescents accounted for self-continuity (Chandler et al., 2000). In particular, most adolescents of western European descent gave *essentialist* accounts of self-continuity. That is, they believed that they were the same person throughout time because some *essential* feature of their identity remained unchanged—their fingerprints, or basic personality structure, for example: "I have always been competitive. When I was little I wanted to win races, now I want to get the best grades" (p. 35). The Native adolescents, in contrast, gave *narrative* accounts of self-continuity, arguing that they were the same person throughout time because they were able to tell a story that linked together their past, present, and future selves: "I used to be quiet and stuff . . . but I had a change . . . I just realized that . . . okay . . . I don't know how to explain it . . . I guess it would

be a shock to others. . . . It is not as much of a shock to me because I know my life . . . and if they want to know out of curiosity, they could ask me . . . and I could tell them" (Chandler et al., 2003, p. 41).

These two distinct ways of understanding self-continuity reflect the two different cultural traditions. Western European culture tends to emphasize individual characteristics of the self, whereas Native culture is based on a storytelling tradition. What is particularly interesting in light of adolescent mental health issues is that the two ways of understanding self-continuity may result in profoundly different levels of suicidal risk, especially under conditions of radical social change such as those affecting Native American communities.

Over the course of just a few generations, Native culture has been crushed. Tribal lands have been taken, hunting and fishing practices have been outlawed, families have been broken up and relocated to reservations, and Native languages and cultural practices have

disappeared. In a manner of speaking, Native stories have been silenced. For adolescents struggling to establish a narrative-based account of self-continuity, the consequences of having no cultural stories can be dire. In fact, given the current statistical trends, 1 out of every 20 Native adolescents will die by his or her own hand (Chandler et al., 2003).

But how can we be sure that the suicides are due to the devastation of Native culture and not some other factor, such as genetic vulnerability to depression, for example? As it happens, Native suicides are not equally distributed throughout all tribes. In many tribes suicides are quite rare, in fact much less common than the national average. In other tribes, in contrast, adolescents are killing themselves at prodigious rates.

What accounts for these astonishing differences? The answer lies in each tribe's efforts to reconstruct its culture and reclaim its heritage. Chandler and his colleagues identified six *cultural continuity factors* that are present in the tribes with lower suicide rates and absent from the tribes with higher suicide rates. As shown in the above figure, suicide rates are greatly reduced if the tribe is self-governing, fights legal battles to win back traditional lands, and exercises some control over its own public health services and schools.

It appears, moreover, that the effects of the cultural reconstruction factors are cumulative. That is, the presence of each additional factor further decreases suicide risk, as shown in the figure on p. 650.

Chandler's work demonstrates that tribal efforts to reclaim a cultural heritage can provide adolescents with a safety net while they work through the normative developmental task of establishing a sense of self-continuity. It also underscores the importance of understanding development in the context of culture and history.

Researchers have found that ethnic identity is positively related to several psychological variables, including self-esteem, personal identity, and school involvement. It may also be a protective factor against particular risks. An example comes from a study of 434 seventh-grade students living in a large Southwestern city who self-identified as American Indian. It was found that students who had a greater sense of ethnic pride also had stronger antidrug norms, compared with their peers whose ethnic pride was less intense (Kulis et al., 2002). (For a discussion of the challenges to ethnic identity formation, see the box "Suicide among Native American Adolescents.") Naturally, developmentalists have been interested in identifying the factors that may facilitate ethnic identity formation. In a recent study of immigrant Armenian, Vietnamese, and Mexican families, Jean Phinney and her colleagues found that identity formation is strongest when the native language is maintained and used in the home, and when adolescents spend significant amounts of time with peers who share their ethnic heritage (Phinney & Ong, 2002). Parents who deliberately maintain and instruct their children in cultural traditions seem also to foster positive ethnic identity formation.

Many families that emigrate to the United States settle in established communities that share their ethnic heritage. For example, established Latino communities have been present in certain areas, including the Southwest, for generations. Adolescents growing up in these communities may be more likely to develop a positive ethnic identity if their peers, families, and communities embrace Latino cultural traditions. Increasingly, however, Latinos are settling in new areas where there are no preexisting communities—for example, Maine, Indiana, Arkansas, and North Carolina (Hamann, 2002). The absence of a community creates new identity challenges within one's own emerging community, as well as within the settled community of long-time residents who have little understanding of Latinos.

In an ethnographic study, Karen Grady (2002) documents efforts to establish a sense of shared identity in a group of immigrant and migrant Latino students who had recently arrived in rural Indiana. Grady describes the students as being marginalized and isolated in the high school on the basis of English proficiency tests that placed most of them together in lower-track and ESL classes with limited bilingual resources and teaching personnel. Most of the "instruction" involved doing unchallenging worksheets. After a while, the students established their own routines for occupying the day. Specifically, they worked on *lowrider art,* a contemporary art form that combines a variety of ethnic themes (religious symbols, pre-Columbian motifs, symbols of the Mexican revolution) into a celebration of Latino heritage (see Figure 16.5). One girl, Xochitl, told Grady that she got her ideas for her art from *Lowrider* magazine: "I like to read that magazine because it talks about my culture and I feel so proud when I read that my people are doing good things and not going out in the streets and selling drugs or getting into trouble" (p. 176). The drawings were photocopied, carried around in binders, talked about and asked about by students and teachers. The art teacher incorporated the art form into her curricula in much the same way that she included Greco-Roman art and Impressionism, requiring students to learn the symbols and meanings of the images. Grady argued that through lowrider art, Latino students were able to make themselves visible to the dominant culture as proud members of an ethnic group with a remarkable history. Her work stands as an example of how adolescents use art and music in the process of identity formation (for another example, see the box "The Hip-Hop Generation: Keeping It Real and Disturbing the Peace," p. 654).

Fig. 16.5 Popular among U.S. adolescents of Hispanic descent, lowrider art often includes symbols of both American and Mexican culture.

Danny Villescas/The Castro Collection, www.castrocollection.com

Cross-Cultural Variations in Identity Formation

Many researchers have claimed that cross-cultural differences in identity formation can be profound (Markus & Kitayama, 1998; Miller, 1997; Shweder et al., 2002). In discussions of cultural variations in concepts of the self, it is common for cultures to be considered along a continuum describing the degree to which either individuals or social groups provide the anchor for concepts of the self and identity (Greenfield et al., 2003; Kagitçibasi, 2003). At one end are cultures whose members see themselves primarily as individuals, as most middle-class Americans do. At the other

table 16.7

Key Differences between an Independent and an Interdependent Construal of Self		
Feature Compared	**Independent**	**Interdependent**
Definition	Separate from social context	Connected with social context
Structure	Bounded, unitary, stable	Flexible, variable
Important features	Internal, private (abilities, thoughts, feelings)	External, public (statuses, roles, relationships)
Tasks	Be unique	Belong, fit in
	Express self	Occupy one's proper place
	Realize internal attributes	Engage in appropriate action
	Promote own goals	Promote others' goals
	Be direct; "say what's on your mind"	Be indirect; "read other's mind"
Role of others	Self-evaluation: others important for social comparison, reflected appraisal	Self-definition: relationships with others in specific contexts define the self
Basis of self-esteem*	Ability to express self, validate internal attributes	Ability to adjust, restrain self, maintain harmony with social context

*Esteeming the self may be primarily a Western phenomenon, and the concept of self-esteem should perhaps be replaced by that of self-satisfaction or by a term that reflects the realization that one is fulfilling the culturally mandated task.

Source: Markus & Kitayama, 1991.

end are cultures, such as Japan's, whose members see themselves primarily in relation to the larger social group. Members of the first kind of culture are said to perceive themselves as independent, while members of the second kind see themselves as interdependent (see Table 16.7).

According to Hazel Markus and Shinobu Kitayama, people whose cultures encourage an independent sense of self are oriented to being unique, to promoting their individual goals, and to expressing their own thoughts and opinions. People whose cultures emphasize an interdependent sense of self, or *collectivist cultures,* by contrast, seek to fit into the group, to promote the goals of others (that is, of the group), and to develop the ability to "read" the minds of others.

As Markus and Kitayama point out, this difference in orientation to the self creates different sets of problems for the young person who is forging a unified sense of identity. For one thing, the American emphasis on the autonomous self presupposes that identity formation is an individual, personal process. In societies in which the self is seen in relation to others, by contrast, others are included as an integral part of the self. Thus adolescents in collectivist societies do not have to make many of the decisions and choices that American adolescents must face in order to resolve their identity. It makes little sense to assert that healthy identity formation requires adolescents to make a "commitment to a sexual orientation, an ideological stance, and a vocational choice" (Marcia, 1980, p. 160) in societies in which marriages are arranged by the family, one's vocation is whatever one's father or mother does, and strict subordination to one's elders is a moral imperative (Grotevant, 1998). The most distinctive fact about identity formation in such societies is that it involves little of the cognitive deliberation and personal choice that play such large roles in accounts of identity formation in Western cultures. There are so few distinct adult roles in such societies that a young person has few decisions to make.

Elliot Turiel (2002) has argued against grouping cultures into two broad categories—those that foster an independent sense of self versus those that foster interdependence. He argues that cultures, and the people who live them, are much more diverse in

In Balinese society, tooth filing is a significant ceremony that marks the age of puberty. The ceremony involves a slight filing of the upper canine teeth, and is meant to symbolically eradicate the "wild" nature of the individual.

© Arnie Hodalic/Corbis

The Hip-Hop Generation: Keeping It Real and Disturbing the Peace

Regardless of your own race, ethnic background, and social status, it is highly likely that you know that *B-Boying* is break dancing, *MCing* is rapping, and that these activities, along with *DJing* and *graffiti,* are key features of hip hop. And it is just as likely that the adults in your life are only dimly, if at all aware of these terms. Hip hop, which emerged initially during the 1970s from urban, lower-income African American youth, has swept through North America to such an extent that many developmentalists believe it defines a large segment of contemporary youth culture, hence the label: the hip-hop generation.

Throughout history, the music, dance, books, styles of dress, and speech that define youth culture have been accused of poisoning the minds and bodies of otherwise innocent adolescents, and eroding the social and moral standards of the day. Those who speak against hip hop argue that it encourages and glamorizes violence, consumerism, and sexism. You don't need to look hard for examples.

Others point out, however, that from its infancy, hip hop has expressed the damage and injustice of growing up poor—especially black and poor. According to many researchers, hip hop, rap music in particular, is a form of social commentary on police brutality, drugs, sex, and poverty (Dyson, 1996; Richardson & Scott,

2002). When Niggas With Attitude (N.W.A.) released their 1988 album *Straight Outta Compton,* their lyrics of violence, death, drugs, and despair—the daily bread of many poor, urban youth—marked the birth of Gangsta rap (Richardson & Scott, 2002).

Hip-hop lyrics often focus on the current incarceration rates for African American males (Garland, 2003; Ruth & Reitz, 2003). Despite an overall reduction in crime, the imprisonment of Americans is at an all-time high, with approximately 2 million people in jail today—four times as many as 30 years ago. According to the Justice Department, 12 percent of African American men between the ages of 20 and 34 are behind bars (the highest rate ever), compared with 1.6 percent of white men. Most disturbing is the statistic that fully 28 percent of black men will be sent to prison in their lifetime (Bruner, 2003).

Beyond providing commentary on social conditions through its music, dance, and graffiti, hip hop includes film and video, as well as particular styles of dress and speech. It also communicates particular values, most notably being authentic, or "keeping it real." As you know from Chapter 1, art, language, and values are all aspects of *culture* as it is usually defined. Researchers of hip hop argue that it constitutes a genuine culture that impacts the formation of identity

among adolescents (Lloyd, 2002), particularly those of African and Latino descent (Richardson & Scott, 2002; Watts et al., 2002).

Murray Forman's (2002) ethnographic study of Somali immigrant adolescents provides a telling example of how minority youth push back the frontiers of their own identity through the medium of music. Since the early 1990s, Somali youth and their families have fled the political violence and oppression of their homeland, and have emigrated to the United States in unprecedented numbers. Uprooted from their traditional ways of life, and transplanted to an entirely foreign environment, many Somali adolescents face a clash of cultures. Forman notes that as they learn to negotiate their new surroundings—new schools, neighborhoods, language, and customs—immigrant Somali adolescents begin to drift away from core values of the family and their traditional Islamic religion. An important means of coping with the cultural transition is to seek out a sense of self and belonging in peer groups. "Somali teens often stake out deliberately rebellious positions, in which hip hop is strategically influential, though in doing so they are also signaling to their peers that they are 'cool,' unafraid of possible repercussions, and willing to test the system for

their practices, struggles, and ambitions than can be captured by a two–category system. Even in America, it is unlikely that the "rugged individualist" could ever have "won the West"—much less survived it—in the absence of collectivist practices such as barn raising. There is, in fact, little cross-cultural research on the development of identity except in industrialized societies or in those small segments of the population in nonindustrial societies that have entered the modern,

These new graduates of a vocational school in Japan are participating in a rite of passage that celebrates their transition from school to the job market.

AP Photo/Junji Kurokawa

Music and dance play important roles in adolescent identity development and peer culture. Originated by African American teenagers in the 1970s, break dancing swept the North American continent and crossed the ocean to Asia.

flaws or weaknesses." (Forman, 2002, p. 100). Hip hop is thus a means of connecting with peers and expressing authenticity.

Interestingly, it is only upon their arrival in North America that "being black" becomes an issue for Somali youth. Cultural codes of race are simply not relevant in countries like Somalia, where virtually the entire popula-

tion is black. Hip hop, Forman argues, provides an important vehicle for understanding the racial basis of the adolescents' new social status because the music generates an awareness of *blackness,* and the current state of black, urban-dwelling youth. Foreman writes that, "there is a sense of comfort—even a sense of security—in the

students' identification with hip hop" (Forman, 2002, p. 110).

Whereas Forman focused on why black youth may be drawn to hip hop, others have sought to use the music as a teaching tool. For example, Stephens and his colleagues (1998), have argued that hip hop can provide a culturally relevant and peer-endorsed medium for teaching teens about HIV/AIDS prevention (today, AIDS is the leading cause of death for African American men, ages 25 to 44, and the third-leading cause of death for African American women of the same age). Focusing on the social commentary inherent in much of hip-hop music and film, Roderick Watts and his colleagues (2002) used hip hop as part of a youth program intended to foster the development of "critical consciousness," that is, adolescents' understanding of the social forces and oppression that challenge African Americans.

Thus, hip hop seems to play several roles in the lives and development of black adolescents. Shared with peers, it provides a sense of belonging and social identification built upon the core value of authenticity—"keeping it real." It also provides raw commentary and insight on the prejudices, economic inequities, and political oppression of blacks in contemporary America. As the noted author James Baldwin (1992) pointed out, it is often the role of artists and musicians to give voice to injustice, and "disturb the peace."

industrialized sector (Marcia, 1999). Consequently we have to turn to the reports of anthropologists who have concerned themselves with identity formation in small hunter-gatherer or agricultural societies, such as those found in parts of West Africa, the Arctic regions, and New Guinea (Schlegel & Barry, 1991). The transition to adult identity in such societies is often made in ritual initiation ceremonies that are obligatory and painful.

The term **rites of passage** was coined in 1908 by Arnold van Gennep, an influential anthropologist who was attempting to explain the role of cultural rituals and ceremonies in marking changes in the life cycle of individuals. Van Gennep argued that all rites of passage share a particular structure composed of three parts: *separation* from old ways of being, *transition* to new practices and knowledge, and *incorporation* into the new role. For example, among the Kpelle in Liberia and in several other West African tribes, boys undergo a ceremonial "death" at puberty and are then spirited away by older men to an isolated grove deep in the forest. There the boys are taught the secret lore of the men, as well as the farming and other skills they will need to earn a living. When they emerge from "behind the fence," in some cases several years later, they have a new name and a new identity (Gay, 1984).

There are many examples of rites of passage in the United States, which together reflect the ethnic and religious diversity of the country. Adolescents experience confirmations and bar or bat mitzvahs to mark their passage into full membership

rites of passage Cultural ceremonies and events that mark a transition in status from child to adult.

in their respective religious groups. High school graduation in a rite of passage shared by most adolescents in the United States. Other rites of passage are specific to particular interest groups; and not all of them are considered to be in the best interests of those being initiated. Hazing, for example, is a means of initiating new students into university fraternities. Hazing has received a lot of recent public attention because it employs methods that can be humiliating and emotionally and even physically painful for the initiates. Cultures and subcultures nurture the process of identity development in a variety of ways. Formal rituals and rites of passage, as well as socialization practices and belief systems, help adolescents find answers to the age-old question "Who am I?"

Self and Society

Adolescents throughout the world are witnessing seismic shifts in the cultural, political, and economic structures of their neighborhoods, communities, and countries. In many places they are not silent witnesses, but actively attempting to take part in the process of change. They volunteer in community organizations; they participate in demonstrations and politically oriented youth groups; they take up arms as soldiers and as suicide bombers (Park, 2004). Yet political activism among youth is more the exception than the rule (van Hoorn et al., 2000; Youniss & Yates, 1999). Despite the dizzying whirl of major sociopolitical events during the past few decades, most adolescents show little interest in news and political affairs. Given that "adolescents are the last children of the old system and the first adults of the new" (van Hoorn et al., 2000, p. 4), it is important to understand the development of their sociopolitical knowledge and interests, and how they respond emotionally to the global changes going on around them.

The ways that adolescents experience and are affected by the sociopolitical forces in their lives are determined by all of the other domains of adolescent development, including adolescents' abilities to reason abstractly and hypothetically, their understanding of moral issues, and their answer to the question "Who am I?" We can also suppose that sociopolitical events have important consequences for how adolescents feel about themselves as persons, about their lives, and about their futures.

Adolescents' Subjective Well-Being

Developmentalists have recently attempted to learn about adolescents' sense of well-being in relation to the broader contexts of their social lives. **Subjective well-being** is a concept that encompasses self-esteem as well as satisfaction with one's life (Grob et al., 1999). Interestingly, it seems that most adolescents are satisfied and optimistic. In fact, cross-national studies conducted in eastern and western European countries and the United States find that a positive sense of subjective well-being is typical of adolescents.

Table 16.8 presents the results of a large, cross-national study that examined the relationship among subjective well-being, stress, and feelings of control. In light of the massive sociopolitical changes underway in the former socialist countries of eastern Europe, we might reasonably wonder whether adolescents' well-being is lower in some countries than in others. Although the differences are not large, the researchers found nevertheless that adolescents from eastern Europe reported lower levels of subjective well-being than their peers from western Europe and the United States. In summarizing their results, the researchers speculate that sociohistorical conditions, such as greater security and economic stability, affect the sense of well-being in adolescents; but other factors, including everyday stress and a sense of personal control, are also influential.

subjective well-being A concept that encompasses self-esteem and satisfaction with one's life.

table 16.8

Adolescents' Well-Being in Cross-National Context				
	Stress	**Personal Control**	**Emotion-Oriented Coping**	**Problem-Oriented Coping**
Bulgaria	−.39	.25	−.34	n/a
Czech Republic	−.30	.28	−.40	n/a
Hungary	−.47	.25	−.39	.22
Poland	−.45	.22	−.26	.38
Romania	−.48	.22	−.26	.38
Russia	−.37	.18	−.30	n/a
Eastern Countries	−.41	.21	−.31	.18
Finland	−.49	.16	−.44	.21
France	−.42	n/a	−.38	.18
Germany	−.46	.22	−.27	.24
Norway	−.47	.21	−.40	.19
German Switzerland	−.51	.13	−.24	.27
French Switzerland	−.50	n/a	−.38	.26
United States	−.47	.42	−.39	.28
Western Countries	−.46	.20	−.34	.25
Total Sample	−.44	.20	−.30	.20

p of all correlations < .05.

Source: Grobet et al., 1999.

The first column reports correlations between stress and subjective well-being. As you can see, all of the correlations are negative, meaning that subjective well-being decreases as stress increases (see Chapter 1, "Correlation and Causation," to review correlations). The second column shows the correlations between well-being and feelings of control. Here, all of the correlations are positive: adolescents feel better when they have a greater sense of personal control.

Thinking about Politics and the Political Process

Given that adolescents' well-being is affected by larger sociopolitical systems, and that many such systems throughout the world are undergoing radical transitions, it makes sense to ask about how adolescents reason about political systems and ideologies. According to many influential theories of adolescence, young people are often drawn to *ideologies,* systems of ideas on which particular political systems are formed (Adelson, 1991; Erikson, 1963; Inhelder & Piaget, 1958). Again, recall Anchee Min's adolescent devotion to communist ideology (p. 619).

In the United States, adolescents' enthusiasm for more perfect social and political systems was especially visible during the civil rights and commune movements of the 1960s, both of which drew heavily on support from adolescents (Berger, 1981). This same tendency to seek ideal systems of life is reflected currently in the attraction that various cults hold for their adolescent followers (Miller et al., 1999), in the appeal of the environmental movement, and in the eagerness with which some will go to the extreme of sacrificing their lives in order to make political statements.

Existing evidence shows that adolescents' thinking about political matters is, for the most part, immature. In one early study, Joseph Adelson and his colleagues asked middle-class young people, 11 to 18 years old, in the United States, Germany, and Great Britain to imagine how they thought a new society should be organized. The results revealed a major change in adolescents' reasoning about politics sometime around the age of 14 (Adelson, 1991; Adelson et al., 1969). This change occurred for members of both sexes and in all three countries, prompting Adelson to remark that "a twelve-year-old German youngster's ideas of politics are closer to those of a twelve-year-old American than to those of his fifteen-year-old brother" (Adelson, 1986, p. 206). For example, the 12- to 13-year-olds answered questions about society and its laws in terms of concrete people and events, whereas 15- to 16-year-olds answered in terms of abstract principles. Likewise, the 12- to 13-year-olds viewed crime, punishment, and retribution in severe, authoritarian terms. One 13-year-old boy who was asked how to teach people not to commit crimes in the future answered:

> Jail is usually the best thing, but there are others. . . . In the nineteenth century they used to torture people for doing things. Now I think the best place to teach people is in solitary confinement. (p. 213)

In addition to finding age differences in understanding crime and punishment, Adelson's study also demonstrated differences in understanding social and political regulation as a continually evolving process. In contrast to 12- and 13-year-olds, the older adolescents seem capable of reasoning about modifiable, flexible, well-balanced political systems. Adelson points out that this shift in reasoning about politics corresponds to changes that Inhelder and Piaget found in their studies of formal operational thinking.

Sociopolitical Identity Development

Whereas Adelson's study identified links between adolescents' reasoning about political issues and emerging cognitive developmental abilities, more recent work has focused on how identity processes affect the way that adolescents understand and respond to the sociopolitical events in their personal lives. An example is provided in an intensive study of adolescents living in Hungary and Poland, two eastern European countries that experienced radical shifts during the 1980s and 1990s from a totalitarian communist regime toward democracy and a free market economy.

The international team of researchers used Erikson's theory of identity development and Bronfenbrenner's ecological perspective (see Chapter 1, p. 17). As you are aware, both Bronfenbrenner's and Erikson's theories emphasize the importance of historical and social contexts to human development. As Erikson wrote, "[t]rue identity . . . depends on the support which the young individual receives from the collective sense of identity characterizing the social groups significant to him: his class, his nation, his culture" (1964, p. 93).

In in-depth interviews, the adolescents were asked to discuss their knowledge, values, concerns, experiences, and interests in the sociopolitical process in a variety of historical and social contexts. In general, and consistent with previous studies of adolescents' interest in political processes, the majority of the subjects interviewed believed that the recent changes in their countries had little significant impact on their personal lives. A few spoke of new freedoms and opportunities:

- Thank God there is democracy. Now not only one party can appear on the scene, but many parties can be formed. Luckily, the party that won the election wants something else, wants a free country and free people. The time that one person can do anything and another can do nothing is over. There is equality between people. Laws apply to everybody equally. (17-year-old girl)

- Finally we live in a constitutional state. A policeman cannot beat a person just because he likes doing it. (16-year-old boy)

- Today everything can appear in the press. You can criticize even the Minister. (19-year-old boy)

Most adolescents, however, were at best uninterested in, if not downright cynical about, the political process:

- I'm not much interested in politics. My parents and friends are also not interested. I would not get involved with politics at any level. I don't talk with my friends about politics. I don't know much about it. (16-year-old girl)

Similar to their North American peers, over the course of the adolescent years, the Polish and Hungarian youths became increasingly disengaged from sociopolitical

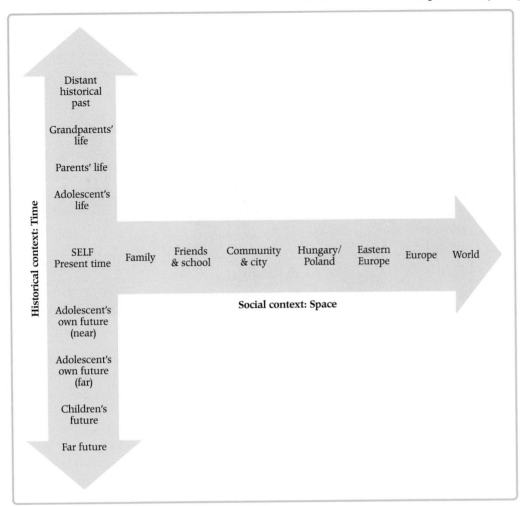

Fig. 16.6 Interviews with Hungarian and Polish adolescents indicate that their sociopolitical identities can be described in terms of two dimensions. The time dimension reflects how adolescents understand themselves to be rooted in the historical context of their family identity. The space dimension reflects their awareness that they are influenced by social contexts and national and international systems.

concerns. Ironically, at the same time that their interest waned, and again like their North American age-mates, their reasoning about political affairs became much more complex.

To capture some sense of the process through which adolescents develop a sociopolitical identity, the researchers discussed two contrasting identity patterns in the adolescents' responses (see Figure 16.6). All of the adolescents defined themselves in terms of their relationships with family. The authors reported that "these Hungarian and Polish adolescents' sense of self was deeply rooted in their positive feeling about their family identity. They explicitly discussed the significance of their family when describing their own sense of self" (van Hoorn et al., 2000, p. 259). Some adolescents, however, also viewed their personal development in terms of their membership and participation in community groups and their sense of connection to more global national and international systems. Interestingly, families played an important role in the process. Some parents attempted to shield their youth from the effects of the transitions by downplaying the negative consequences and making personal sacrifices in order to meet their children's needs. When their families diluted the significance of, or failed to openly discuss sociopolitical issues, adolescents were less likely to link their own experiences to broader social systems.

Fostering Sociopolitical Engagement

The foregoing discussion provides ample evidence for the role of significant others in facilitating the sociopolitical identity and engagement of adolescents. Concerned that too many adolescents reach adulthood uninterested in sociopolitical issues

These adolescent volunteers are participating in a community improvement program. Such activities allow young people to confront social problems through personal experience, in addition to learning about them through the popular press and textbooks.

©Jim West/ The Image Works

and/or unable to reason about them effectively, some developmentalists have urged that high schools offer classes—often called **service-learning classes**—that allow young people to confront social problems through personal experience, in addition to reading about them in textbooks (Leming, 2001). For example, Miranda Yates and James Youniss studied the effect that helping out at a soup kitchen for the homeless had on a large group of African American high school juniors (Youniss & Yates, 1999). On the basis of group discussion sessions and essays written by the students before and after their experiences, Youniss and Yates found that the direct experience of severe social problems not only stimulated the students to think more deeply about social problems but resulted in more complex reasoning over the course of time as they made increasingly clear connections between different policies and social problems.

In addition to affecting the sociopolitical identity development of adolescents, it seems that community engagement can also change communities. For example, one study explored whether adolescents living in low-income neighborhoods could participate effectively in community activities intended to reduce the advertising, availability, and use of tobacco, alcohol, and other drugs in their schools and neighborhoods (Winkleby et al., 2001). The adolescents attended weekly meetings after school throughout an academic year. The after-school course focused on teaching the participants how environmental factors contribute to substance abuse, strategies for creating change in their schools and neighborhoods, and skills for initiating advocacy projects. For part of the program, the adolescents chose a substance abuse issue and designed a plan to initiate change in their school or community.

The researchers found that participation in the course led to a four fold increase in the adolescents' participation in substance abuse prevention advocacy activities. These activities, in turn, resulted in a number of policy-level changes in schools and neighborhoods, including the following (Winkleby et al., 2001):

- Four state legislators pledged not to accept tobacco contributions.

- The underage tobacco purchasing rate was reduced from 10 percent to 0 percent in 50 stores, following a merchant education campaign.

- One hundred and one stores reduced the number of their alcohol and tobacco advertisements.

- Drug-free Zone signs were posted by the city in a neighborhood park.

service-learning classes Classes that allow young people to confront social problems through personal experience.

Erikson believed that the historical forces driving cultural and social change are vitally related to the identity of each new generation. "To remain vital," he wrote, "societies must have at their disposal the energies and loyalties that emerge from the adolescent process" (1987, p. 676). Many neighborhoods, many nations, are attempting to reinvent themselves in ways that grant their citizens freedom from a variety of oppressive forces, including drug abuse, crime, poverty, illiteracy, racism, sexism, and corruption. Erikson understood that successful historical change requires a new alignment of self and society. The research presented here indicates that adolescents are in many ways prepared to contribute to this process, if the adults in their lives are prepared to provide them with tools that foster their sociopolitical involvement and sense of efficacy.

emerging adulthood A developmental stage describing the unique developmental challenges facing individuals between the ages of 18 and 25 in technologically advanced societies.

Reconsidering Adolescence

Bodily changes that signal sexual maturity; wholly new ways of thinking, deciding, and processing information; a new sense of who one is, and who one can become; the increasing weight of responsibility for self and for others: all of these are markers of the bio-social-behavioral shift that defines adolescence (see p. 620). Evidence presented in this chapter, as well as in Chapter 15, indicates that the transition universally involves conflict, anxiety, and uncertainty. At the same time, however, the data indicate just as strongly that the adolescent experience—how individuals navigate the passage to adulthood, and how the transition is structured by families, communities, and institutions—depends to a large extent on the cultural context in which it occurs.

Perhaps the most significant way that culture impacts the adolescent experience is its influence on how the biological, behavioral, and social domains coincide with each other. Unlike previous stages in which the three domains developed more or less simultaneously, in adolescence they can be out of synch. This is particularly apparent in technologically advanced societies that encourage prolonged education and delayed marriage and childbearing. In such societies, adolescents often continue to rely on their parents for support, engage in an extended period of identity exploration, and feel unprepared for the roles and responsibilities typically associated with adulthood. Does this capture how you feel about yourself? If so, are you experiencing a prolonged adolescence or an entirely new stage of development?

If you resist describing yourself as an "adolescent," you are not alone. Based in part on how college students feel about themselves, some developmentalists have argued for the existence of a new stage of development. Called emerging adulthood, this stage is meant to characterize the unique developmental challenges facing individuals between the ages of 18 and 25 in technologically advanced societies (Arnett, 2002; Eccles et al., 2003; Nelson et al., 2004). Although the term is relatively new, the idea behind it—that changing social conditions have set the stage for the emergence of a distinctive period in the life cycle—was suggested decades ago (Keniston, 1963; Parsons, 1963).

Kenneth Keniston, for example, proposed that we adopt the term "youth" to describe individuals in their late teens and early twenties who are coming of age in rapidly changing societies (1963). He argued that societies in the clutch of fast-paced technological advances experience a high degree of social, political, and cultural change as they adapt to new technologies. Such societies tend to value innovation over tradition. The past grows increasingly distant from the present; the future grows remote and uncertain. As a consequence, the connections that once bound generations are weakened: the knowledge and values of the parent generation feel less relevant to their children's interests and concerns. According to Keniston, under such conditions youth turn to each other, rather than their elders, to sort out fundamental identity issues. They create their own "youth culture" separate and distinct from the culture of the prior generation. The cultural discontinuity between generations contributes to a number of attitudes and behaviors that Keniston observed in youth, including their sense of powerlessness to make a personal difference in their societies, and their lack of interest and involvement in politics.

Both Keniston and modern developmentalists claim that emerging adulthood is not a universal stage, but depends on the cultural context in which children develop. Much the same argument has been made about the stage of adolescence itself. Many of the questions that concern adolescents—Who am I? Who will I become? Who will be my mate? What is right and just?—may be less significant in cultures where identity, career, and social role possibilities are mapped out in advance according to long-standing cultural traditions, and where traditional beliefs and values are rarely open to question.

Whether the challenges and psychological changes of adolescents and youth are determined to be sufficiently unique to define specific stages in the life course, we can be sure that the transition to adulthood, however prolonged or abrupt, reflects a special relationship between developing individuals and the cultures they will transform and carry into the future.

S U M M A R Y

Research on Adolescent Thought

- The thinking of adolescents often manifests four characteristics not usually observed in the thinking of younger children:

    1. Reasoning hypothetically

    2. Thinking about thinking

    3. Planning ahead

    4. Thinking beyond conventional limits

- Piagetian theory attributes these characteristics to the emergence of formal operations, in which all possible logical aspects of a problem are thought about as a structured whole. The core of Piaget's evidence comes from observations of adolescents working on problems modeled on scientific experiments and formal logical reasoning.

- Not everyone proves capable of solving Piagetian formal operational tasks consistently, even in adulthood.

- Environmental conditions play a role in the development of formal operations; sociocognitive conflict in particular may encourage its emergence.

- Large cultural variations in formal operational thinking have been observed in traditional, nontechnological societies among children who have not experienced relatively high levels of education. However, ability to reason in terms of formal operations appears in specific culturally valued domains in all cultures.

- Difficulties with Piaget's explanations of adolescent thought processes have inspired attempts at alternative explanations.

    1. Information-processing theorists hypothesize that increased memory capacity and increased efficiency in the use of strategies and rules, rather than changes in the logic of thought, account for adolescents' new thought processes.

    2. Cultural-context theorists propose that involvement in new activities creates the conditions for a new level of systematic thought. Systematic thought is assumed to occur in all societies but is always bound to the demands of particular contexts.

    Developmentalists are particularly interested in the process of adolescent decision making. Generally, adolescents manifest less competent decision-making skills than do adults, which raises questions about whether they should be tried as adults in courts, or are competent to make informed decisions about medical treatments.

Adolescent Thinking about Moral Issues

- Adolescents' thinking about moral issues undergoes several changes:

    1. The ability to reason about all existing factors relevant to moral choices is supplemented by the ability to think about all possible factors.

    2. Reasoning about moral issues begins to go beyond social conventions to encompass more abstract principles of right and wrong.

- According to Kohlberg, during adolescence most children progress from stage 3 moral reasoning ("good-child morality") to stage 4 ("law-and-order stage") and only rarely move on to stage 5 (postconventional reasoning) in early adulthood. He has been criticized for underestimating children's ability to distinguish between social conventions and moral beliefs, and for utilizing a narrow conception of morality.

- Variability in the way males and females respond to some moral-reasoning problems has led to proposals that there are sex differences in moral orientations rather than a single sequence of moral development. The current consensus is that both sexes are equally capable of reasoning from different moral orientations.

- Members of small, face-to-face, traditional cultures generally do not engage in postconventional reasoning about moral issues but sometimes do attain the level associated with the Golden Rule.

- Adolescents in all cultures distinguish moral issues from social conventions and personal issues, but the border between these categories of social rules varies from one culture to the next.

- Though some developmental psychologists assume that increased intellectual capacity results in a higher level of moral and political behavior, the evidence linking reasoning ability with actual behavior shows that many other factors are involved.

- Authoritative, democratic parenting has been related to higher levels of moral maturity. The quantity and quality of peer relationships can also have a positive impact on moral development.

Integration of the Self

- Personality development during adolescence requires that new sexual capacities and new social relations be integrated with the personality characteristics accumulated since birth.

- Adolescents describe themselves in more varied, generalized, and abstract ways than they did during middle childhood, an indication of the need to reconcile their "multiple selves."

- In the United States, self-esteem declines at the onset of adolescence, especially among girls, reflecting the difficulties of adjusting to social and biological changes. It then rises throughout the remainder of adolescence.

- According to Erikson, adolescence is the time when individuals must initiate the process of identity formation, attempting to resolve their identity in both the personal and social spheres in order to form an adult identity.

- Marcia divided the process of identity formation into four categories arising from the possible combinations of crisis/exploration and commitment: identity achievement, foreclosure, moratorium, and identity diffusion.

- Families that encourage adolescents to express their own views enhance their children's identity formation.

- Supportive friendships enhance identity formation.

- There is little evidence for the existence of sex differences in the sequence of changes that lead to identity formation, although there are sex differences in the salience of different domains of experience within which identities are formed.

- A key issue in the process of forming a sexual identity is one's sexual orientation.

- According to the Freudian view, the adolescent's shift from indifference to attraction regarding opposite-sex peers begins when new sexual desires reawaken the Oedipus complex, requiring the individual to find an appropriate person to love.

- There is currently considerable uncertainty about the factors leading to homosexual identity formation. Both heredity and experience, including exposure to androgens during the prenatal period and to socializing experiences during childhood, have been implicated in homosexual identity formation.

- The formation of homosexual identity appears to go through four stages:
    1. Sensitization: a feeling of being different
    2. Self-recognition and identity confusion
    3. Identity assumption
    4. Commitment

- The formation of ethnic identity in adolescence appears to go through three stages:
    1. Unexamined ethnic identity
    2. Ethnic identity search
    3. Ethnic identity achievement

- There is ample evidence that the process of identity formation varies with sociocultural circumstances.

Self and Society

- Developmentalists study adolescents' subjective well-being to determine the impact of the broader contexts of their social lives.

- With respect to thinking about politics:
    1. Conceptions of the law become more abstract.
    2. An appreciation of the positive value of laws appears.
    3. Adolescents show increasing ability to consider both individual and social contributions to conditions such as poverty and homelessness.
    4. Adolescents desire ideal political systems, but at the same time they are increasingly cynical about the possibilities of solving social problems.

- Teens have been encouraged to become engaged in sociopolitical issues; service-learning classes have been found to be an effective means.

Key Terms

emerging adulthood p. 661
formal operations p. 622
hypothetical-deductive reasoning p. 625
I-self p. 637
logical necessity p. 624
me-self p. 637

morality of care p. 632
morality of justice p. 632
oppositional identity formation p. 649
rites of passage p. 655
saturated self p. 637
second-order operation p. 623

service-learning classes p. 660
sexual orientation p. 646
sociocognitive conflict p. 626
subjective well-being p. 656

Thought Questions

1. Monitor your activities for a day and make a list of all those in which you engaged in formal operational thinking to any extent. What characteristics seem to differentiate the contexts in which you use formal operational thinking from those in which you don't?

2. Draw comparisons among Troiden's stages of homosexual identity formation, Erikson's four preadolescent developmental crises, and Marcia's four patterns of identity development. What accounts for the similarities and differences among them?

3. Increasing numbers of young adults in the United States are remaining in their parents' homes long after they have finished college and found employment. On the basis of material covered in Chapters 15 and 16, what can you hypothesize about the psychological consequences of this trend?

4. What are some activities or events that connect you to your cultural traditions? Do you think that such activities may be more important for ethnic minority or immigrant adolescents than for others? Why?

5. Why do you think adolescents are largely uninterested in political issues? Do you think there are developmental advantages to being politically involved?

Epilogue

You have just finished what we hope was a stimulating journey through the story of human development from conception through adolescence. Although journeys are valuable in their own right, it is often rewarding to take a moment and think about what lessons they have taught us, and how this newly acquired knowledge connects to other lessons and other journeys. The ultimate goal is to form a coherent understanding of ourselves in relation to those close to us and the worlds we live in.

From our years of teaching, we have encountered many examples of the ways students form connections between the material presented in this book and the experiences they have had with their own family and friends in their own homes, schools, and neighborhoods. Do you have a better sense now of your parents' child-rearing practices? Maybe now that you know the relationship between the development of children's competence and firm, yet loving, parenting, you are less critical of the curfews and seemingly unreasonable demands your parents placed on you as an adolescent. And what about the kid in fifth grade that nobody got along with—the one who had turned into such a bully by seventh grade? Do you now have more insight into how his lack of social skills, or his egocentrism—that is, his immature ability to coordinate his own perspective with those of his peers—may have undermined his success in joining peer activities, thus contributing even further to his social isolation and aggression?

While it is our hope that you have made a number of connections between your past experiences and what you have read in this book, we also hope that you will take away from your reading a few general principles of development that will serve you as tools for thinking about developmental issues that you will encounter in the future.

Development Emerges from Multiple Sources

We have emphasized throughout this book that development takes place within dynamic, interacting systems. Our use of the notion of a bio-social-behavioral shift to describe apparent turning points in development emphasizes the error of assigning causal priority to one or another source of development. It is tempting, for example, to envision the appearance of social smiling as the result of a sequence of factors: first, biological changes in the infant's visual system reorder the potential for social interaction; then smiles become linked to social feedback; then changes occur in the emotional tone of child–caregiver relations. However, when Robert Emde and his colleagues examined the relation between changes in brain waves and the advent of social smiling, they could find no strict sequence. Each kind of change—biological, cognitive, and social—is necessary for the others to occur.

This view is particularly pertinent when considering the traditional form of the nature–nurture debate. As data presented in Chapters 2 and 13 indicate, when statistical procedures are used to tease apart genetic and environmental contributions to an individual trait such as personality or intelligence, roughly half the observed variations are attributed to genetic factors and half to the specific environments that individuals encounter after birth. Even these kinds of estimates are fraught with uncertainty because they assume those two sources of variation to be independent contributors to development, when in reality each contributes in subtle ways to the other.

Sequence Is Fundamental

At the core of the definition of development we offered in Chapter 1 (p. 2) is the idea that developmental changes follow one another in an orderly sequence: there must be one cell before there can be two; muscles and bones must be present before nerves can coordinate arm and leg movement; gonads must secrete testosterone before the genitalia characteristic of genetically male embryos can emerge. The same principle is equally apparent after birth. The primary emotions evident at or near birth must be present in order for the secondary emotions to arise with the acquisition of language. Children must be able to think operationally before they can develop the ability to think formally.

Owing to the sequential nature of development, the old proverb that an ounce of prevention is worth a pound of cure is especially relevant where children are concerned. When expectant mothers receive inadequate health care and give birth to premature and underweight babies, or when children begin their schooling without benefit of appropriate intellectual socialization at home, the long-term costs to society, as well as to the children, are vastly greater than the costs of preventing the problem in the first place.

Timing Is Important

Recall that fetuses who were exposed to thalidomide later than 3 months after conception were unlikely to be affected by the drug, whereas many of those exposed during the first 2 to 3 months of pregnancy experienced disastrous developmental effects. The timing of developmental change after birth is just as important. Children's ability to acquire language depends on their having linguistic input during the first few years of life. In modern societies, adolescents' self-esteem depends in part upon the timing of their experience of puberty relative to their peers' and the timing of their transition from elementary to middle to high school. Timing is also significant in a broader sense, in that the developmental impact of many life events—from a change in residence to the loss of a parent—is affected by when in the child's life those events occur.

Development Is Culturally Mediated

Children born into one culture may have a long, almost exclusive relationship with their mothers during the day but sleep in a crib by themselves at night, and therefore must wake their caregivers with their cries before they are fed. In another culture, children soon spend their days under the care of older siblings and other family members and their nights nestled in their mothers' arms, nursing at will while their mothers continue to sleep. Parents may place different kinds of controls on their children, and have different expectations for their behavior, according to whether they are living in safe or dangerous neighborhoods. In immigrant families, parents may work hard to ensure that their children remain connected to the language, beliefs, and practices of their native culture while helping them to succeed in the new culture. Every cultural pattern sets up a workable means of coordinating children's developmental needs with adult activities, beliefs, and values, but each culture does so in a fashion consistent with the particular demands and customs of the local group. The cultural diversity of our species promotes a rich array of developmental possibilities.

Throughout their development, children spend their time engaged in activities that have been scripted for them by adults who have well-fixed ideas about the roles, skills, knowledge, and values children should be expected to have mastered by the time they reach adulthood. The experiences arranged for young children growing up in technologically advanced "information societies" are vastly different from experiences arranged for children growing up in agrarian or nomadic societies. The considerable effort that human societies invest in teaching their children is apparent in how parents interact with and raise their children, and how social institutions such as schools, religious bodies, and youth organizations try to influence children's development.

The Science of Human Development Affects Children's Lives

In addition to organizing experiences to help children become masters of the skills, knowledge, and beliefs that are valued in a particular culture, many human societies are committed to understanding how processes of children's development and socialization can be supported most effectively. It is this desire to identify the conditions in which children develop well, as well as to understand how and why they do poorly, that inspires developmental science and its applications to education, therapy, and social policy. The people who assume professional responsibility for promoting children's development—the child-development practitioners who work in schools, hospitals, clinics, youth clubs, family services, and the like—use information from developmental science in a variety of ways. Psychologists who work with visually impaired children, for example, have scientifically derived methods at their disposal that enable them to test vision, intellectual development, language development, and so on. They can also draw on other developmental research for guidance in organizing the child's social life, literacy, and access to other valued cultural resources.

The realization that children's lives are greatly affected by the developmental niches that they inhabit and the larger social contexts that shape those niches puts developmental science to use at a broader level of social policy. For example, developmental research has shown that when adults are under stress, their ability to provide optimal conditions for their children's development suffers. This understanding gives added importance to programs based on contemporary research that are designed to provide parents with employment, safe housing, good health care, and supportive social networks. Similarly, when a politician advocates a simple plan for improving the reading scores of schoolchildren, we know that the children's performance is the result of a convergence of factors and is not likely to improve in response to any one-dimensional program.

Many of you will go on to become teachers, counselors, doctors, nurses, lawyers, policy makers, even developmental scientists. Many more of you will become parents. If your view of children's development is now a bit sharper and more informed, if you have a better sense of children's developmental needs and how children experience the world, and, especially, if what you have learned here inspires your own personal efforts to create contexts in which children can live well, then we consider our own work here well done.

Appendix: Guide to Discussions of Specific Aspects of Development

Guide 1	Discussions of Physical Development	
Period	**Characteristic**	**Page Numbers**
Early infancy	Hearing capacities at birth	pp. 121–122
	Early visual capacities	pp. 123–127
	Taste and smell	pp. 127–128
	Detection of touch, temperature, and position	p. 128
	Reflexes present at birth	pp. 128–132
	Maturation of sleeping patterns	pp. 139–143
	Maturation of the nervous system	pp. 146–151
	Growth and weight gain in first year	pp. 166–168
	Sex differences in rate of growth	p. 168
	Brain development in first year	pp. 168–169
	Development of reaching and grasping	pp. 169–170
	Development of locomotion	pp. 171–173
	Effect of practice on early motor development	pp. 173–174
Later infancy	Height and weight during second year	p. 206
	Changes in brain during second year	pp. 206–207
	Transition from crawling to walking	pp. 207–208
	Manual dexterity during second year	pp. 209–210
	Control during elimination	pp. 210–211
Early childhood	Biological prerequisites for language	pp. 303–307
	Physiological growth and behavior	p. 321
	Brain maturation	pp. 321–322
Middle childhood	Physical growth	pp. 451–452
	Motor development	pp. 452–454
	Brain maturation	pp. 454–456
Adolescence	Puberty	pp. 583–594

Guide 2   Discussions of Social Development

Period	Characteristic	Page Numbers
Early infancy	Infant's preference for facelike figures	pp. 126–127
	Coordination of infant's needs and caretaker's responses	pp. 143–145
	Role of mother's response in sensorimotor substages	pp. 153–155
	Emergence of social smiling	pp. 157–159
Later infancy	Help-seeking behavior in infants	pp. 195–199
	The origins of social play	p. 223
	Self-recognition	pp. 235–237
	Self-reference	p. 237
	Developing a sense of standards	pp. 237–238
	Effects of separation from parents	pp. 251–255
	Effects of isolation	pp. 255–256
	Recovery from deprivation and isolation	pp. 266–270
Early childhood	Environmental support of language	pp. 307–309
	Scripts	pp. 348–350
	Cultural and social influences on development	pp. 347–348, 352–353
	Mechanisms of identification	p. 362
	Acquiring a sex-role identity	pp. 362–369
	Acquiring an ethnic or racial identity	pp. 369–371
	Personal identity	pp. 371–373
	Morality of constraint	pp. 373–375
	Internalization of social standards	p. 375
	Self-regulation	pp. 376–384
	Aggression	pp. 385–393
	Prosocial behavior	pp. 393–398
	Family structure and dynamics	pp. 402–407
	Parenting styles	pp. 407–410
	Relations with siblings	pp. 410–412
	Family diversity	pp. 413–414
	Distressed families	pp. 415–422
	Child care	pp. 422–429
	Effects of media	pp. 429–440
Middle childhood	Education and apprenticeship	pp. 484–486
	Social organization of classroom instruction	pp. 493–500
	Rule-based games	pp. 533–537
	Behavior and morality	pp. 537–543
	Peer relations	pp. 544–560
	Relations with parents	pp. 560–564
	Self-concept	pp. 565–566
	Self-esteem	pp. 567–569
Adolescence	Consequences of early and late maturation	pp. 592–594
	Peer relations	pp. 594–602
	Sexual activity	pp. 602–609
	Relations with parents	pp. 609–612
	Work	pp. 612–615
	Thinking about morality	pp. 629–636
	Identity formation	pp. 636–656
	Gender variations in identity formation	pp. 642–648
	Minority-group status and identity formation	pp. 646–652
	Rites of passage	pp. 655–656
	Self and society	pp. 656–661

Guide 3   Discussions of Language Development

Period	Characteristic	Page Numbers
General	Questions about language acquisition	pp. 282–284
	Language subsystems	pp. 284–297
	Theories of language acquisition	pp. 297–302
	Biological prerequisites	pp. 303–307
	Environmental prerequisites	pp. 307–314
	Relation between language and thought	pp. 309–310
	Cultural and social influences	pp. 301–302, 311–312
Infancy	Language preferences at birth	pp. 121–123
	Intersubjectivity and social referencing	p. 198
	Beginnings of speech: cooing, babbling, jargoning	pp. 198–200
Early childhood	Prelinguistic communication	pp. 280–281
	Distinguishing phonemic differences	pp. 284–285
	First words	pp. 285–286
	Pointing	p. 286
	Earliest vocabulary	pp. 286–287
	Early word meanings	pp. 287–291
	Constructing sentences	pp. 291–295
	Learning the uses of language	pp. 295–297
	Associations between early language development and early cognitive development	p. 300
Middle childhood	Language of schooling	pp. 493–500

Guide 4   Discussions of Emotional Development

Period	Characteristic	Page Numbers
Early infancy	Evidence of emotions at birth	pp. 134–135
	Evidence of temperament differences at birth	pp. 136–139
	Crying and parents' responses	pp. 144–145
Later infancy	The onset of wariness	pp. 193–195
	Beginnings of attachment	pp. 195–198
	Explanations of attachment	pp. 223–225
	Patterns of attachment	pp. 226–235
	Emergence of secondary emotions	pp. 238–239
	Developing attachment	pp. 246–250
	Vulnerability and resilience	pp. 256–259
Early childhood	Regulation of emotions	pp. 382–384
	Empathy and understanding others	pp. 394–396
Middle childhood	Emotional control and social status	pp. 544–549
	Emotional maturity	p. 561
Adolescence	Traditional and modern conceptions of adolescents' emotions	pp. 579–583
	Psychological responses to puberty	pp. 588–592
	Emotional consequences of early and late maturation	pp. 592–594

Guide 5 Discussions of Cultural Influences on Development

Period	Characteristic	Page Numbers
General	Culture in language development	pp. 301, 312–314
	Family organization	pp. 404–412
Early infancy	Coordination of feeding and sleep schedules	pp. 139–144
	Nursing behaviors	pp. 153–156
	Motor skills	p. 174
Later infancy	Attachment	pp. 233–234, 263–265
	Effects of temperamental traits	pp. 259–260
	Language	pp. 301–302, 312–314
Early childhood	Scripts	pp. 348–350
	Role of language	pp. 350–352
	Unevenness of development	pp. 352–353
	Acquiring a sex-role identity	pp. 362–369
	Acquiring ethnic and racial identity	pp. 369–371
	Internalization of adult standards	p. 375
	Regulation of emotion	pp. 383–384
	Causes of aggression	pp. 388–389
	Family structure and roles	pp. 407–422
Middle childhood	Concrete operations	pp. 473–475
	Information processing and memory	pp. 475–476
	Schooling and intelligence	pp. 505–516
	Intelligence testing	pp. 506–509
	Learning	pp. 519–528
	Moral reasoning	pp. 541–542, 546–549
	Competition and cooperation among peers	pp. 550–553
	Physiological responses to puberty	pp. 589–592
Adolescence	Friendships	pp. 595–597
	Sexual activity	p. 597
	Parent-child relations	pp. 604–608
	Work and leisure	pp. 612–615
	Formal operations	pp. 621–629
	Formal operations and adolescent thinking	pp. 628–629
	Moral reasoning	pp. 632–636
	Identity formation	pp. 646–656
	Rites of passage	pp. 655–656
	Self and society	pp. 656–661

guide 6 Discussions of Cognitive Development

Period	Characteristic	Page Numbers
Early infancy	Learning	pp. 147–153
	Imitation in newborns	pp. 148–149
	Piagetian substages 1 and 2	pp. 151–152
	Piagetian substages 3 and 4	pp. 175–177
	Appearance/stages of object permanence	pp. 177–179
	Criticisms/challenges of Piaget's theory	pp. 179–183
	Cross modal perception	pp. 183–184
	Perception of number	p. 186
	Categorizing by perceptual features	pp. 187–191
	Memory	pp. 192–195
Later infancy	Piagetian substages 5 and 6	pp. 212–213
	Mastery of object permanence	pp. 214–215
	The beginnings of systematic problem solving	pp. 215–216
	The origins of symbolic play	pp. 216–217
	Deferred imitation	pp. 217–219
	Categorizing by conceptual features	pp. 219–220
	Understanding visual representations and models	pp. 220–221
	The influence of language on thought	pp. 221–222
	Studies of cognitive continuity between infancy and childhood	pp. 246–250
	Effects of extended separation and isolation	pp. 250–256
Early childhood	Maturation of the brain	pp. 321–322
	Preoperational thinking	pp. 322–324
	Egocentrism	pp. 324–325
	Confusing appearance and reality	pp. 325–327
	Precausal reasoning	pp. 327–329
	Uneven levels of performance	pp. 329–332
	Information processing and memory	pp. 332–337
	Domain-specific approaches and theory of mind	pp. 337–347
	Role of cultural context	pp. 347–353
	Empathy	pp. 395–396
Middle childhood	Concrete operations	pp. 456–460
	Information processing and memory	pp. 461–466
	Logical problem solving	pp. 465–466
	Cognitive development as the evolution of strategies	pp. 466–468
	Additional cognitive binding mechanisms	pp. 468–473
	Learning to read	pp. 488–490
	Learning mathematics	pp. 491–493
	Effects of schooling on cognition	pp. 500–505
	Aptitude for schooling (intelligence)	pp. 506–509
	Learning disabilities	pp. 516–518
	Motivation to learn	pp. 518–519
	Cultural and social influences on learning	pp. 519–528
	Ability to play rule-based games	pp. 533–537
	Reasoning about rules and morality	pp. 537–543
	Cognitive importance of peer interactions	pp. 549–550
Adolescence	Puberty brain development	pp. 584–585
	Formal operations and reasoning	pp. 621–629
	Cultural-context explanations for adolescent thought	pp. 628–629, 632–634
	Morality	pp. 629–636

academic motivation The ability to try hard and persist at school tasks in the face of difficulties.

accommodation In Piagetian terms, a modification of a previous schema so that it can be applied to both old and new experiences.

adaptation Piaget's term for the twofold process involving assimilation and accommodation.

adoption study A study in which genetically related individuals who are raised in different family environments or genetically unrelated individuals living in the same family are compared to determine the extent to which heredity or environment controls a given trait.

aggression The committing of an act intended to hurt another.

allele The specific form of a gene coded for a particular trait.

amnion A thin, tough, transparent membrane that holds the amniotic fluid.

anxious/avoidant attachment The attachment pattern in which infants are indifferent to where their mothers are sitting, may or may not cry when their mothers leave, are as likely to be comforted by strangers as by their mothers, and are indifferent when their mothers return to the room.

anxious/resistant attachment The attachment pattern in which infants stay close to their mothers and appear anxious even when their mothers are near. They become very upset when their mothers leave but are not comforted by their return. They simultaneously seek renewed contact with their mothers and resist their mothers' efforts to comfort them.

Apgar Scale A quick, simple test used to diagnose the physical state of newborn infants.

apprenticeship A form of activity combining instruction and productive labor that is intermediate between the implicit socialization of family and community life and the explicit instruction of formal education.

assimilation Piaget's term for the process by which various experiences are mentally taken in by the organism and incorporated into existing schemas.

attachment An enduring emotional bond between babies and specific people.

autism A mental condition defined primarily by an inability to relate normally to other people and low scores on intelligence tests.

autobiographical memory A personal narrative that helps children acquire an enduring sense of themselves.

axon The main protruding branch of a neuron that carries messages to other cells in the form of electrical impulses.

babbling A form of vocalizing by babies that includes consonant and vowel sounds like those in speech.

behavioral geneticist A researcher who studies how genetic and environmental factors combine to produce individual differences in behavior.

bio-social-behavioral shift A transition point in development during which a convergence of biological, social, and behavioral changes gives rise to cause distinctively new forms of behavior.

biological drives States of arousal, such as hunger or thirst, that urge the organism to obtain the basic prerequisites for its survival.

blastocyst The hollow sphere of cells that results from the differentiation of the morula into the trophoblast and the inner cell mass.

brain stem The base of the brain, which controls such elementary reactions as blinking and sucking, as well as such vital functions as breathing and sleeping.

Brazelton Neonatal Assessment Scale A scale used to assess the newborn's neurological condition.

canalization The process that makes some traits relatively invulnerable to environmental events.

categorizing The process of responding to different things as equivalent because of a similarity between them.

catharsis A general term for the release of fear, tension, or other intense negative emotions.

causation When the occurrence of one event depends upon the occurrence of a prior event.

cephalocaudal pattern The pattern of development that proceeds from the head down.

cerebral cortex The brain's outermost layer. The networks of neurons in the cerebral cortex integrate information from several sensory sources with memories of past experiences, processing them in a way that results in human forms of thought and action.

child development The sequence of physical, cognitive, psychological, and social changes that children undergo as they grow older.

child-care center An organized child-care facility supervised by licensed professionals.

chorion One of the membranes that develops out of the trophoblast. It forms the fetal component of the placenta.

chromosome A threadlike structure made up of genes. In humans, there are 46 chromosomes in every cell, except sperm and ova.

classical conditioning Learning in which previously existing behaviors come to be elicited by new stimuli.

cleavage The series of mitotic cell divisions that transform the zygote into the blastocyst.

clinical method A research method in which questions are tailored to the individual, with each question depending on the answer to the preceding one.

clique A group of several young people that remains small enough to enable its members to be in regular interaction with one another and to serve as the primary peer group.

codominance Outcome in which a trait that is determined by two alleles is different from the trait produced by either of the contributing alleles alone.

coevolution The combined process that emerges from the interaction of biological evolution and cultural evolution.

cognitive processes Psychological processes through which children acquire, store, and use knowledge about the world.

cohort A group of persons born about the same time who are therefore likely to share certain experiences.

cohort sequential design An experimental design in which the longitudinal method is replicated with several cohorts.

compensation A mental operation in which the child realizes that changes in one aspect of a problem are compared with and compensated for by changes in another aspect.

conceptual knowledge The ability to understand the principles that underpin a problem.

concrete operations Coordinated mental actions that fit into a logical system in a way that creates greater unity of thinking.

conditional response (CR) In classical conditioning, a response to the conditional stimulus (CS).

conditional stimulus (CS) In classical conditioning, a stimulus that elicits a behavior that is dependent on the way it is paired with the unconditional stimulus (UCS).

conservation Piaget's term for the understanding that some properties of an object or substance remain the same even when its appearance is altered in some superficial way.

constraining interactions Those that limit and restrict communication through detachment, lack of curiosity, and other forms of discouragement.

control group The group in an experiment that is treated as much as possible like the experimental group except that it does not participate in the experimental manipulation.

conversational acts Actions that achieve goals through language.

cooperative principle The conversational principle to make your contributions to conversation at the required time and for the accepted purpose of the talk exchange.

coregulation A form of indirect social control in which parents and children cooperate to reinforce the children's understandings of right and wrong, what is safe and unsafe, when they are not under direct adult control.

correlation The condition that exists between two factors when changes in one factor are associated with changes in the other.

critical period A period during which specific biological or environmental events are required for normal development to occur.

cross-fostering A system of child exchange within families; it is a traditional practice in many African societies.

cross-sectional design A research design in which children of various ages are studied at the same time.

crossing over The process in which genetic material is exchanged between chromosomes containing genes for the same characteristic.

crowd A large, reputation-based and mixed-gender social network observed when cliques interact.

cultural style A dominant way of thinking about and relating to the world that arises from a people's common historical experience.

culture A people's design for living as encoded in their language and seen in the physical artifacts, beliefs, values, customs, and activities that have been passed down from one generation to the next.

decoding The process of establishing letter–sound correspondences when reading.

deep structure In Chomskian terms, the basic set of rules of a language from which the actual sentences that people produce are derived.

deferred imitation The ability to imitate an action observed in the past.

dendrite The protruding part of a neuron that receives messages from the axons of other cells.

deoxyribonucleic acid (DNA) A long double-stranded molecule that makes up chromosomes.

detachment The state of indifference to others that children manifest when there is a continuing separation from their caregivers.

developmental niche The physical and social context in which a child lives, including the child-rearing and educational practices of the society and the psychological characteristics of the parents.

developmental stage A qualitatively distinctive, coherent pattern of behavior that emerges during the course of development.

deviancy training Positive reactions to discussions of rule breaking.

differential reinforcement The process by which girls and boys are differently rewarded for engaging in gender appropriate behavior.

discrete traits Traits involving a single gene that operate as "either-or" traits because a person either has one or does not.

dishabituation The term used to describe the situation in which an infant's interest is renewed after a change in the stimulus.

dizygotic twins Twins that come from two zygotes.

dominant allele The allele that is expressed when an individual possesses two different alleles for the same trait.

dual representation The mental representation of both a symbol and its relationship to the thing it depicts.

dyadic friendships Close relationships between two individuals.

ecological validity The extent to which behavior studied in one environment (such as a psychological test) is characteristic of behavior exhibited by the same person in a range of other environments.

ecology The range of situations in which people are actors, the roles they play, the predicaments they encounter, and the consequences of those encounters.

ectoderm Cells of the inner cell mass that develop into the outer surface of the skin, the nails, part of the teeth, the lens of the eye, the inner ear, and the central nervous system.

education A form of socialization in which adults engage in deliberate teaching of the young to ensure that they acquire specialized knowledge and skills.

EEG coherence The synchronization of electrical activity in different areas of the brain.

effortful control The inhibition of an action that is already underway.

ego In Freudian theory, this is the mental structure that develops out of the id as the infant is forced by reality to cope with the social world. The ego's primary task is self-preservation, which it accomplishes through voluntary movement, perception, logical thought, adaptation, and problem solving.

egocentrism In Piaget's terms, to "center on oneself," to consider the world entirely in terms of one's own point of view.

elaboration A memory strategy in which children identify or make up connections between two or more things they have to remember.

embryonic period The period that extends from the time the organism becomes attached to the uterus until the end of the eighth week of pregnancy, when all the major organs have taken primitive shape.

emerging adulthood A developmental stage describing the unique developmental challenges facing individuals between the ages of 18 and 25 in technologically advanced societies.

emotion A feeling state produced by the distinctive physiological responses and cognitive evaluations that motivate action.

emotional tone The degree to which a person experiences a sense of well-being versus depression and anxiety.

enabling interactions Those that facilitate and enhance communication through explaining, empathizing, expressing curiosity, and encouraging mutual problem solving.

endoderm Cells of the inner cell mass that develop into the digestive system and the lungs.

endogenous The term applied to causes of development that arise as a consequence of the organism's biological heritage.

environment The totality of conditions and circumstances that surround the organism.

environmental hypothesis of intelligence The hypothesis that intelligence is both specific and heavily dependent on experience.

epigenesis The process by which a new form emerges through the interactions of the preceding form and its current environment.

equilibration The Piagetian term for the back-and-forth process of the child's seeking a fit between existing schemas and new environmental experiences.

ethnography The study of the cultural organization of behavior.

ethology An interdisciplinary science that studies the biological and evolutionary foundations of behavior.

eugenics A policy of attempting to rid the gene pool of genes considered undesirable by preventing individuals who have the genes from reproducing, thereby ensuring that these genes are not passed on to the next generation.

exogenous The term applied to causes of development that come from the environment, particularly from the adults who shape children's behavior and beliefs.

experience–dependent Development of neural connections that is initiated in response to experience.

experience–expectant Development of neural connections under genetic controls that occurs in any normal environment.

experiment In psychology, research in which a change is introduced in a person's experience and the effect of that change is measured.

experimental group The persons in an experiment whose experience is changed as part of the experiment.

explicit memory The ability to recall absent objects and events without any clear reminder.

explicit modeling The kind of modeling in which adults behave in ways they desire the child to imitate.

extended family A family in which not only parents and their children but other kin—grandparents, cousins, nephews, or more distant family relations—share a household.

exuberant synaptogenesis The rapid growth in synaptic density that occurs between 3 and 12 months of age.

family A group of people traditionally defined by *shared ancestry* (blood relations), *shared residence,* and/or *marital ties.*

family care Child care provided in someone else's home, that of either a relative or a stranger.

family dynamics Refers to how families function, specifically, patterns of interaction and communication among members.

family structures Refers to how the family unit is socially organized.

family study A study that compares members of the same family to determine how similar they are on a given trait.

fast mapping The way in which children quickly form an idea of the meaning of an unfamiliar word they hear in a familiar and highly structured social interaction.

fetal alcohol syndrome A syndrome found in babies whose mothers were heavy consumers of alcohol while pregnant. Symptoms include an abnormally small head and underdeveloped brain, eye abnormalities, congenital heart disease, joint anomalies, and malformations of the face.

fetal growth retardation The term for newborns who are especially small for their gestational age.

fetal period This period begins the ninth week after conception, with the first signs of the hardening of the bones, and continues until birth.

formal operations In Piaget's terms, a kind of mental operation in which all possible combinations are considered in solving a problem. Consequently, each partial link is grouped in relation to the whole; in other words, reasoning moves continually as a function of a structured whole.

format Recurrent socially patterned activities in which adult and child do things together.

gender schema A mental model containing information about males and females that is used to process gender-relevant information.

gender segregation The term for the preference of girls to play with other girls, and boys to play with other boys.

gene pool The total variety of genetic information possessed by a sexually reproducing population.

genes The segments on a DNA molecule that act as hereditary blueprints for the organism's development.

genotype The genetic endowment of an individual.

germ cells The sperm and ova, which are specialized for sexual reproduction and have half the number of chromosomes normal for a species.

germinal period The period that begins at conception and lasts until the developing organism becomes attached to the wall of the uterus about 8 to 10 days later.

gestational age The time that has passed between conception and birth. The normal gestational age is between 37 and 43 weeks.

gonads The primary sex organs—ovaries in females and testes in males.

grammar The rules of a given language for the sequencing of words in a sentence and the ordering of parts of words.

grammatical morphemes Words and parts of words that create meaning by showing the relations between other elements within the sentence.

habituation The process in which attention to novelty decreases with repeated exposure.

heritability A measure of the degree to which a variation in a particular trait among individuals in a specific population is related to genetic differences among those individuals.

heterochrony Variability in the rates of development of different parts of the organism.

heterogeneity Variability in the levels of development of different parts of the organism at a given time.

heterozygous Having inherited two genes of different allelic forms for a trait.

holophrase A term for babies' simple-word utterances that some believe stand for entire phrases or sentences.

home care Child care provided in the child's own home, primarily by the father or a grandmother, while the mother is at work.

homophily The degree to which friends are similar to each other.

homozygous Having inherited two genes of the same allelic form for a trait.

hostile aggression Aggression that is aimed at hurting another person as a way of establishing dominance, which may gain the aggressor advantages in the long run.

hypothetical–deductive reasoning The ability to formulate and evaluate the logical implications of a set of premises, even if it is imaginary or contradicts the real world.

I-self (subject-self) The part of the system that reflects on, guides, and directs the self.

id In Freudian theory, the mental structure present at birth that is the main source of psychological energy. It is unconscious and pleasure-seeking and demands that bodily drives be satisfied.

identification A psychological process in which children try to look, act, feel, and be like significant people in their social environment.

identity A mental operation in which the child realizes that a change limited to outward appearance does not change the substances involved.

implantation The process by which the blastocyst becomes attached to the uterus.

implicit memory The ability to recognize objects and events that have been previously experienced.

induction A means of promoting children's prosocial behavior in which adults give explanations of what needs to be done and why children should behave in a prosocial manner.

information-processing approach A strategy for explaining cognitive development based on an analogy with the workings of a digital computer.

initiation-reply-feedback sequence An instructional discourse pattern in which the teacher initiates an exchange, usually by asking a question; a student replies; and then the teacher provides feedback.

innatist hypothesis of intelligence The hypothesis that some people are born generally smarter than others and no amount of training or variation in the environment can alter this fact.

inner cell mass The collection of cells inside the blastocyst that eventually becomes the embryo.

instructional discourse A distinctive way of talking and thinking that is typical in school but rarely encountered in everyday interactions in the community or home.

instrumental aggression Aggression that is directed at obtaining something.

intelligence quotient (IQ) The ratio of mental age to chronological age, calculated as IQ = (MA/CA)100. Calculation of IQ in this fashion ensures that when children are performing precisely as expected for their age, the resulting score will be 100; thus 100 is an "average IQ" by definition.

intentionality The ability to engage in behaviors directed toward achieving a goal.

intermodal perception The understanding that a certain object or event can be simultaneously perceived by more than one sensory system.

internal working model A mental model that children construct as a result of their experiences with their caregivers and that they use to guide their interactions with their caregivers and others.

internalization The process by which external, culturally organized experience becomes transformed into internal psychological processes that, in turn, organize how people behave.

jargoning Babbling with the stress and intonation of actual utterances in the language that the baby will eventually speak.

kinship studies The use of naturally occurring conditions provided by kinship relations to estimate genetic and environmental contributions to a phenotypic trait.

language acquisition device (LAD) Chomsky's term for an innate language-processing capacity that is programmed to recognize the universal rules that underlie any particular language that a child might hear.

language acquisition support system (LASS) Bruner's term for the parental behaviors and formatted events within which children acquire language. It is the environmental complement to the innate, biologically constituted LAD.

learning A relatively permanent change in behavior brought about by experience of events in the environment; or the process by which an organism's behavior is modified as a result of experience.

locomotion The ability to move around on one's own.

logical necessity When the conclusions of reasoning are set entirely by the rules of logic; example: if the cow jumped over the moon, then we *must conclude* (it is logically necessary) that the moon was under the cow.

long-term memory Memory that is retained over a long period of time.

longitudinal design A research design in which data are gathered about the same group of children as they grow older over an extended period of time.

low birth weight The term used to describe babies weighing 2500 grams or less at birth whether or not they are premature.

maturation A sequence of changes that are strongly influenced by genetic inheritance and that occur as individuals grow older.

me-self (object-self) Includes all of the things that people know about themselves.

meiosis The process that produces sperm and ova, each of which contains only half of the parent cell's original complement of 46 chromosomes.

meme A basic unit of cultural inheritance. Like genes, memes evolve and are transmitted over time, but they are passed down through social, rather than biological, processes.

memory organization A memory strategy in which children mentally group the materials to be remembered in meaningful clusters of closely associated items.

memory span The number of randomly presented items of information that can be repeated immediately after they are presented.

menarche The first menstrual period.

mental age (MA) The measure of intelligence proposed by Binet and Simon to describe the test performance of an average child of a given age.

mental modules Innate mental faculties that receive inputs from particular classes of objects and produce corresponding information about the world.

mental operations In Piaget's theory, the mental process of combining, separating, or transforming information in a logical manner.

mesoderm The cells of the inner cell mass that give rise to the muscles, the bones, the circulatory system, and the inner layers of the skin.

metacognition The ability to think about one's own thought processes.

metamemory The ability to think about one's memory processes.

microgenetic design A research method in which children's development is studied intensively over a relatively short period of time.

mitosis The process of cell duplication and division that generates all the individual's cells except sperm and ova.

modeling The process by which children observe and imitate individuals of the same sex as themselves.

monozygotic twins Twins that come from one zygote and therefore have identical genotypes.

morality of care A morality that stresses relationships, compassion, and social obligations.

morality of justice A morality that emphasizes issues of rightness, fairness and equality

morpheme The smallest unit of meaning in the words of a language.

morula The cluster of cells inside the zona pellucida.

motherese Speech directed to young children that is characterized by a special high-pitched voice, an emphasis on the boundaries between idea-bearing clauses and a simplified vocabulary.

mutation An error in the process of gene replication that results in a change in the molecular structure of the DNA.

myelin A sheath of fatty cells that insulates axons and speeds transmission of nerve impulses from one neuron to the next.

naturalistic observation Observation of the actual behavior of people in the course of their everyday lives.

nature The inherited biological predispositions of the individual.

neuron A nerve cell.

neurotransmitter A chemical secreted by a cell sending a message that carries the impulse across the synaptic gap to the receiving cell.

nuclear family A family consisting of a husband, a wife, and their children.

nurture The influences of the social and cultural environment on the individual.

object permanence The understanding that objects have substance, maintain their identities when they change location, and ordinarily continue to exist when out of sight.

objective view of responsibility An understanding that responsibility depends on objective consequences alone.

objectivity The requirement that scientific knowledge not be distorted by the investigator's preconceptions.

Oedipus complex In Freudian theory, the fear, guilt, and conflict evoked by a little boy's desire to get rid of his father and take the father's place in his mother's affections.

ontogeny The development of an individual organism during its lifetime.

operant conditioning Learning in which changes in behavior are shaped by the consequences of that behavior, thereby giving rise to new and more complete behaviors.

oppositional identity formation The process of rejecting the patterns of dress, speech, mannerisms, and attitudes associated with one's society, and adopting an identity that opposes them.

overextension A term for the error of applying verbal labels too broadly.

peers Others of one's own age and status.

perseveration Young infants' tendency to repeat a movement rather than shift movements to fit events.

personality The unique pattern of temperament, emotions, interests, and intellectual abilities that a child develops as the child's innate propensities and capacities are shaped by his or her social interactions with kin and community.

personality formation The process through which children develop their own unique patterns of feeling, thinking, and behaving in a wide variety of circumstances.

phallic stage In Freudian theory, the period around the fourth year when children begin to regard their own genitals as a major source of pleasure.

phenotype The organism's observable characteristics that result from the interaction of the genotype with the environment.

phonemes The smallest sound categories in human speech that distinguish meanings. Phonemes vary from language to language.

phonemic awareness The ability to "hear phonemes" (for example, to recognize that "balloon" begins with a *b*).

phylogeny The evolutionary history of a species.

placenta An organ made up of tissue from both the mother and the fetus that serves as a barrier and filter between their bloodstreams.

plan Cognitive representations of the actions needed to achieve a specific goal.

plasticity The degree to which, and the conditions under which, development is open to change and intervention.

polygenic trait A genetic trait that is determined by the interaction of several genes.

pragmatic uses of language The ability to select words and word orderings that are appropriate to their actions in particular contexts.

precausal thinking Piaget's description of the reasoning of young children that does not follow the procedures of either deductive or inductive reasoning.

preoperational stage According to Piaget, the stage of thinking between infancy and middle childhood in which children are unable to decenter their thinking or to think through the consequences of an action.

preterm The term for babies born before the thirty-seventh week of pregnancy.

prevention science An area of research that examines the biological and social processes that lead to maladjustment as well as those that are associated with healthy development.

primacy The idea that early experiences can significantly shape later development.

primary circular reaction The term Piaget used to describe the infant's tendency to repeat pleasurable bodily actions for their own sake.

primary intersubjectivity The emotional sharing that occurs between very young infants and their caregivers. It is restricted to face-to-face communication.

primary motor area The area of the brain responsible for nonreflexive, or voluntary, movement.

primary sensory areas The areas of the cerebral cortex responsible for the initial analysis of sensory information.

primary sex organs The organs directly involved in reproduction.

privileged domains Cognitive domains that call upon specialized kinds of information, require specifically designated forms of reasoning, and appear to be of evolutionary importance to the human species.

procedural knowledge The ability to carry out a sequence of actions to solve a problem.

prosocial behavior Behavior such as sharing, helping, caregiving, and showing compassion.

prosocial moral reasoning The thinking that is involved in deciding whether to share with, help, or take care of other people when doing so may prove costly to oneself.

prospective study A forward-looking research method in which children are studied as they grow older.

protective factors Environmental and personal factors that are the source of children's resilience in the face of hardship.

proximodistal pattern The pattern of development that proceeds from the middle of the organism out to the periphery.

puberty The series of biological developments that transforms individuals from a state of physical immaturity into one in which they are biologically mature and capable of sexual reproduction.

racial socialization The race-related messages communicated to children by their parents.

range of reaction All the possible phenotypes for a single genotype that are compatible with the continued life of the organism.

recessive allele The allele that is not expressed when an individual possesses two different alleles for the same trait.

reciprocal teaching A method of teaching reading in which teachers and children take turns reading text in a manner that integrates decoding and comprehension skills.

recursion The embedding of sentences within each other.

reflex A specific, well-integrated, automatic (involuntary) response to a specific type of stimulation.

rehearsal The process of repeating to oneself the material that one is trying to memorize.

reinforcement A consequence, such as a reward, that increases the likelihood that a behavior will be repeated.

relational aggression Actions that threaten the relationships and social standing of peers.

reliability The scientific requirement that when the same behavior is measured on two or more occasions by the same or different observers, the measurements be consistent with each other.

replicability The scientific requirement that other researchers can use the same procedures as an initial investigator did and obtain the same results.

representation The ability to picture the world mentally and think about an object or event in its absence

research design The overall plan describing how a study is put together; it is developed before conducting research.

resilience The ability to recover quickly from the adverse effects of early experience or persevere in the face of stress with no apparent special negative psychological consequences.

retrospective study A follow-back research method that starts with developmental outcomes in later childhood and looks back at the individual's early life for predictive signs of those later outcomes.

reversibility A mental operation in which the child realizes that one operation can be negated, or reversed, by the effects of another.

risk factors Personal characteristics or environmental circumstances that increase the probability of negative outcomes for children. Risk is a statistic that applies to groups, not individuals.

rites of passage Cultural ceremonies and events that mark a transition in status from child to adult.

saturated self A self full to the brim with multiple "me's" that have emerged as a consequence of needing to conform to social roles and relationships that demand different, and sometimes contradictory, selves.

schema In Piagetian terms, a mental structure that provides an organism with a model for action in similar or analogous circumstances.

school-cutoff strategy A means of assessing the impact of education while controlling for age by comparing children who are almost the same age but begin schooling a year apart because of school rules that set a specific cutoff date for starting school.

schooling A form of education that is characterized by special forms of motivation, social relations, social organization, and communication using written language.

scientific hypothesis An assumption that is precise enough to be tested as true or false through properly planned comparison.

scripts Event schemas that specify who participates in an event, what social roles they play, what objects they are to use during the event, and the sequence of actions that make up the event.

second-order operations Another term for formal operations, since children at this stage can apply operations to operations.

secondary circular reactions The behavior characteristic of the third substage of Piaget's sensorimotor stage, in which babies repeat actions to produce interesting changes in their environment.

secondary emotions Emotions such as embarrassment, pride, shame, guilt, and envy that depend on children's ability to recognize, talk about, and think about themselves in relation to others.

secondary intersubjectivity The sharing between infants and their caregivers of understandings and emotions that refer beyond themselves to objects and other people.

secondary sex characteristics The anatomical and physiological signs that outwardly distinguish males from females.

secure attachment A pattern of attachment in which children play comfortably and react positively to a stranger as long as their mothers are present. They become upset when their mothers leave and are unlikely to be consoled by a stranger, but they calm down as soon as their mothers reappear.

secure base Bowlby's term for the people whose presence provides the child with the security that allows him or her to make exploratory excursions.

selection The process by which adolescents seek out other teenagers who seem similar to themselves on important traits and behaviors, most generally those that are relevant to the adolescent's social reputation.

self-concept The way in which children come to conceive of themselves in relation to other people.

self-esteem One's evaluation of one's own self-worth.

semenarche The first ejaculation. It often occurs spontaneously during sleep and is called a nocturnal emission.

sensitive period A time in an organism's development when a particular experience has an especially profound effect.

sensorimotor stage Piaget's term for the stage of infancy during which the process of adaptation consists largely of coordinating sensory perceptions and simple motor behaviors to acquire knowledge of the world.

sensory register That part of the information-processing system that stores incoming information for a fraction of a second before it is selectively processed.

separation anxiety The distress that babies show when the person to whom they are attached leaves.

service–learning classes Classes that allow young people to confront social problems through personal experience.

sex-linked characteristics Traits determined by genes that are found on only the X or the Y chromosome.

sexual orientation The sex toward which one has erotic feelings.

short-term (working) memory That part of the information-processing system that holds incoming sensory information until it is taken up into long-term memory or forgotten.

single-parent family A family that is headed by one parent, usually the mother.

skeletal principles Domain-specific principles that get particular cognitive processes started and provide some initial direction, but require subsequent experience in order to realize their potential.

social comparison The process of defining oneself in relation to one's peers.

social competence The set of skills that collectively result in successful social functioning with peers.

social development A two-sided process in which children simultaneously become integrated into the larger social community and differentiated as distinctive individuals.

social domain theory The moral domain, the social conventional domain, and the personal domain have distinct rules that vary in how broadly the rules apply, and what happens when they are broken.

social referencing Babies' tendency to look at their caregivers for some indication of how they should feel and act when they encounter something unfamiliar.

social repair mechanisms Strategies that allow friends to remain friends even when serious differences temporarily drive them apart.

social roles Categories that reflect adult expectations about the child's rights, duties, and obligations, as well as appropriate forms of behavior.

social structure A complex organization of relationships between individuals.

socialization The process by which children acquire the standards, values, and knowledge of their society.

sociocognitive conflict Cognitive conflict that is rooted in social experience.

sociodramatic play Make-believe play in which two or more participants enact a variety of related social roles.

socioemotional competence The ability to behave appropriately in social situations that evoke strong emotions.

somatic (body) cells All the cells in the body except for the germ cells (ova and sperm).

specific learning disabilities A term used to refer to the academic difficulties of children who fare poorly in school despite having normal intelligence.

spinal cord The part of the central nervous system that extends from below the waist to the base of the brain.

stem cells The cells of the morula, every one of which has the potential to grow into an embryo and a normal, healthy baby.

strange situation A procedure designed to assess children's attachment on the basis of their responses to a stranger when they are with their mothers, when they are left alone, and when they are reunited with their mothers.

strategy A deliberate, controllable cognitive operation performed for the purpose of attaining a particular goal.

subjective view of responsibility An understanding that responsibility depends on both intentions and consequences.

subjective well-being A concept that encompasses self-esteem and satisfaction with one's life.

superego In Freudian terms, the conscience. It represents the authority of the social group and sits in stern judgment of the ego's efforts to hold the id in check. It becomes a major force in the personality in middle childhood.

surface structure In Chomskian terms, the actual sentences that people produce.

symbolic play (pretend, fantasy play) Play in which one object stands for, or represents, another.

synapse The tiny gap between axons and dendrites.

synaptic pruning The process of selective dying off of nonfunctional synapses.

synaptogenesis The process of synapse formation.

temperament The term for the individual modes of responding to the environment that appear to be consistent across situations and stable over time. Typically included under the rubric of temperament are such characteristics as children's activity level, their intensity of reaction, the ease with which they become upset, their characteristic responses to novelty, and their sociability.

teratogens Environmental agents that cause deviations from normal development and can lead to abnormalities or death.

tertiary circular reactions The fifth stage of the sensorimotor period, which is characterized by the deliberate variation of action sequences to solve problems and explore the world.

theory A broad framework or set of principles that can be used to guide the collection and interpretation of a set of facts.

theory of mind The ability to think about other people's mental states and form theories of how they think.

transactional models Models of development that trace the ways in which the characteristics of the child and the characteristics of the child's environment interact across time ("transact") to determine developmental outcomes.

triangulation When two or more methods are combined to confirm conclusions about factors causing a particular behavior.

trophoblast The outer layer of cells of the blastocyst that develop into the membranes that protect and support the developing organism.

twin study A study in which groups of monozygotic (identical) and dizygotic (fraternal) twins of the same sex are compared to each other and to other family members for similarity on a given trait.

umbilical cord A soft tube containing blood vessels that connects the developing organism to the placenta.

unconditional response (UCR) In classical conditioning, the response, such as salivation, that is invariably elicited by the unconditional stimulus (UCS).

unconditional stimulus (UCS) In classical conditioning, the stimulus, such as food in the mouth, that invariably causes the unconditional response (UCR).

underextension A term used for applying verbal labels in a narrower way than adults do.

utilization knowledge The ability to know when to apply particular problem-solving procedures.

validity The scientific requirement that the data being collected actually reflect the phenomenon being studied.

X and Y chromosomes The two chromosomes that determine the sex of the individual. Normal females have two X chromosomes, while normal males have one Y chromosome inherited from their fathers and one X chromosome inherited from their mothers.

zona pellucida The thin envelope that surrounds the zygote and later the morula.

zone of proximal development The gap between what children can accomplish independently and what they can accomplish when they are interacting with others who are more competent.

zygote The single cell formed at conception from the union of the sperm and the ovum.

REFERENCES

Abbott, S. (1992). Holding on and pushing away: Comparative perspectives on an Eastern Kentucky child rearing practice. *Ethos, 20,* 33–65.

Aber, J. L., Brooks-Gunn, J., & Maynard, R. A. (1995). Effects of welfare reform on teenage parents and their children. *Future of Children, 5*(2), 53–71.

Abrams, R., Gerhardt, K., & Antonelli, P. J. (1998). Fetal hearing. *Developmental Psychobiology, 33*(1), 1–3.

Adair, L. S. (1987). *Nutrition in the reproductive years.* New York: Alan R. Liss.

Adams, M. J. (1990). *Learning to read: Thinking and learning about print.* Cambridge, MA: MIT Press.

Adams, M. J., Treiman, R., & Pressley, M. (1998). Reading, writing, and literacy. In W. Damon, I. E. Sigel & K. A. Renninger (Eds.), *Handbook of child psychology: Vol. 4. Child psychology in practice* (5th ed., pp. 275–355). New York: Wiley.

Adamson, L. B. (1995). *Communication development during infancy.* Madison, WI: Brown & Benchmarks.

Addams, J. (1910). *The spirit of youth and the city streets.* New York: Macmillan.

Adelson, J. (1986). *Inventing adolescence: The political psychology of everyday schooling.* New Brunswick, NJ: Transaction Books.

Adelson, J. (1991). Political development. In R. Lerner, A. C. Petersen, & J. Brooks-Gunn (Eds.), *Encyclopedia of adolescence.* New York: Garland Publishers.

Adelson, J., Green, B., & O'Neil, R. P. (1969). Growth of the idea of law in adolescence. *Developmental Psychology, 1,* 327–332.

Adolph, K. (1997). Learning in the development of infant locomotion. *Monographs of the Society for Research in Child Development, 62*(3), 1–140.

Adolph, K. E., & Eppler, M. A. (2002). Flexibility and specificity in infant motor skill acquisition. In J. W. Fagen & H. Hayne (Eds.), *Progress in infancy research: Vol. 2.* (pp. 121–167). Mahwah, NJ: Erlbaum.

Adolph, K. E., Eppler, M. A., & Gibson, E. J. (1993). Crawling versus walking infants: Perceptions of affordances for locomotion over sloping surfaces. *Child Development, 64,* 1158–1174.

Adolph, K. E., Vereijken, B., & Denny, M. A. (1998). Learning to crawl. *Child Development, 69*(5), 1299–1312.

Ahadi, S. A., & Rothbart, M. K. (1993). Children's temperament in the U. S. and China: Similarities and differences. *European Journal of Personality, 7,* 359–377.

Ahiadeke, C. (2000). Breast-feeding, diarrhoea and sanitation as components of infant and child health: A study of large scale survey data from Ghana and Nigeria. *Journal of Biosocial Science, 32*(1), 47–61.

Ahnert, L., & Lamb, M. (2000). The East German child care system: Associations with caretaking and caretaking beliefs, children's early attachment and adjustment. *American Behavioral Scientist, 44,* 1843–1863.

Ahnert, L., & Lamb, M. (2003). Shared care: Establishing a balance between home and child care settings. *Child Development, 74,* 1044–1049.

Ahnert, L., Pinquart, M., & Lamb, M. (2003). Security of children's relationships with non-parental care providers: A meta-analysis.

Ainsworth, M. D. S. (1967). *Infancy in Uganda: Infant care and the growth of love.* Baltimore, MD: Johns Hopkins University Press.

Ainsworth, M. D. S. (1982). Attachment: Retrospect and prospect. In C. M. Parkes & J. Stevenson-Hinde (Eds.), *The place of attachment in human behavior.* New York: Basic Books.

Ainsworth, M. D. S., & Bell, S. M. (1969). Some contemporary patterns of mother–infant interaction in the feeding situation. In A. Ambrose (Ed.), *Stimulation in early infancy.* New York: Academic Press.

Ainsworth, M. D. S., Bell, S. M., & Stayton, D. J. (1971). Individual differences in strange-situation behavior of one-year-olds. In H. R. Schaffer (Ed.), *The origins of human social relations.* New York: Academic Press.

Ainsworth, M. D. S., Blehar, M. C., Waters, E., & Wall, S. (1978). *Patterns of attachment: A psychological study of the strange situation.* Mahwah, NJ: Erlbaum.

Ainsworth, M. D. S., & Wittig, B. A. (1969). Attachment and exploratory behavior of one-year-olds in a strange situation. In B. M. Foss (Ed.), *Determinants of infant behavior: Vol. 4.* London: Methuen.

Akers, J. F., Jones, R. M., & Coyl, D. D. (1998). Adolescent friendship pairs: Similarities in identity status development, behaviors, attitudes, and intentions. *Journal of Adolescent Research, 13*(2), 178–201.

Alan Guttmacher Institute. (1994). *Sex and America's teenagers.* New York: Author.

Alan Guttmacher Institute. (1999). Teen sex and pregnancy. Facts in brief. Retrieved from http://www.agi-usa.org/pubs/fb_teen_sex.html.

Alan Guttmacher Institute. (2004). U.S. teenage pregnancy statistics. Retrieved from www.guttmacher.org.

Aldrich, C. A., & Hewitt, E. S. (1947). A self-regulating feeding program for infants. *Journal of the American Medical Association, 35,* 341.

Allen, K. E., Turner, K. D., & Everett, P. M. (1970). A behavior modification classroom for Head Start children with problem behavior. *Exceptional Children, 37,* 119–127.

Alsaker, F. D. (1996). Annotation: The impact of puberty. *Journal of Child Psychology and Psychiatry and Allied Disciplines, 37*(3), 249–258.

Altabe, M. (1998). Ethnicity and body image: Quantitative and qualitative analysis. *International Journal of Eating Disorders, 23*(2), 153–159.

Amato, P. (2000). The consequences of divorce for adults and children. *Journal of Marriage and the Family, 62,* 1269–1287.

American Academy of Childhood and Adolescent Psychiatry. (2000). Children and TV Violence. Retrieved from http://www.parenthoodweb.com/articles/phw247.htm.

American Academy of Pediatrics (2003). Policy statement. *Pediatrics 112*(2), 424–430.

American Academy of Pediatrics Committee on Psychosociological Aspects of Child and Family Health. (1998). Guidance for effective discipline. *Pediatrics, 101,* 723–728.

Ames, E. (1997). *The development of Romanian orphanage children adopted to Canada: Final report to the National Welfare Grants Program: Human Resources Development Canada.* Burnaby, British Columbia: Simon Fraser University.

Ames, E., & Chisholm, K. (2001). Social and emotional development in children adopted from institutions. In D. Bailey, J. Bruer, F. Symons, & J. Lichtman (Eds.), *Critical thinking about critical periods.* Baltimore, MD: Paul H. Brookes Publishing.

Amerman, R. T., Kolko, D. J., Kirisci, L., Blackson, T. C., & Dawes, M. A. (1999). Child abuse potential in parents with histories of substance use disorder. *Child Abuse and Neglect, 23,* 1225–1238.

Ampofo-Boateng, K., Thornson, J. A., Grieve, R., Pitcairn, T., Lee, D. N., & Demetre, J. D. (1993). A developmental training study of children's ability to find safe routes to cross the road. *British Journal of Developmental Psychology, 11,* 31–45.

Anderman, E. M., Austin, C. C., & Johnson, D. (2001). The development of goal orientation. In A. Wigfield & J. S. Eccles (Eds.), *Development of achievement orientation* (pp. 197–221). San Diego: Academic Press.

Anderman, E. M., Griesinger, T., & Westerfield, G. (1998). Motivation and cheating during early adolescence. *Journal of Educational Psychology, 90,* 84–93.

Anderson, E. (1990). *Streetwise: Race, class, and change in an urban community.* Chicago: University of Chicago Press.

Anderson, G. (1995). Touch and the kangaroo care method. In T. Fields (Ed.), *Touch in early development.* Mahwah, NJ: Erlbaum.

Anderson, R. E., & Dexter, S. L. (2000). *School technology leadership: Incidence and impact. Teaching, learning, and computing* (1998 National Survey, Rep. No. 6). Irvine, CA: University of California, Irvine.

Anglin, J. M. (1977). *Word, object, and conceptual development.* New York: W. W. Norton.

Anglin, J. M. (1985). The child's expressible knowledge of word concepts: What preschoolers can say about the meanings of some nouns and verbs. In K. E. Nelson (Ed.), *Children's language: Vol. 5.* Mahwah, NJ: Erlbaum.

Anglin, J. M. (1993). Vocabulary development: A morphological analysis. *Monographs of the Society for Research in Child Development, 58* (10, Serial No. 238).

Anisfeld, M., Turkewitz, G., Rose, S. A., Rosenberg, F. R., Sheiber, F. J., Couturier-Fagan, D. A., et al. (2001). No compelling evidence that newborns imitate oral gestures. *Infancy, 2*(1), 111–122.

Annis, R. C., & Corenblum, B. (1987). Effect of test language and experimenter race on Canadian Indian children's racial and self-identity. *Journal of Social Psychology, 126,* 761–773.

Antonov, A. N. (1947). Children born during the siege of Leningrad in 1942. *Journal of Pediatrics, 30,* 250.

Apgar, V. (1953). A proposal for a new method of evaluation of the newborn infant. *Current Researches in Anesthesia and Analgesics, 32,* 260–267.

Archer, J. (1992). *Ethology and human development.* New York: Wheatsheaf.

Arey, L. B. (1974). *Developmental anatomy: A textbook and laboratory manual of embryology* (7th ed.). Philadelphia: Saunders.

Arias-Camison, J. M., Lau, J., Cole, C. H., & Frantz, I. D. (1999). Meta-analysis of dexamethasone therapy started in the first 15 days of life for prevention of chronic lung disease in premature infants. *Pediatric Pulmonology, 28*(3), 167–174.

Ariel, J., & McPherson, D. (2000). Therapy with lesbian and gay parents and their children. *Journal of Marital and Family Therapy, 26,* 421–432.

Ariès, P. (1962). *Centuries of childhood.* Translated from the French by Robert Baldick. London: Cape.

Arnett, J. J. (1996). Sensation seeking, aggressiveness, and adolescent reckless behavior. *Personality and Individual Differences, 20*(6), 693–702.

Arnett, J. J. (1999). Adolescent storm and stress. *American Psychologist, 54*(5), 317–326.

Arnett, J. J. (2002). The psychology of globalization. *American Psychologist, 57*(10), 774–783.

Arterberry, M. E., & Yonas, A. (2000). Perception of three-dimensional shape specified by optic flow by 8-week-old infants. *Perception and Psychophysics, 62*(3), 550–556.

Asher, S. R., & Coie, J. D. (Eds.). (1990). *Peer rejection in childhood.* New York: Cambridge University Press.

Asher, S. R., Rose, A. J., & Gabriel, S. W. (2001). Peer rejection in everyday life. In M. R. Leary (Ed.), *Interpersonal rejection* (pp. 105–142). London: Oxford University Press.

Aslin, R. N., Jusczyk, P. W., & Pisoni, D. B. (1998). Speech and auditory processing during infancy: Constraints on and precursors to language. In D. Kuhn & R. S. Siegler (Eds.), *Handbook of child psychology: Vol. 2* (pp. 147–198). New York: Wiley.

Astington, J. W. (1993). *The child's discovery of the mind.* Cambridge, MA: Harvard University Press.

Atkinson, C. C. (1997). Another baby walker injury. *Journal of Emergency Nursing, 23*(4), 302–325.

Atkinson, J. (1998). The "where and what" or "who and how" of visual development. In F. Simion & G. Butterworth (Eds.), *The development of sensory, motor and cognitive capacities in early infancy: From perception to cognition.* Hove, UK: Psychology Press/Erlbaum.

Atkinson, R. C., & Shiffrin, R. M. (1968). Human memory: A proposed system and its control processes. In K. W. Spence & J. T. Spence (Eds.), *The psychology of learning and motivation: Advances in research and theory: Vol. 2.* Orlando, FL: Academic Press.

Atran, S. (1998). Folk biology and the anthropology of science: Cognitive universals and cultural particulars. *Behavioral & Brain Sciences, 21*(4), 547–609.

Augusta, D., & Hakuta, K. (1998). *Educating language-minority children.* Washington, D.C: National Academy Press.

Avis, J., & Harris, P. L. (1991). Belief-desire reasoning among Baka children: Evidence for a universal conception of mind. *Child Development, 62,* 460–467.

Azmitia, M. (2002). Self, self-esteem, conflicts, and best friendships in early adolescence. In T. M. Brinthaupt & R. P. Lipka (Eds.), *Understanding early adolescent self and identity: Applications and interventions. SUNY series: Studying the self* (pp. 167–192). Albany, NY: State University of New York Press.

Azmitia, M., & Hesser, J. (1993). Why siblings are important agents of cognitive development: A comparison of siblings and peers. *Child Development, 64,* 430–444.

Bachman, J. G., & Schulenberg, J. (1993). How part-time work intensity relates to drug use, problem behavior, time use, and satisfaction among high school seniors: Are there consequences or merely correlates? *Developmental Psychology, 29,* 220–235.

Bagwell, C. L., Coie, J. D., Terry, R. A., & Lochman, J. E. (2000). Peer clique participation and social status in preadolescence. *Merrill Palmer Quarterly, 46*(2), 280–305.

Bahrick, L. E. (2002). Generalization of learning in three-and-a-half-month-old infants on the basis of amodal relations. *Child Development, 73*(3), 667–681.

Baillargeon, R. (1987). Young infants' reasoning about the physical and spatial properties of a hidden object. *Cognitive Development 2*(3): 179–200.

Baillargeon, R. (1993). The object concept revisited: New directions in the investigation of infants' physical knowledge. In C. Granrud (Ed.), *Visual perception and cognition in infancy. Carnegie Mellon symposia on cognition.* Mahwah, NJ: Erlbaum.

Baillargeon, R. (1998). Infants' understanding of the physical world. In M. Sabourin & F. Craik (Eds.), *Advances in psychological science, Vol 2: Biological and cognitive aspects* (pp. 503–529). Hove, England: Taylor & Francis.

Baillargeon, R. (2000). Reply to Bogartz, Shinskey, and Schilling; Schilling; and Cashon and Cohen. *Infancy, 1*(4), 447–462.

Baillargeon, R. (2001). Infants' physical knowledge: Of acquired expectations and core principles. In E. Dupoux (Ed.), *Language, brain, and cognitive development: Essays in honor of Jacques Mehler* (pp. 341–361). Cambridge, MA: MIT Press.

Baillargeon, R. (2002). The acquisition of physical knowledge in infancy: A summary of eight lessons. In U. Goswami (Ed.), *Blackwell's handbook of childhood cognitive development* (pp. 47–83). Oxford, UK: Blackwell..

Baillargeon, R., Spelke, E., & Wasserman, S. (1985). Object permanence in five-month-old infants. *Cognition, 20,* 191–208.

Baker, M. (1993). Long term love: Discover the magic. *Parents, 73,* 89–91.

Bakker, E., & Wyndaele, J. J. (2000). Changes in the toilet training of children during the last 60 years: The cause of an increase in lower urinary tract dysfunction? *British Journal of Urology International, 86*(3), 248–252.

Baldwin, J. (1992). Letter: Luanne. In N. Phillip (Ed.), *Frontiers: Essays and writings on racism and culture.* Stratford, Canada: Mercury.

Baldwin, J. M. (1902). *Social and ethical interpretations in mental development* (3rd ed.). New York: Macmillan.

Bale, J. F. J. (2002). Congenital infections. *Neurological Clinic, 20*(4), 1039–1060.

Bandstra, E. S., Morrow C. E., Anthony J. C., Accornero V. H., & Fried, P. A. (2001). Longitudinal investigation of task persistence and sustained attention in children with prenatal cocaine exposure. *Neurotoxicol Teratology, 23*(6):545–559.

Barcus, F. E. (1986). The nature of television advertising to children. In E. L. Palmer & A. Dorr (Eds.), *Children and the faces of television* (pp. 273–285). New York: Academic Press.

Bargelow, P., Vaughn, B. E., & Molitor, N. (1987). Effects of maternal absence due to employment on the quality of infant–mother attachment in a low-risk sample. *Child Development, 58,* 945–953.

Barker, R. G., & Wright, H. F. (1955). *One boy's day: A specimen record of behavior.* New York: Harper Brothers.

Barkley, R. (1997). Behavioral inhibition, sustained attention, and executive function: Constructing a unifying theory of ADHD. *Psychological Bulletin, 121,* 65–94.

Barnett, D., Manly, J. T., & Cicchetti, D. (1993). Defining child maltreatment. In D. Cicchetti & S. L. Toth (Eds.), *Child abuse, child development, and social policy: Advances in applied developmental psychology, Vol. 8.* Norwood, NJ: Ablex.

Barnett, O. W., Miller-Perrin, C. L., & Perrin, R. D. (1997). Physical child abuse. In O. W. Barnett (Ed.), *Family violence across the lifespan: An introduction* (pp. 39–67). Thousand Oaks, CA: Sage.

Barnett, W. S. (1996). *Lives in the balance: Benefit-cost analysis of the Perry Preschool Program through age 27.* Monographs of the High/Scope Educational Research Foundation. Ypsilanti, MI: High/Scope Press.

Baron-Cohen, S., Leslie, A. M., & Frith, U. (1986) Mechanical, behavioural, and intentional understanding of picture stories in autistic children. *British Journal of Developmental Psychology, 4,* 113–125.

Baron-Cohen, S., Wheelwright, S., Lawson, J., Griffin, R., & Hill, J. (2002). The exact mind: Empathizing and systematizing in autism spectrum conditions. In U. Goswami (Ed.), *Blackwell handbook of childhood cognitive development* (pp. 491–508). Oxford, UK: Blackwell.

Baroody, A. J. (2003). The development of adaptive expertise and flexibility: The integration of conceptual and procedural knowledge. In A. J. Baroody & A. Dowker (Eds.), *The development of arithmetic concepts and skills: Constructing adaptive expertise.* Studies in mathematical thinking and learning (pp. 1–33). Mahwah, NJ: Erlbaum.

Barr, D. (1997). Friendship and belonging. In R. Selman, C. Watts, & L. Schultz (Eds.), *Fostering friendship: Pair therapy for treatment and prevention.* New York: Aldine de Gruyter.

Barrett, J. (2001). Do children experience God as adults do? In J. Andressen (Ed.), *Religion in mind: Cognitive perspectives on religious belief, ritual, and experience.* Cambridge: Cambridge University Press.

Barrett, M. (1995). Early lexical development. In P. Fletcher & B. McWhinney (Eds.), *The handbook of child language* (pp. 362–392). Cambridge, MA: Blackwell.

Barth, R. P. (1998). Abusive and neglecting parents and the care of their children. In M. A. Mason & A. Skolnick (Eds.), *All our families: New policies for a new century* (pp. 217–235). New York: Oxford University Press.

Bartlett, E. (1977). The acquisition of the meaning of color terms. In P.T. Smith & R. N. Campbell (Eds.), *Proceedings of the Sterling Conference on the psychology of language.* New York: Plenum Press.

Bates, E. (1976). *Language and context: The acquisition of pragmatics.* New York: Academic Press.

Bates, E. (1999). On the nature and nurture of language. In E. Bizzi, P. Calissano, & V. Volterra (Eds.), *Frontiere della biologia* [Frontiers of biology]. Rome: Giovanni Trecanni.

Bates, E., Benigni, L., Bretherton, I., Camaioni, L., & Volterra, V. (1979). *The emergence of symbols: Cognition and communication in infancy.* New York: Academic Press.

Bates, E., Camaioni, L., & Volterra, V. (1975). The acquisition of performatives prior to speech. *Merrill Palmer Quarterly, 21,* 205–226.

Bates, E., & Goodman, J. (1999). On the emergence of grammar from the lexicon. In B. MacWhinney (Ed.), *The emergence of language.* Mahwah, NJ: Erlbaum.

Bates, E., O'Connell, B., & Shore, C. (1987). Language and communication. In J. D. Osofsky (Ed.), *Handbook of infant development* (2nd ed.). New York: Wiley.

Bates, E., & Roe, K. (2001). Language development in children with unilateral brain injury. In C. A. Nelson & M. Luciana (Eds.), *Developmental cognitive neuroscience.* Cambridge: Cambridge University Press.

Bauer, P. J., Wiebe, S. A., Carver, L. J., Waters, J. M., & Nelson, C. (2003). Developments in long-term explicit memory late in the first year of life: Behavioral and electrophysiological indices. *Psychological Science, 14*(6), 629–635.

Baumrind, D. (1971). Current patterns of parental authority. *Developmental Psychology Monographs, 4(1, Part 2).*

Baumrind, D. (1980). New directions in socialization research. *American Psychologist, 35,* 639–652.

Bayley, N. (1993). *The Bayley scales of infant development.* San Antonio, TX: Psychological Corporation.

Beal, C. R. (1994). *Boys and girls: The development of gender roles.* New York, NY: McGraw-Hill.

Becker, L. (2000). Garden money buys grain: Food procurement patterns in a Malian village. *Human Ecology, 28,* 219–250.

Behl-Chada, G. (1996). Basic-level and superordinate-like categorical representations in early infancy. *Cognition, 60*(2), 105–141.

Behl-Chadha, G., & Eimas, P. D. (1995). Infant categorization of left-right spatial relations. *British Journal of Developmental Psychology, 13*(1), 69–79.

Beidelman, T. (1997). *The cool knife: Imagery of gender, sexuality, and moral educaion in Kaguru initiation ritual.* Washington, DC: Smithsonian Institution Press.

Beilin, H., & Fireman, G. (2000). The foundation of Piaget's theories: Mental and physical action. In H. W. Reese (Ed.), *Advances in child development and behavior* (pp. 221–246). San Diego, CA: Academic Press.

Bekoff, M., & Colin, A. (Eds.). (2002). *The cognitive animal: Empirical and theoretical perspectives on animal cognition.* Cambridge, MA: MIT Press.

Bell, A. P., Weinberg, M. S., & Hammersmith, S. K. (1981). *Sexual preference: Its development in men and women.* Bloomington, IN: Indiana University Press.

Bell, M. A. (2001). Brain electrical activity associated with cognitive processing during a looking version of the A-not-B task. *Infancy, 2*(3), 311–330.

Bell, M. A., & Fox, N. A. (1997). Individual differences in object permanence performance at 8 months: Locomotor experience and brain electrical activity. *Developmental Psychobiology, 31*(4), 287–297.

Bellmore, A. D., & Cillessen, A. H. N. (2003). Children's meta-perceptions and meta-accuracy of acceptance and rejection by same-sex and other-sex peers. *Personal Relationships, 10*(2), 217–233.

Bellugi, U., Lichtenberg, L., Mills, D., & Galaburda, A. (1999). Bridging cognition, the brain, and molecular genetics: Evidence from Williams syndrome. *Trends in Neurosciences, 22*(5), 197–207.

Bellugi, U., & St. George, M. (Eds.). (2001). *Journey from cognition to brain to gene.* Cambridge, MA: MIT Press.

Belsky, J. (1986). Infant day care: A cause for concern? *Zero to Three, 7*(1), 1–7.

Belsky, J. (1990). Developmental risks associated with infant day care: Attachment insecurity, noncompliance, and aggression? In S. S. Chehrazi (Ed.), *Psychosocial issues in day care* (pp. 37–68). Washington, DC: American Psychiatric Press.

Belsky, J. (1993). Etiology of child maltreatment: A developmental-ecological analysis. *Psychological Bulletin, 114*, 413–434.

Belsky, J. (1999). Interactional and contextual determinants of attachment security. In J. Cassidy & P. R. Shaver (Eds.), *Handbook of attachment: Theory, research, and clinical applications* (pp. 249–264). New York: Guilford Press.

Belsky, J., Fish, M., & Isabella, R. (1991). Continuity and discontinuity in infant negative and positive emotionality: Family antecedents and attachment consequences. *Developmental Psychology, 27*, 421–431.

Belsky, J., Woodworth, S., & Crnic, K. (1996). Trouble in the second year: Three questions about family interaction. *Child Development, 67*(2), 556–578.

Bemak, F., & Young, M. E. (1998). Role of catharsis in group psychotherapy. *International Journal of Action Methods, 50*(4), 166–184.

Ben-Arieh, A., & Ofir, A. (2002). Time for (more) time-use studies: Studying the daily activities of children. *Childhood: A Global Journal of Child Research 9*(2), 225–248.

Bendersky, M., & Lewis, M. (1998). Arousal modulation in cocaine-exposed infants. *Developmental Psychology, 3*, 555–564.

Benjet, C., & Hernandez-Guzman, L. (2001). Gender differences in psychological well-being of Mexican early adolescents. *Adolescence, 36*, 47–65.

Bergen, D. (1998). Development of the sense of humor. In W. Ruch (Ed.), *The sense of humor: Explorations of a personality characteristic. Humor research: 3* (pp. 329–358). Berlin: Walter de Gruyter.

Berger, B. M. (1981). *The survival of a counterculture: Ideological work and everyday life among rural communards.* Berkeley: University of California Press.

Berger, S. E., & Adolph, K. E. (2003). Infants use handrails as tools in a locomotor task. *Developmental Psychology, 39*(3), 594–605.

Berkowitz, L. (2003). Affect, aggression and antisocial behavior. In R. Davidson, K. Scherer, & H. Goldsmith (Eds.), *Handbook of Affective Sciences.* Oxford: Oxford University Press.

Bernal, J. F. (1972). Crying during the first few days and maternal responses. *Developmental Medicine and Child Neurology, 14*, 362–372.

Berndt, T. J. (1979). Developmental changes in conformity to peers and parents. *Developmental Psychology, 15*, 608–616.

Berndt, T. J. (1988). The nature and significance of children's friendships. In R. Vasta (Ed.), *Annals of Child Development, Vol. 5.* Greenwich, CT: JAI Press.

Berndt, T. J., & Keefe, K. (1995). Friend's influence on adolescent's adjustment in school. *Child Development, 66*, 1312–1329.

Berndt, T. J., & Murphy, L. M. (2002). Influences of friends and friendships: Myths, truths, and research recommendations. In R. V. Kail (Ed.), *Advances in child development and behavior: Vol. 30* (pp. 275–310). San Diego: Academic Press.

Berndt, T. J., & Savin-Williams, R. C. (1993). Peer relations and friendships. In P. H. Tolan & B. J. Cohler (Eds.), *Handbook of clinical research and practice with adolescents.* New York: Wiley.

Berry, G., & Asamen, J. (2001). Television, children, and multicultural awareness. In D. Singer & J. Singer (Eds.), *Handbook of children and the media.* Thousand Oaks, CA: Sage.

Bertenthal, B. I., Campos, J. J., & Barrett, K. C. (1984). Self-produced locomotions: An organizer of emotional, cognitive, and social development in infancy. In R. Emde & R. Harmon (Eds.), *Continuities and discontinuities in development.* New York: Plenum Press.

Best, D. L., & Williams, J. E. (1997). Sex, gender, and culture. In M. H. Segall, J. W. Berry, & C. Kagitçibasi (Eds.), *Handbook of cross-cultural psychology: Vol. 3. Social and behavioral application* (pp. 163–212). Boston: Allyn & Bacon.

Bettelheim, B. (1977). *The uses of enchantment: The meaning and importance of fairytales.* New York: Vintage Books.

Beuf, A. H. (1977). *Red children in white America.* Philadelphia: University of Pennsylvania Press.

Bialystok, E. (2001). *Bilingualism in development: Language, literacy, and cognition.* Cambridge, Cambridge University Press.

Bickham, D., Wright, J., & Huston, A. (2001). Attention, comprehension and the educational influences of television. In D. Singer & J. Singer (Eds.), *Handbook of children and the media.* Thousand Oaks, CA: Sage.

Biederman, J., Rosenbaum, J. F., Chaloff, J., & Kagan, J. (1995). Behavioral inhibition as a risk factor for anxiety disorders. In J. S. March (Ed.), *Anxiety disorders in children and adolescents.* New York: Guilford Press.

Biemiller, A., & Slonim, N. (2001). Estimating root word vocabulary growth in normative and advantaged populations: Evidence for a common sequence of vocabulary acquisition. *Journal of Educational Psychology, 93*(3): 498–520.

Bigelow, A. E. (1998). Infants' sensitivity to familiar imperfect contingencies in social interaction. *Infant Behavior and Development, 21*(1), 149–161.

Biggler, R. (1995). The role of classification skill in moderating environmental influences on children's gender stereotyping: A study of the functional use of gender in the classroom. *Child Development, 66*, 1440–1452.

Binet, A., & Simon, T. (1916). *The development of intelligence in children.* Vineland, NJ: Publications of the Training School at Vineland (reprinted by Williams Publishing Co., Nashville, TN, 1980.).

Bisanz, J., & Lefevre, J. (1990). Mathematical cognition: Strategic processing as interactions among sources of knowledge. In D. P. Bjorkland (Ed.), *Children's strategies: Contemporary views of cognitive development.* Mahwah, NJ: Erlbaum.

Bizeul, C., Brun, J. M., & Rigaud, D. (2003). Depression influences the EDI scores in anorexia nervosa patients. *European Psychiatry, 18*(3), 119–123.

Bjorklund, D. F., & Miller, P. H. (1997). New themes in strategy development. *Developmental Review, 17*(4), 407–410.

Bjorklund, D. F., & Pellegrini, A. D. (2002). *The origins of human nature: Evolutionary developmental psychology.* Washington, DC: American Psychological Association.

Blachman, B. A. (2000). Phonological awareness. In M. L. Kamil & P. B. Mosenthal Eds.), *Handbook of reading research.* Mahwah, NJ: Erlbaum.

Blake, J., & De Boysson-Bardies, B. (1992). Patterns in babbling: A cross-linguistic study. *Journal of Child Language, 19*, 51–74.

Blasi, A. (1994a). Bridging moral cognition and moral action: A critical review of the literature. In B. Puka (Ed.), *Fundamental research in moral development* (pp. 123–167). New York: Garland Publishing.

Blasi, A. (1994b). Moral identity: Its role in moral functioning. In B. Puka (Ed.), *Fundamental research in moral development. Moral development: A compendium, Vol. 2.* (pp. 168–179). New York: Garland Publishing.

Bloom, L. (1973). *One word at a time: The use of single word utterances before syntax.* The Hague: Mouton.

Bloom, L., & Tinker, E. (2001). The intentionality model and language acquisition: Engagement, effort, and the essential tension in development. *Monographs of the Society for Research in Child Development, 66*(4), 1–89.

Bloom, P. (2001). Precis of How children learn the meaning of words. *Behavior and Brain Sciences, 24*(6), 1095–1103.

Blos, P. (1972). The child analyst looks at the young adolescent. In J. Kagan & R. Coles (Eds.), *Twelve to sixteen: Early adolescence.* New York: W. W. Norton.

Boaler, J. (2001). Mathematical modelling and new theories of learning. *Teaching Mathematics and Its Applications 20*(3): 121–127.

Boas, F. (1911). *The mind of primitive man.* New York: Macmillan.

Bogartz, R. S., Shinskey, J. L., & Schilling, T. (2000). Object permanence in five-and-a half-month-old infants? *Infancy, 1*(4), 403–428.

Bogin, B. (1999). *Patterns of human growth* (2nd ed.). New York: Cambridge University Press.

Bogin, B. (2001). *The growth of humanity.* New York: Wiley-Liss.

Bogin, B., Smith, P., Orden, A. B., Varela Silva, M. I., & Loucky, J. (2002). Rapid change in height and body proportions of Maya American children. *American Journal of Human Biology, 14*(6): 753–761.

Bohan, J. S. (1996). *Psychology and sexual orientation: Coming to terms.* New York: Routledge.

Bolger, K., & Patterson, C. (2001). Developmental pathways from child maltreatment to peer rejection. *Child Development, 72,* 549–568.

Boone, T. L., Lefkowitz, E. S., Romo, L., Corona, R., Sigman, M., & Au, T. K. F. (2003). Mothers' and adolescents' perceptions of AIDS vulnerability. *International Journal of Behavioral Development, 27*(4), 347–354.

Borke, H. (1975). Piaget's mountains revisited: Changes in the egocentric landscape. *Developmental Psychology, 11,* 240–443.

Bosma, H., & Kunnen, S. (2001). Determinants and mechanisms in ego identity development: A review and synthesis. *Developmental Review, 21,* 39–66.

Botta, R. A. (1999). Television images and adolescent girls' body image disturbance. *Journal of Communication, 49*(2), 22–41.

Bottoms, B. L., Goodman, G. S., Schwartz-Kenney, B. M., & Thomas, S. N. (2002). Understanding children's use of secrecy in the context of eyewitness reports. *Law & Human Behavior, 26*(3), 285–314.

Boulton, M. J. (1996). A comparison of 8- and 11-year-old girls' and boys' participation in specific types of rough and tumble play and aggressive fighting: Implications for functional hypotheses. *Aggressive Behavior, 22*(4), 271–287.

Bourchier, A., & Davis, A. (2002). Children's understanding of the pretence-reality distinction: A review of current theory and evidence. *Developmental Science 5*(4): 397–426.

Bower, T. G. R. (1979). *Human development.* San Francisco: W. H. Freeman.

Bower, T. G. R. (1982). *Development in human infancy.* New York: W. H. Freeman.

Bowlby, J. (1969). *Attachment and loss: Vol. 1. Attachment.* New York: Basic Books.

Bowlby, J. (1973). *Attachment and loss: Vol. 2. Separation.* New York: Basic Books.

Bowlby, J. (1980). *Attachment and loss: Vol. 3. Loss, sadness, and depression.* New York: Basic Books.

Bowman, C., Pieters, B., Hembree, S., & Mellender, T. (2002). Shakespeare, our contemporary: Using technology to teach the Bard. *English Journal, 92*(1), 88–93.

Boyatzis, C. J., Baloff, P., & Durieux, C. (1998). Effects of perceived attractiveness and academic success on early adolescent peer popularity. *Journal of Genetic Psychology, 159*(3), 337–344.

Boykin, A. W., & Cunningham, R. T. (2001). The effects of movement expressiveness in story content and learning context on the analogical reasoning performance of African American children. *Journal of Negro Education, 70*(1–2), 72–83.

Braine, M. D. S. (1963). The ontogeny of English phrase structure: The first phase. *Language, 39,* 3–13.

Bransford, J. D., Brown, A. L., & Cocking, R. R. (1999). *How people learn: Brain, mind, and school.* Washington, DC: National Research Council.

Brazelton, T. B. (1984). *Neonatal behavioral assessment scale* (2nd ed.). London: Spastics International Medical Publications.

Brazelton, T., & Greenspan, S. (2000). *The irreducible needs of children: What every child must have to grow, learn, and flourish.* Cambridge, MA: Perseus Publishing.

Bremner, J. G. (2001). Cognitive development: Knowledge of the physical world. In A. Fogel & J. G. Bremner (Eds.), *Blackwell handbook of infant development* (pp. 99–138). Malden, MA: Blackwell.

Bremner, J. G., & A. Fogel (Eds.). (2001). *Blackwell handbook of infant development.* Malden, MA: Blackwell.

Brennan, P., Hammen, C., Andersen, M., Bor, W., Najman, J., & Williams, G. (2000). Chronicity, severity, and timing of material depressive symptoms: Relationships with child outcomes at age 5. *Developmental Psychology, 36,* 759–766.

Bretherton, I. (1985). Attachment theory: Retrospect and prospect. *Monographs of the Society for Research in Child Development, 50*(1–2, No. 209).

Bretherton, I., Fritz, J., Zahn-Waxler, C., & Ridgeway, D. (1986). Learning to talk about emotions. *Child Development, 57,* 529–548.

Bretherton, I., & Munholland, K. (1999). Internal working models in attachment relationships: A construct revisited. In J. Cassidy and P. Shaver, (Eds.), *Handbook of Attachment: Theory, Research and Clinical Applications.* New York: Guilford Press.

Bretherton, I., & Waters, E. E. (1985). Growing points in attachment theory. *Monographs of the Society for Research in Child Development, 50*(1–2, Serial No. 209).

Bridges, L. J., & Grolnick, W. S. (1995). The development of emotional self-regulation in infancy and early childhood. In N. Eisenberg (Ed.), *Social development: Review of personality and social psychology.* Thousand Oaks, CA: Sage Publications.

Brody, G. H. (1998). Sibling relationship quality: Its causes and consequences. *Annual Review of Psychology, 49,* 1–24.

Brody, G. H., & Murry, V. M. (2001). Sibling socialization of competence in rural, single-parent African American families. *Journal of Marriage and the Family 63*(4), 996–1008.

Bronfenbrenner, U. (1970). *Two worlds of childhood: U.S. and U.S.S.R.* New York: Russell Sage Foundation.

Bronfenbrenner, U. (1979). *The ecology of human development.* Cambridge, MA: Harvard University Press.

Bronfenbrenner, U., & Ceci, S. J. (1993). Heredity, environment, and the question, "How?": A first approximation. In R. Plomin & G. McClearn (Eds.), *Nature, nurture, and psychology.* Washington, DC: American Psychological Association.

Bronfenbrenner, U., & Morris, P. A. (1998). The ecology of developmental processes. In R. M. Lerner (Ed.), *Handbook of child psychology: Theoretical models of human development: Vol. 1* (5th ed., pp. 993–1028). New York: Wiley.

Bronson, G. W. (1991). Infant differences in rate of visual encoding. *Child Development, 62,* 44–54.

Bronson, G. W. (1994). Infants' transitions toward adult-like scanning. *Child Development, 65,* 1243–1261.

Bronson, G. W. (1997). The growth of visual capacity: Evidence from infant scanning patterns. *Advances in Infancy Research, 11,* 109–141.

Brooke, J. (1991, June 15). Cubato journal: Signs of life in Brazil's industrial valley of death. *New York Times,* Pt. 1, p. 2.

Brooks-Gunn, J., Klebanov, P. K., & Duncan, G. J. (1996). Ethnic differences in children's intelligence test scores: Role of economic deprivation, home environment, and maternal characteristics. *Child Development, 67*(2), 396–408.

Brooks-Gunn, J., & Petersen, A. (Eds.). (1983). *Girls at puberty: Biological and psychosocial perspectives.* New York: Plenum Press.

Brooks-Gunn, J., & Reiter, E. O. (1990). The role of pubertal processes in the early adolescent transition. In S. Feldman & G. Elliot (Eds.), *At the threshold: The developing adolescent.* Cambridge, MA: Harvard University Press.

Brookes-Gunn, J., & Warren, M. (1989). Biological and social contributions to negative affect in young adolescent girls. *Child Develoment, 60,* 40–55.

Brotman, L., Gouley, K., Klein, R., Castellanos, F., & Pine, D. (2003). Children, stress and context: Integrating basic, clinical, and experimental prevention research. *Child Development, 74,* 1053–1057.

Broude, G. J., & Green, S. J. (1976). Cross-cultural codes on twenty sexual attitudes and practices. *Ethnology, 15*, 409–429.

Brown v. Board of Education of Topeka. (1954). Paper presented at the 347 U.S. 483; 7455 Ct. 686, Kansas.

Brown, A. L. (1997). Transforming schools into communities of thinking and learning about serious matters. *American Psychologist, 52*(4), 399–413.

Brown, A. L., Campione, J. C., Reeve, R. A., Ferrara, R. A., & Palincsar, A. S. (1992). Interactive learning and individual understanding: The case of reading and mathematics. In L. T. Landsmann (Ed.), *Culture, schooling, and psychological development*. Mahwah, NJ: Erlbaum.

Brown, A. L., Palinscar, A. S., & Arbruster, B. B. (1994). Instructing comprehension-fostering activities in interactive learning situations. In R. B. Ruddell, M. R. Ruddell, & H. Singer (Eds.), *Theoretical models and processes of reading* (pp. 757–787). Newark, DE: International Reading Association.

Brown, B. B. (1990). Peer groups and peer cultures. In S. S. Feldman & G. R. Elliott (Eds.), *At the threshold: The developing adolescent*. Cambridge, MA: Harvard University Press.

Brown, B. B. (1999). Measuring the peer environment of American adolescents. In S. L. Friedman & T. D. Wachs (Eds.), *Measuring environment across the life span*. Washington, DC: American Psychological Association.

Brown, B. B., Clasen, D. R., & Eicher, S. A. (1986). Perception of peer pressure, peer conformity dispositions, and self reported behavior among adolescents. *Developmental Psychology, 22*, 521–530.

Brown, B. B., & Huang, B. (1995). Examining parenting practices in different peer contexts: Implications for adolescent trajectories. In L. J. Crockett & A. C. Crouter (Eds.), *Pathways through adolescence: Individual development in relation to social contexts* (pp. 151–174). Mahwah, NJ: Erlbaum.

Brown, B. B., & Klute, C. (2003). Friendships, cliques, and crowds. In G. R. Adams & M. D. Berzonsky (Eds.), *Blackwell handbook of adolescence. Blackwell handbooks of developmental psychology* (pp. 330–348). Malden, MA: Blackwell Publishers.

Brown, B. B., Mory, M. S., & Kinney, D. (1994). Casting adolescent crowds in a relational perspective: Caricature, channel, and context. In R. Montemayor, G. Adams, & T. Gullotta (Eds.), *Personal relationships in adolescence: Advances in adolescent development, Vol. 6*. Thousand Oaks, CA: Sage.

Brown, L. M., Way, N., & Duff, J. L. (1999). The others in my I: Adolescent girls' friendships and peer relations. In N. G. Johnson, M. C. Roberts, & J. Worell (Eds.), *Beyond appearance: A new look at adolescent girls*. Washington, DC: American Psychological Association.

Brown, P., & Elliot, R. (1965). Control of aggression in a nursery school class. *Journal of Experimental Child Psychology, 2*, 103–107.

Brown, R. (1973). *A first language: The early stages*. Cambridge, MA: Harvard University Press.

Brown, R., & Bellugi, U. (1964). Three processes in the child's acquisition of syntax. *Harvard Educational Review, 34*, 133–151.

Brown, R., & Herrnstein, R. J. (1975). *Psychology*. Boston: Little, Brown.

Bruer, J. T. (2001). A critical and sensitive period primer. In D. B. J. Bailey, J. T. Bruer, F. J. Symons, & J. W. Lichtman (Eds.), *Critical thinking about critical periods*. Baltimore, MD: Paul H. Brookes.

Bruer, J. T., & Greenough, W. T. (2001). The subtle science of how experience affects the brain. In D. B. J. Bailey, J. T. Bruer, F. J. Symons, & J. W. Lichtman (Eds.), *Critical thinking about critical periods* (pp. 209–232). Baltimore, MD: Paul H. Brookes.

Bruner, J. S. (1966). On cognitive growth. In J. S. Bruner, R. R. Olver, & P. M. Greenfield (Eds.), *Studies in cognitive growth*. New York: Wiley.

Bruner, J. S. (1982). Formats of language acquisition. *American Journal of Semiotics, 1*, 1–16.

Bruner, J. S. (1996). *The culture of education*. Cambridge, MA: Harvard University.

Bryant, P., & Nunes, T. (1998). Learning about the orthography: A cross-linguistic approach. In S. G. Paris & H. M. Wellman (Eds.), *Global prospects for education: Development, culture, and schooling* (pp. 171–191). Washington, DC: American Psychological Association.

Buhrmester, D., & Furman, W. (1987). The development of companionship and intimacy. *Child Development, 58*, 1101–1113.

Bulik, C., Wade, T. D., & Kendler, K. S. (2001). Characteristics of monozygotic twins discordant for bulimia nervosa. *International Journal of Eating Disorders, 29*, 1–10.

Bullock, M. (1984). Preschool children's understandings of causal connections. *British Journal of Developmental Psychology, 2*, 139–142.

Bullock, M., & Gelman, R. (1979). Preschool children's assumptions about cause and effect: Temporal ordering. *Child Development, 50*, 89–96.

Bullock, M., & Lutkenhaus, P. (1989). The development of volitional behavior in the toddler years. *Child Development, 59*, 664–674.

Burgess, K. B., Marshall, P. J., Rubin, K. H., & Fox, N. A. (2003). Infant attachment and temperament as predictors of subsequent externalizing problems and cardiac physiology. *Journal of Child Psychology and Psychiatry and Allied Disciplines, 44*(6), 819–831.

Bushman, B., & Anderson, C. (2001). Media violence and the American public. *American Psychologist, 56*, 477–489.

Bushnell, E. W., & Boudreau, J. P. (1991). The development of haptic perception during infancy. In W. Schiff (Ed.), *The psychology of touch* (pp. 139–161). Mahwah, NJ: Erlbaum.

Bushnell, I. W. R. (2001). Mother's face recognition in newborn infants: Learning and memory. *Infant and Child Development, 10*(1–2), 67–74.

Butterworth, G. (2001). Joint visual attention in infancy. In G. Bremner & A. Fogel, (Eds.), *Blackwell handbook of infant development. Handbooks of developmental psychology* (pp. 213–240). Malden, MA: Blackwell Publishers.

Butterworth, G. (2003). Pointing is the royal road to language for babies. In K. Sotaro (Ed.) *Pointing: Where language, culture, and cognition meet*. Mahwah: Erlbaum.

Butterworth, G. & Morissette, P. (1996). Onset of pointing and the acquisition of language in infancy. *Journal of Reproductive & Infant Psychology, 14*(2), 219–231.

Cairns, E. (1996). *Children and political violence*. Oxford, UK: Blackwell.

Cairns, E., & Dawes, A. (1996). Children: Ethnic and political violence—A commentary. *Child Development, 67*, 129–139.

Cairns, R. B. (1979). *Social development: The origins of interchanges*. New York: W. H. Freeman.

Cairns, R. B. (1998). The making of developmental psychology. In W. Damon & R. M. Lerner (Eds.), *Handbook of child psychology: Vol. 1. Theoretical models of human development* (5th ed.). New York: Wiley.

Cairns, R. B., & Cairns, B. D. (1994). *Lifelines and risks: Pathways of youth in our times*. Cambridge: Cambridge University Press.

Calabrese, L. H., Kirkendall, D. T., Floyd, M., Rapoport, S., Williams, G. W., Weiker, G. F., & Bergfeld, J. A. (1983). Menstrual abnormalities, nutritional patterns and body composition in female classical ballet dancers. *Physician and Sports Medicine, 11*, 86–98.

Caldji, C., Tannenbaum, B., Sharma, S., Francis, D., Plotsky, P. & Meaney, M. (1998) Maternal care during infancy regulates the development of neural systems mediating the expression of fearfulness in the rat. *Proceedings of the National Academy of Science, 95*, 5335–5340.

California Department of Education. (2003). Educational demographics. Retrieved from www.cde.ca.gov.

Call, K., Riedel, A., Kein, K., McLoyd, V., Petersen, A., & Kipke, M. (2002). Adolescent health and well-being in the twenty-first century: A global perspective. *Journal of Research on Adolescence, 12*, 69–98.

Cameron, N. (Ed.) (2002). *Human growth and development*. New York: Academic Press.

Campbell, D. (1997). *The Mozart effect: Tapping the power of music to heal the body, strengthen the mind, and unlock the creative spirit.* New York: Avon.

Campbell, F., Pungello, E., Miller-Johnson, S., Burchinal, M., & Ramey, C. (2001). The development of cognitive and academic abilities: Growth curves from an early childhood educational experiment. *Developmental Psychology, 37,* 231–242.

Campos, J. J., Anderson, D. I., Barbu-Roth, M. A., Hubbard, E. M., Hertenstein, M. J., & Witherington, D. (2000). Travel broadens the mind. *Infancy 1*(2), 149–219.

Campos, J. J., Benson, J., & Rudy, L. (1986). *The role of self-produced locomotion in spatial behavior.* Unpublished Posterpaper presented at the meeting of the International Conference for Infant Studies, Beverly Hills, CA.

Campos, J. J., Kermoian, R., & Zumbahlen, M. R. (1992). Socioemotional transformations in the family system following infant crawling onset. In N. Eisenberg & R. A. Fabes (Eds.), *Emotion and its regulation in early development (New directions for child development, 55).* San Francisco: Jossey-Bass.

Cantor, J. (1998). *"Mommy, I'm scared": How TV and movies frighten children and what we can do to protect them.* New York: Harcourt Brace & Co.

Caplan, N., Choy, M. H., & Whitmore, J. K. (1991). *Children of the boat people: A study of educational success.* Ann Arbor: University of Michigan Press.

CARE. (2003). Changing childbirth practices.

Carey, S. (1978). The child as word learner. In M. Halle, J. Bresnan, & G. A. Miller (Eds.), *Linguistic theory and psychological reality.* Cambridge, MA: MIT Press.

Carey, W. B., & McDevitt, S. C. (1995). *Coping with children's temperament: A guide for professionals.* New York: Basic Books.

Carpendale, J. (2000). Kohlberg and Piaget on stages and moral reasoning. *Developmental Review, 20,* 181–205.

Carpenter, M., Call, J., & Tomasello, M. (2002). A new false belief test for 36-month-olds. *British Journal of Developmental Psychology, 20*(3), 393–420.

Carpenter, M., Nagell, K., & Tomasello, M. (1998). Social cognition, joint attention, and communicative competence from 9 to 15 months of age. *Monographs of the Society for Research in Child Development, 63*(4), 176.

Carro, M. G., Grant, K. E., Gotlib, I. H., & Compas, B. E. (1993). Postpartum depression and child development: An investigation of mothers and fathers as sources of risk and resilience. *Developmental Psychopathology, 5,* 567–579.

Case, R. (1998). The development of conceptual structures. In D. Kuhn & R. S. Siegler (Eds.), *Handbook of child psychology, Vol 2: Cognition, perception and language* (5th ed., pp. 745–800). New York: Wiley.

Case, R., Kurland, D. M., & Goldberg, J. (1982). Operational efficiency and growth of short-term memory span. *Journal of Experimental Child Psychology, 33,* 386–404.

Case, R., & Okamoto, Y. (1996). The role of central conceptual structures in the development of children's thought. *Monographs of the Society for Research in Child Development, 61*(1–2).

Cashon, C. H., & Cohen, L. B. (2000). Eight-month-old infants' perception of possible and impossible events. *Infancy, 1,* 429–446.

Casper, C. (1997). *The reconstruction.* New York: St. Martin's Press.

Casper, R. C. (1996). Carbohydrate metabolism and its regulatory hormones in anorexia nervosa. *Psychiatry Research, 62*(1), 85–96.

Caspi, A. (1995). Puberty and the gender organization of schools: How biology and social context shape the adolescent experience. In L. J. Crockett & A. C. Crouter (Eds.), *Pathways through adolescence: Individual development in relation to social contexts* (pp. 57–74). Mahwah, NJ: Erlbaum.

Caspi, A. (1998). Personality development across the life course. In W. Damon & N. Eisenberg (Eds.), *Handbook of child psychology: Vol. 3. Social, emotional, and personality development* (5th ed., pp. 311–388). New York: Wiley.

Caspi, A., Lynam, D., Moffitt, T. E., & Silva, P. A. (1993). Unraveling girls' delinquency: Biological, dispositional, and contextual contributions to adolescent misbehavior. *Developmental Psychology, 29,* 19–30.

Caspi, A., & Roberts, B. W. (2001). Target article: Personality development across the life course: The argument for change and continuity. *Psychological Inquiry, 12*(2), 49–66.

Cassell, J. (2004). Towards a model of technology and literacy development: Story listening systems. *Journal of Applied Developmental Psychology, 25,* 75–105.

Cassell, J., & Jenkins, H. (1998). Chess for girls? Feminism and computer games. In J. Cassell & H. Jenkins (Eds.), *From Barbie to Mortal Combat: Gender and Computer Games.* Cambridge: MIT Press.

Cassidy, J., & Shaver, P. R. (Eds.). (1999). *Handbook of attachment.* New York: Guilford Press.

Cauffman, E., & Steinberg, L. (1996). Interactive effects of menarcheal status and dating on dieting and disordered eating among adolescent girls. *Developmental Psychology, 32,* 631–635.

Caughy, M., Campo, P., Randolph, S., & Nickerson, K. (2002). The influence of racial socialization practices on the cognitive and behavioral competence of African American Preschoolers. *Child Development, 73,* 1611–1625.

Cazden, C. B. (1965). *Environmental assistance to the child's acquisition of grammar.* Unpublished doctoral dissertation, Harvard University.

Ceballo, R., & McLoyd, V. (2002). Social support and parenting in poor, dangerous neighborhoods. *Child Development, 73,* 1310–1321.

Ceci, S. J., & Bruck, M. (1993). Suggestibility of child eyewitnesses: A historical review and synthesis. *Psychology Bulletin, 113,* 403–439.

Ceci, S. J., & Bruck, M. (1998). The ontogeny and durability of true and false memories: A fuzzy trace account. *Journal of Experimental Child Psychology, 71*(2), 165–169.

Centers for Disease Control. (1998). *CDC Surveillance Summaries.*

Centers for Disease Control. (1999a). Achievements in public health, 1900–1999: Healthier mothers and babies. *Mortality and Morbidity Weekly Report, 48*(38), 849–858.

Centers for Disease Control. (1999b). Infant mortality statistics from the linked birth/infant death data set—1997 period data. *Mortality and Morbidity Weekly Report, 48.*

Centers for Disease Control. (2000). Trends in the attendant, place, and timing of births and in the use of obstetric interventions in the United States, 1989–1997. *Mortality and Morbidity Weekly Report, 49.*

Centers for Disease Control. (2004). *National vital statistics report* (Vol. 52, no. 3, 9/18/2003). Washington, DC: Department of Health and Human Services.

Chan, A., Keane, R. J., & Robinson, J. S. (2001). The contribution of maternal smoking to preterm birth, small for gestational age and low birthweight among Aboriginal and non-Aboriginal births in South Australia. *Medical Journal of Australia, 174*(8), 389–393.

Chan, A., McCaul, K. A., Keane, R. J., & Haan, E. A. (1998). Effect of parity, gravidity, previous miscarriage, and age on risk of Down's syndrome: Population based study. *British Medical Journal (Clinical Research Ed.), 3*(17), 923–924.

Chandler, M., Lalonde, C., Sokol, B., & Hallett, D. (2003). Personal persistency, identity, and suicide: A study of Native and non-Native North American adolescents. *Monographs for the Society for Research in Child Development, 68*(2, Series No. 273).

Chao, R. K. (1994). Beyond parental control and authoritarian parenting style: Understanding Chinese parenting through the cultural notion of training. *Child Development, 65,* 1111–1119.

Chao, R. K. (1996). Chinese and European American mothers' beliefs about the role of parenting in children's school success. *Journal of Cross-Cultural Psychology, 27*(4), 403–423.

Charpak, N., Ruiz-Pelaez, J. G., Figueroa de Calume, Z., & Charpak, Y. (2001). A randomized, controlled trial of kangaroo mother care: Results of follow-up at 1 year of corrected age. *Pediatrics, 108*(5), 1072–1079.

Chase, W., & Simon, H. (1989). Perception in chess. *Cognitive Psychology, 4,* 55–81.

Chase-Lansdale, P. L., Brooks-Gunn, J., & Zamsky, E. S. (1994). Young African-American multigenerational families in poverty: Qualities of mothering and grandmothering. *Child Development, 65,* 394–403.

Chavajay, P., & Rogoff, B. (2002). Schooling and traditional collaborative social organization of problem solving by Mayan mothers and children. *Developmental Psychology, 38*(1): 55–66.

Chen, C., & Stevenson, H. W. (1988). Cross-linguistic differences in digit span of preschool children. *Journal of Experimental Child Psychology, 46,* 150–158.

Chen, X., & Rubin, K. H. (1994). Family conditions, parental acceptance, and social competence and aggression in Chinese children. *Social Development, 3*(3), 269–290.

Chen, Z., & Siegler, R. S. (2000). Intellectual development in childhood. In R. J. Sternberg (Ed.), *Handbook of intelligence* (pp. 92–116). New York: Cambridge University Press.

Chess, S., & Thomas, A. (1982). Infant bonding: Mystique and reality. *American Journal of Orthopsychiatry, 52,* 213–221.

Chess, S., & Thomas, A. (1996). *Temperament: Theory and practice.* New York: Brunner-Mazel.

Chesterton, G. K. (1908/1957). The logic of elfland. In M. Gardner (Ed.), *Great essays in science.* New York: Washington Square Press.

Chi, M. T. H. (1978). Knowledge structures and memory development. In R. S. Siegler (Ed.), *Children's thinking: What develops?* Mahwah, NJ: Erlbaum.

Chi, M. T. H., Hutchinson, J. E., & Robin, A. F. (1989). How inferences about novel domain-related concepts can be constrained by structured knowledge. *Merrill-Palmer Quarterly, 35*(1), 27–62.

Chi, M. T. H., & Koeske, R. D. (1983). Network representation of a child's dinosaur knowledge. *Developmental Psychology, 19,* 29–39.

Chicz-DeMet, A., Barbaro, T. G., Doan, P. H., Glynn, L. M., Garite, T., Wadhwa, P. D., et al. (2001). Maternal stress hormone changes during pregnancy associated with preterm births. *Society for Neuroscience Abstracts, 27*(2), 1942.

Children Now. (1998). *A different world: Children's perceptions of race and class in the media.* Oakland, CA: Children Now.

Chirkov, V., & Ryan, R. (2001). Parent and teacher autonomy-support in Russian and U.S. adolescents. *Journal of Cross-Cultural Psychology, 32,* 618–635.

Chisholm, K. (1998). A three year follow-up of attachment and indiscriminate friendliness in children adopted from Romanian orphanages. *Child Development, 69*(4), 1092–1106.

Choi, S., & Gopnik, A. (1995). Early acquisition of verbs in Korean: A cross-linguistic study. *Journal of Child Language, 22*(3), 497–529.

Chomsky, N. (1959). Review of verbal behavior by B. F. Skinner. *Language, 35,* 26–58.

Chomsky, N. (1980). Initial states and steady states. In M. Piatelli-Palmerini (Ed.), *Language and learning: The debate between Jean Piaget and Noam Chomsky.* Cambridge, MA: Harvard University Press.

Chomsky, N. (1988). *Language and problems of knowledge.* Cambridge, MA: MIT Press.

Chomsky, N. (1999). On the nature, use, and acquisition of language. In W. C. Ritchie & T. K. Bhatia (Eds.), *Handbook of child language acquisition* (pp. 33–54). San Diego, Academic Press.

Chouinard, M. M., & Clark, E. V. (2003). Adult reformulations of child errors as negative evidence. *Journal of Child Language, 30,* 637–669.

Christian Aid. (2001). *No excuses: Facing up to sub-Saharan Africa's AIDS orphans crisis.* London: Christian Aid.

Christian, K., Bachman, H. J., & Morrison, F. J. (2001). Schooling and cognitive development. In R. J. Sternberg & E. L. Grigorenko (Eds.), *Environmental effects on cognitive abilities* (pp. 287–336). Mahwah, NJ: Erlbaum.

Christian, P. (2002). Maternal nutrition, health, and survival. *Nutritional Review, 60,* S59–S63.

Chugani, H., Behen, M., Muzik, O., Juhász, C., Nagy, F., & Chugani, D. (2001). Local brain functional activity following early deprivations: A study of postinstitutionalized Romanian orphans. *NeuroImage, 14,* 1290–1301.

Chukovsky, K. (1968). *From two to five.* Berkeley: University of California Press.

Cicchetti, D., & Toth, S. L. (1993). Child maltreatment research and social policy: The neglected nexus. In D. Cicchetti & S. L. Toth (Eds.), *Advances in applied developmental psychology series: Vol. 8. Child abuse, child development, and social policy.* Norwood, NJ: Ablex.

Cicchetti, D., & Toth, S. L. (1998). The development of depression in children and adolescents. *American Psychologist, 53*(2), 221–241.

Cicchetti, D., & Toth, S. L. (2003). Child maltreatment: Past, present, and future perspectives. In R. P. Weissberg, H. J. Wahlberg, & M. V. O'Brien (Eds.), *Long-term trends in the well-being of children and youth: Issues in children's and families' lives* (pp. 181–205). Washington, DC: Child Welfare League of America.

Cicchetti, D., Toth, S. L., & Maughm, A. (2000). An ecological-transactional model of child maltreatment. In A. Sameroff, M. Lewis, & J. Miller (Eds.), *Handbook of developmental psychology* (2nd ed.). New York: Plenum.

Cillessen, A. H. N., Vanijzendoorn, H. W., Van Lieshorst, C. F. M., & Hartup, W. W. (1992). Heterogeneity among peer-rejected boys: Subtypes and stabilities. *Child Development, 63,* 893–905.

Clark, C. (2003). *In sickness and in play: Children coping with chronic illness.* New Brunswick, NJ: Rutgers University Press.

Clark, E. V. (1995). Later lexical development and word formation. In P. Fletcher & B. MacWhinney (Eds.) *The handbook of child language* (pp. 393–412). Oxford, UK: Blackwell.

Clark, E. V., & Wong, A. D.-W. (2002). Pragmatic directions about language use: Words and word meanings. *Language in Society, 31,* 181–212.

Clark, K. B., & Clark, M. P. (1939). The development of consciousness of self and the emergence of racial identity in Negro pre-school schoolchildren. *Journal of Social Psychology, 10,* 591–599.

Clark, K. B., & Clark, M. P. (1950). Emotional factors in racial identification and preference in Negro children. *Journal of Negro Education, 19,* 341–350.

Clarke, A. M., & Clarke, A. D. B. (1986). Thirty years of child psychology: A selective review. *Journal of Child Psychology and Psychiatry, 27,* 719–759.

Clarke, A. M., & Clarke, A. D. B. (2000). *Early experience and the life path.* London: Jessica Kingsley.

Clarke-Stewart, A. (1984). Day-care: A new context for research and development. In M. Perlmutter (Ed.), *Parent-child interaction and parent-child relations in child development: The Minnesota Symposia on Child Psychology, Vol. 17.* Mahwah, NJ: Erlbaum.

Clarke-Stewart, A. (1993). *Daycare* (2nd ed.). Cambridge, MA: Harvard University Press.

Clarke-Stewart, A., & Koch, J. B. (1983). *Children: Development through adolescence.* New York: Wiley.

Clausson, B., Granath, F., Ekbom A., Lundgren, S., Nordmark, A., Signorello, L. B., et al. (2002). Effect of caffeine exposure during pregnancy on birth weight and gestational age. *American Journal of Epidemiology, 155*(5), 429–436.

Cloud, N., Genesee, F., & Hamayan, E. (2000). *Dual language instruction: A handbook for enriched education.* Boston: Heinle & Heinle.

Coates, S., & Wolf, S. (1997). Gender identity disorders in children. In P. F. Kernberg & J. R. Bemporad (Eds.), *Handbook of child and adolescent psychiatry: Vol. 2* (pp. 595–609). New York: Wiley.

Cobb, P., Gravemeijer, K., Yackel, E., McClain, K., & Whitenack, J. (1997). Mathematizing and symbolizing: The emergence of chains of signification in one first-grade classroom. In D. Kirshner & J. A. Whitson (Eds.), *Situated cognition: Social, semiotic, and psychological perspectives* (pp. 151–234). Mahwah, NJ: Erlbaum.

Cobb, P., & McClain, K. (2002). Supporting students' learning of significant mathematical ideas. In G. Wells & G. Claxton (Eds.) *Learning for life in the 21st century: Sociocultural perspectives on the future of education* (pp. 154–166). Malden, MA, Blackwell.

Cochran, M., & Niego, S. (1995). Parenting and social networks. In E. Marc H. Bornstein (Ed.), *Handbook of parenting: Vol. 3. Status and social conditions of parenting* (pp. 393–418). Mahwah, NJ: Erlbaum.

Cohen, L. B. (2002). Extraordinary claims require extraordinary controls: Reply. *Developmental Science, 5*(2), 210–212.

Cohen, L. B., Chaput, H. H., & Cashon, C. H. (2002). A constructivist model of infant cognition. *Cognitive Development, 17,* 1323–1343.

Cohen, L. B., & Marks, K. S. (2002). How infants process addition and subtraction events. *Developmental Science, 5*(2), 186–201.

Coie, J. D., & Dodge, K. A. (1998). Aggression and antisocial behavior. In N. Eisenberg (Ed.), *Handbook of child psychology: Vol. 3. Social, emotional, and personality* (5th ed., pp. 779–882). New York: Wiley.

Coie, J. D., Lochman, J. E., Terry, R., & Hyman, C. (1992). Predicting early adolescent disorder from childhood aggression and peer rejection. *Journal of Consulting & Clinical Psychology, 60*(5), 783–792.

Colby, A., & Kohlberg, L. (1987). *The measurement of moral judgment.* New York: Cambridge University Press.

Colby, A., Kohlberg, L., Gibbs, J., & Lieberman, M. (1983). A longitudinal study of moral development. *Monographs of the Society for Research in Child Development, 48* (1–2, Serial No. 200).

Cole, M. (1996). *Cultural psychology: A once and future discipline.* Cambridge, MA: Belknap Harvard.

Cole, M. (1999a). Culture-free versus culture-based measures of cognition. In R. J. Sternberg, Ed. *The nature of cognition* (pp. 645–664). Cambridge, MA: MIT Press.

Cole, M. (1999b). Culture in development. In M. H. Bornstein & M. E. Lamb (Eds.) *Developmental Psychology: An advanced textbook: Vol. 4* (pp. 73–123). Mahwah, NJ: Erlbaum.

Cole, M., & Subbotsky, E. (1993). The fate of stages past: Reflections on the heterogeneity of thinking from the perspective of cultural-historical psychology. *Schweizerische Zeitschrift füer Psychologie 52*(2): 103–113.

Cole, M., Gay, J., Glick, J. A., & Sharp, D. W. (1971). *The cultural context of learning and thinking.* New York: Basic.

Cole, P. M. (1986). Children's spontaneous control of facial expression. *Child Development, 57*(6), 1309–1321.

Coleman, J. S. (1962). *The adolescent society.* Glencoe, IL: Free Press.

Coley, R. L., & Chase-Lansdale, P. L. (1998). Adolescent pregnancy and parenthood. *American Psychologist, 53*(2), 152–166.

Collins, W. A. (2002). Historical perspectives on contemporary research in social development. In P. K. Smith, & C. H. Hart (Eds.), *Blackwell handbook of childhood social development. Blackwell handbooks of developmental psychology* (pp. 3–23). Malden, MA: Blackwell.

Collins, W. A., & Laursen, B. (2004). Changing relationships, changing youth: Interpersonal contexts of adolescent development. *Journal of Early Adolescence, 24*(1), 55–62.

Collins, W. A., Laursen, B., Mortensen, N., Luebker, C., & Ferreira, M. (1997). Conflict processes and transitions in parent and peer relationships: Implications for autonomy and regulation. *Journal of Adolescent Research, 12*(2), 178–198.

Collins, W. A., Maccoby, E., Steinberg, L., Hetheringon, E., & Bornstein, M. (2000). Contemporary research on parenting: The case for nature *and* nurture. *American Psychologist, 55,* 1–15.

Colon, A., & Colon, P. (2001). *A history of children.* Westport, CT: Greenwood Press.

Colwell, J., Grady, C., & Rhaiti, S. (1995). Computer games, self-esteem, and gratification of needs in adolescents. *Journal of Community and Applied Social Psychology, 5,* 195–206.

Compas, B., Hinden, B., & Gerhardt, C. (1995). Adolescent development: Pathways and processes of risk and resilience. *Annual Review of Psychology, 46,* 265–293.

Comstock, G., & Scharrer, E. (1999). *Television: What's on, who's watching, and what does it mean?* New York: Academic Press.

Condry, K. F., Smith, W. C., & Spelke, E. S. (2000). Development of perceptual organization. In F. Lacerda, C. von Hofsten, & M. Heiman (Eds.), *Emerging cognitive abilities in early infancy.* Mahwah, NJ: Erlbaum.

Conel, J. L. (1939/1967). *The postnatal development of the human cerebral cortex* (8 vols.). Cambridge, MA: Harvard University Press.

Conger, J. J., & Petersen, A. C. (1984). *Adolescence and youth: Psychological development in a changing world.* New York: Harper & Row.

Conger, R. D., & Ge, X. (1999). Conflict and cohesion in parent-adolescent relations: Changes in emotional expression from early to midadolescence. In M. J. Cox & J. Brooks-Gunn (Eds.), *Conflict and cohesion in families.* Mahwah, NJ: Erlbaum.

Connolly, J., Furman, W., & Konarski, R. (2000). The role of peers in the emergence of heterosexual romantic relationships in adolescence. *Child Development, 71,* 1395–1408.

Connolly, K., & Dalgleish, M. (1989). The emergence of a tool using skill in infancy. *Developmental Psychology, 25,* 539–549.

Connor, J. M., & Ferguson-Smith, M. A. (1991). *Essential medical genetics* (3rd ed.). London: Blackwell Scientific Publications.

Consortium for Longitudinal Studies. (1983). *As the twig is bent.* Mahwah, NJ: Erlbaum.

Coopersmith, S. (1967). *The antecedents of self-esteem.* New York: W. H. Freeman.

Corbin, P. F., & Bickford, R. G. (1955). Studies of the electroencephalogram of normal children. *Electroencephalography and Clinical Neurology, 7,* 15–28.

Cormier, K., Mauk, C., & Repp, A. (1998). Manual babbling in deaf and hearing infants: A longitudinal study. In E. V. Clark (Ed.), *The Proceedings of the Twenty-Ninth Annual Child Language Research Forum* (pp. 55–61). Chicago: Center for the Study of Language and Information.

Cornell, E. H., Heth, C. D., & Broda, L. S. (1989). Childrens' wayfinding: Response to instructions to use environmental landmarks. *Developmental Psychology, 25,* 755–764.

Cornell, E. H., Heth, C. D., & Rowat, W. L. (1992). Wayfinding by children and adults: Response to instructions to use look-back and retrace strategies. *Developmental Psychology, 28,* 328–336.

Corsaro, W. A. (1985). *Friendship and peer culture in the early years.* Norwood, NJ: Ablex.

Cortés, C. (2000). *The children are watching: How the media teach about diversity.* New York: Teachers College Press.

Costello, D. (2000, June 9). Spanking makes a comeback. *Wall Street Journal.*

Costello, E. Compton, S., Keeler, G., & Angold, A. (2003). Relationships between poverty and psychopathology. *Journal of the American Medical Association, 290,* 2023–2030.

Cottrell, J. (1996). *Social networks and social influences in adolescence.* London: Routledge.

Cowan, W. M. (1979). The development of the brain. *Scientific American, 241,* 112–133.

Cowen, E. (1973). Long-term follow-up of early detected vulnerable children. *Journal of Consulting & Clinical Psychology., 41*(3), 438–446.

Craig, W. M. (1998). The relationship among bullying, victimization, depression, anxiety, and aggression in elementary school children. *Personality & Individual Differences, 24*(1), 123–130.

Crick, N. R., Casas, J. F., & Mosher, M. (1997). Relational and overt aggression in preschool. *Developmental Psychology, 33*(4), 579–588.

Crick, N. R., & Dodge, K. A. (1999). "Superiority" is in the eye of the beholder: A comment on Sutton-Smith and Swettenham. *Social Development, 8*(1), 128–131.

Crick, N. R., Grotpeter, J. K., & Bigbee, M. A. (2002). Relationally and physically aggressive children's intent attributions and feelings of distress for relational and instrumental peer provocations. *Child Development, 73*(4), 1134–1142.

Crick, N. R., & Ladd, G. W. (1993). Children's perceptions of their peer experiences: Attributions, loneliness, social anxiety and social avoidance. *Developmental Psychology, 29,* 244–254.

Crick, N. R., & Rose, A. J. (2000). Toward a gender-balanced approach to the study of social-emotional development: A look at relational aggression. In P. H. Miller, & E. K. Scholnick (Eds.), *Toward a feminist developmental psychology* (pp. 153–168). Florence, KY: Taylor & Francis/Routledge.

Crockenberg, S. (1987). Support for adolescent mothers during the postnatal period. In C. Boukydis (Ed.), *Research on support for parents and infants in the postnatal period.* Norwood, NJ: Ablex.

Crook, C. (1987). Taste and olfaction, *Handbook of Infant Perception: Vol. 1* (pp. 237–264). New York: Academic Press.

Crook, C. (1996). Schools of the future. In T. Gill (Ed.), *Electronic children : How children are responding to the information revolution.* London: National Children's Bureau.

Cross, W. E. (2003). Tracing the historical origins of youth delinquency and violence: Myths and realities about black culture. *Journal of Social Issues, 59*(1), 67–82.

Cross, W. E., & Gore, J. S. (2003). Cultural models of the self. In M. R. Leary & J. P. Tangney (Eds.), *Handbook of self and identity* (pp. 536–564). New York: Guilford.

Cross, W. E., & Phagen-Smith, P. (1996). Nigrescence and ego identity development. In P. B. Pedersen, J. G. Draguns, W. J. Lonner, & J. E. Trimble (Eds.), *Counselling across cultures* (pp. 108–123). Thousand Oaks, CA: Sage.

Crowley, K., & Siegler, R. S. (1993). Flexible strategy use in young children's tic-tac-toe. *Cognitive Science, 17*(4), 531–561.

Crowther, B. (1999). Writing as performance: Young girls' diaries. In R. Josselson & A. Lieblich (Eds.), *Making meaning in the narrative study of lives.* Thousand Oaks, CA: Sage Publications.

Csaba, A. (2003). Ethical dimensions of genetic counseling. *Clinics in Perinatology, 30,* 81–93.

Csibra, G., & Gergely, G. (1998). The teleological origins of mentalistic action explanations: A developmental hypothesis. *Developmental Science, 1*(2), 255–259.

Csikszentmihalyi, M., & Larson, R. (1984). *Being adolescent: Conflict and growth in the teenage years.* New York: Basic.

Cunningham, F. G., MacDonald, P. C., Gant, N. F., Leveno, K. J., Gilstrap, L. C., III, Hankins, G. D. V., & Clark, S. L. (2001). *Williams obstetrics* (21st ed.). Stamford, CT: Appleton & Lange.

Curtis, H. (1979). *Biology.* New York: Worth.

D'Amico, R. (1984). Does employment during high school impair academic progress? *Sociology of Education, 57,* 152–164.

D'Angiulli, A., & Siegel, L. S. (2003). "Cognitive functioning as measured by the WISC-R: Do children with learning disabilities have distinctive patterns of performance?" *Journal of Learning Disabilities, 36*(1): 48–58.

Daley, B. J. (1999). Novice to expert: An exploration of how professionals learn. *Adult Education Quarterly, 49*(4), 133–147.

Dalton, S., & Bielby, D. (2000). "That's our kind of constellation": Lesbian mothers negotiate institutionalized understandings of gender within the family. *Gender & Society, 14,* 36–61.

Damasio, A. (1999). *The feeling of what happens: Body and emotion in the making of consciousness.* New York: Harcourt Brace.

Damerow, P. (1998). Prehistory and cognitive development. In J. Langer & M. Killen (Eds.), *Piaget, evolution, and development* (pp. 247–270). Mahwah, NJ: Erlbaum.

Damon, W. (1977). *The social world of the child.* San Francisco: Jossey-Bass.

Damon, W., & Hart, D. (1988). *Self-understanding in childhood and adolescence.* Cambridge: Cambridge University Press.

Daniels-Beirness, T. (1989). Measuring peer status in boys and girls: A problem of apples and oranges. In B. H. Schneider, G. Attili, J. Nadel, & R. P. Weissberg (Eds.), *Social competence in developmental perspective.* Boston: Kluwer Academic Publishers.

Darwin, C. (1859/1958). *The origin of species.* New York: Penguin.

Dasen, P. R. (1972). Cross-cultural Piagetian research: A summary. *Journal of Cross-Cultural psychology, 3,* 29–39.

Dasen, P. R. (1973). Preliminary study of sensori-motor development in Baoule children. *Early Child Development & Care, 2*(3), 345–354.

Dasen, P. R. (1999). Rapid social change and turmoil in adolescence: A cross-cultural perspective. *World Psychology, 5.*

Dasen, P. R., Lavallee, M., & Retschitzki, J. (1979). Training conservation of quantity (liquids) in West Africa (Baoule) children. *International Journal of Psychology, 14*(1), 57–68.

David, H. P. (1981). Unwantedness: Longitudinal studies of Prague children born to women twice denied abortions for the same pregnancy and matched controls. In P. Ahmed (Ed.), *Pregnancy, childbirth, and parenthood.* New York: Elsevier.

Davies, M. M. (1997). *Fake, fact, and fantasy: Children's interpretations of television reality.* Mahwah, NJ: Erlbaum.

Davis, B. E., Moon, R. Y., Sachs, H. C., & Ottolini, M. C. (1998). Effects of sleep position on infant motor development. *Pediatrics, 102*(5), 1135–1140.

Davis, D. L., Wooley, J. D., & Bruell, M. J. (2002). Young children's understanding of the roles of knowledge and thinking in pretense. *British Journal of Developmental Psychology, 20*(1), 25–45.

Day, R., Peterson, G., & McCracken, C. (1998). Predicting spanking of younger and older children by mothers and fathers. *Journal of Marriage and the Family, 60,* 79–94.

De Villiers, J. G., & de Villiers, P. A. (1978). *Language acquisition.* Cambridge, MA: Harvard University Press.

De Vries, J. I., Hay V. G., & Prechtl, H. F. (1982). The emergence of fetal behaviour. I. Qualitative aspects. *Early Human Development, 7*(4), 301–322.

De Vries, M. W. (1987). Cry babies, culture, and catastrophe: Infant temperament among the Masai. In N. Scheper-Hughes (Ed.), *Child survival: Anthropological approaches to the treatment and maltreatment of children.* Boston: Reidel.

De Vries, M. W. (1994). Kids in context: Temperament in cross-cultural perspective. In W. B. Carey & S. C. Devitt (Eds.), *Prevention and early intervention: Individual differences as risk factors for the mental health of children.* New York: Brunner/Mazel.

De Vries, R. (1969). Constancy of genetic identity in the years three to six. *Monographs of the Society for Research in Child Development, 34* (Serial No. 127).

de Vrijer, B., Harthoorn-Lasthuizen, E. J., & Oosterbaan, H. P. (1999). The incidence of irregular antibodies in pregnancy: a prospective study in the region of the 's-Hertogenbosch. *Nederlands Tijdschrift voor Geneeskunde, 143*(5), 2523–2527.

de Waal, F. (2001). *The ape and the sushi master: Cultural reflections of a primatologist.* New York: Basic Books.

De Wolff, M., & van Ijzendoorn, M. H. (1997). Sensitivity and attachment: A meta-analysis on parental antecedents of infant attachment. *Child Development, 68*(4), 571–591.

Deak, G. O., Ray, S. D., & Brenneman, K. (2003). Children's perseverative appearance-reality errors are related to emerging language skills. *Child Development, 74,* 944–964.

Deater-Deckard, K., Pike, A., Petrill S. A., Cutting A. L., Hughes C., & O'Connor T. G. (2001). Nonshared environmental processes in social-emotional development: An observational study of identical twin differences in the preschool period. *Developmental Science, 4,* F1–F6.

DeCasper, A. J., & Spence M. J. (1986). Prenatal maternal speech influences newborn's perceptions of speech sounds. *Infant Behavior and Development, 3,* 133–150.

Delacour, J. (1999). The memory system and brain organization: From animal to human studies. In H. J. Markowtsch (Ed.), *Cognitive neuroscience of memory* (pp. 239–270). Kriland, WA: Hogrefe & Huber.

della Cava, M. R. (2002, June 25). The race to raise a brainier baby. *USA Today.*

DeLoache, J. S. (1995a). Early symbolic reasoning. In D. Medin (Ed.), *The Psychology of Learning and Motivation: Vol. 32.* New York: Academic Press.

DeLoache, J. S. (1995b). Early understanding and use of symbols: The model model. *Current Directions in Psychological Science, 4,* 109–113.

DeLoache, J. S. (2000). Dual representation and young children's use of scale models. *Child Development, 71*(2), 329–338.

DeLoache, J. S. (2002). The symbol-mindedness of young children. In W. Hartup & R. A. Weinberg (Eds.), *Child psychology in retrospect and prospect: In celebration of the 75th anniversary of the Institute of Child Development* (pp. 73–101). Mahwah, NJ: Erlbaum.

DeLoache, J. S., & Burns, N. M. (1994). Symbolic functioning in preschool children. *Journal of Applied Developmental Psychology, 15*(4), 513–527.

Denham, S., Caverly, S., Schmidt, M., Blair, K., DeMulder, E., Caal, S., Hamada, H., & Mason, T. (2002). Preschool understanding of emotions: Contributions to classroom anger and aggression. *Journal of Child Psychology and Psychiatry, 43,* 901–916.

Dennis, M., Sugar, J., & Whitaker, H. A. (1982). The acquisition of tag questions. *Child Development, 53,* 1254–1257.

Dennis, W. (1973). *Children of the creche.* New York: Appleton-Century-Crofts.

Dennis, W., & Dennis, M. (1940). The effect of cradling practices upon the onset of walking in Hopi children. *Journal of Genetic Psychology, 56,* 77–86.

Dent-Read, C. (1997). A naturalistic study of metaphor development: Seeing and seeing as. In C. Dent-Read & P. Zukow-Goldring (Eds.), *Evolving explanations of development* (pp. 255–296). Washington, DC: American Psychological Association.

Denzin, N. K., & Lincoln, Y. S. (2000). Introduction: The discipline and practice of qualitative research. In N. K. Denzin & Y. S. Lincoln (Eds.), *Handbook of qualitative research* (2nd ed., pp. 1–28), Thousand Oaks, CA: Sage Publications.

Desmond, R. (2001). Free reading: Implications for child development. In D. Singer & J. Singer (Eds.), *Handbook of children and the media.* Thousand Oaks, CA: Sage.

Devaney, B. L., Ellwood, M. R., & Love, J. M. (1997). Programs that mitigate against poverty. *The Future of Children, 7*(2), 88–112.

Diamond, A. (1991). Neuropsychological insights into the meaning of object concept development. In R. Gelman (Ed.), *The epigenesis of mind: Essays on biology and cognition* (pp. 67–110). Mahwah, NJ: Erlbaum.

Diamond, A. (2000). Close interrelation of motor development and cognitive development and of the cerebellum and prefrontal cortex. *Child Development, 71*(1), 44–56.

Diamond, A. (2002). A model system for studying the role of dopamine in prefrontal cortex during early development in humans. In M. H. Johnson & Y. Munakata (Eds.), *Brain development and cognition: A reader* (pp. 441–493). Malden, MA: Blackwell.

Dick, D., Rose, R., Viken, R., & Kaprio, J. (2000). Pubertal timing and substance use: Associations between and within families across late adolescence. *Developmental Psychology, 36,* 180–189.

Dickens, W. T., & Flynn, J. R. (2001). Heritability estimates versus large environmental effects: The IQ paradox resolved. *Psychological Review 108*(2): 346–369.

Diener, M. L., Nievar, M. A., & Wright, C. (2003). Attachment security among mothers and their young children living in poverty: Associations with maternal, child, and contextual factors. *Merrill-Palmer Quarterly, 49*(2), 154–182.

Dietz, T. (2000). Disciplining children: Characteristics associated with the use of corporal punishment. *Child Abuse and Neglect, 24,* 1529–1542.

Dietz, W. H., & Gortmacher, S. L. (1985). Do we fatten our children at the television set: Obesity and television viewing in children and adolescents. *Pediatrics, 75,* 807–812.

Dimant, R. J., & Bearison, D. J. (1991). Development of formal reasoning during successive peer interactions. *Developmental Psychology, 27*(2), 277–284.

Dishion, T. J. (1990). The family ecology of boys' peer relations in middle childhood. *Child Development, 61,* 874–892.

Dishion, T., Capaldi, K., Spracklen, K., & Li, F. (1995). Peer ecology of male adolescent drug use. *Development and Psychopathology, 7,* 803–824.

Dishion, T., McCord, J., & Poulin, F. (1999). When interventions harm. *American Psychologist, 54,* 755–764.

Dixon, A. C., Schoonmaker, C. T., & Philliber, W. W (2000). A journey toward womanhood: Effects of an Afrocentric approach to pregnancy prevention among African-American adolescent girls. *Adolescence, 35,* 425–429.

Dobbs, S. E. (1992). Conceptions of giftedness and talent: A Q-methodological study. *Dissertation Abstracts International, 52*(7).

Dodge, K. A. (1990). Developmental psychopathology in children of depressed mothers. *Developmental Psychology, 26,* 3–6.

Dodge, K. A., Lansford, J. E., Burks, V. S., Bates, J. E., Pettit, G. S., Fontaine, R., & Price, J. M. (2003). Peer rejection and social information-processing factors in the development of aggressive behavior problems in children. *Child Development, 74*(2), 374–393.

Domino, G. (1992). Cooperation and competition in Chinese and American children. *Journal of Cross-Cultural Psychology, 23*(4), 456–467.

Donald, M. (1991). *Origins of the modern mind: Three stages in the evolution of culture and cognition.* Cambridge, MA: Harvard University Press.

Donald, M. (2001). *A mind so rare: The evolution of human consciousness.* New York: Norton.

Dondi, M., Simion, F., & Caltran, G. (1999). Can newborns discriminate between their own cry and the cry of another newborn infant? *Developmental Psychology, 35*(3), 323–334.

Dore, J. (1979). Conversational acts and the acquisition of language. In E. Ochs & B. B. Schieffelin (Eds.), *Developmental Pragmatics.* New York: Academic Press.

Dore, J., Gearhart, M., & Newman, D. (1979). The structure of nursery school conversation. In K. E. Nelson (Ed.), *Children's language: Vol. 1.* Mahwah, NJ: Erlbaum.

Dorr, A. (1983). No shortcuts to judging reality. In P. E. Bryant & S. Anderson (Eds.), *Watching and understanding TV: Research on children's attention and comprehension.* New York: Academic Press.

Dorval, B. (Ed.). (1990). *Conversational organization and its development*. Norwood, NJ: Ablex.

Dossett, D., & Burns, B. (2000). The development of children's knowledge of attention and resource allocation in single and dual tasks. *The Journal of Genetic Psychology 16*(2), 216–234.

Douvan, E., & Adelson, J. (1966). *The adolescent experience*. New York: Wiley.

Dromi, E. (1999). Early lexical development. In M. Barrett (Ed.), *The development of language* (pp. 99–131). Philadelphia: Psychology Press/Taylor & Francis.

Duncan, G. J., & Brooks-Gunn, J. (Eds.). (1997). *Consequences of growing up poor*. New York: Russell Sage Foundation.

Duncan, G., & Raudenbush, W. (1999). Assessing the effects of context in studies of children and youth development. *Educational Psychology, 34,* 29–41.

Duncan, P. D., Ritter, P. L., Dornbusch, S. M., Gross, R. T., & Carlsmith, J. M. (1985). The effects of pubertal timing on body image, school behavior, and deviance. *Journal of Youth and Adolescence, 14,* 227–235.

Dunkel, C., & Anthis, K. (2001). The role of possible selves in identity formation: A short-term longitudinal study. *Journal of Adolescence, 24,* 765–776.

Dunn, J. (1988). *The beginnings of social understanding*. Cambridge, MA: Harvard University Press.

Dunn, J. (2002). Sibling relationships. In P. Smith and C. Hart (Eds.), *Blackwood handbook of childhood social development*. Malden, MA: Blackwell.

Dunn, J., Deater-Deckard, K., Pickering, K., & O'Connor, T. G. (1998). Children's adjustment and prosocial behavior in step-, single-parent, and non-stepfamily settings: Findings from a community study. *Journal of Child Psychology and Psychiatry & Allied Disciplines, 39*(8), 1083–1095.

Dunphy, D. C. (1963). The social structure of urban adolescent peer groups. *Sociometry, 26,* 230–246.

Durston, S., Hulshoff, P., Hilleke, E., Casey, B. J., Giedd, J. N., Buitelaar, J. K., & van Engeland, H. (2001). Anatomical MRI of the developing human brain: What have we learned? *Journal of the American Academy of Child and Adolescent Psychiatry, 40*(9), 1012–1020.

Dweck, C. S. (1999). *Self-theories: Their role in motivation, personality, and development*. Philadelphia, PA: Psychology Press/Taylor & Francis.

Dweck, C. S. (2001). The development of ability conceptions. In A. Wigfield & J. S. Eccles (Eds.), *The development of achievement motivation* (pp. 57–91). San Diego: Academic Press.

Dybdahl, R. (2001). A psychosocial support programme for children and mothers in war. *Clinical Child Psychology and Psychiatry, 6,* 425–436.

Dyson, A. (2003). "Welcome to the Jam": Popular culture, school literacy, and the making of childhoods. *Harvard Educational Review, 73,* 328–361.

Dyson, M. E. (1996). *Between God and gangsta rap: Bearing witness to black culture*. New York: Oxford University Press.

Eagly, A., Wood, W., & Diekman, A. (2000). Social role theory of sex differences and similarities: A current appraisal. In T. Eckes & H. Trautner (Eds.), *The developmental social psychology of gender*. Mahwah, NJ: Lawrence Erlbaum.

Eccles, J., Templeton, J., Barber, B., & Stone, M. (2003). Adolescence and emerging adulthood: The critical passageways to adulthood. In M. H. Bornstein, L. Davidson, C. L. Keyes, K. A. Moore, & the Center for Child Well Being (Eds.), *Well-being: Positive development across the life course. Crosscurrents in contemporary psychology* (pp. 383–406). Mahwah, NJ: Erlbaum.

Eckenrode, J., Laird, M., & Doris, J. (1993). School performance and disciplining problems among abused and neglected children. *Developmental Psychology, 29,* 53–62.

Eckert, P. (1995). Trajectory and forms of institutional participation. In L. J. Crockett & A. C. Crouter (Eds.), *Pathways through adolescence: Individual development in relation to social contexts* (pp. 175–195). Mahwah, NJ: Erlbaum.

Eckes, T., & Trautner, H. (Eds.). (2000). *The developmental social psychology of gender*. Mahwah, NJ: Erlbaum.

Edelman, G. M. (1992). *Bright air, brilliant fire: On the matter of the mind*. New York: Basic Books.

Edwards, C. P., & Whiting, B. B. (1993). "Mother, older sibling and me": The overlapping roles of caregivers and companions in the social world of two- to three-year-olds in Ngeca, Kenya. In K. MacDonald (Ed.), *Parent-child play: Descriptions and implications* (pp. 305–329). Albany, NY: State University of New York Press.

Edwards, V. J., Holden, G. W., Felitti, V. J., & Anda, R. F. (2003). Relationship between multiple forms of childhood maltreatment and adult mental health in community respondents: Results from the Adverse Childhood Experiences study. *American Journal of Psychiatry, 160,* 1453–1460.

Eggebeen, D. J. (2002). The changing course of fatherhood: Men's experiences with children in demographic perspective. *Journal of Family Issues, 23,* 486–505.

Eimas, P. D. (1985). The perception of speech in early infancy. *Scientific American, 252*(1), 66–72.

Eisen, M., Zellman, G. I., Leibowitz, A., Chow, W. K., & Evans, J. R. (1983). Factors discriminating pregnancy resolution decisions of unmarried adolescents. *Genetic Psychology Monographs, 108,* 69–95.

Eisenberg, N. (1992). *The caring child*. Cambridge, MA: Harvard University Press.

Eisenberg, N., & Fabes, R. A. (1992). Emotion, regulation, and the development of social competence. *Review of Personality and Social Psychology, 14,* 119–150.

Eisenberg, N., & Fabes, R. (1998). Prosocial development. In W. Damon & N. Eisenberg (Eds.), *Handbook of child psychology: Vol. 3. Social, emotional, and personality development* (5th ed., pp. 701–778). New York: Wiley.

Eisenberg, N., Fabes, R., Murphy, B., Karbon, M., Smith, M., & Maszk, P. (1996). The relations of children's dispositional empathy-related responding to their emotionality, regulation, and social functioning. *Developmental Psychology, 32,* 195–209.

Eisenberg, N., Fabes, R., Shepard, S., Murphy, B., Jones, J., & Guthrie, I. (1998). Contemporaneous and longitudinal prediction of children's sympathy from dispositional regulation and emotionality. *Developmental Psychology, 34,* 910–924.

Eisenberg, N., Losoya, S., & Spinrad, T. (2003). Affect and prosocial responding. In R. Davidson, K. Scherer, & H. Goldsmith (Eds.), *Handbook of affective sciences*. Oxford: Oxford University Press.

Eisenberg, N., Zhou, Q., & Koller, S. (2001). Brazilian adolescents' prosocial moral judgement and behavior: Relationships to sympathy, perspective taking, gender-role orientation, and demographic characteristics. *Child Development, 72,* 518–534.

Ekman, P. (1999). Facial expressions. In T. Dalgleish & M. J. Power (Eds.), *Handbook of cognition and emotion* (pp. 301–320). Chichester, England: Wiley.

Elder, G. H. J. (1998). The life course and human development. In W. Damon & R. M. Lerner (Eds.), *Handbook of child psychology: Vol 1. Theoretical models of human development* (5th ed., pp. 939–992). New York: Wiley.

Eley, T. C., Lichtenstein, P., & Stevenson, J. (1999). Sex differences in the etiology of aggressive and nonaggressive antisocial behavior: Results from two twin studies. *Child Development, 70*(1), 155–168.

Elfenbein, H. A., & Ambady, N. (2003). Universals and cultural differences in recognizing emotions. *Current Directions in Psychological Science, 12*(5), 159–164.

Elias, C., & Berk, L. (2002). Self-regulation in young children: Is there a role for sociodramatic play? *Early Childhood Research Quarterly, 17,* 216–238.

Ellis, L. (1996a). The role of perinatal factors in determining sexual orientation. In R. C. Savin-Williams & K. M. Cohen (Eds.), *The lives of lesbians, gays, and bisexuals: Children to adults.* (pp. 35–70). Fort Worth, TX: Harcourt-Brace College Publishers.

Ellis, S. A., & Gauvain, M. (1992). Social and cultural influences on children's collaborative interactions. In L. T. Winegar & J. Valsiner (Eds.), *Children's development within social context* (pp. 155–180). Mahwah, NJ: Erlbaum.

Ellis, S. J., Kitzinger, C., & Wilkinson, S. (2002). Attitudes towards lesbians and gay men and support for lesbian and gay human rights among psychology students. *Journal of Homosexuality, 44*(1), 121–138.

Ellis, S., & Siegler, R. S. (1997). Planning as a strategy choice, or why don't children plan when they should? In S. L. Friedman & E. K. Scholnick (Eds.), *The developmental psychology of planning: Why, how, and when do we plan?* (pp. 183–208). Mahwah, NJ: Erlbaum.

Ellis, S., Rogoff, B., & Cromer, C. (1981). Age segregation in children's interactions. *Developmental Psychology, 17,* 399–407.

Elman, J. L., Bates, E. A., Johnson, M. J., Karmilof-Smith, A., Parsi, D., & Plunkett, K. (1996). *Rethinking innateness: A connectionist perspective on development.* Cambridge, Mass: MIT Press.

Emde, R. N., Gaensbauer, T. J., & Harmon, R. J. (1976). Emotional expression in infancy: A behavioral study. *Psychological Issues Monograph Series, 10*(1, No. 37).

Emde, R. N., & Hewitt, J. K. (Eds). (2001a). *Infancy and early childhood.* Oxford: Oxford University Press.

Emde, R. N., & Hewitt, J. K. (Eds). (2001b). *Infancy to early childhood: Genetic and environmental influences on developmental change.* New York: Oxford University Press.

Emde, R. N., & Robinson, J. (1979). The first two months: Recent research in developmental psychobiology and the changing view of the newborn. In J. Noshpitz & J. Call (Eds.), *Basic handbook of child psychiatry.* New York: Basic Books.

Engel, G. L., Reichman, F., Harway, V. T., & Hess, D. W. (1985). Monica: Infant-feeding behavior of a mother gastric fistula-fed as an infant: A 30-year longitudinal study of enduring effects. In E. J. Anthony & G. H. Pollack (Eds.), *Parental Influences in Health and Disease* (pp. 29–90). Boston: Little, Brown & Co.

Epstein, L. H., McCurley, J., Wing, R. R., & Valoski, A. (1990). A five-year follow-up of family-based behavioral treatments for childhood obesity. *Journal of Consulting and Clinical Psychology, 58,* 661–664.

Epstein, L. H., Valoski, A., & McCurley, J. (1993). Compliance and long-term follow-up for childhood obesity: Retrospective analysis. In N. A. Krasnegor, L. H. Epstein, S. B. Johnson, & S. J. Yaffe (Eds.), *Developmental aspects of health compliance behavior.* Mahwah, NJ: Erlbaum.

Erel, O., Margolin, G., & Joh, R. S. (1998). Observed sibling interaction: Links with the marital and mother–child relationship. *Developmental Psychology, 34*(2), 288–298.

Erickson, F., & Mohatt, G. (1982). Cultural organization of participation structures in two classrooms of Indian students. In G. Spindler (Ed.), *Doing the ethnography of schooling: Educational anthropology in action* (pp. 132–175). Prospect Heights, IL: Waveland Press.

Erikson, E. (1959). *Identity and the life cycle: Selected papers.* New York: International Universities Press.

Erikson, E. H. (1964/1993). *Childhood and society.* New York: Norton.

Erikson, E. H. (1968a). *Identity: Youth and crisis.* New York: W. W. Norton.

Erikson, E. H. (1968b). Life cycle. In D. L. Sills (Ed.), *International encyclopedia of the social sciences, Vol. 9.* New York: Crowell, Collier.

Erikson, E. H. (1987). *A way of looking at things: Selected papers from 1930 to 1980* (S. Schlein, Ed.). New York: Norton.

Erikson, M. F., Sroufe, L. A., & Egeland, B. (1985). The relationship between the quality of attachment and behavior problems in preschool in a high-risk sample. *Monographs of the Society for Research in Child Development, 50,* 1–2, No. 209.

Estell, D. B., Farmer, T. W., Cairns, R. B., & Cairns, B. D. (2002). Social relations and academic achievement in inner-city early elementary classrooms. *International Journal of Behavioral Development, 26*(6), 518–528.

Estes, D. (1998). Young children's awareness of their mental activity: The case of mental rotation. *Child Development, 69*(5), 1345–1360.

Estevez, P. A., Held, C. M., Holtzmann, C.A., Perez, C. A., Perez, J. P., Heiss, J., Garrido, M., & Peirano, P. (2002). Polysomnographic pattern recognition for automated classification of sleep-waking states in infants. *Medical and Biological Engineering and Computing, 40*(1), 105–113.

Eyer, D. E. (1992). *Mother-infant bonding: A scientific fiction.* New Haven, CT: Yale University Press.

Eyler, F. D., & Behnke, M. (1999). Early development of infants exposed to drugs prenatally. *Clinical Perinatology, 26*(1), 107–150.

Fabes, R. A., Eisenberg, N., Nyman, M., & Michealieu, Q. (1991). Young children's appraisals of others' spontaneous emotional reactions. *Developmental Psychology, 27*(5): 858–866.

Fabricus, W. V., & Hagen, J. W. (1984). Use of casual attributions about recall performance to assess metamemory and predict strategic memory behavior in young children. *Developmental Psychology, 20,* 975–987.

Fagot, B. I. (1995). Psychosocial and cognitive determinants of early gender-role development. *Annual Review of Sex Research, 6,* 1–31.

Fan, G. X., Qing, L. X., Jun, Y., & Mei, Z. (1999). Molecular studies and prenatal diagnosis of phenylkletonuria in Chinese patients. *Southeast Asian Journal of Tropical Medicine & Public Health, 30* (Supplement 2), 63–65.

Fanaroff, A. A., & Martin, R. J. (Eds.). (1997). *Neonatal-perinatal medicine: Diseases of the fetus and infant.* St. Louis, MO: Mosby.

Fant, L. (1972). *Ameslan.* Silver Springs, MD: National Association for the Deaf.

Fantz, R. L. (1961). The origins of form perception. *Scientific American, 204* (5) 66–72.

Fantz, R. L. (1963). Pattern vision in newborn infants. *Science, 140,* 296–297.

Fantz, R. L., Ordy, J. M., & Udelf, M. S. (1962). Maturation of pattern vision in infants during the first six months. *Journal of Comparative Physiological Psychology, 55,* 907–917.

Farver, J. M., & Wimbarti, S. (1995). Indonesian children's play with their mothers and older siblings. *Child Development, 66,* 1493–1503.

Feiring, C. (1996). Lovers as friends: Developing couscious views of romance in adolescence. *Journal of Research on Adolescence, 7,* 214–224.

Feiring, C., & Taska, L. S. (1996). Family self-concept: Ideas on its meaning. In B. A. Bracken (Ed.), *Handbook of self-concept: Developmental, social, and clinical considerations.* New York: Wiley.

Feldman, H., Goldin-Meadow, S., & Gleitman, L. (1978). Beyond Herodotus: The creation of language by linguistically deprived, deaf children. In A. Lock (Ed.), *Action, symbol, and gesture: The emergence of language.* New York: Academic Press.

Fenson, L., Dale, P. S., Reznick, J. S., Bates, E., Thal, O. J., & Pettnick, S. J. (1994). Variability in early communicative development. *Monographs for Research in Child Development, 59*(5, Serial No. 242).

Fernald, A. (1991). Prosody in speech to children: Prelinguistic and linguistic functions. In R. Vasta (Ed.), *Annals of child development, Vol. 8.* London: Kingley.

Fernald, A. (2001). Hearing, listening, and understanding: Auditory development in infancy. In G. Bremner & A. Fogel (Eds.), *Blackwell handbook of infant development* (pp. 35–70). Malden, MA: Blackwell.

Ferrer-Wreder, L., Lorente, C. C., Kurtines, W., Briones, E., Bussell, J., Berman, S., & Arrufat, O. (2002). Promoting identity development in marginalized youth. *Journal of Adolescent Research, 17*(2), 168–187.

Field, A., Camargo, C., Taylor, C., Berkey, C., & Colditz, G. (1999). Relation of peer and media influences to the development of purging behaviors among preadolescent and adolescent girls. *Archives of Pediatric and Adolescent Medicine, 153,* 1184–1189.

Field, T. (1995). Infants of depressed mothers. *Infant Behavior & Development, 18*(1), 1–13.

Field, T. (1997). The treatment of depressed mothers and their infants. In L. Murray & P. J. Cooper (Eds.), *Postpartum depression and child development* (pp. 221–236). New York: Guilford Press.

Field, T. M., Diego, M., Dieter, J., Hernandez-Reif, M., Schanberg, S., Kuhn, C., et al. (2001). Depressed withdrawn and intrusive mothers' effects on their fetuses and neonates. *Infant Behavior and Development, 24,* 27–39.

Field, T. M., Diego, M., & Sanders, C. (2001). Exercise is positively related to adolescents' relationships and academics. *Adolescence, 36,* 106–110.

Field, T. M., Woodson, R., Greenberg, R., & Cohen, D. (1982). Discrimination and imitation of facial expressions by neonates. *Science, 218,* 179–182.

Fifer, W. P., & Moon, C. M. (1995). The effects of fetal experience with sound. In J. P. Lecanuet, W. P. Fifer, N. A. Krasnegor, & W. P. Smotherman (Eds.), *Fetal development: A psychobiological perspective.* Mahwah, NJ: Erlbaum.

Finch, M. D., Mortimer, J. T., & Ryu, S. (1997). Transition into part-time work: Health risks and opportunities. In J. Schulenberg & J. L. Maggs (Eds.), *Health risks and developmental transitions during adolescence* (pp. 321–344). New York: Cambridge University Press.

Fine, G. A. (1987). *With the boys: Little League Baseball and preadolescent culture.* Chicago: University of Chicago Press.

Finkelhor, D., & Dziuba-Leatherman, J. (1995). Victimization prevention programs: A national survey of children's exposure and reactions. *Child Abuse & Neglect, 19*(2), 129–139.

Finnegan, R. A., Hodges, E. V. E., & Perry, D. G. (1998). Victimization by peers: Associations with children's reports of mother–child interaction. *Journal of Personality & Social Psychology, 75*(4), 1076–1086.

Fischer, K. W., Bullock, D., Rotenberg, E. J., & Raya, P. (1993). The dynamics of competence: How context contributes directly to skill. In R. H. Wozniak & K. W. Fischer (Eds.), *Development in context: Acting and thinking in specific environments* (pp. 93–117). Mahwah, NJ: Erlbaum.

Fischer, K. W., & Pare-Blagoev, J. (2000). From individual differences to dynamic pathways of development. *Child Development 71*(4): 850–853.

Fischer, K. W., & Rose, S. P. (1996). Dynamic growth cycles of brain and development. In R. Thatcher, G. R. Lyon, J. Rumsey, & N. Krasnegor (Eds.), *Developmental neuroimaging: Mapping the development of brain and behavior.* New York: Academic Press.

Fischer, K. W., & Yan, Z. (2002). The development of dynamic skill theory. In R. Lickliter & D. Lewkowicz (Eds.), *Conceptions of development: Lessons from the laboratory.* Hove, UK: Psychology Press.

Fishbein, H. D. (1976). *Evolution, development and children's learning.* Pacific Palisades, CA: Goodyear.

Fivush, R. (1998). Gendered narratives: Elaboration, structure, and emotion in parent–child reminiscing across the preschool years. In P. Thompson & D. J. Herrmann (Eds.), *Autobiographical memory: Theoretical and applied perspectives* (pp. 79–103). Mahwah, NJ: Erlbaum.

Flammer, A., Alsaker, F. & Noak, P. (1999). The case of leisure activities. In F. Alsaker & A. Flammer (Eds.), *The adolescent experience: European and American adolescents in the 1990s.* Mahwah, NJ: Erlbaum.

Flavell, J. H. (1971). Stage-related properties of cognitive development. *Cognitive Psychology, 2,* 421–453.

Flavell, J. H., Flavell, E. R., Green, F. L., & Korfmacher, J. E. (1990b). Do young children think of television images as pictures or real objects? *Journal of Broadcasting & Electronic Media, 34,* 339–419.

Flavell, J. H., Friedrichs, A. G., & Hoyt, J. D. (1970). Developmental changes in memorization processes. *Cognitive Psychology, 1,* 324–340.

Flavell, J. H., Green, F. L., & Flavell, E. R. (1986). Development of knowledge about the appearance-reality distinction. *Monographs of the Society for Research in Child Development, 51*(1, Serial No. 212).

Flavell, J. H., Green, F. L., & Flavell, E. R. (1995). Young children's knowledge about thinking. *Monographs of the Society for Research in Child Development, 60*(1, Serial No. 243), 1–95.

Fletcher, A. C., Darling, N. E., Steinberg, L., & Dornbusch, S. (1995). The company they keep: Relation of adolescents' adjustment and behavior to their friends; perceptions of authoritative parenting in the social network. *Developmental Psychology, 31,* 300–310.

Flowers, P., & Buston, K. (2002). "I was terrified of being different": Exploring gay men's accounts of growing up in a heterosexist society. *Journal of Adolescence, 24,* 51–65.

Flynn, J. R. (1999). Searching for justice: The discovery of IQ gains over time. *American Psychologist, 54*(1), 5–20.

Fodor, J. (1983). *The modularity of mind.* Cambridge, MA: MIT Press.

Fonagy, P. (2001). *Attachment theory and psychoanalysis.* New York: Other Press.

Forbus, K. D, & Feltovich P. J. (Eds.). (2001). *Smart machines in education: The coming revolution in educational technology.* Cambridge, MA: MIT Press.

Fordham, S., & Ogbu, J. U. (1986). Black students' school success: Coping with the "burden of 'acting white.'" *Urban Review, 18*(3), 176–206.

Foreman, N., Fielder, A., Minshell, C., Hurrion, E., & Sergienko, E. (1997). Visual search, perception, and visual–motor skill in "healthy" children born at 27–32 weeks' gestation. *Journal of Experimental Child Psychology, 64*(1), 27–41.

Forgays, D. G., & Forgays, J. W. (1952). The nature of the effect of free-environmental experience in the rat. *Journal of Comparative and Physiological Psychology, 45,* 322–328.

Forman, M. (2002). Keeping it real: African youth identities and hip hop. In R. Young (Ed.), *Critical Studies, 19, Music, popular culture, identities.* New York: Rodopi.

Fox, N., & Bell, M. A. (1990). Electrophysiological indices of frontal lobe development. *Annals of the New York Academy of Sciences, 608,* 677–704.

Fraiberg, S. H. (1959). *The magic years: Understanding and handling the problems of early childhood.* New York: Scribner.

Fraiberg, S. H. (1974). Blind infants and their mothers: An examination of the sign system. In M. Lewis & L. Rosenblum (Eds.), *The effect of the infant on its caregiver.* New York: Wiley.

Frankel, K., & Bates, J. (1990). Mother-toddler problem solving: Antecedents in attachment, home behavior, and temperament. *Child Development, 61,* 810–819.

Frankenburg, W. K., Fandal, A. W., Sciarillo, W., & Burgess, D. (1981). The newly abbreviated and revised Denver Developmental Screening Test. *Behavioral Pediatrics, 99*(6), 995–999.

Freed, K. (1983, March 14). Cubatao—a paradise lost to pollution. *Los Angeles Times,* pp. 1, 12, 13.

Freud, S. (1905/1953a). Three essays on the theory of sexuality. In J. Strachey (Ed.), *The standard edition of the complete psychological works of Sigmund Freud: Vol. 7.* London: Hogarth Press.

Freud, S. (1920/1924). The psychogenesis of a case of homosexuality in a woman (B. Low and R. Gabler, Trans.). *Collected papers: Vol. 2.* London: Hogarth Press.

Freud, S. (1920/1955). Beyond the pleasure principle. In J. Strachey (Ed.), *The standard edition of the complete psychological works of Sigmund Freud: Vol. 18.* London: Hogarth Press.

Freud, S. (1921/1949). Group psychology—The analysis of the ego. In J. Strachey (Ed.), *The standard edition of the complete psychological works of Sigmund Freud: Vol. 18.* London: Hogarth Press.

Freud, S. (1925/1961). Some psychical consequences of the anatomical distinctions between the sexes. In J. Strachey (Ed.), *The standard edition of the complete psychological works of Sigmund Freud: Vol. 19.* London: Hogarth Press.

Freud, S. (1933/1964). *New introductory lectures in psychoanalysis.* New York: W. W. Norton.

Freud, S. (1940/1964). An outline of psychoanalysis. In J. Strachey (Ed.), *The standard edition of the complete psychological works of Sigmund Freud: Vol. 32.* London: Hogarth Press.

Freud, S. (1963). *Jokes and their relation to the unconscious.* Oxford, UK: W. W. Norton.

Frid, C., Drott, P., Lundell, B., Rasmussen, F., & Anneren, G. (1999). Mortality in Down's syndrome in relation to congenital malformations. *Journal of Intellectual Disability Research, 43*(3), 234–241.

Friedman, H. S., Tucker, J. S., Schwartz, J. E., Tomlinson–Keasey, C., Martin, L. R., Wingard, D. L., & Criqui, M. H. (1995). Psychosocial and behavioral predictors of longevity. *American Psychologist, 50(2),* 69–78.

Frith, U. (1989). *Autism.* Oxford: Oxford University Press.

Frith, U. (2003). *Autism: Explaining the enigma* (2nd ed.). Oxford, UK: Blackwell.

Fry, D. P. (1988). Intercommunity differences in aggression among Zapotec children. *Child Development, 59,* 1008–1018.

Frye, D. (2000). Theory of mind, domain specificity, and reasoning. In K. J. Riggs & P. Mitchell, *Children's reasoning and the mind* (pp. 149–167). Hove, UK: Psychology Press/Taylor & Francis.

Fuligni, A. (1998). Authority, autonomy, and parent-adolescent conflict and cohesion: A study of adolescents from Mexican, Chinese, Filipino, and European backgrounds. *Developmental Psychology, 34,* 782–792.

Fuligni, A. J., & Eccles, J. S. (1993). Perceived parent–child relationships and early adolescents' orientation toward peers. *Developmental Psychology, 29,* 622–632.

Fuligni, A. J., & Stevenson, H. W. (1995). Time use and mathematics achievement among American, Chinese, and Japanese high school students. *Child Development, 66*(3), 830–842.

Fullard, W., & Reiling, A. M. (1976). An investigation of Lorenz's babyness. *Child Development, 47,* 1191–1193.

Furman, L., & Kennell, J. (2000). Breastmilk and skin-to-skin kangaroo care for premature infants: Avoiding bonding failure. *Acta Paediatrica, 89,* 1280–1283.

Furman, W. (1999). The role of peer relationships in adolescent romantic relationships. In W. A. Collins & B. Larsen (Eds.), *Minnesota Symposium on Child Development: Vol 29. Relationships as developmental contexts* (pp. 133–154). Mahwah, NJ: Erlbaum.

Furman, W., Rahe, D. F., & Hartup, W. W. (1979). Rehabilitation of socially withdrawn preschool children through mixed-age and same-age socialization. *Child Development, 50(4),* 915–922.

Furstenberg, F. (1998). Social capital and the role of fathers in the family. In A. Booth & N. Crouter (Eds.), *Men in families: When do they get involved? What difference does it make?* Mahwah, NJ: Erlbaum.

Furstenberg, F. F., Jr., Hughes, M. E., & Brooks-Gunn, J. (1992). The next generation: The children of teenage mothers grow up. In M. Rosenheim & M. F. Testa (Eds.), *Early parenthood and coming of age in the 1990's.* New Brunswick, NJ: Rutgers University Press.

Futuyma, D. J. (1998). *Evolutionary biology* (3rd ed.). Sunderland, MA: Sinauer Associates.

Gagnon, J. H., & Simon, W. (1973). *Sexual conduct: The social sources of human sexuality.* Chicago: Aldine.

Gallego, M. A., Cole, M., & Laboratory of Comparitive Human Cognition. (2000). Classroom culture and culture in the classroom. In V. Richardson (Ed.), *The Handbook of Research on Teaching.* Washington, DC: American Educational Research Association.

Gallup, G. G. J. (1970). Chimpanzees: Self-recognition. *Science, 167,* 86–87.

Gamper, E. (1926). Bau and Leistungen eines menschichen Mitteilhirnwesens (Arhinencephalie mit Encephalocele). Zugleich ein Beitrag zu Teratologie und Fasersystematik. *Zeitschr. f.d.ges. Neurol. u. Psychiat, vii*(154, civ. 149).

Garcia, M., Shaw, D., Winslow, E., & Yaggi, K. (2000). Destructive sibling conflict and the development of conduct problems in young boys. *Developmental Psychology, 36,* 44–53.

Gardner, H. (1983). *Frames of mind: The theory of multiple intelligences.* New York: Basic Books.

Gardner, H. (1999). *Intelligence reframed: Multiple intelligences for the 21st century.* New York: Basic Books.

Gardner, H., Wolf, D., & Smith, A. (1982). Max and Molly: Individual differences in early artistic symbolization. In H. Gardner (Ed.), *Art, mind and brain: A cognitive approach to creativity.* New York: Basic Books.

Gardner, W., & Rogoff, B. (1990). Children's deliberateness of planning according to task circumstances. *Developmental Psychology, 26,* 480–487.

Garland, D. (2003). *The culture of control: Crime and social order in contemporary society.* Chicago: University of Chicago Press.

Garrod, A., Smulyan, L., Powers, S., & Kilkenny, R. (Eds.). (1999). *Adolescent portraits: Identity, relationships, and challenges.* Boston: Allyn & Bacon.

Garrow, I., & Werne, J. (1953). Sudden apparently unexplained death during infancy: III. Pathological findings in infants dying immediately after violence, contrasted with those after sudden apparently unexplained death. *American Journal of Pathology, 29*(5), 833–851.

Garton, A., & Pratt, C. (1998). *Learning to be literate: The development of spoken and written language.* Oxford: Blackwell.

Garvey, C., & Berndt, R. (1977). Organization of pretend play. *Catalog of Selected Documents in Psychology, 7,* 107.

Gaskins, S. (1999). Children's daily lives in a Mayan village: A case study of culturally constructed roles and activities. In A. Göncü (Ed.), *Children's engagement in the world: Sociocultural perspectives* (pp. 25–61). New York: Cambridge University Press.

Gaskins, S. (2000). Children's daily activities in a Mayan village: A culturally grounded description. *Cross-Cultural Research: The Journal of Comparative Social Science. Special Issue in Honor of Ruth H. Munroe: Part I, 34*(4), 375–389.

Gay, J. (1984). *Red dust on the green leaves: A Kpelle twins' childhood.* Yarmouth, ME: Intercultural Press.

Gay, J., & Cole, M. (1967). *The new mathematics and an old culture.* New York: Holt, Rinehart, and Winston.

Geertz, C. (1984). From the native's point of view: On the nature of anthropological understanding. In R. Shweder & R. Levine (Eds.), *Culture theory.* Cambridge, UK: Cambridge University Press.

Geiger, B. (1996). *Fathers as primary caregivers.* Westport, CT: Greenwood.

Gelis, J. (1991). *History of childbirth.* Cambridge, UK: Polity Press.

Gelman, R. (1990). First principles affect learning and transfer in children. *Cognitive Science, 14,* 79–107.

Gelman, R. (1998). Domain specificity in cognitive development: Universals and nonuniversals. In M. Sabourin & F. Craik (Eds.), *Advances in psychological science: Vol. 2. Biological and cognitive aspects* (pp. 557–579). Hove, UK: Psychology Press/Erlbaum.

Gelman, R., & Lucariello, J. (2002). Role of learning in cognitive development. In R. Gallistel (Ed.), *Stevens' handbook of experimental psychology: Vol. 3* (pp. 395–444). New York: Wiley.

Gelman, R., Meck, E., & Merkin, S. (1986). Young children's mathematical competence. *Cognitive Development, 1,* 1–29.

Genovese, E. D. (1976). *Roll, Jordan, roll.* New York: Random House.

George, C., & Solomon, J. (1999). Attachment and caregiving: The caregiving behavioral systems. In J. Cassidy & P. R. Shaver (Eds.), *The handbook of attachment: Theory, research, and clinical applications* (pp. 649–670). New York: Guilford Press.

Georgieff, M. K., & Raghavendra, R. (2001). The role of nutrition in cognitive development. In C. A. Nelson and M. Luciana (Eds.), *Handbook of developmental cognitive neuroscience* (pp. 491–504). Cambridge, MA: M.I.T. Press.

Gergely, G. (2002). The development of understanding self and agency. In U. Goswami (Ed.), *Blackwell handbook of childhood cognitive development* (pp. 26–46). Malden, MA: Blackwell.

Gesell, A. (1940). *The first five years of life* (9th ed.). New York: Harper & Row.

Gesell, A., & Ilg, F. L. (1943). *Infant and child in the culture of today.* New York: Harper & Row.

Gewirtz, J. L., & Pelaez-Nogueras, M. (1992). B. F. Skinner's legacy in human infant behavior and development. *American Psychologist, 47*(11), 1411–1422.

Gibson, E. J. (1988). Exploratory behavior in the development of perceiving, acting, and the acquiring of knowledge. *Annual Review of Psychology, 39,* 1–41.

Gibson, E. J., & Pick, A. D. (2000). *An ecological approach to perceptual learning and development.* London: Oxford University Press.

Giedd, J. N., Blumenthal, J., Jeffries, N. O., Castellanos, F. X., Liu, H., Zijdenbos, A., et al. (1999a). Brain development during childhood and adolescence: A longitudinal MRI study. *Nature Neuroscience, 2*(10), 861–863.

Giedd, J. N., Blumenthal, J., Jeffries, N. O., Rajapakse, J. C., Vaituzis, A. C., Liu, H., et al. (1999b). Development of the human corpus collosum during childhood and adolescence: A longitudinal MRI study. *Progress in Neuro-Psychopharmacology & Biological Psychiatry, 23,* 571–588.

Gielen, U. P., & Markoulis, D. C. (2001). Preference for principled moral reasoning: A developmental and cross-cultural perspective. In L. L. Adler & U. P. Gielen (Eds.), *Cross-cultural topics in psychology* (2nd ed., pp. 81–101). Westport, CT: Praeger.

Gilbert, S. F. (2001). Ecological developmental biology: Developmental biology meets the real world. *Developmental Biology, 233*(1), 1–12.

Giles, J., & Heyman, G. (2003). Preschoolers' beliefs about the stability of antisocial behavior: Implications for navigating social challenges. *Social Development, 12,* 182–197.

Gilligan, C. (1982). *In a different voice: Psychological theory and women's development.* Cambridge, MA: Harvard University Press.

Gilman, S., Kawachi, I., Fitzmaurice, G., & Buka, S. (2003). Family disruption in childhood and risk of adult depression. *The American Journal of Psychiatry, 160,* 939–946.

Ginsburg, H. (1977). *Children's arithmetic.* New York: Van Nostrand.

Gleitman, H. (1963). *Psychology.* New York: W. W. Norton.

Godfrey, K. M., & Barker, D. J. P. (2000). Fetal nutrition and adult disease. *American Journal of Clinical Nutrition, 71*(Suppl. 5), 1344S–1352S.

Golan, M., Fainaru, M., & Weizman, A. (1998). Role of behaviour modification in the treatment of childhood obesity with the parents as the exclusive agents of change. *International Journal of Obesity and Related Metabolic Disorders, 22*(12), 1217–1224.

Goldin-Meadow, S. (2003). *The resilience of language: What gesture creation in deaf children can tell us about how all children learn language.* New York: Psychology Press.

Goldin-Meadow, S., & Mylander, C. (1998). Spontaneous sign systems created by deaf children in two cultures. *Nature, 391,* 279–281.

Goldsmith, H. H., & Campos, J. J. (1982). Toward a theory of infant temperament. In R. N. Emde & R. Harmon (Eds.), *The development of attachment and affiliative systems.* New York: Plenum Press.

Goldstein, A. P., Glick, B., & Gibbs, J. C. (1998). Aggression replacement training: a comprehensive intervention for aggressive youth (Rev. ed.). Champaign, IL: Research Press.

Golinkoff, R. M., Hirsh-Pasek, K., & Schweisguth, M. A. (1999). A reappraisal of young children's knowledge of grammatical morphemes. In J. Weissenborn & B. Hoehle (Eds.), *Approaches to bootstrapping: Phonological, syntactic, and neurophysiological aspects of early language acquisition.* Amsterdam and Philadelphia: John Benjamins.

Golinkoff, R. M., Mervis, C. B., & Hirsh-Pasek, K. (1994). Early object labels: The case for a developmental lexical principles framework. *Journal of Child Language, 21,* 125–155.

Golinkoff, R. M., Shuff-Bailey, M., Olguin, R., & Ruan, W. (1995). Young children extend novel words at the basic level: Evidence for the principle of categorical scope. *Developmental Psychology, 31*(3), 494–507.

Golledge, R. G. (1999). *Wayfinding behavior: Cognitive mapping and other spatial processes.* Baltimore: Johns Hopkins University Press.

Golombok, S. & Hines, M. (2002). Sex differences in social behavior. In P. Smith & C. Hart (Eds.), *Blackwell handbook of childhood social development.* Malden, MA: Blackwell.

Goncu, A. E. (Ed.). (1999). *Children's engagement in the world: Sociocultural perspectives.* New York: Cambridge University Press.

Gonsiorek, J. C. (1996). Mental health and sexual orientation. In R. C. Savin-Williams & K. M. Cohen (Eds.), *The lives of lesbians, gays, and bisexuals: Children to adults* (pp. 462–478). Orlando, FL: Harcourt Brace College.

Gooden, A., & Gooden, M. A. (2001). Gender representation in notable chidren's picture books: 1995–1999. *Sex Roles, 45,* 89–101.

Goodman, G. S., Emery, R. E., & Haugaard, J. J. (1998). Developmental psychology and the law: Divorce, child maltreatment, foster care, and adoption. In I. E. Sigel & K. A. Renninger (Eds.), *Handbook of child psychology: Vol 4. Child psychology in practice* (5th ed., pp. 775–876). New York: Wiley.

Goodman, G. S., Rudy, L., Bottoms, B. L., & Aman, C. (1990). Children's concerns and memory: Issues of ecological validity in the study of children's eyewitness testimony. In R. Fivush & J. A. Hudson (Eds.), *Knowing and remembering in young children.* New York: Cambridge University Press.

Goodman, K. S. (1998). Reading, writing, and written texts: A transactional sociopsycholinguistic view. In R. B. Ruddell & M. R. Ruddell (Eds.), *Theoretical models and processes of reading* (4th ed., pp. 1093–1130). Newark, DE: International Reading Association.

Goodman, M., Stormshak, E., & Dishion, T. (2001). The significance of peer victimization at two points in development. *Applied Developmental Psychology, 22,* 507–526.

Goodnow, J. J. (1998). Beyond the overall balance: The significance of particular tasks and procedures for perceptions of fairness in distributions of household work. *Social Justice Research, 11*(3), 359–376.

Goodnow, J. J., Cashmore, J., Cotton, S., & Knight, R. (1984). Mothers' developmental timetables in two cultural groups. *International Journal of Psychology, 19,* 193–205.

Goodwin, M. H. (in press). Participation. In A. Duranti (Ed.), *A companion to linguistic anthropology.* Oxford, UK: Blackwell.

Goodwin, M. H. (2002). Exclusion in girls' peer groups: Ethnographic analysis of language practices on the playground. *Human Development, 45*(6), 392–415.

Goodwyn, S. W., Acredolo, L. P., & Brown, C. (2000). Impact of symbolic gesturing on early language development. *Journal of Nonverbal Behavior, 24*(2), 81–103.

Goossens, L. (2001). Global versus domain-specific statuses in identity research: A comparison of two self-report easures. *Journal of Adolescence, 24,* 681–699.

Gopnik, A., & Choi, S. (1990). Do linguistic differences lead to cognitive differences? A cross-linguistic study of semantic and cognitive development. *First Language, 10*(3), 199–215.

Gopnik, A., & Meltzoff, A. N. (1997). *Words, thoughts, and theories.* Cambridge, MA: MIT Press.

Gopnik, A., Meltzoff, A. N., & Kuhl, P. A. (1999). *The scientist in the crib: Minds, brains, and how children learn.* New York: William Morrow.

Gopnik, A., & Wellman, H. M. (1994). The theory theory. In L. A. Hirschfeld & S. A. Gelman (Eds.), *Mapping the mind: Domain specificity in cognition and culture* (pp. 257–293). New York: Cambridge University Press.

Gordon, R. A., Savage, C., Lahey, B. B., Goodman, S. H., Jensen, P. S., Rubio-Stipic, M., et al. (2003). Family and neighborhood income: Additive and multiplicative associations with youths' well-being. *Social Science Research, 32,* 191–219.

Gortmaker, S. L., Must, A., Perrin, J. M., & Sobol, A. M. (1993). Social and economic consequences of overweight in adolescence and young adulthood. *New England Journal of Medicine, 329*(14), 1008–1012.

Gortmaker, S. L., Must, A., Sobol, A. M., Peterson, K., Colditz, G. A., & Dietz, W. H. (1996). Television viewing as a cause of increasing obesity among children in the United States, 1986–1990. *Archives of Pediatrics and Adolescent Medicine, 150*(4), 356–362.

Goswami, U. (1999). The relationship between phonological awareness and orthographic representation in different orthographies. In M. Harris & G. Hatano (Eds.), *Learning to read and write: A cross-linguistic perspective.* New York: Cambridge University Press.

Goswami, U. (Ed.). (2002). Blackwell handbook of childhood cognitive development. Oxford, UK: Blackwell.

Gottardo, A., Chiappe, P., Siegel, L. S., & Stanovich, K. E. (1999). Patterns of word and nonword processing in skilled and less-skilled readers. *Reading & Writing, 11*(5–6), 465–487.

Gottesman, I. I., & Erlenmeyer-Kimling, L. (2001). Family and twin strategies as a head start in defining prodomes and endophenotypes for hypothetical early interventions in schizophrenia. *Schizophrenia Research, 51*(1), 93–102.

Gottlieb, G. (2002a). Developmental-behavioral initiation of evolutionary change. *Psychological Review, 109*(2), 211–218.

Gottlieb, G. (2002b). *Individual development and evolution: The genesis of novel behavior.* Mahwah, NJ: Erlbaum.

Gottman, J. M. (1983). How children become friends. *Monographs of the Society for Research in Child Development, 48*(3, Serial No. 201).

Gould, S. J. (1977). *Phylogeny and ontogony.* Cambridge, MA: Harvard University Press.

Graber, J. A., Brooks-Gunn, J., & Galen, B. R. (1998). Betwixt and between: Sexuality in the context of adolescent transitions. In R. Jessor (Ed.), *New perspectives on adolescent risk behavior* (pp. 270–316). New York: Cambridge University Press.

Graber, J. A., Brooks-Gunn, J., Paikoff, R. L., & Warren, M. P. (1994). Prediction of eating problems: An 8-year study of adolescent girls. *Developmental Psychology, 30,* 823–834.

Graber, J. A., Brooks-Gunn, J., & Warren, M. (1995). The antecedents of menarcheal age: Heredity, family environment, and stressful life events. *Child Development, 66,* 346–359.

Graber, J. A., Lewinsohn, P. M., Seeley, J. R., & Brooks-Gunn, J. (1997). Is psychopathology associated with the timing of pubertal development? *Journal of the American Academy of Child & Adolescent Psychiatry, 36*(12), 1768–1776.

Grady, K. (2002). Lowrider art and Latino students in the rural Midwest. In S. Wortham, E. Murillo, & E. Hamann (Eds.), *Education in the new Latino diaspora.* Westport, CT: Ablex.

Graham, F. K., Leavitt, L. A., Stroch, B. D., & Brown, J. W. (1978). Precocious cardiac orienting in human anencephalic infants. *Science, 199,* 322–324.

Graham, J. A., Cohen, R., Zbikowski, S. M., & Secrist, M. E. (1998). A longitudinal investigation of race and sex as factors in children's classroom friendship choices. *Child Study Journal, 28*(4), 245–266.

Graham, M. J., Larsen, U., & Xu, X. (1999). Secular trend in age at menarche in China: A case study of two rural counties in Anhui province. *Journal of Biosocial Science, 31*(2), 257–267.

Granic, I., Hollenstein, T., Dishion, T. J., & Patterson, G. R. (2003). Longitudinal analysis of flexibility and reorganization in early adolescence: A dynamic systems study of family interactions. *Developmental Psychology, 39*(3), 606–617.

Grant, B. F., & Dawson, D. A. (1997). Age at onset of alcohol use and its association with DSM-IV alcohol abuse and dependence: Results from the National Longitudinal Alcohol Epidemiologic Survey. *Journal of Substance Abuse, 9,* 103–110.

Greco, C., Rovee-Collier, C., Hayne, H., & Griesler, P. (1986). Ontogeny of early event memory: I. Forgetting and retrieval by 2- and 3-month-olds. *Infant Behavior Development, 9,* 441–460.

Green, G. (1984). On the appropriateness of adaptations in primary-level basal readers: Reactions to remarks by Bertran Bruce. In R. C. Anderson, J. Osborn, & R. J. Tierney (Eds.), *Learning to read in American schools.* Mahwah, NJ: Erlbaum.

Greenberg, B. S., & Brand, J. E. (1994). Minorities and the mass media. In J. Bryant & D. Zillman (Eds.), *Media effects: Advances in theory and research.* Mahwah, NJ: Erlbaum.

Greenfield, P. M. (1984). *Mind and media: The effects of television, video, games and computers.* Cambridge, MA: Harvard University Press.

Greenfield, P. M. (2002). The mutual definition of culture and biology in development. In H. Keller & Y. H. Poortinga (Eds.), *Between culture and biology: Perspectives on ontogenetic development. Cambridge studies in cognitive perceptual development* (pp. 57–76). New York: Cambridge University Press.

Greenfield, P. M., Brazelton, T. B., & Childs, C. P. (1989). From birth to maturity in Zinacantan: Ontogenesis in cultural context. In V. Bricker & G. Gossen (Eds.), *Ethnographic encounters in southern Mesoamerica: Celebratory essays in honor of Evon Z. Vogt.* Albany: Institute of Mesoamerican Studies, State University of New York.

Greenfield, P. M., Keller, H., Fuligni, A., & Maynard, A. (2003). Cultural pathways through universal development. *Annual Review of Psychology, 54,* 461–490.

Greenfield, P. M., & Smith, J. H. (1976). *The structure of communication in early language development.* New York: Academic Press.

Greenspan, S. I. (2003). Child care research: A clinical perspective. *Child Development, 74*(4), 1064–1068.

Greenwood, D., & Levin, M. (2000). Reconstructing the relationships between universities and society through action research. In N. K. Denzin & Y. S. Lincoln (Eds.), *Handbook of qualitative research* (2nd ed., pp. 85–106). Thousand Oaks, CA: Sage.

Gregor, J. A., & McPherson, D. A. (1966). Racial preference and ego identity among White and Bantu children in the Republic of South Africa. *Genetic Psychology Monographs, 73,* 218–253.

Grice, H. P. (1975). Logic and conversation. In P. Cole & J. L. Morgan (Eds.), *Syntax and semantics: Vol. 3. Speech acts.* New York: Academic Press.

Griffin, P. (1983). Personal communication.

Grigorenko, E. L., Geissler, P., Wenzel, P. R., Okatcha, F., Nokes, C., Kenny, D. A., et al. (2001). The organization of Luo conceptions of intelligence: A study of implicit theories in a Kenyan village. *International Journal of Behavioral Development, 25*(4), 367–378.

Grisso, T., Steinberg, L., Woolard, J., Cauffman, E., Scott, E., Graham, S., et al. (2003). Juveniles' competence to stand trial: A comparison of adolescents' and adults' capacities as trial defendants. *Law and Human Behavior, 27*(4), 333–363.

Griswold Del Castillo, R. (1984). *La familia: Chicano families in the urban southwest, 1848 to the present.* Notre Dame, IN: University of Notre Dame Press.

Grob, A., Stetsenki, A., Sabatier, C., Botcheva, L., & Macek, P. (1999). A cross-national model of subjective well-being in adolescence. In F. Alsaker & A. Flammer (Eds.), *The adolescent experience: European and American adolescents in the 1990s* (pp. 115–129). Mahwah, NJ: Erlbaum.

Grolnick, W. S., McMenamy, J. M., & Kurowski, C. O. (1999). Emotional self-regulation in infancy and toddlerhood. In L. Balter & C. S. Tamis-LeMonda (Eds.), *Child psychology: A handbook of contemporary issues.* Philadelphia: Psychology Press/Taylor & Francis.

Gronlund, N. E. (1959). *Sociometry in the classroom.* New York: Harper Brothers.

Grossmann, K., Grossmann, K. E., Fremmer-Bombik, E., Kindler, H., Scheuerer-Englisch, H., & Zimmermann, P. (2002). The uniqueness of the child–father attachment relationship: Fathers' sensitive and challenging play as a pivotal variable in a 16-year longitudinal study. *Social Development, 11*(3), 307–331.

Grossmann, K., Grossmann, K. E., Spangler, S., Suess, G., & Unzner, L. (1985). Maternal sensitivity and newborn orientation responses as related to quality of attachment in northern Germany. In I. Bretherton & E. Waters (Eds.), *Growing points of attachment theory. Monographs of the society for research in child development: Vol. 50.* (1–2, Serial No. 209).

Grotevant, H.D. (1998). Adolescent development in family contexts. In W. Damon & N. Eisenberg (Eds.), *Handbook of child psychology: Vol. 3. Social, emotional, and personality development.* (5th ed., pp. 1097–1150). New York: Wiley.

Grotevant, H. D., & Cooper, C. (1985). Patterns of interaction in family relationships and the development of identity exploration in adolescence. *Developmental Psychology, 56,* 415–428.

Grotevant, H. D., & Cooper, C. R. (1998). Individuality and connectedness in adolescent development: Review and prospects for research on identity, relationships, and context. In E. E. A. Skoe & A. L. von der Lippe (Eds.), *Personality development in adolescence: A cross national and life span perspective* (pp. 3–37). New York: Routledge.

Grusec, J. E. (1991). Socializing concern for others in the home. *Developmental Psychology, 27,* 338–342.

Grusec, J. E., Davidov, M., & Lundell, L. (2002). Prosocial and helping behavior. In P. Smith & C. Hart (Eds.), *Blackwell handbook of childhood social development.* Malden, MA: Blackwell Publishers.

Guilford, J. P. (1967). *The nature of human intelligence.* New York: McGraw-Hill.

Guinn, B., Semper, T., & Jorgensen, L. (1997). Mexican American female adolescent self-esteem: The effect of body image, exercise behavior, and body fatness. *Hispanic Journal of Behavioral Sciences, 19*(4), 517–526.

Guttler, F. (1988). Epidemiology and natural history of phenylketonuria and other hyperphenylalaninemias. In R. J. Wurtman & E. Ritter-Walker (Eds.), *Dietary phenylaline and brain function.* Boston: Birkhauser.

Haith, M. M. (1980). *Rules that babies look by: The organization of newborn visual activity.* Mahwah, NJ: Erlbaum.

Haith, M., & Benson, J. B. (1998). Infant cognition. In D. Kuhn & R. S. Siegler (Eds.), *Handbook of child development, Vol 2. Cognition, perception, and language* (5th ed., pp. 199–254). New York: Wiley.

Hakuta, K. (1999). The debate on bilingual education. *Journal of Developmental & Behavioral Pediatrics, 20*(1), 36–37.

Hakuta, K., Bialystok, E., & Wiley, E. (2003). Critical evidence: A test of the critical-period hypothesis for second-language acquisition. *Psychological Science, 14*(1), 31–38.

Halberstadt, A., Denham, S., & Dunsmore, J. (2001). Affective social competence. *Social Development, 10,* 79–119.

Hall, G. S. (1904). *Adolescence.* New York: Appleton.

Halpern-Felsher, B., & Cauffman, E. (2001). Costs and benefits of a decision: Decision-making competence in adolescents and adults. *Applied Developmental Psychology, 22,* 257–273.

Halverson, H. M. (1931). An experimental study of prehension in infants by means of systemic cinema records. *Genetic Psychology Monographs, 10,* 107–286.

Hamann, E. (2002). *Un paso adelante?* The politics of bilingual education, Latino student accommodation, and school district management in Southern Appalachia. In S. Wortham, E. Murillo, & E. Hamann (Eds.), *Education in the new Latino diaspora.* Westport, CT: Ablex.

Hammen, C. (1991). *Depression runs in families: The social context of risk and resilience in children of depressed mothers.* New York: Springer-Verlag.

Hammen, C. (1999). Children of affectively ill parents. In H. C. Steinhausen & F. Verhulst (Eds.), *Risks and outcomes in developmental psychopathology.* Oxford, UK: Oxford University Press.

Hanna, E., & Meltzoff, A. N. (1993). Peer imitation by toddlers in laboratory, home, and day-care contexts: Implications for social learning and memory. *Developmental Psychology, 29*(4), 701–710.

Hareven, T. (2000). *Families, history, and social change: Life course and cross-cultural perspectives.* Boulder, CO: Westview.

Harkness, S., & Super, C. M. (1983). The cultural construction of child development: A framework for the socialization of emotion. *Ethos, 11,* 221–231.

Harlow, H. F. (1959). Love in infant monkeys. *Scientific American, 200*(6), 68–74.

Harlow, H. F., & Harlow, M. K. (1962). Social deprivation in monkeys. *Scientific American, 207*(5), 136–146.

Harlow, H. F., & Harlow, M. K. (1969). Effects of various mother-infant relationships on rhesus monkey behaviors. In B. M. Foss (Ed.), *Determinants of infant behavior: Vol. 4.* (4th ed.). London: Methuen.

Harlow, H. F., & Novak, M. A. (1973). Psychopathological perspectives. *Perspectives in Biology and Medicine, Spring,* 461–478.

Harrington, M. (1963). *The other America: Poverty in the United States.* New York: Macmillan.

Harris, J. R. (1998). *The nurture assumption: Why children turn out the way they do.* New York: Free Press.

Harris, P. L., Brown, E., Marriot, C., Whittall, S., & Harmer, S. (1991). Monsters, ghosts and witches: Testing the limits of the fantasy-reality distinction in young children. *British Journal of Developmental Psychology, 9*(1), 105–123.

Harrison, H., Algea, O., McLoyd, V. C., & Smedley, B. (2004). Racial and ethnic status: Risk and protective processes among African American families. In K. I. Maton, C. J. Schellenbach, B. J. Leadbetter, & A. L. Solarz (Eds.), *Investing in children, youth, families, and communities: Strengths-based research and policy* (pp. 269–283). Washington, DC: American Psychological Association.

Hart, B., & Risley, T. R. (1999). *The social world of children learning to talk.* Baltimore: Brookes.

Hart, C., Young, C., Nelson, D., Jin, S., Bazarskaya, N., Nelson, L., et al. (1999). Peer contact patterns, parenting practices, and preschoolers' social competence in China, Russia, and the United States. In P. Slee & K. Rigby (Eds.), *Children's peer relationships* (pp. 3–30). London: Routledge.

Hart, D., Atkins, R., & Ford, D. (1999). Family influences on the formation of moral identity in adolescence: Longitudinal analyses. *Journal of Moral Education, 28,* 375–386.

Hart, S., Field, T., & Roitfarb, M. (1999). Depressed mothers' assessments of their neonates' behaviors. *Infant Mental Health Journal, 20*(2), 200–210.

Harter, S. (1982). The perceived competence scale for children. *Child Development, 53*, 87–97.

Harter, S. (1987). The determinants and mediational role of global self-worth in children. In N. Eisenberg (Ed.), *Contemporary topics in developmental psychology.* New York: Wiley.

Harter, S. (1998). The development of self-representation. In N. Eisenberg (Ed.), *Handbook of child psychology: Vol. 3. Social, emotional, and personality development* (5th ed., pp. 553–617). New York: Wiley.

Harter, S. (1999). *The construction of the self: A developmental perspective.* New York: Guilford.

Harter, S. (2003). The development of self-representations during childhood and adolescence. In M. R. Leary & J. P. Tangney (Eds.), *Handbook of self and identity* (pp. 610–642). New York: Guilford.

Harter, S., & Pike, R. (1984). The pictorial scale of perceived competence and social acceptance for young children. *Child Development, 55,* 1969–1982.

Hartshorn, K., & Rovee-Collier, C. (1997). Infant learning and long-term memory at 6 months: A confirming analysis. *Developmental Psychobiology, 30*(1), 71–85.

Hartshorn, K., Rovee-Collier, C., Gerhardstein, P., Bhatt, R. S., Wondoloski, T. L., Klein, P., Gilch, J., et al. (1998). The ontogeny of long-term memory over the first year-and-a-half of life. *Developmental Psychobiology, 32*(2), 69–89.

Hartup, W. W. (1978). Children and their friends. In H. McGurk (Ed.), *Issues in childhood social development.* London: Methuen.

Hartup, W. W. (1984). The peer context in middle childhood. In A. Collins (Ed.), *Development during middle childhood: The years from six to twelve.* Washington, DC: National Academy Press.

Hartup, W. W. (1992). Friendships and their developmental significance. In H. McGurk (Ed.), *Childhood social development: Contemporary perspectives.* London: Erlbaum.

Hartup, W. W. (1993). Adolescents and their friends. In B. Laursen (Ed.), *Close friendships in adolescence* (pp. 3–22). San Francisco: Jossey-Bass.

Hartup, W. W., & Silbereisen, R. K. (Eds.). (2002). *Growing points in developmental science: An introduction.* New York: Psychology Press.

Hashima, P. Y., & Amato, P. R. (1994). Poverty, social support, and parental behavior. Special issue: Children and poverty. *Child Development, 65,* 394–403.

Haskett, M. E., & Kistner, J. A. (1991). Social interactions and peer perception in young physically abused children. *Child Development, 62,* 979–990.

Hatano, G., & Inagaki, K. (2000). Domain-specific constraints of conceptual development. *Internationl Journal of Behavioral Development, 24*(3), 267–275.

Hatano, G., & Inagaki, K. (2002). Domain-specific constraints of conceptual development. In W. W. Hartup & R. K. Silbereisen (Eds.), *Growing points in developmental science: An introduction* (pp. 123–142). Philadelphia: Psychology Press.

Hauck, F. R., Herman, S. M., Donovan, M., Iysau, S., Moore, C. M., Donoghue, E., et al. (2003). Sleep environment and the risk of sudden infant death syndrome in an urban population: The Chicago Infant Mortality Study. *Pediatrics, 111*(5, Part 2), 1207–1214.

Hauser, M. D., & Chomsky, N. (2002). The faculty of language: What is it, who has it, and how did it evolve? *Science, 298,* 1569–1579.

Hauser, S., Powers, S., & Noam, G. (1991). *Adolescents and their families: Paths of ego development.* New York: Free Press.

Haviland, J. M., & Kramer, D. A. (1991). Affect-cognition relationships in adolescent diaries: The case of Anne Frank. *Human Development, 34*(3), 143–159.

Hawley, P. H., & Little, T. D. (1999). On winning some and losing some: A social relations approach to social dominance in toddlers. *Merrill Palmer Quarterly, 45*(2), 185–214.

Hawley, P. H., Little, T. D., & Pasupathi, M. (2002). Winning friends and influencing peers: Strategies of peer influence in late childhood. *International Journal of Behavioral Development, 26*(5), 466–474.

Hayes, K., & Hayes, C. (1951). The intellectual development of a home-raised chimpanzee. *Proceedings of the American Philosophical Society, 95,* 105–109.

Hayflick, L. (1994). *How and why we age.* New York: Ballantine Books.

Hayne, H., Boniface, J., & Barr, R. (2000). The development of declarative memory in human infants: Age-related changes in deferred imitation. *Behavioral Neuroscience, 114*(1), 77–83.

Hayne, H., & Rovee-Collier, C. (1995). The organization of reactivated memory in infancy. *Child Development, 66,* 893–906.

Haywood, K., & Getchell, N. (2002). *Life span motor development.* Champaign, IL: Human Kinetics.

Haywood, K. (1986). *Life span motor development* (pp. 130–131). Champaign, IL: Human Kinetics.

Haywood, K., & Getchell, N. (2001). *Lifespan motor development* (3rd ed.). Champaign, IL: Human Kinetics.

Heath, S. B. (1983). *Ways with words: Language, life, and work in communities and classrooms.* Cambridge, UK: Cambridge University Press.

Heights, R. (1999). Identity development of homosexual youth and parental and familiar influences on the coming out process. *Adolescence, 34,* 597–601.

Heimann, M. (2002). Notes on individual differences and the assumed elusiveness of neonatal imitation. In A. N. Meltzoff & W. Prinz (Eds.), *The imitative mind: Development, evolution, and brain bases* (pp. 74–84). New York: Cambridge University Press.

Held, R., & Hein, A. (1963). Movement-produced stimulation and the development of visually guided behaviors. *Journal of Comparative and Physiological Psychology, 56,* 872–876.

Heller, J. (1987). What do we know about the risks of caffeine consumption in pregnancy? *British Journal of Addiction, 82,* 885–889.

Helmuth, L. (2001). From the mouths (and hands) of babes. *Science, 293*(7), 1758–1759.

Hendren, R. L., & Berenson, C. K. (1997). Adolescent impulse control disorders: Eating disorders and substance abuse. In L. T. Flaherty & R. M. Sarles (Eds.), *Handbook of child and adolescent psychiatry: Volume 3. Adolescence: Development and syndromes.* New York: Wiley.

Henington, C., Hughes, J. N., Cavell, T. A., & Thompson, B. (1998). The role of relational aggression in identifying aggressive boys and girls. *Journal of School Psychology, 36*(4), 457–477.

Hennessy, K. D., Rabideau, G., Cicchetti, D., & Cummings, E. M. (1994). Responses of physically abused and nonabused children to different forms of interadult anger. *Child Development, 65,* 815–828.

Hepper, P. G., & Shahidullah, S. (1994). The beginnings of mind: Evidence from the behavior of the fetus. *Journal of Reproductive and Infant Psychology, 12*(3), 143–154.

Herdt, G. (2001). Social change, sexual diversity, and tolerance for bisexuality in the United States. In A. R. D'Augelli & C. J. Patterson (Eds.), *Lesbian, gay, and bisexual identities and youth: Psychological perspectives* (pp. 267–283). London: Oxford University Press.

Herlihy, D. (1985). *Medieval household.* Cambridge, MA: Harvard University Press.

Herman-Giddens, M., Slora, E., Wasserman, R., Bourdony, C., Bhapkar, M., Koch, G., & Hasemeier, C. (1997). Secondary sex characteristics and menses in young girls seen in office practice: A study from the Pediatric Research in Office Settings network. *Pediatrics, 99,* 505–512.

Herman–Giddens, M., Wang, L., & Koch, G. (2001). Secondary sex characteristics in boys: Estimates from the National Health and Nutrition Examination Survey III, 1988–1994. *Archives of Pediatric and Adolescent Medicine, 155,* 1022–1028.

Hernàndez Blasi, C., & Bjorklund, D. F. (2003). Evolutionary developmental psychology: A new tool for better understanding human ontogeny. *Human Development, 46,* 259–281.

Herrnstein, R. J., & Murray, C. (1994). *The bell curve: Intelligence and class structure in American life.* New York: Free Press.

Herskovitz, M. J. (1948). *Man and his works: The science of cultural anthropology.* New York: Knopf.

Hespos, S. J., & Rochat, P. (1997). Dynamic mental representation in infancy. *Cognition, 64*(2), 153–188.

Hetherington, E. M. (1988). Parents, children, and siblings: Six years after divorce. In R. A. Hinde & J. Stevenson-Hinde (Eds.), *Relationships within families: Mutual influences.* Oxford: Oxford University Press.

Hetherington, E. M. (1999). Should we stay together for the sake of the children? In E. Hetherington (Ed.), *Coping with divorce, single parenting, and remarriage: A risk and resiliency perspective.* Mahwah, NJ: Erlbaum.

Hetherington, E. M., Bridges, M., & Insabella, G. M. (1998). What matters? What does not? Five perspectives on the association between marital transitions and children's adjustment. *American Psychologist, 53*(2), 167–184.

Hetherington, E. M., Collins, W. A., & Laursen, E. (1999). Social capital and the development of youth from nondivorced, divorced and remarried families. In W. A. Collins (Ed.), *Relationships as developmental contexts* (pp. 177–209). Mahwah, NJ: Erlbaum.

Hewlett, B. S. (1992). The parent-infant relationship and socio-emotional development among Aka pygmies. In J. L. Roopnarine & D. B. Carter (Eds.), *Parent-child socialization in diverse cultures: Vol. 5.* (pp. 223–244). Norwood, NJ: Ablex.

Heywood, C. (2001). *A history of childhood: Children and childhood from medieval to modern times.* Malden, MA: Polity Press.

Hickling, A. K., & Wellman, H. M. (2001). The emergence of children's causal explanations and theories: Evidence from everyday conversation. *Developmental Psychology, 37*(5), 668–683.

Hicks, L. E., Langham, R. A., & Takenaka, J. (1982). Cognitive and health measures following early nutritional supplementation: A sibling study. *American Journal of Public Health, 72,* 1110–1118.

Hiebert, J., Gallimore, R., Garnier, H., Given, K. B., Hollingworth, H., Jacobs, J., et al. (2003). *Teaching mathematics in seven countries: Results from the TIMSS 1999 video study.* Washington, DC: U.S. Department of Education.

Hill, W. H., Borovsky, O. L., & Rovee-Collier, C. (1988). Continuities in infant memory development over the first half-year. *Developmental Psychobiology, 21,* 43–62.

Hindman, H. D. (2002). *Child labor: An American history.* Armonk, NY: Sharpe.

Hodges, E., & Perry, D. (1999) Personal and interpersonal antecedents and consequences of victimization by peers. *Journal of Personality and Social Psychology, 76,* 677–685.

Hodges, J., & Tizard, B. (1989a). IQ and behavioral adjustments of ex-institutional adolescents. *Journal of Child Psychology and Psychiatry, 30,* 53–75.

Hodges, J., & Tizard, B. (1989b). Social and family relationships of ex-institutional adolescents. *Journal of Child Psychology and Psychiatry, 30,* 77–97.

Hodgkinson, S., Mullan, M., & Murray, R. M. (1991). The genetics of vulnerability to alcoholism. In P. M. R. Murray (Ed.), *The new genetics of mental illness.* London: Mental Health Foundation.

Hoff, E. (2001). *Language development.* Belmont, CA: Wadsworth.

Hoff-Ginsberg, E., & Tardiff, T. (1995). Socioeconomic status and parenting. In M. H. Bornstein (Ed.), *Handbook of parenting: Biology and ecology of parenting: Vol. 2.* (pp. 161–188). Mahwah, NJ: Erlbaum

Holcroft, C. J., Blakemore, K. J., Allen, M. A., & Graham, E. M. (2003). Prematurity and neonatal infection are most predictive of neurologic morbidity in very low birthweight infants. *Obstetrics & Gynecology, 101*(6), 1249–1254.

Holden, G. W. (2002). Perspectives on the effects of corporal punishment: Comment on Gershoff (2002). *Psychological Bulletin, 128,* 590–595.

Holden, G. W., & Buck, M. J. (2002). Parental attitudes toward childrearing. In M. H. Bornstein (Ed.), *Handbook of parenting: Being and becoming a parent: Vol. 3* (2nd ed., pp. 537–562). Mahwah, NJ: Erlbaum.

Hollos, M., & Richards, F. A. (1993). Gender-associated development of formal operations in Nigerian adolescents. *Ethos, 21,* 24–52.

Holmbeck, G. N. (1996). A model of family relational transformations during the transition to adolescence: Parent-adolescent conflict and adaptation. In J. A. Graber & J. Brooks-Gunn (Eds.), *Transitions through adolescence: Interpersonal domains and context* (pp. 167–199). Mahwah, NJ: Erlbaum.

Holmbeck, G. N., Paikoff, R. L., & Brooks-Gunn, J. (1995). Parenting adolescents. In M. H. Bornstein (Ed.), *Handbook of parenting: Children and parenting: Vol. 1* (pp. 91–118). Mahwah, NJ: Erlbaum.

Holowaka, S., & Petitto, L. A. (2002). Left hemisphere cerebral specialization for babies while babbling. *Science, 297,* 1515.

Holsti, L., Grunau, R. V. E., & Whitfield, M. F. (2002). Developmental coordination disorder in extremely low birth weight children at nine years. *Journal of Developmental and Behavioral Pediatrics, 23*(1), 9–15.

Honwana, A. (2000). Children of war: Understanding war and war cleansing in Mozambique and Angola. Retrieved from http://cas.uchicago.edu/workshops/African/papers/honwana.htm.

Hopkins, B., & Westen, T. (1988). Maternal handling and motor development: An intracultural study. *Genetic Psychology Monographs, 14,* 377–420.

Horgen, K. B. (2001). Promoting healthy food choices: A health message and economic incentive intervention. *Dissertation Abstracts International: Section B. The Sciences & Engineering, 62*(3-B), 1560.

Horn, T. S. (Ed.). (2002). *Advances in sport psychology.* Champaign, IL Human Kinetics.

Houpt, M. I. (2003). Childhood obesity—A growing epidemic. *Pediatric Dentistry, 25*(5), 42.

Howell, S. (1984). Equality and hierarchy in Chewong classification. *Journal of the Anthropological Society of Oxford, 15*(1), 30–44.

Howes, C. (1999). Attachment relationships in the context of multiple caregivers. In J. Cassidy & P. R. Shaver (Eds.), *Handbook of attachment: Theory, research, and clinical applications* (pp. 671–687). New York: Guilford Press.

Huang-Pollack, C. L., Carr, T. H., & Nigg, J. T. (2002). Development of selective attention: Perceptual load influences early versus late attentional selection in children and adults. *Developmental Psychology, 38*(3), 363–375.

Huelsken, C., Sodian, B., et al. (2001). Distinguishing between appearance and reality in a dressing-up game—a problem of dual coding or preserving identity? *Zeitschrift für Entwicklungspsychologie und Paedagogische Psychologie, 33*(3), 129–137.

Hughes, D. (2003). Correlates of African American and Latino parents' messages to children about ethnicity and race: A comparative study of racial socialization. *American Journal of Community Psychology, 31,* 15–33.

Hughes, D., & Chen, L. (1999). The nature of parents' race-related communications to children: A developmental perspective. In L. Balter & C. S. Tamis-LeMonda (Eds.), *Child psychology: A handbook of contemporary issues* (pp. 467–490). Philadelphia: Psychology Press.

Hughes, F. P. (1995). *Children, play, and development* (2nd ed.). Boston: Allyn & Bacon.

Hughes, H., Graham-Bermann, S., & Gruber, G. (2001). Resilience in children exposed to domestic violence. In S. Graham-Bermann & J. Edleson (Eds.), *Domestic violence in the lives of children: The future of research, intervention and social policy*. Washington, DC: American Psychological Association.

Hulbert, A. (2003). *Raising America: Experts, parents, and a century of advice about children*. New York: Knopf.

Hulme, C., & Joshi, R. M. (Eds.). (1998). *Reading and spelling: Development and discourse*. Mahwah, NJ: Erlbaum.

Human Genome Project. (2004). An introduction to genomics: The human genome and beyond. Retrieved from http://www.jgi.doe.gov/programs/hgp.html.

Hunsley, M., & Thoman, E. B. (2002). The sleep of co-sleeping infants when they are not co-sleeping: Evidence that co-sleeping is stressful. *Developmental Psychobiology, 40*(1), 14–22.

Huston, A. C., & Wright, J. C. (1996). Television and socialization of young children. In T. M. MacBeth (Ed.), *Tuning in to young viewers: Social science perspectives on television* (pp. 37–60). Thousand Oaks: Sage Publications.

Huttenlocher, P. R. (1994). Synaptogenesis in human cerebral cortex. In G. Dawson & K. W. Fischer (Eds.), *Human behavior and the developing brain*. New York: Guilford Press.

Huttenlocher, P. R. (2002). *Neural plasticity*. Cambridge, MA: Harvard University Press.

Huttenlocher, P. R., & Dabholkar, A. S. (1997). Regional differences in synaptogenesis in human cerebral cortex. *Journal of Comparative Neurology, 387*(2), 167–178.

Hymel, S., Vaillancourt, T., McDougall, P., & Renshaw, P. D. (2002). Peer acceptance and rejection in childhood. In P. K. Smith & C. H. Hart (Eds.), *Blackwell handbook of childhood social development* (pp. 265–284). Malden, MA: Blackwell.

Hymel, S., Wagner, E., & Butler, L. J. (1990). Reputational bias: View from the peer group. In S. R. Asher & J. D. Coie (Eds.), *Peer rejection in childhood*. Cambridge: Cambridge University Press.

Inagaki, K. (1990). The effects of raising animals on children's biological knowledge. *British Journal of Developmental Psychology, 8*, 119–129.

Inagaki, K., & Hatano, G. (2002). *Young children's naive thinking about the biological world*. New York: Psychology Press.

Inhelder, B., & Piaget, J. (1958). *The growth of logical thinking from childhood to adolescence*. New York: Basic Books.

Inoue-Nakamura, N. (2001). Mirror self-recognition in primates: An ontogenetic and a phylogenetic approach. In T. Matsuzawa & U. Kyoto (Eds.), *Primate origins of human cognition and behavior: I. Primate Research* (pp. 297–312). New York: Springer-Verlag.

Itard, J. M. G. (1801/1982). *The wild boy of Aveyron*. New York: Appleton-Century-Crofts.

Ivey, P. (2000). Cooperative reproduction in Ituri Forest huntergatherers: Who cares for Efe infants? *Current Anthropology, 41*, 856–866.

Izard, C. E. (1994). Innate and universal facial expressions: Evidence from developmental and cross-cultural research. *Psychological Bulletin, 115*, 288–299.

Izard, C. E., Huebner, R. R., Risser, D., McGinnes, G. C., & Dougherty, L. M. (1980). The young infant's ability to produce discrete emotion expressions. *Developmental Psychology, 16*, 132–140.

Izawa, E.-I., Yanagihara, S., Atsumi, T., & Matsushima, T. (2001). The role of basal ganglia in reinforcement learning and imprinting in domestic chicks. *Neuroreport: For Rapid Communication of Neuroscience Research, 12*(8), 1743–1747.

Jackson, J. S., McCullough, W. R., & Gurin, G. (1997). Family, socialization environment, and identity development in Black Americans. In H. P. McAdoo (Ed.), *Black families* (3rd ed., pp. 251–266). Thousand Oaks, CA.: Sage.

Jacob, F. (1982). *The possible and the actual*. New York: Pantheon Books.

Jacobs, N., Van Gestel, S., Derom, C., Thiery, E., Vernon, P., Derom, R., & Vlietinck, R. (2001). Heritability estimates of intelligence in twins: Effect of chorion type. *Behavior Genetics, 31*(2), 209–217.

Jahoda, G. (1980). Theoretical and systematic approaches in cross-cultural psychology. In H. C. Triandis & W. W. Lambert (Eds.), *Handbook of cross-cultural psychology: Vol. 1*. Boston: Allyn & Bacon.

James, D., Pillai, M., & Smoleniec, J. (1995). Neurobehavioral development in the human fetus. In J. P. Lecanuet & W. P. Fifer (Eds.), *Fetal development: A psychobiological perspective* (pp. 101–128). Mahwah, NJ: Erlbaum.

James, W. T. (1890). *The principles of psychology*. New York: Holt, Rinehart and Winston.

James, W. T. (1951). Social organization among dogs of different temperaments: Terriers and beagles reared together. *Journal of Comparative and Physiological Psychology, 44*, 71–77.

Jang, K. L., Livesley, W. J., & Vernon, P. A. (1998). A twin study of genetic and environmental contributions to gender differences in traits delineating personality disorder. *European Journal of Personality, 12*, 331–344.

Janowsky, J. S., & Carper, R. (1996). Is there a neural basis for cognitive transitions in school-age children? In Arnold J. Sameroff & M. M. Haith (Eds.), *The five to seven year shift: The age of reason and responsibility*. Chicago: University of Chicago Press.

Jarrett, R. (2000). Voices from below: The use of ethnographic research for informing public policy. In J. Mercier, S. Garasky, & M. Shelly (Eds.), *Redefining family policy: Implications for the 21st century*. Ames: Iowa State University Press.

Jason, L., & Hanaway, L. K. (1997). *Remote control: A sensible approach to kids, TV, and the new electronic media*. Sarasota, FL: Professional Resource Press.

Jennings, K. D., & Dietz, L. J. (2003). Mastery motivation and goal persistence in young children. In M. H. Bornstein, L. Davidson, C. L. Keyes, K. A. Moore, & the Center for Child Well Being (Eds.), *Well-being: Positive development across the life course. Crosscurrents in contemporary psychology* (pp. 295–309). Mahwah, NJ, Erlbaum.

Jessor, R. (1992). Risk behavior in adolescence: A psychosocial framework for understanding and action. *Developmental Review, 12*, 374–390.

Jessor, R. (1998). *New perspectives on adolescent risk behavior*. New York: Cambridge University Press.

Jocklin, V., McGue, M., & Lykken, D. (1996). Personality and divorce: A genetic analysis. *Journal of Personality and Social Psychology, 71*, 288–299.

Jodl, K. M., Michael, A., Malanchuk, O., Eccles, J., & Sameroff, A. (2001). Parents' roles in shaping early adolescents' occupational aspirations. *Child Development, 72*, 1247–1265.

Joh, A., Sweeney, B., & Rovee-Collier, C. (2002). Minimum duration of reactivation at 3 months of age. *Developmental Psychobiology, 40*(1), 23–32.

John, V. P. (1972). Styles of learning—styles of teaching: Reflections on the education of Navajo children. In C. Cazden, V. P. John, & D. Hymes (Eds.), *Functions of language in the classroom* (pp. 331–343), New York: Teachers College Press.

Johnson, D. (2001). Parental characteristics, racial stress, and racial socialization processes as predictors of racial coping in middle childhood. In A. M. Neal-Barnett, J. Contreras, & K. Kerns (Eds.), *Forging links: African American children–clinical and developmental perspectives*. Westport, CT: Praeger.

Johnson, D., Jaeger, E., Randolph, S., Cauce, A., Ward, J., & NICHD (2003). Studying the effects of early child care experiences on the development of children of color in the United States: Toward a more inclusive research agenda. *Child Development, 74*, 1227–1244.

Johnson, M. (2001). Functional brain development during infancy. In G. Bremner & A. Fogel (Eds.), *Blackwell handbook of infant development.* (pp. 169–190). Oxford, UK: Blackwell.

Johnson, W., Emde, R. N., Pannebecker, B., Stenberg, C., & Davis, M. (1982). Maternal perception of infant emotion from birth through 18 months. *Infant Behavior and Development, 5,* 313–322.

Jolly, A. (1999). *Lucy's legacy: Sex and intelligence in human evolution.* Cambridge, MA: Harvard University Press.

Jones, M., Yonezawa, S., Ballesteros, E., & Mehan, H. (2002). Shaping pathways to higher education. *Educational Researcher, 3,* 3–17.

Jones, R. E. (1997). *Human reproductive biology.* San Diego: Academic Press.

Jones, S. M., & Zigler, E. (2002). The Mozart effect: Not learning from history. *Journal of Applied Developmental Psychology, 23*(3), 355–372.

Jordan, B. (1993). *Birth in four cultures: A crosscultural investigation of childbirth in Yucatan, Holland, Sweden, and the United States.* Prospect heights, IL: Waveland Press.

Jorde, L. B., Carey, J. C., Bamshad, M. J., & White, R. L. (1999). *Medical genetics.* St. Louis: Mosby.

Joseph, J. (2001). Separated twins and the genetics of personality differences: A critique. *American Journal of Psychology, 114*(1), 1–30.

Joshi, M. S., & MacLean, M. (1994). Indian and English children's understanding of the distinction between real and apparent emotion. *Child Development, 65*(5), 1372–1384.

Juang, L. P., & Silbereisen, R. K. (2002). The relationship between adolescent academic capability beliefs, parenting and school grades. *Journal of Adolescence, 25,* 3–18.

Jusczyk, P. W. (1997). *The discovery of spoken language.* Cambridge, MA: MIT Press.

Jusczyk, P. W. (2001). Finding and remembering words: Some beginnings by English-learning infants. In E. Bates (Ed.), *Language development: The essential readings* (pp. 19–25). Malden, MA: Blackwell.

Jusczyk, P. W. (2002). How infants adapt speech-processing capacities to native language structure. *Current Directions in Psychological Science, 11*(1), 15–18.

Justice, E., Lindsey, L., & Morrow, S. (1999). The relation of self-perceptions to achievement among African American preschoolers. *Journal of Black Psychology, 25,* 48–60.

Kafai, Y., & Resnick, M. (1996). *Constructionism in practice: Designing, thinking, and learning in a digital world.* Mahwah, NJ: Erlbaum.

Kagan, J. (1981). *The second year.* Cambridge, MA: Harvard University Press.

Kagan, J. (1984). *The nature of the child.* New York: Basic Books.

Kagan, J. (1998). *Three seductive ideas.* Cambridge, MA: Harvard University Press.

Kagan, J. (2000). Human morality is distinctive. *Journal of Consciousness Studies, 7*(1–2), 46–48.

Kagan, J. (2001). Biological constraint, cultural variety, and psychological structures. In A. Harrington (Ed.), *Unity of knowledge: The convergence of natural and human science* (pp. 177–190). New York: New York Academy of Sciences.

Kagan, J., Kearsley, R. B., & Zelazo, P. (1978). *Infancy: Its place in human development.* Cambridge, MA: Harvard University Press.

Kagan, S., & Madsen, M. C. (1971). Cooperation and competition of Mexican, Mexican-American, and Anglo-American children of two ages under four instructional sets. *Developmental Psychology, 5,* 32–39.

Kagan, S., & Madsen, M. C. (1972). Experimental analyses of cooperation and competition of Anglo-American and Mexican children. *Developmental Psychology, 6*(1), 49–59.

Kagitçibasi, C. (1997). Individualism and collectivism. In J. Berry, M. H. Segall, & C. Kagitçibasi (Eds.), *Handbook of cross-cultural psychology: Vol. 3* (pp. 1–50). Needham Heights, MA: Allyn & Bacon.

Kagitçibasi, C. (2003). Autonomy, embeddedness and adaptability in immigration contexts. *Human Development, 46*(2–3), 145–150.

Kail, R. (2000). Speed of information processing: Developmental change and links to intelligence. *Journal of School Psychology, 38*(1): 51–61.

Kaltenbach, K., Berghella, V., Finnegan, L., & Woods, J. R., Jr. (1998). Opioid dependence during pregnancy: effects and management in substance abuse in pregnancy. *Obstetrics and Gynecology Clinics of North America, 25*(1), 139–152.

Kaltiala-Heino, R., Kosunen, E., & Rimpela, M. (2003). Pubertal timing, sexual behaviour and self-reported depression in middle adolescence. *Journal of Adolescence, 26*(5), 531–545.

Kamara, A. I., & Easley, J. A. (1977). Is the rate of cognitive development uniform across cultures? A methodological critique with new evidence from Themne children. In P. R. Dasen (Ed.), *Piagetian psychology: Cross-cultural contributions.* New York: Gardner.

Kandel, D. (1978). Homophily, selection, and socialization in adolescent friendships. *American Journal of Sociology, 84,* 427–436.

Kaplan, H., & Dove, H. (1987). Infant development among the Ache of Eastern Paraguay. *Developmental Psychology, 23,* 190–198.

Kaplan, M., Eidelman, A. I., & Aboulafia, Y. (1983). Fasting and the precipitation of labor: The Yom Kippur effect. *Journal of the American Medical Association, 250*(10), 1317–1318.

Kaplowitz, P., Slora, E., Wasserman, R., Pedlow, S., Herman-Giddens, M. (2001). Earlier onset of puberty in girls: Relations to increased body mass index and race. *Pediatrics, 108,* 347–353.

Kaprio, J., Rimpela, A., Winter, T., Viken, R.J., Rimpela, M., & Rose, R. (1995), Common genetic influences on BMI and age at menarche. *Human biology, 67,* 739–753.

Karmiloff, K., & Karmiloff-Smith, A. (2001). *Pathways to language: From fetus to adolescent.* Cambridge, MA: Harvard University Press.

Karniol, R. (1989). The role of manual manipulative stages in the infant's acquisition of perceived control over object. *Developmental Review, 9,* 205–233.

Kaslow, F. (2001). Families and family psychology at the millennium. *American Psychologist, 56,* 37–46.

Katch, J. (2001). *Under deadman's skin: Discovering the meaning of children's violent play.* Boston: Beacon Press.

Katchadourian, H. A. (1977). *The biology of adolescence.* San Francisco: Freeman.

Kaufman, C., Maharaj, P., & Richter, L. (1998). Fosterage and children's schooling in South Africa. In L. Richter (Ed.), *In view of school: Preparation for and adjustment to school under rapidly changing social conditions.* Johannesburg: Goethe Institut.

Kaufman, J., & Zigler, E. (1989). The intergenerational transmission of child abuse. In D. Cicchetti & V. Carlson (Eds.), *Child maltreatment: Theory and research on the causes and consequences of child abuse and neglect.* Cambridge, UK: Cambridge University Press.

Kaul, C. (2002). *Statistical handbook on the world's children.* Westport, CT: Oryx.

Kaye, K. (1982). *The mental and social life of babies.* Chicago: University of Chicago Press.

Keating, D. (1990). Adolescent thinking. In S. S. Feldman & G. R. Elliott (Eds.), *At the threshold: The developing adolescent.* Cambridge, MA: Harvard University Press.

Keel, P. K., Dorer, D. J., Eddy, K T., Franko, D., Charatan, D. L., & Herzog, D. B. (2003). Predictors of mortality in eating disorders. *Archives of General Psychiatry, 60*(2), 179–183.

Keel, P. K., & Klump, K. L. (2003). Are eating disorders culture-bound syndromes? Implications for conceptualizing their etiology. *Psychological Bulletin, 129*(5), 747–769.

Keeney, T. J., Cannizzo, S. D., & Flavell, J. H. (1967). Spontaneous and induced verbal rehearsal in a recall task. *Child Development, 38,* 935–966.

Keller, H. (2003). Socialization for competence: Cultural models of infancy. *Human Development, 46*(5), 228–311.

Kellman, P. J., & Banks, M. S. (1998). Infant visual perception. In R. Siegler & D. Kuhn (Eds.), *Handbook of child psychology: Vol. 2* (5th ed., pp. 103–146). New York: Wiley.

Kellman, P. J., & Spelke, E. S. (1983). Perception of partly occluded objects in infancy. *Cognitive Psychology, 15*(4), 483–524.

Kellogg, W. N., & Kellogg, L. A. (1933). *The ape and the child: A study of environmental influences upon early behavior.* New York: Whittlesey House.

Keniston, K. (1963). Social change and youth in Americal. In E. Erikson (Ed.), *Youth: Change and challenge.* New York: Basic Books.

Kennell, J. H., Jerauld, R., Wolfe, H., Chester, D., Kreger, N., McAlpine, W., Steffa, M., & Klaus, M. H. (1974). Maternal behavior one year after early and extended post-partum contact. *Developmental Medicine and Child Neurology, 16,* 172–179.

Kenyatta, J. (1938). *Facing Mt. Kenya: The tribal life of the Kikuyu.* London: Secker & Warburg.

Kermayer, L. (1994). Suicide among Canadian aboriginal people. *Transcultural Psychiatric Research Review, 31,* 3–57.

Kesmodel, U. (2001). Binge drinking in pregnancy: Frequency and methodology. *American Journal of Epidemiology, 154*(8), 777–782.

Kesmodel, U., Wisborg, K., Olsen S. F., Henriksen T. B., & Secher, N. J. (2002). Moderate alcohol intake in pregnancy and the risk of spontaneous abortion. *Alcohol and Alcoholism, 37*(1), 87–92.

Kesner, J., & McKenry, P. (2001). Single parenthood and social competence in children of color. *Families in Society, 82,* 136–144.

Kett, J. F. (1977). *Rites of passage: Adolescence in America 1790 to the present.* New York: Basic Books.

Kiell, N. (1959). *The adolescent through fiction: A psychological approach.* New York: International Universities Press.

Killen, M., McGlothlin, H., & Lee–Kim, J. (2002). Between individuals and culture: Individuals' evaluations of exclusion from social groups. In H. Keller, Y. Poortinga, & A. Schoelmerich (Eds.), *Between biology and culture: Perspectives on ontogenetic development.* Cambridge: Cambridge University Press.

Killen, M., & Stangor, C. (2001). Children's social reasoning about inclusion and exclusion in gender and race peer group contexts. *Child Development, 72*(1), 174–186.

Kim, I.-K., & Spelke, E. S. (1999). Perception and understanding of effects of gravity and inertia on object motion. *Developmental Science 2*(3): 339–362.

Kim, J., & Cicchetti, D. (2003). Social self-efficacy and behavior problems in maltreated children. *Journal of Clinical Child and Adolescent Psychology, 32,* 106–117.

Kim, J. M. (1998). Korean children's concepts of adult and per authority and moral reasoning. *Developmental Psychology, 34,* 947–955.

Kim, K., & Rohner, R. (2002). Parental warmth, control and involvement in schooling: Predicting academic achievement in Korean American Adolescents. *Journal of Cross-Cultural Psychology, 33,* 127–140.

Kirsten, G. F., Bergman, N. J., & Hann, F. M. (2001). Kangaroo mother care in the nursery. *Pediatric Clinics of North America, 48*(2), xvi, 443–452.

Kisilevsky, B. S., Hains, S. M., & Low, J. A. (2001). Maturation of fetal heart rate and body movement in 24–33-week-old fetuses threatening to deliver prematurely. *Developmental Psychobiology, 38*(1), 78–86.

Kisilevsky, B. S., & Low, J. A. (1998). Human fetal behavior: 100 years of study. *Developmental Review, 18,* 1–29.

Kitamura, C., Thanavishuth, C., Luksaneeyanawin, S., & Burnham, D. (2002). Universality and specificity in infant-directed speech: Pitch modifications as a function of infant age and sex in a tonal and nontonal language. *Infant Behavior & Development, 24*(4), 372–392.

Klahr, D. (1982). Nonmonotone assessment of monotone development: An information processing analysis. In S. Strauss (Ed.), *U-shaped behavioral-growth.* New York: Academic Press.

Klahr, D. (1989). Information-processing approaches. In R. Vasta (Ed.), *Annals of child development: Vol. 6. Six theories of child development: Revised formulations and current issues.* Greenwich, CT: JAI Press.

Klaus, M. H., & Kennell, J. H. (1976). *Maternal-infant bonding: The impact of early separation or loss on family development.* St. Louis: Mosby.

Klaus, M. H., Kennell, J. H., & Klaus, P. H. (1995). *Bonding: Building the foundations of secure attachment and independence.* Reading, MA: Addison-Wesley.

Klaus, M. H., Kennell, J. H., Plumb, N., & Zuehlke, S. (1970). Human maternal behavior at the first contact with her young. *Pediatrics, 46,* 187.

Klebanoff, M. A., Levine, R. J., Clemens, J. D., & Wilkins, D. G. (2002). Maternal serum caffeine metabolites and small-for-gestational age birth. *American Journal of Epidemiology, 155*(1), 32–37.

Klein, A., & Starkey, P. (2000). Enhancing low-income children's early achievement in an academically enriched after-school program: The UC Links program. In N. H. Gabelko (Ed.), *Toward a collective wisdom: Forging successful educational partnerships* (pp. 43–55). Berkeley, CA: ECO Center, University of California.

Kleitman, N. (1963). *Sleep and wakefulness.* Chicago: University of Chicago Press.

Klesges, R. C., Klesges, L. M., Eck, L. H., & Shelton, M. L. (1995). A longitudinal analysis of accelerated weight gain in preschool children. *Pediatrics, 95*(1), 126–130.

Klineberg, O. (1935). *Race differences.* New York: Harper & Row.

Klinger, J., Vaughn, B., & Schumm, J. (1998). Collaborative strategic reading during social studies and heterogeneous fourth–grade classrooms. *The Elementary School Journal, 96,* 275–293.

Klopfer, P. H., Adams, D. K., & Klopfer, M. S. (1964). Maternal imprinting in goats. *Proceedings of the National Academy of Sciences, 52,* 911–914.

Kluckhohn, C., & Kelly, W. H. (1945). The concept of culture. In R. Linton (Ed.), *The science of man in the world crisis.* New York: Columbia University Press.

Klump, K. L., McGue, M., & Iacono, W. G. (2003). Differential heritability of eating attitudes and behaviors in prepubertal versus pubertal twins. *International Journal of Eating Disorders, 33*(3), 287–292.

Klumpp, A., Domingos, M., & Klumpp, G. (2002). Foliar nutrient contents in tree species of the Atlantic rain forest as influenced by air pollution from the industrial complex of Cubatao, SE-Brazil. *Water Air and Soil Pollution, 133*(1–4), 315–333.

Kochanska, G. (2002a). Committed compliance, moral self, and internalization: A mediational model. *Developmental Psychology, 38,* 339–351.

Kochanska, G. (2002b). Mutually responsive orientation between mothers and their young children: A context for the early development of conscience. *Current Directions in Psychological Science, 11,* 191–195.

Kochanska, G., & Askan, N. (1995). Mother-child mutually positive affect, the quality of child compliance to requests, and prohibitions, and maternal control as correlates of early internalization. *Child Development, 66,* 236–254.

Koedinger, K. R. (2001). Cognitive tutors as modelling tools and instructional models. In K. D. Forbus & P. J. Feltovich (Eds.) *Smart machines in education,* Cambridge, MA: MIT Press.

Kohlberg, L. (1966). A cognitive-developmental analysis of children's sex role concepts and attitudes. In E. E. Maccoby (Ed.), *The development of sex differences*. Stanford, CA: Stanford University Press.

Kohlberg, L. (1969). Stage and sequence: The cognitive-developmental approach to socialization. In D. A. Goslin (Ed.), *Handbook of socialization theory and research*. Chicago: Rand McNally.

Kohlberg, L. (1976). Moral stages and moralization: The cognitive-developmental approach. In J. Lickona (Ed.), *Moral development behavior: Theory, research and social issues*. New York: Holt, Rinehart and Winston.

Kohlberg, L. (1984). *The psychology of moral development: The nature and validity of moral stages: Vol. 2*. New York: Harper & Row.

Kokko, K., & Pulkkinen, L. (2000). Aggression in childhood and long-term unemployment in adulthood: A cycle of maladaptation and some protective factors. *Developmental Psychology, 36*, 463–472.

Kolata, G. (1986). Obese children: A growing problem. *Science, 232*, 20–21.

Kolb, B., & Whishaw, I. Q. (2001). *An introduction to brain and behavior*. New York: Worth.

Koluchova, J. (1972). Severe deprivation in twins: A case study. *Journal of Child Psychology and Psychiatry, 13*, 107–114.

Koluchova, J. (1976). A report on the further development of twins after severe and prolonged deprivation. In A. M. Clarke & A. D. B. Clarke (Eds.), *Early experience: Myth and evidence*. London: Open Books.

Konner, M. (1977). Evolution in human behavior development. In P. H. Leiderman, S. Tulkin, & A. Rosenfeld (Eds.), *Culture and infancy: Variations in human experience*. New York: Academic Press.

Koopmans-van Beinum, F. J., Clement, C. J., & van den Dikkenberg-Pot, I. (2001). Babbling and the lack of auditory speech perception: A matter of coordination? *Developmental Science, 4*(1), 61–70.

Korner, A. F., & Constantinou, J. C. (2001). The neurobehavioral assessment of the preterm infant: Reliability and developmental and clinical validity. In L. T. Singer & P. S. Zeskind (Eds.), *Biobehavioral assessment of the infant* (pp. 381–397). New York: Guilford.

Krappmann, L. (1989). Family relationships and peer relationships in middle childhood: An exploratory study of the associations between children's integration into the social network of peers and family development. In K. Kreppner & R. Lerner (Eds.), *Family systems and life-span development*. Mahwah, NJ: Erlbaum.

Krashen, S. (1996). *Under attack: The case against bilingual education*. Culver City, CA: Language Education Associates.

Krashen, S. D. (1999). *Condemned without a trial: Bogus arguments against bilingual education*. Portsmouth, NH,: Heinemann.

Krasnogorski, N. I. (1907/1967). The formation of artificial conditioned reflexes in young children. In Y. Brackbill & G. G. Thompson (Eds.), *Behavior in infancy and early childhood: A book of readings*. New York: Free Press.

Kreutzer, M. A., Leonard, S. C., & Flavell, J. H. (1975). An interview study of children's knowledge about memory. *Monographs of the Society for Research in Child Development, 40*(1, Serial No. 159).

Krevans, J., & Gibbs, J. C. (1996). Parent's use of inductive discipline: Relations to children's empathy and prosocial behavior. *Child Development, 67*(6), 3263–3277.

Kroger, J. (2003). What transists in an identity status transition? *Identity, 3*(3), 197–220.

Kuhl, P. K. (2001). Speech, language, and developmental change. In F. Lacerda, C. von Hofsten, & M. Heimann (Eds.), *Emerging cognitive abilities in early infancy* (pp. 111–133). Mahwah, NJ: Erlbaum.

Kulis, S., Napoli, M., Marsiglia, F. (2002). Ethnic pride, biculturalism, and drug use norms of urban American Indian adolescents. *Social Work Research, 26*, 101–112.

Kumra, S., Giedd, J., Vaituzis, A., & Jacobsen, L. (2000). Childhood-onset psychotic disorders: Magnetic resonance imaging of volumetric differences in brain structure. *American Journal of Psychiatry, 157*, 1467–1474.

Kupersmidt, J. B., Coie, J. D., & Dodge, K. A. (1990). The role of poor peer relationships in the development of disorder. In S. R. Asher & J. D. Coie (Eds.), *Peer rejection in childhood*. New York: Cambridge University Press.

Kupperman, J. & Fishman, B. J. (2002). Academic, social, and personal uses of the Internet: Cases of students from an urban Latino classroom. *Journal of Research on Technology in Education, 34*(2), 189–215.

Kusiako, T., Ronsmans, C., & Van der Paal, L. (2000). Perinatal mortality attributable to complications of childbirth in Matlab, Bangladesh. *Bulletin of the World Health Organization, 78*(5), 621–627.

Kuther, T., & Higgins–D'Alessandro, A. (2000). Bridging the gap between moral reasoning and adolescent engagement in risky behavior. *Journal of Adolescence, 23*, 409–422.

Laboratory of Comparative Human Cognition. (1983). Culture and cognitive development. In P. Mussen (Ed.), *Handbook of child psychology: Vol. 1, History, theory, and methods* (4th ed.). New York: Wiley.

Lacereda, F., von Hofsten, C., & Heimann, M. (Eds.). (2001). *Emerging cognitive abilities in early infancy*. Mahwah, NJ: Erlbaum.

Lacombe, A. C., & Gay, J. (1998). The role of gender in adolescent identity and intimacy decisions. *Journal of Youth & Adolescence, 27*(6), 795–802.

Ladd, G. W. (1999). Peer relationships and social competence during early and middle childhood. *Annual Review of Psychology, 50*, 333–359.

Ladd, G. W., & Troop-Gordon, W. (2003). The role of chronic peer difficulties in the development of children's psychological adjustment problems. *Child Development, 74*(5), 1344–1367.

Lagercrantz, H., & Slotkin, T. A. (1986). The "stress" of being born. *Scientific American, 254*, 100–107.

Lake, A., Staiger, P., & Glowinski, H. (2000). Effect of Western culture on women's attitudes to eating and perceptions of body shape. *International Journal of Eating Disorders, 27*, 83–89.

Lamb, M. (1998). Nonparental child care: context, quality, correlates, and consequences. In I. E. Sigel & K. A. Renninger (Eds.), *Handbook of child psychology, Vol 4: Child psychology in practice* (5th ed., pp. 73–133). New York: Wiley.

Lamb, M. E. (Ed.). (1987). *The father's role: Cross-cultural perspectives*. Mahwah, NJ: Erlbaum.

Lamb, M. E., Hwang, C. P., Ketterlinus, R. D., & Fracasso, M. P. (1999). Parent-child relationships: Development in the context of the family. In M. H. Bornstein & M. E. Lamb (Eds.), *Developmental psychology: An advanced textbook* (pp. 411–450). Mahwah, NJ: Erlbaum.

Lamb, M. E., Pleck, J. H., Charnov, E. L., & Levine, J. A. (1987). A biosocial perspective on paternal behavior and involvement. In J. B. Lancaster, J. Altmann, A. Rossi, & L. R. Sherrod (Eds.), *Parenting across the lifespan: Biosocial perspectives*. Hawthorne, NY: Aldine de Gruyter.

Lamborn, S. D., Dornbusch, S. M., & Steinberg, L. (1996). Ethnicity and community context as moderators of the relations between family decision making and adolescent adjustment. *Child Development, 67*(2), 283–301.

Lampert, M., & Blunk, M. L. (Eds.). (1998). *Talking mathematics in school: Studies of teaching and learning*. Cambridge, UK: Cambridge University Press.

Lane, H. (1976). *The wild boy of Aveyron*. Cambridge, MA: Harvard University Press.

Langlois, J. (1986). From the eye of the beholder to behavioral reality: Development of social behaviors and social relations as a function of physical attractiveness. In C. P. Herman, M. P. Zanna, & E. T. Higgins (Eds.), *Physical appearance, stigma, and social behavior: The Ontario Symposium: Vol. 3*. Mahwah, NJ: Erlbaum.

Langlois, J. H., Kalakanis, L., Rubenstein, A. J., Larson, A., Hallam, M., & Smoot, M. (2000). Maxims or myths of beauty? A meta-analytic and theoretical review. *Psychological Bulletin, 126*(3), 390–423.

Langlois, J. H., Ritter, J. M., Casey, R. J., & Sawin, D. B. (1995). Infant attractiveness predicts maternal behaviors and attitudes. *Developmental Psychology, 31*, 464–472.

Largo, R. H., Molinari, L., von Siebenthal, K., & Wolfensberger, U. (1996). Does a profound change in toilet-training affect development of bowel and bladder control? *Developmental Medicine and Child Neurology, 38*, 1106–1116.

Larsen, B. (1996). Closeness and conflict in adolescent peer relationships: Interdependence with friends and romantic partneter. In W. Bukowski, A. Newcomb, & W. Hartup (Eds.), *The company they keep: Friendship in childhood and adolescence*. New York: Cambridge University Press.

Larson, R., & Richards, M. (1991). Daily companionship in late childhood and early adolescence: Changing developmental contexts. *Child Development, 62*, 284–300.

Laslett, P. (1972). *Household and family in past time*. Cambridge University Press.

Latour, B. (1987). *Science in action*. Cambridge, MA: Harvard University Press.

Laumann, E., Gagnon, J. H., Michael, R. T., & Stuart Michaels, S. (1994). *The social organization of sexuality: Sexual practices in the United States*. Chicago: University of Chicago Press.

Laupa, M., Turiel, E., & Cowan, P. (1995). Obedience to authority in children and adults. In M. Killen & D. Hart (Eds.), *Morality in everyday life: Developmental perspectives* (pp. 131–165). Cambridge, UK: Cambridge University Press.

Laursen, B., Coy, K. C., & Collins, W. A. (1998). Reconsidering changes in parent–child conflict across adolescence: A meta-analysis. *Child Development (Chicago), 69*(3), 817–832.

Laursen, B., Finkelstein, B., & Betts, N. (2001). A developmental meta-analysis of peer conflict resolution. *Developmental Review, 21*, 423–449.

Lave, J., & Wenger, E. (1991). *Situated learning: Legitimate peripheral practice*. New York: Cambridge University Press.

Lavelli, M., & Fogel, A. (2002). Developmental changes in mother–infant face-to-face communication: Birth to 3 months. *Developmental Psychology, 38*(2), 288–305.

Lebra, T. S. (1994). Mother and child in Japanese socialization: A Japan–U.S. comparison. In P. M. Greenfield & R. R. Cocking (Eds.), *Cross-cultural roots of minority child development* (pp. 259–274). Mahwah, NJ: Erlbaum.

Lecanuet, J. P., & Schaal, B. (1996). Fetal sensory competencies. *European Journal of Obstetrics, Gynecology, and Reproductive Biology*.

Lecanuet, J. P., Graniere-Deferre, C., Jacquet, A-Y., & DeCasper, A. J. (2000). Fetal discrimination of low-pitched musical notes. *Developmental Psychobiology, 36*(1), 29–39.

Lecanuet, J.-P., & Jacquet, A.-Y. (2002). Fetal responsiveness to maternal passive swinging in low heart rate variability state: Effects of stimulation direction and duration. *Developmental Psychobiology, 40*(1), 57–67.

Lee, C. D. (1995). Signifying as a scaffold for literary interpretation. *Journal of Black Psychology, 21*(4): 357–381.

Lee, C. D. (2001). Is October Brown Chinese? A cultural modeling activity system for underachieving students. *American Educational Research Journal, 38*(1): 97–141.

Lee, L. (1965). *Cider with Rosie*. London: Hogarth Press.

Lee, M. (1998). Marijuana and tobacco use in pregnancy. *Obstetrics and Gynecology Clinics of North America, 25*(1), 65–83.

Lefeber, Y., & Voorhoeve, H. W. A. (1998). *Indigenous customs in childbirth and child care*. Assen, Netherlands: Von Gocum.

Lefkowitz, E., Romo, L., Corona, R., Au, T., & Sigman, M. (2000). How Latino American and European American adolescents discuss conflicts, sexuality, and AIDS with their mothers. *Developmental Psychology, 36*, 315–325.

Legault, F., & Strayer, F. F. (1990). The emergence of sex-segregation in preschool peer groups. In F. F. Strayer (Ed.), *Social interaction and behavioral development during early childhood*. Montreal: La Maison D'Ethologie de Montreal.

Legerstee, M. (1991). The role of person and object in eliciting early imitation. *Journal of Experimental Child Psychology, 51*(3), 423–433.

Legerstee, M. (2001). Domain specificity and the epistemic triangle: The development of the concept of animacy in infancy. In F. Lacereda, C. von Hofsten, M. Hermann (Eds.), *Emerging cognitive abilities in early infancy* (pp. 193–212). Mahwah, NJ: Erlbaum.

Leighton, D., & Kluckhohn, C. (1947/1969). *Children of the people; the Navaho individual and his development*. Cambridge: Harvard University Press.

Lemaire, P., & Siegler, R. S. (1995). Four aspects of strategic change: Contributions to children's learning of multiplication. *Journal of Experimental Psychology: General, 124*, 83–97.

Lemerise, E., & Arsenio, W. (2000). An integrated model of emotion processes and cognition in social information processing. *Child Development, 71*, 107–118.

Leming, J. (2001). Integrating a structured ethical reflection curriculum into high school community service experiences: Impact on students' sociomoral development. *Adolescence, 36*, 33–45.

Lemish, D., & Rice, M. L. (1986). Television as a talking picture book: A prop for language acquisition. *Journal of Child Language, 13*, 251–274.

Leoni, L. (1964). *Tico and the golden wings*. New York: Pantheon.

Lerner, R. M., Anderson, P. M., et al. (2003). Applied developmental science of positive human development. In R. M. Lerner, M. A. Easterbrooks, & J. Mistry (Eds.), *Handbook of psychology: Developmental psychology: Vol. 6* (pp. 535–558). New York: Wiley.

Leslie, A. M. (1994). To MM, to BY, and agency: Core architecture and domain specificity. In L. A. Hirschfeld & S. Gelman (Eds.), *Mapping the mind: Domain specificity in cognition and culture*. New York: Cambridge University Press.

Leslie, A. M. (2002). Pretense and representation revisited. In N. L. Stein, P. J. Bauer, & M. Rabinowitz (Eds.), *Representation, memory, and development: Essays in honor of Jean Mandler* (pp. 103–114). Mahwah, NJ: Erlbaum.

Lesser, G. S. (1974). *Children and television*. New York: Random House.

Lester, B. M., Boukydis, C. Z., Garcia-Coll, C. T., Hole, W., &Peucker, M. (1992). Infantile colic: Acoustic cry characteristics, maternal perception of cry, and temperament. *Infant Behavior & Development, 15*(1), 15–26.

Lester, B. M., & Tronick, E. Z. (1994). The effects of prenatal cocaine exposure and child outcome. Special issue: Prenatal drug exposure and child outcome. *Infant Mental Health Journal, 15*, 107–120.

LeVine, R. A. (1974). Parental goals: A cross-cultural view. In H. J. Leichter (Ed.), *The family as educator*. New York: Teachers College Press.

LeVine, R. A. (1998a). Child psychology and anthropology: An environmental view. In P.-B. Catherine (Ed.), *Biosocial perspectives on children* (pp. 102–130). New York: Cambridge University Press.

LeVine, R. A. (1988b). Human parental care: Universal goals, cultural strategies, individual behavior. In R. A. LeVine, P. M. Miller, & M. M. West (Eds.), *Parental behavior in diverse societies. New directions for child development, No. 40: The Jossey-Bass social and behavioral sciences series*. San Francisco: Jossey-Bass.

LeVine, R. A., Dixon, S., LeVine, S., Richman, A., Leiderman, P. H., Keefer, C. H., & Brazelton, T. B. (1994). *Child care and culture: Lessons from Africa*. New York: Cambridge University Press.

LeVine, R. A., LeVine, S. E., & Schnell, B. (2001). "Improve the women": Mass schooling, female literacy, and worldwide social change. *Harvard Educational Review, 71*(1): 1–50.

Levy, E. (1989). Monologue as development of the text-forming function of language. In K. Nelson (Ed.), *Narratives from the crib*. Cambridge, MA: Harvard University Press.

Levy, G. D., & Fivush, R. (1993). Scripts and gender: A new approach for examining gender-role development. *Developmental Review, 13,* 126–146.

Lewis, M. (1997). *Altering fate: Why the past does not predict the future.* New York: Guilford.

Lewis, M. (1998). The development and structure of emotions. In M. F. Mascolo & S. Griffin (Eds.), *What develops in emotional development?* (pp. 29–50). New York: Plenum Press.

Lewis, M. (2001). Origins of the self-conscious child. In W. R. Crozier & L. E. Alden (Eds.), *International handbook of social anxiety: Concepts, research and interventions relating to the self and shyness* (pp. 101–118). New York: Wiley.

Lewis, M., & Feiring, C. (1989). Infant, mother, and mother–infant interaction behavior and subsequent attachment. *Child Development, 60,* 831–837.

Lewontin, R. C. (1976). Race and intelligence. In N. J. Block & G. Dworkin (Eds.), *The IQ controversy.* New York: Pantheon.

Liaw, F.-R., Meisels, S. J., & Brooks-Gunn, J. (1995). The effects of experience of early intervention on low birth weight, premature children: The Infant Health and Development Program. *Early Childhood Research Quarterly, 10*(4), 405–431.

Liben, L., & Bigler, R. (2002). The developmental course of gender differentiation. *Monographs for the Society for Research in Child Development, 67,* 1–147.

Lichter, S. R., Lichter, L. S., & Amundson, D. (1997). Does Hollywood hate business or money? *Journal of Communication, 47*(1), 68–84.

Liddell, C. (2002). Emic perspectives on risk in African childhood. *Developmental Review, 22,* 97–116.

Lifter, K., & Bloom, L. (1989). Object knowledge and the emergence of language. *Infant Behavior and Development, 12,* 395–424.

Lightfoot, C. (1997). *The culture of adolescent risk taking.* New York: Guilford Press.

Lightfoot, C. (2004). Risk-taking, carnival, and the novelistic self: Adolescents' avenues to moral being and integrity. In L. Nucci (Ed.), *Conflict, contradiction, and contrarian elements in moral development and education.* Mahwah, NJ: Erlbaum.

Lillard, A. (1998). Ethnopsychologies: Cultural variations in theories of mind. *Psychological Bulletin, 123*(1), 3–32.

Lillard, A. (2002). Pretend play cognitive development. In U. Goswami (Ed.), *Blackwell handbook of childhood cognitive development* (pp. 188–205). Marten, MA: Blackwell.

Linn, M. C., & Hyde, J. S. (1991). Cognitive and psychosocial gender differences trends. In R. Lerner, A. C. Petersen, & J. Brooks-Gunn (Eds.), *Encyclopedia of Adolescence.* New York: Garland Publishers.

Linnenbrink, E. A., & Pintrich, P. R. (2003). The role of self-efficacy beliefs in student engagement and learning in the classroom. *Reading & Writing Quarterly: Overcoming Learning Difficulties, 19*(2), 199–137.

Lipsitt, L. P. (1990). Learning and memory in infants. *Merrill-Palmer Quarterly, 36*(1), 53–66.

Lipsitt, L. P. (2003). Crib death: A biobehavioral phenomenon. *Current Directions in Psychological Science, 12*(5), 164–170.

Lloyd, B. T. (2002). A conceptual framework for examining adolescent identity, media influence, and social development. *Review of General Psychology, 6*(1), 73–91.

Loeber, R., & Hay, D. (1993). Developmental approach to aggression and conduct problems. In M. Rutter & D. Hay (Eds.), *Development through life: A handbook for clinicians* (pp. 488–516). Oxford, England: Blackwell.

Loehlin, J. C. (1992). *Genes and environment in personality development, Vol. 2.* Newbury Park, CA: Sage Publications.

Loftus, E. F. (1996). *Eyewitness testimony.* Cambridge, MA: Harvard University Press.

Lopez, G. (2001). The value of hard work: Lessons on parent involvement from an (im)migrant household. *Harvard Educational Review, 71,* 416–437.

Lorberbaum, J. P., Newman, J. D., Horwitz, A. R., Dubno, J. R., Lydiard, R. B., Bohning, D. E., & George, G. S. (2002). A potential role for the thalamocingulate circuitry in human maternal behavior. *Biological Psychiatry, 51,* 431–445.

Lorch, E. P. (1994). Measuring children's cognitive processing of television. In A. Lang (Ed.), *Measuring psychological responses to media.* Mahwah, NJ: Erlbaum.

Lorenz, J. M. (2001). The outcome of extreme prematurity. *Seminars in Perinatology* (Philadelphia), *25*(5), 348–359.

Lorenz, K. (1943). Die Angebornen Formen mogicher Erfahrung. *Zeitschrift fur Tierpsychologie, 5,* 233–409.

Lorenz, K. (1966). *On aggression.* New York: Harcourt, Brace & World.

Lourenco, O., & Machado, A. (1996). In defense of Piaget's theory: A reply to 10 common criticisms. *Psychological Review, 103*(1), 143–164.

Love, J., Harrison, L., Sagi-Schwartz, A., van IJzendoorn, M., Ross, C., Ungerer, J., et al. (2003). Child care quality matters: How conclusions may vary with context. *Child Development, 74,* 1021–1033.

Lovitt, T. C. (2000). Preventing school failure: tactics for teaching adolescents. Austin, TX: Pro-Ed.

Lowry, J. (1999, March 7). Gay adoption backlash growing. *San Francisco Examiner,* p. 20.

Lucas, C. J. (1972). *Our western educational heritage.* New York: Macmillan.

Luhrmann, T. M. (1989). Persuasions of the witch's craft: Ritual magic and witchcraft in present-day England. Oxford: Basil Blackwell.

Lundqvist, C., & Sabel, K.-G. (2000). Brief report: The Brazelton Neonatal Behavioral Assessment Scale detects differences among newborn infants of optimal health. *Journal of Pediatric Psychology, 25*(8), 577–582.

Lunthar, S., Cicchetti, D., & Becker, B. (2000). The construct of resilience: A critical evaluation and guidelines for future research. *Child Development, 71,* 543–562.

Luria, A. R. (1973). *The waking brain.* New York: Basic Books.

Luria, A. R. (1981). *Language and cognition.* New York: Wiley.

Luria, Z., & Herzog, E. W. (1991). Sorting gender out in a children's museum. *Gender and Society, 5*(2), 224–232.

Luster, T., Bates, L., Figtzgerald, H., Vandenbelt, M., & Key, J. (2000). Factors related to successful outcomes among preschool children born to low-income adolescent mothers. *Journal of Marriage and the Family, 62,* 133–146.

Luthar, S., & Becker, B. (2002). Privileged but pressured? A study of affluent youth. *Child Development, 73,* 1593–1610.

Lutz, C. (1987). Goals, events, and understanding Ifaluk emotion theory. In D. Holland & N. Quinn (Eds.), *Cultural models in language and thought.* Cambridge: Cambridge University Press.

Lyn, H., Greenfield, P., & Savage-Rumbaugh, S. (2004, March 31). *Semiotic combination in Pan: Evolutionary implications of proto-syntax.* Leipzig, Germany: Fifth International Conference on the Evolution of Language.

Lyons-Ruth, K., & Jacobvitz, D. (1999). Attachment disorganization. In J. Cassidy & P. R. Shaver (Eds.), *Handbook of attachment: Theory, research, and clinical applications* (pp. 520–554). New York: Guilford Press.

Maccoby, E. E. (1980). *Social development: Psychological growth and the parent-child relationship.* New York: Harcourt Brace Jovanovich.

Maccoby, E. E. (1984). Middle childhood in the context of the family. In W. A. Collins (Ed.), *Development during middle childhood: The years from six to twelve.* Washington, DC: National Academy Press.

Maccoby, E. E. (1998). *The two sexes.* Cambridge, MA: Havard Univeristy Press.

Maccoby, E. E. (2000). Parenting and its effects on children: On reading and mistrading behavior genetics. *Annual Review of Psychology, 51,* 1–27.

Maccoby, E. E. (2003). The gender of child and parent as factors in family dynamics. In A. C. Crouter & A. Booth (Eds.), *Children's influence on* *family dynamics: The neglected side of family relationships* (pp. 191–206). Mahwah, NJ: Erlbaum.

MacFarlane, A. (1977). *The psychology of childbirth.* Cambridge, MA: Harvard University Press.

Mackintosh, N. J. (1998). *IQ and human intelligence.* Oxford: Oxford University Press.

MacWhinney, B. (2000). *The CHILDES project: Tools for analyzing talk: Vol 1: Transcription format and programs.* Mahwah, NJ: Erlbaum.

Magai, C., & Haviland-Jones, J. (2002). *The hidden genius of emotion: Lifespan transformations of personality.* Cambridge: Cambridge University Press.

Maguen, S., Floyd, F., Bakeman, R., & Armistead, L. (2002). Developmental milestones and disclosure of sexual orientation among gay, lesbian, and bisexual youths. *Applied Developmental Psychology, 23.*

Main, M., & Solomon, J. (1990). Procedures for identifying infants as disorganized/disoriented during the Ainsworth strange situation. In M. Greenberg, D. Cicchetti, & E. M. Cummings (Eds.), *Attachment in the preschool years: Theory, research, and intervention* (pp. 121–160). Chicago: University of Chicago Press.

Maleta, K., Virtanen, S., Espo, M., Kulmala, T., Ashorn, P. (2003). Timing of growth faltering in rural Malawi. *Archives of Disease in Childhood, 88,* 574–578.

Malina, R. M. (1998). Motor development and performance. In S. J. Ulijaszek, F. E. Johnston, & M. A. Preece (Eds.), *The Cambridge encyclopedia of human growth and development* (pp. 247–250). Cambridge: Cambridge University Press.

Malina, R. M., & Bouchard, C. (1991). *Growth, maturation and physical activity.* Champaign, IL: Human Kinetics Books.

Mandler, J. M. (1998). Representation. In D. Kuhn & R. S. Siegler (Eds.), *Handbook of child psychology: Vol. 2. Cognition, perception and language* (5th ed., pp. 255–308). New York: Wiley.

Mandler, J. M. (2000). Perceptual and conceptual processes in infancy. *Journal of Cognition and Development, 1*(1), 3–36.

Mandler, J. M., & McDonough, L. (1993). Concept formation in infancy. *Cognitive Development, 8,* 291–318.

Mandler, J. M., Scribner, S., Cole, M., & de Forest, M. (1980). Cross-cultural invariance in story recall. *Child Development, 51,* 19–26.

Mandoki, M. W., Sumner, G. S., Hoffman, R. P., & Riconda, D. L. (1991). A review of Klinefelter's syndrome in children and adolescents. *Journal of the American Academy of Child & Adolescent Psychiatry, 30*(2), 167–172.

Manning, W. D. (1990). Parenting employed teenagers. *Youth and Society, 22*(2), 184–200.

Manns, W. (1997). Supportive roles of significant others in African American families. In H. P. McAdoo (Ed.), *Black families* (3rd ed., pp. 198–213). Thousand Oaks, CA: Sage.

Manstead, A. S. R. (1995). Children's understanding of emotion. In J. A. Russell & J. M. Fernandez-Dols (Eds.), *Everyday conceptions of emotion: An introduction to the psychology, anthropology and linguistics of emotion.* Boston: Kluwer Academic Publishers.

Mappes, T. A., & DeGrazia, D. (Eds.). (2001). *Biomedical ethics.* Boston: McGraw-Hill.

Maratsos, M. (1973). Nonegocentric communication abilities in preschool children. *Child Development, 44,* 697–700.

Maratsos, M. (1999). Some aspects of innateness and complexity in grammatical acquisition. In M. Barrett (Ed.), *The development of language: Studies in developmental psychology* (pp. 191–228). Philadelphia, PA: Psychology Press.

Marcia, J. E. (1966). Development and validation of ego identity status. *Journal of Personality and Social Psychology, 3,* 551–558.

Marcia, J. E. (1980). Identity in adolescence. In J. Adelson (Ed.), *Handbook of adolescent psychology.* New York: Wiley.

Marcia, J. E. (1999). Representational thought in ego identity, psychotherapy, and psychosocial developmental theory. In I. E. Sigel (Ed.), *Development of mental representation: Theories and applications* (pp. 391–414). Mahwah, NJ: Erlbaum.

Marcia, J. E. (2002). Identity and psychosocial development in adulthood. *Identity, 2*(1), 7–28.

Marcus, G. F., Vijayan, S., Bandi Rao, S., & Vishton, P. M. (1999). Rule learning by seven-month-old infants. *Science, 283,* 77–79.

Markovitz, H., & Barrouillet, P. (2002). The development of conditional reasoning: A mental model account. *Developmental Review, 22,* 5–36.

Marks, J. (2002). *What it means to be 98% chimpanzee: Apes, people, and their genes.* Berkeley: University of California Press.

Markus, H. R., & Kitayama, S. (1991). Culture and the self: Implications for cognition, emotion, and motivation. *Psychological Review, 98,* 224–253.

Markus, H. R., & Kitayama, S. (1998). The cultural psychology of personality. *Journal of Cross-cultural Psychology, 29*(1), 63–87.

Marlier, L., Schaal, B., & Soussignan, R. (1998). Neonatal responsiveness to the odor of amniotic and lacteal fluids: A test of perinatal chemosensory continuity. *Child Development, 69*(3), 611–623.

Marshall, W. A., & Tanner, J. M. (1974). Puberty. In J. A. Davis & J. Dobbing (Eds.), *Scientific foundations of pediatrics.* Philadelphia: Saunders.

Marsiglio, W., Amato, P., Day, R., & Lamb, M. (2000). Scholarship on fatherhood in the 1990s and beyond. *Journal of Marriage and the Family, 62*(1), 1173–1191.

Martin, C. B., Jr. (1998). Electronic fetal monitoring: A brief summary of its development, problems and prospects. *European Journal of Obstetrics & Gynecology and Reproductive Biology, 78,* 133–140.

Martin, C. H., & Halverson, C. F. (1981). A schematic processing model of sextyping and stereotyping in children. *Child Development, 52,* 1119–1134.

Martin, C. H., & Halverson, C. F. (1987). The roles of cognition in sex role acquisition. In D. B. Carter (Ed.), *Current conceptions of sex roles and sex typing: Theory and research.* New York: Praeger Publishers.

Martin, J. A., Park, M. M., & Sutton, P. D. (2002). Births: Preliminary data for 2001. *National Vital Statistics Reports, 50*(10), 1–20.

Martin, K. (1996). *Puberty, sexuality and the self: Boys and girls at adolescence.* New York: Routledge.

Martineau, W. H. (1972). A model of the social functions of humor. In J. H. Goldstein & P. E. McGhee (Eds.), *The psychology of humor: Theoretical perspectives and empirical issues* (pp. 116–119). New York: Academic Press.

Mascolo, M., Fischer, K., & Li, J. (2003). Dynamic development of component systems of emotions: Pride, shame and guilt in China and the United States. In R. Davidson, K. Scherer, & H. Goldsmith (Eds.), *Handbook of affective sciences.* Oxford: Oxford University Press.

Mason, M. A., Skolnick, A., & Sugarman, S. D. (1998). *All our families: New policies for a new century.* New York: Oxford University Press.

Massey, C. M., & Gelman, R. (1988). Preschooler's ability to decide whether a photographed unfamiliar object can move itself. *Developmental Psychology, 24*(3), 307–317.

Massimini, F., & Delle Fave, A. (2000). Individual development in a bio-cultural perspective. *American Psychologist, 55*(1), 24–33.

Massoni, G. A., Vannuccci, M., & Loftus, E. F. (1999). Misremembering story material. *Legal & Criminological Psychology, 4*(1), 93–110.

Matturri, L., Biondo, B., Suarez-Mier, M. P., & Rossi, L. (2002). Brain stem lesions in the sudden infant death syndrome: Variability in the hypoplasia of the arcuate nucleus. *Acta Neuropathology* (Berlin), *104,* 12–20.

Maurer, D., Stager, C. L., & Mondloch, C. J. (1999). Cross-modal transfer of shape is difficult to demonstrate in one-month-olds. *Child Development, 70*(5), 1047–1057.

Mazur, A., & Booth, A. (1998). Testosterone and dominance in men. *Behavioral & Brain Sciences, 21*(3), 353–397.

McAdoo, H. P. (1985). Racial attitude and self-concept of young black children over time. In H. P. McAdoo & J. L. McAdoo (Eds.), *Black children: Social, educational, and parental environments.* Beverly Hills, CA: Sage.

McCabe, D. (1999). Academic dishonesty among high school students. *Adolescence, 34,* 681–687.

McCarty, M. E., Clifton, R. K., & Collard, R. R. (1999). Problem solving in infancy: The emergence of an action plan. *Developmental Psychology, 35*(4), 1091–1101.

McCarty, M. E., Clifton, R. K., & Collard, R. R. (2001). The beginnings of tool use by infants and toddlers. *Infancy, 2*(2), 233–256.

McCarty, M. E., Clifton, R. K., Ashmead, D. H., Lee, P., & Goubet, N. (2001). How infants use vision for grasping objects. *Child Development, 72*(4), 973–987.

McDonough, L., & Mandler, J. M. (1994). Very long-term memory in infancy: Infantile amnesia reconsidered. *Memory, 2,* 339–352.

McDonough, L., & Mandler, J. M. (1998). Inductive generalization in 9- and 11-month-olds. *Developmental Science, 1*(2), 227–232.

McGhee, P. (1979). *Humor: Its origin and development.* San Francisco: Freeman.

McGilly, K., & Siegler, R. S. (1989). How children choose among serial recall strategies. *Child Development, 60*(1), 172–182.

McGraw, M. B. (1975). *Growth: A study of Johnny and Jimmy.* New York: Arno Press. (Original work published 1935)

McGue, M. (1993). From proteins to cognitions: The behavioral genetics of alcoholism. In R. Plomin & G. E. McClearn (Eds.), *Nature, nurture & psychology* (pp. 245–268). Washington, DC: American Psychological Association.

McGue, M. (1995). Mediators and moderators of alcoholism inheritence. In J. R. Turner, L. R. Cardon, & J. K. Hewitt (Eds.), *Behavior genetic approaches to behavioral medicine* (pp. 17–44). New York: Plenum Press.

McGuire, S. (2002). Nonshared environment research: What is it and where is it going? *Marriage & Family Review, 33*(1), 31–56.

McGuire, S., & Roch-Levecq, A.-C. (2001). Mother's perceptions of differential treatment of infant twins. In R. N. Emde & J. K. Hewitt (Eds.), *Infancy to early childhood: Genetic and environmental influences on developmental change* (pp. 247–256). New York: Oxford University Press.

McHale, S., & Crouter, A. (1996). The family contexts of children's sibling relationships. In G. H. Brody (Ed.), *Sibling relationships: Their causes and consequences.* Norwood, NJ: Ablex.

McKelvie, P., & Low, J. (2002). Listening to Mozart does not improve children's spatial ability: Final curtains for the Mozart effect. *British Journal of Developmental Psychology, 20,* 241–258.

McKenna, J. J. (1996) Sudden infant death syndrome in cross-cultural perspective: Is infant-parent cosleeping protective? *Annual Review of Anthropology, 25,* 201–216.

McKinney, M. L. (1998). Cognitive evolution by extending brain development: On recapitulation, progress, and other heresies. In J. Langer & M. Killer (Eds.), *Piaget, evolution, and development.* Mahwah, NJ: Erlbaum.

McLoyd, V. C. (1998a). Children in poverty: Development, public policy, and practice. In I. E. Sigel & K. A. Renninger (Eds.), *Handbook of child psychology: Vol. 4. Child psychology in practice* (5th ed., pp. 135–210). New York: Wiley.

McLoyd, V. C. (1998b). Socioeconomic disadvantage and child development. *American Psychologist, 53*(2), 185–204.

McLoyd, V.C., & Smith, J. (2002). Physical discipline and behavior problems in African American, European American, and Hispanic children: Emotional support as a moderator. *Journal of Marriage and Family, 64,* 40–53.

McNamara, F., Lijowska, A. S., & Thach, B. T. (2002). Spontaneous arousal activity in infants during NREM and REM sleep. *Journal of Physiology, 538,* 263–269.

McNeill, D. (1966). Developmental psycholinguistics. In S. Smith & G. A. Miller (Eds.) *The genesis of language: A psycholinguistic approach.* Cambridge: MIT Press.

McNeill, D. (1970). *The acquisition of language: The study of developmental psycholinguistics.* New York: Harper & Row.

McPhee, C. (1970). Children and music in Bali. In J. Belo (Ed.), *Traditional Balinese culture* (pp. 212–239). New York: Columbia University Press.

Mead, M., & Macgregor, F. C. (1951). *Growth and culture.* New York: Putnam.

Meaney, M. (2001). Maternal care, gene expression, and the transmission of individual differences in stress reactivity across generations. *Annual Review of Neuroscience, 24,* 1161–1192.

Meara, E. (2001). *Why is health related to socioeconomic status? The case of pregnancy and low birth weight.* Cambridge, MA: National Bureau of Economic Research.

Meeus, W., & Dekovic, M. (1995). Identity development, parental and peer support in adolescence: Results of a national Dutch survey. *Adolescence, 30*(120), 931–944.

Meeus, W., Iedema, J., & Maassen, G. H. (2002). Commitment and exploration as mechanisms of identity formation. *Psychological Reports, 90*(3, Pt. 1), 771–785.

Mehan, H. (1979a). *Learning lessons.* Cambridge, MA: Harvard University Press.

Mehan, H. (1979b). What time is it, Denise? Asking known information questions in classroom discourse. *Theory into Practice, 18,* 285–294.

Mehan, H. (1998). The study of social interaction in educational settings: Accomplishments and unresolved issues. *Human Development, 41*(4), 245–268.

Melot, A.-M., & Houde, O. (1998). Categorization and theories of mind: The case of the appearance/reality distinction. *Cahiers de Psychologie Cognitive/Current Psychology of Cognition 17*(1), 71–93.

Meltzoff, A. N. (1988a). Imitation of televised models by infants. *Child Development, 59,* 1221–1229.

Meltzoff, A. N. (1988b). Infant imitation and memory: Nine-month-olds in immediate and deferred tests. *Child Development, 59,* 217–225.

Meltzoff, A. N. (1995). Understanding the intentions of others: Re-enactment of intended acts by 18-month-old children. *Development Psychology, 66,* 838–850.

Meltzoff, A. N. (2002). Elements of a developmental theory of imitation. In A. N. Meltzoff & W. Prinz (Eds.), *The imitative mind* (pp. 19–41). Cambridge: Cambridge University Press.

Meltzoff, A. N., & Moore, M. K. (1977). Imitation of facial and manual gestures by human neonates. *Science, 198,* 75–78.

Meltzoff, A. N., & Moore, M. K. (1994). Imitation, memory, and the representation of persons. *Infant Behavior and Development, 17,* 83–99.

Meltzoff, A. N., & Prinz, W. (Eds). (2002). *The imitative mind.* New York: Cambridge University Press.

Meyer, L. H., Park, H.-S., Grenot-Scheyer, M., Schwartz, I. S., & Harry, B. (1998). *Making friends.* Baltimore: Paul H. Brooks.

Meyers, S. (2001). *Everywhere babies.* San Diego: Harcourt.

Mezzich, A. C., Giancola, P. R., Tarter, R. E., Lu, S., Parks, S. M., & Barrett C. M. (1997). Violence, suicidality, and alcohol/drug use involvement in adolescent females with a psychoactive substance use disorder and controls. *Alcoholism Clinical and Experimental Research, 21*(7), 1300–1307.

Michael, R. T. (1994). *Sex in America: A definitive survey.* Boston: Little Brown.

Michalson, L., & Lewis, M. (1985). What do children know about emotions and when do they know it? In M. Lewis & C. Saarni (Eds.), *The socialization of emotions*. New York: Plenum Press.

Miller, B. C., Bgenson, B., & Galbraith, K. (2001). Family relationships and adolescent pregnancy risk: A research synthesis. *Developmental Review, 21*, 1–38.

Miller, D., & Byrnes, J. (2001). Adolescents' decision making in social situations: A self-regulation perspective. *Journal of Applied Developmental Psychology, 22,* 237–256.

Miller, G. A. (1991). *The science of words*. New York: Scientific American Library.

Miller, J. G. (1997). Theoretical issues in cultural psychology. In J. W. Berry & Y. H. Poortinga (Eds.), *Handbook of cross-cultural psychology: Theory and method* (pp. 85–128). Boston: Allyn & Bacon.

Miller, J. G., & Schaberg, L. (2003). Cultural perspectives on personality and social psychology. In T. Millon, & M. J. Lerner (Eds.), *Handbook of psychology: Vol. 5. Personality and social psychology* (pp. 31–56). New York: Wiley.

Miller, K. (1996). The effects of state terrorism and exile on the indigenous Guatemalan refugee children: A mental health assessment and an analysis of children's narratives. *Child Development, 67*, 89–106.

Miller, P. (1982). *Amy, Wendy and Beth: Learning language in south Baltimore*. Austin: University of Texas Press.

Miller, P. (2002). *Theories of developmental psychology* (4th ed.). New York: Worth.

Miller, P. H. (1990). The development of strategies of selective attention. In D. F. Bjorklund (Ed.), *Children's strategies: Contemporary views of cognitive development* (pp. 157–184). Mahwah, NJ: Erlbaum.

Miller, P., Wang, W., Sandel, T., & Cho, G. (2002). Self–esteem as folk theory: A comparison of European American and Taiwanese mothers' beliefs. *Parenting, 2,* 209–239.

Miller, T. W., Veltkamp, L. J., Kraus, R. F., Lane, T., Heister, T. (1999). An adolescent vampire cult in rural America: Clinical issues and case study. *Child Psychiatry & Human Development, 29*(3), 209–219.

Milson, A. J. (2002). The Internet and inquiry learning: Integrating medium and method in a sixth grade social studies classroom. *Theory & Research in Social Education, 30*(3), 330–353.

Minoura, Y. (1992). A sensitive period for the incorporation of a cultral meaning system: A study of Japanese children growing up in America. *Ethos, 20,* 304–339.

Minton, H. L. & Schneider, F. W. (1980). *Differential psychiatry*. Monterey, CA: Brooks/Cole.

Miyake, K., Campos, J., Bradshaw, D. L., & Kagan, J. (1986). Issues in socioemotional development. In H. Stevenson, H. Azuma, & K. Hakuta (Eds.), *Child development and education in Japan*. New York: W. H. Freeman.

Miyake, K., Chen, S., & Campos, J. J. (1985). Infant temperament, mother's mode of interaction, and attachment in Japan. An interim report. *Monographs of the Society for Research in Child Development, 50*(1–2, Serial No. 209).

Mizukami, K., Kobayashi, N., Ishii, T., & Iwata, H. (1990). First selective attachment begins in early infancy: A study using telethermography. *Infant Behavior and Development, 13,* 257–273.

Moely, B. E., Santulli, K. A., & Obach, M. S. (1995). Strategy instruction, metacognition, and motivation in the elementary school classroom. In F. E. Weinert & W. Schneider (Eds.), *Memory performance and competencies: Issues in growth and development* (pp. 301–321). Mahwah, NJ: Erlbaum.

Moffit, T. E., Caspi, A., Belsky, J., & Silva, P. A. (1992). Childhood experience and the onset of menarche: A test of a sociobiological model. *Child Development, 63,* 47–58.

Mondloch, C. J., Lewis, T. L., Budreau, D. R., Maurer, D., Dannemiller, J. L., Stephens, B. R., & Kleiner-Gathercoal, K. A. (1999). Face perception during early infancy. *Psychological Science, 10*(5), 419–422.

Moon, C., Cooper, R. P., & Fifer, W. P. (1993). Two-day-olds prefer their native language. *Infant Behavior Development, 16,* 495–500.

Moore, C. (1996). Theories of mind in infancy. *British Journal of Developmental Psychology, 14*(1), 19–40.

Moore, K. L., & Persaud, T. V. N. (1993). *The developing human: Clinically oriented embryology* (5th ed.). Philadelphia: Saunders.

Moore, K. L., & Persaud, T. V. N. (1998). *The developing human: Clinically oriented embryology*. Philadelphia: Saunders.

Moore, R., & Young, D. (1978). Childhood outdoors: Toward a social ecology of the landscape. In I. Altman & J. Wahlwill (Eds.), *Human behavior and environment: Vol. 3*. New York: Plenum Press.

Mora, J. O., & Nestel, P. S. (2000). Improving prenatal nutrition in developing countries: Strategies, prospects, and challenges. *American Journal of Clinical Nutrition, 71* (Suppl. 5), 1353S–1363S.

Moran, J. P. (2000). *Teaching sex: The shaping of adolescence in the 20th century*. Cambridge: Harvard University Press.

Morelli, G. A., Rogoff, B., Oppenheim, D., & Goldsmith, D. (1992). Cultural variation in infants sleeping arrangements: Questions of independence. *Developmental Psychology, 28,* 604–613.

Morelli, G. A., Tronick, E., & Beeghly, M. (1999). *Is there security in numbers? Child care in a hunting and gathering community and infants' attachment relationships*. Albuquerque, NM: Society for Research in Child Development.

Morgan, G., & Woll, B. (Eds.). (2002). *Directions in sign language acquisition*. Philadelphia: John Benjamins.

Morrison, F. J., Smith, L., & Dow-Ehrensberger, M. (1995). Education and cognitive development: A natural experiment. *Developmental Psychology, 31,* 789–799.

Morrongiello, B. A., Fenwick, K. D., Hillier, L., & Chance, G. (1994). Sound localization in newborn human infants. *Developmental Psychobiology, 27*(8), 519–538.

Morrow, C. E., Bandstra, E. S., Anthony, J. C., Ofir, A. Y., Xue, L., & Reyes, M. B. (2003). Influence of prenatal cocaine exposure on early language development: Longitudinal findings from four months to three years of age. *Journal of Developmental and Behavioral Pediatrics, 24*(1), 39–50.

Mortimer, J. T., & Johnson, M. K. (1998). Adolescent part-time work and educational achievement. In K. Borman & B. Schneider (Eds.), *The adolescent years: social influences and educational challenges* (pp. 183–206). Chicago: National Society for the Study of Education.

Mortimer, J. T., Finch, M. D., Ryu, S., & Shanahan, M. J. (1996). The effects of work intensity on adolescent mental health, achievement, and behavioral adjustment: New evidence from a prospective study. *Child Development, 67*(3), 1243–1261.

Moshman, D. (1998). Cognitive development beyond childhood. In D. Kuhn & R. S. Siegler (Eds.), *Handbook of child psychology: Vol. 2. Cognition, perception, and language* (5th ed., pp. 947–978). New York: Wiley.

Moshman, D. (1999). *Adolescent psychological development: Rationality, morality and identity*. Mahwah, NJ: Erlbaum.

Moshman, D. (2004). Theories of self and selves as theories: Identity in Rwanda. In C. Lightfoot, C. Lalonde, & M. Chandler (Eds.), *Developing conceptions of psychological life*. Mahwah, NJ: Erlbaum.

Moss, N. E., & Carver, K. (1998). The effect of WIC and Medicaid on infant mortality—the United States. *American Journal of Public Health, 88,* 1354–1361.

Müller, U., Sokol, B., & Overton, W. F. (1999). Developmental sequences in class reasoning and propositional reasoning. *Journal of Experimental Child Psychology, 74,* 69–106.

Murray, L., & Cooper, P. J. (1997). Postpartum depression and child development. *Psychological Medicine, 27*(2), 253–260.

Nagler, J. (2002). Sudden infant death syndrome. *Current Opinion in Pediatrics, 14*(2), 247–250.

Naigles, L. G., & Gelman, S. A. (1995). Overextensions in comprehensions and production revisited: Preferential-looking in a study of dog, cat, and cow. *Journal of Child Language, 22*(1), 19–46.

Nakamura, K., Hoshino, Y., Watanabe, A., Honda, K., Niwa, S., Tominaga, K., Shimai, S., & Yamamoto, M. (1999). Eating problems in female Japanese high school students: A prevalence study. *International Journal of Eating Disorders, 26,* 91–95.

Nassaji, H., & Wells, G. (2000). What's the use of triadic dialogue?: An investigation of teacher-student interaction. *Applied Linguistics, 21*(3), 376–406.

Natali, R., Nasello-Paterson, C., & Conners, G. (1988). Patterns in fetal breathing activity in the human fetus at 24 to 28 weeks of gestation. *American Journal of Obstetrics and Gynecology, 158,* 317–321.

National Center for Educational Statistics. (2003). Adult literacy. Retrieved from http://nces.ed.gov/fastfacts/display.asp?id=69.

National Center for Health Statistics. (2000). *Health, United States, 2000, with adolescent health chartbook.* Hyattsville, MD: National Center for Health Statistics.

National Center for Health Statistics. (2003). *Healthy people, 2000, review.* Hyattsville, MD: National Center for Health Statistics.

National Child Abuse and Neglect Data System. (2002). Child maltreatment 2001. Retrieved from www.acf.hhs.gov/programs/cb/publications/cm01/outcover.htm.

National Clearinghouse on Child Abuse and Neglect (NCCAN). (1997). *National Child Abuse and Neglect Data System.* Retrieved from http://www.acf.hhs.gov/programs/cb/publications/congress/ncands.htm.

National Clearinghouse on Child Abuse and Neglect (NCCAN). (1999). *National Clearing House on Child Abuse and Neglect Data System.* Retrieved from: http://www.calib.com/nccanch/pubs/factsheets/infact.htm.

National Council of Teachers of Mathematics. (2000). *Principles and standards for school mathematics.* Reston, VA: National Council of Teachers of Mathematics.

Nazzi, T., Kemler Nelson, D. G., Jusczyk, P. W., & Jusczyk, A. M. (2000). Six-month-olds' detection of clauses embedded in continuous speech: Effects of prosodic well-formedness. *Infancy, 1*(1), 123–147.

Needham, A., & Baillargeon, R. (1993). Intuitions about support in 4.5-month-old infants. *Cognition, 47*(2), 121–148.

Needham, A., Barrett, T., & Peterman, K. (2002). A pick-me-up for infants' exploratory skills: Early stimulated experiences reaching for objects using "sticky mittens" enhances young infants' object exploration skills. *Infant Behavior and Development, 25,* 279–295.

Neisser, U. (1976). *General, academic, and artificial intelligence.* Mahwah, NJ: Erlbaum.

Nelson, C. A. (2001). The development and neural bases of face recognition. *Infant and Child Development, 10*(1–2), 3–18.

Nelson, C. A., & Bloom, F. E. (1997). Child development and neuroscience. *Child Development, 68,* 970–987.

Nelson, C. A., & Luciana, M. (Eds.). (2001). *Handbook of developmental cognitive neuroscience.* Cambridge, MA: MIT Press.

Nelson, K. (1977). The syntagmatic-paradigmatic shift revisited: A review of research and theory. *Psychological Bulletin, 84,* 93–116.

Nelson, K. (1981). Social cognition in a script framework. In J. H. Flavell & L. Ross (Eds.), *Social cognitive development.* Cambridge: Cambridge University Press.

Nelson, K. (1996). *Language in cognitive development.* New York: Cambridge University Press.

Nelson, K. (2003). Co-constructing the cultural person through narratives in early childhood. In C. Daiute & C. Lightfoot (Eds.), *Narrative analysis: Studying the development of individuals in society.* New York: Sage Press.

Nelson, K., & Fivush, R. (2000). Socialization of memory. In E. Tulving & F. I. M. Craik (Eds.), *The Oxford handbook of memory* (pp. 283–295). London: Oxford University Press.

Nelson, K., Skwerer, D. P., Goldman, S., Henseler, S., Presler, N., & Walkenfeld, F. F. (2003). Entering a community of minds: An experimental approach to "theory of mind." *Human Development, 46*(1), 24–46.

Nelson, L., Badger, S., & Wu, B. (2004). The influence of culture in emerging adulthood: Perspectives of Chinese college students. *International Journal of Behavioral Development, 28*(1), 26–36.

Nemeroff, C., & Rozin, P. (2000). The makings of magical mind: The nature and function of sympathetic magical thinking. In K. S. Rosengren, C. N. Johnson & P. L. Harris (Eds.), *Imagining the possible: Magical, scientific, and religious thinking in children* (pp. 1–34). Cambridge, UK: Cambridge University Press.

Netter, F. H. (1965). *The CIBA collection of medical illustrations.* Summit, NJ: CIBA Pharmaceutical Products.

Newcomb, A. F., Bukowski, W. M., & Pattee, L. (1993). Children's peer relations: A meta-analytic review of popular, rejected, controversial and average sociometric status. *Psychological Bulletin, 113,* 99–128.

Newman, D. L., Caspi, A., Moffitt, T. E., & Silva, P. A. (1997). Antecedents of adult interpersonal functioning: Effects of individual differences in age 3 temperament. *Developmental Psychology, 33*(2), 206–217.

Newport, E. L., Bavelier, D., & Neville, H. J. (2001). Critical thinking about critical periods: Perspectives on a critical period for language acquisition. In E. Dupoux, (Ed.), *Language, brain, and cognitive development: Essays in honor of Jacques Mehler* (pp. 481–502). Cambridge, MA: MIT Press.

Newton, N., & Newton, M. (1972). Lactation: Its psychological component. In J. G. Howells (Ed.), *Modern perspectives in psycho-obstetrics.* New York: Brunner/Mazel.

NICHD Early Child Care Research Network. (1996). Characteristics of infant child care: Factors contributing to positive caregiving. *Early Childhood Research Quarterly, 11,* 296–307.

NICHD Early Child Care Research Network. (1998a). Characteristics and quality of child care for toddlers and preschoolers. *Applied Developmental Science, 4,* 116–135..

NICHD Early Child Care Research Network. (1998b). Relations between family predictors and child outcomes: Are they weaker for children in child care? *Developmental Psychology, 34*(5), 1198–1128.

NICHD Early Child Care Research Network. (2001). Child care and children's peer interaction at 24 and 36 months: The NICHD Study of Early Child Care. *Child Development, 72,* 1478–1500.

NICHD Early Child Care Research Network. (2002). Structure, process, outcome: Direct and indirect effects of caregiving quality on young children's development. *Psychological Science, 13,* 199–206.

NICHD Early Child Care Research Network. (2003a). Child care and common communicable illnesses in children aged 37 to 54 months. *Archives of Pediatrics and Adolescent Medicine, 157,* 196–201.

NICHD Early Child Care Research Network. (2003b). Does quality of care affect child outcomes at age 4? *Developmental Psychology, 39,* 451–469.

NICHD Early Child Care Research Network. (2003c). Does amount of time spent in child care predict socioemotional adjustment during the transition to kindergarten? *Child Development, 74,* 976–1005.

NIH. (2002). *Stem cells: Scientific progress and future research directions.* Retrieved from http://stemcells.nih.gov/stemcell/scireport.asp.

Nikken, P., & Peters, A. L. (1988). Children's perceptions of TV reality. *Journal of Broadcasting and Electronic Media, 32*(4), 441–452.

Ninio, A., & Snow, C. E. (1999). The development of pragmatics: Learning to use language appropriately. In W. C. Ritchie & T. K. Bhatia (Eds.), *Handbook of child language acquisition* (pp. 347–383). San Diego, CA: Academic Press.

Nkata, M. (2001). Perinatal mortality in breech delivery. *Tropical Doctor, 31*(4), 222–223.

Noland, J. S., Singer, L. T., Arendt, R. E., Minnes, S., Short, E. J., & Bearer, C. F. (2003). Executive functioning in preschool-age children prenatally exposed to alcohol, cocaine, and marijuana. *Alcohol and Clinical Experimental Research, 27*(4), 647–656.

Nucci, L. (1996). Morality and the personal sphere of actions. In E. Reed, E. Turiel & T. Brown (Eds.), *Values and knowledge* (pp. 41–60). Mahwah, NJ: Erlbaum.

Nucci, L. (2001). *Education in the moral domain*. Cambridge: Cambridge University Press.

Nucci, L. (2004). The promise and limitations of the moral self construct. In C. Lightfoot, C. Lalonde, & M. Chandler (Eds.), *Developing conceptions of psychological life*. Mahwah, NJ: Erlbaum.

Nünes, T., Schliemann, A. D., & Carraher, D. W. (1993). *Street mathematics and school mathematics*. Cambridge: Cambridge University Press.

Nussbaum, M. (2001). *Upheavals of thought*. Cambridge: Cambridge University Press.

Nussbaum, M. (2004, January 11). My so-called blog. *The New York Times Magazine*.

Nyiti, R. M. (1976). The development of conservation in the Meru children of Tanzania. *Child Development, 47*, 1122–1129.

O'Brien, K. M., & Vincent, N. K. (2003). Psychiatric comorbidity in anorexia and bulimia nervosa: Nature, prevalence and causal relationships. *Clinical Psychology Review, 23*(1), 57–74.

O'Brien, M., Peyton, V., Mistry, R., Hruda, L., Jacobs, A., Caldera, Y., et al. (2000). *Sex Roles, 42*, 1007–1025.

O'Connor, T., Deater-Deckard, K., Fulker, D., Rutter, M., & Plomin, R. (1998). Genotype-environment correlations in late childhood and early adolescence: Antisocial behavioral problems and coercive parenting. *Developmental Psychology, 34*, 970–981.

O'Connor, T., Rutter, M., Beckett, L., Keaveney, J., Kreppner, J. & the English and Romanian Adoptees Study Team. (2000). The effects of global severe privation on cognitive competence: Extension and longitudinal follow-up. *Child Development, 71*, 376–390.

Oakes, L. M., & Cohen, L. B. (1990). Infant perception of a causal event. *Cognitive Development, 5*, 193–207.

Ochs, E. (1982). Talking to children in Western Samoa. *Language in Society, 11*, 77–104.

Ochs, E., & Schieffelin, B. (1995). The impact of language socialization or grammatical development. In P. Fletcher & B. MacWhinney (Eds.), *The handbook of child language*. Cambridge, MA: Blackwell.

Office of Science: Department of Energy. (2003). All goals achieved: New vision for genome research unveiled. Retrieved from http://www.genome.gov/11006929.

Ogbu, J. U. (1997). Understanding the school performance of urban Blacks: Some essential background knowledge. In H. J. Walberg & O. Reyes (Eds.), *Children and youth: Interdisciplinary perspectives* (pp. 190–222). Thousand Oaks, CA: Sage.

Okamoto, Y., & Case, R. (1996). Exploring the microstructure of children's central conceptional structures on the domain of numbers. *Monographs of the Society for Research on Child Development, 61*(1–2), 27–58.

Oldberg, C. (1998, December 15). Children and violent video games: A warning. *New York Times*, p. 6.

Oliner, S. B., & Oliner, P. (1988). *The altruistic personality: Rescuers of Jews in Nazi Germany*. New York: Macmillan.

Ollendick, T. H., Weist, M. D., Borden, M. C., & Greene, R. W. (1992). Sociometric status and academic, behavioral, and psychological adjustment: A five-year longitudinal study. *Journal of Consulting & Clinical Psychology, 60*(1), 80–87.

Olweus, D. (1993). *Bullying at school: What we know and what we can do*. Oxford, England: Blackwell.

Orioli, I. M., & Castilla, E. E. (2000). New associations between prenatal exposure to drugs and malformations. *American Journal of Human Genetics, 67*(4, Suppl. 2), 175.

Ornstein, P. A., Shapiro, L. R., Clubb, P. A., Follmer, A., & Baker-Ward, L. (1997). The influence of prior knowledge on children's memory for salient medical experiences. In N. Stein, P. A. Ornstein, B. Tversky, & C. J. Brainerd (Eds.), *Memory for everyday and emotional events* (pp. 83–112). Mahwah, NJ: Erlbaum.

Ortony, A. (1993). *Metaphor and thought* (2nd ed.). New York: Cambridge University Press.

Osofsky, J., & Fitzgerald, H. (Eds.). (2000). *Handbook of infant mental health. World Association for Infant Mental Health*. New York: Wiley.

Ovando, C. J., & McLaren, P. (Eds.). (2000). *The politics of multiculturalism and bilingual education : students and teachers caught in the cross fire*. Boston: McGraw-Hill.

Page-Goertz, S., McCamman, S., & Westdahl, C. (2001). Breastfeeding promotion. Top tips for motivating women to breastfeed their infants. *AWHONN Lifelines, 5*(1), 41–43.

Paikoff, R. L., & Brooks-Gunn, J. (1991). Do parent-child relationships change during puberty? *Psychological Bulletin, 110*, 47–66.

Paley, V. G. (1981). *Wally's stories*. Cambridge, MA: Harvard University Press.

Paley, V. G. (1984). *Boys & girls: Superheroes in the doll corner*. Chicago: The University of Chicago Press.

Pan, B. A., & Snow, C. E. (1999). The development of conversational and discourse skills. In M. Barrett (Ed.), *The development of language* (pp. 229–250). Hove, UK: Psychology Press.

Papert, S. (1980). *Mindstorms, children, computers and powerful ideas*. New York: Basic Books.

Papert, S. (2002). The turtle's long slow trip: Macro-educational perspectives on microworlds. *Journal of Educational Computing Research, 27*(1 & 2), 7–27.

Park, B. C. B. (2004). Sociopolitical contexts of self-immolations in Vietnam and South Korea. *Archives of Suicide Research, 8*(1), 81–97.

Parke, R. D. (1995). Fathers and families. In M. H. Bornstein (Ed.), *Handbook of parenting: Status and social conditions of parenting: Vol 3* (pp. 27–66). Mahwah, NJ: Erlbaum.

Parke, R. D., & Buriel, R. (1998). Socialization in the family: Ethnical and ecological perspectives. In W. Damon & N. Eisenberg (Eds.), *Handbook of child development: Vol 3: Social, emotional, and personality development* (5th ed., pp. 463–552). New York: Wiley.

Parke, R. D., & Ladd, G. W. (1992). Family-peer relationships. *Merrill-Palmer Quarterly, 40*, 1–20.

Parke, R., O'Neil, R., Spitzer, S., Isley, S., Welsh, M., Wang, S., et al. (1997). A longitudinal assessment of sociometric stability and the behavioral correlates of children's social acceptance. *Merrill-Palmer Quarterly, 43*, 635–662.

Parker, J. G., & Asher, S. R. (1993). Friendship and friendship quality in middle childhood: Links with peer acceptance and feelings of loneliness and social dissatisfaction. *Developmental Psychology, 29*, 611–621.

Parker, J. G., Rubin, K. H., Price, J. M., & De Rosier, M. E. (1995). Peer relationships, child development, and adjustment: A developmental psychopathology. In D. Cicchetti & D. J. Cohen (Eds.), *Developmental Psychopathology*. New York: Wiley.

Parmalee, A. H., Jr., Akiyama, Y., Schultz, M. A., Wenner, W. H., Schulte, F. J., & Stern, E. (1968). The electroencephalogram in active and quiet sleep in infants. In P. Kellaway & I. Petersen (Eds.), *Clinical electroencephaly of children*. New York: Grune & Stratton.

Parsons, T. (1963). Youth in the context of American society. In E. Erikson (Ed.), *Youth: Change and challenge*. New York: Basic Books.

Patrick, J., Anderman, L. H., & Ryan, A. M. (2002). Social motivation and the classroom social environment. In C. Midgley (Ed.), *Goals, goal structures, and patterns of adaptive learning* (pp. 85–108). Mahwah, NJ: Erlbaum

Patterson, G. R., Crosby, L., & Vuchinich, S. (1992). Predicting risk for early police arrest. *Journal of Quantitative Criminology, 8*(4), 335–355.

Patterson, G. R., Littman, R. A., & Bricker, W. (1967). Assertive behavior in young children: A step toward a theory of aggression. *Monographs of the Society for Research for Child Development, 32*(Serial No. 113).

Patterson, G. R., Reid, J. B., & Dishion, T. J. (1998). Antisocial boys. In J. M. Jenkins, K. Oatley, & N. L. Stein (Eds.), *Human emotions: A reader* (pp. 330–336). Malden, MA: Blackwell.

Paus, T., Collins, D. L., Evans, A. C., Leonard, G., Pike, B., & Zijdenbos, A. (2001). Maturation of white matter in the human brain: A review of magnetic resonance studies. *Brain Research Bulletin, 54*(3), 255–266.

Paus, T., Zijdenbos, A., Worsley, K., Collins, D. L., Blumenthal, J., Giedd, J. N., et al. (1999). Structural maturation of neural pathways in children and adolescents: In vivo study. *Science 283*(5409): 1908–1911.

Pavlov, I. P. (1927). *Conditioned reflexes*. Oxford, England: Oxford University Press.

Pellegrini, A. D. (2002). Rough-and-tumble play from childhood through adolescence: Development and possible functions. In P. K. Smith & C. H. Hart (Eds.), *Blackwell handbook of childhood social development* (pp. 437–453). Malden, MA: Blackwell.

Pellegrini, A. D., & Bartini, M. (2001). Dominance in early adolescent boys: Affiliative and aggressive dimension and possible functions. *Journal of Educational Psychology, 92*, 360–366.

Pellegrini, A. D., & Long, J. (2002). A longitudinal study of bullying, dominance, and victimization during the transition from primary through secondary school. *British Journal of Developmental Psychology, 20*, 259–280.

Pellegrini, A. D., & Long, J. D. (2003). A sexual selection theory longitudinal analysis of sexual segregation and integration in early adolescence. *Journal of Experimental Child Psychology, 85*(3), 257–278.

Penchaszadeh, V. B. (2001). Genetic counseling issues in Latinos. *Genetic Testing, 5*(3), 193–200.

Peplau, L. A., DeBro, S. C., Veniegas, R. C., & Taylor, P. L. (1999). *Gender, culture, and ethnicity: Current research about women and men*. Mountain View, CA: Mayfield.

Perez-Granados, D. R., & Callanan, M. A. (1997). Parents and siblings as early resources for young children's learning in Mexican-descent families. *Hispanic Journal of Behavioral Sciences*, 3–33.

Persaud, T. V. N. (1977). *Problems of birth defects: From Hippocrates to thalidomide and after*. Baltimore: University Park Press.

Pescosolido, B. A., Grauerholz, E., & Milkie, M. A. (1997). Culture and conflict: The portrayal of Blacks in U.S. children's picture books through the mid- and late-twentieth century. *American Sociological Review, 62*(3), 443–464.

Petersen, A., Sarigiani, P., Leffert, N. & Camarena, P. (1998). Resilience in adolescence. In A. Schwartzberg (Ed.), *The adolescent in turmoil*. Westport, CT: Praeger.

Petitto, L. A, Katerlos, M., Levy, B. G., Gauna, K., Tétreault, K., & Ferraro, V. (2001). Bilingual signed and spoken language acquisition from birth: Implications for the mechanisms underlying early bilingual language acquisition. *Journal of Child Language, 28*, 453–496.

Pettit, G. S., Bates, J. E., Dodge, K. A., & Meece, D. W. (1999). The impact of after-school peer contact on early adolescent externalizing problems is moderated by parental monitoring, perceived neighborhood safety, and prior adjustment. *Child Development, 70*(3), 768–778.

Phinney, J. S., & Haas, K. (2003). The process of coping among ethnic minority first-generation college freshmen: A narrative approach. *Journal of Social Psychology, 143*(6), 707–726.

Phinney, J. S., & Ong, A. D. (2002). Adolescent-parent disagreements and life satisfaction in families from Vietnamese- and European-American backgrounds. *International Journal of Behavioral Development, 26*(6), 556–561.

Phinney, J. S., Romero, I., Nava, M., & Huang, D. (2001). The role of language, parents, and peers in echnic identity among adolescents in immigrant families. *Journal of Youth and Adolescents, 30*, 135–153.

Piaget, J. (1926). *The language and thought of the child*. New York: Meridian Books.

Piaget, J. (1928). *Judgment and reasoning in the child*. London: Routledge & Kegan Paul.

Piaget, J. (1929/1979). *The child's conception of the world*. New York: Harcourt Brace.

Piaget, J. (1930). *The child's conception of physical causality*. New York: Harcourt Brace.

Piaget, J. (1932/1965). *The moral judgment of the child*. New York: Free Press. (Original work published 1932)

Piaget, J. (1952a). *The child's conception of number*. New York: W. W. Norton.

Piaget, J. (1952b). *The origins of intelligence in children*. New York: International Universities Press.

Piaget, J. (1954). *The construction of reality in the child*. New York: Basic Books.

Piaget, J. (1962). *Play, dreams and imitation*. New York: W. W. Norton.

Piaget, J. (1964). Development and learning. In R. E. Ripple & V. N. Rockcastle (Eds.), *Piaget rediscovered. Conference on cognitive studies and curriculum development*. Cornell University and University of California.

Piaget, J. (1966/1974). Need and significance of cross-cultural studies in genetic psychology. In J. W. Berry & P. R. Dasen (Eds.), *Culture and cognition: Readings in cross-cultural psychology*. London: Metheun.

Piaget, J. (1973). *The psychology of intelligence*. Totowa, NJ: Littlefield & Adams.

Piaget, J. (1977). *The development of thought: Equilibration of cognitive structure*. New York: Viking.

Piaget, J. (1987). *Possibility and necessity: Vol. 1. The role of possibility in cognitive development*. Minneapolis: University of Minnesota Press.

Piaget, J. (1995). *Sociological studies*. New York: Routledge.

Piaget, J., & Inhelder, B. (1956). *The child's conception of space*. London: Routledge & Kegan Paul.

Piaget, J., & Inhelder, B. (1969). *The psychology of the child*. New York: Basic.

Piaget, J., & Inhelder, B. (1973). *Memory and intelligence*. New York: Basic Books.

Pick, A. D. (1997). Perceptual learning, categorizing, and cognitive development. In C. Dent-Read & P. Zukow-Golding (Eds.), *Evolving explanations of development: Ecological approaches to organism environment systems* (pp. 335–370). Washington, DC: American Psychological Association.

Pien, D., & Rothbard, M. K. (1976). Incongruity and resolution in children's humor: A reexamination. *Child Development, 47*, 966–971.

Pierroutsakos, S. L., & DeLoache, J. (2003). Infants' manual exploration of pictorial objects varying in realism. *Infancy, 4*(1), 141–156.

Pinker, S. (2002). *The blank slate: The modern denial of human nature*. New York: Viking.

Pipher, M. (1994). *Reviving Ophelia: Saving the selves of adolescent girls.* New York: Putnam.

Pittman, R., & Oppenheim, R. W. (1979). Cell death of motoneurons in the chick embryo spinal cord. *Journal of Comparative Neurology, 187,* 425–446.

Plato. (1945). *The republic.* London: Oxford University Press.

Pleck, J. H., & Masciadrelli, B. P. (2003). Paternal involvement in U.S. residential fathers: Levels, sources, and consequences. In M. Lamb (Ed.), *The role of the father in development.* New York: Wiley.

Plomin, R., De Fries, J. C., McClearn, G. E., & Rutter, M. (2001). Behavioral genetics: A primer (4th ed.). New York: Worth.

Plotkin, H. (2001). Some elements of a science of culture. In H. Whitehouse (Ed.), *The debated mind* (pp. 91–112). New York: Oxford University Press.

Pnevmatikos, D. (2002). Conceptual changes in religious concepts of elementary schoolchildren: The case of the house where God lives. *Educational Psychology, 22*(1), 93–112.

Polikoff, B. (1999). *With one bold act: The story of Jane Addams.* Chicago: Boswell Books.

Polivy, J., & Herman, C. P. (2004). Sociocultural idealization of thin female body shapes: An introduction to the special issue on body image and eating disorders. *Journal of Social and Clinical Psychology, 23*(1), 1–6.

Pollack, H. A., & Frohna, J. G. (2002). Infant sleep placement after the back to sleep campaign. *Pediatrics, 109*(4), 608–614.

Pollack, S., Cicchetti, D., Horung, K., & Reed, A. (2000). Recognizing emotion in faces: Developmental effects of child abuse and neglect. *Developmental Psychology, 36,* 679–688.

Pollack, W. (2000). *Real boys' voices.* New York: Random House.

Pollitt, E. (2001). Statistical and psychobiological significance in developmental research. *American Journal of Clinical Nutrition, 74*(3), 281–282.

Pollitt, E., Saco-Pollitt, C., Jahari, A., Husaini, M. A., & Huang, J. (2000). Effects of an energy and micronutrient supplement on mental development and behavior under natural conditions in undernourished children in Indonesia. *European Journal of Clinical Nutrition, 54*(Suppl. 2), S80–S90.

Pomerantz, E. M., Ruble, D. N., Frey, K. S., & Greulich, F. (1995). Meeting goals and confronting conflict: Children's changing perceptions of social comparison. *Child Development, 66,* 723–738.

Pontius, K., Aretz, M., Griebel, C., Jacobs, C., LaRock, K., et al. (2001). Back to sleep—Tummy time to play. *Newsletter of the Children's Hospital, 4*(4), 1–3.

Portes, A., & Rumbaut, R. (2001). *Legacies: The story of the second generation.* Berkeley: University of California Press.

Poulin, F. & Boivin, M. (2000). The role of proactive and reactive aggression in the formation and development of boys' friendships. *Developmental Psychology, 36,* 233–240.

Poulin, F. & Boivin, M. (2000a). The formation and development of friendship in childhood: The role of proactive and reactive aggression. *Developmental Psychology, 36,* 233–240.

Poulin, F., & Boivin, M. (2000b) Proactive and reactive aggression: Evidence of a two-factor model. *Psychological Assessment, 12,* 115–122.

Poulin-Dubois, D. (1995). Object parts and the acquisition of the meaning of names. In K. Nelson & Z. Réger (Eds.), *Children's language, Vol. 8.* Mahwah, NJ: Erlbaum.

Powers, J. (2003). An analysis of performance-based accountability: Factors shaping school performance in two urban school districts. *Educational Policy, 17*(5), 558–585.

Pratt, M. W., Arnold, M. L., Pratt, A. T., & Diessner, R. (1999). Predicting adolescent moral reasoning from family climate: A longitudinal study. *Journal of Early Adolescence, 19*(2), 148–175.

Prechtl, H. (1977). *The neurological examination of the full-term newborn infant* (2nd ed.). Philadelphia: Lippincott.

Preisser, D. A., Hodson, B. W., & Paden, E. P. (1988). Developmental phonology: 18–29 months. *Journal of Speech and Hearing Disorders, 53,* 125–130.

Prentice, A. M., & Jebb, S. A. (2003). Fast foods, energy density and obesity: A possible mechanistic link. *Obesity Review 4*(4), 187–194.

Prescott, E., & Jones, E. (1971). Day care of children—assets and liabilities. *Children, 18,* 54–58.

Prevatt, F. F. (2003). The contribution of parenting practices in a risk and resiliency model of children's adjustment. *British Journal of Developmental Psychology, 21*(4), 469–480.

Preyer, W. (1888). *The mind of the child.* Leipzig, Germany: Grieben.

Preyer, W. T. (1890). *The mind of the child ... observations concerning the mental development of the human being in the first years of life.* New York: Appleton.

Pueschel, S. M., Craig, W. Y., & Haddow, J. E. (1992). Lipids and lipoproteins in persons with Down's syndrome. *Journal of Intellectual Disability Research, 36*(4), 365–369.

Putallaz, M., & Wasserman, A. (1990). Children's entry behavior. In S. R. Asher & J. D. Coie (Eds.), *Peer rejection in childhood: Cambridge studies in social and emotional development.* New York: Cambridge University Press.

Quadrel, M. J., Fischoff, B., & Davis, W. (1993). Adolescent (in) vulnerability. *American Psychologist, 48,* 102–116.

Quinn, P. C. (2002). Early categorization. In U. Goswami (Ed.), *Blackwell handbook of childhood cognitive development* (pp. 85–101). Oxford, UK: Blackwell.

Quinn, P. C., & Eimas, P. D. (1996). Perceptual organization and categorization in young infants. In C. Rovee-Collier & L. P. Lipsitt (Eds.), *Advances in infancy research: Vol. 10* (pp. 1–36). Norwood, NJ: Ablex.

Quinn, P. C., Eimas, P. D., & Rosenkrantz, S. L. (1993). Evidence for representations of perceptually similar natural categories by 3-month-old and 4-month-old infants. *Perception, 22,* 463–475.

Quinn, P. C., Slater, A. M., Brown, E., & Hayes, R. A. (2001). Developmental change in form categorization in early infancy. *British Journal of Developmental Psychology, 19*(2), 207–218.

Quinton, D., & Rutter, M. (1976). Early hospital admissions and later disturbances of behavior: An attempted replication of Douglas' findings. *Developmental Medicine and Child Neurology, 18,* 447–459.

Quinton, D., & Rutter, M. (1985). Parenting behavior of mothers raised "in care." In A. R. Nicol (Ed.), *Longitudinal studies in child psychology and psychiatry: Practical lessons from research experience.* New York: Wiley.

Rabin, A. J. (1965). *Growing up in the kibbutz.* New York: Springer-Verlag.

Rakison, D. H., & Oakes, L. M. (Eds.). (2003). *Early category and concept development: Making sense of the blooming, buzzing confusion.* London: Oxford University Press.

Rao, U., Lutchmansingh, P., & Poland, R. E. (2000). Contribution of development to buspirone effects on REM sleep: A preliminary report. *Neuropsychopharmacology, 22*(4), 440–446.

Rapoport, J., Castellanos, R., Gogate, N., Janson, K., Kohler, S., & Nelson, P. (2001). Imaging normal and abnormal brain development: New perspectives for child psychiatry. *Australian and New Zealand Journal of Psychiatry, 35,* 272–281.

Rauscher, F. H., Shaw, G. L., & Ky, K. N. (1993). Music and spatial task performance. *Nature, 365,* 611.

Raven, J. C. (1962). *Coloured progressive matrices.* London: H. K. Lewis.

Raymond, D. (1994). Homophobia, identity, and the meanings of desire: Reflections on the culture construction of gay and lesbian adolescent sexuality. In J. Irvine (Ed.), *Sexual cultures and the construction of adolescent identities* (pp. 115–150). Philadelphia: Temple University Press.

Read, M. (1960/1968). *Children of their fathers: Growing up among the Ngoni of Malawi.* New York: Holt, Rinehart & Winston.

Read, M. (1983). *Children of their fathers: Growing up among the Ngoni of Malawi.* New York: Irvington.

Reed, M. D., & Roundtree, P. W. (1997). Peer pressure and adolescent substance abuse. *Journal of Quantitative Criminology, 13*(2), 143–180.

Reese, E., & Cox, A. (1999). Quality of adult book reading affects children's emergent literacy. *Developmental Psychology, 35*(1), 20–28.

Reichel-Domatoff, G., & Reichel-Domatoff, A. (1961). *The people of Aritama.* London: Routledge & Kegan Paul.

Relier, J.-P. (2001). Influence of maternal stress on fetal behavior and brain development. *Biology of the Neonate, 79*(3–4), 168–171.

Renz-Polster, H., & Buist, A. S. (2002). Being born by cesarean section increases the risk of asthma and hay fever as a child. *Journal of Investigative Medicine, 50*(1), 29a.

Resnick, M. (1998). Technologies for lifelong kindergarten. *Educational Technology Research and Development, 46*(4), 43–55.

Rest, J., Narvaez, D., Bebeau, M. l. J., & Thoma, S. J. (1999). *Postconventional moral thinking: A neo-Kohlbergian approach.* Mahwah, NJ: Erlbaum.

Rice, C., Koinis, D., Sullivan, K., & Tager-Flusberg, H. (1997). When 3-year-olds pass the appearance-reality test. *Developmental Psychology, 33*(1), 54–61.

Richardson, J., & Scott, K. (2002). Rap music and its violent progency: America's culture of violence in context. *The Journal of Negro Education, 71*(3), 175–192.

Richters, J. E., & Martinez, P. E. (1993). Violent communities, family choices, and children's chances: An algorithm for improving the odds. Special issue: Milestones in the development of resilience. *Development & Psychopathology, 5,* 609–627.

Riel, M. (1998). Learning communities through computer networking. In G. James & S. V. Goldman (Eds.), *Thinking practices in mathematics and science learning* (pp. 369–398). Mahwah, NJ: Erlbaum.

Rimoin, D. L., Connor, J. M., & Pyeritz, R. E. (1997). *Emery and Rimoin's principles and practice of medical genetics* (3rd ed.). New York: Churchill Livingstone.

Rivera, S. M., Wakeley, A., & Langer, J. (1999). The drawbridge phenomenon: Representational reasoning or perceptual preference? *Developmental Psychology, 35*(2), 427–435.

Robbins, W. J., Brody, S., Hogan, A. G., Jackson, C. M., & Greene, C. W. (Eds.). (1929). *Growth.* New Haven, CT: Yale University Press.

Roberts, D., Foehr, U., Rideout, V., & Brodie, M. (1999). *Kids and media at the new millennium: A comprehensive national analysis of children's media use.* Menlo Park, CA: Kaiser Family Foundation.

Robinson, J. (2000). Are there implications for prevention research from studies of resilience? *Child Development, 71,* 570–572.

Robinson, J. L., Emde, R. N., & Corley, R. P. (2001). Dispositional cheerfulness: Early genetic and environmental influences. In R. N. Emde & J. K. Hewitt (Eds.), *Infancy to early childhood: Genetic and environmental influences on developmental change* (pp. 163–177). New York: Oxford University Press.

Robson, K. S., & Moss, H. A. (1970). Patterns and determinants of maternal attachment. *Journal of Pediatrics, 77,* 976–985.

Rochat, P. (2000). *The infant world: Self, objects, people.* Cambridge, MA: Harvard University Press.

Rodkin, P. C., Farmer, T. W., Pearl, R., & Van Acker, R. (2000). Heterogeneity of popular boys: Antisocial and prosocial configurations. *Developmental Psychology, 36*(1), 14–24.

Rodriguez, C., & Sutherland, D. (1999). Predictors of parents' physical disciplinary practices. *Child Abuse and Neglect, 23,* 651–657.

Rogoff, B. (2000). *Culture and development.* New York: Oxford University Press.

Rogoff, B. (2003). *The cultural nature of human development.* Oxford: Oxford University Press.

Rogoff, B., & Waddell, K. J. (1982). Memory for information organized in a scene by children from two cultures. *Child Development, 53,* 1224–1228.

Romans, S. E., Martin, M., Gendall, K., & Herbison, G. P. (2003). Age of menarche: The role of some psychosocial factors. *Psychological Medicine, 33*(5), 933–939.

Roopnarine, J. L., & Carter, D. B. (Eds.). (1992). *Parent-child socialization in diverse cultures: Vol. 5..* Norwood, NJ: Ablex.

Roosa, M. (2000). Some thoughts about resilience versus positive development, main effects versus interactions, and the value of resilience. *Child Development, 71,* 567–569.

Rosen, W. D., Adamson, L. B., & Bakeman, R. (1992). An experimental investigation of infant social referencing: Mothers' messages and gender differences. *Developmental Psychology, 28*(6), 1172–1178.

Rosenblatt, R. A., Dobie, S. A., Hart, L. G., Schneeweiss, R., Gould, D., Raine, T. R., et al. (1997). Interspecialty differences in the obstetric care of low-risk women. *American Journal of Public Health, 87*(3), 344–351.

Rosenblum, G. D., & Lewis, M. (1999). The relations among body image, physical attractiveness, and body mass in adolescence. *Child Development, 70*(1), 50–64.

Rosengren, K. S., & Brasswell, G. S. (2001). Variability in children's reasoning. In H. W. Reese and R. Kail (Eds.), *Advances in child development and behavior, Vol. 28* (pp. 2–41). New York: Academic Press.

Rosenkoetter, L. (2001). Television and morality. In D. Singer & J. Singer (Eds.), *Handbook of children and the media.* Thousand Oaks, CA: Sage.

Rosenstein, D., & Oster, H. (1988). Differential facial responses to four basic tastes in newborns. *Child Development, 59,* 1555–1568.

Rosenthal, D. A., & Feldman, S. S. (1999). The importance of importance: Adolescents' perceptions of parental communication about sexuality. *Journal of Adolescence, 22*(6), 835–851.

Rosenzweig, M. R. (1984). Experience, memory, and the brain. *American Psychologist, 39,* 365–376.

Ross, H. E., & Ivis, F. (1999). Binge eating and substance use among male and female adolescents. *International Journal of Eating Disorders, 26*(3), 245–260.

Rossell, C. H., & Baker, K. (1996). The educational effectiveness of bilingual education. *Research in the Teaching of English, 30*(1), 7–74.

Rosso, P. (1990). *Nutrition and metabolism in pregnancy.* Oxford: Oxford University Press.

Rothbart, M. K. (1988). Temperament and the development of inhibited approach. *Child Development, 59,* 1241–1250.

Rothbart, M. K., Ahadi, S. A., & Evans, D. E. (2000). Temperament and personality: Origins and outcomes. *Journal of Personality and Social Psychology, 78*(1), 122–135.

Rothbart, M. K., Chew, K. H., & Gartsetin, M. A. (2001). Assessment of temperament in early development. In L. T. Singer & P. S. Zeskind (Eds.), *Biobehavioral assessment of the infant* (pp. 190–208). New York: Guilford Press.

Rothbaum, F., Weisz, J., Pott, M., & Morelli, G. (2000). Attachment and culture: Security in the United States and Japan. *American Psychologist, 55*(10), 1093–1104.

Rousseau, J. J. (1762/1911). *Emile; Or on education.* London: Dent.

Rovee-Collier, C. (1997). Dissociations in infant memory: Rethinking the development of implicit and explicit memory. *Psychological Review, 104*(3), 467–498.

Rovee-Collier, C., & Barr, R. (2001). Infant learning and memory. In G. Bremner & A. Fogel (Eds.), *Blackwell handbook of infant development* (pp. 139–168). Malden, MA: Blackwell.

Rovee-Collier, C., Hartshorn, K., & DiRubbo, M. (1999). Long-term maintenance of infant memory. *Developmental Psychobiology, 35*(2), 91–102

Roy, P., Rutter, M., & Pickles, A. (2000). Institutional care: Risk from family background or pattern of rearing? *Journal of Child Psychology and Psychiatry, 41,* 139–149.

Rubin, J. Z., Provezano, F. J., & Luria, Z. (1974). The eye of the beholder: Parents' view on sex of newborns. *American Journal of Orthopsychiatry, 44,* 512–519.

Rubin, K. H., Bukowski, W., & Parker, J. G. (1998). Peer interactions, relationships, and groups. In W. Damon & N. Eisenberg (Eds.), *Handbook of child psychology: Vol. 3. Social, emotional, and personality development* (5th ed., pp. 619–700). New York: Wiley.

Rubin, K. H., Burgess, K. B., Kennedy, A. E. & Stewart, S. L. (2003). Social withdrawal in childhood. In E. J. Mash & R. A. Barkley (Eds.), *Child psychopathology* (2nd ed., pp. 372–406). New York: Guilford.

Rubin, K. H., Coplan, R. J., Nelson, L. J., & Cheah, C. S. L. (1999). Peer relationships in childhood. In M. H. Bornstein & M. E. Lamb (Eds.), *Developmental psychology: An advanced textbook* (4th ed., pp. 451–501). Mahwah, NJ: Erlbaum.

Rubin, K. H., Lynch, D., Coplan, R., Rose-Krasnor, L., & Booth, C. L. (1994). "Birds of a feather . . .": Behavioral concordance and preferential personal attraction in children. *Child Development, 64,* 1778–1785.

Rubin, Z. (1980). *Children's friendships.* Cambridge, MA: Harvard University Press.

Rubinowitz, L. S., Rosenbaum, J. E., Dvorin, S., Kulieke, M., McCareins, A., & Popkin, S. (2000). *Crossing the class and color lines: From public housing to white suburbia.* Chicago: University of Chicago Press.

Ruble, D. N., & Dweck, C. S. (1995). Self conceptions, person conceptions, and their development. In N. Eisenberg (Ed.), *Review of personality and social psychology: Vol. 15.* Thousand Oaks, CA: Sage.

Ruble, D. N., & Martin, C. L. (1998). Gender development. In W. Damon & N. Eisenberg (Eds.), *Handbook of Child Development: Social, emotional, and personality development: Vol. 5* (pp. 933–1016). New York: Wiley.

Ruble, D. N., & Martin, C. L. (2002). Conceptualizing, measuring and evaluating the developmental course of gender differentiation. *Monographs of the Society for Research in Child Development, 67,* 148–166.

Ruch, W. (Ed.) (1998). *The sense of humor: Exploration of a personality characteristics.* New York: Mouton de Gruter.

Ruel, M. T., & Menon, P. (2002). Child feeding practices are associated with child nutritional status in Latin America: Innovative uses of the demographic and health surveys. *Journal of Nutrition, 132*(6), 1180–1187.

Ruff, H. A., & Capozzoli, M. C. (2003). Development of attention and distractibility in the first 4 years of life. *Developmental Psychology, 39*(5), 877–890.

Ruiz, S., Roosa, M., & Gonzales, N. (2002). Predictors of self-esteem for Mexican American and European American youths: A reexamination of the influence of parenting. *Journal of Family Psychology, 16,* 70–80.

Rumbaugh, D. M., & Washburn, D. A. (2003). *Intelligence of apes and other rational beings.* New Haven, CT: Yale University Press.

Rumbaugh, D. M., Savage-Rumbaugh, E. S., & Sevcik, R. A. (1994). Biobehavioral roots of language: A comparative perspective on chimpanzee, child, and culture. In R. W. Wrangham, W. C. McGrew, F. B. M. de Waal, & P. G. Helthe (Eds.), *Chimpanzee cultures.* Cambridge, MA: Harvard University Press.

Rust, J., Golombok, S., Hines, M., & Johnston, K. (2000). The role of brothers and sisters in the gender development of preschool children. *Journal of Experimental Child Psychology, 77,* 292–303.

Ruth, H., & Reitz, K. (2003). *The challenge of crime: Rethinking our response.* Harvard: Harvard University Press.

Rutter, M. (1987). Continuities and discontinuities from infancy. In J. D. Osofsky (Ed.), *Handbook of infant development* (2nd ed.). New York: Wiley.

Rutter, M. (1995). Clinical implications of attachment concepts: Retrospect and prospect. *Journal of Child Psychology and Psychiatry and Allied Disciplines, 36*(4), 549–571.

Rutter, M., Dunn, J., Plomin, R., & Simonoff, E. (1997). Integrating nature and nurture: Implications of person-environment correlations and interactions for developmental psychopathology. *Development & Psychopathology, 9*(2), 335–364.

Rutter, M., and the English and Romanian Adoptees Study Team. (1998). Developmental catch-up, and deficit, following adoption after severe global early privation. *Journal of Child Psychology and Psychiatry, 39,* 465–476.

Rutter, M., & Plomin, R. (1997). Opportunities for psychiatry from genetic findings. *British Journal of Psychiatry, 171,* 209–219.

Rutter, M., Quinton, D., & Hill, J. (1990). Adult outcome of institution-reared children. In L. Robins & M. Rutter (Eds.), *Straight and devious pathways from childhood to adulthood.* Cambridge: Cambridge University Press.

Rutter, M., & Sroufe, L. (2001). Developmental psychopathology: Concepts and challenges. *Development and Psychopathology, 12,* 265–296.

Ryan, S. (2000). Examining social workers' placement recommendations of children with gay and lesbian adoptive parents. *Families in Society, 81,* 517–528.

Rymer, R. (1993). *Genie: A scientific tragedy.* New York: Harper Collins.

Saarni, C. (1998). Issues of cultural meaningfulness in emotional development. *Developmental Psychology, 34*(4), 647–652.

Saarni, C. (1999). *The development of emotional competence.* New York: Guilford Press.

Saarni, C. (2000). Emotional competence: A developmental perspective. In R. Bar-On & J. Parker (Eds.), *The handbook of emotional intelligence.* San Francisco: Jossey-Bass.

Sachs, J., Bard, B., & Johnson, M. (1981). Language learning with restricted input: Case studies of two hearing children of deaf parents. *Applied Psycholinguistics, 2,* 33–54.

Sachs, J., & Devin, J. (1973). *Young children's knowledge of age-appropriate speech styles.* Paper presented to the Linguistic Society of America.

Sadovsky, A., & Troseth, G. (2000). Aspects of young children's perceptions of gender-typed occupations. *Sex Roles, 42,* 993–1006.

Sagi, A., Lamb, M. E., Lewkowicz, K. S., Shoham, R., Dvir, R., & Estes, D. (1985). Security of infant-mother, -father, and metapelet attachments among kibbutz reared Israeli children. *Monographs of the Society for Research in Child Development, 50*(1–2, Serial No. 209).

Sagi, A., van IJzendoorn, M. H., Aviezer, O., Donnell, F., & Mayseless, O. (1994). Sleeping out of home in a kibbutz communal arrangement: It makes a difference for mother-infant attachment. *Child Development, 65,* 992–1004.

Sale, R. (1978). *Fairy tales and after.* Cambridge, MA: Harvard University Press.

Salomon, G. L. (1984). Television is "easy" and print is "tough": The differential investment of mental effort in learning as a function of perceptions and attributions. *Journal of Educational Psychology, 76,* 647–658.

Salzarulo, P., & Ficca, G. (Eds.), (2002). *Advances in consciousness research: Vol. 38. Awakening and sleep-wake cycle across development.* Amsterdam: John Benjamins.

Salzinger, S., Feldman, R. S., Hammer, M., & Rosario, M. (1993). The effects of physical abuse on children's social relationships. *Child Development, 64,* 169–187.

Sameroff, A. J. (1983). Developmental systems: Contexts and evolutions. In P. H. Mussen (Ed.), *Handbook of child psychology: Vol. 1. History, theory and methods.* New York: Wiley.

Sameroff, A. J., Bartko, W. T., Baldwin, A., Baldwin, C., & Seifer, R. (1998). Family and social influences on the development of child competence. In M. Lewis & C. Feiring (Eds.), *Families, risk, and competence* (pp. 161–186). Mahwah, NJ: Erlbaum.

Sameroff, A. J., & Haith, M. M. (1996). *The five to seven year shift: The age of reason and responsibility.* Chicago: University of Chicago Press.

Sameroff, A. J., & MacKenzie, M. J. (2003). Research strategies for capturing transactional models of development: The limits of the possible. *Development & Psychopathology, 15*(3), 613–640.

Sameroff, A. J., Seifer, R., Baldwin, A., & Baldwin, C. (1993). Stability of intelligence from preschool to adolescence: The influence of social and family risk factors. *Child Development, 64,* 80–97.

Sampaio, R. C., & Truwitt, C. L. (2001). Myelination in the developing human brain. In C. Nelson and M. Luciana (Eds.), *Handbook of developmental cognitive science* (pp. 35–44). Cambridge, MA: MIT Press.

Sanson, A., Hamphill, S., & Smart, D. (2002). Temperament and social development. In P. Smith & C. Hart (Eds.), *Blackwell handbook of childhood social development.* Malden, MA: Blackwell.

Sapp, F., Lee, K., & Muir, D. (2000). Three-year-olds' difficulty with the appearance-reality distinction: Is it real or is it apparent? *Developmental Psychology, 36*(5): 547–560.

Sartor, C., & Youniss, J. (2002). The relationship between positive parental involvement and identity achievement during adolescence. *Adolescence,* 221–234.

Savage-Rumbaugh, E. S. (1993). How does evolution design a brain capable of learning language? *Monographs of the Society for Research in Child Development 58*(3–4), 243–252.

Savage-Rumbaugh, S., Shanker, S. G., & Taylor, T. J. (1998). *Apes, language, and the human mind.* New York: Oxford University Press.

Savin-Williams, R. C. (2001a). A critique of research on sexual-minority youths. *Journal of Adolescence, 24,* 5–13.

Savin-Williams, R. C. (2001b). *Mom, dad, I'm gay. How families negotiate coming out.* Washington, DC: American Psychological Association.

Savin-Williams, R. C., & Diamond, L. (2001). Sexual identity trajectories among sexual-minority youths: Gender comparisons. *Archives of Sexual Behavior, 29,* 419–440.

Saxe, G. B. (1981). Body parts as numerals: A developmental analysis of numeration among the Oksapmin in Papua, New Guinea. *Child Development, 52,* 306–316.

Saxe, G. B. (2002). Children's developing mathematics in collective practices: A framework for analysis. *Journal of the Learning Sciences, 11*(2–3), 275–300.

Saxon, T. F., Gollapalli, A., Mitchell, M. W., & Stanko, S. (2002). Demand feeding or schedule feeding: Infant growth from birth to 6 months. *Journal of Reproductive and Infant Psychology, 20*(2), 89–100.

Saxton, M. (1997). The contrast theory of negative input. *Journal of Child Language, 24*(1), 139–161.

Scarr, S., & Salapatek, P. (1970). Patterns of fear development during infancy. *Merrill-Palmer Quarterly, 16*(1), 53–90.

Schafer, G., & Plunkett, K. (1998). Rapid word learning by fifteen-month-olds under tightly controlled conditions. *Child Development, 69*(2), 309–320.

Schaffer, R. (1977). *Mothering.* Cambridge, MA: Harvard University Press.

Schaller, S. (1991). *A man without words.* New York: Summit.

Scheper-Hughes, N. (1992). *Death without weeping: The violence of everyday life in Brazil.* Berkeley: University of California Press.

Scheuermann, B. (2002). Autism: Teaching does make a difference. Belmont, CA: Wadsworth Thomson Learning.

Schlagmueller, M., & Schneider, W. (2002). The development of organizational strategies in children: Evidence from a microgenetic longitudinal study. *Journal of Experimental Child Psychology, 81,* 298–319.

Schlegel, A., & Barry, H. (1991). *Adolescence: An anthropological inquiry.* New York: Free Press.

Schmitt, K. L., Anderson, D. R., & Collins, P. A. (1999). Form and content: Looking at visual features of television. *Developmental Psychology, 35*(4), 1156–1167.

Schmitt-Rodermund, E., & Vondracek, F. (1999). Breadth of interests, exploration, and identity development in adolescence. *Journal of Vocational Behavior, 55,* 298–317.

Schneider, B. (2000). *Friends and enemies: Peer relations in childhood.* New York: Oxford University Press.

Schneider, B., Richard, J., Younger, A., & Freeman, P. (2000). A longitudinal exploration of the continuity of children's social participation and social withdrawal across socioeconomic status levels and social settings. *European Journal of Social Psychology, 4,* 497–519.

Schneider, B., & Stevenson, D. (1999). *The ambitious generation: America's teenagers, motivated, but directionless.* New Haven, CT: Yale University Press.

Schneider, W. (1999). The development of metamemory in children. In D. Gopher & A. Koriat (Eds.), *Attention and performance XVII: Cognitive regulation of performance: Interaction of theory and application. Attention and performance* (pp. 487–517). Cambridge, MA: MIT Press.

Schneider, W., & Bjorklund, D. F. (1998). Memory. In D. Kuhn & R. S. Siegler (Eds.), *Handbook of child psychology: Vol. 2. Cognition, perception, and language* (5th ed., pp. 467–522). New York: Wiley.

Schneider, W., Gruber, H., Gold, A., & Opwis, K. (1993). Class expertise and memory for chess positions in children and adults. *Journal of Experimental Child Psychology, 56,* 328–349.

Scholes, R. J. (1998). The case against phonemic awareness. *Journal of Research in Reading, 21*(3), 177–218.

Schonert-Reichl, K. A. (1999). Relations of peer acceptance, friendship adjustment, and social behavior to moral reasoning during early adolescence. *Journal of Early Adolescence, 19,* 249–279.

Schuler, M. E., & Nair, P. (1999). Frequency of maternal cocaine use during pregnancy and infant neurobehavioral outcome. *Journal of Pediatric Psychology, 24*(6), 511–514.

Schultz, T. R. (1972). Role of incongruity and resolution in children's appreciation of cartoon humor. *Journal of Experimental Child Psychology, 13*(3), 456–477.

Schum, T. R., Kolb, T. M., McAuliffe, T., Simms, M. D., Underhill, R. L., & Marla, L. (2002). Sequential acquisition of toilet-training skills: A descriptive study of gender and age differences in normal children. *Pediatrics, 109*(3), e48.

Schwartz, D., McFadyen-Ketchum, S. A., Dodge, K. A., & Pettit, G. S. (1998). Peer group victimization as a predictor of children's behavior problems at home and in school. *Development & Psychopathology, 10*(1), 87–99.

Schwartz, M. B., & Puhl, R. (2003). Childhood obesity: A societal problem to solve. *Obesity Review 4*(1), 57–71.

Scott, J. O. (1997). Genetic analysis of social behavior. In N. L. Siegel, G. E. Weisfeld, & C. C. Weisfeld (Eds.), *Uniting psychology and biology: Integrative perspectives on human development.* Washington DC: American Psychological Association.

Scribner, S., & Cole, M. (1981). *The psychology of literacy.* Cambridge, MA: Harvard University Press.

Scripps Howard News Service. (2002). Americans "overwhelmingly" believe in angels; survey says one in five claim personal sightings. Ohio State University School of Journalism.

Segal, N. L. (1999). *Entwined lives: Twins and what they tell us about human behavior.* New York: Dutton/Penguin Books.

Segall, M. H., Dasen, P., Berry, J. W., & Poortinga, Y. (1999). *Human behavior in global perspective: An introduction to cross-cultural psychology* (2nd ed.). Needham Heights, MA: Allyn & Bacon.

Segall, M. H., Ember, C., & Ember, M. (1997). Aggression, crime, and warfare. In J. W. Berry, M. H. Segall, & C. Kagitçibasi (Eds.), *Handbook of cross-cultural psychology: Vol. 3. Social and behavioral applications* (pp. 213–254). Boston: Allyn & Bacon.

Selman, R. & Adalbjarnardottir, S. (2000). A developmental method to analyze the personal meaning adolescents make of risk and relationship: The case of "drinking." *Applied Developmental Science, 4,* 47–65.

Selman, R., Levitt, M. & Schultz, L. (1997). The friendship framework: Tools for the assessment of psychosocial development. In R. Selman, C. Watts, & L. Schultz (Eds.), *Fostering friendship: Pair therapy for treatment and prevention.* New York: Aldine de Gruyter.

Senghas, A., & Coppola, M. (2001). Children creating language: How Nicaraguan sign language acquired a spatial grammar. *Psychological Science, 12*(4), 323–328.

Serpell, R. (2000). Intelligence and culture. In R. J. Sternberg and E. L. Grigorenko (Eds.), *Handbook of intelligence.* New York: Cambridge University Press.

Serpell, R., & Hatano, G. (1997). Education, schooling, and literacy. In J. W. Berry, P. R. Dasen, & T. S. Saraswathi (Eds.), *Handbook of cross-cultural psychology (Vol. 2).* Boston: Allyn & Bacon.

Serra, M., Loth, F. L., van Geert, P. L. C., Hurkens, E., & Minderaa, R. B. (2002). Theory of mind in children with "lesser variants" of autism: A longitudinal study. *Journal of Child Psychology & Psychiatry & Allied Disciplines, 43*(7), 885–900.

Serwach, J. J. (2003, March). 20 years after "A Nation at Risk": Why national education reform failed. *The University Record Online.* Retrieved from http://www.umich.edu/~urecord/0203/Mar17_03/04.shtml.

Sfard, A., & Kieran, C. (2001). Cognition as communication: Rethinking learning-by-talking through multi-faceted analysis of students' mathematical interactions. *Mind, Culture, & Activity, 8*(1), 42–76.

Shapira, A., & Madsen, M. C. (1969). Cooperative and competitive behavior of kibbutz and urban children in Israel. *Child Development, 4,* 609–617.

Shatz, M. (1978). Children's comprehension of question-directives. *Journal of Child Language, 5,* 39–46.

Shaw, D. S., Winslow, E. B., Owens, E. B., & Hood, N. (1998). Young children's adjustment to chronic family adversity: A longitudinal study of low-income families. *Journal of the American Academy of Child and Adolescent Psychiatry, 37*(5), 545–553.

Shaw, G. B. (1963). *George Bernard Shaw on language.* London: Peter Owen.

Sherif, M., & Sherif, C. W. (1956). *An outline of social psychology.* New York: Harper & Row.

Shonkoff, J., & Phillips, D. (Eds.). (2000). *From neurons to neighborhoods: The science of early childhood development.* Washington, DC: National Academy Press.

Shopen, T. (1980). How Pablo says "love" and "store." In T. Shopen & J. M. Williams (Eds.), *Standards and dialects in English.* Cambridge, MA: Winthrop.

Shostak, M. (1981). *Nissa: The life and words of a !Kung Woman.* Cambridge, MA: Harvard University Press.

Shultz, T. R. (1972). The role of incongruity and resolution in children's appreciation of cartoon humor. *Journal of Experimental Child Psychology, 13*(3), 456–477.

Shweder, R. A., Goodnow, J., Hatano, G., LeVine, R. A., Markus, H., & Miller, P. (1998). The cultural psychology of development: One mind, many mentalities. In R. M. Lerner (Ed.), *Handbook of child psychology: Vol. 1. Theoretical models of human development* (5th ed., pp. 865–938). New York: Wiley.

Shweder, R. A., Jensen, L. A., & Goldstein, W. M. (1995). Who sleeps by whom revisited: A method for extracting the moral goods implicit in practice. *New Directions for Child Development, 67,* 21–39.

Shweder, R. A., Mahapatpa, M., & Miller, J. G. (1987). Culture and moral development. In J. Kagan & S. Lamb (Eds.), *The emergence of morality in young children.* Chicago: University of Chicago Press.

Shweder, R. A., Minow, M., & Markus, H. R. (Eds.). (2002). *Engaging cultural differences: The multicultural challenge in liberal democracies.* New York: Russell Sage Foundation.

Siegal, M. (1991). *Knowing children: Experiments in conversation and cognition.* Mahwah, NJ: Erlbaum.

Siegel, L. S., & Ryan, E. B. (1988). Development of grammatical-sensitivity, phonological, and short-term memory skills in normally achieving and learning disabled children. *Developmental Psychology, 24*(1), 28–37.

Siegler, R. S. (1996). *Emerging minds: The process of change in children's thinking.* New York: Oxford University Press.

Siegler, R. S. (1998). *Children's thinking* (3rd ed.). Upper Saddle River, NJ: Prentice Hall.

Siegler, R. S. (2000). The rebirth of children's learning. *Child Development, 71*(1), 26–35.

Siegler, R. S., & Stern, E. (1998). Conscious and unconscious strategy discoveries: A microgenetic analysis. *Journal of Experimental Psychology: General, 127*(4), 377–397.

Silbereisen, R. & Kracke, B. (1997). Self-reported maturational timing and adaptation in adolescence. In J. Schulenbert, J. Maggs, & K. Hurrelmann (Eds.), *Health risks and developmental transitions during adolescence* (pp. 85–109). Cambridge, England: Cambridge University Press.

Simmons, R. (2002). *Odd girl out: The hidden culture of aggression in girls.* New York: Harcourt.

Simmons, R. G., & Blyth, D. A. (1987). *Moving into adolescence: The impact of pubertal change in school context.* New York: Aldine de Gruyter.

Simmons, R. G., Burgeson, R., Carlton-Ford, S., & Blyth, D.A. (1987). The impact of cumulative change in early adolescence. *Child Development, 58,* 1220–1234.

Simon, K. (1982). *Bronx primitive: Portraits in a childhood.* New York: Viking.

Simpson, J. A. (2001). Attachment theory in modern evolutionary perspective. In J. Cassidy & P. R. Shaver (Eds.), *Handbook of attachment: Theory, research, and clinical applications* (pp. 115–140). New York: Guilford.

Simpson, J. L., & Golbus, M. S. (1993). *Genetics in obstetrics and gynecology* (2nd ed.). Philadelphia: W. B. Saunders.

Sinclair, D. C., & Dangerfield, P. (1998). *Human growth after birth.* New York: Oxford University Press.

Singer, D. G., & Singer, J. L. (1990). *The house of make believe.* Cambridge, MA: Harvard University Press.

Singer, L. T., & Zeskind, P. S. (Eds.). (2001). *Biobehavioral assessment of the infant.* New York: Guilford Press.

Singleton, J. (Ed.). (1998). *Learning in likely places: Varieties of apprenticeship in Japan.* New York: Cambridge University Press.

Siqueland, E. R. (1968). Reinforcement patterns and extinction in human newborns. *Journal of Experimental Child Psychology, 6,* 431–432.

Skinner, B. F. (1938). *The behavior of organisms.* New York: Appleton-Century-Crofts.

Skinner, B. F. (1953). *Science and human behavior.* New York: Macmillan.

Skoe, E. E. (1999). Care-based moral reasoning in Norwegian and Canadian early adolescents: A cross-national comparison. *Journal of Early Adolescence, 19,* 280–291.

Skuse, D. H. (1984a). Extreme deprivation in early childhood: I. Diverse outcomes for three siblings from an extraordinary family. *Journal of Child Psychology & Psychiatry & Allied Disciplines, 25*(4), 523–541.

Skuse, D. H. (1984b). Extreme deprivation in early childhood: II. Theoretical issues and a comparative review. *Journal of Child Psychology and Psychiatry, 25,* 543–572.

Smetana, J. G. (2000). Middle class African American adolescents' and parents' conceptions of parental authority and parenting practices: A longitudinal investigation. *Child Development, 71,* 1672–1686.

Smith, E., & Udry, J. (1985). Coital and non-coital sexual behaviors of white and black adolescents. *American Journal of Public Health, 75,* 1200–1203.

Smith, K. (2002). *Who's minding the kids? Child care arrangements: Spring 1997.* Current Population Reports, P70–86, U.S. Census Bureau. Washington, DC: U.S. Government Printing Office.

Smith, N. V. (1973). *The Acquisition of Phonology: A Case Study.* Cambridge: Cambridge University Press.

Smith, P. K., Morita, Y., Junger-Tas, J., Olweus, D., Catalano, R., & Slee, P. (1999). *The nature of school bullying: A cross-national perspective.* London: Routledge.

Smits, W., & Stromback, T. (2001). *The economics of the apprenticeship system.* Cheltenham, UK: E. Elgar.

Smitsman, A. W. (2001). Action in infancy—Perspectives, concepts, and challenges: The development of reaching and grasping. In A. Fogel (Ed.), *Blackwell handbook of infant development* (pp. 71–98). Malden, MA: Blackwell.

Smotherman, W. P., & Robinson, S. R. (1996). The development of behavior before birth. *Developmental Psychology, 32* (3), 425–434.

Smyth, C. M., & Bremner, W. J. (1998). Klinefelter syndrome. *Archives of Internal Medicine, 158*(12), 1309–1314.

Snarey, J. R. (1995). Cross-cultural universality of social moral development: A critical review of Kohlbergian research. *Psychological Bulletin, 97,* 202–232.

Snow, C. (1995). Issues in the study of input: Finetuning, universality, individual and developmental differences, and necessary causes. In P. Fletcher & B. MacWhinney (Eds.), *The handbook of child language.* Oxford: Blackwell.

Snow, C. E. (1972). Mother's speech to children learning language. *Child Development, 43,* 549–565.

Snow, C. E., Burns, M. S., & Griffin, P. (Eds.). (1998). *Preventing reading difficulties in young children.* Washington, DC: National Academy Press.

Sommer, K., Whitman, T., Gorkowski, J., & Gondoli, D. (2000). Prenatal maternal predictors of cognitive and emotional delays in children of adolescent mothers. *Adolescence, 35,* 87–112.

Soussignan, R., Schaal, B., Marlier, L., & Jian, T. (1997). Facial and autonomic responses to biological and artificial olfactory stimuli in human neonates: Re-examining early hedonic discrimination of odors. *Physiology and Behavior, 62*(4), 745–758.

Sowell, E. R., Delis, D., Stiles, J., & Jernigan, T. L. (2001). Improved memory functioning and frontal lobe maturation between childhood and adolescence: A structural MRI study. *Journal of the International Neuropsychological Society, 7*(3): 312–322.

Sowell, E. R., Trauner, D. A., Gamst, A., & Jernigan, T. L. (2002). Development of cortical and subcortical brain structures in childhood and adolescence: A structural magnetic resonance imaging study. *Developmental Medicine Child Neurology, 44,* 4–16.

Spearman, C. (1927). *The abilities of man.* New York: Macmillan.

Spelke, E. S. (2000). Core knowledge. *American Psychologist, 35,* 1233–1234.

Spelke, E. S., Breinlinger, K., Macomber, J., & Jacobson, K. (1992). Origins of knowledge. *Psychological Review, 99*(4), 605–632.

Spencer, M. B. (1988). Self-concept development. *New Directions for Child Development, 42,* 59–72.

Spencer, M. B., Icard, L., Harachi, T., Catalano, R., & Oxford, M. (2000). Ethnic identity among monoracial and multiracial early adolescents. *Journal of Early Adolescence, 20,* 265–387.

Spencer, M. B., & Markstrom-Adams, C. (1990). Identity processes among racial and ethnic minority children in America. *Child Development, 61,* 290–310.

Spiro, M. E. (1965). *Children of the kibbutz.* New York: Schocken Books.

Spitz, H. H., Minsky, S. K., & Besselieu, C. L. (1985). Influence of planning time and first move strategy on Tower of Hanoi problem solving performance of mentally retarded young adults and nonretarded children. *American Journal of Mental Deficiency, 90*(1), 46–56.

Sroufe, L. A. (1979). Socioeconomic development. In J. Osofsky (Ed.), *Handbook of infant development.* New York: Wiley.

Sroufe, L. A., Carlson, E. A., Levy, A. K., & Egeland, B. V. (1999). Implications of attachment theory for developmental psychopathology. *Development & Psychopathology, 11*(1), 1–13.

Sroufe, L. A., Carlson, E., & Shulman, S. (1993). Individuals in relationships: Development from infancy through adolescence. In D. C. Funder, R. D. Parke, C. Tomlinson-Keasey, & K. Widaman (Eds.), *Studying life through time: Personality and development.* Washington: American Psychological Association.

Sroufe, L. A., Egeland, B., & Carlson, E. A. (1999b). One social world: The integrated development of parent-child and peer relationships. In W. A. Collins & B. Laursen (Eds.), *Relationships as developmental contexts* (pp. 241–261). Mahwah, NJ: Erlbaum.

Sroufe, L. A., & Fleeson, J. (1986). Attachment and the construction of relationships. In W. W. Hartup & Z. Rubin (Eds.), *Relationships and development.* Mahwah, NJ: Erlbaum.

St. James-Roberts, I., Conroy, S., & Wilshir, K. (1996). Bases for maternal perceptions of infant crying and colic behavior. *Archives of Disease in Childhood, 75,* 375–381.

St. Onge, M. P., Keller, K. L., Heymsfield, S. B. (2003). Changes in childhood food consumption patterns: A cause for concern in light of increasing body weights. *American Journal of Clinical Nutrition 78*(6), 1068–1073.

Stanovich, K. E. (2000). *Progress in understanding reading: Scientific foundations and new frontiers.* New York: Guilford Press.

Stattin, H., & Magnusson, D. (1990). *Pubertal maturation in female development.* Mahwah, NJ: Erlbaum.

Stauder, J. E., Molenaar, P. C., & Van Der Molen, M. W. (1993). Scalp topography of event-related brain potentials and cognitive transition during childhood. *Child Development, 64,* 769–788.

Stauder, J. E., Molenaar, P. C., & Van Der Molen, M. W. (1999). Brain activity and cognitive transition during longitudinal event-related brain potential study. *Child Neuropsychology, 5,* 44–59.

Steele, H. (2003). Attachment and human development. *Attachment and Human Development, 5*(1), 1.

Stein, J. H., & Reiser, L. W. (1994). A study of white middle-class adolescent boys' responses to "semenarche" (the first ejaculation). *Journal of Youth and Adolescence, 23,* 373–384.

Steinberg, L. (1996). *Beyond the classroom: Why school reform has failed and what parents need to do.* New York: Simon & Schuster.

Steinberg, L. (2001). We know some things: Parent-adolescent relationships in retrospect and prospect. *Journal of Research on Adolescence, 11,* 1–19.

Steinberg, L., & Duncan, P. (2002). Work group IV: Increasing the capacity of parents, families, and adults living with adolescents to improve adolescent health outcomes. *Journal of Adolescent Health, 31*(Suppl. 6), 261–263.

Steinberg, L., Fegley, S., & Dornbusch, S. M. (1993). Negative impact of part-time work on adolescent adjustment: Evidence from a longitudinal study. *Developmental Psychology, 29,* 171–180.

Steinberg, L., & Silk, J. S. (2002). Parenting adolescents. In M. H. Bornstein (Ed.), *Handbook of parenting: Vol. 1. Children and parenting* (2nd ed., pp. 103–133). Mahwah, NJ: Erlbaum.

Steiner, J. E. (1979). Human facial expressions in response to taste and smell stimulation. In H. W. Reese & L. P. Lipsitt (Eds.), *Advances in child development and behavior: Vol. 13.* New York: Academic Press.

Stern, D. N. (1977). *The first relationship.* Cambridge, MA: Harvard University Press.

Stern, D. N. (2002). *The first relationship: Infant and mother.* Cambridge, MA: Harvard University Press.

Stern, W. (1910). Abstracts of lectures on the psychology of testimony and on the study of individuality. *American Journal of Psychology, 21,* 273–282.

Stern, W. (1912). *Psychologische methoden der intelligenz-prufung.* Leipzig: Barth.

Sternberg, R. J. (1990). *Metaphors of mind: Conceptions of the nature of intelligence.* New York: Cambridge University Press.

Sternberg, R. J. (1999). A triarchic approach to the understanding and assessment of intelligence in multicultural populations. *Journal of School Psychology, 37*(2), 145–159.

Sternberg, R. J., Forsythe, G. B., Hedlund, J., Horvath, J. A., Wagner, R. K., Williams, W. A., et al. (2000). *Practical intelligence in everyday life.* Cambridge, UK: Cambridge University Press.

Sternberg, R. J., & Grigorenko, E. L. (Eds.). (2001). *Environmental effects on cognitive abilities.* Mahwah, NJ: Erlbaum.

Stevens, J., Quittner, A. L., Zuckerman, J. B., & Moore, S. (2002). Behavioral inhibition, self-regulation of motivation, and working memory in children with attention deficit hyperactivity disorder. *Developmental Neuropsychology, 21*(2), 117–140.

Stevenson, H. C., Davis, G., & Abdul-Kabir, S. (2001). *Stickin' to, watchin' over, and gettin' with: An African American parent's guide to discipline.* San Francisco: Jossey Bass.

Stevenson, H. W., Chen, C. S., & Lee, S. (1993). Mathematics achievement of Chinese, Japanese, and American children—10 years later. *Science, 259*(5091), 53–58.

Stevenson, H. W., & Stigler, J. W. (1992). *The learning gap: Why our schools are failing and what we can learn from Japanese and Chinese education.* New York: Summit.

Stevenson, H. W., Stigler, J. W., Lee, S., Lucker, G. W., Kitamura, S., & Hsu, C. (1985). Cognitive performance and academic achievement of Japanese, Chinese, and American children. *Child Development, 56,* 718–734.

Stevenson, R. (1977). The fetus and newly born infant: Influence of the prenatal environment (2nd ed.). St. Louis: Mosby.

Stigler, J. W., Gallimore, R., & Hiebert, J. (2000). Using video surveys to compare classrooms and teaching across cultures: Examples and lessons from the TIMSS video studies. *Educational Psychologist, 35*(2), 87–100.

Stigler, J. W., & Perry, M. (1990). Mathematics learning in Japanese, Chinese, and American classrooms. In J. W. Stigler, R. A. Shweder, & G. Herdt (Eds.), *Cultural psychology: Essays on comparative human development.* New York: Cambridge University Press.

Stipek, D. (2001). Pathways to constructive lives: The importance of early school success. In A. C. Bower & D. J. Stipek (Eds.), *Constructive & destructive behavior: Implications for family, school, & society* (pp. 291–315). Washington, DC: American Psychological Association.

Stoltzfus, R. J., Kvalsvig, J. D., Chwaya, H. M., Montresor, A., Albonico, M., Tielsch, J. M., et al. (2001). Effects of iron supplementation and anthelmintic treatment on motor and language development of preschool children in Zanzibar: Double blind, placebo controlled study. *British Medical Journal, 323*(7326), 1389–1393.

Stone, J. E., & Clements, A. (1998). Research and innovation: Let the buyer beware. In R. R. Spillane & R. Regnier (Eds.), *The superintendent of the future* (pp. 59–97). Gaithersburg, MD: Aspen.

Stone, J. L., & Church, J. (1957). *Childhood and adolescence: A psychology of the growing person.* New York: Random House.

Strathearn, L., Gray, P. H., O'Callaghan, M. J., & Wood, D. O. (2001). Childhood neglect and cognitive development in extremely low birth weight infants: A prospective study. *Pediatrics, 108*(1), 142–151.

Stratton, K., Howe, C., & Battaglia, F. (1996). *Fetal alcohol syndrome: Diagnosis, epidemiology, prevention, and treatment.* Washington, DC: National Academy Press.

Straus, M., & Stewart, J. (1999). Corporal punishment by American parents: National data on prevalence, chronicity, severity, and duration, in relation to child and family characteristics. *Clinical Child and Family Psychology Review, 2,* 55–70.

Strauss, R. (1999). Childhood obesity. *Current Problems in Pediatrics, 29*(1), 1–29.

Strayer, F. F. (1991). The development of agonistic and affiliative structures in preschool play groups. In J. Silverberg & P. Gray (Eds.), *To fight or not to fight: Violence and peacefulness in humans and other primates.* Oxford, UK: Oxford University Press.

Strayer, F. F., & Santos, A. J. (1996). Affiliative structures in preschool peer groups. *Social Development, 5,* 117–130.

Streri, A., & Spelke, E. S. (1988). Haptic perception of objects in infancy. *Cognitive Psychology, 20,* 1–23.

Striano, T., & Rochat, P. (2000). Emergence of selective social referencing in infancy. *Infancy, 1*(2), 253–264.

Striegel-Moore, R. H., & Cachelin, F. M. (1999). Body image concerns and disordered eating in adolescent girls: Risk and protective factors. In N. G. Johnson, M. C. Roberts, & J. Worell (Eds.), *Beyond appearance: A new look at adolescent girls.* Washington, DC: American Psychological Association.

Stunkard, A. J., Sorenson, T. I., Hanis, C., Teasdale, T. W., Chakraborty, R., Schull, W. J., & Schulsinger, F. (1986). An adoption study of human obesity. *New England Journal of Medicine, 314,* 193–198

Suarez-Orozco, C. (2000). Identities under siege: Immigration stress and social mirroring among the children of immigrants. In A. Robben & M. Suarez-Orozco (Eds.), *Cultures under siege: Collective violence and trauma.* New York: Cambridge University Press.

Suarez-Orozco, M. (2001). Globalization, immigration, and education: The research agenda. *Harvard Educational Review, 71,* 345–365.

Subbotsky, E. (2001). Causal explanations of events by children and adults: Can alternative causal modes coexist in one mind? *British Journal of Developmental Psychology 19*(1): 23–45.

Subbotsky, E. V. (1993). *The birth of personality: The development of independent and moral behavior in preschool children.* New York: Harvester Wheatsheaf.

Subbotsky, E., & Quinteros, G. (2002). Do cultural factors affect causal beliefs? Rational and magical thinking in Britain and Mexico. *British Journal of Psychology 93*: 519–543.

Subrahmanyam, K., & Greenfield, P. (1998). Computer games for girls: What makes them play? In J. Cassell & H. Jenkins (Eds.), *From Barbie to Mortal Combat: Gender and computer games.* Cambridge, MA: MIT Press.

Subrahmanyam, K., Kraut, R., Greenfield, P., & Gross, E. (2001). New forms of electronic media: The impact of interactive games and the Internet on cognition, socialization, and behavior. In D. Singer & J. Singer (Eds.), *Handbook of children and the media.* Thousand Oaks, CA: Sage.

Sugarman, S. (1983). *Children's early thought: Developments in classification.* New York: Cambridge.

Sullivan, H. S. (1953). *The interpersonal theory of psychiatry.* New York: W. W. Norton.

Sullivan, K., & Winner, E. (1993). Three-year-olds' understanding of mental states: The influence of trickery. *Journal of Experimental Child Psychology, 56*(2), 135–148.

Summerfield, D. (1999). A critique of seven assumptions behind psychological trauma programmes in war-affected areas. *Social Science and Medicine, 48,* 1449–1462.

Sun, L.-C., & Roopnarine, J. L. (1996). Mother–infant, father–infant interaction and involvement in childcare and household labor among Taiwanese families. *Infant Behavior and Development, 19*(1), 121–129.

Sun, Y. (2001). Family environment and adolescents' well-being before and after parents' marital disruption: A longitudinal analysis. *Journal of Marriage and Family, 63,* 697–713.

Sun, Y., & Li, Y. (2002). Children's well-being during parents' marital disruption process: A pooled time-series analysis. *Journal of Marriage and Family, 64,* 472–488.

Sunseth, K., & Bowers, P. G. (2002). Rapid naming and phonemic awareness: Contributions to reading, spelling, and orthographic knowledge. *Scientific Studies of Reading, 6*(4): 401–429.

Suomala, J., & Alajaaski, J. (2002). Pupils' problem-solving processes in a complex computerized learning environment. *Journal of Educational Computing Research, 26*(2): 155–176.

Suomi, S. (1995). Influences of attachment theory on ethological studies of biobehavioral development in nonhuman primates. In S. Goldberg & R. Muir & J. Kerr (Eds.), *Attachment theory: Social, developmental, and clinical perspectives* (pp. 185–202). Mahwah, NJ: Analytic Press.

Suomi, S. J. (1997). Early determinants of behavior: Evidence from primate studies. *British Medical Bulletin, 53,* 170–184.

Suomi, S. J. (2000). A biobehavioral perspective on developmental psychopathology: Excessive aggression and serotonergic dysfunction in monkeys. In A. Sameroff, M. Lewis, & S. M. Miller (Eds.), *Handbook of developmental psychopathology* (2nd ed., pp. 237–256). Dordrecht, Netherlands: Kluwer Academic.

Suomi, S. J., & Harlow, H. F. (1972). Social rehabilitation of isolate-reared monkeys. *Developmental Psychology, 6,* 487–496.

Suomi, S. J., Harlow, H. F., & McKinny, W. T., Jr. (1972). Monkey psychiatrists. *American Journal of Psychiatry, 128,* 927–932.

Super, C. M. (1976). Environmental effects on motor development: A case of African infant precocity. *Developmental Medicine and Child Neurology, 18,* 561–567.

Super, C. M., & Harkness, S. (1972). The infant's niche in rural Kenya and metropolitan America. In L. Adler (Ed.), *Issues in cross-cultural research.* New York: Academic Press.

Super, C. M., & Harkness, S. (2002). Culture structures the environment for development. *Human Development, 45,* 270–274.

Suppes, P. (1966). The uses of computers in education. *Scientific American, 215*(3), 206–220.

Susman, E. J., Nottlemann, E. D., Inhoff-Germain, G. E., Dorn, L. D., Cutler, G. B., Jr., Loriaux, D. L., & Chrousos, G. P. (1985). The relation of development and social-emotional behavior in young adolescents. *Journal of Youth and Adolescence, 14,* 245–264.

Susman, E. J., Schmeelk, K. H., Ponirakis, A., & Gariepy, J. L. (2001). Maternal prenatal, postpartum, and concurrent stressors and temperament in 3-year-olds: A person and variable analysis. *Development and Psychopathology, 13*(3), 629–652.

Sutton, J., Smith, P. K., & Swettenham, J. (1999). Bullying and "theory of mind": A critique of the "social skills deficit" view of anti-social behavior. *Social Development, 8*(1), 117–127.

Sutton-Smith, B., & Roberts, J. M. (1973). The cross-cultural and psychological study of games. In B. Sutton-Smith (Ed.), *The folkgames of children.* Austen, TX: University of Texas Press.

Sweeney, J., & Bradbard, M., R. (1988). Mothers' and fathers' changing perceptions of their male and female infants over the course of pregnancy. *Journal of Genetic Psychology, 149*(3), 393–404.

Sweet, A., & Snow, C. E. Eds. (2003). *Rethinking reading comprehension.* New York: Guilford Press.

Szkrubalo, J., & Ruble, D. N. (1999). "God made me a girl": Sex-category constancy judgments and explanations revisited. *Developmental Psychology, 35*(2), 392–402.

Tager-Flusberg, H. (1999). *Neurodevelopmental disorders.* Cambridge, MA: MIT Press.

Tallal, P. (2003). Language learning disabilities: Integrating research approaches. *Current Directions in Psychological Science, 12*(6): 206–211.

Tallal, P., Merzenich, M., Miller, S., & Jenkins, W. (1998). Language learning impairment: Integrating research and remediation. *Scandanavian Journal of Psychology, 39*(3), 197–199.

Tamis-LeMonda, C. S., Bornstein, M. S., Cyphers, L., Toda, S., & Ogino, M. (1992). Language and play at one year: A comparison of toddlers and mothers in the United States and Japan. *International Journal of Behavioral Development, 15,* 19–42.

Tani, C. R., Chavez, E. L., & Deffenbacher, J. L. (2001). Peer isolation and drug use among while non-Hispanic and Mexican American adolescents. *Adolescence, 36,* 127–139.

Tanner, J. M. (1978). *Fetus into man: Physical growth from conception to maturity.* Cambridge, MA: Harvard University Press.

Tanner, J. M. (1990). *Fetus into man: Physical growth from conception to maturity (revised).* Cambridge, MA: Harvard University Press.

Tanner, J. M. (1998). Sequence, tempo, and individual variation in growth and development of boys and girls aged twelve to sixteen. In D. P. Harriet (Ed.), *Adolescent behavior and society: A book of readings* (5th ed. pp. 34–46). New York: McGraw-Hill.

Tardif, T., Gelman, S. A., & Xu, F. (1999). Putting the "noun bias" in context: A comparison of English and Mandarin. *Child Development, 70*(3), 620–635.

Telzrow, R. W., Campos, J. J., Kermoian, R., & Bertenthal, B. I. (1999). *Locomotor acquisition as an antecedent of psychological development: Studies of infants with myelodysplasia.* Berkeley, CA: University of California.

Temple, E., Deutsch, G. K., Poldrack, R. A., Miller, S. L., Tallal, P., Merzenich, M. M., & Gabrieli, J. D. (2003). Neural deficits in children with dyslexia ameliorated by behavioral remediation: Evidence from functional MRI. *Proceedings of the National Academy of Sciences, 100*(5), 2860–2865.

Tenenbaum, H. R., Callanan, M., Alba-Speyer, C., & Sandoval, L. (2002). The role of educational background, activity, and past experiences in Mexican-descent families' science conversations. *Hispanic Journal of Behavioral Sciences, 24*(2), 225–248.

Terman, L. M. (1925). *Genetic studies of genius.* Stanford: Stanford University Press.

Tessier, R. M. C., Velez, S., Girón, M.S.W., Figueroa de Calume, Z., Ruiz-Paláez, J. G., Charpak, Y., & Charpak, N. (1998). Kangaroo mother care and the bonding hypothesis. *Pediatrics, 102,* e17.

Teti, D. M., Gelfand, D. M., Messinger, D. S., & Isabella, R. (1995). Maternal depression and the quality of early attachment: An examination of infants, preschoolers, and their mothers. Special Section: Parental depression and distress: Implications for development. *Developmental Psychology, 31,* 364–376.

Thapan, M. (2000). Adolescence, embodiment and gender identity in contemporary India: Elite women in a changing society. *Women's Studies International Forum, 24,* 359–371.

Tharp, R., & Yamauchi, L. (2000). Instructional conversations in Native American classrooms: Rural, urban and minority education. *Journal of Early Education and Family Review, 7*(5): 33–37.

Thatcher, R. W. (1991). Maturation of the human frontal lobes: Physiological evidence for staging. *Developmental Neuropsychology, 7(3),* 397–419.

Thatcher, R. W. (1994). Cyclic cortical reorganization. In G. Dawson & K. W. Fischer (Eds.), *Human behavior and the developing brain.* New York: Guilford Press.

Thatcher, R. W. (1997). Human frontal lobe development: A theory of cyclical cortical reorganization. In N. A. Krasnegor, G. R. Lyon, & P. S. Goldman-Rakic, (Eds.), *Development of the prefrontal cortex: Evolution, neurobiology, and behavior* (pp. 85–116). Baltimore, MD: Paul H. Brookes.

Thelen, E. (1995). Motor development: A new synthesis. *American Psychologist, 50,* 79–95.

Thelen, E. (2002). Self-organization in developmental processes: Can systems approaches work? In M. H. Johnson & Y. Munakata (Eds.), *Brain development and cognition: A reader* (2nd ed., pp. 336–374). Malden, MA: Blackwell.

Thelen, E., Fisher, D. M., & Ridley-Johnson, R. (2002). The relationship between physical growth and a newborn reflex. *Infant Behavior and Development, 25*(1), 72–85.

Thelen, E., Schoener, G., Scheier, C., & Smith, L. B. (2001). The dynamics of embodiment: A field theory of infant perseverative reaching. *Behavioral and Brain Sciences, 24*(1), 1–86.

Thelen, E. & Smith, L. B. (1998). Dynamic systems theory. In W. Damon & R. M. Lerner (Eds.), *Handbook of child psychology: Vol. 12* (5th ed., pp. 563–634). New York: Wiley.

Thelen, E., & Ulrich, B. D. (1991). Hidden skills. *Monographs of the Society for Research in Child Development, 56*(1, Serial No. 223).

Thiessen, E. D., & Saffran, J. R. (2003). When cues collide: Use of stress and statistical cues to word boundaries by 7 to 9-month-old infants. *Developmental Psychology 39*(4): 706–716.

Thoman, E. (1999). *Some good habits to acquire.* Los Angeles: Center for Media Literacy. Retrieved from http://www.medialit.org/ReadingRoom/childrenTV/goodTVhabits.htm

Thoman, E. B., Hammond, K., Affleck, G., & Desilva, H. N. (1995). The breathing bear with preterm infants: Effects on sleep, respiration, and affect. *Infant Mental Health Journal, 16*(3), 160–168.

Thoman, E. B., & Ingersoll, E. W. (1993). Learning in premature infants. *Developmental Psychology, 29*(4), 692–700.

Thoman, E. B., & Whitney, M. P. (1989). Sleep states of infants monitored in the home: Individual differences, developmental trends, and origins of diurnal cyclicity. *Infant Behavior & Development, 12*(1): 59–75.

Thomas, A., & Chess, S. (1984). Genesis and evaluation of behavioral disorders: From infancy to early adult life. *American Journal of Psychiatry, 141*, 1–9.

Thomas, A., & Chess, S. (1989). Temperament and personality. In G. A. Kohnstamm, J. E. Bates, & M. K. Rothbart (Eds.), *Temperament in childhood.* New York: Wiley.

Thompson, G. B., & Nicholson, T. (Eds.). (1999). *Learning to read: Beyond phonics and whole language.* New York: Teachers College Press.

Thompson, M., Cohen, L., & Grace, C. (2001) *Best friends, worst enemies: Understanding the social lives of children.* New York: Ballantine.

Thompson, R. A. (1998). Early sociopersonality development. In N. Eisenberg (Ed.), *Handbook of child psychology: Vol. 3. Social, emotional, and personality development* (5th ed., pp. 25–104). New York: Wiley.

Thompson, R. A. (2001). Sensitive periods in attachment? In D. Bailey, J. Bruer, F. Symons, & J. Lichtman (Eds.), *Critical thinking about critical periods.* Baltimore, MD: Paul H. Brookes.

Thompson, R. A., & Nelson, C. A. (2001). Developmental science and the media: Early brain development. *American Psychologist, 56*, 5–15.

Thomson, J. A. (2001). Primate embryonic stem cells. Official Gazette of the United States Patent and Trademark Office Patents, 1244(2), n.p.

Thorne, B. (1993). *Gender play: Girls and boys in school.* New Brunswick, NJ: Rutgers University Press.

Thorne, B., & Luria, Z. (1986). Sexuality and gender in children's daily worlds. *Social Problems, 33*, 176–190.

Thrasher, F. (1927). *The gang: A study of 1,313 gangs in Chicago.* Chicago: University of Chicago Press.

Thurstone, L. L. (1938). *Primary mental abilities.* Chicago, IL: University of Chicago Press.

Tienari, P., Wynne, L., Moring, J., & Lahti, I. (1994). The Finnish adoptive family study of schizophrenia: Implications for family research. *British Journal of Psychiatry, 164*, 20–26.

Tizard, B., & Hodges, J. (1978). The effect of early institutional rearing on the development of eight-year-old children. *Journal of Child Psychology and Psychiatry, 19*, 99–118.

Tizard, B., & Rees, J. (1975). The effect of early institutional rearing on the behavioral problems and affectional relationship of four-year-old children. *Journal of Child Psychology and Psychiatry, 16*, 61–73.

Tolchinsky, L., & Teberosky, A. (1998). The development of word segmentation and writing in two scripts. *Cognitive Development, 13*(1), 1–24.

Tomasello, M. (1999). *The cultural origins of human cognition.* Cambridge, MA: Harvard University Press.

Tomasello, M. (2000). First steps toward a usage-based theory of language acquisition. *Cognitive Linguistics. Special Issue: Language Acquisition 11*(1–2): 61–82.

Tomasello, M., & Mannle, S. (1985). Pragmatics of sibling speech to one-year-olds. *Child Development, 56*, 911–917.

Tonneau, F., & Thompson, N. S. (Eds.). (2000). *Evolution, culture and behavior.* New York: Kluwer Academic/Plenum Press.

Travis, F. (1998). Cortical and cognitive development in 4th, 8th and 12th grade students: The contribution of speed of processing and executive functioning to cognitive development. *Biological Psychology, 48*(1): 37–56.

Tremblay, R. (2000). The development of aggressive behavior during childhood: What have we learned in the past century? *International Journal of Behavioral Development, 24*, 129–141.

Trevarthen, C. (1998). The concept and foundations of infant intersubjectivity. In S. Braten (Ed.), *Intersubjective communication and emotion in early ontogeny* (pp. 15–46). New York: Cambridge University Press.

Trevarthen, C. (2001). Does developmental cognitive neuroscience promise too much? *Trends in Neurosciences, 24*, 424–425.

Troiden, R. R. (1993). The formation of homosexual identities. In L. D. Garnets & D. C. Kimmel (Eds.), *Psychological perspectives on lesbian and gay male experiences* (pp. 191–217). New York: Columbia University Press.

Tronick, E. Z., Thomas, R. B., & Daltabuit, M. (1994). The Quechua manta pouch: A caretaking practice for buffering the Peruvian infant against the multiple stressors of high altitude. *Child Development, 65*, 1005–1113.

Troseth, G. L. (2003). Getting a clear picture: Young children's understanding of a televised image. *Developmental Science, 6*, 247–253.

Tuchmann-Duplessis, H. (1975). *Drug effects on the fetus.* Acton, MA: Publishing Science Group.

Tuchmann-Duplessis, H., David, G., & Haegel, P. (1971). *Illustrated human embryology: Vol. 1.* New York: Springer-Verlag.

Tucker, G. R. (1999). *A global perspective on bilingualism and bilingual education.* Washington, DC: ERIC Clearinghouse on Languages and Linguistics.

Tulving, E., & Craik, F. I. M. (Eds.). (2000). *The Oxford handbook of memory.* London: Oxford University Press.

Tulviste, P. (1991). *The cultural-historical development of verbal thinking.* Commack, NY: Nova Science.

Turati, C., Simion, F., Milani, I., & Umilta, C. (2002). Newborn's preference for faces: What is crucial? *Developmental Psychology, 38*(6), 875–882.

Turiel, E. (1983). *The development of social knowledge: Morality and convention.* Cambridge: Cambridge University Press.

Turiel, E. (1998). The development of morality. In W. Damon & N. Eisenberg (Eds.), *Handbook of child psychology, Vol. 3: Social, emotional, and personality development* (5th ed., pp. 863–932). New York: Wiley.

Turiel, E. (2002). *The culture of morality.* Cambridge: Cambridge University Press.

Turiel, E., Killen, M., & Helwig, C. C. (1987). Morality: Its structure, functions, and vagaries. In J. Kagan & S. Lamb (Eds.), *The emergence of morality.* Chicago: Chicago University Press.

Turksen, K. (Ed.) (2002). *Embryonic stem cells: Methods and protocols.* Clifton, NJ: Humana Press.

Turnbull, E., Rothstein-Fisch, C., Greenfield, P. M., & Quiroz, B. (2001). *Bridging cultures between home and school.* Mahwah, NJ: Erlbaum.

U. S. Bureau of the Census (1991). Daily disruption and economic hardship: The shortrun picture for children. *Current Population Report,* Series P-70, No. 3.

U. S. Bureau of the Census (1995). *Statistical abstract of the United States: 1995* (115th ed.). Washington, DC: U. S. Government Printing Office.

U. S. Bureau of the Census (1998). Who's minding our preschoolers. *Current Population Reports,* Series P70–53. Washington, DC: U. S. Government Printing Office.

U. S. Bureau of the Census (1999). Child support for custodial mothers and fathers: 1995. *Current Population Reports.* Washington, DC: U. S. Government Printing Office.

U. S. Bureau of the Census (2000). *Money income in the United States: 2000.* Washington, DC: U. S. Department of Commerce.

U. S. Bureau of the Census. (2001). *Statistical abstract of the United States: 2001* (121st ed.). Washington, DC: U. S. Government Printing Office.

U. S. Bureau of the Census (2002). *Statistical abstract of the United States: 2002* (122nd ed.). Washington, DC: U. S. Government Printing Office.

U. S. Department of Health and Human Services. (1999). *Trends in the well-being of America's children and youth: 1999.*

U. S. Department of Justice. (2002/2000) *Sourcebook of criminal justice statistics, 2000.* Washington, DC.: Congressional Information Service.

U. S. Office of Education. (1977). *Procedures for evaluating specific learning disabilities:* Federal Register 42. Washington, DC: U. S. Government Printing Office.

Underwood, M. (2002). Aggression among boys and girls. In P. Smith & C. Hart (Eds.*), Blackwell handbook of childhood social development.* Malden, MA: Blackwell.

UNESCO (2003). Institute for Statistics: Gross net and gross enrollment ratios–secondary education. Montreal, Canada: UNESCO.

UNICEF/United Nations Children's Fund. (1999). *The state of the world's children.* Oxford: Oxford University Press.

UNICEF. (2000). The progress of nations, 2000. Retrieved from www.unicef.org/pon00 on March 15, 2004.

UNICEF. (2003). Prevention of mother-to-child transmission of HIV.

United Nations Commission on Population and Development. (1996). Report of the Secretary-General on world population monitoring, focusing on international migration, with special emphasis on the linages between migration and development on gender issues and the family. United Nations: Official Records of the Economic and Social Council, Supplement No. 5 (E/1996/25).

United Nations Security Council (2002). Report of the Secretary-General on children and armed conflict (S/2002/1299). Retrieved from http//www.un.org/Docs/scinfo.htm

University of Michigan Institute for Social Research (1996). *Monitoring the future: 1981, 1991, and 1992.*

Urberg, K. A., Degirmencioglu, S. M., & Tolson, J. M. (1998). Adolescent friendship selection and termination: The role of similarity. *Journal of Social & Personal Relationships, 15*(5), 703–710.

Ursitti, F., Klein, J., & Koren, G. (2001). Confirmation of cocaine use during pregnancy: A critical review. *Therapeutic Drug Monitoring, 23*(4), 347–353.

Uzgiris, I. C., & Hunt, J. (1975). *Assessment in infancy: Ordinal scales of psychological development.* Champaign: University of Illinois Press.

Valian, V. (1999). Input and language acquisition. In W. C. Ritchie & T. K. Bhatia (Eds.), *Handbook of child language acquisition* (497–530). San Diego: Academic Press.

Valsiner, J. (1998). Editorial: Culture and psychology on the move. *Culture & Psychology, 4,* 5–9.

Valsiner, J. (2000). *Culture and human development.* London: Sage.

Valsiner, J., & van der Veer, R. (2000). *The social mind: Construction of the idea.* Cambridge, UK: Cambridge University Press.

van den Boom, D. C., & Hoeksma, J. B. (1995). "The effect of infant irritability on mother–infant interaction: A growth-curve analysis": Correction. *Developmental Psychology, 31*(2), 197.

Van Der Put, N. M. J., Thomas, C. M. G., Eskes, T. K., Trijbels, F. J., Steegers-Theunissen, R. P., Mariman, E. C., et al. (1997). Altered folate and vitamin B-12 metabolism in families with spina bifida offspring. *Quarterly Journal of Medicine, 90*(8), 505–510.

Van Evra, J. P. (1998). Television and child development (2nd ed.). Mahwah, NJ: Erlbaum.

van Heteren, C. F., Boekkooi, P. F., Jongsma, H. W., & Nijhuis, J. G. (2000). Fetal learning and memory. *Lancet* (North American Edition), *356*(9236), 1169–1170.

Van Hoorn, J., Komlosi, A., Suchar, E., & Samelson, D. (2000). *Adolescent development and rapid social change: Perspectives from Eastern Europe.* New York: State University of New York Press.

van IJzendoorn, M. H., & Sagi, A. (2001). Cross-cultural patterns of attachment: Universal and contextual dimensions. In J. Cassidy, & P. R. Shaver (Eds.), *Handbook of attachment: Theory, research, and clinical applications* (pp. 713–734). New York: Guilford Press.

Van Roosmalen, E. (2000). Forces of patriarchy: Adolescent experiences of sexuality and conceptions of relationships. *Youth and Society, 32,* 202–227.

Vander Linde, E., Morrongiello, B. A., & Rovee-Collier, C. (1985). Determinants of retention in 8-week-old infants. *Developmental Psychology, 21*(4), 601–613.

Vangelisti, A., Reis, H., & Fitzpatrick, M. (Eds.). (2002). *Stability and change in relationships.* Cambridge: Cambridge University Press.

Vasquez, O. (2002). *La classe magica.* Mahwah, NJ, Erlbaum.

Vaughn, B. E., & Bost, K. K. (1999). Attachment and temperament. In J. Cassidy & P. R. Shaver (Eds.), *Handbook of attachment: Theory, research, and clinical applications* (pp. 198–225). New York: Guilford Press.

Vickerstaff, S. A. (2003). Apprenticeship in the "golden age": Were youth transitions really smooth and unproblematic back then? *Work, Employment & Society, 17*(2), 269–287.

Vinden, P. G. (1998). Imagination and true belief: A cross-cultural perspective. In de Rivera, J. & Sarbin, T. R., *Believed-in imaginings: The narrative construction of reality.* Memory trauma, dissociation, and hypnosis series (pp. 73–85). Washington, DC: American Psychological Association.

Vinden, P. G. (2002). Understanding minds and evidence for belief: A study of Mofu children in Cameroon. *International Journal of Behavioral Development, 26*(5), 445–452.

Vintzileos, A. M., Ananth, C. V., Smulian, J. C., Scorza, W. E., & Knuppel, R. A. (2002). Prenatal care black-white fetal death disparity in the United States: Heterogeneity by high-risk conditions. *Obstetrics and Gynecology, 99*(3), 483–489.

Violato, C. & Wiley, A. (1990). Images of adolescence in English literature: The middle ages to the modern period. *Adolescence, 25,* 253–264.

von Hofsten, C. (1982). Eye-hand coordination in the newborn. *Developmental Psychology, 18*(3), 450–461.

von Hofsten, C. (1984). Developmental changes in the organization of prereaching movements. *Developmental Psychology, 20*(3), 378–388.

von Hofsten, C. (2001). On the early development of action, perception, and cognition. In F. Lacerda, C. von Hofsten, & M. Heimann (Eds.), *Emerging cognitive abilities in early infancy* (pp. 73–89). Mahwah, NJ: Erlbaum.

von Hofsten, C., & Roennqvist, L. (1993). The structuring of neonatal arm movements. *Child Development, 64*(4), 1046–1057.

Vurpillot, E. (1968). The development of scanning strategies and their relation to visual differentiation. *Journal of Experimental Child Psychology, 6,* 632–650.

Vygotksy, L. S. (1978). *Mind in society.* Cambridge, MA: Harvard University Press.

Wachs, T. D. (1999). The what, why, and how of temperament: A piece of the action. In L. Balter & C. S. Tamis-LeMonda (Eds.), *Child psychology: A handbook of contemporary issues* (pp. 23–44). Philadelphia: Psychology Press/Taylor & Francis.

Wachs, T. D. (2000). *Necessary but not sufficient: The respective roles of single and multiple influences on individual development* (pp. 69–96). Washington, DC: American Psychological Association.

Wachs, T. D., & Bates, J. E. (2001). *Temperament.* In G. Bremmer & A. Fogel (Eds.), *Blackwell handbook of infant development: Vol. 12.* Handbooks of developmental psychology (pp. 465–501). Malden, MA: Blackwell.

Waddington, C. H. (1947). *Organizers and genes.* Cambridge: Cambridge University Press.

Wade, T. D., Bulik, C. M., Neale, M. C. & Kendler, K. S. (2000). Anorexia nervosa and major depression: An examination of shared genetic and environmental risk factors. *American Journal of Psychiatry, 157,* 469–471.

Wagner, D. A. (1974). The development of short-term and incidental memory: A cross cultural study. *Child Development, 48,* 389–396.

Wagner, D. A. (1978). Memories of Morocco: The influence of age, schooling, and environment on memory. *Cognitive Psychology, 10,* 1–28.

Wainryb, C. (1995). Reasoning about social conflicts in different cultures: Druze and Jewish children in Israel. *Child Development, 66*(2), 390–401.

Wakely, A., Rivera, S., & Langer, J. (2000). Can young infants add and subtract? *Child Development, 71*(6), 1525–1534.

Walker, L. J., Hennig, K., & Krettenauer, T. (2000). Parent and peer contexts for children's moral reasoning development. *Child Development, 71,* 1033–1048.

Walker, L. J., Pitts, R. C., Henning, K. H., & Matsuba, M. K. (1995). Reasoning about morality and real-life moral problems. In M. Killen & D. Hart (Eds.), *Morality in everyday life: Developmental perspectives.* New York: Cambridge University Press.

Walker, S., Irving, K., & Berthelsen, D. (2002). Gender influences on preschool children's social problem-solving strategies. *The Journal of Genetic Psychology, 163,* 197–209.

Walker-Andrews, A., & Kahana-Kahana, R. (1999). The understanding of pretence across the second year. *British Journal of Developmental Psychology, 17,* 523–536.

Walsh, W. (2002). Spankers and nonspankers: Where they get information on spanking. *Family Relations, 51,* 81–88.

Wandersman, A. & Florin, P. (2003). Community interventions and effective prevention. *American Psychologist, 58*(6–7), 441–448.

Wang, A. O. (2001). Multicultural genetic counseling: Then, now, and in the 21st century. *American Journal of Medical Genetics, 106*(3), 208–215.

Wang, X., Zuckerman, B., Pearson, C., Kaufman, G., Chen, C., Wang, G., et al. (2002). Maternal cigarette smoking, metabolic gene polymorphism, and infant birth weight. *Journal of the American Medical Association, 287*(2), 195–202.

Ward, K. (1994). Genetics and prenatal diagnosis. In J. R. Scott, P. J. DiSaia, C. B. Hammond, & W. N. Spellacy (Eds.), *Dansforth's obstetrics and gynecology* (7th ed.). Philadelphia: J.B. Lippincott.

Warner, T. D., Dede, D. E., Garvan, C. W., & Conway, T. W. (2002). One size still does not fit all in specific learning disability assessment across ethnic groups. *Journal of Learning Disabilities, 35*(6), 501–509.

Warren, A. R., & McCloskey, L. A. (1997). Language in social contexts. In J. B. Gleason (Ed.), *The development of language* (pp. 210–258). Boston, MA: Allyn & Bacon.

Warren, M. P., Brooks-Gunn, J., Fox, R., Lancelot, C., Newman, D., & Hamilton, W. G. (1991). Lack of bone accretion and amenarchea in young dancers: Evidence for a relative osteopenia in weight bearing bones. *Journal of Clinical Endocrinology and Metabolism, 72,* 847–853.

Warschauer, M. (2003). *Technology and social inclusion: Rethinking the digital divide.* Cambridge, MA: MIT Press.

Watamura, S., Donzella, B., Alwin, J., & Gunnar, M. (2003). Morning-to-afternoon increases in cortisol concentrations for infants and toddlers at child care: Age differences and behavioral correlates. *Child Development, 74,* 1006–1020.

Waterman, A. S. (1985). Identity in the context of adolescent psychology. In A. S. Waterman (Ed.), *Identity in adolescence: Progress and contents (New directions for child development, No. 30).* San Francisco: Jossey-Bass.

Waters, E., & Cummings, E. M. (2001). A secure base from which to explore close relationships. *Child Development, 71*(1), 164–175.

Waters, E., Hamilton, C., & Weinfield, N. (2000a) The stability of attachment security from infancy to adolescence and early adulthood: General introduction. *Child Development, 71,* 678–683.

Waters, E., Merrick, S., Treboux, D., Crowell, J., & Albersheim, L. (2000b). Attachment security in infancy and early adulthood: A twenty-year longitudinal study. *Child Development, 71,* 684–689.

Waters, M. (1999). Black identities: West Indian immigrant dreams and American realities. Cambridge, UK: Cambridge University Press.

Watson, J. B. (1930). *Behaviorism.* Chicago: University of Chicago Press.

Watson, M. W., & Fischer, K. W. (1980). Development of social roles in elicited spontaneous behavior during the preschool years. *Developmental Psychology, 16,* 483–494.

Watts, Abdul-Adil, J., & Pratt, T. (2002). Enhancing critical consciousness in young African American men: A psychoeducational approach. *Psychology of Men and Masculinity, 3*(1), 41–50.

Waxman, S. R. (2002). Early word learning. In U. Goswami (Ed.), *Blackwell's handbook of childhood cognitive development* (pp. 102–126). Malden, MA: Blackwell.

Waxman, S. R., & Gelman, R. (1986). Preschoolers use of superordinate relations in classification. *Cognitive Development, 1,* 139–156.

Way, N., & Chen, L. (2000). The characteristics, quality, and correlates of friendships among African American, Latino, and Asian American adolescents. *Journal of Adolescent Research, 15,* 274–301.

Way, N. & Pahl, K. (2001). Individual an contextual predictors of perceived friendship quality among ethnic minority, low-income adolescents. *Journal of Research on Adolescence, 11,* 325–349.

Webb, S. J., Monk, C. S., & Nelson, C. A. (2001). Mechanisms of postnatal neurobiological development: Implications for human development. *Developmental Neuropsychology, 19*(2), 147–171.

Wechsler, D. (1939). *The measurement of adult intelligence.* Baltimore: Williams & Wilkins.

Wechsler, D. (1974). *Manual for the Wechsler intelligence scale for children.* New York: Psychology Corporation.

Weill, B. C. (1930). *Are you training your child to be happy? Lesson material in child management.* Washington, DC: U.S. Government Printing Office.

Weinberg, M. K., & Tronick, E. Z. (1997). Maternal depression and infant maladjustment: A failure of mutual regulation. In J. D. Noshpitz (Ed.), *Handbook of child and adolescent psychiatry. Vol 1. Infants and preschoolers: Development and syndromes.* New York: Wiley.

Weisfeld, G. (1999). *Evolutionary principles of human adolescence.* New York: Basic Books.

Weisner, T. S. (1996). The 5-to-7 transition as an eccocultural project. In A. J. Sameroff & M. M. Haith (Eds.), *Reason and responsibility: The passage through childhood.* Chicago: University of Chicago Press.

Weiss, M. (1997). Parents' rejection of their appearance-impaired newborns: Some critical observations regarding the social myth of bonding. *Marriage & Family Review, 27*(3–4), 191–209.

Weisz, A. N., & Black, B. M. (2003). Gender and moral reasoning: African American youths respond to dating dilemmas. *Journal of Human Behavior in the Social Environment, 6*(3), 17–34.

Weitoft, G., Hjern, A., Haglund, B., & Rosen, M. (2003). Mortality, severe morbidity, and injury in children living with single parent in Sweden: A population-based study. *Lancet, 361,* 289–295.

Wellman, H. M., Cross, D., & Watson, J. (2001). Meta-analysis of theory of mind development: The truth about false beliefs. *Child Development, 72,* 655–684.

Wellman, H. M., & Gelman, S. A. (1998). Knowledge acquisition in foundational domains. In D. Kuhn & R. S. Siegler (Eds.), *Handbook of child psychology: Vol. 2. Cognition, perception, and language* (5th ed., pp. 523–574). New York: Wiley.

Wellman, H. M., Hickling, A. K., & Schult, C. A. (1997). Young children's psychological, physical, and biological explanations. In H. M. Wellman & K. Inagaki (Eds.), *The emergence of core domains of thought: Children's reasoning about physical, psychological, and biological phenomena* (pp. 7–26). San Francisco: Jossey-Bass.

Wellman, H. M., & Lempers, J. D. (1977). The naturalistic communication abilities of two-year-olds. *Child Development, 48,* 1052–1057.

Wellman, H. M., Phillips, A. T., & Rodriguez, T. (2000). Young children's understanding of perception, desire, and emotion. *Child Development, 7*(4), 895–912.

Wellman, H. M., & Woolley, J. D. (1990). From simple desires to ordinary beliefs: The early development of everyday psychology. *Cognition 35*(3): 245–275.

Wells, G. (2001). *Action, talk, and text: Learning and teaching through inquiry.* New York: Teachers College Press.

Wentzel, K. R., & Asher, S. R. (1995). The academic level of neglected, rejected, popular, and controversial children. *Child Development, 66,* 754–763.

Werker, J. F., Pegg, J. E., & McLeod, P. J. (1994). A cross-language investigation of infant preference for infant-directed communication. *Infant Behavior and Development, 17*(3), 323–333.

Werner, E. E., & Smith, R. S. (1982). *Vulnerable but invincible: A longitudinal study of resilient children and youth.* New York: McGraw-Hill.

Werner, E. E., & Smith, R. S. (1992). *Overcoming the odds: High-risk children from birth to adulthood.* Ithaca, NY: Cornell University Press.

Whaley, S., Sigman, M., Beckwith, L., Cohen, S., & Espinosa, M. (2002). Infant-caregiver interaction in Kenya and the United States. *Journal of Cross-Cultural Psychology, 33,* 236–247.

Whitaker, R. C., Wright , J. A., Pepe, M. S., Seidel, K. D., & Dietz, W. H. (1997). Predicting obesity in young adulthood from childhood and parental obesity. *New England Journal of Medicine, 337*(13), 869–873.

White, B. L. (1975). *The first three years of life.* Englewood Cliffs, NJ: Prentice-Hall.

White, L. A. (1949). *The science of culture.* New York: Grove Press.

White, M. (1987). *The Japanese education challenge: A commitment to children.* New York: Free Press.

White, S. (1991). Three visions of educational psychology. In L. Tolchinsky-Landsmann (Ed.), *Culture, schooling and psychological development* (pp. 1–38). Norwood, NJ: Ablex.

White, S. H. (1996). The relationship of developmental psychology to social policy. In E. F. Zigler & S. L. Kagan (Eds.), *Children, families, and government: Preparing for the twenty-first century* (pp. 409–426). New York: Cambridge University Press.

Whiting, B. B. (1980). Culture and social behavior: A model for the development of social behavior. Ethos, 8, 95–116.

Whiting, B. B., & Whiting, J. W. M. (1975). *Children of six cultures: A psycho-cultural analysis.* Cambridge, MA: Harvard University Press.

Whiting, J. W. M., Burbank, V. K., & Ratner, M. S. (1986). The duration of maidenhood across cultures. In J. W. M. Whiting, V. K. Burbank, & M. S. Ratner (Eds.), *School-age pregnancy and parenthood: Biosocial dimensions* (pp. 273–302). New York: Aldine de Gruyer.

Wigfield, A., & Eccles, J. S., Eds. (2001). *Development of achievement motivation.* San Diego: Academic Press.

Wilcox, A. J., Baird, D. D., & Weinberg, C. R. (1999). Time of implantation of the conceptus and loss of pregnancy. *New England Journal of Medicine, 340*(23), 1796–1799.

Williams, T. M. (1986). *The impact of television: A natural experiment in three communities.* Orlando, FL: Academic Press.

Wilson, E. O. (1975). *Sociobiology: The new synthesis.* Cambridge, MA: Harvard University Press.

Wilson, J. D. (1995). Editorial: Sex hormones and sexual behavior. *New England Journal of Medicine, 300*(22), 121–134.

Wilson, M. N., & Saft, E. W. (1993). Child maltreatment in the African-American community. In D. Cicchetti & S. L. Toth (Eds.), *Child abuse, child development, and social policy: Advances in applied developmental psychology: Vol. 8.* Norwood, NJ: Ablex.

Wimmer, H. & Hartl, M. (1991). Against the Cartesian view on mind: Young children's difficulty with own false beliefs. *British Journal of Developmental Psychology, 9,* 125–138.

Winchester, A. M. (1972). *Genetics.* Boston: Houghton Mifflin.

Winkleby, M., Feighery, E., Altman, D., Kile, S., & Tencati, E. (2001). Engaging ethnically diverse teens in a substance use prevention advocacy program. *American Journal of Health Promotion, 15,* 433–436.

Winner, E. (1998). *The point of words: Children's understanding of metaphor and irony.* Cambridge, MA: Harvard University Press.

Winnicott, D. W. (1971). *Playing and reality.* London: Tavistock.

Witherington, D. C., Campos, J. J., & Hertenstein, M. (2002). Principles of emotion and its development in infancy. In G. Bremner & A. Fogel (Eds.), *Blackwell handbook of infant development* (pp. 427–464) Oxford: Blackwell.

Witter, F. R., & Keith, L. G. (Eds.). (1993). *Textbook of prematurity: Antecedents, treatment, & outcome.* Boston: Little, Brown & Company.

Wolf, A. W., Lozoff, B., Latz, S., & Paludetto, R. (1996). Parental theories in the management of young children's sleep in Japan, Italy, and the United States. In S. Harkness & C. M. Super (Eds.), *Parents' cultural belief systems: Their origins, expressions, and consequences* (pp. 364–384). New York: Guilford Press.

Wolfenstein, M. (1953). Trends in infant care. *American Journal of Orthopsychiatry, 33,* 120–130.

Wolff, P. H. (1966). The causes, controls, and organization of behavior in the neonate. *Psychological Issues, 5,* 1–105.

Wolff, P. H. (1969). The natural history of crying and other vocalizations in infancy. In B. M. Foss (Ed.), *Determinants of infant behavior: Vol. 4.* London: Methuen.

Wong, Y., Bennink, M., Wang, M., & Yamamoto, S. (2000). Overconcern about thinness in 10- to 14- year old schoolgirls in Taiwan. *Journal of the American Dietetic Association, 100*(2), 234–236.

Wood, J., Cowan, P., & Baker, B. (2002). Behavior problems and peer rejection in preschool boys and girls. *Journal of Genetic Psychology, 163,* 72–88.

Woodruff-Pak, D. S., Logan, C. G., & Thompson, R. F. (1990). Neurobiological substrates of classical conditioning across the life-span. *Annals of the New York Academy of Sciences, 608,* 150–178.

Woodward, A. L. (1998). Infants selectively encode the goal object of an actor's reach. *Cognition, 69*(1), 1–34.

Woodward, A. L., & Markman, E. M. (1998). Early word learning. In D. Kuhn & R. S. Sigler (Eds.), *Handbook of child psychology: Vol. 2. Cognition, perception, and language* (5th ed., pp. 371–420). New York: Wiley.

Worchel, F. F., & Allen, M. (1997). Mothers' ability to discriminate cry types in low-birthweight premature and full-term infants. *Children's Health Care, 26*(3), 183–195.

World Health Organization. (2002). HIV/AIDS statistics and features by world region. UNAID. Retrieved from www.unaids.org.

Worthman, C. M., & Whiting, J. W. M. (1987). Social change in adolescent sexual behavior, mate selection, and premarital pregnancy rates in a Kikuyu community. *Ethos, 15*, 145–165.

Wright, D. B., & Loftus, E. F. (1998). How misinformation alters memories. *Journal of Experimental Child Psychology, 71*(2), 155–164.

Wright, J. C., Huston, A. C., Reitz, A. L., & Pienyat, S. (1994). Young children's perceptions of television reality: Determinants and developmental differences. *Developmental Psychology, 30*, 229–239.

Wright, J. C., Huston, A. C., Vandewater, E. A., Bickham, D. S., Scantlin, R. M., Kotler, J. A., et al. (2002). American children's use of electronic media in 1997: A national survey. In S. L. Calvert, A. B. Jordan, & R. R. Cocking (Eds.), *Children in the digital age: Influences of electronic media on development* (pp. 35–54). Westport, CT: Praeger.

Wynn, K. (1992). Addition and subtraction by human infants. *Nature, 358*, 749–750.

Yanai, J., Steingart, R. A., Snapir, N., Gvaryahu, G., Rozenboim, I., & Katz, A. (2000). The relationship between neural alterations and behavioral deficits after prenatal exposure to heroin. *Annals of the New York Academy of Sciences, 914*, 402–411.

Yerkes, R. M. (Ed.). (1921). *Psychological examining in the United States Army. Memoirs of the National Academy of Sciences, 15*, 1–890..

Yeung, W., Sandberg, J., Davis-Dean, P., & Hofferth, S. (2001). Children's time with fathers in intact families. *Journal of Marriage and the Family, 63* (1), 136–154.

Yoshikawa, H., Rosman, E., & Hsueh, J. (2001). Variation in teenage mothers' experiences of child care and other components of welfare reform: Selection processes and developmental outcomes. *Child Development, 72*, 299–317.

Young, M., Miller, B., Norton, M., & Hill, E. (1995). The effect of parental supportive behaviors on life satisfaction of adolescent offspring. *Journal of Marriage and the Family, 57*, 813–822.

Youniss, J., & Yates, M. (1999). Youth service and moral-civic identity: A case for everyday morality. *Educational Psychology Review, 11*(4), 361–376.

Zafeiriou, D. I., Tsikoulas, I. G., Kremenopoulos, G. M., & Kontopoulos, E. E. (1999). Moro reflex profile in high-risk infants at the first year of life. *Brain and Development, 21*(3), 216–217.

Zahavi, S., & Asher, S. R. (1978). The effects of verbal instruction on preschool children's aggressive behavior. *Journal of School Psychology, 16*, 146–153.

Zahn-Waxler, C., Radke-Yarrow, M., & King, R. (1979). Child rearing and children's prosocial initiations toward victims of distress. *Child Development, 50*, 319–330.

Zarbatany, L., Hartmann, D. P., & Rankin, D. B. (1990). The psychological functions of preadolescent peer activities. *Child Development, 61*(4), 1067–1080.

Zeanah, C. (Ed.) (2000). *Handbook of infant mental health.* New York: Guilford Press.

Zech, L., Vye, N. J., Bransford, J. D., Goldman, S. R., Barron, B., Schwartz, D., et al. (1998). An introduction to geometry through anchored instruction. In R. Lehrer & D. Chazan (Eds.), *Designing learning environments for developing understanding of geometry and space* (pp. 439–463). Mahwah, NJ: Erlbaum.

Zeifman, D. M. (2001). An ethological analysis of human infant crying: Answering Tinbergen's four questions. *Developmental Psychobiology, 39*(4), 265–285.

Zelazo, P. R. (1983). The development of walking: New findings and old assumptions. *Journal of Motor Behavior, 15*, 99–137.

Zero to Three. (2003). Choosing quality child care. Retrieved from http://www.zerotothre.org/choosecare.htm.

Zeskind, P. S., Klein, L., & Marshall, T. R. (1992). Adults' perceptions of experimental modifications of durations of pauses and expiratory sounds in infant crying. *Developmental Psychology, 28*(6), 1153–1162.

Zeskind, P. S., & Lester, B. M. (2001). Analysis of infant crying. In L. T. Singer & P. S. Zeskind (Eds.), *Biobehavioral assessment of the infant* (pp. 149–166). New York: Guilford Press.

Zigler, E. F., & Finn-Stevenson, M. (1999). Applied developmental psychology. In M. H. Bornstein & M. E. Lamb (Eds.), *Developmental psychology: An advanced textbook* (4th ed., pp. 555–598). Mahwah, NJ: Erlbaum.

Zigler, E. F., & Hall, N. W. (1989). Physical child abuse in America: Past, present, and future. In D. Cicchetti & V. Carlson (Eds.), *Child maltreatment: Theory and research on the causes and consequences of child abuse and neglect.* New York: Cambridge University Press.

Zimmermann, P., & Becker-Stoll, F. (2002). Stability of attachment representations during adolescence: The influence of ego-identity status. *Journal of Adolescence, 25*, 107–124.

Zukow-Goldring, P. (1995). Sibling caregiving. In M. Bornstein (Ed.), *Handbook of parenting: Vol. 3. Status and social conditions of parenting.* Mahwah, NJ: Erlbaum.

NAME INDEX

Siegler, R. S., 27, 333, 334, 336, 337, 338, 354, 465, 468, 469, 470, 472, 478, 491
Silbereisen, R. K., 2, 594, 611
Silk, J. S., 609
Simion, F., 127
Simmons, R. G., 531, 544, 594
Simms, M. D., 211
Simon, H. A., 628
Simon, K., 452
Simon, T., 506, 507, 508, 509, 516, 529
Simon, W., 608, 609
Simons, J. A., 593
Simpson, J. L., 62, 223
Sinclair, D., 119, 583, 584
Singer, D. G., 434, 533
Singer, J. L., 434, 533
Singer, L. T., 99, 100, 101
Singleton, J., 486
Siqueland, E. R., 149
Skinner, B. F., 34, 149
Skoe, E. E., 632
Skuse, D. H., 255
Slater, A. M., 190
Slonim, N., 280
Slotkin, T. A., 99
Smetana, J. G., 375, 610
Smith, E., 606
Smith, J., 292, 389
Smith, K., 407
Smith, L. B., 130, 180
Smith, N. V., 285
Smith, P. K., 545
Smith, R. S., 260
Smith, W. C., 10
Smits, W., 485
Smitsman, A. W., 169
Smotherman, W. P., 80
Smulian, J. C., 84
Smyth, C. M., 65
Snarey, J. R., 632
Snow, C. E., 295, 297, 487, 488, 489
Snow, C., 313
Solomon, J., 230, 231
Sommer, K., 418
Soussignan, R., 128
Sowell, E. R., 23, 456, 457, 463
Spearman, C., 509, 510
Spelke, E. S., 10, 125, 184, 337, 339
Spence, M. J., 81
Spencer, M., 648
Spencer, M. B., 13, 370
Spiro, M. E., 551
Spitz, H. H., 472
Sroufe, L. A., 194, 244, 246, 271, 377, 553, 554, 563
St. George, M., 57
St. James-Roberts, I., 145
St.-Onge, M. P., 455
Stager, C. L., 133

Stangor, C., 542 , 632
Stanko, S., 144
Stanovich, K. E., 488
Starkey, P., 441
Stattin, H., 593
Stauder, J. E. A., 457
Steele, H., 197
Stein, J. H., 589
Steinberg, L., 416, 593, 609, 612, 614
Steiner, J. E., 127
Stephens, T., 655
Stern, D. N., 113, 124, 205
Stern, E., 491
Stern, W., 328, 508
Sternberg, R. J., 478, 510, 511, 513, 515
Stevens, J., 169
Stevenson, D., 595, 610, 614
Stevenson, H. W., 67, 90, 389, 464, 520, 595
Stewart, J., 389
Stigler, J. W., 520, 521
Stipek, D., 417
Stoltzfus, R. J., 84
Stone, J. E., 493
Stone, J. L., 325, 493
Strathearn, L., 103
Stratton, K., 87
Straus, M., 389
Strauss, R., 455
Strayer, F. F., 16, 386, 388
Streri, A., 184
Striano, T., 198
Striegel-Moore, R. H., 590
Stromback, T., 485
Stunkard, A. J., 454
Suarez-Orozco, C., 416
Suarez-Orozco, M., 416
Subbotsky, E. V., 327, 352, 541
Subrahmanyam, K., 440, 441, 442
Sugarman, S., 219
Sullivan, H. S., 556
Sullivan, K., 341
Summerfield, D., 265
Sun, L.-C., 231
Sun, Y., 419, 421
Sunseth, K., 489
Suomala, J., 499
Suomi, S., 138, 224, 268, 269, 270
Super, C. M., 17, 142, 173, 353, 451
Suppes, P., 498
Susman, E. J., 83, 594
Sutherland, D., 389
Sutton, J., 545
Sutton-Smith, B., 554
Sweeney, B., 106
Sweet, A., 488
Szkrubalo, J., 367

Tager-Flusberg, H., 23, 346
Tallal, P., 517, 518
Tamis-Lemonda, C. S., 217

Tani, C. R., 599
Tanner, J. M., 20, 57, 99, 118, 167, 583, 587, 615
Tardif, T., 18, 287
Taska, L. S., 568
Teberosky, A., 488
Telzrow, R. W., 189
Tenenbaum, H. R., 347
Terman, L. M., 507
Tessier, R. M. C., 104
Teti, D. M., 262
Thach, B. T., 140
Thanavishuth, C., 121
Thapan, M., 645
Tharp, R. G., 527
Thatcher, R. W., 207, 321, 457
Thelen, E., 130, 167, 180, 207
Thiessen, E. D., 280
Thoman, E. B., 102, 140, 141, 439
Thomas, A., 136, 137, 260, 266, 361
Thomas, S., 328
Thompson, B., 386
Thompson, G. B., 488
Thompson, N. S., 16
Thomson, J. A., 75
Thompson, R. A., 23, 232, 248, 254, 271, 382, 383, 531, 585
Thorne, B., 554, 555, 589
Thrasher, F., 599
Thurstone, L. L., 510
Tienari, P., 261
Tinker, E., 221, 222
Tizard, B., 253, 254
Toda, S., 217
Tolchinsky, L., 488
Tomasello, M., 8, 66, 198, 238, 299, 301, 303, 311, 330, 341
Tonneau, F., 16
Toth, S. L., 258, 422, 423
Trautner, H., 362
Travis, F., 463
Tremblay, R., 385
Trevarthen, C., 23, 158, 235
Triandis, H. C., 522
Troiden, R. R., 646, 648
Tronick, E. Z., 66, 89, 262
Troop-Gordon, W., 550
Troseth, G., 365, 434
Trudeau, G., 16
Truwitt, C. L., 321
Tsikoulsa, I. G., 130
Tuchmann-Duplessis, H., 73, 92
Tucker, G. R., 302
Tulving, E., 320
Tulviste, P., 503
Turati, C., 127
Turiel, E., 360, 361, 374, 375, 538, 541, 542, 610, 629, 631, 632, 633, 653
Turksen, K., 75
Turnbull, E., 521

Udry, J., 606
Ullah, M. Z., 534
Ulrich, B. D., 207
Umilta, C., 127
Underhill, R. L., 211
Underwood, M., 385
Urberg, K. A., 599
Ursitti, F., 88
Uzgiris, I. C., 179

Valian, V., 299, 314
Valsiner, J., 13, 36, 404
van den Boom, D. C., 54
van den Dikkenberg-Pot, I., 200
Van der Paal, L., 97
Van der Put, N. M. J., 83
van der Veer, R., 13
Van Evra, J., 439
Van Gennep, A., 655
van Heteren, C. F., 80
Van Hoorn, J., 656, 659
van IJzendoorn, M. H., 232, 233, 234
Van Roosmalen, E., 644, 645
Vander Linde, E., 193
Vandross, L., 413
Vangelisti, A., 421
Vasquez, O., 523
Vaughn, B. E., 233
Vickerstaff, S. A., 485
Victor, the Wild Boy of Averon, 1, 2, 3, 11, 39, 255, 257
Vincent, K., 590
Vinden, P., 351
Vintzileos, A., 84
Violato, C., 580
von Hofsten, C., 132, 169, 181, 192
Vondracek, F., 639
Voorhoeve, H. W. A, 80, 83, 95
Vurpillot, E., 470, 471
Vygotsky, L. S., 27, 36, 37, 196, 291, 301, 378, 379, 381, 432, 496

Wachs, T. D., 54, 136, 138, 139
Waddell, K. J., 478, 503
Waddington, C. H., 55, 403
Wade, T., 591
Wagner, D. A., 502, 503
Wainryb, C., 633, 634
Wakely, A., 186
Walker, L. J., 632, 636
Walker, S., 385
Walker-Andrews, A., 216
Walsh, W., 389
Wandersman, A., 256
Wang, A. O., 64
Wang, X., 87
Ward, K., 61
Warner, T. D., 516
Warren, A. R., 475